THE TENTH AIR FORCE
IN WORLD WAR II

STRATEGY, COMMAND,
AND OPERATIONS 1942-1945

EDWARD M. YOUNG

SCHIFFER MILITARY
4880 Lower Valley Road Atglen, PA 19310

Copyright © 2020 by Edward M. Young

Library of Congress Control Number: 2019947414

All rights reserved. No part of this work may be reproduced or used in any form or by any means—graphic, electronic, or mechanical, including photocopying or information storage and retrieval systems—without written permission from the publisher.

The scanning, uploading, and distribution of this book or any part thereof via the Internet or any other means without the permission of the publisher is illegal and punishable by law. Please purchase only authorized editions and do not participate in or encourage the electronic piracy of copyrighted materials.

"Schiffer," "Schiffer Publishing, Ltd.," and the pen and inkwell logo are registered trademarks of Schiffer Publishing, Ltd.

Designed by Justin Watkinson
Type set in Engravers MT/Minion Pro/Univers LT Std

ISBN: 978-0-7643-5932-3
Printed in India

Published by Schiffer Publishing, Ltd.
4880 Lower Valley Road
Atglen, PA 19310
Phone: (610) 593-1777; Fax: (610) 593-2002
E-mail: Info@schifferbooks.com
Web: www.schifferbooks.com

For our complete selection of fine books on this and related subjects, please visit our website at www.schifferbooks.com. You may also write for a free catalog.

Schiffer Publishing's titles are available at special discounts for bulk purchases for sales promotions or premiums. Special editions, including personalized covers, corporate imprints, and excerpts, can be created in large quantities for special needs. For more information, contact the publisher.

We are always looking for people to write books on new and related subjects. If you have an idea for a book, please contact us at proposals@schifferbooks.com.

IN MEMORY OF
ALL THE MEN AND WOMEN
WHO SERVED IN THE
TENTH AIR FORCE
DURING WORLD WAR II,

AND TO MY UNCLE,
1ST LT. CHARLES W. YOUNG,
1ST PROVISIONAL TANK GROUP,
BURMA, 1944–45.

My intention in writing this history of the Tenth Air Force in World War II was to provide, for those interested in the air war over Burma, a companion volume to Air Commodore Henry Probert's study *The Forgotten Air Force: The Royal Air Force in the War against Japan, 1941–1945*. The title of Probert's book applies equally to the Tenth Air Force and the Army Air Force units that served in Air Command, Southeast Asia, during the final years of the Burma war. The Tenth Air Force at times appears to be a "forgotten air force," consigned to living in the shadow of its more illustrious neighbor, the famous "Flying Tigers" of the Fourteenth Air Force in China. While there are a number of memoirs of airmen who served in the Tenth Air Force and histories of some Tenth Air Force units, since the publication of the relevant volumes of Wesley Craven and James Cate's monumental *The Army Air Forces in World War II* in the 1950s, there have been few attempts to write a history of the Tenth Air Force using material that was unavailable to Craven and Cate and their contributors. My effort is by no means a definitive history, but I have tried to put the operations of the Tenth Air Force into a larger context of Allied strategy in China and Southeast Asia and the ground campaigns that ultimately led to victory.

My interest in pursuing a history of the Tenth Air Force dates back to the years I spent in Bangkok, Thailand, as a boy who had a love of airplanes and a keen interest in World War II. I remember seeing rusting locomotives damaged in Allied strafing attacks still lying in the railroad yard at Bangsue—then on the outskirts of Bangkok—and being shown fragments of American 500 lb bombs that had landed in the yard of a Thai friend of my parents. Why the Americans had dropped bombs on Thailand was then a mystery to me. Returning to Thailand ten years later as a Peace Corps volunteer stimulated an interest in the history of aviation in Thailand. This led to my first book, *Aerial Nationalism: A History of Aviation in Thailand*, and in the process my first research into the operations of the Tenth Air Force during World War II.

In the years that followed, this interest in the Tenth Air Force and the war in Burma led me to work on histories of the Air Commando fighter squadrons that flew in Burma, monographs on Gen. Sir William Slim's brilliant capture of Meiktila in March 1945, and the operations of Merrill's Marauders in Stilwell's northern Burma campaign, as well as a history of the 7th Bombardment Group that flew missions into Burma and Thailand from 1942 to 1945.

A good number of people have helped me along the way. My great regret in writing this history is that I did not take more opportunities to meet with veterans of the Tenth Air Force before they passed on. I did have the great good fortune to meet with a number of veterans of the Air Commando fighter squadrons. I would like to acknowledge with thanks the support and encouragement I received from William Burghardt, Olin Carter, Jack Klarr, and Roland Lynn, who served with the 5th and 6th Fighter Squadrons (Commando); and W. R. Eason, Kevin Mallen, and Bob Spann from the 1st and 2nd Fighter Squadrons (Commando). These men and several of their squadron mates graciously gave me time at their reunions for interviews and provided personal photographs. I would also like to thank Col. Thomas Sledge (USAF, Ret'd), who served as a bombardier with the 7th Bomb Group during 1943, for allowing me to interview him on his experiences and sharing his diary and photos. Jim Augustus, whose father served with the 7th Bomb Group, gave me access to a substantial amount of material and photographs he had accumulated working with the 7th Bombardment Group Historical Foundation.

I would like to thank three good friends who have helped me in innumerable ways: Steve Ellis, Peter Pedersen, and Osamu Tagaya. A fellow volunteer at the Museum of Flight in Seattle and a former intelligence officer in the Air Force, Steve's interest in military history and issues of strategy and command, and his questions on the Tenth Air Force, have stimulated my own thinking. Steve kindly read sections of an early draft of this history and made several invaluable suggestions for improvements. Peter Pedersen, an accomplished military historian, has provided encouragement and support for my writing this history in many ways, for which I am profoundly grateful, particularly his insistence that the neglected aspects of the air war in Burma needed more-detailed coverage. Over many years Sam Tagaya has been exceptionally generous in sharing his extensive knowledge of Japanese military aviation in World War II. His insights into the doctrines and tactics of the Japanese Army Air Force, and his explorations of the links between Japanese industrial capacity and airpower, have been enlightening. Sam has also been an enthusiastic supporter of writing a history of the Tenth Air Force.

I would also like to thank my professors in the MA History of Warfare Program at King's College, London, particularly Professor Philip Sabin, my dissertation supervisor; Dr. Alan James, my academic supervisor; and Professor Joe Maiolo. I am indebted to all three for their efforts to make me a better historian.

Several institutions and individuals have been the sources of documents and photographs without which this history could not have been written and illustrated. I am grateful to all for their efforts to preserve the archival records in their care. First and foremost, my thanks to the staff of the Air Force Historical Research Agency at Maxwell AFB in Montgomery, Alabama, and especially to Ms. Tammy Horton, who cheerfully and promptly responded to my many requests for Tenth Air Force records. At the National Archives and Records Administration in Washington, DC, Ms. Holly Reed and her capable staff in the Still Pictures Branch were exceptionally patient with my requests for boxes of photos from the Army Air Force collection and directed me to other record groups that held photos of operations in Burma. The staff of the National Archives at Kew, in London, were equally professional and helpful. I would also like to thank Dr. Mary Elizabeth Ruwell, academic archivist and chief, Special Collections, at the US Air Force Academy Library for giving me access to materials in the 7th Bombardment Group Historical Foundation Collection. At the Museum of Flight in Seattle, Amy Heidrick provided copies of photographs from the Peter M. Bowers collection. I would also like to thank the staffs of the Imperial War Museum and the San Diego Air & Space Museum for permission to use photographs from their collection. Carl Molesworth kindly offered a number of photographs from his extensive collection on American fighter groups that fought in China and Burma. Maria Brown, chief cartographer at the Kroll Map Company in Seattle, did a superb job creating many of the maps that accompany the text.

I save my deepest thanks for my wife, Candis, who has watched this history evolve over the four decades of our marriage. Without her love, support, and encouragement I could not have completed this or any other project.

TABLE OF CONTENTS

6 INTRODUCTION

9 CHAPTER 1. Formation and Early Operations:
December 1941–June 1942

33 CHAPTER 2. The China Air Task Force:
July 1942–March 1943

55 CHAPTER 3. The India Air Task Force:
October–December 1942

78 CHAPTER 4. From Casablanca to Trident:
Tenth Air Force Operations, January–May 1943

112 CHAPTER 5. Trident, Command Changes,
and Operations during the Monsoon:
June–August 1943

132 CHAPTER 6. Air Command, Southeast Asia:
Integrating the Allied Air Forces,
August–December 1943

150 CHAPTER 7. Combat Resumed: Operations,
October–December 1943

177 CHAPTER 8. American Fighter Operations
under Eastern Air Command:
December 1943–June 1944

208 CHAPTER 9. Strategic Bombing and Air Supply
Operations under Eastern Air Command:
December 1943–June 1944

234 CHAPTER 10. Myitkyina and Beyond:
Operations, Plans, and Preparations,
May–August 1944

255 CHAPTER 11. Supporting the NCAC Advance:
August 1944–April 1945

281 CHAPTER 12. Army Air Force Units Supporting
14th Army Operations:
June 1944–May 1945

311 CHAPTER 13. Victory in Burma:
February–April 1945

339 CHAPTER 14. Endgame

354 GLOSSARY

355 APPENDIXES

364 NOTES

406 REFERENCES CITED

414 INDEX

INTRODUCTION

The Tenth Air Force fought a long, difficult war in a theater beset with unique challenges. From tenuous beginnings in the early months of the war, the Tenth grew to a sizeable force that contributed in no small measure to the defeat of the Imperial Japanese Army in Burma. The China-Burma-India (CBI) theater, as it was designated, was a theater of war in which airpower was the predominant American contribution to the fight against Japanese forces. British and American airpower played a vital role in the war in Burma.

In an area where few roads existed, air supply became the only reliable means of getting supplies to forward troops, while fighters providing close air support made up for a lack of heavy artillery. Light planes pioneered aeromedical evacuation, giving the badly wounded a chance for survival. Heavy and medium bombers pounded the Japanese line of communications into and within Burma, bombing railroad yards, mining harbors, and busting bridges. Royal Air Force and Tenth Air Force fighters broke the back of the Japanese Army Air Force to establish air superiority over Burma, enabling transports and light planes to perform their tasks relatively unhindered from interception. All the techniques and applications of airpower employed in the war in Burma had to be learned through experience, tried and tested over months of combat. Allied airpower grew slowly in strength and capability. Following the humiliating defeat and withdrawal from Burma in 1942, it took nearly two years for the Allies to return to the offensive. As will be seen, three factors influenced the course of the campaign in Burma from its beginning to the very end: the geography and climate of the India-Burma area; logistics and the continual problem of obtaining supplies of aircraft, men, and materials; and the divergent and often-conflicting national interests of the three Allies—America, Britain, and China—that made agreement on a coherent strategy and objectives for the prosecution of the war in Burma difficult to achieve.[1]

The China-Burma-India theater encompassed a broad sweep of the Asian mainland, stretching from Karachi—then still part of India—in the west to the China coast in the east. For most of its existence, Burma was the focus for Tenth Air Force operations. The country of Burma—now Myanmar—lies on the western edge of Southeast Asia. Burma shares a border with India to the west, with China to the north and east, and with Thailand to the southeast. The country stretches roughly 1,200 miles from north to south, and 575 miles from east to west. The great Irrawaddy River runs from the foothills of the Himalayas down to a broad delta emptying into the ocean south of Rangoon and Bassein. To the east, the Salween River flows down to enter the Gulf of Martaban at Moulmein. To the west, the Chindwin River follows the mountain ranges along the border with India before cutting south to join the Irrawaddy

A view of the Naga Hills in northern Burma. Ranging from 2,000 to 5,000 feet, the Naga Hills formed part of the mountain chain running along the India-Burma border down to the Arakan. Difficult to traverse in the dry season, these mountain ranges became nearly impassable during the heavy rains of the monsoon. *3A-36155, Record Group 342FH (RG342FH), Army Air Forces, National Archives and Records Administration (NARA)*

China - Burma - India Theater

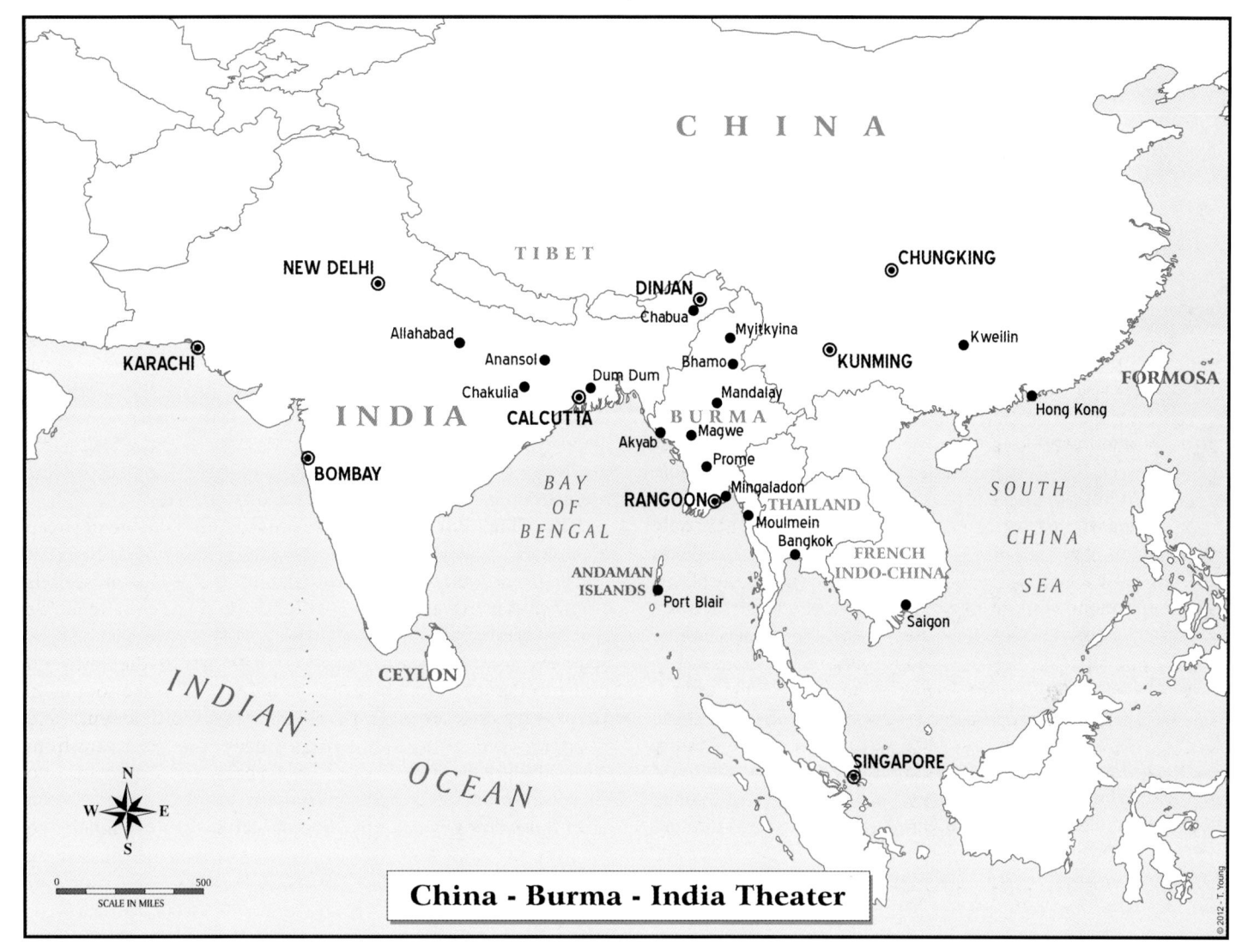

River west of Mandalay. All three of these rivers featured prominently in the reconquest of Burma. Mountain ranges to the west, north, and east surround the drier central plain and the rich rice fields of the Irrawaddy River delta, much like a thumb and forefinger. Burma was rich in resources, producing rice, timber, minerals, and oil.

Terrain and weather proved to be formidable obstacles to the conduct of the air war and the reconquest of Burma. Along the border with India, a series of mountain ranges rise up from the Bay of Bengal in the Arakan to follow the India-Burma border for some 500 miles northward to Burma's border with China. The hills range in height from 1,000 to 3,000 feet at the southern end in the Arakan, from 5,000 to 11,000 feet in the central Chin and Naga Hills, and from 2,000 to 8,000 feet at the northernmost section. Another range follows the Burmese border with China, rising to 12,000–15,000 feet in the beginnings of the Himalayas.[2]

These steep jungle and forested mountain ranges are 40 miles to more than 100 miles wide, presenting a formidable barrier to any attempt to mount an overland campaign from India into Burma. To reach the front lines along the India-Burma border and beyond, and to penetrate deeper into Burma, airplanes had to fly over these mountain ranges and return the same way. Bailing out over the mountains meant walking back through jungle and on mountain paths to Allied lines, if possible. Prior to World War II, communication through these mountain ranges was next to nonexistent. Roads ran up from Rangoon through the central plains to where the mountain ranges began, connecting at Lashio to link up with the Burma Road that ended at Kunming, across the border in China. Other roads reached up to Kalewa, on the Chindwin River, and to Myitkyina in the northeast, but not beyond. Between Burma and India there were no roads; only a few tracks leading up from the Chindwin through the mountains to Imphal in Assam. The Burmese railway system ran from Rangoon to the end of the Burmese central plain near Myitkyina and Lashio. On the Indian side, there were few roads through Assam. The Indian railroad system had limited capacity—adequate for peacetime, but not for war.

For both the Allies and the Japanese, getting supplies to their forward troops was an arduous ordeal even in the best of weather. During the southwest monsoon, which lasts from May to September, torrential rains hit the mountains nearly every day. Movement through the hills becomes exceptionally difficult and flying dangerous, with thick clouds covering the mountains for weeks on end. For men on the ground, high temperatures and humidity add to the discomfort and the risk of debilitating diseases. The central Burmese plains are drier, but rainfall is heavy along the coastal areas and in the Irrawaddy River delta. From the perspective of terrain and climate, as a place to conduct an overland campaign, northern Burma was "among the worst for that purpose in the world."[3]

The Allied decision to defeat Germany first gave the European theater of war priority in the allocation of supplies of all kinds. The Pacific theater came next, leaving the China-Burma-India theater a distant third. Shortages of men and materials—but especially shipping—and the demands of higher-priority theaters of war limited the amount of supplies and the number of aircraft and men that could be spared for the CBI in the first two years of the war.[4]

It took time for America's productive capacity to expand to the point where all theaters of war could be supplied, but even in the last stages of the war, Europe and the Pacific had first call on resources. Getting supplies to the CBI was a huge problem. The Tenth Air Force had one of the longest supply lines of any American air force. Only the Fourteenth Air Force in China had a longer one. For the first few years of the war the supplies that did arrive from the United States were off-loaded at Karachi (then part of India) after a journey of 12,000 miles that took the better part of two months. From Karachi, supplies had to travel another 1,000 miles over the inadequate Indian railroad system to bases in Assam, in northeastern India, near the border with Burma. From there, supplies for China went on transport aircraft and traveled over what came to be called the Hump route, flying over the lower, eastern end of the Himalayan mountain range to Kunming—covering another 700 miles. As a comparison, it was as if all supplies were delivered to Kansas City, put on a train to New York, and then flown on to Nova Scotia.

The more intractable problem was the clash of national interests and objectives among the Allies, a problem that was never fully resolved. As one observer put it, contrasting the harmonious relationship Britain and America established in Europe with the heated debates and disagreements over strategy for China and Southeast Asia, "in South-East Asia on the other hand, the British and Americans were fighting two wars for different purposes, and the Kuomintang Government of China was fighting a third war for purposes largely of its own."[5] In essence, the American objective was to provide support for China to ensure that China continued to resist Japan and contain the more than half a million Japanese soldiers tied down in China.[6] American strategy was based on delivering supplies to China to sustain the Chinese war effort, though there would be an intense debate within the Roosevelt administration and the War Department on how best to accomplish this mission. With the loss of Burma in early 1942, cutting the last overland route to China, America's options became the air route over the Hump or the reconquest of Burma to reopen a land route from India to China. For Britain, the loss of Singapore and Malaya outweighed the loss of Burma. The magnitude of the defeat was a shattering blow to British prestige in Asia.[7] As a result, Prime Minister Winston Churchill and British high command tended to look toward the capture of Rangoon and lower Burma, and beyond to the reconquest of the British colonies in Malaya and Singapore. The idea of using limited British resources for an overland campaign from India into upper Burma became anathema.[8] The British had little faith in the ability of China to play a more active role in the war against Japan.[9]

For the government of China the goal was survival. Nearly five years of protracted war with Japan had devastated Chinese society, the economy, and government administration. Since 1937, the Chinese Nationalist army had lost more than one million men fighting the Japanese, with another one and a quarter million wounded.[10] The cost to Japan had been far greater than expected. What had been planned as a short, decisive conflict (three divisions, three months, and a cost of ¥100 million) had turned into a stalemated quagmire that by 1941 had cost the Japanese army 1.8 million casualties and nearly half a million dead, with the continued commitment of 21 divisions and 40 mixed brigades.[11] Generalissimo Chiang Kai-shek—China's head of state and commander of the Nationalist army—governed as *primes inter pares* (first among equals), playing off factions within the ruling Kuomintang Party and rival military leaders whose loyalty he could not always command through adroit manipulation of funds and military supplies.[12] By 1941, China's battered army consisted of some 2.9 million men in 244 "first line" divisions, with an additional 900,000 men in 70 "second line" formations, but almost all these divisions were for the most part poorly trained, poorly equipped, and badly led.[13]

Compounding the problem of resisting the Japanese was the loss of a major portion of China's industrial base to the Japanese advance. As a predominantly agricultural nation, China had only a limited ability to produce the materials needed for modern warfare to begin with, and the situation only got worse as the war continued.[14] In going to war against Japan, Chiang had gambled that at some point Japan would come into direct conflict with the great powers—America, Britain, and the USSR—who had the resources to defeat Japan that China lacked.[15] Chiang's gamble was rewarded on 7 December 1941, when Japan attacked Pearl Harbor. He now had an ally in the United States, but America's wartime relationship with China would be one of strains and tensions over goals and strategies, perceptions of time, and ways of making war.

The goal of the United States was straightforward: to defeat the Japanese Empire as quickly as possible. American political and military leaders looked to China to contribute to Japan's defeat. Chiang Kai-shek's objectives were different, as was his approach to war against Japan. While he was determined to liberate China from Japanese occupation, Chiang's principal concern was the reunification of China under the rule of the Kuomintang after decades of political disintegration following the collapse of the Qing dynasty, and the need to emerge victorious from the civil war with the Communist Party of China, which he knew would resume after the Japanese defeat. He labored under severe political, military, economic, and financial constraints, which he had limited ability to resolve.

For the men of the Tenth Air Force, dealing with this host of geographic, climatic, logistic, political, and strategic challenges began as soon as the Tenth came into existence in February 1942, and continued until the end of the war. While fighting out of India over and into Burma, the Tenth had always to be cognizant of developments in China, since support for China continued to be the Tenth's principal mission. China's pull would influence the conduct of the Tenth Air Force's air war in numerous and often-unpredictable ways. How the Tenth undertook its mission in a war that was little heralded at the time and is little known today is the subject of this history.

CHAPTER 1
FORMATION AND EARLY OPERATIONS
December 1941–June 1942

American Support for China

The American government was slow to provide material support to China in its war against Japan. American views of China were "a curious, usually glib amalgam of missionary zeal, reformist interest, and dreams of a boundless market."[1] Although many Americans felt that America had a special relationship with China, the United States had acquired the special privileges of other foreign powers in China, particularly the rights of extraterritoriality the Chinese people despised, and had been a party to the 1922 Nine Power Treaty, which called for the European nations, Japan, and the United States to engage in "peaceful competition for economic and political influence in China."[2] The outbreak of the Sino-Japanese War in July 1937 did not change US government policy toward China, particularly given the strong isolationist sentiment in Congress and among the public. During 1938–39, public opinion within America began to change with reports of Japanese brutality against the Chinese people and news of indiscriminate bombing of Chinese cities. Public support for aiding China in its resistance to Japan became more widespread. President Franklin Roosevelt decided to show more support for China by granting China credits to purchase materials in America.[3]

American support for China became more direct following the fall of France in June 1940, and Japan's occupation of northern French Indochina in September, which directly threatened British colonies in Burma, Malaya, and Singapore; the Netherlands East Indies; and America's Philippine colony. That same month, Japan signed the Tripartite Pact with Germany and Italy, openly signaling its alliance with the expansionist fascist powers. Fear of further Japanese designs on the rest of Asia prompted a change in US policy toward China. Supporting Chinese resistance to Japan was now seen as a cornerstone of American policy. American military planners recognized the benefit of containing Japanese troops in China and the drain this put on Japanese resources. In addition, the War Department considered China's manpower and its geographic proximity to Japan as potential advantages in a war with Japan.[4] In October 1940, the United States granted China an additional credit of $25 million, followed in December by a larger credit of $100 million, for the first time allowing the Chinese to purchase weapons with a portion of the loan.[5] On 11 March 1941, Congress passed the Lend-Lease Act, allowing for the transfer of weapons and material to countries fighting against Germany, Italy, and Japan. Five days later President Roosevelt gave a speech pledging aid to China and on May 6 stated clearly that the defense of China was vital to the defense of the United States.[6]

Japanese army officers at the railroad station at Tientsin in China in summer 1936. Japanese designs on northern China and its resources led inexorably to the Sino-Japanese War. *Kenneth T. Young via the author*

Japanese bombers attacking the Chinese wartime capital Chunking. Scenes of death and destruction turned American public opinion against Japan. 03_01375, San Diego Air & Space Museum Collection (SDAMC)

Even before passage of the Lend-Lease Act, the Roosevelt administration had quietly taken steps to provide airplanes to China. In November 1940, Generalissimo Chiang Kai-shek had sent a mission to the United States to request combat planes. Maj. Gen. Mao Pang-tzo, director of the operations division of the Chinese air force, headed the mission, accompanied by retired Army Air Corps captain Claire L. Chennault, now a Chinese air force colonel and a technical advisor to the generalissimo.[7] The Chinese delegation asked for 250 Brewster F2A or Grumman F4F fighters, 100 Curtiss-Wright P-40s, 50 Douglas B-23 bombers, and 100 Lockheed Hudsons.[8]

The needs of the American Army and Navy and Britain were deemed to have higher priority, but through negotiations the British Purchasing Commission in the United States agreed to the release of 100 P-40Bs from British orders for shipment to China.[9] At the same time, the Roosevelt administration gave its approval for the Chinese to recruit American pilots from the Army Air Corps, the Navy, and the Marine Corps to fly the P-40s on behalf of the Chinese air force under the auspices of William Pawley's Central Aircraft Manufacturing Company (CAMCO).[10] This became the American Volunteer Group (AVG), with Chennault as its commander. With the cooperation of British authorities, the AVG set up training facilities at Toungoo, in

After retiring from the Army Air Corps in 1937, Claire Chennault served as an air advisor to Generalissimo Chiang Kai-shek and the Chinese government, where he observed Japanese air operations firsthand. A brilliant tactician, Chennault trained his American Volunteer Group pilots in tactics that countered the maneuverability of Japanese fighter planes. 02_C-00249, SDAMC

The Republic P-43 Lancer was the precursor of the far more capable Republic P-47 Thunderbolt. While able to climb to high altitude, the P-43's lack of armor and self-sealing fuel tanks made it decidedly inferior to contemporaneous Japanese fighter planes. Despite these deficiencies, the Lancer was all that could be spared at a time when the American Army Air Force was desperately rearming and expanding. Historical Record and Activities of US Army Air Forces in Area of Karachi, India, Book I, Miscellaneous, March 1942 to December 31, 1942, 828.08, Air Force Historical Research Agency (AFHRA), Maxwell AFB, AL

Burma, where American and Chinese mechanics assembled the P-40s and the former Air Corps, Navy, and Marine Corps volunteer pilots underwent training in Chennault's tactics.[11]

Lend-Lease aid also began to be shipped to China. The American government arranged for the Chinese to receive under Lend-Lease 144 Vultee P-66 Vanguard fighters the British were happy to release from their own orders, and 125 Republic P-43 Lancers to supplement the P-40s already en route for China.[12] The Chinese presented proposals to the War Department for arms, ammunition, and artillery sufficient to equip 30 divisions, as well as requests for several thousand trucks to transport supplies from the port of Rangoon up to China over the Burma Road.[13] To advise the Chinese on the procurement of Lend-Lease equipment, to train the Chinese in the use of the equipment they would receive, and to assist in developing the line of communications into China from Burma, at Army Chief of Staff Gen. George Marshall's suggestion, President Roosevelt agreed to the creation of an American military mission to China, establishing the first direct relationship between the American and Chinese armed forces.[14]

Germany's invasion of the Soviet Union in June 1941 and Japan's occupation of southern French Indochina in July gave a new sense of importance to the growing American military support for China. In response to Japan's latest move, the American government placed an embargo on all trade with Japan—including oil—while continuing negotiations to seek a way out of the impasse between the two countries. With Britain hard-pressed in the Middle East, and the Soviets facing a dire threat, any further Japanese expansion into the rest of Asia had to be prevented, or at least delayed. While having few illusions about the quality of the Chinese army and its ability to take offensive action in its then-current state against Japanese forces in China, American officials hoped that supplying more arms and aircraft might cause the Japanese to reconsider attacking Southeast Asia out of concern for their position in China.[15] Such hopes proved to be in vain. But regardless of what China could or could not do, America was now firmly committed to supporting China. President Roosevelt now saw China as a valuable ally in the event of war with Japan, and possibly beyond in the postwar world that would emerge with victory over the Axis.[16]

American Airpower for China

The outbreak of war with Japan on 7 December 1941 brought the question of China's potential role in the war into urgent, sharper focus. There were sound strategic reasons for ensuring that China remained in the war and continued its resistance to Japan. Prime among them remained the vital necessity of containing the Japanese army's divisions based in China. Remarkably, in launching its conquest of Southeast Asia, the Imperial Army deployed only 10 of its 50 divisions for the Southeast Asia campaign. In China, the Army kept 22 divisions, 20 brigades, and 16 air squadrons in the *China Expeditionary Army*, totaling 620,000 men, with an additional 13 divisions and 56 air squadrons guarding Manchuria from the Soviet Union.[17] It was imperative that these Japanese forces remain where they were and not reinforce Japanese formations in Southeast Asia.[18]

For the American airpower advocates, as the Allied nation closest to Japan, China appeared to be a logical base for a strategic bombing campaign against Japanese industry.[19] China was also considered as a possible route to the ultimate invasion of Japan, which military planners considered to be the only means of forcing Japan's surrender. A captured port on the China coast could potentially serve as the base for an invasion force.[20] With an eye to a possible

The Japanese swiftly established air superiority over the Philippines with heavy attacks on the main American Far East Air Force base at Clark Field and other installations. Many of the B-17s the United States had hoped would serve as a deterrent to Japanese aggression ended up wrecked on their airfields, as did this B-17D probably belonging to the 19th Bombardment Group. *From Koku Asahi via the author*

invasion of Japan, China's reserves of manpower seemed to hold considerable potential. Despite the many real inadequacies of the Chinese army, some planners thought that with proper training, American equipment, and possibly American leadership, an effective Chinese army could be built and brought to bear against Japan.[21]

There was a further political dimension to America's support for China. China's continued participation in the war against Japan as one of the four Allied powers was an effective counter to Japan's argument that this was a war to leave "Asia for the Asiatics," and Japan's sole mission was to rid Asia of the Western imperial powers.[22] What would drive Chinese-American relations over the next several years would be a clash in expectations and conflicting objectives. While the Americans sought to give China the resources to take an active role in the war against Japan, in reality Chiang Kai-shek's regime had only a limited ability to deal with the many intractable problems his government and military administration faced after four years of bitter warfare. Many Americans involved in China came to believe that Chiang's sole motivation was to accumulate and preserve these same resources to ensure the KMT's supremacy over its domestic rivals, prime among them the Chinese Communist Party.[23]

The first task facing the Allies was to determine where and how the war in the Far East fit into overall Allied strategy, and then to establish a structure of command for the direction of Allied forces. Shortly after the attack on Pearl Harbor, Chiang Kai-shek proposed that the Allies develop a plan for joint action against Japan.[24] President Roosevelt agreed and suggested conferences in Chungking and Singapore with British and American representatives to discuss proposals. The War Department appointed as its representatives Maj. Gen. George H. Brett, Army Air Force, who was then on a tour of the Far East examining the flow of Lend-Lease supplies and the possibility of basing American heavy bombers in China, and Maj. Gen. John Magruder, head of the American Military Mission to China.[25] At the Chungking conference on 17 and 23 December 1941, Chiang agreed to provide the American Volunteer Group and Chinese armies for the defense of Burma, while stressing the need for the Allies to establish air superiority over the Japanese from bases in Alaska and the coast of China.[26] The Singapore conference on December 18 and 20 among British, American, Australian, and Dutch representatives called for a single Allied commander with a combined staff to coordinate Allied operations against the Japanese.[27]

FORMATION AND EARLY OPERATIONS

Prior to taking up his position as commander of Allied air forces in ABDACOM, Air Chief Marshal Sir Richard Peirse (*center*) had commanded Royal Air Force Bomber Command. He would go on to become Air Officer Commanding, Royal Air Forces India, and subsequently Allied Air Commander in Chief, Southeast Asia Command, in 1943. *CI_000002, Imperial War Museum (IWM)*

Final decisions on strategy and command came out of the ARCADIA Conference held in Washington from 22 December 1941 to 14 January 1942, between President Roosevelt and the Joint Chiefs of Staff and Prime Minister Winston Churchill and the British Chiefs of Staff. The conference reaffirmed that American and British grand strategy in the war would be based on the defeat of Germany as the main objective of the Allied war effort.[28] Allied strategy against Japan would be defensive, to hold the Japanese advance and prepare bases for future operations. The Chiefs of Staff agreed that the Allies would attempt to hold the Malay Barrier (a line running from Malaya through the Netherlands East Indies) and hold Burma and Australia to support the Allied position in Southeast Asia. The defense of Burma was deemed essential to sustain the flow of supplies to China and for the defense of India as a base.[29] Overall Allied command would rest with the combined British and American Chiefs of Staff in a new, unified structure to be known as the Combined Chiefs of Staff, which combined the top Allied military leaders with a joint British and American Combined Planning Staff.[30] Following the principle of unity of command, the ARCADIA conference decided to set up a joint Allied command to coordinate the war in Southeast Asia as the Australian-British-Dutch-American Command (ABDACOM), with British Lt. Gen. Sir Archibald Wavell as Allied commander and Maj. Gen. George Brett as his deputy.[31] Maj. Gen. Lewis Brereton, commander of what were now the remnants of the American Far Eastern Air Forces in the Philippines, was appointed deputy chief of the air staff for ABDACOM under Air Chief Marshal Sir Richard Peirse, Royal Air Force.[32] ABDACOM was charged with defense of the Philippines, the Netherlands East Indies, Malaya and Singapore, and Burma with what limited resources the Allies could provide.[33]

With regard to China, Roosevelt and Churchill wanted to support China's continued resistance to Japan. Roosevelt particularly wanted some means of aiding the Generalissimo in his conduct of the war.[34] The Combined Chiefs of Staff recommended setting up a China theater command—similar to ABDACOM—to be responsible for all of China, Thailand, and French Indochina, with the Generalissimo as supreme commander.[35] The proposal was put to

Lt. Gen. Joseph Stilwell—shown here with Lt. Gen. Sun Li-jen, then commanding the 38th Chinese Division—became a controversial participant in the complex Allied command structure in Asia. Irascible, impatient for results, and often intolerant of those who did not agree with his position, he shouldered a heavy burden trying to implement American objectives for conducting the war against the Japanese in Asia. *SC274247, Record Group 111, US Army Signal Corps, NARA*

THE TENTH AIR FORCE IN WORLD WAR II

the Chinese, and in early January, Chiang Kai-shek agreed to become supreme commander of the China theater.[36] He asked Roosevelt to send a high-ranking American officer to serve as his chief of staff. There was some question within the War Department whether this officer would serve as the head of military mission, or whether there would also be a command component as part of an American theater of war.[37] Gen. George Marshall's first choice for the position, Lt. Gen. Hugh Drum, had reservations about these differing points of view, and this hesitation caused Drum to lose the support of Secretary of War Henry Stimson. Marshall then proposed a man he served with in China and at the Army's Infantry School: Maj. Gen. Joseph W. Stilwell. Stilwell was the only high-ranking American officer with extensive experience in China as an infantry commander and as military attaché from 1935 to 1939. Stilwell was no diplomat; his acerbic tongue had won him the nickname "Vinegar Joe," but Marshall valued his abilities as a tactician and trainer of troops—qualities he would need in China.[38] Having been designated as the commander of American forces for the planned invasion of North Africa, Stilwell now faced the most challenging assignment of his career. No doubt reluctant to give up a combat role, when Marshall asked him if he would go to China, Stilwell replied, "I'll go where I'm sent."[39]

The War Department's orders to Stilwell were broad in scope, and without much detail. He was to "increase the effectiveness of United States assistance to the Chinese Government for the prosecution of the war and to assist in improving the combat efficiency of the Chinese Army."[40] In addition to serving as the Generalissimo's chief of staff, Stilwell would also command all US Army forces in the China theater and in Burma and India.

Through discussions with War Department planners, Lend-Lease officials, and Chinese representatives in Washington, Stilwell began to formulate plans for his mission to China. To build up the effectiveness of the Chinese army, Stilwell focused on War Department plans to train and equip 30 Chinese divisions. Stilwell asked Marshall to approve shipping equipment for these divisions and to ensure that supplies for China would continue to be shipped from India—by air if necessary—and that sufficient transport aircraft be allocated for the task.[41] Promoted to lieutenant general, Stilwell left for China on 14 February 1942.

It was clear to many of the participants in the Allied conferences and Allied planning staffs at the time that American airpower would play a key role in supporting China's war effort and in prosecuting the war against Japan from China. China appeared to be an excellent base for the bombing of Japan. Even before the attack on Pearl Harbor, T. V. Soong, Chinese minister of foreign affairs, and William Pawley had begun recruiting for a second American Volunteer Group (AVG) that would be a bomber unit equipped with Lockheed Hudsons and Douglas A-20 light bombers.[42]

At the ARCADIA Conference, President Roosevelt had supported Lt. Gen. Henry "Hap" Arnold, commanding the Army Air Force, when he argued for the need to establish air bases in China for American bombers.[43] Once war with Japan had begun, American Army Air Force units could be stationed in China, and the War Department initiated steps to bring this about. The American Volunteer Group appeared to many to be the nucleus for an American Army Air Force presence in China. The AVG had been structured to get around American neutrality laws, but now that America was at war, the government and the War Department felt uncomfortable with a unit of Americans fighting as civilians—who would not be subject to the articles of war or military command—in the employ of a foreign government.[44] At the end of December, the War Department gave Maj. Gen. Magruder authority to establish American Army units in China and contemplated the induction of the American Volunteer Group into the Army Air Force as the 23rd Pursuit Group if Magruder could get Chiang Kai-shek's approval. These initial discussions came to nothing.[45]

When in early January the Generalissimo requested a senior American officer to serve as his chief of staff, T. V. Soong recommended that a high-ranking Army Air Force officer be appointed as well to organize air operations, apparently thinking of Claire Chennault.[46] Maj. Gen. Magruder apparently recommended Chennault to the War Department because of Chennault's experience and his close relationship with the Generalissimo.[47] However, on 23 January 1942, Assistant Secretary of War John McCloy informed Soong that Chiang's American chief of staff should have an officer with the rank of general as his air advisor, and that then Col. Clayton L. Bissell had been chosen for the post.[48]

Clayton Bissell was a long-serving officer who had joined the Army Air Service in World War I. He had flown Sopwith Camels with the 148th Aero Squadron in France, claiming six victories and winning the Distinguished Service Cross and a British Distinguished

A long-serving Army Air Corps officer, Clayton Bissell was a capable staff officer with broad administrative experience. Appointed as air advisor to Stilwell, Bissell would replace Brereton as commander of the Tenth Air Force after Brereton departed for the Middle East. Bissell soon found himself in conflict with Claire Chennault. Unfortunately, he and Chennault were unable to overcome their personal animosity stemming from their days as instructors at the Army Air Corps Tactical School in the early 1930s. *Author's collection*

FORMATION AND EARLY OPERATIONS

Flying Cross.[49] He remained in the Army after the war and during the interwar years acquired broad experience as a pursuit squadron and group commander and staff officer. He graduated from the Navy War College in 1939 and spent the next two years as a member of the War Plans Division in the War Department.[50]

While Bissell was an instructor at the Air Corps Tactical School in 1930–31, Claire Chennault had been one of Bissell's students, and the two men had some heated clashes that unfortunately had a long-lasting impact on their relationship. They had come into conflict over their differing views on pursuit tactics. Chennault was a forceful advocate for pursuit aircraft at a time when the senior leadership of the Army Air Corps was pushing the importance of strategic bombardment. From his experiences with Bissell at the Air Corps Tactical School, Chennault came to see him as overly focused on the rule book and the details of administration.[51] Chennault protested the appointment, believing that his command of the AVG, his long years in China, and his understanding of the air war against the Japanese made him the logical choice to be the senior American airman in the China theater.[52]

Stilwell, the War Department, and, importantly, Hap Arnold did not want the Chinese dictating who could or should be on Stilwell's staff. Arnold appreciated Bissell's qualities as a staff officer and his attention to detail. He overruled Chennault and told him to "play ball or else."[53] Chennault backed down, but his animosity toward Bissell remained. The tension between the two men would later affect the Tenth Air Force. Relations between Bissell and Chennault were not helped when Bissell was promoted to brigadier general on 21 April 1942—a day ahead of Chennault's promotion—to give him seniority over Chennault.[54]

The Tenth Air Force Is Activated

Having assigned a senior Army Air Force officer as Stilwell's air advisor, the War Department took the next step toward providing American airpower for China: creating an American air force for the China theater. Under President Roosevelt's direction, the Combined Chiefs of Staff approved the establishment of an American air force in India with the mission of conducting air operations in China.[55] There were few illusions about the difficulties involved in operating an American force in a British colony lacking almost all the requirements for supporting a modern air force that was 12,000 miles from the United States. In a memo to Arnold, the then Assistant Chief of the Air Staff, Col. Harold L. George, Air War Plans Division, outlined the challenges the new air force would face. The ability to organize and maintain the air force would depend, in George's view, on seven factors:

1. The ability of the Allies to hold satisfactory operating areas in India
2. The need to construct strategically located air bases that would provide effective air operations
3. The ability to provide the necessary logistical support services to these bases and the units operating from them
4. The need to provide necessary maintenance and local security forces
5. The necessity of maintaining sea communications between the United States and India
6. The need to provide the necessary amount of shipping to transport the supplies needed to sustain air operations
7. Integration of the US air force in India with other Allied military operations[56]

The reality of the situation in the Far East called all these factors into question. As George pointed out, India lacked the infrastructure a modern air force needed for operations. The military organization in India was, he noted, "critically deficient in supporting air forces and in the necessary air bases and services to support any air reinforcement dispatched to this theater. India has never been organized for major military operations of either an offensive or defensive character."[57] George's assessment was correct. During the interwar years Britain had invested little money for the Royal Air Force (RAF) in India. The RAF's orientation was to the northwest of India, where RAF squadrons had supported the Indian army in suppressing recalcitrant hill tribes during the interwar years.[58] In March 1942, there were a mere 16 all-weather airfields in all of India. The critical northeastern area of India, where bases for operations in support of China would have to be located, had very few airfields.[59] Moreover, the internal communications system needed to move supplies from ports in western India to the northeast was barely adequate in peacetime. The northeastern area of India had several large rivers with no bridges, a railway system with a different gauge from the rest of India, and few roads.[60] It was a depressing picture. In a letter to Air Chief Marshal Sir Charles Portal, Chief of the Air Staff, Air Chief Marshal Sir Richard Peirse, who had taken command of the Royal Air Force in India in March 1942, wrote this:

Everything in India is unbelievably primitive—the totally inadequate staff and complete lack of most things essential is quite devastating, and much of the personnel is past praying for—the government of India is an Alice in Wonderland hierarchy.[61]

As if the Indian infrastructure, or lack of it, was not problem enough, George was even more concerned with the ability of the Army Air Force to get supplies to India in adequate amounts to sustain air operations. "Our ability," he noted, "to maintain sea communications of sufficient tonnage to support operations in India is probably the most vital requirement involved in the planned air operations in India."[62] George stated emphatically: "If the required delivery of fuel, ammunition and supplies cannot be effected the entire plan collapses."[63] With the Battle of the Atlantic unabated and shipping losses increasing, this did not seem beyond the range of possibility in February 1942. George recommended sending 30 B-17s from the United States to supplement the 19 bombers then en route to India, but he argued for a logical progression in the deployment of an air force to India: build the necessary air bases, establish a reliable logistical supply service, move the ground echelon to the area, and when all was prepared, move the combat aircraft and crews.[64] George stated that there was seldom a military justification for deviating from this process, but in February 1942, the need to have an air force in India as soon as possible was just such an exception. With the Japanese rampaging throughout Southeast Asia, there wasn't time to build a solid foundation before deploying an American air force to support China.

With the forces of ABDACOM trying in vain to stem the Japanese advance, Maj. Gen. George Brett had also recognized the need for an American air force in India and China. By early February 1942 the Japanese had captured Malaya, had sealed the fate of the Philippines, and had seized strategic positions on Borneo and the Celebes in the

Robert Neale (*standing, right*) with fellow American Volunteer Group (AVG) pilots at Mingaladon airfield in early 1942. Neale commanded the AVG's 1st Pursuit Squadron and became the AVG's top-scoring pilot. The AVG's record against the Japanese provided one of the few bright spots in a season of disasters for the Allies. *CF_000027, IWM*

Netherlands East Indies. With the fall of Singapore on 15 February, the invasion of Java was imminent and the Allies had little means of stopping the Japanese.[65] Brett had proposed to the War Department that Burma, China, and Australia should be built up as bases to strike back at the Japanese.[66] On his own initiative, Brett sent the chief of staff of the Far East Air Force, Col. Francis M. Brady, to Burma on February 5 to survey airfields for heavy bombers.[67] Brady reported to Brett that heavy bombers could operate from the airfield at Akyab, on the Bay of Bengal, and could use the airfields at Magwe and Toungoo in Burma as advanced bases.[68] Brett informed Arnold that

A B-17E destroyed in the 20 February 1942 Japanese attack on the airfield at Singorsari on Java. Shortly thereafter, all Army Air Force bombers withdrew from Java to Australia. *7th Bombardment Group Historical Foundation, McDermott Special Collections Library, US Air Force Academy (USAFA)*

FORMATION AND EARLY OPERATIONS

he was making plans to divert B-17E bombers coming from the United States and flying across India on their way to Java to Akyab and to withdraw B-17s and maintenance personnel from Java and Australia to be sent to India as well.[69] To command this force, Brett proposed sending Maj. Gen. Lewis Brereton, who in addition to serving as deputy chief of air staff for ABDACOM commanded what remained of the Far East Air Force operating in Java.[70]

Taking command of an American air force in India would be the third challenging assignment Brereton had undertaken in as many months. Like Clayton Bissell—a veteran of the Army Air Service in France in World War I—Brereton had remained in the Army after the war and had gained extensive experience as a commander of bombardment units and in staff assignments.[71] While serving as commander of the Third Air Force in the United States, in October 1941 Brereton took command of the soon-to-be-established Far East Air Force in the Philippines, comprising the 5th Bomber Command and the 5th Interceptor Command.[72] Brereton arrived in the Philippines in early November.

As a deterrent to Japan, the War Department planned to base four heavy-bomber groups and two pursuit groups in the Philippines by April 1942; by the time of Brereton's arrival, only the 19th Bombardment Group had arrived with its 35 B-17s, with the 7th Bombardment Group preparing to leave the United States in early December.[73] On the morning of 8 December 1941, a Japanese attack destroyed 13 of these B-17s at Clark Field. Within 10 days the Japanese had established air superiority over the Philippines, and Gen. Douglas MacArthur had agreed to the withdrawal of the remaining B-17s.[74] Brereton continued to command the Far East Air Force in the defense of the Netherlands East Indies, but despite reinforcements from the United States, including B-17s and LB-30 bombers flown out to Java by squadrons of the 7th Bombardment Group, Allied forces could not stand up to Japan's carefully thought-out and brilliantly executed plan of conquest. At an ABDACOM commanders meeting on 8 February 1942, Brereton stated that because of losses and the inability to reinforce his bomber squadrons, who by this point had only 16 to 18 serviceable B-17s and LB-30s, he proposed withdrawing the Far East Air Force to Australia or Burma.[75] Brett, who had initially been critical of Brereton's pessimistic view of the situation, came to agree, and when Brereton received permission to withdraw the Far East Air Force from Java following the dissolution of ABDACOM on February 23, Brett ordered Brereton to India.[76]

Realizing that bombers operating from India, Burma, or China would need fighter cover for their bases, Brett decided to send the 51st Pursuit Group with its 16th, 25th, and 26th Fighter Squadrons to India, as well as the 51st Air Base Group and the Headquarters and Headquarters Squadron (HQ and HQ Squadron) of the 35th Pursuit Group.[77] At the same time, with the fall of Java now imminent, Brett ordered several Army Air Force ground echelons that had been en route to Java to join their units to go to India instead. These consisted of the HQ and HQ Squadron of the 7th Bombardment Group, the maintenance personnel of the 9th Bombardment Squadron, the 88th Reconnaissance Squadron, the 51st Air Base Group, and a number of other air service units; in all, these units totaled 146 officers and 2,870 enlisted men.[78] These units left Melbourne in three transports on February 12 for Java, carrying supplies of bombs and ammunition and 10 crated P-40s, in company with the USS *Langley*, with 32 P-40s on its deck, and the *Sea Witch*, carrying an additional 27 P-40s in its hold. The convoy made its way to Fremantle, on Australia's west coast, setting sail again on February 22. The three transports carrying Army Air Force personnel were directed to sail to India, but Gen. Wavell overruled Brett and ordered the *Langley* and the *Sea Witch* to Java, where the *Langley* was sunk on February 27.[79] The *Sea Witch* made it to Tjilatjp in Java to unload its P-40s, but they remained on the docks to be captured when the Japanese took the port, thus depriving American forces in India of badly needed fighters.[80]

The War Department rapidly took steps to organize and equip an air force for India and China. In early February the War Department informed the commanding general of the Army Air Force's Air Service Command that the Headquarters and Headquarters Squadron, Tenth Air Force, had been constituted. On 12 February 1942, HQ and HQ Squadron, Tenth Air Force, was activated at Patterson Field, Ohio, under the command of Col. Harry A. Halverson and temporarily assigned to the Air Force Combat Command prior to overseas embarkation.[81] It was intended that the Tenth Air Force would be assigned to India. On February 20, Col. Caleb V. Haynes—an experienced bomber pilot who had pioneered air routes across the Atlantic to Britain and from South America to the Middle East via Africa—received orders to organize the transfer of bomber aircraft to India for operations in China under the code name AQUILA, which also applied to the Tenth Air Force.[82] The next day, more-detailed instructions arrived for Haynes.

In a letter from Arnold, Haynes learned that he would command the heavy bombardment group to be assigned to the US Army Air Force in India, reporting to Maj. Gen. Lewis Brereton, now designated its commander.[83] Haynes's mission was to ensure the line of communications between India and China remained open and to prepare for operations from China at a later date. Until facilities in China were ready, Haynes was instructed to cooperate with British military authorities in India for operations. The forces available to him in India would be the Army Air Force ground elements diverted from Java to India.[84] Col. George prepared a memo for Arnold, summarizing these actions for Arnold's approval, noting the intention to establish an American air force in India with the ultimate purpose of conducting air operations in China; the objectives were building up a force of 50 heavy bombers under command of Col. Haynes, the movement of units from ABDACOM to India, and the assignment of the newly activated HQ and HQ Squadron, Tenth Air Force, to AQUILA.[85] One more important message went out from the War Department over the next few days. On February 25, Arnold sent Brereton a cable informing him that Stilwell would be appointed commander of all US Army forces in China, India, and Burma, and that Brereton would be designated commander of the US Army Air Force in India, with headquarters in Karachi. The cable added that HQ and HQ Squadron, Tenth Air Force, and the 3rd Air Depot Group were being transferred to his command.[86]

The new Tenth Air Force's first month was chaotic. Only a few of the men assigned to the new unit were at Patterson Field. By early March, 17 officers and 23 enlisted men had gathered in the corner of a hangar, using whatever equipment they could borrow, all under the command of Col. Harry Halverson, who was then organizing a project to fly 24 B-24D bombers to bomb Japan from bases in eastern China under the code name HALPRO.[87] Embarkation of the new unit couldn't wait until all assigned personnel—76 officers and 389 enlisted men—had gathered at Patterson Field. On March 8, the unit received orders to move to Charleston, South Carolina, their port of embarkation for India. Two days later, Maj. Walter Urbach replaced Col. Halverson and took command of HQ and HQ Squadron, Tenth Air Force. The 3rd Air Depot, with 62 officers and 869 enlisted men in the 3rd and 26th Depot Repair Squadrons and the 3rd Air Depot Supply Squadron, left its base in San Antonio, Texas, for Charleston. Both units scrambled to acquire men and equipment, drawing from HQ and HQ squadrons at Bolling Field and Savannah Air Base. Many men arrived with only the clothes they were wearing. Short of equipment and the last few personnel, the first units from the United States assigned to the Tenth Air Force set sail for Bombay, India, on 18 March 1942.[88]

Col. Haynes put out a call for volunteers to fly 13 heavy bombers to India—12 B-17Es and a single B-24D—via Africa. One of the men who did so was Col. Robert L. Scott Jr., a pursuit pilot who had never flown a B-17 before, but who flagrantly exaggerated his experience for the chance to fly to India to get into combat with a chance to bomb Japan.[89] Haynes's pilots set off from Florida toward the end of March, with Haynes piloting the single B-24D, flying down to Natal in Brazil and then across the South Atlantic to Africa, and from there to Karachi.[90] Col. Halverson was working up planes and crews for HALPRO. A third project was a plan to fly 33 Lockheed A-29 bombers for delivery to the Chinese air force under Lend-Lease, with the American crews remaining with the Tenth Air Force. It was also expected, at the time, that the 16 B-25s assigned to Lt. Col. James Doolittle's mission to bomb Japan from US Navy carriers would also go on to join the Tenth. Last, 35 C-47 transports would be sent out to India to ferry supplies to China. Col. Clayton Bissell, who left for China on February 22—eleven days after Stilwell's departure—had to coordinate these projects.[91] This was the beginning: a numbered air force, a commander, combat aircraft, and supporting units all underway to India. The road to victory would be long, hard, and not without frustration.

Brereton Takes Command

Brereton received permission from Gen. Marshall to withdraw the Far East Air Force from Java on February 22. After making arrangements for the evacuation of his staff, Brereton said goodbye to Gen. Wavell on February 24 and that evening boarded an LB-30 bomber from the 11th Bomb Squadron for the flight from Java to Colombo, in Ceylon.[92] He took with him several experienced officers from the Far East Air Force to serve in his new command. He chose Lt. Col. Emmett O' Donnell, FEAF operations officer, and, from the 19th Bomb Group, Maj. Cecil Combs, group commander, and Capts. Elmer Parsel, Donald Keiser, Earl Tash, and George Schaetzel; from the 7th Bomb Group came Maj. Conrad Necrason and Capts. William Bayse and Horace Wade.[93] Two days later, another LB-30 flew Gen. Wavell to Colombo, along with Brig. Gen. Earl Naiden, Brereton's chief of staff.[94] Having suffered two defeats at the hands of the Japanese, Brereton was not sorry to leave Java. As he recorded in his diary, "my desire for some time had been to give the Japs territory and get back where we could reorganize the striking forces, and I didn't much care whether it was India or Australia. Brett gave me my choice and I picked India, maybe because I was sick of islands, even one as big as Australia."[95]

The day after Wavell's arrival in Colombo, Brereton flew to New Delhi with Wavell and with ACM Peirse, who had also left Java to take command of the Royal Air Force in India. In his bedroll, Brereton carried a package of $250,000 in cash given to him by a young B-17 pilot that had been intended for ABDACOM; this money would help cover expenses for the Tenth Air Force in India.[96] There followed a hurried round of conferences in New Delhi and Calcutta—where Brereton met Stilwell for the first time—on the military situation in Burma. At these meetings Brereton insisted that he did not want to commit the Tenth Air Force in a piecemeal fashion as circumstances had forced the Far East Air Force to do in Java, but instead to build up a trained force with striking power.[97] Brereton then accompanied Gen. Wavell to Magwe in Burma for meetings with the commander of British forces in Burma, where Brereton learned that the military situation was dire.[98]

Burma was strategically important to the American objective of sustaining China's war effort, as well as vital to the defense of India. Burma was the last remaining connection between China

Rangoon was China's last lifeline to the Allied nations, supplying China with war material. Ships wait in the Rangoon River to offload supplies. Trucks carried the material up to Lashio to connect with the Burma Road to China. A major objective of the Japanese invasion of Burma was to cut this link in the hope of forcing China out of the war.
Author's collection

FORMATION AND EARLY OPERATIONS

Knowing its importance, the Japanese Army Air Force began bombing Rangoon on 23 December 1941. Here, Kawasaki Ki-48 Type 99 light bombers—later given the Allied code name "Lily"—from the 8th *Hikōsentai* (Air Regiment) are on their way to Burma. *Via the author*

and the outside world. Lend-Lease supplies and other war materials were offloaded at the port of Rangoon and shipped by truck north to Lashio to connect with the Burma Road. If this link was severed, China had no other means of obtaining these supplies. Two days after the attack on Pearl Harbor, Dr. Lauchlin Currie, an advisor to President Roosevelt who had been placed in charge of the Lend-Lease program for China, wrote a memo to the president, pointing out the strategic importance of Burma to the Japanese. If the Japanese could cut China's lifeline, it could lead to the end of Chinese resistance and free Japan from its China quagmire, providing hundreds of thousands of Japanese soldiers for service elsewhere.[99] In addition, the Japanese would gain access to Burma's resources of rice, oil, and other raw materials and a base to threaten the British position in India. For Britain and America, loss of Burma would present a host of problems, not least of which was the need to somehow resume the flow of supplies to China. The dilemma for the Allies was that there were precious few troops and airplanes available for Burma's defense. Burma had been low on the list of British priorities, and there had been no definitive plan for its defense prior to the attack on Pearl Harbor.[100] The British Air Ministry had determined that the aerial defense of Burma required six fighter squadrons, seven bomber squadrons, and two army cooperation squadrons, yet during

In one of the first instances in the Burma campaign of using aircraft to transport troops, the 7th Bombardment Group's B-17s flew 474 soldiers from the 1st Royal Inniskillen Fusiliers from India into Burma. *CF_000017, IWM*

THE TENTH AIR FORCE IN WORLD WAR II

the Burma campaign in early 1942 there were only one AVG squadron, three Royal Air Force fighter squadrons, three bomber squadrons, and two army cooperation squadrons in operation in Burma.[101]

Japan's Imperial General Headquarters had assigned responsibility for the invasion of Burma to the *15th Army*, comprising the *33rd* and *55th* divisions with air support from the *10th Hikōdan* (Air Brigade). After the fall of Manila on 5 January 1942, the *5th Hikōshidan* (Air Division) took over the air support role, bringing with it the *4th Hikōdan*.[102] The Japanese offensive against Burma began with air attacks on Rangoon, beginning on 23 December 1941 and continuing into January 1942, until heavy losses forced the *5th Hikōshidan* to abandon daylight raids.[103] The *15th Army* started its advance into Burma on 15 January 1942. Moving rapidly forward, the Japanese reached the Sittang River on February 24—the day Brereton left Java for Colombo—and once across the river were in reach of Rangoon. The British had hoped to stop the Japanese advance with more reinforcements but could not hold. On March 6, Gen. Sir Harold Alexander, who had arrived to take command of British forces in Burma the day before, realized that Rangoon had to be abandoned, and ordered his remaining troops to withdraw to the north, beginning a long retreat to India.[104]

There was little Brereton could do to support the British in their defense of Burma. The War Department planned an initial establishment for the Tenth Air Force of one heavy bombardment group and one pursuit group (as fighter groups were still then called), with required service units.[105] Personnel from the 7th Bomb Group and the 51st Pursuit Group were on their way from Australia, and Col. Haynes was gathering pilots and crews to fly more heavy bombers out to India, but when Brereton formally took command of the Tenth Air Force on 5 March 1942, he had available five B-17s that had been held back in India on their way to Java, two more B-17s that had flown in from Africa, one LB-30 that had flown him to Colombo, and ten crated P-40s coming in the convoy to Australia.[106] When a recently arrived British battalion (the 1st Royal Inniskillen Fusiliers) needed transportation to Burma from India, Brereton volunteered his heavy bombers to serve as transports.[107] From March 8 to 13, the B-17s and the single LB-30 flew in 474 troops and 29 tons of supplies from Asansol, outside Calcutta, to Magwe in Burma, evacuating 423 civilians on their return flights to India.[108]

Brereton decided to establish the headquarters of the Tenth Air Force in New Delhi to be close to Stilwell's offices and to his counterparts in the Royal Air Force and the government of India, whom he would depend on for much of the material he needed to build his air force. The day after he assumed command, he wrote a long letter to Arnold, laying out the challenges he faced and some of the steps he was taking to address them. Prime among his requirements was a directive on strategy: it was essential, he wrote Arnold, "that I receive as soon as possible the most complete plan as to what is intended by the United States in the way of air and ground forces in India for the next year."[109] Brereton had given Wavell and Peirse his conception of American strategy as offensive operations toward northeastern China and from there to Japan. With this as the primary mission, he determined that "it is necessary to establish an American direct line of communications by the most convenient and direct route from whatever base of debarkation is selected on the west coast to the northeast."[110] Brereton recognized that setting up an air ferry route from India to China would be enormously challenging, with the difficulty of getting fuel to the Assam area (where the air ferry service would likely be based), the shortage of airfields and the labor to build them, and the imminent onset of the monsoon in India. Although the British were initially reluctant to agree, Brereton wanted to develop Karachi as a major American base for receiving supplies and for operational training. And he wanted senior Army Air Force staff to assist him. Brereton had, he wrote, gone through severe campaigns without experienced and trained staff, to the detriment of operating efficiency. He asked Arnold for permission to appoint Brig. Gen. Naiden as his chief of staff and to assign Brig. Gen. Elmer Adler—then in the Middle East—to set up an air service command. In conclusion, Brereton told Arnold, "I am thoroughly confident that with the support I know will be forthcoming, that we have at last in the Far East the opportunity

The large dirigible hangar the British built at the airport outside Karachi. This became home to the first units of the Tenth Air Force to arrive in India. *7th Bombardment Group Historical Foundation, USAFA*

of developing direct air action in a vital direction against Japan. This is the opportunity I have been waiting for since December 8."[111]

The British agreed to allow the Americans to set up base facilities at Karachi. With the likely fall of Burma, the Japanese could threaten any shipping heading toward the port of Calcutta on India's east coast, making Karachi the safer option as a port for American transport ships. The drawback to Karachi was that it was 1,000 miles from northeastern India—the likely area for Tenth Air Force operations—but after inspecting facilities in Karachi and noting the number of ships waiting to unload at the port of Bombay, Brereton reaffirmed his decision to make Karachi his initial base of operations for setting up the Tenth Air Force.[112] The British provided areas for camps outside the city and facilities at the Karachi airport, including the giant hangar built for the R101 dirigible. The convoy from Australia arrived on 12 March 1942, bringing the first American units to reach the theater. The men disembarked two days later, with the HQ and HQ Squadron of the 51st Pursuit Group and the 25th Pursuit Squadron joining the 51st Air Base Group and the 7th Bombardment Group's HQ and HQ Squadron and 9th Bombardment Squadron at the Karachi airport, where they were assigned quarters in the dirigible hangar, while the 26th and 16th Pursuit Squadrons and the 88th Reconnaissance Squadron went to camps nearby.[113] On the way, the men encountered new sights, sounds, and smells, and a mass of people and vehicles they likened to a circus.[114]

For the rest of the month the men of the 7th Bomb Group and the 51st Pursuit Group worked to get organized and prepared for combat. They set up a new tent camp west of the dirigible hangar and brought the squadrons of the two groups together. Over the next several weeks the facilities improved gradually, with floors added to the tents, showers built, messes arranged, and kitchens, offices, and supply rooms built from airplane packing crates.[115] In addition to the ten crated P-40s, the convoy from Australia had carried with it 4,503 bombs of various sizes and 405,000 rounds of .50-caliber and 600,000 rounds of .30-caliber ammunition, but only 50 vehicles of various kinds—far fewer than needed.[116] Diligent searching and reverse Lend-Lease helped make up for these and other shortages. Sources in the Karachi area came up with 102 sedans for the AAF units at the air base, while 172 truck chassis turned up in Bombay; shipped to Karachi, they were fitted out with wooden truck beds and cabs made in the city of Lahore and sent down to Karachi.[117] With this mismatched collection of vehicles, men from the 7th and 51st Groups made repeated trips to the Karachi docks to bring supplies and equipment back to the airfield.

The 7th Bomb Group received new commanding officers from the men Brereton had brought with him from Java. On 15 March 1942, Maj. Cecil Combs, who had flown with the 19th Bomb Group in Java, became commander of the group. Two other 19th Bomb Group veterans were assigned to the group that same date: Capt. Donald Keiser taking over the 9th Bomb Squadron and Capt. William Bayse the 88th Reconnaissance Squadron.[118] After completing the transfer of the Royal Inniskilling Fusiliers into Burma, the B-17Es that had been used to transport the troops flew to Karachi for assignment to the 7th Bomb Group.[119] This gave the group eight B-17s and the one LB-30, enabling a training program to begin for pilots and crews. More B-17s did not arrive from the United States until the end of the month. Then in April the bombers transferred under Col. Haynes's command began to arrive, with Haynes bringing his B-24D into Karachi on 7 April 1942.[120] In the days that followed, five B-17s and five C-47s arrived in Karachi, with the bombers going to the 7th Bomb Group. More B-17s would follow in May. Maintenance crews found that sand and dust blown in from the Sindh desert around Karachi made it difficult to keep the airplanes in commission.[121] The HALPRO Project was still in the process of formation, delaying the arrival of its bombers to the theater.

After their arrival the men of the 51st Group helped move their crated P-40s from the port of Karachi to the dirigible hangar, where they set up a production line to assemble the aircraft. The first assembled P-40 flew on March 19, and by the end of the month the group had all ten of its P-40s in operation. Group Commander Lt. Col. Homer Sanders started an intensive flying training course for the group's pilots, who had not flown for several months.[122] Sadly, on 1 April 1942, 2nd Lt. George Chipman from the 16th Fighter Squadron became the first Tenth Air Force pilot to be killed, when his P-40 failed to pull out of a dive during practice at a gunnery

The men of the 7th Bomb Group and the 51st Fighter Group set up temporary living quarters inside the dirigible hangar near the assembly line for Lend-Lease aircraft for China. Note the Vultee P-66s Vanguard undergoing assembly in the background. *Historical Record and Activities of US Army Air Forces in Area of Karachi, India, Book I, Miscellaneous, March 1942 to December 31, 1942, 828.08, AFHRA*

Shortly after their arrival, the 51st Fighter Group began assembling the P-40s that had come from Australia. Karachi became the receiving and assembly point for more P-40s sent out from the United States. The P-40K-1 shown in the foreground lasted until 30 June 1943. *Historical Record and Activities of US Army Air Forces in Area of Karachi, India, Book I, Miscellaneous, March 1942 to December 31, 1942, 828.08, AFHRA*

Short of nearly everything, the men assigned to units in the Karachi area made use of whatever materials came to hand. Wood from the packing crates used to ship P-40 fighters to India went to building offices, mess halls, and even clubs, as shown here, named after the famous Stork Club in New York City. *Historical Record and Activities of US Army Air Forces in Area of Karachi, India, Book I, Miscellaneous, March 1942 to December 31, 1942, 828.08, AFHRA*

range set up east of Karachi Air Base. By the end of April only five P-40s were serviceable.[123] More P-40s for the Tenth Air Force arrived a few months later, when Lt. Col. John Barr led a group of 68 P-40Es from the United States to Karachi as Project 157. Traveling on the USS *Ranger* to Africa, the P-40s flew across the African continent to Karachi, losing nearly 18 airplanes along the way to damage and maintenance problems. Twenty-eight airplanes arrived in Karachi during May, with another 22 P-40s apparently arriving later in June. Many of the pilots joined the 51st Group.[124] In his report to Brereton, Barr noted that one of his difficulties was theft on route. "Theft of tools, parts off airplanes and personal belongings," he wrote, "was atrocious—I personally so lost three separate Allison engine kits, two screwdrivers, two pairs pliers, and throat microphones aside from all my cigarettes, toilet articles, and a large portion of my clothes."[125] Pilferage along the ferry route from the United States to India was a problem that would plague the Tenth Air Force for months to come. The AVG had priority for the P-40s, so most from Barr's delivery flight went on to China. The redesignated 51st Fighter Group (all Army Air Force pursuit groups were redesignated fighter groups in May 1942) did receive thirteen more P-40s in June.[126]

Brereton had a challenging time trying to get his new command prepared for combat in the face of shortages of men and equipment, a lack of adequate base facilities, conflicts over command and strategy, and the relentless Japanese advance through Burma. In preparing his command, Brereton drew on what he had learned from his experiences in the Philippines and Java, lessons learned in war that he summarized in a long cable to Arnold at the end of March.[127] The principal lesson he had learned was that all operations in war—in the air, on the ground, or at sea—depended on establishing and maintaining air superiority. This required unrelenting operations against an enemy air force in the air and on the ground. Brereton believed that the Army Air Force's tactics were generally sound; the problem was execution. Proper execution depended, in turn, on two areas: properly trained air crews and adequate equipment. The Japanese attack had caught the Army Air Force unprepared. Brereton had witnessed how difficult it was to get results when untrained pilots and crews were thrown into combat. He now recommended that crews not be sent out from the United States until they were thoroughly trained in pilotage, gunnery, and bombardment and were familiar with their equipment. Variations in tactics and techniques could be taught once crews were in the theater.[128] Brereton appointed newly promoted Brig. Gen. Francis Brady to command and build an operational training center at Karachi; this later became the Karachi American Air Base Command.[129]

With regard to equipment, Brereton wanted a fighter that would be superior to current and future Japanese aircraft. Brereton noted in his long cable that while the P-40 had a faster dive and top speed than Japanese fighters, the Japanese airplanes had a better rate of climb and a higher operating altitude. He also wanted P-38s for photoreconnaissance—vitally important for strategic-bombing operations to identify targets and document damage after bombing raids. And instead of more heavy bombers, he wanted medium bombers assigned to the theater. Brereton recognized that weather conditions over Burma and China often made high-altitude bombing ineffective and difficult to sustain. There were few truly strategic targets in the area, but many interdiction and counterair targets suitable for medium bombers. In addition, his P-40 fighters did not have the range to escort B-17s on longer-range missions. If bombing missions had to be conducted by night, better to use faster medium bombers to reduce the risk of interception.[130]

A Gurkha soldier stands guard next to a Tenth Air Force B-17E. Maj. Gen. Lewis Brereton, commanding the Tenth Air Force, decided to convert the 7th Bomb Group into a composite group with two squadrons of B-17 heavy bombers and two squadrons of B-25 medium bombers. *3A-37372, RG342FH, NARA*

FORMATION AND EARLY OPERATIONS

During March, Brereton made several requests for medium bombers and photoreconnaissance P-38s.[131] In early April the Joint Chiefs of Staff agreed to allocate 30 B-25 Mitchell bombers to the Tenth Air Force. Five were already underway, and the War Department authorized 10 more to leave in the first half of April, with a further 15 to depart the US during May and early June, as well as one P-38 photoreconnaissance squadron.[132] Later in April, Brereton received permission to convert the 7th Bomb Group into a composite group of two heavy and two medium-bomber squadrons. When the 7th Group transferred to India it left two of its component squadrons, the 11th and 22nd Bomb Squadrons, in Australia. On 26 April 1942, the War Department activated the 11th Bombardment Squadron (M) and the 22nd Bombardment Squadron (M) at Columbia Army Air Base in South Carolina.[133] In the middle of April, crews and airplanes arrived at the base, where they joined the 17th Bombardment Group (Medium) for training. On 1 May 1942, the first B-25s left the United States for the long flight across the South Atlantic to Africa, then to Egypt and on to Karachi, overloaded with extra parts and equipment. More followed at intervals as part of Project 157, helping to escort flights of P-40s along the way. Although several airplanes were lost in transit, by the end of May, 18 B-25s had reached Karachi, though the ground echelons of the two squadrons would not arrive until late July.[134]

There was much more that needed to be done to build a foundation for the Tenth Air Force. The Tenth needed airfields in eastern India, especially in Assam, for operations into Burma and China. While American forces in India could obtain what was needed through reverse Lend-Lease—the supply of materials or services to the United States—the British colonial administration in India had responsibility for organizing construction and providing materials, labor, and engineering staff, with support from the British army engineer units. American needs were considerable. At a March 15 meeting of the Administrative Planning Committee Brereton had organized, Brig. Gen. Naiden told his RAF counterparts that the Tenth Air Force expected to have one pursuit group and four bomb groups in India by the end of 1942, and that the Tenth had requested three more pursuit groups.[135] These groups would require all-weather runways, and the bomber groups would need concrete runways to take the weight of heavy bombers (requiring 9,000 tons of concrete per airfield), as well as taxiways, hardstands, and accommodation for up to 2,000 men in each group.[136] In addition, for the air ferry route to China then under discussion, the Tenth would need three all-weather airfields in the Dinjan area in Assam—the British were preparing the existing airfields at Dinjan and Chabua for this, but a third would be needed nearby—plus three airfields around Myitkyina in Burma (at the time still under British control) as staging grounds for the route to China.[137] The Tenth would also need airfields in other areas of India for repair and maintenance and for operational training, and all these airfields would have to be linked to the Indian rail and road system to bring in fuel and supplies. Balancing the competing demands of British and American forces was a challenge. The British army was in desperate need of all-weather roads into Assam to move supplies for the defense of India, while the Royal Air Force was planning to build 215 airfields in India to support its own expansion.[138] Brereton was frustrated with the pace at which the problem of airfields was being addressed, complaining to Wavell about the lack of progress in developing airfields for the Tenth, blaming "the inertia of the Indian Government in the construction of aerodromes."[139]

To sustain air operations, the Tenth Air Force needed its own Air Service Command, paralleling the structure of the Army Air Force commands. The US Army had established the Services of Supply command for the China theater at Karachi under Maj. Gen. Raymond Wheeler in March to oversee supply of Lend-Lease material to China and supplies to all US Army units in India and China, and Army Air Force units as needed.[140] Brig. Gen. Adler arrived on 26 April 1942 and activated the Tenth Air Service Command on May 1, consisting of himself and two staff officers.[141] In late May the 3rd Air Depot Group arrived in Karachi after the two-month ocean voyage from the United States and moved to Agra, in India, the site chosen as the main base for the Air Service Command. The new command drew personnel from other units already in Karachi to set up operating units at Dinjan and Chabua, at Bangalore, and at Kunming for maintenance and repair and distribution of supplies. The Tenth Air Force negotiated a contract with the Hindustan Aircraft Ltd. plant in Bangalore—then assembling aircraft for the Chinese air force and for the RAF—to overhaul American aircraft and aircraft engines, manufacture spare parts, and build metal drop tanks for P-40s.[142]

The Tenth was far from ready—short of aircraft, trained crews, supplies, and personnel at every level—but when Stilwell asked Brereton at a meeting on March 24 when his force could begin operations, Brereton said that depending on the arrival of more aircraft, his heavy bombers would be ready on May 1.[143] Discussing the War Department's plans to bomb Japan from bases in China, Stilwell commented, "What the hell are we doing trying to go to Japan to bomb when we have a war on our hands right here?"; Brereton agreed that the priority should be to support Allied operations in Burma.[144] Brereton still hoped to obtain many more aircraft for his command. Following the Japanese attack on the Royal Navy base at Colombo, in Ceylon, Brereton cabled Washington to ask the War Department for two more pursuit groups, two heavy bomb groups, a medium bomb group, and three squadrons of P-38 reconnaissance aircraft with supporting antiaircraft and aviation engineer units, and 80 P-39Fs.[145] He wanted to use one bomb group and one pursuit group to protect the Dinjan area and for offensive operations into Burma, one bomb group and one pursuit group for the Myitkyina-Bhamo-Loiwing area, and one bomb group and one pursuit group for operations in the Bay of Bengal and against Japanese shipping in Rangoon.[146] Gen. Marshall replied a few days later, telling Brereton he would have to make do with what he had already been allocated: one pursuit group with 80 pursuits, one composite bomb group with the two heavy and two medium bomb squadrons, and one photoreconnaissance squadron. Marshall indicated that the number of medium bombers assigned to the Tenth would be gradually increased to 57 from 30, but Brereton could expect no more heavy bombers beyond what had already been promised, nor any more pursuits. Marshall stated clearly that the medium-bomber squadrons and the P-38 reconnaissance squadron were "contemplated as the maximum reinforcements for the 10th Air Force.... Additional pursuit units for the 10th Air Force are unable to be furnished."[147]

Early Operations

Brereton had hoped for more time to prepare his crews and gain more aircraft for his command, but time was running out. The military situation in Burma was deteriorating rapidly, despite the efforts of the Allies to halt the Japanese advance. Following the loss of Rangoon and the withdrawal of British army units to the north,

A burned-out Hawker Hurricane IIb at the airfield at Moulmein, with a damaged Lockheed Hudson in the background. Japanese air attacks severely damaged the RAF squadrons operating in Burma, forcing them back to India. *Via the author*

the Japanese *15th Army* had kept up a relentless pursuit against the retreating British forces and the Chinese 5th and 6th Armies that Chiang Kai-shek had sent to Burma to help defend the Burma Road. The Japanese brought in more reinforcements of troops and aircraft, with the *5th Hikōshidan* gaining two more air brigades—the *7th* and *12th Hikōdan* from Malaya and the Netherlands East Indies— bringing Japanese Army Air Force strength in Burma to around 420 aircraft.[148] On March 21–22, the Japanese raided the RAF base at Magwe, where the RAF's BURWING had No. 17 Squadron, with 16 Hurricane II fighters; No. 45 Squadron, with 20 Blenheim IV bombers; a flight of three Lysanders; and the 3rd Pursuit Squadron of the AVG, with six serviceable P-40Bs.[149] In successive raids the Japanese smashed what remained of Allied airpower in Burma, destroying nine Blenheims, three Hurricanes, and three P-40s and leaving the remaining aircraft unserviceable.[150] The RAF withdrew its remaining aircraft temporarily to Akyab while the three AVG P-40Bs flew to Loiwing. British and Chinese forces were now without air support, and the *5th Hikōshidan* had complete control of the skies over Burma.

Japanese forces captured the Andaman Islands in the Bay of Bengal on 23 March 1942. That same day the RAF base at Akyab came under heavy attack, continuing the next day; the destruction caused the RAF to abandon Akyab on March 27 and withdraw back to Calcutta.[151] Wavell was now extremely anxious about the risk of a Japanese air offensive against Calcutta, as well as threats to other parts of India, and asked the Air Ministry in London to sound out the War Department's willingness to allow him to use Brereton's few B-17s to supplement his own meager bombers and to urgently send more heavy bombers to India.[152] In Washington, Air Marshal DCS Evill went to see Arnold on March 28 to ask what the US could do to strengthen the bomber force in India, and to confirm that Brereton had the authority to use his B-17s in support of the defense of India, which Arnold did.[153] Evill communicated his understanding to the Air Ministry, which informed Wavell and Peirse that while Stilwell's orders were to move his air forces to China as soon as possible for operations against Japan, until this was possible he was authorized to employ the Tenth Air Force in support of Wavell.[154]

An aerial reconnaissance photograph of Port Blair, in the Andaman Islands in the Bay of Bengal. From the Andamans the Imperial Japanese Navy could threaten the vital port of Calcutta and shipping along the east coast of India. *Historical Record and Activities of US Army Air Forces in Area of Karachi, India, Book I, Miscellaneous, March 1942 to December 31, 1942, 828.08, AFHRA*

FORMATION AND EARLY OPERATIONS

At a meeting with Wavell on March 27, Brereton learned that RAF reconnaissance airplanes had found that Japanese naval vessels and transports were being brought in to Port Blair, in the Andaman Islands, and to Rangoon. Wavell believed there was a strong possibility of a Japanese attack on Colombo (in Ceylon) or on Calcutta.[155] Knowing that no RAF bombers had the range to reach Port Blair or Rangoon with a decent load of bombs, Brereton responded positively to a query from Wavell and decided to use the 9th Bomb Squadron's few available heavy bombers—amounting to nine B-17Es—to attack Port Blair and Rangoon.[156] Lt. Col. O'Donnell (Brereton's G-3) drew up a plan to have the 9th Bomb Squadron use the RAF airfield at Asansol, 100 miles northwest of Calcutta, as a base for attacks on three successive nights—night attacks being deemed to present the least risk.[157] The bombers would carry four 500 lb bombs and one bomb bay tank for the 1,600-mile trip to Port Blair and back, attacking in two flights of six aircraft. Brereton decided the attack would be made on the night of April 2, with a simultaneous attack on shipping at Rangoon.[158]

The six B-17s assigned to the Port Blair attack took off from Dum-Dum airfield at 21:50 on the night of April 2 into a moonlit sky. Maj. Cecil Combs led the mission, with Brereton as his copilot. Brereton described the mission in his diary:

At 3:30, as we neared the northwest shore of the Andaman Islands, I took my post as co-pilot. Watch stations or shipping had reported our approach because an occasional searchlight flash could be seen from 50 miles distant. We were to bomb at 3,000 feet, and as we lost height to meet the altitude, the main details of the harbor could be seen clearly. Inside the harbor were five large ships, transports, large freighters, or naval ships. In the shadow near the shore were a number of smaller craft, probably destroyers. We approached from the east in order to get a good silhouette target against the moon and to avoid presenting a target for the antiaircraft gunners.

Passing over the harbor mouth we spotted a large ship heading out to sea. Our target showed beautifully in the moon path, but unfortunately we had turned too short and the bombardier, Lt. Bruno Delmissier, reported the sighting run too short. The antiaircraft guns on shore opened up and the rear gunner reported enemy fighters on our port quarter. We turned north to make another run. This time, as we turned into our approach, the bombardier reported "on the target" and as we came closer the decks, turrets, and guns of the cruiser could be seen clearly. As the ship passed out of view beneath the cockpit a glare flared from under and Lt. Delmissier scrambled up to the cockpit hatch, grinning, and shouted, "Direct hits, sir!" We landed at Asansol at 11:40 AM on Good Friday, April 3.[159]

The other bombers in the attack claimed a hit on a transport and near misses against several other ships in the harbor.[160] The antiaircraft fire damaged two of the B-17s. Unfortunately the mission to Rangoon was unsuccessful. On takeoff, Capt. Elmer Parsel's B-17 hit a large tree stump, tearing off the elevator. The plane climbed to 100 feet before plunging into the ground, killing the entire crew and Maj. Norman Lewellyn—Brereton's aide—who had insisted on going on the mission. The second B-17 assigned to the mission developed mechanical problems and had to return to base. The 9th Bomb Squadron tried again the next night, and this time six B-17s made it to Rangoon, dropping bombs and incendiaries in the dock area, with one bomber failing to return.[161] The *New York Times* reported that American planes based in India had made "a smashing attack on Rangoon," setting off three large fires, but in reality six bombers bombing at night could do little damage.[162]

While this first American bombing mission against the Japanese was good for morale, Stilwell was not pleased. Having directed Brereton to put priority on attacking targets in Burma, particularly against the Japanese Army Air Force, Stilwell was angered to learn of the mission to bomb shipping at Port Blair.[163] He sent a message

Lewis Brereton awards decorations to the men of the 7th Bomb Group who participated in the raid on Port Blair on the night of 2 April 1942. *3A-34310, RG342FH, NARA*

to Brereton that said: "Much surprised at Reuters report of action by B-17s near the Andaman Islands. At the Maymyo meeting March 24 you assured me that the Tenth Air Force could not be ready for one month and I indicated to you priority for its use. If the Tenth Air Force is prepared to operate I want to know it so that its action can be coordinated with the critical ground operations in this theater. Report at once the present capabilities of the Tenth Air Force and possibility of its use against hostile aviation in Burma."[164] When Brereton explained the constraints he was working under—his lack of bombers and trained crews and the lack of fighters for escort all contributing to his inability to undertake daylight missions, and that his actions were in accord with directions from Washington—Stilwell was mollified.[165] Soon after, following a further British inquiry to determine if Brereton had the authority to use his heavy bombers in the defense of India, Arnold replied that because of the critical situation in Burma and the threat of Japanese naval attacks on India, Brereton had been authorized to use his force, under British direction, over the Bay of Bengal from Ceylon to Calcutta, and that Stilwell had been so informed.[166] Still unsure of where he stood, Brereton cabled Arnold on April 23, saying he had received no direct instructions to cooperate with the British either from Stilwell or the War Department.[167] In reply, Brereton was told that he was to cooperate with the British as requested, though Stilwell complained that these instructions were given without reference to him as theater commander.[168] Concerned with the possible Chinese reaction to the apparent diversion of American air forces to supporting the British, Stilwell insisted that control of the Tenth Air Force should remain with him and not be transferred to the British command in India. In a cable to the War Department, Stilwell said, "It is imperative that command and final decision relative to use of American air forces not—repeat, *not*—be passed to the British but remain with me."[169] Stilwell informed Brereton that the Tenth Air Force could operate in cooperation with the British in the areas the War Department had designated, pending further orders.[170] With the threat of Japanese naval attacks on India or elsewhere diminishing after the Battle of the Coral Sea, Marshall informed Stilwell on May 24 that he was rescinding the order for the Tenth Air Force to cooperate with the RAF for the defense of India, telling him that operations of the Tenth Air Force in India, Burma, and China were "completely at your discretion."[171] Questions over the Tenth Air Force's mission and priorities between operations in support of China and the defense of India would remain an issue for months to come.

The 9th Bomb Squadron did not fly another mission into Burma until April 16. That night, six B-17s were assigned to bomb shipping on the Irrawaddy River at Rangoon. Only three aircraft made it off from Dum-Dum airport near Calcutta without problems, with Maj. Donald Keiser, commanding the 9th Bomb Squadron, leading Maj. Edward Carmack and Lt. Col. Robert Tate. The bombers were to go in at low altitude—between 3,500 and 4,000 feet—dropping flares to illuminate the target area, with Maj. Keiser going in first. Keiser dropped his flares south of the city, thinking he was over Rangoon. This alerted the antiaircraft guns and searchlights. Carmack dropped his flares over the Irrawaddy River, near the dock area, but could find no ships; he dropped his 14 250-pound bombs on the docks without seeing the result. Col. Tate also mistook another area for Rangoon and dropped four flares, only to find nothing below him. Realizing his error, Tate flew to the mouth of the Irrawaddy and turned north to follow the river up to Rangoon. He dropped four more flares but saw no ships on the river. The searchlights picked out his airplane, so he headed to the northwest to avoid them. Turning around, he came in again from the northwest and went back to bomb the dock area, dropping 14 300-pound bombs despite searchlights blinding the bombardier and the pilot. With bombs gone, the three airplanes turned for home.[172]

After this mission Maj. Combs pulled his bombers and crews back to Karachi for two weeks of intensive training, concentrating on high-altitude formation flying, bombing, gunnery, and night landings, with extra ground school classes for combat crews.[173] Long reconnaissance flights out over the Arabian Sea searching for Japanese submarines provided additional training for some of the newer crews who arrived from the United States during April. In the middle

Ground crew at the RAF base at Asansol, India, preparing a 7th Bomb Group B-17E for a raid into Burma. Note the RAF Blenheim light bomber across the way. At the time, the Blenheim was the only RAF bomber available to RAF India. *7th Bombardment Group Historical Foundation, USAFA*

FORMATION AND EARLY OPERATIONS

In April 1942, several more B-17s and crews arrived in India for the 7th Bomb Group. 2nd Lt. Harry Burkhart stands near a later model B-17E equipped with the Sperry ball turret. *Author's collection*

of the month, five more B-17s arrived from Project Aquila and went to the 7th Bomb Group.[174] To comply with the reconfiguration of the 7th Bomb Group into two heavy-bomber squadrons and two medium-bomber squadrons, on April 22 the 88th Reconnaissance Squadron received a new designation, becoming the 436th Bombardment Squadron (H).[175] To ease the burden of operating missions out of Karachi, that same day the ground echelon of the 9th Bomb Squadron left for a new base at Allahabad, 456 miles west of Calcutta, with the air crews and available B-17s following five days later.[176] From Allahabad, the B-17s would fly to Dum-Dum airport at Calcutta to refuel before going off on missions into Burma.

Operations began again at the end of April, when a single B-17E made a daylight attack against shipping at Rangoon on April 29, with another B-17E undertaking a night attack on the same target the day after.[177] The B-17s, with their greater range, concentrated on targets in and around Rangoon, while the shorter-range RAF Blenheim, Hudson, and Wellington bombers went after the recently captured Japanese airfields at Magwe and Akyab and rivercraft carrying supplies to the advancing Japanese armies.[178] Getting enough serviceable B-17s was a problem. One B-17E flew a daylight mission to the Rangoon docks on May 1, but of the three B-17s scheduled for a mission on the night of May 2, only one made it to the target. One bomber couldn't take off due to engine trouble, and a second had to return after two hours for the same reason. The sole bomber that reached the target found 15 ships in the river alongside the dock area but couldn't see the ships clearly through the bombsight, dropping six 500-pound bombs on the docks instead.[179] Another night mission to the Rangoon docks followed, with two B-17s reaching the target, then the 9th Bomb Squadron switched to attacks on the airfield at Mingaladon, outside Rangoon. On the night of May 5, two flights of two B-17s bombed the airfield, claiming hits on a hangar and aircraft parked nearby and reporting an estimated 40 aircraft destroyed and 25 more damaged, but the Japanese reported no losses on this date.[180] Three B-17s returned to Mingaladon the next night, starting fires around the airfield. Several Japanese fighters attacked Lt. Long's B-17 after he made his bomb run at 10,000 feet, putting 11 holes in his ship to add to damage from antiaircraft fire.[181] On the night of May 8, the 9th Bomb Squadron sent out six B-17s. Five bombed the Rangoon dock area without observing any results, while a single B-17 bombed Mingaladon again.[182]

Events then forced a change in target. On May 8 the Japanese captured the important airfield at Myitkyina, a staging field for the ferry flights to China. Myitkyina's capture brought Japanese fighter planes within range of the airfield at Dinjan, the base for the flights to China. Six B-17s took off from Dum-Dum airfield on May 12 for a predawn attack on the Myitkyina airfield. Two had to turn back due to engine trouble, and the formation of four had to separate due to thunderstorms in the area, bombing the target individually. The planes dropped 40 300-pound bombs and observed hits on the runway and among several airplanes parked alongside.[183] Four B-17s went to Myitkyina two days later, bombing from 24,000 feet in clear weather. They dropped 40 100-pound bombs and 20 300-pound bombs, most of which fell in the target area across the runway and among some of the 28 fighters and two bombers parked on the field. Four more B-17s went out again on May 16, but an overcast covering the airfield made it difficult to observe results.[184]

More B-17s for the Tenth Air Force arrived during May, bringing the total up to 20 aircraft, but serviceability and a lack of trained crews continued to limit the number of bombers available for missions. On May 30, out of 19 B-17s in India only five were serviceable: two in Karachi and three at Allahabad.[185] B-25s also arrived with the air echelons of the 11th and 22nd Bomb Squadrons. The 11th Bomb Squadron prepared to move to China, drawing crews from the 22nd to bring it up to full strength, while the remaining crews of the 22nd went temporarily to the HQ and HQ Squadron of the 7th Bomb Group for coastal patrols and reconnaissance missions into Burma.[186] After a delay of nine days, four B-17s returned to the Rangoon dock area on the night of May 25, dropping bombs on barges in the Irrawaddy River and the dock area, without observing the results due to haze. Later that same night, two out of three B-17s sent off bombed Mingaladon airfield, starting several fires. The bombers went back to Myitkyina, with four B-17s attacking during the afternoon of May 29 and three more making a morning attack the next day. A B-25 from the 22nd Bomb Squadron undertook a reconnaissance of the Rangoon area on May 31—possibly the first B-25 mission in the theater. The crew found nine ships—transports or tankers—on the Irrawaddy River, with six in the river and three at the docks. That night (different sources put this mission on May 31 or June 1), five B-17s went after the six ships in the river, dropping 15 500-pound bombs from 10,000 feet in two bombing runs. On the first run the crews saw bombs hit near what they identified as a tanker, with steam escaping from the ship. On their second run they observed the ship listing. This may have been the *Kofuku Maru*, which was lost to American aircraft on this date in this area. Japanese fighters came up after the bombers but did no damage.[187]

Six 500-pound bombs waiting to be loaded onto a 7th Bomb Group B-17E for a mission over Rangoon in early June 1942. The onset of the monsoon in the middle of the month halted bombing operations. *7th Bombardment Group Historical Foundation, USAFA*

A mission to Rangoon scheduled for June 2 had to be called off when two out of the three B-17s developed engine trouble before taking off from Allahabad. The next day's attempt had to be called off because of bad weather.[188] Two B-17s went back to Rangoon on June 4 for a daylight attack on shipping but bombed without result. Unfortunately they ran into Japanese fighters. The Type 1 fighters (Ki-43 Oscar) of the *64th Hikōsentai* took off from Mingaladon to intercept the two B-17s, making repeated attacks on the bombers before they reached cloud cover.[189] As the B-17s flew back to India, Type 97 fighters (Ki-27 Nate) from the *77th Hikōsentai*, flying out of Magwe, intercepted the bombers. Lt. Junichi Ogata claimed one of the B-17s shot down.[190] Capt. Frank Sharp was flying the B-17 that came under attack. After making two runs on two freighters in the river, Sharp turned his B-17 to make his getaway when the Japanese fighters intercepted his airplane. As he recalled later:

Jap fighters now swarmed up. They hovered around on the edge of the ack-ack, waiting for us. We came out of the cloud, trying to climb back into the overcast. They jumped us. The first attack got my number 3 engine. Oil from it spewed back, covering up the ball turret so that the gunner couldn't see, and put it out of action. The next attack got my number 4 engine. It began going out. We had to salvo the last three bombs. Then the doors were hit and wouldn't close. There we were, with only two good engines and bomb bay doors open! We couldn't climb. I stuck the nose down to pick up speed. I saw a low overcast ahead and made for it.

Our side gunner, Teehan, was killed by an explosive bullet. It hit him in the chest. His gun jammed. Our top turret gunner, Malok, was wounded. The hydraulic system, radio, and rudder controls were shot up. Smoke began pouring from the navigator's compartment. Smoke came so thick from the nose I could not see the instruments. We finally made the overcast at 1,500 feet. I had to carry full left rudder, trim tab, and fly left wing down to hold course. . . .

We were in combat for thirty-five minutes. For about twenty minutes we had no guns to shoot back except one waist gun and the .30-caliber nose gun. The Japs attacked us simultaneously from left and right beam. We could look out at about 45° on the tail and from full left and right beam on the nose. From the side windows we could see them coming in, smoke pouring from their guns as they fired.[191]

With two engines out, controls damaged, and crew wounded, Sharp's B-17 came under attack from Lt. Ogata's Type 97 fighter. He flew into a cloud and ordered the crew to bail out. His copilot, 1st Lt. Herbert Wunderlich, volunteered to stay with him while Sharp attempted a crash landing. Seeing a small river valley ahead of him, Sharp brought the damaged B-17 down onto rice paddies along the river, ripping off two engines in the process. Local Burmese helped them link up with a British army officer working with local hill tribes, who passed them on to British government officials in Assam. They finally reached Calcutta a month after being shot down.[192]

The onset of the monsoon and continued maintenance problems brought bombing operations to a halt for 11 days. Shortages of spare parts and excessive wear on the Wright Cyclones in the B-17s from the sand and dust played havoc with serviceability. As Brereton wrote plaintively to Arnold on June 24, "Motors are whipping us. The Ferry Command will be on the ground soon and I have no B-17s in commission."[193] The 9th Bomb Squadron flew only two more missions into Burma in June: a single B-17 bombing the town of Homalin by day on June 15, while two out of four B-17s dispatched bombed the airfield at Myitykina on June 19.[194] Crews from the 22nd Bomb Squadron carried out a number of missions during the month. On June 7 a single B-25 took off to attack Akyab. The pilot, 2nd Lt. Clarke Johnston, brought his airplane down to 50 feet to strafe the town, but antiaircraft fire killed one of the crew in the nose and knocked out the left engine. The plane struggled back to base, only to crash-land into the Bay of Bengal some 21 miles off the coast of India. The crew rowed their rubber life raft to shore, where they lived for six days on coconut milk and emergency ration bars until Lt. Col. Conrad Necrason, executive officer of the 7th Bomb Group, rescued the crew by landing a transport plane borrowed from the China National Aviation Corporation on a nearby beach.[195] When the weather permitted, single B-25s went out on reconnaissance

B-17E "Jungle Jim" at Karachi with the airplane's maintenance crew. B-17s suffered from the constant dust and sand at Indian airfields, which together with a shortage of spare parts left many bombers unserviceable. *7th Bombardment Group Historical Foundation, USAFA*

flights to cover the area around Mandalay and Rangoon. On a mission over Rangoon late in June, the B-25 showed its worth when three Japanese fighters attacked while it was taking photographs of Mingaladon airfield at 15,000 feet. The fighters made two passes without damaging the B-25, with the bomber getting away at top speed, outrunning the pursuing Japanese fighters.[196]

The first three months of combat operations for the Tenth Air Force were an exercise in frustration. There was little its units could do to strike back effectively against the Japanese. By the end of May the Japanese had captured all of Burma, with the last British units of 1 Burma Corps withdrawing across the Chindwin River in northern Burma on 20 May 1942.[197] In a review of operations he prepared for Brereton, Col. William D. Old, appointed operations officer of the Tenth Air Force on 5 May 1942, summarized the problems facing the Tenth. The harsh reality was that "the lack of suitable operating aircraft, effective communications, suitable reconnaissance over possible objective[s], the lack of strategically located aerodromes, and the approaching monsoons make the employment of the Tenth Air Force a most difficult problem."[198] Too many of the Tenth's B-17s were out of commission. There were 18 serviceable B-25s in India, but these lacked the range to reach targets deep in Burma from the available air bases. It was generally believed that the Japanese would use the pause granted to them by the monsoon to build up their supplies for future operations in Burma or into India once good weather returned. Supplies for the Japanese armies in Southeast Asia flowing in to the ports at Rangoon, Bangkok, and Haiphong would be important targets for the Tenth Air Force if suitable aircraft could be obtained, and if there could be adequate reconnaissance of potential targets. Old argued that the few B-17s available should be reserved for these more-distant targets. Supply routes to the front along the Irrawaddy and the Chindwin Rivers in Burma and via the rail lines to important towns in central Burma could become targets for the medium bombers. To protect the Tenth's few air bases in northeastern India—especially the bases for the ferry route to China—Japanese Army Air Force bases in Burma would have to be attacked and neutralized.[199] Though the objectives were clear-cut, the means to attain them were not available, and what limited resources the Tenth Air Force had available would soon be denuded even further.

The Assam-Burma-China Ferry

American objectives in the China theater were twofold: to ensure that China remained in the war so that Chinese forces could contain Japanese troops, and to prepare China as a base for air and possibly ground operations against Japan in the future. These objectives required a much-greater flow of supplies to China. One of the main tasks of the American Military Mission to China in 1941 was to improve the movement of Lend-Lease supplies from Rangoon to

With the loss of Burma, the air route from Assam to China over the Himalayan mountains that became famous—or infamous—as the "Hump" became the only means of getting supplies to China. The C-47 was the backbone of the Assam-Burma-China Ferry operation that pioneered the route during 1942. The Army Air Force lent some C-47s to the China National Aviation Corporation (CNAC), China's domestic airline. These C-47s carry CNAC markings. *Box 12, China-Air, folder FX-26, Record Group 208AA, Office of War Information, NARA*

THE TENTH AIR FORCE IN WORLD WAR II

China. The possibility that the Japanese might capture Burma and cut China's last lifeline to the Allies caused serious concern among Chinese and American leaders. As previously related, shortly after the attack on Pearl Harbor, Dr. Laughlin Currie had warned President Roosevelt of Burma's strategic importance to China, arguing that cutting off China from her source of supplies could lead to the collapse of Chinese resistance against Japan. Fearing this eventuality, on 1 January 1942, Chinese officials asked the American government to provide equipment under Lend-Lease to build a road from Ledo, in India, across northern Burma to link up with the Burma Road.[200] The War Department concurred with the Chinese proposal and recommended the plan to Allied representatives in Chunking. On a visit to India, Generalissimo Chiang Kai-shek received the approval of the government of India to undertake the project, and with the Allies in agreement the American government agreed to provide material support through Lend-Lease.[201]

At the same time, there was an equally rapid realization of the need to establish an air route to China to transport supplies. President Roosevelt had expressed this during the first meeting of the Combined Chiefs of Staff in Washington in December 1941.[202] On 31 January 1942, T. V. Soong sent a memorandum to the president expressing Chinese concern with the prospect of the loss of the Burma Road.[203] Building on earlier air transport projects for China, Soong stated that the alternative was an air route from the terminus of the Indian railroad at Sadiya, in northeastern Assam, to Kunming in China. Soong informed the president that Pan American Airways had explored the route and found it feasible. Flying a route from India to China via Myitkyina, in Burma, planes could fly at an altitude of 10,000 feet and avoid the Himalayan mountains to the northwest.[204] Soong added that the Douglas Aircraft Company had calculated that 100 DC-3 airplanes could transport 12,000 tons a month over the route to China, nearly making up for the loss of the Burma Road.[205] President Roosevelt approved the plan and informed Generalissimo Chiang Kai-shek that the American government would ensure that an air route to carry supplies from India to China would be maintained if Rangoon fell to the Japanese.[206] Before his departure for China, Stilwell received instructions to organize the air route to China after his arrival in the theater.[207] Plans called for allocating DC-3s to the China National Aviation Corporation (CNAC)—China's national airline and a subsidiary of Pan American Airways—and for an American Army Air Force transport operation to be run out of northeastern Assam to China, using 75 C-47s.[208]

When Brereton took command of the Tenth Air Force in early March, he was told that one of the most important immediate tasks was to set up the air transport operation between India and China. This was to be his first priority.[209] He requested that the ferry operation be assigned to the Tenth Air Force, believing that as Tenth Air Force commander he should have responsibility for all air operations within his area.[210] Instead, to Brereton's annoyance, the War Department instructed Brig. Gen. Earl Naiden, Brereton's chief of staff, to begin setting up the air ferry operation separate from his duties for the Tenth Air Force. On March 20, following the Japanese capture of Rangoon, President Roosevelt approved creation of the Assam-Burma-China Ferry Command, and the War Department instructed Brereton to organize the operation "as seemed best to accomplish the desired ends."[211] When Brereton again brought up the issue of command over the Assam-Burma-China Ferry in early April, requesting that all equipment and personnel in India be assigned to the Tenth Air Force, he received a reply from Gen. Marshall that control of the air transport route from Sadiya to China "will be for the 1st Air Force Ferrying Group and Stilwell will control these operations."[212] The Tenth Air Force would have responsibility for protecting the air ferry route and for sustaining it but would not control its operations. The War Department's concern was that the commander of the Tenth Air Force might be tempted to divert transports for their own needs rather than follow directions based on American national interests. The air ferry to China would be controlled from Washington and not India. This split in the command structure would become a continuing source of tension until the end of the war.[213]

As instructed, Naiden began planning for the air ferry operation soon after his arrival in India. His first task was to survey the proposed route, which he did, flying from Assam to Kunming, in China. Naiden recommended that the route should run between Dinjan, in northeast Assam, and Myitkyina. At the time there was still some thought that the Japanese might be content with their capture of Rangoon and lower Burma and would not advance as far north as Myitkyina. From Myitkyina, supplies could be taken by rail or river to link up with the Burma Road. He proposed that three all-weather airfields with taxiways and hardstands be built in the area around Dinjan, and three more around Myitkyina. The air ferry operation would have to share the Dinjan airfield with the RAF until these new airfields could be built, which would likely not be completed until after the monsoon season ended in early November. It was doubtful that more than 25 transports could operate over the route in its current state until more airfields and facilities had been built at either end.[214]

With the survey completed, Brereton ordered Naiden to begin operating the air ferry route. Naiden realized that with the distances involved from Karachi to China, the operation really needed two ferry routes: one running from Karachi to Dinjan, and the second from Dinjan to Myitkyina and China. He activated the Trans-India Ferry Command (TIFC) on 7 April 1942 to operate from Karachi to Dinjan, where it would shift cargos to the Assam-Burma-China Ferry Command (ABCFC), connecting with the China National Aviation Corporation's own service from China to the Indian airfield at Allahabad. The Army Air Force Ferry Command in the United States had activated the 1st Ferry Group in early March and had assigned it to the proposed India-China air transport route. Brig. Gen. Clinton Russell arrived in India in early April with the advance party of the 1st Ferry Group, and Naiden placed the Trans-India Ferry under Russell, only to have to transfer command to Col. Robert M. Tate when Russell fell ill. Fortuitously, a commander for the Assam-Burma-China Ferry arrived the same day the Trans-India Ferry was activated. Col. Haynes landed in Karachi on April 7 with the first two airplanes from the Project AQUILA force: his own B-24D and a C-47 flown by Capt. Julian Joplin. The next morning Col. William Old, who had flown in with Haynes, was ordered to fly to Dinjan with eight enlisted men to begin working on the ferry operation. With the situation in Burma now desperate, the original mission of Project AQUILA was canceled and Brereton and Naiden ordered Haynes to take command of the Assam-Burma-China Ferry, with Old as his executive officer. Haynes flew to Dinjan and, after conducting his own survey of the proposed route between Assam and China, flew back to New Delhi to meet with Brereton and Naiden, after which Brereton and Naiden issued a directive formally activating the Assam-Burma-China Ferry Command on 17 April 1942.[215]

Aircraft for the ferry operation had already begun to arrive. For the ABCFC, the government requisitioned 25 DC-3s from

American airlines and arranged for them to be flown to India, but it would take time for them to make the long trip to Karachi, so 10 Pan American Airways DC-3s were pulled off the trans-Africa service Pan American was operating and sent to India at the end of March.[216] The first two Pan American DC-3s to arrive were immediately put to work transferring gasoline and engine oil for the Doolittle B-25s that were expected to land in China following their raid on Tokyo, scheduled for April 18. There was 8,000 gallons of gasoline stored in Calcutta, with an additional 22,000 gallons at Dinjan. Since Calcutta was considered under threat following the Japanese attack on Ceylon, the priority was to move the gasoline to a safer area. Over April 6 and 7, the two DC-3s flew the gasoline to the airfield at Asansol. From there it was flown to Dinjan. The remaining eight Pan American DC-3s arrived shortly thereafter. One airplane got lost trying to find Dinjan and ended up landing in a riverbed; Capt. Joplin flew the airplane out successfully. These airplanes went to work flying the gasoline for Doolittle's airplanes to China.[217]

Haynes arrived at Dinjan on April 23 with Col. Robert L. Scott and several other Project AQUILA pilots to take formal command of the ABCFC. A few more Army Air Force C-47s had arrived, giving him a total of 13 DC-3s and C-47s. The Americans shared the now-crowded airfield with two RAF units—No. 31 Squadron with DC-2s and DC-3s and No. 5 Squadron with Curtiss Mohawks (Army P-36)—as well as with CNAC DC-3s flying in from China. There was no early-warning system to alert the fighters of impending attack, no antiaircraft guns to defend the airfield, and nowhere to disperse the airplanes if there was an attack. Accommodations for officers and men consisted of local bashas 14 miles from the airfield, with only the most-basic facilities and decidedly unfamiliar food. The only way to protect the transports was to get them into the air at dawn. Soon the ground crews were working 16-hour days without relief.[218]

By this time the military situation in Burma had become so desperate that the immediate need was to fly badly needed supplies to the retreating British and Chinese troops and evacuate the wounded and any refugees that could be taken out. The ABCFC airplanes began making two or three trips a day to Myitkyina and other fields as long as they were in Allied hands. All too soon other airfields fell to the Japanese. The Japanese army captured Lashio on April 29, and Mandalay quickly followed. Japanese air attacks forced the AVG to withdraw from Loiwing on May 1. Some of the Pan American pilots refused to fly into Burma because as civilians they had no rights if captured.[219] More Army Air Force C-47s arrived so that by May 24 there were 19 American transports operating in India, providing badly needed capacity working alongside the RAF's five serviceable transports from No. 31 Squadron.[220] The pilots filled their planes with as many wounded soldiers or refugees as they could squeeze in. As Col. Robert Scott recalled in his memoir *God Is My Co-pilot*:

The C-47, or DC-3, as the airlines called the Douglas transport, was constructed to carry a full load of twenty-four passengers or six thousand pounds. . . . Carrying the refugees, we broke all the rules and regulations because we had to. There were women and children, pregnant women, and women so old that they presumably couldn't have gone to the altitude that was necessary to cross into India. There were hundreds of wounded British soldiers with the most terrible gangrenous infections. At the beginning we used to load the wounded first, those who were worst off; but later, when we realized that with our few transports we'd never get them all out, we took only the able-bodied. That was a hard decision to make, but we looked at it finally from the theory that those must be saved who could someday fight again.

But as I say, at first we carried the terribly wounded, piling them in until the ship groaned and the door would hardly close. I always carried out fifty or more in this ship that had been designed for twenty-four, and one day I counted seventy-three getting out of one ship. A young pilot by the name of Lieutenant Sartz broke all records, as far as I know. One morning he took off with seventy-three, and on landing British customs counted seventy-four. In route over the Naga Hills a baby had been born, and now Sartz holds the world's record.[221]

By the end of the Burma campaign, American, British, and CNAC transport aircraft had evacuated 8,600 people from Burma, of which 2,600 were wounded.[222]

When Myitkyina fell to the Japanese on 8 May 1942, the transports shifted to dropping supplies to retreating British and Chinese troops and resumed flying supplies into China. The original plan had been for the Trans-India Ferry Command to fly supplies from Karachi, where all supplies from the United States were delivered, to Dinjan, where the supplies would be offloaded from a TIFC transport plane and loaded onto an ABCFC transport plane. Haynes immediately recognized that with the limited personnel he had available, this was completely impractical. On his own authority he simply ordered TIFC and ABCFC airplanes to fly wherever needed. Planes carried supplies into China, returning with tungsten ore, tin, and pig bristles for export abroad to earn China badly needed foreign currency. The planes were loaded to capacity, with a normal load to China weighing up to 5,000 pounds. On one flight Haynes carried 7,200 pounds to China, including two Ryan training planes. Haynes persuaded Chennault to lend him two P-40s and acquired two P-43s from the Chinese air force. Haynes, Scott, Maj. Dalene Bailey, and two pilots from the recently completed Doolittle mission—Capts. R. M. Gray and R. O. Joyce—flew these fighters on reconnaissance missions into Burma to keep track of the Japanese advance.[223]

After crossing the Chindwin River, the British and Indian troops in 1 Burma Corps, under the command of Lt. Gen. William Slim, withdrew to India, completing a retreat of nearly 1,000 miles—the longest retreat in British history.[224] The divisions of the Chinese 5th and 6th Armies retreated as well, some to Yunnan in China and some to India.[225] As they made their way out of Burma, transport planes flew in supplies as long as there were airfields to land on, and when the Japanese captured the last of these, the transports switched to air-dropping supplies. Neither the American nor the British transports had any special containers for supply dropping, and there were few parachutes available. The pilots of the ABCFC found that they could fill a small burlap bag with rice, salt, canned food, and medical supplies; put the small bag into a larger one; and drop this from low altitude into a clearing in the jungle or near a village to waiting British or Chinese troops or refugees. While the smaller bag might burst when it hit the ground, the larger bag didn't, containing the supplies within.[226] Pilots also found that they could get into smaller and rougher airfields than they had ever thought possible. When Chinese troops nearing Ft. Hertz, in the northernmost part of Burma near the border with Assam, desperately needed food, Capt. John Payne flew a C-47 loaded with 4,200 pounds of rice onto a dirt-and-grass landing strip 900 feet in length—an exceptional feat of piloting that became routine.[227]

From 8 April to 14 June 1942, the combined Trans-India Ferry and Assam-Burma-China Ferry carried 1,401,950 pounds of passengers and freight eastward into Burma and China, and 758,826 pounds westward into India.[228] The efforts of the American and British transport units, halting, desperate, and inadequate as they were, were nonetheless of critical importance for the future. As the British official history of the war against Japan noted:

> *Perhaps the greatest lesson learnt from the campaign was the possibility of air supply for an army cut off from all other means of support. The history of air supply in the Far East can be traced from the modest beginnings on the Burma front to the colossal army/air supply organization based in India, which was destined to revolutionize support for land forces and have a profound influence on the future conduct of the war against Japan.*[229]

Although few Americans involved in the ferry operation at the time could have predicted it, this was a revolution in which the Tenth Air Force would play a prominent role in the years ahead.

Brereton Departs

The Japanese conquest of Burma added new difficulties to the mission of the Tenth Air Force. The Tenth's original mission had been to conduct offensive operations against Japan from bases in China, but now China was completely isolated, its only source of supply the rudimentary air link from one inadequate airfield in Assam to Kunming. The limited supplies that could be carried over this route with the few transports available put constraints on the type and level of operations the Tenth Air Force could carry out in China. The Tenth could operate in China only the number of aircraft it could keep fueled, armed, and maintained with supplies flown in from India. With the loss of Myitkyina the air route had to be moved north to avoid the risk of Japanese fighters, meaning flying at higher altitudes to get over higher mountains, using more fuel, and putting more strain on men and planes. More critically, the Tenth now had to provide for the defense of the air ferry route at both ends in China and Assam, something that had not been contemplated in early planning for operations in China. The airfield at Dinjan, and the other airfields planned for the area, lay only 200 miles from Myitkyina and were within easy reach of Japanese bombers. Allied air bases in and around Calcutta were also now potentially vulnerable to Japanese attack. For the foreseeable future the Tenth Air Force's supply base would remain at Karachi—1,000 miles from Assam—over the inadequate Indian domestic rail system. It took two months for supplies to reach Karachi from the United States and then six weeks to reach American bases in Assam. To get these supplies to Kunming took an additional two weeks or more.[230] And now India—the Tenth Air Force's base—was itself under threat of attack. The British were wholly concerned with India's defense and would look to American forces for support.

It is not surprising that at a conference with his small staff on 8 June 1942, Brereton gave vent to his frustrations. He was most upset with the lack of serviceable heavy bombers, his principal means of striking back against the Japanese. He told his staff that he was upset to realize that "he had an Air Force that was practically all grounded on account of a lack of engines and spares."[231] At the time, there were ten B-17s at Karachi all out of commission for lack of engines and spare parts, while the 7th Bomb Group at Allahabad had only four serviceable B-17s out of seven assigned to the group.[232] New engines and spare parts were on the way from the United States but would not arrive until late July. Brereton ordered his Air Service Command to prepare a plan of maintenance to get more aircraft in the air, if necessary cannibalizing parts from one aircraft to get another flying. He also pushed for planned engine overhaul facilities at Agra and at the Hindustan Aircraft factory to begin work as soon as possible.[233]

Nevertheless, there had been progress. A command and administrative structure for the Tenth Air Force was slowly being put in place. In addition to the two ferry commands, the X Air

Maj. Gen. Lewis Brereton (*right*) stands next to Maj. Max Fennell underneath Fennell's B-17 in North Africa after Brereton's transfer to the Middle East. *7th Bombardment Group Historical Foundation, USAFA*

For several months in 1942, the RAF's No. 5 Squadron, equipped with Curtiss Mohawk fighters, provided the only air defense of the airfield at Dinjan, base for the transports flying the Hump route. *CI_001892, IWM*

FORMATION AND EARLY OPERATIONS

Service Command had been activated on May 1, and on May 19 Brereton had activated the Karachi Air Defense Command to take on responsibility for running the Operational Training Center and the defense of American facilities in the Karachi area. More units and personnel had arrived, including the original HQ and HQ Squadron cadre for the Tenth Air Force and the 3rd Air Depot Group, bringing the total strength of the Tenth Air Force to 651 officers and 5,586 enlisted men. More P-40s arrived via the Africa route and on ships, and medium bombers and more transports were arriving, giving the Tenth Air Force a nominal strength of 136 airplanes, even if not all were serviceable. Moreover, Brereton's tactical units were moving eastward, closer to the front lines in Burma. The 7th Bomb Group had transferred from Karachi to Barrackpore in Calcutta, while the redesignated 436th Bomb Squadron had gone to join the 9th Bomb Squadron at Allahabad. The two medium-bomber squadrons were preparing for combat, with the 11th Bomb Squadron sending a detachment to join Chennault at Kunming while the 22nd Bomb Squadron was moving to bases in Assam. The 51st Fighter Group planned to send one of its fighter squadrons to China to join the soon-to-be-activated 23rd Fighter Group, while its remaining two fighter squadrons prepared to move to Dinjan for the defense of the air ferry route.[234]

Brereton wrote a long letter to Arnold on 24 June 1942, outlining his continuing frustrations and his plans for deploying his limited forces. Above all, Brereton asked Arnold for a strategic plan for his air force and some indication of when this plan could be implemented. Brereton believed that Burma should be retaken, and that offensive operations should begin after the end of the monsoon. He assumed that the initial effort would be air operations aimed at reducing Japanese air strength in Burma through attacks from India and China. He told Arnold that because of the greater demands his heavy bombardment airplanes would put on the supply system for fuel, bombs, ammunition, and crews, and with the limitations of the air ferry to China, he intended to use his bases in China for pursuit aircraft, and dive-bombers if Arnold could supply them. Fighters from China could cover the Japanese airfields at Loiwing, Lashio, and Myitkyina, as well as support whatever Chinese armies that might be fighting in China. If the capabilities of the air ferry improved, he could base medium bombers in China. He would keep his heavy bombers in India and expected that his heavy-bomber force would increase to more than 60 aircraft when more of the Project AQUILA and Project HALPRO bombers arrived. As to his fighter strength, activation of the 23rd Fighter Group to replace the AVG would give him—with the 51st Fighter Group—six fighter squadrons. He planned to deploy five to China, leaving one of the 51st Group's squadrons to defend Dinjan, but warned Arnold that this left Karachi and his heavy-bomber base around Calcutta undefended. He wanted an additional pursuit group to defend Calcutta and Karachi, or at least more pursuits he could assign to the Operational Training Center for defense of the area. He hoped to receive his promised P-38 reconnaissance squadron, since his need to use his few B-25s for reconnaissance reduced the number available for offensive operations. While frank in his expression of his problems and needs, the tone of the letter was upbeat. Brereton wanted to fight the Japanese. He understood that he was in a secondary theater of war, but he would do the best he could with what he had available.[235]

At this juncture, events in the Middle East forced Brereton to abandon his own plans for the Tenth Air Force. On 26 May 1942, Gen. Erwin Rommel launched an attack on British positions in North Africa in what became the Battle of Gazala. The battle was a disaster for the British, who were forced to withdraw to El Alamein—only 60 miles from Alexandria and the Suez Canal—surrendering Tobruk on June 21.[236] There was at the time real concern that the German and Italian armies under Rommel might continue their advance to capture the canal. The Combined Chiefs of Staff had recognized that India and the Middle East were interdependent. Had the Middle East fallen, the repercussions on the Allied position in India would have been enormous, since the line of communications from the United States and England would have come under threat.[237] The British needed reinforcements urgently, particularly American heavy bombers. In response, President Roosevelt agreed that the Project HALPRO bombers would remain in Egypt for operations against the Germans, while the A-29s on their way to China would also be shifted to the Middle East.[238] In addition, to get more heavy bombers to Egypt, Brereton received orders to transfer immediately to Egypt with all the Tenth Air Force's available heavy bombers, together with sufficient transport planes to fly the men and equipment his force would need.[239]

Brereton appended a short note to his June 24 letter to Arnold, dated June 25:

Since writing the above I have received my radio orders to proceed to Middle East. I am now in route and expect to deliver in M.E. about ten heavy bombers—including one LB-30 and four B-24s. As stated above, not more than four or five B-17s will be available due to engines. I will send an air estimate as soon as possible, but from what information I have had from G-2 India, it sounds like another tough job. However, that's what we're out here for.[240]

Brereton left for the Middle East on June 26; he took with him several senior staff officers. Shortly thereafter the 9th Bomb Squadron left Allahabad with the 7th Bomb Group's most experienced combat crews and maintenance personnel. More B-17s followed as soon as their engines could be repaired, along with ten transports and their crews from the two ferry commands. This left the Tenth Air Force with "a crippled air transport system, a skeleton staff, and almost totally stripped of its already meager striking power."[241]

CHAPTER 2

THE CHINA AIR TASK FORCE

July 1942–March 1943

Organizing American Airpower in China

With the departure of the Tenth Air Force's heavy bombers to the Middle East, the Tenth's main effort over the following few months would be in China. Since the beginning of America's war with Japan, the War Department had planned to place American air units in China. Projects AQUILA and HALPRO had been early products of these intentions, but there had also been plans to induct the AVG into the American armed forces and replace it with an Army Air Force fighter group under an American air commander in China. In his memo to President Roosevelt of 9 December 1941, Dr. Laughlin Currie suggested that the AVG could serve as the nucleus for an American air task force for the defense of Burma.[1] President Roosevelt had approved in principle the induction of the AVG, subject to Generalissimo Chiang Kai-shek's concurrence, on 18 December 1941, and the 23rd Pursuit Group had been constituted the day before with the intention of sending the group to China to incorporate the AVG.[2] In the event there were delays, the AVG would not be inducted in the Army Air Force until 4 July 1942, nearly seven months after the Pearl Harbor attack. For political reasons, command relationships, personal antagonisms, and geographic and logistical difficulties, the organization of American airpower in China and its relationship with the Tenth Air Force would be complicated from its very beginnings.

The Chinese were not surprisingly reluctant to agree to the induction of the AVG—the only effective air unit in China—preferring to delay the induction in the hopes of gaining more Lend-Lease aid as a quid pro quo.[3] On 2 April 1942, Generalissimo Chiang Kai-shek finally agreed to the induction of the AVG on 4 July 1942—when most of the pilots' contracts with CAMCO would expire—in return for Stilwell's promise that an American fighter group would replace the AVG and remain in China for China's air defense.[4] Claire Chennault was also opposed to induction of the AVG into the Army Air Force. He was reluctant to give up command of the force he had raised and trained, or the freedom to act independently. He thought the best alternative was to allow the AVG to continue as an independent force under his leadership, with the Army Air Force supplying him with more airplanes and pilots.[5] This was impossible for the War Department to agree to, since any volunteer pilots would not have been subject either to military discipline or the articles of war.[6] For his part, Brereton was concerned that there would be an air unit in the China theater that would not be under his control. In March he asked that the AVG be inducted into the Tenth Air Force and placed under his command, hoping to use the unit for the defense of Burma and India, only to be told that the 23rd Pursuit Group, when activated, would remain in China and would not be assigned to the Tenth Air Force in India.[7] There were also logistical problems to consider. At a March 15 meeting of the Administrative Planning Committee with the Royal Air Force to discuss Army Air Force requirements in India, Brig. Gen. Naiden, who had just begun examining the challenges of setting up the air ferry route to China, told his RAF counterparts that he did not expect to be able to operate an air force in China for at least six months due to the impossibility of bringing in adequate supplies to support air operations.[8]

Despite hesitations and reservations on the part of several of the parties involved, and the many unresolved logistical problems, plans for induction of the AVG went forward. On 9 April 1942, the War Department recalled Chennault to active duty with the temporary rank of colonel and promoted him to brigadier general 13 days later.[9] Brereton decided to create an air task force for China under the Tenth Air Force—designated the China Air Task Force (CATF)—to include a medium-bomber squadron as well as the fighters of the now 23rd

Claire Chennault stands next to his two patrons, Generalissimo Chiang Kai-shek and his wife, Soong Mei-ling. In the heated debates over which military strategy to pursue in China, Chiang came to favor Chennault's strategy of emphasizing airpower over reform of the Chinese armies, in part because airpower posed no threat to Chiang's political position within China. 02_C-00227, SDAMC

China Battle Area 1942-1943

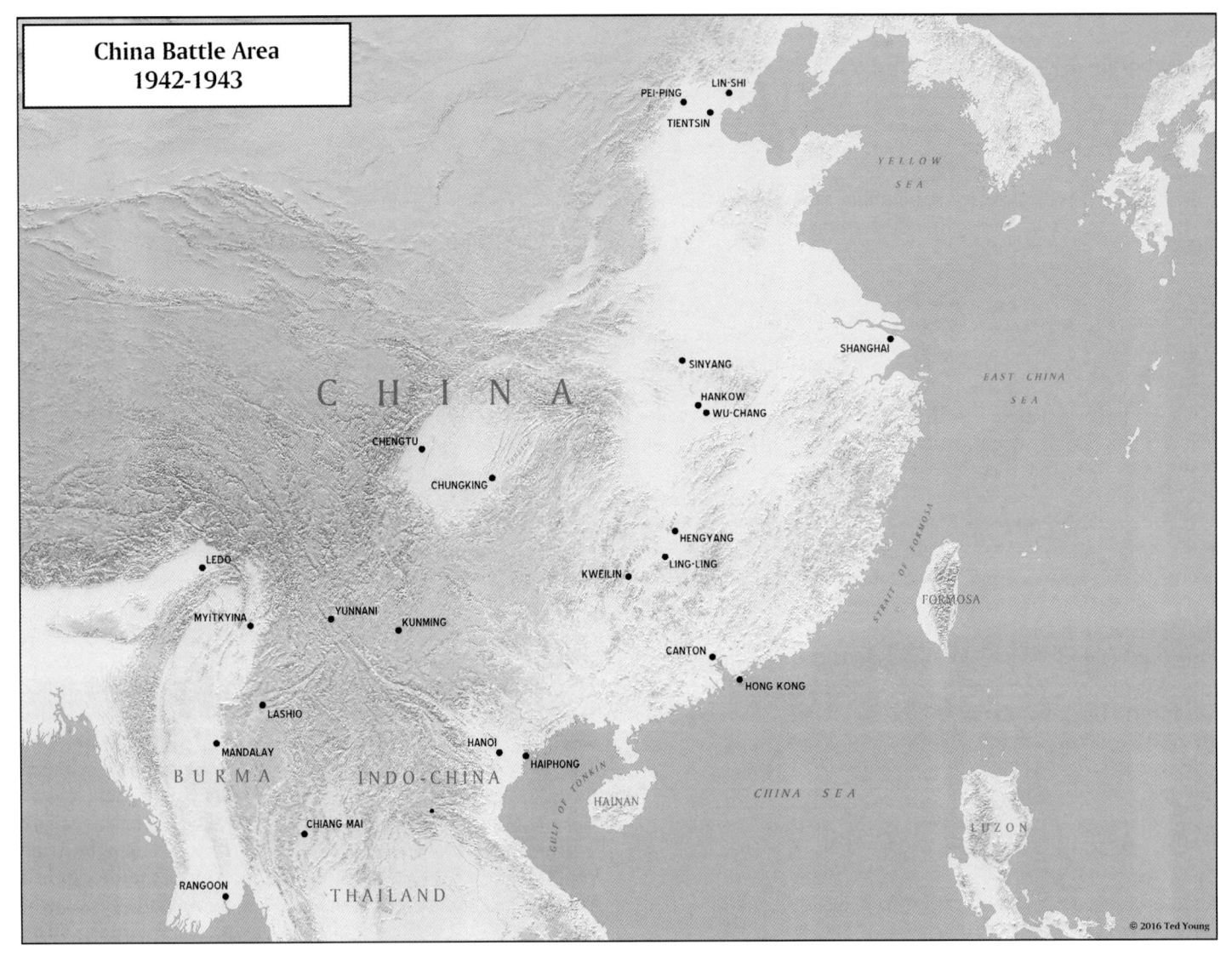

In China the AVG had its main base at Kunming. Here an AVG Curtiss P-40B (*left*) and P-40E (*right*) undergo maintenance with a P-43 (*behind*) around the time of the transfer of the AVG to the US Army Air Force as the 23rd Fighter Group. *Courtesy, Carl Molesworth*

THE TENTH AIR FORCE IN WORLD WAR II

Fighter Group.[10] Brereton selected the newly arrived 11th Bomb Squadron to serve in China.[11] Brereton had planned to appoint Naiden to command the CATF, placing Col. Caleb Haynes in command of the bomber force and Chennault in charge of the fighters, but this would have had serious repercussions within China.[12] As his aeronautical advisor for nearly five years, Chennault had established a close relationship with Generalissimo Chiang Kai-shek and his wife. Chennault's successful command of the AVG had made him a hero in China and a renowned figure in the American press. To have placed Chennault in anything less than command of American air units in China would have incurred the generalissimo's ill will, as Stilwell recognized. He recommended that Chennault be placed in command of the CATF upon its activation.[13] This became possible when Brereton left the Tenth Air Force for the Middle East and Naiden, as Brereton's chief of staff and the most senior officer in the Tenth Air Force, assumed command of the Tenth in his absence, which was at the time expected to be temporary. Haynes received orders on June 9 ordering him to his new command, departing for China on June 17 and leaving Col. Scott in command of the Assam-Burma-China Ferry, but a few days later Scott was appointed commander of the 23rd Fighter Group and also left for China.[14]

Toward the end of June, Naiden informed Chennault that he would become commander of the CATF and receive a directive outlining his responsibilities. The primary mission of the Tenth Air Force, Naiden told him, was "the maintenance and operation of the Assam-Burma-China Ferry and air transport route under the strategic direction of Stilwell with a secondary mission of conducting operations against suitable and proper enemy installations and targets of opportunity in eastern and southeastern China."[15] Chennault had "the widest latitude" in carrying out this directive and in the conduct of his operations as long as the primary eastern terminus of the air ferry route at Kunming was defended at all times. In addition to the soon-to-be-activated 23rd Fighter Group, Chennault gained the 16th Fighter Squadron from the 51st Fighter Group, 50 officers and 125 enlisted men drawn from the 88th Reconnaissance Squadron, and an additional 10 officers and 100 men from various service units in the Tenth Air Force. Two hundred enlisted men for the 23rd Fighter Group would be flown to China as soon as air transport was available. Because of the difficulty of supplying men and equipment over the air route to China, Naiden urged Chennault to use Chinese sources of labor and equipment to the greatest extent possible, to keep to a minimum the number of Americans assigned to his command.[16]

Planning for the induction of the AVG took place during a period of tension between the Chinese and American governments—a tension arising out of what were emerging as diametrically opposed strategic visions of China's role in the war against Japan, which would intensify over the following years. This divergence would have a direct impact on the mission and operations of the Tenth Air Force. Following the debacle in Burma and his retreat from India, Stilwell had said, "I claim we got a hell of a beating. We got run out of Burma and it is humiliating as hell. I think we ought to find out what caused it, go back and retake it."[17] On his return to Chungking in early June, Stilwell prepared a report on events in Burma for the Generalissimo and a proposal for the reform of the Chinese army. Noting the army's weakness in equipment, but more critically in leadership and organization, Stilwell proposed reorganizing the army into 30 new divisions to create a better-armed and better-led force with competent commanders. The plan he was envisioning was to create a Chinese force of several divisions in India and a force in Yunnan that the Americans would train and equip, and to use this force to retake Burma and reopen a land link to China. But a plan for the reorganization of the Chinese army was not what the Generalissimo wanted to hear.[18]

The level of support they were receiving from the Allies and their lack of any position within Allied councils frustrated the

In the first few months after its formation, the 23rd Fighter Group continued using several of the remaining AVG P-40Bs until they could be replaced with newer P-40 models. A P-40B, now with USAAF markings under the wing, lands at Kunming in early September 1942. *3A-1011, RG342FH, NARA*

Brereton assigned the 11th Bombardment Squadron (M) and its B-25s to the newly formed China Air Task Force under Chennault's command. This gave Chennault—recalled to active duty and promoted to brigadier general—a small force of bombers to begin offensive operations against the Japanese in China. *3A-1000, RG342FH, NARA*

Chinese. A request for Chinese representation on the Combined Chiefs of Staff had been politely but firmly turned down, the Tenth Air Force had been diverted to support the British withdrawal from India, and the level of Lend-Lease supplies delivered over the air route was far less than the Chinese expected.[19] There were more disappointments in store. At this juncture Stilwell had to inform the Generalissimo not only that the Tenth Air Force's heavy bombers were being withdrawn to the Middle East, but other aircraft intended for China (under Project HALPRO and the 33 A-29s in route) would also go to the Middle East. An angry Chiang Kai-shek presented the Americans with three demands: first, that America send three combat divisions to China for operations with the Chinese army; second, that beginning in August the air forces in the China theater be brought up to 500 aircraft and sustained at that level; and third, that the tonnage of supplies carried over the Hump should be brought up to 5,000 tons a month, hinting that if China did not receive American support as a commitment to maintaining a China theater it would seek a separate peace with Japan.[20] Over the next few months, Stilwell, the War Department, and officials in Washington struggled to work out a compromise that would go some way toward meeting Chiang's demands. But views on China's role were beginning to diverge. Stilwell, with the War Department's backing, was looking to reform of the Chinese army for operations in Burma, while the Generalissimo wanted more American airpower in China and more Lend-Lease supplies for the army as it was.

In the weeks leading up to the induction of the AVG, the units designated for China began moving to their new assignments. The 11th Bomb Squadron was the first of the Army Air Force units to move to China. On 27 May 1942, Maj. Gordon Leland, newly appointed 11th Bomb Squadron commander, led the first of two flights of six B-25s to Allahabad, departing for Dinjan on June 2.[21] Leland and his pilots had only recently arrived in India and had no experience flying during the monsoon that had begun. At Dinjan, Col. Haynes spoke with Leland and suggested that one of Haynes's experienced transport pilots could fly with Leland to guide him to Kunming.[22] Leland declined the offer, since he would have had to leave one of his own crew at Dinjan. Carrying six 500-pound bombs each, the six B-25s took off the next morning intending to bomb the airfield at Lashio on the way to Kunming during the 11th Bomb Squadron's first combat mission. The formation ran into bad weather before reaching Lashio, and one airplane became separated. The five remaining airplanes bombed the airfield from 1,500 feet, hitting the runway. The sixth ship caught up and bombed the runway just after the first formation, only to run into two Japanese fighters that had taken off to intercept the formation. The top turret gunner damaged one fighter, which broke away, but the second fighter made 10 passes against the B-25, killing the radio operator. Maj. Leland was leading the other five ships in a formation of two elements at 10,000 feet through heavy cloud on their way to Kunming when he ran into the side of a mountain, with his wingman crashing a few seconds later, followed by the number 1 ship in the second element. The two surviving B-25s missed the mountain by only a few feet, the crews getting a glimpse of grass and trees and the explosions of their comrades crashing as they flew past—a brutal demonstration of the dangers of flying what became known as the "Hump." Only two bombers made it to Kunming, the third running out of fuel before finding the airfield and the crew bailing out and walking back to Kunming.[23]

Maj. William Bayse, a veteran of the 19th Bomb Group in Java, replaced Leland as squadron commander. Three more B-25s came to Kunming on June 10, and another three eight days later, giving Bayse eight aircraft—less than a full squadron. Twenty-five ground crew arrived by plane and began working on the bombers to prepare them for combat. The crews found the Bendix ventral turret, operated through a periscope, to be of little use, so the armorers removed the turret and rigged up two .30-caliber machine guns in the opening in a mounting

THE TENTH AIR FORCE IN WORLD WAR II

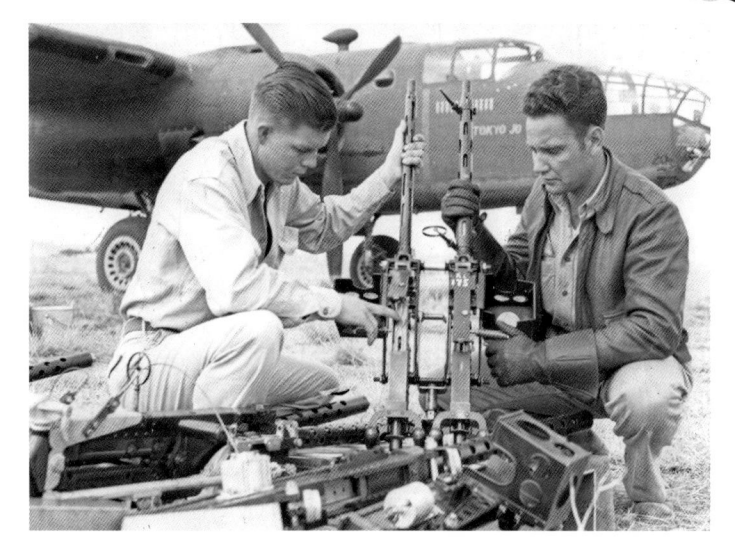

TSgt. Norton Stubblefield (*left*) and TSgt. Adam Williams—a veteran of the Doolittle raid on Tokyo—examine two .30-caliber machine guns. The 11th Bomb Squadron removed the Bendix remote control turret from its B-25s and put in two .30-caliber machine guns. *Box 12, China-Air, folder FX-47, RG208AA, NARA*

the squadron armaments officer designed.[24] Removing the turret increased the speed of the B-25C by 10 miles per hour and improved the flying characteristics.[25] These eight B-25s composed the bomber force that Haynes would have for his CATF bomber command.

The fighter squadrons for the CATF came together slowly as men and planes reached Karachi via different routes. Brereton's withdrawal of transport aircraft from the Assam-Burma-China Ferry for the Middle East made getting men to China more difficult. The 23rd Pursuit Group had begun forming on 1 March 1942, when a group of officers and men arrived at Langley Field, Virginia, as the initial cadre for the group, leaving the United States on March 17 on the convoy carrying other units designated for the Tenth Air Force.[26] The men for the 23rd Group arrived in Karachi on May 17, where they were attached temporarily to the 51st Fighter Group. The first contingent of Army Air Force pilots for China (seven in total) arrived in Kunming on 1 June 1942 to begin training with the AVG to learn Chennault's combat tactics.[27] Nineteen enlisted men from the 23rd Group traveled to Kunming by air on June 15 to begin working with AVG maintenance crews. Three days later, nine more Army pilots arrived at Kunming and by the end of June, 22 Army pilots had arrived in China.[28] Twenty-two officers and 125 enlisted men transferred from the 51st Group on July 1 to bring the 23rd Group up to strength, also heading to China by air.[29] The 16th Fighter Squadron, consisting of 30 officers and 48 enlisted men, left Karachi on June 29, with the pilots flying their P-40s to Kunming over the Hump and Col. Homer Sanders, 51st Group commander, leading the formation.[30] The problem for the soon-to-be-activated China Air Task Force was that many of these pilots had only a limited number of hours flying P-40s, and none had any combat experience, making the planned induction of pilots from the AVG all the more important.

Unfortunately, the induction of members of the AVG into the Army Air Force did not go well. Only five pilots, 22 ground crew, and five staff officers agreed to accept positions in the Army Air Force and remain in China. There were reasons why so few men chose to remain with the CATF. Almost all had been away from the United States for nearly a year and were worn out after months of intense combat and hard work with limited tools and facilities in often-trying conditions. They needed, and were looking forward to, some rest. Others who had served in the Navy or the Marine Corps wanted to return to their original services rather than join the Army Air Force, while some were reluctant to return to formal military discipline. An induction board, with Chennault as president, the AVG's surgeon, and four officers from the Tenth Air Force as members, interviewed AVG pilots and maintenance men but had limited authority in what they could offer. The AVG men resented the way the Army Air Force conducted the induction process, many feeling that the Army Air Force representatives applied pressure and not persuasion, including apparently Clayton Bissell. Since so few AVG pilots agreed to continue their service in China, Tenth Air Force officers were greatly concerned that without more experienced fighter pilots the soon-to-be-activated 23rd Fighter Group would be vulnerable to Japanese attacks. Sixteen pilots and 37 ground crew agreed to extend their contracts for an additional two weeks after 4 July 1942 to give the 23rd Group more time to gain experience and more men and planes.[31]

The transition took place as planned on July 4, with the activation of the 23rd Fighter Group and its three component squadrons: the

The Chinese government agreed to transfer the AVG's 31 P-40Bs and 20 P-40Es to the 23rd Fighter Group, joining the small number of P-40s that had flown in after assembly at Karachi. *03_01548, SDAMC*

THE CHINA AIR TASK FORCE

Chennault arranged to borrow 10 P-43 Lancers from the Chinese air force and had them converted to reconnaissance airplanes by fitting an aerial camera inside the fuselage. Flying at high altitudes to avoid Japanese fighters, these P-43s brought back photos of potential targets for the CATF's B-25 bombers. *3A-02211, RG342FH, NARA*

74th, 75th, and 76th Fighter Squadrons. With that the AVG passed into history. On July 6 Chennault became commander of the China Air Task Force, reporting to the Tenth Air Force. He had only a meager force of aircraft available to him. The 23rd Fighter Group had 47 P-40s—a mix of P-40Es and older P-40Bs from the AVG purchased through reverse Lend-Lease from the Chinese government—and only 30 of these P-40s were serviceable (Claire Chennault states in his memoir that there were 51 P-40s available, 31 P-40B Tomahawks, and 20 P-40E Kitty Hawks, of which 29 were serviceable).[32] The 16th Fighter Squadron had brought 25 P-40Es to China, and Chennault had arranged to borrow 10 P-43 Lancers from the Chinese air force for reconnaissance.[33] His bomber force consisted of the 11th Bomb Squadron's eight B-25s.[34] Chennault spread his force across several airfields east of Kunming so that the most-important Japanese targets could be brought within range of his bombers and fighters.[35] Fortunately, three of his experienced AVG pilots—David Lee "Tex" Hill, Ed Rector, and Frank Schiel Jr.—agreed to accept commissions as majors in the Army Air Force and remain with the CATF. Maj. Schiel took command of the 74th Fighter Squadron, which remained in Kunming for the defense of the eastern terminus of the air ferry route and served as a mini-operational training unit for the newly arrived Army Air Force pilots.[36] Chennault sent his remaining squadrons to three Chinese air bases far to the east. Maj. David Hill commanded the 75th Fighter Squadron and was assigned to Hengyang, on the CATF's northern flank. The 16th Fighter Squadron, under Maj. Harry Young, went to the base at Lingling in the center, while Maj. Ed Rector took on the 76th Fighter Squadron and moved to Kweilin, 400 miles east of Kunming at the southern end of the arc of Chinese airfields.[37] At the time these fields were basic—a single runway made of crushed rock and mud, with only the most rudimentary facilities, few tools, and hardly any spare parts.[38] The 11th Bomb Squadron remained at Kunming, flying to forward bases as required.

Although his means were limited, Chennault planned to use the few aircraft he had aggressively against a range of Japanese targets, continuing the pattern of success he had established with the AVG. In a memo he sent to Stilwell on July 16, Chennault argued for the potential of airpower in China, telling Stilwell that "the opportunities here are too many and too productive of results to neglect."[39] If given 100 new P-51 fighters and 30 B-25s the China Air Task Force could accomplish the following:

1) Destruction of Japanese aircraft in much-greater numbers than the CATF's entire strength
2) Destruction of enemy military and naval establishments in China to encourage Chinese resistance
3) Disruption of Japanese shipping in the interior of China and off the coasts of China
4) Interdiction of Japanese air concentrations being ferried from Chinese bases across Indochina and Thailand into Burma
5) Destruction of Japanese air force morale by destroying rear depots and production facilities[40]

Chennault refined his ideas in a memo prepared at Naiden's request two months later, titled "Plan for Employment of U.S. Air Forces in China."[41] Chennault had accepted Stilwell's modification of his plans to make the defense of the air ferry route his priority, with operations against Japanese forces and installations his secondary mission. To accomplish this mission, he believed he would require a minimum of 100 fighters and 30 medium bombers, with six long-range reconnaissance airplanes to monitor Japanese air force activity. With this same force he believed he could carry out his second mission of attacking Japanese installations and targets of opportunity in China, Indochina, and Burma, using the range and mobility of his aircraft whenever and wherever there was a chance of inflicting heavy losses. With air reconnaissance, American aircraft in China could be rapidly concentrated to attack targets across a wide arc, responding to any threats from Japanese air forces in China or Burma. There were requirements, however, particularly for better facilities at Chinese airfields and above all an ensured supply of gasoline, ammunition, and bombs. This was the plan. Although the CATF had half the forces he considered the minimum he required, he began putting his plan into effect.

China Air Task Force Operations, July–December 1942

At the time, the Japanese Army Air Force had the *1st Hikōdan* (1st Air Brigade) in central China opposing the Chinese air forces. The *1st Hikōdan* had on strength several independent squadrons for reconnaissance, the *44th Hikōsentai* for army cooperation, and two fighter and two bomber *sentai* as its main striking force. The *54th Sentai* was based at Hankou and Nan Ching with the Type 97 Fighter (Ki-27 Nate), along with the *10th Dokuritsu Hikōchutai* with the Type 1 Fighter (Ki-43 Oscar), while the *24th Hikōsentai* had recently been transferred from Manchuria to Canton with Type 1 fighters. Of the Air Brigade's two bomber *sentai*, the *62nd Hikōsentai* had the Type 97 Heavy Bomber (Ki-21 Sally), while the *90th Hikōsentai* had the Type 99 Light Bomber (Ki-48 Lily). These units had supported the Japanese army's campaign in Chekiang-Kiangsi to destroy Chinese airfields intended for the Doolittle raiders. To strengthen Japanese Army Air Force units in China, the *3rd Hikōshidan* (3rd Air Division) moved from Singapore to Canton in August. Later in the year the *33rd Hikōsentai* arrived to replace the *24th Hikōsentai*, and with the China Air Task Force's growing attacks and the withdrawal of the *54th Hikōsentai* back to Japan to reequip with the Type 1 Fighter, the *10th Dokuritsu Hikōchutai* was expanded to

A formation of Type 99 light bombers from the *90ʰ Hikōsentai* heading out on a mission over China during 1942–43. *Author's collection*

become the *25th Hikōsentai*. These forces were charged with destroying the CATF and its bases at Kweilin, Lingling, and Hengyang.[42]

American Army Air Force combat operations in China began before the CATF was activated. Chennault sent out the 11th Bomb Squadron while he still had AVG pilots available to provide an escort, switching the bombers between different targets and different airfields to keep the Japanese guessing on his strength and intentions.[43] Chennault scheduled several missions during the second half of June to bomb Hanoi and Hankow, but bad weather prevented the B-25s from flying. On 1 July 1942, with somewhat better weather predicted, Maj. Bayse took four B-25s off from Hengyang to bomb shipping on the Yangtze River, 40 miles from Hankow, with Ed Rector leading five AVG P-40s in the first American Army Air Force bombing mission in China. Poor visibility over the river and inexperience on the part of bombardiers caused near misses, but no hits on the ships.[44] The next day, Bayse led three bombers back to Hankow to bomb shipping at the docks on the river, getting hits on warehouses and some near misses on the ships alongside. Continuing their assault on Japanese targets, Bayse and four other B-25s went out on July 3 to bomb the Japanese Army Air Force base at Nan Chang, southeast of Hankow, with an escort of four AVG P-40s from the 3rd AVG Squadron, led by Squadron Leader James Howard. Approaching the target above an overcast, the bombers found a hole in the clouds right over the airfield. They came in at 2,500 feet, dropping demolition and fragmentation bombs on the runway and onto two hangars, claiming several airplanes on the ground destroyed. Three of the P-40s went down to strafe the airfield. As the B-25s pulled away from the target, one of the pilots radioed Bayse, "I see red spots and they are right over us!" A formation of around a dozen Type 97 fighters (Nates) came after the bombers, but the P-40 pilots kept them away, with Harry Bolster and Robert Raines claiming one each. S/Sgt. Adam Williams claimed one fighter probably destroyed when it flew too close to his B-25.[45]

Over the following few days, Chennault sent his small force to bomb Canton, switching them to the airfield at Kweilin. On the morning of July 4, five bombers took off to attack the Japanese airfield at Tien Ho near Canton. One airplane had to head back for Kweilin with engine trouble, but the four continued on, without escort, reaching the target a little after 7 a.m. to drop their bombs on the runway and airplanes alongside and claiming seven to ten destroyed. The formation then flew back to their new temporary base at Kweilin. After a day for needed maintenance, the bombers went back to Canton on July 6 to attack an oil storage facility. Five B-25s went on the mission, this time with an escort of four Army Air Force P-40s from the 75th Fighter Squadron, with Maj. "Tex" Hill leading his fighters on their first escort mission and the 23rd Fighter Group's first offensive mission. The bombers came in at 2,500 feet but couldn't see any oil storage tanks, so they bombed warehouses, starting large fires before withdrawing at high speed. A formation of Nates tried to intercept the bombers, but the P-40s were there to intercept them, with Hill claiming one shot down, while John Petach—one of the AVG pilots who had agreed to stay on for an additional two weeks—claimed a second destroyed and another probable. After another hiatus for maintenance of 10 days, during which time Haynes went out in a single B-25 to bomb a Japanese headquarters on July 8, five B-25s took off from Kweilin on the morning of July 16 and flew to Hengyang for another mission against Hankow. Haynes led the mission, with Hill again leading six P-40s from the 75th Squadron as escort. The targets were the docks and warehouses along the river. The B-25s carried a mix of half 50 kg demolition and half 50 kg incendiary bombs, with each ship also having six small Chinese-made 18 kg bombs that the crew threw out a rear window when they were over the target. After refueling at Hengyang and getting a final briefing, the bombers took off for the trip to Hankow, where they bombed from 12,000 feet, starting numerous fires in the target area. After returning to Hengyang the bombers were refueling when the alert sounded. They took off for Lingling—the designated dispersal field—but in poor weather one of the B-25s was accidentally shot down by Freeman Ricketts, an AVG pilot who had agreed to stay on. Fortunately the crew all bailed out safely, but the 11th Bomb Squadron had lost a precious B-25.[46] There were further raids over the next several days—an attack on Tien Ho airfield on July 18, a mission in support of the Chinese army on July 19, and an attack on shipping in the Yangtze River on July 20—and then the bombers withdrew back to Kunming for needed maintenance.[47]

This would be the pattern of bomber operations over the next few months. The bombers would fly a few missions interspersed with delays due to weather, maintenance, or a lack of gasoline. Chennault used his bomber force in a form of aerial guerrilla warfare, striking widely dispersed targets in a series of hit-and-run raids, shifting his bombers between his advanced airfields as needed until lack of parts, bombs, or fuel ended the series of missions, and then withdrawing back to Kunming to regroup, his bombers protected by the Chinese air-warning net he had built and his P-40s.[48] Spare parts were particularly hard to come by. It could take weeks for

THE CHINA AIR TASK FORCE

A high-altitude photo of the Japanese Army Air Force base at Tien Ho, near Canton. Tien Ho was the JAAF's main base in southern China and covered the important ports of Canton and Hong Kong. It would be a frequent target for the CATF. *3A-2629, RG342FH, NARA*

parts to arrive from the depot in Karachi. The 11th Bomb Squadron had to resort to setting aside the B-25C damaged in the mission of June 2 to supply spare parts so the other bombers could keep flying. A major headache for the armament crews was the variety of bombs supplied to the 11th Squadron. Only a small number of Army Air Force 300-pound and 500-pound bombs could be carried over the Hump route, so the squadron had to rely on older stocks of Chinese and foreign bombs that had accumulated over the years. These ranged from 100 kg (220 lb.) Chinese demolition and incendiary bombs to French-made 50 kg (110 lb.) bombs and Russian 200 kg and 50 kg bombs. None of these bombs would fit the standard bomb racks on the B-25s, so the armament crews were constantly welding attachments onto the bombs to get them to fit.[49] The squadron armaments officer, Lt. Elmer Tarbox, who had removed the Bendix turrets and replaced them with two .30-caliber machine guns, installed another .30-caliber machine gun in the tail of the B-25s that could be fired remotely—although without accuracy—to cover the tail.[50]

The newly arrived Army Air Force fighter pilots soon had their own baptism of fire. The first Japanese fighters the CATF claimed not surprisingly fell to the more experienced former AVG pilots. 1st Lt. Henry Elias of the 75th Fighter Squadron was the first of the

THE TENTH AIR FORCE IN WORLD WAR II

To increase the number of fighters in the CATF, Bissell transferred the 16th Fighter Squadron from the 51st Fighter Group to the 23rd Fighter Group. Lt. D. D. Bryant sits in the cockpit of his 16th Fighter Squadron P-40E while the ground crew refuel his airplane. *3A-1999, RG342FH, NARA*

new arrivals to score a victory, claiming a Type 97 fighter (Nate) shot down over Hankow on July 10 and another over Nan Chang airfield 16 days later.[51] Many of the air combats over the next several months, by day and by night, took place over the CATF's airfields as the *1st Hikōshidan* tried to knock out these bases. The Japanese launched a major attack on Hengyang on July 30 and 31. As a preliminary to the main daytime attack, the Japanese sent a small formation of bombers to bomb the airfield at night, a tactic they had used on several previous nights in attacks on Lingling, Kweilin, and Hengyang. At Hengyang, Maj. John Alison and Capt. Ajax Baumler, both experienced fighter pilots assigned to the 75th Fighter Squadron, had watched the night attack on Hengyang the night of July 29. Alison decided that if the Japanese bombers came back the next night, he would try to intercept them in his P-40. Baumler said he would go with him, and on the night of July 29 the two pilots prepared their two P-40s on the runway. In the early hours of July 30, the Chinese warning net alerted them to an incoming raid. The two pilots climbed to 12,000 feet to get above the Japanese bombers. Seeing exhaust lights above him, Alison climbed to attack, coming in on a formation of three Type 97 bombers. He fired on one, knocking it out of formation; coming up from below, Baumler attacked this airplane and shot it down. Although his P-40 was damaged by enemy fire, Alison continued his attack, knocking down two bombers before bringing his P-40 in for a crash landing in a nearby river. Baumler had pursued a fourth bomber, knocking this aircraft down north of Hengyang.[52]

A few hours later the Japanese sent out a large fighter force to attack Hengyang, with Ki-27 fighters, apparently from the *54th Sentai*, and Ki-43 fighters from the *24th Sentai* and the *10th Dokuritsu Hikōchutai*, arriving over the airfield around 9:00 a.m. Ten pilots from the 16th and 75th Fighter Squadrons took off to intercept, with Maj. "Tex" Hill leading the formation. Hill found himself approaching one of the Ki-27s head on and, when he judged himself in range, fired, sending the Japanese fighter down to crash at the end of the Hengyang runway. Maj. John Bright, who had scored two victories with the AVG, attacked one of the Ki-43s and shared its destruction with his wingman. He then found himself, like Hill, making a head-on pass at a Ki-27, knocking this down for his second claim. Capt. Baumler also claimed a fighter shot down in the battle. Two other 75th Squadron pilots and one from the 16th Squadron claimed victories, although these were later assessed as probable victories, not confirmed. The Japanese squadrons claimed four P-40s shot down for the loss of one pilot.[53]

The *24th Sentai* returned to Hengyang early the next morning with its Ki-43s on a sweep over the airfield. With good warning, the 16th Fighter Squadron sent six P-40s from Lingling to cover Hengyang

1st Lt. Dallas Clinger's P-40E with other 16th Fighter Squadron P-40s at the CATF base at Kweilin in October 1942. Clinger became an ace flying with the CATF and the Fourteenth Air Force. *3A-986, RG342FH, NARA*

THE CHINA AIR TASK FORCE

under Maj. Hal Young, while Maj. Bright led a formation of the 75th Squadron from Hengyang. Bright's formation was the first to run into the Japanese fighters, with Bright exploding a fighter he identified as a Zero (for many Allied pilots at the time, any radial-engine Japanese fighter with retractable landing gear was a Zero) and sending a second down smoking for a probable. 1st Lt. John Lombard and his wingman, 2nd Lt. Dallas Clinger from the 16th Squadron, found themselves in a swirling fight with a large formation of Ki-43s. Lombard shot down one Ki-43, while Clinger claimed another destroyed and a probable. The results were even that day, with each squadron claiming three victories and a probable. The *24th Sentai* claimed six P-40s shot down for the loss of three Ki-43s.[54]

The Japanese went after Hengyang again on August 5 and September 3 and made two attacks on Kweilin in November. The raid on August 5 saw the Japanese sending around 50 fighters to attack Hengyang shortly after dawn. John Alison led eight P-40s from the 16th and 75th Squadrons. This fight appears to have been more difficult, since only Alison and 1st Lt. Lauren Barnebey managed to score, each claiming one fighter shot down. The 75th Squadron lost 2nd Lt. Lee Minor, who was shot down and killed—the 23rd Fighter Group's first pilot to be killed in action. The *24th Sentai*, in turn, claimed nine P-40s shot down. On September 3, the *24th Sentai* and the *10th Dokuritsu Hikōchutai* went out to strafe the CATF's three airfields at Hengyang, Lingling, and Kweilin, claiming 10 P-40s destroyed on the ground, though none were in fact lost. Intercepting these raids, the 75th Squadron claimed two fighters shot down over Hengyang and two over Lingling.[55]

By this time, the CATF was down to 34 serviceable P-40s and 38 pilots.[56] There was a growing consensus that the P-40 was no longer adequate to take on the latest Japanese fighters. In early September, "Tex" Hill and John Alison submitted their evaluations of the P-40 in combat over China. In his report addressed to Chennault, Hill stated:

> *In the early stages of the war the P-40, with its superior speed and diving characteristics, gave us the tremendous advantage of choosing the time and place for combat and also of breaking off an engagement at will. This enabled us to engage an enemy force many times our size with good results.*
>
> *As time went on the Japanese had an opportunity to study and learn well our tactics in the air, which basically have remained the same. At the same time their tactics have improved and are becoming better as time goes on. Their pursuit has become better to such an extent that we are now at a decided disadvantage. On the morning of July 30th the Japanese appeared with a new type of pursuit ("971") which could outmaneuver, out climb, and almost out run the P-40. The P-40 has very little chance operating against a type such as this, especially when the enemy is always numerically superior.*[57]

John Alison supported Hill's criticisms of the P-40, noting that the P-40 had difficulty combating the latest Japanese fighters and intercepting high-flying Japanese twin-engine reconnaissance airplanes, which he called the Japanese Army "45" (probably the Army Type 100 Command Reconnaissance Plane, the Mitsubishi Ki-46, code-named Dinah, which equipped the *18th Dokuritsu Hikōchutai* in the *1st Hikōdan*). Alison also referred to the "Army 971," saying that the airplane had the characteristic climb and maneuverability of Japanese fighters, but a speed that was close to that of the P-40. Alison stated his position unequivocally:

> *The P-40, even with its superior armament, protection for the pilot, and strong construction, is not suitable for operations against Japanese aircraft now in use in this theater. To properly exploit superior fire power it is absolutely necessary to have a definite advantage in either climb, maneuverability, or high speed. In weighing these conditions the advantage goes to the Japanese. . . . The Japanese have always met us in greatly superior numbers. To engage them at low altitudes where we are unable to dive away is to go into the fight with the weight on the side of the enemy. If the Japanese should attack from high altitudes it would be impossible to meet the enemy until he decided to come down and fight. The advantage of deciding when to fight would not be ours. The service ceiling of the fully loaded P-40 is for practical purposes 20,000 feet and the absolute ceiling is 25,000 feet or less. The Japanese have been attacking us from medium altitudes, and when we have been able to dive through their formations our results have been good because of the advantage of fire power. It is reasonable to believe that as a result of their recent losses when using these tactics the Japanese will go high or low altitude attacks, or a combination of both.*[58]

Part of the problem was the poor quality of the P-40s the CATF had available and the difficulty of maintenance with shortages of spare parts and tools. Hill and Alison complained that many of the P-40Es that had arrived in China were already worn out. They had been used in the United States for training and then shipped to Africa to be flown to Karachi and then on to China, arriving with more than 150 hours on their Allison engines, which was considered to be the useful life of the engine before major overhaul. As a result, performance was less than optimal, and the planes suffered from a high rate of mechanical failure. Hill noted that on the mission of September 2 he had begun the day with 16 P-40s, only to end the day with 10, having six airplanes—40 percent of his available force—out of commission not through enemy action, but through mechanical problems.[59] The other problem the squadron commanders were dealing with was the poor quality of some of the pilots who had been assigned to the CATF. Many lacked flying experience and had difficulty flying the formations that combat required. As Alison bluntly stated in his report, "the proficiency of pilots assigned to this group was far below that considered acceptable for training squadrons in peace time operations and certainly not acceptable in an active theater."[60]

Fortunately, over the coming months the situation began to improve. As Chennault wrote in his postwar memoir, "flying accidents weeded out our worst pilots, and the summer fighting tempered the best newcomers into confident veterans."[61] In mid-September, newer model P-40Ks began to arrive to replace the worn-out P-40Es. The P-40K had a more powerful Allison engine (V-1710-73), which gave the K model an additional 175 horsepower and a slightly higher maximum speed than the E model.[62] While the pilots appreciated any increase in power, they remained concerned over the apparent decline in the P-40's margin of performance over the Japanese fighters. What the "Army 971" that Hill and Alison referred to is unclear, since the Japanese fighter *sentai* in the area at the time were all equipped with the first model of the Type 1 fighter (Ki-43-I), which the AVG pilots had already encountered over Burma. The later model of the Type 1 fighter, the Ki-43-II, did not come into service until early 1943. It may simply have been that the margin of performance between a worn-out P-40E and a Ki-43 had narrowed considerably. Fortunately for the CATF, the Japanese did not adopt

A P-40K of the 23rd Fighter Group in China. Newer P-40 models gradually replaced older AVG P-40B and P-40E aircraft. *Box 12, China-Air, folder FX-37, RG208AA, NARA*

high-altitude tactics as John Alison feared they would. The Ki-43 pilots found that their best tactical altitude was around 9,000 feet. They always tried to engage the P-40s at lower altitudes.[63] This proved difficult, since the P-40s stuck to Chennault's tactics of maintaining an altitude advantage and using hit-and-run attacks against the more maneuverable Japanese fighters. The Chinese early-warning net that Chennault had built before the war often gave the CATF the advantage of having time to climb to altitude before the Japanese formations arrived.

More pilots arrived in September, and, to Chennault's delight, they turned out to be pilots who had spent considerable time flying fighters defending the Panama Canal. The "Panama pilots," as he called them, were exactly the kind of pilots he wanted for the CATF. As he later wrote,

All of them learned to fly in the rigorous prewar Air Corps training regime. They were expert fighter boys with ample experience in long range navigations, gunnery, dive-bombing, and tight formation flying. . . . This group of Panama postgraduates produced some of the finest pilots ever to fight in China. . . . For more than a year they were the backbone of the China fighter squadrons. After they arrived the C.A.T.F. smacked less of a primary training school and more of a combat group. The Japanese soon felt the difference.[64]

In November the Japanese launched a series of raids against the CATF's base at Kweilin, which had not been subject to many attacks. The first attack took place on November 2, when the *25th and 33rd Sentai* escorted 12 bombers to bomb the airfield. The 16th Fighter Squadron had adequate warning, and 12 P-40s took off to intercept the raid, climbing for the advantage of altitude. When the Japanese formation neared the airfield, the P-40s dove down to attack. 1st Lts. John Lombard, Robert Mooney, and Llewellyn Couch each claimed a Ki-43, while Capt. Clyde Slocumb and 2nd Lt. Walter Lacy both shot down one of the bombers. The Ki-43s claimed three P-40s shot down, but the 16th Squadron lost only one airplane when 2nd Lt. Lacy was killed during his attack on the bombers. Bad weather delayed the next attack until November 9, when eight Japanese fighters came over Kweilin and the 16th Squadron claimed another three shot down, with 1st Lt. Lombard getting his second kill in a week. Three days later the Japanese attacked Kweilin once again, this time sending six waves of eight to twelve fighters, with each wave beginning shortly after dawn and continuing until late in the morning. The Japanese fighters went first to Kweilin, then to Lingling about two hours later, perhaps in the hope of catching the P-40s on the ground refueling after the first attack. The 16th Squadron rose up to defend their field, and in battles over Kweilin and Lingling the 11 pilots who got off claimed four Ki-43s destroyed, six probably destroyed, and five damaged. 2nd Lt. Melvin Kimball claimed two probables and two damaged during the course of a busy morning. This was the last daylight attack on Kweilin for some months, although several bombers carried out a night attack on November 23, hoping to catch the 11th Bomb Squadron's B-25s that had flown to Kweilin in preparation for attacks on Hong Kong and Canton. Maj. Harry Pike, 1st Lt. John Lombard, and 1st Lt. Joseph Griffin took off in the early hours and shot down three bombers, though Lombard's P-40 was hit in the gasoline tank by return fire and burst into flames, with Lombard bailing out and landing safely.[65]

With its limited planes and pilots, the CATF fighter squadrons had done remarkably well in defending their bases. In the battles over Hengyang, Kweilin, and Lingling, the 16th, 75th, and 76th Squadrons had claimed around 35 Japanese fighters and bombers for the loss of three P-40s in air combat. On escort missions for the B-25s the fighters did equally as well, including their best day in a fierce air battle over Canton. The 11th Bomb Squadron had spent 12 days at Kunming on needed maintenance and additions to the armament on their B-25s. On August 2, six bombers flew to Kweilin for an operation against Tien Ho airfield at Canton. After waiting four days for the weather to break, Maj. Bayse led four bombers to the target, with an escort of seven P-40s getting hits on the runways and aircraft parked alongside, claiming 10 destroyed. Five bombers returned to Tein Ho on August 8, getting good hits on the airfield again. Japanese fighters intercepted the formation, and Capt. Charles Sawyer, leading the P-40s, claimed one fighter (identified as an I-97-II) and 2nd Lt. Patrick Daniels got another. The next day Haynes took five B-25s on the first mission to Haiphong, in French Indochina, with an escort of three P-40s. Because of the range, the bombers landed at the Chinese airfield at Nanning, close to the border, to refuel. Finding clear weather over the target, the bombers hit the docks and warehouses and got one hit on a large freighter. The P-40s carried 17 kg incendiary bombs and went down to bomb and strafe after the B-25s had finished bombing.[66]

THE CHINA AIR TASK FORCE

A B-25 flies over Haiphong on 9 August 1942. Col. Caleb V. Haynes, commanding the CATF bomber force, led five 11th Bomb Squadrons on the mission to bomb the docks and warehouse in the port. *3A-2803, RG342FH, NARA*

Bad weather prevented any flying for the next two weeks. In the last few days of August, as the Japanese seemed to be preparing for an attack across the Salween River into Yunnan, the bombers went to attack Lashio and other targets in Burma and northern French Indochina in support of Chinese forces. Five bombers attacked Myitkyina on August 30, flying on to land at Dinjan to rearm and returning to Kunming the next day, bombing Myitkyina again on the way. Then, on September 3, Bayse undertook a reconnaissance flight over Hanoi to gather information for future missions. Coming in at 20,000 feet, the B-25 dropped bombs on Gialam airfield at Hanoi, getting hits on the runway. Nine Type 2 twin-engine fighters (Ki-45 Nick) from the *21st Sentai* took off to intercept as Bayse dove away from the target. His top turret gunner sent one fighter down with a smoking engine. The B-25s returned to Hanoi three weeks later, when Bayse led four B-25s to bomb Gialam airfield on September 25 with an escort of nine P-40s from the 76th Fighter Squadron, led by Maj. Ed Rector and Col. Robert Scott, who tagged along. Over the target a mixed formation of Ki-45s and Ki-43s came up to intercept the bombers. The Ki-45s suffered heavily, with the P-40s claiming six shot down and two damaged. Rector claimed two destroyed and Scott received credit for one shot down and another damaged.[67] In *God Is My Co-pilot* Scott described his combat:

I caught a flight of three I-45s [as the American pilots called the Ki-45 at the time] going hell-bent for the bombers from below and to the rear and shot the last one in the formation with a short burst. It was point-blank range and occurred very fast. I first saw a thin trail of gray smoke that looked like the usual condensation cloud that forms behind the wings of fighter ships doing maneuvers at high altitude, when the atmospheric conditions are just right. And then flame poured from the right engine. It spread up over the cockpit and stretched thirty feet back in the slipstream. I moved up towards the second enemy fighter and didn't see the flamer go down.

With my first burst the next ship rolled over and dove, with one engine shot-up. By now I had caught up to the lead I-45, who was shooting at the bombers from exceedingly long range. I methodically aimed for his engines, putting a short burst into one and then into the other. The Jap must have felt the fire, for he went into a steep, climbing turn—which incidentally is very good if you have a ship that will outclimb your opponent. I thought this climbing turn might be a trick so I watched closely for him to turn on me. But when he rolled over he dove not for me but for the clouds. I kept going after him and must have put two hundred shots into him before he got out of my sight in the cumulus clouds. Pieces had begun to come from his fuselage and smoke was trailing behind. I believe his engines were hit and were failing, for his props seemed to be "windmilling." And yet I could only claim a "probable" for I didn't see it catch fire or crash.[68]

After a month of missions in support of the Chinese army and having received reinforcements in the shape of five more B-25s and crews, the 11th Bomb Squadron prepared for the first American attack on Hong Kong. Chennault wanted to wear down the Japanese fighter force in China by using the B-25s as bait, putting in the bombers at 15,000 feet with the P-40s flying above to allow the diving attacks they had found so successful against the Japanese fighters.[69] Hong Kong was considered to be an important target bound to be defended. On October 24, the 11th Bomb Squadron sent 11 B-25s, including one from the 22nd Bomb Squadron—one of several sent to China temporarily to work with the 11th Squadron—to Kweilin. After a final briefing the next morning from Haynes, who led the mission, 12 B-25s took off to bomb the docks at Kowloon in the largest CATF bombing mission to date. Nine P-40s took off as escort, with Col. Scott in the lead and "Tex" Hill leading the second flight of four airplanes. Two P-40s had to return to Kweilin with engine problems, leaving only seven to accompany the bombers. Making a wide detour around Canton, the formation came in on Hong Kong in perfect weather with the Kowloon docks clearly visible. The B-25s bombed from 17,000 feet, getting hits in the target area. Haynes then took his formation into a diving turn to avoid antiaircraft fire. Haynes made another turn in the opposite direction, directly into a formation of Japanese fighters he had seen waiting to attack the bombers. As the bombers raced past flying in tight formation at full throttle, the gunners opened fire as the Japanese fighters came around into the attack.[70]

The P-40s flying above were already diving down in their own attacks on the Japanese fighters, identified as Navy Zeros (these were almost certainly Ki-43 Oscars from the *33rd Sentai*, which arrived in Canton in September, since the Imperial Japanese Navy had no fighter units based at Hong Kong at this time) and twin-engine Ki-45s. "Tex" Hill came out of his dive behind an enemy fighter that had not seen his approach, blowing it up for his 17th victory. Hill then went after other Japanese fighters, firing quick bursts to keep them off the bombers and damaging at least three. Capt. John Hampshire Jr.—one of the newly arrived Panama pilots—returned with claims for two Zeros shot down, his first victories in China. Scott claimed one Zero and one Ki-45 shot down and two more Zeros as probables. Other pilots claimed four more Zeros shot down and two more damaged. The bomber gunners claimed four Japanese fighters shot down and four probables, Staff Sgt. W. C. Stubblefield, flying in Haynes's B-25, received credit for one Zero and one Ki-45 shot down and two Zeros probably destroyed. 2nd Lt. Morton Sher's P-40 was hit during the combat, but he managed to get back for a crash landing in Chinese territory, returning several weeks later. The CATF lost its first B-25 to Japanese fighters. Coming off the target, the B-25 of Capt. Howard Allers fell behind the formation and came under intense attack, setting the right engine on fire. Then the left engine was hit and quit. Allers gave the order to bail out and the flight engineer and radio operator did so, but soon the B-25 was too low for the rest of the crew to bail out, so Allers brought the B-25 down in some rice paddies. Of the six-man crew, only Lt. Marich, the copilot, and Lt. Cunningham, the navigator, made it back through Japanese lines to Kweilin after a journey of two weeks, with the others being captured.[71] The B-25s flew a night mission to Hong Kong on October 25 and to Canton on October

B-25s from the 11th Bomb Squadron flying over Hong Kong, with smoke rising from their target, Japanese navy installations. During fall 1942 the squadron flew several missions to Hong Kong and Canton. *3A-2672, RG342FH, NARA*

26, and then on October 28 the 16th Fighter Squadron sent 17 P-40s to bomb and strafe shipping in Kowloon harbor. Six P-40s carried one 500-pound bomb each, with 11 more flying above as escort. Using dive bombing, the P-40s hit one large freighter and got a near miss on a second, losing one P-40 in the attack, possibly to one of several Japanese fighters who took off to intercept the raid.[72]

After more missions supporting the Chinese army and several raids on targets in Burma, toward the end of November, Chennault marshaled his meager force at Kweilin for a series of return attacks on French Indochina, Hong Kong, and Canton. Nine B-25s with an escort of seven P-40s went to bomb shipping and the dock areas at Hon Gay and Haiphong on November 22, claiming one large 12,000-to-14,000-ton freighter sunk and another smaller freighter severely damaged (the French freighter *Khai Dinh*, of 5,110 tons, which the Japanese had seized in 1941, was sunk on this date).[73] The next day, six B-25s with an escort of 17 P-40s went to bomb Tien Ho airfield, getting hits on the runway and airfield installations and destroying a number of aircraft on the airfield. Approaching the airfield, 1st Lt. Robert Davis—bombardier in the lead aircraft—saw many Japanese aircraft on the field and signaled his pilot for a change of course through the pilot's direction indicator. The six bombers had just finished their turn when they dropped their bombs, but many fell among the parked aircraft. The bombers went back to the area on November 24 to bomb shipping in the Pearl River between Canton and Hong Kong, with some of the P-40s carrying 17 kg fragmentation bombs. The bombers and fighters claimed two direct hits and three near misses on one freighter, which sank, and another damaged. One P-40 force landed with a damaged wing when one of the fragmentation bombs went off prematurely. Chennault shifted his attacks north and sent seven B-25s to attack a target near Hankow on November 25, using Hengyang as their base before bringing them back to Kweilin.[74]

Col. Robert L. Scott helping reload his P-40E. Scott commanded the 23rd Fighter Group and became an ace over China. He went on to write *God Is My Co-pilot*, an account of his experiences fighting in China that became a bestseller during the war. *3A-1073, RG342FH, NARA*

The mission of November 27 to bomb the Whampoa docks at Canton—the biggest CATF mission to date—resulted in the CATF's largest victory against their Japanese fighter opponents. Once again using B-25s as bait to draw up the Japanese fighters, Chennault sent 10 B-25s on the mission, with Col. Scott leading an escort of 21 P-40s from the 16th, 75th, and 76th Fighter Squadrons. As the bombers neared Canton they split into three formations: one to attack an aircraft factory, one to attack Tien Ho airfield, and one to attack shipping in the Pearl River. Japanese fighters came up in large numbers to intercept the American formation. The American pilots identified both Ki-27s (called I-97s) and Ki-43s (which they called

Japanese fighters damaged this 11th Bomb Squadron B-25 during one of the squadron's missions over China, narrowly missing the top turret gunner. *3A-73963, RG342FH, NARA*

THE TENTH AIR FORCE IN WORLD WAR II

Zeros). The combats began soon after the B-25 formation split up. In the fights that followed, nearly every P-40 pilot would have a run-in with a Japanese fighter. The bombers hit the airfield and sank one ship in the Pearl River, claiming this as an 8,000-ton freighter, although it was more likely the 1,907-ton *Ryokusei Maru*, sunk that day by American aircraft (demonstrating the difficulty Army Air Force pilots had determining the size of ships they attacked). High-scorer fighter for the day was Capt. John Hampshire, who was credited with three "Zeros" (Ki-43s) shot down. This gave him ace status, the first Army Air Force pilot in the 75th Fighter Squadron to achieve this distinction. By coincidence, 1st Lt. Charles Dubois of the 16th Fighter Squadron and 1st Lt. John Lombard of the 76th Fighter Squadron also became aces that day. Col. Scott claimed two fighters shot down, as did Capt. Edmund Gross and 1st Lt. William Druwing from the 16th Squadron, and 1st Lt. Charles Dubois and Maj. Bruce Holloway from the 76th Squadron, who also received credit for a probable.[75] The fighters claimed 23 Japanese airplanes destroyed, with another four probables and one damaged. The bomber gunners put in claims for two fighters confirmed destroyed and two probables.[76]

Maj. Holloway recorded his impressions of the mission in his diary:

By this time I was right over Tien Ho Airdrome, so I dived down into the fight. It was really going strong and my flight pitched right into the middle of it. I made a pass at a Zero and it burst into flames. Didn't see it hit the ground but started to look for others. They were all over the place, and you could see burning tracer bullets going in every direction. I saw burning Japanese airplanes falling all over the sky.

I made several more runs on Zeros and I-97s and finally got into a good position on an I-97 and gave him a long burst. I don't know whether he went down or not—claimed him as a probable. After this I climbed back up for a little altitude on the outside of the fighter, expecting to be jumped on from above at any instant. I got back to about 8,000 feet and barged in again. By this time I could see only about three Japs left milling around over the field like mosquitoes. All the P-40s had either left or were chasing some Jap out over the countryside. The three that were left were very elusive and I didn't get a good pass at any of them. Finally two of them got on my tail so I left the vicinity in somewhat of a hurry and started for home. I could hear everybody talking about how many they shot down, and it certainly sounded good.

I proceeded toward home all by myself, looking around behind me all the time, when I saw an aircraft off to my left going back toward Canton. It was a twin-engine light bomber and was very low over the hills. I turned in behind him and gave chase. Apparently he never did see me. I pulled on up to within about 100 yards behind him, expecting the rear gunner to open up on me at any instant. Either there was no rear gunner or he was asleep. I opened up from directly astern and poured the lead into him. The whole right side of the plane burst into flames and immediately thereafter there was an explosion which tore off the entire right wing. The flaming wreckage fell off to the left and crashed into the ground. It made a beautiful fire and the whole thing took less time than it takes to tell about it [instead of a light bomber, Holloway was given credit for a Ki-45 fighter].[77]

Chennault sent the B-25s back to Hon Gay on November 29, then pulled his force back to Kunming, since the force was short on gas and on drop tanks for the P-40s and needed maintenance after an intensive week of operations.[78] Arnold sent Chennault the following message in early December:

You have my commendation and hearty congratulations for the remarkable succession of ably planned and brilliantly executed raids conducted against Japanese shipping, troop concentrations, and gun emplacements on November 25, 26, and 27. . . . Your complete success on all missions attempted and the impressiveness of your destruction of Japanese shipping has brought home to the American people the effectiveness of the air arm against surface craft and has emphasized that the Air Forces are superior to the enemy even in our most remote zone of combat. Congratulations to you and your men on a job well done.[79]

On December 23, Chennault was awarded the Distinguished Service Medal for his leadership of the China Air Task Force. The commendation read:

Chennault has demonstrated keen knowledge of Japanese air tactics and techniques, and though greatly outnumbered in planes and essential needs has succeeded in protecting large portions of unoccupied China from hostile air attack and caused severe losses to the enemy. His understanding of the problems of the China theater has resulted in a high degree of good will between US forces and the people of China.[80]

The CATF's fighters had one more good day before the end of the year. Chennault had sent the 16th Fighter Squadron down to the airfield at Yunnanyi, west of Kunming and closer to the Burmese border, to support attacks on Japanese forces across the Salween River. On Christmas Day the Japanese sent over a force of bombers before the 16th Squadron could get off the ground, but the Japanese bombs missed the airfield. Expecting the Japanese to return the next day, Col. Scott, who had flown down from Kunming the evening before, ordered all pilots on alert and sent up a patrol shortly after dawn. By chance, two 74th Squadron pilots returning to Kunming from escorting the bombers to Lashio encountered a twin-engine Japanese reconnaissance airplane likely on its way to Yunnanyi and shot it down. At 2:00 p.m. in the afternoon, Scott sent the 16th Squadron up on patrol in expectation of an afternoon attack. An hour later a Japanese formation of nine bombers with an escort of ten fighters approached the airfield. These were nine Type 99 (Ki-48 Lily) bombers from the *8th Sentai* with an escort of ten Type I fighters (Ki-43 Oscars) from the *50th Hikōsentai*.[81] Maj. Hal Pike led his flight of four P-40s down in an attack on the escort while Scott and Maj. George Hazlett took the rest of the pilots to attack the bombers. Scott claimed one bomber shot down and two more as probables, while other pilots claimed six "Zeros" and two bombers destroyed, with three more probably destroyed. Two P-40s were shot down: 1st Lt. Llewellyn Couch bailed out successfully; Sgt. Kazuo Fujii shot down 1st Lt. Robert Mooney, who bailed out but died from his wounds. It appears that only one of the Ki-43s was lost, with a further Ki-43 and two of the Ki-48 bombers damaged but able to return to their base.[82]

While their clashes with Japanese fighters received the most notice, Chennault regularly employed his fighters on strafing missions and reconnaissance. Many of these missions during September and October were to search for Japanese activity along the old Burma Road west of the Salween River down to Lashio, sometimes by a pair of P-40s and sometimes by a single airplane. As an example, on 22 September 1942, four P-40s on a reconnaissance over the area came upon Japanese convoys on the road around Lungling and destroyed between 12 and 20 trucks during repeated strafing attacks. On October 30, two P-40s went out from Kunming on a reconnaissance of Lashio, Loiwing, and Myitkyina. They found two Ki-43s at the airfield and went down to strafe them. One P-40 failed to return from the mission. In early December, four P-40s went out to bomb an airfield under construction at Dong Coung, in northern French Indochina, northwest of Hanoi. Each P-40 carried six 17 kg fragmentation bombs and used these to damage two steamrollers and the barracks. For reconnaissance, Chennault sent out his modified P-43s to photograph key targets. The P-43s flew frequent sorties over Hanoi, Haiphong, Canton, Hong Kong, and Japanese-occupied towns in Burma. Most of these missions were carried out at medium altitudes without interception. On one occasion on September 18, while flying at a higher altitude over Hanoi, a P-43 pilot noticed two Japanese fighters climbing up to intercept him. He took the P-43 from 26,000 to 28,000 feet and easily completed his reconnaissance and made his escape. In November the 9th Photographic Reconnaissance Squadron, which had recently arrived in India for service with the Tenth Air Force, sent a small detachment of three F-4 airplanes (the photoreconnaissance version of the Lockheed P-38) to operate out of Kunming, giving Chennault a much more capable reconnaissance aircraft.[83]

The 11th Bomb Squadron finished the year with several raids on Japanese installations around the Lashio area after a final mission on Gia Lam airport at Hanoi on December 14. The bombers hit Lashio on December 26 and 27. On the 27th, Capt. John Ruse made an individual attack on a small-walled town where he had noticed a lot of Japanese activity. Returning to Kunming, he recommended going back to the town for a second attack. This was approved and Ruse went back, leading three B-25s with an escort of three P-40s. Ruse decided to bomb from low level, since heretofore the bombers had not encountered much antiaircraft fire over small targets. On this occasion the Japanese were expecting another attack and opened up on the B-25s with machine gun fire as they came over the town. Ruse's B-25 had an engine knocked out, and he had to find his way back to Yunnanyi through a series of valleys, since he couldn't climb his B-25 high enough to get over the 10,000-foot-tall mountains in the surrounding area. On the flight home his navigator demonstrated exceptional bravery, as the squadron history recorded:

It was during this flight that Lt. Rowland Hill, Captain Ruse's navigator, exhibited that character of selfless devotion to duty that histories are written about. While over the target a large fragment of shell came through the floor of his compartment, hitting him in the back. It made a deep, gaping wound, through which blood poured unhindered, but Lt. Hill did not lose consciousness. The wound was too grave to respond to first aid treatment and Lt. Hill was forced to lie on the floor with his life blood flowing out of him while the limping plane sought a way home. During this period, and up until the landing at Yunnanyi, Lt. Hill attempted to continue his duties as navigator, passing on advice to Captain Ruse and aiding materially in the plane's safe arrival at the field. He died shortly after the landing.[84]

At the end of the year, Chennault had Col. Scott and Capt. Everett Holstrom—who had assumed command of the 11th Bomb Squadron after Maj. Bayse was promoted to lieutenant colonel and transferred back to India—prepare reports summarizing the activities of the fighters and bombers of the China Air Task Force. The reports made impressive reading. Scott reported that between its July 4 activation and 31 December 1942, the 23rd Fighter Group and the attached 16th Fighter Squadron had claimed 109 Japanese airplanes destroyed in aerial combat, with another 39 probably destroyed and 72 more damaged in 839 combat missions of all types. Most of the time the 23rd Group had only one-third of its strength in men and

B-25 gunners play a game of cards while waiting to take off on another mission over China. The .30-caliber machine gun the 11th Bomb Squadron's armament officer fitted into the tail of the squadron's B-25s can just be made out to the left. *Box 12, China-Air, folder FX-19, RG208AA, NARA*

THE TENTH AIR FORCE IN WORLD WAR II

planes in operation. The CATF had lost 17 airplanes to enemy action, with five pilots killed in combat and four more killed through other causes—a ratio of six to one in favor of the CATF. Nine airplanes were lost due to mechanical failures, but, frustratingly, 15 fighters were damaged or lost through accidents, mostly due to inexperienced pilots. Scott recommended that more pilots be assigned to the CATF so that they could be trained and made ready to replace pilots coming to the end of their tours. He also recommended that a second fighter group be assigned to the CATF, activated with personnel from the 23rd Fighter Group and the 16th Fighter Squadron to provide opportunities for promotion.[85]

The 11th Bomb Squadron completed 58 missions, sending out an average of five B-25s on each mission despite having only six aircraft available from July to October. The arrival of more aircraft after October 5, bringing the squadron up to 12, allowed at least nine aircraft to be kept in commission despite a constant shortage of spare parts and, for much of the time, maintenance crews. The flight crews had to fuel and prep their own airplanes and fuse and load their own bombs for most missions. The bomber gunners claimed nine Japanese fighters shot down and another 11 as probables. As a result of their bombing, the squadron believed they had destroyed 45 Japanese aircraft on the ground and damaged 30 more. The squadron claimed good results against Japanese shipping, claiming four large freighters sunk and damaged and possibly three more. This record was achieved with the loss of just two B-25s in combat, with four men captured, one killed, and four injured. The squadron's greatest handicap was the shortage of gasoline, which frequently restricted operations, as well as a shortage of bombs. Out of the 2,461 bombs over 100 lbs. in weight dropped during the squadron's 58 missions, only 389 were American.[86]

The China Air Task Force had accomplished much—perhaps not as much as Chennault would have liked, but "much more than could reasonably have been expected" from the limited resources he had available.[87] He had successfully executed both missions that Stilwell had set out for him: he had protected the Chinese end of the ferry route from India, and he had conducted effective operations against Japanese forces in China when those opportunities had become available. Despite this success, there was one area that continued to be a source of strain, and that was the CATF's relations with the Tenth Air Force in India.

Relations with the Tenth Air Force

There were any number of factors that led to the strained relationship between the China Air Task Force and the Tenth Air Force in the months following the CATF's activation, but among them were the complex command relationships in what was coming to be called the China-Burma-India (CBI) theater; the distances and difficulty of communications between headquarters; frustrations over shortages of men, equipment, and airplanes; and personality conflicts between commanders. The harsh reality was that during 1942, American production of all armaments and training of military forces, while building on the expansion begun in 1941, never came close to meeting the demands of all the theaters of war. The CBI theater was a distant third in priority after Europe and the Pacific and, with the Allied strategy of defeating Germany first, would remain so for some time to come. There simply were not enough men and planes available. All Arnold could do at the time was reassure his commanders in the CBI theater that reinforcements would come in time. But as a history of the American air war in Asia commented, "it does not require any great imagination to see that the authorities of the Tenth Air Force must have felt that they had been given a war to fight and were then being denied the men and equipment with which to fight it."[88] But as the history went on to say, "It requires great courage to neglect a sorely pressed theater, month after month, in pursuit of a

Claire Chennault takes Stilwell on an inspection of the CATF's P-40s a few months after the CATF's activation. Stilwell's support of Bissell to be head of the Tenth Air Force did not endear him to Chennault. Chennault and Stilwell would clash repeatedly over the next two years. *Box 12, China-Air, folder FX-36, RG208AA, NARA*

strategy which will eventually reduce a two-front war to a one-front war. And it requires great wisdom on the part of theater authorities to accept such a situation with patience."[89]

When Brereton left for the Middle East at the end of June 1942, Brig. Gen. Earl Naiden, his chief of staff, took over command of the Tenth Air Force, with the expectation that Brereton would soon return when the crisis in the Middle East was resolved. Chennault's initial dealings with the Tenth Air Force as commander of the China Air Task Force were with Naiden, who was carrying out decisions already made regarding the organization and missions of the CATF. Naiden's tenure as commander of the Tenth did not last long. Stilwell was apparently not happy with having Naiden as an acting commander of the principal Army Air Force unit in his command. Stilwell wanted Brig. Gen. Bissell appointed as commander of the Tenth instead of Brereton or Naiden, and asked for the War Department's approval. The War Department was hesitant about Stilwell's choice, since Bissell's earlier appointment as his air advisor over Claire Chennault had angered the Chinese. Stilwell persisted, arguing that Bissell's experience in the China theater, particularly his understanding of the logistical problems besetting the Tenth Air Force, made him a good candidate. In recommending Bissell he also had "Hap" Arnold's support.[90] The War Department finally agreed to Stilwell's request on August 4. Bissell replaced Naiden as commander of the Tenth Air Force, and Naiden took over command of the air ferry operation.[91]

Unfortunately, the friction between Bissell and Chennault soon reemerged and only intensified in the months following Bissell's assumption of command of the Tenth Air Force. The personality clash reflected differences in temperament, outlook, experience, and approach to the complicated situation the two men found themselves thrust into. In her biography of Claire Chennault, Martha Byrd observed that Chennault had found in the AVG "the niche in which he functioned best, working with strong and independent men of action, free from administrative impediments, in an environment that encouraged creativity and expressed appreciation."[92] His forte was the tactics of air warfare, and his strength the leadership of men in battle. His approach was to select "aggressive, innovative men who were eager to fight, training them well, then turning them loose by eliminating most of the restraints under which conventional Western military force operates."[93] Chennault had little patience with administration, seeing it as interfering with his ability to devote his time to "tactics and operations."[94] Nor did he seem to have an understanding of logistics and the complexity of the supply problems that affected the Tenth Air Force.[95] As the Air Force history commented, while no one doubted his qualities as a leader or his fighting record, "his administrative ability has been called into question many times and the thought that he lacked the necessary efficiency to manage his own headquarters seems to have been present in the minds of 10th Air Force officials from the beginning."[96] His desire to fight the Japanese and his firm ideas on how to fight them made him impatient when the United States failed to provide him with the tools he needed. He came to put the blame for this situation on Bissell and the Tenth Air Force.[97] There also remained his resentment that a man for whom he had little respect, and who had none of Chennault's experience in China, should have been promoted over him.[98]

Bissell, for his part, had the demanding responsibility of coordinating the activities of all the commands under the Tenth Air Force. His command stretched from Kunming to Karachi, with bases, units, and operations expanding slowly but steadily in between. The chain-of-command structure was awkward and communications between commands difficult and often slow. Chennault, for example, reported to Bissell in New Delhi as commander of the Tenth Air Force; Bissell in turn reported to Stilwell in Chungking as commander of all American Army forces in the CBI theater. Sometimes decisions had to go to Bissell in New Delhi, then to Stilwell in Chungking, back to Bissell, and then on to Chennault in Kunming, a time-

11th Bomb Squadron B-25s getting refueled before a mission in December 1942. Practically every bullet, bomb, and gallon of gasoline the bombers used had to come over the Hump. The CATF's logistical difficulties were a severe constraint on operations. *3A-1994, RG342FH, NARA*

consuming process.⁹⁹ Chennault criticized Bissell as a "fanatic for meticulous staff work and detailed reports."¹⁰⁰ But an argument could be made that with all the problems of communication in the theater—not least of which was the inadequate Indian telephone system—and the complexities of moving aircraft, men, and supplies along the long line of communications from Karachi to Kunming, Bissell had to insist on meticulous staff work. What Bissell seems to have understood was a key principle of military effectiveness; that is, "the most potent and ingenious operational capabilities are worthless unless a network of supporting activities buttresses them."¹⁰¹ This was what he was trying to build in the Tenth Air Force. Arnold observed that Bissell did not have "the 'We'll-get-it-done-in-spite-of-hell-or-high-water' attitude that Chennault had."¹⁰² Bissell "was an excellent staff officer who carefully worked out every operation before he undertook it, or said he could not do it," while Chennault "had the originality, initiative, and drive the Chinese liked."¹⁰³ Given this difference in temperament and outlook, it is not surprising that the two men came into conflict. Chennault could, at times, "sense slights where none were intended" and appear "unduly sensitive to his personal position and authority."¹⁰⁴ In his interactions with Chennault, Bissell did not always use the tact that might have smoothed the turbulent waters between them. While at first "exercising great patience with someone who seemed persistently to misjudge the motives of the 10ᵗʰ Air Force," later Bissell's patience "betokened tolerant and patronizing superiority."¹⁰⁵ Bissell "became ever more critical, Chennault ever more irascible, the messages darting back and forth ever more barbed in tone."¹⁰⁶

Their disagreements were over problems large and small. As the writer of the Air Force history commented, "it is not a pleasing correspondence to study."¹⁰⁷ Two areas in particular have a bearing on the outcome of this friction between Bissell and Chennault and its effect on the subsequent history of the Tenth Air Force: issues relating to the organization of Chennault's staff in the China Air Task Force and the attitudes that developed within the CATF toward the Tenth Air Force in the closing months of 1942. Regarding staff for the CATF, Bissell appears to have initially responded to a request from Chennault for assistance but then taken his concern further than Chennault intended or wanted. At the end of August, Chennault had asked Bissell to assign a competent A-1 officer, responsible for personnel and administrative matters. Bissell transferred Col. Strickland, his own adjutant general, to Chennault's command. A month later, without a formal request from Chennault, Bissell assigned Col. Birrell Walsh—serving as A-4 (logistics and supplies) for the Tenth Air Force—to be Chennault's A-4. Bissell then decided to replace Col. Marion Cooper, Chennault's chief of staff, with a capable, younger, West Point–trained officer—Lt. Col. Casey Vincent from the Karachi Air Base Command—and proposed that Chennault appoint Maj. Bruce Holloway as the CATF's A-3 (operations). On arrival in China, Chennault made Vincent his A-3 instead and later appointed Holloway to command the 76ᵗʰ Fighter Squadron. When in early January 1943 Bissell attempted to appoint a new group commander for the 23ʳᵈ Fighter Group upon Col. Scott's return to the United States, Chennault replied with a blistering letter asserting his right to appoint his own commanders, forcefully reminding Bissell that he himself had earlier given Chennault this authority.¹⁰⁸

Understandably, within the CATF there was a great frustration with the continued shortages of spare parts, personnel, airplanes, gasoline, and much else, but the blame came to be placed on the Tenth Air Force in India—as the apparent source of much of CATF's needed supplies—and not on the immense logistical problems the CBI theater faced at the time, much less the low priority Allied leaders had given the theater. Delays in promotion, in the award of decorations, and in the delivery of PX supplies and winter clothing were all laid at the feet of the Tenth Air Force, and by implication Bissell and Stilwell. This led to a "sense of being the victims of discrimination" among many personnel within the CATF, and by

Chinese and American ground crew clean the guns on a P-40 in China. Shortages of parts and gasoline also affected the CATF's fighter force. These shortages unfortunately led to resentment against Bissell and the Tenth Air Force. *3A-1077, RG342FH, NARA*

THE CHINA AIR TASK FORCE

the fall of 1942 this had become a topic of open discussion.[109] At the end of November, Bissell wrote to Chennault to complain about the comments an observer recently returned from Kunming had reported to him. According to this observer, pilots at Kunming, while proud of being part of the CATF, had a "feeling of kinship with the rest of the Tenth Air Force [that] was very close to nil . . . most of the pilots . . . seemed to have the firm conviction that the Tenth Air Force existed for the sole purpose of denying equipment to the China Air Task Force. Delhi is to them a place where the CATF's pet schemes are regularly sabotaged."[110] Bissell pointed out to Chennault that sentiment within the CATF reflected the leadership of its commanding general, perhaps a not-so-subtle hint pointing to Chennault's own views. He reminded Chennault that the Tenth Air Force had given the CATF the best personnel and most of the aircraft and supplies that arrived in the theater as soon as possible. He wanted Chennault's officers to understand the limitations of the air transport service and the fact that the Chinese were demanding supplies to be flown over the route as well as the CATF. He also wanted to ensure that the men in China knew about the conditions their counterparts in India were facing, saying, "they should know that there is more dysentery and malaria in India than in China; that the heat in India frequently runs 20 degrees greater than in China; that the seasonal dust makes living and flying conditions in India more difficult than they are [encountered] elsewhere."[111] There is no record of Chennault's response to Bissell's letter.

If Chennault's postwar memoir can be taken to reflect his feelings at the time, he appears to have been immensely frustrated with the situation that kept his force, as he saw it, on "a starvation diet" under the command of a man who, in his eyes, "prized a snappy salute from a perfectly uniformed staff officer more than a Japanese plane shot down in flames."[112] It is a pity that the souring of the relationship between Bissell and Chennault distracted them from trying to work out solutions together to what were in fact difficult problems with no easy or immediate solutions. Chennault believed he knew the best way to fight the Japanese and beat them. What he needed were "the means and the freedom to fight": a bigger air force under his own command, out from under Bissell's strictures, with adequate numbers of well-trained pilots, the most-modern aircraft, and ensured supplies.[113]

Ground or Air? The Debate on a Strategy for China

During the fall of 1942 a debate began among American military and political authorities over the most-effective means of prosecuting the war against Japan in China. The debate would intensify during the first half of 1943 and would lead to strains and bitterness within the American command in the China-Burma-India theater. The outcome of the debate would have a direct impact on the organization and mission of the Tenth Air Force. In essence, the debate revolved around the issue of how the American effort and resources devoted to China could best be employed: building an effective Chinese army to reopen a land route through northern Burma to provide supplies for later offensives against the Japanese in China, or organizing an air campaign from bases in China against the Japanese forces there, and potentially beyond. Stilwell, with the support of Gen. Marshall and the War Department, was on one side of the debate, favoring the development of the Chinese army, with Chennault, his patron Generalissimo Chiang Kai-shek, and several of President Roosevelt's closest advisors on the other supporting arguments for an air campaign, with President Roosevelt making the final decision.

The proposals Stilwell submitted to the Generalissimo in July 1942 recommended a major reorganization of the Chinese army. The War Department had given specific instructions to Stilwell that his mission was to "increase the effectiveness of United States assistance to the Chinese Government for the prosecution of the war and to assist in improving the combat efficiency of the Chinese Army."[114] To Stilwell, this meant reorganizing, retraining, and reequipping the Chinese army's nearly 300 existing divisions along the lines of the War Department's earlier Thirty Division plan. He recommended reducing the number of divisions by 50 percent and amalgamating troops and weapons into the remaining divisions to bring them up to strength.[115] The key to any aid for China and for improving the combat efficiency of the Chinese army was to greatly increase the flow of Lend-Lease supplies to China. Stilwell, as did most Allied strategists at the time, believed that the most-efficacious means of getting large volumes of supplies to China was to reopen a land route through Burma. Stilwell saw the alternatives either as retaking all of Burma; using the retrained and reequipped Chinese divisions from Yunnan together with Chinese, British, and American divisions from India; or building the road from Assam across northern Burma to link up with the old Burma Road—also employing Chinese divisions trained and armed in India for the task. By the fall of 1942, Stilwell had 45,000 Chinese troops training in India as his X-force and was trying to persuade the Generalissimo to agree to training 27 divisions in Yunnan as Y-Force. Using X-force from India and Y-Force from Yunnan, Stilwell hoped to open the land route through Burma as a precursor to operations in China. Both Stilwell and Marshall wanted to clear Burma and reestablish the land route to China before beginning the air offensive against Japan from Chinese bases. With adequate supplies and a strong Chinese army to defend the air bases, American bombers could undertake the planned bombing campaign against Japan from air bases in China secure from Japanese attack and without concern about logistics. The difficulty with Stilwell's plans was that they would take time to complete: time to train the Chinese forces in India and China, time to bring in the new weapons and supplies needed, and time to capture northern Burma and build a road across it.[116]

In contrast, Chennault held the firm belief that airpower offered a unique opportunity to inflict heavy damage on the Japanese, thereby sustaining China's war effort and morale at considerably lower cost in resources and time than Stilwell's plan. He had first articulated his ideas in 1940, when he helped develop plans for a 500-plane air force for China.[117] Chennault, like many of his contemporaries in the Army Air Corps in the 1930s, had implicit faith in the potential of airpower to be decisive in future wars. Chennault's area of expertise was pursuit aviation, which put him at odds with those disciples of William Mitchell who argued for strategic bombardment as the true role of airpower, but he recognized that the role of pursuit was "decisive only when exploited by other forces."[118] He came to believe that the critical factor in air warfare was the achievement of air superiority through the actions of pursuit aviation to enable bombardment aviation to achieve its mission, "the destruction of such strategical objectives as industrial centers, rail and marine transport facilities, and munitions and fuel production plants."[119] These ideas formed the basis for his air plan for China. Using bombers against key Japanese targets in China to force the Japanese to defend them, he believed he could defeat the Japanese air forces in China. With air superiority over China, he would use his bombers to attack Japanese shipping on the sea lanes off the

Loading a drop tank onto a P-40. Drop tanks gave P-40s the ability to escort B-25s to Hong Kong and Hanoi, increasing the reach of the CATF's striking power. Chennault came to believe that with a relatively small number of bombers and fighters, he could destroy the Japanese in China. *3A-2000, RG342FH, NARA*

China coast, disrupting the flow of raw materials back to Japan. Bombers based in China could strike at the industrial heartland of Japan, denying the Japanese armies the materials they would need to combat Chinese and American armies, who could then advance at lower cost in men and materials.[120]

For Generalissimo Chiang Kai-shek, Chennault's air plan became the preferred alternative. Even if the Generalissimo had wanted to reform and rebuild the Chinese army, political realities within China made it extremely unlikely that he could have done so. Within the Chinese government, "the division of political power was determined by the scale of military power directly held by each party."[121] The various factions making up the Kuomintang Party (KMT) and the provincial warlords that supported the Generalissimo to varying degrees would have stoutly resisted any diminution in their military strength through a reduction in the number of divisions in the Chinese army. The distribution of weapons and supplies was a form of patronage the Generalissimo used to ensure loyalty and obedience. For his part, the Generalissimo was loathe to see modern arms and training go to build up any of his political rivals, nor did he want to sacrifice divisions loyal to him in the jungles of Burma, or remove commanders who may have been militarily incompetent but who were politically loyal.[122] Chennault's air plan had the advantages that it would meet the American objectives of striking back against Japan, but with minimal use of Chinese resources and no disruption to the system of patronage that helped ensure the KMT's position within China, nor the risk of giving a foreigner (Stilwell) command over Chinese armies.[123] In addition, Chiang Kai-shek had a strong belief in airpower and modern machines as the means to defeat Japan, and confidence in Chennault's ability and vision.[124]

Chennault's air plan reached President Roosevelt in a roundabout way. In early October 1942, Wendell Willkie, the Republican Party's presidential nominee in 1940, arrived in China as a special representative of President Roosevelt. Willkie met with Chennault and, impressed with Chennault's ideas, asked him to prepare a letter for the president. In the letter Chennault laid out his air plan, with the astonishing statement that if given complete freedom of action he could cause the downfall of Japan if he was given 105 modern fighters, 30 medium bombers, and 12 heavy bombers.[125] Upon his return to the United States, Willkie showed Chennault's letter to the president. Chennault won another important advocate in Harry Hopkins, one of Roosevelt's closest and most trusted advisors. The difference in strategy between Stilwell and Chennault was now directly in front of the president. Over the next few months, more advocates among American and Chinese officials pressed Chennault's case with the president to the point where in the new year President Roosevelt proposed to Gen. Marshall that Chennault be given his own separate air force.[126]

Toward the end of the year, Generalissimo Chiang Kai-shek came to favor Chennault's plan over Stilwell's. During the fall, Chiang had moderated his Three Demands and responded positively to Stilwell's proposals for a combined Chinese and British offensive to begin the reconquest of Burma in spring 1943 under the code name ANAKIM, agreeing to Stilwell's training a Chinese force in India (X-Force) and preparing a force in Yunnan (Y-Force). But as Chennault's air plan gained momentum in Chungking and Washington, Stilwell's own plans began to unravel. The British, for a variety of reasons, were reluctant to go ahead. Observing British hesitation and presented with Chennault's alternative air plan, Chiang withdrew his support for ANAKIM, suggesting instead that the Allies pursue an air offensive from Chinese bases. At the Casablanca Conference in January 1943, the Combined Chiefs of Staff confirmed the postponement of ANAKIM until fall 1943 to support Allied efforts in the Mediterranean and the Pacific. Although President Roosevelt spoke in favor of providing more airplanes for the Army Air Force in China, no firm commitments of aid to China came out of the conference, a great disappointment to the Chinese.[127]

After the Casablanca Conference, Arnold and Field Marshal Sir John Dill, chief of the British joint staff mission in Washington, traveled to Chungking to brief the Generalissimo on conclusions reached at the conference and Allied plans for operations in Burma.

THE CHINA AIR TASK FORCE

Chennault shows Gen. Henry "Hap" Arnold one of the 23rd Fighter Group's P-40s during Arnold's visit to China in February 1943. *Courtesy, Carl Molesworth*

At the meeting with the Generalissimo the subject of air support for China was a key topic. Chiang brought up the Chinese government's desire to have an independent air force under Chennault, and their frustration with Bissell. Initially, Arnold was not opposed in principle to the idea of establishing a separate air force in China, since he recognized the problems the command structure in the CBI presented to operations, though he felt such a move was premature until the logistical problems had been dealt with to ensure an adequate flow of supplies to sustain operations.[128] There was no point in sending more aircraft to China if there was no gasoline available. Arnold's visit to China and his discussions with Chennault, whom he found to his astonishment had an unrealistic appreciation of the logistical problems he faced, made Arnold realize that the CATF could never be completely independent of the Tenth Air Force and the India base.[129] Arnold did promise more help for the CATF, including the assignment of a heavy-bomber group and a doubling of the number of transports for the Hump route to increase the monthly tonnage to 4,000 tons a month, but this was not what the Generalissimo wanted.[130] Chiang presented Arnold with a new ultimatum, demanding an independent American air force in China under Chennault's command reporting directly to the Generalissimo, 500 airplanes to be operated by American or Chinese pilots, and an increase in Hump tonnage to 10,000 tons a month.[131] The Generalissimo put these demands in a letter to President Roosevelt and gave the letter to Arnold to deliver to the president on his return to Washington.

Overruling his military commanders, President Roosevelt agreed to much of what the Generalissimo wanted: an independent air force under Chennault, a buildup to 10,000 tons a month over the Hump route, and 500 aircraft for Chennault as soon as he believed he could support this number in China.[132] On 3 March 1943, Chennault was informed of his promotion to major general (Bissell had been promoted to the same rank a day earlier to preserve his seniority). A week later, the War Department activated the new Fourteenth Air Force to replace the China Air Task Force, but while this freed Chennault from Bissell, he remained under the command of Stilwell as commander of the China-Burma-India theater and did not report to the Generalissimo as Chiang had wanted.[133] At one stroke the Tenth Air Force had lost half its combat strength and part of its reason for being: to conduct the bombing of Japan from Chinese bases. Although organizationally independent from the Tenth Air Force, Chennault and the Fourteenth Air Force would remain dependent on the Tenth for many services and for the defense of the western terminus of the Hump route in Assam. Until the end of the war, the Tenth would have to carry out its own assigned mission always with an eye on events in China, remaining always on call to support America's strategic objectives in China as the priority. Creation of the Fourteenth Air Force divided the American air effort in Asia into two areas—China and India/Burma—though a formal division took some months to achieve. Nor did acquiescence to the Generalissimo's wishes settle the debate on strategy for China. The debate would intensify over the coming months and remain a source of strain within American military and political circles—and between American and British military and political leaders—until the end of the war. As the months went on, the operations of the Tenth Air Force would focus exclusively on Burma, an effort that had begun with the organization of the one combat command Bissell was left with: the India Air Task Force.

Chennault with Col. Casey Vincent. Appointed operations officer of the CATF, Vincent went on to become executive officer but continued to fly combat missions. On the formation of the Fourteenth Air Force, Vincent became chief of staff under Chennault. *02_C-00230, SDAMC*

CHAPTER 3

THE INDIA AIR TASK FORCE

October–December 1942

Not Single Spies, but in Battalions

The summer of 1942 was the Tenth Air Force's nadir. Brereton's sudden departure for the Middle East and the withdrawal of the few available heavy bombers and experienced crews in the 9th Bomb Squadron removed the Tenth Air Force's most potent striking force. Using overhauled engines, the 7th Bomb Group maintenance crews put 11 B-17Es back in commission, and these bombers, together with the lone LB-30 that had come with Brereton from Java and four B-24Ds that had just arrived in Karachi, departed for the Middle East in early July.[1] This left eight B-17Es in India, most of which were either out of commission due to the lack of engines and spare parts or limited to short flights.[2] For some reason—perhaps the heat and the dust—the B-17s continued to suffer from excessive oil consumption, contributing to the engine problems. The Tenth arranged to borrow two Fortress I aircraft (B-17C) from the Royal Air Force. These aircraft were two of the original batch of B-17C Flying Fortresses sent to the Royal Air Force in 1941. After service in the United Kingdom and a brief stint in the Middle East, they ended up in India, where they had been unserviceable for much of the time. With replacement engines from Army Air Force stocks in Karachi, the 7th Bomb Group got the airplanes flying again and used them as training aircraft to give the air crews at least some practice in a B-17.[3]

The Tenth had 23 B-25s available in June but lost five aircraft on operations (four on the 11th Bomb Squadron's first mission in route to China, and one out of India) and another through an accident, leaving only 17 medium bombers in operation. The 11th Bomb Squadron had eight in China, with a detachment of two bombers at Dinjan in Assam. The understrength 22nd Bomb Squadron, assigned to the 7th Bomb Group's HQ and HQ Squadron, had the remaining seven B-25s. More B-25s did not arrive until September, though the ground echelons both of the 11th and 22nd Bomb Squadrons arrived at Karachi in July. More fighters arrived in small batches, bringing the total number of P-40s in the theater up from 55 in May to 112 in August. Most of the fighters went to China, leaving some with the 51st Fighter Group's 25th and 26th Fighter Squadrons in Karachi for operational training. The number of transports available for the Tenth Air Force grew slowly, from 38 C-47s and C-53s in May to 51 in August. The Tenth was expanding, if ever so slowly, with the total number of aircraft assigned reaching 195 in August, up from 115 in May. The 11th Bomb Squadron and the 16th Fighter Squadron moved to China for service with the China Air Task Force. The remaining units of the Tenth were starting to move eastward. The 51st Fighter Group sent three P-40s to Dinjan on June 23 to undertake reconnaissance missions over Burma, while the 22nd Bomb Squadron deployed its B-25s to Calcutta for reconnaissance missions out over the Bay of Bengal and into Burma.[4]

It was fortunate for the Allies that the monsoon weather over much of eastern India and Burma during these months made operations difficult not just for the Tenth Air Force and the Royal Air Force, but also for the Japanese Army Air Force units in Burma. The reduction in Allied air operations allowed the JAAF to withdraw some of its units to Malaya and Thailand for rest, reequipment, and

The Tenth Air Force borrowed two RAF Flying Fortress I aircraft (B-17C) that had served in the United Kingdom and the Middle East before finding their way to India. With replacement engines, these two airplanes allowed the 7th Bomb Group to continue training in Karachi. Author's collection

As more P-40s arrived in Karachi, the 51st Fighter Group gained enough airplanes to continue training pilots in the 25th and 26th Fighter Squadrons and to send a small number of fighters to Dinjan in Assam. At Dinjan the fighters stayed under cover to keep them from the prying eyes of Japanese photoreconnaissance airplanes. 3A-33948, RG342FH, NARA

Burma and Thailand

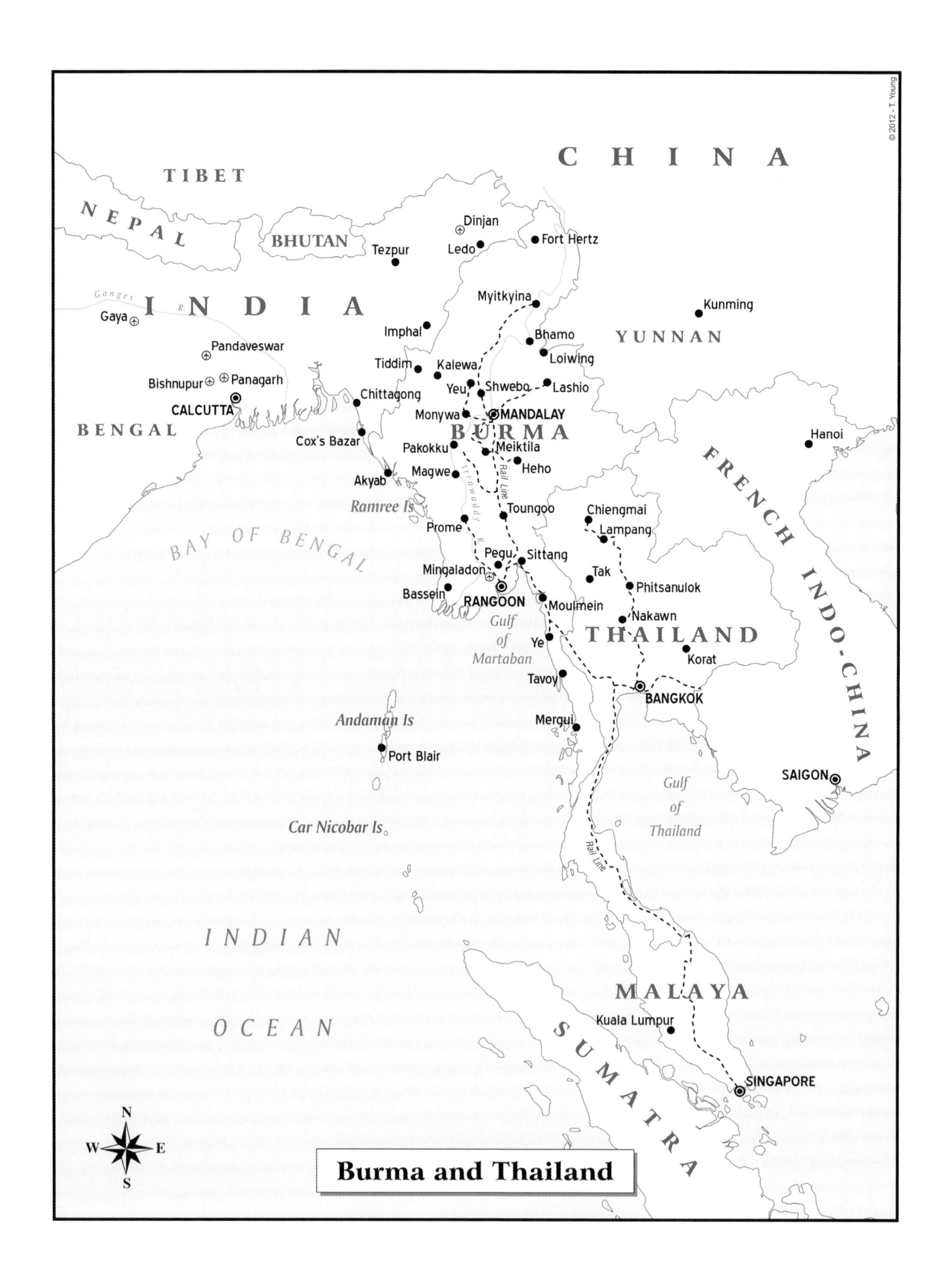

After Brereton departed for the Middle East with the 9th Bomb Squadron and most of the serviceable B-17s, the 7th Bomb Group could maintain a only small number of B-17s in commission. To combine training with operational requirements, the available bombers sometimes flew reconnaissance sorties out over the approaches to the port of Karachi, covering Allied shipping on the way to the port. *7th Bombardment Group Historical Foundation, USAFA*

training.[5] Neither the Allies nor the Japanese were able to take much action, and not just because of the monsoon weather. The Allies lacked the resources, while the Japanese had no immediate need to do so, though resources also acted as a constraint on Japanese abilities. Having forced the British out of Burma, the Japanese now had a formidable barrier in the hills and mountains along the India-Burma border to give them protection for some period. The British and American Joint Intelligence Committee believed that Japan's strategy with regard to India was to ensure that India could not be used as a base for an Allied counterattack to regain Burma.[6] Ironically, Japanese forces in Burma were also subject to logistical problems, since they, too, were at the end of a long line of communication back to Japan. Japan's lack of shipping acted as a constraint on further operations, limiting the supplies for the *15th Army* in Burma. Allied intelligence believed that the logistical problems of supplying the Japanese army would limit the Japanese to conducting air raids on Allied targets in India to prevent Allied advances into Burma.[7]

While Stilwell was setting out his own proposals for the reconquest of Burma, or at least the construction of a new road link from Assam through northern Burma to China, Gen. Wavell, as commander in chief in India, was working on his own plans for a counteroffensive into Burma, with Prime Minister Churchill urging him on. The seemingly insurmountable difficulties of an advance into Burma from Assam led British planners to focus instead on a limited advance to the Chindwin River (code-named Operation RAVENOUS) and amphibious operations to capture lower Burma and Rangoon, a plan that came to be designated Operation ANAKIM.[8] The obstacles to carrying out this plan in 1942 were as formidable as the mountain barriers between India and Burma. British forces would need trained troops, an adequate air force to ensure air superiority, and landing craft and naval support craft—none of which were available, particularly since plans for Operation TORCH, the invasion of North Africa planned for November, had the priority for shipping.[9] With all the logistical and supply problems and the demands of other theaters, it soon became obvious that ANAKIM, or some version of it, could not be mounted during the 1942–43 dry season following the end of the monsoon. Instead, Wavell and his staff began planning for a more limited advance to capture the town of Akyab, on the Burma coast, and a long-range penetration mission behind Japanese lines with a brigade under the command of Brig. Orde Wingate, while Stilwell organized two divisions of Chinese troops in India for a planned advance from Ledo to Myitkyina.[10]

Planning for future operations into Burma brought up the issue of command and control of American Army Air Force units in India. An advance into Burma depended, in part, on the availability of strong air support. There were now two air forces in India: the British Royal Air Force and the American Tenth Air Force, with one committed to the defense of India and potentially the reconquest of Burma, and the other to supporting China but needing India as a base. How they were to interact, to what extent, and for what mission was a question that had not been formally addressed. There was no unified command over the two air forces. The fall of Burma had complicated the Tenth Air Force's mission. Support for China now meant defending the air route across the Hump and the air route bases in Assam. The Tenth Air Force needed a secure base in India to ensure the flow of supplies to China across India to Assam and then over the Hump to China, but to what extent was the Tenth responsible for helping to secure and defend all or part of that base? And under whose command?

The issue of command and control of American air forces in India came up briefly during the scramble to respond to the Japanese offensive into Burma and the Bay of Bengal. In April, following the Japanese naval attack on Ceylon, the British had asked that American heavy bombers be made available for the defense of India under

Wavell as commander in chief, India. Neither Stilwell nor Brereton wanted the Tenth Air Force to come under Wavell's control, so the War Department worked out a compromise. The Tenth remained under Stilwell's command, but Marshall instructed Stilwell that he was to order the Tenth Air Force to cooperate with the British for the protection of northeastern India and the British navy's eastern fleet under British direction.[11] Marshall rescinded this instruction on 24 May 1942, when the crisis had passed, advising Stilwell that employment of the Tenth Air Force was under his discretion.[12] At the end of May, Arnold and Rear Adm. John Towers, representing the US Navy, met with Air Chief Marshal Sir Charles Portal, Chief of the Air Staff, to work out an allocation policy for American Army Air Force units and American aircraft to each theater of war.[13] These negotiations ended with the Arnold-Portal-Towers agreement (the Arnold-Portal agreement, as it came to be called), signed on June 21 and approved by the Combined Chiefs of Staff soon after. The agreement stated that America would assign certain Army Air Force units to theaters of war where Britain had strategic responsibility, such as India, and that these would be homogeneous American organizations, but serving under the control of the British commander in chief in the theater.[14]

Significantly for the Tenth Air Force, the Arnold-Portal agreement contained plans for an increase in the number and strength of units assigned to the Tenth. Instead of having the 7th Bomb Group as a composite group with two heavy and two medium bomb squadrons, the agreement called for the Tenth Air Force to have one full heavy-bomber group with four squadrons and 35 heavy bombers, and one medium-bomber group of four squadrons with 57 aircraft, to be made up from two additional squadrons added to the 11th and 22nd Bomb Squadrons already in India.[15] The plan called for these two bomber groups to be established and brought up to full strength by September 1942. The two fighter groups assigned to the Tenth—the 23rd and 51st—would be brought up to full strength (160 airplanes) by October. The agreement stated that "the role of these groups will include collaboration in offensive operations in Burma to relieve pressure on China. In the event of a threat to India they will be used to defeat that threat."[16]

The control issue came up again with the movement of the Tenth Air Force's squadrons to China, as Wavell was beginning to formulate his plans for operations in Burma. Portal had informed Wavell of the substance of the Arnold-Portal agreement. Considering the agreement, Wavell found the Tenth Air Force's transfer of the 11th Bomb Squadron and the 16th Fighter Squadron to China disconcerting, particularly since neither the Tenth Air Force command nor Stilwell apparently informed Wavell of these transfers. The movement of these squadrons to China appeared to contradict the terms of the Arnold-Portal agreement. Wavell requested that the status of the Tenth Air Force and its role in the defense of India be more clearly defined. In a message to Portal, Wavell said:

> *Any arrangement which does not place American Air Forces under my command means that I either cannot count on their availability in plans for offensive operations or make myself responsible for the special training and preparation required to that end. Same applies to the participation of American Fighters or American bombers in the defense of India. . . . If I am to rely on American air forces as part of the defense forces of India, I cannot do so on the basis of collaboration. I require to know what Air Forces I can definitely count on and have them placed under my orders and those of A.O.C-in-C [Air Officer Commander in Chief].[17]*

Portal had the Royal Air Force delegation in Washington propose to Arnold that the Tenth be placed under the strategic control of the air officer, commander in chief, India, and that American units be made available for the defense of India and whenever possible for offensive operations in Burma, as well as support for China.[18] Instructions to that effect could be issued to Stilwell and to Wavell. Arnold replied that the American Joint Chiefs of Staff felt it was unwise to remove the Tenth Air Force from Stilwell's command due to the negative impact this would have on Chinese morale, given Chiang Kai-shek's concern that the Tenth Air Force should be used only for the support of China, and his suspicion of British motives. The Joint Chiefs believed that Marshall's directive to Stilwell from May, which included language instructing Stilwell

With the crisis in the Middle East during the summer of 1942 taking first claim on available aircraft, replacements for the Tenth Air Force were hard to come by. This early-model B-17E was equipped with the Bendix remote control belly turret that was removed in later models. *Author's collection*

to ensure the Tenth Air Force cooperated with Wavell's command, provided him with adequate guidance. The debate over control went on for another two months without a change in the American position. The British Chiefs of Staff told Wavell that the American Chiefs of Staff "have been exceedingly tiresome" about the issue, suggesting that in lieu of a new directive Wavell should arrange for support from the Tenth Air Force through a conference with Stilwell.[19] Field Marshal Sir John Dill, head of the British Joint Staff Mission in Washington, advised the Chiefs of Staff not to press the issue, but presciently noted that "the real battle will be to ensure a satisfactory solution to command question when re-conquest of Burma begins."[20] A solution to the command problem would emerge a year later, but the tension between the Tenth Air Force's role in supporting China and supporting offensive action in Burma would remain an issue.

With most of the Tenth Air Force's effort devoted to operations in China, there was little the units in India could undertake against the Japanese in Burma. The monsoon weather and lack of aircraft limited the combat missions flown out of India during July and August. The 11th Bomb Squadron's detachment of two B-25s at Dinjan flew almost all of the 45 sorties recorded over the two months. During July the B-25s, flying as a pair and sometimes singly, flew two reconnaissance missions into Burma and carried out 11 bombing missions to attack the airfield and railway stations at Myitkyina and nearby Mogaung. Even with the monsoon weather hindering attacks, the airfield at Myitkyina remained a direct threat to the airfields in Assam and needed to be kept out of action if possible. August saw more attacks on the same targets, with a single B-25 going out on six missions to targets around Myitkyina and Mogaung, and two B-25s going out on four missions to the same targets. The much-reduced 7th Bomb Group flew only two combat missions during July and August: a single B-24 apparently bombing Myitkyina on July 28, and a single B-17E going back to the Andaman Islands in search of a reported Japanese aircraft carrier, without result. The 51st Fighter Group's small detachment of three P-40s at Dinjan carried out a number of reconnaissance flights into Burma, losing Capt. Thrashley Hardy, commander of the detachment, on July 8 when he failed to return from a strafing mission carried out on his own.[21]

The steady erosion of the Tenth Air Force's combat strength was of great concern to Naiden. The War Department had promised to deliver replacement aircraft to the Tenth, but these had not arrived. The War Department had planned for the medium-bomber force in the Tenth Air Force to be maintained at 26 aircraft for two squadrons, but the Tenth did not receive 26 B-25s from the United States, or the promised replacements to keep the force at the planned level. Instead of three heavy bombers and crews for June and July, the Tenth received one B-17. The same was true for replacements of fighter aircraft. With the wastage from operations, accidents, and planes grounded for lack of parts, Naiden was worried about how strong the Tenth would be at the end of the monsoon, when he expected the Japanese to resume their air offensive. What Naiden now saw happening was exactly what he and Brereton had hoped to avoid: using their aircraft in small numbers—in dribbles—instead of in a concentrated force that could hit the Japanese hard, even if infrequently. As he commented in a letter to Stilwell, "it seems to me we are playing a game right now which is precisely what the Japanese would wish us to do. In other words, in my opinion, we are frittering away our handful of airplanes while the Japanese are concentrating their efforts for a better day. If we had definite promises of an augmentation in bombers and pursuit by September, I would not feel so concerned about this. As you know, the information from the War Department is that they cannot afford to allocate any more units or planes to this theater."[22]

Over the summer of 1942, the Tenth Air Force's other operation, the air ferry route to China, did little better. Multiple problems dogged the operation: "the monsoon, lack of spare parts and maintenance facilities, loss of transport bases in Burma, and transfer of cargo planes to the Middle East combined to prevent even an approximation of the desired 800 tons a month to China."[23] The

A row of C-53s and C-47s in Assam later in 1943. Short of transport aircraft in the summer of 1942, the India-China Ferry operation could carry only limited amounts of supplies over the Hump to China in its C-47s and C-53s. The C-53 in the background (42-6470) remained in India after the end of the war, flying for domestic Indian airlines.
3A-33680, RG342FH, NARA

THE INDIA AIR TASK FORCE

War Department had allocated 75 C-47 and C-53 transports to the air ferry route, but not all of these had arrived (ten C-53s had gone to the China National Aviation Corporation and the Chinese government); of the 52 transports available in early July, ten were with CNAC, seven were flying with the Assam-Burma-China Ferry, eight were with the Trans-India Ferry, twelve were out of commission, and twelve were about to depart for the Middle East with Gen. Brereton.[24] To keep the airplanes flying, the maintenance crews took Pratt & Whitney R-1830 engines from Chinese Lend-Lease P-43s and adapted them to the C-47s and C-53s.[25] After taking command of the Tenth Air Force, Naiden formally adopted Caleb Haynes's de facto combination of the Trans-India Ferry and the Assam-Burma-China Ferry into one organization, creating the India-China Ferry on 15 July 1942 under the command of Col. Robert Tate.[26] The shipments that Army Air Force transports carried over the Hump route during May through July were minimal: 79 tons in May, 106 tons in June, and 85 tons in July. August saw a jump to 284 tons carried to China as 14 more transport aircraft became available.[27]

Bissell Takes Command

These were the challenges Clayton Bissell faced when he took over command of the Tenth Air Force from Naiden on 18 August 1942: the need to get aircraft, men, and supplies to Chennault's China Air Task Force; build up an offensive force to protect the India-China Ferry bases in Assam; and increasing the monthly tonnage over the air route to China. His first priority was to improve the flow of supplies over the Hump route.[28] Four days after taking command, Bissell appointed Naiden commander of the India-China Ferry, with the objective of increasing the delivery to China to 5,000 tons a month. He told Naiden that "Successful operation of the India-China Ferrying Command is vital to the prosecution of the war in this theater. Unless munitions can be delivered by air to the Chinese and the American forces in China, neither can long continue effective operations against the enemy."[29] Naiden felt aggrieved at being placed in what he considered to be a less important position, and asked to be relieved. Shortly thereafter his health broke and he was sent to the United States, with Col. Tate assuming command in his place.[30]

Bissell immediately took several actions to improve the India-China Ferry, although he realized full well the near impossibility of the task. He sent more service troops to Assam, made maintenance of the available transport planes a high priority, and put every available transport plane on the route from Assam to Kunming.[31] By early October three more airfields in Assam—Chabua, Mohanbari, and Sookerating—were ready to accept airplanes from the 1st Ferrying Group, greatly relieving the pressure on Dinjan, which the India-China Ferry was still sharing with RAF squadrons and CNAC transports.[32] In a letter to Arnold in response to a critical inspection report of Tenth Air Force operations and organization, Bissell gave a frank explanation of the supply problems the Tenth Air Force faced:

From the base port at Karachi to the combat units in China is a distance greater than from San Francisco to New York. From Karachi, supplies go by broad gauge railroad a distance about as far as from San Francisco to Kansas City. They are then transshipped to meter gauge and to narrow gauge and go on a distance by rails as far as from Kansas City to St. Louis. They are then transshipped to water and go down the Ganges and up the Brahmaputra, a distance about equivalent to that from St. Louis to Pittsburgh. They are then loaded on transports of the Ferrying Command in the Dinjan area and flown to Kunming—a distance greater than from Pittsburgh to Boston. From Kunming, aviation supplies go by air, truck, rail, bullock cart, coolie, and river to operating airdromes—a distance about equivalent from Boston to Newfoundland. With interruption of this communication system due to sabotage incident to the internal political situation in India [that broke out in August 1942], you can readily appreciate that regular supply presents difficulties.[33]

Getting supplies over the Hump to China was a logistical nightmare. Ships had to travel more than 10,000 miles from the United States to India—a journey of over two months—to the ports at Karachi and later Calcutta, where they were offloaded. *3A-37163, RG342FH, NARA*

THE TENTH AIR FORCE IN WORLD WAR II

From the docks at Calcutta, Army trucks carried supplies of all kinds to the railroad station to be loaded on train cars and transported north to the railhead on the west bank of the Brahmaputra River. *3A-37169, RG342FH, NARA*

With the end of the monsoon, more personnel, and more experience throughout the India-China Ferry Command, monthly tonnage did increase to 434 tons flown to China in September and to 602 tons in October, despite having fewer serviceable aircraft available in the latter month.[34] This was an improvement, but still well below the target Bissell had set for the command. By this time, the War Department had decided that the India-China Ferry Command properly belonged as part of the newly activated Air Transport Command. The belief was that Air Transport Command could provide a sharper focus on the problem of getting supplies to China, since this would be its only mission, without the distractions facing the theater command.[35] It was also felt that shipments to the CBI that were part of an integrated transportation system would be less subject to the pilfering along the way that had hindered getting supplies to India.[36] The transfer of the India-China Ferry Command to the Air Transport Command would also relieve Stilwell and Bissell of the responsibility of operating this service among all the other demands and challenges facing them. Arnold agreed with the transfer of the India-China Ferry Command to the Air Transport Command, and, accordingly, on 31 October 1942 the War Department activated the India-China Wing, Air Transport Command, and advised Stilwell that this new organization would take over the 1st Ferrying Group on 1 December 1942. From then on, the Air Transport Command in Washington had responsibility for operating the air route to China and using the transport aircraft assigned to the India-China Wing exclusively for this mission.[37]

The transfer of the India-China Ferry Command to the Air Transport Command did not change the Tenth Air Force's responsibility for the defense of the air ferry route. As long as support for the Chinese military effort remained the primary mission of the Tenth Air Force, the air route to China—China's only remaining source of supplies—had to be kept open. Even before Bissell's appointment to command the Tenth, and despite all the delays in providing the Tenth with adequate numbers of aircraft, the Army Air Force planners in Washington had begun to develop a concept of defense of the air ferry route that went beyond the simple defense of the airfields in Assam against attack. The first priority was to attack the Japanese airfields that threatened the security of the air ferry route and the bases in Assam and Kunming, particularly the airfields at Toungoo, Myitkyina, Magwe, and Lashio in Burma and the airfields around Hanoi in French Indochina, all of which Japanese bombers could use to reach either Assam or Kunming. The second priority was to attack the Japanese lines of communication and transshipment points that supported the Japanese airfields in Burma and French

Once at the Brahmaputra River, ferries carried supplies for China across to the east bank, where the supplies went on to a narrow-gauge railroad line up to the airfields in Assam. Barely adequate for peacetime traffic, the increasing flow of supplies north put a severe strain on the system until American railroad engineers arrived to reorganize the entire operation. *3A-37176, RG342FH, NARA*

THE INDIA AIR TASK FORCE

Indian laborers loading aircraft tires and boxes of supplies onto a C-46 at one of the Assam airfields for the flight over the Hump. Once at Kunming, supplies for the Fourteenth Air Force and the Chinese armies had to travel over an even more inadequate transportation system to get to southern and eastern bases. *3A-37182, RG342FH, NARA*

Indochina and facilitated the movement of personnel and supplies to the area. Rangoon was an important target because as the port of entry for all Japanese shipping, it was the main transshipment point for Japanese supplies entering Burma. Shipping, the dock areas, and the railroads leading north would be the main objectives. Similarly, the ports of Hong Kong and Bangkok in Thailand were significant because these ports were also important transshipment points. The third priority was industrial installations that supported the Japanese war effort in Burma and China. The broader definition of defense of the air ferry route created a wider list of potential targets for Tenth Air Force fighters, medium bombers, and heavy bombers. The difficulty was getting adequate numbers of aircraft

Serviceability problems with B-17s and the need for longer range persuaded the War Department to agree to replacing the 7th Bomb Group's Flying Fortresses with the Consolidated B-24D Liberator. The group would fly the Liberator for the remainder of the war, moving progressively from the B-24D to the B-24J, and the B-24L and B-24M in the final months of the war. *3A-33645, RG342, NARA*

THE TENTH AIR FORCE IN WORLD WAR II

7th Bomb Group crews stand by one of their newly arrived B-24Ds. The group remained short of its full complement of B-24s until well into 1943, forcing the squadrons to borrow aircraft from each other and limiting the number of B-24s that could be sent on bombing missions into Burma. *3A-34837, RG342FH, NARA*

to the theater so the Tenth could conduct an air offensive against these objectives.[38]

The Arnold-Portal agreement called for an increase in the bomber units assigned to the Tenth Air Force. Accordingly, on 15 September 1942 the War Department authorized activation of the 341st Bombardment Group (Medium) at Karachi, India, under the command of Lt. Col. Torgils G. Wold, an experienced bomber pilot. That same date saw the activation of the 490th and 491st Bombardment Squadrons (Medium) and the transfer of the 11th and 22nd Bomb Squadrons to the new 341st Group. Cadre for the new 490th Bomb Squadron came from the 11th Bomb Squadron, while the 22nd Bomb Squadron provided men for the new 491st Squadron. More aircrews and enlisted men would have to come from the United States. The following month the War Department activated two additional heavy-bomber squadrons for the 7th Bomb Group—the 492nd and 493rd Bombardment Squadrons—on October 25. With the planned return of the 9th Bomb Squadron from the Middle East, this would bring the 7th Bomb Group up to full strength in assigned units (the 9th, 436th, 492nd, and 493rd Bomb Squadrons), but aircrews and ground staff for the two new heavy-bomber squadrons would also have to come from the United States. With serviceability problems keeping so many B-17s out of commission, and the need for longer range to reach targets in southern Burma and Thailand, the Army Air Force decided to reequip the 7th Bomb Group with the Consolidated B-24 Liberator as these airplanes became available. On paper this appeared to be an impressive force, but the key question was how quickly these new units could be brought up to strength in airplanes and men.[39]

In mid-September the War Department wrote to Bissell to confirm the allocation of these new squadrons and other service units for his command. With regard to aircraft, the War Department told Bissell that eight B-25Ds were en route to India, with a further 32 B-25Ds expected to arrive by October 31 to supplement the 17 B-25Cs he had in the Tenth Air Force, bringing the total up to the 57 medium bombers specified in the Arnold-Portal agreement. As to heavy bombers for the 7th Bomb Group, the War Department said that thirteen B-24Ds would depart the United States in late September, eight in early October, and five more in late October to join the nine B-24Ds that had already been assigned to the Tenth (though only two were on hand in September). This would bring the group to the planned strength of 35 heavy bombers. In addition, the Tenth would receive an additional air service group and quartermaster, signal, transportation, and antiaircraft units. But as the letter admitted, "the problem of meeting all requests from the Asiatic Theater for communication, equipment, and personnel has been and continues to be a most difficult one."[40] The harsh reality was that the China-Burma-India theater was still low in priority. As the War Department's letter said, "while the Asiatic Theater has a priority high on the list it means little due to the demands made on available transportation by those theaters higher on the list."[41] In the event, the Tenth did not receive its full complement of either heavy or medium bombers until March 1943.[42]

Soon after taking command of the Tenth Air Force, Bissell recognized that with the activation of the China Air Task Force the command structure was unbalanced. The combat units in India needed closer coordination and control. Bissell proposed to Stilwell setting up an India Air Task Force to provide a task force on either side of the air ferry route. This would also allow the headquarters of the Tenth Air Force to devote its effort to policy and administrative issues, particularly coordination with the Army's Services of Supply organization in India. Stilwell recommended this change in command structure to the War Department and proposed that Col. Caleb Haynes be promoted to brigadier general and placed in command of the India Air Task Force. With War Department approval, on 24 September 1942 Bissell announced that the Tenth Air Force would be composed of five subordinate commands: the China Air Task Force under Chennault, the India Air Task Force under Haynes, the Karachi American Air Base Command under Brady (formerly

THE INDIA AIR TASK FORCE

Promoted to brigadier general, Caleb Haynes brought a wealth of experience to the India Air Task Force. During the interwar years he commanded fighter and bomber squadrons. After arriving in India he took on the Assam-China-Burma Ferry operation, then moved to China to be Chennault's bomber commander in the CATF. *India Air Task Force, 10th USAAF, November 1942–May 1943, 827.306-1, vol. 1, AFHRA*

the Karachi Air Defense Area), the India-China Ferry under Tate, and the X Air Service Command under Col. Robert Oliver. The India Air Task Force would be activated on October 2.[43]

Bissell sent Haynes a directive on October 2—the date of the activation of Haynes's new command—outlining the mission and responsibilities of the India Air Task Force (IATF). The force's primary mission was the defense of the India-China Ferry route in cooperation with the China Air Task Force. The IATF was to take responsibility for the area to the west of a north–south line drawn through the town of Myitkyina, with the CATF responsible for the area to the east of this line. The secondary mission was the destruction of Japanese aircraft, installations, and shipping, but Bissell stressed in his directive that while the secondary mission was desirable, the primary mission was mandatory. The secondary mission would be undertaken "when suitable aircraft and munitions are available and when its execution does not jeopardize the primary mission."[44] Haynes was also charged with maintaining close relations with the British Royal Air Force and Royal Army units in his area. The IATF would have the following units assigned: the 51st Fighter Group, less the 16th Fighter Squadron; the 7th Bomb Group (H) with the 9th and 436th Squadrons and the soon-to-be-activated 492nd and 493rd Squadrons; the 341st Bomb Group (M) with the 22nd, 490th, and 491st Squadrons and one flight from the 11th Bomb Squadron (at Dinjan); and the 9th Photographic Reconnaissance Squadron, less one flight assigned to the CATF, in addition to antiaircraft and signal units to be deployed to the Dinjan area.[45]

On activation, the IATF's actual strength was less than it appeared on paper, since few of the assigned units were up to their full complement of aircraft or established at their designated bases. Within the 51st Fighter Group, the 26th Fighter Squadron began moving to Dinjan on September 16, when 12 P-40s left Karachi for Assam. The 51st Group Headquarters left for Dinjan on October 10. The 25th Fighter Squadron remained at Karachi to train 26 newly arrived pilots fresh from the United States, ferry P-40s to China, and defend the Karachi air base. The 7th Bomb Group had two B-24Ds that had recently arrived in India for the 436th Bomb Squadron at Allahabad, joining the squadron's eight B-17s, with two more B-17s at Karachi waiting for spare parts. The 9th Bomb Squadron's ground echelon would return from the Middle East later in the month, with the aircrews to follow after. Bissell told Haynes

The first headquarters of the India Air Task Force at Barrackpore, near Calcutta. Haynes moved his command here from Dinjan in Assam. *India Air Task Force, 10th USAAF, November 1942–May 1943, 827.306-1, vol. 1, AFHRA*

THE TENTH AIR FORCE IN WORLD WAR II

Lockheed F-4 Lightning reconnaissance airplanes being unloaded at the port of Karachi for the 9th Photo Reconnaissance Squadron. Once assembled and tested, the squadron sent a small detachment of F-4s to support the CATF. *Historical Record and Activities of US Army Air Forces in Area of Karachi, India, Book I, Miscellaneous, March 1942 to December 31, 1942, 828.08, AFHRA*

Assembling F-4 Lightnings at Karachi. Photoreconnaissance was a vital aspect of daylight precision strategic bombing. Aerial reconnaissance identified potential targets, aided in the assessment of bomb damage, and monitored enemy repairs to determine when a return bombing mission would be needed. *Historical Record and Activities of US Army Air Forces in Area of Karachi, India, Book I, Miscellaneous, March 1942 to December 31, 1942, 828.08, AFHRA*

that the arrival date for the group's remaining B-24D bombers was unknown. The 341st Bomb Group's two new squadrons were at Karachi with the 22nd Bomb Squadron, all three squadrons awaiting officers, men, and aircraft from the United States to bring them to full strength. The 9th Photographic Reconnaissance Squadron's F-4 aircraft had arrived at Karachi on September 10, but the squadron was still assembling and test-flying the aircraft in preparation for operations expected to begin in mid-November. Bissell also informed Haynes that one of his first tasks would be to expand and improve the early-warning system at Dinjan, which had only just begun to operate. Bissell ended his directive to Haynes on a more encouraging note, saying:

> *All units of the AFCBI [Air Forces China-India-Burma theater] have but a single purpose: Successful prosecution of the war. It is essential that all elements cooperate to the fullest extent. Long lines of communication and the size of the theater require initiative, ingenuity, and cooperation to the maximum degree. You have my fullest confidence in your ability successfully to accomplish your mission.*[46]

Over the next few months Bissell pressed the War Department repeatedly for the aircraft, equipment, men, and units the Tenth Air Force needed to be effective. The squadrons lacked equipment and transport vehicles (at Dinjan the 51st Group had a single sedan, a few jeeps, and a few trucks), and there was an urgent need for communications and air-warning squadrons, more men for headquarters squadrons, spare engines and parts to keep aircraft in commission, and a host of other requirements. Bissell also wanted better aircraft. He wrote to Arnold that the B-17 had proven to be unacceptable, with excessive oil consumption, while the B-25s in the theater lacked sufficient range, the bomb bays of the B-25Cs being unable to accommodate bomb bay tanks and bombs at the same time. Experience with the P-40E/K in China indicated that the small margin of superiority the P-40 had over Japanese fighters with its armament, speed, and diving ability was likely to disappear as the Japanese introduced more-capable fighter airplanes. Col. Homer Sanders, commanding the 51st Fighter Group, had urged Bissell to request P-51 Mustangs as replacements for the P-40s, but three requests to the War Department came back with the same reply: P-51s were not available for the Tenth Air Force at this time. This was the War Department's standard reply to Bissell's requests: aircraft or men or units could not be sent now, but in six months to a year. Marshall sent Stilwell a frank message in December saying that "Bissell should be informed . . . [his requests] cannot be fulfilled as the units are not available."[47]

Combat: October to December 1942

Activation of the IATF coincided with the end of the monsoon and the expectation of renewed Japanese attacks in northeast Burma against the air ferry route. There was a concern that the Japanese might try to cross the Salween River into Yunnan or attempt an advance up the Hukawng Valley to Ledo. While the *15th Army* did draw up plans for such operations, a realization of the logistical difficulties caused these plans to be abandoned.[48] *Southern Army*, commanding the *15th Army*, ordered Japanese forces in Burma to remain on the defensive behind Burma's mountain and river barriers. The Japanese army did consider the growing Tenth Air Force presence in Assam to be a major threat and ordered the *5th Hikōshidan* to annihilate the air bases in the area around Dinjan. The *5th Hikōshidan* assigned the task to the *4th Hikōdan* (composed of the *50th Hikōsentai* [Ki-43 fighter], *8th Hikōsentai* [Ki-48 light bomber], and *14th Hikōsentai* [Ki-21 heavy bomber]) and the *7th Hikōdan* (with the *64th Hikōsentai* [Ki-43 fighter], *12th Hikōsentai* [Ki-21 heavy bomber], and *98th Hikōsentai* [Ki-48 light bomber]), all returned from Malaya. The *5th Hikōshidan* also had a reconnaissance unit (*81st Hikōsentai*) equipped with the Type 100 command reconnaissance airplane (Ki-46 Dinah), with a detachment based at the airfield at Meiktila, in central Burma, to carry out reconnaissance flights over Assam.[49]

Pilots from the 51st Fighter Group's 26th Fighter Squadron stand in front of a heavily camouflaged P-40 at Dinjan in late 1942. Japanese Type 100 command reconnaissance airplanes (Mitsubishi Ki-46 Dinah) from the *81st Hikōsentai* began flying reconnaissance missions over Dinjan during September 1942. *India Air Task Force, 10th USAAF, November 1942–May 1943*, 827.306-1, vol. 1, AFHRA

When an alert sounded, the bamboo branches and other plants covering a P-40 in its revetment could be hurriedly stripped off and the plane made ready for takeoff. *3A-33969, RG342FH, NARA*

Haynes left China for Dinjan in early October to set up IATF headquarters, though he continued to fly bombing missions in China for a few more weeks. The 26th Fighter Squadron had begun patrols and reconnaissance flights into Burma soon after arriving at Dinjan, despite poor weather. Toward the end of September, the *81st Hikōsentai* began sending single Type 100 reconnaissance airplanes out to photograph Dinjan and nearby bases. Pairs of P-40s undertook defensive patrols over the area from dawn to dusk but couldn't gain altitude in time to intercept the Japanese reconnaissance airplanes when the warning net reported sightings. Seven air-warning stations had started operating in the area around Dinjan, and British antiaircraft units also reported Japanese aircraft, but the early-warning system was still rudimentary. The Tenth Air Force arranged for two P-43s—which had a higher ceiling than the P-40—to join the 26th Squadron to intercept the Japanese reconnaissance flights. The P-40s carried out their patrols at 15,000 to 20,000 feet, with a single P-43 flying above at 25,000 feet. The Mohawks of No. 5 Squadron, RAF, joined the P-40s on patrols over Dinjan and maintained alerts on the ground.[50]

Although the P-43 had a better performance at high altitude than the P-40, a P-40 pilot from the 26th Fighter Squadron was the first to claim one of the Japanese reconnaissance airplanes. Late in the morning on October 19, reports came in of an unidentified airplane flying at high altitude. British antiaircraft guns picked up the airplane and fired bursts to help the patrolling P-40s locate the airplane, but the patrol failed to see these. At 1115, 1st Lt. Alvin Watson saw a twin-engine airplane flying above him at 24,000 feet that he identified as a Type 97 bomber (Ki-21) or an I-45 (Ki-45). It was in fact a Ki-46 from the *81st Hikōsentai* on a reconnaissance mission. Watson climbed his P-40 up toward the Ki-46, firing a burst from long range that set fire to the left engine. As the Ki-46 slowed down and started to descend, Watson closed in and fired another long burst that set the right engine on fire, sending the Japanese airplane down smoking toward the clouds below. The Japanese pilot made a crash landing in Burma, and both he and his observer survived. Watson received credit for the 26th Fighter Squadron's first victory.[51] More Japanese reconnaissance airplanes came over during the next few days. The P-40s and P-43s tried for interceptions but without success.

These reconnaissance flights were clearly a harbinger of an attack, but when the first Japanese attack on the airfields came on October 25, it caught the defenses unprepared. Around 1340 one of the radio stations reported to Dinjan that a large force of Japanese aircraft were heading north toward Dinjan and Chabua. They arrived over the two airfields at 1350 to begin simultaneous attacks. The force comprised 24 Ki-21 bombers from the *14th Hikōsentai* with an escort of 32 Ki-43 fighters from the *64th Hikōsentai* that went after Dinjan, while 30 Ki-48 bombers from the *8th Hikōsentai*

26th Fighter Squadron pilots get an informal briefing before heading off on a mission. The Americans soon learned that Japanese reconnaissance flights were often the harbinger of an attack a few days later. *India Air Task Force, 10th USAAF, November 1942–May 1943, 827.306-1, vol. 1, AFHRA*

THE INDIA AIR TASK FORCE

One of the three P-40s the 26th Fighter Squadron lost in the 25 October 1942 Japanese air raid on the airfields around Dinjan. At this time the Tenth Air Force had only just begun to set up an early-warning net. The mountains to the east of Assam blocked the range of American radar sets. *3A-36929, RG342FH, NARA*

attacked Chabua with an escort of 30 Ki-43s from the *50th Hikōsentai*. The bombers came over at 8,000 to 12,000 feet with demolition, fragmentation, and incendiary bombs on the runways and installations alongside. At Dinjan the bombing destroyed the 26th Fighter Squadron's engineering, communications, operations, supply, and armament sections and cratered the runway. At Chabua the runway was badly damaged. When the bombers had finished their runs the fighters came down in strafing attacks on Dinjan, Chabua, and nearby Mohanbari and Sookerating. The bombing and strafing destroyed five transports, three P-40s, and the two P-43s and left four more transports and 13 P-40s unserviceable. Included in this total were an RAF DC-3, Lysander Army Cooperation airplane, and a Blenheim bomber.[52]

There were three P-40s on patrol as the raids began, and six more managed to get off during the strafing attacks. Capt. Yasuhiko Kuroe, leading the *64th Hikōsentai*'s *3rd Chutai*, and his wingman, Sgt. Maj. Yasuda, fired on the last of the six scrambled P-40s, sending it down to crash-land on the airfield, the pilot escaping unharmed. Col. Homer Sanders and his wingman, Capt. Charles Dunning, attempted to intercept the Ki-43s attacking Chabua. Sanders engaged several Japanese fighters over the next twenty to thirty minutes, claiming two shot down, but losing Capt. Dunning, who was shot down and killed by Sgt. Anabuki of the *50th Hikōsentai*. 2nd Lt. William Rogers claimed a third fighter, while antiaircraft fire claimed several more fighters shot down as they were strafing the airfields, as well as several of the higher-flying bombers as destroyed, probably destroyed, and damaged. The *50th Hikōsentai* did lose three Ki-43s, possibly through a combination of the antiaircraft fire and fighter attacks, while the bombers suffered no losses.[53]

The next morning, 26 October 1942, the Japanese sent over another Type 100 reconnaissance airplane. Lt. Ira Sussky, a pilot from the 25th Fighter Squadron temporarily attached to the 26th Squadron, claimed a Type 97 bomber destroyed at 0930, although

Col. Homer Sanders, 51st Fighter Group commander, briefs his pilots around the time of the Japanese air raids on the Assam airfields. Sanders claimed two Type 1 fighters (Ki-43 Oscar) during the raid on 25 October 1942. *India Air Task Force, 10th USAAF, November 1942–May 1943, 827.306-1, vol. 1, AFHRA*

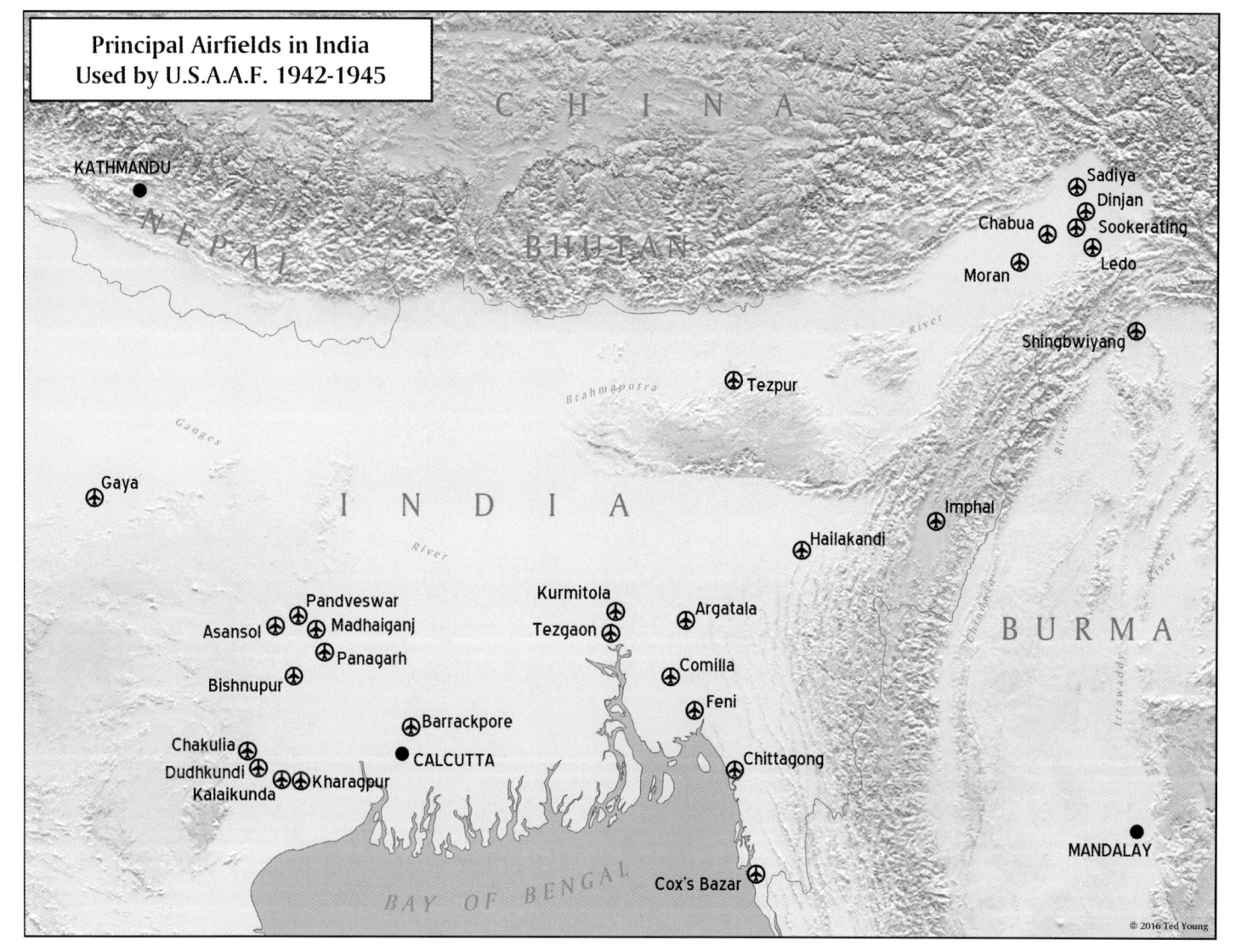

Principal Airfields in India Used by U.S.A.A.F. 1942-1945

a British heavy antiaircraft battery submitted a similar claim that may have been against the same aircraft, or possibly another later in the afternoon. The *81st Hikōsentai* did record the loss of one Ki-46 during the day. The *50th* and *64th Hikōsentai* sent more than 50 Ki-43s to strafe the airfields in the early afternoon, apparently with five reconnaissance aircraft to record the results of the attack. The fighters damaged a grounded P-40 at Mokalbari and another at Sookerating. Several P-40s had been on patrol when the attack began, and 1st Lt. Edward Nollmeyer claimed a fighter shot down south of the airfields, though neither of the Japanese fighter units suffered a loss that day. The Japanese paused for a day, then launched another major raid on October 28, with the *64th Hikōsentai* escorting the Ki-48s of the *8th Hikōsentai* and the Ki-21s from the *14th Hikōsentai* to bomb Chabua, Mohanbari, Dinjan, and Sookerating. Once again there was only a short warning of the attack, but fortunately the Japanese bombs did only minor damage to the airfields, instead destroying a service-of-supply depot full of Lend-Lease supplies for China. Seven 26th Squadron P-40s got off and five intercepted the raid, with 2nd Lt. Kermit Hyndes claiming a bomber and a fighter shot down, while 1st Lt. John Yantis claimed a probable bomber. Three other pilots claimed four fighters and two bombers damaged. Four of the Ki-21s did receive damage—one crash-landing on its return to base—while the *64th Hikōsentai* lost one Ki-43 and its pilot. These were the last Japanese attacks for some months.[54]

Reinforcements soon arrived to strengthen the defenses, with advance echelons of three antiaircraft units ironically arriving at Dinjan shortly after the air raid. On October 31 the 25th Fighter Squadron, less one flight, arrived in Assam, stationing one flight at Sookerating and one flight at nearby Sadiya airfield, both east of Dinjan. With more fighters available, the 25th and 26th Squadrons maintained overlapping patrols of two P-40s from dawn till dusk, spreading their 35 P-40s around the five airfields in the Assam area. The squadrons kept up these patrols until early December with only one interception. The *5th Hikōshidan* did not launch any further attacks against the Assam bases and apparently cut back reconnaissance missions, pulling the *4th Hikōdan* back to counter the British army's advance down the Mayu peninsula toward Akyab. On November 15, two P-40s attempted an interception of what was most likely a Ki-46 flying at 27,000 feet. One of the pilots got in one burst before stalling out in a climbing turn. The two followed the airplane south but couldn't climb high enough to intercept. With the threat of Japanese air attack apparently diminishing, the squadrons turned their efforts to other operations.[55]

The reconnaissance patrols that the P-40s started flying into Burma after their arrival at Dinjan soon turned into armed reconnaissance missions. At first this was simple strafing of military buildings and other installations along their routes following the roads leading out of Myitkyina and along the rail line, but the pilots

THE INDIA AIR TASK FORCE

A P-40K from one of the 51st Fighter Group squadrons sits in a bamboo grove on an airfield in Assam. Two Japanese flags can just be made out under the cockpit. *Peter M. Bowers Collection, Museum of Flight (MoF)*

A pilot suits up for an armed reconnaissance mission over Burma. This P-40 has yet to have the shark mouth applied to its nose. The original caption for this photo states that the mission was to search for pack elephants the Japanese were using to transport supplies through the jungle. *India Air Task Force, 10th USAAF, November 1942–May 1943, 827.306-1, vol. 1, AFHRA*

soon began going out armed with 20-pound fragmentation bombs to do more damage. In mid-November the squadrons began sending out flights of P-40s to attack specific targets. On November 11, nine P-40s went off to bomb and strafe the town of Shingbwiyang with 500-pound demolition bombs and 20-pound fragmentation bombs, starting fires in four buildings. Two days later, nine P-40s with the same bombload attacked the town of Maingkwan. At the end of the month the P-40s went back to Maingkwan, 12 aircraft again dropping 500- and 20-pound bombs on what were believed to be Japanese supply dumps, starting large fires. These bombing and strafing missions continued into December, mixed with escort missions for bombers and transport planes.[56]

December witnessed what was likely the first example of an airborne rescue of downed aircrew in the CBI. The copilot and radio operator had bailed out of a C-47 that appeared to be on the verge of crashing. They spent 12 days wandering in the jungle before coming to a friendly village near Japanese lines. The villagers got word to an American air base, and on December 10, Maj. Paul Droz, with the 25th Fighter Squadron, volunteered to take a PT-17 trainer assigned to the base to rescue the two men. Droz first flew to the area in a P-40 to find a landing ground, locating a small field about a mile from the village. He returned in the PT-17, landing in the small field, about 300 yards long, then walked to the village to find the two reported American air crewmen. He first took out the lighter of the two men, leaving an ax for the villagers to cut down some of the trees at the edge of the field to give him a little more clearance. He returned to get the second crewman, taking off again successfully. Each time he had to climb in a tight circle to 3,000 feet to get above the surrounding hills. On the last day of December, 2nd Lt. Willard Wendt from the 26th Fighter Squadron had to bail out near the Chindwin River when his engine lost power, but radioed in his approximate location. Maj. Droz went out in a P-40 and found Wendt, dropping food and a note that he would be back the next day. Droz again took a PT-17 and flew down to the Chindwin, landing on a sandy area near the river. He took Wendt onboard and flew him back to Dinjan. For his bravery on both occasions, Droz was awarded the Distinguished Flying Cross.[57]

The IATF's bomber force took a bit longer to get into action. The 7th Bomb Group undertook the IATF's first bombing missions with its new B-24 Liberator bombers, but the group's first mission

THE TENTH AIR FORCE IN WORLD WAR II

Maj. Paul Droz—getting out of the front cockpit of a PT-17—rescued 2nd Lt. Willard Wendt—sitting in the rear cockpit—from behind Japanese lines at the end of December 1942. Crew chief Sgt. Lynn Hansen takes a Thompson submachine gun from Wendt that Droz brought along for protection. *3A-36841, RG342FH, NARA*

was not into Burma but to China—the target was the Lin-his coal mines in northern China. The mines produced 14,000 tons of coking coal a day for the iron and steel plants the Japanese operated in Manchuria and on the home islands. The objective of the mission was to destroy the power plant and pumping station to knock the mines out of action. The group selected five newly arrived crews assigned to the 9th and 436th Bomb Squadrons and placed them under the command of Maj. Max Fennell, who had experience flying over China before going to the Middle East with the 9th Squadron. Recalled to Karachi, Fennell put his crews through an intensive two-day training session to sharpen their bombing. On 11 October 1942 Fennell and his team flew their six B-24Ds to the 7th Group's base at Allahabad and then on to Dinjan, the jumping-off point for Kunming. From Kunming the B-24s flew to Hsinching, near the city of Chengdu. After a wait for good weather over the target area, the bombers took off on October 20 carrying 750-pound Russian-made bombs, but a cold front forced their return to Hsinching. The weather improved the next day, and the bombers went off again. One returned with engine trouble, but the five remaining bombers reached the mines and, in the B-24D's combat debut in the CBI, bombed individually from 14,000 feet. The bombing damaged the mines but failed to destroy the vital power plant and pumping station. Returning to India via Kunming, the B-24s bombed the Japanese airfield at Myitkyina on their way back to Allahabad on October 27.[58]

Maj. Max Fennell's crew stand with Chinese soldiers in front of their B-24D in China before undertaking the raid on the Lin-hsi coal mines in October 1942. *7th Bombardment Group Historical Foundation, USAFA*

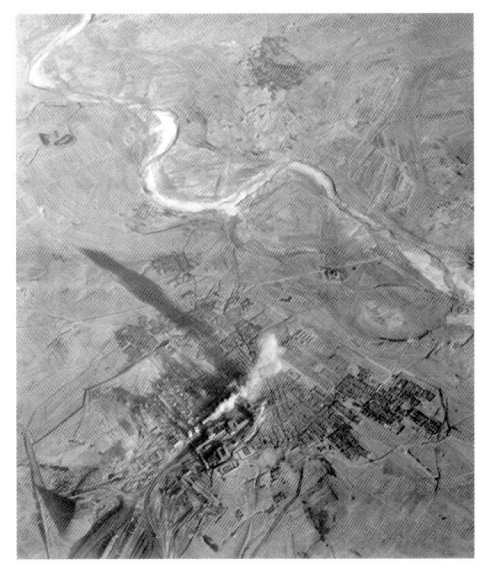

An aerial view of the Lin-hsi coal mine complex in northern China. The raid on the coal mines was the B-24's combat debut in the China-India-Burma theater, using Russian-made bombs for the occasion. *7th Bombardment Group Historical Foundation, USAFA*

THE INDIA AIR TASK FORCE

The 7th Bomb Group's base at Gaya, where the 9th and 436th Squadrons began flying missions into Burma. A lone B-24 sits on the ramp with two of the 9th Bomb Squadron's B-17s brought back from the Middle East. The 7th Group retained a number of B-17s on strength for several more months. *3A-33635, RG342FH, NARA*

In preparation for operations into Burma, the 7th Bomb Group began moving to new bases in eastern India to avoid the difficulties of operating out of Karachi and Allahabad while using advanced bases near Calcutta for refueling. At the end of October the air echelon of the 436th Bomb Squadron left Allahabad for the air base at Gaya—farther to the east and some 260 miles from Calcutta—with the ground staff following a few weeks later. The 9th Bomb Squadron's ground crews had flown back to India during October, with the air crews arriving during November in new B-24Ds. The 9th Squadron also went temporarily to Gaya with the 7th Bomb Group headquarters, before moving to a more permanent station at Pandaveswar—130 miles from Calcutta—in December. The 7th Group's newest squadrons (492nd and 493rd) remained at Karachi at Camp New Malir, training new air crews for the 9th and 436th Squadrons and gradually accumulating officers and enlisted men arriving from the United States to bring the squadrons up to full strength. The group still had ten B-17Es on strength, though few were in commission. New B-24Ds arrived in small numbers, with 16 aircraft on strength in November and an additional six bombers arriving for the group in December.[59]

While undertaking these moves of aircraft, men, and equipment to new bases, the 7th Bomb Group started regular operations to targets in southern Burma and beyond. On the group's second mission on 5 November 1942 the 436th Squadron sent six aircraft to bomb the dock area at Rangoon, but the force couldn't locate the target due to poor weather. The squadron sent six aircraft back to Rangoon on November 9, in what would become a regular feature of 7th Bomb Group operations for the next year. The bombers would take off from their bases and fly down the Bay of Bengal well off the coast of Burma at lower altitudes. Approximately 100 miles from Rangoon, the bombers would begin to climb to their bombing altitude of 23,000 to 27,000 feet. The bombers would tighten their formation as they approached Rangoon from the west, coming in across the Irrawaddy delta. After bombs away, the formation would make a sharp turn and descent to pick up speed and get out over the Gulf of Martaban, south of the delta, for the long haul up the Bay of Bengal and back to base in India. To ensure a return to base before dark, the missions to Rangoon most often left India in the early morning, usually arriving over Rangoon around noon. This routine prompted some crews in the 9th Bomb Squadron to form

7th Bomb Group pilots get a briefing beside a B-24 before heading off for a mission against Rangoon. To return to their airfields in India before nightfall, the squadrons had to take off early in the morning, reaching Rangoon around noon, leading the 9th Bomb Squadron to form the "Goon at Noon" Club for anyone who had flown a mission over the city at that hour. *India Air Task Force, 10th USAAF, November 1942–May 1943, 827.306-1, vol. 1, AFHRA*

Smoke rises up from an attack on the dock area at Rangoon as the B-24s make their withdrawal. The Rangoon River flows south to empty into the Gulf of Martaban. After bombing the city, the 7th Group's squadrons would head for the gulf to get away from intercepting Japanese fighters, who were often reluctant to follow the bombers far out over the water. *Courtesy, Col. Thomas Sledge, USAF (Ret'd)*

THE INDIA AIR TASK FORCE

the "'Goon at Noon" Club, an elite organization open to anyone who had flown over Rangoon at this hour. On the November 6 mission the bombers dropped 20 1,000-pound bombs on the warehouses in the dock area and one bomb on a freighter in the river, which sank. The bombers went back to Rangoon again three days later, getting another 20 bombs into the dock area and five on the Syriam oil refinery, starting large fires. On this mission, three Japanese fighters rose to intercept but only one attacked, without damaging any of the bombers. The 436th next went to bomb the railroad yards at Mandalay on November 20 with eight B-24s. The 9th Bomb Squadron made its return debut two days later, sending six aircraft out on another attack on the Mandalay rail yards, having to circle the target for 45 minutes waiting for clouds to clear. On November 25, Lt. Col. Conrad Necarson, the group commander, led a night-bombing mission to bomb an oil refinery and power plant at Bangkok, Thailand—a round trip of 2,700 miles, the longest American bombing mission of the war up to that date. At the end of the month, six B-24s went back to Port Blair in the Andaman Islands to bomb a Japanese naval vessel reported there, getting hits, while six B-24s undertook a night raid on the Rangoon dock area. Japanese fighters rose up to intercept with the aid of searchlights from the ground, but only one fighter attacked without doing any damage. One bomber failed to return from the mission, most likely a victim of heavier antiaircraft fire.[60]

During December, the 9th and 436th Bomb Squadrons flew another six missions into Burma and a single mission to Port Blair

Bombs exploding in the Rangoon dock area on the Rangoon River, with several Japanese freighters tied up alongside. The 7th Bomb Group carried out an extended and ultimately successful campaign to prevent the Japanese from using Rangoon as a port of entry for supplies coming into Burma. *India Air Task Force, 10th USAAF, November 1942–May 1943, 827.306-1, vol. 1, AFHRA*

Crews unload equipment after returning from one of the early missions to Bangkok in December 1942. At the time, the raids on Bangkok were some of the longest combat missions the Army Air Force had yet flown. *India Air Task Force, 10th USAAF, November 1942–May 1943, 827.306-1, Vol. 1, AFHRA*

in search of shipping. The main targets continued to be the dock area in Rangoon and shipping in the Rangoon River—the bombers hitting the docks on three missions and the Rangoon railway yards on one mission—while a single flight of three aircraft bombed the Japanese airfield at Mingaladon. In the largest mission to date, Necrason led 12 bombers from the 9th and 436th Squadrons back to Bangkok on the night of December 26. The 9th Squadron sent three airplanes to hit the main railroad station, while three went to bomb a naval shipyard on the Chao Phraya River. Necrason led the 436th Squadron's aircraft to bomb the Bangkok arsenal that manufactured weapons of various kinds. On the last mission of the month, the 436th Squadron sent out two flights of six aircraft to attack shipping approaching Rangoon, damaging a larger tanker and a freighter. The 7th Bomb Group ended the year below its assigned strength, with only 22 of a planned 35 B-24s on hand and the 492nd and 493rd Squadrons still at Camp New Malir awaiting airplanes and air crews. The 9th and 436th Squadrons had settled into their bases at Pandaveswar and Gaya, but neither squadron could reliably send out more than six aircraft on a mission. The 9th Squadron had nine B-24s available while the 436th had 11, with 10 combat crews each. The squadrons suffered from the standard problems affecting all the units in the IATF: shortages of spare parts, aircraft, and personnel.[61]

From the activation of the IATF in early October until mid-December, the 11th Bomb Squadron's two-aircraft detachment at Dinjan was the only active American medium-bomber unit flying regular bombing missions into Burma. The detachment would send out one B-25C—and sometimes both its aircraft—on reconnaissance missions, usually with an escort of one or two P-40s. These missions often included bombing military targets such as barracks, supply dumps, or bridges. Often the pilot would drop down to low level to strafe targets with the .30-caliber and .50-caliber machine guns in the nose, since antiaircraft fire was rarely encountered. On October 25, the detachment was called back to Kweilin to take part in the CATF's raid on Hong Kong. One of the bombers developed engine trouble 30 minutes out of Dinjan, and in the crash landing that followed, the entire crew was killed, including Capt. Robert Gray—commanding the Dinjan detachment—who was a veteran of the Doolittle raid on Tokyo. Only one B-25 returned to Dinjan after the Hong Kong mission, flying four reconnaissance missions over Burma during November.[62]

The other medium-bomber squadrons of the 341st Bomb Group took even longer to get into combat than the 7th Bomb Group's squadrons. The 22nd, 490th, and 491st Squadrons had to spend time waiting in Karachi for personnel to arrive from the United States by sea and for aircraft to be flown along the route across Africa to India. Finally, on 3 December 1942, the 22nd Bomb Squadron moved from Karachi to a new station at Chakulia, a little more than 100 miles west of Calcutta. At this time the squadron had seven B-25Cs and seven crews ready for operations. This would be the squadron's base for the next year, though missions often went out of air bases closer to Burma. The B-25s would take off from Chakulia, land at the RAF base at Argartala to refuel, carry out the mission, and return to Argartala to refuel before returning to Chakulia. Maj. Frank Sharp, squadron commander, led the first mission on December 14, taking six B-25s to bomb the Myohaung railroad junction near Mandalay with an escort of five P-40s, according to the records of the mission. The squadron went back to the Myohaung railroad junction on December 21, this time on their own, getting hits on boxcars and the rail line. The next day, five B-25s bombed the railroad-marshaling yards at Sagaing, on the Irrawaddy River, 12 miles southwest of Mandalay. The squadron flew one more mission before the end of the year, with three B-25s bombing the Japanese airfield at Shwebo, getting hits on the hangars and revetment areas.[63]

At the end of December, with the necessary personnel having arrived from the United States, the ground echelons of the 341st Group headquarters and the 490th and the 491st Bomb Squadrons

THE INDIA AIR TASK FORCE

The crew of a 490th Bomb Squadron get a briefing before a flight out of Karachi. The 341st Bomb Group's squadrons had to wait for several months for sufficient aircraft, crews, and ground staff before they could begin combat operations. *3A-36256, RG342FH, NARA*

left Karachi by train to travel across India to their new bases. The 341st Group headquarters and the 491st Squadron joined the 22nd Squadron at Chakulia, the 491st air echelon arriving in early January 1943. The 490th Bomb Squadron's ground echelon went to the base at Ondal, 100 miles northwest of Calcutta, the air echelon not arriving until mid-February. Like the 7th Bomb Group, the 341st ended the year short of aircraft and combat crews, with only one squadron actively engaged in combat.[64] Reinforcements were on the way. Bissell learned in mid-December that the Army Air Force was preparing 11 more B-24s and 17 more B-25s for the CBI, while 13 B-25s were en route. Another 101 P-40s were on their way to Karachi by boat, with three more F-4 reconnaissance airplanes.[65]

IATF operations from its activation to the end of 1942 were designed to "feel out the enemy, survey his lines of communications

Toward the end of 1942, the 9th Photo Reconnaissance Squadron began flying reconnaissance missions to southern Burma with their F-4 Lightnings, providing vital intelligence on Japanese shipping at Rangoon. *India Air Task Force, 10th USAAF, November 1942–May 1943, 827.306-1, vol. 1, AFHRA*

and test his defenses."[66] The results of these operations were in no way significant, but they pointed toward a steadily increasing capability and the potential, when the IATF was at full strength, of inflicting more-lasting damage. The trend was in the right direction. During October the IATF dropped 52.4 tons of bombs on targets in Burma; during November, 86.5 tons; and during December, 153.9 tons, a near doubling of the tonnage on targets.[67] The Royal Air Force was also increasing its bombing effort, the RAF tonnage rising from 65 tons in October to 146 tons in December.[68] The targets themselves varied, but a pattern was beginning to emerge: 91.2 tons against docks and shipping, 82.5 tons against military targets, 75.6 tons against railways, and 43.6 tons against airfields. To weaken the Japanese hold on Burma, the Allies had to establish air superiority. A way to achieve this was to deny the supplies the Japanese army and army air force needed to conduct operations, by bombing the means of transporting these supplies to the front and destroying them along the way. The Allies did not yet have the fighter aircraft with the quality and in the quantity needed to achieve air superiority, but repeated attacks on Japanese airfields would help degrade the Japanese Army Air Force units operating in Burma. Fortunately for the heavy and medium bombers, the Japanese Army Air Force's reaction to Allied bombing raids had been hesitant. So far the bombers, especially the B-24s who flew without fighter escort deep into southern Burma, could carry out their attacks with little risk of interception.

CHAPTER 4

FROM CASABLANCA TO TRIDENT

Tenth Air Force Operations, January–May 1943

The Casablanca Conference and an Air Plan for Burma

At the turn of the year there were a few signs that the strategic situation for the Allies in Burma and China, if not actually improving, was at least more stable than just a few months before. Rommel's defeat at the Battle of El Alamein, the Allied invasion of North Africa, and the Russian defeat of the German army at Stalingrad had ended the threat to Allied positions in the Middle East and thus the threat to India. In the Pacific, while mounting a tenacious defense against Allied offensives in New Guinea and Guadalcanal, the Japanese had failed in their attempts to capture New Guinea and were on the verge of withdrawing from Guadalcanal after a brutal attritional battle. It seemed, for the first time, that the Allies would soon be in a position to undertake more offensive actions against Germany and Japan and possibly seize the strategic initiative, but where and to what extent remained a subject of intense debate and sharply opposing views within Allied councils.[1] At the Casablanca Conference in January 1943—the first of five Allied conferences to be held that year—President Roosevelt, Prime Minister Churchill, and the Combined Chiefs of Staff met to work out Allied strategies for the coming year. After intense debate the Casablanca Conference reaffirmed the strategy of defeating Germany first, with the American Joint Chiefs of Staff reluctantly accepting British proposals for the Mediterranean to be the focus of operations during 1943, postponing the proposed cross-Channel attack into Europe the Americans preferred.[2]

There was a sharp division of opinion on a strategy toward Japan. While the British Chiefs of Staff advocated allocating the minimum force necessary to contain Japan, the American Joint Chiefs of Staff wanted a combination of offensive and defensive measures to ensure that the Japanese could not solidify their hold on their captured territories or threaten the security of Allied communications.[3] The American concern was that the defeat of Japan could not, as the British appeared to believe, be postponed indefinitely. Delay, the Americans believed, "would enable the Japanese to entrench themselves in Asia and the Pacific sufficiently to make U.S. re-conquest of the area extremely difficult if not impossible."[4] A delay would also work against the US objective of supporting China and keeping China in the war.[5] In particular, the American chiefs expressed the view that Burma and China presented a vulnerable flank from which to attack the Japanese, and were strongly in support of Operation ANAKIM.[6] Gen. Marshall said that he was "most anxious to open the Burma Road, not so much for the morale effect on China as for the need to provide air support to China for operations against Japan and Japanese shipping."[7] The

Allied leaders at the Casablanca Conference in January 1943. Generalissimo Chiang Kai-shek sits next to President Franklin Roosevelt, with Madam Chiang (Soong Mei-ling) on Prime Minister Winston Churchill's left. Standing behind them are (*left to right*) Chinese general Chang Chen, Gen. Ling Wei, American lieutenant general Brehon Somerville, Lt. Gen. Joseph Stilwell, Lt. Gen. Henry Arnold, British field marshal Sir John Dill, Vice-Admiral Lord Louis Mountbatten, and Maj. Gen. de Wiart. *SC 338025, RG111, NARA*

THE TENTH AIR FORCE IN WORLD WAR II

Chinese troops undergoing training in the use of a heavy mortar at one of the training bases in India. The Chinese government supplied the manpower to form five divisions, while the Americans provided equipment and American Army instructors. *Box 161, folder V, RG208AA, NARA*

American Joint Chiefs of Staff recommended a series of limited offensives to put pressure on Japanese lines of communication between Japan and its captured territories in Southeast Asia and the Pacific, in particular to increase the flow of supplies to China for the air campaign against Japan. The British chiefs argued in return that ANAKIM, with its planned amphibious operations against southern Burma, would draw landing craft from the cross-Channel attack the Americans wanted. In a compromise, the British agreed to continue planning for ANAKIM with a target date of 15 November 1943, but with the Combined Chiefs of Staff making a final decision in July.[8]

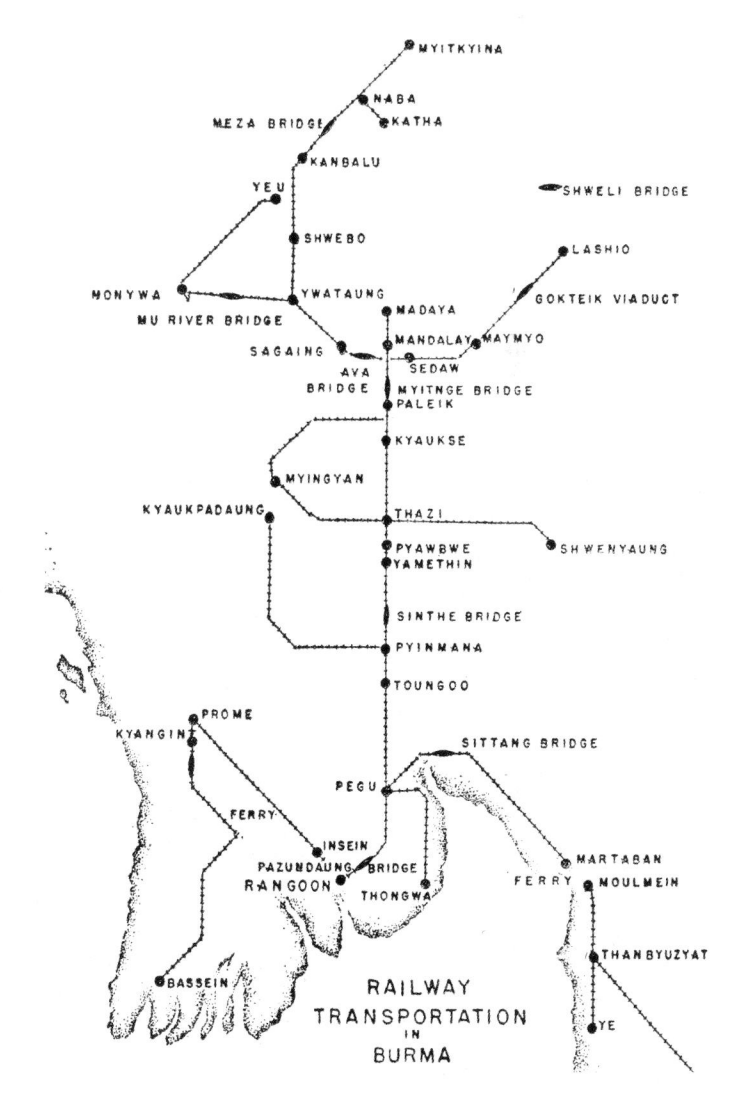

The final report of the Combined Chiefs of Staff at the Casablanca Conference called for several limited advances in the Pacific, and in Burma continuing the operation to capture Akyab, and a limited advance from Assam to secure the air route to China.[9] The main effort for China would be to increase the flow of supplies to enable intensified air attacks on Japanese shipping and to build up the capacity for direct air attacks on Japan. This would be accomplished by providing more transport aircraft, though there was support for Stilwell to begin work on a road out of Ledo, in Assam. The report made clear that there would be no major Allied offensive in Burma until late in the year, and possibly not even then. In the coming months Gen. Wavell planned to continue his offensive in the Arakan to capture Akyab and launch Wingate's Long Range Penetration Group's mission behind Japanese lines in February. Stilwell would concentrate on preparing his Chinese forces training in India (X-Force) and the Chinese armies in Yunnan (Y-Force) for operations in support of ANAKIM while developing a base at Ledo to continue construction of the road into Burma.[10] It was evident from the plans outlined at the Casablanca Conference that much of the American contribution to the war in Burma would be from and through the air. Clearly the air ferry route required more transport aircraft, which the India-China Wing of the Air Transport Command would receive in the months ahead. The priority for the IATF remained defense of the air route to China, with the additional task of supporting Chinese forces in Yunnan from any Japanese offensive across the Salween River or a northward advance toward Ledo. The ITAF's main effort up to the start of the monsoon season at the end of May was against the Japanese army's line of communications into Burma.

The Japanese army and army air forces in Burma also faced logistical challenges. While Burma could provide the Japanese with supplies of food, clothing, and some petroleum products, weapons, ammunition, and spare parts for vehicles and airplanes had to come from Japan. The sea journey from Japan to Burma via the South China Sea to Singapore and then up the Straits of Malacca to the port of Rangoon covered more than 4,000 miles. Rangoon provided access to the Burmese railroad system, which in 1943 comprised around 2,000 miles of single-track rail lines running principally to the north, with branch lines connecting Rangoon to the smaller port of Moulmein to the east and to Bassein to the west. But the main railroad line ran 356 miles north to Mandalay, where it split off, with one branch line heading 175 miles east to Lashio while another branch line went farther north, ending at Myitkyina, 337 miles away. Lacking adequate numbers of motor vehicles and a poor road system in Burma, the Japanese army was heavily dependent on the railroad to move supplies to its forward bases, and units nearer the borders with India and China.[11]

The Japanese line-of-communications system had four potentially vulnerable elements: shipping, ports, and storage facilities; rail centers; bridges; and rolling stock. Japan did not have an adequate margin of merchant shipping available to cover its now-far-flung empire. As the war progressed, shipping losses, or even damage to shipping, compounded the disruption in shipping schedules above and beyond the losses of supplies and equipment. Using airpower and sea power to destroy enemy supplies before they could be deployed on the battlefield was a much more efficient means of destruction.[12] Once a ship reached port, supplies had to be offloaded at the dock area, then stored until moved to the railroad system for transport. Burma had four principal ports—Rangoon, Moulmein, Bassein, and Akyab—although Rangoon was by far the most important. Mandalay was an important inland port on the Irrawaddy River for riverboat traffic. Additionally there were an estimated 15 or more key storage centers along or near the rail line where supplies could accumulate pending shipment. The railroad system had around 21 rail centers that served as storage and transshipment points, moving supplies from boats to trains, or from trains to trucks. These rail centers also served as collection points for rolling stock. There were many bridges all along the main railroad line and the branch lines, many with spans more than 100 feet long. Locomotives were the most important component of the railroad system, since there were not many available in Burma. Prior to the Japanese invasion there were 355 locomotives operating over the railroad system, but the British army had put many of these out of commission during the retreat, leaving about half this number available to the Japanese. There was only one main locomotive repair facility in Burma, the shops at Insein in Rangoon. The Japanese had several thousand railroad cars available to ship goods over the rail system, and while these were relatively easy to repair, any damaged cars were unusable until they could be repaired.[13]

All of these elements had to be functioning to make the line-of-communications system work reliably, and all were vulnerable to air attack. More importantly, damage, or the elimination of one element, had a ripple effect through the entire system. Sinking or damaging a ship meant a loss of supplies. Destruction of the docks made it difficult to offload cargo. Destruction of warehouses or storage facilities meant further losses of supplies. Destruction of a rail center and transshipment point meant that supplies coming up from Rangoon could not get through, nor could rolling stock return to Rangoon for more supplies. Damage or destruction of a bridge meant the entire system could be shut down for some period, leading to backups in supplies at storage or rail centers, delaying the delivery of supplies to the front and making these centers even more vulnerable to attack and even more-serious losses. Destruction of locomotives disrupted railroad schedules and limited the number of trains that could be put in use. The challenge for the IATF was that to deny these facilities to the Japanese, they had to be attacked again and again, relentlessly. The Japanese became adept at repairing railroad yards and railroad bridges, forcing the medium and heavy bombers to return repeatedly to the same targets. The campaign against the Japanese line of communications system would continue until the liberation of Burma two and a half years later.

Brig. Gen. Haynes employed his heavy bombers, medium bombers, and fighters to the task of disrupting Japanese communications in ways that fit their range and capabilities.[14] With their longer range and heavier bombload, the 7th Bomb Group's B-24s took responsibility for targets in southern Burma south of Mandalay, concentrating on Japanese shipping and the port of Rangoon, and targets in between Rangoon and Mandalay. Haynes assigned targets in central Burma to the 341st Group's B-25s. The medium bombers went after rail centers, storage areas, and especially bridges, as well as Japanese airfields. The P-40s from the 51st Group maintained defensive patrols over the Assam air bases but continued their sweeps and bombing missions as far south as Myitkyina, covering the roads leading north from this end of the railroad line, the railroad line itself, storage facilities and warehouses, and airfields in their assigned area. For the first few months of 1943, until the activation of the Fourteenth Air Force, the China Air Task Force covered the area around Lashio with the 11th Bomb Squadron's B-25s—if fuel was available—and the 23rd Fighter Group's P-40s. In this way, the IATF could cover the Japanese communications system from Rangoon to the border with India.[15]

The mission the IATF had taken on complemented the work of the Royal Air Force. Having only a small number of longer-range Liberator bombers (the RAF's designation for the Consolidated B-24) and medium-range Wellington bombers for night bombing, the RAF reached an agreement with the Tenth Air Force where the Tenth took on responsibility for flying most of the missions greater than 250 miles from Allied air bases.[16] This left the RAF's squadrons of light Blenheim bombers available for supporting the British army's advance in the Arakan and for attacks on Japanese airfields nearer to the front lines. In November, Haynes had moved the headquarters of the IATF to Barrackpore, near Calcutta, to be closer to RAF Air Headquarters, Bengal, responsible for No. 221 Group (based at Calcutta) and No. 224 Group (operating out of Chittagong). No. 221 Group had five squadrons of Hurricane fighters available for the defense of Calcutta and controlled one squadron of Wellington bombers and one squadron of Liberators. No. 224 Group, closer to the British front lines, had five Hurricane squadrons and two Mohawk squadrons, with four squadrons of Blenheim IV and Bisley light bombers (later in 1943, American Vultee Vengeances procured through Lend-Lease replaced the Blenheims in several RAF squadrons). Cooperation between the IATF and the RAF was informal, with daily conferences covering planned operations and a sharing of intelligence on Japanese activity, but each force operated independently of the other.[17]

An RAF Bisley light bomber (Blenheim Mk V) taxis past an older Blenheim Mk IV. In early 1943 the RAF in India had four squadrons equipped with the Bisley and the Blenheim Mk IV. These continued on operations until the squadrons converted to the Hurricane IIc later in 1943. CI_000024, IWM

The Hurricane IIb, armed with 12 .303 machine guns, and the Hurricane IIc, with four 20 mm cannon, were the RAF's main fighters until the arrival of the first Spitfires in late 1943. The Hurricanes did not have the performance to establish dominance over the Japanese Ki-43s but proved to be an excellent ground attack airplane, serving in this capacity until the very end of the war in Burma. IND _002143, IWM

The Japanese *5th Hikōshidan* was well aware that the Allies were reinforcing their air units in India and increasing their air operations into Burma. The *5th Hikōshidan* had the twofold mission of maintaining air supremacy over Burma through attacks on Allied aircraft and airfields and providing support for the *15th Army*'s ground operations. To defend Burma the *5th Hikōshidan* retained the *4th* and *7th Hikōdan*, each with one fighter and two bomber *sentai*, but lost the *12th Hikōdan* with its two fighter regiments—the *1st* and *11th Hikōsentai*—when this air brigade left for the Southwest Pacific in December 1942. During the first few months of 1943, Japanese fighters and bombers flew missions against the British advance toward Akyab in coordination with the *15th Army*, fighting to maintain air superiority over the area. This meant fewer operations against the American airfields in the Dinjan area, though interceptions of American transport aircraft continued. The *5th Hikōshidan* also had to deal with the growing number of American heavy-bomber raids against Rangoon and Japanese shipping. Initially the *4th Hikōdan*'s *50th Hikōsentai* provided support for the *15th Army* in the defense of the Akyab area, while the *7th Hikōdan*'s *64th Hikōsentai* defended the Rangoon area, the two fighter *sentai* sending squadrons

FROM CASABLANCA TO TRIDENT

to airfields in other parts of Burma as needed. To avoid losses, the *5th Hikōshidan* based the bomber *sentai* in Thailand and Malaya, with the bombers flying up to airfields in Burma when required. The two fighter *sentai* converted to the more capable Type 1 Fighter Model 2 (Ki-43-II), with the *64th Hikōsentai* undertaking the conversion in Japan in December 1942, returning to Burma in February 1943 to allow the *50th Hikōsentai* to convert to the new fighter in Java between February and March. Thus, for some months in early 1943, the *5th Hikōshidan* had to defend Burma with a single fighter *sentai*.[18]

Fighter Operations: January to May 1943

The priority mission for the Tenth Air Force, and for the India Air Task Force, remained the defense of the air route to China, but the resources available were less than satisfactory and barely adequate for the task. The 51st Fighter Group's two squadrons—the 25th Fighter Squadron at Sookerating and the 26th Fighter Squadron at Dinjan—had between them 26 P-40Es and 14 P-40Ks.[19] Neither the P-40E nor the P-40K had a rapid rate of climb or the performance to reach Japanese aircraft flying at higher altitudes. Nor was there an adequate supply of fighters to defend the expanding number of American airfields in Assam that were finally coming into commission. As a result, the fighter squadrons had to split their forces into smaller flights to cover all the airfields in Assam. The more difficult problem was the limited early-warning network then available. One of the first visual-observation posts, designated KC-8, went into operation in November 1942 in the Naga Hills east of Ledo. Radar proved to have limited utility. The airfields in the Dinjan area lay in the valley of the Brahmaputra River, but, to the east, hills rose steeply all the way to the Burma border and beyond, limiting the ability of radar to locate and track incoming Japanese air raids in time to give fighters a chance to climb to altitude.[20] The 679th Signal Company

Supplies go down from a C-47 for an isolated early-warning station in the mountains east of the Assam Valley. Small teams of Army Air Force officers and men manned these stations to give warning of approaching Japanese aircraft. The stations had to rely on air drops for all their supplies and equipment.
3A-36187, RG342FH, NARA

(Air Warning) arrived in Assam in January 1943 as a radar-warning unit, only to find that its radar equipment had limited utility.[21] The 679th gave up its radar and converted to a Visual Air Warning Company organized into four platoons with six reporting teams, each with 10 men and an SCR-177 radio. These teams went into the mountains east of the Assam Valley to set up additional observation posts to warn of approaching Japanese aircraft. Reporting directly into the 51st Fighter Group's 51st Fighter Control Headquarters, these posts reported any unidentified aircraft and alerted the fighter squadrons to incoming raids. Their isolated locations and the lack of any roads meant they had to depend on air supply for all their needs. While the early-warning system—basic as it was—did help protect the Assam airfields from air attack, the 51st Group's fighters also had to provide protection to the transports flying the Hump route into China and to transports dropping supplies to forward Allied units and the 679th Signal Company's observation posts in the hills. There were too few fighters to defend the airfields and escort the transports. Because of the lack of an adequate number of airfields, the transports had to fly individually to and from China, and not in formation, which would have been easier to escort. As a result, the fighter squadrons resorted to maintaining alert flights on their airfields and flying regular patrol missions over Assam and northern Burma to at least be in the air if the observation posts or a transport called in a Japanese attack. Whenever weather permitted, the fighter squadrons flew small patrols between their Assam bases and Ft. Hertz, along the route the transports took to Kunming.[22]

Fortunately, with only one fighter *sentai* available for escort work and commitments to the *15th Army*, the *5th Hikōshidan* carried out few bombing missions against the Assam airfields or Yunnanyi— the westernmost airfield on the Chinese side of the Hump route— during the first half of 1943. The first Japanese raid of the year took place on 16 January 1943, when the *50th Hikōsentai* escorted Ki-48 bombers from the *8th Hikōsentai* to attack the China Air Task Force's airfield at Yunnanyi, base for the 16th Fighter Squadron. Two P-40 pilots up on an early patrol (Capt. Robert Liles and 2nd Lt. Aaron Liepe) spotted the Japanese formation and reported 18 bombers with 12 Ki-43s flying as close escort, with another dozen fighters flying behind the bomber formation.[23] Liles and Liepe went after the escorts, with Liles claiming two destroyed and Liepe a third. Eight more P-40s took off and reached the Japanese bombers as

A P-40K undergoing maintenance at Lilibari airfield in Assam in March 1943. Maintenance facilities were barely adequate. Here a tarpaulin stretched over a wooden post frame serves as a makeshift hangar, with the repair shack behind built out of local bamboo. *3A-35802, RG342FH, NARA*

Another P-40 undergoing engine repairs in a grove of trees at Lilibari. In the dry season these arrangements were passable, but the monsoon rains could turn the ground into a sea of mud. *3A-35745, RG342FH, NARA*

FROM CASABLANCA TO TRIDENT

they flew over the airfield. The bombing did little damage to the field. In the combat that followed, both 1st Lt. George Barnes and 1st Lt. James Little claimed two "Zeros," and Capt. Robert Smith claimed another "Zero" and one of the bombers.[24] The *50th Hikōsentai* lost one fighter during the raid, and a second when the pilot had to make a forced landing returning to base, while the *8th Hikōsentai* had one bomber damaged.[25] The 16th Squadron lost one pilot during the combat. These turned out to be the last claims of the China Air Task Force as part of the Tenth Air Force.

The next month the Japanese went back to Assam. On 23 February 1943 the *5th Hikōshidan* launched a raid on Chabua, but both sides escaped serious damage. In the late afternoon the early-warning net picked up the approach of 12 aircraft: seven bombers (most likely Type 97 bombers [Ki-21] from the *98th Hikōsentai*) with an escort of five Ki-43 fighters from the recently returned *64th Hikōsentai* heading toward Chabua airfield. The 25th Fighter Squadron sent off 14 P-40s while the 26th Fighter Squadron got off 17, but neither formation found the Japanese aircraft due to hazy conditions in the area and a mix-up with Fighter Control, which sent the 26th Squadron in the wrong direction. By the time the fighters reached Chabua, the Japanese had bombed the field and left without doing any damage. Bomb fragments killed one American officer from an antiaircraft unit when he left his slit trench to warn some Indian laborers to leave the field.[26]

The Japanese returned two days later on February 25, when the *98th Hikōsentai* sent out nine Ki-21 bombers with an escort of 21 fighters from the *64th Hikōsentai*. On this occasion the early-warning stations gave the alert in time. At 0620, station KC-8 radioed a warning of a large Japanese formation heading for the Assam airfields. The 25th and 26th Fighter Squadrons went to red alert, and by 0640 the 26th Squadron had three flights of 18 P-40s in the air and climbing, while the 25th Squadron sent off 12 P-40s. The P-40s found the Japanese formation attacking the airfields at Digboi and Sookerating. Clouds over the airfields forced the Japanese bombers to turn and make a second attack, giving the P-40s more time to climb and intercept, with heavy antiaircraft fire guiding the American pilots to the Japanese formation. One of the intercepting pilots reported seeing three fighters flying ahead of the bomber formation making S turns, with the rest of the escort flying 1,000 feet behind and also making S turns. As the P-40s attacked the Ki-43s rose up to do battle, leaving the bombers undefended. Antiaircraft fire hit one of the bombers, knocking it down. The American fighters attacked the leader of the bomber formation, shooting down Capt. Tadao Hara, commanding the *98th Hikōsentai's 1st Chutai*. The *64th Hikōsentai* lost its commanding officer when two P-40s shot down Maj. Takeo Akera's Ki-43 in a head-on attack. The P-40s damaged a second Ki-43, forcing the pilot to withdraw. In the confused fighting, the pilots of the 25th and 26th Fighter Squadrons claimed six Japanese bombers and six fighters shot down, 14 probably shot down, and seven airplanes damaged, with the 26th Squadron claiming five bombers and four fighters destroyed, nine probables, and five damaged. Once again, the Japanese attack failed to do much damage, leaving 40 bomb craters on the airfield at Sookerating that were easily repaired.[27]

Capt. Tadao Hara may have been the victim of Capt. Earl Livesay of the 25th Fighter Squadron, who claimed one bomber shot down and one fighter as a probable. Livesay came across a bomber flying apart from the main bomber formation, possibly damaged in an earlier attack. He reported his encounter as follows:

During the enemy raid on 25 February 1943, I first sighted the Japanese bomber formation approximately five miles south of Digboi proceeding on a course of 140 degrees. There was a dog fight in progress at the rear of this formation, and I noticed 3 black trails of smoke from airplanes going down and one that was leaving a large trail of white smoke and in a tight spiral or spin.

Pilots of the 26th Fighter Squadron at Lilibari Field on 17 March 1943. Several of these pilots participated in the combat with Japanese fighters and bombers on 25 February 1943. *Front row, kneeling*: Capt. William Moore, Lt. Horace Adkins, and Lt. John Harrington, chaplain; *standing*: 1st Lt. John Ferguson, Lt. John Coonan, 1st Lt. Arthur Gregg, Lt. Virgil Burge, 1st Lt. Alfred Wipf, and Lt. William Rogers; and *on the wing*: Lt. Leonard Hicks, 1st Lt. Larry Howie, and 1st Lt. Charles Evans. *3A-34909, RG342FH, NARA*

The main flight of bombers seemed to be drawing away; I gradually drew ahead of the bomber formation and about one-half mile from its left flank and started to turn into the flight when I saw a lone bomber about the same distance from the flight as myself. I immediately turned into this airplane for a quartering frontal attack and shot out his starboard engine. I then closed in from the rear, firing a long burst from very close range which set the bomber's fuselage on fire and started him down. I then pulled off to the side and saw a fighter plane flying abreast of me on the left and out about 600 yards. We turned into each other for a head-on pass and I started firing from long range and succeeded in hitting the Japanese ship when the range was shortened. The ship poured out black smoke from the engine cowling and fuselage, then passed below me; as I turned to get another look at this ship another Zero fighter was coming into my quartering rear so I dove my airplane to the tree tops and came home.[28]

The Japanese did not launch attacks on the Assam airfields again, though they kept up reconnaissance flights over the area. The 25th and 26th Squadrons scrambled on several occasions when the early-warning net radioed in reports of Japanese aircraft, but had no success intercepting the high-flying Japanese reconnaissance airplanes. The P-40s could not climb high enough or fast enough to reach them. In early April the 26th Squadron took one P-40E and stripped out four of the six .50-caliber machine guns, leaving one gun in each wing. To lighten the airplane even further, the squadron removed all armor plate and all but one radio, filled the fuel tanks only half full, and put in only half the regular load of ammunition.[29] At 1140 on April 8, station KC-14 reported an unidentified airplane flying at high altitude. Further plots confirmed that the airplane was a Japanese reconnaissance airplane. 1st Lt. Charles Streit took off in the stripped P-40 at 1200 and climbed rapidly, catching up with what he identified as a Type 100 reconnaissance airplane (Ki-

Brig. Gen. Clayton Bissell awards the Distinguished Flying Cross to Col. Homer Sanders for his leadership of the 51st Fighter Group. Sanders relinquished command of the group in May 1943. He went on to serve in the European theater, commanding the 7th Photo Reconnaissance Group in the Eighth Air Force and the 100th Fighter Wing in the Ninth Air Force. *3A-34179, RG342FH, NARA*

The men of the India Air Task Force learned to make do with what was available. Bamboo proved to be a versatile material with all sorts of uses. Woven split bamboo provided cover for soft areas of sand or dirt in the fighter dispersal areas. *3A-33967, RG342FH, NARA*

46 Dinah). Seeing the approaching fighter, the Ki-46 pilot tried to dive away, but Streit followed him down to 5,000 feet, where he opened fire from 100 yards behind the Japanese airplane, only to have both his guns jam. He recharged his guns six times and finally got his right-wing gun firing, hitting the Ki-46 in the right engine, which started smoking. Streit made four more passes, setting the right wing on fire. The Ki-46 did a slow roll and went down into the jungle.[30] This would be the 51st Fighter Group's last air victory as part of the Tenth Air Force.

Bissell's repeated requests for a fighter plane with performance superior to the P-40 finally brought about a response from Washington, but the results turned out to be less than he had hoped. Although Bissell and others in the Tenth Air Force wanted the P-51, in March 1943 Gen. Arnold agreed to assign the 80th Fighter Group, equipped with the new Republic P-47, to the Tenth Air Force. What transpired is illustrative of the problems with priorities and production levels that continued to limit what could be made available for the Tenth Air Force. As Arnold explained in a letter to Bissell, "no other action at the present time was possible under the existing schedules and commitments of fighter aircraft. I realize that the P-47 may not be ideally suited for your operations, but feel strongly that it will provide you with a high speed, high altitude weapon which can profitably be employed."[31] Arnold told Bissell that the 80th Group's commander, Maj. Albert Evans, was a superior leader and that the group's pilots had an average of 175 hours on the P-47, had excellent morale, and were confident that at high altitudes the P-47 was unbeatable. Arnold said 100 P-47s would be shipped to India for the 80th Group. While the P-47 had yet to encounter enemy fighters, Arnold felt that "the P-47 can and will prove itself in combat."[32] Bissell replied that "we are all very happy about the dispatch of the 80th Fighter Group. We hope that everything practicable will be done to expedite its sailing."[33]

The 80th Fighter Group had already been alerted that it would soon be sent overseas.[34] The pilots expected they would take their P-47s to England to fight the Luftwaffe, even going to the Republic Aviation plant on Long Island to test-fly new production airplanes, but in April the group received the astonishing news that their destination was not England but India, and instead of P-47s they would go into combat with the latest version of the P-40 (P-40N). The European and Pacific theaters had priority over the China-Burma-India theater and would have first claim for the superior P-47. Those 80th Fighter Group pilots who did not have at least 30 flying hours on the P-40 went to a field in Virginia to get in the required flying time. The P-40N—lighter, faster, and with a better rate of climb than the earlier P-40E/K models—was an improvement, but not significantly so. Conversion of the Curtiss Airplane Company's plants to the newer P-40N caused delays in production, so commitments to the different theaters of war and to Lend-Lease could not be met on time, as Arnold explained in a later letter to Bissell.[35] The 80th Fighter Group would not reach its bases in Assam until the end of August.

The secondary mission for the 51st Fighter Group was the destruction of Japanese forces and installations in Burma in support of the air plan against Japanese lines of communications and Allied ground units in northern Burma. The fighters covered the last stage of the line-of-communications system: the delivery of supplies to the Japanese army's frontline units in northern Burma. The Japanese *15th Army* had assigned the task of defending this area to the *18th Division*. The division garrisoned the towns around Myitkyina and the smaller villages on the roads and tracks leading north to the border with India. Myitkyina and Mogaung were the *18th Division*'s main bases. From Myitkyina, the road and rail line ran southwest to Mogaung and on to Indaw and south to Mandalay. From Mogaung, a road worked north up through the Hukawng Valley toward the border with India. The Japanese occupied the towns of Kamaing, Maingkwan, and Shingbweyang and used them as bases and supply points. Another road led north from Myitkyina to Nsopzum, where the road changed to a track leading to Sumprabum—where the British maintained a small outpost—and on to Fort Hertz, in the northernmost corner of Burma, another British post with a small airstrip. From the beginning of the year, the 25th and 26th Fighter Squadrons had the task of attacking Japanese army buildings, storage areas, and supply dumps in the area, as well as keeping roads and rail lines clear of any motor vehicles or railroad equipment. Because the roads and the rail line from Myitkyina to Indaw crossed a number of small rivers and streams, the numerous existing and newly built bridges the Japanese army installed along the route became important targets to disrupt the flow of supplies to the north. Operating out of Dinjan and Sookerating, the 25th and 26th Squadrons could cover the entire area. In January 1943, in reaction to Kachin guerrilla activity in the area, Lt. Gen. Renya Mutaguchi, commanding the *18th Division*, sent columns of troops north to push the British out of Sumprabum and to move up the Hukawng Valley toward the road then under construction from Ledo.[36] When the Japanese columns started their advance north, the squadrons added harassing these columns and their supply lines to their regular missions.

During January the 25th and 26th Fighter Squadrons carried out nine bombing and strafing attacks into Burma. Most of the missions involved a flight of three to six P-40s, sometimes with a few aircraft flying top cover while the rest went down to bomb and strafe the target with 20-pound fragmentation bombs and 100-, 300-, and 500-pound demolition bombs. The first attack of the year took place on January 4, when the 26th Squadron sent seven P-40s to bomb the railroad yard at Naba, on the rail line from Myitkyina to Indaw. On several missions, B-25s from a 22nd Bomb Squadron detachment at Dinjan that had replaced the 11th Bomb Squadron detachment accompanied the fighters. On January 18, eight 25th Squadron P-40s flew to the town of Kamaing with one B-25, bombing and strafing the town and starting large fires. The 26th Squadron sent 14 P-40s

In early January 1943 the 51st Fighter Group began flying bombing and strafing missions against the Japanese lines of communications in northern Burma, using a mix of bombs of different weights carried under the belly of their P-40s and smaller 20-pound fragmentation bombs under the wings. *3A-34907, RG342FH, NARA*

THE TENTH AIR FORCE IN WORLD WAR II

Col. Homer Sanders prepares to take off on a bombing mission over northern Burma in early 1943. This photo shows the standard bomb load on a 51st Fighter Group P-40 in more detail. *Author's collection*

back to Kamaing the next day, again with a B-25, dropping demolition, fragmentation, and incendiary bombs in the target area and destroying a Japanese headquarters building, a barracks, and several warehouses. Railroads were the target a week later. Four P-40s went back to the railroad yard at Naba on January 25 to strafe locomotives, damaging eight or nine they found in the yard. The next day, eight P-40s escorted two B-25s back to Naba to bomb the railroad yard more thoroughly, getting hits on the roundhouse and damaging several railroad cars. Another technique to disrupt the railroad was to bomb a hillside above the tracks and cause a landslide, with a single B-25 causing a partial block on the railroad line near Meza, south of Indaw, on February 5. The two escorting P-40s found a train stopped above the block and strafed it.[37]

February brought several comparatively large attacks on Japanese-occupied towns and facilities. The first took place on February 13, when 12 P-40s from the 25th Squadron bombed and strafed a Japanese barracks complex at Lonkin, west of Kamaing. The next day, the 26th Squadron sent 14 P-40s to attack Japanese barracks around the town of Maingkwan, dropping 300-pound demolition bombs and 20-pound fragmentation bombs and firing 5,000 rounds of .50-caliber ammunition into the barracks areas. A very successful attack took place on February 16; the two squadrons combined forces to attack the town of Nsopzup, on the track from Myitkyina to Sumprabum. Nine P-40s from the 25th Squadron and seven from the 26th Squadron attacked the town, dropping 11 300-pound bombs and 66 20-pound fragmentation bombs, then returning to strafe the town. The pilots estimated that 90 percent of their bombs fell in the target area, starting large fires and damaging 20 trucks that were in the town. Kachin guerrillas later reported that the attack had destroyed a gasoline and ammunition dump, killed more than 130 Japanese soldiers, and wounded 120. The two squadrons went out together again on February 20, with 10 P-40s from the 25th Squadron and seven from the 26th, to attack the town of Sahmaw, a short distance southwest of Mogaung. Once again the bombing was excellent, with 85 percent of the 12 500-pound bombs and the 72 20-pound fragmentation bombs hitting the target area. Hits on oil tanks near the railroad spread burning oil and contributed to the fires the bombing and strafing had started. The 51st Fighter Group's largest mission to date took place on February 27, when 24 P-40s bombed the town of Waingmaw, 4 miles south of Myitkyina. The 25th Squadron supplied 12 aircraft, with three more pilots joining nine P-40s from the 26th Squadron. Four P-40s flew as top cover while the other flights bombed and strafed the target area, starting large fires in another gasoline and ammunition storage area and sending up a column of black smoke that was visible 60 miles away on their return flight to base. The squadrons were fortunate that the Japanese forces in these small towns lacked antiaircraft guns. Occasionally the P-40s would run into ground fire but suffered little damage.[38]

This was the pattern of operations for the 25th and 26th Fighter Squadrons over the next few months: two to four P-40s carrying out regular offensive reconnaissance missions over northeastern Burma, with larger numbers of fighters attacking Japanese facilities and the communications infrastructure. This was in addition to flying regular patrols in the area, standing alert for air raids, and escorting American and British transports dropping supplies to forward observation posts. The two squadrons flew all these various missions with rarely more than 40 airplanes between them. The demands on the two squadrons increased as Japanese troops advanced up the tracks toward Fort Hertz and through the Hukawng Valley toward Hklak-ga, north of Shingbwiyang, where the important KC-8 early-warning station had its base. To defend the Fort Hertz area, the British had 750 local Kachin fighters and a company of Gurkha troops, while Chinese troops training at Ramgarh went to defend the road from Ledo, providing support to other Kachin guerrillas operating in the Hukawng Valley.[39] Both forces called on American fighters to help delay the Japanese advance.

51st Fighter Group pilots get a briefing before a mission in April 1943. *Kneeling left to right:* 2nd Lt. John Keith, Col. John Barr, 2nd Lt. William Bertram, and Capt. Edward Nollmeyer; and *standing left to right:* 2nd Lt. Hazen Helvey and 2nd Lt. Robert McClurg. *3A-36240, RG342FH, NARA*

To delay the Japanese in their advance north, the 51st Fighter Group employed tactics that complemented the work the fighter squadrons were already doing to deny supplies to the Japanese.[40] The fighters flew regular patrols along the tracks and trails the Japanese were using to move north, strafing and dropping fragmentation bombs in areas where Kachin guerrillas had located Japanese troops. The squadrons followed this with repeatedly bombing and strafing nearby villages the Japanese were using as advance bases, and the towns where the Japanese stored supplies for their forward units. Daily reconnaissance missions kept a close watch on any trucks or riverboats brave enough to move in daylight, while the ongoing attacks on bridges helped delay the movement of supplies north. The Kachin guerrillas provided intelligence on the location of Japanese troops and supply dumps and could often assess the damage after a strike—a real benefit to the morale of the pilots, who often couldn't determine the results of their missions.[41]

In early March the Japanese were nearing Sumprabum, forcing the British to withdraw their outpost. To support the withdrawal on March 1, the 25th and 26th Squadrons flew 15 missions bombing and strafing targets in the area, expending 17,000 rounds of .50-caliber ammunition on multiple targets. Offensive reconnaissance missions kept a watchful eye on the trails over the next several days. The situation in the Hukawng Valley became even more tense when the Kachins guarding the KC-8 station reported a force of 400 Japanese soldiers advancing on Hklak-Ga.[42] The American 10-man air-warning team could hear the sounds of machine guns and mortars in the distance as they prepared to join in the defense of their base. Calls to the 51st Fighter Group brought in P-40s for strikes against the Japanese positions, with the Kachin passing on the Japanese troop locations to the KC-8 team, who directed the P-40s onto their targets.[43] On March 8, the 26th Squadron flew four missions in defense of Hklak-ga, with pairs of P-40s coming in to strafe and drop fragmentation bombs. With the dense jungle in the area it was difficult for the pilots to identify their targets and determine where the Japanese positions were, even with help from the Kachins. To get a better idea of the area, a 1st Lt. Gammas from the 26th Squadron went out in a PT-17 with a P-40 as escort to reconnoiter the area around Hklak-ga—a remarkably brave thing to do—but poor weather over the area prevented close observation. The next day, the squadrons received word that the Japanese had pulled back from Hklak-ga.[44] For the rest of the month the two squadrons flew regular reconnaissance missions over the Hukawng Valley and around Sumprabum, looking for any Japanese activity.

During one of these missions at the end of March, a pilot from the 25th Fighter Squadron used one of the 51st Group's PT-17s to make another daring rescue behind Japanese lines. Late in the afternoon of March 29, Capt. Charles Colwell and 1st Lt. Ferguson from the 26th Fighter Squadron were flying back to Dinjan after carrying out an offensive reconnaissance over Burma. Flying near the Japanese-held town of Maingkwan, Colwell saw below him a P-40 that had landed in a field near the town. Going down to investigate, Colwell saw that the pilot was in the cockpit and apparently conscious. He immediately radioed back to Dinjan, reporting his sighting, and received orders to circle the downed P-40 until a relief flight could arrive to provide protection for the pilot while the group organized a rescue mission. As the group learned later, 1st Lt. Melvin Kimball from the 16th Fighter Squadron had been flying a P-40E from China back to India for overhaul but became lost and was running low on fuel. Thinking he was in Allied territory, he landed his P-40 to seek assistance but soon found that there were people shooting at him. Because the radio on his P-40 was tuned to a different frequency, Kimball couldn't communicate with Colwell flying above him. Back at Dinjan, Col. Homer Sanders, who had turned over command of the 51st Fighter Group to Col. John F. Egan the previous day, ordered a transport to be loaded with

THE TENTH AIR FORCE IN WORLD WAR II

1st Lt. Ira Sussky stands on the wing of the PT-17 he flew behind Japanese lines to rescue 1st Lt. Melvin Kimball (in the rear cockpit). Capt. Charles Colwell, who discovered Kimball's downed P-40, shakes Kimball's hand. *3A-36791, RG342FH, NARA*

gasoline to drop to the pilot if it turned out he was out of fuel. 1st Lt. Ira Sussky volunteered to take a PT-17 and fly the 100 miles to the field to attempt a rescue. Five P-40s went off immediately to relieve Colwell, and two circled above Kimball while the other three flew top cover above, waiting for the PT-17 and its escort to arrive. At 1718, Sussky landed the PT-17 on what proved to be a boggy and badly rutted field. Kimball climbed aboard, but the trainer kept getting stuck in ruts and boggy ground. Japanese troops began to fire on the rescue plane, fortunately missing Sussky and Kimball, who had to jump out of the PT-17 eight times to get it unstuck. Finally, on the ninth attempt, Sussky got the PT-17 off the ground and flew back to Dinjan with a greatly relieved Kimball. As soon as the PT-17 took off, the covering P-40s dropped down and strafed Kimball's airplane, setting it on fire. Back at the airfield, Kimball related how he happened into his predicament, explaining that he had been lost and running out of gas. "I knew I was south of the course," he explained, "but thought it was friendly country so landed to find out where I was. Then somebody started shooting in my direction. I wanted to shoot back but couldn't find them—they were hidden in the jungle. They put about twenty holes in my plane; hit the fuel line and put it out of commission. P-40s showed up, then the Japs—or whoever it was—made themselves scarce. But damn it, I didn't realize how lucky I am until I got here and found out just what a hotspot I had picked to land in."[45] For his bravery that day, 1st Lt. Sussky was awarded the Distinguished Service Cross.[46]

Attacks on road and rail bridges in northern Burma and the need for more-lasting damage led to a new technique that few would have thought possible: arming a P-40 with a 1,000-pound bomb. The 26th Squadron was the first to make an attack on a bridge target when three pilots dropped 100-pound demolition bombs on the bridge at Shaduzup on 26 January 1943, doing only minor damage. The fighters went out again on February 19, this time with 500-pound bombs, but missed the bridge. They had more success on February 23, knocking out a 200-foot-long railroad bridge 10 miles west of

bridges on February 26, on March 1, and on March 9, when six P-40s got six hits on the railroad bridge at Mogaung with 500-pound bombs, knocking out the north span of the bridge and causing the center span to sag. Offensive reconnaissance flights over the area showed that the Japanese were rapidly repairing these damaged bridges, often within 48 hours of an attack. With Japanese columns now advancing up the Hukawng Valley and around Sumprabum, there was some consideration to bringing in the B-25 bombers from the 341st Group, diverting them from their own attacks on targets in central Burma to do more-lasting damage to the bridges.[47]

When transports delivered some 1,000-pound bombs to Dinjan for the B-25s, Col. John E. Barr, the 51st Fighter Group's executive officer, looked at the bombs and wondered if it might be possible to fit one to a P-40. The 25th Squadron's most recent attacks on a railroad bridge 4 miles west of Myitkyina on March 17 with 12 500-pound bombs had knocked out the rail line approaching the bridge but had done no damage to the bridge itself.[48] Barr spent an afternoon "under his P-40 with his eye on the rivets and his conscience with his God."[49] Having worked out how to attach a 1,000-pound bomb to his P-40, Barr took off on the morning of March 19, with one other P-40 flying top cover, to put his idea to the test. To lighten his airplane he had the standard ammunition load reduced to 100 rounds per gun but found that his takeoff was normal. The heavy bomb had only a modest impact on the P-40's performance, reducing the climbing speed by 10 miles an hour and the top speed by only 7 miles an hour. Barr had picked a bridge a few miles south of Mogaung as his target and came in at 8,000 feet. He found the dive on the target and the release of the bomb to be about the same as with a standard 500-pound bomb. His bomb fell just north of the bridge, doing no damage to the target, but he had proved that it was possible for a P-40 to carry and drop a 1,000-pound bomb.[50]

Encouraged by the results of his first test, Barr chose five experienced pilots—1st Lts. John Keith, Robert McClurg, and William Bertram from the 25th Fighter Squadron and 1st Lts. Edward Nollmeyer and Hazen Helvey from the 26th Squadron—and taught them how

Col. John Barr, executive officer of the 51st Fighter Group, decided to try loading a 1,000-pound bomb under a P-40 to inflict greater damage on Japanese bridge targets than the group had achieved using standard 500-pound bombs. *3A-33866, RG342FH, NARA*

Myitkyina by getting a direct hit on each approach span, and again on February 24, when four P-40s bombed another railroad bridge northeast of Pinbaw, getting good hits. The squadrons hit more

Armorers attaching a 1,000-pound bomb—suitably inscribed—underneath a 51st Fighter Group P-40 while the pilot watches the procedure. On his left hip the pilot is wearing a Gurkha kukri knife, a versatile tool in the jungles of northern Burma. *3A-33870, RG342FH, NARA*

With the 1,000-pound bomb firmly attached, a pilot prepares to take off for another mission against a bridge in northern Burma. The 51st Fighter Group dubbed their airplanes "B-40s" for their ability to carry such a heavy bombload. *3A-33647, RG342FH, NARA*

to bomb successfully with a 1,000-pound bomb. For their first test as a flight, Barr took his pilots back to Mogaung, but this time their target was the town itself—a lot easier to bomb than a narrow bridge. All six pilots placed their bombs directly in the target area, destroying two blocks in the town. Regular offensive reconnaissance and attack missions took precedence over the next few weeks, so Barr and his flight did not go out again with their big bombs until April 14, when Barr took the flight out to bomb the airfield at Manywet in the morning and returned to bomb Myitkyina airfield in the afternoon, taking two P-40s as top cover each time. The 1,000-pound bombs blew huge craters in each airfield. The flight went after bridges for the first time on April 16. They went first to a bridge 10 miles northeast of Pinbaw, on the railroad line between Mogaung and Indaw. Three of the P-40s dropped their bombs on the railroad bridge, getting two direct hits that destroyed the bridge. The flight and their escort then went to a second railroad bridge south of Mogaung, getting one direct hit on the corner of the bridge, knocking it sideways. Three days later, Barr took Nollmeyer, Helvey, McClurg, and two other pilots from the 25th Squadron on their first 1,000-pound bomb mission to attack a railroad bridge at Namti, destroying the southern approach and getting one direct hit in the middle, damaging one of the spans. By now Barr and his flight had proven 1,000-pound bombs could be used effectively, and began training other squadron pilots in the technique. A mission on May 2 showed that the 1,000-pound bomb was not a complete solution to knocking out bridges, when Barr and five other pilots dropped six 1,000-pound bombs but failed to hit their bridge target, though on a second mission that afternoon to the same target, the pilots got direct hits that destroyed two spans of the bridge. Two missions took place on May 3, when flights from the two squadrons knocked out two more railroad bridges, and a third bridge went down on May 8, when six P-40s got four direct hits on a bridge with their 1,000-pound bombs, setting off a huge explosion from a dud bomb dropped on a previous mission.[51]

The missions of May 3 were the last 1,000-pound bomb missions until July, in what the pilots jokingly called their "B"-40s. As 1st Lt. Hazen Helvey recalled:

Flying the bomb off the ground was the simple part. The targets assigned for destruction by this group were specific, difficult to hit, and well protected. A near miss was worthless, especially when dive-bombing railroad bridges and key buildings, or skip-bombing tunnels. Delay fuses were used in skip-bombing, but all bridges required instantaneous fuses. The key was to get as close as you could without getting involved in the explosion. In several

Clayton Bissell awards Col. John Barr the Silver Star and the Distinguished Flying Cross for developing the technique of adapting the 1,000-pound bomb to the P-40 and making it a regular practice for the 51st Fighter Group's squadrons. *3A-34157, RG342FH, NARA*

instances pilots' concentration on their target was so intense that they flew low enough for their planes to be damaged from their own bomb blast.

We tried to dive at about a 60-degree angle, and the speed of the P-40 was usually between 350 and 400 mph. You never saw the instant results of your dive, as you were too busy taking evasive action, and also too blacked out from pulling out of the dive. However, you could hear the exclamations of your comrades— or the lack of exclamations (if you missed the target)! We did not have bombsights—just the regular gunsight. You just placed the vertical line of the gunsight onto the target and flew exactly down that path. Your degree of success depended upon how well you did just that.[52]

Neither the 25th nor the 26th Squadron lost any P-40s on these missions. For successfully adapting the 1,000-pound bomb to the P-40 and developing the techniques of using these heavy bombs against actual Japanese targets, Barr and each of the five members of his flight received the Silver Star.[53]

During April, replacement aircraft began to arrive in India for the 51st Fighter Group. The group gained 21 new P-40s in April, taking the number of aircraft in the 25th and 26th Fighter Squadrons from 40 at the beginning of the month to 59 at the end of April (the group lost two on operations during the month).[54] The group was flying a mix of older P-40Es and P-40Ks but apparently received a small number of newer P-40M models during May. More pilots arrived, enabling the squadrons to fly more missions each day with more fighters. During the first weeks of April, the squadrons flew several strafing and bombing missions against Japanese forces in the Hukawng Valley and around Sumprabum on the basis of intelligence from Chinese and British forces in the area. A reconnaissance mission on April 15 demonstrated the value of these regular missions. Two P-40s on a reconnaissance of the railroad line south of Mogaung found five large locomotives under some camouflage. A strafing attack blew up two of the locomotives and damaged three more.[55] The reconnaissance and bombing and strafing missions continued in May, but the approaching monsoon made bad weather begin to be a factor, with the group flying no offensive missions between May 12 and 24. The monsoon had one benefit: forcing the Japanese to withdraw from their positions at Sumprabum and in the Hukawng Valley. There were a few more missions flown to the end of May and in the first days of June before the full monsoon arrived, forcing a halt to all but a few weather reconnaissance missions between June 11 and July 8.[56]

From January to the end of May, the 51st Fighter Group had carried out what some viewed as "a nearly impossible task."[57] The group had to defend the Assam air bases and the transports flying over the Hump route, as well as support Allied units on the ground with constant attacks on Japanese troops and facilities in northern Burma, and their lines of communications. Until the end of April the group had little more than 40 P-40s to accomplish all these varied missions. It is surprising that the Japanese *5th Hikōshidan* did not make a greater effort against the American airfields in Assam during the dry season in the first half of 1943—carrying out only the two raids on February 23 and 25 with few losses—and even more surprising that the Japanese did not make more of an effort to disrupt the transports flying the Hump route during the same period. Defending the unarmed transports on their way to China would have placed an enormous strain on the 51st Fighter Group's limited resources. The *15th Army*'s defense against the British advance in the Arakan did draw off the *4th* and *7th Hikōdan* from other missions, while the increasing frequency of raids on Rangoon tied down numbers of Japanese fighters for the defense of the city.[58] It is highly likely that the presence of American fighter planes and

Bombing with a 1,000-pound bomb became standard procedure for the 51st Fighter Group. When the 80th Fighter Group reached Assam later in the year, the 51st Group passed on the technique to the new arrivals.
3A-33648, RG342FH, NARA

the supporting early-warning network did serve as a deterrent to further Japanese air raids.

With the air threat diminished, the fighter squadrons could devote more missions to supporting the Allied forces in northern Burma and attacking Japanese units in the field and their facilities—the third and final stage of the campaign to disrupt the flow of supplies to the front. From February through April 1943, the 25th and 26th Fighter Squadrons flew 1,899 sorties of all kinds. During 84 bombing missions into Burma, the squadrons dropped 92 tons of bombs and on all offensive missions fired off more than 220,000 rounds of .50-caliber ammunition.[59] Remarkably, the squadrons lost only two airplanes on these missions, but none to enemy fire. The same targets had to be attacked again and again, especially bridges. A reconnaissance of the Hukawng Valley and the railroad leading south from Myitkyina following the 12 days of bad weather in May reported that under cover of the weather the Japanese had repaired all the bridges along the railroad line. As the heavy and medium-bomber squadrons were also learning, the effort against the Japanese communication system in Burma was continuous and had to be unrelenting.

Bomber Operations: January to May 1943

The major effort of Tenth Air Force bomber operations through to the end of the war was aimed at destroying the vulnerable Japanese communications system between Japan and Burma, and within Burma. This effort involved two principal tasks: first, "to sever the long-distance water communications back to the homeland, blockading enemy forces in Burma"; second, "to destroy the enemy's power of resistance to Allied armies within Burma by disorganizing his railway and roadway communications and razing his dumps, stores, troops, and limited industrial areas."[60] Severing the long-distance water communications was itself a two-part endeavor: first, to destroy Japanese shipping on the way to Burma, or approaching or in the harbors, principally at Rangoon, Martaban, and Moulmein in Burma and Bangkok in Thailand; second, to destroy the dock facilities in these ports. Locating shipping approaching Rangoon was found to be time consuming and not productive, so the effort tended to concentrate on ships in the harbors.[61] Rangoon was the main Burmese harbor, with docking facilities for 20 to 40 oceangoing vessels covering 2 miles of the Rangoon River in the city, with many warehouses near the docks.[62] Moulmein was smaller, with only six wharves for large vessels. There were other important targets in and around Rangoon, including the Insein railroad workshops; the Mahlwagon and Botataung railroad yards; the Pazundaung Creek Bridge, carrying the rail line from Rangoon north to Mandalay; and the Syriam Oil Refinery, producing petroleum products, including aviation gasoline.[63] The India Air Task Force assigned all these long-range targets to the 7th Bomb Group. From January until the onset of the monsoon in late May, the majority of the 7th Bomb Group's missions were against shipping and targets in the Rangoon area. At the start of the year, the 7th Bomb Group had two squadrons fully operational: the 9th Bomb Squadron at Pandaveswar and the 436th Bomb Squadron at Gaya. The group's two remaining squadrons (492nd and 493rd Bomb Squadrons) were still in cadre status—waiting for more aircraft and air crews—and did not begin combat operations until near the end of the month. In early January the 9th Photographic Reconnaissance Squadron moved to Pandaveswar to provide photographic intelligence to the 7th Bomb Group on its prospective targets and bomb damage assessments after bombing missions—a vital requirement for long-range bombing. The 9th Photo Reconnaissance Squadron's F-4 Lightnings could reach Rangoon and other parts of southern Burma and flew regular photoreconnaissance missions over Rangoon to monitor Japanese shipping.

Missions directed against Japanese shipping during this period brought mixed results. The group carried out sea sweeps every few weeks but found few Japanese ships on their own. The group had

A B-24D from the 9th or 493rd Bomb Squadrons taxis in at the 7th Bomb Group base at Pandaveswar after a mission. A fixed, forward-firing machine gun has been added on the lower left side of the nose to defend against head-on Japanese fighter attacks. *3A-33641, RG 342FH, NARA*

FROM CASABLANCA TO TRIDENT

Contrary to prewar expectations, moving ships at sea proved extremely difficult to hit from high altitude. On 29 December 1942, six aircraft from the 9th and 436th Squadrons went after a large Japanese freighter, getting several near misses. *India Air Task Force, 10th USAAF, November 1942–May 1943, 827.306-1, vol. 1, AFHRA*

Bombing ships moored in the Rangoon River had the benefit that a near miss might well fall in the dock area alongside, doing additional damage. This illustrates what a difficult target even stationary ships proved to be from altitudes of more than 20,000 feet. *Courtesy, Jim Augustus*

better luck when Allied intelligence provided information on Japanese shipping movements. Intelligence reported a Japanese convoy heading for Rangoon in mid-January, probably from radio intercepts of Japanese merchant shipping schedules. The 9th Bomb Squadron sent out seven B-24s on 15 January 1943 to search for the convoy and found two merchant ships with several small naval escort vessels 130 miles south of Rangoon. The bombers got near misses on one ship but badly damaged the second merchant vessel, leaving it disabled. This was the *Nichimei Maru*, of 4,700 tons, which sank. As it turned out, the 9th Squadron had another success at the end of February. On February 27 four B-24s went out to photograph railroad construction southeast of Moulmein and to search for shipping along the coast. Returning from their photo run, the formation found a large cargo ship south of Moulmein harbor and heading north a little before 1 o'clock in the afternoon. The bombers proceeded to attack, but heavy haze made it difficult to pick up the ship, and most of the bombs missed. Finally 1st Lt. George Sloan went down to low altitude and, after making four practice passes over the Japanese ship, came back for a final run, getting four direct hits and leaving the ship burning and listing heavily. The ship was the 8,700-ton *Asakasan Maru*, which sank later that day. These were the 7th Bomb Group's only successful attacks on Japanese ships at sea.[64]

Missions that combined attacks on the Rangoon dock areas with attacks on shipping in the Rangoon River were more profitable. Sometimes bombs aimed at vessels in the river missed the ships but hit nearby dock areas—another prime target. The first of these missions in the new year took place on January 4, when three B-24s bombed a large cargo vessel in the Rangoon River, claiming two direct hits and three near misses out of 18 bombs dropped, and leaving the ship with smoke billowing upward, though the Japanese lost no cargo ships in the area around this date. On January 24 the 492nd Bomb Squadron made its combat debut with a mission to the Rangoon docks, borrowing four B-24s and one combat crew from the 436th Squadron to make up a formation of nine aircraft. The formation dropped 81 500-pound bombs, getting 27 direct hits in the Sule Pagoda Wharf area—one of the major dock and warehouse complexes along the Rangoon River—and two direct hits on a large cargo vessel in the river, as well as damage to other dock areas. The

The Mark 13 Aerial Mine. Mining proved to be an effective means of destroying Japanese shipping and disrupting Japanese shipping schedules. The presence of mines in a harbor halted any movement of ships until mine sweepers could clear the area. Ships had to sometimes wait for days to unload their cargo. *Via the author*

493rd Bomb Squadron flew its first combat mission to the same target two days later, on January 26. The squadron's seven B-24s dropped 61 500-pound bombs, getting nine more hits on the Sule Pagoda Wharf complex. The 9th Bomb Squadron was the next to go back to Rangoon, with seven aircraft bombing the dock areas and a naval vessel in the river on February 1. A week later the 436th Bomb Squadron went to Rangoon with six aircraft, but on this occasion all the bombs fell into the Rangoon River, doing no damage. The dock areas were the target again on March 3 and 26, while on March 7 four B-24s from the 9th Bomb Squadron attacked two cargo ships coming up the Rangoon River, their bombs straddling the ships with near misses and leaving one ship smoking. The dock areas suffered more attacks at the end of April and in early May. On April 26, the 493rd Squadron got seven aircraft to Rangoon and dropped 54 bombs, getting hits on buildings just north of the target area. Three days later the 492nd Squadron went after shipping in the Rangoon River, missing the ships tied up alongside the Sule Pagoda Wharves but doing more damage to the dock area. The 9th Squadron tried for shipping in the Rangoon River on April 30, on this mission dropping 15 1,000-pound bombs and seven 2,000-pound bombs, but again the bombs missed the ships, hitting the docks instead. The 7th Group also went after other ports, bombing Moulmein twice in March and the small port at Bassein once in April. On none of these missions did the squadrons send more than nine aircraft, and usually only six or seven. Throughout this period, and well into 1944, the 7th Bomb Group suffered from a shortage of aircrews that limited the number of aircraft that could be sent out on a single mission. Some of the targets the group attacked were small in area, and it was felt at the time that sending a full group out to bomb would result in too many misses.[65]

On 3 January 1943 the 436th Squadron bombed the railroad yards at Mandalay, with excellent results. The Mandalay railroad yards became a regular target for the AAF and RAF heavy and medium bombers. *India Air Task Force, 10th USAAF, November 1942–May 1943, 827.306-1, vol. 2, AFHRA*

Minelaying was a valuable supplement to attacks on shipping and port facilities. Placing mines in harbors and river channels had the dual benefit of possibly sinking ships as they passed over a mine, but also disrupting shipping schedules. Once the enemy detected the presence of mines in waters close to a harbor, all shipping had to stop until the mined areas could be cleared. Using mines with delayed settings compounded the clearance problem. Mines could be set so that they would not go off until there had been up to a dozen sweepings over the mine, adding to the delays in clearing a river or harbor of mines. Until enemy minesweepers could clear the area, no ships could enter or leave the harbor, throwing shipping schedules into confusion, delaying the delivery or offloading of supplies, and cascading these delays throughout the shipping system. In early January 1943, Col. Harold B. Wright, Tenth Air Force A-2 (Intelligence) officer—having done some preliminary research—recommended to Brig. Gen. Bissell that the Tenth Air Force begin a program of mining the Rangoon River. Wright had made inquiries to the Royal Air Force and found that the Royal Navy (RN) had a supply of 1,000-pound type A Mark V mines in Ceylon and that the RAF believed its technicians could mount these mines in a B-24D. The RAF also had specialists in India who could mount the mines and personnel trained in aerial mining in Europe. In addition, the Royal Navy had precise charts for the Rangoon River and could recommend where to place the mines for maximum effectiveness.[66]

Bissell gave his approval to the plan and urged Wright to follow up aggressively with the British.[67] Wright began working out the technical and operational details with the RAF and the Royal Navy (RN) on what became designated as "Project Low." The commander in chief of the Royal Navy's Eastern Fleet gave his approval to transferring the navy's mines to the Tenth Air Force. The RN had stored the mines in Ceylon, where fortunately the RAF had a Liberator II bomber available for a trial fitting of the mines. RAF technicians found that with a slight modification to the Army Air Force's standard B-9 bomb shackle, the mines could be carried in the bomb bay of a B-24. They recommended placing four mines in the rear section of the bomb bay so that the mine parachutes would not catch on any bulkheads when they dropped out. The RAF did a test drop of a mine with the Liberator in Ceylon to ensure the fittings worked, which they did. After Bissell made a formal request to Gen. Wavell, the RN allocated 50 mines to the 7th Bomb Group and had them shipped to Calcutta, and on to the airfield at Alipore. The RN also drew up charts showing the best areas for placing the mines, while the RAF worked up technical manuals on the mines and minelaying to give to the 7th Bomb Group. A full moon over Rangoon and a low tide in the Rangoon River were the ideal conditions for the mission. The IATF selected the night of February 22–23—two days after the full moon and two days before the lowest tide—for the first minelaying mission to Rangoon.[68]

To divert attention from the minelaying aircraft, the 436th Bomb Squadron sent six B-24s out to fly over Rangoon between the hours of 0215 and 0243. These arrived over the city and dropped bombs intermittently on the dock areas, starting several fires. At the same time, two Liberators from No. 159 Squadron attacked Mingaladon airfield to add to the diversion. Col. Conrad Necrason, 7th Bomb Group commander, led 11 aircraft from the 493rd Bomb Squadron and the 492nd Bomb Squadron to mine the lower sections of the Rangoon River where it entered the Gulf of Martaban. The release mechanism on one of the bombers failed, but the other 10 dropped 40 mines in the river from an altitude of 500 feet. The mines had delayed fuses from one to seven days to disrupt the minesweeping effort. The first mining mission appears to have been a success, since no Japanese ships entered or left Rangoon between February 27 and March 3. Even if the mines sank no ships, this was the kind of delay that disrupted Japanese shipping schedules. As Wright informed Bissell in a report on the results of Project Low, "if the 'Low' project has resulted in the closing of RANGOON HARBOR, the obvious follow up is for us to drop small numbers of mines with widely varied arming delays and continue to drop them occasionally. Thus we would force the enemy to continue to deny himself his best harbor."[69] Bissell agreed and requested more mines from the British. The ITAF scheduled the next mining mission for the night of March 26–27, with the 436th Squadron again sending out six airplanes as a diversion while the 492nd sent six to mine the Rangoon River. The 493rd Squadron had prepared seven aircraft to mine the Rangoon River that same night, but the first bomber to take off from the field at Alipore, where the mission began, hit a tree and crashed, killing all but one of the crew and blocking the airfield. The 493rd completed the mission the following night.[70]

These first mining missions were the beginning of a campaign the Tenth Air Force would wage for the next two years, extending mining operations to other ports along the Burmese coast, to Bangkok, and to islands in the Gulf of Thailand. Mining the Rangoon River added to the cumulative impact of the attacks on Japanese shipping and the destruction of the Rangoon dock areas. Through these attacks the IATF slowly denied the Japanese use of Rangoon as a major port. In August 1942, before any attacks on Rangoon had begun, Japanese shipping using Rangoon reached close to an estimated 60,000 tons for the month. By March 1943 the monthly tonnage had declined to below 5,000 tons a month.[71] The regular attacks on Rangoon forced the Japanese to develop an alternative means of transporting supplies into Burma. This became the infamous Burma-Thailand railroad—built with the labor of Allied prisoners of war and forced labor—resulting in thousands of deaths. The Tenth would undertake a separate campaign against this rail line later in the war with a new weapon and outstanding success.

Disorganizing the railway facilities the Japanese used depended on attacks on railroad yards and railroad bridges, and the 7th Bomb Group's B-24s went after both. The group's first mission of 1943 saw the 9th and 436th Squadrons sending 10 B-24s to bomb the railroad yards at Mandalay on January 4, getting nearly all their bombs into the railway yard and hitting a concentration of freight cars. The RAF followed this up, sending eight Blenheim bombers to bomb the Mandalay railroad yards the next day with an escort of Mohawk fighters and doing more damage to the facilities. Two weeks later, the 7th Group bombed the railroad yards at Thazi, on the Rangoon-Mandalay line, but the group's main effort was against the main Mahlwagon railroad yard in Rangoon, beyond the range of the medium bombers. From February to May the group bombed Mahlwagon six times, with each mission several weeks apart. The 436th Squadron went first, sending seven B-24s to bomb the railroad yard on February 12, while the 492nd Squadron bombed the main Rangoon railroad station. Two airplanes had to turn back with mechanical problems, but the remaining five got 34 bombs into the target area. The 436th went back to Mahlwagon on March 3 with six B-24s, trying to hit the roundhouse in the yards, but this proved to be a small, difficult target to bomb from 21,000 feet, and only four bombs made direct hits, the remainder falling in the general area and no doubt doing more damage. Seemingly assigned to this target, the 436th Squadron returned to Mahlwagon on April 5 and again on May 7, inflicting heavy damage on the yards and rolling stock and on the last mission getting 15 direct

The infamous Myitnge Bridge south of Mandalay. Destroying a bridge only 15 to 20 feet wide proved to be exceedingly difficult from high or medium altitudes. The 7th Bomb Group dropped hundreds of bombs on the Myitnge Bridge and the Pazundaung Bridge in Rangoon without inflicting serious damage to either. *India Air Task Force, 10th USAAF, November 1942–May 1943, 827.306-1, vol. 1, AFHRA*

Left to right: Joe Murray, bombardier, Robert McIntosh, bombardier, Earl Rainbow, navigator, and Edward McCoy, pilot, all from the 492nd Squadron, sitting on a 2,000 lb bomb. When 1,000 lb. bombs failed to damage key bridge targets, the 7th Bomb Group tried using the larger 2,000 lb. bombs, but without much success. *7th Bombardment Group (H) Historical Foundation, USAFA*

hits on the roundhouse. In addition, the 7th Group undertook a night mission to bomb the Bangkok railroad station on the night of April 20–21, though only three of the sixteen aircraft reached the target due to bad weather, and in May carried out raids against the railroad yards at Toungoo, Pyinmina, and Prome. Most of these missions to the Rangoon area involved nine to twelve hours of flying covering a distance greater than from England to Berlin (1,600 miles on average). The crews had the added psychological burden of knowing that if they had to bail out over Burma, their chances of making it back to Allied lines were practically nil, with every likelihood that if they survived they would end up in a Japanese prisoner-of-war camp under cruel treatment.[72]

In the battle to disrupt the Japanese communications, the greatest number of missions, if not the greatest tonnage of bombs, went after railroad bridges. The Burmese railroad system depended on a few key bridges. Knocking these out could disrupt rail service for days or weeks at a time, but these bridges proved to be exceptionally difficult targets for the heavy and medium bombers to destroy. The Japanese soon became adept at making rapid repairs. The 7th Group concentrated its efforts mainly on two bridges: the Myitnge Bridge south of Mandalay and the Pazundaung Bridge in Rangoon. The 436th Squadron was the first to go after the Myitnge Bridge, with six aircraft bombing the bridge on January 10, a week after the 341st Bomb Group's attack was thought to have destroyed the bridge. On this mission six B-24s dropped 27 500-pound bombs and 15 1,000-pound bombs, getting three direct hits with the 1,000-pound bombs on the third span of the bridge and knocking it down into the river below. The bombers went back to the Myitnge Bridge on February 4 and 5, dropping more bombs for a few hits, but noting that repairs to the bridge were nearly completed. The 493rd Squadron went out on February 12 to attack the bridge with 2,000-pound bombs, the first time these heavy bombs had been used in the CBI.

The big bombs demolished one span of the bridge and damaged the approaches to the bridge. The bridge drew the B-24s back three more times before monsoon weather intervened. On a mission on February 25, eight B-24s dropped 57 1,000-pound bombs in two runs on the bridge, getting a possible hit on only one section. On March 24 the group sent three squadrons back to the bridge, bombing at different altitudes. The 9th Squadron went in at 16,500 feet, while the 436th and 492nd Squadrons bombed from 20,000 feet and 16,800 feet; all three squadrons dropped 2,000-pound bombs that damaged the approaches to the bridge but did not appear to hit the bridge structure.[73]

The attacks on Pazundaung Bridge were even more frustrating. The bridge crossed a small creek that emptied into the Rangoon River, carrying the rail line north to Mandalay. The bridge was 700 feet long but only 15 feet wide. The 7th Group made a first attempt on the bridge on February 27. Eleven B-24s dropped 55 1,000-pound bombs on the bridge, with the first flight bombing from 24,000 feet and the second flight from 15,600 feet. The first flight's bombs landed short of the target, as did most of the second flight's bombs, with a few straddling the bridge, leaving it undamaged. The 493rd Squadron tried to hit the bridge on March 3, with nine B-24s dropping 45 1,000-pound bombs but hitting only the southern and northern approaches to the bridge, not the bridge structure. Six more attacks during March had similar results: near misses but no damage to the bridge. The 493rd Squadron went back to the bridge on April 17 for another try, this time using 2,000-pound bombs, but once again the bombs failed to hit the bridge.[74]

In addition to these main bridge targets, from time to time the 7th Group flew missions to support the medium bombers in their efforts to destroy bridges in their area of responsibility in central Burma. On one of these missions to the Ava Bridge near Mandalay, the 7th Group tried a different tactic. Timed to coincide with the group's attack on the Myitnge Bridge on March 24, Col. Conrad

Col. Conrad Necrason, 7th Bomb Group Commander (*center*), and Capt. Wesley Werner (*right*), commanding the 493rd Bomb Squadron, attempted a low-level attack on the Ava Bridge by using two of the group's remaining B-17Es, in what proved to be the 7th Group's last Flying Fortress mission.
3A-48884, RG342FH, NARA

FROM CASABLANCA TO TRIDENT

Necrason, group commander, and Capt. Wesley Werner, commanding the 493rd Squadron, took two of the squadron's elderly B-17Es to attack the Ava Bridge from low level. The Ava Bridge was a massive stone structure. The British army had blown up the bridge during the retreat from Burma, but the attack was to ensure the Japanese could not repair it. Necrason and Werner took their B-17s down to 50 feet and flew up the Irrawaddy River toward the bridge. One of the bombers dropped its bombs just short of the bridge, and the other airplane's bombs got hung up in the bomb bay and failed to release, leaving the bridge undamaged.[75]

What became apparent after these successive but unsuccessful missions was that the attempt to bomb bridges from high or even medium altitude was not worth the effort in terms of the number of sorties flown and the number of bombs dropped, as an operational analysis of the 7th Bomb Group's effort against the bridges demonstrated.[76] During the course of 29 missions against bridges flown between February 1943 and February 1944, the 7th Group dropped 1,140 bombs on eight bridges, damaging three bridges a total of five times. The group flew 10 missions against the Myitnge Bridge, dropping 221 tons of bombs and damaging the bridge twice. Against the Pazundaung Bridge the results were similar: 174 tons of bombs dropped over nine missions, with damage on two missions. An analysis of these missions came to the conclusion that it would take on average 200 bombs to get one hit on a bridge, which meant 1,000 bombs would be required to get five hits on a bridge. That number of bombs would require 200 aircraft sorties with each aircraft carrying five 1,000-pound bombs, and with six aircraft the usual number dispatched, approximately 33 missions to destroy a single bridge target. The lack of success resulted in fewer attacks on bridge targets as the year went on, and the gradual realization that bridges were targets better suited to the medium bombers. The medium bombers would have similar frustrations attacking these targets, though it would be a medium-bomber pilot who would find the first solution to destroying bridges.

The 7th Bomb Group's bombing effort expanded steadily as the months went on, particularly after the 492nd and 493rd Squadrons began operations, even though none of the squadrons had more than a dozen airplanes and were short of a full complement of combat crews. For the month of February the 9th Squadron averaged eight serviceable B-24s and 11 combat crews, while the 436th and 492nd had seven serviceable aircraft and 11 and 10 crews, respectively. During February the 493rd Squadron had no B-24s assigned and had to borrow airplanes from the 9th Squadron to fly missions. The group received more airplanes over the following months in small numbers until each of the squadrons had around a dozen B-24s. For the first half of the year the group had fewer than 50 complete crews, compared to a normal complement of 72 crews for a full group.[77] The 7th Group flew 10 missions during January, but 19 in February, as the 492nd and 493rd began operations. As a result, the number of sorties doubled from 59 in January to 126 in the following month. March saw 25 missions and 172 sorties completed, covering 13 targets. After a small decline during April, the month of May saw the group flying 41 missions with 252 sorties against 26 targets. Bomb tonnage delivered followed a similar pattern, rising from 117 tons in January to 662 tons in May. The shortage of combat crews meant fewer missions could be flown and fewer airplanes could be dispatched on each mission. The squadrons dispatched on average six planes per mission, and sometimes as few as three. The crews considered a mission with nine airplanes a "big thing." If one or more airplanes sent on a mission had to return due to mechanical difficulties, the damage the mission could inflict on Japanese targets diminished accordingly.[78]

During this period, the 9th Photographic Squadron flew regular missions to targets in southern Burma in support of the 7th Bomb Group's efforts, as well as the medium bombers of the 341st Group. At the end of December 1942 the squadron moved to Pandaveswar—base for the 9th and 493rd Bomb Squadrons—with seven F-4 airplanes.

Ground staff removing the cameras from 9th Photo Reconnaissance Squadron F-4 "Stinky" after a mission over Burma. The long range of the 9th Squadron's F-4s allowed Allied intelligence to monitor Japanese shipping coming into Rangoon. *3A-36295, RG342FH, NARA*

THE TENTH AIR FORCE IN WORLD WAR II

Fellow pilots of the *64th Hikōsentai* admire a comrade's new haircut. One of the air regiment's Type 1 fighters (Ki-43 Oscar) sits behind, with the *64th Sentai*'s arrow marking on the tail. The *64th Hikōsentai* served in Burma from 1942 until Burma's reconquest in 1945. *Author's collection*

The 9th Photo Squadron flew missions out of Pandaveswar, refueling at forward RAF bases to enable longer flights down to the area around Rangoon. Having begun combat operations in December, the squadron had spent most of its time covering northern Burma, photographing the key Japanese-occupied towns and the roads and rail lines in the area. The squadron flew its first reconnaissance mission to Rangoon on February 16, when two aircraft went out to cover Rangoon and Bassein. From then on, the F-4s provided regular cover of the Rangoon River and the dock areas, the railroad yards, and nearby airfields. In central Burma the reconnaissance pilots covered the bridge and railroad targets for the medium bombers. This photographic coverage was critical for damage assessment and mission planning to determine whether the bombers had destroyed their target or whether another mission to the same target was required. This coverage was especially important for monitoring Japanese shipping activity at Rangoon, tracking the number, arrival, and departure of cargo ships. During March the F-4s had several encounters with Japanese fighters over Rangoon. Two single-engine fighters—likely Ki-43 Oscars—attempted to intercept two F-4s flying a photoreconnaissance mission over the city on March 4, but the F-4s easily evaded them. A few weeks later, on March 26, a single F-4 completed coverage of the Rangoon River and dock areas and was heading back to base, flying at 20,000 feet and 200 mph, when two Oscars climbed up to intercept. One fighter, flying 1,000 feet below and around 1,000 yards on the right, attempted a climbing turn to come in on the F-4 from the front, while the second fighter approached from the front and below, attempting to turn in behind the F-4. The F-4 pilot quickly increased speed, climbed to 25,000 feet, and then dove down to 22,000 feet, getting his speed up to 320 mph and soon outdistancing the two Oscars. The F-4s continued to range over central and southern Burma without interception until May 6, when Lt. Hirao Yukimoto from the *64th Hikōsentai* intercepted an F-4 on a mission over southern Burma. Making a frontal attack, Yukimoto shot out one of the F-4's engines. Yukimoto's guns jammed, but the American pilot, 2nd Lt. Donald Humphrey, did not know this, and when Yukimoto flew alongside, gesturing for Humphrey to land, he had little choice, since he could not have returned to Allied lines on one engine. Humphrey crash-landed his F-4 at Mingaladon and was taken prisoner. By this time the 9th Photo Squadron had only two serviceable F-4 aircraft available.[79]

The 7th Bomb Group's losses on these long missions to the Rangoon area were surprisingly light. Between January and May 1943, the group lost four bombers to Japanese fighters and none to Japanese antiaircraft fire; a loss rate of less than 1 percent. The Japanese were by no means indifferent to the growing depredations of the American bombers striking Rangoon, but the *5th Hikōshidan* had only a limited ability to inflict losses that the IATF might have considered prohibitive. For part of this period (January to March), while the *5th Hikōshidan*'s two fighter regiments successively converted to the Ki-43-II, there was only one fighter regiment available for offensive and defensive missions over all of Burma. A Japanese Army Air Force fighter *sentai* had a normal complement of 42 to 49 Type 1 fighters in three *chutai* (equivalent to a squadron), so that the single *sentai* had to provide fighters to support the Japanese army's defense against the British advance in the Arakan, operations in northern Burma and over Yunnan in southern China, and the defense of the Rangoon area. With the return of the full *50th Hikōsentai* in March 1943, the *5th Hikōshidan* once again had around 80 fighters available and could afford to base more in southern Burma to defend Rangoon.

A further handicap to defending Burma against American bombers was the very airplane equipping the *5th Hikōshidan*'s fighter regiments. The JAAF's Type 1 Fighter was less than adequate as a bomber interceptor. The newer Ki-43-II had a more powerful engine, giving an increase in top speed, but its armament of two 12.7 mm machine guns left it at a disadvantage when coming up against American heavy bombers. The JAAF had intended the Type 1 to be a pure air superiority fighter, and Nakajima had designed the fighter to have superlative maneuverability at the sacrifice of heavier armament. As a bomber interceptor it proved to be weak. As former lieutenant Yohei Hinoki, a pilot with the *64th Hikōsentai*, recalled, "by the time the Hayabusa had become a good attack aircraft, things were changing. It was now to be used for defense, as an interceptor. So again its firepower was insufficient. And it lacked the speed needed for attacking bombers. The Hayabusa was coming to the end of its time."[80] In March the *21st Hikōsentai* arrived in Burma equipped with the Type 2 Two-Seat Fighter Toryu (Kawasaki Ki-45-I Dragon Slayer, code-named Nick). This twin-engine fighter had a heavier armament than the Ki-43, with one 20 mm and one 37 mm cannon in the nose and a ventral tunnel, but even the Ki-45s had a difficult time with the B-24s.

The Japanese fighter pilots in Burma found their initial encounters with the B-24s immensely frustrating. The first clash took place on 26 January 1943, when three Ki-43 pilots intercepted a flight of seven bombers from the 9th and 493rd Squadrons. Although Sgt. Maj. Satoshi Anabuki—the *50th Hikōsentai*'s leading ace—claimed one B-24 shot down, in reality, after repeated attacks the Japanese fighters inflicted only minor damage to two of the 493rd Squadron's aircraft. Return fire from the bombers damaged all three of the attacking Oscars, who one by one had to leave the fight. Following the return of the *64th Hikōsentai* to Burma in early February, the *50th Hikōsentai* returned to Japan to convert to the Ki-43-II, leaving the *64th* to confront the B-24s. During February there were three encounters between the American bombers and the *64th*'s fighters over the Rangoon area. On February 8, during a joint mission to Rangoon with the 492nd Squadron attacking the Rangoon railroad station and Mingaladon airfield and the 493rd bombing the Mahlwagon marshaling yards, the 436th Squadron went to bomb the dock area, where a flight of six Japanese fighters (identified as three Zekes, two Mikes [believed to be the Japanese version of the Bf 109], and a single Nate [Ki-27]) intercepted the formation. The Japanese fighters made repeated attacks for a half hour, inflicting only minor damage. The bombers claimed one Zeke shot down, but it appears the *64th* suffered no losses. Four days later the 492nd Squadron went back to Rangoon to bomb the railroad station, encountering five fighters who continued to attack the formation for nearly an hour, but it suffered no damage. The bombers claimed one fighter destroyed and one damaged, but again it appears the *64th* had no losses. It may have been on one of these missions that Lt. Yohei Hinoki watched as he and four other fighters fired more than 1,000 rounds at one of the B-24s, only to see the bomber fly serenely on as if nothing had happened.[81]

Gradually the *64th Hikōsentai*'s pilots worked out tactics that would give them a chance against the B-24s. During two interceptions on March 3 and 10, it appeared that the fighters were still working out tactics. In the battle on March 10, 10 to 12 Oscars attacked a formation of four B-24s from the 492nd Bomb Squadron just after they bombed the airfield at Mingaladon. The fighters made several attacks from the front and from the rear, coming in from the 4 o'clock and 6 o'clock positions, with the fighters coming in singly, but clearly in coordinated attacks. The bombers claimed three "Zekes" (in the early years of the war, many American air crews typically identified all Japanese single-engine fighters as Zekes, the Imperial Navy's A6M Zero-sen) destroyed and three damaged, though it again appears the bomber gunners were overly optimistic in their claims. Capt. Yasuhiko Kuroe, commanding the *3rd Chutai* (and soon to be promoted to executive officer of the *64th*), frustrated with what he considered a "miserable battle" with the B-24s, came to the realization that the Hayabusas had the best chance of shooting down or damaging a B-24 through frontal attacks, even though this form of attack was difficult to carry out successfully.[82] The *64th* worked out a tactic using two fighters flying on either side of the B-24 formation, about 1,000 feet below the bombers. One fighter would then climb to a position 3,000 feet higher and ahead of the bombers and make a diving 180-degree turn to come down in a head-on attack, concentrating its fire on one airplane before diving

The 7th Bomb Group's squadrons flew down to Rangoon over the Bay of Bengal in a loose formation parallel to the Burmese coast, but far enough out to sea to avoid fighter interception. Attacking targets in Rangoon, the bombers would try to minimize their time over land, turning back toward the sea as soon as they had finished their bombing run. *7th Bombardment Group (H) Historical Foundation, USAFA*

A Ki-43 Oscar fighter circles around the 7th Bomb Group formation to line up for another frontal attack. Hayabusa pilots found that with their limited armament of two 12.7 mm machine guns, their best chance of inflicting damage on a B-24 was to make a frontal attack in the hope of hitting the crew or one or more engines. *7th Bombardment Group (H) Historical Foundation, USAFA*

away beneath or climbing above the formation to the opposite side. While this attack was underway, the fighter on the opposing side of the formation would cross over so that the bomber formation was always bracketed with two fighters on either side, with the second fighter beginning its climb and dive attack soon after.[83]

While Kuroe and his fellow pilots appear to have been the ones to work out the tactics for combating the B-24s, it was the newly arrived *21st Hikōsentai* that had the first success using the frontal-attack approach. On 13 March 1943 the 9th Bomb Squadron sent out four B-24s to bomb the Pazundaung Bridge at Rangoon. Just before starting the bomb run at 1200 hours, five to seven Ki-45s dived on the formation in a frontal attack. Over the next 45 minutes the Japanese fighters made 15 to 20 determined passes against the B-24s, coming in from the 10 o'clock and 2 o'clock positions and diving down through the formation after completing their runs. When the bombers turned into the attack coming from one quarter, another fighter would dive down to attack from the opposite quarter, catching the top turret gunners off guard. The attackers heavily damaged two of the B-24s as they raced out over the Gulf of Martaban to the south of Rangoon: Capt. James Baldwin's plane and that of 1st Lt. William Short both crashed in the sea. The two surviving bombers made it back to base, one with a gunner killed and two wounded aboard. The bomber gunners claimed one fighter destroyed, one probable, and one damaged in the encounter.[84]

The *64th Hikōsentai* claimed their next bomber when a group of Ki-43s ran into a 7th Bomb Group formation on March 31 as the bombers were on their way to bombing the railroad station and rail bridge at Pyinmana. This was the group's largest mission to date, with each of the four squadrons sending out six airplanes, but severe haze and cloud near the target forced the squadrons apart just as Kuroe was leading a dozen *64th Hikōsentai* fighters on a mission to Chittagong. Kuroe immediately led his fighters into an attack on the B-24s, making coordinated attacks from the front and the rear quarter. The bombers claimed two Oscars destroyed, two probables, and three damaged but lost one B-24 to the fighters. The group lost one more B-24 on May 1, its last combat loss until October. In a

mission to bomb shipping in Rangoon River, eight 492nd Squadron B-24s came under attack. On this occasion the four attacking Oscar fighters made frontal attacks from below the bomber formation. The first pass knocked out two engines on 1st Lt. Robert Kavanagh's B-24, sending the bomber down with engines smoking and three fighters following behind. Sgt. Miyoshi Watanabe attacked Kavanagh's airplane as it descended, and when he ran out of ammunition he rammed the tail turret. Kavanagh's airplane was already badly damaged, and he brought it in for a crash landing in a field.[85]

The American pilots were also learning and soon adopted defensive tactics to counter the Japanese head-on attacks. The 7th Bomb Group typically flew in the Army Air Force's standard "Javelin Down" formation, with the second element of bombers stepped down behind the lead element. This formation brought the maximum number of guns to bear for attacks from the rear but, in the small formations the 7th Bomb Group usually flew, proved to be both

Once in the target area, B-24s would pull in tight for better defense. The squadrons found that small numbers of bombers in the "javelin down" formation could throw off Japanese fighter attacks with well-timed evasive maneuvers. *Courtesy, Col. Thomas Sledge, USAF (Ret'd)*

maneuverable and controllable, allowing a small formation to execute evasive maneuvers in the face of head-on attacks, using determined air discipline to maintain the integrity of the formation at all times. Formation leaders found that if they lowered the noses of the bombers just as a fighter came in, it would allow the top turrets to acquire the incoming fighter and open fire. Another tactic the group developed to counter the Japanese fighters on their approach was to alter their course 10 degrees away from the Japanese fighters as they flew parallel to the bombers and were maneuvering into position for the attack.[86] This maneuver could spoil the Japanese fighter's approach, forcing the pilot to begin all over again. In an explanation of the 7th Bomb Group's tactics written after his return to the United States, Col. Necrason commented that "the only thing lethal about a fighter is its nose. If you plan your maneuvers so that you reduce to a minimum the length of time that the nose of the fighter is pointed toward your formation, evasive tactics are a success. It is a great mistake to fly straight and level in order to maintain a steady shooting platform for bombardment gunners. The gunners just aren't that good!"[87]

FROM CASABLANCA TO TRIDENT

This still taken from a movie shot on an actual combat mission shows a silver Oscar fighter diving past a B-24 formation over Burma. After making a pass against the bombers, the Japanese fighters would dive away to avoid the bomber gunners and reposition their aircraft for another attack. At higher altitudes the speed advantage the Oscars had over the B-24s was not enough to allow for more than a few passes before the bombers went out over the Gulf of Martaban. *Courtesy, Col. Thomas Sledge, USAF (Ret'd)*

The fighter attacks were intense, as 1st Lt. Alfonso B. Perez, a bombardier with the 9th Bomb Squadron, wrote in a diary he kept during his time in India. Perez was on a mission to bomb the Toungoo railroad yards on May 7 when fighters intercepted the formation:

We were out of the target area when someone called, "Pursuit at 9 o'clock." I peered out, but couldn't see a thing; still someone kept reporting it, "It's up at ten o'clock now and is climbing. It looks like he's coming in!" Then all of a sudden I saw him. A speck in the distance, moving parallel to us and apparently trying to make up his mind whether to come in or not. He was at about eleven o'clock when he made his turn to come in. I could see our tracers reaching out for him. He kept coming; he was high—it seemed like he was going to crash right into the formation, bullets were flying at him from all directions. He came straight, straight. Suddenly, just as he seemed about to crash into the second element he flipped on his back and miraculously went through the second and third elements. He came out directly underneath our right wing, trailing black smoke. All possible guns were on him, including ours. He headed back and later, our rear gunner reported the pilot had bailed out and the plane spun in. That was all for him, but there were more around to reckon with.[88]

In the air battles between the 7th Bomb Group's B-24s and the 50th and 64th *Hikōsentai*'s fighters between February and May 1943, the two sides came out roughly even, with the 7th Group losing four bombers and the two Japanese fighter units four Ki-43s, though the *21st Hikōsentai* may also have had some losses. But this period was a clear victory for the India Air Task Force. The Japanese were never able to prevent the 7th Bomb Group from operating over southern Burma, even though the bombers flew without a fighter escort on every one of their missions. With the Ki-43's limited armament there were simply too few fighters to make an impact. As their brother *Hikōsentai* in China would determine a few months later, it took many more fighters than the 64th *Hikōsentai* had available—making repeated attacks—to bring down a B-24. For the Japanese,

A B-25C/D from the 490th Bomb Squadron ("Skull and Wings") flying over Burma during 1943. Brig. Gen. Caleb Haynes assigned targets in central Burma to the 341st Bomb Group that were within the range of the group's B-25C and D aircraft. *3A-33768, RG342FH, NARA*

THE TENTH AIR FORCE IN WORLD WAR II

greater success would come in the following dry season, when the *5th Hikōshidan* received additional fighter *sentai* as reinforcements.

The India Air Task Force's medium bombers in the 341st Bomb Group flew in parallel with their colleagues in the heavy bombers. In many ways their experiences during this period were similar. Haynes had assigned to the 341st Group the task of conducting the second phase of the attack on the Japanese line of communications in Burma, "to destroy the enemy's power of resistance to Allied armies within Burma by disorganizing his railway and roadway communications and razing his dumps, stores, troops, and limited industrial areas."[89] Given their more limited range with a useful bombload, the B-25 medium bombers covered central Burma, concentrating on the area around Mandalay as far south as Thazi. This was a large area with many important targets that needed to be hit repeatedly, but like the 7th Bomb Group, for much of the first half of 1943 the 341st Bomb Group lacked airplanes and combat crews. At the beginning of the year the 341st Group had only the 22nd Bomb Squadron flying operations from the base at Chakulia. The 491st Bomb Squadron, also based at Chakulia, flew its first combat mission on January 10, but the 490th Bomb Squadron at Ondal did not enter combat until February 18. At the beginning of February the group had 21 combat crews and 26 B-25Cs available, with another 12 crews training in Karachi.[90] Most of the group's targets in its assigned area were small and did not lend themselves to area bombing, instead requiring careful precision bombing.[91] As a result, like the 7th Bomb Group, the 341st tended to fly single-squadron missions of three to nine bombers, though sometimes the squadrons would fly joint missions to get up to 12 aircraft over the target. Leaving their bases at Chakulia and Ondal, the B-25s would land at the RAF base at Agartala to refuel before climbing up over the Chin Hills to fly to the Mandalay area in central Burma—a distance of about 330 miles. For the most part the targets for the mediums were less heavily defended, with fewer antiaircraft guns or fighters. The B-25s ran into Japanese fighters about half as many times as the B-24s bombing targets around Rangoon.

By far the greater part of the 341st Group's missions was to railroad yards, bombing the yard facilities, warehouses nearby, and especially rolling stock.[92] Between January and May 1943 the group flew approximately 77 missions against railroad facilities in the area around Mandalay, concentrating on the larger railroad facilities that serviced the main rail line from Rangoon north to Myitkyina and the branch lines that ran northeast to Lashio and northwest to Yeu. The principal targets were Mandalay, which had the largest rail facilities in the area, holding on average over 400 rolling stock; Maymyo, to the east; Thazi, to the south, which averaged around 250 rolling stock in its yards; and Ywataung, to the west, but there were another dozen or so rail targets that also needed to be attacked. The railroad yards could be profitable targets. The Japanese often used the yards as storage areas for locomotives and rolling stock as well as supply centers, so that a mission to a railroad yard might often destroy railroad cards in addition to damaging the railroad facilities and warehouses nearby. Most of these attacks went in at medium altitudes (8,000 to 12,000 feet), especially if the bombers expected to run into antiaircraft fire, but where the antiaircraft defenses were weak, the bombers would drop down to lower altitudes for better accuracy. The squadrons would fly in flights of three B-25s, the flights sometimes having slightly different aiming points to get a spread of bombs across the target. For railroad yards and buildings the bombload typically consisted of M-30 100-pound, M-31 300-pound, or M-43 500-pound General Purpose bombs. The group got off to a slow start due to the lack of crews and airplanes, flying only four missions against railroad targets in January, then ten in February and nine in March. During March and April, more combat crews arrived for the 341st Group's squadrons, enabling more missions to be flown. During April the group made 24 attacks against railroad targets and five missions against warehouses and other installations in several towns, in addition to five attacks against Japanese airfields. The group flew even more missions during May, hitting the railroad system on 31 missions and flying another 12 missions on towns and warehouses. In the course of these missions, the squadrons hit Maymyo eleven times, Ywataung ten times, Thazi nine times, and the rail yards at Mandalay eight times. Often these missions were the result of the 9th Photo Squadron's photoreconnaissance flights over the railroad yards. When the reconnaissance pilots noted a

Railroad yards became a frequent target for the medium bombers. During the first half of 1943, the 341st bombed the rail yards at Mandalay (*shown*) eight times. The objective was to disrupt the flow of supplies to Japanese army divisions on the front lines by destroying railroad facilities, tracks, rolling stock, and locomotives. *3A-37626, RG342FH, NARA*

buildup of rolling stock in a railroad yard, the medium bombers would schedule a mission to that target.[93]

The bombers returned to the same targets repeatedly because the Japanese became adept at rapidly repairing the damage that bombers inflicted. Occasionally the mediums got lucky and returned to the target before the Japanese completed repairs. On 7 April 1943, the 22nd and 491st Squadrons each sent nine aircraft to bomb the railroad yards at Ywataung. The 22nd Squadron bombed first at 1300, arriving over the target to find the yards full of 350 freight cars. The B-25s got most of their bombs into the target area, getting hits on the main railroad tracks and engine sheds, starting many fires and destroying many of the rolling stock in the yard. When the 491st Squadron arrived half an hour later the fires in the yard were still burning. Malfunctioning bombsights caused many of the 491st Squadron's bombs to miss the target area. The 490th Squadron went back to Ywataung two days later to find that the Japanese had not completed repairs and that many freight cars remained in the railroad yards as the squadron's bombs went down.[94]

The cumulative damage from this successive bombing—with the American B-25s going out by day and RAF Wellingtons and Liberators bombing the larger railroad yards by night—began to have an impact. As the frequency of attacks across the railroad system in central Burma increased during April and May, the repair effort began to lag. Using local labor and their own engineers, the Japanese had to concentrate on keeping the main lines open, leaving aside repairs to sidings, buildings, engine sheds, and nearby warehouses.[95] Photographic coverage of the Mandalay rail yard revealed damage to the buildings in the goods yards alongside the station, derailed freight cars lying on their sides, and only a few tracks through the station serviceable. Coverage of the Ywataung yards showed that a month after the B-25s bombed the target on April 12, two of the eight tracks running through the yard—destroyed in the bombing—had yet to be repaired and five remained blocked with damaged and overturned railroad cars. Though the Japanese could still get trains through, the rail system's efficiency began to decline as rolling stock became stuck in stations until the tracks opened up again, and as the Japanese took to camouflaging and dispersing their locomotives away from the main railroad yards into smaller stations and operating only during nighttime. Although the damage was increasing, the Allied bombing effort still had not choked off the flow of supplies to the Japanese army. Unlike their American and British equivalents, the daily requirements of a Japanese division in the field were minimal—probably amounting to around 50 tons a day, primarily for ammunition and fuel, since the Japanese troops in Burma could obtain almost all their food locally. Fuel and supplies for Japanese aircraft added another 80 tons a day, so that all the divisions and aircraft in Burma had a requirement of around 700 tons a day, which in 1943 was still within the capability of the Burmese railroad system despite all the damage done, even if the delivery of supplies had slowed appreciably.[96]

As the B-25s flew more missions into central Burma, they inevitably ran into Japanese fighters. A notable encounter took place on 24 March 1943, when the 490th Bomb Squadron went out to bomb targets around Meiktila the squadron had noticed while returning from a mission to bomb the railroad yards at Thazi the day before. Taking off at 0910, the bombers reached Meiktila around noon, hitting the runway on the airfield at Meiktila, a Japanese barracks area, and the Meiktila railroad yards. That morning, three pilots from the *50th Sentai*'s *3rd Chutai* were on patrol in the area in their new Ki-43-II fighters, the *50th Sentai* having just returned from reequipping with the new model fighter in Thailand. The fighters were ordered to intercept the B-25 formation and did so, claiming one B-25 shot down. The entire *sentai* scrambled to go after the bombers and, in a running battle that was widely publicized in Japan, claimed to have shot down all eight remaining bombers for the loss of one fighter whose pilot had to bail out. In fact the 490th Squadron suffered no losses. After completing their bomb run, the crews reported that they had come under attack from a formation of five fighters, with one making a pass at the formation from above and one in a head-on attack. Three of the fighters continued to shadow the formation as it flew back to India, but made no further attacks. The bomber gunners claimed two fighters probably shot down and apparently did get one.[97]

On a mission in early April, 2nd Lt. David Hayward, a newly arrived pilot in the 22nd Bomb Squadron, had his first experience running into Japanese fighter aircraft. On this occasion the fighters did no damage, apart from scaring Hayward, though in the weeks that followed, the B-25s would have several sharp encounters. Hayward had arrived at Chakulia in early April and on April 8 was flying his first mission as a copilot with an experienced crew to get some seasoning before taking over his own crew. The mission that day was to bomb the Japanese airfield at Meiktila, southwest of Mandalay. After dropping their bombs the B-25s headed back to their base. As Hayward recalled years later:

Normally that was a happy time, the first real feeling of relief for the day. Even the sandwiches that were provided to us tasted good, although we always wondered whether those black specks in the bread were bugs of some kind. Indeed, often they were.

I looked out and down through my co-pilot's window and saw to my great alarm a formation of Japanese aircraft below us, heading in the same direction as we were. I counted twenty-one of them. There might have been more. I picked up the radio mike and tried to spread the word, but by that time a lot of other people were trying to do the same thing, none very effectively.

Every minute or two (probably every few seconds) I looked down. I soon recognized that the Japanese formation was comprised of both fighters and bombers, and even worse, they were gaining altitude on us fast and would soon be alongside of us. LG Brown [Hayward's pilot] and I were flying "Old Number 13," the oldest and slowest plane in the 22nd Bomb Squadron—certainly the slowest plane that day—and we were flying as "tail end Charlie." The pilot of the lead plane must have pushed his throttles forward nearly to the firewall, because all of the planes except ours took off for home base, leaving us behind.

Due to the meaningless screaming and confusion on the radio, the lead ship was apparently unaware that "Old 13" was being left behind without the protective shield of all the guns that could be brought to bear from the other planes in the formation. A lone bomber amidst a swarm of Zeros does not have much of a chance of survival.

Before long our turret gunner called on the intercom to report that a Jap Zero was doing a slow roll in the blind spot of our tail. A little while later I looked out my window and could see right into the cockpit of a Zero. I'll tell you, I did some praying and philosophizing about that time.

Well, as far as I know there was not a shot fired. The Japs went away. . . . Perhaps the Jap pilot thought we weren't worth the trouble, or he was just trying to show off. Perhaps the Japs had something else on their minds. It could have been all of the

A B-25 C/D from one of the 341st Bomb Group's squadrons undergoes maintenance in an open-air revetment. The ground crews had to work in blistering hot sun—which sometimes made the metal skin of the aircraft they were working on too hot to touch—and in the drenching rains of the monsoons. In India and later in Burma they did a magnificent job in often-trying circumstances.
3A-35734, RG342FH, NARA

above. My guess is that the formation of Japanese planes had taken off just before our arrival, on its way to bomb a target in India, and we stumbled upon them accidently [sic]. If so, it is likely that their fighters had been instructed to avoid possible decoys and to fight only if their own bombers were attacked.

When we finally returned to home base at Chakulia, I kissed the ground. Were all the rest of the missions going to be this bad? If so, how could I possibly make it through? LG Brown tried to be consoling, saying that this mission wasn't so bad considering some he had been on.[98]

Hayward's assumption was correct. The 22nd Bomb Squadron happened to pass a formation of 23 Ki-21 bombers with an escort of 12 Ki-43 fighters on their way to bomb the RAF base at Dohazari. Likely the fighters had orders to remain as escorts to the bombers and not attack the B-25s above them.[99]

By chance, the 22nd Bomb Squadron ran into another Japanese formation later that same month. On the morning of April 20, the *5th Hikōshidan* sent out 27 Ki-21 heavy bombers from the *12th* and *98th Hikōsentai* with an escort of 19 Ki-43s from the *50th Hikōsentai* and another 19 from the *64th Hikōsentai* to bomb British bases in India, switching targets at the last minute to Imphal. Early that morning, eight 22nd Squadron B-25s had taken off on a mission to bomb the engine sheds at Thazi. While over the target, the B-25s ran into a formation of 18 Ki-43s, but on this occasion three of the fighters broke off to attack the American bombers. The gunners fired back and claimed to have damaged two of the attackers, one going down smoking.[100] A week later the 22nd Squadron went back to Thazi with seven aircraft (three had returned to base with engine trouble), and on the way back after bombing, three Ki-43s attacked the formation, slightly damaging one of the B-25s. The 490th Bomb Squadron sent eight aircraft to join the 22nd Squadron in bombing Thazi at the same time. Five minutes after the B-25s finished their bombing, six Ki-43s attacked, continuing their attacks for half an hour. The fighters made six attacks: the 490th Squadron reported two "half-hearted" attacks from the 4 o'clock and 6 o'clock positions, and four attacks from the 10 o'clock position when a fighter went through, raking the entire formation. The 490th claimed one enemy fighter as probably destroyed and two damaged, against minor damage to three of the B-25s.[101]

With experience the combat crews made changes to improve the B-25's basic armament. By this time, more B-25s were arriving in the CBI theater. From 56 airplanes in March, the total B-25s available climbed to 62 in April and 95 in May.[102] The IATF started to receive some newer B-25Ds, comparable to the B-25C. The crews found that in action, the B-25C/D's Bendix ventral turret, which used a periscopic sight for the radio operator gunner, was "virtually useless."[103] The 490th Bomb Squadron's ground crews removed the turret, leaving a 30-inch opening in the underside of the fuselage. They placed an L-shaped steel angle iron across the hole and rigged up a mounting for two .30-caliber machine guns on a ball joint. For additional protection, the ground crews cut holes in the two small observation windows on the sides of the fuselage, just behind the wings, and inserted a ball socket to hold a .30-caliber machine gun in each window.[104]

It may well be that the increase in the number of raids on railroad yards in central Burma and the extent of the damage prompted the *5th Hikōshidan* to respond more aggressively. The 490th Bomb Squadron had the misfortune of twice running into Japanese fighters during May. Capt. Robert McCarten had been in command of the 490th Squadron for four days when he led a mission to bomb the railroad yards at Thazi on 13 May 1943. The nine B-25s were just about to start their bombing run at 10,500 feet when 15 Ki-43s from the *50th Hikōsentai* intercepted the formation. At 0847 the men in McCarten's lead ship saw a fighter climbing up on the left to begin an attack. After completing the bombing run, McCarten ordered the squadron to shift into a Javelin Down formation, and the fight began in earnest. The Japanese fighters used the same tactics that their colleagues in the *64th Hikōsentai* had started using against the B-24s: flying ahead and above the bombers, then turning in a half roll to come in on the lead ship, raking the entire formation as the fighter flew past. The fighters kept up the attacks for over an hour, coming in on the

A crew from the 490th Bomb Squadron stands next to their B-25, with 33 missions marked under the cockpit. The 490th painted the squadron insignia (a skull with wings) on the noses of their B-25s. *3A-34789, RG342FH, NARA*

formation from nearly every direction, including a few attacks from the rear. McCarten had his top turret knocked out in the first pass, with the engineer gunner wounded. McCarten's radio operator, S/Sgt. Cook, got the gunner out of the turret, fixed the damage, and began firing again, only to have another shell put the turret out of action. The crews later reported that the fighter attacks were well coordinated and were pressed home "with considerably more determination than previously encountered."[105] In response, the B-25s found that turning into the attack was an effective defense, since it threw off the attacker's aim and increased the closure rate, limiting the time the fighter had to fire. 2nd Lt. Toshio Yamashita attacked one bomber from the rear and watched as it dropped out of the formation. This was the lead ship of B Flight, which was last seen flying close to the ground with five fighters attacking. Capt. A. DeLapp and his crew failed to return from the mission. A few minutes later, the Ki-43s knocked out an engine of a B-25 in C Flight. The other two pilots in the flight dropped back to give the cripple protection, and McCarten slowed the entire formation down to 155 mph to stay together. The crippled bomber crash-landed at the RAF base at Palel, near Imphal, wrecking the airplane, but the crew survived without harm. Four other B-25s were damaged in the attack. The bombers claimed two fighters destroyed, two probables, and three damaged. Return fire did bring down Sgt. Yukio Shimokawa, who had to bail out of his damaged fighter.[106]

McCarten was leading the squadron again eight days later when they ran into another formation of Japanese fighters. That morning, 17 Ki-43s from the *64th Hikōsentai* went on a fighter sweep over RAF bases in the Cox's Bazaar area with 13 Ki-43s from the *50th Hikōsentai*. The Japanese fighters strafed the airfield and became involved in dogfights with RAF Hurricanes scrambled to intercept the raid. It appears the 490th Bomb Squadron ran into this battle on its return from bombing workshops at Chauk. The B-25s saw 16 fighters above and ahead of them, which they identified as Zeros, and nine more fighters, identified as Oscars, approaching from the rear 1,000 feet below. Once again the fighters used coordinating attacks from multiple directions, taking advantage of the blind spots to the left and right of the B-25 rudders and coming up from below the bombers. In a new tactic, as many as 15 fighters would turn in together, apparently on a signal from the leader, and make a raking attack on the entire B-25 formation. After 25 minutes under attack, Lt. R. A. Coon's B-25D, flying as part of C Flight, dropped out of the formation and immediately drew several fighters who went after the crippled bomber. The bomber appeared to regain control when it was down around 2,000 feet and the crew started bailing out, only to have the Japanese fighters start firing on them as they floated down under their parachutes. The crews in the remaining bombers reported seeing three chutes collapse as the Japanese fighters flew around them. Only one man from this crew—Cpl. Marvin Beckman, flying as engineer/gunner—survived after a harrowing ordeal, as he reported on his return to Chakulia:

Approximately ten minutes after we were attacked, my guns jammed. Shortly afterward one of the rear guns also jammed. The rear gunner was killed and I took his place using the one good gun. The tail section of our plane was almost completely shot off. Our plane started to lose altitude and the pilot gave orders for us to bail out. I bailed out as directed. The co-pilot left the plane directly after I jumped. His pack opened but I doubt very much if it had opened enough to bring him down safely. As far as I know the pilot and the bombardier remained with the plane. Because I had one bullet wound in the right leg, one in the right arm, two in the left hand, and one in the forehead, I was in a state of semi-consciousness that made it difficult for me to see exactly what was occurring after I left the plane. When approximately 5,000 feet from the ground I regained consciousness and saw three Zeros that began to fire at me. I began to slide-slip

THE TENTH AIR FORCE IN WORLD WAR II

my chute to avoid the bullets. When I went down to 1,000 feet they continued after the other planes in our squadron. I landed in the jungle about thirty miles the other side of Rankin, in enemy territory. Upon landing I began shouting for the co-pilot. Because of the denseness of the trees and underbrush I finally had to give up my search for the co-pilot. The loss of blood from my wounds left me weak.

I then found a small water hole and proceeded to wash and dress my wounds with the material of the parachute as best I could. Whenever I used my left hand for climbing it would start to bleed. While traveling through the jungle, which was from 1100 hours on May 21 to 1200 hours on May 24, the only food I had was one bar of chocolate. At 1300 hours on May 24 I reached the river, and on the morning of the 25th, while walking downstream, I met two natives who gave me fish and rice. I continued to walk with them down the river for approximately one-half mile, but they were too damn slow to suit me, so I left them because I couldn't wait till I reached civilization. That evening I met an Indian policeman who took me to an Indian village where I met the Indian police officer in charge. The Indian police officer in charge lent me three Rupees so that I might hire two villagers to take me by boat down the river to Lama.

With the help of the Indian police along the way, Beckman reached a British army unit and made his way to Chittagong, where British medical staff treated his wounds. An RAF mail plane flew him back to Calcutta on 29 May 1943.[107]

The air battle of May 21 took place just after the IATF had cooperated with the RAF in Operation WIMPOLE, an intensive combined attack by day and by night on the Japanese lines of communications leading to the Arakan, where the British army was now withdrawing after a failed attempt to capture Akyab. The operation covered three days (May 18 to 20) and involved the heavy and medium bombers of the IATF and No. 221 and No. 224 Groups of the RAF. The IATAF took responsibility for targets to the east of longitude 94°30'—essentially the Irrawaddy Valley—while the RAF took on targets to the west of this line, closer to the Arakan peninsula. The B-24s and B-25s carried out 132 sorties over the three days, dropping 332 tons of bombs on the towns of Magwe, Minbu, and Thaetmyo—most hit for the first time—as well as railroad facilities at Prome and the refinery complex around Chauk. The RAF sent out Beaufighters, Hurricanes, and Mohawk fighters on sweeps looking for motor vehicles and rivercraft while Blenheim and Vultee Vengeances went after supply dumps closer to the Arakan front. At night, RAF Wellington bombers went out to bomb towns along the supply route. Although it was difficult to determine the extent of the destruction, British intelligence deemed the operation a success on the basis of the number of motor vehicles and rivercraft the fighters destroyed over the three days and the damage the IATF bombers had done to several of their targets.[108]

A vital aspect of the campaign against the Japanese line of communications was the goal of paralyzing railroad traffic in the railroad yards through the destruction of key bridges along the rail line.[109] If rolling stock and locomotives backed up in the yards, the yards themselves became even more-lucrative targets. Attacks on bridges became an important part of the medium-bomber effort in central Burma, but the mediums found bridges just as difficult to hit—much less destroy—as did their colleagues in the heavy bombers. The narrow width of the bridges made them difficult to hit even from the lower altitudes the medium bombers typically used for bombing. As one inspection report on the IATF bomber units noted, a further technical problem was the characteristics of the M-43 500-pound and M-44 1,000-pound bombs the mediums and the heavy bombers used. According to this report, "natural errors inherent in the bomb due to methods used in its fabrication will give it a dispersion error greater than the width of the target."[110] In other words, even if aimed perfectly the small imperfections in the bomb's construction and finish would cause it to deviate from its intended path. An imperfect approach to the target from a turn onto the approach a bit too late, or a speed a bit faster than predicted as wingmen tried to catch up with the lead aircraft, could throw off a bombing approach. The other problem was the open construction of most of the bridges, which dissipated the blast effect of the bombs dropped on or nearby the bridge structure, so that a near miss did little if any damage, and even a direct hit might cause only damage that was easily repairable. The only solution appeared to be saturating the target with bombs in the hope of getting enough direct hits that would do damage to the structure.[111]

There were more than 100 bridges in Burma of 200 feet in length or greater, but for the medium bombers there were four key bridges in central Burma that if knocked out would have had the greatest impact on operations of the railroad system. These were

B-25C 42-32263 "Wham Bam" from one of the 341st Bomb Group's squadrons flying over India or Burma in 1943. *Author's collection*

The B-25s went after bridges with somewhat better success than the heavy bombers achieved. This attack on the Myitnge Bridge took place on 15 March 1943. The photo shows what difficult targets the bridges were to bomb from high or medium altitudes. Ultimately, successful attacks would come through new techniques of low-level bombing and new technology. *3A-37701, RG342FH, NARA*

the Myitnge Bridge south of Mandalay, the Mu River Bridge on the rail line to Yeu, the Meza Bridge below Naba (on the line north to Myitkyina), and the Gokteik Viaduct on the rail line to Lashio. Of these, the Myitnge Bridge became the most heavily bombed target in Burma outside Rangoon. The bridge was an all-steel structure with four spans 600 yards in length. The record of the attacks on the Mytnge Bridge is representative of the IATF's attacks on almost all bridges during the first half of 1943. Between January and May, the 341st Bomb Group's squadrons flew 21 missions against the Myitnge Bridge, making it unserviceable just once. On these 21 missions, the B-25s dropped 200 tons of bombs on the bridge, including 64 tons dropped during one intense assault on the bridge over six days in March. The squadrons tried different techniques to see what might work, bombing from as low as 2,000 feet and as high as 13,000 feet and using different combinations of bombs before standardizing on the 1,000-pound bomb. The B-25s also used different types of fuses, sometimes during the same mission, with some bombs having instantaneous fuses and some with a ¹⁄₁₀ of a second delay. Experience did prove that the medium bombers were more effective than the B-24s bombing from higher altitude. Whereas the B-24s obtained one hit on a bridge for every 81 sorties, the B-25s recorded one hit for every 15 sorties.[112] The strategic importance

Brig. Gen. Caleb Haynes, commanding the India Air Task Force (*left*), stands next to Col. John Egan—who took over command of the 51st Fighter Group from Col. Homer Sanders—after awarding a Distinguished Flying Cross to Maj. Paul Droz, who flew some of the earliest rescue missions behind enemy lines in a PT-17. Haynes had operational command of the IATF during its formative early months. *3A-34024, 342FH, NARA*

of the bridge made it somewhat easier for the Japanese to defend. Knowing its importance and the likelihood of continued attacks, the Japanese brought in antiaircraft guns, but fortunately for the medium bombers, antiaircraft damaged only eight B-25s, although the 7th Bomb Group lost two B-24s bombing the bridge. Results against the Gokteik Viaduct—a narrow steel structure spanning a 2,260-foot-wide gorge—were distressingly similar. The 341st Bomb Group carried out 11 missions against the viaduct, inflicting only minor damage before the monsoon.[113]

From January to May 1943 the 7th and 341st Bomb Groups flew 2,577 sorties over Burma. As shown in table 1, the weight of bombs dropped increased steadily over the period, while table 2 shows the tonnage dropped on the main targets. The IATF's two bomb groups dropped 40 percent of their bombs on just five targets: Rangoon, the Myitnge Bridge, the Gokteik Viaduct, the Pazundaung Bridge in Rangoon, and Mandalay. The two groups dropped a combined total of 3,048 tons of bombs during the period, with the B-24s dropping 60 percent of the total. In comparison, the RAF, with fewer medium and heavy bombers, dropped 1,656 tons of bombs by day and night.[114] While the near tripling of tonnage was an impressive achievement given all the constraints the IATF faced regarding lack of aircraft and especially lack of combat crews, the impact the bombing had on the Japanese line-of-communications system is difficult to assess. Clearly by the end of May the IATF heavy bombers had made Rangoon too dangerous for the Japanese to use as a major port facility. The effort of the medium bombers in central Burma did reduce the efficiency of the railroad system, but the inability to destroy the major bridges reduced the effect of the raids on railroad yards. Damaged they were, but goods could still get through. In the judgment of the Royal Air Force's history of the campaign up to this point, the bomber offensive "up to the end of June 1943 was neither heavy nor sustained and it is unlikely that the enemy regarded the threat as a serious one."[115] But as the history goes on to say, "air operations are continuous affairs and are rarely endowed with graphic battle names. Although in Burma during the first half of 1943 the bomber offensive reached no conclusion, it was the beginning of a war of attrition which continued until the last shot was fired in August 1945."[116]

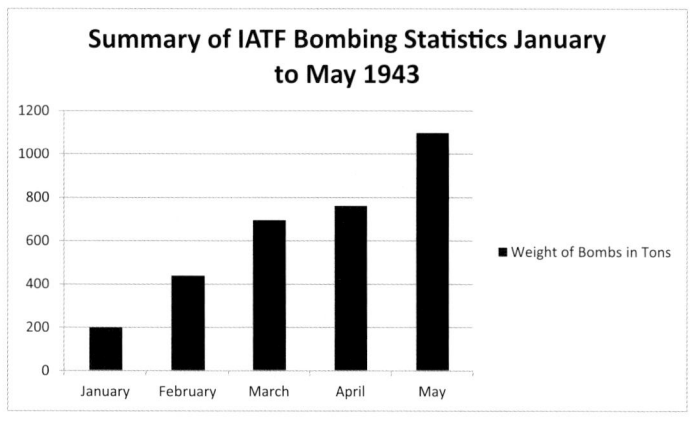

Summary of IATF Bombing Statistics January to May 1943 (Weight of Bombs in Tons)

Month	Weight of Bombs in Tons
January	~200
February	~440
March	~700
April	~760
May	~1090

Table 1 Source: Narrative History India Air Task Force November 1942-May 31, 1943

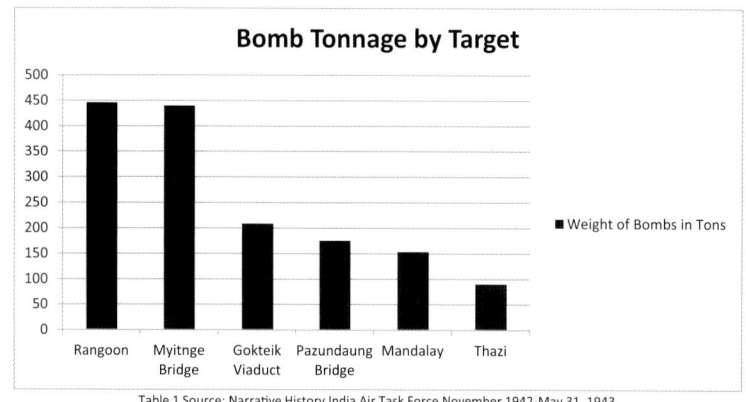

Bomb Tonnage by Target (Weight of Bombs in Tons)

Target	Weight of Bombs in Tons
Rangoon	~445
Myitnge Bridge	~440
Gokteik Viaduct	~205
Pazundaung Bridge	~175
Mandalay	~150
Thazi	~90

Table 1 Source: Narrative History India Air Task Force November 1942-May 31, 1943

CHAPTER 5

TRIDENT, COMMAND CHANGES, AND OPERATIONS DURING THE MONSOON

June–August 1943

The Trident Conference

As the Allies prepared for their second strategic planning session—the Trident Conference to be held in Washington, DC, in mid-May (sometimes referred to as the Washington Conference)—the situation in Burma was not encouraging. The British army's advance in the Arakan to capture Akyab would soon end in a dismal failure (news of the defeat arrived during the Trident Conference). Despite early numerical superiority in men, artillery, and tanks, Gen. Wavell "paid the penalty for committing inexperienced troops to a difficult operation at the end of a tenuous line of communication."[1] Once again the Japanese launched a successful counterattack, threatening the British line of communications and ultimately forcing an ignominious retreat back to the positions from where the British forces had started in October 1942. The defeat—another blow to British prestige—had a serious impact on the morale of the British and Indian troops involved in the abortive campaign, reinforcing the view that the Japanese were far superior in jungle warfare and were, in fact, invincible.[2]

American preparations for the reconquest of Burma under the planned ANAKIM operation continued to move forward, but at a slow pace. Two Chinese divisions (22nd and 38th) had completed their training and reequipment at the Ramgarh training center. Training of a third (30th Division) was getting underway. The 38th Division had moved up to Ledo, where American Army Air Force aviation engineers were building a base to support construction of the road from Ledo into Burma, with the 22nd Division preparing to move to Ledo in support. The road project itself had made little progress. In February the road had crossed the border into Burma at mile 43.2 from Ledo, but by the onset of the monsoon in May, construction had pushed the road only about 4 miles farther. Stilwell's attempts to build a similar American-trained force in Yunnan—his planned Y-Force—had made only halting progress. The effort to build up tonnage over the Hump, now under the control of the Air Transport Command, had also run into difficulties. The tonnage carried over the Hump during March, April, and May was well below the 4,000-ton-a-month goal that Arnold had set for the India-China Wing, averaging just over 1,800 tons a month.[3] The reasons were many: shortages of air crews, insufficient numbers of airplanes even with the additions Arnold had provided, bad weather over Assam, and the slow pace of airfield construction.[4]

The one development from this period that did have a profound effect on the war in Burma was the success, such as it was, of Orde Wingate's long-range penetration mission into Burma with his

C-47 transports on a muddy airfield in Assam. American efforts in the China-Burma-India theater concentrated on building the tonnage carried over the Hump route. A shortage of aircraft, crews, and facilities restricted the ability of the India-China Wing to meet the monthly tonnage promised to China during the first half of 1943. *3A-33678, RG342FH, NARA*

Similar shortages of men and equipment confronted the American engineers working to extend the Ledo Road into Burma. Two African American units—the 45th Engineers General Service Regiment and the 823rd Engineer Aviation Battalion—shifted from building airfields in Assam to working on the Ledo Road, taking over from British engineers and local labor. Ultimately, African Americans would make up 60 percent of the 15,000 American troops working on the road.
Author's collection

British, Burmese, and Gurhka battalions—the famous Chindits—who marched overland deep behind Japanese lines. While the strategic value of the first Chindit expedition was minimal and the casualties inflicted on the Japanese were small in comparison to the Chindits' losses, the expedition had a profound psychological impact on British and Indian troops because it demonstrated that they, too, could fight in the jungles just as well as the Japanese, and defeat them. More importantly, Wingate's expedition demonstrated that a large body of troops could be maintained entirely through air supply. Wingate showed that "provided air superiority could be retained and sufficient transport aircraft made available, an offensive into Burma across the grain of the country [i.e., through the mountain ranges along the Burma-India border] was no longer of necessity tied to roads which could only be built slowly and with great difficulty. Given these two conditions, commanders were to find themselves once again with strategical and tactical freedom."[5] Relying on air supply pointed to a way of overcoming the Japanese encirclement tactics aimed at cutting an enemy's lines of communications, which had proven so successful in earlier Japanese campaigns.[6] In the campaigns in Malaya and Burma, the British and Indian divisions had been heavily dependent on roads and motor vehicles for all their supplies, leaving them vulnerable to Japanese roadblocks cutting off supplies and invariably forcing the British forces to retreat to reopen their supply routes. If an Allied force could rely on air supply instead of roads, Japanese encirclement would become less of a threat.

The Chindit expedition also had a profound effect on the Japanese army in Burma and the Japanese commanders' appreciation of how to defend Burma from Allied attack. The *15th Army* had adopted a defensive posture in northern Burma on the basis of the belief that it would be difficult, if not impossible, for a British army to cross over the mountainous area along the Assam-Burma border and sustain a campaign in Burma in the absence of a network of roads to carry supplies. The Chindits had shown that a large force could cross the mountain barrier and enter Burma even without a fully developed road network through the mountains. And if the British could do it once, they could do it again, and possibly on an even-larger scale. The *15th Army* determined that a purely defensive policy might well be unsound, and that a Japanese offensive into Assam to prevent a British offensive into Burma might well be necessary and possible. This change in Japanese strategy would have dramatic repercussions.[7]

With regard to future operations in Burma to be discussed at the Trident Conference, the two Allies approached the problem from completely different perspectives. Reviewing Wavell's own assessment of the needs for the success of ANAKIM, an operation he himself felt was "a gamble involving great difficulties and risks," the British Chiefs of Staff came to the conclusion that ANAKIM could not be undertaken as planned during the 1943–44 dry season.[8] The Chiefs of Staff concluded that the amphibious requirements for ANAKIM would take shipping away from operations in the Mediterranean after the planned invasion of Sicily, while an amphibious assault on Rangoon against prepared Japanese positions could be a disaster. But more importantly, ANAKIM would "commit British forces to a major operation not essential towards the ultimate defeat of Japan, in some of the worst campaigning country in the world" and, even if successful, would not accelerate the opening of the Burma Road to full capacity before 1945.[9] The Chiefs of Staff proposed instead a plan favoring air operations, putting all available resources to developing the air bases in Assam to increase the supplies to China, building up the Fourteenth Air Force in China for operations against the Japanese forces in China and Japanese shipping, and more-intensive air operations against the Japanese in Burma.[10] Ground operations would be limited to supporting the air bases in Assam and capturing Akyab and Ramree Islands to use as air bases to attack Japanese facilities in central and southern Burma. Churchill himself was apparently beginning to consider the idea of bypassing Burma altogether, arguing that "going into swampy jungles to fight the Japanese is like going into the water to fight a shark. It is better to entice him into a trap or catch him on a hook and then demolish him with axes after hauling him out on dry land."[11]

For the Americans, the debate over a ground or air strategy for China had only intensified, pitting Stilwell, Marshall, and the War

Gen. Henry Arnold stands next to Clayton Bissell in front of Tenth Air Force Headquarters in New Delhi. Arnold met with Bissell and his staff to review air operations in India and Burma before going on to Chungking to meet with Generalissimo Chiang Kai-shek during his official mission to China. *Author's collection*

Department against Generalissimo Chiang Kai-shek and Chennault. Creation of the Fourteenth Air Force had gone only partway toward what the latter wanted. Chennault wanted to implement his air plan in its entirety, for which he would need the greater proportion of tonnage over the Hump route. His plan envisioned three phases of operations: in Phase One, the Fourteenth Air Force would gain air superiority over China by defeating the Japanese Army Air Force in the air and destroying its airfields; in Phase Two, the Fourteenth Air Force's heavy and medium bombers would undertake an intensive campaign against Japanese shipping off the China coast while the air superiority campaign continued; and Phase Three would see air attacks on the Japanese home islands from bases in China and an extension of the antishipping campaign from Korea to French Indochina.[12] Chennault admitted that such an extensive air campaign might well provoke a major Japanese response to take over the Fourteenth Air Force's bases in central China, but he did not believe that such an offensive would be any more effective than past attempts, and to mount such a sizeable offensive the Japanese would have to draw men, airplanes, and shipping from other theaters, weakening their defensive positions. He listed his minimum requirements to implement his plan as two fighter groups, one medium-bombardment group, one heavy-bombardment group, and one photoreconnaissance squadron totaling 150 fighters, 48 medium and 35 heavy bombers, and 15 reconnaissance airplanes with enough Hump tonnage to sustain this force in action. In addition, Chennault called for the Chinese air force to have two fighter groups with American P-40s and one medium-bomber group with B-25s. As his air plan advanced, he would require an additional fighter group and an additional medium-bomber group for the Fourteenth Air Force.[13]

Stilwell had no doubt about the possibilities of an air campaign and the damage it could do to the Japanese in China and Japanese shipping. He further believed that bases in China were necessary to bomb Japan. His concern remained the possible Japanese reaction

Lt. Gen. Joseph Stilwell (*far right*) stands with a group of Chinese and American officers at an airfield in India. Stilwell's commitment to the War Department's plan to improve the effectiveness of the Chinese army and his concern with the probable Japanese reaction to air attacks on the Japanese home islands from China put him into direct conflict with Chennault and the generalissimo. *Author's collection*

to Chennault's proposed air campaign and how to defend the Fourteenth Air Force's bases against a Japanese offensive. As he told Marshall, "What Chennault says about available targets is quite true. The Japs could be done considerable injury. Just one point about the whole thing and that is, as we found out last spring [during the Chekiang Expedition], any attempt to bomb Japan is going to bring a prompt and violent reaction on the ground and somebody has to decide how far we can sting them before that reaction appears. . . . If we start an air campaign, they may decide they are being hurt to the extent that it would be advantageous for them to take Chungking and Kunming. If that is done, we will have to fold up out there."[14] What China needed to defend the air bases was a reformed, well-trained, and effective Chinese army. From Stilwell's perspective, an air campaign should not be undertaken until China had the means to halt a Japanese offensive. The problems the India-China Wing was having getting Hump tonnage up to 4,000 tons may have influenced Stilwell's view that the air route could never fulfill all of China's needs. He continued to argue for building a land route from India through Burma to reopen the Burma Road.

Chiang Kai-shek urged Roosevelt to recall Chennault to Washington to present his case for his air plan, which Chiang strongly supported and argued was vitally necessary to keep up Chinese morale and continued participation in the war. Marshall insisted that Stilwell be called as well, and both Chennault and Stilwell flew to Washington at the end of April to meet with the president. After listening to both presentations, and with T. V. Soong conveying Chiang's wishes, Roosevelt chose to support Chennault's air plan because of his concern with providing more-immediate support to Chiang to sustain China's participation in the war. He ordered that Chennault should receive the first 4,700 tons of supplies flown over the Hump, with the next 2,000 tons to be allocated for other purposes. The difficulty with Stilwell's plan was that it would take time to implement, and the president did not want to wait. He wanted immediate support for China without the complications Stilwell's plan for reforming the Chinese army would involve, and that could come only through Chennault's air plan.[15] To Roosevelt and his political advisors, the air plan seemed to provide a means of hitting the Japanese, and especially Japanese shipping, at low cost, creating the impression that China was making a valuable contribution to the war effort while supporting the generalissimo but not involving the United States in Chinese internal politics, which a major reform of the Chinese army would have required.[16] But in backing Chennault's air plan, the president left open the possibility of supporting a modified and more limited version of ANAKIM.

At the Trident Conference, the British Chiefs of Staff presented their view that the full ANAKIM plan could not be implemented during the 1943–44 dry season, and gave their proposals for devoting greater resources to American airpower in China and Burma, with only limited ground operations in Assam to contain the Japanese army and defend the Assam air bases. The British argued that there were not enough resources available to improve the Hump route and at the same time initiate a ground campaign to recapture all of Burma. Building capacity over the Hump route was the better choice, since it promised more-immediate support for China, as Roosevelt wanted. Delaying any ground offensive in Burma was their preferred choice. Churchill brought up his idea of bypassing Burma altogether in favor of amphibious operations to seize northern Sumatra, much as the Americans were planning to bypass certain Japanese bases in the Pacific. Seeing this as merely a cover for Churchill's desire to retake Singapore, the American Joint Chiefs of Staff argued that any operation away from Burma would do little to support China, and that even if more resources went to building up the Hump route, the air bases in Assam and at Kunming would still remain vulnerable to a Japanese offensive. A ground campaign in Burma would help keep Japanese forces occupied and not available for an offensive against the air bases. The result of the debate was a compromise agreement to a modified and much-reduced ANAKIM focusing only on northern Burma, with priority given instead to building up the capacity of the Hump route to 10,000 tons a month by September 1943. The Combined Chiefs of Staff recommended concentrating resources on developing the air bases in Assam, increasing air operations over Burma, and increasing the American air forces in China, with limited ground operations by Stilwell's Chinese forces from Ledo, by the Chinese armies in Yunnan, and by the British army's IV Corps from Imphal to contain the Japanese in northern Burma and as a preliminary step to opening a road to China, as well as amphibious operations to capture Akyab and Ramree Islands, as the British chiefs had proposed. This became the agreed-on plan for operations in Burma.[17]

Changes in Command

The agreement reached at the Trident Conference did not change the Tenth Air Force's mission. In April, following the formation of the Fourteenth Air Force, Stilwell had written to Bissell to restate the Tenth's missions. The Tenth's primary mission remained the defense of the India-China ferry route and its bases in Assam. The secondary mission was the destruction of Japanese aircraft, installations, and shipping in the Burma area. As part of the Tenth's secondary mission, Stilwell stated that the Tenth also had responsibility for providing air support to Allied ground units under his direction. The Tenth continued to have many other duties to perform, including providing all aviation and related logistical support for all American aviation units in the theater, delivering aviation materiel and personnel to these units, maintaining the weather service and Army Airways Communications System, coordinating the activities of all American and Chinese operations out of bases in India, and providing intelligence on all Japanese aircraft that might threaten American operations. In addition, the Tenth was responsible for cooperation with the Royal Air Force, British army, and Royal Navy in India.[18]

The Tenth Air Force was now in a far-better position to fulfill its primary and secondary missions and the multiple tasks Stilwell had assigned to it. By June 1943 the Tenth had 1,196 officers and 7,624 enlisted men assigned, though this was still 537 officers and 2,049 enlisted men short of requirements under established tables of organization.[19] Bissell had worked constantly to build the Tenth Air Force's strength and efficiency. Bissell "sent many messages to Washington, always showing the inadequacies of the supplies for the task assigned, always requesting more material, more men, and more planes."[20] Despite the fact that American production was rapidly expanding, many of Bissell's requests went unanswered because the defeat of Germany was still the priority. The Tenth Air Force now had its full complement of airplanes as agreed to in the Arnold-Portal-Towers agreement of 1942, but Bissell not surprisingly wanted more units, more men, and more planes for more offensive operations against the Japanese. Bissell had acquired the 1st and 2nd Troop Carrier Squadrons for the Tenth Air Force, but Arnold turned down Bissell's pleas for an additional heavy-bomber group. At the end of March, Arnold did agree to add another fighter group (selecting the 80th Fighter Group) and another medium- or light-bombardment group to the Tenth, as well as another photoreconnaissance squadron and a photographic-mapping squadron by the end of the year.[21] Bissell repeatedly asked for more service units for the Tenth, given the geographic breadth of the Tenth's operations stretching from Karachi to Assam. Flying more missions meant using more fuel, ammunition, and parts, with planes requiring more maintenance, creating a need for more maintenance and repair units and more supply units to acquire and deliver more spare parts to the combat units. The War Department agreed to send the 52nd Service Group to India in July, with the 12th Service Group and the 23rd Air Depot Group following in October.[22] With these service groups came more signals, ordnance, and quartermaster companies, and more aviation engineer battalions and hundreds of vehicles for all these units. By July the War Department had sent or committed to send seven service groups, seven air depot groups, and ten depot repair and supply squadrons to the Tenth Air Force.[23]

To get firsthand knowledge of conditions in the China-Burma-India theater, achieve a better understanding of the needs of the Tenth and Fourteenth Air Forces, and provide an objective assessment, in May the War Department ordered Maj. Gen. George Stratemeyer, Army Air Force chief of staff, to make an extensive tour of the region. Stratemeyer was an Army Air Force officer of long experience and a former commander of the 7th Bomb Group during the 1930s. He had been serving as Arnold's chief of staff since June 1942.[24] As chief of staff, Stratemeyer was already familiar with many of the issues confronting the Tenth Air Force in the CBI, having corresponded with Bissell on Arnold's behalf. More than a month spent in India and China meeting with commanders at different levels and discussing their operations and conditions made Stratemeyer sympathetic to their continued demands for more men and equipment and how important it was to meet at least some of these requests.[25] In one of his first reports back to Army Air Force headquarters in Washington, Stratemeyer stated that both the Tenth and the Fourteenth Air Forces urgently needed a minimum of one squadron of fast, high-altitude fighters—preferably P-38s or P-51As—because of the similarity of their Allison engines to those in the P-40.[26] A small but vital contribution Stratemeyer made on his return to Washington was to order an increase in PX supplies of cigarettes, tobacco, and magazines to the CBI to help boost morale.[27] Stratemeyer's familiarity with the air forces in the CBI gained on his trip would become even more important just a few months later.

The outcome of the Trident Conference did lead to some organizational changes in the Tenth Air Force. The plans to devote more resources to the Hump operation implied that more aircraft, personnel, and airfield facilities would be needed to expand the operation. There was already frustration with the failure of the India-China Wing to meet the goal of 4,000 tons a month to China, and recognition—on the basis of reports from Stratemeyer and Capt. Eddie Rickenbacker, who was reviewing the India-China Wing's operations—that the problems in Assam were serious.[28] Part of the difficulty was the confusing command arrangements in Assam. The India-China Wing reported to the Air Transport Command in Washington; Bissell, as commander of the Tenth Air Force, had no responsibility for the India-China Wing but was responsible for working with British authorities to provide air bases for the India-China Wing; and the Services of Supply and local troops had responsibility for loading and unloading ATC aircraft in Assam, while a committee in New Delhi determined priorities for shipment.[29] To compound the problem, American, RAF, and Chinese aircraft all used the Assam airfields for various purposes. The likelihood that this confusion would only worsen led to the creation of the Assam American Air Base Command, which later became American Air Base Command 1. The function of this new command was the coordination and integration of all American air activities in Assam, including Tenth Air Force units in the area, the India-China Wing, the X Air Service Command, the Army Airways Communications System, the weather service, any Fourteenth Air Force units operating out of Assam, and also the Chinese National Aviation Corporation. In addition, the new command had responsibility for the defense of

One outcome of the Trident conference was a decision to allocate more resources to the China-Burma-India theater. Gen. Arnold had already decided to send the larger Curtiss C-46 transport to India. The C-46 could carry considerably more cargo than the C-47, though mechanical problems plagued the airplane during its initial months of operations over the demanding Hump route. This photo shows early-model C-46s, with the three-bladed propeller, with other CNAC and Army Air Force C-47s on a rain-soaked field in Assam. *Author's collection*

the India-China Wing in Assam and, as a secondary mission, the destruction of Japanese aircraft, installations, and troops in the assigned area and the support of Allied ground forces. Because of his varied experience in the theater, Bissell appointed Brig. Gen. Caleb Haynes as commander of the Assam American Air Base Command. Haynes's new command consisted of the 51st Fighter Group (less the 16th Fighter Squadron, still with the Fourteenth Air Force in China), the 679th Air Warning Company, the 2nd Troop Carrier Squadron (then on loan to the India-China Wing), and all American antiaircraft units in Assam. This left the India Air Task Force as a pure bomber command, with the 7th Bomb Group, the 341st Bomb Group, and the 9th Photographic Reconnaissance Squadron. To command the IATF, Bissell appointed Col. Cecil Combs, one of Brereton's original cadre of officers brought from Java.[30]

At the Trident Conference, the Combined Chiefs of Staff agreed to assign an additional medium-bomber group and another fighter group to Chennault's Fourteenth Air Force, with the medium group provided once the India-China Wing reached 10,000 tons per month.[31] In July, Arnold proposed to Stilwell that these units for the Fourteenth Air Force could come from shifting units from the Tenth Air Force to China. With the 80th Fighter Group on its way to India, Arnold suggested that the 51st Fighter Group could move to China, where it would regain the 16th Fighter Squadron. Arnold had assigned the 311th Bombardment Group (Dive)—equipped with A-36 Invader dive-bombers and P-51A fighters—to the Tenth Air Force and offered that when this unit reached India, the 341st Bomb Group could move to China, though this would leave the Tenth without a medium-bomber group for some months until a group from the Middle East could move to the CBI—a transfer the Combined Chiefs of Staff had already approved.[32] The 51st Fighter Group would move to China in September, but the 341st Group would not depart the Tenth Air Force until January 1944, leaving behind the 490th Bomb Squadron when it did.[33]

A more fundamental change that took place over these months was the reorganization of the structure of Army Air Force units in the China-Burma-India theater and the appointment of new commanders. The organizational structure that had evolved by June 1943 was a function both of military necessity and political realities.[34] As theater commander, Stilwell had control over all Army Air Force units in the CBI except for the India-China Wing in Assam. The headquarters of all these units were spread out across the region. Stilwell maintained his headquarters in Chungking, with his rear-echelon headquarters in New Delhi. Chennault had the headquarters of the Fourteenth Air Force in Kunming, while Bissell had the headquarters of the Tenth Air Force in New Delhi, near his RAF and British army counterparts, while his combat units were in Assam and Bengal. Since from the standpoint of numbers of personnel the CBI was an air theater, senior Army Air Force leaders were concerned with the lack of a senior air officer on Stilwell's staff, particularly with the prospect that Stilwell's focus would increasingly be drawn to ground operations in northern Burma in the months ahead.[35]

On his own initiative, fearing that the generalissimo would try to persuade Roosevelt to appoint Chennault as commander of all air forces in the CBI, Stilwell had requested in March that the War Department appoint a theater air commander to command both the Tenth and the Fourteenth Air Forces.[36] Stilwell had a strong argument. A single air commander would provide unity of command, an important principle of war that Carl von Clausewitz had emphasized in his great work *On War*. Clausewitz stressed the concentration of force, the need of keeping one's forces concentrated so as to always be very strong at the decisive point.[37] Clausewitz also emphasized what he termed economy of force, the principle that all forces available were involved and "always to make sure that no part of the whole force remains idle.... When the time for action comes, the first requirement should be that all parts must act."[38] With a single commander, all units of a force could be allocated to the task and concentrated as needed for maximum effectiveness. This principle was central to Army Air Force doctrine, as described in FM 100-20, *Command and Employment of Air Power*, which stated:

> *The inherent flexibility of air power is its greatest asset. This flexibility makes it possible to employ the whole weight of the available air power against selected areas in turn; such concentrated use of the air striking force is a battle winning factor of the first importance. Control of available air power must be centralized and command must be exercised through the air force commander if this inherent flexibility and ability to deliver a decisive blow are to be fully exploited.*[39]

But at this time, unity of command for American air forces in the CBI proved impossible to achieve.

With his recent exposure to the conditions and problems in the CBI and the breadth of his experience as chief of staff of the Army Air Force, the War Department selected Maj. Gen. Stratemeyer for the position of senior air commander in the CBI. There was some expectation that in this new position Stratemeyer would exercise control over both the Tenth and the Fourteenth Air Force, but since the Generalissimo had previously rejected proposals to place a senior officer over Chennault, President Roosevelt deferred to his wishes. In advising Chiang of Stratemeyer's appointment, Roosevelt stated that Stratemeyer's mission was to improve the effectiveness of the air effort in China. There were issues of maintenance, aircraft, training, logistics, and air force administration that could be dealt with more efficiently with a senior officer in the theater rather than having to wait for a decision from Washington. Roosevelt assured Chiang that Stratemeyer would not be placed over Chennault but would instead focus on improving the capacity of the Fourteenth Air Force and the flow of men, aircraft, and supplies to China. Stratemeyer could advise but would not command Chennault.[40] The inability to appoint a single air commander for the CBI led to the decision to split the Army Air Forces in the theater into two separate commands: Army Air Forces, India-Burma Sector (IBS), and Army Air Forces, China Sector. Stratemeyer would command the Army Air Forces, India-Burma Sector.[41]

The Generalissimo used the opportunity of Stratemeyer's appointment to request Bissell's replacement as commander of the Tenth Air Force with someone who would work well with Chennault.[42] Establishment of the Fourteenth Air Force had done nothing to reduce the personal animosity between Bissell and Chennault, and relations between the two air forces remained strained. Chennault insisted on his independence from the Tenth Air Force but continued to rely on the Tenth for many services without reciprocity, at one point suggesting that pilots who had proven unfit for combat in the Fourteenth Air Force should be assigned to the Karachi training base in exchange for experienced instructors.[43] Word of this tension, and squabbles with other organizations in the CBI, reached Gen. Marshall through a letter from an enlisted man, prompting Stilwell to have Bissell and Brig. Gen. Edgar Glenn, Fourteenth Air Force chief of staff, to write letters to their commands reminding them, as Stilwell said, that "our job is too big to be jeopardized by petty squabbles,

Clayton Bissell escorts Maj. Gen. Howard Davidson (*on Bissell's right*) after Davidson's arrival at New Delhi on 15 August 1943. Davidson would remain in command of the Tenth Air Force and, for a time, the Allied Strategic Air Force for two years. *Personal collection of Maj. Gen. Howard C. Davidson, 168.7266-233, AFHRA*

and for that reason, if no other, we cannot afford to let them arise."[44] The Generalissimo coupled his request for Bissell's replacement with a recommendation that Chennault become chief of staff of Army Air Forces in the theater or chief of staff to the Chinese air force. President Roosevelt agreed to the latter and to Bissell's replacement initially with Caleb Haynes, but the Pentagon brought pressure to have Brig. Gen. Howard Davidson, who was senior to Haynes, appointed instead.[45] Davidson had served as commander of the VII Fighter Command in the Seventh Air Force, was then serving as special projects officer at the Proving Ground Command at Eglin Field, and had recently returned from a tour of China done at Arnold's request.[46] On 24 July 1943, Bissell was informed that he would be relieved of his command of the Tenth Air Force upon Davidson's arrival in the theater the following month.[47]

In a letter to Stilwell on 20 July 1943, Marshall elaborated his conception of Stratemeyer's role in the CBI theater, which Stratemeyer took as a definition of his mission:

Regarding the assignment of General Stratemeyer to your command, a review of the train of events that led to the decision is desirable as well as a statement of the mission he should accomplish.

As you indicated in a message dated March 20, you need a theater air commander. The soundness of this requirement was evident, but the appointment of such a commander could not be made for the reasons which were stated in our reply. In the meantime, we considered that the next best solution would be to provide you with a senior and very experienced air officer to coordinate the many complicated air problems that arise due to the peculiar situation in your theater. Some of these problems as you know come into the War Department direct from the several air headquarters involved. This of course is due to the air set up which, for reasons familiar to you, has been allowed to develop. In some cases submitted here your views are not known to us. In other cases where there is perhaps a theater solution, submission by one of the air headquarters direct to the War Department invites interference from us in local affairs which may lead to an unsatisfactory result from your viewpoint. . . .

I anticipate that Stratemeyer's supervision of all those logistical matters in India in support of the 14th A.F., which have, right or wrong, been the grounds for so much controversy, will go a long way toward solving these troubles. He hopes in carrying out this difficult task to effect locally a more complete coordination of all your theater air matters.[48]

Stratemeyer arrived in New Delhi on 5 August 1943, shortly after the War Department—through the air adjutant general—had authorized activation of "The Headquarters of the Commanding General, Army Air Force Units, India-Burma Theater and Air Advisor to the Asiatic Theater Commander," even though neither an India-Burma theater nor an Asiatic theater existed.[49] Meeting with Stilwell a few days later, Stratemeyer recommended that the X and XIV Air Service Commands in the Tenth and Fourteenth Air Forces be combined into one command to serve both air forces and that a new training command be set up to train Chinese pilots. Stratemeyer also proposed moving the Tenth Air Force headquarters farther east to be closer to its combat units. Stilwell approved all these suggestions and advised Stratemeyer that he not try to establish himself as commander of all the air forces in the theater, as apparently Marshall and Arnold wanted, but rather to concentrate on his advisory role to the Fourteenth Air Force while carrying out his responsibilities in India.[50] Shortly thereafter, Stratemeyer flew to China to meet with the Generalissimo and with Chennault, obtaining Chennault's agreement to combining the air service commands and setting up a training center for the Chinese.[51]

On August 18, Stratemeyer issued several directives setting up his new command structure. Stilwell formally announced these directives two days later. Stratemeyer activated the Headquarters, Army Air Forces, India-Burma sector; the China-Burma-India Air Service Command; and the China-Burma-India Training Command to take over training Chinese pilots from the Karachi American Air Base Command. At the same time, Stratemeyer issued directives inactivating the X and XIV Air Service Commands and the Karachi American Air Base Command, and absorbing the India Air Task Force into Headquarters, Tenth Air Force, as soon as the Tenth could move from New Delhi to Calcutta. The China-Burma-India Air Service Command had three area commands: in China, the 5308th Air Service Area Command (Provisional) at Kunming; in Assam, the 5309th Air Service Command (Provisional) at Chabua; and the 5317th Air Depot Headquarters (Provisional) at Calcutta. Howard Davidson arrived in New Delhi that same day and immediately began meetings with Stratemeyer and Bissell, formally taking over command of the Tenth Air Force on 19 August 1943. Stratemeyer began setting up a small staff of his own for his headquarters, AAF India-Burma sector, appointing Col. Charles B. Stone III as his chief of staff.[52] Stratemeyer's command (AAF India-Burma sector) comprised the following units: Tenth Air Force (India Air Task Force and Assam American Air Base Command), China-Burma-India Air Service Command, China-Burma-India Air Forces Training Unit, 10th Weather Squadron, 10th Army Airways Communications Squadron, and 22nd Statistical Control Unit.[53]

On relinquishing command of the Tenth Air Force, Bissell issued the following farewell to all his units:

1. Since August 18, 1942, it has been my privilege and honor to command the Tenth Air Force. During this year the Tenth Air Force has developed from a skeleton organization with three airplanes operating against the Japanese from India into the most powerful and effective aviation striking force in this Theater. It has virtually denied the port of Rangoon to the enemy. It has effectively attacked Japanese communications and installations from Tientsin, China, to Bangkok, Siam, and throughout the length and breadth of Burma from Sumprabum to Rangoon. It has successfully defended the vital air route to China. It has repeatedly attacked and sunk enemy shipping in the Gulf of Martaban between the Andamans and Malaya. The Tenth Air Force has accomplished its mission with the smallest combat losses of any American Air Force. It has carried out the longest bombing raids on record with both its medium and heavy bombers. It has won the respect and commendation of our Allies, the Theater commander, the Army Air Forces, and the War Department.

2. In relinquishing this command for another assignment, I desire to thank you, the officers, enlisted men, and civilian employees of the Tenth Air Force for your loyalty, courage, teamwork, determination, and devotion to duty. It is these factors which have made possible our success. The difficulties and handicaps of weather, language, customs, communications, and material shortages which you have overcome makes your accomplishment more outstanding and demonstrates again the initiative and resourcefulness which everywhere characterizes the American Air Force.

3. Good luck, Tenth Air Force! To all personnel my best wishes during the war and in the years ahead.[54]

It is unfortunate that Clayton Bissell is better known for his harsh treatment of the AVG during the attempt to recruit its members into the Army Air Force and for his acrimonious relationship with Claire Chennault than for his achievements as commander of the Tenth Air Force. Bissell apparently did not have the interpersonal skills that might have allowed him to come to some accommodation with Chennault's often-defiant tone toward his superiors to work constructively with him.[55] He had a similarly tempestuous relationship with Brig. Gen. Edward Alexander—commanding the India-China Wing—over the issue of control of the air ferry operation, oftentimes appearing reluctant to relinquish control over an operation he apparently believed belonged under the Tenth Air Force.[56] But he did prove to be a capable administrator and an excellent staff officer, as Arnold judged him to be.[57] He worked tirelessly to obtain the aircraft, men, and supplies he believed the Tenth Air Force needed to fulfill its mission, and, despite repeated rejections and postponements from Washington, never cast blame. Bissell clearly lacked Chennault's charisma and his natural leadership, which engendered strong loyalty on the part of many of his subordinates, but Bissell's attention to the details of administration and his understanding of the need to build a strong logistical organization to support the combat units was perhaps what the Tenth Air Force needed during its formative first year. Howard Davidson took over an Air Force with a sound foundation.

Operations during the Monsoon

In Burma, the southwest monsoon begins in May and lasts until October, bringing with it heavy clouds and rain that cover much of the country for most of the time. The weather is worst along the coast, with rainfall in the Arakan and the Irrawaddy delta averaging 3–5 inches a day. The effect of the monsoon is less in the dryer central plain. Mandalay will average 19 inches of rain between June

Clayton Bissell awards a Distinguished Flying Cross to Caleb Haynes. Regrettably, Bissell is better known for his acrimonious relationship with Claire Chennault than for the work he did building up the Tenth Air Force. 3A-34178, RG342FH, NARA

The 7th Bomb Group's B-24D "Destiny's Tot" flying over jungle-covered hills. The monsoon weather severely restricted operations to southern Burma. Crews often found that after flying on instruments for several hours, when they reached the Rangoon area it would be covered with cloud. *3A-33754, RG342FH, NARA*

and September, compared to more than 82 inches of rain in Rangoon during the same period. The mountains of northern Burma and Assam have less rainfall than the coastal areas, but often fog and heavy cloud cover make flying during the monsoon difficult and often dangerous, since the clouds can range from 300 feet up to 30,000 feet over the mountains.[58] The monsoon weather limited air operations over most of the country from its onset in May until the end of September or early October. Neither side had an adequate number of all-weather airfields available near the battlefront, so both the Royal Air Force and the Japanese Army Air Force withdrew some of their units to rest and refit in preparation for the following dry season, leaving other units in place to conduct operations at a much-reduced rate.

The India Air Task Force decided to continue operations when possible. Writing to Bissell shortly after taking command of the IATF, Col. Combs indicated his intention to hit the Japanese as often as possible. "My plan of operation," he wrote Bissell,

is to continue frequent sweeps south of Rangoon, except when local depressions make flying too hazardous, as when there is a low in the Bay of Bengal. . . . Also I shall send the heavies against the usual targets in central Burma where possible and especially when the weather down in the south is too difficult. In the medium group a technique of frontal penetration is being perfected which will enable a majority of efforts to succeed in crossing the Chin Hills into the dry zone of central Burma. . . . During the next few months we shall undoubtedly accomplish less, but there will be no slackening of our efforts.[59]

The priority targets continued to be Japanese shipping and the Burmese railroad system. In expectation that the Japanese would take advantage of the monsoon weather to get ships into Rangoon undetected, the 7th Bomb Group took on the task of flying shipping sweeps as often as possible over the Gulf of Martaban, looking for Japanese shipping. The battle against the railroad system continued whenever possible. During the dry season the Japanese could utilize motor vehicles and the road network to overcome, to a certain extent, damage to the railroad system, but during the monsoon season, heavy rains made road travel difficult, forcing supplies back to the railroad lines.[60] The medium bombers were fortunate in that the weather was less of a problem over central Burma, enabling the mediums to fly more missions than the heavy bombers, who often had to abort a mission due to poor weather. This enabled the 341st Group's squadrons to continue their bombing of railroad yards,

THE TENTH AIR FORCE IN WORLD WAR II

engine sheds, and railroad bridges, adding more targets to their regular repertoire to spread the destruction.

The sea sweeps that began in June and continued into September were hard work, often involving hours of instrument flying through clouds and rain and turbulence, only to have to abandon the mission when the target couldn't be located. Lt. Charles Duncan, a copilot in the 9th Bomb Squadron, later recalled what these missions were like:

Formation flying had been hard physical work, with no power assists on the B-24. Instrument flying began to replace formation flying as the sweat job. Stewart [his pilot] and I would take ten or fifteen minute turns at it in the most turbulent air. This sometimes went on for over four hours without a break. The automatic pilot was of no use for either formation or instrument flying in rough air. At times we would be forced to fly only a few hundred feet off the water of the Bay of Bengal for several hours.[61]

The crews now received a primary target, a secondary one, and often a third possible target should the weather prove difficult over the first two.

June saw the 7th Bomb Group's squadrons flying missions on only 11 days due to the onset of the monsoon. The seven shipping sweeps flown that month brought no results. The squadrons flew more missions to other targets during July but returned to sea sweeps at the end of the month. The first success came when Maj. Wesley Werner, commanding the 493rd Bomb Squadron, went out with two other B-24s to search the area around Tavoy—on the Gulf of Martaban, where Allied intelligence had reported the presence of Japanese shipping—as part of a larger sea sweep mission, the 9th Bomb Squadron also sending nine airplanes to the Gulf of Martaban while the 436th Bomb Squadron sent nine to search for shipping at Port Blair in the Andaman Islands. Despite the poor weather, Werner and his flight found a Japanese freighter off the coast with a naval escort. The two wingmen went in first under a 4,000-foot ceiling, dropping their bombs and getting several near misses and one or two direct hits on the freighter. With the ship heading toward the coast with smoke pouring out, Werner came in at low altitude, his bombs hitting amidships. The *Tamiskima Maru*, of 1,931 tons, sank a few minutes later. Werner and his flight flew back to their base at 700 feet through heavy rain and turbulence, completing a mission of 12 hours and 40 minutes.[62] After several more sea sweeps during August that found but failed to sink several Japanese ships, the 493rd Squadron again had success when two pilots on a sweep to the Nicobar Islands, south of the Andamans, found a large Japanese freighter on 23 August 1943. The B-24s bombed successfully from 3,000 feet, getting at least three direct hits and setting the 4,468-ton *Heito Maru* on fire, with the ship sinking a few hours later. The bombers ran into Japanese fighters on only a few of the sea sweeps. No doubt the Japanese had as hard a time finding the bombers in the monsoon weather as the bombers did trying to find Japanese ships. On July 27, nine B-24s from the 492nd Bomb Squadron went out on a sea sweep, but the weather was so bad the formation had to split up. Capt. Disher and 1st Lt. Bonsteel ran into three Ki-43s who shot up Bonsteel's ship, with Bonsteel's top turret gunner claiming one Oscar destroyed and one damaged. Four 436th Squadron B-24s attacked a small freighter off Pagoda Point, at the southwest tip of the Irrawaddy delta, on August 13, when they ran into a single Ki-43 shortly after their attack. The Ki-43 dove in from the 1 o'clock position, running into fire from all the top turrets and the nose guns in the four B-24s. The Oscar never recovered from the dive, Lt.

Bombs exploding on the 4,468-ton Japanese freighter *Heito Maru*. Two 493rd Bomb Squadron B-24s found the freighter during a sea sweep to Car Nicobar on 23 August 1943. *3A-37550, RG342FH, NARA*

Koichi Mori of the *64th Hikōsentai* apparently having been killed instantly at the start of his attack.[63]

On September 4, six B-24s from the 492nd Squadron went after a freighter moored in the Rangoon River, but their bombs hit the warehouses nearby, missing the ship. The next day a 9th Photographic Squadron (the squadron's designation after February 1943) F-4 on a photoreconnaissance mission over Rangoon returned with photos of four large freighters in the Rangoon River: two estimated to be 425 feet in length and two at 325 feet.[64] A target this lucrative called for a major effort. On September 6, the 7th Bomb Group sent out all four of its squadrons. Flying as one formation, the 25 bombers who reached Rangoon took separate targets, trying to get hits on all four ships. The crews reported 13 direct hits on the two larger vessels and one of the smaller ones, with many near misses, though it is possible the squadrons attacked the same ships. The attack sank the *Milan Maru*, of 5,467 tons, and the *Annan Maru*, of 2,941 tons. Intense and accurate antiaircraft fire damaged six of the B-24s. At the end of the bombing run the fighters came in—a group of four to five Ki-45 Toryu twin-engine fighters from the *21st Hikōsentai* attacking with three to six Ki-43 Hayabusas from the *64th Hikōsentai*. The fighters made repeated passes at the B-24 formation, making 25 to 30 attacks over 45 minutes. Most of the attacks were from the 10 o'clock and 2 o'clock positions, with the fighters diving down under their targets to come in on the formation below. Crews in the 492nd Squadron reported that the attacks "were pressed relentlessly

The Kawasaki Type 2 two-seat fighter (Ki-45 Nick) was relatively well armed for a Japanese army fighter of the middle war years, with two 12.7 mm machine guns and either a 20 or 37 mm cannon in the nose. Despite having heavier armament than the Type 1 fighter, the Ki-45 did not do as well against B-24s over southern Burma. *Author's collection*

from all quarters above and below and all around the clock. All told around 30 passes were made, some being pressed to within 50 yards."[65] The bombers claimed two of the Ki-45s and one Ki-43 destroyed, one Ki-43 probably destroyed, and one Ki-45 damaged. Remarkably, only four of the B-24s received any damage during this lengthy assault, despite repeated firing passes that many of the crews thought was the most intense opposition they had yet faced over Rangoon.[66]

The sea sweep missions continued during the rest of September without result. Even though the weather was starting to improve, the 7th Group's squadrons had to abandon six sea sweep missions because of poor weather, completing 13 successfully. It is possible that some ships slipped into Rangoon under cover of poor weather over the Gulf of Martaban. The importance of Japanese shipping meant that Rangoon remained a high-priority target for the 9th Photographic Squadron. During June the squadron received several new F-5 Lightnings (equivalent to the Lockheed P-38G model) to replace its worn-out F-4s. Missions to the Rangoon area were frustrating, as pilots would fly long missions (some as long as nine hours) only to find their target areas covered in cloud. Going underneath the cloud cover carried the risk of running into antiaircraft fire or, worse, Japanese fighters, but the reconnaissance pilots often took the risk to get photographs of their targets. For the Japanese fighters, intercepting reconnaissance aircraft over Rangoon also became a priority. With the 9th Photographic Squadron sending out an F-4 or F-5 to Rangoon every three to four days, the Japanese had several opportunities. The reconnaissance pilots avoided interceptions during July and August but lost two airplanes to Japanese fighters in the first half of September. On September 10, Capt. Don Webster—an experienced pilot who had set records for flying exceptionally long missions—went out to cover Rangoon following a B-24 raid and had the misfortune to come out of the cloud cover right into a group of Japanese fighters. Sgt. Maj. Shigeru Takura from the *64th Hikōsentai* quickly shot Webster down. Three days later Capt. Yasuhiko Kuroe—now the *64th Hikōsentai*'s executive officer—intercepted 1st Lt. Frank Tilcock over Rangoon and, after a 30-minute pursuit, shot Tilcock down. It is possible that Takura and Kuroe were flying the Type 2 single-engine fighter Shoki (Ki-44 Tojo), the *64th Hikōsentai* having received four Ki-44s during the monsoon season.[67]

By far the greater portion of the bombs the B-24s and B-25s dropped during the monsoon went against the railroad system. As tables 3 and 4 indicate, the weather affected the B-24 squadrons—whose targets were mostly in southern Burma—more than the B-25 squadrons flying to targets in the drier central plains. On average the B-24s completed a little over 70 percent of their missions, while the B-25 squadrons completed over 90 percent. With the monsoon

The 9th Photo Reconnaissance Squadron received a few new Lockheed F-5 reconnaissance airplanes during the monsoon season but continued flying older F-4s on missions to southern Burma, where they also encountered problems with the monsoon weather. *3A-35801, RG342FH, NARA*

Monthly Bomb Tonnage May-September 1943

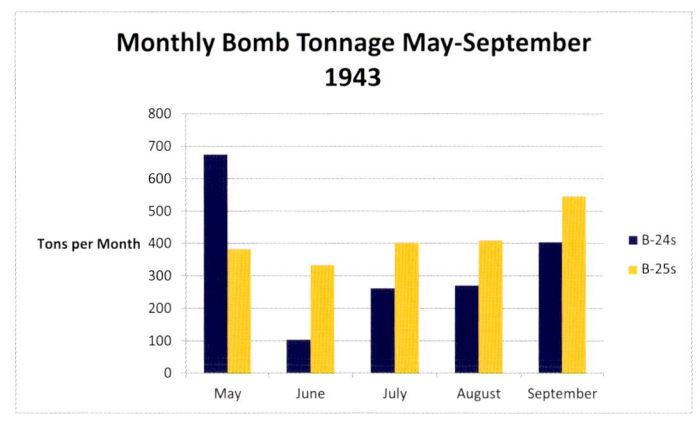

Table 3 Source: India Air Task Force Operations November 1942-September 1943

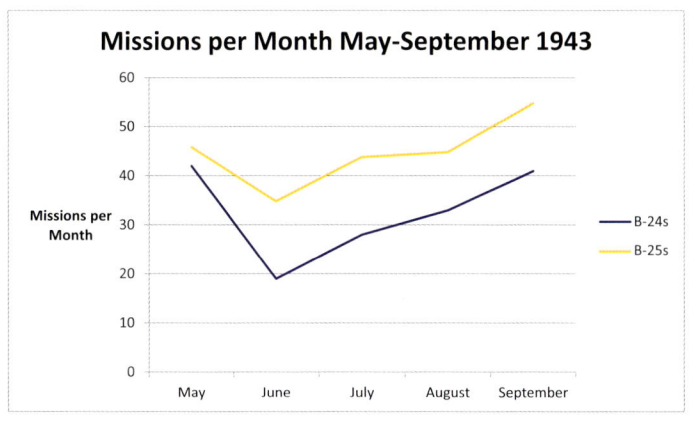

Missions per Month May-September 1943

Table 4 Source: India Air Task Force Operations November 1942-September 1943

in full force during June, the weather did affect both the heavy and the medium bombers to a greater extent than in the following months, with the heavies flying missions on only 11 days during the month, while the mediums flew missions on 19 days. While the weather didn't begin to improve until September, both the 7th and the 341st Bomb Groups found they could send out more aircraft on more missions on the days when the weather was acceptable. During June the B-24 squadrons flew 70 sorties, completing 19 missions on 11 days, while the B-25s flew 275 sorties over 35 missions on 19 flying days. In September the B-24s flew 223 sorties, completing 41 missions on 18 flying days, while the B-25s were even more productive, flying 482 sorties and completing 55 missions on 26 flying days. The greater number of missions flown during September enabled the IATF to nearly match the number of bombs dropped in May, with the B-24s and B-25s dropping 955 tons of bombs on targets in Burma.[68]

For the medium bombers of the 341st Bomb Group, missions during the monsoon were more of the same, just with bad weather thrown in. Taking off from their bases in India, the squadrons had to fly through cloud and rain until they could break out into the central plain, though even in this drier area they often found some of their targets covered in cloud, forcing diversions to secondary targets. To be closer to their area of operations, the 490th Bomb Squadron moved to a new base at Kurmatola, near Dacca in eastern Bengal. The B-25s went back to familiar targets, hitting Mandalay, Thazi, Sagaing, and the Ywataung railroad junction, and that old favorite, the Myitnge Bridge. During June the 491st Squadron flew two missions against the bridge—which the Japanese had repaired since previous attacks—severely damaging the northern and southern approaches to the bridge and putting the bridge out of action again. The 490th and 491st Squadrons flew repeated missions to bomb the Myitnge Bridge during July and August. On July 3 the two squadrons went to the bridge on the same day, getting hits on the approaches,

The medium bombers of the 341st Bomb Group fared better during the monsoon than their 7th Bomb Group colleagues flying down to southern Burma. The monsoon weather had less of an impact in the drier central plains of Burma, though B-25s had their share of missions aborted due to weather. *Author's collection*

TRIDENT, COMMAND CHANGES, AND OPERATIONS DURING THE MONSOON

The 22nd and 490th Bomb Squadrons bombed the Mu River Bridge on 29 July 1943, getting several direct hits that knocked out two spans of the bridge—not an everyday occurrence. *10th Air Force Miscellaneous Photos, 830.08, AFHRA*

with the 490th knocking out one span of the bridge off its pier to rest in the river below. The 491st Squadron went back to Myitnge Bridge on July 9 as part of a multitarget attack, bombing the Myitnge, Mu River, and Sagaing Bridges, while the 490th attacked the Mu River Bridge the same day. The two squadrons went back to the Myitnge Bridge on July 20, with eight aircraft from the 491st Squadron getting hits on one span and the approaches, while three bombers from the 490th got two direct hits and several near misses before the flight went on to bomb the Mu River Bridge. On this occasion, five B-24s from the 493rd Bomb Squadron joined the mediums attacking the Myitnge Bridge, the bombs bracketing the bridge. Four of the B-25s and one of the B-24s received hits from the antiaircraft guns surrounding the bridge. The 490th made one more attack on the bridge in late August before the squadrons shifted to other targets. The mediums had equal success with the Mu River Bridge, with the 22nd and 490th Squadrons flying a joint mission on July 29, knocking out two spans of the bridge.[69]

Railroad yards received attention both from the medium and the heavy bombers, with the 7th Bomb Group flying 14 missions to bomb railroad installations in central Burma, hitting the rail yards at Mandalay and Ywataung three times each. The B-24s made a major effort to knock out the railroad facilities at Thanbyuzayat, on the southern coast of Burma, where the Japanese had established a base for constructing a railroad line to the south to link up with the Burma-Thailand railroad then under construction to link Bangkok with Moulmein. The 493rd Bomb Squadron made the first attack on Thanbyuzayat on June 12 with six aircraft, but a three-squadron mission three days later saw only five B-24s battling through the bad weather to reach the target. The squadrons tried again at the end of the month, with the 9th Squadron sending out six aircraft and the 436th Squadron four (only one of which reached the target due to weather) on June 26. Despite poor visibility over the target, the bombers got most of their bombs into the railroad yard, blowing a train on the tracks literally up into the air. The 492nd and 493rd Squadrons went back the next day, the 493rd hitting the warehouses on the west side of the railroad yards while the 492nd got all its bombs onto the yard area, causing extensive damage. The next attacks took place on July 1 and July 2, when the 7th Group's primary target, the Syriam Oil Refinery at Rangoon, proved to be covered with cloud. On the July 1 mission the 9th and 492nd Squadrons headed to Thanbyuzayat—the secondary target—where they bombed successfully, with the 492nd fighting off a lone Ki-45 fighter. The next day the 436th Squadron made it to the primary target but lost one airplane—that of Capt. Vic Winter—on the return flight for unknown

During June and July 1943 the 7th Bomb Group flew several missions to bomb the railroad yards at Thanbyuzayat. The bombers got a good strike on June 26, when seven aircraft battled bad weather to reach the target deep in southern Burma. *10th Air Force Miscellaneous Photos, 830.08, AFHRA*

reasons. The 493rd found the refinery covered in cloud, so they went on to Thanbyuzayat, inflicting heavy damage to the railroad yards. On this occasion another single Ki-45 attacked the formation, the determined Nick pilot making six passes during a 30-minute attack. The Nick pressed home the attack, and the gunners noticed that the Nick's rear gunner would fire on the B-24s as the fighter flew past the B-24s. While admiring the Japanese pilot's daring and skillful flying, the same could not be said for his aim, since only one B-24 received any damage. On several occasions the B-24s followed up the mediums, attacking the same target a few days later to sustain the damage, and on August 27, the 436th and 492nd Squadrons joined the 22nd, 490th, and 491st Squadrons in an attack on the railroad yards at Thazi, the five squadrons placing 55 tons of bombs on the railroad yards and doing considerable damage. The next day the 9th, 492nd, and 493rd Squadrons joined the three medium squadrons on an attack on the town of Akyab.[70]

During July and August the medium-bomber squadrons began flying more joint missions, with two and sometimes all three squadrons bombing the same target. The objective was to increase the level of damage at key rail targets and to destroy supplies kept in warehouses near the railroad yards. On August 17 the 341st flew one of its first three squadron missions when the three squadrons

Medium-bomber squadrons began adding machine guns to the noses of their B-25s to convert them into strafers to go after targets of opportunity during sweeps along the railroad lines in central Burma. This 490th Bomb Squadron B-25C or D had six .50-caliber machine guns mounted in the nose. *3A-01075, RG342FH, NARA*

A photograph of the inside of the nose of the B-25, showing the welded-tube mounting for the .50-caliber machine guns. These locally made adaptations remained in use until the arrival of the dedicated B-25H and B-25J strafer models in 1944, which mounted pairs of .50-caliber machine guns on the sides of the fuselage and combinations of four or eight guns in the nose. *3A-01074, RG342FH, NARA*

flight of nine aircraft taking turns to bomb yards, sidings, buildings, rolling stock, or tracks, each flight dropping only a few bombs at a time to spread out the damage along the route. By this time the squadrons had begun adding fixed .50-caliber machine guns in the nose of their B-25s so that the pilots would occasionally go down and strafe a target after bombing. The weather sometimes served to send the B-25s to different targets. If cloud obscured the primary, the bombers would go on to another, often-smaller target, compounding the problems for the Japanese repair crews. Sometimes these diversions had unexpectedly good results. Rolling stock was always an important target, and a mission on August 22 saw considerable destruction when weather forced the 22nd and 490th Bomb Squadrons to divert from their primary target, the ferry facility and railroad yard at Sagaing. Only one flight from the 490th Squadron bombed the railroad yards at Sagaing together with one B-25 from the 22nd Squadron, destroying 60 to 70 at the yards at Sagaing, while four planes from the 22nd that couldn't bomb at Sagaing flew to the railroad yards at Ywataung, where they found more than 250 freight cars in the yard. Their bombs destroyed an additional 50 to 60 cars—a profitable day.[71]

A new target for the mediums was river shipping on the Irrawaddy River. The RAF's Beaufighter squadrons made regular sweeps along the Irrawaddy, strafing river traffic, but to keep more pressure on the Japanese the 341st Group began sending out squadrons to bomb river ships and ferries and the wharf facilities at towns along the river. These missions appear to have become something of a specialty for the 490th Bomb Squadron. Between June and September the 490th undertook twelve missions to bomb shipping and the wharf areas, hitting Mandalay, which was an important inland port on the Irrawaddy River in addition to a rail center, on seven missions. The 22nd Bomb Squadron carried out seven missions against shipping, concentrating on the port of Katha, farther up the Irrawaddy River to the north. Most of the missions involved bombing rivercraft tied up near the wharves, with the benefit that bombs that

went to bomb the railroad yards and buildings in the town of Meiktila, with 27 aircraft bombing in succession over the course of 25 minutes. The bombs hit around the railroad station area, damaging tracks and the buildings alongside. After the missions to Thazi and Akyab, the 341st Group flew four multiple-squadron missions in July, seven in August, and five in September, almost all to railroad targets. A new tactic was the railroad sweep, where a squadron would cover several targets along a section of the rail line, with a

Medium bombers from one of the 341st Bomb Group's squadrons bombing rivercraft in the Irrawaddy River. The Irrawaddy River was navigable for a considerable part of its length, allowing the transport of supplies into central Burma. Disrupting shipping along this important river route became part of the battle against Japanese lines of communication in Burma. *3A-37624, RG342FH, NARA*

Capt. McCarten and his crew after their return to the 490th Bomb Squadron's base at Kurmitola after bailing out of their damaged B-25. They were fortunate to land in Allied territory near friendly local villages. Many other Allied air crews were not so fortunate. *10th Air Force Miscellaneous Photos, 830.08, AFHRA*

missed the ships often hit the wharf and warehouse facilities alongside. During July the squadrons destroyed five large river steamers, probably destroyed six, and damaged a further twelve. The destruction continued during August. While many of these attacks were from medium altitude, on August 12 the 490th and 491st Squadrons went out on a low-level shipping sweep along the Irrawaddy River. The 491st sent out six aircraft to cover the river from Myingyan, southwest of Mandalay, all the way to Katha in the north. The B-25s destroyed five 50-foot-long barges and three 75-foot-long river steamers and hit three locomotives and more than 20 freight cars. Automatic-weapons fire damaged one of the B-25s as it flew low along the river. One airplane from a flight of four from the 22nd Squadron that could not bomb its primary target went after shipping on its own, sinking a 200-foot-long river steamer with two 1,000-pound bombs.[72]

The 490th Bomb Squadron also had a successful mission but nearly lost its commanding officer, Capt. McCarten. That morning McCarten led two other B-25s on a river sweep of the Irrawaddy southwest of Mandalay. The flight approached their target area at 10,000 feet, letting down to 500 feet to sweep the river, but because of cloud cover McCarten decided to split up the formation to make individual sweeps. One bomber sank a large riverboat and damaged a second on its sweep, while another attacked a railroad bridge. McCarten found a riverboat and bombed from low altitude but couldn't see the result. As he flew past, machine gun fire damaged his airplane. Going on, McCarten saw another riverboat near Monywa and went into attack, running into heavy medium- and light-antiaircraft fire on his bomb run. Four 40 mm cannon shells hit the B-25: one in the left outboard fuel tank, a second in the left engine accessory section, the third in the left main fuel tank, and the fourth in the bombardier's compartment. At the same time, 12 more shells—probably from an Army Type 93 13.2 mm antiaircraft machine gun—hit the bomber, with two hitting the pilot's instrument panel, one hitting the right main fuel tank, and seven or eight hitting the left horizontal and vertical stabilizers. By great good fortune, none of these hits were fatal and McCarten immediately undertook evasive action, dropping his last bombs on another riverboat a few miles beyond. He then headed for Palel, an RAF base near Imphal, but bad weather made him decide to chance flying back to the 490th's base at Kurmatola. The crew could see oil leaking from the left engine, and fuel leaking from the left and right wing tanks. McCarten had only the manifold pressure gauge, the altimeter, and the air speed indicator working on the damaged instrument panel. About an hour after being hit, while flying at 15,500 feet, the engines ran out of fuel. McCarten could see a large clearing ahead of him, so he glided the B-25 toward it, ordering the crew to bail out when he reached 4,000 feet. Luck was with the crew as they bailed out over Allied territory, coming down near some friendly villagers who soon put them in touch with the local Indian police. The police arranged for a boat to carry the crew down a nearby river the next day, the crew arriving at Chittagong late in the afternoon of August 16. The following morning a plane flew them back to Kurmatola.[73]

The 341st Bomb Group's losses during the monsoon were remarkably light. While the B-25s regularly returned with minor damage from antiaircraft fire, the group lost only four B-25s during these months. The monsoon weather helped, since the *5th Hikōshidan* had withdrawn most of its fighter units from Burma. The *50th Hikōsentai* pulled back to Singapore and Bandoeng in Java, while the *64th Hikōsentai* sent its *2nd Chutai* to Palembang in Sumatra and its *3rd Chutai* to Sungei Patani in Malaya, leaving only the *1st Chutai* at Mingaladon to defend Rangoon.[74] Thus there were far fewer fighters available to attempt interceptions over central Burma. The B-25s saw enemy fighters on six occasions, but the few attempted interceptions were unsuccessful. By one of those strange quirks of fate, while the 491st Squadron had no losses and the 490th had only one loss with the crew returning, the other three losses for the 341st Group were all from the 22nd Bomb Squadron. 2nd Lt. Dunham and his crew failed to return from a sweep over the ocean that was aborted due to bad weather, while 1st Lt. McCook and his crew were lost on a mission over Meiktila. The squadron's third loss occurred on September 10, when 1st Lt. Greenstein failed, for unknown reasons, to return from a mission to bomb shipping near Katha.[75]

The 9th Photographic Squadron provided support to the medium bombers with regular photoreconnaissance missions over central Burma whenever weather permitted. The coverage kept track of rail and shipping activity and provided vital intelligence for damage assessment. The squadron's F-4 and newer F-5 airplanes flew most of these missions, but the demand for photographic coverage was always greater than the available aircraft could provide. To supplement the Lightnings, the squadron obtained some B-25s that the 341st Bomb Group had declared war weary but were still flyable. The first of these aircraft arrived at the end of May, after the Third Air Depot had completed modifications, removing most of the guns and adding extra fuel tanks and provision for cameras. The crew consisted of a pilot, copilot, navigator, and two photographers. The squadron had 14 enlisted men trained as photographers and flight engineers to have more crews available as more pilots checked out on the B-25. The B-25s went only to central Burma, where there was less risk of fighter interception, though they often had to contend with Japanese antiaircraft fire.[76]

The monsoon weather had a severe impact on operations of the 24th and 26th Fighter Squadrons in Assam. From June 11 to July 8 the 25th and 26th Fighter Squadrons flew no offensive missions into Burma, conducting mostly local patrols, weather reconnaissance, and a few escort missions because of the adverse weather. July saw some improvement, then the weather closed in again from July 29 to August 19, and again from August 22 to September 14, with the two squadrons flying only 12 offensive missions during August. September was little better, with weather limiting operations during the beginning and the end of the month. The weather and the withdrawal of many Japanese units to other parts of Southeast Asia did mean that there was little risk of a Japanese attack on the Assam airfields. The ground situation was more stable, with the Japanese having withdrawn their units from beyond Sumprabum and on the trails to Shingbywiyang, and the heavy rains making the jungle tracks practically impassable. When the weather in early July allowed more local patrols and offensive missions to resume, the two squadrons had 62 P-40s available for operations. They returned to what they had been doing since the beginning of the year: protecting the air bases in Assam with regular local patrols, escorting C-47s on supply-dropping missions to Allied outposts, and continuously hammering Japanese positions and installations in northern Burma. When the weather cleared sufficiently, flights of three to six P-40s would go out to bomb and strafe Japanese-held towns and villages with 500-pound bombs and fragmentation bombs, usually flying with two P-40s as top cover. Often a photo P-40 or a B-25 with photographers would accompany the mission to record the damage. On a mission on July 29, Col. Egan, 51st Fighter Group CO, went out to bomb and strafe the town of Manywet with eight other pilots, dropping nine 500-pound bombs and 54 fragmentation bombs on the town. After dropping their bombs the fighters went back to strafe the town, expending 33,000 rounds of .50-caliber ammunition, which must have been something of a record. The pounding of the Japanese garrison at Sumprabum continued, with six attacks in July dropping 16,000 pounds of bombs on the town, blowing up many buildings. In response to requests from the Kachin Levies and from the British IV Corps at Imphal, the squadrons carried out bombing and strafing missions against specific areas the Kachins and British army intelligence had identified as locations of Japanese units, though often this meant simply attacking areas of jungle. The P-40s rarely encountered much antiaircraft fire, and when they did it was

Refueling and rearming a 51st Fighter Group P-40 on one of the airfields in Assam during August 1943. Bad weather over the mountain ranges between Assam and northern Burma during the monsoon restricted fighter operations.
3A-35871, RG342FH, NARA

THE TENTH AIR FORCE IN WORLD WAR II

The 26th Fighter Squadron bombed the railroad bridge at Loilaw, south of Mogaung, on 11 July 1943 with 1,000-pound bombs, getting several direct hits. The attack knocked the central span of the bridge out of line. *3A-37611, RG342FH, NARA*

mostly from small-arms fire, which would occasionally do slight damage to the aircraft.[77]

During a period of somewhat better weather in July, the 25th and 26th Squadrons went back to bombing road and rail bridges, concentrating on the road linking Sumprabum with Myitkyina and the rail line from Katha to Myitkyina—all within range of a P-40 carrying a 1,000-pound bomb. The squadrons had particular success against the road bridge at Nsopzup—on the road from Myitkyina to Sumprabum—and the rail bridges at Namti and Loilaw, 4 miles south of Mogaung. The 26th Squadron took out the 360-foot-long rail bridge at Loilaw on July 11 with five 1,000-pound bombs, getting direct hits on the south span and knocking the north end of the center span into the river, and destroying 200 feet of railroad track south of the bridge. The nearby Namti bridge took three missions to knock out. The first mission—on July 20 with 1,000-pound bombs—did some damage, but a return mission the next day failed to hit the bridge. The pilots noticed that the Japanese had already repaired a section of track damaged the day before. Finally, on July 24, the 26th Squadron sent out six P-40s with 1,000-pound bombs, getting two direct hits that moved two spans of the bridge off their abutments while near misses did further damage, making the bridge unserviceable. The 25th Squadron was the first to go after the road bridge at Nsopzup, sending out four P-40s with 500-pound bombs but getting only near misses. The 26th Fighter Squadron tried on July 21 with four P-40s carrying 1,000-pound bombs, but again the bridge escaped damage. The 25th Squadron went back to the bridge on July 22, and on this mission four P-40s got two direct hits on the center span with 500-pound bombs and one direct hit on the south span, destroying the bridge. The 25th Squadron damaged another road bridge that day and a third the day after. By early September the Japanese had still not repaired these bridges. Kachin patrols around Sumprabum during August determined that due to the problem of supplying the Japanese garrison in the town with the road bridges knocked out, the Japanese had withdrawn one of the two companies in the town back to Myitkyina.[78]

During September the 51st Fighter Group began its planned transfer to the Fourteenth Air Force. The 51st Group was officially relieved from the Tenth Air Force on 12 September 1943.[79] The 25th Fighter Squadron left for Yunnan-yi on September 14, while the 26th Fighter Squadron remained at Dinjan to help the newly arrived 80th Fighter Group take over responsibility for the defense of the Assam air bases from the 51st Group. The 80th Group had arrived in Karachi at the end of June. As new P-40Ns arrived during July, the group's squadrons (88th, 89th, and 90th Fighter Squadrons) resumed training after several weeks at sea, with the pilots getting around 18 hours of flying time, including practice bombing. At this time, Col. Ivan McElroy replaced Maj. Albert Evans as group commander. McElroy chose the 89th Fighter Squadron as the first to move to Assam, though the squadron spent several weeks at a base west of Calcutta for more training flights. To provide the 80th Group with some experienced pilots, American Air Base Command Number One (as the Assam American Air Base Command had been renamed on 26 August 1943) arranged to transfer some of the 51st Group's pilots to the 80th Group in exchange for some of the newly arrived 80th Group pilots: 12 pilots going from the 89th Fighter Squadron to the 25th Fighter Squadron in exchange for 16 pilots from the 25th Squadron, with Capt. John Svenningsen taking over as commander of the 89th Squadron. The 89th arrived in Assam in early September, setting up at Nagaghuli, 30 miles west of Sookerating, also with flights at Sadiya, while the 90th Squadron followed a week later to Jorhat, the 88th Squadron reaching Assam in early October. The weather during September was poor for most of the month, with the 26th Fighter Squadron flying offensive missions on only six days during the middle of the month. The 89th and 90th Squadrons began flying local patrol missions and weather check flights, as well as flying top cover for the 26th Squadron on bombing missions. The 26th Squadron flew its last offensive mission as part of the Tenth Air Force on September 21, leaving for China in early October.[80]

As the monsoon neared its end, the men of the Tenth Air Force could look back over four months of intensive but, more often than not, frustrating effort. The weather had affected the fighter squadrons

Col. John Egan helps Brig. Gen. Haynes award the air medal to pilots of the 51st Fighter Group. Receiving the awards (*left to right*) are Maj. Wright, assistant group operations officer; Capt. Moore, 26th Fighter Squadron; and Capt. Simpson, 25th Fighter Squadron. *3A-34136, RG342FH, NARA*

the most, severely limiting operations for much of June, August, and September. The B-24s of the 7th Bomb Group had spent many hours battling through rain and cloud, only to find their primary targets in southern Burma covered over. While the sea sweeps had sunk and damaged several Japanese ships, overall these missions were not profitable in terms of benefit compared to the cost of wear and tear on airplanes and crews. Overall, an operational analysis of the 7th Bomb Group's missions suggested that during the monsoon it would be better to limit flying hours, given the results obtained, or even switch the bombers to carrying supplies instead of bombs.[81] Benefiting from the better weather over central Burma, the medium bombers of the 341st Bomb Group had fared the best, completing

A 491st Bomb Squadron B-25 releasing its bombload on a target in Burma, with clouds covering most of the area—not atypical in the monsoon season. A bomb can just be seen coming out of the bomb bay. Close inspection of the photo reveals that the squadron removed the remote control Bendix belly turret and put what appears to be a single machine gun in its place. *Author's collection*

THE TENTH AIR FORCE IN WORLD WAR II

more missions with more aircraft and dropping more bombs than their colleagues in the B-24s. But all the missions of the heavy and medium bombers, and even the fighters, contributed to the relentless pressure on the Japanese, which, even if diminished due to the weather, when added to the damage the RAF bombers and fighters inflicted made the lives of the Japanese in Burma that much more difficult. In the months ahead, the Tenth Air Force would fly even more missions, drop more bombs, and take heavier losses under a new command and a new commander as the Allies began their long-delayed advance into Burma.

CHAPTER 6

AIR COMMAND, SOUTHEAST ASIA: INTEGRATING THE ALLIED AIR FORCES

August–December 1943

The Quadrant Conference

The Trident Conference had concluded with an outline of the first stage of operations in Burma, but without a clear idea of what was to follow, nor how these operations would contribute to the ultimate defeat of Japan.[1] While the Tenth Air Force and the Royal Air Force struggled with the monsoon over Burma, American and British military planners worked on a more comprehensive plan for Japan's defeat. The planners were agreed that Japan's strategy was likely to be defensive, seeking to secure the areas in China, Southeast Asia, and the Pacific now under its control but responding to Allied attempts to pierce this barrier. There was further agreement that ultimately Japan might have to be invaded to bring about its defeat, but that an air offensive aimed at crippling Japan's war industries together with a campaign to cut Japan off from the resources of Southeast Asia and wear down its air, naval, and military forces would be necessary precursors to an invasion. The key question remained where the Allies should establish bases for the air offensive and an invasion. China remained high on the list of alternatives, seizing a base either through a march across the Pacific or through a land campaign on the China mainland, using Chinese divisions. The planners saw the need to capture either Luzon in the Philippines, Formosa, or Hainan Island—the latter possibly through a British campaign coming up from Singapore—as a preliminary step to establishing a presence on the Chinese mainland. But there remained the question of how the possible reconquest of Burma fit into this larger strategic plan, if at all.[2]

There was a recognition among both American and British planners that Chinese morale and the Chinese economy were deteriorating after six years of war, but while China's disintegration and withdrawal from the war would hurt the Allied cause and make establishing a base on the Chinese mainland difficult, to the British planning staff, China's possible collapse "did not appear to them quite so catastrophic as their American colleagues feared."[3] Since it was also generally accepted that improving the efficiency of the Chinese army would take years, the British believed that while opening the Burma Road would have a significant impact on Chinese morale, it would have little military benefit for some years to come. The British agreed with the idea of a limited offensive in northern Burma, as outlined at the Trident Conference, but, rather than going on to recapture all of Burma, recommended the capture of northern Sumatra and then Singapore as a more effective means of damaging Japan.[4] A British thrust northward from Singapore could open the South China Sea and meet up with an American attack coming across the Central Pacific. This seemed a far-worthier prize than the recapture of all or part of Burma. As Churchill put it, the alternative to capturing northern Sumatra was "Akyab and the right to toil through the swamps of Southern Burma."[5]

American and British military commanders meeting during the Quebec Conference in August 1943. Vice-Admiral Lord Louis Mountbatten, soon to be appointed Allied supreme commander in chief, Southeast Asia Command, stands on the left, facing American Army chief of staff Gen. George Marshall. *SC178136, RG111, NARA*

The difficulty for the American planners and Joint Chiefs of Staff was that the resources that would be necessary to capture northern Sumatra and then Singapore would not be available until the defeat of Germany, then projected for sometime in 1945.[6] This would mean no major offensive in Burma for at least two dry seasons (1943–44 and 1944–45) and further delays in opening a road to China—a delay the Americans could not accept. The American planners wanted to ultimately recapture all of Burma to reopen the route from Rangoon north to the Burma Road, since it would greatly simplify the logistical problems of shipping goods from Calcutta through Assam to a road from Ledo to China. A road from Ledo to China would be a first but not the final step toward assisting China through Burma. This divergence of views of China and objectives between the British and Americans remained central to the debate on the place of operations in Burma in the plan for the defeat of Japan, a debate that the Quadrant Conference would not resolve.

Churchill did see the need for the British to make some effort in Burma to accommodate American wishes, but the question was how best to do this. The British army high command in India was pessimistic. Gen. Sir Claude Auchinleck, who had replaced Gen. Wavell as commander in chief, India, on June 18—two months before the Quadrant Conference—had sent Churchill his appreciation of the requirements for executing the objectives set at Trident. Auchinleck believed that the line-of-communications system in Assam could not support an extensive ground campaign either by Stilwell's Chinese forces or the British IV Corps and the planned increased flow of supplies for the Hump operations—especially after recent damaging floods—nor did he think it possible to launch successful attacks on Akyab or Ramree Islands with the forces available. Two months later he urged a delay in all offensive operations for the coming dry season. This was not what Churchill wanted to hear. While equally skeptical of the value of attacking Akyab and Ramree, he wanted the British army to undertake some offensive. Auchinleck's appreciations, Churchill wrote to the Chiefs of Staff, "would rightly excite the deepest suspicions in the United States that we are only playing and dawdling with war in this theater."[7] He wanted "to be able to put across to the Americans, who were likely to criticize our lack of enterprise and drive, a bold project for the summer of 1944 on the lines of the Sumatra operation."[8]

There was an alternative "bold project" that appealed to Churchill that was based on Orde Wingate's plans for even larger long-range-penetration operations. Wingate's successful mission prompted Churchill to recall him to London and to travel with Churchill and the Chiefs of Staff to the Quadrant Conference in Washington. Onboard the *Queen Mary*, Wingate outlined a plan to form long-range-penetration groups to be introduced behind Japanese lines to disrupt Japanese communications and draw off Japanese troops prior to the advance of the British and Chinese main forces from Imphal, Ledo, and Yunnan to help open the road to China. Wingate's plans were what Churchill had been looking for: "positive proposals for attacking the enemy, proving our zeal in this theater of war, which by its failure and sluggishness is in a measure under reasonable reproach."[9] Wingate appeared to provide Churchill with what Chennault had provided for Roosevelt—"a savior whose bold and unorthodox ideas might bring about decisive results for an economical outlay of force in a theater whose difficulties had so far baffled the commanders on the spot and where national prestige was rapidly ebbing."[10] The Chiefs of Staff agreed to propose the maximum use of Wingate's long-range-penetration groups in the coming offensive in northern Burma.[11]

Roosevelt and the Joint Chiefs of Staff met with Churchill and the Chiefs of Staff in Quebec from 14 to 24 August 1943. The discussions covered strategy against Germany and Italy, as well as Japan. Regarding the Far East, the two sides presented their different points of view, but there was no agreement on long-term strategy. Marshall and the other American Chiefs of Staff continued to press for opening a road link to China and for the capture of Akyab and Ramree to serve as bases for operations against Rangoon a year later. The Americans continued to insist that ultimately all of Burma would need to be recaptured, since this was the likeliest route to China and the shortest route to Japan. The American side proposed that all of Burma be taken following the capture of northern Burma, with the campaign to begin in November 1944.[12] Churchill's proposed operations against northern Sumatra and Singapore would inevitably divert resources away from aiding China. The conference participants decided to simply postpone a decision on what would follow operations in northern Burma: the reconquest of all of Burma or the capture of Singapore. The Combined Chiefs of Staff ordered the planners to study several options for future operations, including the capture of northern Sumatra, a move into southern Burma in November 1944, the capture of Akyab and Ramree, and possible operations against Malaya and Singapore. All agreed that the capture of northern Burma would be the priority for the coming dry-season offensive to begin in February 1944. The other actions mirrored the decisions taken at the Trident Conference: to prepare for a possible amphibious operation in spring 1944, possibly to capture Akyab and Ramree, to prepare India as a base for future operations, and to build the air route and amount of supplies delivered to China to keep China in the war and increase air operations against Japan.[13] In support of this effort, the Combined Chiefs agreed to develop the communications links to Assam with greater urgency. All these decisions were subject to the availability of resources, with Europe always having the priority, especially for landing craft and naval forces that would be required for any amphibious operations in Burma or beyond. Operations in Burma would fall within the longer-term strategy for the war against Japan, a key part of which was the "continuing need for applying the maximum attrition to Japan's air force, naval forces, and shipping by all possible means in all possible areas."[14]

At the Quadrant Conference, the Combined Chiefs of Staff approved Wingate's proposal for a greatly expanded long-range-penetration operation in support of the main forces' advance into northern Burma.[15] This was to be a division-size force of 26,000 men known as Special Force (and later designated 3rd Indian Division), to be formed into eight independent groups operating behind Japanese lines to disrupt Japanese communications and to draw off Japanese forces as the main forces began their movement into northern Burma. Wingate's groups were intended to operate for 12 weeks and then be withdrawn (this time limit would become a source of controversy later on). Because the columns would have to be supplied entirely by air, Wingate requested that transports be assigned to his force, as well as bombers to provide close air support. At Quadrant, Wingate met with Marshall and Hap Arnold, both of whom were intrigued with Wingate's ideas. Marshall proposed contributing American troops to form one of Wingate's groups, a proposal that resulted in the formation of the 5307th Composite Unit (Provisional), better known as Merrill's Marauders. Wingate's ideas for air support resembled a proposal Gen. George Kenny, then commanding the Fifth Air Force in the Pacific, had put to Arnold in early 1942 for a composite air unit that would combine fighters,

Maj. Gen. Orde Wingate talking with Col. Phil Cochran, who commanded the 1st Air Commando Group, supporting Wingate's Special Force during its long-range-penetration operation in Burma in 1944. At the Quebec Conference, the Combined Chiefs of Staff agreed to Wingate's proposal for a greatly enlarged long-range mission behind Japanese lines. After meeting with Wingate, Gen. Hap Arnold promised to provide him with his own air support and ordered Cochran and his good friend, Col. John Alison, to organize the new unit. *3A-36092, RG342FH, NARA*

Mountbatten speaking with Hap Arnold in Quebec. During the conference, Arnold agreed to support Mountbatten's proposal to integrate the two Allied air forces in India into a single Allied command, as the Allies had done successfully in the Mediterranean. *SC178073, RG111, NARA*

bombers, and transport aircraft and would be highly mobile. Arnold saw in Kenny's proposal the idea of an offensive air unit "capable of advancing by 'fire and movement.'"[16] Wingate's plans gave Arnold an opportunity to try out these ideas. He offered to provide Wingate with several hundred aircraft of different types to support his operation. On his return to Washington, DC, after the Quadrant Conference, Arnold began setting up an air unit to work alongside Wingate's force. He chose two young lieutenant colonels newly returned from combat overseas to build the unit: Lt. Col. Philip Cochran, who had fought with the 33rd Fighter Group in North Africa, and Lt. Col. John Alison, who had become an ace flying with the 23rd Fighter Group in China. This unit would become the 1st Air Commando Group, which became part of the Tenth Air Force after its service with Wingate's force.[17]

It had become clear at the Trident Conference in May that any expansion of Allied operations in Burma would require a new command structure.[18] The commander in chief, India, charged with the defense of India and managing the Indian base of the British and Indian armies, could not also take on responsibility for conducting operations in Burma, especially since those operations now seemed likely to involve not just British and Indian forces, but also Chinese and American units. What was needed was a supreme allied commander who could coordinate all Allied forces—a role that Gen. Dwight Eisenhower was fulfilling in North Africa and Gen. Douglas MacArthur had in the Southwest Pacific. When he appointed Auchinleck as the new commander in chief, India, on June 18, Churchill also announced the formation of a new Southeast Asia Command to take over responsibility for operations against the Japanese in Burma.[19] Exactly how this command would be structured, and who would command it, was the subject of further studies, discussions among the members of the Combined Chiefs of Staff, and correspondence between Churchill and Roosevelt. The British Chiefs of Staff wanted to pattern the proposed Southeast Asia Command after the structure of MacArthur's command in the Southwest Pacific, where MacArthur reported to the Combined Chiefs of Staff for matters of strategy and to his own Joint Chiefs of Staff on operational policy.[20] Roosevelt and the American Joint Chiefs of Staff acquiesced to the British preference but insisted on appointing Gen. Stilwell as the deputy supreme commander. This would make Stilwell commander in chief of all American air and ground forces in Southeast Asia Command, commander in chief of Chinese forces in India, chief of staff to Chiang Kai-shek, and commander in chief, China-Burma-India theater, as well as deputy supreme commander, Southeast Asia Command, a multiple command seemingly impossible for one individual to take on. Yet, it was important to have Stilwell in a senior position in the new command structure to ensure that Chinese forces and the Fourteenth Air Force would contribute to future operations. As Marshall pointed out to his British counterparts, "politically all United States forces in China or in the proposed South East Asia Command were regarded as being there for the sole purpose of supporting China. A system had therefore to be evolved whereby, without sacrifice of this political principle, the maximum support could be provided for operations in Burma."[21] There was further debate on who should be the new supreme allied commander, but on 25 August 1943—the day after the Quadrant Conference ended—a press release announced the formation of a new Southeast Asia Command, and that Vice-Admiral Lord Louis Mountbatten had been appointed supreme allied commander, Southeast Asia.[22]

To say that the structure of the new Southeast Asia Command was complicated would be an understatement. As Marshall explained to Stilwell, the new command arrangement was composed of three geographic theaters: India, under the command of Auchinleck; the China Theater, under the Generalissimo; the American China-Burma-India theater, under Stilwell, which operated in all three areas; and one operational theater, Southeast Asia Command (SEAC), under Mountbatten.[23] SEAC would be a joint Anglo-American command with a combined British and American staff that would have responsibility for operations only in Burma, Ceylon, Malaya, and Sumatra. China was outside Mountbatten's area of responsibility. Although forces in India would provide administrative and logistical support to SEAC, command over these forces would remain with Auchinleck, while command of Chinese forces in India and Yunnan and control over the Fourteenth Air Force rested with the Generalissimo. Control of the Chinese divisions in India would be through Stilwell in his capacity as the Generalissimo's chief of staff, but these divisions would not come under Mountbatten's direct command, though their operations would conform to the British army commander's overall plan.[24] There was no pretense, as Marshall told Stilwell, that these complex command relationships represented "sound administrative practice"; they had been set up instead to reflect the political realities of the government in India and the position of the Generalissimo.[25] Under Mountbatten as supreme allied commander would be Air, Army, and Navy commanders in chief to exercise control over all forces specifically assigned to SEAC and to direct the operations of these units.[26]

As the Allies were wrestling with issues of strategy and command for operations in Southeast Asia, so too were the Japanese. The Japanese had also recognized a need to change the structure of command for the defense of Burma. The basis of Japanese strategy in Burma was defensive. It was logical to assume that any Allied counteroffensive to retake Burma would come through Assam, down the Hukawng Valley in northern Burma, and from Yunnan, with the possibility of amphibious operations along the Arakan coast. The ideal defense would be to have three Japanese armies positioned to counter any Allied moves from Assam, Yunnan, and the Arakan. To coordinate the defense of Burma, the Japanese *Imperial General Headquarters* established a higher command in Burma (*Burma Area Army Headquarters*) under Lt. Gen. Masakazu Kawabe on 27 March 1943.[27] The Japanese high command would not provide three armies for Burma but did reinforce the *15th Army* (composed of the *18th*, *33rd*, and *56th Divisions*) with a fourth division (*31st*) during the monsoon season. Lt. Gen. Renya Mutaguchi, who had been promoted to command the *15th Army*, came to the belief that even with reinforcements the Japanese army's plan for the defense of Burma was flawed.[28]

Mutaguchi concluded that to defend Burma from the Kabaw Valley beyond the Chindwin River, where the Chin Hills began, was insufficient. Having studied Wingate's operation, he was convinced that the hills no longer provided an adequate barrier to a British offensive from Assam. Far better, he believed, to take the offensive, push into Assam, and capture the British bases around Imphal, then push deeper into Assam to forestall a British invasion. As head of *Burma Area Army*, Kawabe was also looking at the problem of Burma's defense. He considered Mutaguchi's plan of an offensive deep into Assam much too ambitious but came to the conclusion that the capture of Imphal and Kohima nearby would allow the Japanese to set up strong defensive positions in the hills west of the Imphal plain, presenting the British army with a far more difficult and prolonged campaign to remove Japanese forces. Plans for the offensive won the approval of *Southern Army*, commanding the *Burma Area Army* and *Imperial General Headquarters*, who agreed to reinforce the *15th Army* with the *15th Division*, *54th Division*, and *24th Independent Mixed Brigade*, as well as other engineer and transport units with their vehicles. To provide air support for this planned offensive (designated Operation *U-GO*), the *5th Hikōshidan* realized that it would need more fighter aircraft for air defense, escort, and close air support for the *15th Army*. With increasing Allied air strength, the *5th Hikōshidan* was losing air superiority over Burma. *Imperial General Headquarters* agreed to provide more fighter units before the commencement of Operation *U-GO*, tentatively scheduled for early 1944. The main Japanese offensive during 1944 would be toward Imphal, with Japanese units in the Hukawng Valley and the Salween remaining on the defensive. Mutaguchi's insistence on switching from a defensive to an offensive strategy in Burma would dramatically change the fortunes of the Japanese and the Allies, though not in the manner he had intended.[29]

Integrating the Allied Air Forces: Creating Air Command, Southeast Asia

As the monsoon season came to an end, the Tenth Air Force and the Royal Air Force were stronger than they had ever been. The Tenth Air Force's expansion had been more modest, but it was a vast improvement over the struggling, near-impotent force of the year before. In July the 80th Fighter Group had arrived with three squadrons of P-40N fighters and by September had begun to replace the 51st Fighter Group as the 51st moved on to China. The group would soon adopt a new name, becoming the "Burma Banshees." In mid-September the 311th Bombardment Group (Dive) arrived in India with four squadrons: the 382nd, 383rd, 384th, and 385th Bombardment Squadrons (Dive).[30] The 311th Group had been activated as a bombardment group (light) in March 1942 with dive-bombers, being redesignated the 311th Bombardment Group (Dive) in July 1942.[31] The group began training on the Vultee A-31 Vanguard dive-bomber but converted to the North American A-36 Invader before going overseas. The group moved to a temporary base at Nawadih, India, before moving up to Assam. Shortly after the group's arrival on 19 September 1943, Headquarters, Army Air Forces, India-Burma sector, issued an order redesignating the group and its component squadrons to become effective on September 30. The group became the 311th Fighter-Bomber Group, while the 382nd, 383rd, and 384th Squadrons became the 528th, 529th, and 530th Fighter-Bomber Squadrons, respectively.[32] The 528th and 529th Squadrons went into combat with the A-36, while the 530th Squadron was equipped with the P-51A. At the same time, Headquarters, AAF, India-Burma sector, disbanded the 385th Bombardment Squadron (Dive) and assigned its personnel to the newly activated 459th Fighter Squadron, formed in the theater to receive, at long last, long-range P-38 fighters. The Tenth Air Force headquarters had activated the 459th at Karachi on 1 September 1943 as the 80th Fighter Group's fourth squadron, with an initial cadre of nine officers and 54 enlisted men drawn from the 80th Group. Another 10 officers and 228 enlisted men came from the 385th Squadron.[33] These additions gave the Tenth Air Force five fighter and two dive-bomber squadrons.

The 80th Fighter Group arrived in India in July 1943. Although one of the first fighter groups to receive the Republic P-47 Thunderbolt, the Eighth Air Force in Europe had first call on these fighters. The 80th Group went to war flying the Curtiss P-40N; something of a disappointment to the pilots, who had expected to take the more capable P-47 into combat. *3A-33654, RG342FH, NARA*

Although the 341st Bomb Group would be moving to China to the Fourteenth Air Force, this transfer did not take place until early 1944, leaving the Tenth Air Force with three medium-bomber squadrons and the four heavy-bomber squadrons of the 7th Bomb Group. While the squadrons had the normal complement of aircraft assigned, neither the 7th Group nor the 341st Group had its full complement of air crews. The Tenth had two troop carrier squadrons (the 1st and 2nd Troop Carrier Squadrons) now returned from service with the India-China Wing, Air Transport Command. A new type of squadron joined the Tenth Air Force when the 71st Liaison Squadron arrived in August with L-4 and L-5 liaison airplanes. With the 9th Photographic Squadron, the Tenth now had a total of 18 squadrons with around 290 aircraft. In the entire China-Burma-India theater the Army Air Force now had 3,852 officers and 28,598 enlisted men.[34]

The 311th Bombardment Group (Dive) arrived in India with squadrons but was soon reorganized as a standard fighter group of three squadrons, with its fourth squadron used to form the 459th Fighter Squadron. The 311th Group's A-36 Invader dive-bombers and P-51A Mustangs did valuable work in northern Burma, providing close air support to Stilwell's Chinese and American force. *3A-35760, RG342FH, NARA*

The Tenth Air Force received enough Lockheed P-38H Lightnings to form the 459th Fighter Squadron, drawing pilots from the 80th and 311th Groups. The arrival of P-38s and P-51As finally gave the Tenth Air Force the more-capable and longer-range fighters the theater had been asking for since 1942. *SC267016, RG111, NARA*

The Royal Air Force had undergone an even more significant expansion, with the total number of aircraft of all types in India Command growing from 1,388 in January 1943 to 2,760 in some 54 squadrons by October, although not all these squadrons were operational, nor were all the aircraft under RAF Bengal Command.[35] Under RAF Bengal Command, No. 221 Group, supporting the British IV Corps at Imphal, now had seven squadrons of fighters: one night-fighter squadron for the defense of Calcutta, four squadrons of Vengeance dive-bombers, two squadrons of Wellington medium bombers, and two squadrons of heavier Liberator bombers, while No. 224 Group, supporting the XV Corps in the Arakan, had eight squadrons of fighters and a Vengeance squadron, and two squadrons of longer-range Beaufighter twin-engine fighters.[36] The Royal Air Force had improved the quality of its aircraft as well as the quantity. Five of the light-bomber squadrons had given up their Blenheim IV and Bisley light bombers for Hurricane Mk IIc fighter-bombers. While most of the fighter squadrons still had the Hurricane Mk II, with one squadron still flying Mohawks, the arrival of the Spitfire Mk Vc in India—enough to convert three squadrons—gave promise for the coming battles with the Japanese Ki-43s.

It was clear that with the Allied ground forces going over to the offensive in the coming dry season, the Allied air forces in India would be taking on an even-greater role: providing air support to the ground forces while continuing the battles for air superiority and against the Japanese lines of communications in Burma. The air forces were also shifting from the defensive to the offensive. With the fighting likely to cover a large area of Burma from the far north to the Arakan, there was a need to ensure coordination of the air effort for maximum effectiveness. Prior to the formation of SEAC, the RAF in India under Air Chief Marshal Peirse had reported to the commander in chief, India, a system of command that would not work as the RAF intensified offensive operations over Burma.[37] Likewise, an increasing American air effort logically called for joint control over Allied air operations. Up to the formation of SEAC, cooperation between the RAF and the Tenth Air Force had been informal and not subject to any agreed-on structure of command. Bissell, as commander of the Tenth Air Force, attended a daily commander's conference with Gen. Wavell, commander in chief, India, with the head of the Army, Navy, Intelligence, and Peirse.[38] In a similar manner, Brig. Gen. Haynes, as commander of the IATF, met daily with his RAF counterpart, Air Vice-Marshal T. M. Williams, commanding RAF Bengal Command. These meetings had produced an overall bombing policy for the RAF and the IATF, but there had been only one coordinated mission (Operation WIMPOLE) during

The American Army Air Force never used the Vultee Vengeance in combat, but the RAF was happy to take the aircraft through Lend-Lease to replace obsolete Blenheim bombers still serving in India. With a slightly greater bombload than the Blenheim, one fewer crewman, and four .30-caliber machine guns in the wings, the Vengeance proved valuable in providing close air support to British and Indian troops fighting in the jungles of Burma. *CF_00204, IWM*

AIR COMMAND, SOUTHEAST ASIA: INTEGRATING THE ALLIED AIR FORCES

By the end of the 1943 monsoon, the RAF had two squadrons of Lend-Lease Liberator bombers (equivalent to the B-24D) for night-bombing missions into Burma. The older Wellington bombers soldiered on in two of the RAF's medium-bomber squadrons. *CI_000123, IWM*

The arrival of the Bristol Beaufighter in India gave the RAF a powerful weapon for long-range interdiction. Heavily armed with cannon and machine guns, Beaufighters ranged deep into central Burma to strike at locomotives, rolling stock, and rivercraft. *CI_000162, IWM*

Maj. Gen. George Stratemeyer meets Adm. Mountbatten for the first time during Mountbatten's visit to Chungking, shortly after his arrival to take up his new command. Although philosophically in favor of integrating the Allied air forces, Stratemeyer felt compelled to follow Stilwell's view that integration was contrary to the guidance he had received from the Combined Chiefs of Staff at the Quebec Conference. *CI_000428, IWM*

Organization of Allied Air Power
February 18, 1943

- Mediterranean Air Command
  ACM Tedder RAF
  - Northwest African Air Forces
    L/G Spaatz
    USAAF
    - Northwest African Strategic Air Force
      M/G Doolittle
      USAAF
    - Northwest African Tactical Air Force
      AM Cunningham RAF
    - Northwest African Coastal Air Force
      AVM Lloyd RAF
    - Northwest African Photo Reconnaissance Wing
      L/C Roosevelt
      USAAF
  - Malta Air Command
    AVM Park RAF
  - Middle East Command
    ACM Sholto Douglas RAF
    - RAF Middle East
    - Ninth Air Force
      M/G Brereton
      USAAF

Chart 1 Source: Davis, Richard G.: *Carl A. Spaatz and the Air War in Europe*, (Washington, D.C., 1992), P. 179.

AIR COMMAND, SOUTHEAST ASIA: INTEGRATING THE ALLIED AIR FORCES

the British withdrawal in the Arakan in May. In effect, each air force went its own separate way.

When Mountbatten arrived in India in early October, he was not satisfied with this arrangement. "British and American aircraft," he later wrote, "were functioning in an undivided common element [the air]; and there was no logical reason why their operations should not have been fully coordinated from the beginning."[39] Mountbatten found that the command relationships with regard to the Tenth Air Force made coordination difficult. Under the structure for the new Southeast Asia Command, which the Combined Chiefs of Staff had agreed to at the Quadrant Conference, operational control of the Tenth Air Force was vested in Stilwell as commander of all US Army forces in the CBI and deputy supreme allied commander of SEAC. Thus Stratemeyer, as commander of Army Air Force, India Burma sector (including the Tenth Air Force), took orders from Mountbatten through Stilwell, and not through the air commander in chief, SEAC. As Mountbatten explained this complicated command structure, "the position was, therefore, that a subordinate air commander in my theater was responsible to me for his air operations through a senior officer other than my Air Commander-in-Chief. I considered this situation was certain to entail an over-lapping of effort—or, worse, gaps in our air defense; that it would lead to a lack of co-ordination, and an impairment of general efficiency; and that these might, at a time of crisis, have very serious consequences."[40] The only solution, Mountbatten decided, was to integrate the two air forces, though this proved to be a challenging process. In coming to this decision, Mountbatten had the support of Marshall and Arnold, who had suggested that he should try to integrate the American and British air forces in his new theater.[41]

The Mediterranean theater provided a precedent for the integration of Allied air forces. Following the invasion of North Africa in November 1942, the Army Air Force's Twelfth Air Force and Royal Air Force's Eastern Air Command—both under Maj. Gen. Carl Spaatz, commander of Allied air forces—had operated separately with minimal coordination, "running separate air wars."[42] To the east, the Western Desert Air Force operated separately under Air Chief Marshal Arthur Tedder, air officer commanding in chief, Middle East Forces. Tedder found the command structure and airpower's poor performance in Tunisia disturbing and won Gen. Dwight Eisenhower's and Air Chief Marshal Sir Charles Portal's agreement to form a combined air command for all Allied air forces in the Mediterranean.[43] This became the Mediterranean Air Command under Tedder, which combined all Allied air forces under one command. Army Air Force and Royal Air Force wings, groups, and squadrons retained their integrity as American or British units but were grouped together according to their respective roles, strategic or tactical.[44] The Mediterranean Air Command and its component units had integrated and alternating American and British command and staff positions in combined headquarters. This reorganization of Allied air forces established a fundamental principle of airpower, that "a single airman must command all the air forces committed to the ground battle, because aircraft, unlike other combat arms, had free rein over the combat zone and should deploy with overwhelming force at the decisive points and not fritter away their strength in penny-packet formations at the ground commander's whim."[45] This principle was later incorporated into a new War Department manual, FM 100-20, titled *Command and Employment of Air Power*, issued in July 1943, which confirmed that airpower had to be unified under the control of the air force commander.[46]

Stratemeyer had a more-than-passing familiarity with the issues of Allied air force integration. As Army Air Force chief of air staff, Stratemeyer had followed these developments closely and corresponded regularly with Spaatz, a former West Point classmate.[47] On his way to India in May, Stratemeyer visited Tunisia and reported back to Arnold that the British viewed the concentration of airpower in an air commander positively.[48] Stratemeyer was also among a small number of senior Army Air Force officers who read and approved the principles incorporated in FM 100-20.[49] The peculiarities of the American command in the CBI made the question of the integration of American Army Air Force and Royal Air Force units particularly challenging. First and foremost was the American commitment to China, which carried the explicit understanding that all Army Air Force units in the CBI had as their first priority the support of China and could be called on at any time to provide that support. The Fourteenth Air Force was clearly intended for service in China and did not come under Army Air Forces, India-Burma sector, at all. The second complication was the presence of Army Air Force units controlled directly from Washington, and not through Stilwell or Stratemeyer. This was the case with the India-China Wing of the Air Transport Command, but an added complication was the proposal Gen. Arnold raised at the Quadrant Conference: to base very long-range B-29 bombers in China for a strategic air offensive against Japan. The initial conception of this plan—Operation TWILIGHT (later MATTERHORN)—called for basing the B-29s and supporting transport aircraft in India for operations out of airfields in China.[50] What role the Army Air Force, India-Burma sector, would perform for TWILIGHT was then uncertain, but it was clear that this operation would be focused entirely on bombing Japan. In addition, there were service units in the AAF, India-Burma sector, that had a dual role of servicing the Tenth and Fourteenth Air Forces. How these could be integrated into an Allied air command was also uncertain.

Arnold's instructions to Stratemeyer after the announcement of the formation of Southeast Asia Command gave only the broadest guidance on how to proceed. In an August 28 letter to Stratemeyer (and similar letters to Stilwell and Chennault), Arnold told Stratemeyer that he would command all US air units that may be assigned to Southeast Asia Command in addition to his current duties as commanding general, Army Air Forces, India-Burma sector.[51] Since operational control of the Tenth Air Force would remain with Stilwell, it would be "necessary for Stilwell, Mountbatten, and yourself to work out plans for its operational control and use in the Southeast Asia Command. It is contemplated that some or all of the combat units will be employed in the Southeast Asia Theater."[52] In an obvious understatement, Arnold closed his letter to Stratemeyer with the following point:

> *This new command setup and your relationships with Generals Stilwell, Mountbatten, and Chennault is somewhat complicated and will have to be worked out to a great extent among yourselves. We feel that it can and it must be made to work efficiently. The success of this complicated command setup depends in great measure on personalities. If a true spirit of cooperation is engendered throughout the command, it will work. If the reverse is true, it is doomed to failure. I know I can count on you to play your part and to pass the word right down the line.*[53]

The first issue to be resolved was the choice of the new commander in chief, Air Forces, Southeast Asia Command. The Americans believed that Stratemeyer should be considered for the position because of his broad experience and the important contribution the Tenth Air Force had made to the war against the Japanese in Burma. Brig. Gen. Benjamin Ferris, commanding Stratemeyer's rear-echelon headquarters in New Delhi, had Col. Stone, Stratemeyer's chief of staff, prepare a memo arguing the case for Stratemeyer's appointment, pointing out that over the previous three months the Tenth had dropped over 2,200 tons of bombs on targets in Burma while the RAF had dropped less than 600 tons.[54] This proposal ignored the reality that the RAF outnumbered the Tenth Air Force both in number of squadrons and aircraft. There was also an apparent concern on the part of the British that appointing an American officer to the position might be taken as an implication of British weakness and might damage British prestige.[55] The British would not agree to give the position to Stratemeyer, so in November it was announced that Air Chief Marshal Sir Richard Peirse had been appointed commander in chief, Air Force, Southeast Asia Command, with Stratemeyer as his deputy commander.[56]

In the absence of firm guidance from Washington, it was clear that Stratemeyer would have to work out the new command structure and his responsibilities within it on his own. Despite considerable efforts, the "process of clarification dragged on for weeks."[57] Stratemeyer's staff began working on the problems of integration. The difficulty was that under the command system then in force, only part of Stratemeyer's command would theoretically come under Mountbatten's command. All or part of the Tenth Air Force might come under Mountbatten's command through his Southeast Asia air commander, but large areas that came under Stratemeyer's control or supervision—the CBI Air Services Command, CBI Air Forces Training Command, and the India-China Wing, Air Transport Command—would not.[58] There remained the vexing problem of the Fourteenth Air Force, where Stratemeyer had an extensive administrative role, but operational control only through his position as air officer and air advisor to Stilwell's staff. Stratemeyer's staff in an initial attempt, "Plan for System of Operational Command in Southeast Asia," focused on what would be the ideal structure and not what was practical. The plan made some basic assumptions that ignored the political realities in the CBI. The first major assumption was that the command would be a true combined command, integrating the personnel and units to create "a unity of purpose, a unity of organization and a unity of command whose sole mission is the destruction of a dangerous enemy."[59] The plan further assumed that the new Southeast Asia Command would be divided into two operational theaters (India-Burma and China), but the two would need to be coordinated and integrated into one unified air command with Stratemeyer as the commander. This air command would consist of the following:

1 China Air Force
2 India-Burma Air Force
3 Southeast Asia Coastal Command
4 Southeast Asia Training Command
5 Southeast Asia Air Service Command[60]

Each of these would incorporate the Allied air units according to their roles, with the China Air Force and India-Burma Air Force being subdivided into a Strategic Air Force and a Tactical Air Force, and within these organizations a Bomber Command and a Fighter Command. While this initial plan may have represented an ideal command structure that provided the elusive goal of unity of command, the political reality was that Generalissimo Chiang Kai-shek was not likely to agree to neither the Chinese Air Force nor the Fourteenth Air Force coming under an Allied air command. Nor were the British keen to accept an American as overall air commander.

This plan apparently served as the basis for Stratemeyer's first proposals to his RAF counterparts on integrating the two air forces, particularly the idea of a unified air command structured along the lines of the Mediterranean Air Command that Stratemeyer was familiar with. Stratemeyer met with Peirse, and possibly with Air Marshal Sir Guy Garrod, deputy air officer commanding in chief, on October 11 to discuss the new air force structure under Southeast Asia Command.[61] From these discussions Garrod drew up a tentative organizational chart and sent it to Stratemeyer for his comments.[62] Stratemeyer made a few revisions but kept to the basic intent of obtaining "the closest possible integration of American and British air forces under the Air Commander-in-Chief, S.E. Asia Command."[63] Stratemeyer had been suggested as the deputy air commander in chief, but since this was equivalent to a chief-of-staff position—Stratemeyer wanted an active command, not a staff position—he proposed that he be appointed commander of the Indo-Burma Air Forces, a position analogous to Maj. Gen. Spaatz as commander of the Northwest African Air Forces within Mediterranean Air Command. The Indo-Burma Air Forces would have three component units: a Strategic Air Force under an American commander, which would include all American and British heavy bombers; a Tactical Air Force under a British commander, with No. 221 and No. 224 Groups and Calcutta Defense units from the RAF and the American units assigned to American Air Base No. 1 that would have an American commander; and a Photographic Reconnaissance Wing of American and British units. Peirse would have direct control over all general reconnaissance units under a Coastal Command. Staffing at the Southeast Asia Air Command and the Indo-Burma Air Forces Command would combine American and British staffs.[64] Stratemeyer submitted this plan to Mountbatten for his approval shortly before he and Mountbatten left for meetings in Chunking with the Generalissimo and Gen. Stilwell.

In this initial proposal for a command structure, Stratemeyer included the Fourteenth Air Force as a component unit of the Southeast Asia Air Force. In conversations with Peirse and Garrod, Stratemeyer apparently pressed for this. A draft message prepared for Mountbatten to send to the Combined Chiefs of Staff says, "Stratemeyer strongly urges that Major-General Chennault and the 14th U.S. Air Force should come under Peirse's command so that all air forces within South East Asia Command should be integrated and coordinated to the maximum extent. Stratemeyer makes very strong point of this and we naturally agree."[65] Stratemeyer's plan did not last beyond his visit to Chungking from October 16 to 20. As he recorded in his diary:

> [A]s a result of all the conferences and my conversations with Somervell [Lt. Gen. Brehon Somervell, commander, Army Service Forces, whom Roosevelt had sent to China to inform the Generalissimo of the formation of Southeast Asia Command] and Generals Chennault and Stilwell, the plan for command of the Air Forces that I had submitted to Lord Louis was not considered feasible. Therefore, I am drawing up another plan which sets up parallel organizations in India; the Army Air Forces

**System of Operational Command
South-East Asia Air Force**

```
                    South East Asia Commander-in-Chief
                           Lord Mountbatten
                                  │
                       South-East Asia Air Command
                              ACM Peirse
                                  │
        ┌─────────────────────────┼─────────────────────────┐
   Air Commander            Air Commander              Air Commander
  Coastal Command         Indo-Burma Air Forces       Air Forces in China
                             M/G Stratemeyer             M/G Chennault
                                  │
        ┌─────────────────────────┼─────────────────────────┐
   Air Commander            Air Commander              Air Commander
  Strategic Air Force     Tactical Air Force        Reconnaissance Wing
                                  │
                ┌─────────────────┴─────────────────┐
            221 Group                        American Air Base
             Imphal                               No. 1

            224 Group                         Calcutta Defense
           Chittagong
```

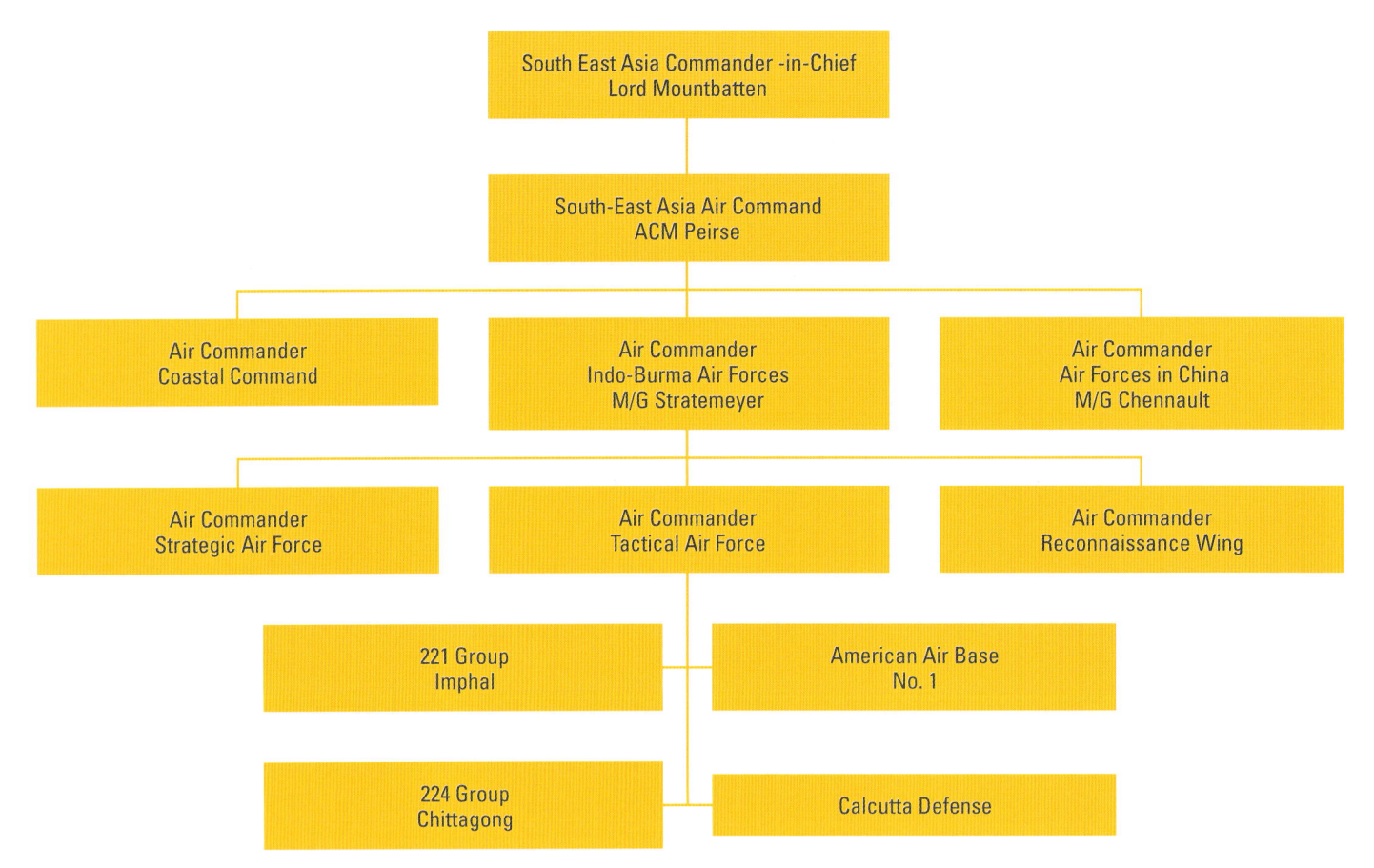

Chart 2 Source: Air 23/2167, Air Ministry and Ministry of Defence: Royal Air Force Overseas Commands: Reports and Correspondence: Air Command, South-East Asia. Integration of British and American Air Forces under S.E.A.C.

---

to be commanded by me and the Royal Air Forces to be commanded by an R.A.F. officer. Both of these to be headed up by Lord Louis Mountbatten's Air Commander. General Chennault in this picture will operate in cooperation under Stilwell and me and in turn under Lord Louis Mountbatten.[66]

Stratemeyer added that he thought Mountbatten would "be disappointed in my concept in the use of Air Forces as we must use them under this bastard command set up that now exists."[67]

It appears that Stilwell may have been the driving force behind Stratemeyer's change of heart on integrating the Allied air forces, since Stratemeyer noted in his diary that on his return to New Delhi, he ordered his staff to draw up a new organization chart "in accordance with General Stilwell's wishes."[68] Apparently Stilwell believed that if there were no Allied plans for an offensive to retake all of Burma, there was no need for integrating the Army Air Force with the Royal Air Force under a single air commander.[69] More importantly, he believed that the proposed integration was contrary to the guidelines decided at the Quadrant Conference, as well as directives from Washington that insisted on the primacy of the American commitment to support China.[70] As a follow-up to his meetings in Chungking with Stilwell, Stratemeyer sent Stilwell an outline for his approval of what Stratemeyer believed were the specific missions of the commanding general, Army Air Forces, India-Burma sector:

a To assure and protect the flow of supplies and personnel by air transport to designated Chinese and American units in China-Burma-India.
b To control and coordinate the activities of the India-China Wing, Air Transport Command, with other Theater activities concerned.
c To provide and distribute supplies peculiar to the Army Air Forces within the Theater.
d To maintain Theater aircraft and equipment.
e To plan and execute operations of available airpower to its maximum capability against the enemy.
f To train Chinese and American Air Force units and personnel within the Theater.
g To assist in improving the combat effectiveness of Chinese ground and Air Forces.
h To provide tactical air support to the Ledo and Yunnan forces.[71]

Stilwell approved this list on October 24.

Over the next several days, Stratemeyer had meetings with Peirse, Garrod, Maj. Gen. Albert Wedemeyer [US Army, who had been assigned to Mountbatten as deputy chief of staff], and his own staff to discuss the organization and integration of the Army Air Forces within Southeast Asia Command.[72] Meeting with Garrod on October 26, Stratemeyer discussed a revised organization chart he had given Peirse earlier in the day that had Stilwell's approval, showing parallel, but not integrated, American and British air organizations, though still under Peirse's operational control.[73] Stratemeyer had backed away completely from the Mediterranean Air Command model. He no longer believed there should be an integrated command at any level, nor that given his commitments to support the Fourteenth Air Force should he take on the role of air commander of the Indo-Burma Air Forces as he had originally proposed. He did agree that there should be the closest possible coordination between the two air forces, but this could be achieved through the exchange of a small number of staff officers at Peirse's new headquarters.[74]

Stratemeyer met with Garrod again the next day, together with Wedemeyer, to review an organization chart that Peirse had prepared laying out the ideal organization for integrating the two air forces without any restrictions that the Quadrant Conference or previous directives might have imposed on Stratemeyer.[75] The chart was almost the same as Stratemeyer's early proposal, calling for the creation of an air commander, Eastern Front (Stratemeyer's Indo-Burma Air Forces), with a Strategic and Tactical Air Force combining American and British units, but with the Fourteenth Air Force removed from under the air commander in chief and placed under Stilwell as deputy commander, Southeast Asia Command. Garrod conveyed Peirse's view that air operations in the India-Burma sector had to be coordinated through a single commander who had authority over both the strategic and the tactical air forces. As overall air commander, Peirse would be too far removed to exercise this authority. He proposed setting up an air commander, Eastern Front, like Stratemeyer's idea for air commander, Indo-Burma Air Forces, as an essential for the efficient control of operations. Peirse said it would be appropriate for an American to take up this position. At this meeting, Stratemeyer made clear his objection, believing the proposed command structure ran counter to the directives he had received from Arnold. Stratemeyer's concern was that under these directives, he might at some point in time be forced to withdraw all or part of the Tenth Air Force to defend the air ferry route to China, and therefore he could not regard himself as wholly under the command of the air commander in chief of Southeast Asia Command.[76] Once again, the dominance of China in American thinking came to the fore. Wedemeyer gave his opinion that the proposed organizational structure seemed sound but did conflict with the decisions adopted at the Quadrant Conference. Stilwell, Wedemeyer said, would adhere to these decisions until they were amended. He proposed a meeting among Mountbatten, Stilwell, Peirse, Stratemeyer, and himself so that Mountbatten could decide what steps he wanted to take to get the Quadrant decisions altered.[77]

At this meeting, held on October 28, Mountbatten, Stilwell, Peirse, Stratemeyer, Garrod, and Wedemeyer met to consider the integration of American and British air forces into Southeast Asia Command. The participants reviewed Peirse's organizational chart, which was intended to set out "the ideal organization for command and administration of the American and British air forces within South East Asia Command, regardless of the decisions at the Quadrant Conference on this subject, and regardless of directives that may have been issued to the Air Commanders. The sole consideration in mind was the organization that would provide the most effective control of Allied Air Forces for the defeat of the enemy."[78] The factors that went into determining the proposed command structure reflect the evolving views on the command and control of airpower and the lessons that had come out of experience in the Mediterranean:

a The Allied Air Squadrons engaged in the Tactical role on the Eastern Front of India should be under one commander who should live with the General Officer Commanding the Allied Army Forces operating on that front.
b The Allied Air Squadrons engaged in the Strategical role over Burma should be under one Air Commander who should be distinct from the Air Commander of the Tactical Air Force.
c The coordination of the Tactical and Strategical Air Forces cannot be effectively carried out from Delhi, which is too remote from the area of operations.
d Thus an Air Commander for the Eastern Front becomes essential for the most effective control of the Allied Air Forces operating over Burma and eastward thereof.[79]

Operational control of the planned Strategical and Tactical Air Forces would be carried out through a combined American and British staff at the higher levels of command, while administrative control would remain with the respective air forces. Peirse recommended that Stratemeyer take on the role of air commander, Eastern Front, in addition to his duties as commanding general, Army Air Forces, India-Burma sector, which would remain under the proposed command structure. There was general agreement that command of the Fourteenth Air Force should remain as is— reporting to Stilwell, who could arrange for any coordination with the air commander, Eastern Front. Stratemeyer noted that he could not agree to the proposed command structure since it ran counter to his directives. The meeting concluded that Mountbatten should write to Portal, Marshall, and Arnold to apprise them of these proposals, seeing if amendments to the Quadrant Conference decisions could not be put in place to remove the conflicts and get their concurrence to integrate the air forces.[80] For the time being, Mountbatten did not push the integration of the two air forces but decided to continue with the existing structure until he could get a decision from the Combined Chiefs of Staff.

Reviewing the notes of the meeting a few days later, Stratemeyer spelled out his current views to Wedemeyer. He asked Wedemeyer to insert an amendment to the notes as follows:

It was agreed that the diagram would represent the ideal organization which should be aimed at if the primary mission given to the American Commander of protecting American commitments to China did not stand in the way. Major General Stratemeyer stressed Lieutenant General Stilwell's obligation to withdraw any part or all of the Tenth Air Force from the Southeast Asia Command in order to protect those commitments if such a course became necessary. He was, therefore, unable to concur in the proposed organization in view of present directives in Quadrant.[81]

As Stratemeyer explained to Wedemeyer,

Particularly in view of Twilight, I believe it important that the American Air Commander should be in a position to concentrate all available American Air Forces in China without being embarrassed by commitments to the Southeast Asia Command. He must also be sufficiently independent of British control to be able to insist upon obtaining adequate facilities and equipment for Twilight in India. I believe I can achieve these results more effectively if I am not personally responsible to Air Chief Marshal Peirse for all air operations over Burma. I, therefore, prefer the plan which I submitted, calling for separate American A.A.F. and R.A.F. Air Forces fighting on a cooperative basis on the eastern front.[82]

Stratemeyer went on to say that he thought the plan discussed at the October 28 meeting was "entirely workable and I have no objections to it" as long as it included a note to the effect that Stilwell as deputy commander, Southeast Asia Command, would withdraw any or all of the American Air Forces to protect American commitments to China.[83]

In a long letter to Arnold, Stratemeyer spelled out what had happened to change his point of view. He had hoped, he said, to obtain an agreement for one unified command of all air forces in the CBI along the lines of the Mediterranean Air Command model, but his meetings with Stilwell in Chungking and further study of the Quadrant Conference decisions convinced him it was not possible.[84] He and Stilwell had then insisted that they retain the right to withdraw all or part of any American units assigned to Southeast Asia Command if needed for the defense of the Hump route or China. This led to his plan for parallel but not integrated air forces, which would make withdrawal of American units easier but still under Peirse's operational control, with the promise of full cooperation with the RAF. As he reported to Arnold, "The British were disappointed at this suggestion. Peirse is anxious to have one integrated air force under his command and wants to be assured that the American units assigned to him will remain under his control."[85] He told Arnold that Peirse had proposed appointing him as air commander for the Eastern Front with a Strategic Air Force, a Tactical Air Force, and a reconnaissance wing all composed of mixed British and American units. Mountbatten would be writing to Arnold, Stratemeyer said, to ask him to reconsider the Quadrant decisions. A major factor in this protracted debate was Washington's failure to provide Stilwell and Stratemeyer new directives following the Quadrant Conference. Having insisted on the primacy of providing support to China, the War Department did not amend earlier directives when the mission shifted to concentrate on offensive operations in Burma.[86]

Mountbatten wrote a long letter to Arnold on November 1, enclosing a chart of his proposed organization of the Allied air forces and sending copies to Marshall, Portal, and Field Marshal Sir John Dill in Washington.[87] Mountbatten described how the plans for integrating the two air forces had evolved from Stratemeyer's original conception of a fully integrated force to his subsequent reluctance to place himself in an organization that he believed conflicted with his directives from Washington. Mountbatten told Arnold that he fully respected Stratemeyer's position and believed that while Stratemeyer was seeking "an organization which would ensure the most effective employment against the enemy," he was reluctant to criticize the current command structure and directives. Mountbatten had decided to leave the current structure as it was, with the two air forces operating separately until he could get a change in directives. He then stated his case for full integration:

> *At present, for instance, Stratemeyer is charged with the responsibility of defending the air ferry route to China and, in theory, the fact that the route has been attacked frequently during the last few weeks and that we have had a fair number of transport aircraft shot down is nothing whatever to do with me. I am sure you will agree that this is wrong and that I should be charged with all operational activities in my own theatre. I feel that I should be responsible for defending the air ferry route and feel that I should place at the disposal of Stratemeyer any Royal Air Force squadrons he requires for the purpose, as well as directing the land campaign towards improving the security of the air ferry route. I am sure you will agree that the position between Stratemeyer and myself is unsatisfactory to both of us as matters now stand, and it will be much worse when I am responsible for fighting a campaign in Northern Burma which is designed to clear the ferry route and yet have not the power to move Air Forces freely to help in achieving this object.*[88]

Reviewing Mountbatten's letter for Arnold, Maj. Gen. Barney Giles, chief of the air staff, concluded that Mountbatten's proposal on air force integration was satisfactory provided that it allowed Stratemeyer to maintain the right to withdraw Army Air Force units to support operations in China.[89] But as Giles pointed out, "if Stratemeyer maintains this right to move his units to China and does so it may leave Mountbatten with a job to do and nothing to do it with."[90]

For his part, Peirse wrote to Portal seeking his support for the proposed integration.[91] Peirse told Portal that at the date of the activation of Southeast Asia Command, the Tenth Air Force would come under his command but would continue as a parallel organization to the Royal Air Force. Peirse was in favor of full integration, and he told Portal in his telegram, "if you and Washington can agree to

Mountbatten with his two American Army Air Force commanders: George Stratemeyer, who would become the first commander of the Allied Eastern Air Command after Mountbatten ordered the AAF and RAF to integrate, and Howard Davidson, who would remain commander of the Tenth Air Force as an administrative unit and take on operational command of the new Strategic Air Force, combining AAF and RAF heavy and medium bombers. *3A-48793, RG342FH, NARA*

proposed set-up we have suggested I believe we shall achieve first-class integrated Allied air force. Very best relationship exists throughout between Americans and ourselves and I would welcome anything you can do to accelerate a decision."[92] Air Command, Southeast Asia, came into being on 16 November 1943, with Peirse as Allied air commander in chief, and Air Marshal Guy Garrod as deputy Allied air commander in chief. On activation the Air Command had forty-six RAF squadrons, six squadrons of the Royal Indian Air Force, one Royal Canadian Air Force squadron, one squadron from the Netherlands, and seventeen Army Air Force squadrons with an operational strength of 723 aircraft, including 204 American aircraft.[93] Geographically the command ranged as follows: No. 222 Group in Ceylon for reconnaissance and defense of the Eastern Fleet; No. 221 Group, moving to bases in central Assam to support IV Corps; No. 224 Group, supporting XV Corps in the Arakan; and Tenth Air Force units in northern Assam and elsewhere in India. But there was no more progress on integration until the Sextant Conference later in the month.

The Sextant Conference—also known as the Cairo Conference—took place on 22–26 November 1943 and resumed on December 3 to 7, after the Allies met with Stalin in Tehran. An objective of the conference was to reach a final decision on operations in Burma over the coming dry season, since this had a bearing on China's role in the approach to Japan—a topic still under much discussion.[94] Discussions on the integration of the Allied air forces took place around the debates on operations and meetings with Roosevelt, Churchill, and their respective military staffs, and with Generalissimo Chiang Kai-shek, who was present for the first series of meetings. Mountbatten and his planning staff had produced a plan for seven interrelated operations for the 1943–44 dry season:

a A seaborne operation to capture the Andaman Islands (Operation BUCCANEER).
b An advance with one Corps along the Arakan coast and the Mayu Peninsula leading eventually to the capture of Akyab.
c An advance with one Corps on the central front across the Chindwin River.
d An advance by Stilwell's three divisions on the northern front.
e An advance by the Chinese force in Yunnan (Y-Force) to Bhamo and Lashio, to secure the Chinese end of the Ledo Road.
f Operations in support of d) and e) by Wingate's long-range-penetration Special Force.
g Airborne operations to capture Indaw, on the railway from Mandalay to Myitkyina (Operation TARZAN).[95]

An amphibious operation in Southeast Asia was important, since Chiang Kai-shek had made that a precondition for Y-Force's participation in operations in northern Burma, believing that the Allies had to have control over the Bay of Bengal to prevent the Japanese from sending in reinforcements.[96] But BUCCANEER proved to be a victim of requirements for the war against Germany. The Combined Chiefs of Staff, after some intense debate, decided that the landing craft that would be required for BUCCANEER were needed more for Operation OVERLORD—the invasion of Europe planned for May 1944—and the follow-on invasion of southern France, Operation ANVIL. TARZAN, too, seemed overly ambitious and would have to be scaled back if BUCCANEER was to be postponed. In their final report to the president and the prime minister, the Combined Chiefs of Staff recommended to continue with the planned ground operations to capture northern Burma and to continue these operations during fall 1944 with the forces that were available. The CCS decided to continue preparations for TARZAN, but to postpone a major amphibious operation in the Bay of Bengal until after the 1944 monsoon. TARZAN might possibly be postponed, providing more transport airplanes for the Hump operation and for the buildup of long-range B-29 operations from China (TWILIGHT/MATTERHORN). The choice between these two alternatives would depend on the opinions of the Generalissimo and Mountbatten. With regard to Allied air operations, the report recommended the continued buildup of American and Chinese air forces in China for intensified air attacks on the Japanese, the planned buildup of the B-29 force in India with advance bases in the Chengtu area, and the start of operations against the Burma-Thailand railroad and the port of Bangkok.[97] This left SEAC with the planned advances of Stilwell's force, the advance to the Chindwin and in the Arakan, and the possible advance of the Yunnan force if the Generalissimo approved, with Wingate's force supporting some part of these operations.[98]

Stratemeyer accompanied Mountbatten, Stilwell, Wedemeyer, and Chennault to Cairo for the Sextant Conferences. He recorded in his diary that the topic of integration of the Allied air forces came up in conferences during Sextant.[99] On November 23 he participated in a meeting with the president, the prime minister, and the Combined Chiefs, at which Stratemeyer noted there was a tentative decision not to integrate the air forces, but to continue on the basis of cooperation. At a meeting two days later, Stratemeyer was asked whether he preferred the organizational chart showing the two air forces working in parallel or integrated. He replied that he preferred the former but could make the latter work if that was the decision. At this meeting Mountbatten insisted that integration take place, and Arnold and Marshall received memos outlining the two proposed command structures for their decision. At some point during these meetings, the arguments in favor of integration appeared to become generally acceptable, as in a November 29 memo to Arnold requesting a final decision in which Stratemeyer wrote, "although it apparently has been generally agreed that the United States Army Air Force units in Southeast Asia Command will be integrated with the Royal Air Force units and that I will have operational air command of the integrated forces under the A.O. C-in-C, a final decision in writing has not been rendered."[100]

Although Stratemeyer left Cairo on December 8 without the definitive directive on integration he had been hoping for, he was sure enough of the direction the directive would take that he had already alerted his staff to begin planning accordingly. On November 26, Stratemeyer sent a radio message to Col. Stone, his chief of staff, saying that contrary to his radio of just two days earlier, he now understood that Army Air Force units would be integrated with the RAF along the lines of earlier plans and that he would have operational command of all these air units.[101] He asked Stone to begin planning for staffing his new command and locating a headquarters. Stratemeyer further communicated to his staff that although he had been strongly against such an organization, "if the decision is made we will all give it our full support and we will make it work."[102] Mountbatten had also passed on instructions to Air Marshal Sir John Baldwin—then serving at the headquarters of Air Command, Southeast Asia, but who was the prospective commander of the Tactical Air Force in the new command—to begin planning for the integration pending the arrival of a new directive.[103]

A new factor in the planning for integration was the prospect of a greatly enhanced transport force if TARZAN was given the go-ahead. The War Department had committed to sending 35 C-47s to India to equip the 27th Troop Carrier Squadron to be sent from the United States, and the 315th Troop Carrier Squadron, to be activated in the theater, though TARZAN would require many more aircraft if it was approved.[104] Peirse had suggested that all troop carrier squadrons be placed under Baldwin's Tactical Air Force, but Stratemeyer disagreed. He wanted to set up a Troop Carrier Command equal in status to the Strategic and Tactical Air Forces and independent of both. No doubt because he realized most of the transport units assigned to this command would be American, he wanted an American commander and was considering Brig. Gen. William Old, who had replaced Haynes as commander of American Air Base No. 1, for the position.[105] He instructed Stone to begin planning for this new command, as well as the Strategic Air Force under the command of Brig. Gen. Howard Davidson and the Tactical Air Force under Air Marshal John Baldwin.

At the Sextant Conference, Arnold, Marshall, and Portal all agreed with Mountbatten's proposal to integrate the two air forces. Over the course of several informal conversations outlining what Mountbatten's operational control over Army Air Force units would mean in practice, Arnold and Marshall added several stipulations that Mountbatten agreed to: first, that the integrity of American units would be maintained; second, that American commanders would retain administrative control; third, that American commanders would also retain responsibility for supply; and fourth, that Mountbatten would become responsible for defending all Air Transport Command facilities within SEAC.[106] Arnold and Marshall also told Mountbatten that he must get the agreement of the Generalissimo before going forward.[107] Mountbatten met with Chiang, who was in Cairo for the Sextant Conference, and told him of the proposed integration of the American and British air forces in India, with Stratemeyer to command the operational units under Air Command, Southeast Asia. Mountbatten assured Chiang that the Fourteenth Air Force would remain under Chiang's command through Stilwell, and that if China required any units of the Tenth Air Force, these would be made available by having Stilwell contact Washington.[108] Arnold was delighted to learn of the Generalissimo's agreement, writing to Mountbatten that "your characteristic tact and force have produced the usual excellent results!"[109] After Mountbatten's return to India at the end of November, Marshall wrote the following to him concerning their discussions on integration:

The command relationship paper which embodies your ideas concerning operational control of forces involved in the Burma operations has been explained to me by General Wedemeyer. I fully recognize that you, as the responsible commander, must be vested with operational control as envisioned in the paper and will gladly lend my support when this subject is presented to the U.S. Joint Chiefs of Staff and the Combined Chiefs of Staff.[110]

Advice from Arnold and Marshall and a small—but illustrative—incident determined Mountbatten's next steps in achieving the integration of the two air forces. At one of their meetings in Cairo, Arnold and Marshall explained to Mountbatten that as supreme allied commander and theater commander for Southeast Asia Command, he had the right to organize the air forces in his command as he wished, and that this right applied equally to American forces and British forces.[111] Apparently at one of their meetings, Arnold said to Mountbatten, "You are the supreme commander, and if I were you, I would go back to India and order integration."[112] On his return from the Sextant Conference, Mountbatten learned of an incident that exemplified the problems with the existing command relationships and confirmed his belief in the need to have a fully integrated air command. Prior to leaving for Sextant, Mountbatten had learned that a Japanese force was moving from Sumprabum toward Fort Hertz. He had ordered a force from the Burma regiment to be flown to Fort Hertz to reinforce the garrison there, and since this was in defense of the American airfields in Assam, he had further ordered the Tenth Air Force to undertake the fly-in. On his return to India, Mountbatten learned that Stilwell's headquarters had canceled the order without informing Mountbatten's headquarters, and the troops were turned back while they were in the air. When he learned of this, Mountbatten drafted orders for the integration of the two air forces.[113]

Stratemeyer returned to New Delhi from Cairo on 9 December 1943. The next day he met with Mountbatten, who told Stratemeyer that he was ordering the integration to go forward. Stratemeyer said he objected to integration and wanted to send a reply to the War Department. Mountbatten asked Stratemeyer to outline for him the reasons for his protest, and said that he would incorporate the objections in his message to the Combined Chiefs of Staff, informing them of his intention to order the integration. Stratemeyer worked up a list of his objections to integration and presented the list to Stilwell on the morning of December 11 for Stilwell's approval before he left for Chunking, passing the list under Stilwell's name to Wedemeyer for Mountbatten. The essence of Stilwell's and Stratemeyer's objections were still that integration conflicted with their directives from Quadrant, and that no new directives had emerged from the Sextant Conference to change the basis of the Quadrant directives. Moreover—and these points may have reflected more of Stilwell's opinions than Stratemeyer's—if Operation TARZAN was not approved and if there were no operations in northern Burma to achieve the objectives set forth at Quadrant, there was no reason for integrating the two air forces. If there were to be no operations to open a land route for China, they felt the better use of American air units was to defend and support the expansion of the air route to China, and that the current system of having the American and British air forces operate in parallel, as was done in England, was perfectly adequate for this purpose.[114]

In his diary entry for 11 December 1943 Stratemeyer recorded that after presenting his and Stilwell's list of objections to Wedemeyer he had lunch with Mountbatten, "where we talked over the whole matter of integration very frankly."[115] Mountbatten saw the interaction somewhat differently, as he explained in a letter to Portal written later in the month:

As I explained in my telegram the situation was truly electric after Stilwell and Stratemeyer had threatened to telegraph Washington rather than carry out my orders to integrate. I read the Riot Act to both of them and drew their attention to the fact that I was an American as well as a British Commander and that their protest to Washington could only be passed through their senior officer, i.e. myself.

I told Stratemeyer I should pass on the protest but with my own comments. I then gave him direct orders to carry on with the integration, which he said he would do. In view of this I asked whether he still wished the protest to be forwarded and he replied that he did.

You can imagine my feelings because I felt that failure on the part of the U.S. Chiefs of Staff to back me would have rendered my position here quite impossible. Failure on the part of Stratemeyer to carry out the orders wholeheartedly would have nullified the value we were going to get from integration. And yet I absolutely had to integrate because the two Air Forces were running in watertight compartments with friction which occasionally came to a head.[116]

After getting Stilwell's and Stratemeyer's objections, Mountbatten prepared a telegram for the Combined Chiefs of Staff outlining their objections with his own comments, noting in the telegram that they had both agreed to loyally carry out his directive on air force integration.[117] Mountbatten pointed out that with regard to the Quadrant directives, he had brought this issue up with Arnold and Marshall and received their agreement to implementing new directives for Stilwell and Stratemeyer. With regard to whether or not TARZAN or other operations would go forward, Mountbatten said that "even if TARZAN is not carried out I intend to fight with all the resources left to me and require the most effective coordination of my air forces in support and obviously this can best be accomplished by integration."[118] Mountbatten reiterated how it was impossible for him to have a subordinate commander in his theater who had independent command over air operations. He finally said that he thought Stilwell and Stratemeyer should be released from the previous Quadrant or War Department directives that conflicted with this new directive.

Later that day he sent a conciliatory but firm letter to Stratemeyer, enclosing a copy of his telegram to the Combined Chiefs, saying that unless he heard back from Stratemeyer he would send out the telegram at midnight that night. Mountbatten's letter read:

My dear Strat,
It is always difficult going against the advice of a Commander whom one likes and admires and has faith in, but it is less difficult for me in this instance than usual, because I know that you once held strong views in favor of integration, and, if I have judged your character correctly, you will throw yourself as enthusiastically into the new set-up now as you would then.

As regards General Stilwell, I again do not feel too guilty, because when he saw Pownall [Lt. Gen. Sir Henry Pownall, SEAC chief of staff], Wedemeyer, and myself, he agreed to accept the directive and let me send it to Washington without comment. The comments are in fact the outcome of my suggestion to you that you should see Stilwell and agree your comments with him. . . .

The R.A.F. in the Bengal Command will be delighted at coming under your command, and I feel confident that you will do great things in the coming fighting, whether we do TARZAN or whether we do some plain straightforward fighting.

Best of luck to you in your vital new job, which will become effective forthwith.[119]

The next day, 12 December 1943, Mountbatten issued Southeast Asia Command Directive No. 5, integrating elements of the Tenth Air Force and the RAF under the air commander in chief, Southeast Asia Command, to form a new subordinate air command (Eastern Air Command) and appointing Stratemeyer as commander. The directive outlined the structure of the new Eastern Air Command and reiterated that unit integrity would continue and that administrative control of operational units would remain with their respective air forces. Eastern Air Command would initially have two components: a Tactical Air Force under Air Marshal John Baldwin, commander of RAF, Bengal Command; and a Strategic Air Force under Brig. Gen. Howard Davidson, commanding the Tenth Air Force. Other groups would be formed as the commander of Eastern Air Command

Maj. Gen. George Stratemeyer presents the Air Medal to Brig. Gen. Robert Oliver in his office in New Delhi in February 1944. On the wall behind are portraits of all the commanders that Stratemeyer reported to as commander of the Army Air Forces, India-Burma theater, and commander of Eastern Air Command. *3A-34166, RG342FH, NARA*

directed. The directive stated clearly that the air commander in chief, SEAC, would take on responsibility for the defense of the Air Transport Command's facilities within SEAC, as Arnold and Marshall had requested, and that Stilwell would continue to command the Fourteenth Air Force and coordinate operations through his position as deputy supreme allied commander, as Mountbatten had promised the generalissimo (for the full text of the directive, see appendix 3).[120] It is interesting to note that in a response to Mountbatten's telegram to the Combined Chiefs incorporating his directive, Marshall said that he wholeheartedly approved of Mountbatten's actions but reminded him of the ever-present reality of America's commitment to China. Mountbatten's proposal was a sound basis for integrating the Allied air forces, but Marshall noted that "in view of our commitments to China, however, we consider the integration of the 10th Air Force with the Royal Air Force on the eastern front of India may have to be re-examined by the Combined Chiefs of Staff at some future time when the situation permits us to move a large part of the 10th Air Force into China."[121]

Stratemeyer now had his orders and he followed them loyally, as Mountbatten expected he would, throwing himself into his new command. The day Mountbatten issued his directive on integration, Stratemeyer met with his staff for five hours to work through the problems that integration would create.[122] The group looked at issues around Stratemeyer's position in the command structure of Air Command, Southeast Asia; the structure of Eastern Air Command and staff integration; and the location of Stratemeyer's headquarters.[123] Stratemeyer presented the recommendations from this meeting to Peirse in a memo on December 14. He began by stating that he saw his primary mission as cooperating with Peirse in the employment of American airpower in the theater to the maximum effect.[124] He then listed six activities that this mission required:

a   Protecting the flow of supplies and personnel by air transport to China
b   Planning and executing air operations against the enemy in Burma
c   Planning and executing very long-range American strategic bombing attacks on Japan from China
d   Meeting the commitments of the American government respecting tonnage over the Hump to China
e   Supplying and maintaining American-built aircraft and Army Air Force units in China and India
f   Training Chinese and American air force units and personnel for combat

As commander of Eastern Air Command, Stratemeyer did not propose to become involved in daily operations, but to delegate that responsibility to his subordinate commanders in the Strategic and Tactical Air Forces with full authority to conduct operations under broad directives. To ensure the full integration that Mountbatten wanted, it would be important to have a full exchange of British and American personnel to establish integrated staffs at Air Command, Southeast Asia; at Eastern Air Command; and in the Strategic and Tactical Air Forces. But since supply and administration would not be subject to integration, he proposed that the exchange of staff concentrate on filling positions relating to plans, operations, intelligence, photography, weather, and communications. His initial thoughts were that the Strategic Air Force would consist of all Allied heavy and medium bombers, while the Tactical Air Force would include fighters, light and dive-bombers, troop carriers, and reconnaissance airplanes. American air units in Assam, as well as Cochran's force for Wingate (then known as Project 9), and the troop carrier squadrons would all be placed with the Tactical Air Force, which would accordingly take on responsibility for the defense of the Calcutta area and the air bases in Assam. He would place his headquarters, at least initially, close to Peirse and Mountbatten but at a later date would likely move closer to the combat zone. Peirse approved these recommendations and on 15 December 1943 issued Air Command, Southeast Asia, Policy Directive No. 1, appointing Stratemeyer as air commander, Eastern Air Command, with RAF Bengal Command and the Tenth Air Force to be reorganized into the Tactical Air Force, with a British commander, and a Strategic Air Force, with an American commander.[125]

Simultaneously, Stratemeyer issued his own directive as commander of Eastern Air Command as General Orders No. 1 (see appendix 4 for the full text).[126] His own thinking on the structure of his new command had already changed, and instead of two subordinate commands he now had four, having added two seemingly overnight:

a   A Strategic Air Force under Brig. Gen. Howard Davidson
b   A Tactical Air Force under Air Marshal Sir John Baldwin
c   A Troop Carrier Command under Brig. Gen. William Old
d   A Photographic Reconnaissance Force with a commander to be announced

The directive spelled out the mission of each of these forces and the organizing principles of Eastern Air Command, and the American and British units that would make up the command (for the Eastern Air Command Order of Battle, see appendix 5). There was much more to be done—more meetings, more plans, more movement of staff—but the integrated air command that Mountbatten had argued for was, after much debate, finally in place. The Allied air forces had achieved unity of command, at least to a degree, While the Fourteenth Air Force and the Air Transport Command remained outside Air Command, Southeast Asia, the bombers, fighters, and

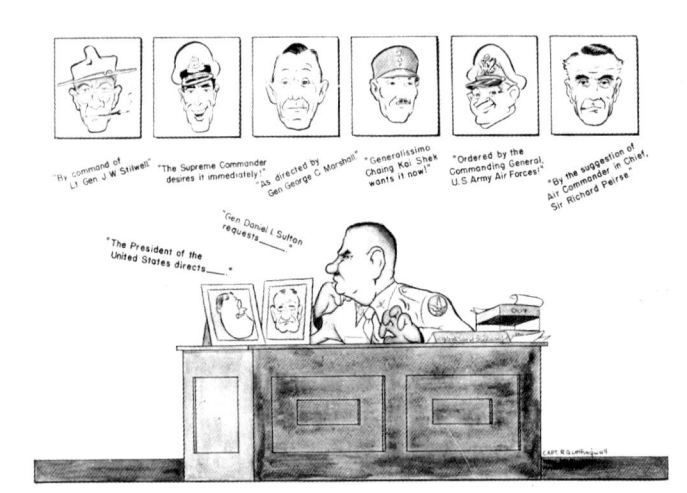

The portraits in Stratemeyer's office prompted this amusing cartoon illustrating the complex, confusing, and often-contradictory Allied command arrangements in the China-Burma-India theater that he had to work with. *Wesley Frank Craven and James Lea Cate, eds., The Army Air Forces in World War II, vol. 4, The Pacific: Guadalcanal to Saipan, August 1942 to July 1944 (Chicago: University of Chicago Press, 1950), p. 438*

Mountbatten excelled at traveling throughout his command to visit Allied units to boost morale and encourage a spirit of enthusiasm and belief in ultimate victory over the Japanese in Burma. Here he addresses a group of Tenth Air Force officers and men of a transport squadron. *SE_008129, IWM*

transport planes of the Tenth Air Force would now work as part of a coordinated team with their counterparts in the Royal Air Force. Stratemeyer ended his directive with a stirring call:

A resourceful, wily and able enemy must be blasted from the jungles of Burma and driven from its skies in the days to come. His line of communication must be obliterated, his shipping destroyed, his will to resist crushed. Against the inevitable day of retribution when Japan's cities will meet the fate of Berlin, our life line to China must be strengthened and protected. Every ounce of energy of every man in this Command will be required to accomplish this purpose. We must merge into one unified force, in thought and in deed—a force neither British nor American, with the faults of neither and the virtues of both. There is no time for distrust or suspicion.

I greet the forces of the Bengal Air Command, and their Commander, Air Marshal Baldwin, as comrades in battle, as brothers in the air. A standard of cooperation which we must strive to surpass has been set by the inspiring example of joint achievement of our colleagues in the Northwest African Air Force. We must establish in Asia a record of Allied victory of which we can all be proud in the years to come. Let us write it now in the skies over Burma.[127]

AIR COMMAND, SOUTHEAST ASIA: INTEGRATING THE ALLIED AIR FORCES

CHAPTER 7

COMBAT RESUMED

Operations, October–December 1943

The End of the Monsoon

The monsoon weather began to taper off during the first weeks of October as the dry season began. There would be good flying weather until the monsoon arrived again the following May. Over the next two and a half months, until its absorption into Air Command, Southeast Asia, the Tenth Air Force would fly a record number of sorties and drop a record number of tons of bombs but lose more aircraft to Japanese fighters than ever before. While the debates on integration of the Allied air forces were going on, there were several command changes within the Tenth Air Force's components. Col. Cecil Combs relinquished command of the India Air Task Force on 11 September 1943 to Col. Torgils Wold, commander of the 341st Bomb Group. Wold's tenure was short, since on October 5, as planned, the IATF was absorbed into the Tenth Air Force and the IATF Headquarters was redesignated Forward Echelon, Tenth Air Force, with Col. John Sutherland commanding.[1] Another long-serving veteran left the Tenth in September, when Caleb Haynes returned to the United States. Brig. Gen. William Old, who had worked with the Assam-Burma-China Ferry and served as Tenth Air Force chief of staff, replaced Haynes as commander of the renamed American Air Command No. 1.[2] With the 26th Fighter Squadron about to leave for China, the American Air Command now had the 80th Fighter Group and the 311th Fighter-Bomber Group under its command, with the 311th Group's three squadrons scheduled to arrive in Assam around mid-October. The missions assigned to the Tenth Air Force remained essentially the same: to protect the air ferry route to China and continue the campaign against the Japanese line of communications in Burma.

A new mission was on the horizon. When Stilwell and his Chinese divisions began their march into Burma from Ledo later in the year, the Tenth would be charged with providing air support.

With the arrival of the 311th Group, American Air Base Command No. 1 had six fighter squadrons, an increase of four squadrons from

An early-model P-40N-1 flying over the jungles of Assam. The 80th Fighter Group's squadrons carried out patrols throughout the day along the routes the transports took on their way across the Hump to China. The P-40s would often escort C-47s dropping supplies to forward units in Burma, to protect them from Japanese fighters. *3A-33758, RG342FH, NARA*

P-40Ns from the 80th Fighter Group wait to take off on patrol. The Tenth Air Force lost the 51st Fighter Group to the Fourteenth Air Force but gained the 80th and the 311th Groups. The 80th took over the air defense of the Assam air bases. *3A-33656, RG342FH, NARA*

two months before. More importantly, the addition of new A-36 dive-bombers and P-51A fighters allowed something of a division of labor between the two fighter groups. The 80th Group's P-40Ns took over defense of the airfields and patrol duties over northern Burma in addition to bombing and strafing missions, while the 311th Group concentrated its efforts on interdiction and, as the months went on, close air support.[3] The interdiction missions followed the pattern the 51st Group had established earlier in the year and covered the following:

1 Regular strafing and fragging the roads and trails leading to Sumprabum and up the Hukawng Valley toward Shingbywiyang
2 Repeated bombing and strafing of Japanese forward positions and supply dumps that supported these positions
3 Offensive reconnaissance sweeps along the roads and rail lines leading from Myitkyina to Sumprabum and from Mogaung up the Hukawng Valley to destroy motor vehicles, locomotives, and rolling stock
4 Repeated bombing of road and rail bridges along these routes to disrupt the flow of supplies to the front lines
5 Bombing and strafing attacks against the key centers at Myitkyina and Mogaung and the towns in the area that served as supply bases[4]

In addition, during their offensive reconnaissance missions the fighter squadrons regularly flew over the Japanese forward airfields at Myitkyina, Bhamo, and other locations, checking the state of repair and keeping a lookout for Japanese airplanes.

The 80th Group's two squadrons closest to the Hump route—the 88th Fighter Squadron, with two flights at Lilibari and one flight at Mokalbari, and the 89th Fighter Squadron, with two flights at Nagahuli and one at Sadiya—had primary responsibility for flying the patrols over the area between Dinjan and Fort Hertz. The squadrons would send out flights of four P-40s several times a day for two-hour-long patrol missions to protect the transports, though complete coverage of this large area was practically impossible. The squadrons alternated patrol duties; for example, the 89th Squadron carried out 143 patrol sorties during the 20 days in October when the weather permitted flying. When not on patrol, the squadrons went on bombing and strafing missions against Japanese-held towns and villages in the area. Bridges were important targets, and the 80th Group quickly adopted the 51st Group's practice of loading up their P-40s with 1,000-pound bombs. The squadrons made it a practice to provide several P-40s as top cover for the P-40 "bombers" with their heavy loads. Bridges were hard targets to knock out, even for fighters bombing from low altitude, and Japanese repair crews worked quickly. The group sent 12 P-40s out to bomb the railroad bridge at Namkwin, 25 miles south of Mogaung on the way to Indaw, in the early afternoon of October 7, and 12 more two hours later, but neither mission took out the bridge, only damaging the northern approach to the bridge. The 90th Fighter Squadron went back to the bridge on October 24, sending out five P-40Ns and a single P-40K with 1,000-pound bombs, but again missed the bridge. The Japanese had already repaired the northern approach to the bridge, but the bombing on this date missed that area and instead hit the tracks leading to the bridge from the south. The 90th Squadron went back again the next day with six P-40 bombers and four as top cover but again missed the bridge, but they tore up the northern and southern approaches. The 89th Squadron tried on October 26 without much more luck.[5]

The 311th Fighter-Bomber Group headquarters and the 528th Fighter-Bomber Squadron arrived at Dinjan on October 11, with the 530th Fighter-Bomber Squadron arriving there on October 18 and the 529th Fighter-Bomber Squadron reaching Dinjan the next

The 80th Fighter Group soon began arming its P-40s with bombs for offensive reconnaissance missions over northern Burma and attacks on Japanese-held towns and villages and road and rail bridges in the area. Armorers load a 250-pound bomb under the wing of a P-40N. *3A-33913, RG342FH, NARA*

A formation of A-36 Invaders flying on patrol over the hills of northern Burma after the end of the monsoon. The 528th and 529th Fighter-Bomber Squadrons both entered combat with the A-36. As attrition took its toll, the 311th Group concentrated the A-36As in the 528th Squadron, with the 529th Squadron taking on P-51As as replacements. *GP-80-SU-PH, AFHRA*

day. The squadrons soon split up, with the 528th Squadron going to Sookerating and the 530th Squadron to Mohanbari, leaving the 529th Squadron at Dinjan. The group flew its first mission on October 16, when eleven A-36s went out to bomb Sumprabum, eight airplanes getting their bombs into the target area in the town. Three pilots from the 529th Squadron who went on the mission failed to return, losing their way in poor visibility as evening came on. The three made forced landings, but the Japanese captured 2nd Lts. Melville Bowman and Christopher Morgan, who became prisoners of war.[6] When all three squadrons had settled into their bases, they began flying regular missions to bomb and strafe ammo dumps, barracks, and other facilities in Mogaung, Hopin, Kamaing, and other towns, as well as the airfield at Myitkyina. The 528th and 529th Squadrons would send out six to eight A-36s on a mission, with four to six P-51As from the 530th Squadron flying top cover. The A-36s usually carried two M-31 300-pound or M-43 500-pound General Purpose bombs, but the squadrons also used M-30 100-pound General Purpose bombs, 120-pound fragmentation clusters, and M-47 100-pound incendiary bombs. The missions rarely encountered more than light and inaccurate antiaircraft fire—often from small arms—so after bombing, the fighter-bombers would go down to strafe their targets.[7]

During November the weather was excellent and both groups flew many more missions. Although the 80th Group had to devote most of its effort to patrols in defense of the Hump route, the 311th Group often sent out three or four offensive missions a day. In total, the Tenth Air Force's fighter squadrons flew 2,057 sorties during the month.[8] When not flying patrols, the 80th Group's squadrons continued their attacks on bridges. The 90th Squadron went back to the Namkwin railroad bridge on November 13 but apparently missed hitting the bridge structure. The 89th Squadron, which flew most of the offensive missions during the month, tried again four days later, damaging the northern approach to the bridge. On November 19 the 89th Squadron went back to the Namkwin Bridge, and on this mission seven P-40s dropped their 1,000-pound bombs to good effect, getting two direct hits that knocked out the bridge's central span and another hit on a trestle that damaged the railway tracks, making the bridge unserviceable. The 311th Group also went after bridges, bombing the bridge at Loilaw—which the 80th Group's P-40s had bombed three times in October—on November 2. Eight A-36s from the 529th Squadron, with six P-51s from the 530th as top cover, bombed the bridge, getting 15 500-pound bombs on the bridge or nearby and getting a direct hit on the central span and knocking out the southern section of the bridge. The 311th Group took its turn at the Namkwin railroad bridge, hitting the bridge on November 2 and again on November 10, getting one direct hit on the bridge and near misses on the approaches. The 529th Squadron took out the road bridge near Mogaung over two missions, the second mission on November 17 getting six direct hits on the bridge and knocking out the west span.[9]

Motor vehicles, locomotives, and rolling stock were important targets but were not often found, since the Japanese had become cautious about using the roads in the area by day or leaving locomotives without camouflage. Yet, occasionally the fighters came across these lucrative targets. The squadrons regularly flew offensive reconnaissance patrols covering the roads and railroad lines. In a rare find on a mission in early October, two pilots from the 89th Squadron flying a patrol south of Sumprabum came upon five trucks 6 miles north of Nsopzup and strafed them, then found four more south of the town and strafed those as well. During November the 311th Group began combining bombing missions with these offensive reconnaissance patrols. After bombing and strafing a target, the A-36s and P-51s would continue covering a section of the railroad line between the target and the next-largest town. On the morning of November 7, four A-36s from the 529th Squadron went out to bomb the railroad junction at Naba, with four P-51As from the

THE TENTH AIR FORCE IN WORLD WAR II

The Japanese became adept at using camouflage to hide their locomotives and rolling stock from prowling Allied fighters. Camouflage covers this entire train on a stretch of railroad line passing through an area of jungle. *3A-33933, RG342FH, NARA*

To protect valuable locomotives, the Japanese built special shelters on short spurs off a rail line, where a locomotive could be pulled off and hidden during the day. As Allied fighters became more active, the Japanese had to restrict their rail and road movements by day to avoid destruction. *3A-33935, RG342FH, NARA*

530th Squadron as top cover. After bombing the junction the two flights followed the rail line north to Mogaung. On the way they found five camouflaged locomotives and strafed them, four emitting clouds of steam indicating hits in the boilers. Later that afternoon the squadrons sent four A-36s with two P-51As to the same area and remarkably found three more locomotives in addition to the four strafed and damaged earlier. The pilots strafed these three new targets, getting hits and sending up more gouts of steam. The 529th and 530th Squadrons flew exactly the same mission five days later on November 12 and found five more locomotives on their sweep of the railroad north from Naba to Mogaung. The planes went down to strafe, leaving four of the five with steam streaming out of the boilers. The pilots found around 120 railcars along the route that they also strafed. Damage to the locomotives was particularly valuable, since the Japanese had fewer and fewer available, and every locomotive damaged meant one less available for pulling freight. During October and November, the groups lost only one fighter pilot on these offensive missions over northern Burma. Capt. John Ruckstuhl was part of a three-plane formation strafing the town of Maingkwan on November 2 when the number three man in the flight saw his airplane slow down sharply after pulling up from their first strafing run. After the second run, Ruckstuhl's airplane had disappeared, but the remaining two airplanes found a column of smoke and flames 2 miles southeast of the town and speculated that Ruckstuhl had engine problems, since they had not seen any antiaircraft fire.[10]

During October, Japanese attacks on the transport aircraft flying the Hump route forced a shift in missions for the 80th and 311th Groups, adding counterair operations to their repertoire. The Japanese were aware from aerial reconnaissance and naval intelligence that the Allies were building up their airpower in India and making heavy use of the ports of Calcutta and Chittagong, clearly intending an attack on Burma. An increasing amount of supplies were going to China over the Hump route.[11] Japanese plans for the dry season were to attack Allied air bases and port facilities to delay this attack. Seeing the increase in capacity over the Hump route, the Japanese decided their second priority would be to strike the air bases in Assam and destroy transport aircraft.[12] The arrival of the *33rd Hikōsentai* in mid-October as the first of the fighter reinforcements for the *5th Hikōshidan* allowed the *50th Hikōsentai* to send eight Ki-43 fighters to the airfield at Myitkyina—repaired during the monsoon—to undertake attacks on the transports, an operation the *sentai*'s pilots called "Tsuzigiri" (Street Murder).[13] The first of these missions took place on 13 October 1943 and was a success, the Japanese fighters shooting down an Air Transport Command C-87 and C-46 and a CNAC transport and damaging a Fourteenth Air Force B-24 and one C-47 from the 2nd Troop Carrier Squadron.[14] The fighters struck again on October 23, shooting down two ATC C-46s and getting a third C-46 the next day.[15] On October 27 the *50th Hikōsentai* went out again, shooting down another ATC C-46, but then saw a formation of B-24 bombers they mistakenly took for unarmed C-87s. These were six B-24Ds from the 308th Bomb Group that Chennault had sent to fill in for the transports lost over recent days in the hope that the Japanese fighters would mistake them for unarmed transports, which the Japanese did. The *50th Hikōsentai* lost three Ki-43s to the bomber gunners, although one pilot managed to make it back to Japanese lines on foot. The gunners on the B-24s claimed eight fighters shot down and more damaged.[16]

After the first attack on the transport aircraft, the 80th Fighter Group had stepped up its patrols over the area between Fort Hertz

An aerial reconnaissance photograph of the Japanese airfield at Lashio, taken in April 1943. The Japanese fighter *sentai* used these airfields as forward bases for attacks on the transports flying over the Hump. Over time, these airfields came under frequent fighter and medium-bomber attacks to limit their use. *Air Headquarters, India, Notes on Japanese Airfields, 802.323, AFHRA*

and Sumprabum, sending out flights of eight aircraft instead of four and maintaining patrols from dawn till dusk.[17] These attacks demonstrated that even with air patrols and the early-warning net in Assam, Japanese fighters could still penetrate the defenses with relative ease since the area the patrols had to cover was so large.[18] In response to the Japanese fighter threat, during November the 80th Group tripled the number of patrols over the Fort Hertz / Sumprabum area, flying 993 patrol sorties.[19] American Air Command No. 1 worked to push the early-warning net as far forward as possible to give the Assam airfields more time for fighters to respond to an incoming attack and set up a radio control station at Fort Hertz to contact the transports and the fighters.[20] As an added precaution, all transport pilots received instructions to fly from Chabua to Kunming along a route farther north of Fort Hertz and away from the areas around Sumprabum, where the transports had run into Japanese fighters.[21] The 80th and 311th Fighter Groups took on the task of carrying out counterair operations, ensuring that Japanese forward airfields, especially at Myitkyina, remained unserviceable.[22]

The first attack on Myitkyina took place a few hours after the Japanese fighters had claimed their last transport plane at 1045 on October 13. Four P-40s from the 80th Fighter Group went to Myitkyina and thoroughly strafed the airfield, but the *50th Hikōsentai*'s fighters had already pulled back to Mingaladon, so the P-40s found nothing. It seems likely that the Japanese were beginning to use these forward airfields as staging posts for short missions, flying into a field in the late afternoon, taking off on a mission early the next morning, and flying directly back to an airfield farther south to limit the risk of losing airplanes to Allied strafers and bombers. The P-40s went back to Myitkyina again, possibly on October 21, while the 88th Squadron carried out a reconnaissance of the main airfield (Myitkyina #1) southwest of the town and nearby landing ground (Myitkyina #2) to the north on October 26 and 27 but saw no aircraft. Both groups went back to Myitkyina on November 8. The 89th Squadron sent out seven P-40s: six as bombers and one as top cover. The flight dropped six 1,000-pound bombs on the airfield, getting two direct hits just south of the center of the runway and two more on a concrete strip nearby. The 311th Group sent out all three squadrons: the 528th and 529th Squadrons provided eight A-36s each for the mission, while the 530th Squadron provided the top cover with six P-51As. The 311th Group's main target was Myitkyina #2, and the A-36s got 14 hits on the runway before going on to bomb Myitkyina town. The 80th Group went back to Myitkyina on November 25, dropping more 1,000-pound bombs and getting hits on the south end of the runway. An offensive reconnaissance on November 30 revealed that Myitkyina #2 still had unfilled bomb craters, while the main airfield was serviceable. To be safe, the groups bombed the airfield at Bhamo and the landing ground at Katha and continued coverage of the Myitkyina airfields into early December. The India-China Wing did not lose any transports to Japanese fighters during November, probably due to the combination of pulling the transports back to a more northerly route, the increased patrols, and the attacks on the forward base at Myitkyina, and the likelihood that the *50th Hikōsentai* had more-pressing duties covering central and southern Burma from Allied air attacks.[23]

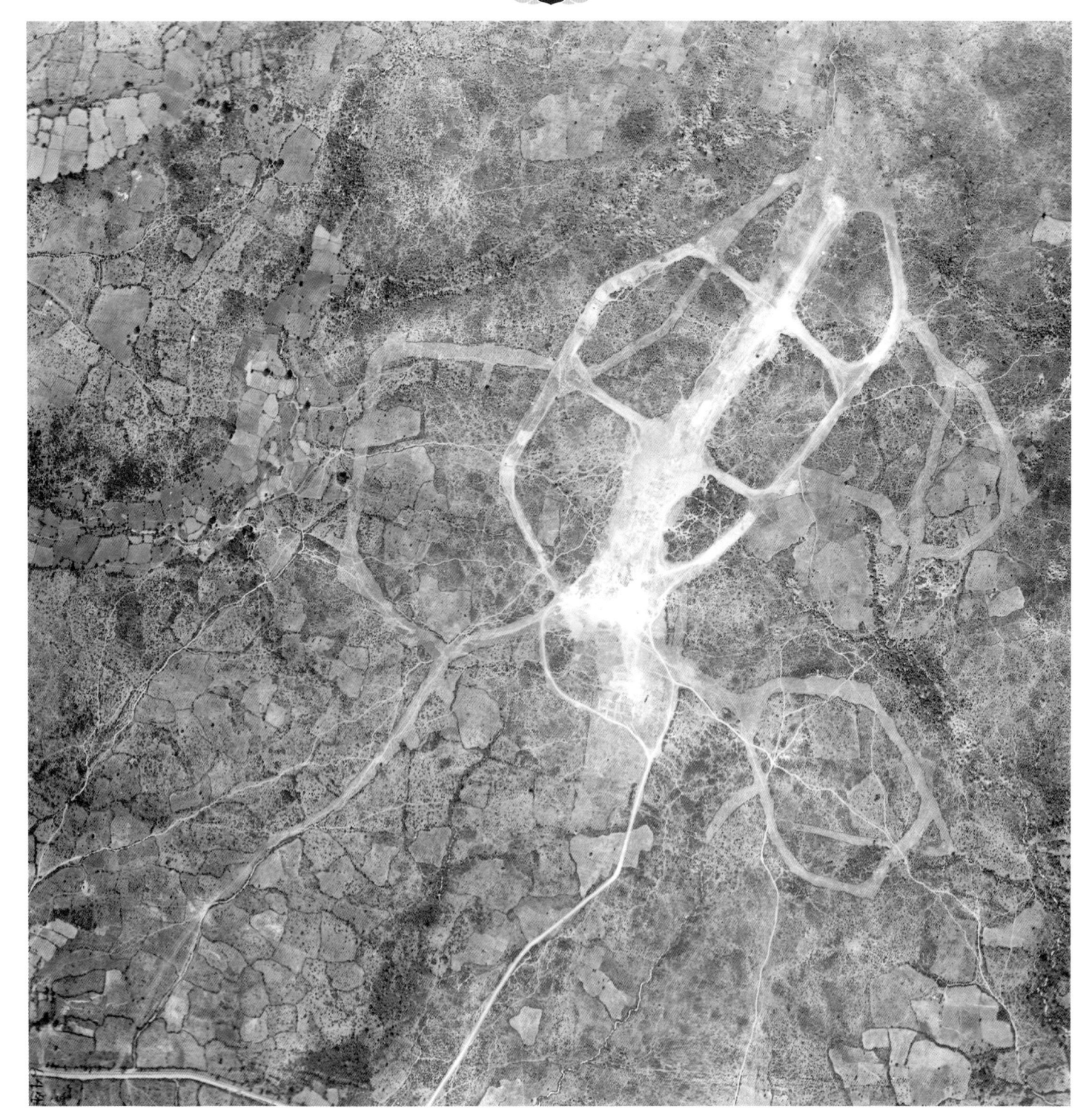

The Japanese airfield at Onbauk, in central Burma, would become a frequent target for American long-range fighters during 1944. *Air Headquarters, India, Notes on Japanese Airfields, 802.323, AFHRA*

The *5th Hikōshidan* launched two raids to Assam in December, combining the first raid on December 10 with a large fighter sweep of the Sumprabum area, sending 25 Ki-43s from the *50th Hikōsentai* out hunting for transport aircraft. That morning the *8th Hikōsentai* sent three Type 99 light bombers (Ki-48 Lily) to carry out a reconnaissance around the Fort Hertz area with an escort of three Ki-43s from the *33rd Hikōsentai* in coordination with the *50th Hikōsentai*'s fighter sweep. Capt. William Harrell was leading a patrol of four P-40Ns from the 89th Fighter Squadron east of Fort Hertz when he saw the Japanese formation flying to the west of Fort Hertz: three bombers he identified as Sallys (Type 97 Ki-21) flying in a V formation with the fighters flying above the bombers. He ordered his flight to drop their belly tanks and started climbing to get above the Japanese. As the P-40s commenced their attack, the three escorting Ki-43s pulled up to meet the American fighters. Harrell fired at one of the fighters and saw smoke come out of the engine as the Oscar rolled over and dived down toward the ground. Harrell continued on toward the bombers and fired at the right-hand bomber in the V, seeing the right engine explode and the left engine begin to smoke badly, and the bomber dived down to the ground.

COMBAT RESUMED

Harrell's wingman, 2nd Lt. Robert McCarty, followed his leader into the attack, firing on the lead bomber before diving beneath the bomber formation. Harrell and McCarty came back in on the bombers, with Harrell firing a burst and then breaking away. McCarty came in after him, firing on the lead bomber, seeing the bomber burst into flame and pieces fly off. Climbing away, he saw an Oscar coming down on him from 1,000 feet above, so he dove down steeply, pulling out at 5,000 feet and then climbing back up to support the leader of the second element, 1st Lt. Charles Whiteley. Coming into attack the bombers, Whiteley found a fighter on his tail and had to dive away, but he pulled back up and attacked the bombers from below, seeing the lead bomber smoking badly from its right engine. He came up under the left-hand bomber and continued firing until both the bomber's engines caught fire, watching as the bomber went into a dive. Whiteley followed the bomber down to see it crash in the jungle below. Whiteley's wingman, 2nd Lt. Dodd Shepard, had joined him in the pass on the bombers but on pulling up saw two Oscars going after McCarty, so he dove down in support, coming in directly behind the Japanese fighter trying to get on McCarty's tail. Shepard gave the fighter two short bursts and saw the Oscar smoke and roll away, bursting into flames. The pilots claimed three bombers and two fighters destroyed for light damage to two of the P-40s. This was close to the mark, since the *8th Hikōsentai* lost all three of the Ki-48s, but all of the *33rd Hikōsentai*'s fighters returned safely, having claimed three P-40s shot down. Two other 89th Squadron pilots claimed two Oscars damaged around the same time, though these may have belonged to the *50th Hikōsentai*, flying near the same area.[24]

That same morning, the 529th Squadron sent out four A-36s and two P-51As to escort eight C-47s from the 2nd Troop Carrier Squadron dropping supplies in the Fort Hertz area. 2nd Lts. Charles Chrismer and Leslie Sturgis broke off to escort two of the C-47s to their drop zone nearby, covering the transports from 3,000 feet as the C-47s went down to the treetops to make their drops. The two pilots spotted eight to ten Japanese fighters that they identified as Oscars and Zekes circling above the transports and about to attack. The two A-36s dived down to break up the enemy formation, easily outdistancing the Oscars and climbing back up before coming in for another pass. Chrismer damaged one Oscar on his second pass, getting hits in the engine, while Sturgis hit one fighter in the cockpit area. Both Oscars broke away. Climbing back up to 6,000 feet, the pilots saw another eight Oscars near a single C-47 and again dove down to the attack, with five of the Oscars turning to meet them head-on. Chrismer fired and got hits in the engine of one of the Oscars, passing underneath the Japanese fighter. Sturgis also hit one of the Oscars on this pass, but the two A-36s then became separated and each found three Oscars coming after them, so they broke down to low level and made their escape. The pilots found that at 350 mph the A-36s could pull away from the Japanese fighters without trouble.[25]

The other two A-36s and the two P-51As remained with the main C-47 formation, flying above at 3,000 feet. Just as the transports began their drop, Japanese fighters attacked, quickly shooting down one of the C-47s. The C-47 went down and exploded in the jungle, killing 2nd Lt. Lynn Harrison and his crew. That morning, 2nd Lt. George Laben—a recent arrival—was flying on the mission as copilot to 1st Lt. Charles Lawton in Lawton's regular C-47, which he had named "Lawton's Limited." Years later, Laben recalled his experiences that morning:

Chuck Lawton and I were one of six C-47s on a mission to Sumprabum, Fort Hertz area. I was flying co-pilot for Chuck and Leo Deruntz was the navigator. . . . We had flown to the area in formation and all of the planes had just gotten into line to start the drop. We were either third or fourth in line. I looked out the side window and saw what I thought to be an AT-6 with fire coming out the front of it. I said to Chuck, "What's an AT-6 doing out here shooting at us?" (How stupid—only a greenhorn at the

The Tenth Air Force's early-warning stations in the mountains east of the Assam airfields were often so isolated they had to depend entirely on air drops for their supplies. The men of this station have put out panels indicating their station number and stand ready to receive the air drop from a C-47 circling above. *3A-36186, RG342FH, NARA*

Lt. Gayda and his crew were lucky to have survived their encounter with Japanese fighters on 10 December 1943. The crew stands near their wrecked and burned-out C-47 (*left to right*): Sgt. Nodoll, PFC Goldberg, PFC Owens, Pvt. Blossom, Lt. Gayda, and Lt. Cahen, his copilot. *3A-34739, RG342FH, NARA*

time.) Chuck yelled, "That's no AT-6, that's a Zero!" and we peeled off. He said, "I'll work the controls, you keep the throttle, prop pitch, etc., full forward and keep me posted on the instrument readings." We instructed the food droppers to dump the load. They did this in record time. Leo kept us posted on where the Zeros were by going from rear side windows to the navigator's dome. I think we had a Zero after us at least three different times. The last one had us lined up pretty good. Chuck dived down sharply and we were well over the instrument red lines; then, at the last second, pulled up sharply over a small mountain ridge. The Zero apparently didn't see the ridge and hit the top of it. The food droppers in the back said they saw the Zero explode. We didn't go back to find out. We continued hedge hopping thru the mountains to the Hukawng Valley and then thru the mountains north of Shingbwiyang into Ledo and back to Dinjan.[26]

Seeing the C-47s under attack, 1st Lt. Harold Paige dived down on the Ki-43, which he identified as a Japanese navy Hamp, as it climbed back up from its attack on the C-47. Paige fired and got hits near the cockpit. The Oscar pilot did a split-S, and as he did so, Flt. Off. Hoyt Hensley, in the second A-36, fired on him, hitting the Oscar in the wing roots. The Oscar did a second split-S, and the third fighter in the string—one of the P-51As—fired without result. The pilots saw the Oscar diving at very low altitude and claimed it as probably destroyed. The four American fighters then climbed back up to 6,000 feet and circled, searching for the remaining five C-47s. The transports had scattered, but Capt. Ivan Hirshburg's C-47 had taken hits during the first attack that killed his radio operator and wounded his copilot and navigator. Seeing two enemy fighters coming at him in a head-on attack, he deliberately crash-landed his plane in the jungle to save his remaining crew. A C-47 rescue ship was also shot down, but Lt. Gayda and his crew survived. One more C-47 suffered heavy damage but made it back to base.[27]

The 529th Squadron fighters couldn't locate the C-47s but saw two enemy fighters a few miles away and went after them. As the A-36s came in, the Oscars went up in a chandelle, with one dropping down on Paige. Following close behind, Hensley fired on this Oscar, hitting the Japanese fighter and seeing parts come off and smoke and flame break out. When last seen, the Oscar was diving steeply toward the ground at 500 feet. Hensley was given credit for shooting the Oscar down. At this point the flight became separated. 2nd Lt. Wilbert McEvoy closed on a fighter he thought was friendly, only to find it was an Oscar. McEvoy came in from behind and opened fire, closing to 50 yards and seeing flames come out of the engine. The Oscar turned to the right, as did McEvoy, meeting the Oscar head-on and firing a long burst. He saw the Oscar go into a river below him and explode. This may have been Wt. Off. Oshima, who failed to return from the mission; he was the *50th Hikōsentai*'s only loss that day.[28]

On their return to base, the American pilots praised their opponents:

The enemy pilots in all encounters were not overly aggressive but displayed a high degree of skill in handling their aircraft. They used the chandelle, and the Split S maneuvers chiefly, and in two instances came in for head on attacks in an inverted position, rolling into an upright position as they passed over the A/C attacked. It is to be noted that they attacked the C-47s at very low altitude, and one interesting maneuver was the Split S, done twice under 1000 feet altitude. There was no apparent formation plan in any of the Jap attacks, but each enemy pilot did coordinate well with his fellow pilots.[29]

As part of their plan to forestall Allied efforts to invade Burma, the Japanese launched a major raid against Calcutta on December 5, involving the reinforced *5th Hikōshidan*, the Imperial Japanese Navy's G4M bombers from the *705th Kōkutai*, and the A6M Zero-sen fighters of the *331st Kōkutai*.[30] A force of 30 bombers, 18 army Ki-21s, and nine G4Ms, with an escort of 101 Ki-43s and 27 A6Ms, struck the dock areas, hitting three merchant ships and starting a large fire in the dock area, but fortunately the damage was not severe. While the RAF lost a number of fighters in the raid, the Japanese did not repeat the attack. On December 13, the *5th Hikōshidan* launched a large raid against Dinjan airfield involving 24 Ki-48 bombers from the *8th* and *34th Hikōsentai*, with an escort of 35 Type 1 fighters from the *33rd*, the *50th*, and the recently arrived *204th*

Pilots from the 80th Fighter Squadron get their ID photos taken. 2nd Lt. Philip Adair (*lower left*) claimed one Oscar fighter shot down, two damaged, and a Sally bomber (Type 97 heavy bomber, Ki-21) damaged during the fighting on 13 December 1943. *GP-80-SU-PH, AFHRA*

Hikōsentai. The raid appeared on the radar screens only 12 minutes before the Japanese formation showed up over Dinjan. The bombers approached the field in two waves, with 12 to 14 bombers in each wave at an altitude of 25,000 feet, with the fighters weaving 2,000 feet above and 500 feet behind the bomber formation. That morning, 2nd Lt. Philip Adair, a member of the 89th Fighter Squadron, was sitting in the alert tent when the red alert warning came on. Adair hurriedly took off in his P-40 and climbed for altitude, expecting per standard procedure to rendezvous with other fighters over the airfield at 20,000 feet. He saw what he thought was a flight of four aircraft, but as he drew closer he realized it was the largest formation of aircraft he had ever seen. He climbed higher and came in from the rear of the Japanese formation on his own, deciding to attack the bomber formation to disrupt their bombing run. He made a pass across the formation, firing as he went, coming in behind one of the bombers on the right side of the formation. He saw hits on the left engine and the fuselage before he had to dive away. Trying to get in at the bombers again, he kept running into the fighter escort, damaging two Oscars. Coming in on his third Oscar, he fired and saw the fighter's landing gear drop and the airplane go down in a spiral to crash in the Naga Hills. He tried for the bombers one more time, but the fighters came in on him and damaged his P-40, forcing him to head home. 2nd Lt. James May Jr. got off in time to attack the bomber formation and claimed one of the Ki-48s as a "Sally," but several other P-40s that scrambled to intercept the raid could not climb to altitude in time. Fortunately the Japanese bombing was poor, and most of the bombs did little damage.[31]

The 311th Group's squadrons also took off to intercept the Japanese formation. The 528th Squadron sent up 19 A-36s from Sookerating, but these failed to make contact with the Japanese. Six P-51As from the 529th Squadron took off from Dinjan, but tragically two collided, killing 1st Lt. Harold Paige. The remaining four planes from this squadron also failed to intercept the Japanese. The 530th Squadron had the only success, with nine P-51As climbing out of Mohanbari 10 minutes after the Japanese had completed their bombing and were heading southeast, back into Burma. The pilots began to attack the formation, apparently as soon as they reached a higher altitude. 2nd Lt. Gordon Cruikshanks climbed above the bombers and, seeing the escorting fighters engaged in combat with P-40s, came down on the right side of the formation, closing in on one bomber and setting the right engine on fire with two long bursts. The bomber left the formation, and another pilot saw a bomber going down in flames. F/O Michael Demos also claimed one of the bombers. He, too, made an attack on the right side of the formation, closing to 50 yards and setting the right engine on fire. The flames spread and the bomber fell off to the right, out of control. Lt. Kenneth Granger made a frontal attack on the bombers, coming in from 12 o'clock on the leading bomber in the first wave, his fire raking the fuselage of the second airplane and then passing on to the second wave, where he damaged two more of the bombers. 2nd Lt. Paul Lucier claimed a "Zero" in the same combat.[32]

The P-40s Cruikshank saw fighting the Oscars were most likely from the 88th Fighter Squadron, which had attacked the Japanese formation slightly earlier. The 88th Squadron had sent out six fighters to escort a B-25 on a mission to bomb Bhamo. On their way to Bhamo, while flying near Shingbwiyang, they heard a call from the KC1 early-warning station, "Payday today," alerting them to the approaching Japanese aircraft and giving them a plot. The B-25 cleared them to break away from providing top cover, and flight leader Capt. George Hamilton ordered the flight to drop their belly tanks and climb for altitude. After flying to the northeast at 21,000 feet for 35 minutes, they headed west and saw the Japanese formation flying south with about 18 bombers at 19,000 feet and the fighter escort of 25 to 30 Oscars flying 2,000 feet above the bombers. As the P-40s came in on the bombers, the Oscars turned into the oncoming Americans to head them off. Hamilton and his wingman, 1st Lt. Patrick Randall, claimed an Oscar that was seen to go down and explode. The leader of the second element, Capt. Owen Allard, fired at an Oscar, hitting the Japanese fighter in the engine, which was seen to explode, the fighter then going down smoking, while his wingman hit another Oscar in the wing roots and saw this Oscar crash as well. The flight claimed one more Oscar destroyed and two damaged. In the confused combat it appears the American pilots undoubtedly fired on the same aircraft, since the Japanese lost just two Ki-48 bombers—one from each of the two bomber *Hikōsentai* on the raid—while the *50th* and *204th Hikōsentai* lost one fighter each. In return, the Japanese fighter pilots claimed 18 American fighters shot down. This was the last attack on Dinjan and the Assam

THE TENTH AIR FORCE IN WORLD WAR II

As Stilwell's Chinese divisions began their advance down the Hukawng Valley, the Tenth Air Force's fighter squadrons began flying close-air-support missions. During the last few months of 1943, the air and ground liaison staffs began working out the basic techniques of close air support that would become standard procedures in the coming fighting in Burma. This row of 80th Fighter Group P-40Ns are armed with 1,000-pound bombs, which were more often used against bridges and towns. *3A-35879, RG342FH, NARA*

airfields for the year, since the Japanese switched their attention to the Fourteenth Air Force airfields at Kunming and Yunnanyi and to British forces in the Arakan in preparation for the planned Japanese offensive.[33]

During the last months of 1943 there were developments in two applications of airpower—close air support and air supply—that would prove vital to the prosecution of the war in Burma. During the war, close air support often served as a substitute for artillery, which in jungle terrain was hard to bring forward.[34] While the RAF squadrons in the Arakan had been providing close air support to British and Indian troops advancing against the Japanese, the Tenth Air Force's fighter squadrons had not been called upon for this mission until after the monsoon, when Stilwell's Chinese force began their advance down the Hukawng Valley toward the end of October.

Air supply and air movement of troops became the key to overcoming the natural and logistical barriers facing the Allied armies as they began their advance into Burma. One of the earliest examples of the rapid movement of troops by air was the transport of Indian troops to reinforce the garrison at Ft. Hertz in northern Burma in June 1943, when the area came under threat from advancing Japanese troops. *3A-37368, RG342FH, NARA*

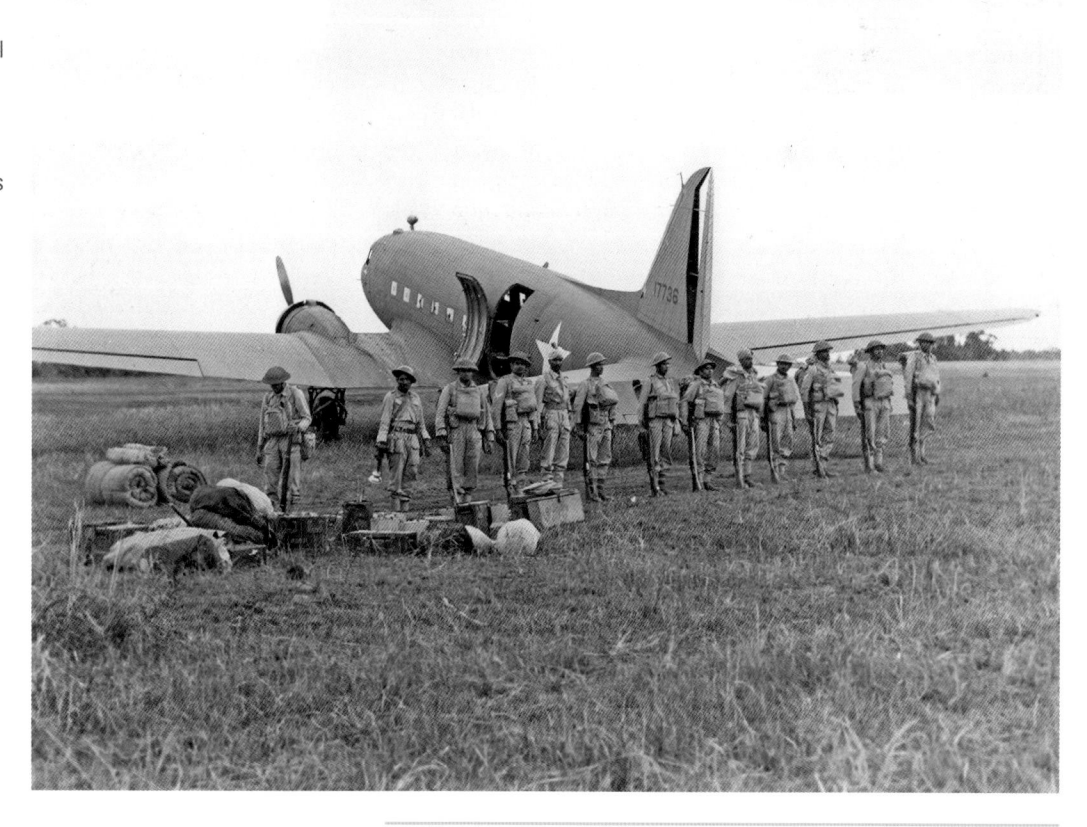

COMBAT RESUMED

Regiments of the Chinese 38th Division began the advance but ran into veteran troops of the *Burma Area Army*'s *18th Division*, charged with fighting a delaying action.[35] Neither the 80th Fighter Group nor the 311th Fighter-Bomber Group had experience with close air support, and up to the months before the advance began there was no joint Army Air Force–Chinese New First Army in India air-to-ground-operations organization in the CBI.[36] Brig. Gen. Haydon Boatner, chief of staff and deputy commander of the Chinese army in India, set up a series of conferences with the Tenth Air Force to begin working out the techniques of close air support and the necessary organizational structure. What was needed was a system that would

1) receive all requests for close air support,
2) screen requests and eliminate those not suitable for air attack,
3) convey the accepted requests with all necessary information to air headquarters to assign a mission to execute the request, and
4) establish effective liaison between Air Intelligence and Ground Intelligence so that Air Headquarters would know the location of friendly and enemy troops at all times.[37]

To establish liaison between air and ground units, an air intelligence officer went to the G-2 (Intelligence) staff with the New First Army, and an air operations officer to the G-3 (Operations) staff. The air intelligence officer kept the air units updated on the current ground situation, while the air operations officer did the screening and forwarding of requests for close air support from the units on the front lines.[38] The first means that was tried to indicate the target to the close support aircraft overhead was with colored, arrow-shaped panels pointing toward the target, sometimes combining this with a system that specified the number of yards to the target.

The frontline troops would place the panels out before the time on target. The results of this early system were uneven. In the dense jungle that was typical of the Hukawng Valley, it was often difficult and sometimes impossible for a pilot flying overhead to see the panel through the jungle's foliage. To make the panels easier to locate, the Chinese troops started placing smoke pots at the point of the arrow to make them more visible.

During November the squadrons of the 311th Fighter-Bomber Group began flying close-support missions for the Chinese troops in the Hukawng Valley, referring to these as "request missions." As an example, on November 10, the 528th Squadron sent out 12 A-36s in flights A, B, and C at intervals in the late morning, armed with M-30 100-pound bombs with instantaneous fuses. The mission was to bomb and strafe an area north of the village of Yubang Ga, where the Japanese *18th Division* was resisting the 112th Regiment of the Chinese 38th Division from strong positions. Mission A found the panels and smoke pots without difficulty, bombing and strafing in the target area and knocking out one Japanese machine gun. Mission B came into bomb but didn't strafe the area, since the pilots saw that the Chinese troops were too close to the Japanese positions. Mission C also did not strafe, but the four A-36s bombed and destroyed another machine gun position and started several fires in the area. The 528th Squadron went back to the same area the next day, with 14 A-36s bombing and strafing the Japanese positions by using M-31 300-pound bombs, this time with 45-second-delay fuses. A frustration for the pilots was that often they could not see the results of their strikes other than explosions in the jungle and occasional fires that erupted after their bombing. As the months went on, the group would fly many more close-support missions, and over time the methods of locating and indicating targets would improve.[39]

Air supply would become one of the keys to Allied victory in the war in Burma. The terrain and weather from the Arakan up through northern Burma made building and maintaining roads difficult and time consuming. There were few to begin with, and

Men from the Quartermaster trucking companies served as kickers on C-47s, kicking out supply packages over the drop zone. These men served for months, taking the same risks as the air crews but without flight pay or any recognition. Nor did they fly a set number of missions. Some of the long-serving men built up more than 1,400 flying hours, according to the Army's official history of the China-Burma-India theater. *3A-37134, RG342FH, NARA*

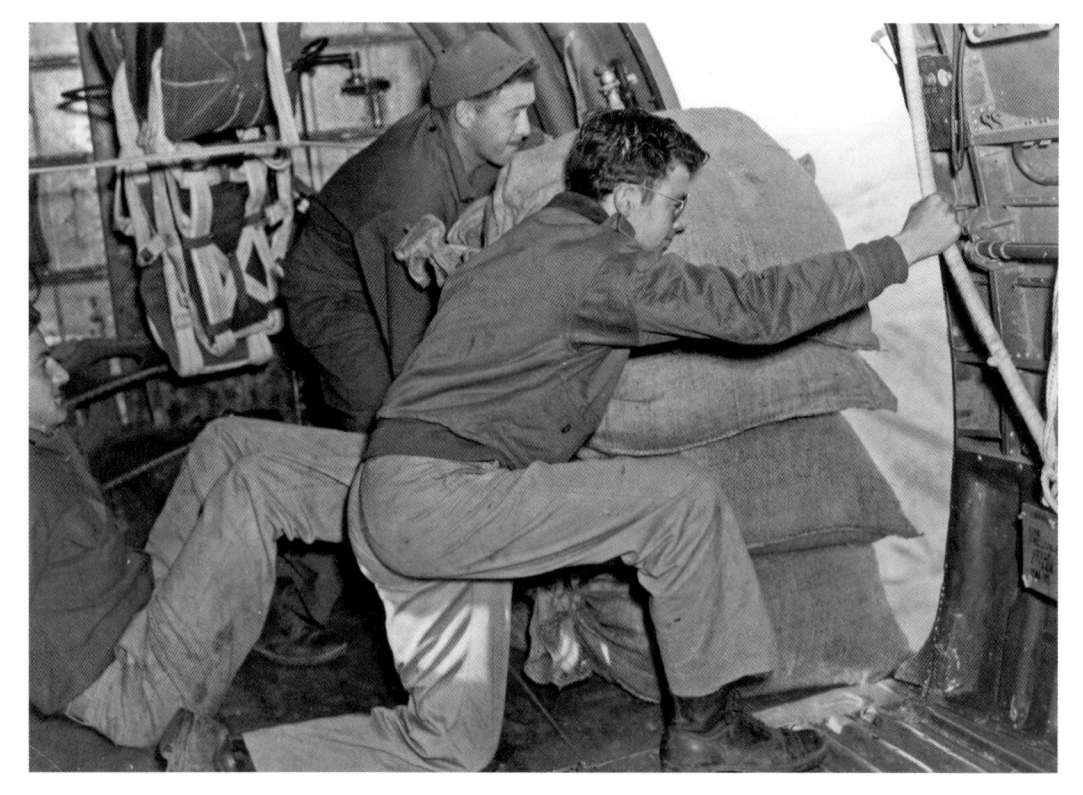

B-25s from one of the 341st Bomb Group's squadrons line up for takeoff on a mission in the last months of 1943. The group's 22nd and 491st Bomb Squadrons were preparing to move to China, leaving the 490th Bomb Squadron as the only Tenth Air Force medium-bomber squadron in India. *3A-33708, RG342FH, NARA*

enlarging the road network involved a great deal of effort and the commitment of significant engineering resources. Air supply provided an answer that was far more economical. There had been a few air drops to columns of refugees during the retreat from Burma in 1942, but the first Wingate expedition demonstrated the potential of air supply. Stilwell decided in early 1943 that the isolated early-warning stations in the Naga Hills and Chinese outposts guarding approaches to the Ledo Road could be supplied by air, and the initial experiments using some C-47s borrowed from the India-China Wing were successful.[40] By summer 1943, the American advisors to the Chinese divisions in India had accepted that air supply would be the method for supplying forward units in their advance down the Hukawng Valley.[41] In July 1943, the 2nd Troop Carrier Squadron moved to Dinjan to provide air supply to the early-warning stations and Stilwell's Chinese troops, with the 1st Troop Carrier Squadron arriving at Sookerating in October to add more C-47s.[42] Slowly an organization built up to put air supply on a regular basis. The G-4 (Logistics) working with the Chinese divisions determined what supplies the troops needed and where the air drop zones would be. Quartermaster companies arranged for the supplies to be gathered, packed, and delivered to the airfields, where they would be loaded onto the C-47s of the 1st and 2nd Troop Carrier Squadrons.[43] Men from Quartermaster Truck companies flew with the aircrews as kickers, kicking the supply bundles out the open door of the C-47 as the airplane flew over the drop zone. By the end of 1943, the amount of supplies delivered by air had grown from 638 tons in October to 1,699 tons in December.[44]

In early December, American Air Command No. 1 underwent a change in name to better reflect its primary mission: the defense of the India-China Wing, Air Transport Command, and its bases in Assam. Brig. Gen. Davidson informed Stratemeyer on 20 November 1943 that as of December 1 the command would be redesignated the Tenth Wing (Provisional), but this designation was only temporary. Stilwell's Rear Echelon headquarters approved a new designation, the 5320th Air Defense Wing (Provisional), activated on 4 December 1943 under the command of Brig. Gen. William Old. When Old became commander of the new Troop Carrier Command, Col. John Egan, who had commanded the 51st Fighter Group up to September 1943, replaced him. The new 5320th Air Defense Wing (Prov.), also known as the Northern Air Sector Force, now controlled the 80th Fighter Group, the 311th Fighter-Bomber Group, the 1st and 2nd Troop Carrier Squadrons, the 51st Fighter Control Squadron, and various signal, early-warning, and antiaircraft units assigned to its bases in Assam. By the end of the year the wing had 692 officers and 5,472 enlisted men under command.[45]

COMBAT RESUMED

Bombs going down on the railroad yards at Naba in central Burma during the 490th Bomb Squadron's mission of 9 October 1943. More than 30 rolling stock are sitting on the tracks and the sidings, possibly waiting to be unloaded or to be moved to the next station. *3A-37709, RG342FH, NARA*

During the last few months of 1943, the 341st Bomb Group received a few B-25G aircraft fitted with a 75 mm cannon and two .50-caliber machine guns in the nose. Under the Tenth Air Force's code system for its aircraft, the B-25G was dubbed "Fisher."
Personal collection of Maj. Gen. Howard C. Davidson, 168.7266-230, AFHRA

Bombing Resumed

For the medium bombers, for whom the monsoon weather had not been as troubling, the clearer skies of October brought more missions and a record both for number of sorties and tons of bombs dropped on targets in central Burma. The planned transfer of the 341st Bomb Group to the Fourteenth Air Force would disrupt the medium-bombing effort during November, cutting the number of sorties by two-thirds. The battle against the Japanese line-of-communications system continued unabated. Most of the missions flown during October and November were against railroad targets, blasting railroad junctions, railroad yards, the buildings nearby, and locomotives and rolling stock. With more Japanese fighters in Burma but more long-range Allied fighters available, the mediums now often went to Burma with an escort of P-51As from the 530th Fighter-Bomber Squadron or the P-38s from the 459th Fighter Squadron, though encounters with Japanese fighters were infrequent.

On some targets the flights would bomb in sequence, coming in from different directions to spread the bomb pattern over the target area. The squadrons also used a greater variety of bombs, with each flight carrying a different bombload. In an attack on the railroad junction at Naba on 9 October 1943, 12 B-25s from the 490th Bomb Squadron dropped 96 M-30 100-pound bombs, 24 M-57 250-pound bombs, and five M-43 500-pound bombs, destroying many railroad cars and the tracks. The next day the squadron sent 12 B-25s to bomb the town of Natchaung—the alternate target—with 648 M-41 20-pound fragmentation bombs and 2,488 M-50 4-pound incendiary bombs. A and B flights went across the target area first, dropping fragmentation bombs, followed by C and D flights dropping incendiaries. In addition to bombing railroad facilities, the squadrons went on rail sweeps, dropping bombs directly onto the railroad tracks, with the flights taking different sections of a line. The aircraft would bomb individually, dropping one M-43 500-pound bomb at a time. Though sometimes the bombs would bounce off the tracks, a hit on the tracks or alongside on the embankment could rip open a wide section of track.[46]

Despite the regular bombing of the line-of-communications system, supplies were still getting through. Attacks on railroad yards, junctions, sidings, workshops and warehouses, and tracks "gave promise of favorable returns, and all were tried with varying degrees of success. But the Japanese became amazingly adept at making repairs and unsnarling traffic. Hence it was ultimately recognized that these methods were achieving little permanent damage, and that only by destroying locomotives and rolling stock could progressive and cumulative dividends be realized."[47] The 341st Group's squadrons had for some months armed their B-25s with fixed machine guns mounted in the nose of the airplane for strafing, but in late October the 490th Squadron received a more powerful weapon when several B-25G aircraft arrived for the squadron. The B-25G carried a 75 mm cannon and two .50-caliber machine guns in the nose, the cannon fitting into what was the bombardier's compartment. The B-25G carried 21 rounds of high-explosive or armor-piercing 75 mm rounds for the cannon that had to be hand-loaded by a "cannoneer." The Tenth Air Force had assigned bird names to all the different types of American aircraft operating in India, designating the B-25C a "Gull" and the B-25D a "Crow" (see appendix 1 for the full list of designations). When the B-25Gs arrived in India they received the code name "Fisher." The first mission with the B-25s appears to have taken place on November 15, when Maj. Robert McCarten, commanding the 490th Squadron, led three B-25Gs with an escort of four fighters to go after two locomotives reported in a small town on the railroad line. Each airplane carried six M-43 500-pound bombs and 11 shells for the 75 mm cannon. One of the B-25s hit one of the locomotives with a 75 mm shell, causing severe

Bombs hitting directly on the railroad tracks and the rolling stock in the yard. The bombers had to attack these railroad targets repeatedly to ensure the yards remained out of service. *3A-37710, RG342FH, NARA*

Crews from the 490th Bomb Squadron get a briefing before their next mission near one of the squadron's B-25s at their base at Kurmitola. The rain has let up enough to hold the briefing outside. *3A-36150, RG342FH, NARA*

All the Tenth Air Force's squadrons learned to make do with what was available. The briefing officer for this 490th Bomb Squadron mission has tacked a map of central Burma, showing the target for the day's mission, to a piece of wood and hung it from a metal repair stand. *3A-36151, RG342FH, NARA*

damage, then the bombers came in at low level, with two 500-pound bombs demolishing the locomotives. The B-25Gs went back after locomotives on November 17 and 18, the 75 mm shells proving to be devastating and knocking out two more locomotives, one of which was destroyed with a 500-pound bomb. On a mission in early December the B-25Gs damaged three locomotives and a riverboat, having severely damaged two others a few days earlier. The B-25Gs also flew on regular bombing missions, apparently dropping on the lead aircraft. These early missions demonstrated that the 75 mm cannon was a potent weapon.[48]

The squadrons flew fewer missions against bridges, with limited results. During October the squadrons went after bridges on the 20th, 22nd, and 23rd without inflicting much damage. On the 23rd the 491st Squadron sent 12 B-25s against the Meza Bridge, and although observations and photos deemed the bombing excellent, the bridge remained undamaged. The 490th Squadron also tried the same day, dropping 21 M-44 1,000-pound and 11 M-43 500-pound bombs: the A flight got only near misses, B flight got one hit on one of the approaches, C flight straddled the bridge, and D flight found its lead bombsight inoperative and had to drop by an estimated angle—cloud covered the target, preventing any indication of the result. While the medium bombers were still more accurate bombing from medium altitude than the B-24s bombing from higher up, bridges remained an especially difficult target to hit, and the Japanese repair crews were exceptionally good at making rapid repairs.

COMBAT RESUMED

Medium bombers attacking the Myitnge Bridge, a frequent target both for the 341st Bomb Group's B-25s and the 7th Bomb Group's B-24s. With the departure of the 22nd and 491st Bomb Squadrons to China, the 490th Bomb Squadron took on the task of destroying the bridges. *3A-37617, RG342FH, NARA*

Pilots from one of the 341st Bomb Group's squadrons get a hurried briefing before boarding their B-25s. Two of the pilots wear prominent American flags and a "blood chit" in Chinese on the back of their flight jackets to identify themselves as American fliers. *3A-36201, RG342FH, NARA*

THE TENTH AIR FORCE IN WORLD WAR II

Frustrated with their relative lack of success destroying bridges with medium-altitude bombing, the 490th Bomb Squadron began experimenting with other techniques, including bombing from low level. This B-25 has just flown a practice skip-bombing run at low level. While not the final answer, skip bombing led to the discovery of the technique that did work. *3A-33674, RG342FH, NARA*

Responsibility for the bridge campaign fell to the 490th Squadron during November. In preparation for the planned move to China, the Tenth Air Force ordered the 22nd and 491st Bomb Squadrons to cease operations after November 7. This left the 490th Squadron as the Tenth Air Force's only medium bomber for the following month, until administrative problems relating to the transfer caused the 341st Group's move to China to be delayed until January.[49] The 341st Bomb Group, with the 22nd and 491st Bomb Squadrons, was relieved of assignment to the Tenth Air Force on 25 October 1943 and reassigned to the Fourteenth Air Force, regaining the 11th Bomb Squadron in the process. The 490th Squadron remained assigned to the Tenth Air Force. As the group history recorded, "everyone wanted to go to China due to the unanimous hate of the Indian climate."[50] At Kurmitola, home to the group headquarters and the 490th Bomb Squadron, the men experienced the blistering heat and heavy rains of the monsoon while living in thatched and woven bamboo bashas, with only an occasional trip to Calcutta as a diversion. The two China-bound squadrons stood down on November 7 and did not fly missions again until December 4.

Within the 490th Squadron there was great frustration with the apparent inability to knock out bridges. The 490th and its sister squadrons had tried bombing at different altitudes, using different approaches to a bridge, and using different weights of bombs from 2,000 to 500 pounds, all seemingly to no avail. Some new tactic was

B-24D "Sittin' Bull" heads for the Rangoon docks during a mission after the end of the monsoon. After flying 56 missions over Burma and renamed "Rangoon Rambler," this B-24D took a veteran 7th Bomb Group crew back to the United States for a bond tour. *3A-33755, RG342FH, NARA*

COMBAT RESUMED

needed to destroy a bridge, and if medium altitude didn't work, possibly a low-level attack might. After a conversation he had with Brig. Gen. Davidson, Lt. Col. James Philpott, who had recently relinquished command of the 341st Group, decided to try a new approach: skip bombing. Borrowing a B-25 and with two P-51As as escort, Philpott went to the Zigon railroad bridge to try his luck from 50 feet with a single 1,000-pound bomb. His aiming point was the connecting approach between the bridge structure and the riverbank. He came in on the railroad track at a 45-degree angle at 320 mph to release his bomb. The bomb had a ten-second-delay fuse, giving Philpott time to pass over the bridge and farther away before the bomb went off. Circling back to view the result, Philpott saw that while the bridge was still standing, his bomb had blown apart the approach to the bridge. As a further experiment, Philpott went back the next day to try releasing two 1,000-pound bombs at the same time, but this did not work. While one bomb hit the approach, the other bomb sailed right through the bridge structure, landing and exploding nearly a mile away. As Philpott concluded in his report to Davidson on his experiment, "it is impossible to miss with low level tactics, and on an undefended target this appears to be the way to destroy an objective."[51]

Skip bombing proved to be only a partial answer. When the 490th Squadron tried the technique on November 7 on several bridges on the railroad line south of Wuntho, seven B-25s, bombing individually with M-44 1,000-pound bombs, failed to do any damage to the bridges. In almost every case the bombs went over the bridge. On the one definite hit on the approach to a bridge, the bomb failed to detonate. The only consolation was finding a number of railroad cars that the bombers strafed. The squadron tried again on November 15. Six B-25s went after smaller bridges along the rail line, bombing from 150 feet, and on this mission got one good hit that knocked out the southern approach to one bridge, but most of the bombs went over their targets. On November 17, three B-25C/Ds and three B-25Gs went to bomb bridges and attack locomotives, with similar results. There were a few direct hits on approaches, but no damage to the bridges themselves. Success came the next day when a low-altitude attack knocked out the northern half of a small railroad bridge by using M-43 500-pound bombs dropped in individual runs. The technique was difficult, but Maj. McCarten decided to keep experimenting to find a method that would work against the bridges and instituted a training program. The answer, as it happened, was just a few weeks away.[52]

Despite all the efforts of the medium and heavy bombers, the campaign against the Japanese lines of communication during 1943 could not be judged a success.[53] The bombing had not stopped the flow of supplies into Burma, though it had made the task considerably more difficult. But this campaign was a battle of attrition without a single decisive victory, and in that sense what was accomplished during 1943 was a considerable achievement. The bombing of railroad yards, warehouses, and bridges and the destruction of locomotives and rolling stock had cut the daily average traffic over the Burmese railroad system from 337 cars a day in January to 218 cars in December. What the air crews couldn't see, but was the result of their efforts, was "upset train schedules, delays caused by damage to bridges and trackage, loss of supplies, and the necessity of employing so much equipment and so many laborers in repair work. . . . Repaired bridges [that] could no longer bear normal loads, and rebuilt locomotives [that] were not up to standard."[54] The Tenth Air Force lacked the numbers of aircraft and the weapons required to do the job, but these would arrive in the months ahead.

The Rangoon Missions

As the monsoon weather receded, targets in southern Burma became open again, and the B-24s went back to the Rangoon area. During October the heavy bombers added their weight to the battle against the lines of communication, bombing several railroad facilities in central Burma. Still short of its full complement of aircrews, the 7th Bomb Group began flying more multisquadron missions to get more aircraft to the target. At the end of September the 436th Bomb Squadron moved to join the 492nd Bomb Squadron at Panagarh, while the 9th and 493rd Bomb Squadrons remained at Pandaveswar. This move allowed an easier pairing of squadrons for joint or group missions. The group had several sharp encounters with Japanese fighters, losing several airplanes. More losses would follow during November, when the reinforced Japanese fighter units attacked in greater strength. Newer B-24J aircraft with nose turrets, which the group received toward the end of October, did not prove to be as effective as had been hoped, but the presence, at long last, of escort fighters did provide a stronger defense. At the end of November the 7th Group participated in the largest bombing raids the CBI theater had yet seen: a coordinated effort to knock out key targets in Rangoon involving the 7th Bomb Group, the 341st Bomb Group, RAF bombers, and the 308th Bomb Group, loaned from the Fourteenth Air Force.

Japanese shipping remained the priority target, and the 7th Group's first mission to Rangoon in nearly a month was to bomb ships in the Rangoon River. On October 3 the group sent 26 bombers to Rangoon, with 19 bombing a larger freighter, getting two direct hits and several near misses. Antiaircraft fire damaged three bombers and another was slightly damaged when four Ki-43s made a half-hearted attack on the formation after the bombing run. The group went back to Rangoon the next day, but the 22 B-24s that bombed shipping missed the ships and hit the docks alongside. After leaving the target, five Ki-43s and two Ki-45 fighters intercepted the formation and kept up a running fight for 40 minutes, though the 9th Bomb Squadron described the attacks as "displaying no great eagerness for battle."[55] In this combat the *50th Hikōsentai*, which had returned to Rangoon from Malaya two days before, lost the commander of the *1st Chutai*, Capt. Yoshihiro Takanarita, to the bomber gunners.[56] The group ran into a hornet's nest 10 days later when all four squadrons went back to Rangoon to bomb shipping, with the Pazundaung works as the secondary target—the 9th and 493rd Squadrons as one pair with the 436th and the 492nd as the second. After bombing Pazundaung, the 9th and 493rd Squadrons ran into 12 Oscars from the *64th Hikōsentai* and seven Nick fighters from the *21st Hikōsentai*. During a battle that lasted over an hour, the 493rd Squadron lost one B-24 to the fighters. The group returned to Rangoon again on October 26, still going after shipping in the Rangoon River. The 9th, 436th, and 493rd Squadrons bombed a large freighter (*Dover Maru*, of 3,212 tons), getting direct hits and near misses that sank the vessel. The 492nd Squadron bombed the docks nearby. The interception followed, with the *64th Hikōsentai* sending up nine and possibly as many as fifteen fighters and the *21st Hikōsentai* sending five to seven Ki-45s. The 493rd Squadron had four bombers damaged, and the 492nd Squadron lost one aircraft.[57]

During October and November the 7th Group flew 13 missions to bomb railroad facilities in central Burma, building on the work of the medium bombers but also going to targets farther to the south, beyond the range of the mediums. The B-24s went to the Sagaing railroad yards and to Naba, Myingyan, Myitnge, and Prome, as well as to Toungoo, Pyinmana, and Kanbalu, adding to the destruction. Following the attacks on the Hump transports, the

The railroad yards at Thazi under attack. The station, warehouses, engine sheds, and tracks received heavy damage during this 7th Bomb Group attack on the yards. Although the Japanese became adept at making repairs to bridges and railroad yards, repeated attacks on the rail yards in Burma diverted Japanese engineering resources away from other tasks. *3A-37779, RG342FH, NARA*

The 7th Bomb Group received new B-24J models in November 1943, but these proved to be less effective than hoped, since the gunners did not have enough time to train thoroughly in using the new nose turret. A fighter attack on a November 11 mission to Heho hit Lt. Robert Graves's new B-24J, wounding Graves, killing his copilot, and knocking out his hydraulic system and one engine. TSgt. Doug Labat, the flight engineer, flew the damaged bomber most of the way back to India, where Graves revived to make a successful landing. *3A-33583, RG342FH, NARA*

COMBAT RESUMED

group bombed several Japanese airfields in northern Burma, hitting Heho, Lashio, and Loiwing to keep these forward airfields unserviceable. A mission to bomb the Japanese barracks at Maymyo on 14 November 1943 together with B-25s from the 490th Bomb Squadron proved costly. The 493rd Bomb Squadron went out with the 9th Bomb Squadron with an escort of P-51As from the 530th Fighter Squadrons on the group's second mission with fighter escort. Clouds over Maymyo led the squadron commander to go to the alternate, but confusion led to the 9th and 493rd Squadrons splitting up, the Mustangs remaining with the 9th Squadron. The six new B-24Js of the 493rd continued on their own to the alternate, where they ran into seven and possibly more Ki-43s from the *50th Hikōsentai*. Making concentrated frontal attacks on the bombers, they shot down one B-24 and inflicted mortal damage on two others, including that of the squadron commander, Maj. William Werner, a veteran of 52 combat missions. The Oscars did not get away unscathed, with the bombers shooting down two fighters and damaging a third so badly that the pilot had to crash-land on the way back to his base. In a little over a month the 7th Bomb Group had lost six B-24s, more than in any previous month.[58]

Planning for a major operation against Rangoon began early in November. Since arriving in India, Stratemeyer had wanted to work for greater cooperation between the Army Air Forces in the CBI and the RAF in the prosecution of the air war over Burma.[59] He suggested to Peirse that the AAF and the RAF coordinate in attacking key targets in the Rangoon area to inflict severe damage, the AAF attacking by day and the RAF by night, to which Peirse agreed. Stratemeyer then proposed to Chennault that the Fourteenth Air Force join the RAF and the Tenth Air Force and send the 308th Bomb Group to India for the raids. Stratemeyer met with Chennault at Kunming on 12 November 1943 and secured his agreement.[60] At the time, a shortage of gasoline in China limited the number of missions Chennault's bombers could fly, and a series of missions from India could damage Japanese air and ground strength in Burma, which would also potentially benefit China.[61] The planning staffs at RAF Bengal Command and the Tenth Air Force worked out the details of the operation. The planners decided the locomotive works at Insein would be the priority target. As the only facility in Burma capable of repairing locomotives, destruction of the Insein works would have a significant impact on the Burmese railroad system and the limited number of locomotives the Japanese had available already subject to air attack from AAF and RAF fighters and bombers. The second priority was the Mahlwagon marshaling yards, since this target would be relatively straightforward for RAF bombers to locate at night. The third target was the dock areas of Rangoon, in the hopes that a major raid would devastate the docks, rendering them unusable for a significant period.[62]

Because the 308th Bomb Group could stay in India only a short time, the operational plan had a tight schedule over six days and five nights. The plan called for the 7th Bomb Group to attack the Insein works on November 25, while the 308th Bomb Group and the 490th Bomb Squadron would provide a second wave to attack airfields around Rangoon. RAF Wellington and Liberator bombers would attack the Mahlwagon marshaling yards that night, with a follow-up attack the next day with the combined 7th and 308th Bomb Groups. The RAF would begin the attack on the dock area by night, the 7th and 308th Groups attacking by day for a period of days. Because of expected Japanese air opposition, the daylight attacks would have an escort of P-38s from the 459th Fighter Squadron and P-51As from the 530th Fighter-Bomber Squadron, the first time Allied fighters would fly over Rangoon since a year and a half earlier. A complication was that the B-25s and the fighters did not have the range to reach Rangoon from their staging base at Kurmitola, so the plan called for the bombers to refuel at Chittagong and the fighters at Ramu, near Cox's Bazar.[63]

Loading drop tanks under the wings of a 459th Fighter Squadron P-38H Lightning. P-38s had the range to escort B-24s all the way to Rangoon—a novel but welcome experience for the bomber crews. *SC267015, RG111, NARA*

P-51As from the 530th Fighter-Bomber Squadron joined the 459th Fighter Squadron's P-38s on the missions to Rangoon, the first time Allied fighter aircraft had appeared over the city.
3A-35834, RG342FH, NARA

The Rangoon missions got off to a bad start. The 9th Bomb Squadron lost two B-24s in succession on the day of the first mission, 25 November 1943. The crashes of the heavily laden B-24s killed both crews.
Courtesy, Jim Augustus

The weather on 25 November 1943—the first day of the operation—did not cooperate. The mission got off to a bad start when the 9th Bomb Squadron lost two B-24s in successive takeoffs, killing the two crews and delaying takeoff for the mission. After takeoff, seven aircraft from the 7th Bomb Group and seven from the 308th Group had to turn back due to mechanical difficulties. The 7th Group headed for Insein, only to find the target covered in cloud, so they aborted the mission, some of the aircraft bombing Akyab on the return flight. The 308th Group also found heavy cloud over its target (Zayatkwin airfield), but 10 airplanes bombed as best they could through the cloud, losing one bomber to antiaircraft fire. There had been a mix-up with the fighter escort. Since the bombers were late getting off, they missed their rendezvous with the P-38s who were to escort the 7th Group. Six P-51As from the 530th Squadron detailed to escort the 308th Group had delays refueling at Ramu, taking off later than planned, and had to speed to Rangoon to catch up with the bombers. While the P-51s were searching for the bomber formation over Rangoon, a flight of *64th Hikōsentai* Ki-43s jumped them,

COMBAT RESUMED

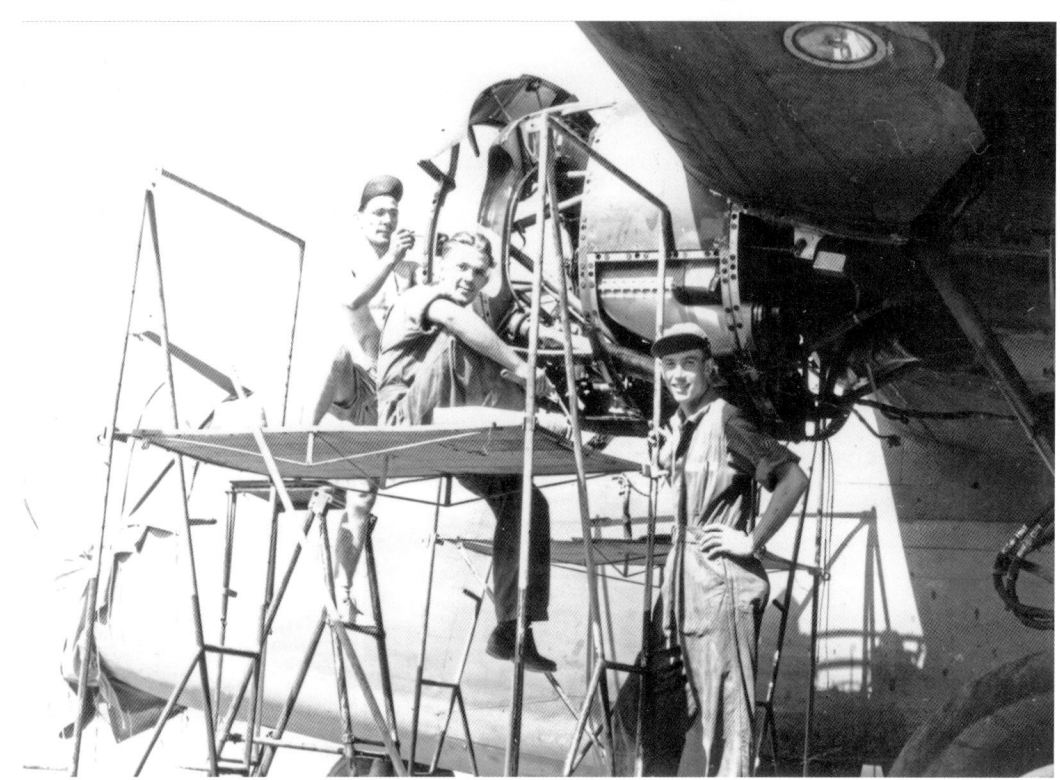

The 308th Bomb Group flew to India to join the 7th Bomb Group for the series of missions to Rangoon. The hard-pressed 7th Bomb Group ground crews had to do double duty servicing and repairing twice the number of B-24s they normally maintained. *7th Bombardment Group Historical Foundation, USAFA*

shooting down two of the Mustangs, while Mustang pilot 1st Lt. James England claimed one Ki-45 shot down and another pilot claimed a Ki-43 as probably shot down. An hour later the 490th Bomb Squadron attacked Mingaladon airfield with an escort of 12 P-51As from the 530th Squadron, with Col. Harry Melton, the 311th Group commander, leading the fighters. Once again the Japanese fighters rose up to intercept, with 12 Ki-43s and six Ki-45s attacking. 2nd Lt. Clifton Bray went after a Ki-45 flying at 8,000 feet, closing in to point-blank range. The Ki-45's left engine exploded and the twin-engine fighter went into a spiral that turned into a dive, and it crashed and exploded below. Two other pilots claimed Ki-45s, and 2nd Lt. Geoffrey Neal claimed a Ki-43 probable, but the Japanese lost only a single Ki-45. Col. Melton's P-51 took a hit in the cooling system, and after flying 150 miles north of Rangoon he had to bail out, becoming a prisoner of war. The next day bad weather over southern Burma caused the planned missions to be canceled, but that night RAF Wellingtons and Liberators bombed the Mahlwagon yards.[64]

With the original schedule thrown off, the 7th and 308th Groups went back to bomb the Insein works on November 27 with an escort of eleven P-38s and five P-51s. A total of 49 B-24s reached the target, the largest force of bombers yet to fly over Rangoon. In a letter to Gen. Arnold reporting the offensive against Rangoon, Davidson described the two bomb groups as having done "an almost perfect job on this mission. At least 70% of the repair shops were destroyed in ten minutes."[65] Just before starting the bomb run, the Japanese fighters came in: eight Ki-43s and one Ki-44 from the *64th Hikōsentai* and four Ki-45s from the *21st Hikōsentai*. Capt. Kuroe, leading the attack, had ordered his pilots to attack the escorting fighters first, then go after the bombers. The escorts had a hard fight, with the 459th Squadron making no claims but losing two P-38s to the Oscars. The 530th Squadron did better. 1st Lt. James England attacked a fighter he identified as a Zeke, opening fire at 150 yards and watching as the Japanese fighter exploded. This was most likely the sole Ki-44. 2nd Lt. Robert Mulhollem fired on an Oscar from 100 yards, the Oscar bursting into flames and diving down out of control. Mulhollem

During the mission to Rangoon on 17 November 1943, Capt. Sydney Newcomb from the 530th Fighter-Bomber Squadron claimed one Ki-45 Nick and one single-engine fighter damaged. Two days later Newcomb claimed two Oscars destroyed. Newcomb would go on to claim two more Japanese fighters shot down during May 1944. This dates this photo of his airplane, "Sis the Second"—showing four victory markings—to late May 1944. *Jack Lambert Collection, MoF*

then attacked a second Oscar, sending it down smoking, and knocked pieces off a third. 2nd Lt. Geoffrey Neal claimed a probable Ki-45, but the 530th Squadron lost two pilots in the encounter.[66]

The *64th Hikōsentai* had absorbed the lessons of past combats with the B-24s and now knew how to attack the big American bombers. During the monsoon the *64th* had withdrawn to Singapore, where Capt. Kuroe had arranged for his pilots to practice head-on attacks against a B-17 captured in Java.[67] The answer was to launch repeated attacks from the front, and the *64th Hikōsentai* now had enough planes to make an impact. When the Japanese fighter pilots went after the bombers, they made repeated frontal attacks from the 10 o'clock and 2 o'clock positions. Their closing speed made it

The Botataung Docks at Rangoon were the target for the mission of 18 November 1943. Both the 7th and 308th Bomb Groups hit the target area with excellent results and on this occasion did not lose any bombers to attacking Japanese fighters. *3A-37743, RG342FH, NARA*

difficult for the gunners, new to the nose turrets on the B-24J, to track them. The 9th Squadron had nine aircraft damaged, one so severely that it crashed in the Bay of Bengal on the return flight. The 308th Group lost two bombers shot down, with Sgt. Horoji Morio of the *21st Hikōsentai* claiming one of the bombers with the 37 mm cannon in his Ki-45. The 7th Bomb Group claimed one Nick and three Oscars shot down, while the 308th Group claimed one Nick and five Oscars. The Japanese lost one Ki-43 and a second damaged, the single Ki-44, and one Ki-45 in this fight. Shortly thereafter the 490th Squadron came in to bomb Insein from medium altitude, and over the target the fighters came in on them, the bomber gunners claiming one Oscar shot down. The 530th Squadron had provided 10 P-51As as escort to the B-25s, and they quickly engaged the enemy fighters. 2nd Lt. Thomas Wilson Jr. claimed one Ki-45 shot down and an Oscar probably destroyed, while Capt. Sidney Newcomb damaged a Ki-45 and a single-engine fighter and 2nd Lt. Harry Wray claimed another fighter damaged that he identified as a Zeke. Pilots saw one of the escorting Mustangs going down in flames, while a second Mustang failed to return. The returning pilots from both escort missions rated the ability of the Japanese pilots they encountered highly and were equally impressed with the maneuverability of the Japanese fighters.[68]

November 28 the B-24s went back to Rangoon. The 7th Group's target was the Botataung wharves and the nearby rail depot. The 23 bombers that reached Rangoon dropped 115 M-44 1,000-pound bombs, a third falling directly in the target area and some nearby. One bomb missed the wharves but got a direct hit on a 150-foot-long boat in the river, completely destroying it. The 308th Group got 22 bombers over the target, and they dropped another 105 M-44 bombs on the wharves, with excellent results. The Japanese intercepted the formation with two Ki-45s and a reported eight to ten Ki-43s. Although the fighters made 25 passes against the 7th Group and four against the 308th Group in a fight lasting 50 minutes, they failed to shoot down any bombers, inflicting moderate damage on one bomber and minor damage on eight others. The bomber gunners claimed one fighter destroyed, five probably destroyed, and one

The B-24s went after the Insein locomotive repair works for the second time on 1 December 1943. The distinguishing locomotive roundhouse can be made out on the upper left side of the photograph. *Courtesy, Jim Augustus*

damaged. The 530th Squadron sent 10 P-51s as escort, and these engaged the Japanese fighters, claiming four Ki-43s shot down and four damaged for the loss of one P-51, though the Japanese apparently had no losses that day. That night RAF Wellingtons and Liberators bombed the Insein works. One Wellington bomber failed to return, but the Liberators shot down one pilot from the *64th Hikōsentai*. On November 30 the RAF bombers attacked Mingaladon and Zayatkwin airfields near Rangoon and the Rangoon dock areas.[69]

After two days for needed maintenance the bombers went back to Rangoon on December 1 to bomb the Insein works again. The 459th Squadron sent 15 P-38s as escort, but the 530th Squadron was delayed again—fog at Kurmitola delaying takeoff and refueling at Ramu so that the P-51s missed their rendezvous with the bombers. When the bomb groups arrived over Rangoon, only the P-38s were there to help. Allied intelligence was apparently unaware that the *5th Hikōshidan* had brought in the *204th Hikōsentai* to reinforce the *64th* and *21st Hikōsentai*. When the alert sounded, the *64th* sent up all three of its *chutai*, joining the *204th* and *21st Hikōsentai* over Rangoon. More than 50 Japanese fighters attacked the 7th Bomb Group formation head-on as it approached the target. The 9th Bomb

1st Lt. Hampton Boggs in his P-38H, named "Melba Lou." During the mission of 1 December 1943, Boggs claimed a single-engine fighter he identified as a Hamp, shot down over Rangoon for the 459th Fighter Squadron's first victory. Boggs went on to become the 459th Fighter Squadron's second-highest-scoring ace, with claims for nine aerial victories. *SC267025, RG111, NARA*

Squadron was leading the formation that day, flying their B-24Js at 19,000 feet since the heavier J model could not bomb easily from higher altitude. To avoid antiaircraft fire over the city, the formation elected to approach the target from north to south, but this meant heading into the sun. The Japanese fighters came out of the sun and were on the B-24s almost before the formation spotted them, and not in time for the gunners to put up an adequate defense. The fighters came in a string of 14 to 15, one close behind the other in determined attacks. Within minutes the Oscars had shot down Capt. Bill Wright, the squadron's operations officer, who was leading that day, and his two wingmen, one of whom (2nd Lt. Carl Carpenter) was on only his second mission. One airplane went down with all its crew. Wright and five of his crew bailed out of their stricken airplane, while only the bombardier and the navigator made it out of Carpenter's airplane. Of these eight, six survived the war as prisoners of the Japanese. This was the 9th Bomb Squadron's worst mission of the war.[70]

The 436th and 493rd Bomb Squadrons each lost a bomber to a combination of antiaircraft fire and fighters. The damaged bombers fell out of their formations and the fighters jumped them, shooting down both airplanes. The attacks on the 7th Bomb Group went on for more than an hour, with the fighters making between 30 and 40 passes against some of the bomber formations. The bomber gunners claimed nine fighters destroyed and five probables. As the 308th Bomb Group came in, 10 or more Ki-43s went for the formation leader, Maj. Paul O'Brien, whose B-24 exploded under the concentrated fire of repeated attacks. In the confusion, the flight passed over the primary target without bombing, as did another nearby flight. The following formation did bomb the Insein works with good results. The fighter attacks continued, damaging nine of the 308th Group's bombers in what the returning crews called very aggressive attacks. The bomber gunners claimed six Oscars shot down. The P-38s protecting the formation claimed several fighters shot down, with 1st Lt. Hampton Boggs, a future 459th Squadron ace, claiming a single-engine fighter he identified as a Hamp (Allied code name for the A6M3 Zero-sen), while his colleague 1st Lt. Walter Thompson claimed a Ki-45. The P-51s arrived after the B-24s had completed their bombing run and were 20 miles west of Rangoon on their way home, with two Ki-43s still attacking the formation. 2nd Lt. Aloysius Hiltgen saw a P-51 under attack with an Oscar on its tail and dove down to drive the Oscar off. The Oscar turned into the attack and came in head-on, Hiltgen firing from 400 yards until the Oscar pulled up and to the right, giving Hiltgen a chance to rake the Oscar's belly. He claimed the Oscar as destroyed on the basis of others seeing two airplanes crash below, one of which was the P-51 Hiltgen had been trying to save, flown by Lt. Allan DuBose. The 64th *Hikōsentai* lost one Ki-43 shot down and four more damaged, while losses for the other two *sentais* that day are not known. The Japanese fighters claimed ten B-24s shot down, two P-38s, and two P-51s. In the confused combat among around 100 airplanes, it is not surprising that both sides claimed more than the number of actual losses.[71]

What was painfully obvious from these missions was that the B-24s could no longer go to Rangoon without fighter escort and that the bomber gunners needed more training. As Davidson said to Arnold in his review of the mission, "if we are going to put long-range bombers out here, we had better count on furnishing our own fighter protection."[72] A meeting of senior commanders the day after the December 1 mission discussed the need for 50 to 60 fighter escorts for the bombers—a ratio of three fighters to every bomber—and expressed a clear preference for the P-51 over the P-38.[73] Although the overall loss rate on the Rangoon missions was 6 percent, which was not deemed excessive, the losses on the mission of December 1 were 12 percent of the bomber force, a rate of loss difficult for a small air force such as the Tenth to absorb.[74] The missions had not accomplished all their intended objectives, though the damage to the Insein repair works alone may have justified the missions and

COMBAT RESUMED

the losses incurred.[75] The cooperation among the RAF, the Tenth Air Force, and the Fourteenth Air Force represented the benefit that unity of command could provide, concentrating all available forces at the decisive point as Clausewitz had argued was fundamental. One of the problems of the strategic air effort during 1943 was the absence of such coordination. The RAF and AAF bombing operations "were conducted without the advantages of a unified air command and with no over-all strategic direction."[76] This would soon change when the Strategic Air Force came into being under Eastern Air Command two weeks later.

The last of the Rangoon missions for the Army Air Force bomb groups was a night mining mission of the Rangoon River and the harbor at Moulmein the 9th and 493rd Bomb Squadrons flew on the night of December 4. The 308th Bomb Group returned to China on December 7. For the next week the 7th Bomb Group effectively stood down, flying only one mission until December 12. In the final months of operations before the integration of the two air forces, the 7th and 341st Bomb Groups set a new record for bomb tonnage dropped on targets in Burma, dropping 1,212 tons of bombs during October. When combined with the growing RAF effort, in the last three months of 1943 the Allies dropped nearly twice the average monthly bomb tonnage of the prior nine months.[77] Over the coming year the Allied bombing effort would nearly triple the amount of bombs dropped over Burma, with the American effort more than doubling.

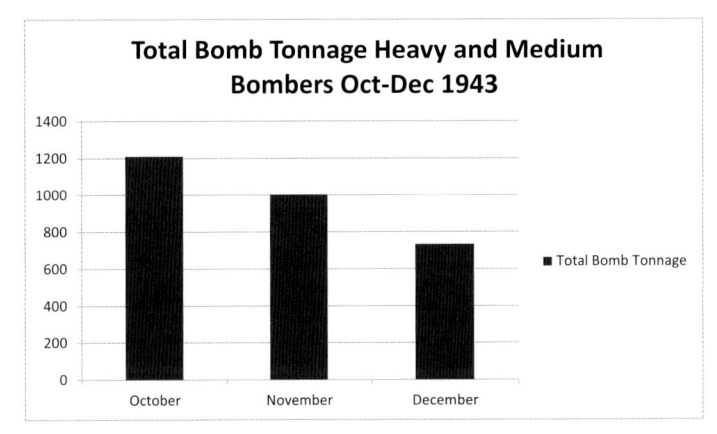

Total Bomb Tonnage Heavy and Medium Bombers Oct-Dec 1943

Month	Total Bomb Tonnage
October	~1200
November	~1000
December	~740

Table 1 Source: Air 23/4884, Air Ministry and Ministry of Defence: Royal Air Force Overseas Commands: Reports and Correspondence: Air Command, South-East Asia. Operational Effort by R.A.F. and U.S.A.A.F. for Period of Japanese War.

CHAPTER 8

AMERICAN FIGHTER OPERATIONS UNDER EASTERN AIR COMMAND

December 1943–June 1944

Plans and Preparations

Within weeks of the Sextant Conference in Cairo, Mountbatten's ambitious plans for SEAC had to be revised. The new objectives for the 1943–44 dry season were less ambitious. After the Combined Chiefs of Staff canceled Operation BUCCANEER, Mountbatten's staff came up with a smaller amphibious operation called PIGSTICK for a landing on the Mayu Peninsula in the Arakan. Mountbatten hoped this operation, though much reduced compared to BUCCANEER, would still meet Chiang Kai-shek's requirement for an amphibious operation in the Bay of Bengal as a precondition for his agreement to the advance of Y-Force from Yunnan into northern Burma. In this he was to be disappointed. In response to a radio from Roosevelt at Cairo informing him of the cancellation of BUCCANEER, Chiang replied that what China needed most was financial assistance and more airpower, and suggested postponing major operations in Burma until late 1944.[1] Chiang requested a loan of $1 billion, an increase in the Hump tonnage to 20,000 tons a month, and a doubling of the number of aircraft assigned to the Fourteenth Air Force.[2] The president responded with a careful negative to Chiang's requests, urging action in northern Burma to reopen land communications as the best means of supporting China, since these operations would provide greater protection for the Hump route. Chiang did not change his view, and although he agreed to allow Stilwell to use the Chinese forces in India for the advance down the Hukawng Valley, he said that Y-Force would not advance unless the Allies took the Andaman Islands, Rangoon, or Moulmein or captured Mandalay or Lashio.[3] In early January 1944 the British Chiefs of Staff canceled PIGSTICK. Instead of the seven operations approved at Sextant, Mountbatten was left with four:

1. The advance of Stilwell's Chinese divisions down the Hukawng Valley to Shaduzup and then to Mogaung-Myitkyina
2. A limited advance by IV Corps south of Imphal to the area west of the Chindwin River to contain Japanese troops in that area
3. A limited overland advance by XV Corps in the Arakan, still with the intention of seizing Akyab
4. Wingate's long-range penetration operation to support these other advances[4]

The plan to open a land route to China from India involved building a road from Ledo in Assam to connect with the Burma Road at the Burma-China border north of Lashio. Clearing the Japanese from northern Burma would require the Chinese divisions to advance down the Hukawng Valley in phases to Shaduzup, with American engineers building the road behind their advance. After clearing the Hukawng Valley the Chinese forces would enter the Mogaung Valley, and then on to capture Mogaung. From Moguang the road from Ledo would push east below Myitkyina to cross the Irrawaddy River to link up with an existing road that went to Bhamo, and then on to link up with the Burma Road. Capture of the Japanese base at Myitkyina became critical to the success of the campaign. From Myitkyina the Japanese controlled passage along the Irrawaddy River and the road south to Bhamo. The airfield at Myitkyina directly threatened the Hump air route and the air bases in Assam, as the loss of the transport planes had demonstrated. Capturing the airfield not only would remove this threat but would allow the transports to fly to Kunming over a shorter route at lower altitudes, saving wear and tear on airplanes and crews. Myitkyina's airfield could also be developed into a major staging base to support air supply operations. For the initial advance Stilwell had two American-trained and American-equipped Chinese divisions, the 22nd Division and the 38th Division, with American service and medical units attached. At the Quebec Conference in August, Marshall had promised Wingate an American regimental-size force for his long-range-penetration operation. This force, initially known as GALAHAD, arrived in India at the end of October and began training in jungle

Joseph Stilwell discusses plans with two of his Chinese commanders: Lt. Gen. Sun Li-jen (*left*), commanding the Chinese 38th Division, and Lt. Gen. Liao Yao-hsiang (*right*), commanding the Chinese 22nd Division. These two divisions formed the spearhead for the advance down the Hukawng Valley. *SC190517, RG111, NARA*

warfare under Wingate's supervision. In December GALAHAD was redesignated the 5307th Regiment (Provisional) but became better known as Merrill's Marauders after its commander, Brig. Gen. Frank Merrill. These forces, and attached British and Indian army units, would be designated the Northern Combat Area Command (NCAC).[5]

British and Indian army forces had undergone a reorganization to prepare for the coming offensive. To relieve the commander in chief, India, from responsibility for operations in Burma, in October 1943 the British formed the 14th Army under the command of Lt. Gen. William Slim, one of the greatest British generals of the Second World War.[6] The new 14th Army consisted of XV Corps in the Arakan with two Indian and one West African divisions, and IV Corps in the central front at Imphal with three Indian divisions, with a fourth division and a tank brigade in reserve.[7] A new formation (XXXIII Corps) with one British and three Indian divisions and a tank brigade temporarily came under India command but was assigned to SEAC on its formation. Slim and the 14th Army reported to 11th Army Group under Gen. Sir George Giffard, a purely British formation. In one of the many quirks of command, Stilwell, whose command of the two Chinese divisions made him equivalent to a corps commander, refused to come under Giffard's command, since Stilwell had no confidence in Giffard.[8] Out of his respect for Slim's abilities, Stilwell chose instead to come under Slim's command until his Chinese forces had reached Kamaing, near Moguang, even though Stilwell was the senior officer.[9]

With the creation of Air Command, Southeast Asia (ACSEA), and the integration of the Royal Air Force and the Tenth Air Force, the Allies now had a combined force of 48 RAF, RIAF (Royal Indian Air Force), RCAF (Royal Canadian Air Force), and Netherlands squadrons and 17 American squadrons.[10] This force had a total of around 850 aircraft, of which some 260 were American. With integration the Tenth Air Force ceased to be an operational command

Field Marshal Sir William Slim, perhaps the greatest British general of the Second World War. As a lieutenant general, Slim took on command of the new 14th Army in late 1943. Slim would lead his British and Indian divisions back into Burma to defeat the Japanese *Burma Area Army*. IND_003595, IWM

Air Marshal Sir John Baldwin, commanding Third Tactical Air Force, listens intently to the comments of one of Stilwell's Army Air Force liaison officers. Baldwin had flown with the Royal Flying Corps in World War I and held command and staff positions in the Royal Air Force during the interwar years. He served with RAF Bomber Command in the first years of World War II, before becoming deputy air officer commanding in chief, India, under Air Chief Marshal Sir Richard Peirse in late 1942. *Author's collection*

but retained administrative responsibilities for all the American air units previously assigned to the Tenth. The principal Allied operational air command was now Eastern Air Command (EAC) under Stratemeyer, organized into four components:

The Third Tactical Air Force under Air Marshal Sir John Baldwin, organized on 18 December 1943, comprised three principal units: the 5360th Air Defense Wing, with the American 80th Fighter Group and the 311th Fighter-Bomber Group for the defense of the Assam air bases and support of Stilwell's Chinese divisions; RAF No. 221 Group at Imphal, supporting IV Corps; and RAF No. 224 Group at Chittagong, supporting XV Corps.[11] Altogether there were a total of 576 RAF and AAF fighters in the Third Tactical Air Force, of which 357 RAF fighters and 129 AAF fighters were operational.[12] On 17 January 1944 Cochran's and Alison's force organized to support Wingate's Special Force, initially designated Project 9 and then re-designated the 5318th Provisional Air Unit (which would become, subsequently, the No. 1 Air Commando Force and then the 1st Air Commando Group), came under the operational control of the Third Tactical Air Force.[13] The force Cochran and Alison had assembled was multifaceted to provide Wingate's force with a range of applications of airpower. The Air Commandos, as they became known, comprised a fighter section with P-51A fighters; a transport section with C-47s; a light-plane section with UC-64s, L-5s, and YR-4 helicopters; and 100 CG-4 gliders. After their arrival in India, the Air Commandos acquired a bomber section of B-25H bombers when the RAF found it couldn't provide Wingate with the light bombers it had promised.[14]

The Tenth Air Force's contribution to the Strategic Air Force (SAF) was the 7th Bomb Group and the 341st Bomb Group, with the prospect that another full medium-bomber group would be transferred from the Middle East to India in early 1944 to replace the 341st Group, slated to move to China. The group's 490th Bomb Squadron would remain assigned to the Strategic Air Force until moving to China to rejoin the

Organization of Eastern Air Command

- Eastern Air Command — M/G Stratemeyer
- Third Tactical Air Force — AM Baldwin
- Strategic Air Force — B/G Davidson
- Troop Carrier Command — B/G Old
- Photo Reconnaissance Force — G/C Wise

Chart 3 Source: Air Ministry. Air Historical Branch: *The Campaigns in the Far East, Volume IV: South East Asia November 1943 to August 1945*

341st Group in April 1945. The RAF element in the Strategic Air Force comprised No. 231 Group, newly formed to command RAF bomber units in India, then consisting of two squadrons with Wellington medium bombers and two squadrons with Liberators. Air Commodore F. J. W. Mellersh became commander of No. 231 Group and deputy air officer commanding, Strategic Air Force. The new Troop Carrier Command under Brig. Gen. Old began with the RAF's No. 31 Squadron from Bengal Command and the Tenth Air Force's 1st and 2nd Troop Carrier Squadrons from Assam. Within a few months, three more RAF transport squadrons joined Troop Carrier Command. Two more AAF transport squadrons—the 27th and 315th Troop Carrier Squadrons—arrived in India to join the 1st and 2nd Troop Carrier Squadrons in forming the 443rd Troop Carrier Group, which then came under Troop Carrier Command. The Photographic Reconnaissance Force—formed somewhat later—combined RAF and AAF photoreconnaissance squadrons (see appendix 5 for the complete Eastern Air Command Order of Battle on 12 December 1943). Eastern Air Command and each of its four components had integrated British and American senior staff, which Stratemeyer believed contributed greatly to the smooth transition to an integrated force.[15]

Peirse set six tasks for his new command, basically continuing the previous objectives that Bengal Command and the Tenth Air Force had been pursuing but would now do so in cooperation:

a   To conduct a strategic air offensive in conformity with the general plan to destroy enemy air forces and installations; selected rail, road, and river communications; and depots and maintenance facilities
b   To ensure the air defense of the US Air Transport Command airfields in Northeast India and to provide for the defense against air attack of Calcutta and adjacent industrial areas
c   To provide support for the operations of 14th Army
d   To provide support for the Chinese-American forces under command of Gen. J. W. Stilwell, which were operating from bases in the Ledo area
e   To support the operations of Long Range Penetration forces
f   To conduct photographic reconnaissance and survey[16]

Peirse assigned these tasks to Eastern Air Command, where Stratemeyer, in turn, issued broad directives to his operational commanders, leaving them to work out and issue more-detailed operational orders to the units under their command. This preserved their operational freedom, as long as their operations were in conformity with the overall objectives of Air Command, Southeast Asia, and EAC.[17]

A key objective for Eastern Air Command was to obtain air superiority not just over the battlefield, but over as much of Burma as possible. Eastern Air Command had to defend an arc running 700 miles from Assam to the Arakan.[18] Patrolling this vast area required many more fighter aircraft than EAC had available, particularly considering the need for fighter aircraft for close air support and interdiction. During the first six months of 1944, air supply would become even more critical to the land battle than close air support. AAF and RAF transports had to be able to deliver their vital cargos unimpeded. The Japanese had the advantage of having the initiative, launching attacks where and when they chose. In the weeks leading up to the announcement of EAC on 15 December 1943, the Japanese had launched a major raid against Calcutta and had attacked the Assam airfields. The *5th Hikōshidan* had the added advantage of using its forward airfields to stage these and other raids, pulling its aircraft back to their bases in central and southern Burma—out of range of most Allied fighters and bombers—when a raid was over. Peirse and Stratemeyer understood that the best

The air commando force assigned to support Wingate's Special Force included a fighter section with P-51A Mustangs, adding to the number of long-range fighters available to Air Command, Southeast Asia. The Mustangs of the Air Commandos and the redesignated 530th Fighter Squadron and the Lightnings of the 459th Fighter Squadron would range deep into Burma, looking for Japanese fighters in the air and on the ground. *3A-33713, RG342FH, NARA*

way to defend this vast area, provide close air support, and defend air transport operations was to deny the Japanese the initiative by destroying Japanese airplanes in the air and on the ground, damaging airfield facilities, and limiting the use of Japanese forward air bases. Toward the end of 1943, Allied fighter strength was undergoing a qualitative improvement and soon a quantitative superiority as well. By the end of the year the RAF had received its first squadrons of Spitfire Mk. Vs: one squadron with No. 221 Group at Imphal and four squadrons with No. 221 Group at Chittagong and Calcutta. Within a few months, two more Spitfire squadrons would arrive, and all would convert to the more capable Spitfire Mk. VIII—superior to the Japanese Ki-43.[19] The Spitfire was a superlative defensive fighter but lacked the range to penetrate central Burma, where the Japanese based their fighters and bombers. While the Spitfires could win a defensive battle that would bring air superiority over the battlefront, they could not achieve air superiority over Burma. This would still leave the Allies with the problem of defending their long defensive arc from air attack.

The problem of maintaining an extensive air defense coupled with difficulties afflicting the Allied early-warning system made counterair operations that much more critical to the achievement of air superiority.[20] The arrival of American long-range fighters—the P-38s of the 459th Fighter Squadron and the P-51As of the 530th Fighter-Bomber Squadron and the Air Commando force's Fighter Section—was particularly timely. These fighters had the range to attack the Japanese airfields in central Burma as well as provide escort to Allied bombers on their raids into southern Burma. Peirse planned to undertake offensive counterair operations with these long-range fighters against Japanese airfields in Burma as much as possible, consistent with their other tasks.[21] The campaign for air superiority the American fighter squadrons conducted during March to May 1944 was one of the most important air battles of the air war over Burma. Supplementing the damage the RAF's Spitfires inflicted on the Japanese in air battles over the Arakan and Imphal, these long-range counterair missions would help the Allies win air superiority, which was vital to two of the most important applications of airpower in the war in Burma: close air support and air supply.

During the first half of 1944, ground operations reached a new scale and level of intensity not seen previously as the British, Chinese American, and Japanese forces launched and responded to their different offensives. Close air support became even more critical in some of these desperate battles. The terrain where much of the fighting took place made it difficult to deploy heavy artillery. Close air support had to supplement artillery, but the terrain also remained a major obstacle for the fighters providing close air support to the

The 530th Fighter Squadron's P-51s joined the Air Commandos and the 459th Fighter Squadron in the battle to wrest air superiority from the Japanese. RAF Spitfire squadrons inflicted losses on the Japanese fighter units flying in support of *Burma Area Army*'s advances in the Arakan and Imphal, but it was the American long-range fighters that did the most damage to the 5th *Hikōshidan*'s fighter *sentai*. *Courtesy, Carl Molesworth*

1st Lt. Maxwell Glenn was another of the pilots who became aces flying the P-38 with the 459th Fighter Squadron. Glenn scored regularly during the air battles over central Burma that took place from April to June 1944, rising to the rank of major. He named his P-38s "Sluggo"; this airplane is "Sluggo-II." *SC267026, RG111, NARA*

Allied armies. The heavily wooded and jungle-covered hills made it difficult for pilots to recognize targets. The Japanese became adept at camouflaging their positions and dumps and learned to build bunkers that could withstand bombardment apart from a direct hit. For some battles the ground forces had to call in the medium and heavy bombers to counter the problems of terrain and concealment, but for the most part the close-air-support role was a task for the fighters and dive-bombers using a variety of techniques and weapons. Over time the air and ground forces developed more-effective tactics and techniques for identifying and marking targets. Air superiority freed AAF and RAF fighters from defensive patrols and escort duties to allow more close-air-support missions, and as the risk of Japanese fighter interception diminished, more fighters could carry bombs on every mission.[22]

Perhaps no application of airpower was as critical to the war in Burma as air supply, nor was any application of air more dependent on air superiority. Air supply transformed the ground war in Burma and was the answer to the problems of terrain and the lack of a reliable road system between India and Burma, giving ground forces vital mobility. As Dr. Joe Taylor's history of the role of air supply in the Burma campaign states, "The Allied ground campaign in Burma from mid-1943 to the end of the war was made possible by air supply."[23] And as Peirse said in his dispatch on air operations during the first half of 1944, "it is not too much to say that their [the transport squadrons'] services were instrumental in preserving the existence of the 14th Army as a striking force on the Burma frontier."[24] Taylor went on to say that "without goods delivered by air the Wingate expeditions could not have been launched, the second Arakan campaign would have been a disaster, Imphal would have fallen to the Japanese, Stilwell would not have taken Myitkyina, and the final Allied conquest of Burma would not have taken place until amphibious resources had been provided for a major amphibious assault in the south."[25] Over time the air forces and the armies developed the techniques of air supply to a fine art, to the point where the ground forces could undertake major operations in areas where there were no roads available for surface transport.[26] The difficulty with air supply during this critical period of the Burma war was that there were never enough transport planes to meet the requirements of the Allied armies. During the crucial battle for Imphal, shortages of transports forced Peirse and Stratemeyer to divert bombers from the SAF to transport supplies and for Mountbatten to "borrow" transports from the India-China Wing of the Air Transport Command, and to make desperate appeals to the Combined Chiefs of Staff for more transport aircraft. Air supply would have been impossible without air superiority, as the damaging but relatively infrequent Japanese fighter attacks on Allied transport aircraft demonstrated.[27] The Allies simply did not have enough fighter aircraft to escort every air supply mission, but during the last year of the war, transport aircraft could fly close to the Allied front lines with relative impunity. The inability of the Japanese Army Air Force to understand the importance of air supply to the Allied armies in Burma and to take measures to counter air supply operations was arguably not only its greatest failure in the conduct of air operations in Burma, but a priceless gift to the Allies.

Peirse planned to use the Strategic Air Force in the counterair campaign, putting Japanese airfields at the top of the SAF's list of priority targets.[28] The other priorities for the bombers continued to be shipping and harbor installations; the destruction of railroad transportation, including railroad yards, repair depots, and especially bridges; attacks on road communications; and the destruction of industrial facilities and military stores areas.[29] New additions to the target list were port facilities in Bangkok and shipping in the Gulf of Thailand, and the recently completed Burma-Thailand railway. The railway ran from Ban Pong in Thailand west of Bangkok to Thanbyuzayat, a small town in Burma on the railroad line from Ye to Moulmein. With the opening of the Burma-Thailand railroad,

Air supply became vital to the success of the Allied armies in all the campaigns to defeat the Japanese in Burma. Air transport enabled the Allies to overcome the barriers that terrain had previously imposed on the armies. Air superiority was the necessary prerequisite for air supply. *3A-37078, RG342FH, NARA*

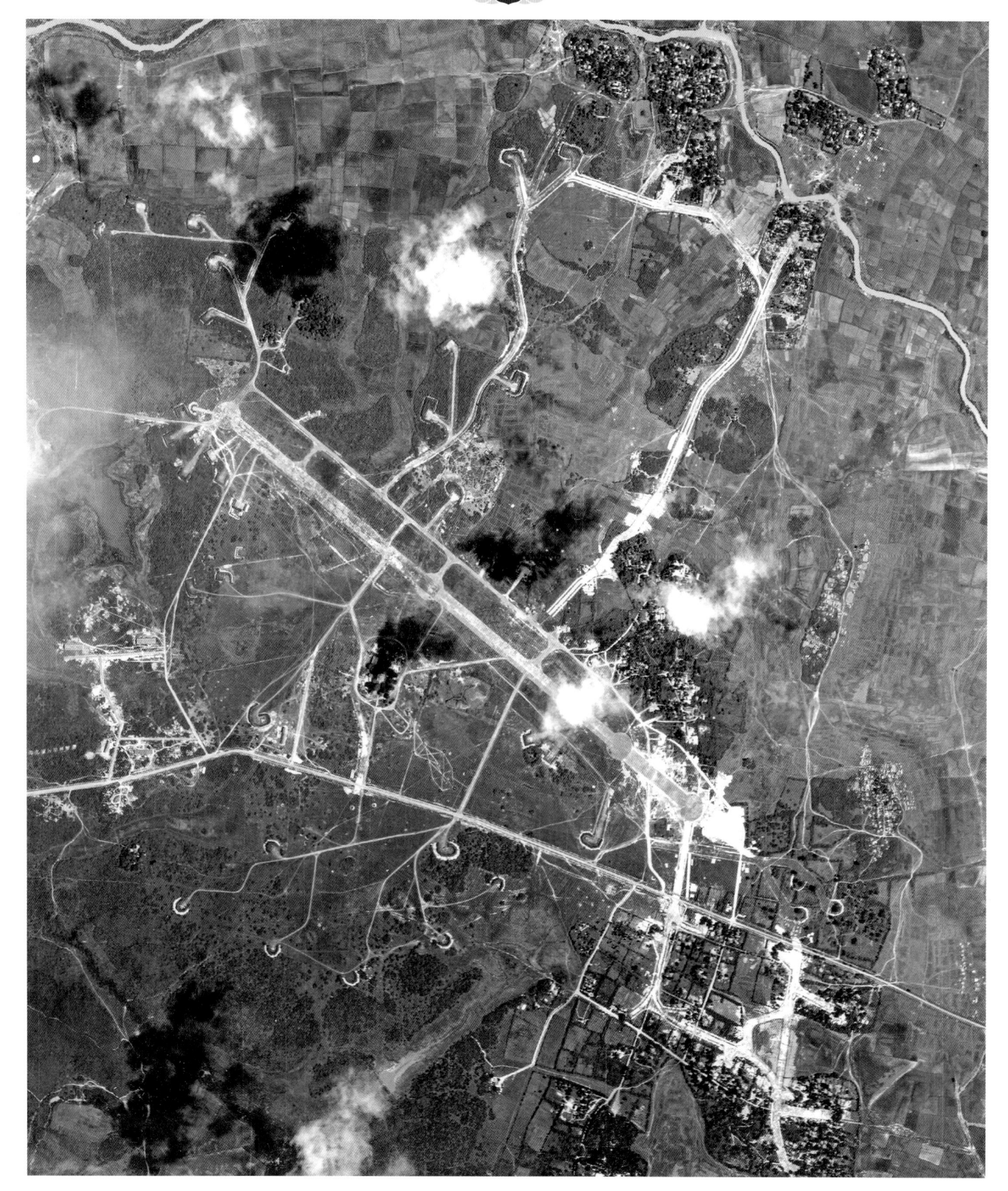

An aerial reconnaissance photo of the Japanese airfield at Zayatkwin, near Rangoon. Note the extensive number of airplane revetments well away from the main runway, to avoid damage from Allied bombing and strafing. *Courtesy, Jim Augustus*

AMERICAN FIGHTER OPERATIONS UNDER EASTERN AIR COMMAND

the Japanese army could now bypass Rangoon, shipping supplies to Bangkok or bringing them up from Singapore on the railroad line through Malaya and southern Thailand and sending them over the newly built route to Moulmein. At Moulmein, ferries carried supplies across the mouth of the Salween River to Martaban to connect with the railroad line to Rangoon and Mandalay. Attacks on the Japanese lines of communication now had to extend into Thailand, and the aerial-mining campaign now included Moulmein, Ye, Mergui, and Tavoy in Burma and Bangkok and Sattahib Bay in the Gulf of Thailand. In time the Burma-Thailand railway itself would become a key target, since this single-line railroad was vulnerable to breaks anywhere along the line. To accomplish all these tasks, the SAF had on 1 January 1944 48 AAF B-24s, 37 B-25s, 31 RAF Liberators, and 33 RAF Wellingtons, of which 61 heavy bombers and 57 medium bombers were operational.[30] In early January 1944 the 341st Bomb Group moved to China with the 22nd and 491st Bomb Squadrons, leaving the SAF with only 16 medium bombers in the 490th Bomb Squadron—which remained in Burma—until the Army Air Force's 12th Bomb Group arrived from the Middle East and began operations in April.[31] The heavy B-24s by day and Liberators by night took on the larger railroad targets, particularly those in southern Burma and long-range mining operations to the ports in southern Burma and Thailand, while the Wellingtons flew night missions to railroad targets in central Burma.[32] The 490th Bomb Squadron conducted rail sweeps and came to specialize in the destruction of bridges. Daylight missions now had the benefit of fighter escort from the P-38s and P-51s.

While the Allies were making plans for operations in the coming dry season, the Japanese were making theirs. In August 1943 Lt. Gen. Kawabe, commanding *Burma Area Army*, issued operational instructions for *15th Army's* planned offensive. Lt. Gen. Mutaguchi was to take three divisions of his *15th Army* (*15th*, *31st*, and *33rd Divisions*) and advance to Imphal to gain control of the mountain passes leading from Imphal to Assam, designated Operation *U-GO*. To tie down British forces in the Arakan and prevent their reinforcing the British and Indian divisions at Imphal, the *55th Division* would launch a smaller operation in the Arakan, designated Operation *HA-GO*, a few weeks before the advance on Imphal, with support from the *54th Division*. In northern Burma, the *18th Division* was to delay the Chinese advance down the Hukawng Valley while the *56th Division* guarded the right flank opposite Yunnan. The Japanese planners expected that once cut off from their road network, the British and Indian divisions in the Arakan and at Imphal could not hold out and would be forced to retreat as they had done so often in the past. Optimistic Mutaguchi estimated that his divisions could complete the first phase of their operations in three weeks, and instructed the divisions to carry only enough supplies to cover themselves for that period of time. But a quick success was vital, since Japanese logistical support for *U-GO* was weak. There were shortages of administrative units and motor vehicles. Ironically, the *15th Army* would face the same problem advancing north to Imphal that the British army faced advancing south from Imphal: a poor and vulnerable road network. Despite this critical weakness, *Imperial General Headquarters* approved the plans for Operation *U-GO* and *HA-GO* in January, with *HA-GO* set to begin in early February and *U-GO* to follow in mid-March. To control the upcoming operations in the Arakan and the defense of southern Burma, *Imperial General Headquarters* ordered the formation of the *28th Army*. In April a new *33rd Army* command took control of the *18th* and *56th Divisions* to coordinate operations in northern Burma.[33] The role of the *5th Hikōshidan* in the Japanese offensive was to provide air support to both the planned operations, maintaining air superiority over the battlefront and attacking British positions and Allied airfields. The *5th Hikōshidan* assigned the task of supporting *28th Army* in the *HA-GO* operation to the *7th Hikōdan*, which had available the *64th* and *204th Hikōsentai* and the *12th Hikōsentai* with Type 97 heavy bombers (Ki-21 Sally). The *7th Hikōdan* could also call on the *50th Hikōsentai* from the 4th *Hikōdan*. For operation *U-GO*, the *5th Hikōshidan* had the three fighter *sentai* from the *4th* and *7th Hikōdan* (the *33rd Hikōsentai* having transferred to New Guinea) that could move rapidly to airfields in central Burma from the Arakan; the *8th Hikōsentai* flying the Type 99 light bomber (Ki-48 Lily) with the *4th Hikōdan*; the *12th Hikōsentai*; and the reconnaissance airplanes of the *81st Hikōsentai* from the *7th Hikōdan*. This gave the *5th Hikōshidan* approximately 120 fighter aircraft, 20 medium bombers, 30 heavy bombers, and 30 reconnaissance aircraft. In March the *62nd Hikōsentai* would arrive with the new Type 100 heavy bomber (Ki-49 Helen) to support the *U-GO* operation. The *5th Hikōshidan* moved its headquarters to Kalaw, south of Mandalay, and sent its flying units to forward bases in the area around Mandalay and Meiktila with airfield companies, maintenance, and supply units.[34]

Air Support for Northern Combat Area Command

Stilwell's staff designated their plan for the advance down the Hukwang Valley to Myitkyina Operation ALBACORE. The plan called for an advance in phases. ALBACORE ONE and TWO involved securing the Ledo base and the area around Shingbwiyang at the northern end of the Hukawng Valley. ALBACORE THREE had four stages: A, B, C, and D. Phase 3A would see the 38th Division seize the ridge at Jambu Bum, at the southern end of the Hukawng Valley, and advance to capture Shaduzup. Phase 3B would advance to capture the town of Kamaing. Phase 3C would involve the capture

Soldiers of the 114th Regiment, Chinese 38th Division, crossing a river at Taipa Ga, in the Hukawng Valley, in February 1944. The Japanese *18th Division* fought stubbornly to slow the Chinese advance and retain control of the valley. *SC263238, RG111, NARA*

THE TENTH AIR FORCE IN WORLD WAR II

of Mogaung and the advance to Myitkyina, with the 22nd Division moving on Myitkyina while the 38th Division pushed south of Mogaung. A British force was to advance on Myitkyina from the Fort Hertz area. In Phase 3D the 38th Division would advance south to the west of the Irrawaddy River to seize Katha, while the 22nd Division went south to the east of the Irrawaddy to seize Bhamo. To provide his forces with close air support and air supply, Stilwell planned to build an airfield at Shingbywiyang once the Chinese had consolidated the area and the Ledo road had reached the town.[35]

The decision to cancel the amphibious operations planned for 1944 led to the further decision to cancel TARZAN, the proposed airborne operation to capture Indaw, in central Burma. And with no planned amphibious operations, Chiang Kai-shek canceled Y-Force's advance across the Salween River into Burma. These cancellations changed the mission of Wingate's Special Force brigades, including the American GALAHAD force. The initial plan had been to fly in GALAHAD to the area west of the Salween River to support the Y-Force advance, but since this was no longer possible, Stilwell asked Wingate in early January if GALAHAD could be transferred to Stilwell's control for operations in support of his Chinese divisions. Wingate agreed to Stilwell's request, since his own new mission was to support Stilwell's advance on Myitkyina. The plans worked out for Wingate's Special Force of British and Indian army units— designated Operation THURSDAY—called for two of his brigades (77th and 111th Brigades) to be flown into Burma behind Japanese lines to operate in an area forming a rough triangle from Indaw to Mogaung to Bhamo, while his third brigade entered Burma overland. Once in the operating area, Wingate's force was to concentrate on breaking the rail line north to Myitkyina to prevent the movement of Japanese reinforcements to *18th Division* and cause maximum confusion and losses to Japanese forces. GALAHAD would now support the 38th and 22nd Chinese divisions in their advance, with the expectation that the force would begin operations later in February after completing training under Wingate's supervision.[36]

To provide air support for the ground forces, the 5320th Air Defense Wing had the 80th Fighter Group, the 311th Fighter-Bomber Group, and a small detachment of B-25D and B-25G medium bombers from the 341st Bomb Group.[37] In March the 20th Tactical Reconnaissance Squadron would join the 5320th Wing, flying from Dinjan with P-40Ns mounted with cameras to supplement the work of the 9th Photo Reconnaissance Squadron's detachment operating F-4/F-5 aircraft and B-25s over northern Burma.[38] Until mid-March the primary responsibility of the 80th Fighter Group remained the defense of the Assam airfields, including patrols over the Fort Hertz area to protect the transports flying the Hump route to China. While the 90th Fighter Squadron at Jorhat spent most of its time on alert duty, all three of the group's squadrons contributed to the 11 overlapping patrols flown daily around Fort Hertz.[39] Patrols made up around 80 percent of the group's missions until March. The 311th Fighter-Bomber Group, in contrast, concentrated almost exclusively on providing support for the ground forces. In December 1943 the 5320th Wing had defined the 311th Group's primary mission as "to provide air support to the ground forces in the area. In addition to direct support of the ground forces they will be utilized against enemy lines of communications, supply dumps and concentrations within their operating range."[40] The 80th Group's three squadrons continued flying the P-40N. Within the 311th Group it appears that from some point in early December 1943 the 529th Squadron began transferring its A-36s to the 528th Squadron, since the flight intelligence reports from mid-December stop recording the 529th Squadron flying missions with the A-36. Apparently there was a shortage of A-36s, given attrition rates in the A-36 groups operating in Italy,

A line of P-40Ns from the 80th Fighter Group. The group painted the skull motif on the nose of its P-40s after taking the name the "Burma Banshees." Over northern Burma the P-40s gave excellent service as fighter-bombers. *3A-33659, RG342FH, NARA*

P-51A "Ole Nipper" from the 529th Fighter Squadron, armed with two 250-pound bombs. Toward the end of 1943, the 529th Squadron began transferring its A-36s to the 528th Squadron and replacing its Invaders with P-51A Mustangs. *Jack Lambert Collection, MoF*

and with more P-51A replacement aircraft coming into the CBI, there appears to have been a decision made to convert the 529th Squadron to the P-51A, giving the 311th Group one squadron of A-36s and two squadrons of P-51As.[41] This gave the 5320th Wing around 150 fighters, with an additional 20 or more P-40Ns of the 20th Tactical Reconnaissance Squadron who combined bombing and strafing with their tactical reconnaissance missions. Wingate's Special Force had the 5318th Unit (Provisional)—becoming better known as the No. 1 Air Commando Force—with its fighter and bomber sections to provide close air support.

The Tenth Air Force's fighter squadrons flew two types of missions in support of the Chinese divisions: interdiction and close air support. For the first few months of the year, interdiction missions outnumbered close-air-support missions by a substantial margin, and even when the balance shifted to close air support as the ground combat intensified after March 1944, interdiction missions continued

The variety of bombs the 80th Fighter Group used for close air support and interdiction missions, ranging from 100- to 1,000-pound demolition bombs, depth charges, and incendiary bombs. The P-40s used a combination of these bombs, depending on the nature of the target. *3A-33903, RG342FH, NARA*

THE TENTH AIR FORCE IN WORLD WAR II

Depth charges proved to be effective for close air support in the jungles of Burma. First used on Guadalcanal, the blast effect of a depth charge would level the surrounding jungle, revealing enemy defensive positions for follow-on attacks. *3A-33905, RG342FH, NARA*

the relentless hammering of Japanese forces in northern Burma. Although the 80th Group devoted most of its effort to patrolling over Assam, the group's three squadrons did fly interdiction missions when possible and continued to specialize in bombing bridges by using their P-40Ns to carry M-44 1,000-pound bombs in the technique they had learned from the 51st Fighter Group. Against buildings and railroad yards, and sometimes bridges, the P-40s would also carry one M-43 500-pound demolition bomb under the belly and two M-57 250-pound demolition bombs under the wings, or sometimes M-31 300-pound demolition bombs. In December the squadrons began using Mk. 17 325-pound depth charges for targets in the jungle. The blast effect of a depth charge could level a large section of jungle growth, revealing Japanese positions. The 80th Group found that flights of four aircraft were best for bombing precision targets, with flights alternating in providing top cover. Since the fighters rarely encountered antiaircraft fire over their targets in northern Burma, they had the luxury of making longer approaches to their targets, beginning their dives at 5,000 feet, with each plane flying at an interval sufficient to allow the dust and debris from the previous plane's bombs to clear before the next pilot entered his bomb run. The P-40s would dive at a 45-degree angle to their target, normally releasing their bombs at 1,500 feet, or 2,000 feet if dropping a 1,000-pound bomb. The narrow rail and road bridges in northern Burma presented a difficult target, even for a 1,000-pound bomb. The squadrons found that even a near miss with the 1,000-pound bomb would do little damage to a bridge. When the P-40s did damage a bridge, the Japanese repair crews could often get it working again in one or two days, requiring another bombing mission. On some missions a few of the aircraft would carry delayed-action bombs set to go off several hours later to disrupt the work of the repair crews.[42]

By the end of 1943 the 311th Group—especially the 528th and 529th Fighter-Bomber Squadrons—had also accumulated considerable experience and perfected tactics for aerial interdiction. Between the group's first combat mission on 16 October 1943 and the end of the year, the group had completed 1,133 bombing and strafing sorties over 239 missions and dropped 316 tons of bombs on targets in northern Burma.[43] With the A-36, the 311th Group had a true dive-bomber that could dive on a target from directly overhead at an angle of 70 to 90 degrees for much-greater accuracy. Approaching the target area, the leader of an A-36 flight would concentrate on finding the target, usually after a thorough briefing before the mission. The A-36s would start their dives from at least 6,000 feet, retarding their throttles and popping the dive breaks just before beginning their dive onto the target at a signal from the flight leader, who would be the first to go in on the target. If there were no friendly aircraft in the way, pilots would often fire their machine guns at the target as they dove down. The P-51As also used dive bombing as a tactic, but at a lower angle (usually 60 degrees), beginning their dives between 6,000 and 8,000 feet—the smaller the target, the higher the initial altitude, to give the pilots more time to pick out the target. The P-51s would release their bombs at around 2,500 feet and complete their pullout above 1,500 feet. Like the 80th Group, the 311th Group's squadrons operated in flights of four, with one or more flights acting as top cover and taking turns bombing so that at least one flight always provided cover during the bombing or strafing of a target. The interval between planes varied with the size of the target. The standard procedure was to execute a rolling pushover once the target had passed under the wing root, and then acquire the target when it appeared over the nose, placing the bottom of the ring on the gunsight on the target. The 311th Group pilot preferred to drop their bombs while still in a dive, rather than as they began their pullout. The squadrons also used glide bombing—approaching the target at an angle between 30 and 70 degrees and releasing the bomb at a minimum of 600 feet—although this approach required more judgment and was often less accurate than dive-bombing. Another technique the 311th Group used was buzz bombing, which resembled a strafing pass, with the airplane coming in at a slower speed and lower, flatter altitude than glide bombing to release the bomb between 200 and 400 feet. The dive angle was critical, since too steep an angle would make recovery difficult, while too flat an angle meant the bomb would often bounce over the target. Given the lower bombing altitude, delayed fuses had to be used to give the fighter a chance to get away from the blast. The benefit of the buzz-bombing approach was that it could be used in poorer weather when there was a low ceiling over the target. Skip bombing was an alternative, but the pilots found that the target had to be strong enough to stop the weight of the bomb; otherwise it would simply plow through a building to explode beyond the target.[44]

With little in the way of antiaircraft fire except for small arms and machine guns, the fighters routinely went down to strafe their targets after completing their bombing. The flights alternated so that at least one flight stayed high as top cover. A greater danger was Japanese explosive devices triggered as a low-flying aircraft passed over them. The 311th Group experienced these explosions on several occasions and changed tactics to avoid strafing at low levels below 500 feet, instead coming in on a target at a 45-degree angle and pulling up above 500 feet. Like their counterparts in the 80th Group, the 311th Group squadrons carried a variety of different weights of bombs. The 311th Group appears not to have used the 1,000-pound bomb on the A-36 or the P-51A. The normal bombload was two M-43 500-pound bombs, two M-31 300-pound or M-57 250-pound bombs, or 100-pound gasoline incendiary bombs. The squadrons also employed the Mk. 17 325-pound depth charge for jungle targets, as did the 80th Fighter Group.[45]

The objective of the interdiction missions was to do as much damage to Japanese facilities, supplies, and troops as possible, and to make it difficult for reinforcements and supplies to be brought

Preparing to load .50-caliber rounds for the wing machine guns on a 528th Fighter Squadron A-36. The Invader carried two additional .50-caliber machine guns in the nose, making it an effective strafer. On close-air-support missions, the fighters would often return to strafe a target area after bombing. *Courtesy, Carl Molesworth*

forward to the front lines. The pressure applied to the Japanese forces had to be, and was, constant, with the groups flying missions whenever the weather and other tasks allowed. Often the squadrons would combine missions, escorting C-47s on a supply-dropping mission, then breaking off to bomb and strafe a nearby target. Many of the targets were by now familiar—Mogaung, Shaduzup, Myitkyina, Kamaing, Maingkwan, Hopin, and Mohnyin—and many smaller villages less so. These targets were easy for the fighter-bombers to find, and the bombing was straightforward. Often, several flights of aircraft would attack the same target, with a dozen or more P-51As flying top cover for a similar number of A-36s to bomb a section of a town, or a flight of A-36s or P-51s would escort one or two B-25s to bomb the same town or village a few days later. But in the first few months of 1944 the squadrons flew an increasing number of missions against Japanese supply dumps, bivouacs, and troop concentrations in the jungles around and leading to the Hukawng Valley. Sometimes the targets were sections of trail going through the jungle. These targets were more difficult to locate in a broad swath of jungle-covered hills or valleys. The 9th Photo Squadron's B-25s went out regularly to photograph the areas likely to hold Japanese dumps or troops to provide photographs for the fighter pilots to study and aid target location. When the 20th Tactical Reconnaissance Squadron arrived in the area, the squadron's P-40s could go down to take low-level oblique photos for better references. The American Office of Strategic Service's Detachment 101 recruited local Kachin and built an intelligence network behind Japanese lines, providing key intelligence on the location and composition of Japanese positions that the OSS passed on to the fighter and bomber groups.[46] For these targets the pilots would have a map reference and a description of the target area, often something like this:

Bomb and strafe the Japanese camp and stable areas at SC-4738, approx. 2 miles SE of Swang Hka (SC-4142). These areas lie south of the Manywet-Kamaing road; one in a large clump of trees, a trail running through it; a larger area in the hills just S; and the third in a cleared area SE of the first mentioned clump of trees, at the foot of the hills.[47]

Two flights of eight P-51As from the 529th and 530th Squadrons went after this target on 3 February 1944.

The description of one of these missions on 12 January 1944 gives a flavor of what these operations were like:

At 1545 hours fifteen A-36's and twelve P-51's attacked specific areas along the Mogaung-Kamaing road which had been reported by ground sources to contain storage dumps, cavalry and approximately four thousand Japanese troops. Our planes dropped twenty-eight 250 lb. quarter second delayed action demos, eight 300 lb. instantaneous bombs and fourteen 100 lb. gasoline incendiaries over their objective areas from altitudes ranging between 2,000 and 2,500 feet. Five designated areas were heavily hit with bombs and were then subjected to strafing which caused seven fires near Hapaotut, five near Seton and six others about the Labang Ga vicinity. Heavy foliage obscured further results, but a P-38 photo ship later noted several of the above mentioned

The 20th Tactical Reconnaissance Squadron's P-40Ns flew missions over northern Burma in support of the fighters flying close-air-support and interdiction missions. The 20th Squadron provided pre- and poststrike photos of targets for the fighter-bombers. The squadron's P-40s made their own contribution to the interdiction campaign, strafing targets of opportunity whenever they appeared. *Peter M. Bowers Collection, MoF*

THE TENTH AIR FORCE IN WORLD WAR II

The P-40N of Col. Ivan McElroy, 80th Fighter Group commander, loaded with a 1,000-pound bomb—the preferred armament for bombing bridges. McElroy commanded the 80th Group from its arrival in India in July 1943 until April 1944. Note the individual touches to the group's skull motif. *3A-33655, RG342FH, NARA*

fires still burning one hour following the raid. A total of 11,000 rounds of fifty caliber were expended.[48]

These missions went on day after day. Since it was dedicated to the support role, the 311th Group flew most of the interdiction missions during the first two months of 1944, though poor weather in both months limited the number of flying days. By flying missions with more aircraft, the group doubled the bomb tonnage in February over January. The squadrons often flew three or four missions a day, sending out flights of four to eight aircraft per mission, with the P-51As of the 529th and 530th Squadrons flying top cover for the A-36s of the 528th Squadron. As an example, on 12 February 1944 the day began with a flight of four A-36s and four P-51As going out to bomb and strafe Japanese stores at 0825. At 0840 four more A-36s and four P-51As escorted a 490th Bomb Squadron B-25 to bomb a Japanese camp and supply dump. At 1300 eight P-51As went out to bomb and strafe the town of Namting. Ten minutes later, four A-36s and four P-51As went out to bomb and strafe a Japanese bivouac area. At 1500 four P-51As went out to strafe a convoy of 15 trucks on the Myitkyina-Sumprabum road that the 88th and 89th Fighter Squadrons had hit a few hours earlier, completing the destruction. At 1515 four A-36s and four P-51As went out to bomb the town of Chishudu. On the last mission of the day at 1655, two P-51As escorted a B-25 on an offensive reconnaissance, bombing suspected troop areas.[49]

During this period, the 80th Group, when not flying patrol missions, went after bridges, concentrating on the railroad bypass bridges at Namkwin and Loilaw—built next to the original bridge structures—on the railroad line from Indaw up to Myitkyina. These were difficult targets to knock out, and rapid repairs meant frequent follow-up missions. From January 21 to March 1 the squadrons hit each of these bridges six times. The attacks began on January 21, when the 89th Squadron went after the Loilaw railroad bypass bridge, getting one hit near an approach to the bridge with one 1,000-pound bomb. The next day the 88th Squadron bombed the Namkwin railroad bypass bridge, with one 500-pound bomb hitting directly on the southern end of the bridge, knocking it out. The 89th Squadron went back to the Loilaw bypass bridge on January 23 with 12 P-40s and this time knocked out the bridge with three direct hits on the north end of the bridge with one 1,000-pound and two 500-pound bombs, and two direct hits on the southern end, rendering the bridge unserviceable. After the Japanese had completed repairs on the Namkwin railroad bridge and the nearby bypass bridge, the 89th Squadron returned with 12 P-40s on February 21, dropping 1,000-pound bombs and getting two direct hits on the south end of the bridge, blasting two spans into the river below, while near misses on the bypass bridge failed to do any damage. The 88th Squadron bombed the Loilaw railroad bypass bridge the next day, getting one direct hit on the southern abutment, but the 11 other 1,000-pound bombs were all near misses. Another mission that same day got hits on the northern approach to the bridge, but all other bombs were again near misses. Two attacks on the Namkwin bypass bridge on February 24 failed to do any damage. In a change of tactics, the 88th Squadron tried skip bombing the Namkwin bypass bridge on February 28. Four P-40s came in on the bridge, releasing their 1,000-pound bombs with seven-to-eleven-second-delay fuses at between 50 and 100 feet, but all the bombs went through the bridge structure to explode some 100 to 200 feet beyond the bridge. A second flight tried the same tactic from an even lower altitude, releasing their bombs from 20 to 30 feet, but with the same result.[50]

The 89th Squadron had better luck on March 9, destroying not one but two bridges that day, as the intelligence report recorded:

At 1230 hours and again at 1550 hours separate flights of eight P-40's each, attacked the Namkwin railroad by-pass bridge by

Maj. Stanton Smith, 89th Fighter Squadron operations officer, briefing pilots for the next mission sometime in February 1944. One of the key elements of providing close air support was a thorough familiarity with the target area. This was often a challenge in an area where one section of jungle looked exactly the same as another. *3A-36202, RG342FH, NARA*

expending a total of fifteen 1,000 lb. delayed action general purpose bombs from two thousand feet. The first flight dropped its eight bombs in a very close pattern but the bridge sustained no damage although the south approach was severely torn up. One plane of the second flight jettisoned its bomb unarmed, returned early because of a broke oil line, then crash landed five miles from CHABUA without injury to the pilot. The remaining seven planes of No. 2 flight continued to their target and completely knocked out the bridge with their first three bombs, which scored direct hits. The four other 1,000 pounders were dropped on the main railroad line at the North and South intersections leading to the by-pass—direct hits were scored at both location and resulted in much torn up trackage and large craters.

The road bridge at Kamaing was our next target. This structure was blown out at 1445 hours when four P-40 fighters released for 1,000 lb. demolition bombs with ten second delayed fuses. Bombing was accomplished from an altitude of fifteen hundred feet and resulted in two direct bridge hits plus extensive damage to the North approach.[51]

While poor weather limited operations during the first part of the month, toward the end of February the focus of missions both for the 80th Fighter Group and the 311th Fighter-Bomber Group shifted to providing close air support to Stilwell's Chinese forces as they pushed farther down the Hukawng Valley. At the end of January, the Chinese 22nd Division had brought up two regiments to join the 38th Division and the Chinese American 1st Provisional Tank Group in the Hukawng Valley. By mid-February this force was about 10 miles north of the town of Maingkwan and facing two regiments of the *18th Division*.[52] Brig. Gen. Merrill's GALAHAD force (the 5307th Unit) arrived at Shingbwiyang on February 17 to begin operations.[53] Stilwell intended to use GALAHAD as a blocking force, sweeping around and behind the Japanese lines to set up blocks on the Japanese lines of communication while the Chinese forces pushed down from the north to either destroy the Japanese units or force them to retreat.[54] Stilwell ordered Merrill to take his force on a wide sweep around the *18th Division*'s left flank to set up a block at the village of Walawbum, at the southern end of the Hukawng Valley, while the Chinese divisions attacked from the north. Stilwell was hoping to envelop the *18th Division* and destroy it. The 80th and 311th Groups would provide close air support for the advance.

The techniques of close air support had advanced in just a few months, on the basis of more practical experience. Colored panels had proven to be difficult for pilots to locate in the jungle, so the ground forces switched to identifying targets with smoke shells fired from mortars nearby. But this system also had drawbacks, since it was sometimes difficult to coordinate firing the smoke shells with the arrival of the fighters over the target area. On one mission the 528th Squadron did not see the smoke shells until after the pilots had completed their bombing runs. A more effective system was the use of photographs of the target area—provided both to the ground forces and the pilots—that had a grid system to provide a commonly understood method of pinpointing a target. The A-2 section divided a photograph into 20 squares, with a system of letters on the horizontal lines and numbers on the vertical lines so that a particular square could be labeled with a letter and a number and the coordinates of a target more precisely located within the grid of squares. The ground forces could identify on a photograph the targets they wanted bombed or strafed, and provide a description of the surrounding area in detail. The squadrons provided pilots with these same photographs of the target areas to study before a mission to familiarize them with the area. The pilots would take the photos with them on the mission to help identify the target from the air.[55]

Merrill's GALAHAD force introduced radio control of close-air-support missions in northern Burma.[56] Because the Marauders were completely dependent on air supply when operating behind

THE TENTH AIR FORCE IN WORLD WAR II

89th Fighter Squadron pilots studying aerial photographs of their target. Through experience, the practice developed of having both the air liaison teams on the ground and the pilots in the air using photos of the target area with a grid reference system. This allowed a more precise identification of the exact target in relation to the position of Allied troops on the ground. *3A-36203, RG342FH, NARA*

Japanese lines, each battalion had a communications platoon maintaining radio contact with the rear echelon to arrange for supply drops and to communicate with the C-47 pilots from the 1st and 2nd Troop Carrier Squadrons who flew the supply drop missions. The GALAHAD force added an air liaison team to each battalion—consisting of a communications officer and an air intelligence officer—to direct airstrikes on Japanese positions. When a flight of fighters arrived over the area, the air liaison team would describe the target and its location by using landmarks the pilots could identify from above. The pilots would make dry runs over the target to confirm its location and, when the air liaison team gave the go-ahead, would return to bomb and strafe the target area. The air liaison teams could radio corrections if needed. Often the liaison team selected a target only once the fighters were overhead, on the basis of reports from units in contact with the Japanese. The system worked well, and soon air liaison teams went to work with each of the Chinese divisions. In a further refinement, the A-2 staffs soon began combining when possible ground-to-air direction through the air liaison teams with reconnaissance photographs and the grid system. Pilots could study photos prior to a mission to familiarize themselves with the location of friendly troops and Japanese positions. The flights would arrive over the target area at a specified time, contact the air liaison team on the ground, and confirm the location of targets by using the grid references on their target photographs before beginning their attack. The system worked well when the targets were areas in the jungle and could not be readily identified from the air.[57]

The fighting in this area lasted from March 3 to 9.[58] The Marauders were heavily engaged from March 4 to 6, fighting off repeated Japanese attacks on their positions and inflicting heavy casualties on the Japanese battalions sent against them. The *18th Division*'s commander skillfully withdrew his regiments from between the Chinese "hammer" and the Marauder "anvil," but at the cost of giving up Maingkwan to the 22nd Division on March 5 and Walawbum to units of the 22nd and 38th Divisions on March 9, retreating to positions farther south. Air support for the advance began on March 1, when five P-51As from the 529th Squadron went to bomb suspected artillery positions near Maingkwan. On March 2 the 88th Fighter Squadron sent out three flights of four P-40s to bomb and strafe Japanese artillery positions between Maingkwan and Walawbum with 250- and 300-pound bombs. The P-40s returned to bomb the same areas the next day in the morning and again in the afternoon. On March 4 the 88th Squadron went to the area around Walawbum for two missions, following directions apparently from the 5307th's air liaison team to attack suspected Japanese areas in the heavily wooded jungle. The 311th Group took over the next day, striking the Japanese units now withdrawing from Maingkwan to the south. The 528th and 529th Squadrons together flew what was called an offensive shuttle mission to support the ground troops, sending out five flights of A-36s and P-51As at intervals of around 45 minutes to bomb and strafe trails and wooded areas along the road south of Maingkwan. The flights contacted the ground forces by radio and attacked areas the ground troops had identified with smoke shells from their mortars. As so often happened, the pilots could not see the results of their attacks apart from explosions in the jungle, but the ground troops radioed that the fighters had done an excellent job. Two B-25Gs from the 490th Bomb Squadron accompanied the fighter-bombers to the area to add their weight in bombs. The P-40s came back on March 6, again bombing targets identified with smoke shells. The 311th Group squadrons flew two more offensive shuttle missions on March 8 and 9 to attack the Japanese forces now withdrawing from Walawbum. The air liaison teams directed the flights to their targets by using smoke shells. When the pilots couldn't contact the ground forces, they went looking for targets 10 miles south of Walawbum on the road to Shaduzup to avoid bombing friendly troops. When not flying missions in direct support of the

AMERICAN FIGHTER OPERATIONS UNDER EASTERN AIR COMMAND

Chinese troops advancing in the jungle during the Hukawng Valley campaign. Stilwell had his Chinese divisions push down the valley while using the GALAHAD force—better known as Merrill's Marauders—to sweep around the Japanese to set up blocks in a "hammer and anvil" tactic. *Box 160, China–Armed Forces–Burma, folder B-1, RG208AA, NARA*

ground forces, the squadrons of both groups continued bombing Japanese supply dumps and troop concentrations to the south of Walawbum and as far east as Myitkyina. For their close support work over these few days the squadrons received a commendation from Stilwell:

Fighter action on the 4th and 5th of March was a fine job. You cannot imagine how much easier it is for the ground troops to advance when our planes are overhead since as soon as the engine sounds disappear the Japs start up again with their shooting.[59]

That same week, Wingate's Special Force began Operation THURSDAY—their mission deep behind Japanese lines. The operations of the Air Commando units (officially designated the 1st Air Commando Group on 25 March 1944) in support of Special Force have been well documented.[60] Beginning on the night of

Maj. Gen. Orde Wingate and Col. Phil Cochran briefing American and British officers on Operation THURSDAY, the aerial invasion of Burma. The Air Commandos supported the initial glider-borne landings behind Japanese lines. *3A-36091, RG342FH, NARA*

THE TENTH AIR FORCE IN WORLD WAR II

Refueling Maj. Robert Petit's P-51A. Petit served as deputy commander of the fighter section in the Air Commandos. He had previously served a combat tour on Guadalcanal, where he flew a P-38H named "Miss Virginia" for his then girlfriend. On his return to the United States they were married, leading to his naming his P-51A "Mrs. Virginia." *3A-35880, RG342FH, NARA*

March 5, Air Commando gliders flew in elements of the 77th Brigade to a landing site 50 miles northeast of Indaw, dubbed BROADWAY. When the troops had carved out a rough landing strip, Air Commando C-47s and transports from the 27th and 315th Troop Carrier Squadrons and Nos. 31, 62, 117, and 194 Squadrons began flying in the rest of 77th Brigade. Over the next seven days the squadrons completed the fly-in of 77th Brigade and the 111th Brigade to BROADWAY and a second landing site dubbed CHOWRINGHEE. The 77th Brigade set up a block along the Indaw-Myitkyina railroad line, creating a strongpoint designated "White City" north of Mawlu, around 17 miles northeast of Indaw, thereby cutting the line of communications to the north. The 111th Brigade harassed Japanese communications farther south toward Indaw while 16th Brigade set up a second strongpoint (ABERDEEN) 15 miles west of Mawlu. Although the *18th Division* had stockpiled supplies in northern Burma, having an Allied force across its line of communications to *Burma Area Army* created longer-term problems for the division.[61]

The Air Commando Fighter Section with some 25 P-51As, and the Bomber Section with 12 B-25H medium bombers, provided air support to Special Force. The Air Commando fighters and bombers flew interdiction missions, combat air patrols over the Chindit strongpoints, counter airstrikes, reconnaissance, and close air support. The fighters and bombers began their operations in February before the fly-in, ranging over central Burma to become familiar

The Air Commando Fighter Section's P-51As carried 1,000-pound bombs, as well as the standard 500-pound bomb and 325-pound depth charges commonly used in Burma for close air support. The Air Commandos were the first AAF unit in Burma to employ the 4.5-inch bazooka rocket, carried in tubes of three under the wings. *3A-33702, RG342FH, NARA*

with the area where Special Force would be operating. After the Chindits flew into Burma and set up their blocking strongpoints, the Air Commandos flew regular close-air-support missions against Japanese forces attacking the strongpoints, providing a form of "flying artillery." Each Special Force brigade had an air liaison officer who would forward requests for air supply, casualty evacuation, and close air support to the Air Commandos. For close air support, the air liaison officer would direct the airstrike through direct radio contact with the fighters and bombers. As the fighters or bombers neared the Chindit position, the air liaison officer instructed the ground forces to fire smoke shells from their mortars onto the desired target area. Often the pilots had photographs with them to help identify and locate the target. An innovation the Air Commandos pioneered was the use of light airplanes as forward air controllers when the target was beyond the range of mortars. On at least two occasions an L-5 flew over the target with the air liaison office onboard, dropping smoke grenades on the target for the bombers and fighters flying above. The Fighter Section added 1,000-pound bombs and 4.5-inch bazooka rockets to the P-51As' armament. The pilots found their Mustangs could carry two 1,000-pound bombs at a time as an alternative to the standard 500-pound demolition bombs or 325-pound depth charges. Even with this load the fighters could carry six bazooka rocket projectiles—three tubes under each wing—which proved effective against large targets such as warehouses, supply dumps, and rolling stock. From March until mid-May the Air Commandos supported Special Force as the columns disrupted communications along the railroad line to Myitkyina and then moved north toward Mogaung in support of Stilwell's Chinese forces advancing on Myitkyina. The Air Commando attacks on supply dumps, warehouses, railroad facilities, bridges, motor vehicles and rolling stock, locomotives, and rivercraft all added to the destruction of Japanese supplies and disruption of the line of communications system leading to northern Burma.[62]

The *15th Army* launched its advance on Imphal on March 8, three days after Operation THURSDAY began. Gen. Mutaguchi refused to delay the advance to deal with the Special Force landings. Instead, he and Gen. Kawabe pulled together a mixed force of battalions from several Japanese units to deal with the Chindits, drawing off forces that might otherwise have gone to reinforce *15th Army* or the *18th Division* opposing Stilwell.[63] By this time, Operation *HA-GO*, launched on 4 February 1944, had ended. The Japanese high command in the *15th Army* and *Burma Area Army* believed that the operation, despite heavy losses to the *55th Division*, had achieved its objective of tying down 14th Army's reserves in the Arakan. They failed to realize that the Allies were employing new tactics and how effective these tactics would be going forward. The *55th Division* had moved around the flank of the 7th Indian Division—one of two forward XV Corps divisions advancing in the Arakan—cutting its lines of communication, but instead of retreating in confusion as British and Indian units had done in the past, the 7th Division held fast. AAF and RAF transports dropped supplies to the surrounded British and Indian troops, enabling the division to hold off repeated Japanese attacks. By the end of February the *55th Division* was a shattered force.[64] This new pattern of operations, whereby an Allied unit surrounded by the Japanese could rely entirely on air supply while letting the Japanese batter against well-supplied defenses like a wave against a concrete breakwater, would soon be repeated on a much-larger scale in the battles of Imphal and Kohima.

Slim and Lt. Gen. G. A. P. Scoones, commanding IV Corps at Imphal, had expected the Japanese attack on Imphal on the basis of reports of Japanese troop movements and had planned accordingly. Their plan called for IV Corps' divisions to withdraw slowly back to the Imphal plain, where the British and Indian units could rely on air transport of supplies and reinforcements flown in from the Arakan. The attacking Japanese would be at the end of a very tenuous supply

Loading 4.5-inch rockets into their launch tubes on an Air Commando P-51A. The rockets were not particularly accurate weapons but proved useful against large targets, such as warehouses or supply dumps. *3A-33845, RG342FH, NARA*

THE TENTH AIR FORCE IN WORLD WAR II

line, and when worn down, IV Corps would go on the offensive. The *15th Army* attacked with greater speed and force than expected. While two Japanese divisions advanced on Imphal, forcing the 17th and the 20th Indian Divisions to withdraw rapidly back to Imphal, a third Japanese division cut the road from Imphal to Kohima—the only road from Imphal to Assam—and besieged the British garrison at Kohima. This placed Japanese forces a mere 25 miles from Dimapur in Assam, where the Bengal and Assam Railway carried supplies from Calcutta to the Hump airfields and to Stilwell's Chinese divisions advancing down the Hukawng Valley. Stilwell considered the threat to his line of communications serious. Alarmed at developments around Imphal, Stilwell proposed shifting the 38th Division to aid Slim's defense of Dimapur and Kohima. At a conference Stilwell had with Slim and Mountbatten on April 3, Slim reassured Stilwell that he believed he could hold Kohima and Imphal, though there was still much hard fighting to be done. Slim told Stilwell that he had brought up XXXIII Corps to defend the Dimapur area. Slim and Mountbatten recommended that Stilwell continue with his advance toward Mogaung and Myitkyina to keep pressure on *18th Division*.[65]

Having captured Walawbum, the next stage of Stilwell's advance was just about to get underway when the Japanese started their advance on Imphal. Stilwell planned another envelopment of *18th Division*, using the 5307th and a Chinese regiment to set up blocking positions on the road from Shaduzup to Kamaing, while two more Chinese regiments and the Chinese American tank unit captured the Jambu Bum range—the gateway to the Mogaung Valley—and pushed beyond to capture Shaduzup. The advance required air support, and the 80th and 311th Groups made some adjustments to improve what they could deliver to the ground forces. In February, American aviation engineer battalions had completed an all-weather airstrip at Shimbwiyang so transports could fly in supplies for the Chinese troops, supplementing the road from Ledo, which had reached the town the previous December. In early March the 88th Fighter Squadron transferred its A Flight from its base in Assam to Shimbwiyang, becoming the first AAF fighter contingent to operate from Burma. This brought the fighters closer to the front, shortening flying time, and allowed missions to be flown when the weather in Assam prevented flying. The A Flight flew its first bombing-and-strafing mission from its new base on March 9. B Flight shifted to Shimbwiyang 20 days later, and the rest of the squadron the following month. The 311th Group decided to have the 528th Squadron with its A-36s concentrate on providing air support to GALAHAD, since the dive-bombers could deliver their bombs more accurately than the P-51As.[66]

For the advance on the Jambu Bum and Shaduzup, Stilwell sent one battalion of GALAHAD and one Chinese regiment to set up a block below the town, and a second GALAHAD battalion to set up another block farther south at Inkangahtawng. The tanks and regiments of the 22nd Division began a frontal attack on Japanese positions on the Jambu Bum. To soften up the area, the 80th Group sent out flights of P-40s to bomb Japanese positions and supply dumps around Shaduzup and in the Mogaung Valley south of the town, flying seven missions on March 13 and another four the next day. The fighters kept up a steady bombing of targets around Kamaing and Mogaung for the rest of the month in an attempt to deny supplies to the Japanese. On one of these missions on March 19, the 90th Squadron lost a pilot, Lt. Irvin Jenkins Jr. Jenkins's bombs had failed to release over the target, but when he returned to make a strafing pass he apparently jarred the bombs loose. The bombs exploded below him, seriously damaging his P-40 and forcing him to bail out. He returned to the squadron a few weeks later after walking out of the jungle. The 311th Group added to the destruction of Japanese supply dumps, storage areas, gun positions, and troop concentrations, flying three or more missions a day. During the last

The airfield at Shinbwiyang nearing completion in December 1943. American aviation engineer battalions carved these airfields out of the jungle. They were not all-weather airfields, but they could accommodate C-47 transports, liaison aircraft, and a few fighters. *Author's collection*

Bombs exploding on Japanese positions during a close-air-support strike for the Chinese divisions moving down the Hukawng Valley. The 80th Fighter Group flew regular close-air-support missions for the Chinese and for Merrill's Marauders, working closely with air liaison teams attached to forward ground units. *GP-80-SU-PH, AFHRA*

week of the month, the 311th Group began flying regular shuttle missions to the area, sending out flights of four A-36s or P-51As at regular intervals to patrol over the front lines. As the flights arrived over the area they would contact the air liaison teams, who would assign specific targets and guide the pilots onto the targets by radio.[67]

The 22nd Division's regiments ran into heavy resistance from the Japanese forces defending their positions on the Jambu Bum, losing a number of tanks, but the GALAHAD and Chinese roadblock below Shaduzup weakened Japanese resistance, and a battalion of the 22nd Division entered Shaduzup on March 29. The Marauders had to abandon their second roadblock at Inkangahtawng when Japanese pressure became too great. The 2nd Battalion withdrew into the hills on the eastern side of the Mogaung Valley, setting up a defensive position along a ridgeline at the tiny village of Nhpum Ga. The Marauders' 3rd Battalion set up another defensive position a few miles away, guarding a small airstrip. The Japanese decided to attack the Marauder position in force to push the Americans back as far as possible to protect the *18th Division*'s right flank, sending in two battalions to attack the Marauders at Nhpum Ga. The Japanese continued their assault on the 2nd Battalion's position at Nhpum Ga from March 29 to April 9. The 80th Group's P-40s provided close air support during the first few days of April, bombing and strafing suspected Japanese artillery and troop positions near Nhpum Ga with directions from the air liaison team and smoke shells marking the targets. From April 5 to 9 the 528th Squadron maintained patrols over the area from morning until late afternoon, sending out a flight of four A-36s at intervals of 45 minutes to an hour. Arriving near Nhpum Ga, the flight leader would contact the GALAHAD air liaison team for instructions. The air liaison team would indicate the target to be bombed, providing a map reference and sometimes smoke bombs. After dropping their bombs, the flights would contact the air liaison team again to receive instructions for a strafing attack on the same or a nearby target, often making dry runs to ensure they were strafing in the right location. During these four days of close air support, all the flights dropped Mk. 17 325-pound depth charges, which were more effective in the jungle-covered hills in this area. On the second day of these patrols the GALAHAD air liaison team called the flight leader of the sixth flight of the day to compliment him and his pilots on the accuracy of their bombing, and stressed the immense value of the squadron's air support. Since the pilots could rarely see any results of their bombing, these messages were welcome. By now the 528th Squadron's pilots could place a bomb within 100 feet of the Marauders' positions, although most missions bombed targets farther from the Marauders' lines. On April 9—the last day of the siege—the 528th Squadron put up 11 patrols beginning at 0615 and lasting until 1530, bombing and strafing targets the air liaison teams assigned to them. Later that month, Brig. Gen. Merrill sent a message of thanks to the 311th Group, saying, "Bushel of orchids for your unequaled support—many thanks from men and officers."[68]

Stilwell's next objectives were to capture Mogaung and the all-important town of Myitkyina. At their conference on April 3, Mountbatten reaffirmed that these objectives were in accord with

A P-40N from the 89th Fighter Squadron returns from a mission over northern Burma. With constant practice and close coordination with the air liaison teams on the ground, the fighter-bomber pilots learned to place their bombs within a short distance of Allied ground troops, greatly aiding their advance. *GP-80-SU-PH, AFHRA*

Stilwell's directives from the Combined Chiefs of Staff, though within the SEAC staff there was doubt as to whether Myitkyina could be captured and held, and even whether its capture was worth the effort.[69] Stilwell's dilemma was that there was little time to capture either objective before the monsoon started sometime in May. He decided on a bold plan. While the 22nd and 38th Divisions continued their drive down the Mogaung Valley, a force consisting of the now-much-depleted GALAHAD (the Marauders were down to around 1,400 men from the 2,997 men at the start of their campaign) and two Chinese regiments would cross over the Kumon mountain range and seize the airfield at Myitkyina in an operation dubbed END RUN. This force began their march over the mountains on April 28. The general commanding the *18th Division* hoped to keep the Chinese penned up in the Mogaung Valley until the monsoon rains turned the valley into a quagmire, preventing their capture of Myitkyina. The Chinese continued their advance, with Stilwell constantly prodding his Chinese commanders to move faster. By the end of May the Chinese regiments were around 12 miles from Kamaing. The 38th Division sent its 112th Regiment around the Japanese right flank to set up a block at the village of Seton, between Kamaing and Mogaung. The Chinese held the village despite fierce Japanese counterattacks, further weakening the *18th Division*, which now had only 30 men per infantry company.[70] In a controversial move, the Chindits, now also reduced in numbers through battle and disease, came under Stilwell's command in mid-May, and he ordered the 77th and 111th Brigades to push north toward Mogaung despite their evident exhaustion.[71]

Throughout these weeks, despite worsening weather, the fighter squadrons flew hundreds of close-air-support and interdiction sorties to support the Chinese American offensive, providing support to the Chindits as well as they moved north toward Mogaung. During April, several 80th and 311th Group squadrons set records for the number of missions or sorties flown, and collectively the two groups set a record for the number of tons of bombs they dropped during the month. To provide more aircraft for close support and interdiction missions, during April the 80th Group cut back the number of patrol missions flown over the Fort Hertz area from eleven to six per day, and later in May the 89th Squadron stopped flying patrol missions completely, switching over to flying only offensive sorties. For the 80th Group, during April and May, Japanese supply dumps and troop concentrations around Kamaing and Mogaung became the main targets for the squadrons. The final capture of these two towns in June proved to be a real boost to pilot morale. In the 311th Group, the 528th Squadron continued to take on the close-air-support missions, while the 529th Squadron went back to flying interdiction missions and attacks on supply dumps and troop concentrations as with the 80th Group squadrons. During May, Eastern Air Command pulled the 530th Squadron out of flying close support and interdiction missions to join the counterair campaign. Both groups lost pilots supporting the ground forces; the 80th Group lost two pilots on successive days in April. On April 20, a lucky Japanese gunner hit 89th Squadron pilot 1st Lt. Robbins's P-40 in the coolant system. Robbins bailed out and walked back successfully to Allied lines. The next day a flight of four aircraft from the 90th Squadron bombed an area northeast of Kamaing and, after dropping their bombs, went back to the target area to strafe. Pulling up from their strafing runs, the pilots noticed the number three man in the flight, 2nd Lt. George Weller Jr., was missing. The flight could find no trace of his aircraft. Returning from a mission on May 16, 1st Lt. Cecil Blow spun in after running into some bad weather and crashed. While there were losses, there were also new aircraft coming in for both groups. The 311th Group was first to begin the transition. In mid-April the 529th Squadron transferred all its P-51As to the 530th Squadron and went back to Bangalore in India to pick up new P-51B airplanes, ending the month with 18 airplanes on strength. The squadron began operations with its new fighters in early May. In May the 80th Group began pulling pilots out of combat to go to Karachi to convert to the P-47. The 90th Squadron would be the first to take the P-47 into combat, beginning operations with their new fighter in June.[72]

After a grueling trek over the Kumon mountains, the Marauders and the 150th Regiment from the Chinese 50th Division arrived at a position 2 miles from the main airfield at Myitkyina on May 16. The next morning, Col. Charles Hunter, commanding the force, ordered an attack at 1000. While the 150th Regiment seized the lightly held airfield, the Marauders captured a ferry terminal on the Irrawaddy River. With the airfield in his hands Hunter sent the password MERCHANT OF VENICE back to Merrill to begin flying in supplies and reinforcements. Within hours a force of gliders landed a company of aviation engineers to begin preparing the airfield for transports, which landed a battalion of Chinese troops before dark. The next day, Gen. Stratemeyer ordered a British light antiaircraft unit to be flown in to Myitkyina instead of the additional infantry and supplies that were desperately needed. More Chinese

An 89th Fighter Squadron P-40N sits on a rain-soaked airfield during the monsoon. Assam gets as much as 110 inches of rainfall during the year, most of which comes during the monsoon from May to October. The rain turned dirt fields into seas of mud. *GP-80-SU-PH, AFHRA*

Aviation engineers offload a small tractor from a glider at Myitkyina airfield a few hours after the Chinese American force had captured the field. The next day, C-47s began flying in supplies and reinforcements while under fire from Japanese machine guns. *SC190519, RG111, NARA*

AMERICAN FIGHTER OPERATIONS UNDER EASTERN AIR COMMAND

troops arrived over the next two days, but the chance for a quick seizure of the town slipped away due to poor organization and bad intelligence on the strength of the Japanese force in Myitkyina. The Japanese rapidly reinforced their positions in Myitkyina, bringing in hundreds more troops and converting the houses in the town into strongpoints. Dislodging the Japanese and capturing the town would take two and a half months and would bring a new meaning to the words "close air support." The capture of the airfield was a coup for Stilwell and the climax of his campaign in north Burma. Even though his troops would not capture the town until early August after much hard fighting, the Chinese and American force was now sitting astride the key town in northern Burma, and their very presence denied its use to the Japanese.[73]

Close air support and interdiction made a vital contribution to the Allied advance in northern Burma. The Chinese divisions lacked heavy artillery and had only light tanks in support of their advance down the Hukawng and Mogaung Valleys. The Marauders had no artillery until Merrill obtained two 75 mm pack howitzers for them at the siege of Nhpum Ga. The 80th and 311th Groups compensated for this lack of artillery, helping Chinese units overcome Japanese strongpoints and, in the case of the Marauders, fend off Japanese attacks. The continued assault on Japanese supplies, troop concentrations, camps, bridges, transportation facilities, motor vehicles, and railroad equipment had a cumulative effect. Once the Chindits set up their blocks along the railroad line to the south, the *18th Division* became ever more dependent on the supplies the division had built up in northern Burma. Maintaining these supplies and getting them to the frontline units became more and more difficult under progressive air attack. By early June 1944, the daily rice ration for the men of the *18th Division* had dropped from 860 grams per day to 100 grams, there was little gasoline for the remaining trucks, and air attacks had destroyed an estimated 40 percent of the *18th Division*'s supplies.[74] A key aspect of the air support to the ground campaign in northern Burma during the first half of 1944 was the ability of the 80th Fighter Group to gradually reduce its patrol duties and shift fighters to ground attack missions. Similarly, though both groups regularly sent out missions with one flight as top cover, they carried out their close-air-support and interdiction missions with little risk of interception, enabling more fighters to carry more bombs on every mission. The fighter squadrons operating in northern Burma benefited from growing Allied air superiority and the *5th Hikōshidan*'s focus on supporting the *15th Army*'s attack on Imphal.

Counter Air Force Operations, January to June 1944

When Eastern Air Command came into being on 15 December 1943 the Japanese *5th Hikōshidan* could still be said to have held air superiority over Burma and the ability to harass Allied air and ground operations from the Arakan to Assam.[75] The planned Allied offensives for 1944 required the broad application of airpower: defense of Allied bases and the air route to China, strategic-bombing operations over Burma, air supply to forward areas, and close air support, all of which needed freedom from Japanese interception to succeed.[76] This made the establishment of Allied air superiority through counter air force operations a priority for Eastern Air Command. These operations were a joint effort between AAF and RAF units, though the areas of operation differed due to the capabilities of the aircraft employed. The objective was to destroy the capability of the Japanese air units in Burma to interfere with Allied operations, and this could be achieved only by destroying and damaging Japanese aircraft. Where the Allies destroyed these aircraft mattered less than the fact that they were destroyed. Counter air force operations were thus twofold: defensive operations countering Japanese air raids on Allied positions and air activities, and offensive operations to seek out and destroy Japanese aircraft in the air, and especially on the ground at their bases in Burma. To be effective, counter air force operation had to be "concentrated and sustained for long enough that an effect in replacing losses can be imposed."[77] Fortunately for the Allies, the RAF and AAF in India finally had the resources with which to undertake a sustained and concentrated campaign. The arrival of the Spitfire in India, especially the Spitfire VIII, gave the RAF a fighter superior to the Ki-43 Oscar, turning the defensive air battles in the Allies' favor. Similarly, the P-38s of the 459th Fighter Squadron and the P-51As of the 311th Fighter-Bomber Group and the Air Commandos Fighter Section meant the Allies finally had fighter planes with the range to strike deep into central Burma to attack the *5th Hikōshidan*'s forward air bases. Over the first half of 1944, the combination of defensive battles and long-range counter air force operations would tilt the balance of air superiority over Burma toward the Allies.

At the end of 1943 the *5th Hikōshidan* had what Allied intelligence estimated to be 370 airplanes in Burma and Thailand available for operations in Burma, with around 200 fighter aircraft in five single-

Tons of Bombs Dropped by AAF Fighters 1944

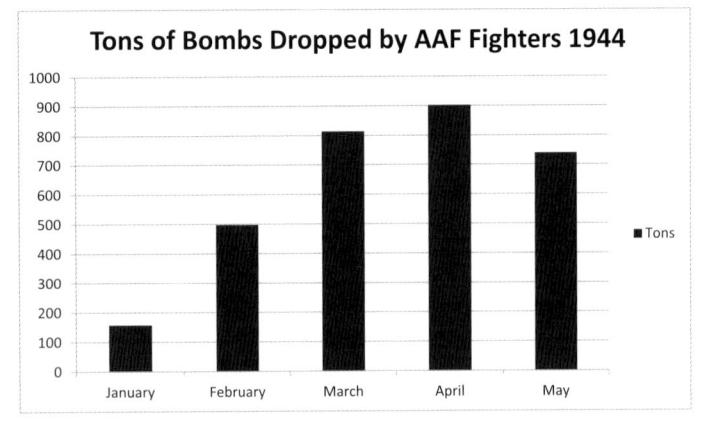

Month	Tons
January	~160
February	~500
March	~820
April	~910
May	~750

Table 6: (Source: History of United States Army Air Force Operations in the India Burma Theater 1 January 1944 to 2 September 1945)

The *5th Hikōshidan* employed small numbers of the Type 2 single-engine fighter (Ki-44 Tojo) during fall 1943 but did not convert any of the fighter *sentai* stationed in Burma onto the new type. The Type 2 was a more heavily armed interceptor fighter intended to complement the lighter Type 1 (Ki-43 Oscar). *Author's collection*

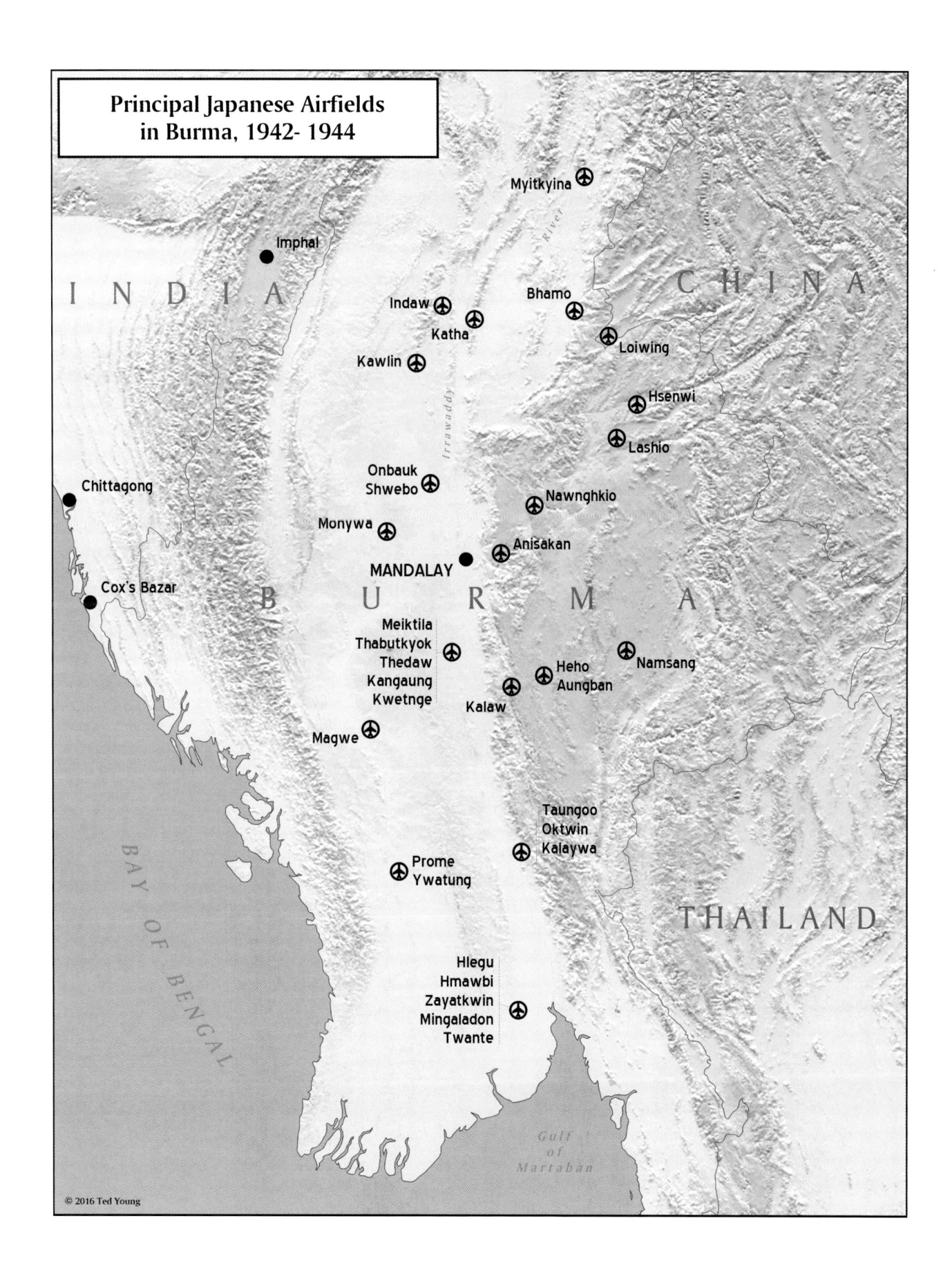

Principal Japanese Airfields in Burma, 1942-1944

AMERICAN FIGHTER OPERATIONS UNDER EASTERN AIR COMMAND

engine and one twin-engine fighter *sentai*, 110 bomber aircraft in two light- and two heavy-bomber *sentai*, and 80 reconnaissance aircraft in two reconnaissance *sentai*.[78] The *5th Hikōshidan* could also draw on units of the *9th Hikōshidan* in Sumatra, which it would do in May 1944, calling on the *87th Hikōsentai* as reinforcements after the *33rd* and *77th Hikōsentai* departed for New Guinea in February.[79] The *5th Hikōshidan* stationed around 40 single-engine and 9 twin-engine fighters at airfields in central and upper Burma and kept around 50 single-engine and 9 twin-engine fighters around Rangoon for the defense of the city.[80] The *5th Hikōshidan*'s advantage over the Allied air forces at this time was its great mobility. The *5th Hikōshidan* could base its fighters and bombers in the Rangoon area, beyond the range of Allied fighters, and deploy these aircraft to numerous landing strips in upper and central Burma for operations.[81] Typically the units involved would fly their aircraft to one of these landing strips a day or two before an operation, carry out the operation, and on the return flight fly to a different landing strip to confuse Allied intelligence. The spread of landing strips across Burma gave the *5th Hikōshidan* the initiative, allowing the Japanese to choose the time and location of their attacks on Allied forces.[82]

Opposing the *5th Hikōshidan* was the Third Tactical Air Force, which carried out most of the counter air force operations; it had around 357 operational RAF fighters in No. 221 and No. 224 Groups while the 5320th Air Defense Wing had around 129 AAF fighters.[83] Although numerically superior to the *5th Hikōshidan*, not all these fighters could be brought to bear against the Japanese, since Allied air defense had to cover such a large area and many fighters had to be available for escorting transports to the front lines and for close air support. For the first few months of its existence, Third Tactical Air Force counter air force operations were almost all defensive, as Allied fighters countered Japanese attacks in Assam and over the Arakan. In December 1943 and for part of January 1944 the *5th Hikōshidan* continued its operations against the Hump route, flying more "Tsujigiri" missions and striking at the Chinese end of the route with raids on Kunming and Yunnan-yi. The missions to China cost the *5th Hikōshidan* seven bombers and nine fighters.[84] The Japanese army generally did not favor strategic air operations and utilized the Japanese Army Air Force as a tactical air force. Official Japanese army doctrine specified that the mission of the air force was to ensure destruction of the enemy air force over the battlefield and to provide close support of the ground forces through attacks on enemy ground forces.[85] As a result, the *5th Hikōshidan* shifted its efforts away from attacks on Allied air transports to supporting Operation *HA-GO* in the Arakan during January and February and Operation *U-GO* beginning in March.[86]

During this defensive period the 5320th Air Defense Wing's fighters had two encounters with Japanese aircraft. The 89th Fighter Squadron sent out 10 P-40Ns to bomb Myitkyina airfield on 28 December 1943, with eight aircraft armed with bombs and two flying as top cover. Two of the bomb-carrying aircraft had to turn back to base. When the remaining aircraft arrived over Myitkyina, the six bombing aircraft went into a line to bomb the airfield. Just before the last two aircraft could peel off for their bombing runs, two Ki43s from the *33rd Hikōsentai* got past the top cover and attacked, damaging one of the P-40s. Having completed their bombing runs, two of the P-40s engaged the two Oscars, making a head-on pass at the first Japanese fighter and turning on the second, following the Oscar down in a dive and seeing the Japanese fighter dive straight into the ground. Another pair of P-40s attacked a third Oscar in head-on and stern attacks. 1st Lt. Freeling Clower and 2nd Lt. Charlie Hardy each claimed an Oscar shot down, but in the fight, one of the Japanese fighters set Clower's P-40 on fire and he was forced to bail out. Clower walked back to Allied lines, but 2nd Lt. Masanobu Nakamura went down to the guns of one of the P-40s.[87]

On 18 January 1944 the *50th* and *77th Hikōsentai* went out on "Tsuzigiri" missions looking for supply-dropping transports around the Fort Hertz area—possibly together. The *77th Hikōsentai* apparently sent out 25 Ki-43s on the mission. That morning the 2nd Troop Carrier Squadron sent out three C-47s to drop supplies to a station to the southeast of Sumprabum with an escort of four P-51As from the 529th Squadron and four more from the 530th Squadron, with one flight of fighters flying 3,000 feet above the transports as medium cover and the other flight flying high cover at 3,000 feet above them. There were clouds in the area, and on route to the drop zone, two

Although not the best quality, this shows a rare air-to-air shot of a flight of 80th Fighter Group P-40Ns on patrol over the mountains of northern Burma. The 80th Group had several encounters with Japanese fighters during the 1943–44 dry season. *GP-80-SU-PH, AFHRA*

of the high-cover Mustangs lost contact with the transports. 1st Lt. John Clay was leading the medium-cover flight flying at 6,000 feet when he saw three Oscars suddenly appear to his left and above. Clay turned into the attack but the Oscars went underneath him. He climbed for altitude and saw two more Oscars beneath him, diving down on these and firing at one, getting hits in the fuselage. He then dove down on an Oscar he saw attacking the C-47s. As he opened fire, three of his guns jammed, but he continued firing with his one remaining gun, claiming a second Oscar damaged. Clay's wingman, 2nd Lt. Hubert Loosen, claimed a second fighter damaged. 1st Lt. Robert Mulanax, leading the second element, followed Clay in the first attack, getting hits on one Oscar in a head-on attack as the Oscar dove down on him. Diving down on another Japanese fighter, Mulanax's fire hit the Oscar's engine. Climbing back up to altitude, Mulanax saw a flight of airplanes a few miles away that turned out to be 15 Oscars and attacked them, claiming one as probably destroyed, with his wingman also claiming a probable. The two pilots flying top cover came down on several Oscars, and 1st Lt. Cecil Blow claimed one as damaged, while F/O Hoyt Hensley came in on one Oscar from the 11 o'clock position, continuing to fire until he was at point-blank range, watching the Oscar go straight into the ground. There were more Ki-43s than the Mustang pilots could handle, and the Oscars shot down two of the C-47s immediately, then damaged a third that crash-landed a few miles away. Of the 24 men flying on the C-47s, only two survived. About an hour later four P-40s from the 89th Fighter Squadron ran into another formation of Japanese fighters escorting six Ki-21 bombers, claiming one Oscar destroyed and two Oscars and a Ki-44 Tojo damaged in the encounter.[88]

As the battles in the Arakan unfolded, the *5th Hikōshidan* had the fighter *sentais* mount large fighter sweeps, with around 70 Ki-43s carrying out a sweep on February 4 and this same number of fighters returning again the next day. Over the next month the RAF's Hurricane and Spitfire squadrons in No. 224 Group saw almost constant action fighting off Japanese fighter attacks and raids on British army positions. During January and February, RAF fighters claimed 35 Japanese aircraft shot down—mostly Ki-43 fighters—15 probably destroyed, and 87 damaged, this last figure a tribute to the Ki-43's astonishing maneuverability.[89] Actual losses were more likely to have been around 16 aircraft destroyed with several more damaged.[90] Overclaiming was common to all sides, not surprisingly in the heat of combat, though the claims the *50th* and *204th Hikōsentai* submitted appear to have astonished their fellow pilots in the *64th Hikōsentai*.[91] The *5th Hikōshidan* could make good the losses in aircraft, but it was harder to replace the veteran pilots who fell.

Offensive counter air force operations began in early March, when 12 P-51As from the Air Commando Fighter Section bombed and strafed Shwebo airfield on March 3—two days before Wingate's Special Force operation began—though no Japanese aircraft were on the field at the time. The Air Commando fighters and bombers next went to the airfield at Bhamo on March 7, bombing the runway but finding no aircraft. On a reconnaissance of the airfields around Mandalay, Anisakan, and Heho later that day, Lt. Col. Grant Mahony, commanding the Fighter Section, saw six Ki-43s flying near Anisakan. He and his wingman attacked, damaging one Oscar, but the others flew away. Early on March 8, 16 P-51s from the Fighter Section armed with two 1,000-pound bombs accompanied 12 of the Air Commando Bomber Section's B-25Hs to bomb the airstrips at Indaw and Katha near the BROADWAY landing area, once again without finding any aircraft on the fields. Mahony apparently decided to revisit the airfields where he had encountered the Ki-43s the day before. That afternoon he led 22 P-51s to Anisakan, each P-51 carrying one 500-pound bomb and a drop tank to get extra range. In preparation for an attack on Imphal, the *5th Hikōshidan* had sent the *62nd Hikōsentai*, newly equipped with the Type 100 heavy bomber (Nakajima Ki-49 Helen), with the *50th*, *64th*, and *204th Hikōsentai* sent to airfields in the Mandalay area. The bombers and the fighters from the *64th* and *204th Hikōsentai* went to the airfield at Shwebo and nearby Onbauk, while the *50th Hikōsentai* went to Anisakan. A mix-up at Shwebo caused the raid on Imphal—planned for March 8—to be canceled, and the *50th Hikōsentai* returned to Anisakan to find the Air Commando Mustangs attacking their airfield. The Ki-43s immediately went after the top cover and, in the fight that followed, claimed three Mustangs shot down, although only one was lost when Capt. Erle Schneider crashed into an Oscar he was pursuing, both airplanes crashing and killing Schneider and Cpl. Harumi Watanabe. Capt. Holly Keller claimed another Oscar shot down, probably Lt. Takumi Takagi. The *50th* lost another five Ki-43s destroyed in strafing attacks.[92]

On the way back to the Fighter Section's base at Hailakandi, Mahony led his force to the airfields at Shwebo and Onbauk, where they found both fields covered in Japanese airplanes. The high scorer that day was 1st Lt. Hubert Krug, who made repeated strafing runs against the *62nd Hikōsentai*'s Type 100 bombers, as he recalled much later:

Going back, we came across this airfield [Onbauk] that had been deserted earlier, and it was just covered with airplanes. So that's when we started, and I don't know how many of us there were. I thought that I counted six airplanes that I had shot, but it wasn't my airplane I was flying, it was one of the flight leader's, and it had a gun camera in it. There weren't many that had gun cameras in them. I didn't know that I even had a camera. When we were being interrogated the crew chief came in and handed me my film. I was as surprised as anybody. Well, they developed them real quick and saw exactly what kind of planes there were on the ground. I think at the time I told them I thought they were Betty bombers. It showed five destroyed. So that was quite exciting. No one was shooting back. I didn't see anybody on the ground, just the airplanes.[93]

In the strafing attack, the *50th* and *204th Hikōsentai* each lost five Ki-43s. The *64th Hikōsentai* got off several Ki-43s, claiming one Mustang shot down, with 1st Lt. Martin O'Berry failing to return from the mission, but lost one Ki-43 to Capt. Lester Murray, who claimed two Oscars shot down. In the confusion of repeated strafing runs, the Air Commando pilots claimed 27 Ki-43s, six Dinahs (Ki-49 Helens, most likely), a Ki-21, and a transport plane destroyed.[94]

The 459th Fighter Squadron began its offensive counterair missions on March 11. During February the squadron completed a gunnery course at Wing Commander Frank Carey's Air Fighting Training Unit at Armada Road near Calcutta. Instead of returning to their base at Kurmitola, the squadron moved to the RAF base at Chittagong on March 1, coming under the command of No. 224 Group. Capt. Verl Luehring took 12 P-38s on a sweep over the Japanese airfields at Heho and Aungban early in the morning of March 11. Eight P-38s arrived over Aungban just as a number of Ki-43s—apparently from the *50th Hikōsentai*—were taking off (the 459th Squadron history states that Aungban was the first airfield hit that morning, while the ACSEA Weekly Intelligence Summary 18 for the week of 19 March 1944 says the attack was on Heho). The P-38 pilots later reported seeing 20 fighters taking off and 12 bombers on the airfield, which they identified as Sallys and Helens. The P-38s came in at low altitude and attacked the Ki-43s, claiming seven shot down over the airfield and another three damaged, together with three bombers and a fighter destroyed on the ground for the loss of one P-38. Four Lightnings sent to attack Aungban couldn't find the field, so they went on to Heho, apparently also encountering Oscars taking off. Attacking these fighters at 100 to 500 feet, the P-38s claimed two Ki-43s shot down and five damaged for no loss, adding one bomber destroyed on the ground and one damaged. Capts. William Webb and Maxwell Glenn and 1st Lt. Walter Duke—all future 459th aces—claimed two fighters each. Which units the P-38s attacked is unclear, since only the *50th Hikōsentai* reported the loss of a pilot that day.[95]

Whatever losses the Japanese fighter units sustained in these attacks did not prevent them from flying several joint missions with large numbers of fighters. Later in the day on March 11, the *50th*, *64th*, and *204th Hikōsentai* marshaled 60 Ki-43s to cover the *15th Army*'s crossing of the Chindwin River for the attack on Imphal.[96] The three fighter *sentai* sent out 60 fighters to escort six Ki-48 bombers in an attack on Silchar airfield on March 12, and some 55 fighters escorted three bombers to bomb the landing ground at BROADWAY on March 13. In the attack on Silchar, RAF radar posts directed two Air Commando Mustangs onto the Japanese fighters, with 1st Lt. Olin Carter claiming one Ki-43 as a probable (Cpl. Shigeo Ishiyama of the *64th Hikōsentai* actually failed to return from the encounter). The next day, Spitfires based at BROADWAY took off to intercept the Japanese raid, shooting down one Oscar and damaging another that force-landed back at Mandalay for the loss of one Spitfire. The Japanese sent out another large force to BROADWAY on March 18, with 54 fighters escorting Ki-21 and Ki-49 bombers from the *12th* and *62nd Hikōsentai*. In response, the next day the Air Commandos went to attack the airfields in central Burma in coordination with Beaufighters of No. 211 Squadron. The Mustangs bombed Shwebo and Onbauk fields but found no aircraft at either, while the Beaufighters went to the airfields at Meiktila and Anisakan, destroying one Ki-43 on the ground and shooting down a twin-engine aircraft.

To disrupt the Allied air forces, the *5th Hikōshidan* launched major attacks against the airfields at Chittagong and Cox's Bazaar on March 25 and against Ledo and the Assam airfields on March 27. The 459th Squadron went after the attackers on March 25, while the 5320th Air Defense Wing took on the raid on Ledo. Early in the morning on March 25 the *5th Hikōshidan* sent out three Ki-48 bombers from the *8th Hikōsentai* with an escort of 24 Ki-43s from the *50th*, *64th*, and *204th Hikōsentai*. RAF fighter control sent up Spitfires, Hurricanes, and 10 P-38s from the 459th Squadron. The Allied fighters missed the Japanese formation, but Fighter Control ordered the 459th to fly to Shwebo and Onbauk to intercept the Japanese fighters as they returned from the raid. Finding nothing at either field, the Lightnings went on to Anisakan, where the *50th* and *204th Hikōsentai* were landing. 1st Lt. Hampton Boggs saw the sky full of Japanese fighters as he came near the airfield. He put his Lightning into a dive and came down on four Oscars approaching to land, shooting two down on his pass over the field and making a head-on attack against a third that he also claimed as destroyed. The other Lightnings went after more fighters, with 2nd Lts. John Whitescarver and Robert Hargis each claiming one destroyed, while 1st Lt. Walter Duke shared a fighter with his wingman. The problem of aircraft recognition remained, since some pilots claimed these fighters as Hamps and some as Oscars.[97] 2nd Lt. William Behrns claimed a probable, as he recalled in a memoir he wrote years later:

> *Nothing presented itself as a target for me, so as Boggs pulled up from the mayhem he had caused, I followed him right straight into a flock of Zeros and Hamps. I was able to get a bead on a Hamp and poured rounds into him. The roar of machine gun fire was accented by the heavy wump, wump, wump of the 20 mm cannon as my two-second burst went outward toward the target. I saw my tracers strike near the left wing root, but I suddenly became aware of a pair of Zekes bearing down on me*

Capt. Olin Carter claimed an Oscar fighter probably destroyed and another damaged during combat on 12 March 1944. It is likely that one of his victims was in fact destroyed. Carter went on to destroy several more Japanese aircraft in strafing attacks on Japanese airfields. *Courtesy, 1st Air Commando Association*

Capt. John England in his P-51A "Jackie" talking with his crew chief, TSgt. Eugene Crawford. England rose to command the 530th Fighter Squadron. He claimed two Oscars and one Helen bomber destroyed on 27 March 1944, making him an ace. England scored eight victories over Burma and added two more after the 311th Fighter Group moved to China. *3A-34896, RG342FH, NARA*

from my right and slightly above. I got very busy with evasive action and shortly lost them both. Unfortunately while thus occupied I had to take my eyes off of my Hamp and did not see what finally became of him. A teammate saw me on my target and saw tracers going home, but he too became involved in survival activities and did not see a crash either. That is how you wind up with a "probable" on your action report.[98]

The P-38 pilots claimed seven fighters destroyed in the air, one on the ground, three probably destroyed, and two damaged, but lost 1st Lt. Guy Freeman and 2nd Lt. Anthony Greco in the fighting. The *204th Hikōsentai* lost two pilots and the *50th* one pilot, with another Ki-43 destroyed on the ground as the P-38s claimed. The *204th Hikōsentai* claimed eight P-38s shot down.[99]

On March 27 *62nd Hikōsentai* sent nine Ki-49 bombers to attack targets in the Ledo area—probably the airfields around Dinjan following the raids on airfields at Chittagong—with an escort of 60 Ki-43s from the *50th*, *64th*, and *204th Hikōsentai*. For the hapless *62nd Hikōsentai* the mission turned into a disaster. With clouds covering the target area, the leader of the bombers decided to circle, apparently hoping for a break in the cloud cover. Two circuits consumed 40 minutes, allowing more time for fighters from the 80th and 311th Groups and the 20th Tactical Reconnaissance Squadron to intercept the Japanese formation. Fighter Control scrambled 16 A-36s from the 528th Squadron, five P-51As from the 529th Squadron, and five from the 530th. Only five of the A-36s reached the Japanese formation, reporting nine bombers the pilots identified as Bettys (Mitsubishi G4M) and 20 to 30 fighters. The A-36s attacked immediately and claimed one Oscar and a Betty as probably destroyed, and damage to five more Bettys. The 529th Squadron's flight failed to contact the Japanese, but Capt. James England, leading the 530th Squadron's flight of five P-51As, went after the formation, England claiming a Helen and two Oscars shot down and one of each damaged,

while the other members of his flight claimed another Helen destroyed and an Oscar probably destroyed. The 530th lost 1st Lts. Glen Paradise and Harry Wray to the escorting fighters. Eight P-40Ns from the 89th and 90th Squadrons attacked the Japanese formation shortly after the 528th and 530th Squadrons began their attack, claiming 11 Ki-49 Helen bombers destroyed and five damaged, as well as seven fighters for the loss of one P-40. From the 89th Fighter Squadron, 1st Lt. Robert Bell claimed one Helen bomber, a Zeke, and an Oscar, while 2nd Lt. Herbert Doughty claimed two Zekes and a Helen destroyed and one Helen damaged. The 90th Fighter Squadron had

In the combat on 27 March 1944, then 2nd Lt. Herbert Doughty claimed two "Zeke" fighters and a Helen bomber (Type 100 Nakajima Ki-49) destroyed and another Helen damaged. The *62nd Hikōsentai* lost nine bombers in the raid—a heavy loss. *Courtesy, Herbert Doughty via Bob Miller*

concentrated on the bombers. 1st Lt. Ralph Ward, 2nd Lt. Lyon, and Flt. Off. Samuel Hammer claimed two bombers each, with Ward adding a probable and two bombers damaged to his total and Lyon also claiming two more bombers damaged. Another 529th Squadron flight of four P-51s on a bombing mission ran into six Ki-43s after completing their bombing. Climbing to 10,000 feet to get above the Japanese fighters, the four came down to attack. 1st Lt. Cecil Blow made a head-on pass at a fighter he identified as a Zeke, raking the fighter from the engine to the tail, noting pieces of the tail assembly coming off and the engine bursting into flame. Flt. Off. Hoyt Hensley came in behind an Oscar and raked the enemy fighter, watching as it fell out of control to crash into the jungle below. He then attacked a second fighter he claimed as a Zeke, coming in from astern and seeing part of the tail assembly come off as the airplane burst into flames (possibly the same fighter Blow was attacking). Two other members of the flight claimed two more Zekes damaged. Two Oscars attacked eight P-51As from the 530th Squadron while they were flying a mission over Myitkyina, with 1st Lt. Robert Mulanax claiming one destroyed and 2nd Lt. Clifton Bray a second damaged. The *64th Hikōsentai* lost two pilots killed on the mission, while the *204th Hikōsentai* lost another. The *62nd Hikōsentai* lost all nine of its Ki-49 bombers and apparently had to leave Burma shortly thereafter to reequip, taking no further part in the *5th Hikōshidan*'s operations.[100]

At the start of April the offensive counter air force operations resumed. For the rest of the month the 459th Squadron and the Air Commando Fighter Section made regular sweeps over the Japanese airfields in central Burma. Bad weather washed out a sweep of Aungban and Heho on April 1, so 14 P-38s went back the next day to find a group of Ki-43s preparing to land at Heho, the pilots claiming two Ki-43 fighters and two Ki-48 bombers shot down and five bombers and three fighters destroyed on the ground, with the loss of one P-38 pilot to antiaircraft fire. The *8th Hikōsentai* lost one Ki-48 shot down and two destroyed on the ground, while the *50th Hikōsentai* lost a Ki-43 on the ground. On April 3 the Air Commandos bombed Anisakan, claiming one airplane destroyed and several damaged. On April 4 both the 459th and the Air Commandos attacked the airfield at Aungban. Radio intercepts had indicated that the Japanese would have aircraft at Aungban and Heho that morning. The 459th went in first early in the morning, claiming seven airplanes destroyed and three probably destroyed in two passes over the field. The Air Commandos came in shortly thereafter, Mahony leading 19 P-51As carrying a drop tank and bazooka rockets under the wing. Leaving seven Mustangs above as top cover, Mahony took 11 planes down and made repeated strafing attacks, calling the top cover down when no Japanese fighters appeared over the field. The pilots claimed four Ki-21 bombers, 19 Ki-43s, and one Ki-61 (one of which had arrived for the *50th Hikōsentai* to test) destroyed, two fighters as probably destroyed, and eight Ki-43s damaged. In this attack the *50th Hikōsentai* lost 15 Ki-43s and had to withdraw from Burma for a few weeks to reequip.[101]

The 459th Squadron returned to Heho on April 15, finding some 20 Japanese aircraft on the field and claiming six destroyed and two damaged, though Japanese records say only one aircraft was damaged, the rest possibly being airplanes already wrecked. The 12 P-38s also strafed installations on the airfield. The next day, now Maj. Luehring, newly appointed commanding officer of the 459th, led ten Lightnings on the longest fighter sweep yet undertaken out of India, flying 460 miles to strafe the Japanese airfield at Zayatkwin, outside Rangoon. Diving down from 27,000 feet to attack, the pilots found their windshields fogging up as they came in over the field at more than

Capt. Paul Forcey's P-51A "Bobbie" showing three kill markings under the cockpit. Forcey made his first claim during the Air Commando's strike against the Japanese airfield at Aungban on 4 April 1944 and claimed two more Japanese fighters two weeks later. *Courtesy, William Burghardt*

400 mph. Despite this handicap, Luehring and four other pilots claimed three bombers destroyed between them; Japanese records show that the P-38s did destroy two bombers of an undetermined type. That same day, two Air Commando Mustangs made a reconnaissance over Anisakan and claimed two Ki-43s destroyed on the ground. Continuing their attacks on airfields, the 459th Squadron went back to Heho on April 17, and on this occasion, the nine P-38 pilots found around a dozen Ki-43s over the airfield. The squadron made one pass over the field, shooting at the Oscars as they went through and strafing down on the deck. The pilots claimed seven destroyed and two damaged in the air and two destroyed and three damaged on the ground. The *50th Hikōsentai*, using Heho as a forward base, lost two pilots killed in the fighting. Later that afternoon the Air Commando Mustangs turned back from a bombing mission when they were alerted to a major raid over Imphal. They attacked a formation of Ki-43s on the way back to their base, with Mahony claiming one Oscar destroyed and Capt. Paul Forcey claiming two. That day the *64th Hikōsentai* lost five aircraft and four pilots to Spitfires and the Mustangs.[102]

By now the 459th had developed sound tactics for fighter sweeps over the Japanese airfields. The procedure the squadron developed called for four flights of airplanes to fly deep into central Burma at high altitude (around 20,000 to 25,000 feet), with the third and fourth flights flying 1,000 feet above as top cover. As the P-38s entered areas where there was a chance of interception, they increased speed to at least 220 mph, since speed was the Lightning's principal advantage over the Ki-43. Nearing the target area, the flights would drop down to 16,000 feet, dropping their fuel tanks and increasing speed to 300 mph by the time they were around 3 miles from the target airfield. At 14,000 feet the formation would circle the airfield to look for enemy fighters in the air and to locate targets on the ground, with groups of two flights taking separate target areas. The P-38s would enter a steeper dive, building up speed to 400 mph, and come in on their target areas with the formation spread out so that the second elements in the flights could fire without risk of hitting the first element ahead of them. After making one single pass over the airfield—a July 1944 operational bulletin explaining these tactics stressed the importance of making only one pass—the formations would remain on the deck at high speed until they were

The 459th Fighter Squadron began receiving new P-38Js in late April 1944. The squadron painted a striking dragon design on the engines of its aircraft, after the squadron's nickname, the "Twin Dragons." Armorers attach 4.5-inch bazooka rocket launchers to Maj. Willard Webb's airplane. Webb claimed five aerial and three ground victories over Burma, though this photo shows nine victory flags on his airplane. *3A-33838, RG342FH, NARA*

well away from the enemy field. The 459th Squadron found that maintaining a high speed during the initial attack limited the ability of any airborne Japanese fighters intercepting the P-38s.[103]

The 459th Squadron continued its airfield attacks through April and into May. In late April the squadron began to receive the more capable P-38Js to replace the P-38Hs the squadron was still flying. The squadron hit the airfield at Meiktila on April 23, then Heho again on April 25 and 29, and Kangaung, near Meiktila, on May 7 and 8, and again on May 10, when the P-38s also went back to Aungban. On these missions the 459th claimed 17 Japanese aircraft shot down and nine more destroyed on the ground, though actual Japanese losses were less. The claims on May 10 brought the squadron's total air and ground claims to 101. In an effort to cope with growing numbers of Allied fighters with performance superior to the latest model of the Type 1 fighter, the Model II (Ki-43 II, which the Allies designated Oscar II), in early May the *5th Hikōshidan* requested reinforcements from the *9th Hikōshidan* covering the Sumatra area. The *9th Hikōshidan* agreed to send the *87th Hikōsentai*, equipped with the Type 2 fighter (Ki-44 Tojo), in the hope that the Type 2's superior performance could help counter the Spitfires, Lightnings, and Mustangs the Ki-43s were now regularly encountering. The *87th Hikōsentai* arrived at Meiktila on May 8 with 30 Ki-44s allocated among several satellite airfields.[104] The Ki-44 did have superior performance to the Ki-43, but the *87th Hikōsentai's* pilots lacked combat experience and were soon to find out how important experience was to survival in combat with Allied fighters.[105]

On May 10 the 530th Fighter Squadron sent a detachment to the RAF base at Dohazari, near Chittagong, to join the 459th Squadron in the offensive counter air force sweeps. The 530th flew its first offensive sweep the next day to cover the airfields around Meiktila, with Squadron Commander Maj. Sidney Newcomb leading the formation of 24 Mustangs. Seeing nothing at the Meiktila airfield, Newcomb led his squadron to Aungban. As he told a reporter from the Calcutta *Statement*:

> *"We reached the Irrawaddy River"* he said, *"and went on to Meiktila airfield. We gradually reduced height to 14,000 ft. No Japanese planes were visible, so we went on to Aungban, where I saw two enemy planes in the air. I delegated a section to drop their long range tanks and attack, but quickly realized the Japs were there in force."*

Capt. James England (*left*) with other successful pilots from the 530th Fighter Squadron. With claims for 78 aerial victories, the 530th Fighter Squadron was the highest-scoring Army Air Force squadron in the air war over Burma. *3A-34906*

AMERICAN FIGHTER OPERATIONS UNDER EASTERN AIR COMMAND

During its final weeks in combat, the Air Commando Fighter Section received a few new P-51B-model Mustangs: one that was named "Jungle Jolly" and another painted with a shark mouth design on the nose, which can be seen in the background. *Courtesy, William Burghardt*

"There were about 29 of them," he continued. "They were all flying closely together. The whole squadron then went in to attack them. I noticed that the Japs were of pretty poor caliber and showed a tendency to fly in formations of two and four, presumably for protection. I dived out of the sun on the tail of two of them, and gave one a short burst at 200 yards."

"The enemy plane seemed to belch flame from its engine and cockpit, and explosions shook its wing-roots. It seemed to me that either the skill of the Japanese pilots was very poor or that they were out of ammunition. Not one of my boys got a scratch."[106]

The Mustang pilots submitted claims for 13 Japanese fighters destroyed, two probably destroyed, and six damaged, the pilots listing Oscars, Tojos, and Zekes among their claims. Capt. John England, the 530th Squadron's leading ace, claimed two fighters shot down. In its first combat the *87th Hikōsentai* lost four pilots killed and a fifth, Capt. Hirobumi Nakamitsu—commanding the *1st Chutai*—who had to bail out. Nakamitsu was possibly the victim of 1st Lt. Robert Mulhollem, who damaged a Japanese fighter, sending it down out of control and watching the pilot bail out. The *204th Hikōsentai* also lost one Ki-43 in the fight.[107]

The 530th Squadron went back to the Meiktila area again the next day, the 24 Mustangs finding some 25 Japanese fighters in the air, including some Tojos from the *87th Hikōsentai*. The Mustang pilots claimed eight fighters destroyed, three probables, and six damaged. The *87th Hikōsentai* lost two pilots killed, but possible losses from other units are unknown. A sweep of the airfield at Toungoo on May 13 yielded nothing, but when the 530th went back to Meiktila on May 14, they again ran into the Tojos from the *87th Hikōsentai*, claiming four destroyed, three probables, and two damaged. On their return to base, the pilots noted that the Tojos "were cagier, harder to get in our sights, and inflicted slight damage to 3 of our aircraft."[108] The *87th Hikōsentai* claimed five to seven Mustangs shot down for the loss of one pilot. The 459th Squadron arrived at Meiktila after the 530th Squadron had left the area, claiming one Ki-43 shot down. The next day, the 459th scored again during two sweeps over Heho and Kangaung, claiming eight fighters shot down, two probables, and six damaged, with two more destroyed on the ground. On this day the *64th Hikōsentai* lost three pilots killed in these sweeps.[109]

With the monsoon approaching, weather prevented the 530th Squadron from flying a sweep on May 18, but the 459th Squadron went to Shwebo to try to catch Japanese fighters returning from a raid on Imphal. They found no fighters in the air but claimed several destroyed on the ground. The pattern repeated the next day, the 530th Squadron again running into bad weather while the 459th made it to the Shwebo area, where they ran into the *50th Hikōsentai*, claiming two fighters shot down, with the *50th Hikōsentai* losing one pilot. On this same day the Air Commandos made their final claims before being withdrawn from combat, attacking a formation of Ki-48 bombers and their Ki-43 escort, claiming one bomber and two fighters shot down. On May 21 the *87th Hikōsentai* returned to its base at Palembang on Sumatra, having failed to make a dent against the Allied fighters and losing at least six pilots and more aircraft. The monsoon began on May 22, a day when a Beaufighter from No. 211 dispatched a Ki-43 at Shwebo airfield. The 530th Squadron flew its final fighter sweep on May 23, running into 10 fighters the pilots identified as Tojos over Shwebo but making no claims and losing one P-51A to antiaircraft fire over Anisakan. The 530th Squadron moved to the airfield at Tezgaon the next day, ending its participation in the fighter sweeps and having claimed 25 Japanese fighters destroyed, eight probably destroyed, and 14 damaged.[110] Stratemeyer sent a message of congratulations to the squadron for its excellent work, saying:

Please congratulate the 530 Squadron for its brilliant performance so far in the south. It has contributed materially to our air supremacy and such aggressiveness by allied Air Forces units will win the battle over Burma and help annihilate the Jap air force.[111]

The 459th Squadron flew only two more fighter sweeps before the monsoon weather brought the offensive counter air force campaign to a close. In the afternoon of May 23 the 459th went on another sweep to the Meiktila area following a Japanese fighter attack on the Imphal area, catching the *64th Hikōsentai* as the pilots returned to their field. Capt. Duke and 1st Lt. William Behrns—his wingman—came in behind two Ki-43s and shot them both down, with one of the Japanese pilots being killed and the other bailing out. The 459th Squadron made its final sweep of the counter air force offensive on June 6, when 18 P-38s went to Meiktila and Heho. Over Meiktila the *64th* and *204th Hikōsentai* jumped the P-38s. Maj. Maxwell Glenn and now Capt. Hampton Boggs each claimed a Ki-43 shot down, while other pilots claimed nine more damaged. Lt. Goichi Sumino, one of the *64th Hikōsentai*'s leading aces, shot down 1st Lt. Burdette Goodrich, but Capt. Duke then came in and shot down Sumino. Duke failed to return from the mission and may have fallen foul of the other Ki-43s in the area. Authorization for his return to the United States arrived at the squadron that same day.[112]

The counter air force campaign did not achieve complete Allied air superiority over Burma, but it did place great strain on the Japanese air units in Burma and began to shift the initiative to the Allies. Through the campaign the Allies "had kept in check but not substantially reduced" Japanese air strength.[113] From January to June 1944, the AAF and RAF fighter squadrons claimed 204 Japanese aircraft shot down and an additional 155 aircraft destroyed on the ground. Not surprisingly, the long-range Allied fighters involved in the counter air force campaign—principally the 459th and 530th Fighter Squadrons, the Air Commandos, and No. 211 Squadron—destroyed the majority of Japanese aircraft claimed during the period from March to June 1944, with the 459th Fighter Squadron alone claiming 121 aircraft.[114] The actual number of Japanese airplanes destroyed was less than the number claimed during the heat of combat. One source suggests that the counter air force campaign destroyed around 60 Japanese aircraft, with a further 25 shot down in the air to air battles over Arakan, Imphal, and Assam.[115] In addition, there were a large number of Japanese airplanes damaged in air fighting and strafing attacks, many of which were effectively immobilized for some period of time through a lack of spare parts. The Japanese Army Air Force's organization for the maintenance and repair of airplanes was inadequate, a problem the uneven supply of spare parts from Japan made more challenging.[116] Damaged airplanes could not always be quickly returned to combat, putting added strain on the supply system. At this stage of the war the Japanese could still replace airplanes lost in combat. Although the loss of 85 aircraft represents a fairly high rate of attrition, especially for fighter aircraft, Allied intelligence estimated that the JAAF actually increased the number of aircraft available for combat in Burma from 277 in January 1944 to 342 aircraft in June 1944.[117] It seems that the counter air force campaign did force the Japanese to adopt a policy of conserving their air strength. Even though the number of aircraft available increased, the JAAF kept 40 percent of these airplanes in rear areas—Thailand, Malaya, and Sumatra—to avoid Allied air attacks. Even more important than the loss of airplanes was the loss of experienced pilots. During the counter air force campaign, the *5th Hikōshidan*'s fighter *sentai* lost around 45 pilots killed in action—many of them veterans—at a time when the quality of pilots coming through the JAAF training system was beginning an inexorable decline.[118] The counter air force campaign also appears to have contributed to a change in tactics among the *5th Hikōshidan*'s fighter regiments. During March and April the *50th*, *64th*, and *204th Hikōsentai* regularly flew large combined fighter sweeps with 40 to 50 or more fighters, but after April 28 for some reason the number of airplanes sent on these sweeps and escort missions dropped to 20 to 30 fighters.[119] In addition, losses to Allied fighters convinced the *5th Hikōshidan* that it was too dangerous to send out heavy bombers by day, and the majority went back to bases outside Burma.[120] But perhaps the most important benefit of the counter air force campaign was the freedom it gave to the Troop Carrier Command transports to deliver vital supplies and reinforcements to the ground forces fighting in the Arakan, at Imphal with Wingate's Special Force, and in the campaign in northern Burma. From January to June, Troop Carrier Command flew 26,644 sorties, with an astonishing 10,067 sorties flown in May alone.[121] During this period the AAF lost 20 C-47s to enemy action in the air and on the ground, while the RAF lost nine equivalent Dakotas—a loss rate of 0.1 percent.[122] To look at this another way, the transports arrived safely at their destination on 99.9 percent of their missions.

AAF and RAF Air and Ground Claims January to June 1944

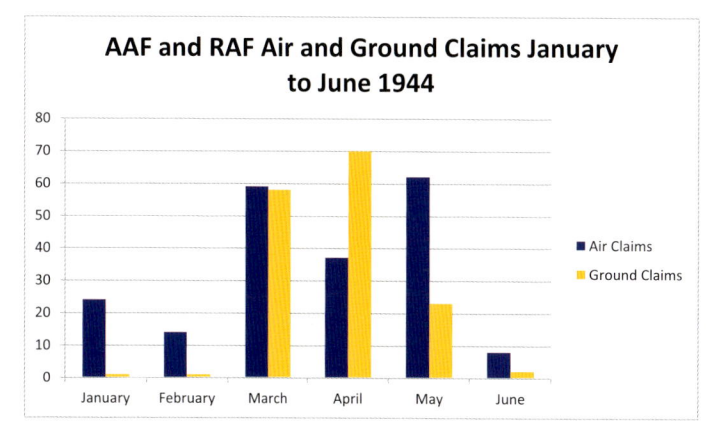

Month	Air Claims	Ground Claims
January	24	1
February	14	1
March	59	58
April	37	70
May	62	22
June	8	0

Table 7 Source: History of United States Army Air Force Operations in the India Burma Theater 1 January 1944 to 3 September 1945

CHAPTER 9

STRATEGIC BOMBING AND AIR SUPPLY OPERATIONS UNDER EASTERN AIR COMMAND

December 1943–June 1944

The Strategic Air Force and the Heavy Bombers

Maj. Gen. Howard Davidson assumed command of the Strategic Air Force on 15 December 1943, with an integrated British and American senior staff. In October, Davidson moved the headquarters of the Tenth Air Force from New Delhi to Calcutta to be closer to the fighting front, so he established the headquarters of the Strategic Air Force there. At its formation the Strategic Air Force consisted of the 7th Bomb Group, with four squadrons of B-24s; the 341st Bomb Group, with three squadrons of B-25s; and the heavy and medium bombers from No. 221 Group. RAF No. 175 Wing had two squadrons of Wellington X bombers, and No. 184 Wing had two squadrons of Liberator III bombers, equivalent to the B-24D. This gave the SAF 48 B-24s, 37 B-25s, 35 Wellingtons, and 31 Liberators, of which 61 heavy and 57 medium bombers were operational. Within a few weeks of its formation the SAF underwent several changes. In January 1944 the RAF created a new group (No. 231 Group) to control its heavy and medium bombers. No. 231 Group took over No. 175 and No. 184 Wings under the command of Air Commodore F. J. W. Mellersh, who became the SAF's deputy air officer commanding under Davidson. In mid-January the 341st Bomb Group transferred to China with the 22nd and 491st Bomb Squadrons, leaving the 490th Bomb Squadron with 16 B-25s for operations with the SAF.[1]

Air Command, Southeast Asia, determined the basic operating principles for its subordinate commands.[2] Eastern Air Command issued operational directives to the SAF, defining functions, general objectives, and areas of operation, and assigned specific missions within overall ACSEA/EAC objectives.[3] In General Order Number 1, EAC defined the purpose of the SAF as "the conduct of strategic air offensive over Burma and adjacent territory in conformity with a plan to destroy enemy air forces and air installations, selected rail, river and road communications, depots and other maintenance facilities."[4] Within this broad objective, the SAF aimed to achieve the following specific objectives:

A. Denial of water transportation
B. Destruction of rail transportation
C. Denial of road communication
D. Destruction of airfields and other military installations
E. Destruction of industrial and stores areas[5]

The SAF then adopted five basic operating principles: "First, there was only sufficient diversity of attacks to confuse the enemy. Second, the most important lines of communication were struck first. Third, the railroads were struck most frequently because they were the most important means of transportation within Burma and Siam. Fourth, in bombing the railroads the attempt was made to isolate segments of the line to prevent transfer of material across a single breach. Fifth, the best target was the most vulnerable and the most difficult to repair, such as railroad bridges."[6] The SAF applied these operating principles flexibly, depending on the situation and intelligence assessments of likely targets. The great benefit of the SAF to the campaign for Burma was that for the first time, operations of the RAF and Tenth Air Force could be coordinated, with the operations staff in Calcutta selecting targets and assigning them to heavy- or medium-bomber squadrons on the basis of the nature of the target and the distance from Allied bases in India.

In the attempt to deny the Japanese the ability to deliver supplies to Burma by sea, attacks on docks and port facilities and aerial mining proved to be more effective than direct attacks on shipping, since it was rare for the Japanese to risk their ships to Allied bombing. By early 1944 the Japanese had effectively abandoned Rangoon as a port and had switched to using smaller coastal vessels to ship supplies to the ports at Moulmein, Mergui, and Tavoy, on the southern coast of Burma in the Gulf of Martaban. From Mergui and Tavoy, supplies could go by rail to the ferry across the Salween River at Moulmein and then by rail to the bridge across the Sittang River and on to Rangoon or Mandalay. With the completion of the Burma-Thailand railway in October 1943, Bangkok became an important transshipment point, as did the anchorages at Sattahip and Koh Si Chang in the Gulf of Thailand, which had access to the railroad line at Bangkok. The SAF assigned these attacks on shipping and the more distant Burmese and Thai ports to the heavy bombers of the 7th Bomb Group and No. 231 Group.

Discussing future operations over Burma and China in February 1944 (*left to right*): Howard Davidson, George Stratemeyer, Claire Chennault, and Maj. Gen. K. B. Wolfe, the first commander of XX Bomber Command. The 58th Bomb Wing, serving under XX Bomber Command, would arrive in India a few months later to begin long-range bombing missions to Japan with the new B-29 Superfortress from bases in China. *3A-36215, RG342FH, NARA*

B-24s from the 436th Bomb Squadron attacking a small Japanese coastal vessel off the Burmese coast near Mergui in January 1944. By early 1944 the Japanese could no longer risk sending their larger freighters into Rangoon, due to the danger of running into mines or Allied air attacks. *Bomb Photos, Tenth Air Force, 830.551-1, AFHRA*

The 7th Bomb Group used two types of aerial mines in the campaign against Japanese shipping in Burma and Thailand. The M-25 aerial mine (*foreground*) weighed 2,000 pounds, while the M-26 aerial mine (*behind*) weighed 1,000 pounds. Both types could be set to activate at different intervals of several hours or several days, compounding the difficulty of sweeping harbors and rivers. *3A-33897, RG342FH, NARA*

The 7th Bomb Group had limited success with direct attacks against shipping. The group had received a "sniffer" aircraft—a B-24 equipped with search radar that accompanied the bombers on sea sweeps—but most attacks on ships came through AAF or RAF photoreconnaissance coverage. On 23 January 1944 the group went after a large freighter reported to be in the harbor at Mergui, a round trip of more than 2,000 miles. The 436th Bomb Squadron attacked first, going in at low level, but all bombs missed the freighter. Coming off the target, the squadron ran into four Ki-43 fighters, losing Capt. Benjamin Joy, squadron operations officer. Only one member of the crew survived the crash landing just offshore. The 9th, 492nd, and 493rd Bomb Squadrons attacked a bit later, with the 9th and 493rd Squadrons getting four to six direct hits on the *Seikai Maru*, sinking the 3,180-ton freighter. In early March the group went out at night to the area around Koh Si Chang, claiming hits on several vessels in the anchorage. Twelve B-24s—three from each squadron—went to bomb shipping reported at Port Blair in the Andaman Islands, but could only get near misses against the ships in the harbor and lost another B-24 to Japanese fighters.[7]

With the Japanese having effectively abandoned Rangoon as a port facility, SAF bombing operations turned to more-distant targets. On one of its first missions under the new command, the 7th Bomb Group joined RAF Liberators for an attack on the government dock areas on the Chao Phraya River at Bangkok on the night of 19 December 1943. A month later, the bombers hit the dock areas at Mergui. In late February the 9th Squadron carried out a night raid on the ferry terminal at Moulmein while the 492nd Squadron attacked the ferry terminals on the opposite side at Martaban. The bombers returned to Moulmein in late April to bomb the jetties. Aerial mining proved to be a far more effective means of denying these harbors to the Japanese than attacks on the port facilities.[8]

ACSEA and EAC drew up a list of approved mining targets—principally Rangoon, Moulmein, Mergui, Tavoy, Bangkok, Sattahip, Koh Si Chang, and later Penang—and gave the SAF permission to mine these targets and renew the mine fields as needed. The SAF conducted these mining operations on the basis of four principles: first, enemy ports in regular use would be mined persistently and the mine fields renewed; second, the bombers would drop different types of mines to make mine sweeping more complicated and time consuming; third, sterilizers that would deactivate a mine would not be used; and fourth, the SAF commander could authorize the use of delayed-arming mechanisms to prolong the effective life of a mine field where weather or long range made regular mining difficult to carry out.[9] Mining operations were always carried out at night to conceal both the bombers and the exact location of the mines dropped. The missions, especially to targets in the Gulf of Thailand, were long and tiring, often requiring flights of fourteen hours or more. Once in the target area, the bombers would have to descend to low altitude to drop their mines in a precise pattern at the designated dropping point.

Maj. David Kellogg (*squatting, right*) and his crew in front of their B-24J "Leaping Lena." Kellogg rose to command the 9th Bomb Squadron but was shot down on a mining mission to the Gulf of Thailand in May 1944, miraculously surviving the ditching of his damaged B-24 to become a prisoner of war. *7th Bombardment Group Historical Foundation, USAFA*

Burma - Thailand Railroad System

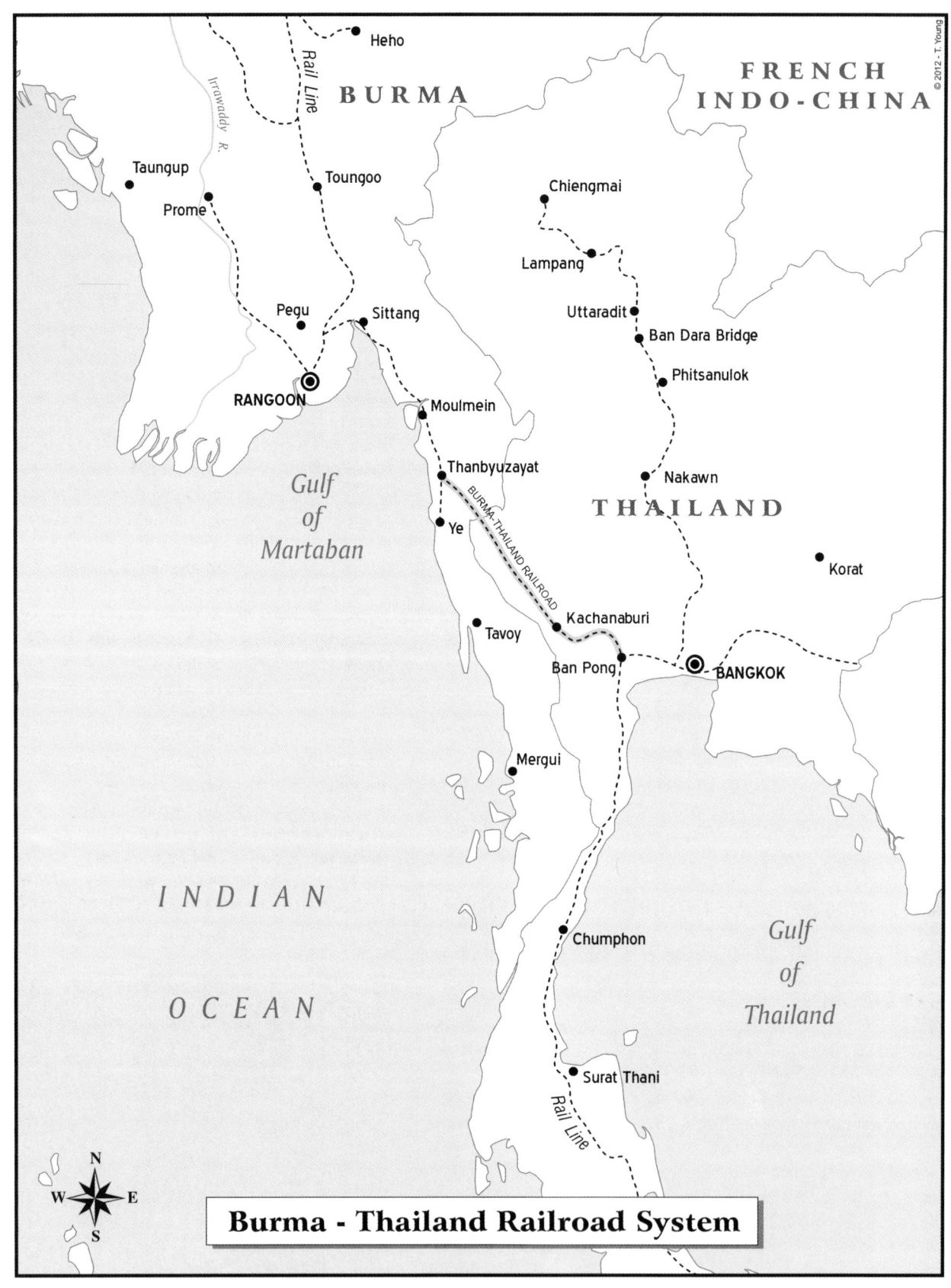

In early January the 7th Bomb Group carried out its first mining mission under the SAF, when the 436th and 492nd Squadrons flew to Thailand to place mines in the Chao Phrya River, which led from the Gulf of Thailand to the docks at Bangkok. The group returned to the Chao Phrya River on April 8, sending three airplanes from the 492nd Squadron to refresh the mine field in the river while one squadron aircraft flew with three from the 436th Squadron and three from the 493rd Squadron to mine Mergui harbor. Over the next two nights the squadrons went back to Mergui and dropped new mines in the harbor at Tavoy. In early May the targets shifted to the anchorages around Sattahip and Koh Si Chang to lay delayed-action mines that would become active during the coming monsoon. On

A 100-pound demolition bomb fitted with a steel spike to impale the bomb on a railroad bed and prevent it from skipping off before exploding. In another example of making do, the Tenth Air Force had the spikes made locally in India, using old truck axles. *3A-33926, RG342FH, NARA*

the night of 7 May 1944, Maj. David Kellogg, 9th Bomb Squadron commander, had the misfortune to fly right over a Japanese gunboat just after dropping his mines. Gunfire knocked out two engines and set one wing on fire. Kellogg put his airplane down in the sea, but only he and one of his gunners survived the ditching. The final mission before the monsoon set in took place on the night of June 8, when the 9th and 436th Squadrons went to drop mines in Mergui and the Chao Phraya River, but only one aircraft from each squadron made it to the target areas. The Strategic Air Force measured the success of the mining campaign not in the number of ships sunk, which was few, but in the decline in shipping. Sinking ships was incidental to the disruption that mining caused to shipping schedules and the delivery of supplies. Photoreconnaissance of the Burmese ports revealed that by early June the Japanese had stopped sending any ships over 200 feet in length to any of the mined Burmese ports in the Gulf of Martaban, and the frequency of even-smaller coastal vessels had become almost negligible. The mining campaign forced the Japanese to offload cargos at the ports of Saigon and Singapore out of reach of SAF bombers, but even farther from the front lines in Burma.[10]

The denial of port facilities forced the Japanese to put even more reliance on the railroad system, making attacks on the railroads, bridges, railroad yards, locomotives, and rolling stock even more damaging. The 7th Bomb Group's B-24s and RAF Liberators took on the larger railroad targets. With Rangoon no longer an important port, the heavy bombers went after the railroad yards at Mandalay, Monywa, and Moulmein and the railroad facilities in and around Bangkok. As the regular pattern of bombing and mining made it increasingly difficult for the Japanese to use any of the ports in Burma, the importance of the Burma-Thailand railroad grew proportionately. The central railroad station in Bangkok and the nearby marshaling yards at Bangsue became prime targets. On the night of 23 December 1943 the 7th Group joined RAF Liberators in an attack on the Bangkok railroad station. The 9th and 493rd Squadrons then followed this with an attack on the Bangsue marshaling yards on 10 January 1944, with the 436th and 492nd Squadrons returning to the central Bangkok station on January 19. The group struck Mandalay and Monywa on several occasions, with RAF Wellington bombers following up with night raids, and hit Moulmein twice in two night attacks in February and April.[11]

Davidson and the SAF operational staff were intent on finding a means of disrupting rail traffic over the Burma-Thailand railroad line and the Burmese lines north to Mandalay. The Burma-Thailand railroad line was particularly vulnerable. The line, running 420 miles from Bangkok to Pegu, had only a single track with no spurs; breaking the track at any point would disrupt the entire system. In a similar fashion, creating multiple breaks in the Burmese rail lines would isolate locomotives and rolling stock, making them vulnerable to the B-25s and RAF Beaufighters flying railroad sweeps. The challenge was to find a weapon that would reliably break up railroad tracks. Conventional bombs had failed to work. Dropped from low level, bombs simply bounced away from the point of impact to explode well beyond the tracks. One attempt at a solution involved attaching metal fins to the rear section of a bomb to act as air brakes, but this didn't work, nor did bombs with concrete weights attached to the nose. Someone then had the idea of putting a steel prong on the nose of a bomb. Using a length of steel taken from an old truck axle, machinists put threads on the end of the steel rod that would screw into the nose of the bomb and tapered the front end so that it would stick in the ground. Tests found that a 24-inch prong fitted to a standard 100-pound demolition bomb proved to be the most effective when dropped from a B-25 flying at 200 mph at low level. The bombs were soon dubbed "spike bombs."[12]

In February the 7th Bomb Group began training for low-level attacks on the Burma-Thailand railroad, using local Indian rail lines as a target for single aircraft and attacks in formation. The first attack

Two spike bombs falling toward a section of railroad track in Burma from the bomb bay of a B-24 or B-25. The bombers came in at low level to drop the spike bombs along the railroad lines in Burma and Thailand to disrupt traffic along the lines. *Personal collection of Maj. Gen. Howard C. Davidson, 168.7266-234, AFHRA*

The result of a spike bomb strike. Previously, standard bombs would often hit the railroad tracks and bounce off to explode alongside, doing no damage. Spike bombs gave a much-greater chance of causing a break in the line. By isolating sections of the railroad lines, locomotives and rolling stock could be immobilized and become targets for medium bombers and the RAF's long-range Beaufighters. *Personal collection of Maj. Gen. Howard C. Davidson, 168.7266-234, AFHRA*

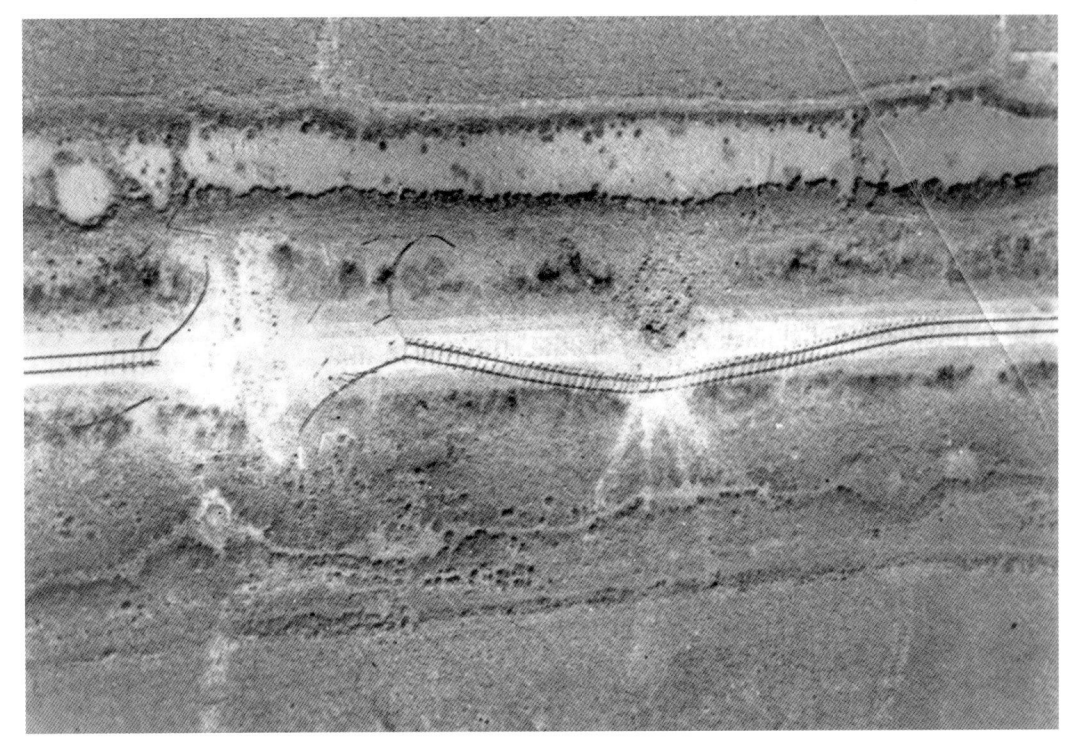

on the Burma-Thailand railroad took place on March 23, when each of the group's four squadrons sent out three airplanes (the group was still short of crews) to bomb a segment of the line between Bangkok and Thanbyuzayat. On this mission, bridges were the main target, the B-24s attacking at low level with 1,000-pound bombs. The 9th Squadron claimed three bridges destroyed. The group went back again on April 5, each squadron taking a different section of the railroad line. On this mission the bombers carried 100-pound spike bombs, destroying more than 20 miles of track along sections of the line and several bridges. After bombing, the B-24s went down to strafe rolling stock and buildings along the rail line. These low-level attacks were not without risk, since the Japanese had brought up 37 mm and 20 mm antiaircraft guns to defend the railroad line and the bridges along it. Antiaircraft fire claimed one B-24 from the 9th Squadron, while the 493rd Squadron's commander, Capt. Robert Bailey, flew his badly damaged bomber back to the Bay of Bengal, where he made a successful ditching; a PBY Catalina rescued Bailey and his surviving crew the next day. Stratemeyer and Peirse sent their congratulations to Davidson and the 7th Bomb Group on an exceptionally well-executed raid on this important rail line.[13]

Operations against Japanese airfields and military installations in Burma and Thailand represented a substantial proportion of the SAF's efforts during January to May 1944, especially as the battles around Imphal intensified. The attacks on airfields formed part of the overall Allied campaign to win air superiority over Burma. The *5th Hikōshidan*'s main bases in Burma were around Rangoon. The Japanese had taken over and expanded the former RAF base at Mingaladon and had built more airfields nearby at Zayatkwin, Hlegu, and Hmawbi. These bases were beyond the range of Allied fighters and served as maintenance and repair centers for the fighters and bombers using the many forward airfields the Japanese had built in central and northern Burma. The Japanese had also greatly expanded the facilities at Don Muang airfield, outside Bangkok. From January to early March the 7th Bomb Group carried out 10 missions against Japanese airfields, mostly by night. The group sent small numbers of B-24s to bomb Don Muang airfield beginning on

One of the first B-24J models to reach the 7th Bomb Group, "Pecker Red" served with the group for 14 months and completed 89 combat missions. In early 1945 the airplane suffered an engine failure while returning from a gas-hauling mission to China. The pilot made an emergency landing at Imphal, where the crew left "Pecker Red" parked on the side of the runway. With newer B-24L and M models arriving regularly, there was no point in recovering an old combat veteran. *Author's collection*

January 10, with six aircraft returning nine days later to hit many of the buildings on the airfield from 10,000 feet. Following the launch of Operation *HA-GO* in the Arakan, the 7th Group went after the Japanese forward airfields at Heho, Aungban, and Akyab, supporting the SAF Wellington bombers who regularly bombed these airfields by night. The bombers occasionally encountered Japanese fighters trying to intercept the bombers flying night missions. The Japanese fighters had no success, but one 9th Squadron B-24 claimed an Oscar destroyed when the crew ran a pursuing Japanese fighter into a mountain in the Chin Hills. The airfields at Loiwing and Lashio were the targets on March 3, and on this occasion the bombers had a welcome escort of P-40s, though the bombers

THE TENTH AIR FORCE IN WORLD WAR II

During the first few months of 1944, the 7th Bomb Group flew a number of missions in support of the 14th Army, fighting the Japanese advance in the Arakan and toward Imphal. This photo shows a Japanese headquarters area under attack in early 1944. *3A-37534, RG342FH, NARA*

didn't encounter any Japanese fighters. The last mission against the airfields took place on March 4, when the 9th and 493rd Squadrons went out on a night attack against Zayatkwin and Hlegu while the 436th and 492nd Squadrons bombed Mingaladon and Hmawbi. One 493rd Squadron pilot over Mingaladon had 15 searchlights follow him for nearly eight minutes, allowing several intercepting Oscar fighters to make repeated passes, fortunately with only minor damage to the B-24. Reluctant to give away their position in the haze and darkness, the B-24 gunners held their fire.[14]

Military installations—especially Japanese army supply dumps—became priority targets during March, April, and May as British and Indian divisions battled the *15th Army* around the Arakan and Imphal, Wingate's Special Force disrupted Japanese rail lines, and Stilwell's American and Chinese forces approached Myitkyina. In support of the ground forces, the SAF dropped 3,687 tons of bombs on Japanese army installations, warehouses, and supply dumps from January to May 1944, amounting to 55 percent of all the bombs the SAF dropped over Burma and Thailand during this period.[15] The SAF directed its effort at the Japanese supply dumps close to the front lines and in southern Burma. In support of Wingate's Special Force, on March 9 the 7th Bomb Group bombed Japanese supply dumps at Mogaung and Kamaing while the landings of Special Force were still in progress. The group sent out 22 airplanes to bomb Mogaung again on March 10—a relatively large mission for the group at the time. On the night of March 14, the 7th Bomb Group sent 22 aircraft to join 10 RAF Liberators and 22 Wellington bombers to attack the large Japanese army supply dumps 9 miles north of Rangoon at Victoria Lake. Coming in at medium altitudes, the bombers had to run a gauntlet of searchlights and antiaircraft fire. Intercepting Japanese fighters badly damaged two B-24s from the 492nd Squadron. The 7th Group then turned to bombing supply dumps supporting *15th Army*'s advance on Imphal. Lt. Gen. Mutaguchi had arranged to build up supplies for the advance at towns along the Chindwin River. The 7th Group carried out several attacks on supply dumps around the town of Kalewa on the Chindwin, with an escort of P-38s to ward off any Japanese fighters. With no risk of antiaircraft fire, the bombers could go in at 10,000 feet, resulting in excellent bombing patterns over their target areas. Toward the end of March the group went back to supporting Special Force, attacking the dumps at Mogaung and Kamaing again. In the first part of May the group flew in support of Stilwell's advance on Myitkyina, flying 15 missions over Myitkyina and the surrounding area. As Stilwell's combined force of Merrill's Marauders and Chinese troops approached Myitkyina, the 7th Group sent out small numbers of bombers to fly over the town at night, dropping bombs at intervals to distract the Japanese from Stilwell's approaching force. At this time the group also responded to a request from IV Corps to bomb specific Japanese positions around Imphal.[16]

On several occasions the 14th Army called on the heavy bombers to provide close air support to British and Indian troops advancing in the Arakan, but the results were mixed. On 17 January 1944 the 7th Bomb Group sent out 13 B-24s to bomb Japanese positions. While aircraft from the 9th and 492nd Squadrons used conventional demolition bombs, the 493rd Squadron dropped 60 Mk-17 325-pound depth charges, getting all of them right on the target area. The 436th Squadron bombed the target the next day and British forces successfully took the position. Nine days later the group sent two formations of eight aircraft to bomb Japanese positions at Razabil holding up the advance. RAF Vengeance dive-bombers marked the target area for the heavy bombers, who came in low at 8,500 feet. On this occasion the follow-up attack did not succeed. The depth of Japanese pill boxes and the terrain enabled the Japanese troops to survive the bombing and repel the British and Indian attack. Using the heavy bombers for saturation bombing generally proved to be unsuccessful. There were too few bombers to put down a really heavy concentration of high explosives with accuracy. Dive-bombers and fighter-bombers proved to be much more effective in providing close air support.[17]

In the first week of June, the 7th Bomb Group flew missions to bomb Japanese supplies around Kalemyo and the railroad yards at Wuntho. Mining missions in preparation for the monsoon continued

Popular movie star Paulette Goddard christens a 7th Bomb Group B-24J named in her honor on a visit to the group in April 1944. With few other diversions available, USO shows were always welcome, and visits of American actors and actresses to far-flung bases in the China-Burma-India theater were much appreciated. *SQ-Bomb-11-SU-PH, AFHRA*

with two night missions to mine the harbor at Mergui and the Chao Phraya River at Bangkok. On June 10 the group bombed the Yenangyaung oil refinery. This would be the 7th Bomb Group's last mission with the SAF until the following October. Three days later, Maj. Gen. Stratemeyer and newly promoted Maj. Gen. Davidson visited all four of the group's squadrons at their bases to inform them that Stratemeyer had ordered the 7th Group to take on a new mission: ferrying gasoline to the Fourteenth Air Force in China. The group would leave the Strategic Air Force temporarily until the completion of its mission. Ironically, this news came just as the 7th Group was finally receiving an influx of new combat crews after months of struggling on with less than a full complement of air crews. The squadrons had begun an intensive training program for the newcomers, stressing formation flying, gunnery, and bombing, with newly built training aids for bombardiers and gunners. To carry out its new mission, bombardiers and gunners would not be necessary, and many would be idle for the next several months.[18]

The pressures that led to the diversion of the 7th Bomb Group from bombing to hauling gas had been building in China for several months. During March, intelligence had begun to come in that the Japanese army in China was building up its forces in what appeared to be preparation for a major offensive. This was indeed what the Japanese were planning. Studies by Japanese army staff in fall 1943 looked at the benefits of capturing the Fourteenth Air Force's airfields in East China to limit the attacks on Japanese shipping and prevent these air bases from being used for air raids against Japan. In addition, capturing the railroad line from North China all the way south to French Indochina would give the Japanese army a means of getting supplies to the *Southern Army* in Southeast Asia overland and not by sea, where Japanese merchant shipping was under increasing threat of American submarine attack. In January 1944 *Imperial Japanese Headquarters* in Tokyo ordered the *China Expeditionary Army* to undertake a campaign (Operation *ICHI-GO*) to achieve these objectives. The *ICHI-GO* plan had two phases: Operation *KO-GO*, scheduled for April–May, would have the Japanese army drive north from Hankow to capture the rail corridor to the north; Operation *TO-GO*, to begin in June, would see Japanese forces drive south to capture the rail corridor to French Indochina and clear the East China airfields, linking up with Japanese forces pushing west from Canton. What Stilwell had feared would happen if the Fourteenth Air Force was as successful as Chennault claimed it would be was about to happen.[19]

In the first weeks of April, Chennault warned of an impending Japanese offensive. Although he initially thought this would be an air offensive, he noted that the Fourteenth Air Force might not have enough airplanes to provide air support to the Chinese armies in the scale that might be needed.[20] Chennault's warning alarmed Stratemeyer, since it came just as final preparations for Project MATTERHORN—the plan to base B-29s in China under the XX Bomber Command for an air offensive against Japan—were nearing completion.[21] If the Japanese were to go on the offensive, the demand for supplies and gasoline would increase dramatically, putting more pressure on ATC operations over the Hump and raising the unpleasant prospect of diverting resources from MATTERHORN to the Fourteenth Air Force. The answer came quickly, since the Japanese launched Operation *KO-GO* on April 19 and advanced rapidly toward their objectives. On May 11 the generalissimo asked that 500 tons of gasoline be diverted from the B-29s to supply fighters supporting the Chinese armies.[22] A week later, with the Japanese threat to his airfields growing, Chennault requested that the Fourteenth Air Force receive adequate supplies, overriding the priority for the B-29 project, submitting in support of his request an intelligence estimate that the Chinese armies would be incapable of defending his airfields in East China.[23] With heavy demands for transport aircraft to support the British and Indian divisions fighting at Imphal and Stilwell's offensive to capture Myitkyina, and unwilling to divert resources from the B-29s, Stratemeyer realized it might be necessary to order some of the Strategic Air Force's units to fly supplies to China.[24] On May 23 Stratemeyer presented a long-range air plan for the Tenth Air Force to Adm. Lord Louis Mountbatten in which he proposed shifting the 7th Bomb Group to transport operations as of July 1, though this would reduce the Strategic Air Force's heavy-bombing effort during the monsoon by 50 percent.[25] Mountbatten agreed to Stratemeyer's proposal, since he did not believe that the loss of this capacity during the monsoon, which would severely limit long-range bombing operations, would be that serious. In fact, at the time the 7th Bomb Group contributed more than 50 percent of the SAF's heavy-bomber force. The 7th Group had 49 B-24s available while the RAF had 32 Liberators, but of this total, only 53 aircraft were fully operational and the 7th Group's aircraft represented 77 percent of that total.[26] Meeting with Stilwell at Shadazup on June 4, Stratemeyer got his agreement to the shift in the 7th Bomb Group's mission. Stilwell agreed to send on Stratemeyer's recommendation to the War Department, and on June 9 Stratemeyer received a directive from Stilwell approving the change in mission.[27] The American command—from Marshall onward—had always insisted that China would be the American priority and that the resources of the Tenth Air Force would always be made available for service in China if needed. With China on the verge of crisis, the Strategic Air Force lost the services of the 7th Bomb Group for the following three months.

The Medium Bombers in the Strategic Air Offensive

The primary objectives for the Strategic Air Force's medium bombers were the Japanese rail and road communications network in central and northern Burma.[28] While the RAF Wellington bombers went out at night to attack railroad stations and marshaling yards, the

A 490th Bomb Squadron B-25D flying over a section of jungle. From January to April 1944, the 490th Squadron was the only B-25 unit operating in Burma after the departure of the rest of the 341st Bomb Group to China. *3A-33770, RG342FH, NARA*

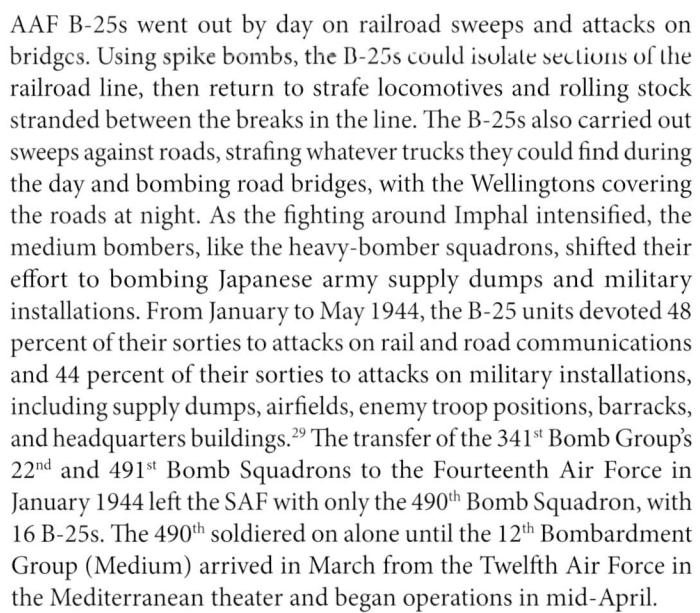

Preparing to load 100-pound demolition bombs onto a 22nd Bomb Squadron B-25C/D. Note the four positions in the nose for .50-caliber machine guns for low-level strafing. In January 1944, the 22nd and 491st Bomb Squadrons transferred to the Fourteenth Air Force in China. *3A-33901, RG342FH, NARA*

AAF B-25s went out by day on railroad sweeps and attacks on bridges. Using spike bombs, the B-25s could isolate sections of the railroad line, then return to strafe locomotives and rolling stock stranded between the breaks in the line. The B-25s also carried out sweeps against roads, strafing whatever trucks they could find during the day and bombing road bridges, with the Wellingtons covering the roads at night. As the fighting around Imphal intensified, the medium bombers, like the heavy-bomber squadrons, shifted their effort to bombing Japanese army supply dumps and military installations. From January to May 1944, the B-25 units devoted 48 percent of their sorties to attacks on rail and road communications and 44 percent of their sorties to attacks on military installations, including supply dumps, airfields, enemy troop positions, barracks, and headquarters buildings.[29] The transfer of the 341st Bomb Group's 22nd and 491st Bomb Squadrons to the Fourteenth Air Force in January 1944 left the SAF with only the 490th Bomb Squadron, with 16 B-25s. The 490th soldiered on alone until the 12th Bombardment Group (Medium) arrived in March from the Twelfth Air Force in the Mediterranean theater and began operations in mid-April.

The 341st Bomb Group's transition to the Strategic Air Force passed unnoticed in the group and squadron monthly histories for December 1943. Missions continued unabated. After a month's hiatus waiting to transfer to China, the 22nd and 491st Bomb Squadrons resumed operations on December 4, joining the 490th Bomb Squadron on a combined group mission to bomb a Japanese army camp. For the rest of the month, all three squadrons flew regularly, bombing targets that were by now familiar: the Myittha and Myitnge railroad bridges, the oil installations at Yenangyaung, a night attack on the Japanese airfield at Heho, Japanese stores at Monywa, a Japanese army camp, and for the last mission of the year, bombing warehouses at Alon. On most of these missions the squadrons bombed from medium altitudes, but often the 490th Squadron's few B-25Gs would go down to strafe with their 75 mm cannon, shooting up antiaircraft emplacements, locomotives, and riverboats on sweeps. There were several encounters with Japanese fighters when small formations of Ki-43s made several passes at the bomber formations, without damage to either side. The 491st Squadron had the misfortune of losing two aircraft on a mission to bomb Monywa on December 20, when antiaircraft fire over the target heavily damaged two airplanes. One crashed near Kalewa on the return flight, while the second airplane crash-landed at the base at Chakulia with damaged hydraulics. Having been reassigned to the Tenth Air Force on 17 December 1943, in early January the 341st was informed that the group and the 22nd and 491st Bomb Squadrons were to transfer to China immediately. The 22nd and 491st Squadrons flew their last mission over Burma on 3 January 1944, attacking the gasoline plant at Yenangyaung refinery. Four days later the advance echelon moved to Yangkai, the group's new base in Yunnan. The 22nd and 491st Squadrons began flying missions over China at the end of the month. The 341st Group would not be reunited until April 1945.[30]

Maj. Robert McCarten and the pilots and bombardiers in the 490th Bomb Squadron were still struggling with the vexing problem of how to knock out bridges. McCarten had the squadron experiment with all known techniques, bombing from medium altitude with the Norden bombsight on long approaches to the target, bombing at low altitudes, bombing on the deck, skip bombing aimed at the bridge structure or the supporting piers, and variations of these techniques—coming in at right angles to a bridge or diagonally—but nothing seemed to work. The squadron had attacked the Myitnge River Bridge on December 1, with the four flights of three aircraft each making a different approach to the bridge at altitudes from 10,200 feet to 11,400 feet, only to record that the "bridge seemed to be standing at last observation."[31] A return attack on December 6 achieved no better results. On December 12 the squadron got two hits on the approach to the Mu River Bridge from medium altitude, but not the bridge itself. Two days later the squadron attacked the Myittha Bridge with similar results. The Myitnge River Bridge was the target on December 21 and 22 in the last bridge attack of the year, but once again the results were a disappointment. In the December 21 attack a problem with the bombsight in B and C Flights sent their 1,000-pound M-44 bombs several hundred yards away from the target, but even with a working bombsight, A Flight could get no closer than 150 yards from the bridge, doing no damage. The mission the next day saw three flights drop 45 500-pound M-43

STRATEGIC BOMBING AND AIR SUPPLY OPERATIONS UNDER EASTERN AIR COMMAND

technique on a practice bombing range he had built near the 490th Squadron's base at Kurmitola. Using different types of bombs, fuse settings, approach altitudes, and speeds, Erdin and Suthpen found that the best method was to approach a bridge along its axis at 300 feet before entering a shallow dive to release the bombs at 100 to 150 feet. The bombs would crash through the bridge decking to hit the pier supporting the bridge below, demolishing the pier and dropping the span into the river. Using a new loading technique, the squadron's armorers later worked out how to put four M-44 1,000-pound bombs into a B-25's bomb bay, providing more bombs for more runs against a bridge. Squadron pilots began practicing the new bombing technique by using the reflector sight on the B-25's cockpit combing as a sighting device. The new method came to be called "glip" bombing, since it was a combination of glide and skip bombing. Although Capt. Erdin's new method worked, it was by no means easy and took time and practice to get right.[34]

The squadron tried the new technique against the Myittha River Bridge on January 23, with Capt. Erdin leading the mission. Six aircraft carried three M-44 1,000-pound bombs each and made individual runs over the bridge at 200 feet. In the first attack, the bombs skipped beyond the bridge to explode on the tracks to the north. The second airplane destroyed one pier and knocked a span out of line, but the third airplane's bombs destroyed the bridge completely, leaving only one span knocked out of line. Three aircraft attacked a second railroad bridge but failed to do any damage. On January 29, Erdin led six airplanes to attack the famous Meza River Bridge and the railroad bridge at Pyintha. Three airplanes went after

B-25s bombing the repaired Mu River Bridge in early 1944 from medium altitude. The shadow of a flight of three bombers can be seen on the river to the left of the bridge. *3A-37678, RG342FH, NARA*

bombs without result. The pilots and bombardiers of the 490th Squadron had long dreaded missions against bridges, since the mission invariably ended in failure. They began to think that Burmese bridges were a "jinx" target.[32]

The solution to the problem of busting bridges came about by a lucky accident on New Year's Day 1944. That morning, having failed to inflict any damage from medium altitude, the squadron sent out two B-25Cs and four B-25Gs to bomb the Mu River Bridge from low level. Capt. Robert Erdin, squadron operations officer, was flying on the mission that morning and decided to try a new approach to the bridge. He was carrying two M-44 1,000-pound bombs armed with an eight-to-eleven-second-delay fuse in the tail. Instead of approaching the bridge from right angles or diagonally, he decided to fly down the railroad track toward the bridge and cross over it lengthwise. Coming in at low altitude, he saw a tall tree directly ahead of him and pulled his B-25 up to miss the tree, but as he started down again on his bomb run he was at the release point for his bombs. Though in a shallow dive, he pressed the bomb release switch on his control wheel and sent his two 1,000-pound bombs down in trail as he passed along the bridge. Looking back, he was astonished to see the first and third spans of the bridge lying in the river below. Apparently Erdin's slight dive before he released the bombs made them fall at an angle and prevented the bombs from skipping over the bridge, as so often had happened with the other methods of low-level bombing.[33]

When McCarten learned of Erdin's success, he immediately assigned Erdin and 1st Lt. Harry Suthpen to experiment with the

The Myittha River Bridge, knocked out on 23 January 1944 by using the new low-level bombing technique that then Capt. Robert Erdin, the 490th Bomb Squadron's operations officer, discovered by accident. This fortuitous discovery proved to be the solution to destroying bridges in Burma. *3A-37708, RG342FH, NARA*

THE TENTH AIR FORCE IN WORLD WAR II

the Meza Bridge, each airplane dropping three bombs in train in individual runs. The first aircraft missed the bridge, but the bombs dropped so close that they destroyed one of the piers supporting the bridge and knocked a span out of line. The second and third aircraft missed but damaged tracks on the approach. At Pyintha the three remaining aircraft bombed with the same result: damage to the approaches but not to the bridge. Erdin took six aircraft back to the Meza Bridge the next day with a slight modification of the method. Each aircraft made two individual runs against the bridge, dropping one 1,000-pound bomb on the first run and two on the second. On its first run the first aircraft to bomb got close to the west pier, but this dislodged the span. On the second run the two bombs shattered the two western piers and the span and the approach fell into the river. The second aircraft demolished the center pier and the center span. The third aircraft missed on its first run but added to the destruction of the west span on its second.[35] As Erdin described the mission:

After crossing the Chin Hills at an altitude of 14,000 feet we let down at 500 feet a minute, arriving just south of the target at 1,000 feet altitude. The three ships were in a V formation. Direction of attack was to be from east to west since a long stretch of the railroad led straight to the bridge, affording an excellent opportunity to kill the drift on the bombing run.

The moment the target came into view I gave a visual signal to the left wing ship, which peeled off to the left, circled to the east and made its planned two runs, both from east to west.

During the few minutes consumed by the first attack, the right wing ship and I circled the target at about 750 feet in a Luftberry circle pattern. This put us in a position to observe results and gave the photographer an opportunity to secure excellent shots of the result of each run.

I made the second run the moment the atmosphere cleared and the left wing ship climbed to 750 feet and circled. This same procedure was followed by the right wing ship. The moment photographs had been taken following the last run we assembled in V formation and headed home.

"Our bombload," Major Erdin explained, "consisted of three 1,000 lb. general purpose bombs, fused 8 to 11 second delay. The first bomb was released select, the remaining two on the second run in train at 100 foot interval. Two runs, as the absence of ground defenses permitted in this case, gave the pilot a chance to correct for any slight error in range made on the first run."

Since no anti-aircraft fire was expected, our runs were made at 300 feet above the target to give the bombs a good downward trajectory and assure their sticking at impact. Indicated air speed was 250 miles per hour. Aiming point was the east pier of the east span. Since the three main spans were approximately 100 feet in length, the interval on the two bombs was set at 100 feet. We held a constant altitude during the runs. Speed was gained by diving plus a slight increase in throttle and pressure settings just prior to the run.

It has been our experience that in attacking targets which do not present a massive vertical surface sufficient to stop the terrific forward motion of the bomb, a shallow dive must be employed. And when ground defenses permit a run at 300 feet above the target is even better.

Referring to bombloads, Major Erdin stated: "The heavier the better. Regardless of pilot efficiency in low-level attacks, there is an element of luck in every successful attack. A near miss with a 1,000 pound bomb often results in complete destruction whereas a similar hit with a 500-pounder usually brings considerably less damage. This applies mainly to operations against bridges. The target itself dictates the bombload and tactics."[36]

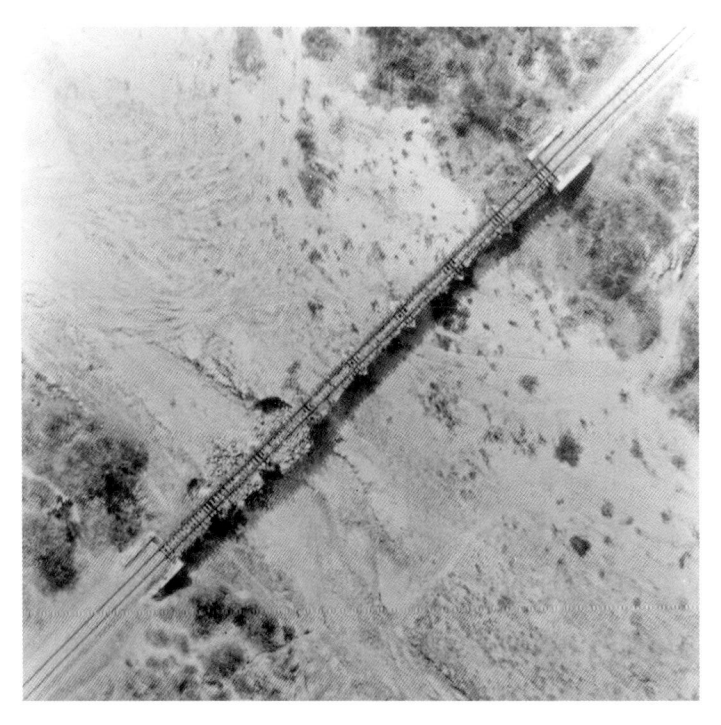

The Myingatha railroad bridge on April 28, just before the 490th Bomb Squadron delivered a low-level attack with 1,000-pound bombs. *3A-37684, RG342FH, NARA*

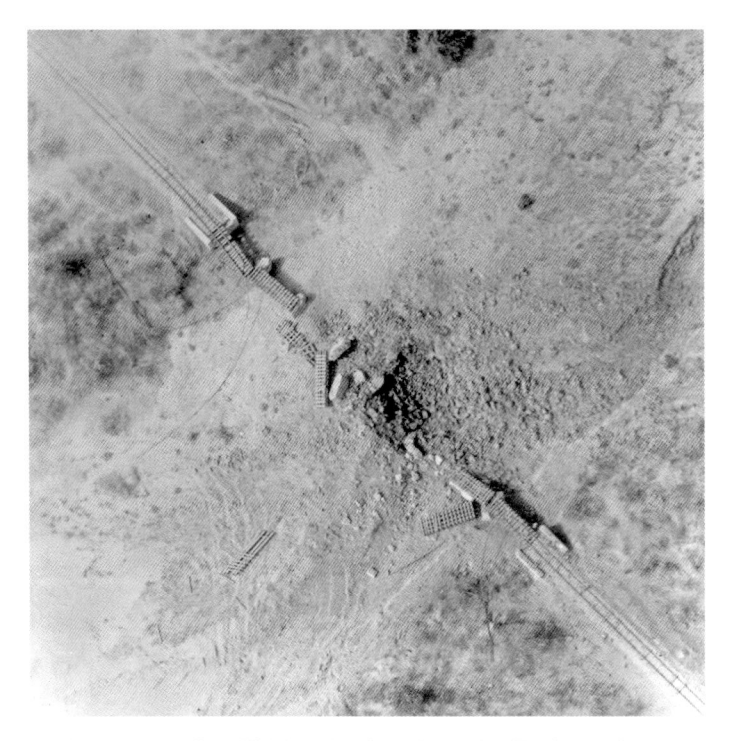

The Myingatha railroad bridge after four direct hits. The bombs have knocked all the spans into the dry riverbed below and shattered the concrete supports. The medium bombers waged a continuous battle with Japanese army engineers, who became adept at rapidly repairing damaged or destroyed bridges, requiring a follow-up attack. *3A-37683, RG342FH, NARA*

During February the squadron attacked 17 bridges, destroying seven and leaving three unserviceable. March saw fewer attacks, with only two bridges destroyed, but the results for April were spectacular. The 490th Squadron flew a record 29 missions during the month and attacked 34 bridges, destroying 14 and leaving another eight unserviceable. May was nearly as productive, with attacks on 23 bridges with 10 destroyed and three unserviceable. From January to May 1944 the 490th Squadron attacked 88 bridges, destroying 39 and rendering 17 unserviceable—a success rate of 64 percent.[37] The squadron broke its previous record of destroying nine bridges over four days between April 21 and 24 by knocking out seven bridges along the main Rangoon-Mandalay line over May 11 and 12. This was a dramatic change from the frustrations of the year before, when only 34 of 2,398 bombs dropped from heavy and medium bombers actually struck a bridge.[38] When he learned of the 490th Squadron's success, Davidson sent a message to McCarten—just promoted to lieutenant colonel—saying, "To you, your Bridge Busters, and all the boys on the ground who keep 'em flying, for their successful accomplishments, my personal congratulations. Your devastating results have been received with glee."[39] This was the first time anyone had used this nickname for the 490th Squadron, but it stuck. For the remainder of the war, the squadron was known as the "Burma Bridge Busters." Formal recognition of the squadron's achievements came later in the year, when the squadron received a Distinguished Unit Citation for its record from January to May 1944.[40]

The 490th Squadron's most important bridge-busting mission was the destruction of the vital Sittang Bridge on the night of 8 April 1944. Built in the early 1900s, the 2,349-foot-long steel bridge over the Sittang River was the longest river bridge in Burma, with 11 150-foot spans. The bridge connected the railroad line from southern Burma to the rail line running south to Rangoon and north to Mandalay. The British had destroyed two spans of the bridge in February 1942 as they retreated to Rangoon. With the completion of the Burma-Thailand railroad in fall 1943, repair of the bridge took on a new importance to speed the flow of supplies coming up from Moulmein and Martaban to the south. The Japanese started major repairs on the bridge to make it serviceable in December 1943, and by early February the bridge was once again open to rail traffic. The 490th Bomb Squadron took on the task of destroying the bridge by using their new low-level bombing techniques. By now the pilots were thoroughly familiar with the method, but the squadron had not yet attempted low-level bombing of a bridge at night. The first attempt took place on March 6, when four B-25H aircraft went out at night to bomb the bridge, carrying four 1,000-pound bombs each, but failed to damage the bridge.

The squadron went back to the Sittang Bridge a month later. This time five B-25s took off from Chittagong the evening of April 8 for the 1,200-mile round trip to the Sittang Bridge. The bombers came in from the west, picking up the railroad line that ran for 5 miles straight to the bridge. It was a moonlit night, making the railroad tracks glisten in the darkness, but ground haze covered the area around the bridge. 1st Lt. William E. Cook, flying a new B-25H, was the second airplane to go in to attack. Coming in on the bridge at 280 mph and 300 feet, Cook dropped two 1,000-pound bombs, knocking out two of the central spans. After dropping his bombs Cook banked sharply left to avoid ground fire that had been tracking him as he made his approach to the bridge. He found himself heading straight for a conical-shaped Burmese Buddhist temple stupa. Instinctively, Cook banked to the right, but not before the tip of his left wing hit the top of the stupa, knocking off 4 feet of the wing and the left aileron. As he straightened out the damaged bomber, the B-25 began to lose altitude, but with full right rudder and aileron Cook got his airplane into a climb, hurriedly telling his crew to put on their parachutes. At 10,000 feet he leveled out with his plane listing to the left and staggered back to Chittagong, where he landed the damaged bomber at 125 mph—15 mph over the normal landing speed. Another crew on the mission had to bail out over friendly territory when their airplane ran out of fuel, but they made it back to base after four days of travel. The other three pilots on the mission returned to Chittagong without incident, having left several more spans on the Sittang Bridge twisted out of line and rendering this important bridge unserviceable.[41]

A great benefit of the new low-level attack method was that it required fewer aircraft to destroy a bridge. Attempts to bomb from medium altitudes had involved nine and sometimes twelve airplanes. With the new method, an attack on a bridge normally required only three bombers, and sometimes just a pair. On May 18, Squadron Operations Officer Erdin—now a major—went back to bomb the Mu River Bridge—the same bridge he had knocked out on New Year's Day, when he discovered the new method of low-level bombing. Regular photographic coverage of the Burmese bridges tracked the state of Japanese repairs. With repairs to the bridge about to be completed, Erdin went back to knock the bridge out again, this time with only one other B-25 instead of the four he had brought with him in January. In two runs over the bridge, Erdin dropped three 1,000-pound bombs and knocked the westernmost span out of line. His wingman, 2nd Lt. Donald Reed—on his first bridge bombing mission—got two bombs directly under the central span on his third bomb run, knocking the two center spans into the river.[42]

From February through April the 490th Squadron alternated attacks on bridges with medium-altitude bombing missions against railroad yards, Japanese supply dumps, strongpoints, and troop concentrations in aid of British and Indian forces fighting around Imphal. To further disrupt the Japanese line of communications and thereby provide indirect support to the British army around

The Air Commandos received a small number of B-25H aircraft to equip the force's Bomber Section under the command of Lt. Col. R. T. Smith, a former AVG ace who returned to combat with Cochran and Alison. The Bomber Section flew in support of Wingate's Special Force, attacking Japanese installations, supply dumps, and lines of communications leading to the areas where Special Force was to operate. *3A-37779, RG342FH, NARA*

Imphal and Stilwell's forces in northern Burma, the squadron flew regular sweeps along the railroad lines in central Burma, seeking out targets of opportunity—especially locomotives and rolling stock—and bombing sections of railroad track. The squadron began combining attacks on bridges with rail sweeps, the B-25s going on to sweep a section of the railroad line after bombing a bridge target. In February the squadron began receiving new B-25H aircraft (code-named "Pigeon" under the Tenth Air Force's system for naming its assigned aircraft) armed with the 75 mm cannon as in the B-25G, but with four .50-caliber machine guns in the nose instead of the two on the B-25G, and two fixed .50-caliber machine gun packages on each side of the fuselage below the cockpit. These low-level missions often encountered automatic-weapons fire, and inevitably there were losses.

On February 22, five B-25Gs with five of the new B-25Hs went out on a sweep to bomb and strafe targets of opportunity, bombing railroad tracks and bridges and destroying two locomotives and a considerable number of rolling stock during an hour's mission. Halfway through the mission the other pilots saw 1st Lt. Harry Stephen's B-25 on fire and then crash and explode in flames, killing all the crew—probably as a result of ground fire. Four days later, three B-25s went out to bomb a bridge and, after dropping their bombs, strafed three trains with 75 mm cannon and .50-caliber machine guns. The returning crews reported inaccurate light machine gun fire but saw 1st Lt. Kenneth Hardy's B-25H crash and burn. The squadron lost two more B-25s on similar missions during March. On April 12, while returning from a bridge-bombing mission, Lt. William Cook's B-25 crashed in friendly territory for unknown reasons—possibly weather or damage from ground fire.[43]

Before the onset of the monsoon and a change in mission, the 490th Squadron continued its attacks on bridges and provided indirect support to IV Corps with attacks on targets on the road leading from Tedium to Imphal. The squadron flew several medium-altitude missions against Japanese supply dumps and strongpoints at the request of IV Corps. In the middle of the month the squadron went back to the Tedium-Imphal road to create roadblocks, dropping 160 500-pound bombs along sections of the road on May 14 and temporarily blocking access. On May 20, the 490th Squadron was suddenly taken off bombing operations and ordered to fly ammunition from Chittagong to British and Indian forces fighting at Imphal, supplementing the transports of Troop Carrier Command. The squadron flew ammunition into Imphal until the end of June through the appalling weather of the monsoon, and not without incident. Despite the weather, the Japanese continued to send fighter sweeps over the Imphal area in support of the Japanese army divisions, fighting what was fast becoming a losing battle. Operating singly out of Chittagong, two of the 490th Squadron's B-25s ran into Japanese fighters over the Imphal area on May 24. At around noon, 10 Oscar fighters attacked 1st Lt. Gary King's B-25. King evaded the attacks while his gunners fought back, with Sgt. Donald Morgan claiming one fighter destroyed. A few minutes later this same formation of fighters came on Lt. Col. McCarten, who was taking his turn on the ammunition run to Imphal. One of the fighters pressed in to attack, setting one of the B-25's engines on fire. With the engine smoking, McCarten evaded the fighters and made his way back to base, where he executed a successful crash landing on one engine, enemy fire having damaged his hydraulics. From May 20 to the end of June, the squadron delivered 1,409 tons of ammunition to the troops at Imphal. The squadron's armorers again found ways to boost the B-25's payload, working out a new rack system that allowed a bomber to carry more than 4,000 pounds of equipment and enabling one bomber to carry what three aircraft had carried before the modification. The monsoon weather and the terrain claimed three aircraft and their crews.[44]

By the time the 490th Bomb Squadron switched to transporting ammunition to Imphal, the 12th Bomb Group and its four squadrons (81st, 82nd, 83rd, and 434th Bombardment Squadrons) had been on operations for over a month. The 12th Bomb Group had gone overseas to North Africa during summer 1942, beginning operations in Egypt as part of Maj. Gen. Lewis Brereton's Middle East Air Force. The group had helped push the Germans and Italians out of North Africa as part of the Ninth Air Force, had flown missions over Sicily and Italy, and, as part of the Twelfth Air Force, had moved to a base in Italy in November 1943 to support the Allied armies moving north toward Rome. At the end of January 1944 the group received orders to prepare for another move overseas. The group went by

The Air Commando Bomber Section's B-25H "Dolly" pulls away after bombing Japanese installations at Wuntho, in central Burma. The Bomber Section removed the .50-caliber gun packages from the fuselage side on many of its B-25H aircraft. 3A-37823, RG342FH, NARA

A battle-worn "Dolly" later in the campaign, with a figure of Bugs Bunny leaning on a cannon that leads to the 75 mm cannon on the B-25H. "Dolly" now has 38 mission symbols on its nose beneath the cockpit. The Air Commando B-25H pilots found the 75 mm cannon especially effective against large structures such as warehouses. Author's collection

A B-25H from the 12th Bomb Group's 81st Bomb Squadron taxis out on a rain-soaked airfield—probably Tezagon—while another B-25H waits its turn. The 12th Bomb Group began flying combat missions in April 1944 with new B-25H and B-25J aircraft. *3A-33703, RG342FH, NARA*

ship from Italy to India, arriving in Bombay on March 12 and taking a four-day train ride to Calcutta, then on to the group's new bases at two former RAF fighter bases near Dacca. The 81st and 82nd Squadrons went to the airfield at Tezgaon, while the 83rd and 434th Squadrons went to nearby Kurmitola. In the first two weeks of April the squadrons flew to Bangalore to pick up new B-25H and B-25J models, flying them back to Tezgaon and Kurmitola for a period of familiarization and training. The arrival of the 12th Bomb Group brought the number of B-25s available to the Strategic Air Force from 15 in March to 85 in May.[45] The 81st Squadron flew the group's first combat mission over Burma to bomb stores at Mogaung on April 16. One airplane failed to return from the mission. Over the next two weeks, the other squadrons began operations. Leaving attacks on bridges to the 490th Bomb Squadron, the 12th Group concentrated on medium-altitude missions to bomb Japanese supplies and troop concentrations around Imphal and along the railroad corridor leading up to Myitkyina. In early May a detachment from the 83rd Squadron flew up to Assam to be closer to Stilwell's American Chinese forces. The arrival of the monsoon weather began to interfere with missions, forcing the bombers to turn back when they found the target covered in cloud. When the weather was too bad over central Burma, the squadrons joined the 490th Squadron in flying ammunition to Imphal. On May 20 the squadrons received a special order to transfer all available pilots to forward areas to relieve C-47 pilots in the transport squadrons. This resulted in the 12th Bomb Group becoming temporarily immobilized, but Stratemeyer intervened to countermand the order and return the group to combat.[46] As May turned into June, the weather was no better. In the middle of the month the 12th Bomb Group exchanged bases with the 7th Bomb Group to bring the 7th Group closer to the route up to the Hump and China for ferrying gasoline. With more missions scrubbed due to weather, the 12th Group's squadrons switched to flying more ammunition to Imphal.[47]

From January to May 1944, the AAF and RAF squadrons in the Strategic Air Force dropped 7,070 tons of bombs on Japanese targets in Burma and Thailand, with the American squadrons contributing 56 percent of this total. Monthly tonnage increased from 957 tons in January to 2,041 tons in May.[48] With the intensive ground fighting during the period ranging from the Arakan to northern Burma, 55 percent of the bombs the AAF and RAF squadrons dropped went against military installations, with the second-highest amount going against railroad installations.[49] While it is difficult to quantify the impact of these attacks, Allied intelligence believed that the continuous bombing of the Japanese communications system from February to the end of May came close to stopping the movement of supplies from Bangkok north to Myitkyina.[50] The effort cost the American squadrons six B-24s and twelve B-25s lost on operations during 1,754 sorties—a loss rate of 1 percent.[51] But as important as the number of bombs dropped and Japanese installations destroyed was the benefit that came from the integration of the two air forces. The Strategic Air Force was an example of the advantages of unity of command and the application of Clausewitz's principles of economy of force and concentration of force. As Maj. Gen. Davidson wrote in his *Dispatch on Operations of Strategic Air Force Eastern Air Command for the Period 15 December 1943 to 31 May 1944*:

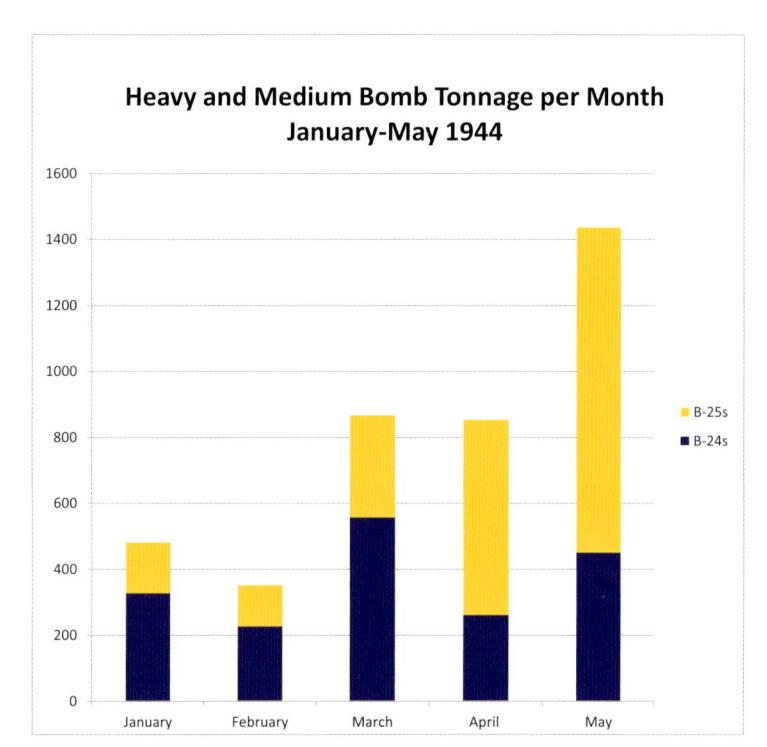

Heavy and Medium Bomb Tonnage per Month January–May 1944

Table 8 Source: Appendix 2, Aircraft in Possession of Strategic Air Force, Dispatch on Operations of Eastern Air Command 15 December 1943–1 June 1945, P. 134.

THE TENTH AIR FORCE IN WORLD WAR II

Throughout the period, a fine spirit of harmony prevailed between British and American personnel which contributed inestimably to the forceful execution of SAF's mission. The combination and coordination of the various units into a single, powerful striking force enabled us to hit the enemy more often and more disastrously than ever before.[52]

Air Supply Operations

Air supply was vital to the success of all the Allied ground operations undertaken in the first half of 1944. Without AAF and RAF transports delivering supplies to the Allied armies, it is doubtful that Allied operations in Burma and the defense of Imphal would have succeeded.[53] Air supply freed Allied units from limited or nonexistent surface supply lines, providing the mobility that enabled Merrill's Marauders and Wingate's Special Force to operate behind Japanese lines, and the ability to withstand and defeat the Japanese tactic of infiltration and envelopment, as demonstrated during the second Arakan campaign and at Imphal. By June 1944, "the techniques of air supply had been developed to an amazing point of perfection in the CBI, where unusual requirements encouraged a wide variety of experimentation in the whole field of air support for ground operations."[54] The demands the ground forces placed on the transport squadrons were exceptional—far more than had been anticipated—and kept the squadrons fully occupied for months.[55] Air Command, Southeast Asia, had to call for additional squadrons from the Air Transport Command's India-China Wing and American and British units from the Mediterranean to meet the needs of the ground forces. The air supply effort during the first six months of 1944 was unprecedented in the China-Burma-India theater. Squadrons set new records in terms of sorties flown and tons of supplies delivered. It was a period of intensive learning, practicing new techniques, and perfecting the methods of air supply, valuable lessons that would be built on during the reconquest of Burma over the following year.

Stratemeyer had planned that one of the components of Eastern Air Command would be an organization to exercise operational control of AAF and RAF transport squadrons operating in Bengal and Assam. In his General Order No. 1, Stratemeyer announced the activation of Troop Carrier Command (TCC) under Brig. Gen. William Old. From its title, Troop Carrier Command, and the definition of its mission, to "provide air transportation for airborne and air transit forces in the support and training of the Army Group and other land or air forces involved in operations in Burma," there was a "certain vagueness" about the assigned mission of the new organization.[56] The focus on carrying troops as opposed to supplies may have reflected the planned second Wingate expedition and the formation of the British army's 50th Parachute Brigade for possible airborne operations in the coming offensive. On 2 January 1944, Old set up his command's headquarters at Camilla, an airbase southwest of Dacca, to be near the headquarters of the Third Tactical Air Force and 14th Army. At its activation, Troop Carrier Command had under its command No. 31 Squadron, RAF, operating in Bengal, and the 1st and 2nd Troop Carrier Squadrons, operating in Assam from Sookerating and Din Jan in support of Stilwell's forces. Of the other RAF transport squadrons, No. 62 Squadron had recently converted to the Dakota and began supply-dropping operations for the 14th Army in early January 1944. Two more RAF Dakota squadrons (No. 117 and No. 194) were training paratroopers in northwestern India and continued in this role until February 1944. All four RAF squadrons soon became part of No. 177 Transport Wing, RAF, and over the next few months moved to bases in Bengal. Two more AAF transport squadrons joined Troop Carrier Command in January 1944. On January 1, the 315th Troop Carrier Squadron (TCS) was activated in the CBI theater with cadre drawn from the 1st and 2nd TCS and assigned to the base at Sylhet in Bengal. Ten days later the 27th Troop Carrier Squadron arrived at Karachi and was quickly assigned to Troop Carrier Command, joining the 315th Squadron at Sylhet. Both squadrons operated the C-47. In March the four American troop carrier squadrons came under the 443rd Troop Carrier Group, brought out hurriedly from the United States the month before without personnel or equipment to form a full troop carrier group. These eight squadrons—four AAF and four RAF—made up Troop Carrier Command from its activation until early June 1944. In early January they had between them some 86 C-47/Dakota aircraft.[57]

Troop Carrier Command's first test began in February in the Arakan, as the Japanese launched Operation *HA-GO*. The transport squadrons had been supporting the advance of IV Corps' two divisions (5th and 7th Divisions), who were moving down the Mayu Peninsula in the Arakan. To the east, the 81st West African Division was moving down the Kaladana Valley, relying on air supply. The Japanese infiltrated around the 7th Division and cut it off from the 5th Division, while at the same time cutting the 5th Division's land communications line to the north. By 8 February 1944, 22,000 British and Indian troops were isolated in their positions with the 7th Division, in what became known as the "Admin Box," with only two days' rations left. At the time, No. 31 Squadron was carrying out air supply operations to IV Corps at Imphal and in the Chin Hills with support from the 27th and 315th Troop Carrier Squadrons, while No. 62 Squadron supported the advance of the 81st W.A. Division. On February 8, No. 31 Squadron flew in supplies to the Admin Box but lost one Dakota to Japanese fighters and another damaged. That evening, Brig. Gen. Old led four 315th TCS C-47s to the box to drop badly needed ammunition, his airplane taking eight hits from Japanese ground fire. With RAF Spitfires battling marauding Japanese fighters during the day, Old decided that air supply missions would have to be flown at night or only with fighter escort during the day. During February, the 27th and 315th TC Squadrons joined

A C-47 takes off from an airfield in Assam during the monsoon, on a flight to Myitkyina after the capture of the airfield. The transports flew in all weather, delivering vital supplies to the Allied armies pushing into Burma. Victory in Burma would not have been possible without air supply. *3A-33781, RG342FH, NARA*

A C-47 from the 2nd Troop Carrier Squadron takes off from a rough dirt strip during the dry season. C-47 pilots would land wherever the engineers could carve out a flat strip of ground that was long enough to land and take off from. *10th Air Force Miscellaneous Photos, 830.08, AFHRA*

British troops of Special Force walk past a damaged Air Commando Waco CG-4 glider at Broadway, one of the landing sites behind Japanese lines chosen for the aerial invasion of Burma. The Air Commandos flew in a small number of gliders for the initial landing during the night of 5 March 1944. *Army Air Force, India-Burma Sector, 825.08, AFHRA*

the four RAF transport squadrons in Troop Carrier Command, flying supplies to British and Indian forces in the Arakan. The 14th Army requested more transport planes to increase the amount of supplies to the divisions in the Arakan, and suggested diverting 63 C-47s from the India-China Wing of the ATC. Transmitting this request to the Chiefs of Staff, on the basis of analysis of base facilities and probable requirements, Stratemeyer reduced the number of aircraft requested to 33 C-47s or 27 C-46s. Adm. Mountbatten formally asked the US Joint Chiefs of Staff to authorize the diversion of the ATC aircraft, and on February 24 the India-China Wing received orders to temporarily transfer 25 C-46s to TCC to support air drops to the 7th Division. The US Joint Chiefs of Staff urged that the C-46s be replaced with C-47s as soon as possible so as not to disrupt tonnage over the Hump for longer than necessary. The ATC C-46s operated from February 26 to March 4, but for a variety of reasons the ATC aircraft were not fully utilized. By then the crisis was over. XV Corps had halted the Japanese attack, severely mauling the Japanese *55th Division*. This was the first significant demonstration that with air supply the Japanese tactic of envelopment through cutting land lines of communication could be defeated. During the crucial month of February, the 27th and 315th Squadrons flew 147 sorties over the Arakan, delivering 424 tons of supplies. For Troop Carrier Command overall, February saw a near doubling of the amount of supplies carried, from 5,459 tons in January to 9,168 tons in February.[58]

Hard on the heels of the Arakan battles came the second Wingate Expedition. The exploits of the 1st Air Commando Group have tended to overshadow the role of the Troop Carrier Command squadrons in supporting Wingate's Special Force, which was considerable. Shortly after setting up his headquarters, Old had dinner with Wingate, during which Wingate mentioned that Troop Carrier Command would need to provide 36 sorties a day in support of Special Force—the first time Old had heard his new command would be required.[59] The Air Commandos Transport Force had 13 C-47s, but for the planned fly-in of two of his brigades, Wingate needed more transport aircraft. On the eve of the operation, TCC prepared 44 Dakotas from its four RAF transport squadrons and 26 C-47s from the 27th and 315th Troop Carrier Squadrons. On the night of March 5 the fly-in to BROADWAY began, with 20 C-47s towing gliders for the initial landing. Having carved out a rough landing strip during the day, on the evening of March 6 the TCC squadrons—RAF and AAF—began flying in men and supplies while

Air Commando gliders brought in small tractors and other equipment that the Air Commandos and British infantry used to hurriedly prepare a rough landing strip for Air Commando and Troop Carrier Command transports bringing in more troops and supplies. The fly-in continued the night of 6 March 1944. *AF-CMDO-1-SU-PH, AFHRA*

more C-47s towed gliders to the second landing area at CHOWRINGEE. Over the next five days the Air Commandos and the TCC Squadrons flew in 9,052 troops, 1,458 horses and mules, and 254 tons of supplies. Of this total, the TCC squadrons flew in 77 percent of the troops, 90 percent of the horses and mules, and 80 percent of the supplies. Although all the air supply operations took place at night, not one transport was lost and only six were damaged.[60]

Once Special Force had landed, the brigade columns set off on their assigned missions. TCC assigned the 27th TC Squadron to support 16th Brigade's columns, while the 315th TC Squadron supported 111th Brigade, and No. 117 Squadron the 77th Brigade. Each column had an air officer attached who requested air supply, located drop zones, and controlled air drops. As an example of the effort involved, between March 13 and 19 the 27th TC Squadron flew 156 sorties supporting 16th Brigade, dropping 408 tons of

British Special Force soldiers struggle to persuade a mule to board a C-47 for the flight into Burma. The crews used bamboo poles to build temporary stalls inside their aircraft to hold several mules at a time. Once inside the mules were, for the most part, docile passengers. 3A-37054, RG342FH, NARA

supplies, and between March 20 and April 4 flew an additional 106 sorties delivering an additional 265 tons. The Air Commandos and the TCC squadrons flew in two more brigades for Special Force at the end of March and the first week of April, in addition to their regular supply runs, flying out the wounded on the return trip. The TCC squadrons supported the Special Force strongpoints at BROADWAY, White City, and farther north at Blackpool, nearer to Mogaung. After May 20, command of Special Force shifted from Gen. Slim and 14th Army to Stilwell in the Northern Combat Area Command. Stilwell kept the exhausted men of Special Force in action beyond the date they had expected to be relieved, using the brigades to push toward Mogaung. The town fell on June 25 to 77th Brigade, with support of the Chinese 114th Regiment. During its final weeks in combat, the TCC squadrons continued to provide all of Special Force's needs through air supply and helped fly out the men in late July, when they were finally withdrawn from combat.[61]

Employment of the Air Commandos in support of Wingate's Special Force was not without controversy. Stratemeyer was hesitant to endorse the concept of assigning an air unit exclusively for one type of operation, particularly since he saw that after Special Force's entry into Burma, its requirements for supplies quickly exceeded the capability of a small air commando transport force. While an air commando unit would be valuable in the initial fly-in of long-range-penetration groups, Stratemeyer saw the role more as one of coordinating the various regular air units that would have to be involved. Writing to Arnold as the second Wingate expedition was underway, Stratemeyer said, "it is our considered opinion that Air Commando function, as such, is not a special branch of aviation and should not be exploited as such. We feel that with some specialized training and some special equipment, elements of regularly constituted units could perform the function just as well. This is particularly true in view of the fact that the Air Commando Force only forms the spear head of the invasion, after which it is not so organized as to be able to continue."[62]

The other issues the Air Commando project created were those of unity of command and economy of force. The Air Commandos were "superimposed upon then existing organizations in the field thus creating a command problem."[63] Arnold had assigned the Air Commandos to Wingate for his operations. Although they were an autonomous unit, the Air Commandos depended on other Third Tactical Air Force and Troop Carrier Command units to fulfill all the requirements of Special Force. The Air Commandos came under the operational control of Third Tactical Air Force for air support operations, but there was no formal arrangement between the Air Commandos and Troop Carrier Command covering air supply operations. As a result, operations had to be worked out in conferences between Old and Cochran as commander of the Air Commandos. In a report on Operation Thursday, Baldwin said that "a commander of all the Air Forces engaged should be appointed to (a) watch training, (b) agree planning and (c) weld the force into a coordinated whole, responsive to his direction."[64] A Special Force report on operations also noted the problem of command and combined planning, noting that "an operation of this nature involves multiplicity of Headquarters and organizations spread over the ample terrain of India and the forward area."[65] That the operation was such a success was due in no small part to the spirit of cooperation that prevailed among all the units involved.

The vexing issue of economy of force related to the idea of assigning an air unit to the exclusive use of one army formation in a theater chronically short of resources and with operations spread over a vast area. While the rapport established between the Air Commandos and Special Force was exceptional and the results of this cooperation were impressive, particularly in developing new techniques of close air support and air supply, "the principle of air commando units gave rise to the danger of tying down air forces permanently and exclusively to one particular army formation with the consequent risks of duplication and lack of flexibility."[66] In his study of air supply in the Burma campaigns, Dr. Joe Taylor made the following observation:

> The assignment of the 1st Air Commando Group to the single task of supporting the second Wingate expedition was in itself a debatable measure. There was no apparent reason why TCC and Third TAF, given the equipment available to the Commandos, could not have carried out the same tasks equally well. The assignment of a private air force to a division commander certainly served to further that commander's operations, but it resulted in a sizable component of the potential Allied airpower in the theater being available only for certain limited operations. . . . Intentionally or otherwise, General Arnold was a party to compartmentalization of airpower when he gave Cochran the sole task of supporting Wingate.[67]

Arnold was delighted with the success of the Air Commandos in executing Operation THURSDAY. In late March he decided to organize four more air commando groups to support long-range-penetration missions. From his participation in discussions with the Joint Chiefs and the Combined Chiefs of Staff, Arnold would have been keenly aware of the need for more transport aircraft for Southeast Asia. To support the new air commando groups, he proposed forming four new transport groups to be known as combat cargo groups, each with 100 C-47 transports and trained in supplying ground forces. Arnold's concept was to have the air commando units provide air support to the long-range-penetration groups, relying on the large combat cargo groups for air supply. He believed that this combination was the answer to the combined handicaps of terrain and logistics that had limited operations in Burma. On 24 March 1944, he wrote a letter to Mountbatten, informing him that Arnold intended to organize the four new air commando units and a wing of four transport groups, providing a total of 400 transports. Arnold intended to have the first air commando unit and the first of the new transport groups arrive in India in July, with three more air commando units and the three transport groups arriving over the following three months. He warned Mountbatten that circumstances might force him to send some of these groups to the Pacific. In making the offer to Mountbatten, Arnold imposed some restrictions for the employment of these units:

1. They shall be known as US Army Air Force Air Commando Unit No. ___.
2. Their operations be directed by the senior US Air Force Commander.
3. Orders and control will employ a US chain of command.
4. The American integrity of the units be maintained
5. The Theater contribute to the support of their operations.[68]

For reasons that will be discussed, Arnold wanted to ensure American control over the Air Commandos. These caveats would become the subject of a later debate between Arnold and the commanders in ACSEA over plans to deploy additional air commando units to Southeast Asia Command. The same day he wrote to Mountbatten, Arnold informed the Combined Chiefs of Staff of his offer of the Air Commandos and 400 transport aircraft and, with Marshall's approval, began organizing the new units.[69]

Ten days after the fly-in of Special Force to BROADWAY, *15th Army* began its advance on Imphal with the *15th, 31st,* and *33rd Divisions*, beginning a siege that would last for three months. The Imphal plain, in the state of Manipur, was a large valley around 50 miles long from north to south and 25 miles wide from east to west. The Imphal plain had only one link to the rest of Assam. A single all-weather road led from Imphal to Kohima and on to Dimapur—a station on the Bengal-to-Assam railroad line, the main line connecting the port of Calcutta with the American air bases in upper Assam. Had the Japanese seized Imphal and Kohima and managed to push on to Dimapur, they would have severed this link and disrupted not just the flow of supplies to Stilwell's forces advancing down the Hukawng Valley toward Myitkyina, but the entire Hump operation. The Imphal plain was the base for IV Corps, Lt. Gen. Geoffrey Scoones commanding, which in mid-March had three divisions (17th, 20th, and 23rd Indian Divisions) and the 50th Parachute Brigade. Imphal was also the headquarters of No. 221 Group, RAF, charged with supporting IV Corps. There were two all-weather airfields in the plain at Imphal and Palel and four fair-weather landing grounds. These airfields held two Spitfire squadrons for the air defense of Imphal and five Hurricane squadrons to provide close air support to the Indian divisions. During March, seven more RAF squadrons would move to Imphal. British and Indian army and RAF forces within the Imphal plain totaled 170,000 men. Aware of the pending Japanese attack, Scoones planned to withdraw his divisions closer in to hold the plain even if encircled, with the expectation that his forces could rely on air supply. But with all three of his divisions committed, Scoones had no reserve available. As the Japanese advance began, the immediate need was to get reinforcements into Imphal.[70]

Gen. Slim decided to bring the 5th Indian Division up from the Arakan, but to transport the division by road and rail would have taken up to two weeks—an unacceptable delay. The only way to get 5th Division to Imphal quickly was by air, but Troop Carrier Command did not have enough transport aircraft available. Although the number of aircraft within the command's eight squadrons had grown to 144, two full squadrons (1st and 2nd TCS) with 32 C-47s were supporting Stilwell's forces in northern Burma, while the 27th and 315th TCS and No. 117 Squadron were fully committed to supporting Wingate's Special Force, leaving TCC with only around 60 aircraft—completely inadequate for flying a full division and needed supplies into Imphal.[71] The only source of transports in the theater was the India-China Wing of the ATC, but only the US Joint Chiefs of Staff could allocate the diversion of these aircraft from the Hump operation,

The process of supplying forward troops by air began with careful packing of supplies into packages that were attached to locally made jute parachutes. Several African American units, such as the 518th Quartermaster Battalion (Mobile), helped procure supplies from warehouses, pack and load them onto transport aircraft, kick them out over a drop zone, and distribute the supplies after they had landed. This was a vital task that received little notice. *3A-37609, RG342FH, NARA*

Transport pilots from the 2nd Troop Carrier Squadron get a briefing on their next air supply mission over northern Burma. Locating the drop zones among the jungle-covered hills was often a challenge. *3A-36104, RG342FH, NARA*

C-47s from the 2nd Troop Carrier Squadron at an advanced base in Assam. Conditions on these fields were basic, and all maintenance had to be carried out in the open, in the heat and the rain. A number of Tenth Air Force squadrons had PT-17s on strength for liaison work, flying parts and personnel between airfields. 3A-37079, RG342FH, NARA

and the request had to come from Mountbatten through Stilwell, as CBI commander, to the Joint Chiefs of Staff. With the urgency of the situation, Mountbatten decided to bypass the approved process and contacted the British Chiefs of Staff and the British Joint Staff Mission in Washington on March 16, stating that on his own authority he would divert 30 C-47s or the equivalent number of C-46s unless this order was countermanded by March 18. At the same time, Mountbatten sent a directive to Stratemeyer ordering him to divert the airplanes from the India-China Wing to fly reinforcements to Imphal. The Joint Chiefs of Staff approved the temporary transfer of 20 C-46s to Troop Carrier Command for a period of one month but denied Mountbatten authority to divert ATC airplanes on his own authority. In some 758 sorties, these C-46s, together with No. 194 Squadron, flew two brigades of 5th Indian Division to Imphal and one to Dimapur. After completing the transfer of 5th Division, Gen. Slim decided to transfer the 7th Indian Division from the Arakan as well. This move began on April 6, with one brigade flying into Imphal. The transports then started flying a brigade from the 2nd Division up to Dimapur to reinforce XXXIII Corps, responsible for the defense of the area. Later in April, TCC flew in a second brigade from 7th Division into Imphal. In total, TCC and the ATC C-46s transported six infantry brigades—the equivalent of two divisions—into Imphal, Dimapur, and Silchar, the largest troop movement by air ever attempted up to that point.[72]

The ATC C-46s flew constantly during their period of detached service with TCC, as did the TCC squadron C-47 crews. The following description could apply equally to both:

C-46 crews put in exhausting days during this operation. Taking off from Amarda Road, they delivered a load of troops to Jorhat. At Jorhat they picked up a load of reinforcements for the Imphal garrison and flew into the Plain. From one of the Imphal strips they took off empty for Silchar, where they loaded bombs for the isolated RAF units. After delivering these bombs, they picked up a load of casualties or evacuees and delivered them to Comilla or Alipore. Then the weary crews flew back to Amarda Road, often arriving after 2100.[73]

Planning for the sustained supply of the Army and RAF forces stationed at Imphal (designated Operation STAMINA) and estimates of the needs of Stilwell's Chinese and American forces indicated that the resources of Troop Carrier Command could not deliver the required supplies to both at the same time. To meet the urgent need for more transport aircraft, Mountbatten asked the Combined Chiefs of Staff to allow the 20 ATC C-46s to remain with TCC for longer than the promised month, and for an additional 70 C-47s or their equivalent from the Hump operation.[74] The Joint Chiefs of Staff would not agree to diverting more aircraft from the Hump, nor to extending the temporary duty of the 20 C-46s operating with TCC. Instead, the Joint Chiefs decided to temporarily loan a C-47 transport group from the Twelfth Air Force, while the RAF agreed to transfer, also on a temporary basis, one Dakota squadron from the Mediterranean. The 64th Troop Carrier Group, with five squadrons of C-47s, arrived in India from the Mediterranean in early April, followed by the RAF's No. 216 Transport Squadron, allowing the 10 ATC C-46s to return to the Hump operation on April 25. Four of these squadrons went to support Operation STAMINA, while two went to Assam to support Stilwell's forces. On May 4, TCC learned that the 64th TC Group and No. 216 Squadron would have to return to the Mediterranean on May 8, leaving TCC short by more than 70 aircraft. At the same time, the 27th Troop Carrier Squadron received orders to transfer to the Fourteenth Air Force to support the Chinese divisions in the Yunnan

A formation of C-47s from the 2nd Troop Carrier Squadron heading out on a supply-dropping mission over northern Burma. The C-47s would fly together to their designated areas, sometimes with a fighter escort, sometimes splitting up to go on to individual drop zones, or sometimes forming a circle over one particular drop zone, with the airplanes taking turns dropping their supplies. 3A-37080, RG342FH, NARA

force, which Chiang had finally agreed could cross the Salween River and advance into Burma. Mountbatten again appealed to the Combined Chiefs of Staff, who agreed that the 64th Group and No. 216 Squadron could remain until June 1, when the first of Arnold's new transport groups (1st Combat Cargo Group) was expected to arrive in India with 100 C-47s. To supplement TCC's air supply effort to Imphal, Stratemeyer suggested diverting the Strategic Air Force's medium-bomber crews and aircraft to haul supplies to Imphal. As previously related, the 490th Bomb Squadron began flying ammunition to Imphal on May 20, with the 12th Bomb Group adding to the effort. The SAF transferred 40 crews from its two Wellington squadrons to TCC's RAF transport squadrons to fly Dakotas, while five Wellington bombers started flying in 250-pound bombs for the Hurricane close-air-support squadrons.[75]

The additional transport aircraft helped TCC get through the crisis at Imphal and meet its commitments just to Stilwell's forces and Wingate's Special Force, although at the cost of fewer deliveries to Imphal. The Japanese cut the road from Imphal to Kohima on the night of March 29. From that date until the road was reopened on June 22, Imphal was cut off from its land line of communication and became entirely dependent on air supply. During Operation STAMINA the transports brought in to Imphal food, ammunition, gasoline, and other supplies as needed. On their return flights the transports evacuated the wounded, carrying out 4,400 men in May and 5,295 in June when the fighting was at its most intense. To reduce the burden on supplies, the transports took out more than 30,000 nonessential personnel from Imphal, in June alone saving around 900 tons of supplies that would have had to be flown in to support this number of personnel. Not surprisingly, there were problems that emerged as the air supply effort ramped up. Often there were delays at rear airfields where transport aircraft had to wait several hours for cargos since there were insufficient trucks to take supplies from depots to the airfields. At Imphal there was only a makeshift organization to unload the transports. In some cases the crews would simply unload their cargo onto the airfield and take off again for another load. The more critical problem was the lack of all-weather airfields in Bengal and especially at Imphal,

A C-47 approaches a drop zone in a clearing in the jungle. Sometimes C-47s had to descend below the level of the surrounding hills to reach the designated drop zone, an exercise that could be harrowing in poor weather when clouds covered the hills. The C-47 proved to be far better at dropping supplies than the larger C-46, since it was easier to maneuver at low altitudes. *3A-37083, RG342FH, NARA*

A C-47 banks low over the jungle-covered terrain to head toward a drop zone. Identifying the drop zones in this featureless terrain took some effort and the presence of air liaison teams on the ground with the forward troops. *3A-37074, RG342FH, NARA*

particularly after the monsoon began in late May. Weather became the most difficult problem of all, forcing the cancellation of many flights. Monsoon winds coming over the high mountains to the west of Imphal along the route the transports took caused severe turbulence and low visibility. Although the Japanese carried out regular fighter sweeps over Imphal during April and May, losses of transport aircraft to Japanese fighters were low, amounting to seven aircraft lost and eight more damaged. The Japanese failure to understand the importance of air supply and *15th Army*'s insistence that Japanese fighters concentrate on supporting the army through attacks on ground installations probably saved many Allied transport aircraft. A concerted effort against the transports might well have altered the outcome of the battle. As it was, the RAF fighters based at Imphal created a protected corridor for the transports. This action reduced the number of transports lost or damaged in Japanese attacks. By the end of the siege of Imphal in June, the transports had carried in sufficient supplies to maintain 118,000 British and Indian troops during the siege.[76]

Seeing the results for April, Gen. Slim wrote the following to Air Marshal Baldwin:

I have just seen that during April, Troop Carrier Command have flown 6,900 sorties, comprising a total lift of 18,371 tons, the movement of 32,312 men and the evacuation of 8,996 casualties. These figures force home the outstanding service that is being

Soldiers from a unit of Merrill's Marauders recovering supplies after an air drop. The air liaison teams with Special Force (the Marauders) would radio the night before a supply drop with a list of supplies needed. Once on the ground, the supplies had to be recovered and distributed as quickly as possible. *RG111, NARA*

One of the most valuable roles Army Air Force and RAF transports performed was the evacuation of casualties. Wounded troops traveled to forward landing strips in light planes, jeeps, or ambulances, where they would be loaded onto the transports and flown to hospitals in the rear area, often arriving within hours of receiving their wound. *Box 11, Air-Planes, folder XX-20470, RG208AA, NARA*

Marauders pick up a package containing several days' rations. Having the quartermaster units prepack rations into these easily distributed packages sped up the process of distribution. Many soldiers took sections of parachutes and lengths of parachute cord with them to build shelters in the jungle. *RG111, NARA*

rendered by transport aircraft to 14th Army. The achievement of Troop Carrier Command and the spirit in which they continue to carry on with the job day and night in all conditions evoke my sincerest admiration and that of all the troops under my command.[77]

Demands from Stilwell's forces in the northern Burma campaign put added pressure on TCC during April and May. To meet these demands and support the efforts of the 1st and 2nd Troop Carrier Squadrons assigned to Stilwell's forces, two of the C-47 squadrons diverted from the Mediterranean (4th and 18th Troop Carrier Squadrons) came under the 443rd Troop Carrier Group and went to Assam. In early April, Stilwell requested Generalissimo Chiang Kai-shek through Mountbatten and the Combined Chiefs of Staff to transfer one of the American-trained Chinese divisions in the Yunnan force to Assam to reinforce the 22nd and 38th Divisions. Both divisions had lost troops in combat and from disease, lowering their effectiveness. Chiang agreed to send the 50th Division. The 1st TC Squadron took on the task of flying the division from Yunnanyi to Maingkwan, where engineers had built an airstrip. Three aircraft from the 27th TC Squadron and two from No. 62 Squadron flew in to help move the troops. The move began on April 5, ending on April 12. To complete the movement the squadrons began flying at night, operating from 0630 to 0200. Fatigue began to affect the pilots, so the 2nd TC Squadron lent four crews and an additional aircraft, while on April 11 the 18th TC Squadron arrived from the Mediterranean to begin operations. Over the week the squadrons flew in 7,842 troops and 1,036 tons of supplies. The 1st TC Squadron and the aircraft from the other squadrons flew 280 sorties during the troop transfer, for an average of more than three trips per day per crew. With the movement of the 50th Division completed, the four American troop carrier squadrons went back to flying in supplies for the Chinese divisions, Merrill's Marauders, and a British and Kachin force moving down toward Myitkyina from the north. During April the 1st, 2nd, and newly arrived 18th Troop Carrier Squadrons completed 2,768 sorties and delivered 8,320 tons of supplies.[78]

The main event in May for the troop carrier squadrons supporting Stilwell's forces was the capture of the airfield at Myitkyina on May 17. Stilwell's plan was to use a combined force of Merrill's Marauders and Chinese troops to seize the airfield, then fly in reinforcements and supplies to consolidate the position. Brig. Gen. Old worked up a plan for the fly-in and went up to Assam on May 15 to brief the pilots and crews of the 2nd and 4th Troop Carrier Squadrons at Dinjan and the 1st and 18th Troop Carrier Squadrons at Sookerating. All four squadrons remained on alert for the operation. Old planned to have gliders land a company of the 879th Aviation Engineer Battalion with equipment to prepare the airfield for the C-47s, who would begin landing as soon as possible. In preparation, on May 12 the 1st and 2nd TC Squadrons towed the gliders to the airfield at Shingbwiyang. On May 17 Col. Charles Hunter, commanding the

The Japanese-built airfield at Myitkyina shortly after its capture on 17 May 1944. A damaged CG-4A glider can be seen at the top of the picture. The gliders brought in engineering equipment to prepare the field for transports bringing in more troops and supplies. *3A-37352, RG342FH, NARA*

Marauders and Chinese force, radioed the code word MERCHANT OF VENICE to start the fly-in. Having received the code signal, nine aircraft from the 1st TC Squadron that had flown into Shingbwiyang that morning took off towing gliders to Myitkyina, with Old leading the formation in his own C-47 towing a tenth glider. Three C-47s from the 2nd TC Squadron took off with more equipment for the airfield. The first TCC airplane to land at Myitkyina was another 2nd TC Squadron C-47 on a supply-dropping mission nearby, who the ground troops contacted and told to land. Coming in through intense ground fire, the pilot found his ship riddled with holes and the hydraulics shot up. The three 2nd TC Squadron C-47s landed next, followed by an L-5 carrying the 2nd TC Squadron's communications officer with a radio and color panels to control the glider landings and subsequent airplanes. Before he could get the panels out, the gliders arrived overhead, four choosing to land at right angles to the runway to avoid the possibility that the Japanese had mined the airstrip. Eight gliders suffered damage in landing, but the engineers recovered most of their equipment and began working on the airfield. As the gliders took off from Shingbwiyang, the 1st, 2nd, 4th, and 18th TC Squadrons took off loaded with troops of the 89th Regiment from the Chinese 30th Division. The C-47s continued landing at the captured airfield, braving Japanese mortar and machine gun fire until 2300, when weather moved in to shut down the field.[79]

The fly-in resumed the next morning, bringing in a British army Bofors antiaircraft unit as Stratemeyer's insistence. That morning the *204th Hikōsentai* sent out six Ki-43s to attack the Myitkyina airfield. Coming in during a gap in the fighter cover over the field, the Oscars shot down an L-5 carrying Capt. Donald Hansen, an officer from the 89th Fighter Squadron who was serving as an air liaison officer. A C-47 from the 2nd Troop Carrier Squadron had just begun its takeoff run when the fighters came in. One of the fighters dropped a small bomb that exploded just ahead of the C-47. 2nd Lt. Richard Henderson braked hurriedly and cut his switches, ordering his crew to get out of their airplane just before another

Local bullock carts carrying wounded soldiers to a waiting C-47 for evacuation to rear-area hospitals. The poor condition of the Myitkyina airfield is readily apparent in the ruts and mud from the early onset of the monsoon. *SC192536, RG111, NARA*

fighter came in to strafe and destroy the C-47. Another 2nd TC Squadron C-47 was also hit in the attack, then received further damage when a C-47 from the 1st TC Squadron collided with it while trying to avoid hitting the first C-47 hit in the attack.[80] The Japanese fighters damaged several more C-47s, losing one Ki-43 to antiaircraft fire. Ground fire from the Japanese in Myitkyina damaged three 2nd TC Squadron aircraft that had to remain on the airfield. Three more 2nd TC Squadron C-47s made it back to their base at Sookerating, where they underwent hurried repairs. The pilots flew day and night, as the 2nd TC Squadron's history recorded:

Some of the crews were so fatigued that they used Benzedrine tablets to stay awake, though beds were set up for them; the beds were never used. Instead, after cigarettes, K-rations, coffee, and sandwiches from the mess hall (running continuously), and doughnuts prepared by the Red Cross, were provided, some fifty to sixty pilots would stretch out on the alert floor, awaiting resumption of Alert operations.[81]

Over three days the four troop carrier squadrons flew most of the sorties into Myitkyina, carrying in the full 89th Regiment and more than 500 tons of supplies.[82]

Transport Operations of Eastern Air Command January to May 1944

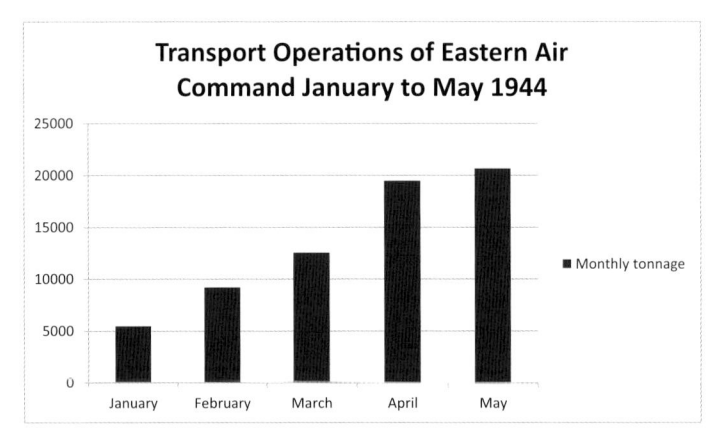

Month	Monthly tonnage
January	~5,500
February	~9,200
March	~12,500
April	~19,500
May	~20,700

Table 9 Source: Appendix 8, Transport Operations of Eastern Air Command, Dispatch on Operations of Eastern Air Command 15 December 1943-1 June 1945, P. 140.

Troop Carrier Command came to an end as a separate command on 4 June 1944 as part of a larger reorganization of Eastern Air Command.[83] Over the five months of its operations, the monthly tonnage delivered to Allied armies had grown fourfold and the number of aircraft in the command had doubled—at least temporarily—thanks to the influx of transports from the Mediterranean and the ATC. The demands placed on Troop Carrier Command from January to June 1944 were enormous, and well beyond the capacity of the command's four American and eight British squadrons. Only the intervention of Mountbatten and the generosity and understanding of the Combined Chiefs of Staff enabled the command to acquire more aircraft through borrowing from other theaters of war and the ATC Hump operation, though the US Joint Chiefs were persistently reluctant to divert airplanes from the Hump. For much of the period, the command had three "masters"—14th Army, Stilwell's Northern Combat Area Command, and Wingate's Special Force—and balancing these competing demands was a trial made possible only through the command's flexibility and its ability to shift squadrons from base to base, from operation to operation, or, more accurately, from emergency to emergency.

Light-Plane Operations

Although not strictly part of the air supply operations under Eastern Air Command, the role of light aircraft in aeromedical evacuation needs more than a passing comment. During the 1920s and 1930s the Army Air Corps gained experience with moving casualties to hospitals in transport planes. Some in the Air Corps medical service recognized that large transport aircraft could operate only from long, prepared fields, but there was clearly a need to evacuate casualties as they came off the front lines. The idea emerged that smaller observation or liaison airplanes might be able to pick up casualties out of small

A Stinson L-5 Sentinel flying over the jungle. The light aircraft of the liaison squadrons became "jacks of all trades" during the war in Burma, ferrying personnel and supplies to the front lines, evacuating casualties, carrying officers over the front on reconnaissance, and serving as forward air controllers for fighter-bombers and artillery. Army Air Forces, India-Burma Sector, 825.04A, AFHRA

fields. In May 1941 the Air Corps modified three Stinson O-49 Vigilant airplanes (later redesignated the L-1) to take a medical attendant and one litter patient as the O-49B. Later, Gen. Arnold agreed with a recommendation that the Air Force had no need for light aircraft for aeromedical evacuation. The Air Force decided not to adopt special aeromedical evacuation aircraft, but to fit modifications to existing transport aircraft, enabling them to be easily converted to carrying litter patients. In November 1942 the Air Force stopped development work on a light aeromedical aircraft.[84]

Following the retreat from Burma in 1942, evacuation of casualties became a subject of importance to the commands in India. During the first Wingate expedition in 1943, the columns had to leave their badly wounded behind. This unpleasant experience stimulated thinking on how to evacuate casualties from the jungles of Burma. The answer appeared to be to use light aircraft that could

The 71st Liaison Squadron was the first light airplane squadron to join the Tenth Air Force, beginning operations in fall 1943. The great advantage of the light planes was that they could take off and land from just about any strip of dry ground. Here a Piper L-4 Grasshopper takes off from a section of the Ledo Road in Assam. SC-274230, RG111, NARA

Loading a wounded soldier into a Stinson L-1 Vigilant from the 71st Liaison Squadron. The bigger L-1s could carry a heavier load than the smaller L-4 and L-5 aircraft. *SQ-LIA-71-HI, AFHRA*

land and take off from hastily prepared fields.[85] In April 1943 a detachment of personnel and some Piper L-4 aircraft from the 77th Observation Group arrived in Karachi without an apparent mission. Stilwell apparently ordered the detachment to move to Ramargh—the training center for his Chinese divisions—with the idea that the L-4s could serve as liaison aircraft for the Chinese.[86] On 15 July 1943 the detachment became the 71st Liaison Squadron, initially as part of the Tenth Air Force, but then coming under US Army Forces, China-Burma-India theater, attached to the 5303rd Area Command—the predecessor of the Northern Combat Area Command.[87] When Stilwell's Chinese divisions advanced to Ledo, the 71st Liaison Squadron followed in October and began flying personnel and mail to jungle outposts from Ledo. When engineers built a small landing strip for the liaison planes at Shingbwiyang, the 71st Squadron modified one of its L-4s to carry a litter and evacuated the first casualty on 25 November 1943.[88] With a complement of around 10 officers and 50 enlisted pilots, the squadron began a regular aeromedical evacuation service from Shingbwiyang, flying wounded Chinese soldiers back to larger airfields where the C-47s would fly them to hospitals in the rear areas. From January to May 1944, the 71st Liaison Squadron flew out 1,065 Chinese and American casualties from Merrill's Marauders, using L-1, L-4, and L-5 aircraft. In addition the squadron delivered mail and medical supplies and ferried passengers between units, sometimes behind enemy lines for the Office of Strategic Services. The liaison airplanes flew artillery adjustment and reconnaissance missions for the Chinese forces and for the Marauders, sometimes carrying ground commanders over the routes their columns were to follow over the next several days. At the end of April the 5th Liaison Squadron arrived at Shaduzup to provide support to the 71st Squadron. The 5th Squadron received several L-1 aircraft, which they preferred to the L-4 and L-5. As one pilot recalled, "The L-1s were as slick as a pair of bug boots to get into and out of short landing strips. They could haul more than twice the number of patients that an L-5 could carry. However, since they were now so obsolete, new parts were very scarce and hard to come by. We really had to make parts recovery patrols to crash sites to help us keep them flying."[89] The two squadrons often operated from a number of small airstrips, using small detachments of liaison aircraft with the pilots rotating between the outlying strips and the main liaison base at Ledo. As an example of the intensity of the flying, one enlisted pilot in the 5th Liaison Squadron flew 88 missions during his 33 days with his detachment.[90]

The Air Commando force also extensively employed light aircraft in its operations with Special Force. Light aircraft capable of evacuating his wounded was Wingate's initial request to Arnold when they met at the Quebec Conference in August 1943.[91] In their planning for Project 9, Cochran and Alison specified their requirement for 100 L-1 and L-5 light aircraft. This became the Light Plane Force under Maj. Andrew Rabori. Once in India, Rabori divided his force into four squadrons with 16 aircraft and 33 pilots each—mostly enlisted men. The Light Plane Force went into operation during February, evacuating casualties from the Admin Box in the Arakan, among other missions.[92] The Air Commandos found many uses for their light aircraft. Because of their ability to carry more patients than the L-5, the Commandos reserved the L-1s for aeromedical evacuation. With their ability to get in and out of short fields, the L-1s could land on just about any stretch of flat ground. The Chindits built a small airstrip next to their stronghold at White City so the L-1s could fly in and take out casualties. The light airplanes flew the standard liaison missions—flying personnel in or out of Burma, carrying documents or medical supplies or mail—but the Commandos also used the L-5s to drop supplies to Chindit columns. Fitted with special racks under the wings, the L-5 could carry two 75-pound parachute packs to drop food or ammunition when needed. In

The liaison squadrons operated out of airstrips that were even more basic than the transport squadrons used. Often these were no more than a few fields or clearings that had been roughly cleared of trees and brush and made more or less level. This is the light-airplane strip at Myitkyina after the capture of the town. *Army Air Forces, India-Burma Sector, 825.04A, AFHRA*

An L-4 with a wounded Marauder onboard in March 1944. Knowing they had a good chance of being evacuated if wounded was a great boost to the morale of American, British, and Chinese soldiers. Most of the light-aircraft pilots were enlisted men, not officers. *SC-263250, RG111, NARA*

addition, the L-5s carried out reconnaissance and, in one example of what must have been an early use of forward air control, spotted targets for the B-25s and the P-51s of the Bomber Section and the Fighter Section.[93] Operating with the 5th and 71st Liaison Squadrons and the Air Commandos, the light aircraft more than proved their worth. Their benefit to the morale of American, British, Chinese, and Indian soldiers was incalculable. The Allied soldiers knew that as long as there was a suitable patch of ground nearby, they had every chance of reaching a hospital for treatment in just a few hours. A third liaison squadron (115th) would join the Tenth Air Force at the end of 1944. When the reformed 1st Air Commando Group returned to operations later in 1944, it would have three liaison squadrons, as did the 2nd Air Commando Group when it began operations in early 1945.

Reorganizing Eastern Air Command

During June 1944, Eastern Air Command underwent a reorganization of its command structure and component units. The impetus for the changes was a concern with the existing command structure and the implications of pending changes in the structure of command of Allied ground forces in Burma. The 14th Army had complained that the current structure of command of Allied air forces was too cumbersome for effective command and control, believing that there were too many channels of communication and a lack of coordination among Air Command, Southeast Asia; Eastern Air Command; Third Tactical Air Force; and Troop Carrier Command.[94] Among the 14th Army's proposals was the idea of eliminating Troop Carrier Command and splitting up its component squadrons between No. 221 and No. 224 Groups and the 5320th Air Defense Wing in the Northern Combat Area Command. There was a certain logic to this, since it would eliminate a separate headquarters and make communications and coordination easier. The mission both of the Third Tactical Air Force and Troop Carrier Command was to support the ground forces. Their operations were interlinked, but the current structure meant that the commander of Third Tactical Air Force had no control over some of the units operating in his area. A single command overseeing and providing centralized control over both operations seemed to be more practical, though at the risk of losing flexibility in the deployment of transport aircraft.[95] This separation of operational commands had been a source of conflict from the establishment of Troop Carrier Command. Air Marshal Baldwin, commanding Third Tactical Air Force, believed that TCC should come under his control—an opinion that Peirse apparently shared.[96] The demands placed on TCC during the February–May operations put a great strain on the organization as it tried to support 14th Army, Stilwell's forces, and Wingate's Special Force. There came a sense that TCC had become too inflexible to cope with all the commitments it faced.[97] Stratemeyer, who had initially supported Old in some of his conflicts with Baldwin, nevertheless transferred operational control of TCC to the Third Tactical Air Force on May 1.[98] Then, on June 4, Stratemeyer, having received Peirse's concurrence, issued a new directive dissolving Troop Carrier Command and transferring control of transport operations directly to Third Tactical Air Force.[99]

The more important issue was the change in the structure of command of Allied ground forces and the objectives the Combined Chiefs of Staff would set for the ground operations going forward. With the formation of Southeast Asia Command, Stilwell's position within the Allied command structure became even more complex. As deputy supreme allied commander he was second only to Mountbatten in the chain of command, but as commanding general, Chinese army in India, he held the subordinate rank of a corps commander. As a corps commander Stilwell should have come under Gen. Sir George Giffard, commanding Eleventh Army Group—effectively commander of all ground forces in SEAC. Stilwell refused to come under Giffard's command, preferring to serve under Slim—his junior by rank, but in whom he had the greatest respect.[100] But Stilwell placed a caveat that once his forces reached Kamaing he would revert to an independent command, which at the time appeared to include the Chinese army in India and the Chinese forces that were expected to advance from Yunnan, which they finally did on the night of 10 May 1944, coming under Stilwell's command.[101] This would create two army commands in Burma—14th Army and Stilwell's Northern Combat Area Command—with Stilwell's operations becoming independent of 14th Army. As the date for this transfer of command approached, the question rose about how best to structure Eastern Air Command to provide the closest cooperation with two soon-to-be-separate army commands. Stratemeyer believed that Third Tactical Air Force, with operations ranging from Assam to the Arakan, was overstretched. It made sense to narrow the span of Third Tactical Air Force's command and control.[102]

Stratemeyer prepared a plan for a proposed reorganization of Eastern Air Command that would improve command channels, presenting his plan to Peirse on 17 May 1944.[103] In his plan he listed seven objectives for the reorganization:

a   The most economic and efficient use of forces available
b   Adaptability to present tactical situation
c   Flexibility in use of forces available
d   Minimizing administrative difficulties
e   Maximum direct support of ground forces
f   Adaptability for expansion upon assignment of additional units
g   Ready adaptation to future strategy for this theater[104]

Stratemeyer also laid out certain basic principles that formed the basis for his proposals, among which were that

a   an air commander should have operational control of all air force units operating within the area for which he is responsible;
b   insofar as is possible, an air commander should have administrative control over all units under his operational control;
c   the chain of command must be simple and direct;
d   integration of combat forces should not obtain for units smaller than USAAF Groups and RAF Wings;
e   RAF units and USAAF units should operate in designated areas, insofar as is feasible, to prevent confusion of logistical problems and to cut down area overhead in maintenance personnel;
f   diffusion of detailed tactical command authority over too wide an area should be avoided;
g   an air commander of any force in the Eastern Air Command, which includes both RAF and USAAF units, should have a fully integrated staff, all members of which hold actual staff positions and are not considered liaison officers; and
h   for the support of ground Task Forces, such as LRP groups, Air Task Forces should be formed. Their organization, chain of command, etc., would depend on the mission of the ground task force and many other considerations.[105]

He proposed that the Tenth Air Force be reconstituted as an operational command and replace the 5320th Air Defense Wing, taking over all responsibility for the defense of the air route to China and providing ground support to Stilwell's Northern Combat Area Command. Stratemeyer argued that his plan would improve the administration and operation of American air units operating in Assam, enable the NCAC commander to negotiate on air matters with a single air commander, give one air commander responsibility for providing support with all the necessary units, and eliminate one headquarters with a savings in personnel. In addition, echoing prior American concerns with integrating Allied air forces, if strategic requirements to support the campaign in the Pacific called for transferring the Tenth Air Force to China, this new structure would allow the move with minimum delay or complications. Stratemeyer then proposed that the Tenth Air Force be composed of the following units:

80th Fighter Group
311th Fighter-Bomber Group
443rd Troop Carrier Group
490th Bomb Squadron (Medium)
All US antiaircraft, early-warning, and signals units
Such additional troop carrier, fighter, or fighter-bomber units as the tactical situation required.

Stratemeyer further proposed that the Third Tactical Air Force consist of all RAF and USAAF units required for the direct support of 14th Army units operating in Imphal and in the Arakan. He recommended transferring the 12th Bomb Group from the Strategic Air Force to the Third Tactical Air Force, leaving the Strategic Air Force with its heavy-bomber and Wellington medium squadrons and allowing the Third Tactical Air Force to retain the 459th Fighter Squadron. This would give the Third Tactical Air Force the following units:

No. 221 Group, RAF
No. 224 Group, RAF
No. 293 Wing, RAF
No. 177 Wing, RAF
12th Bomb Group
459th Fighter Squadron

Thus, each of Eastern Air Command's proposed tactical units would have both fighters, medium bombers, and transport aircraft attached. Contracting Third Tactical Air Force's areas of operational responsibility would make its operations more efficient and reduce its administrative burdens. Other than removing the 12th Bomb Group, the Strategic Air Force would remain the same, as would the Photographic Reconnaissance Force. Stratemeyer recommended releasing Howard Davidson from command of the Strategic Air Force to resume operational as well as administrative control of the Tenth Air Force. He suggested replacing Davidson with Air Commodore Mellersh, commanding No. 231 Group. Stratemeyer also created what was tentatively designated as an Air Task Force to incorporate the new Air Commando and Combat Cargo units expected to arrive in the theater over the following months.[106]

Stratemeyer received Peirse's and Stilwell's approval for the reorganization and implemented the changes on 20 June 1944 with EAC General Orders No. 7, specifying the changes. With respect to the newly reconstituted Tenth Air Force, the general order assigned the Tenth Air Force the following mission:

> *The Commanding General Tenth Air Force is responsible for the protection of the Assam-Myitkyina Area, the India-Burma-China transport route. In addition he is responsible for air supply and air support to the army operating in an area to be defined by Eastern Air Command. He will provide air transportation for airborne and air transit forces in the support and training of the army forces involved in these operations. He is responsible for the maintenance of air superiority over the whole of his operational area.*[107]

Maj. Gen. Howard Davidson escorts Adm. Lord Louis Mountbatten on a tour of Tenth Air Force Headquarters in April 1944, while the Tenth was still an administrative command. At the time Davidson also had command of the Strategic Air Force under Eastern Air Command. Air Commodore Mellersh, Davidson's deputy, is on the right. *Tenth Air Force Miscellaneous Photos, 830.08, AFHRA*

The Eastern Air Command's new command structure reflected these changes:

Eastern Air Command New Command Structure

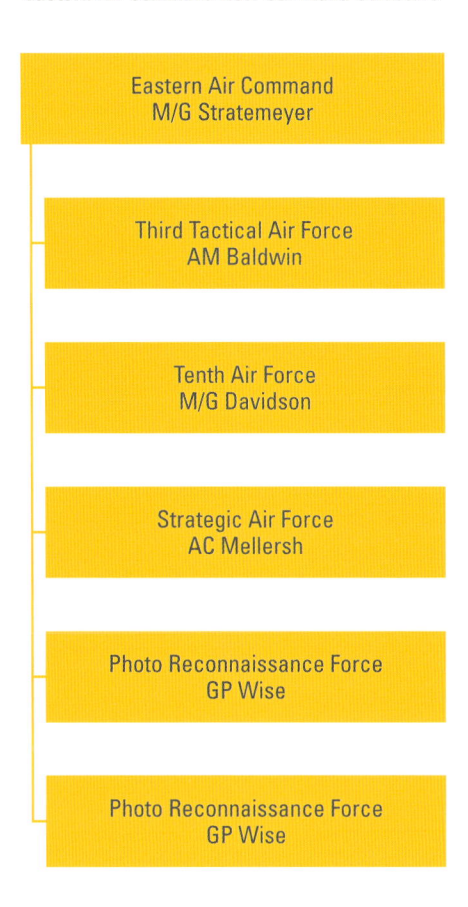

- Eastern Air Command — M/G Stratemeyer
  - Third Tactical Air Force — AM Baldwin
  - Tenth Air Force — M/G Davidson
  - Strategic Air Force — AC Mellersh
  - Photo Reconnaissance Force — GP Wise
  - Photo Reconnaissance Force — GP Wise

Organization Chart 4 Source: Air Ministry. Air Historical Branch: *The Campaigns in the Far East,* Volume IV: *South East Asia November 1943 to August 1945*

After a six-month hiatus as an administrative unit, the Tenth Air Force returned as an operational air force. The Tenth would continue in this role until the end of the war, commanding Army Air Force units supporting American and Chinese forces as they pushed on past Myitkyina to retake northern Burma from the Japanese and open the long-planned road link to China. Other Army Air Force units in the Third Tactical Air Force, the Strategic Air Force, and the Photo Reconnaissance Force under Eastern Air Command would assist RAF units in supporting 14th Army's drive to liberate all of Burma.

CHAPTER 10

MYITKYINA AND BEYOND: OPERATIONS, PLANS, AND PREPARATIONS

May–August 1944

A New Directive For SEAC

Stilwell's assault on Myitkyina in May and the increasing probability of Slim's 14th Army forces defeating the *15th Army* around Imphal brought up the question of what the Allied armies in SEAC should do next. With the situation on the northern and central fronts now fluid, the directive the Combined Chiefs of Staff (CCS) had given Mountbatten in October 1943 was out of date. The issue of resources available to SEAC remained ever present. Mountbatten and his staff still did not believe there were sufficient resources available in airplanes, equipment, and men to support the full development of the air and land routes to China and large-scale operations on the central front and in the Northern Combat Area Command. There seemed to be a choice to be made between halting the advance of Stilwell's forces at Myitkyina to build up the area as a staging base for the Hump operation or continuing ground operations to push through the road and pipeline to China. There was also the possibility that a defeat of the *15th Army* at Imphal might create new opportunities for the 14th Army to exploit. Mountbatten needed a new directive clearly setting out the objectives for SEAC.[1]

The CCS October 1943 directive charged Mountbatten with continuously engaging the Japanese to maintain and broaden contacts with China by air and through a direct land link with China through northern Burma. The directive specified that Mountbatten was to use the forces at his command to seize points that would prompt a strong enemy reaction, and ordered him to "prepare plans for the second phase of your campaign in 1944 contingent upon the reaction extorted from the enemy."[2] The final CCS report on plans for the war against Japan coming out of the Cairo Conference had approved the capture of upper Burma to improve the security of the air route to China and to establish the overland route from India to China, along with amphibious operations, but had also specified "continuance of operations during the autumn of 1944 within the limits of the forces available . . . to extend the position held in Upper Burma."[3] How far to extend this position, what forces would be available, and whether to extend it at all were three important questions to resolve.

Following the Sextant Conference in Cairo, the debate on the appropriate strategy for Burma and how best the CBI theater and SEAC could contribute to the defeat of Japan had continued unabated. With the cancellation in January of SEAC's planned amphibious operations and the Generalissimo's subsequent refusal to allow his Yunnan force to join in the offensive in northern Burma, it had seemed as if the planned capture of upper Burma and construction of the land route to China would be difficult to achieve. Mountbatten and his planning staff came to the view that in any event, the Ledo Road and the pipeline could not be completed in time to make an impact on the war in the Pacific, where the American offensive was gathering momentum as it moved closer to Japan. He and his staff believed the better use of SEAC's resources would be to expand the air route to China in support of Chennault's Fourteenth Air Force and the B-29 air offensive against Japan to be mounted from Chinese bases. To secure the air route, it would be necessary to continue the advance in northern Burma at least as far as Myitkyina, but probably not beyond. Pushing the road and pipeline beyond Myitkyina would be a poor use of resources for little return. It seemed more important for SEAC to coordinate its efforts with Adm. Nimitz's advance across the Central Pacific and Gen. MacArthur's advance in the Southwest Pacific. SEAC could contribute to this advance with an attack on the Malaya–Netherlands East Indies area, pushing north to seize a port on the South China Sea, perhaps in French Indochina or southern China itself, which would provide a more effective solution to China's supply problem. The first step in this campaign would be to seize a position on Sumatra, resurrecting Churchill's cherished Operation CULVERIN. The difficulty with this plan was that the naval forces required for its execution would not become available

Adm. Mountbatten greets Gen. Stilwell during a visit to Stilwell's Northern Combat Area Command. Stilwell disagreed with Mountbatten's proposals for amphibious operations in southern Burma, insisting that the best way to aid China was to push the Japanese out of northern Burma and restore overland communications to China. *SC-263266, RG111, NARA*

until after the defeat of Germany, then estimated to take place in late 1944. Once again SEAC would be postponing operations in Southeast Asia. Mountbatten decided to send members of his staff to London and Washington to present these ideas to the British Chiefs of Staff and the Joint Chiefs of Staff for their consideration. The Axiom Mission, as it was called, left for London in early February.[4]

Stilwell disagreed with Mountbatten and the SEAC planners and objected to the change in long-term strategy, expressing his views at a meeting with the supreme commander on 31 January 1944. Stilwell believed the Ledo Road and the pipeline could be completed sooner than the SEAC planning staff thought possible. He agreed with the benefit of opening a port on the China coast but thought it was far more likely to achieve this through an overland attack using Chinese army divisions in China than through a lengthy campaign up through the Netherlands East Indies and the South China Sea. He did not agree that the route to the China coast would be shorter through Sumatra and Malaya than through Burma and Yunnan. He was also dubious about the merits of advancing through Malaya and the Netherlands East Indies at all. He believed there was no guarantee, even if resources became available with the defeat of Germany, that this route would reach China any quicker than the planned land route via the Ledo Road. Moreover, if the argument was that it was necessary to change the strategy to keep pace with the advance across the Pacific, then waiting an additional six months for resources to possibly come from Europe made little sense. Stilwell argued that the best way for SEAC to contribute to the defeat of Japan was to continue and expand the offensive in northern Burma to complete the road to China.[5]

Stilwell's view corresponded to that of Marshall and the War Department Operations Division, although views within the operations division on China's role in the war against Japan were changing. The War Department still viewed China's continued participation in the war as vital. China could not be abandoned, but there was a growing realization that China's contribution to the war effort would be limited. The Chinese could still tie down the more than half a million Japanese soldiers in the *China Expeditionary Army*, but the War Department no longer held any illusions that Chinese forces could be used in an offensive against the Japanese on the Chinese mainland, certainly not within a reasonable time frame. The War Department had come to accept that China's role in the war against Japan would be to serve as a base to support the American drive across the Pacific to the Formosa-China-Luzon triangle.[6] In February 1944, the War Department developed a strategy to use China as an air base to support American invasions either of Formosa or Luzon, scheduled for February 1945.[7] Air support from bases in China would, it was thought, be critical to the invasion either of Luzon or Formosa. On March 19, Stratemeyer and his planners held a conference to begin working out an air plan to support the planned invasions. Designated ENTERPRISE, the plan envisioned basing thirteen A-26 medium-bomber groups, three P-51B groups, and three P-63 groups in China to begin air support operations on 15 January 1945, a month before the planned invasion.[8] Stratemeyer's plan also called for transferring the bulk of the Tenth Air Force's planned strength—one heavy-bomber group, two medium-bomber groups, one fighter group plus two fighter squadrons, a photoreconnaissance squadron, and a night-fighter squadron—to China to support the Formosa or Luzon invasions, leaving only two AAF fighter squadrons—one tactical and one photoreconnaissance squadron—and the planned air commando units in Burma.[9] Stratemeyer divided his plan into two phases: first, the capture of the Mogaung-Myitkyina area to build a staging area to expand Hump tonnage to 29,000 tons a month by December 1944.[10] This would allow a stockpile of supplies and especially fuel to be built in China for the planned American air units. The second phase, once the stockpile was complete, would have the designated Tenth Air Force units transfer to China.[11] In discussions with Stratemeyer, Mountbatten agreed with the first part of his plan but had reservations about withdrawing the Tenth Air Force, which he believed would leave the Hump route dangerously exposed and reduce air support for the ground forces in Burma.[12]

To build a stockpile for so many air units in China would require a substantial increase in tonnage over the Hump, continued for a number of months. The Joint Chiefs of Staff came to the conclusion that the proposed air effort would require establishing air bases in the Myitkyina area and pushing the land route to China, not so much to transport supplies overland, but to complete the gasoline pipeline to China to provide the supplies of fuel the AAF air units would need.[13] To achieve this objective, the reconquest of all of Burma would not be necessary, but it would require the Allies to clear and hold all of northern Burma to protect the Myitkyina air

Two products of the Curtiss-Wright Corporation that made valuable contributions during their long service in the China-India-Burma theater: a Curtiss P-40N from the 89th Fighter Squadron sits next to a Curtiss C-46 from the India-China Wing, Air Transport Command. *Peter M. Bowers Collection, MoF*

bases and complete the land link to China. The Joint Chiefs of Staff objected to the resurrection of the plans for CULVERIN that the Axiom Mission had brought from SEAC. Instead, the Joint Chiefs pressed the Combined Chiefs of Staff to accept that SEAC's greatest contribution to the war against Japan would be the capture of the Myitkyina area and the buildup of supplies to China.[14] On May 3, the War Department sent a new directive to Stilwell confirming the importance of seizing Myitkyina and building the capacity of the Hump route to carry out the CBI's new mission: providing air support for the planned operations against Formosa and Luzon.[15] The CBI submitted a plan to the War Department and SEAC proposing a three-phased implementation of the new mission. In Phase I, Stilwell's forces would seize the Mogaung-Myitkyina area; in Phase II, engineers would build all-weather airfields in the Myitkyina area by 1 January 1945 and push through the road from Myitkyina to Kunming; and in Phase III, the full communications links between India and China—air, road, and pipeline—would become fully operational.[16] When later in the month Stilwell asked Marshall for clarification of his mission, Marshall informed him that the US did not want to make a major effort in Asia.[17] The plan was to defeat Japan through the advance across the Pacific, not through a major campaign in China. Stilwell's original mission to improve the efficiency of the Chinese army would now be subordinated to the new mission of using China-based airpower to support the Pacific advance. Marshall told Stilwell, "for the present you should devote your principal effort to support of the Hump lift and its security, and the increase in its capacity with the view to the development of maximum effectiveness of the Fourteenth Air Force consistent with minimum requirements for support of all other activities in China."[18]

The new directive sent to Mountbatten from the Combined Chiefs of Staff on 3 June 1944 reflected the American position. The directive read:

> To develop, maintain, broaden and protect the air link to China, in order to provide maximum and timely supply of P.O.L [petroleum, oil & lubricants] and stores to China in support of Pacific operations; so far as is consistent with the above to press advantages against the enemy by exercising maximum effort ground and air, particularly during the current monsoon season, and in stressing such advantages, to be prepared to exploit the development of overland communications to China. All these operations must be dictated by the forces at present available or firmly allocated to S.E.A.C.[19]

The new directive brought a renewed focus on operations in Burma, although it did not clearly define what exactly it meant to "press advantages against the enemy." The immediate needs were to continue the counteroffensive against the *15th Army*'s now-depleted divisions around Imphal and to ensure the capture and consolidation of the Mogaung-Myitkyina area. Events on the ground over the next several months—unforeseen at the time—would bring changes to the directive of June 3.

With the new directive in hand, Mountbatten issued his own directives to his air and ground commanders on their respective missions during the coming monsoon. On June 20 the various command changes went into effect.[20] Stilwell left Slim's command, leaving Slim and 14th Army under the command of Gen. Gifford as commander in chief, Eleventh Army Group. Within Air Command, Southeast Asia, the reconstituted Tenth Air Force formally took over operations of the 5320th Air Defense Wing. Davidson moved his headquarters from Calcutta to Kanjikoah in Assam, near Chabua. The Tenth Air Force's first priority was to support Stilwell's American and Chinese force assaulting Myitkyina.

The Siege of Myitkyina

When Stilwell heard the news that his force of Merrill's Marauders and Chinese troops had captured the airfield at Myitkyina on 17 May 1944, he was ecstatic. Mountbatten and his staff had doubted that Stilwell's forces could capture Myitkyina, which some on the staff considered a risky operation.[21] That day, Stilwell wrote in his diary "WILL THIS BURN UP THE LIMEYS."[22] The seizure of the airfield was the high point of Stilwell's command in Burma and came as a complete surprise to Mountbatten.[23] Stilwell's force had seized the airfield in a coup de main. He had hoped to capture the town itself the same way, with reinforcements rapidly flown in to the airfield, but the attack on the town did not go as Stilwell had hoped. What had been planned to take days turned into a frustrating and grueling two-and-a-half-month siege in which close air support played a pivotal role.

The view from one of the CG-4A gliders carrying aviation engineers to the newly captured airfield at Myitkyina on 17 March 1944. Prepared and ready to go, the gliders and their tow aircraft took off from their bases in Assam as soon as they received word that the American Chinese task force had captured the airfield. *3A-37340, RG342FH, NARA*

"Poor intelligence and faulty organization" characterized the first efforts to take Myitkyina in the days that followed the seizure of the airfield.[24] From the beginning of the battle to near the very end, Stilwell's intelligence staff underestimated the number of Japanese defending the town, believing that there were no more than 500 defenders. The Chinese reinforcements flown in during the first three days came from three different divisions and were not used to working together, making coordinated attacks difficult. The first attacks on Japanese positions in the town were confused and unsuccessful. The 150th Regiment of the Chinese 50th Division suffered more than 650 casualties in four days of fighting.[25] The Marauders themselves were exhausted and too few in number to make a real impact. At the end of three days, the thinly held Allied lines had barely reached the edges of the town, and the airfield was under frequent shelling.

Stilwell meets with his commanders on the Myitkyina airfield shortly after its capture. Col. Charles Hunter, who commanded the American and Chinese units that captured the airfield, stands between Stilwell and Brig. Gen. Frank Merrill, commander of the 5307th Composite Unit (Provisional)—known as GALAHAD, and more popularly as Merrill's Marauders. *3A-37344, RG342FH, NARA*

The Japanese fortified many of the houses in Myitkyina, building bunkers underneath concrete floors, bracing the floors with timber supports, and covering the floors in several feet of earth and debris. Bombing would knock down the structure above, but it took a direct hit or a near miss with a 500- or 1,000-pound bomb to knock out the bunker. *Tenth Air Force, 830.310-1, AFHRA*

A captured Japanese bunker at Myitkyina. The Japanese built strong bunkers of timber and earth. In the absence of tanks, these bunkers were often impervious to anything but a direct hit with a high-explosive bomb. *Tenth Air Force, 830.310-1, AFHRA*

The Japanese won the race to build up reinforcements for the defense of the town. The *56th Division* sent in troops across the Irrawaddy River, while more Japanese soldiers came into the town through the loosely connected Allied lines. Within days there were more than 2,500 troops in the city, in addition to several hundred wounded, who as Stilwell knew were perfectly capable of sitting in a bunker behind a machine gun.[26] The Japanese defenders in Myitkyina had plenty of machine guns and ammunition, four mountain guns, and hurriedly but extremely well-built and well-placed fortifications.[27] Most of the houses in Myitkyina were built of wood, but almost every house had a concrete floor a foot thick.[28] The Japanese dug under this concrete floor to create a fortified position, with small gun ports on three sides. Strong wooden beams supported the floor from below. The Japanese piled lumps of concrete 2 feet thick on the concrete floor above the dugout and covered this with 3 feet of dirt. For buildings without concrete floors, layers of logs covered with dirt provided protection. In the railroad yards, the Japanese filled railroad cars with dirt and rock and dug tunnels and gun pits under them. The Japanese were adept at placing their fortifications to provide interlocking fields of fire. An analysis of bombing after the capture of the town revealed the strength of these fortifications. While a direct hit with a 250-pound bomb would destroy a light- or medium-strength structure, it could not penetrate the concrete floor of the heavier fortifications, nor could it damage the positions built underneath a strengthened railroad car. Only a direct hit or a close near miss with a 500- or 1,000-pound bomb could destroy the strongly built fortifications in the town, though the difference between the 500- and the 1,000-pound bomb in this case was marginal. In an ironic twist, the destruction of buildings in the town provided the Japanese defenders with more building material. Tanks would have been invaluable in the fighting at Myitkyina, but they were unavailable. As a result:

> The problem facing the Allied command was to overcome the combination of machine guns and earthworks which had been so effective on the Western Front in Europe in 1914–18. They would have to do it without tanks, with a final maximum of fourteen artillery pieces, and with air support (the twelve P-40s of the 88th Fighter Squadron, ultimately based at the airstrip itself) which, though devoted and skillful, did not have the weight to drive the Japanese from their positions. To make matters completely uncomfortable and further complicated, after mid-May the rains grew steadily worse, which made air supply very difficult.[29]

Air support for the forces assaulting Myitkyina began the day before the American Chinese force seized the airfield. The 80th Fighter Group and the 311th Fighter-Bomber Group sent out overlapping patrols over Myitkyina on May 16, looking for enemy activity and targets of opportunity. The P-40s and P-51s went out again the next morning, patrolling over the town and waiting for

MYITKYINA AND BEYOND: OPERATIONS, PLANS, AND PREPARATIONS

The Chinese-American force laying siege to Myitkyina lacked tanks and heavy artillery, in a battle that was reminiscent of the trench warfare of World War I. American troops fire a 37 mm antitank gun at Japanese positions, but this was not powerful enough to take out a Japanese bunker. *SC-274320, RG111, NARA*

word from the ground forces before beginning close-support missions. Most of the flights went to alternate targets when they could not contact the ground forces. Around 1300 the ground troops established radio contact with the fighters and designated a bomb line, giving the fighters authority to attack any target beyond this line, but a number of flights still went to alternate targets when they could not get clear instructions from the ground. At the end of the day a patrol of seven P-40s from the 90th Fighter Squadron made contact and received instructions to bomb and strafe an area along the railroad track at the south end of the town.[30]

The fighters were out in force the next day, flying nearly continuous patrols over Myitkyina and carrying out offensive reconnaissance missions over the surrounding area, looking for Japanese reinforcements heading for Myitkyina and knocking out several small bridges along the way. The 88th Fighter Squadron flew most of the missions over Myitkyina during the day, sending out seven flights to the town. The P-40s dropped depth charges and 500-pound bombs on buildings and strafed areas of the town under direction from ground radio. The Mustangs were also active, the 529th Fighter-Bomber Squadron sending three flights to Myitkyina during the day. The P-51s dropped 250-pound bombs on Japanese slit trenches under direction from ground radio, setting fire to several large buildings. Despite the overlapping patrols, at 1420 hours six Ki-43 fighters from the *204th Hikōsentai* slipped in through the overcast and rain to attack the airfield. Four P-40s on patrol saw the Ki-43s through the clouds and went into attack, claiming damage to two of the Japanese fighters, though the pilots do not appear to have received confirmation of their attack. The 706th Anti-Aircraft Machine Gun Battery opened up on the attacking fighters and shot down 2nd Lt. Itsuo Tokutani.[31]

The onset of the monsoon complicated operations, with overcast and rain on and off over the town during the day, but the fighters maintained patrols from dawn until dusk, responding to requests for air support from ground radio whenever the weather cleared. From May 17 to June 1, the fighter squadrons attempted to maintain overlapping patrols of up to eight fighters when weather permitted. When the weather restricted operations, the P-40 flights could land at the airstrip outside Myitkyina to wait, but the poor condition of the field caused three fighters to nose over on landing on May 21. The fighters hit buildings, road and rail junctions, railroad cars, and water transport along the Irrawaddy River, using M-57 250-pound demolition bombs, AN Mk-17 325-pound depth charges, and occasionally M-44 1,000-pound bombs, following up with repeated strafing runs. Toward the end of the month, the P-40s began dropping 1,200-pound mines—possibly the Navy Mark 13 magnetic mine—which could be fused to act as a bomb. On May 29, eight P-40s from the 89th Fighter Squadron dropped eight of these mines on a group of buildings at Myitkyina, completely obliterating four of them.[32]

Whenever possible, the transports flew in supplies and American and Chinese reinforcements, including two battalions of American engineers to replace the exhausted Marauders. The airstrip at Myitkyina was supposedly an all-weather field, but the monsoon rains turned sections of the strip into soft mud, making landings

A P-40N from the 88th Fighter Squadron taxis out from the forward airfield at Tingkawk-Sakan. The 88th Fighter Squadron flew some 80 percent of the close-air-support missions over Myitkyina, moving a flight of P-40s to operate from the captured airfield. *Box 11, Planes, Folder B-23, RG208AA, NARA*

American reinforcements for the Marauders march past a damaged C-47 at Myitkyina airfield. Despite the monsoon weather, the transports flew in men and supplies and evacuated wounded whenever they could get through. *SC-240911, RG111, NARA*

THE TENTH AIR FORCE IN WORLD WAR II

Chinese troops aboard a C-47 en route to Myitkyina. The capture of the airfield allowed Stilwell to fly in reinforcements for his American and Chinese units, but lack of sufficient numbers and inexperience prolonged the battle for the town. *Box 160, China–Armed Forces–Infantry, Folder G, RG208AA, NARA*

inadequate numbers, Brig. Gen. Haydon Boatner, commanding the Myitkyina Task Force, could make little headway. A series of attacks on the town in mid-June made gains that "were not in proportion to the effort expended."[34]

As days and weeks went by, the close-air-support effort became steadily more effective. By this time the techniques of close air support were well established. The air liaison parties consisted of several officers and six to eight enlisted men with portable radios to contact the ground forces and the squadrons in the air. In expectation that the forces at Myitkyina would require intensive close air support, Davidson instructed his A-2 and A-3 officers to send a forward detachment to Myitkyina to work closely with the G-2 and G-3 officers in the Myitkyina Task Force. The Task Force G-3 set up telephone links to the ground forces, down to the level of company commander. A company commander could call in a request for air support to the G-3 with a description of the Japanese strongpoints that were holding up an advance. The G-3 would determine the priority for airstrikes and meet with the Tenth Air Force A-2 and A-3 officers at Myitkyina to determine the suitability of the targets for an airstrike, then arrange a time on target (TOT) that would be communicated to the local commander.[35]

difficult. The field was some 2,000 feet long and 50 feet wide, leaving little room for maneuvering on landing or takeoff, especially when rain turned shell craters into soft bogs. The men of the 879th Engineer Aviation Battalion struggled to keep the field in operation with the limited equipment the gliders had flown in. The engineers filled soft areas with gravel and dug drainage ditches around the field to drain off rainwater. While working constantly to improve the condition of the field, for want of more personnel the engineers helped unload the cargo planes, stack supplies, and carry the wounded to waiting hospital C-47s, often under Japanese artillery and sniper fire. Three transport aircraft cracked up on landing on May 23, with three more damaged the next day. Aircraft coming in to land on the strip often faced a barrage of ground fire from Japanese troops nearby. By the end of May, 11 C-47s sat on the airstrip, victims of landing accidents or Japanese gunfire. To give a modicum of protection against Japanese fighters (or at least a boost in morale for the crews), the 443rd Troop Carrier Group received permission to mount .50-caliber machine guns in the group's C-47s. Air Service Command engineers designed a mounting for a single machine gun, apparently on each side of the fuselage, firing out of an enlarged window. Fortunately these jury-rigged mounts never had to be tested in combat.[33]

Shortly after the capture of the airfield, Stilwell organized his American and Chinese units into the Myitkyina Task Force and appointed a commander to direct and coordinate operations. During June the troops of the Myitkyina Task Force made only small gains against stubborn Japanese resistance. The Marauders were beyond exhaustion, with men falling asleep during engagements with the Japanese, although they remained in combat until finally evacuated in early June. The American engineer battalions and replacements for the Marauders flown into Myitkyina as reinforcements were inexperienced. It took time for these men to gain the combat skills they needed to become effective. The Myitkyina Task Force formed new battalions combining the few remaining Marauders with the new replacements and set up training programs in infantry tactics for the engineers. The Chinese regiments had suffered many casualties without adequate replacements. With inexperienced troops and

Members of an air liaison team at Myitkyina preparing to call in an air strike, using a map of the town and a photomosaic with a grid reference to give the precise location of the target to the fighter-bombers. *Army Air Forces, India-Burma Sector, 825.08, AFHRA*

To ensure an accurate understanding between the air and ground forces of the nature and location of targets, the Tenth Air Force staff prepared a photomosaic of the battle area, including Myitkyina town, at a scale of 1:10,000. A simple grid system overlay the photograph, with letters designating the vertical lines and numbers the horizontal lines. This grid divided the photomosaic into a series of squares, each representing an area of 660 square yards. These individual squares could be broken down into 10 smaller units, allowing local commanders to clearly identify individual buildings or groups of trees as targets, such as ".50 caliber machine gun emplacement at P5-1-8" with a short description of the area around the target: "it's under the left side of the solitary tree which stands just south of the road at that point."[36] Company commanders could use the photomosaic to locate targets for airstrikes and communicate the grid reference to the G-3, who would pass the information on to the A-3 officer, who would in turn pass the

The air liaison team calls in the strike. The air liaison officer would contact the fighter-bombers overhead and give them the grid reference. The pilots carried the same photomosaic in the cockpit with them, allowing them to clearly identify their target. The 88th Fighter Squadron pilots operating out of Myitkyina became thoroughly familiar with the town and the locations of Japanese positions. *Army Air Forces, India-Burma Sector, 825.08, AFHRA*

reference and description on to the pilots in the fighter squadrons. The pilots flew with the photomosaic in the cockpit to help identify the target from the air. To aid in briefing the pilots, the 20th Tactical Reconnaissance Squadron sent a detachment of three P-40s and a small photo lab to Myitkyina in early July to provide both vertical and oblique photos of the town.[37]

With the 89th and 90th Fighter Squadrons converting to the P-47, and the P-51s of the 529th and 530th Fighter Squadrons carrying out longer-range missions, the 88th and 528th Fighter Squadrons took over the bulk of the close-support effort at Myitkyina. On 21 June 1944 a flight of four 88th Squadron P-40Ns moved to the Myitkyina airfield from the squadron's base at Shingbwiyang to begin operations. Five P-40s flew in that day for a close-air-support mission, and after getting a briefing on the target, the flight leader went up in an L-5 to observe the target from the air. With a thorough knowledge of the target, four of the P-40 pilots got direct hits. Four more 88th Squadron pilots flew into Myitkyina the next day. Few fighter squadrons operated as close to their targets as did the 88th Squadron. When the flights arrived at the airfield, the closet Japanese position was only 1,000 yards away. A Japanese machine gun fired on the P-40s every time they took off, until the fighters knocked out the position in a dive-bombing attack. With fighters operating from the airfield, it became common for the P-40s to attack a target in the town within 30 minutes of a request from the ground forces, compared to a typical time of an hour and 40 minutes from Shingbwiyang.[38] Flying repeated missions over the town on the basis of thorough briefings, the P-40 pilots became adept at hitting their targets. On some occasions a company commander would travel to the airfield to personally brief the pilots, giving them the smallest details of the location of his own troops and the Japanese position. The commander of the 88th Squadron's detachment made regular use of the L-5 liaison airplanes to confirm details of the target areas. Once briefed, the fighters were over their targets in minutes. One pilot managed to complete his mission in only 10 minutes, and it was not uncommon for pilots to fly six missions a day out of the Myitkyina airfield. After a briefing the pilots would take off in their P-40s, drop their 250-pound bombs, strafe as requested, then return to the airfield to rearm and be briefed for the next mission. Most importantly, when the monsoon weather made it impossible for the fighters to fly from their bases to Myitkyina, the P-40s on the airfield could often continue flying missions.[39]

With constant practice the pilots became more accurate, bringing new meaning to the term "close air support." Dive-bombing came to be more accurate than artillery fire. A report on air-ground operations recorded the following incident:

On one occasion the Galahad forces [Merrill's Marauders] just north of the town were being held up by a string of six machine

A group of 88th Fighter Squadron pilots get a briefing before their next close-air-support mission from the airfield at Myitkyina. The P-40N behind them appears to be armed with three 100- or 250-pound bombs. It was often possible for a pilot to fly four to six close-air-support missions a day. *SC-274330, RG111, NARA*

An armorer loads .50-caliber rounds on a rain-slick wing of an 88th Fighter Squadron P-40N at Myitkyina. Maintenance went on around the clock in the rain and the mud. *SC-274327, RG111, NARA*

THE TENTH AIR FORCE IN WORLD WAR II

Loading bombs onto a trailer for the 88th Fighter Squadron's P-40s nearby. A C-47 passes overhead, having just taken off. The monsoon rains left the field covered in water and mud. The constant takeoffs and landings left the field covered in ruts, adding to the risk of accidents, as the wrecked C-47 in the background illustrates. *SC-274329, RG111, NARA*

guns, embedded in deep entrenchments that started at the west bank of the Irrawaddy River. The Ground Commander came to the airfield personally and presented his problem directly to the pilots. A mission was set up and the Commander was asked if he wished to withdraw his men during the attack since they were less than 25 yards from the targets. He replied that the men had absolute confidence in the pilots and would stay in their trenches. In the course of the attack the pilots dove to extremely low altitudes before releasing their bombs, using the basin of the Irrawaddy for extra pull-out space. The troops reported that the positions were knocked out by one flight which scored three direct hits. The nearest friendly troops were covered with dirt and debris from the former enemy positions, but none were hurt.[40]

Shortly before the capture of Myitkyina airfield, the 528th Fighter Squadron had moved from Assam to the airfield at Tingkawk-Sakan in Burma to be closer to the front lines. From this base, between May 17 and July 19, the 528th Squadron flew 296 missions to Myitkyina in support of the Myitkyina Task Force. The air liaison team at Myitkyina used a different procedure for fighters flying from other bases. Since the fighters could not land to be briefed on the target, the briefings had to be done before takeoff, using the same photomosaics and grid references. The pilots would fly to Myitkyina, bringing the photomosaic with them, and once over the town would contact the air liaison team as "ground 21." The air liaison team would assign a target over the radio by using the grid reference system, directing the fighter flight on to the target area with a description of the designated target. These flights from other bases normally took on targets that did not require pinpoint bombing in close proximity to Allied troops. At this time the 528th Squadron was still flying the A-36, with a small number of P-51As transferred from the 529th Fighter Squadron when it reequipped with the P-51B. The squadron flew missions to Myitkyina whenever the weather permitted. There were no missions to Myitkyina from June 12 to 20 due to weather, but the squadron more than made up for this when the weather cleared, flying 13 missions to Myitkyina on June 26. The intensity of operations inspired Capt. Henry Pascho to organize an elite club within the 528th Squadron called the "Century Club." Membership was open to any pilot who had flown more than 100 missions against the Japanese. There were six charter members who elected Pascho as the club's first president, on the basis of his record of 162 combat missions flown by the end of June 1944—considered to be a record in the theater. Within weeks the club boasted 26 members—nearly all the pilots in the squadron.[41]

While focused on the capture of Myitkyina, Stilwell also planned to capture the towns Kamaing and Mogaung, which controlled the road and railroad links to Myitkyina and to the south. When Wingate's Special Force came under Stilwell's command in mid-May, there were three brigades to the west of the Myitkyina-Mogaung railroad line disrupting Japanese communications and one brigade (77th Brigade) advancing on Mogaung from the south.[42] Stilwell ordered 77th Brigade to attack Mogaung together with the 38th Chinese Division, while the

The 88th Fighter Squadron's "supply depot" at Myitkyina. The poor condition of the airfield led to many aircraft becoming damaged in landing or taking off. Dragged to the edge of the airfield, these airplanes became a source of spare parts to keep serviceable aircraft flying. *3A-35789, RG342FH, NARA*

MYITKYINA AND BEYOND: OPERATIONS, PLANS, AND PREPARATIONS

other Special Force brigades continued to block any Japanese attempt to interfere. Brig. Michael Calvert, commanding 77th Brigade, had no tanks or artillery to support the advance on the town or the attack. He depended on air support from the Tenth Air Force's fighter squadrons, particularly the 88th, 528th, and 529th Fighter Squadrons. The Special Force brigades and columns were well prepared to direct air support since each column had its own well-trained air liaison team. Requests for close air support went to the Special Force headquarters at Shaduzup, where the staff worked with the headquarters of the Northern Combat Area Command to set priorities and organize air support missions. As was done at Myitkyina, the reconnaissance squadrons prepared photomosaics of Mogaung and the surrounding areas with a similar grid system. The fighter pilots, company commanders, and the air liaison teams all had the same photographs, so that requests for air support could specify a target according to the grid system. Pilots would get a briefing on the designated target, but most often the air liaison teams would talk a flight onto a target, giving corrections on each successive pass. The 528th Squadron worked closely with 77th Brigade's air liaison teams and built a reputation for excellent close support. On one occasion the air liaison team ordered other flights in the area to stay back and observe the 528th at work. The 528th Squadron lost two A-36s supporting the Chindits attacking Mogaung. One pilot had his airplane damaged by a bomb blast and crash-landed, walking back to Allied lines through swamps and jungle. On June 25, while supporting the Chindit attack on Mogaung, 1st Lt. Charles Patterson, a veteran of 132 combat missions, came in on his last strafing pass and while turning close to the ground hit a tree. His airplane crashed and disintegrated instantly. Mogaung fell to the combined forces of the Chindits and the Chinese on June 26. Brig. Calvert sent the following message to the 528th: "This Brigade could not, repeat, not have captured Mogaung without the assistance of direct air support, the results they accomplished were accurate and decisive."[43]

During July the Myitkyina Task Force made slow but steady progress against the Japanese defenders in Myitkyina as the American units became more effective with training and experience and the Chinese received reinforcements. In July the 88th Fighter Squadron provided 80 percent of the close air support.[44] Davidson arranged to have the 12th Bomb Group's B-25s fly several missions in support of Allied attacks on the town, but the mediums proved less adept at providing close air support, since it proved difficult for the bombers to coordinate their bombing with the planned ground attack. Davidson realized they were better employed on interdiction missions.[45] The 490th Bomb Squadron and the 12th Bomb Group did fly missions to Myitkyina to bomb selected areas of the town the Myitkyina Task Force had designated as priority targets: the village of Naungtalaw, on an island in the Irrawaddy River across from Myitkyina, and the nearby Japanese-occupied villages of Maingna and Waingmaw on the east bank of the Irrawaddy River. Flying in close formation and bombing from 5,000 feet or less, one or more squadrons of B-25s could saturate an area with 100- and 500-pound bombs. A squadron of nine aircraft could drop up to 216 M-30 100-pound bombs or 72 M-43 500-pound bombs. The medium-bomber squadrons devoted most of their effort during July to bombing Myitkyina. Eastern Air Command released the 12th Bomb Group from flying ammunition to Imphal on July 1, and the 490th Bomb Squadron four days later. The monsoon weather disrupted many missions. There were days when the 12th Bomb Group's squadrons had missions scrubbed or couldn't get through to Myitkyina. The 490th Bomb Squadron often had better luck with the weather, getting to the target when the 12th Group couldn't. The mediums completed missions to Myitkyina on 16 days during the month. The Japanese at Myitkyina had little in the way of antiaircraft apart from machine guns, so bombing at low altitude became standard, allowing much-greater accuracy. During the final days of the month the 12th Bomb Group flew its last missions to Myitkyina, sending out 34 B-25s on July 28 to drop 67 tons of bombs on the town, and 34 B-25s again the next day to drop 64 tons. The 490th Squadron also completed the last of its 13 bombing missions to Myitkyina on July 29, dropping 72 500-pound bombs on Naungtalaw.[46]

The Japanese made only sporadic efforts to disrupt the Allied effort at Myitkyina through air attacks. The monsoon weather during June no doubt provided some protection for the transport aircraft landing on the Myitkyina airfield daily, as did the regular patrols of

Maj. Gen. Davidson arranged for the medium bombers from the 12th Bomb Group and the 490th Bomb Squadron to fly missions in support of the fighting at Myitkyina. On 29 July 1944 the 12th Bomb Group sent B-25s from all four of its squadrons to bomb assigned areas in Myitkyina. Bombing from around 5,000 feet in the absence of antiaircraft fire, the bombers could saturate an area with 100- and 250-pound bombs. Army Air Forces, India-Burma Sector, 825.08, AFHRA

Fighter pilots getting a briefing before a mission over Burma. A thorough knowledge of the target area was essential for close-air-support missions. 3A-36237, RG342FH, NARA

Over Myitkyina the liaison squadrons began experimenting with new uses for their aircraft. Adding a radio in the rear seat allowed an observation officer to fly over a target area to direct artillery fire onto a target. *SC-274285, RG111, NARA*

Maj. Richard Powell (*right*) commanded the 90th Fighter Squadron in the 80th Fighter Group. On 3 July 1944 Powell led his flight in their new P-47D Thunderbolts on a sweep of the Japanese airfield at Lashio, where they claimed four aircraft destroyed on the ground. *GP-80-SU-PH, AFHRA*

fighter aircraft over the town. The C-47s flew in whenever weather permitted; sometimes as many as 67 transports landed during a single day. But with the fighter squadrons concentrating on close air support for the ground forces when the weather improved, it was impossible to provide fighter protection over the entire area between Myitkyina and Mogaung. As a result, the 443rd Troop Carrier Group lost several transports to Japanese fighters. On June 22 the 11th Combat Cargo Squadron, temporarily attached to the 443rd Group, lost two C-47 aircraft to Japanese fighters of an unknown unit. Only three of the crew survived. Three days later, Ki-43s from the *204th Hikōsentai* who had been dropping supply containers to Japanese troops around Kamaing shot down a C-46 near Maingkwan. On June 29, another group of Ki-43s from the *50th* and *204th Hikōsentai* on a similar supply mission claimed another C-46 flying at 14,000 feet directly over Myitkyina, with three of the crew bailing out and rescued. The next day the 11th Combat Cargo Squadron lost another C-47 to Japanese fighters. But during June the 443rd Group flew 1,302 sorties into Myitkyina, carrying 3,096 tons of supplies and 4,762 troops and evacuating 1,628 casualties. From the Japanese perspective, 99.7 percent of the transport flights arrived safely at Myitkyina; a clear failure to disrupt the Allied effort, especially since the American and Chinese troops fighting at Myitkyina were completely dependent on air supply.[47]

In the first part of July, despite the weather, the Japanese fighter *sentai* made several attacks on Myitkyina. Perhaps in preparation for an attack, an unidentified fighter unit had sent a number of aircraft to the airfield at Lashio. Maj. Richard Powell, commanding the 90th Fighter Squadron, had attempted a sweep of Lashio on July 3 with the squadron's new P-47 Thunderbolts but couldn't get through the weather. Trying again the next day, he and the three other pilots in his flight found around a dozen single-engine fighters on the airfield. Despite intense antiaircraft fire, Powell and the other pilots made several passes over the field, claiming four aircraft destroyed and six damaged. 1st Lt. Paul Eastman went on the mission and recorded his impressions in his diary:

Maj. Powell, myself, Lt. Roane, and Lt. Bell took off with two full 165-gal wing tanks for a four-ship fighter sweep of Jap airfields in central Burma. The weather over the "Hump" was pretty bad, as was it in Burma, but by dodging around we got deeper into Burma. We were way down when suddenly a cloud break showed us we were just a little bit to the left of a Jap airfield (turned out to be Lashio, 20 minutes north of Mandalay) with a whole bunch of Jap Zeros parked. We immediately peeled off from 13,000 feet and went screaming in at almost 500 mph. The Zero I shot at blew up on my first burst. We wheeled around and came in again. By this time, the Nips had awakened and were throwing everything but the guns themselves at us. The air was red with tracers, and every little bit a burst of Ack-Ack would mushroom out below us. We made eight passes however—completely destroyed four ships—and riddled eight others thoroughly with .50 caliber slugs. We also damaged a nice hanger, a truck, and scared hell out of a lone dog loping up the runway. Boy, what a mission.[48]

Two days later, Maj. George Van Duesen, from the 311th Fighter Group Headquarters, was flying an offensive reconnaissance in a P-51B when he sighted three enemy aircraft below him near Indawgyi Lake, southwest of Mogaung. He identified these as two "Zeros" and a Sally bomber. Van Duesen dove down on the higher of the two fighters and closed to 200 yards before opening fire, the fighter exploding. Continuing in his dive, he came in behind the Sally and fired on the right engine, smoke billowing out as he pulled back up to altitude.[49]

The *50th Hikōsentai* attacked the Myitkyina airfield on July 7, catching the 88th Fighter Squadron's P-40Ns on the ground. Six Ki-43s came in from the southeast at 1345, having flown below the radar net. The fighters made a bombing run to the north, dropping around 150 1.5-pound bombs—probably the type of 2⅓ kg cluster bomb carried in containers under the wings. The fighters turned and made a strafing run to the south. The Japanese pilots claimed 23 P-40s and 16 C-47s destroyed in their attack, but only seven fighters and two transports received slight damage from machine gun fire and bomb fragments. By great good fortune, nearly 90 percent of the cluster bombs were duds; corrosion had damaged the wind-driven arming mechanism in the tail of the bombs.[50] The *50th* and *204th Hikōsentai* attacked Myitkyina again on July 9, around 1235. The 24 Ki-43s making the attack approached again from the south, circling the airfield counterclockwise and dropping small cluster bombs over the P-40s parked at the southeastern end of the field, fortunately without doing any damage. On this day, four 88th Fighter Squadron P-40s were in the air patrolling over Myitkyina, there having been an alert the day before. Capt. Owen Allred was climbing up to engage the Oscars when his P-40 lost power. Diving down, an Oscar latched on to his tail. Allred flew down the airfield, waggling his wings as a signal for the antiaircraft gunners to open fire on his assailant, which they did, driving off the Japanese fighter. Getting back into the fight, Allred claimed one fighter destroyed, one probable, and two damaged. 1st Lt. Robert Gale claimed two destroyed and 2nd Lt. Calvin Baldwin one destroyed for the loss of 1st Lt. Thomas O'Connor, who was also given credit for one fighter destroyed.[51]

After 20 minutes the Japanese fighters withdrew to the south, where they ran into a formation of seven B-25 bombers from the 83rd Bomb Squadron on their way to bomb Myitkyina, flying in two formations of three and four bombers. Ten of the Oscars and reportedly two Tojos attacked the formation of four B-25s, setting fire to the port engine on one of the B-25s, which gradually lost altitude and made a crash landing near Myitkyina, with the crew making it back to the airfield. One of the B-25 gunners claimed one Oscar destroyed.[52] Hearing that Myitkyina was under air attack, four P-51s from the 528th Fighter Squadron and four from the 530th Fighter Squadron took off from their base and headed toward the Myitkyina-Mogaung area, though two fighters had to abandon the intercept when they had mechanical problems. A storm in the area made interception difficult. Fighter control vectored two of the 528th Squadron pilots to the area, but because of the storm the pilots had to fly farther south, where they found a single Ki-44 Tojo flying below them. 1st Lt. Jack Decker and his wingman, 1st Lt. Erwin Letak, made a pass on the Japanese fighter, who turned into the attack. Pulling up into the clouds, Decker lost contact with Letak, but on coming out found the Tojo again, flying south. Attacking again, Decker and the Tojo made several passes at each other, with Decker finally getting hits as he dove down in a head-on attack, seeing the Tojo fly away smoking heavily. He claimed this fighter as probably destroyed. Letak, meanwhile, came across a formation of four Japanese fighters flying 2,000 feet below him that he identified as Tojos. As he recorded in his combat report:

During the monsoon season the 528th Fighter Squadron gave up its worn A-36 Invaders for new P-51Bs, giving the squadron a fighter with a substantial performance advantage over their Japanese opponents. *Courtesy, Carl Molesworth*

I dove down choosing the second from the left and opened fire at 500 yards closing in from above to 50 yards, scoring numerous hits on his engine which exploded and fell apart when I was about 100 yards from him. Tracers and incendiary splashes appeared all along the fuselage, and smoke and flame enshrouded the tail. At 75 yards, what was left of the engine burst into flames and fell completely off. At this point he fell off and down through the clouds flaming. I dove down past him and made a 90-degree right turn and headed home.[53]

1st Lt. George Bennett and 2nd Lt. Courtney Richard joined up and flew on to Myitkyina. Around 20 miles southwest of the town, they saw a formation of B-25 bombers (the 83rd Bomb Squadron formation) ahead of them, with four Oscars to the west of the bombers. Bennett and Richard peeled off to go after the fighters, becoming separated as they made their attacks. Bennett damaged one Oscar, then saw another below him:

As I came out of the overcast, I sighted a lone P-51 which joined me on my wing. I immediately sighted a lone Oscar to my left at 5,000 feet and slightly below me. I headed to intercept this plane and my wingman spread out to cover the opposite side. I attacked from his left and slightly above, and the Oscar turned sharply into me. I used my excess speed to chandelle and came down astern of him as he continued in a straight course diving for the clouds. I came astern of him as he went through broken clouds at 1500 feet. I was overtaking him at approximately 50 miles per hour at this point. He started a gradual turn to the right, apparently to clear himself, when I opened fire at 300 yards and continued up to 200 yards at an angle from astern starting at 5° and ending at 15°. There was an explosive spurt of smoke from his engine and flame streamed back along his fuselage. He rolled slowly on his back, then from an altitude of 150 feet dived straight into the ground.[54]

Bennet claimed one more Oscar damaged, while Richard claimed one as probably destroyed.

Separately, Capt. John Emery had led two other 530th Fighter Squadrons off to intercept the Japanese fighters. Fighter direction ordered him to head south from Myitkyina down the Irrawaddy River. Near Mogaung, Emery saw two formations of bombers: one of three airplanes and one of four with fighters milling around them. Emery assumed these were enemy aircraft and ordered an attack, but they were in fact the 83rd Bomb Squadron formation fighting off the Japanese fighters. Flying with Emery, 1st Lt. Ferdinand Wilbourne identified the bombers correctly as B-25s, but when Emery turned into attack the formation of four bombers, he followed. Not surprisingly, the tail gunners in the four bombers opened fire on the approaching Mustangs, hitting Wilbourne's aircraft in the right wing. Passing under the bombers, Wilbourne saw clearly the American insignia on the bombers and broke off his attack. He then saw an Oscar turning to his left, but turned right and down through the overcast where he found a single Oscar flying above the Irrawaddy. Capt. Emery joined him at this point, and together they made passes at the Japanese fighter. Wilbourne lost Emery but continued his own attack, getting hits in the Oscar's tail and along the fuselage. He saw a violent explosion around the Oscar's tail and saw the empennage, rudder, and tail fall off. He did not see the fighter crash, but claimed it as destroyed. In the same combat 1st Lt. Louis Wall claimed an Oscar damaged. Capt. Emery failed to return from the mission, most likely a victim of one of the Oscars.[55] In these combats

THE TENTH AIR FORCE IN WORLD WAR II

the *50th Hikōsentai* lost one pilot, probably to the Mustangs, and the *204th Hikōsentai* lost two, but it is not exactly clear if these two fighters fell to the P-40s over Myitkyina or to the P-51s in the battle to the south.[56]

To guard against a repeat of these attacks, for the next week the 89th and 90th Fighter Squadrons undertook sweeps of the Japanese airfields at Loiwing, Lashio, Bhamo, Shwebo, and Onbauk with their P-47s.[57] The photoreconnaissance squadrons provided regular coverage of these airfields. The 89th Squadron strafed several aircraft at Lashio on July 11, leaving one smoking. The 90th Squadron swept Lashio two days later, claiming two aircraft damaged. During the last part of the month, the 529th Fighter Squadron took over the airfield sweeps, using their longer-range P-51Bs to cover the airfields around Mandalay. The last combat over the Myitkyina battlefield area took place on July 29, in the first clash between the recently arrived P-47s and Japanese fighters. Leading a patrol of four newly arrived Thunderbolts south of Myitkyina, Maj. Robert Becker, CO of the 88th Fighter Squadron, saw four Oscars and over the next 15 minutes ran into six or eight more fighters that he identified as Oscars and Tojos. In the fight that followed, Becker received credit for two fighters damaged, while his element leader, 1st Lt. Wendell Gomo, damaged another. The Japanese shot down 2nd Lt. Lawrence Austin, but he crash-landed in friendly territory. The pilots noted that "in the main, the heavier 47s were able only to get short and snap shots at the much more maneuverable 'zero' types. The Japs could flutter around the '47s like butterflies around a hawk. Two of the Tojos lived up to advance notice by following Maj. Becker in a dive from 9,500 to 2,000 feet, and not losing a foot—although the CO was diving almost vertically and indicating 450 MPH."[58]

Myitkyina finally fell to the American and Chinese force on 3 August 1944. The capture of Kamaing and Moguang toward the end of June cut off the Japanese defenders in Myitkyina from their source of reinforcements and supplies from the south. The Chinese sent fresh regiments to Myitkyina during the first half of July and, together with the American battalions, began to make steady progress

Lt. Philip Adair's P-47D Thunderbolt, which he also named "Lulu Belle" after his P-40N. The three and a half victory flags under the cockpit represent Adair's claims for Japanese aircraft, all scored in his P-40N. *GP-80-SU-PH, AFHRA*

toward the town. Gains now came in hundreds of yards. In the last weeks of July, Tenth Air Force bombers and fighters kept up a relentless pounding of Japanese defenses and made a concerted effort to destroy rail and road bridges south of the town. Unable to hold on, the Japanese commander requested and received permission for his remaining troops to withdraw. American and Chinese troops overcame the last defenders and secured the town at 1545 on August 3.[59] At the end of the campaign, Brig. Gen. Frank Merrill sent the following wire to Eastern Air Command:

> *Fighters, bombers, troop carriers, liaison squadrons, and photo intelligence units have all given us better support than any ground unit could reasonably expect. We feel that with our air-ground team we have caused more serious damage to the Japanese ground forces than is generally believed, and have had a swell time working with all the various air units. My job would have been absolutely impossible without the complete and wholehearted cooperation of your various units.*[60]

The benefits of Allied control of the Myitkyina-Moguang area became evident even before the final capture of Myitkyina itself. Reducing the threat of Japanese fighter interception allowed the transports of the India-China Wing of the ATC (redesignated the India-China Division in July 1944) flying the Hump route to fly a more direct route from the ATC airfields in Assam to Kunming at lower altitudes. This saved gasoline and allowed the C-47s and C-46s flying the route to carry more cargo. Total tonnage over the Hump route rose from 11,383 tons in May 1944 to 18,975 tons in July.[61] In the following months, Myitkyina's airfields, expanded and improved, would become a base supporting the Hump operation. Following a two-month hiatus, the Allied advance from Myitkyina would

Maj. Robert Becker, 89th Fighter Squadron commander, who claimed two Japanese fighters damaged during the last air combat over Myitkyina on 29 July 1944. *GP-80-SU-PH, AFHRA*

MYITKYINA AND BEYOND: OPERATIONS, PLANS, AND PREPARATIONS

continue. For Allied planners, how far to advance into northern Burma became the key question.

Allied Plans and the End of the China-Burma-India Theater

After the capture of Myitkyina, Stilwell ordered the New Chinese First and Sixth Armies to go into training camps around the Mogaung-Kamaing-Myitkyina area to rest and refit.[62] A brigade from the British 36th Division had been flown into Myitkyina to replace the exhausted remnants of Special Force, moving to Moguang and pushing 20 miles farther south down the railway corridor to Indaw to capture the town of Taungi.[63] While allowing 36th Division to push on at a measured pace, Stilwell called a halt to any further advance from Myitkyina to allow all his forces time to reorganize, establishing a defensive line from Taunggyi to Myitkyina. Stratemeyer and Davidson disagreed with Stilwell's decision, arguing that a line only 20 miles from Myitkyina did not give the air-warning system sufficient time to alert fighters to an incoming air raid. They preferred a distance of 70 miles from Myitkyina as the minimum requirement for early warning, which would mean pushing the Japanese farther south to form an Allied defensive line running from Indaw to Katha

Indian troops investigate Japanese trucks abandoned during the Japanese retreat from Imphal. The magnitude of the Japanese defeat became apparent as British and Indian units encountered equipment, guns, and scores of Japanese dead along the trails leading back to the Chindwin River. *IND_003554, IWM*

Howard Davidson discussing plans with Joseph Stilwell at Myitkyina. With Myitkyina secure, Stilwell planned to continue the advance, with the goal of linking up with the old Burma Road, pushing the Japanese out of northern Burma. *Personal collection of Maj. Gen. Howard C. Davidson, 168.7266-233, AFHRA*

to Bhamo. Davidson wrote a letter urging an advance to this line during the rainy season to take advantage of a weakened Japanese army.[64] Stratemeyer forwarded the letter on to Stilwell, but Stilwell would not agree to continuing the advance at this time.[65] Stilwell's troops needed a rest, and the options for the next stage of Allied operations in Burma, and the role of the Northern Combat Area Command, were then under intense discussion.

The Japanese defeats at Imphal and Kohima were the decisive battles of the war in Burma.[66] The magnitude of the Japanese *15th Army*'s defeat at Imphal and Stilwell's capture of Myitkyina ahead of schedule (Mountbatten's directive to Stilwell of 9 June 1944 had called for the capture of the Myitkyina-Mogaung area by October) suggested the possibility of new opportunities that went beyond the Combined Chiefs of Staff directive to Mountbatten of 3 June 1944. This directive had placed emphasis on defending and developing the Hump operation to maximize the flow of supplies to China. The directive had the vague adage to "press advantages against the enemy by exerting maximum effort ground and air" during the monsoon season, but without specifying any geographic objectives.[67] As Slim's IV and XXXIII Corps soldiers pursued the retreating Japanese as they withdrew from the area around Imphal to the Chindwin River, the British and Indian soldiers found evidence of the disaster that had befallen the Japanese divisions. They came across abandoned artillery pieces, motor vehicles, and scores of unburied Japanese dead. As one Japanese historian later described it, "15 Army, once released from battle, was no longer a body of soldiers, but a herd of exhausted men."[68] The *15th Army* had advanced on Imphal with 84,280 troops. In the fighting around Imphal and Kohima, *15th Army* suffered 53,505 casualties, including 30,502 dead, or nearly two-thirds of the army (Louis Allen quotes a figure of 54,879 casualties at Imphal with an additional 5,764 at Kohima and 5,335 during the second Wingate expedition).[69] The men who survived the retreat were exhausted, malnourished, suffering from wounds and disease, and in no shape to mount a spirited counterattack.

With the Japanese army badly weakened and unlikely to launch an offensive before the beginning of 1945, it was vital for the Allies to retain the initiative and continue to press the retreating *15th* and *33rd Armies*.[70] On July 5, Slim ordered IV and XXXIII Corps to vigorously pursue the Japanese divisions retreating from Imphal and destroy them west of the Chindwin River.[71] Mountbatten asked Giffard, Slim, and Stilwell to submit proposals for offensive operations, and had his own SEAC planning staff consider the problem. Mountbatten's planning staff came up with plans for an advance into northern Burma involving 14th Army, the Northern Combat Area Command, the Chinese Yunnan force, and an amphibious operation to capture Rangoon.[72] Toward the end of July, Mountbatten held a series of conferences with his three principal air, ground, and navy commanders, with Stratemeyer attending as commanding general, Eastern Air Command, and Maj. Dan Sultan, Stilwell's deputy commander in the CBI theater, representing Stilwell.[73] Mountbatten and his generals were now beginning to see that crossing the Chindwin was their primary objective to bring *Burma*

Area Army to battle in the Shwebo-Mandalay plain in central Burma, where British tank brigades and mobile infantry would prove decisive.[74] An attack on *15th Army* in the central plain would threaten *33rd Army*'s lines of communication to its supplies in southern Burma, likely forcing *33rd Army* to withdraw from its defense of northern Burma and thus opening the way for Stilwell's forces to advance farther south. Pushing the Japanese armies deeper into Burma and solidifying the reconquest of northern Burma would be in line with Mountbatten's directive to defend and develop the Hump operation and exploit the opening of land communications with China, although the projected advances would entail significant administrative and logistical risks.[75]

The SEAC planning staff came up with two proposals for overland advances, both of which would require heavy reliance on air supply and possible air operations:

Plan "X": An overland advance by NCAC forces, supported by the 10th U.S.A.A.F., from the Mogaung-Myitkyina area to Katha and Bhamo. This would be coordinated with an advance by IV and XXXIII Corps from Imphal to the Chindwin River, with support from No. 221 Group, RAF, to establish a line running from Kalewa on the Chindwin to Lashio in the east.

Plan "Y": A more ambitious advance with IV and XXXIII Corps crossing the Chindwin River to defeat Japanese forces in the Yeu-Shwebo area and advance to Mandalay, with air landings in support, while the NCAC and the Yunnan forces pushed south, jointly establishing a line from Mandalay to Lashio.[76]

An overland advance might be combined with an amphibious assault on Rangoon to destroy Japanese forces in southern Burma and link up with the British, Indian, and Chinese American forces advancing from the north. Mountbatten decided to recommend Plan "Y," which became Operation CAPITAL, and the attack on Rangoon, which became Operation DRACULA, to the Combined Chiefs of Staff.[77] CAPITAL was tentatively scheduled to begin in November 1944 and would be carried out in four phases.[78] In Phase 1, 14th Army would advance to Kalewa and Kalemyo on the Chindwin River between November 1944 and January 1945, while the NCAC and Yunnan forces would advance beyond Bhamo and Hsenwi. This would allow the road from Myitkyina to link up with the old Burma Road, reestablishing the land route to China. In Phase 2, 14th Army would advance to Yeu while the NCAC and Yunnan forces would capture Mogok, Mongmit, and Lashio by mid-March 1945. Phase 3 would see 14th Army capture Mandalay and Pakokku, with the NCAC and Yunnan forces capturing Maymyo. In Phase 4, 14th Army and the NCAC and Yunnan forces would push south to link up with the Rangoon invasion force. Both 14th Army and the NCAC and Yunnan forces would be almost completely dependent on air supply during their respective advances. DRACULA was scheduled for March 1945 but as initially planned would require substantial reinforcements from Europe, which at the time seemed possible. Mountbatten expected that these overland advances would require air-landing operations behind enemy lines, and for these operations he wanted an additional combat cargo group and a second air commando group from the Army Air Force. Ironically, CAPITAL and DRACULA, if the Combined Chiefs of Staff approved both plans, committed SEAC to the reconquest of all of Burma—an objective that had seemed impossible and unnecessary just a few months earlier.[79]

In mid-September, following discussions with Mountbatten in London and his deputy Albert Wedemeyer in Washington, the Combined Chiefs of Staff met with Churchill and Roosevelt in Quebec for the Octagon Conference, where they discussed SEAC's

President Roosevelt and Prime Minister Churchill meeting with the Combined Chiefs of Staff at Quebec in September 1944. Seated (*left to right*) are Gen. Marshall, Adm. Leahy, President Roosevelt, Prime Minister Churchill, Gen. Brook, and Field Marshal Dill; standing (*left to right*) are two unknown officers, Adm. King, Air Chief Marshal Portal, Gen. Arnold, and Adm. Cunningham.
SC-194469, RG111, NARA

MYITKYINA AND BEYOND: OPERATIONS, PLANS, AND PREPARATIONS

proposals for offensive operations. The British Chiefs of Staff argued for a limited CAPITAL, completing the first phase as planned, and part of the second phase, but putting more emphasis on DRACULA in the belief that the capture of Rangoon would cut off *Burma Area Army* from its source of supplies and force it to quit Burma, instead of confronting the Japanese forces in a major battle in central Burma.[80] The American Joint Chiefs agreed but asked that the directive to Mountbatten be amended to specify that opening land communications with China was one of SEAC's missions. Marshall and Arnold pointed out that supplies were accumulating in China because there was no means of transporting them from the airfields to where they were needed.[81] The Chinese urgently needed trucks, and these could come over only the planned Ledo Road. To provide Mountbatten with the air resources he needed, the Joint Chiefs agreed to send the additional combat cargo and air commando groups to SEAC that he had requested.[82] Having received the prime minister and the president's approval, the Combined Chiefs of Staff sent the following directive to Mountbatten on 16 September 1944:

1. Your object is the recapture of all of Burma at the earliest date. Operations to achieve this objective must not, however, prejudice the security of the existing air supply route to China, including the air staging post at Myitkyina and the opening of overland communications.
2. The following are approved operations:
   (a) The stages of Operation "Capital" necessary to the security of the air route, and the attainment of overland communications with China
   (b) Operation "Dracula"
   The Combined Chiefs of Staff attach the greatest importance to the vigorous prosecution of Operation "Capital" and to the execution of Operation "Dracula" before the monsoon in 1945, with a target date of 15th March.
3. If "Dracula" has to be postponed until after the monsoon of 1945, you will continue to exploit Operation "Capital" as far as may be possible without prejudice to preparations for the execution of Operation "Dracula" in November 1945.[83]

Within weeks of receiving this new directive, Mountbatten found that circumstances had changed once again. Stiffening German resistance convinced the British Chiefs of Staff that no reinforcements could be sent to SEAC before Germany's defeat, so that Operation DRACULA would have to be postponed until after the 1945 monsoon. Separately Mountbatten had informed the Chiefs of Staff that the pursuit of *15th Army* was ahead of schedule and that 14th Army was close to achieving the objectives of Phase I of CAPITAL well in advance of the original plans. With this in mind, he argued that it made little sense not to complete Phase II of CAPITAL and that he would explore the possibility of seizing Rangoon with a much-smaller force. With the concurrence of the Joint Chiefs of Staff, Mountbatten was instead ordered to pursue Operation CAPITAL aggressively, with the goal of achieving the objectives outlined in the third phase of the operation: securing the line Pakokku-Mandalay-Maymyo-Lashio with the combined forces of 14th Army, the NCAC, and the Yunnan armies. To coordinate the operations of these separate armies, Mountbatten received approval to set up a new command: Allied Land Forces, Southeast Asia. The new command came into being on 12 November 1944 under Lt. Gen. Sir Oliver Leese.[84]

While the plans and directives for SEAC's future operations were under review and discussion, events in China brought about a complete reorganization of the China-Burma-India theater and Stilwell's recall. The Japanese *ICHI-GO* offensive had proven to be a disaster for the Chinese. Operation *KO-GO*, the capture of the railroad corridor from Hankow to Kaifeng, was a complete success. In late May the Japanese launched the second phase of *ICHI-GO* (Operation *TO-GO*) to capture the railroad corridor from Hankow south to French Indochina and eliminate the Fourteenth Air Force airfields in East China. The town of Changsha fell to the Japanese on June 18. The Japanese then advanced on Hengyang, the Fourteenth Air Force base for the P-40s bombing and strafing the Japanese columns. The Japanese laid siege to the city, which held out until August 9. The Fourteenth Air Force flew constantly in support of the retreating Chinese armies but could not stem the Japanese advance alone. The poorly trained and weakly armed Chinese forces in East China were incapable of mounting a concerted defense, as Stilwell had feared would happen. With Hengyang in Japanese hands, the road to the Fourteenth Air Force bases at Ling-Ling and Kweilin was now open. In early July, Roosevelt urged Chiang to accept Stilwell as overall commander of the Chinese armies. Chiang agreed in principle but delayed a decision. After much political turmoil, in early October Chiang agreed to accept an American commander for China's armies, but not Stilwell. The relationship between the two had deteriorated beyond repair. Long aware of the soured relations between Chiang and Stilwell, Roosevelt decided to order Stilwell's recall to the United States, but not to appoint an American general as commander of the Chinese army. Instead, Roosevelt nominated Albert Wedemeyer, Mountbatten's deputy chief of staff, to be the senior American officer in China and chief of staff to the generalissimo. The War Department used this opportunity to reorganize the theater, splitting the CBI into two

Lt. Gen. Dan Sultan (*left*) meets with Adm. Mountbatten at Myitkyina in early 1945. Mountbatten had argued for the China-Burma-India theater to be split into two separate theaters. When he became commander of the India-Burma theater, Sultan had spent a year as Stilwell's deputy commander in the China-Burma-India theater. *SC-201146, RG111, NARA*

Determined, irascible, and impatient of inaction, Joseph Stilwell did everything he could to achieve the directives the War Department had given him. He had great admiration for the Chinese soldier, but his frustrations with the Chinese military and political leadership contributed to the deterioration of his relationship with Generalissimo Chiang Kai-shek and his recall to Washington. *SC-262251, RG111, NARA*

"there has been between C.B.I., the Chinese and British, up on higher levels, a distrust of each other," but expected that with Sultan's appointment this distrust would be eliminated.[88]

Tenth Air Force Preparations

Prior to Stilwell's recall on 3 October 1944, Mountbatten issued a new directive to Stilwell, outlining his objectives for Phase 1 and Phase 2 of Operation CAPITAL:

Phase 1 (to be completed by mid-December): to destroy and expel the enemy to a line which included the key points Rail Indaw, Kunchang, Sikaw, and Namhkam;

Phase 2 (to be completed by mid-February 1945): to destroy and expel the enemy north of the general line which was to include the key points Thabeikkyin, Mogok, Mongmit, and Lashio, and be prepared to exploit in anticipation of Phases 3 and 4.[89]

Completing these objectives would require an advance of around 50 miles from Myitkyina, east of the Irrawaddy River down the road to Bhamo and Namhkwan, and west of the Irrawaddy overland to Shwegu, and down the Railway Corridor from Mogaung to Indaw and beyond to Thabeikkyin and Mogok. To mount the offensive, Stilwell had American, Chinese, and British units available.[90] Two American regiments—the 475th Infantry, composed of survivors of

parts: the China theater under Wedemeyer and the India-Burma theater under Maj. Gen. Dan Sultan, who had been serving as Stilwell's deputy commander in the China-Burma-India theater. This division of the CBI into two separate theaters was a change that Mountbatten had been recommending, given the impossibility of one individual fulfilling the multiple roles that Stilwell had taken on. Promoted to lieutenant general, Sultan assumed command of the new India-Burma theater on 24 October 1944, taking over command of the Chinese armies in the NCAC and, with the generalissimo's concurrence, the Yunnan forces in Burma.[85]

Before leaving his command, Stilwell paid a handsome tribute to the men of the Tenth Air Force:

I shall always follow the exploits of the 10th and shall feel great pride in its accomplishments. You have developed, from a fledgling force of a few defensive fighters, into a wallop-packing outfit which has severely hampered Jap communications and supply in Burma. Tactically and logistically, you have supported the advance of Allied troops in Burma. Best wishes to all in your continued success.[86]

The reorganization of American forces in the theater did not have an immediate impact on Stratemeyer, in his role as commander, Army Air Forces, India-Burma sector, or Davidson as commander of the Tenth Air Force, apart from they both now reported to Sultan as India-Burma theater commander (in Stratemeyer's case) and commander of the NCAC (in Davidson's case). Stratemeyer hoped that Stilwell's removal as theater commander would see an improvement in relations between the different commands and between the Army Air Force and the ground forces. In a meeting with his senior commanders to discuss the new theater structure, Stratemeyer admitted that in his relations with Stilwell he often didn't know where he stood. He didn't know "whether he [Stilwell] thinks I've done all right and the air forces have done all right."[87] Stratemeyer also noted the problems in relationships within the theater, saying,

After the capture of Myitkyina, Army Air Force engineers worked to improve the facilities at the airfield. To get construction equipment to the airfield faster, the 1888th Engineer Aviation Battalion (Colored) cut truck bodies and other earth-moving equipment into pieces that could fit into a C-47. Here a C-47 of the 12th Combat Cargo Squadron takes on part of a truck for Myitkyina. *3A-37194, RG342FH, NARA*

the original Merrill's Marauders, with newer reinforcements and the 124th Cavalry Regiment newly arrived in India, and the 1st Chinese Separate Regiment, trained in India—formed the 5332nd Brigade (Provisional), in effect a division-size force that became known as the Mars Task Force. Stilwell organized his Chinese divisions into two armies (equivalent to a British or American corps): the New First Army, comprising the 30th and 38th Divisions, and the New Sixth Army, with the 14th, 22nd, and 50th Divisions—all

MYITKYINA AND BEYOND: OPERATIONS, PLANS, AND PREPARATIONS

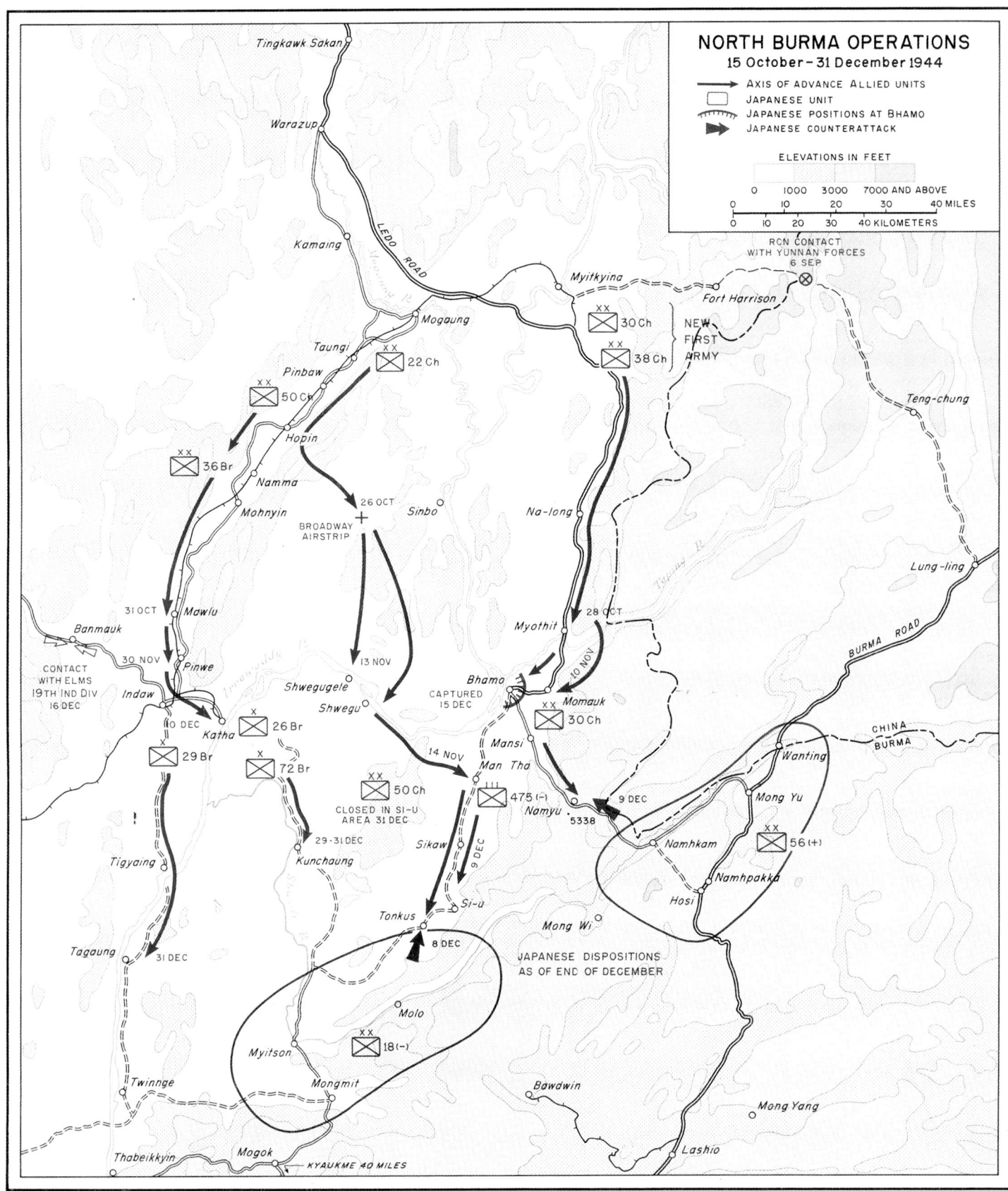

MAP 7

NORTH BURMA OPERATIONS
15 October – 31 December 1944

THE TENTH AIR FORCE IN WORLD WAR II

experienced divisions. The British contribution was the 36th Division, with three brigades, which replaced Wingate's Special Force. The plan that Stilwell developed, but that Lt. Gen. Sultan would carry out, had the 36th Division moving down the Railway Corridor with the Chinese 50th Division in support to capture the Indaw-Katha area, while the Chinese 22nd Division moved down the center of the area to cross the Irrawaddy River at Shwegu. To the east, the Chinese 30th Division would move down the road from Myitkyina to capture Bhamo with the 38th Division in support.[91]

On the Salween front, the Yunnan Force, known as the Chinese Expeditionary Force, had been unable to make a rapid breakthrough into Burma. Beginning the Salween campaign in May, the Expeditionary Force's 12 understrength divisions in the XI and XX Group armies made slow but steady progress, reducing Japanese strongpoints on the route to the old Burma Road with support from the Fourteenth

priority given to the defense of the inner ring of Japanese possessions, *Burma Area Army* could expect little in the way of reinforcements to replace the heavy losses incurred in the failed attack on Imphal. Accordingly, *Imperial General Headquarters* issued a new directive to *Southern Army* stipulating that *Burma Area Army* was to hold the strategic areas of southern Burma at all costs, principally the oil fields at Yenangyaung and the rice-producing areas of the Irrawaddy delta. This meant holding a line across central Burma from Lashio in the east through Mandalay to Yenangyaung and Ramree Island on the Burmese coast—ironically nearly the same line the Allies planned to reach in Phase II of Operation CAPITAL. *Burma Area Army* outlined three operations: *DAN*, to prevent the Allies from establishing the overland route to China; *BAN*, to block 14th Army's expected advance to the Irrawaddy River; and *KAN*, the defense of the Burmese coastal areas. The task of maintaining

Once the C-47s had delivered all the pieces of equipment to Myitkyina, the engineers welded all the parts back together to get the trucks or earth-moving equipment back in operation. Men of the 1888th Engineer Aviation Battalion gather parts to reassemble an Army 6×6 truck at Myitkyina in August 1944. *3A-37227, RG342FH, NARA*

A shovel loads dirt into a 6×6 truck at Myitkyina. Over several months the aviation engineer battalions completely rebuilt the original Japanese airfield at Myitkyina—which became Myitkyina South—and built two more airfields: Myitkyina North and Myitkyina East, across the river from the town. Today the Myitkyina North runway still exists as a road north of the town. *Personal collection of Maj. Gen. Howard C. Davidson, 168.7266-59, AFHRA*

Air Force. A strong Japanese counterattack against the XI and XX Group armies begun in September at Lung-Ling, on the Burma Road, stymied the Chinese advance, but the Chinese forces prevented a Japanese breakthrough. Pausing to allow its divisions to recover, the Chinese XI Group army planned for a new attack from positions around Lung-Ling to begin toward the end of October.[92]

The Japanese were also adjusting their plans for the defense of their shrinking empire. The American capture of the Mariana Islands with the defeat of the Imperial Navy in the Battle of the Philippine Sea, coupled with the first air attacks on the Japanese home islands from China-based B-29s, caused the fall of the Tojo government in mid-July. Recognizing the serious threat to Japan, *Imperial General Headquarters* made preparations for the defense of four key areas—the Philippines, the Formosa-Ryukyu Islands area, the Japanese home islands, and the northeast front—as Operation *Sho-Go*. To provide for the defense of the Philippines and what the Japanese high command expected would be the decisive battle against American forces, *Imperial General Headquarters* withdrew divisions from China, Korea, and Manchuria, though pressing on with Operation *ICHI-GO*. As a result of these deployments and the

the overland blockade of China and holding the line from Lashio to Mandalay under Operation *DAN* fell to the *33rd Army*, with the *18th* and *56th Divisions* and one regiment from the *49th Division*. In the center, the *15th Army*, now under the command of Lt. Gen. S. Katamura (the defeated Mutaguchi having been sent back to Japan), had the *15th*, *31st*, *33rd*, and *53rd Divisions* to defend against 14th Army's advance under Operation *BAN*, while *28th Army*, with two divisions, covered the Arakan coast under Operation *KAN*. In northern Burma, the *33rd Army* intended to delay the advance of the NCAC forces and continue to block the Yunnan force attempting to advance down the old Burma Road for as long as possible, holding the Allies north of Lashio.[93]

The *5th Hikōshidan* now faced the same constraints as *Burma Area Army*: the impossibility of gaining reinforcements. Conserving aircraft became a priority. In July the *7th Hikōdan* and the heavy bombers in the *12th Hikōsentai* transferred to the Netherlands East Indies. This left the *5th Hikōshidan* with the following units:

4th Hikōdan
8th Hikōsentai   Type 99 Light Bomber (Ki-48 Lily)
50th Hikōsentai   Type 1 Fighter Model 2 (Ki-43-II Oscar)
64th Hikōsentai   Type 1 Fighter Model 2 (Ki-43-II Oscar)
204th Hikōsentai Type 1 Fighter Model 2 (Ki-43-II Oscar)
81st Hikōsentai   Type 100 Command Reconnaissance Plane Model 2 (Ki-46 Dinah)

This gave a nominal strength of 60 fighters, 50 bombers, and 15 reconnaissance aircraft in Burma, with more aircraft in Thailand, Malaya, and the Netherlands East Indies under the *3rd Kōkūgun* (3rd Air Army), but the number of operational aircraft available was substantially less. Casualties among experienced aircrew during the Japanese offensives in the first half of 1944 had been heavy, and the replacement pilots who arrived were mostly inexperienced, requiring more training. The superior number and quality of Allied fighter aircraft had made it difficult for the Type 99 light bombers to conduct raids in daylight without prohibitive losses, so the *8th Hikōsentai* began intensive training in night bombing. The lack of adequate numbers of bombers and their inability to operate in daylight put an added burden on the fighter *sentai*, who from now on had to carry out bombing and strafing missions in addition to their responsibility of maintaining air superiority over the battlefront. With Allied numerical superiority allowing regular attacks on Japanese airfields, the *5th Hikōshidan* had to resort to basing its fighters and bombers in southern Burma and even in Thailand, using forward airfields and landing grounds only briefly. Planes would fly to a forward airfield, often in the evening, conduct a dusk or night raid or a mission the following morning, then return to their main base as quickly as possible to avoid being caught on the ground. The fighter *sentai* did gain some newer aircraft, the *64th* and *204th Hikōsentai* reequipping with the Type 1 fighter model 3 (Ki-43 III), while the *50th Hikōsentai* transitioned to the more capable Type 4 fighter (Ki-84 Frank), though maintenance problems with their new fighter plagued the unit for some months. With fewer aircraft the *5th Hikōshidan* still had responsibility for defending a large area of Burma, including the coastal areas from possible invasion. Priority for air support went to the *15th Army* and operation *BAN*, with the *5th Hikōshidan* committing most of its resources to stopping the expected advance of British and Indian infantry and armored units to the Irrawaddy River. There would be no air support for *33rd Army* unless the need was imperative. To make matters worse, at the end of September the *5th Hikōshidan* received orders to transfer the *204th Hikōsentai* to the Philippines, reducing its strength even further. Short of airplanes and trained pilots, the *5th Hikōshidan* could do little to stem the Allied advance into Burma apart from launching what amounted to nuisance raids.[94]

In contrast, the Tenth Air Force continued to grow in strength and capability, adding more units and more-capable aircraft. In the NCAC area the Tenth continued with two fighter groups, but in August the 311th Fighter Group transferred from the Tenth to the Fourteenth Air Force in exchange for the 33rd Fighter Group—one of the two fighter groups protecting the B-29 bases in China.[95] The 311th Group's P-51s required less fuel than the P-47s of the 33rd Group, easing the logistical burden on the Fourteenth Air Force, then desperately short of gasoline from the constant fighting in East China. The 528th and 529th Fighter Squadrons moved to China in early September, with the 530th Fighter Squadron following in early October. The 33rd Group's three squadrons (58th, 59th, and 60th Fighter Squadrons) moved to Nagahuli, in the Dinjan area, and began flying missions in their P-47s toward the end of September after several months of relative inactivity in China. On August 17, the 88th Fighter Squadron's P-40 detachment at Myitkyina returned to Shingbwiyang after 56 days of operating out of the airfield.[96] The 89th Fighter Squadron flew to Myitkyina to replace the 88th Squadron. The P-40s flew their last mission the day before they left Myitkyina. Once back at Shingbwiyang, the P-40s soon went back to India in exchange for more P-47s, the 88th Squadron being the last in the 80th Fighter Group to fully convert to the Thunderbolt. The return of the 88th Squadron's P-40s marked the end of the P-40's two years of hard service over India and Burma. While the pilots considered the P-47 a big improvement over the P-40, Davidson expressed a hint of regret at the P-40's departure in a letter to Arnold, saying "it is going to be very difficult to get along without the old P-40 which seemed to take all airdromes in its stride and did a thorough workmanlike job under adverse conditions."[97]

The Tenth also gained more transport and liaison aircraft. During August the 3rd Combat Cargo Group transferred from operational control of the 3rd Tactical Air Force to the Tenth Air

A P-47D from the 60th Fighter Squadron, 33rd Fighter Group, soon after arriving in northern Burma. The 33rd Group had served in the Mediterranean theater before transferring to China and the Fourteenth Air Force, with the mission of protecting the airfields the B-29s used for their long-range missions to Japan. *Courtesy, Carl Molesworth*

The 88th Fighter Squadron gave up its P-40Ns after the capture of Myitkyina and converted to the P-47D Thunderbolt, which the 80th Fighter Group would fly for the rest of the war on close-air-support and interdiction missions over northern Burma. *GP-80-SU-PH, AFHRA*

C-47s taxi past a line of P-47s from the 89th Fighter Squadron at Myitkyina in September 1944, as the monsoon was coming to an end. The 89th Fighter Squadron replaced the 88th Fighter Squadron at Myitkyina when the 88th Squadron withdrew to reequip with the P-47D. SC-263299, RG111, NARA

Force. The reopening of the road between Assam and Imphal in late June had reduced the need for air transports to supply IV and XXXIII Corps around Imphal, while Stilwell's forces would require more transports for their planned offensive in the coming dry season. This added four combat cargo squadrons with C-47s (9th, 10th, 11th, and 12th) to the three C-47 squadrons of the 443rd Troop Carrier Group. The 5th and 71st Liaison Squadrons, formerly attached directly to the NCAC, became part of the Tenth Air Force in August and were joined together to form the 1st Liaison Group (Provisional). In November the 115th Liaison Squadron arrived in India and became part of the 1st Liaison Group. The 20th Tactical Reconnaissance Squadron returned to the operational control of Eastern Air Command. In total, the number of aircraft assigned to the Tenth Air Force grew from 358 in July (with 300 operational) to 432 in October (with 359 operational), nearly three and a half times the number of aircraft available to the *5th Hikōshidan*.[98]

As of 1 October 1944 the Tenth Air Force had administrative and operational control over the following units supporting the NCAC:

490th Bomb Squadron   B-25H/J Dergaon

33rd Fighter Group, Nagaghuli
    58th Fighter Squadron P-47D   Moran
    59th Fighter Squadron P-47D   Nagaghuli
    60th Fighter Squadron P-47D   Tingkawk Sakan

80th Fighter Group, Tingkawk Sakan
    88th Fighter Squadron P-47D   Shingbwiyang
    89th Fighter Squadron P-47D   Myitkyina
    90th Fighter Squadron P-47D   Tingkawk Sakan

Pilots of the 89th Fighter Squadron stand next to one of the squadron's P-47Ds named "Wahoo" (left to right): Capt. Harold Robbins, 2nd Lt. William Cutler, 1st Lt. Sherry Dare, 1st Lt. Dodd Shepard, and 1st Lt. George Seifert. SC-263303, RG111, NARA

3rd Combat Cargo Group, Tingkawk Sakan
- 9th Combat Cargo Squadron   C-47   Moran
- 10th Combat Cargo Squadron   C-47   Dinjan
- 11th Combat Cargo Squadron   C-47   Dinjan
- 12th Combat Cargo Squadron   C-47   Moran

443rd Troop Carrier Group, Ledo
- 1st Troop Carrier Squadron   C-47   Sookerating
- 2nd Troop Carrier Squadron   C-47   Shingbwiyang
- 315th Troop Carrier Squadron C-47   Ledo

1st Liaison Group, Provisional
- 5th Liaison Squadron   L-1/L-5   Shaduzup
- 71st Liaison Squadron L-1/L-4/L-5 Ledo

The missions of the Tenth Air Force in support of the Northern Combat Area Command were

a to maintain air superiority within assigned areas of responsibility and ensure security of ATC routes to China,
b to give maximum support to land operations of Northern Combat Area Command forces,
c to destroy Japanese lines of communication within the area assigned,
d to ensure air defense of Assam and northern Burma, and
e to provide air transport for airborne and air transit troops, air supplies, and evacuation for units of NCAC.[99]

These missions, in turn, required the following types of operations:

a Fixed air defense of the Assam and Myitkyina areas
b Interdiction of selected enemy lines of communication
c Destruction of enemy supplies and concentrations
d Close air support of engaged ground units
e Counter air force operations
f Air cargo operations
g Liaison aviation operations
h Construction of landing fields[100]

From the fall of Myitkyina in August 1944 until the end of April 1945, the units of the Tenth Air Force undertook all these operations in support of the Allied armies advancing in northern Burma.

CHAPTER 11
SUPPORTING THE NCAC ADVANCE
August 1944–April 1945

Supporting the Advance: Maintaining Air Superiority

Of all the missions assigned to the Tenth Air Force, maintaining air superiority over northern Burma was the most important. All other missions—attacks on lines of communication, attacks on supplies and concentrations, close air support, and air supply—depended on Allied control of the air. The Tenth employed three tactics for ensuring air superiority: extensive patrolling over assigned areas, regular sweeps of Japanese airfields and landing grounds likely to be staging fields for raids, and engaging in air combat with Japanese airplanes whenever possible. The Tenth applied all three tactics continuously. The efforts of the Tenth Air Force formed a part of Eastern Air Command's counter air force effort.[1] EAC assigned responsibility for coverage of Japanese airfields in Burma to the nearest Allied air command. When photographic coverage or radio intercepts alerted EAC to Japanese aircraft staging from forward airfields, EAC would order the appropriate Allied air commands to strike these airfields in coordinated attacks.[2] With the Japanese husbanding their air resources, it was difficult for Allied fighters to draw them into battle, nor could Allied fighters and bombers always catch Japanese airplanes as they staged briefly from forward airfields. As a result, the numerically superior Allied air forces had to devote a considerable effort to containing the smaller *5th Hikōshidan*, which could still threaten unescorted transport aircraft.[3] Fortunately for the Tenth Air Force, the *5th Hikōshidan*'s inability to provide much support to *33rd Army*, together with the Tenth's extensive counterair operations, limited losses to Japanese air attack.

During August and September—the final months of the monsoon—weather and the withdrawal of most Japanese air units to train and reequip limited the ability and the need to carry out counter air force operations. Within the NCAC area the 80th Fighter Group conducted a number of airfield sweeps during August. The 90th Fighter Squadron carried out a sweep of the airfield at Shwebo with six P-47s on August 5, damaging an aircraft covered in a tarp, while the 89th Fighter Squadron covered the airfields at Shwebo, Onbauk, Kawlin, and Indaw two days later with eight Thunderbolts,

An A-24B assigned to the 88th Fighter Squadron at Tingkawk Sakan in fall 1944 next to an F-5 Lighting from the 9th Photo Reconnaissance Squadron. The A-24s served as training planes, flew communications flights between bases, and assisted in searching for downed airmen. *Peter M. Bowers Collection, MoF*

strafing an in-line-engine fighter plane the pilots identified as a Tony. On August 18, the 89th Squadron sent eight aircraft to strafe the airfield at Lashio, leaving several large buildings burning after three strafing passes. This day also saw a rare clash with Japanese fighters. The 89th Squadron sent two P-47s to escort an unarmed Douglas RA-24B searching for a downed 89th Squadron pilot shot down the day before around Kutkai, a small town on the road to Lashio. Spying two trucks, the P-47s went down to strafe, setting one truck on fire. As the P-47s pulled up from their strafing pass, an Oscar flew right between them. The wingman saw an Oscar on the tail of the RA-24. Ordering the RA-24 to head back to base, Capt. McMillan, the element leader, turned to come in on the Oscar behind the RA-24 in a head-on pass, without result. McMillan made another head-on pass at the second Oscar, again without apparent result. His wingman, 1st Lt. James May, turned inside McMillan to get in a deflection shot on this Oscar, then made a 360-degree turn to come in head-on, firing until the Oscar passed beneath him and went off smoking. On September 30 the 89th Squadron sent seven

A P-47D from the 90th Fighter Squadron at Tingkawk Sakan in fall 1944. The Thunderbolts of the 80th Fighter Group, with the newly arrived 33rd Fighter Group, provided air superiority, attacks on Japanese lines of communication, and close air support for the Chinese and American units advancing in northern Burma. *Peter M. Bowers Collection, MoF*

P-47s to sweep the airfield at Lashio and 12 aircraft to cover Anisakan and Nawnghkio, finding no aircraft at any of the airfields.[4]

Once the Allied advance began in mid-October, sweeps of Japanese airfields became a regular mission for the 33rd and 80th Fighter Groups. During October the 33rd Group carried out five airfield sweeps, while the 80th Group conducted two sweeps. At the end of the month, the 89th Fighter Squadron flew to the Japanese airfield at Namsang, 300 miles south of Myitkyina, in the squadron's longest mission to date. These sweeps found no aircraft at any of the airfields covered, but strafed installations around the airfields. The 33rd Group had better luck during November, completing eight sweeps during the month. The 60th Fighter Squadron covered Kawlin East landing ground on November 13 and 14, claiming a Tojo destroyed on each mission. The 80th Fighter Group completed two airfield sweeps early in the month, with the 90th Fighter Squadron also claiming aircraft destroyed—an Oscar and a Tojo—during a sweep of Kawlin East airfield. December saw eight airfield sweeps. The 59th Fighter Squadron made a sweep over three airfields on December 18, possibly destroying one single-engine aircraft and a Dinah. On December 24 the 90th Squadron carried out a sweep over Lashio, strafing four dummy aircraft for the second time, and reported leaving the dummies "unserviceable." The 58th and 60th Fighter Squadrons took over the bombing task in the middle of the month, bombing the runways at Aungban, Meiktila, and Anisakan and rendering them unserviceable. The final airfield sweeps took place during the last week of January, when the P-47s carried out sweeps over Heho, Hsemhsai, and Aungban. Over Heho the 90th Squadron lost 1st Lt. Donald Maxwell, who crashed on the field while on his strafing run. The 490th Squadron made its final bombing missions this week, bombing the same three airfields to knock out the runways.[5]

On missions to Meiktila on January 15, the Tenth Air Force fighter squadrons claimed four Japanese fighters destroyed. In late morning a flight of six P-47s from the 90th Fighter Squadron took off for a sweep to the airfields in the Meiktila area. Flying at 19,000 feet, the flight saw a formation of four Oscar fighters ahead of them at 10 o'clock, flying at 17,500 feet. Dropping their underwing fuel tanks, the P-47s turned to intercept the Japanese fighters, who in turn dropped their wing tanks and broke their formation, each Japanese fighter beginning violent aerobatics. The P-47s had run into four *64th Hikōsentai* fighters sent up to intercept them. Capt. Charles Smith, leading the flight, went after one Oscar, which evaded his fire. He went after another fighter, making three passes and getting strikes into the belly of the Oscar, observing the Japanese fighter beginning to smoke as it broke off the engagement. Smith claimed this fighter as damaged. 2nd Lt. Alex Kostyshak, Smith's wingman, couldn't follow him in his attack but fired at two other Oscars he saw. Seeing another Oscar above two other P-47s, Kostyshak turned into the Japanese fighter and closed to 100 yards, observing hits and claiming the fighter as damaged. 1st Lt. Robert Schoenborn was leading the second element in the flight. He followed Smith in the interception, firing at one Oscar who did an immediate split-S to avoid his fire. Climbing up from this encounter, Schoenborn saw another Oscar above him and approached from the Oscar's blind spot. Schoenborn fired and got hits in the cockpit area and apparently the engine, seeing a burst of flame and then black smoke coming out of the enemy fighter. The Oscar entered a slow spiral, then straightened out into a 30-degree dive. Schoenborn followed, firing again until six of his eight guns jammed. At 4,000 feet he had to break off as his engine began running rough. When last seen, the Oscar was going down in a dive, with more black smoke pouring out. After reviewing the gun camera film, the squadron and group commanders concluded that the Oscar was indeed destroyed, though the *64th Hikōsentai* did not record a loss from this engagement. The Thunderbolt pilots were impressed with the flying skill of their opponents, if not their aggressiveness. In their combat report the pilots made the following comments, which provide an interesting view of the tactics of Japanese Army Air Force fighters:

It is considered that the enemy pilots were above average in skill, especially in acrobatic flying. They consistently used the superior maneuverability of their planes to evade attack. They showed a sure knowledge of the performance characteristics of the P-47, attempting constantly to draw our planes to combat at lower altitudes where the P-47 is at a considerable disadvantage. However, the enemy lacked aggressive spirit, and failed to press home the attack on our planes. They showed a marked absence of cooperation or coordinated action, at times interfering with each other in attack.[6]

The 58th Fighter Squadron also had a mission to Meiktila on January 15, by coincidence the fourth anniversary of the squadron's activation. Two pilots returned claiming three victories against Japanese fighters. During December the 58th Squadron completed its conversion from the P-47 to the Lockheed P-38—the first squadron in the 33rd Group to do so. The P-38 was the third fighter aircraft the squadron had taken into combat, having flown the P-40 in North Africa and the P-47 in China and Burma. That morning, 1st Lt. Daniel Pence was on his way to Meiktila with Maj. Clarence Baker as his wingman, flying at 10,000 feet east of Thazi, when he saw a green-colored Ki-43 flying below him. This was apparently one of the *64th Hikōsentai* fighters scrambled earlier to intercept the P-47s from the 90th Fighter Squadron, and possibly some RAF Thunderbolts in the area. Unable to contact his element leader, who was on a different radio frequency, Pence peeled off with Baker following.

The 58th Fighter Squadron was the first in the 33rd Fighter Group to convert to the P-38, receiving their first Lightning in November 1944 and completing their conversion the following month. Not all pilots were happy with their new fighter. One young pilot was heard to remark, as he watched a P-38 land at the squadron's base at Moran, "Whose coffin will that be?" This P-38 carries the 58th Squadron's insignia—a red gorilla—on the nose. *Courtesy, Carl Molesworth*

Seeing the P-38s approaching, the Oscar dived to the deck. Both pilots gave the Oscar a long burst without effect. The Oscar did a split-S to escape, but Pence got in a 20-degree deflection shot from above, sending the Oscar down to crash into a dry riverbed. Now down on the deck, Pence and Baker saw another Oscar flying near them and attacked. Baker's gunsight failed and his shots went above the Japanese fighter. The Oscar pulled up to come in on Baker, giving Pence an opening. Closing in to 75 yards, Pence fired a 60-degree deflection shot, knocking pieces off the Oscar and pulling up as it rolled inverted and went into the ground. Climbing back up in a chandelle, Pence found a silver Oscar coming in behind him, but Baker came in on the Japanese fighter and, using the path of his bullets as a guide, hit the Oscar around the cockpit area. This fighter crashed below for their third victory, although the *64th Hikōsentai* reported losing only two fighters at the time of this engagement. These claims turned out to be the last victories for the 33rd Fighter Group in World War II, and the last aerial victories for fighter units under the operational control of the Tenth Air Force.[7]

The medium bombers of the 490th Bomb Squadron made their contribution to the counterair effort with three missions to Japanese airfields during October and four during November. During the October missions the 490th Squadron concentrated on the runways at Onbauk, Shwebo, and Nawnghkio. The squadron targeted Onbauk on October 15, but only one flight of B-25s got through the weather to bomb the airfield. The next day 12 aircraft dropped 91 500-pound bombs on the runway at Shwebo. Nawnghkio was the target on the third day of missions against airfields, with eight aircraft dropping 64 500-pound bombs along the runway. One airplane failed to return from the mission. On the November missions the squadron directed its attacks on the airfield installations at Nawnghkio and Lashio. In January 1945 the 490th Squadron kept up the attacks on Japanese airfields. On January 5 the squadron sent out 16 B-25s—the most it had ever sent on a single mission—to bomb three airfields in a daring low-level attack. Four aircraft went after Aungban, dropping 23 500-pound bombs from 300 feet as they roared over the runway. Intense antiaircraft fire damaged three of the bombers. Four aircraft went to Lai-Hka, southeast of Mandalay, dropping 29 500-pound bombs perfectly along the runway. Eight aircraft bombed the two runways at Kunlon, to the east of Mandalay. Four aircraft bombed runway No. 1 with 30 bombs, while the second flight of four bombed runway No. 2 with a mix of 26 500- and 1,000-pound bombs. Intense and accurate machine gun fire hit four of the airplanes. Coming off the target, the right engine on Lt. Quentin Bell's B-25H began smoking and a few minutes later burst into flame, forcing the five crewmen to bail out. Three made it back to the squadron after a harrowing walkout from behind Japanese lines. The mediums went back to airfield bombing on January 18 and followed this up with missions to Heho on January 21 and Aungban on January 23.[8]

To protect the Assam and expanding Myitkyina air bases, the Tenth Air Force set up two defense areas.[9] One was designated the Kanjikosh Air Defense Area—where the Tenth had its headquarters—to cover the Assam airfields. This became the responsibility of the 33rd Fighter Group. The second was the Myitkyina Air Defense Area, which relied on the 80th Fighter Group's units based at Myitkyina, Shingbwiyang, and Tingkawk Sakan. The fighter groups had to keep 12 aircraft on alert at all times—a duty rotated among the squadrons—prepared to take off to intercept any incoming air raids. Once the advance began, the 33rd and 80th Fighter Groups organized overlapping dawn-until-dusk patrols over the forward areas, covering the three prongs of the advance. Between November 1944 and January 1945,

The B-25s of the 490th Bomb Squadron and the 12th Bomb Group contributed to the counterair battle through their regular bombing of Japanese airfields in northern and central Burma to render them unserviceable, even if only for a few days. Here the 12th Group sends its bombs down on the Japanese airfield at Nawngkio in fall 1944. *3A-37630, RG342FH, NARA*

The Fighter Control Section covering the Northern Combat Area Command, probably around the end of 1944. The status board (*background*) lists the three fighter squadrons of the 80th Fighter Group and three from the 33rd Fighter Group with their aircraft type and availability. *3A-36245, RG342FH, NARA*

SUPPORTING THE NCAC ADVANCE

the two fighter groups flew 3,733 patrol sorties over northern Burma.[10] Of particular concern was the need to ensure there were adequate patrols in the forward areas where the transports would be dropping supplies to the advancing troops. Remarkably the Japanese did not attempt interceptions of the vulnerable transports or encounter them on more than a few occasions.

Two 90th Fighter Squadron Thunderbolt pilots demonstrated the importance of these patrols when they encountered Japanese fighters attacking a group of 3rd Combat Cargo Group's C-47s on a supply-dropping mission near Bhamo. 1st Lt. Samuel Hammer and his wingman, 2nd Lt. Steadman Howarth Jr., were on patrol in the area, flying at 10,000 feet when they saw 12 Japanese fighters that they identified as Tojos attacking the transports some 5,000 feet below them. These were a formation of 20 Ki-43s from the *64th Hikōsentai*, which happened to have come across the transports and apparently other P-47s flying missions in the same area. Hammer dived down on a flight of four fighters attacking one of the C-47s, coming in on the leader and firing though his gunsight was inoperative. The lead Oscar pulled up in a climb, with Hammer following and continuing to fire. At the top of the climb the Oscar flipped over and dove into the ground. With two Oscars pursuing him, Hammer pulled up in a vertical reverse, but when the two Oscars tried to follow his maneuver, he saw them collide in midair and crash in the jungle below. Attacked again, Hammer pulled away once more. He then attacked another two Oscars below him, but these came in on his tail. Just then his engine exploded, forcing him to dive away and make an emergency landing at Bhamo landing ground. Howarth had followed Hammer down and found himself in a position behind one of the Japanese fighters going after Hammer. Closing in, Howarth fired as the Japanese fighter began a slight bank, hitting the fuselage and the cockpit area. The fighter went into a steep dive, with Howarth following. Howarth broke off his dive at 700 feet, with the Japanese aircraft diving vertically into the jungle below, but did not apparently see the airplane crash. The *64th Hikōsentai* lost three fighters in the encounter, probably two to Hammer and one to Howarth. Intriguingly, in their combat report both pilots insisted the fighters they encountered were Tojos, but mention the Japanese fighters using only their 20 mm cannon and the fact that on the deck the fighters could gain on the P-47s in level flight, even with the P-47 at war emergency power. This raises the possibility that Hammer and Howarth might have encountered not Tojos or Oscars, but one of the *50th Hikōsentai*'s newer Type 4 fighters, the formidable Frank.[11]

In the clash the 12th Combat Cargo Squadron lost a C-47 and its entire crew to the Japanese fighters, while the 10th Combat Cargo Squadron had another C-47 so badly damaged that after making an emergency landing the plane was a write-off. Four other C-47s received minor damage. 2nd Lt. Robert Severson and his crew of the damaged 10th Combat Cargo Squadron C-47 made a remarkable escape from the Japanese fighters due to the bravery of their radio operator, S/Sgt. James Troglia, as a 3rd Combat Cargo Group report related:

The crew of Sgt. Troglia's plane were not aware of the enemy action, until the rattle of machine gun fire tore through their loaded plane. The scream of a wounded food kicker, who had been in the open doorway preparing to drop the load of supplies, gave testimony that the Japs were on their tail.

The first attack by the enemy resulted in the death of one of the kickers, the wounding of another, Cpl. James Fry of Bedford, Oregon, and the wounding of Sgt. Troglia. Pilot Severson was unable to see the attackers from his position in the cockpit because they were on his tail, and immediately Sgt. Troglia, though hit in the first pass, took a position in the plexiglass astrodome at the top of the plane, facing the attacking Japs.

As bullets continued to plow through the unarmored plane Co-pilot DeVito crawled back to the rear of the plane to aid the injured kickers, but a slug tore through the plane and stopped him. . . . Ducking, dodging, rolling, banking, and other evasive maneuvers of the plane continued, all being done at the direction of Sgt. Troglia as he hung to the cockpit ceiling, his head precariously sticking into the glass dome in the top of the plane.

Bleeding profusely, Co-pilot DeVito yelled for the Radio Operator to look at his wound, but wisely Troglia stuck to his post, and called to his injured crew member, "I've got to stay here," knowing that if he left his post the entire crew would be lost. This proved a wise decision as there was still an enemy Zero on their tail continuing to make passes at the Combat Cargo plane. . . . Troglia's wound continued to bleed, but still he maintained his vigil, shouting directions to his young pilot.

Pilot Severson was then hit. . . . Troglia continued to be the "eyes" of the pilot as they weaved and bobbed in irregular patterns, refusing to be downed by almost a dozen passes of the Japanese fighter. The Zero's guns were finally exhausted of ammunition and he was forced to flee from the threat of American Thunderbolts.

Five of the crew of the transport were wounded, and the sixth killed, but through the brilliant efforts of Sgt. Troglia who out-maneuvered the Jap fighters, and Lt. Severson who skillfully handled the stick of the cargo carrier, the plane landed at an advanced air strip, riddled with countless bullet holes.[12]

Most of the Japanese air attacks on the Tenth Air Force's airfields came at dusk or during the night from small numbers of Type 99 Lily light bombers from the *8th Hikōsentai*. The first of these raids came on October 27, when four bombers raided Myitkyina, coming low to get under the radar and causing minor damage to three P-47s.[13] Just before dawn on November 4, a dozen *64th Hikōsentai* Ki-43s attacked the airfield at Myitkyina, strafing aircraft but apparently doing no damage.[14] The *8th Hikōsentai* went back to Myitkyina again on November 25, when two or three bombers dropped four 50 kg bombs, destroying a P-47 on the field and two trucks. Four days later, two Lily bombers dropped fragmentation bombs on the airfield at Warazup and Sahmaw, again doing little damage, while a third bomber apparently tried to find Myitkyina without success, dropping its bombs to the east. A month later, two Lily bombers attacked the airstrip at Bhamo without doing damage, apparently in the last Japanese air attack against the Tenth Air Force.[15]

Having no defense against night air attacks, the Tenth Air Force arranged for the 427th Night Fighter Squadron to be transferred from Italy to India with its Northrop P-61 night fighters. Arriving in mid-November, the squadron sent detachments to Myitkyina and China, beginning patrols toward the end of the month. On the night of November 25, fighter control scrambled one of the P-61s to intercept the Lily bombers attacking the field. The night fighter made contact with one of the Lilys for two minutes but could not close with the Japanese bomber.[16] During December 1944 and January 1945 the squadron flew regular night patrols over the Myitkyina and Bhamo area, but all interceptions turned out to be Allied aircraft.[17]

During fall 1944, the *5th Hikōshidan* became little more than a nuisance to the Tenth Air Force in the conduct of its operations,

The 427th Night Fighter Squadron arrived in India in November 1944 to provide night-fighter coverage over northern Burma after the Japanese began sending small numbers of bombers out at night to bomb Allied airfields. Although the 427th Squadron carried out a number of interceptions, they did not encounter any Japanese aircraft over Burma. *3A-33771, RG342FH, NARA*

The road bridge at Haipaw, between Mandalay and Lashio, just before a 490th Bomb Squadron B-25 went in to bomb the bridge from low level. By late 1944, the "Burma Bridge Busters"—the nickname the 490th Squadron had acquired—had become adept at destroying bridges with their "glip" bombing technique. *3A-37568a, RG342FH, NARA*

but one that could not be ignored or completely eliminated. The *5th Hikōshidan*'s need to conserve aircraft and its ability to operate from many widely dispersed airfields and landing grounds in Burma made it difficult for the Allied air forces to completely knock out Japanese airpower.[18] The dependence of the Allied armies on air supply and close air support made the counterair effort critical to the success of the land campaign, though this effort required a significant commitment of time and resources from the Tenth's two fighter groups. Referring to the Allied counterair effort as a whole, Air Chief Marshal Sir Keith Park, who replaced Peirse as commander of Air Command, Southeast Asia, said that Allied air dominance during the latter half of 1944 and into 1945 was "the result of hard work with small dividends upon the part of our fighter organization."[19] A measure of the success of the Tenth Air Force's counterair effort, and the relative impotence of the *5th Hikōshidan*, can be gained from a review of air supply and liaison sorties. Neither the C-47s delivering air cargo nor the L-1 and L-5 liaison planes evacuating wounded carried any armament and most often flew unescorted to the front lines, relying on fighter patrols to keep Japanese fighters away. From August 1944 to the end of January 1945, the Tenth Air Force's combat cargo and troop carrier squadrons flew 45,223 air supply sorties over northern Burma for the loss of only two C-47s.[20] From October 1944 to the end of January 1945 the liaison squadrons flew 30,993 sorties without a loss to enemy fighters.[21]

Supporting the Advance: Attacks on the Lines of Communications and Supplies

Destroying the Japanese lines of communications within Burma had been a primary objective of the Tenth Air Force from its beginning. This objective became even more important for the NCAC's planned advance. The goal of the Tenth Air Force was to weaken *33rd Army* and destroy the ability of its divisions to obstruct the Allied advance. There were two aspects to the Tenth Air Force's efforts: first, to restrict the flow of supplies to *33rd Army* by destroying key rail and road bridges and the means of moving supplies to the area by rail, road, or river; second, to destroy the supplies that did reach the area, or that were already present, through the destruction of supply dumps, Japanese buildings, artillery, and troop concentrations. The two aspects of this campaign had to be constant, concurrent, and relentless. To carry out the attacks on the line of communications and Japanese supplies, the Tenth had available the 490th Bomb Squadron and the 33rd and 80th Fighter Groups, with the ability to call on the 12th Bomb Group when needed. Around 50 percent of all Tenth Air Force operations went to attacks on the lines of communication and Japanese supplies.[22]

By this point the Japanese had developed numerous countermeasures to cope with the constant attacks on bridges, in addition to making rapid repairs. Knowing that the Allies relied on photoreconnaissance coverage of bridge targets, the Japanese developed camouflage to make serviceable bridges look damaged

1st Lt. Edmund Kitts releases his bombs in a low-level attack on the Haipaw road bridge. Four 500-pound bombs can be seen in the center of the photograph, going down directly onto the bridge as the B-25 passes overhead. *3A-37568b, RG342FH, NARA*

SUPPORTING THE NCAC ADVANCE

and unserviceable bridges look serviceable, to divert missions away from serviceable bridges. The Japanese would stretch canvas over a wooden framework to make it appear that a bridge was still in use. Another tactic was to remove wooden planking from a bridge during the day to give the impression it was out of service, replacing the planking at night. In some cases the Japanese built a removable pontoon section that fit the center section of a damaged bridge. The Japanese engineers would move the pontoon section downstream and keep it camouflaged during the day, moving it back at night to make the bridge serviceable. The Japanese became adept at quickly building bypass bridges—sometimes more than one—next to a damaged bridge. The movement of supplies took place almost exclusively at night to avoid Allied air attack. As a result, while the Japanese supply effort was often impeded, it could never be completely cut off for any long period of time.[23]

The Haipaw road bridge lies in ruins after the bomb run. Note the many bomb craters on both sides of the river from previous attacks. Despite the extent of the destruction, Japanese engineers became adept at making rapid repairs, requiring another attack to keep the bridge unserviceable. *3A-37568c, RG342FH, NARA*

The history of attacks on the Meza rail bridges during 1944 offers a good illustration of the challenge the Tenth Air Force faced in knocking out a part of the Japanese line-of-communications system:

Mar. 14: Trestle damaged
Mar. 27: East and west approaches damaged
Apr. 3: Approaches severed
Apr. 10 Main and first bypass bridge destroyed
Apr. 15: Main bridge out. 1st bypass serviceable.
June 6: Main bridge out. 1st bypass out.
June 11: 2nd bypass serviceable
July 8: Bypasses gone. Main bridge out.
Aug. 3: 9 B-25—Main and 2nd bypass damaged
Sept. 23: 6 B-25—Main and 2nd bypass severely damaged
Oct. 18: 3 B-25—Approaches and tracks damaged
Nov. 4: 4 P-47—East end of 2nd bypass destroyed. Ferry stage destroyed.
Nov. 12: 4 P-47—Main bridge destroyed
Nov. 14: 4 P-47—Ferry stage destroyed
Nov. 14: Main bridge and bypass out. Ferry out.
Nov. 16: 4 P-47—One hit between main and bypass bridges
Nov. 24: 4 P-47—Six 12-hour-delay fuse bombs in river between ferry landings. Bridge unserviceable.
Nov. 25: 6 B-25—77 fused to 6 to 36 hours delay in ferry area. Rail tracks appear to be well used.
Nov. 29: 7 P-47—Wooden ramp at ferry landing blown up
Dec. 8: Bridge unserviceable[24]

The Tenth Air Force adopted a standard procedure for bridge attacks:

1) Knock out the bridge.
2) Maintain continuous photo coverage of the area.
3) Knock out the bypass bridge when it is built.
4) Drop delayed-action bombs to discourage night-ferrying activity.[25]

Vertical photo coverage did not always reveal Japanese attempts to conceal repairs or deceptive camouflage; coverage of bridge targets had to include oblique photos. To get this coverage and photographs of damage to other targets, the Tenth Air Force arranged for the 20th Tactical Reconnaissance Squadron to move to Myitkyina in November 1944 to carry out photoreconnaissance over northern Burma. During November and December, the squadron flew 544 photoreconnaissance sorties in support of the NCAC forces.[26] It would have been impossible for the Tenth Air Force to keep every bridge knocked out, so Tenth Air Force intelligence identified a number of key bridges that were to be the focus of the bridge-bombing effort. In addition to bridges within the area of the advance, the Tenth created three lines of interdiction that were 50, 100, and 150 miles south of the Katha-Bhamo line, corresponding to the main Japanese lines of rail and road communication to northern Burma. Intelligence identified 29 targets on the primary line of interdiction, 18 targets on the secondary line, and 10 targets on the farthest tertiary line. The objective then became to keep all 49 of these targets—bridges and ferry points—unserviceable or under constant harassment, thereby keeping at least some segment of these main lines of communication broken at all times.[27]

From the beginning of August to the middle of October, when the NCAC forces began their advance, the Tenth Air Force undertook a "softening up" campaign—despite the monsoon weather—to knock out bridges and destroy Japanese supplies before the advance began in the area of a rough triangle stretching from Myitkyina to Katha to Bhamo. On August 1, the 490th Bomb Squadron went back to attacking bridges after a hiatus of 72 days transporting ammunition to Imphal and providing support to the forces at Myitkyina. During two days of operations (August 1 and 3) the squadron destroyed or rendered unserviceable ten bridges and damaged an additional four, using its tactics of low-level "glip" bombing with 1,000-pound bombs. Bridge attacks during the rest of the month contributed another six bridges destroyed, with several more damaged and made unserviceable. Although the monsoon weather during September caused more missions to be aborted, the attacks on bridges continued. By the end of the month, the 490th Squadron had brought its total of destroyed bridges to 76, with a further 28 rendered unserviceable. Having encountered more than normal antiaircraft fire in attacks on three bridges on September 11, which caused the loss of one aircraft, the squadron tried out a new tactic to deal with bridges where antiaircraft fire made low-level attacks more dangerous. This

Two 500-pound bombs from a 490th Bomb Squadron B-25 about to land on a wooden bypass bridge the Japanese built near Lashio. The bombs can just be seen falling toward the bridge on the lower right. Previous attacks have knocked out the main bridge on the left. *3A-37593, RG342FH, NARA*

This veteran 490th Bomb Squadron B-25H has 165 mission markings painted below the cockpit and was responsible for destroying 20 bridges. The 75 mm cannon on the B-25H proved valuable in attacks on large buildings in Japanese-held towns. When there was little risk of antiaircraft fire, the B-25s would drop down to strafe a town after bombing to inflict further damage. *Author's collection*

involved sending in flights of bombers at medium level to saturate the antiaircraft positions with 100-pound bombs before the low-level bombers went in to hit the bridge. The squadron went after the bridge at Hsenwi with these tactics on September 30. Four B-25s went in at 4,000 feet to drop 72 100-pound bombs on the antiaircraft positions around the bridge, then came back to strafe these positions at low level. Eight aircraft bombed the bridge in low-level attacks, doing extensive damage, but the surviving antiaircraft guns damaged four airplanes, one of which had to land at Myitkyina on the return, where it was declared unsafe to fly.[28]

Most of the squadron's missions during August and September went toward attacks on Japanese-held towns and villages, storage areas, headquarters buildings, and troop concentrations. Rarely encountering heavy antiaircraft fire, the B-25s could go in at low level, often bombing from around 2,000 feet. As the squadron had done at Myitkyina, flights of nine or twelve B-25s would saturate the designated target area with up to 216 100-pound bombs. From these low altitudes, the results were most often deemed excellent. For the squadron's 300th mission, on September 8, nine B-25s bombed Katha with 144 100-pound bombs and 1,224 4-pound incendiary bombs. On some targets the bombers would come back to strafe the area with .50-caliber machine guns or 75 mm cannon. In an attack on the Chinese town of Chefang—the squadron's first bombing mission to China—several B-25s carried rocket projectiles for the first time, but the pilots found these to be inaccurate if launched more than 600 yards from a target. The squadron employed rockets on several more missions during the month, with mixed results. In another new tactic, on two missions the B-25s went in to bomb a town at very low level, making individual attacks from 300 to 400 feet with 500-pound bombs. Several times during the month, the Tenth Air Force called on the 12th Bomb Group for support. The 12th sent out several squadrons to bomb Indaw, Katha, and Bhamo, and several towns in China on the Salween front holding supplies for the *56th Division*.[29]

The fighter squadrons contributed their share to the softening-up campaign in addition to their other duties. Until the 33rd Fighter Group arrived in September and began flying missions toward the end of the month, the 80th Fighter Group carried out all the fighter missions against lines of communications and supply targets. The 80th Group began bombing bridges in August, the P-47s dive-bombing

The 80th Fighter Group remained heavily involved in attacks on Japanese lines-of-communication targets and Japanese-held towns, and providing close air support for advancing American, British, and Chinese troops. These 80th Fighter Group pilots stand next to a suitably marked 325-pound depth charge in December 1944. The Thunderbolt squadrons used depth charges against Japanese troop concentrations in jungle-covered areas and to blow apart lightly built wooden buildings in Japanese-held towns. *3A-34904, RG342FH, NARA*

SUPPORTING THE NCAC ADVANCE

their targets with 250- and 500-pound bombs, releasing the bombs from around 2,000 feet above the target. This first month the group's squadrons destroyed one bridge completely and left four unserviceable. During September the record improved, with the squadrons destroying three bridges and leaving two unserviceable. The fighters went after the means of transporting supplies as well as the bridges the supplies moved over. While the monsoon weather limited missions on some days, particularly in September, the 80th Group's squadrons carried out regular road and river sweeps, usually in flights of four P-47s. Sometimes these flights would draw a blank and would end up strafing bashas or warehouses in towns and villages along their route, but they often found small numbers of trucks on the roads that they strafed and left burning. These were not particularly lucrative missions, with claims for only one or two trucks, but the cumulative effect was important, since every truck destroyed was one that the Japanese could not replace. In sweeps of sections of the Irrawaddy and other rivers, the fighters strafed rivercraft and rafts the Japanese used to transport supplies. A few missions saw the fighters go to the larger railroad junctions in the area to search for rolling stock. A particularly profitable pair of railroad sweeps on August 6 saw a flight of six P-47s destroy 36 railroad cars on the railroad line from Shwebo to Indaw, while another flight found and strafed 50 rolling stock at the Naba railroad station, leaving a number burning.[30]

The majority of fighter missions during this period were against Japanese-held towns and villages where the Japanese had stores of supplies. To identify potential targets, Tenth Air Force A-2 intelligence staff studied the routes the Japanese used to supply their forward divisions, pored over photoreconnaissance photographs from the 9th Photo Reconnaissance Squadron and the 20th Tactical Reconnaissance Squadron, and received intelligence from sources behind Japanese lines, often the local Kachin guerrillas working with the British Force 136 and the American OSS Detachment 101. This combined intelligence helped identify the locations of enemy supply dumps, which formed the basis for Tenth Air Force A-3 operations staff to assign bombing and strafing missions to the squadrons. During August and September, when weather permitted, the 80th Group's squadrons would send out several flights of P-47s a day to attack a specific section in a particular town or village. The Thunderbolts would drop 250-or 500-pound bombs on their targets, then return to strafe, with the often-satisfying result of large columns

The 20th Tactical Reconnaissance Squadron flew constantly over northern Burma, searching for Japanese installations and troop locations for the fighter squadrons and the medium bombers to attack. The squadron continued to fly the P-40N modified to carry a camera in the rear fuselage. The squadron's P-40s had a white or all-metal propeller spinner as a recognition marking. *Peter M. Bowers Collection, MoF*

of black or white smoke rising up in the air. The Japanese resorted to dispersing their supplies to smaller villages, but with good intelligence the Tenth Air Force soon identified these locations and sent fighters after them. With limited transport available as strafing attacks claimed more motor vehicles, the dispersion and later collection of supplies became more difficult. The cumulative effect of these constant attacks was debilitating to the Japanese soldier. Allied units patrolling in the weeks before the advance came across Japanese soldiers who were obviously malnourished, poorly supplied, and suffering from a lack of medical care.[31]

When the Allied advance began on 15 October 1944, the attacks on the Japanese lines of communication and on Japanese supplies continued without letup. The two fighter groups concentrated on bridges south of the Railway Corridor ahead of the 36th Division's advance. The fighters normally went after the smaller road and rail bridges, particularly of wooden construction, where 250- and 500-pound bombs had a reasonable chance of knocking out a bridge. By the end of the month the fighters had knocked out 22 bridges and left others unserviceable, leaving Japanese communications in the area paralyzed. The 33rd Group destroyed six bridges during the latter half of the month. The 80th Fighter Group had even better

The 20th Tactical Reconnaissance Squadron's P-40s carried out their own attacks against the Japanese in addition to their tactical reconnaissance duties. The squadron's pilots found these Japanese trucks on the road to Bhamo in late 1944 and left three of them burning. *3A-36918, RG342FH, NARA*

The 90th Fighter Squadron worked out its own technique of bombing bridges at low level. This was labeled "buzz bombing," and the squadron started using the technique in October 1944 to good effect. Here is a railroad bridge the squadron knocked out near Naba in October 1944. *SQ-FI-90-HI, AFHRA*

luck, trying out a new technique the 90th Fighter Squadron had worked out after a frustrating experience with the standard dive-bombing method of attacking bridges. The bridge targets they were after were often less than 100 feet long and around 10 feet wide. Instead of dive-bombing a bridge—coming down in a dive at 400 mph and releasing the bombs at around 2,000 feet, with a greater chance of error because of the altitude of bomb release—the squadron developed a glide-bombing technique the pilots dubbed "buzz bombing." Who first suggested the idea wasn't recorded. The P-47s would approach a bridge at an angle of 30 degrees and a speed of 275 mph, releasing their bombs at approximately 200 feet above the bridge and aiming for the bridge supports, since their destruction caused longer-lasting damage. The squadron used 250- and 500-pound bombs in these attacks, with four-to-five-second-delay fuses and spikes to keep the bombs from skipping over the bridge. The technique was not applicable to all bridge targets, since the topography around the bridge had to be such that the bridge was clearly visible, and trees and hills around a bridge increased the risk of collision. And as the commander of the 80th Fighter Group pointed out, "it cannot be overemphasized that aircraft while making this type of attack are, in reality, 'sitting ducks' for ground fire."[32]

The 90th Squadron first tried out this new technique on October 8, with one pilot knocking out the southern span of a railroad bridge, rendering it unserviceable. The squadron tried again the next day, with the pilots returning enthusiastic about the new method, having completely destroyed one bridge with four direct hits and severely damaging another. Over the rest of the month, the squadron knocked out more bridges, destroying eight of thirteen bridges with the buzz-bombing technique and getting 11 direct hits—a considerably better record of achievement than the squadron had achieved through dive-bombing. For a mission on October 21, two P-47s were stripped of all their guns and ammunition to carry a 1,000-pound bomb under each wing. The pilots tried to release both bombs simultaneously, but with only a manual and not an electrical release mechanism, only one bomb could be dropped at a time, resulting in a dangerous turn in the direction of the wing that still had a bomb attached. Although the damage a 1,000-pound bomb could do to a bridge was considerable, the squadron wisely decided to wait for electrical release mechanisms before trying this again. Not to be outdone, the 88th Squadron knocked out four bridges on October 31 by using conventional dive-bombing tactics.[33]

November brought more bridge attacks, with the two fighter groups knocking out another 19 bridges and making six more unserviceable. The record for December was even better, with 28 bridges destroyed and 24 severely damaged. In almost all cases the fighters used 500-pound bombs to attack the bridge targets, but the squadrons experimented with different types of armament. There were several attacks on lighter wooden bridges with 75-gallon napalm tanks, but the results were less than expected. Another experiment used 1,100-pound depth charges against another smaller wooden bridge, with spectacular results, as the explosion killed large numbers of Japanese soldiers who unfortunately happened to be nearby, but the feeling again was that use of this weight of depth charge wasn't warranted. For the remainder of the year, low-level

SUPPORTING THE NCAC ADVANCE

buzz bombing became the preferred tactic against bridges except where terrain or the threat of antiaircraft fire dictated a dive-bombing attack. During January there were fewer bridge missions, since the Allied advance had limited the number of bridge targets left in the area. As the advance continued, range for the fighters became an issue. During October and November the Tenth Air Force moved a number of squadrons closer to the front. Davidson moved his Tenth Air Force headquarters to Myitkyina. The 80th Fighter Group had been based in Burma for several months, with the 88th Fighter Squadron at Shingbwiyang, the 89th Fighter Squadron at Myitkyina south airfield, and the 90th Fighter Squadron operating out of Tingkawk Sakan. The 33rd Fighter Group kept the 58th and 59th Fighter Squadrons in the Dinjan area but moved the 60th Fighter Squadron to Sahmaw in Burma. Because the 60th Squadron was closer, it took on most of the bridge missions. The 490th Bomb Squadron also moved in November to the air base at Moran.[34]

The 490th Bomb Squadron, by now well known as the "Burma Bridge Busters," kept up its own attacks on bridges. With their longer range, the B-25s worked on the bridges along the old Burma Road farther to the south. During the month, the squadron knocked out 15 bridges and damaged seven more. The squadron lost a B-25H on a bridge-busting mission on October 27 to bomb the road bypass bridge at Lashio, in an example of the dangers of this form of attack. 1st Lt. Herbert Schwarz was an eyewitness to the incident:

While circling the target area at Lashio I watched a B-25 as it made its bomb run on the bridge. A few seconds later I saw a second airplane coming in on a run on the same bridge, much too soon. The second airplane came in very low and flat. Just as he got to the bridge, the bombs of the first plane exploded and he went right through the explosions. The plane was obscured from vision for a fraction of a second.

When the plane emerged it seemed to be wallowing through the air, gaining altitude as it went. Then the plane rolled over on its back and went straight into the ground, about 150 yards from the bridge, exploding on impact and burning.[35]

The crash killed 1st Lt. Willard Johnson and his crew of four.

The squadron's great day came on November 8, when the 490th destroyed its hundredth bridge. Capt. Walter Allen led eight planes to attack the bridge at Bawgyo, which the squadron had attacked on several previous missions without success. The B-25s dropped 28 1,000-pound bombs, destroying the center span of the bridge, the southern approach, and one of the concrete piers supporting the bridge. On November 25 the squadron destroyed two main bridges and a bypass bridge and damaged two more bypass bridges, on this occasion dropping 216 100-pound bombs from 300 feet. During the month, the 490th destroyed 15 bridges, bringing their total to 106, while damaging a further four. December was a record month, with 25 bridges destroyed in total, and a remarkable eight destroyed in one day by nine aircraft. In November, Army Air Force Chief of Staff Lt. Gen. Barney Giles had written to Davidson, saying:

Your "Burma Bridge Busters" will soon run out of their favorite targets at the rate they are going. I don't believe even our engineers could cope with thirteen completely destroyed in two weeks, not to mention those which must have been seriously damaged.[36]

By the end of the year the squadron had destroyed 132 bridges in total. For its development of new techniques for bridge bombing,

Maj. Gen. Davidson awards the Air Medal and the Distinguished Flying Cross to now Lt. Col. Robert Erdin, who rose to command the 490th Bomb Squadron. While a captain and squadron operations officer, Erdin discovered the 490th Squadron's successful bridge-bombing technique by accident. *3A-34042, RG342FH, NARA*

and for the destruction of 56 bridges between January and May 1944, the Army Air Force awarded the 490th Bomb Squadron the Distinguished Unit Citation on 28 December 1944. January was something of an anticlimax, with only nine bridges destroyed.[37]

With so many bridges knocked out, the Tenth Air Force made sure that the fighters and the medium bombers carried out regular road and rail sweeps. On a mission on October 27, the 33rd Fighter Group's squadrons did a sweep of the railroad line in the Railway Corridor between Naba and Mawlu, where they set fire to 55 railroad cars. A few days earlier the 490th Bomb Squadron attacked several railroad yards at low level with 500-pound bombs and 75 mm cannon, destroying and damaging several locomotives, although one airplane was seen to crash into a hillside after the mission. The squadron carried out a similar series of missions in mid-November, damaging a number of locomotives, destroying rolling stock, and tearing up the tracks at several railroad stations. Knowing that the Japanese now traveled almost exclusively by night, at the end of November, when the moon was full, the 490th Squadron sent a detachment of four bombers to Myitkyina to search for targets of opportunity at night along the old Burma Road. Two B-25s went out each night from November 27 to December 6, with excellent results. The bombers found and strafed several motor vehicle convoys and found several trains in stations, damaging locomotives and rolling stock. This success prompted the squadron to repeat the night sweeps during the next period of moonlight at the end of December and into early January, and at the end of January. The bombers found truck convoys on nearly every night, which they hit with fragmentation bombs and strafing.[38]

Throughout the last months of 1944 and into 1945, the attacks on Japanese supplies, occupied towns, and troop concentrations also continued without letup. In carrying out the air offensive in support of NCAC, the Tenth Air Force had to balance sometimes conflicting requirements: "[T]he increased opposition encountered by the troops, the necessity for attacking reported troop concentrations quickly and the desirability of maintaining the enemy's L of C [lines of communications] in a state of disorganization. Every attempt was made to maintain a balanced mission schedule each day—with flexibility retained so that intelligence requiring immediate attack might be favored in preference to a mission already planned."[39] With regard to maintaining a balanced offensive, here were the missions for 14 November 1944:

Three missions to provide close air support to 36th Division. Seven supply dumps and two troop concentrations were attacked.

One road bridge was bombed and an offensive road sweep run in the Shwebo area.

There was an offensive reconnaissance of the Shwebo and Onbauk airfields.[40]

By this point the local Burmese had left their towns and villages to the Japanese and fled into the nearby hills to avoid air attacks. This was fortunate, since the fighter squadrons found new ways of devastating a Japanese-occupied village. In late October the 90th Fighter Squadron tried using a mix of depth charges, incendiary bombs, and napalm to destroy a large section of a town south of Indaw. The P-47s carrying the depth charges went in first to blow apart the buildings in the town. Once the buildings were down, the incendiary bombs set them on fire. The 60th Fighter Squadron carried out a similar attack on the town of Male, on the Irrawaddy River north of Mandalay, on 7 December 1944—the fourth anniversary of the attack on Pearl Harbor. In the course of the day, the 60th Squadron sent out 63 P-47s on nine missions to the town, dropping 76 Mk 17 325-pound depth charges, 48 M-43/M-64 500-pound bombs, magnesium thermite bombs, two 500-pound napalm bombs, and more than 35,000 rounds of .50 caliber. Not surprisingly, the Japanese often abandoned towns and villages by day to seek shelter in the surrounding forests, returning only at night to work on getting supplies through and repairing the damage from air attacks. From October to the end of December, the fighter squadrons carried out 502 attacks on Japanese supply points and troop concentrations. All of these attacks on Japanese lines of communications and Japanese supplies had one end: to aid the advance of the Allied armies.[41]

The 90th Fighter Squadron carried out a devastating attack on the town of Indaw, using depth charges and incendiary bombs to destroy a large section of the town. Here a crew loads an oil-and-gas bomb containing 55 gallons of oil and 5 gallons of 100 octane gasoline onto a P-47 at Myitkyina in October 1944. *3A-33912, RG342FH, NARA*

Chinese troops advancing in the jungle. The Chinese divisions often had a mix of American and British equipment. The soldier on the ground (*center*) is wearing an American helmet and firing a Thompson submachine gun, while the soldier behind him has a British-style helmet and a Bren light machine gun. *Box 160, China–Armed Forces–Burma, Folder N-1, RG208AA, NARA*

Supporting the Advance: Providing Close Air Support

The Allied advance began on 15 October 1944, with the British 36th Division on the right flank moving down the Railway Corridor, the Chinese 22nd Division in the center moving south toward the Irrawaddy River near Shwegu, and the Chinese 38th Division on the left flank following the road to Bhamo. This was a war of movement that called for a different type of close air support than had been employed in the siege of Myitkyina, where there had been direct contact between the ground commanders and the pilots flying overhead.[42] While the problems were different, the organization of close air support in the war of movement built on the lessons learned in the advance down the Hukawng Valley and during the battle for Myitkyina. The key problem was the need "to organize a system whereby controlled and coordinated air attacks could immediately be delivered when and where needed on a constantly moving front."[43] The ground forces normally had two types of requests for close air support: immediate battlefield strikes for or during an attack on Japanese positions, and preplanned missions in preparation for an attack or where intelligence had located Japanese troop or artillery positions, supplies, or troop concentrations.[44] Getting these requests from the ground forces through to the Tenth Air Force was the challenge.

Experience had demonstrated that it was critical to have a knowledgeable air officer attached to the ground unit who could provide an initial screening of requests for air support. To provide this, the Tenth Air Force set up five Joint Operations Air Parties with personnel drawn from the 1st Tactical Air Communications Squadron. The teams consisted of one or two officers with knowledge of fighter-bomber operations—sometimes pilots drawn from the fighter squadrons—with six to eight enlisted men to operate the radios the teams required. Each team had an SCR-284 radio for air–ground communications and an SCR-177 or 188 radio for communicating with the Tenth Air Force. When the Tenth Air Force fighters converted to VHF radio, the Joint Operations teams added this to their standard equipment. All the radios went with the teams

SUPPORTING THE NCAC ADVANCE

by pack mule or Jeep where roads were passable. Working with the ground commander, the Joint Operations Air Party had the responsibility of evaluating all requests for close air support and deciding whether the targets were suitable, the number of aircraft needed, the appropriate types of bombs to use on the target, and the time of the attack. The Joint Operations parties would pass these requests on to Tenth Air Force for approval. After a further evaluation and a determination of the priority of the request, the Tenth Air Force passed the requests and target information to the fighter groups, who would assign the specific mission to one of the squadrons. Confirmation of the request went back to the Joint Operations parties, who would alert the ground commander.[45]

A critical aspect of close air support was the ability to direct the airstrike onto the target, particularly when bombing or strafing in close proximity to Allied troops. The practice of using photomosaics both for the ground commanders and the fighter squadrons continued. The Tenth Air Force arranged for the 9th Photographic Reconnaissance Squadron to send a detachment of F-5 Lighting photoreconnaissance airplanes to the airfield at Tingkawk Sakan in August, moving the detachment to Myitkyina at the end of November. The 9th Squadron, together with the 20th Tactical Reconnaissance Squadron, which

The Tenth Air Force's Thunderbolt squadrons used a wide variety of armament in their attacks on Japanese installations and troop positions. This 80th Fighter Group P-47D carries what appear to be two 500-pound bombs with extended fuses used to detonate the bombs when they hit the ground to expand the blast radius. Peter M. Bowers Collection, MoF

The 9th Photo Reconnaissance Squadron sent a detachment of F-5Es to Tingkawk Sakan to support the Northern Combat Area Command in northern Burma. The reconnaissance pilots provided regular photo coverage of the Japanese airfields for signs of any activity. GP-80-SU-PH, AFHRA

had moved its P-40Ns to Myitkyina from Tingkawk Sakan at the end of October, flew daily reconnaissance missions over northern Burma to keep the mosaics up to date. Knowing the objectives of the ground forces and their probable routes to these objectives, the Tenth Air Force could direct the photoreconnaissance squadrons to the appropriate areas where the ground units and the fighter squadrons would need photographic coverage. As at Myitkyina, the photomosaics had a grid system overlay that provided references for the air officer on the ground to communicate instructions to the pilots in the air, who carried a copy of the appropriate photomosaic with them in the cockpit and who had used the photomosaics in their briefings before the mission. When a flight of fighters arrived overhead, the air party officer would work with the flight leader to ensure he had correctly identified the target from the air, sometimes identifying the target with smoke shells, and then give the OK to begin bombing. Planes bombed individually, with the air party officer giving corrections as needed.[46]

Under some conditions the air party officer could not directly observe the target due to terrain or the tactical situation, making it difficult to direct the fighters onto the designated target. This was the case when the 36th Division was assaulting the town of Pinwe and the 38th Division faced stiff Japanese opposition around Bhamo. In each case the Tenth Air Force assigned an L-5 and pilot to the Joint Operations teams to carry one of the air party officers near to the target for direct observation. The L-5s could not, at least initially, carry the VHF radio required for direct radio communication with the fighters, so they had to contact the other air party officer on the ground, give him corrections, and have him pass these on to the fighters. Still, the use of L-5s helped identify and designate targets and allowed for rapid transmission of enemy movements or new potential targets, as the following description of a close-air-support mission illustrates.[47]

The following provides an example of the close-air-support process, drawn from an actual mission in support of Chinese forces attacking a Japanese bunker position near Bhamo in December 1944. The Joint Operations Air Party officer, radio call sign BANKNOTE, had requested a flight of four P-47s carrying 500-pound bombs to

In contrast, this 88th Fighter Squadron P-47D carries two smaller 250-pound bombs. The Thunderbolt flights would sometimes carry a mix of different weights of bombs, depending on the nature of the target to be attacked. Author's collection

THE TENTH AIR FORCE IN WORLD WAR II

arrive over the target at 0900. The pilots carried a grid-lined mosaic photo of the target area, numbered 1329 for reference. The flight arrived on time, and the following conversation took place:

"Hello, Banknote, this is Ring Up Green. Over."
"Hello, Ring Up Green, this is Banknote. Do you have photo 1329? Over."
"Roger, Banknote. I have 1329. Over."
"Ring Up Green, your target is a bunker position at coordinates G3-15. What do you see? Over.'
"Roger, Banknote, standby."
"Banknote from Ring Up Green. I cannot see the bunker position. All I see is a clump of trees about 100 yards south, 20 yards east of the road junction. At that road junction there is a small building standing. Over."
"Roger, Ring Up Green. The bunker position is underneath the east edge of the northernmost tree in the clump of trees you just described to me. Do you see it now? Over."
"Hello, Banknote; no, I cannot see but I know where it is. Over."
"Roger, Ring Up Green. You are to make your bombing run from south to north. Let me know when you are ready. Over."
"Roger, Banknote. Ring Up Green No. 2, do you have the target?"
"Roger, I have it. No. 2 out."
"Do you have it, No. 3?"
"That's roger. No. 3 out."
"No. 4?"
"Roger, No. 4 out."
"Hello, Banknote, this is Ring Up Green. I am ready to bomb. Over."
"Roger, Ring Up Green; you are clear to go."

Whereupon the flight leader dove at the target and released a bomb. In the meantime the other officer in the air party was observing from a liaison plane. He also had contact with Banknote. Upon seeing the first bomb burst short of the bunker position, he called Banknote and reported that the bomb burst 15 yards to the south. Banknote acknowledged and then called:

"Hello, Ring Up Green No. 2. That bomb fell 15 yards south of the target. Over."
"Roger, Banknote."

The No. 2 airplane then went in to bomb, and his bombs were north of the target. This information was given to No. 3 and 4 planes in the same manner as before, and they laid their bombs squarely on the target. Between the bombs of the second and third planes in the flight, the observer in the liaison plane saw Jap troops running from an area nearby to seek cover in trenches. He called this information immediately to Banknote, and Banknote in turn directed the planes to strafe that trench upon completion of their bombing. Following the air attacks, the Chinese troops assaulted the bunker position, and Banknote directed the fighters on several dry runs (fake strafing passes) to keep the enemy under cover.[48]

This attack was a success, the Chinese commander later sending a message of congratulations to the fighter squadron noting how his troops had seen the arms and legs of Japanese soldiers flying up in the air with other debris. Attacks like this went on day after day, and sometimes several times during a single day, for months. Here

One reason for the excellent close air support the 80th Fighter Group provided Allied troops was the accumulated experience of many of its pilots. Each one of the eight pilots in this photograph had completed 200 combat missions. This high level of experience enabled the pilots to bomb accurately within close range of Allied troops. *GP-80-SU-PH, AFHRA*

are the missions the 80th Fighter Group flew on a typical day in December 1944, probably including the mission described above:

88th Fighter Squadron
a 4 P–47s Bhamo ground support, 8 × 500 lb., 4–5 sec. delay fuse, 2,900 rounds .50 cal.
b 4 P–47s Bhamo ground support, 8 × 500 lb., 4–5 sec. delay fuse, 2,650 rounds .50 cal.
c 4 P–47s Bhamo ground support, 8 × 500 lb., 4–5 sec. delay fuse, 2,700 rounds .50 cal.
d 4 P–47s Bhamo ground support, 8 × 500 lb., 4–5 sec. delay fuse, 2,500 rounds .50 cal.
e 4 P–47s Bhamo ground support, 8 × 500 lb., 4–5 sec. delay fuse, 1,400 rounds .50 cal.
f 4 P–47s Bhamo ground support, 8 × 500 lb., 4–5 sec. delay fuse, 2,300 rounds .50 cal.
g 4 P–47s Bhamo ground support, 8 × 500 lb., 4–5 sec. delay fuse, 1,300 rounds .50 cal.
h 3 P–47s Namhkai bypassbridge, 6 × 500 lb., instantaneous fuse.
i 4 P–47s Bhamo ground support, 8 × 500 lb., 4–5 sec. delay fuse.

89th Fighter Squadron
j 3 P–47s Bhamo ground support, 6 × 500 lb., inst. fuse, 1,500 rounds, .50 cal.
k 4 P–47s escort one B–24.
l 4 P–47s Namhkai bypassbridge, 8 × 500 lb., instantaneous fuse.

90th Fighter Squadron
m 4 P–47s bomb and strafe Namti, 8 × 500 lb., instantaneous fuse, 2,880 .50 cal.
n 4 P–47s bomb and strafe Nawmhkam, 8 × 500 lb., instantaneous fuse.
o 8 P–47s bomb and strafe Namti, 8 × 500 lb., instantaneous fuse, 4 × 500 lb., 8–11 sec. delay fuse, 4 gas and rubber clusters, 4,540 rounds .50 cal.[49]

SUPPORTING THE NCAC ADVANCE

The five Joint Operations Air Parties worked with the following divisions:

36th British Division from August 1944 through January 1945.
38th Chinese Division from late October to mid-December 1944.
30th Chinese Division from mid-December 1944 through January 1945.
22nd Chinese Division from mid-November to mid-December 1944.
50th Chinese Division from mid-December 1944 through January 1945.
Mars Task Force from mid-November through January 1945.[50]

From experience, the Tenth Air Force determined that at least five conditions were necessary for effective close air support:

a Complete air superiority
b Proven bombing accuracy of the pilots
c Thorough orientation of the pilots with the target area
d Reliable communications facilities air to ground and point to point from the air party to the Air Force headquarters
e Gridded aerial photographs prepared in advance
f Air party officers who have good knowledge of fighter-bomber operations and who have microphone experience sufficient to be able to talk the pilots' language[51]

The British 36th Division had begun its advance on October 16, pushing down the Railway Corridor to capture Mawlu on October 31. After waiting for the Chinese 50th Division to advance to protect its flanks, the 36th Division resumed its forward march in November, only to run into strong Japanese resistance around the town of Pinwe. When the 36th Division requested air support, the 80th Fighter Group began five days of close-support missions in and around Pinwe, sending out flights of four P-47s to bomb and strafe targets, with the Joint Operations Air Parties giving directions. On one of the days, an L-5 flew above to give corrections and results. On these missions the pilots often bombed and strafed wooded areas, with little indication of the results. Comments from the air officer on the ground were great for pilot morale. After a flight from the 88th Fighter Squadron got its bombs right on the target, the observer in the L-5 radioed, "Smack in there!" While the 80th Group provided most of the close air support, the 33rd Fighter Group carried out extensive railroad and road sweeps along the Railway Corridor, blasting supply dumps, rolling stock, and stores areas around Indaw and beyond. Gen. Festing launched an attack on Pinwe on November 22 with continued close air support from the 80th Fighter Group. The Japanese abandoned Pinwe on November 29, withdrawing farther south with the 36th Division in pursuit. The division occupied Indaw and Katha between December 9 and 13. On December 16 the division made contact with the 19th Indian Division from the 14th Army—advancing from the west—creating a link between 14th Army and the NCAC. Sultan ordered Festing to continue his advance south, clearing the area east of the Irrawaddy River, with the objective of taking the town of Mogok.[52]

The 80th Group's squadrons provided air support to the 36th Division around Pinwe for 18 days. The Joint Operations Air Party officers coordinated 250 close-air-support sorties, operating with two of the division's brigades. Instead of operating from the brigade headquarters, as was normally the case, the air party officers volunteered to move closer to the Japanese lines to provide more-accurate direction to the fighters, often coming under Japanese fire. When one of the British brigade commanders saw the damage the fighters had inflicted at Pinwe after his troops occupied the town, he said the battle for Pinwe was "definitely an air victory."[53]

The other call for close air support came from the Chinese 38th Division, advancing toward Bhamo on the left flank. The 38th Division had advanced to Myothit by October 28 and reached the plain around Bhamo, which the Japanese had heavily fortified, on November 10. Two Chinese regiments bypassed the town and encircled the Japanese defenders. The Chinese 30th Division moved up to positions on the Bhamo-Namhkam road to block any Japanese attempt to relieve the troops in Bhamo. Having covered the 36th Division at Pinwe, the 80th Fighter Group shifted its attention to the area around Bhamo and attacks on the town itself but continued to provide support to the 36th Division when needed. In and around Bhamo, the fighter squadrons hit bunkers, trenches, and artillery positions, using combinations of 500-pound bombs and 325-pound depth charges with repeated strafing. During November the 80th Group flew 676 missions, including 18 missions on November 28, setting several group records. The group exceeded this record on December 2, flying 20 missions that day. The 33rd Group continued to provide support by shifting its road and rail sweeps and attacks on Japanese supplies to areas supporting Japanese units around Bhamo. The 60th Fighter Squadron joined the 80th Group squadrons providing close air support around Bhamo. Between 18 November and 11 December 1944 the Joint Operations Air Party team directed 490 close-support sorties, again volunteering to move closer to the front lines to better direct the airstrikes. In one case the air party officers had the fighters bomb Japanese positions that were only 35 yards from the Chinese forward troops, enabling the Chinese to occupy the positions immediately after the bombing. The Japanese launched a fierce counterattack against the 30th Division in an attempt to support the

Troops from the British 36th Division advancing toward the town of Pinle in October 1944. The 36th Division covered the right flank of the NCAC's advance into northern Burma. The division received supplies from Tenth Air Force transport planes, and close air support from the Tenth Air Force's fighter squadrons. SC-263341, RG111, NARA

The pilot of this P-47D from an unknown Thunderbolt squadron had completed 59 missions when this photograph was taken. In some of the fighter squadrons the "experienced" pilots were considered to be those with more than 100 missions. *Author's collection*

On 12 October 1944, 1st Lt. Joseph, from the 90th Fighter Squadron, had just begun his bomb run on a bridge near Naba when he had a midair collision with a P-40N from the 20th Tactical Reconnaissance Squadron. Neither pilot had seen the other. The crash tore off Joseph's left aileron and damaged his left flap and left horizontal stabilizer. Joseph flew his crippled P-47 back to base, but the P-40 went down in flames, killing Maj. Angus Lytch, the 20th Squadron's operations officer. By a remarkable coincidence, Lytch was from the same town, attended the same college, and was at the same flight school as the 90th Fighter Squadron's operations officer. The two men had been scheduled to return to the United States the next day. *SQ-FI-90-HI, AFHRA*

Bhamo garrison's breakout from the town, which took place on the night of December 14.[54]

In the center of the advance, the 22nd Division reached the Irrawaddy River on November 3 and crossed the river in rubber boats the C-47s had air-dropped to the troops. By the end of November the division had cut the track running from Bhamo to Si-U and occupied Si-U town. At this juncture, Chiang Kai-shek decided to withdraw two of the Chinese divisions from Burma to help repel a Japanese attack in Kweichow Province that seemed to threaten an advance on Kunming—the terminus for the Hump route—and possibly Chungking. Wedemeyer agreed, since the successful Japanese *ICHI-GO* offensive had shattered the effectiveness of the Chinese armies in eastern China, leaving only poor-quality divisions available for the defense of Kunming. Wedemeyer asked SEAC for the 22nd and 38th Chinese Divisions to be transferred to China. He also wanted the India-Burma theater to send two combat cargo groups to China. This would have greatly interfered with 14th Army's ability to continue its advance and complete the objectives of operation CAPITAL. The India-Burma theater staff found that Wedemeyer's requests put them, and by implication American military and political leadership, in an embarrassing position. After years of pressuring the British to take more offensive action in Burma, "the British Commonwealth was moving toward the climax of the Burma campaign, with its divisions deep in the jungle, and now Wedemeyer was urging, and the Generalissimo demanding, that two Chinese divisions and about one-half of SEAC's resources in transports be sent from Burma to China."[55]

Mountbatten vigorously protested Wedemeyer's requests, especially the demand for the combat cargo groups, which he believed would cause 14th Army's offensive to grind to a halt, given the army's near-complete dependence on air supply. In addition, with the 38th Division heavily involved in combat with the Japanese, its withdrawal would have been devastating to the NCAC's campaign in northern Burma. Mountbatten appealed to the British Chiefs of Staff, who put the question to the Combined Chiefs of Staff for a decision. The American Joint Chiefs were of the opinion that the Generalissimo had every right to request the return of his divisions, but recommended that other Chinese divisions in India be returned to China since the 22nd and 38th Divisions were in combat. The Joint Chiefs also believed that the China theater command had the right to call on any American transport aircraft for operations in China, but modified this position to allow any transports supplying the Allied armies in combat to remain in India and Burma. The Combined Chiefs decided to divert resources from SEAC to China on an emergency basis and worked out a compromise. Mountbatten agreed to the transfer of two Chinese divisions, and Sultan suggested a compromise, sending one of the elite 22nd and 38th Divisions and one division that was in reserve. The choice was to withdraw the 22nd Division, since it was not as heavily engaged, and send the not-yet-committed 14th Chinese Division to China. The Combined Chiefs also directed that some transport aircraft could be diverted to China but would have to return to Burma by 1 March 1945. Sultan replaced the 22nd Division with the Mars Task Force and ordered the Task Force to continue the advance.[56]

By the middle of December, 36th Division and the Mars Task Force had reached the objectives set for Phase 1 of the advance, but the Chinese New First Army on the left flank was still far from Namhkam—its objective for Phase 1. There remained a gap between the NCAC and the Chinese Expeditionary Army's XI Group making slow progress in its advance from Yunnan.[57] Now with two fewer

SUPPORTING THE NCAC ADVANCE

Men from the Mars Task Force marching through a Burmese village at the end of December 1944, heading for the old Burma Road. Mules carried supplies for all the Allied infantry units fighting in Burma. *Box 11, Air, Folder BB, RG208AA, NARA*

divisions, Sultan had to modify his plans for the continued advance. He decided to have 36th Division continue south as planned, but brought up the Chinese 50th Division with orders to advance to the left of 36th Division toward Lashio, while the Mars Task Force aimed for the old Burma Road. The 30th and 38th Divisions still aimed to capture Namhkam and Wanting, southeast of Bhamo, to connect the Ledo Road with the Burma Road.[58] During December the 80th Group flew fewer close-air-support missions, completing around 80 missions to support the 30th and 38th Divisions around Bhamo. Most of the missions for the fighter groups were to bomb and strafe Japanese-held towns and villages, supply dumps, and concentrations of Japanese troops. On some of these attacks the pilots would be rewarded with large secondary explosions and columns of black smoke indicating direct hits on Japanese supplies. The fighter squadrons carried out more patrols over the advancing Allied forces. January brought more of the same, with the fighter squadrons flying missions over the

Trucks from the first overland convoy from Ledo to China crossing over the Burma-China border. Note the sign on the right with the distances from Ledo to Kunming. The convoy arrived at Kunming on 4 February 1945, completing the objective the War Department had set for Stilwell in 1942. *3A-37854, RG342FH, NARA*

SECURING THE BURMA ROAD
January–March 1945

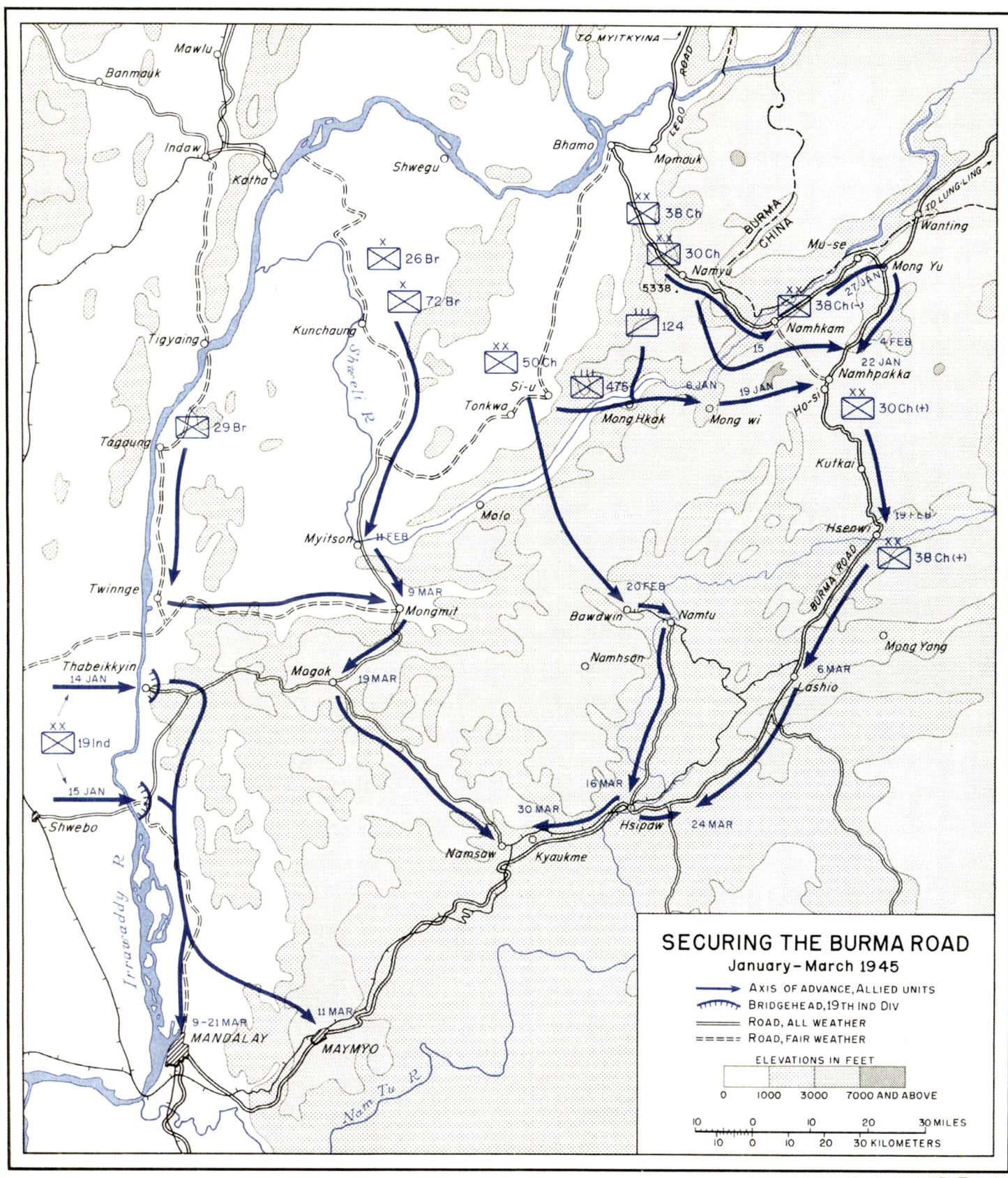

MAP 12

SUPPORTING THE NCAC ADVANCE

Japanese lines of retreat as they withdrew from the area. These missions stretched the range of the P-47s, who often had to add a belly fuel tank when carrying bombs to reach their targets.[59]

By 18 January 1945 the Mars Task Force had reached a position overlooking the Burma Road near the town of Hsenwi, south of Wanting, and began to disrupt Japanese efforts to move supplies along the road. To the north, the 30th and 38th Divisions found Wanting unoccupied on January 20, pushing on to make contact with the XI Group army divisions two days later. When Mountbatten learned this, he sent a cable to the president, the prime minister, and the Combined Chiefs of Staff, saying, "the first part of the order I received at Quebec completely carried out. The land route to China is open."[60] A hastily formed convoy came down the Ledo Road and left Wanting on January 28, arriving at Kunming on February 4, ending the overland blockade of China. On January 22, the Generalissimo ordered the Chinese Expeditionary Force to halt its operations and withdraw back to China, bringing the Salween campaign to an end. With his lines of communication threatened and the 30th and 38th Divisions pressing on, the commander of the *56th Division* requested and received permission to withdraw to Lashio, returning several borrowed regiments to their own divisions. To the west the 36th Division continued its advance, running into Japanese opposition around Twinnge on January 18 and calling for air support. The 80th Fighter Group's squadrons spent the last week of January flying close-air-support missions for 36th Division, the 50th Chinese Division, and the Mars Task Force, winning praise from the air party officers and the ground troops for excellent bombing. Japanese opposition stiffened, preventing 36th Division from capturing Myitson and moving on to Mogok and Mongmit. The 50th Division continued on, making slow progress toward Lashio. By early February, NCAC was still short of its objectives for Phase 2 of its advance: the occupation of Mogok, Mongmit, and Lashio. Sultan could no longer rely on the Chinese Expeditionary Force but would have to cover the area from Mogok to the Chinese border with the forces he had available. Fortunately, 14th Army's advance was putting increasing pressure on the Japanese and causing the *33rd Army* to pull its forces back toward central Burma. Over the next two months, the fighting in the NCAC area would steadily diminish.[61]

Supporting the Advance: Air Supply and Air Evacuation

Until American engineers pushed the Ledo Road to Myiktyina and beyond toward the end of 1944, the NCAC divisions depended almost entirely on air supply. The combat cargo and troop carrier squadrons assigned to the Tenth Air Force flew daily supply missions carrying every conceivable cargo to the troops at the front. An understanding of the extent of this effort can be gained from looking at some of the statistics for the period from September to December 1944. During these four months the Tenth Air Force's transport squadrons

- flew 35,408 air supply sorties,
- flew the equivalent of six times around the world every day,
- lifted 105,568 tons of cargo into Burma,
- flew the equivalent of 40 freight cars every day into Burma,
- flew 90,835 personnel into and out of Burma, and
- flew every transport plane an average of 187 hours per month.[62]

Ground crew loading packages of supplies onto a C-47 from the 2nd Troop Carrier Squadron to be air dropped to advancing American and Chinese troops in early 1945. A truck arriving with more supplies from a depot can be seen on the road in the background. Even with the completion of the Ledo Road, advance Allied units still depended on air supply for nearly all their needs. *3A-37219, RG342FH, NARA*

For the pilots and crews of the combat cargo and troop carrier squadrons, setting these records meant flying more and more hours each day on longer and longer trips to the front. For the first half of 1944 the transport planes flew missions of around 300 miles between their bases in Assam and the front lines in the Hukawng Valley, with flights averaging 2½ hours. As the advance began in October and pushed deeper into Burma, the distances lengthened to upward of 600 miles by the end of the campaign, with flights averaging four or more hours. Crews who had been flying around 100 hours a month before the offensive began were flying nearly 150 hours a month during November and December 1944, with some pilots flying as many as 200 hours a month.[63]

Landing supplies was far more economical than air dropping. As the Allied troops advanced, the transport squadrons flew into hastily prepared landing grounds. This C-47, "The Virgin's Urgeon," was the first airplane to land at a landing ground at Momauk, near Bhamo, in November 1944. *3A-34773, RG342FH, NARA*

This record also required an efficient and effective administration of all phases of air supply. To that end, on the basis of the initial experience of providing air supply to Stilwell's Chinese divisions in their advance down the Hukawng Valley, Davidson as the newly appointed commander of the Tenth Air Force held a meeting in June 1944 with the commander of the Army Services of Supply to work out a better means of fulfilling the requirements of the ground forces. At this meeting, the NCAC G-4 (Logistics) took on responsibility for determining what supplies would be delivered to the forward units, which units would receive these supplies, and in what priority order, and set the delivery schedule for the transport squadrons. The NCAC G-4 set up an Air Control Section at NCAC headquarters to administer all air supply requests and work with the Services of Supply and the Tenth Air Force to arrange preparation and delivery of requested supplies. With the prospect of greatly increased air supply operations for the NCAC advance, the Tenth Air Force activated the Air Cargo Headquarters, Tenth Air Force, on 1 November 1944 to work with the Air Control Section and to serve as an intermediate headquarters between the Tenth Air Force, the 3rd Combat Cargo Group, and the 443rd Troop Carrier Group. The Air Cargo Headquarters had responsibility for overseeing all aspects of air cargo operations, coordinating with the NCAC G-4 and the Services of Supply, scheduling aircraft and ensuring their maximum utilization, setting up flying procedures, and looking after the air crews flying these missions, among other duties. Requests for supplies went to the NCAC G-4 Air Control Section, who would work with the Air Cargo Headquarters to ensure that the schedule of deliveries was within the capacity of the transport squadrons. The system worked well, with monthly tonnage increasing from 13,000 tons in May 1944 to 20,000 tons in September, and to a record 27,607 tons delivered in November.[64]

One of the challenges of the air supply effort in the NCAC area was the need to deliver three different sets of supplies. The 36th Division required British ammunition and British rations, the American regiments in the Mars Task Force required American rations and some types of American ammunition, and the Chinese divisions had their own requirements. In addition, the transport squadrons had to ferry supplies for the engineer units building the road and gasoline pipeline down the Ledo Road. All these conflicting demands had to be carefully balanced if the troops were not to go without the supplies they needed to sustain the advance. To keep 36th Division supplied, the British army seconded British officers to the NCAC Air Control Section and an Indian air supply company to pack supplies for the transport planes dropping supplies to 36th Division's forward units. The ground units in the forward areas had responsibility for picking out the drop zones for the transports. The drop zones ideally were located near enough to the forward units to speed delivery of supplies, were in areas that could be easily marked, and had (it was hoped) few natural obstructions. As the advance moved deeper into Burma and the weather improved, it became possible to build rough landing strips for the C-47s closer to the front lines. This allowed the transports to deliver a greater weight of supplies, since there was no need for the added weight of packaging and parachutes. Air drops were much more flexible than using landing strips, and continued to be used throughout the advance, even if less economical. As the Ledo Road reached Myitkyina and beyond, it became possible to transport supplies by truck from Ledo—the railhead—to Myitkyina, reducing the need for air transport. The expansion of the road network reduced the amount of air cargo delivered in the later months of the campaign.[65]

The transport squadrons found that delivering supplies to the Chinese divisions had its own challenges. The Chinese units were often lax about the placement of drop zones, preferring to set them as close to the front as possible and without regard to obstacles in the way of the transport planes. This often meant that the C-47s

Men from the Mars Task Force load air-dropped supplies onto the backs of their mules, with more supply packages coming down behind them. The need to supply three different armies (American, British, and Chinese) with different rations, ammunition, and equipment complicated the already challenging problem of supplying Allied units in their advance into Burma. *Box 11, Air, folder K, RG208AA, NARA*

Chinese troops load supplies onto their mules after receiving an air drop from the 2nd Troop Carrier Squadron in March 1945. By this point the capture of more roads made supplying the advanced Chinese units somewhat easier. *3A-37225, RG342FH, NARA*

Chinese troops wait to board C-47s from the 1st Air Commando Group's 319th Troop Carrier Squadron and the 3rd Combat Cargo Group during Operation GRUBWORM. The operation called on transports from many American transport groups in India and Burma, including C-46s from the India-China Division of the Air Transport Command. *3A-37128, RG342FH, NARA*

flew within range of the Japanese during their supply drops and risked running into Japanese ground fire. The pilots of the 2nd Troop Carrier Squadron soon learned that certain drop zones carried a high risk of ground fire, with one airplane returning to Myitkyina peppered with Japanese machine gun and rifle fire from a supply mission in mid-December. On occasion the Chinese themselves were the culprits. On another mission a 2nd Squadron airplane returning through Allied territory from a supply-dropping mission received four bursts of tracer fire. An inquiry found that the cause was "just a few of our own boys being playful," although "it scared the daylights out of the plane's crew."[66]

The Tenth Air Force's combat cargo squadrons participated in the move of the two Chinese divisions to China. The movement of these troops and their equipment became Operation GRUBWORM, named after Col. S. D. Grubbs, Tenth Air Force deputy chief of staff who commanded the operation. Between 5 December 1944 and 5 January 1945, transport aircraft from the Tenth Air Force, the Air Transport Command, and the Combat Cargo Task Force flew 25,491 men, more than 1,500 horses and mules, 42 jeeps, 48 howitzers, 48 heavy mortars, and 48 antitank guns to China.[67] The ATC C-46s flew most of the transport flights, since they could carry a greater number of troops than the C-47s. The ATC units maintained a 24-hour schedule out of Myitkyina, which could handle night operations, while the C-47 units flew Chinese troops to China during daylight out of different airfields in India and Burma. The operation made every effort not to disrupt regular supply operations in support of the troops at the front. Operation GRUBWORM demonstrated once again the versatility and flexibility of air supply, and the mobility that air transport provided to Allied ground forces. More importantly, air supply made possible a campaign in terrain where regular means of communication were almost entirely lacking. The work of the transport squadrons in northern Burma "demonstrated clearly and conclusively that sufficient air transport, provided with adequate bases, could, under conditions of air superiority, provide supplies for ground forces with a reliability equal to that of normal ground lines of communication."[68]

The record of the liaison squadrons was in its own way as impressive as that of the transport squadrons. The liaison aircraft were "maids of all work," accomplishing many different tasks with their L-1 and L-5 aircraft. The most important role was in air evacuation, carrying the wounded from any flat stretch of ground near the front lines back to larger airstrips, where they could be transferred to C-47s and flown to rear-area hospitals. The light aircraft carried personnel in and out of the front lines, dropped off mail and special cargo, and performed reconnaissance and spotting for the artillery and for the fighter squadrons, working with the Joint Operations Air Parties. On these reconnaissance missions for the fighter strikes, the Japanese rarely fired on the liaison airplanes, since they knew that to do so would give away their positions. As

TSgt. Herbert Shirer from the 5th Liaison Squadron with his Stinson L-5 "My Duchess" in early December 1944. A number of liaison pilots named their light planes, just as their brethren in the larger fighters, bombers, and transports did. *3A-36230, RG342FH, NARA*

THE TENTH AIR FORCE IN WORLD WAR II

An L-5 from the 5th Liaison Squadron takes off from a rough forward landing strip in December 1944 to carry a wounded soldier back for medical evacuation. A sign on the left warns vehicles that what appears to be a road is actually an airstrip. *3A-33791, RG342FH, NARA*

an example of the variety of missions, during November and December 1944 the 5th Liaison Squadron, in addition to its other duties, flew several mechanics to the old BROADWAY strip to salvage scarce Jeep parts, rescued two pilots from behind Japanese lines, flew a company of aviation engineers to the front lines, evacuated a badly injured American soldier from a jungle strip at night by using the lights of 30 vehicles to illuminate the strip, carried the commanding officer of the 1st Provisional Tank Group so that he could direct his armored units from the air, and delivered Christmas mail and packages to American soldiers of the Mars Task Force. At the end of December, T/Sgt. Clifford Bryan received orders to return to the United States, having completed 608 missions with the 5th Liaison Squadron. Many other pilots had completed more than 500 missions. From September to the end of December, the three liaison squadrons in the 1st Liaison Group completed 26,701 sorties of all kinds over northern Burma, losing only one aircraft to enemy action when Japanese fighters strafed the recently captured airfield at Bhamo, destroying a 5th Liaison Squadron L-1.[69]

One of the most important roles the light aircraft performed was the rescue of downed pilots, particularly from behind Japanese lines. While the India-China Wing of the ATC had a unit for rescuing downed transport crews along the Hump route, up until September 1944 the Tenth Air Force did not have an organization responsible for the rescue of airmen downed in the jungle, especially behind Japanese lines. Rescue efforts were ad hoc and depended primarily on the downed flier's own unit to carry out a search effort. Most aircrews had instructions to head for the nearest hills, where they had a better chance of coming across local people more likely to be friendly to Allied airmen than the lowland Burmese. If a survivor could be located from the air, the searching airplane would try to drop a pack of survival gear with instructions on walking out. Pilots did go through training in jungle survival, and a few did walk out on their own, but the Japanese captured many, and more were simply never heard from. To correct this, on 24 September 1944 the Tenth Air Force activated the Air Jungle Rescue Unit at Tingkawk Sakan and gave the unit full responsibility for carrying out and coordinating search-and-rescue missions, coordinating with other units as necessary. The most important factor was speed. The sooner the unit could be notified of a downed pilot or aircrew, the faster the response and the greater likelihood of a successful rescue. Pilots received instructions to contact Fighter Control stations if they were in difficulty and to provide their location and route of travel. The Fighter Control station would alert the Air Jungle Rescue Unit, who would put a search effort together. Once on the ground, standard procedure was for the downed aircrew to search for a clearing where they could lay out panels or make marks on the ground, using a simple code to indicate their condition and their needs. The rescue unit's initial complement was two B-25s for searches and two L-5s for the rescue effort. This shortly grew to three B-25s and three L-5s, with the ability to call on other aircraft from other squadrons as needed.[70]

1st Lt. Chester Abbot, a P-47 pilot with the 60th Fighter Squadron (*left*), shakes hands with his rescuer, SSgt. Carl Hughes, who rescued Abbot from the top of a mountain after Abbot was shot down some 60 miles behind Japanese lines on 15 November 1944. This was the first official rescue for the newly formed Air Jungle Rescue Unit. *Headquarters, Tenth Air Force, Historical Data for November 1944, 830.01, A8224, reel 100018, AFHRA*

SUPPORTING THE NCAC ADVANCE

The first official rescue began on 15 November 1944, when 1st Lt. Chester Abbot, a pilot with the 60th Fighter Squadron, had to bail out of his P-47 in a mountainous area 63 miles behind Japanese lines. Abbot's flight leader noted his position when he went down, and later that day led one of the Air Jungle Rescue Unit's B-25s to the area. The B-25 dropped a rescue packet and instructions to Abbot, who failed to see the drop. The next day the B-25, the flight leader, and an L-1 returned to the area and signaled to Abbot to go to a clearing on the top of a nearby mountain; S/Sgt. Carl Hughes, with the 5th Liaison Squadron, had volunteered to make the rescue attempt in his L-1. Hughes landed his airplane in a small clearing only a couple of hundred feet long on top of the 5,000-foot mountain, landing uphill to bring his airplane to a halt. While waiting for the pilot to appear, Hughes removed stones and cut down the elephant grass to give himself a better chance of getting off. By late afternoon the pilot had not appeared, having difficulty getting up the jungle-covered mountainside, so Hughes had to take off, running downhill and dropping down 500 feet before his L-1 picked up air speed and recovered. Hughes went back the next morning, despite the increased risk of a Japanese reaction, and successfully picked Abbot up and brought him back safely. For his daring feat, Hughes received the Silver Star.[71]

The unit coordinated the rescue of another 60th Fighter Squadron pilot from behind Japanese lines a week later, and a third in December. During two months of operations the Air Jungle Rescue Unit flew 96 missions responding to reports of crashes, flares, or parachutes sighted, and 14 missions searching for downed aircrew.[72] The rescues were never easy, nor were they without losses. In an attempt to rescue the crew who had bailed out of their B-25H after the 490th Bomb Squadron's mission of 5 January 1945, the Air Jungle Rescue unit lost three L-1s that cracked up trying to land or take off with members of the crew. A Burmese officer who parachuted in to help the crew walk out of the jungle and one of the liaison pilots were both killed in a brief firefight after running into a Japanese patrol. One of the aircrew drowned crossing the Irrawaddy River on makeshift rafts. But four of the crew did make it back to the squadron.[73] The boost the Air Jungle Rescue Unit gave to pilot and aircrew morale was a not insignificant benefit of its operations. As a history of the unit noted:

> *To pilots flying over Northern Burma there is inevitable mental hazard in the realization that beneath them is seemingly endless jungle and mountain terrain, affording few places for forced landings, that walking out through the thick undergrowth is a slow, tortuous process, requiring weeks for what might be a few minutes flying time, that capture by the Japs might mean mistreatment, torture, or death.*
>
> *The presence of the Air Jungle Rescue Detachment, and its work thus far, serve to assure these pilots that speedy, persistent search will be made, that necessary supplies and instructions will be dropped, that every effort made to land a light plane to fly them to safety.*[74]

The End of the Northern Combat Area Command

During February the only Allied force in the NCAC to press the advance was the British 36th Division. The Chinese 30th and 38th Divisions "somewhat discreetly followed up the rearguards of the *56th Division*" as it withdrew to the south, the Chinese occupying Hsenwi on 19 February 1945.[75] The American Mars Force withdrew for a rest period after the first week of February, while the Chinese

Chinese troops entering Bhamo in January 1945. Repeated air attacks had severely damaged the town. With the town's capture, the nearby airfield became available to fly in supplies. *Box 160, China–Armed Forces–Burma, folder N, RG208AA, NARA*

50th Division made its way slowly down to Namtu by the third week of February, where it was still 35 miles short of its objective.[76] The Chinese Expeditionary Force was withdrawing toward Yunnan, having ended its participation in the fighting in Burma. The 36th Division continued its march, reaching the Shweli River near the town of Myitson and fighting a tough battle for the town during the middle of the month. Having occupied Myitson by February 22, 36th Division advanced toward Mongmit, reaching the town on March 7. The day before, the Chinese 38th Division had occupied Lashio without opposition.[77]

The two fighter groups continued to provide support to the Allied divisions. The 80th Fighter Group provided most of the close air support while the 33rd Fighter Group went after Japanese supply areas, troop concentrations, and bridges. The 80th Group had instituted a policy of rotating missions—patrols, close air support, and assigned targets—among the three squadrons, and the pilots

A P-47D from the 89th Fighter Squadron that cracked up on takeoff. The Thunderbolt's rugged construction saved many a pilot's life. This airplane may have previously served with the 33rd Fighter Group, since the 80th Group does not appear to have received camouflaged P-47Ds while serving in India and Burma. *GP-80-SU-PH, AFHRA*

appreciated the diversity. On some days one squadron would send out a dozen missions while the others provided a smaller number, with this obligation also shifting among the three squadrons. The 80th Group kept busy, often sending out a dozen or more missions a day, and on one day reaching 22 missions. During the first week of February the 80th Group flew close support for the American 475th Regiment in the Mars Task Force. On one mission, the ground observer radioed a flight from the 88th Fighter Squadron, "beautiful hit, right on the position," and after the flight completed its bombing and strafing runs, "good bombing; all bombs where we wanted them." For most of the month the 80th Group devoted its effort to supporting the 36th Division. The 90th Fighter Squadron flew 96 close-air-support missions during the month, with 73 missions for the 36th Division, including 53 flown during the division's attack on Myitson. The speed of the advance made it difficult for the photoreconnaissance squadrons to keep up production of photomosaics, so that on some missions only the flight leader would have a photo of the target area. Often the flights had to rely on the Joint Operations Air Party to direct the flight to the correct target. Having L-5s available to give corrections proved invaluable.[78]

The 490th Bomb Squadron made its contribution during the month. While there were fewer bridge targets left, the squadron destroyed 14 bridges, including four knocked out on February 26, bringing its cumulative total to 148 destroyed. Having flown successful dusk offensive reconnaissance missions at the end of the year, the squadron tried out dawn missions, hoping to catch Japanese motor vehicles still on the road. Taking off before dawn, the single B-25s did have some success, catching several Japanese trucks and in one case a convoy of six or more trucks, all of which the B-25s heavily strafed. The squadron continued its effort against Japanese stores with attacks on warehouses and supply areas in several towns and villages ahead of the advance, saturating the target area with demolition and fragmentation bombs. To support 36th Division, the squadron flew three missions to bomb an island in the Shweli River near Myitson, where the Japanese were holding up the division's attempts to cross the river. On February 8, fifteen airplanes dropped 90 325-pound depth charges in the area, on a mission graded excellent. The squadron flew two missions to the island on February 19. During the morning mission, eight aircraft attacked from medium altitude while four aircraft came in at low level, dropping 1,044 small fragmentation bombs and 16 500-pound bombs. In the afternoon, another 12 planes returned to drop 96 500-pound bombs in individual low-level attacks. Afterward the squadron received a message from Mountbatten, who said, "Sultan, Davidson, Festing and I have just looked over your first rate pasting of Myitson. Each of us congratulates you on a splendid job."[79]

While the fighting was still going on as the British and Chinese divisions pushed toward their objectives for Phase 2 of the NCAC's advance, a debate began among Wedemeyer, Mountbatten, and the American and British Chiefs of Staff on the future of the Mars Task Force and the Chinese divisions in Burma.[80] On 3 February 1945, Mountbatten received a new directive from the Combined Chiefs of Staff—coming out of the ARGONAUT Conference at Malta—that for the first time clearly specified that his objective was to liberate all of Burma at the earliest possible date and then plan for the liberation of Malaya.[81] To that end, Slim and 14th Army were about to undertake major battles to capture Mandalay and inflict a punishing defeat on *Burma Area Army* in central Burma. Mountbatten had also instructed his planning staff to begin working on a plan for an amphibious assault on Rangoon before the monsoon—a limited

A wrecked Japanese locomotive damaged beyond repair found near Naba Junction after its capture in December 1944. The locomotive appears to have been the victim of a large bomb, given the size of the nearby crater. Toward the final months of the war, locomotives were illusive targets, since the Japanese did not dare operate them during the day due to the risk of air attack. *Sc-251177, Rg111, NARA*

form of Operation DRACULA. With 14th Army operating deeper into central Burma and almost entirely dependent on air supply into landing grounds that would turn into seas of mud during the monsoon, the capture of Rangoon to provide a port for supplying 14th Army was vital. At this juncture, Wedemeyer informed Mountbatten that he wanted to bring back the Chinese divisions and the Mars Task Force to China for a planned offensive in East China. Once again, having long insisted on the Burma campaign to aid China, the Americans wanted to withdraw forces from the campaign just as it was reaching its most critical point. Sultan subsequently told Mountbatten on February 23 that Wedemeyer needed the Mars Force immediately to serve as training staff for new Chinese divisions, and that he wanted the Chinese divisions to move to China by 1 June 1945. Not surprisingly, Mountbatten objected, since the moves would leave the Burma Road and Slim's left flank unprotected and release Japanese forces for the defense of central Burma.[82]

The American point of view was—as it had been from the creation of the China-Burma-India theater—that all American resources would be devoted to aiding China's war effort. A statement of policy that accompanied Mountbatten's new directive stated the American policy clearly. "The primary military object of the United States in the China and India-Burma theaters is the continuance of aid to China on a scale that will permit the full co-utilization of the area and resources of China for operations against the Japanese. United States resources are deployed in India-Burma to provide direct or indirect support to China."[83] From this perspective, American and Chinese forces in Burma served as a reserve that China could call on at any time. But Marshall and the Joint Chiefs of Staff did not want to take actions that would jeopardize Mountbatten's campaign to liberate Burma, and offered to request that the Generalissimo delay the transfer of the Chinese divisions until after June 1, though they believed that with the likely successful outcome of the attack on Mandalay, SEAC would not need the Chinese forces, and their removal would not jeopardize the outcome of the battle. The Joint Chiefs also agreed that defense of the section of the Burma Road in Burma was the responsibility of the Americans and the Chinese. Separately, Mountbatten and his ground commanders came to the realization that release of the Mars Task Force would reduce the administrative burden on the NCAC, and agreed to its transfer to China immediately. Events on the battlefield influenced Mountbatten and his ground commanders to agree to the transfer of the Chinese divisions on the revised schedule. After the occupation of Lashio on March 6, the Chinese 50th Division occupied Hsipaw on the old Burma Road against fierce Japanese counterattacks that ended on March 20. Four days later the 50th Division linked up with the 38th Division, putting the old Burma Road under Chinese control from Lashio to Kunming. The 36th Division had captured Mogok on March 19 and was now close to reaching Kyaukme—its final objective, where it was due to revert to 14th Army control. The *56th Division* continued its withdrawal to the south and seemed unlikely to contest Allied control over the area along the Burma Road. With the capture of Mandalay at hand, the Allies now had control of the old Burma Road effectively from Mandalay to Kunming, with the Ledo Road now completely secure. Sultan recommended withdrawing the Chinese divisions back to Myitkyina, leaving only a small force to guard the Lashio-Hsipaw area. The Northern Combat Area Command had achieved its objective to establish the overland route to China.[84]

During March, the Tenth Air Force's two fighter groups flew a steadily diminishing number of missions. The 80th Fighter Group flew half the number of missions the group had flown during February. As the Japanese retreat accelerated, there were fewer and fewer profitable targets available. More and more targets were beyond the range of the P-47s, even when flying from Myitkyina, where the entire 80th Group was now based. The lack of strong resistance to the Allied advance meant fewer close-air-support missions. The Tenth Air Force even gave each of the three squadrons six days off during the month. There were some close-air-support missions for 36th Division and 50th Division during the month, with most of the rest of the missions devoted to bombing and strafing the few Japanese supply and troop concentrations that could be found. Gen. Festing paid a visit to the group at the end of the month to present a captured Japanese sword in thanks for the group's superb close air support. In the 33rd Group, by the middle of the month the squadrons were down to flying two missions a day. Most of the 33rd Group's missions were to bomb and strafe Japanese supply and troop concentrations, but as these targets disappeared toward the end of the month, the squadrons shifted to flying road sweeps. The pilots found these monotonous, since they usually found little to bomb or strafe. Unfortunately there were still losses, even with so little Japanese opposition. The 88th Fighter Squadron lost a flight leader when his P-47 spun in after he completed his bomb run, while the 58th Fighter Squadron also lost a flight leader on a road sweep when the pilot's engine cut out and he reported gasoline leaking into the cockpit.

With little risk of Japanese air raids at night, the 427th Night Fighter Squadron began sending out its P-61s on intruder missions over northern Burma, initially by night and then by day. This P-61 served with the squadron in Burma and later transferred to the squadron's detachment in China. *Author's collection*

Gasoline fumes may have caused the pilot to become unconscious, since the plane soon went into a dive and exploded when it hit the ground. At the end of the month, Davidson said of his Tenth Air Force, "we are practically out of business."[85]

In contrast, the 490th Bomb Squadron had a busy month, completing 24 missions. The 427 tons of bombs the squadron dropped during the month set a record, as did the accuracy of its bombing. As with some of the fighter squadrons, the majority of the 490th Squadron's missions were offensive road sweeps. Pairs of B-25s took off every two hours on the days assigned to road sweeps, but found little to bomb or strafe. Attacks on troop concentrations had more success, an attack on one area resulting in the death of 300 Japanese soldiers, which brought a message of commendation from Davidson. Having made its debut as night intruders in February, the P-61s of the 427th Night Fighter Squadron undertook daylight sweeps during March. Armed with two 500-pound bombs and rocket tubes, and with four 20 mm cannon, the P-61s were heavily armed but, like their counterparts, found few targets to bomb or strafe.[86]

By early April it was clear that the Tenth Air Force's war in Burma was coming to an end. The ground campaign effectively came to an end on April 9, when troops captured the last section of the railroad line from Lashio to Mandalay. After that the Tenth Air Force's weekly "Critical Review" had the notation "No reported action on Northern Combat Area Command fronts." As the Japanese retreated east into the Shan States, they came under increasing harassment from Kachin guerrilla units of the Office of Strategic Services Detachment 101

The 80th Fighter Group's Thunderbolts knocked out the main bridge at Lashio and the bypass bridge the Japanese built next to it. With Tenth Air Force's fighters and medium bombers roaming over northern Burma, and being short of men and resources, the Japanese could not keep pace with the destruction. *3A-37226, RG342FH, NARA*

A P-38 from the 60th Fighter Squadron, which converted to the Lightning in early 1945. Baksheesh was the term Indian beggars used to beg money from American GIs. The 60th Squadron remained in combat over Burma until after the monsoon. *Courtesy, Carl Molesworth*

Two Type 1 fighters (Ki-43) from the Japanese Army Air Force, abandoned at Bhamo airfield. One consequence of the constant disruption of Japanese lines of communication was the impact it had on the already inadequate logistical system of the JAAF. As they advanced, the Allies found a large number of damaged aircraft abandoned on captured airfields that the Japanese had been unable to repair. *Personal collection of Maj. Gen. Howard C. Davidson, 168.7266-59, AFHRA*

and British Force 136. The fighter squadrons flew fewer and fewer missions during the month, continuing to bomb and strafe Japanese supplies and troops where these could be found within range of the fighters. On many of these missions the fighters dropped bombs on wooded or jungle areas without observing any results of their efforts, only occasionally getting a secondary explosion or a column of dark smoke indicating a hit on something substantial. Road sweeps, which the pilots found to be increasingly fruitless due to the lack of targets, were the objective of many missions. On one road sweep mission, the pilots of the 58th Fighter Squadron, out of boredom, ended up counting livestock they saw along the route, returning with a count of 100 horses and cows. The fighter groups flew missions on only half the days in April, partly due to weather and partly due to the dearth of worthwhile targets. They flew their last combat missions of the war in the final days of the month. There was time for baseball games and more movies at night, and even a few hours off during midday to avoid the punishing heat. More veteran pilots received their orders to return to the United States. Rumors began flying about possible moves back to India. With no good targets in Burma, the 490th Bomb Squadron transferred to China and the Fourteenth Air Force on 10 April 1945, rejoining its parent 341st Bomb Group. Even the transport and liaison squadrons flew fewer sorties. With the ground forces no longer advancing, the need for daily replenishment of supplies diminished sharply. At the end of April, the Tenth Air Force deactivated Air Cargo Headquarters. For most of the squadrons the end, when it came, came suddenly. In early May the 33rd Fighter Group received orders to transfer to a former B-29 base in India, leaving only the 60th Fighter Squadron, which had converted to the P-38 during the month, to carry on in Burma at Myitkyina as part of the newly organized North Burma Task Force, formed to control the few Tenth Air Force units remaining in Burma. The 80th Fighter Group soon followed, both groups taking up residence at Dudhkundi, west of Calcutta, where the pilots and ground staff were delighted to find an ice-making machine and became reacquainted with fresh food. The 71st Liaison Squadron went to India, while the 115th Liaison Squadron went to Nagaghuli in Assam, as did the 427th Night Fighter Squadron. Many other support units and antiaircraft units also moved to India. The 5th Liaison Squadron stayed at Myitkyina as part of the North Burma Task Force.[87]

Perhaps there is no better way to end this account of the Tenth Air Force's role in the NCAC's campaign in northern Burma then to quote in full Maj. Gen. Davidson's letter of commendation to the personnel in his command:

1. At this the completion of the North Burma campaign and the full accomplishment of the mission of the Tenth Air Force within the India-Burma Theater, I desire to express to all officers and men of my command my profound appreciation for their constant endeavor and highest success in the prosecution of their assigned duties. Without fear of contradiction, I wish to state that the efforts of the organizations of this command given so willingly and freely have been a major contribution not only to the completion of the war in Burma but of World War II as a whole.

2. The Tenth Air Force consists of a variety of types of units, all of whom have executed their functions with extreme determinations and vigor. In the North Burma campaign, it constituted the first major offensive American air effort against the Japanese in South East Asia. Our fighter-bombers opened the way for the advance of American, British and Chinese ground forces in Burma and on the Salween front in China in their advance to open the Ledo-Burma road. Our bombers hit enemy lines of communications and transportation with substantial amounts of bomb tonnage, isolating the battle field and enabling the quicker advance of Northern Combat Area Command troops. Our transports carried enormous quantities of food, supply equipment and ammunition into Burma, thus insuring that all Allied forces in this area would never lack for the essentials of war. Our fighters destroyed the Japanese Air Force in North Burma. Our engineers exhibited keen ingenuity in the breakdown and assembly of heavy engineer equipment and the construction of numerous airfields in minimum time. Our liaison aircraft evacuated casualties and rescued personnel downed far behind enemy lines. Our air evacuation personnel treated the wounded and sick and saw to it that they were transported to safe areas. Our antiaircraft artillery furnished air defense in all areas. Our signal and fighter control troops, many stationed in isolated positions, provided excellent air warning and communications.

3. Despite the severe handicaps of tropical climate, rugged terrain, the jungle and shortages of vital equipment, the Tenth Air Force pressed home the attack to the enemy to the limit. Through a partnership of all arms and services, an entire Japanese army was routed, decimated and forced to give up its hold on North Burma.

4. In whatever task the future holds for the organizations of this command, it is my most firm conviction that you will continue to display equally high devotion to duty and will attain constantly superior results. I know that your successes will be even greater and more numerous in whatever area you are called upon to operate.[88]

Tenth Air Force Statistics, November 1944–April 1945						
	NOV.	DEC.	JAN.	FEB.	MAR.	APR.
Air Supply Sorties	8,463	8,023	7,676	6,531	6,946	1,303
Fighter Sorties	3,595	4,108	4,929	6,579	3,552	1,624
Liaison Sorties	6,792	9,920	11,885	10,997	9,745	5,625
Medium- Bomber Sorties	188	295	296	271	299	18
Total Sorties	19,038	22,346	24,786	24,378	20,542	8,570
Supplies (Tons)	24,266	21,121	21,263	18,061	19,480	9,110
Personnel Carried	20,700	35,172	23,182	27,535	31,983	1,142
Casualties Evacuated	1,508	1,970	2,615	1,847	2,575	1,067

CHAPTER 12

ARMY AIR FORCE UNITS SUPPORTING 14TH ARMY OPERATIONS

June 1944–May 1945

American Air Support for 14th Army

There were a number of Army Air Force units who, while remaining under the administrative control of the Tenth Air Force, came under the operational control of other commands within Eastern Air Command. These units were the 12th Bomb Group and the 459th Fighter Squadron, assigned to the 3rd Tactical Air Force; the 7th Bomb Group, in the Strategic Air Force; the American units in the Photographic Reconnaissance Force; and the American units in a new formation within the 3rd Tactical Air Force—the Combat Cargo Task Force—activated in September 1944. From July 1944 until May 1945 these units provided support for 14th Army's advance into Burma.

By early July the battle of Imphal was effectively over. Reopening the road from Imphal to Kohima and back to Dimpaur—the source of supplies for IV and XXXIII Corps—greatly relieved the 14th Army's logistical problems. To the east of Imphal, XXXIII Corps' divisions were now pushing the battered remnants of the *15th and 31st Divisions* back toward the Chindwin River, fighting the monsoon rains and mud as much as the Japanese. To the south of Imphal IV Corps was fighting against *33rd Division*. As the British and Indian troops advanced, they came across evidence of the disaster that had befallen *15th Army* in its ill-fated attempt at invasion. Abandoned motor vehicles, artillery pieces, and, above all, dead and dying Japanese soldiers, many of whom showed signs of starvation, gave evidence that the Japanese defeat was even greater than British army intelligence realized. The magnitude of the defeat gave rise to new opportunities. Mountbatten had already given Slim, commanding 14th Army, a new directive through Gen. Giffard, commander of 11th Army Group. This required 14th Army to reopen the land route to Dimapur (achieved on June 22), push the Japanese farther back from Imphal, and prepare to exploit across the Chindwin River.[1] Slim had begun to conceive of a campaign that would be much more extensive than a mere exploitation. What he planned was a second decisive battle that would destroy what remained of *Burma Area Army*, and thereby open up Burma to liberation.[2]

Slim believed that the defeats Gen. Kawabe, commanding *Burma Area Army*, had suffered in the Arakan, Imphal, and northern Burma meant that the Japanese would need time to obtain reinforcements to rebuild their shattered divisions. Army intelligence considered the Japanese would be unable to mount an offensive until January 1945 at the earliest, giving the Allies the opportunity to take advantage of this weakness and push deeper into Burma.[3] Slim had long believed that the best means of regaining control of Burma was through an overland advance from the north, and with the Japanese defeat at Imphal, this now seemed a possibility. Slim wanted to send a large force into the Burmese central plain to bring the Japanese to battle around Mandalay and defeat them. This would be the task for IV and XXXIII Corps in the months ahead and corresponded to the plans for Operation CAPITAL, then under development.[4]

In the Arakan, the torrential monsoon rains (up to 20 inches a week in some areas) forced both XV Corps and the Japanese to withdraw to higher ground. XV Corps held advantageous positions that would allow for either a limited or a large-scale advance once the dry season began. Giffard recommended that XV Corps' four divisions not undertake a large advance in the Arakan but should continue with more-limited offensive/defensive operations that would allow some of these forces to move to central Burma to join IV and XXXIII Corps in the main battle.[5] At the end of July, Giffard instructed Slim and Stratemeyer to prepare plans for operations in the Arakan and for the advance into central Burma along the lines of CAPITAL, and to review these plans for their impact on Operation DRACULA.[6]

One of the principal problems that Eastern Air Command and 14th Army planners had to grapple with was the challenge of

By October 1944 the 12th Bomb Group's B-25H "Kid Sister" had flown 93 missions. After shifting from the Strategic Air Force to the 3rd Tactical Air Force, the 12th Group flew many missions in support of the 14th Army's advance into central Burma during 1945. GP-12-HI, AFHRA

supporting a large mechanized force in central Burma over an extended and limited line of communications. The distances from Imphal to the probable areas of battle in central Burma were nearly 200 miles and more. Shwebo, where Slim hoped to meet *Burma Area Army* in battle, was 180 miles from Imphal, while Mandalay was more than 350 miles and Rangoon more than 700 miles. The railhead delivering supplies for IV and XXXIII Corps was at Dimapur in Assam. From there, supplies could be sent via truck to Imphal, but beyond Imphal the roads leading to the Chindwin River and beyond had only limited capacity and were not the all-weather roads that would be needed in the monsoon. It was clear that the advance into central Burma would be heavily dependent on air supply and that even the transport aircraft would be stretched, since the economic range of the transports was around 250 miles.[7] The possibility that Operation CAPITAL might require one or more airborne operations to seize forward areas added to the potential demands on the transport squadrons. Slim's planners estimated that by stretching every fiber and reducing requirements in every way possible, the air and land transportation system could support four and a half divisions and two tank brigades in central Burma, but with little margin for error.[8] The planners estimated that 14th Army's needs for air transports would grow from 57 aircraft in September to 322 aircraft between March and May 1945, and with an airborne operation the maximum number of aircraft required would be 342.[9] As Slim observed in a postwar article:

The main problem was of course to get the aircraft. Gradually they came forward, and as soon as their availability was certain we planned the whole of our strategy for this campaign on air supply. There was no main operational plan made in Fourteenth Army which was not based on air supply.[10]

Fortunately, the Combined Chiefs of Staff had planned for an allocation of 350 transport aircraft—the bulk of them in American squadrons—to be available by January 1945.[11] These Army Air Force and RAF transport squadrons would operate under a new formation, the Combat Cargo Task Force.

The Combat Cargo Task Force

The Combat Cargo Task Force came out of Arnold's 24 March 1944 offer of four air transport groups and four Air Commando groups to Mountbatten and Southeast Asia Command. On the basis of the initial success of the 1st Air Commando Group in Operation THURSDAY, four days earlier Arnold had ordered the activation of these new units, with the intention of sending them to the China-Burma-India theater.[12] Arnold saw the combination of Air Commando units spearheading an aerial invasion behind Japanese lines, with the air transport groups flying in troops and supplies as the air equivalent of "fire and movement." This combination would bring together air mobility and offensive striking power in support of the ground forces.[13] As he wrote to Mountbatten, "the success of this operation is proof of the feasibility and usefulness of this type of unit."[14] Arnold hoped that "out of these operations will come a new air-ground technique that will—I am going to say revolutionize—perhaps that's the right word—modern principles of cooperative warfare."[15] Arnold elaborated on this concept in a letter to Mountbatten, saying:

Within our present capabilities we can visualize the movement by air of large ground forces and the maintenance of these forces for an extended period. I foresee the time when the most effective

An elephant loads fuel drums onto a C-47 from the 1st Combat Cargo Group for a flight into Burma. The 1st Combat Cargo Group was the first of three combat cargo groups that would serve in the India-Burma theater: the 1st and 4th Combat Cargo Groups with the Combat Cargo Task Force, and the 3rd Combat Cargo Group with the Tenth Air Force in the NCAC. *Combat Cargo Task Force, 824.6867, AFHRA*

operations may be conducted in this manner by concentrating against vital enemy installations while small detachments of ground forces are required to fight through the more difficult jungle and mountainous terrain only for the purpose of preventing serious forward movement of Japanese forces.[16]

In Arnold's conception, a new form of warfare required a new form of unit with an energetic and aggressive leadership, a command that would "use our air resources with vigor and imagination."[17] Arnold believed that the Air Commando groups and soon-to-be-designated combat cargo groups that he wanted to send to the CBI should be considered specialized units, with special training in Air Commando tactics, and with commanders who had experience in Air Commando operations. He could not agree to the amalgamation of these units into the existing command structure, as he told Mountbatten:

With this concept I cannot agree. It is a decided step backward. In order to get the maximum value from our Air Commandos, and develop new principles for their participation in air warfare, we must have extreme flexibility. The greatest possible freedom for this development can be secured only by creating a self-contained ground and air command which can accomplish the type of missions we visualize. Particularly at this development stage it is most important that there be no intermediate commanders between the air and ground echelons. It is also essential that all commanders be imbued with the value of bold action and timely execution.[18]

Arnold was skeptical that the leadership in SEAC or ACSEA had the ability and willingness to provide the "bold action and timely execution" he was looking for. He was convinced that the only way to overcome the challenges of terrain and logistics that had seemed to stymie the ability of the Allies to engage the Japanese in Burma was through air assault and air supply behind enemy lines.[19] In a conversation he had with Field Marshal Sir John Dill, head of the British Joint Staff Mission in Washington, Arnold expressed his "anxiety of air affairs in Burma" and what he saw as the "unaggressive leadership" of ACSEA.[20] He wanted the Air Commando and combat cargo units kept apart from ACSEA, insisting that these units be used only for supporting long-range-penetration missions and not have their strength and experience dissipated in day-to-day operations.[21] He did not want the "dead hand" of higher command to interfere with the employment of the Air Commandos, and so resisted putting them under the control of Air Marshal Baldwin and his 3rd Tactical Air Force.[22] Critical of Peirse's and Baldwin's apparent reluctance to wholeheartedly embrace the Air Commando concept, Arnold told Air Marshal Sir William Welsh, head of the RAF delegation in Washington, that he could control Stratemeyer—who was his own senior Army Air Force officer in ACSEA—but not the RAF commanders in the theater.[23] Arnold would resist placing the Air Commandos under men who were not experienced in Air Commando operations; hence his insistence that an American officer would direct the operations of the Air Commando and combat cargo groups and that they would come under an American chain of command. And, as Arnold informed Mountbatten, if SEAC could not come up with concrete plans for the effective use of these units in the type of operations they were designed for, he would turn these units over to another theater that could use them.[24]

Despite their need for many more transport aircraft, Mountbatten and his senior air commanders were reluctant to accept Arnold's offer with the conditions he wanted to impose on command and control of the Air Commando and combat cargo units. It has been argued that their reluctance stemmed from a lack of imagination, from traditional and parochial views, and from the difficulty of accepting new and revolutionary ideas.[25] There is a counterargument that the objections of Mountbatten, Peirse, Stratemeyer, and Portal were based on certain fundamental principles that were the foundation of ACSEA, and on the realities of operations in a theater of war with persistent constraints on available resources. These relate to Clauswitz's principles of the importance of the concentration of force through unity of command, and the economical use of all forces available to a commander. Unity of command and centralized control were foundational principles of ACSEA and key to its formation as an integrated air force. Through unity of command and centralized control, the air forces could maximize the key attributes of airpower: flexibility, versatility, and concentration. In a directive on the principles of joint land/air action, Mountbatten had articulated these points:

2. The greatest asset of airpower is its flexibility which enables it to be switched quickly from one objective to another in the theater of operations. Properly commanded and controlled this enables the whole weight of available airpower to be used in selective areas in turn. This concentrated use of the Air Striking Force is a battle-winning factor of the first importance.

3. In order to exploit the flexibility of air forces to the full, it is essential that their control be centralized and command exercised through Air channels.[26]

Nothing could be more fatal, Mountbatten stated in his directive, "than to dissipate the air resources into small packets placed under the command of Army Formation Commanders with each packet working on its own plan. The soldier must not expect or wish to exercise direct command over Air Striking Forces."[27] In arguing for unity of command and centralized control, Peirse said that an essential aspect of command was the ability of the Allied air commander to move Allied air units within the theater and to allocate them according to operational necessity—a view that Portal strongly supported from London.[28]

Flexibility in the use of available air resources was equally important to ACSEA in a theater where economical use of limited forces was always an issue. ACSEA had to make the best use of the air units assigned to its command, maximizing the number of hours or sorties flown per month. The flexibility of airpower enabled air units to be moved at short notice and over long distances to wherever they were needed, ensuring that they were employed in the air campaign to the fullest extent possible. Arnold's insistence that the Air Commando and combat cargo units be used only for long-range-penetration missions would lead to units that would remain idle when not required for these types of missions—a luxury that

Air supply was vital to the ability of the 14th Army to advance into central Burma. With the lack of adequate roads, the army became almost completely dependent on what transport aircraft could carry into landing grounds in Burma or air drop to forward units (*shown*). A C-47 from the 1st Combat Cargo Group drops supplies to a British unit that had reached the Chindwin River into Burma in December 1944. *3A-37096, RG342FH, NARA*

As well as supplying forward units, Allied transport aircraft flew supplies to bases within India to speed delivery of food and other equipment. This C-47 is taking on a load of long-range drop tanks to be delivered to the 459th Fighter Squadron in late 1944.
Author's collection

ACSEA could ill afford. As Clauswitz wrote, a commander had "always to make sure that all forces are involved—always to ensure that no part of the whole force is idle."[29] In proposing his reorganization of Eastern Air Command to Peirse, Stratemeyer had stressed that one of his primary objectives for the command was to ensure "the most economical and efficient use of forces available."[30] To this point, Portal wrote to Mountbatten as the debate over the Air Commandos continued that he wanted to "avoid the waste of effort which would be entailed by having independent Air Commandos which could be used only in one specialized role."[31] As effective as the 1st Air Commandos had been in supporting Wingate's Special Force, the principle for the operation of Air Commando units that Arnold advocated "gave rise to the danger of tying down air forces permanently and exclusively to one particular army formation with the consequent risks of duplication and the lack of flexibility."[32]

There was a fundamental disagreement between Arnold and Peirse, Stratemeyer, and Portal on the type of unit required for long-range-penetration missions. While Arnold argued that the Air Commando concept required specialized training and expertise incorporated into select units, Peirse, Stratemeyer, and Portal considered that the skills required should be considered part of the normal operations of existing fighter, bomber, and transport squadrons of any tactical air force. The essence of Arnold's Air Commando concept was the use of transport aircraft to insert large numbers of troops behind enemy lines, fighters and bombers to provide close air support in lieu of artillery and tanks, and light aircraft to evacuate the wounded. As Peirse wrote to Portal a few weeks after the launch of Operation THURSDAY:

Experience in support [of] Wingate operations has confirmed my opinion that special air commandos are not necessary and fundamentally unsound. I consider there are no tasks in support of LRPG operations which cannot be undertaken by Tactical Air Force and Troop Carrier Command providing suitable aircraft and equipment available.[33]

Using regular units trained in these types of operations was just as effective and far more economical. With a system of unity of command and centralized control, an air commander could allocate units to special missions as and when required, then return them to regular operations. As Stratemeyer pointed out in a report to Arnold on the initial phase of Operation THURSDAY, since the requirements of Special Force quickly exceeded the capacity of the Air Commando force, regular Tactical Air Force and Troop Carrier Command squadrons took over many of the functions of the 1st Air Commandos and contributed just as much to the success of the operation.[34] During the initial fly-in of Special Force, Troop Carrier Command squadrons airlifted 77 percent of Special Force soldiers to the landing zones behind Japanese lines and delivered 79 percent of the supplies.[35]

By the time of this debate, both air and ground commanders in SEAC had gained an appreciation of the valuable contribution air supply could make to the ground battle in Burma and the mobility it could provide to the ground forces through their own direct experience of battle. In countering the Japanese attacks in the Arakan in early 1944, in resisting the Japanese assault on Imphal when IV Corps units became entirely dependent on air supply, in airlifting two divisions from the Arakan north to join the Imphal battle, and in supplying Stilwell's American and Chinese force advancing on Myitkyina, air supply and air support had made vital contributions to Allied success.[36] As Stilwell pointed out in a letter to Arnold, the operations under his command in northern Burma through the end of June were *[a]n exemplification of the kind of joint air and ground operations which you have in mind on a larger and more demanding basis than has heretofore been undertaken in any Theater. . . . all our Allied ground combat forces now operating in northern Burma and in the Imphal area, American, British, Chinese and Indian, are being logistically sustained almost entirely by air.*[37]

There was no debate on the value of moving large numbers of soldiers by air and sustaining them through air supply. The Allied armies fighting in the Arakan, Assam, and Burma were already employing the concepts of air mobility. How best to employ these concepts, by what type of units, how effectively and economically, and under what form of command and control were the issues.

In some quarters there were also doubts about the effectiveness of Special Force in the campaign in northern Burma. Toward the end of June, Stratemeyer wrote a long letter to Arnold on plans for employing the Air Commandos in which he expressed some reservations. While agreeing that the fly-in of troops behind Japanese lines was "brilliantly conceived and executed" and "opened the eyes of the world to the capabilities of a new form of warfare," Stratemeyer told Arnold that "the operation as whole is not believed to have been worth the effort" for several reasons that he enumerated.[38] Stratemeyer pointed out that once on the ground, the troops of Special Force had limited mobility, but their supply requirements were effectively the same as any other unit in the theater, placing the same level of demand on the air supply system. Operating at a great distance from the squadrons providing them with close air support, Special Force could not get all the close air support the force needed. They had not, he believed, "accomplished the destruction to rear areas, supplies, and lines of communication that was anticipated."[39] Stratemeyer believed that the ground troops in these operations should be "imbued with the necessity for bold strikes and should be able to attack or defend as the situation demands. The Galahad Force is a good example."[40] He was particularly concerned with the ground troops remaining in one place and becoming stagnant, as happened with Special Force through Wingate's concept of the stronghold. "These forces," he argued, "should be lightly equipped and remain mobile, and the air units assigned to their support must have the ability to help them overcome any ground action that might cause them to become stagnant."[41]

Davidson, too, had some reservations. Writing to Brig. Derek Tulloch, Wingate's chief of staff, Davidson said, "I had no intention of questioning their [the Chindits'] valor but was anxious to have your views on the wisdom of sending in lightly armed forces and leaving them for long periods of time in the heart of the enemy country."[42] Davidson made the argument that "if heavily armed troops had been sent in to relieve them I could more readily understand the policy of sending in a force like the Chindits to act as an airborne spearhead to seize ground that following troops, properly armed, would ultimately hold."[43] While agreeing, like Stratemeyer, that the landings had been a magnificent achievement, Davidson wondered if five well-trained brigades with artillery and other heavy equipment had marched into Burma instead of air landing the lightly armed Chindit brigades that the heavily armed brigades "might have been able to fight their way to Indaw by now, whereas the lightly armed Chindits, although having actually gotten to Indaw, have had to fight their way out to Mogaung."[44]

The debate with Arnold placed Stratemeyer in an awkward position. While agreeing philosophically with his RAF colleagues, he nonetheless felt compelled to agree to Arnold's wishes and accept Arnold's conditions.[45] He could not overrule his own Army Air Force commander. He told his staff about Arnold's letter to Mountbatten of March 24 and that the conditions it contained "should be and must be followed despite the wishes of Lord Louis and ACM Peirse to the contrary."[46] In his plan for the reorganization of Eastern Air Command, Stratemeyer proposed creating a new tactical formation with an American commander that would report directly to him, thus satisfying Arnold's requirement for an American chain of command.[47] Stratemeyer's plan was to have the Air Commando and combat cargo groups Arnold had allocated for the CBI come under this new formation to form an air task force that would be responsible for organizing, coordinating, and directing the air units supporting the ground forces in long-range-penetration operations. Peirse was not averse to the creation of a special air task force within Eastern Air Command or an American chain of command as long as he could be sure that once this special task force was established, the assigned units would contribute to regular operations if not required for special missions.[48] This point remained formally unresolved for some months.

Arnold's main concern, which he expressed repeatedly to Mountbatten, Stratemeyer, and Stilwell with support from Marshall, was to have SEAC develop concrete plans for the full utilization of the Air Commando and combat cargo groups. Arnold conveyed his frustration when such plans were not forthcoming.[49] Part of the problem, as Stratemeyer pointed out to Arnold, was that as of July, SEAC had not received a firm directive from the Combined Chiefs of Staff on future operations in Burma.[50] Plans were still in flux, with what would become Operation CAPITAL still in the formative stages. In a long response to Arnold, Mountbatten assured him that "no unnecessary aircraft or formations will be asked for and that the use of every one will be supported by firm plans."[51] Mountbatten went on to explain the evolving view of air supply and air-landing operations in SEAC:

I do not believe that there is any fundamental disagreement between your views and the views held by Stratemeyer, Peirse and myself out here. The dispatch from Air Chief Marshal Peirse to Portal which you mention in your letter sprang from a desire to get people here to regard airborne operations, and the operations of Long Range Penetration Groups supported by Air Commando Groups, as normal operations for this theatre. We felt that there are advantages in getting away from the idea that one can only launch such operations if one has specialized and highly trained personnel on the job. We feel that in this theater our major offensive operations should be of this type. In fact . . . the plans which I am now formulating for operations during the forthcoming winter campaigning season are based on the extensive movement by air of large ground forces, and the maintenance of these forces by air for an extended period. I want to be free to operate land forces where necessary without being tied to land lines of communication. I want it to be regarded as nothing unusual for any unit of the Army to be transported by air and supplied by air during the battle. All minds are ready to accept this point of view, but we need sufficient air resources to give effect to it.[52]

As the planning staffs in SEAC and NCAC explored possibilities for operations under Plan X and Plan Y—the plans that formed the basis for Operation CAPITAL—they proposed two airborne landing operations: one to seize Kalewa, on the Chindwin River, in support of 14th Army's advance, and a second operation to seize Lashio to support the advance of Stilwell's Chinese divisions.[53] There were also plans for airborne operations in support of the operation to capture Rangoon as part of operation DRACULA. On the basis of these plans, and the likelihood that both 14th Army and the NCAC would be heavily reliant on air supply, Mountbatten submitted a request to Arnold and to the Joint Chiefs of Staff for two more combat cargo groups in addition to the two combat cargo groups already allocated to SEAC.[54] Instead of the two combat cargo groups he requested, at the Quadrant Conference the Joint Chiefs of Staff promised to send one additional combat cargo group and one Air Commando group to SEAC to provide more air resources for the planned operations approved at the conference.[55] With the planned magnitude and vital importance of air supply operations in the coming offensives, it became clear that Eastern Air Command would need a new organization to control and coordinate these operations that would be separate from 3rd Tactical Air Force, which controlled air supply operations of the four RAF and seven Army Air Force squadrons assigned.[56] Consequently, Stratemeyer activated the Combat Cargo Task Force (CCTF) on 14 September 1944 to take over the role originally envisioned for the Air Task Force he had set up in June.[57] This was to be a larger, integrated organization with a wider mission than the Air Task Force, encompassing not just air-landing operations, but the full gamut of air supply, incorporating RAF and Army Air Force transport squadrons as well as the Air Commando units. Stratemeyer assigned two missions to the CCTF:

a Delivery of air supplies to units of the Northern Combat Area Command, Fourteenth Army, and such other forces as required, in accordance with plans previously approved by the Air Commander, Eastern Air Command.

b The transport of ground or airborne troops by air and the air evacuation of personnel, in accordance with plans previously approved by the Air Commander, Eastern Air Command.[58]

The 1st Air Commando Light Plane Section also underwent a reorganization, forming three liaison squadrons with the designation (Commando). This L-5 carries the five white bands on the tail (representing each of the 1st Air Commando's first five sections). The aircraft was purchased with donations from students in the United States—one of a number of "Angel of Mercy" light aircraft that flew in Burma. *Box 11, Air, folder H, RG208AA, NARA*

At activation, the Combat Cargo Task Force took command of the 1st Combat Cargo Group (CCG), the newly reorganized 1st Air Commando Group, and No. 177 Wing, RAF, with No. 117 and No. 194 Transport Squadrons.[59] Brig. Gen. Frederick Evans, who had been commanding the 1st Troop Carrier Command in the United States, became commander of the CCTF, reporting directly to Stratemeyer as commander of Eastern Air Command, thus preserving the American chain of command Arnold wanted. Activated on 15 April 1944—just a few weeks after Arnold's offer of the combat cargo groups to Mountbatten—the 1st Combat Cargo Group comprised the 1st, 2nd, 3rd, and 4th Combat Cargo Squadrons. To streamline the

The 1st Air Commando Fighter Section was reorganized into the 5th and 6th Fighter Squadrons (Commando) and equipped with the P-47D Thunderbolt. As part of the Combat Cargo Task Force, the Air Commando fighter squadrons would fly interdiction and close-support missions for the 14th Army. *3A-33721, RG342FH, NARA*

flying units, airdrome squadrons provided maintenance and other services, each paired with one of the combat cargo squadrons. To provide more aircraft for the principal mission, the combat cargo squadrons had an establishment of 25 aircraft as opposed to the 13 to 16 airplanes in a troop carrier squadron. The squadrons operated with smaller crews, consisting of a pilot, copilot, flight engineer, and radio operator, and fewer crews per airplane than an equivalent troop carrier squadron. The 1st Combat Cargo Group had a complement of 100 C-47s. Training in air supply operations began immediately. The group's aircraft began leaving for India on 8 August 1944, arriving at their initial base at Sylhet, India, between August 27 and September 3.[60]

The 1st Air Commando Group had undergone a reorganization, creating squadrons out of what had been the different sections of the 1st Air Commando Force. After completing its assignment to Special Force in May, the Air Commandos had withdrawn to the airfield at Asansol, northwest of Calcutta, and did not participate in combat operations until reforming in September. On 1 September 1944 the group activated the 319th Troop Carrier Squadron (Commando), with C-47s, and the 164th, 165th, and 166th Liaison Squadrons (Commando), with L-1, L-5, and UC-64 aircraft.[61] The Fighter Section became the 5th Fighter Squadron (Commando). During September, Stratemeyer authorized activation of the 6th Fighter Squadron (Commando) to conform to the new table of organization for Air Commando groups that allowed for two fighter squadrons.[62] Both fighter squadrons received new P-47Ds to replace their remaining P-51As and P-51Bs and some war-weary P-40Ns the unit had received for training. The two squadrons received replacement pilots fresh from training in the United States to replace many of the veterans who rotated back. The group retained its bomber section, but for some reason the bomber section did not convert to squadron status, becoming the Bomber, Night Intruder Section, with new B-25H aircraft.[63]

The 1st Combat Cargo Group began operations shortly after the first aircraft arrived at Sylhet, initially evacuating British and Indian casualties and transporting supplies into Imphal.[64] Beginning in mid-September, the group's squadrons began sending detachments to China to work with the India-China Division, Air Transport Command, flying supplies over the Hump and helping transport American and Chinese personnel and equipment where needed in China, including the Fourteenth Air Force airfields at Kweilin and Linchow, which later fell to the Japanese in November 1944. The 319th Squadron and the 164th, 165th, and 165th Liaison Squadrons also began operations soon after their activation. The 319th began flying fresh meat from Calcutta to Imphal, calling themselves the "Mutton Marauders," while the liaison squadrons sent detachments to the airfield at Palel, close to Imphal, and began working with forward units of 14th Army, evacuating casualties back to waiting C-47s for transportation to rear-area hospitals.[65] In both cases the squadrons began flying regular air support missions just as Peirse had wanted them to, and were not held solely for a long-range-penetration operation as Arnold had intended. While there appears to be no formal statement recording Arnold changing his mind on this point, it does seem from the record of operations that the combat cargo and Air Commando squadrons were put to good use in regular operations as soon as possible. It may be that Arnold was willing to compromise and accept the position that Peirse, Portal, and Stratemeyer had advocated for: the most economical use of the resources they had available in return for their acceptance of the American chain of command Arnold wanted. And by this point,

SEAC was on the verge of embarking on what Arnold had wanted all along: an offensive into Burma.[66]

During October the 1st Combat Cargo Group and the Air Commando transport and liaison squadrons steadily expanded their operations. The 1st CCG's detachments in China completed their assignment by the middle of the month, returning to India to continue support for 14th Army. The group operated at a disadvantage since its base at Sylhet was not a 14th Army supply point. This meant the squadrons had to fly to another base to pick up a load of supplies, limiting the amount of supplies the squadrons could deliver. To improve the efficiency of the air supply effort, the CCTF arranged for the 3rd Combat Cargo Squadron to move to the airfield at Tulihal, in the Imphal Valley, where the 14th Army could load supplies directly. Another 1st CCG detachment of eight aircraft from the 2nd Combat Cargo Squadron went to an airfield 9 miles north of Chittagong, in the Arakan, to support XV Corps. With the weather improving, and a full month of operations, the group flew double the number of hours, carrying out 1,632 sorties and delivering 5,125

Loading mules onto a C-47 was always a challenge. Once in the air the mules were normally well behaved and appeared to accept being transported by air without protest. The problem was getting them into the airplane. *3A-37114, RG342, NARA*

tons of combat cargo. The C-47s would fly to the airfield at Agartala or Imphal to pick up cargos, dropping these to the forward units of XXXIII Corps advancing in the Chin Hills toward the Chindwin. These missions were not without risk, or without loss. The group lost three C-47s on air supply missions during the month. Engine failure during supply-dropping missions caused the loss of two aircraft, with the pilot and radio operator in one crew dying from the wounds they sustained in the subsequent crash landing. In a third incident a supply parachute and pack caught on the tail of the airplane, causing it to crash with the loss of the entire crew. The liaison aircraft, flying from an advanced base at Tamu, continued their main work of casualty evacuation, also flying in supplies that could not be air-dropped and carrying Army officers on reconnaissance flights over the forward areas.[67]

In October the 14th Army set up the Combined Army Air Transport Organization (CAATO) to work with the CCTF.[68] CAATO had the task of processing the daily requests for air supply from Army units, determining their priority, and providing a task list to the CCTF, who would then allocate the missions to the squadrons on the basis of available airplanes and crews.[69] CAATO also took over responsibility for the Rear Airfield Maintenance Organizations (RAMO), which oversaw the work of arranging the delivery of supplies to air bases and their packing for supply-dropping missions. Though not without problems, this new combined Air Force and Army structure did improve air transport and supply operations.[70] One of CAATO's first tasks was to increase the flow of supplies from the railhead at Dimapur to the airfields around Imphal. This enabled the 1st CCG squadrons to move from Sylhet to the Imphal area. The 2nd Combat Cargo Squadron went first, transferring to Imphal on November 23. The 1st Combat Cargo Squadron joined the 3rd CCS at Tulihal on November 25, with the 4th CCS and the headquarters of the 1st CCG following at the end of the month. A new unit joined the CCTF this month: the 317th Troop Carrier Squadron (Commando), the first unit from the new 2nd Air Commando Group to arrive in India, went to Imphal, beginning air supply operations to XXXIII Corps soon after arrival.[71]

By mid-November, advance units of 14th Army were closing in on the Chindwin River. The 11th East African Division occupied Kalemyo on November 14, while the next day a brigade from 19th Indian Division reached Sittaung, on the Chindwin River, with a second brigade from the division crossing the Chindwin and setting up a bridgehead on November 16.[72] Slim's plan was to concentrate both IV Corps and XXXIII Corps in the Chindwin area by mid-December in preparation for the second phase of his plan, the advance into central Burma.[73] Army engineers began working to improve the tracks leading from Imphal to the Chindwin, but the forward units of XXXIII Corps remained heavily dependent on air supply. The CCTF transports carried just about everything the troops needed: food, ammunition of all kinds, and gasoline and parts for motor vehicles. In addition, the transports took aviation fuel, parts, and bombs to forward RAF bases and flew the regular fresh-meat run from Calcutta to Imphal. After a few training flights, the 319th Troop Carrier Squadron (Commando) began towing gliders to the front to bring in more supplies, completing 57 glider-towing missions carrying 70 tons of supplies and 37 personnel. Using the glider aerial-retrieval system the Army Air Force had developed, where a C-47 with a hook attached under the fuselage could hook a nylon loop stretched between two poles to pull a glider off the ground, the 319th Squadron snatched gliders to bring out 160 casualties.[74] With improving weather, the squadrons flew twice the number of hours they had flown during October and carried over 50 percent more cargo and passengers. The 3rd Combat Cargo Squadron led the CCTF, flying 1,536 trips and carrying 4,443 tons of cargo—more than a quarter of the total for the CCTF.[75] The Air Commando liaison squadrons were equally busy. The 165th Liaison Squadron had moved to a landing ground at Tamu in October but, to be closer to the front lines, moved to a new airstrip at Yazagyo, farther down the Kawbaw Valley. Squadron engineers found a way to speed up loading a litter into the squadron's L-5s by cutting out part of the rear fuselage to fit a hinged section that could be quickly lifted to insert a litter.[76] During the month the 165th Squadron completed a remarkable 2,569 trips, carrying out 1,264 casualties and bringing in 544 personnel, while the 166th Squadron flew 1,151 trips, carrying 968 casualties and 500 personnel in addition to a combined 53 tons of supplies.[77]

The flying was demanding, with the C-47 crews flying up to three missions a day, each two to three hours in duration into rough landing strips or dropping supplies on forward drop zones. One

A C-47 from the 1st Air Commando Group's 319th Transport Squadron comes in to land at a newly built fair-weather airstrip at Yazagyo, near the Chindwin River, in December 1944, carrying supplies for the advancing units of XXXIII Corps. The airstrip could accommodate C-47s but had little margin for error, as the damaged plane in the background attests. *GP-A-CMDO-HI, AFHRA*

The Combat Cargo Task Force's transports carried everything the troops needed to airstrips close to the front. To supplement the transport planes, the 1st Air Commando Group began using gliders to fly in supplies. After unloading, these same gliders would be loaded with wounded and taken into the air, using a special retrieval system. *3A-35683, RG342, NARA*

A wood, bamboo, and thatch hut served as the Air Commando operations post at the Yazagyo airstrip. In the dry season the men built shelters from whatever materials were at hand, and took wood from shipping crates to make tables and chairs. More-permanent structures were unnecessary, since within a few weeks operations would move to a new airstrip closer to the front as the transport units followed the 14th Army's advance into Burma. *GP-A-CMDO-HI, AFHRA*

The 4th Combat Cargo Group joined the Combat Cargo Task Force in December 1944. The group's larger C-46 Commando aircraft added significantly to the CCTF's cargo capacity just as the 14th Army was beginning its advance into Burma and drawing farther away from its already limited land lines of communication. *File 824.6867, AFHRA*

observer on a supply-dropping flight described the pilots of the C-47 he was riding in:

Coming down from over 3,000' to just over 150' through some very mountainous and wooded defiles, they (and the other aircraft in the formation) dropped their stores with the greatest precision. A field which appeared to be 150 yards square was virtually plastered with the white silk of parachutes . . .

I can honestly say that I never realized that a C-47, with well over three tons of stores, could be maneuvered with such accuracy a few feet over the trees making relatively steep climbing turns directly [over where] the stores were dropped.[78]

There were also more losses. The *64th Hikōsentai* sent 24 Ki-43s on a mission to attack 14th Army artillery positions near Kalemyo on November 8. They found instead transport aircraft dropping supplies without fighter cover, claiming four transports shot down. Returning in the afternoon, 25 Ki-43s again ran into a flight of transports, claiming several more. The 3rd Combat Cargo Squadron lost two C-47s that day. Ground troops saw one of the attacking Oscars shoot down one of the C-47s in flames, with the loss of the entire crew. The second C-47 lost that day simply went missing but was most likely a victim of the Japanese fighters. The RAF squadrons also suffered, with No. 31 Squadron losing two aircraft and No. 62 Squadron losing one in the afternoon combat. The 317th Troop Carrier Squadron (Commando) suffered its first loss when one of the squadron's C-47s lost an engine on takeoff and crashed north of Tulihel, killing the pilot and injuring the rest of the crew. The unfortunate 3rd CCS lost a third C-47 when it crashed trying to land on the airstrip at Yazagyo, losing an engine and then stalling and crashing into the jungle, killing the pilot, copilot, and radio operator.[79]

December brought the welcome and fortuitous arrival of the 4th Combat Cargo Group, the third combat cargo group the Joint Chiefs of Staff had promised for SEAC and Operation CAPITAL. The 4th Combat Cargo Group's four squadrons (13th, 14th, 15th, and 16th Combat Cargo Squadrons) flew the larger Curtiss C-46 Commando, which could carry more than the smaller C-47s. By December 7, all four squadrons had reached their initial base at Sylhet, beginning operations immediately with some 80 available C-46s and bringing the total strength of the CCTF to 209 transport aircraft.[80] Their arrival was timely, since Operation GRUBWORM—moving the Chinese 14th and 22nd Divisions back to China—was about to begin. Wedemeyer had available transport aircraft from the Tenth Air Force and the India-China Division of the ATC but requested more support from the CCTF, given the urgency of conditions in China. The CCTF had already released the two Air Commando transport squadrons, but Wedemeyer asked for two more combat cargo squadrons to speed up movement of the two divisions to China.[81] Mountbatten agreed to give him the two squadrons, the 1st and 2nd Combat Cargo Squadrons moving to bases in China on 11–12 December 1944. When Wedemeyer requested even more transport squadrons to move additional Chinese troops from India to China, Mountbatten again agreed to the loan of an additional combat cargo squadron, with the provision that the squadron had to be returned by 1 February 1945 to support CAPITAL.[82] The 4th Combat Cargo Squadron moved to China on December 21, leaving the 3rd Combat Cargo Squadron at Tulihal to continue supporting 14th Army. Two RAF transport squadrons moved to the Imphal area to replace the American squadrons assigned to China, but the movement of five transport squadrons placed 14th Army on the tightest of air supply margins just as Slim was trying to push IV and XXXIII Corps across the Chindwin. In his great memoir of the war in Burma, Slim recorded his astonishment at the move:

At dawn on the 10th December I was awakened in my headquarters at Imphal by the roar of engines as a large number of aircraft took off in succession and passed low overhead. I knew loaded aircraft were due to leave for 33 Corps later in the morning, but I was surprised at this early start. I sent somebody to discover what it was all about. To my consternation, I learnt that, without warning, three squadrons of American Dakotas (75 aircraft), allotted to Fourteenth Army maintenance, had suddenly been

THE TENTH AIR FORCE IN WORLD WAR II

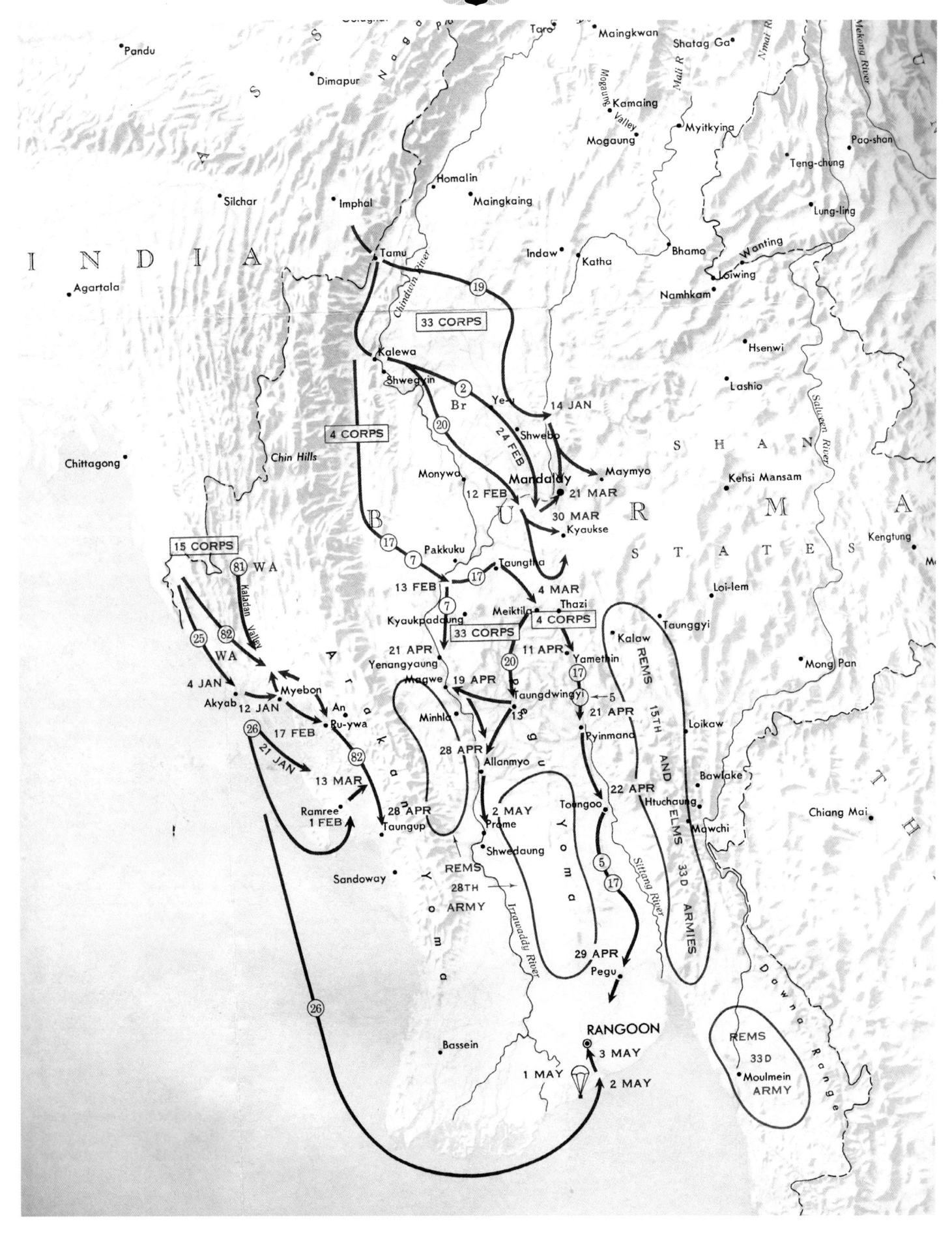

ordered to China, where Stilwell's prophecy had been fulfilled, and the Japanese, galled by Chennault's air attacks on shipping, had begun to overrun the forward American airfields. Passing overhead were the first flights bound for China. The supplies in the aircraft, already loaded for Fourteenth Army, were dumped on the Imphal strip and the machines took off. The noise of their engines was the first intimation anyone in Fourteenth Army had of the administrative crisis now bursting upon us.[83]

Once agreed on, the movement of the American transport squadrons began so quickly that there had not been time to warn 14th Army.[84] This took place just as Slim was having to drastically revise his plans for the coming battle.[85] Slim had intended to fight *Burma Area Army*'s divisions in the Shwebo plain, to the west of Mandalay between the Chindwin and the Irrawaddy Rivers. By mid-December, Slim had received indications that Lt. Gen. Kimura, who had replaced Lt. Gen. Kawabe as commander of *Burma Area Army* in August, had no intention of fighting the battle on ground that would favor 14th Army. Slim now believed that Kimura would withdraw his divisions across the Irrawaddy to fight a battle south of Mandalay, forcing 14th Army to contemplate one of the most difficult of military operations: an opposed river crossing. Slim's challenge was to find a way of forcing the Japanese army to do battle, preventing the Japanese army's further retreat, and giving 14th Army the opportunity to destroy the Japanese divisions in central Burma to open the way to the south and Rangoon. He realized he needed to place a significant force south of Mandalay to threaten the Japanese line of retreat to the south, knowing that Kimura would have to fight to withdraw from central Burma to protect the important rice fields of the Irrawaddy delta. Slim's revised plan, which he designated EXTENDED CAPITAL, called for XXXIII Corps to cross the Irrawaddy and advance on Mandalay—the ancient capital of Burma—to draw Kimura's divisions into battle around the city. While XXXIII Corps drew Japanese attention toward Mandalay, Slim planned to send IV Corps to the west to make a crossing of the Irrawaddy around Pakokku, then send a mechanized and armored force to seize the town of Meiktila, sitting astride the road and rail links to the south. Meiktila was the key administrative and supply center both for *15th* and *33rd Armies*. Slim saw this as an opportunity to have the decisive battle he wanted:

Road and rail routes from the south-east and west converged on Meiktila and Thazi, to spread out again to the north like the extended fingers of a hand, whose wrist was Meiktila. Crush that wrist, no blood would flow through the fingers, the whole hand would be paralyzed, and the Japanese armies on the arc from the Salween to the Irrawaddy would begin to wither. If we took Meiktila while Kimura was deeply engaged along the Irrawaddy about Mandalay, he would be compelled to detach large forces to clear his vital communications. This should give me not only the major battle I desired, but the chance to repeat our old hammer and anvil tactics: 33 Corps the hammer from the north against the anvil of 4 Corps at Meiktila—and the Japanese between.[86]

Slim's concern with the departure of the American transport squadrons is understandable. Logistics would be key to the success of the battle he was planning. He had initially thought of seizing Meiktila with an airborne operation, but the lack of paratroops that could be trained in time for the battle and the withdrawal of the American transport squadrons to China forced him to reconsider his plans. The advance would have to be over land. Slim would have to arrange support for three divisions and an armored brigade in XXXIII Corps, and two divisions and a second armored brigade in IV Corps, with one division in reserve. The daily requirement for this force by the end of January was expected to amount to 788 tons a day, rising to 861 tons a day for the expected peak of operations between March and May 1945.[87] This was theoretically within what the planners estimated to be the CCTF's capacity with the squadrons allocated to the command by January 1945. The unexpected diversion of the American transport squadrons to China had not entered into the planning process. In addition to their daily requirements, Slim's divisions would need several weeks in December and the following January to build up supplies for the advance, putting more demands on the transport squadrons. Once the advance had begun, the divisions would be a long way from their main supply base at Imphal. Army engineers would have to build both an all-weather road down to Kalewa and a fair-weather road from Kalewa to Shwebo, in addition to building a river-borne transport system to supplement road and air supply. Slim's divisions would be reliant on air supply for the bulk of their supplies. As Mountbatten wrote to the Chiefs of Staff on 1 January 1945:

The advance of the Army into Burma depends absolutely on air supply, because the land lines of communication are inadequate. . . . A halt may be forced on 14th Army unless three [American] squadrons are released or replaced from outside the theater by 1 March.[88]

The arrival of the 4th Combat Cargo Group with its C-46s was even more important to the CCTF after the transfer of several of its American transport squadrons to support Operation GRUBWORM, the movement of Chinese divisions from Burma to China by air that began in mid-December 1944.
File 824.6867, AFHRA

C-47s from an American transport squadron on an advance airstrip in Burma, three days after engineers finished carving a rough landing ground out of the surrounding countryside. A makeshift timber tower controlled operations in and out of the airstrip, while trucks carried supplies from the airstrip to the front. *3A-33669, NARA*

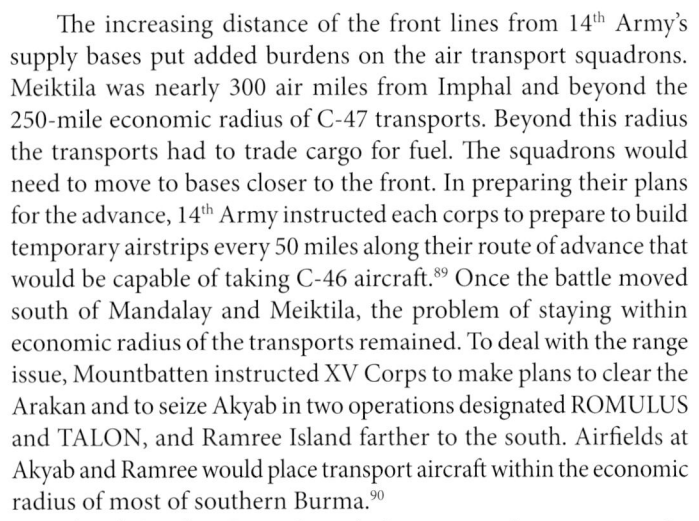

The inside of a C-46 packed with supplies for 14th Army. The C-46 could carry significantly more than a C-47. From 4 December 1944 to 2 January 1945 the 13th Combat Cargo Squadron carried more than 5 million pounds of supplies to the front, as well as passengers, replacement troops, and casualties ferried to rear-area hospitals. *3A-37235, RG342, NARA*

The increasing distance of the front lines from 14th Army's supply bases put added burdens on the air transport squadrons. Meiktila was nearly 300 air miles from Imphal and beyond the 250-mile economic radius of C-47 transports. Beyond this radius the transports had to trade cargo for fuel. The squadrons would need to move to bases closer to the front. In preparing their plans for the advance, 14th Army instructed each corps to prepare to build temporary airstrips every 50 miles along their route of advance that would be capable of taking C-46 aircraft.[89] Once the battle moved south of Mandalay and Meiktila, the problem of staying within economic radius of the transports remained. To deal with the range issue, Mountbatten instructed XV Corps to make plans to clear the Arakan and to seize Akyab in two operations designated ROMULUS and TALON, and Ramree Island farther to the south. Airfields at Akyab and Ramree would place transport aircraft within the economic radius of most of southern Burma.[90]

The 4th Combat Cargo Group's C-46s went a long way to make up for the loss of the 1st Combat Cargo Group's three squadrons and the two Air Commando transport squadrons to Operation GRUBWORM. Despite the loss of five squadrons for half the month, the CCTF flew 28,817 tons of supplies and personnel during December, an increase of 71 percent over November. The 4th CCG delivered 8,479 tons—nearly a third of the total delivered—while the 3rd Combat Cargo Squadron delivered 3,665 tons—more than any other squadron in the CCTF—flying every day during the month and completing 1,705 trips.[91] Remarkably, given the intensity of operations, the 3rd CCS suffered no losses during the month. Since IV Corps was just beginning its advance across the Chindwin River, the bulk of supplies went to XXXIII Corps. Losses were lower and by chance confined to the 4th CCG, which lost four C-46s during supply operations, though none to enemy action.[92]

The 4th CCG found flying from their base at Sylhet uneconomic, since the C-46s would have to leave Sylhet and fly empty to another supply base to pick up their cargo. Often this meant a trip from Sylhet to Comilla—a major 14th Army supply base—where the squadrons loaded cargo for a flight to Imphal, returning to Comilla with casualties, then returning empty to Sylhet at the end of the day. Forward landing strips proved vital to maximizing the carrying capacity of the C-46s, allowing the airplanes to carry in a full load of supplies. The C-46 proved less adept at air-dropping supplies than the C-47, being more difficult to maneuver at the low speeds and low altitudes that airdrops required. Fortunately, 14th Army engineers built more landing strips or repaired captured Japanese airfields as the advance progressed. One of the first of these was the airstrip at Yazagyo, 150 miles south of Imphal. A pilot from the 15th Combat Cargo Squadron carried out test landings on the strip on 13 December 1944 with a 7,000-pound load of cargo and found it acceptable. The transports could fly to Yazagyo from Imphal along a route that had fighter patrols for protection. A few days later a second strip became open for the C-46s a few miles farther south. Among the difficulties in using these forward landing strips was an initial burst of overexuberance on the part of the newly arrived C-46 crews, who would forget their air discipline in a rush to land and offload their cargos. Appointment of formation leaders helped establish more-orderly landings. There were often problems rounding up laborers to offload cargos—more difficult with the larger C-46s than the smaller C-47s. An unforeseen cultural problem was the prohibition on Hindu laborers touching meat. A C-46 with a cargo of meat aboard had to wait for a Muslim labor crew, who faced no such cultural ban. As an example of one squadron's effort, from 4 December 1944 to 2 January 1945 the 13th Combat Cargo Squadron carried in to the forward areas 5,350,042 pounds of military supplies (principally gasoline, food, and ammunition), 408 passengers, and 754 replacement troops and evacuated 75 casualties to rear-area hospitals.[93]

Two Royal Canadian Air Force transport squadrons joined the CCTF late in the year—No. 435 Squadron in December and No. 436 Squadron in mid-January—helping to offset the continued absence of the 1st CCG and bringing the average total of aircraft assigned to the CCTF to 228. Although weather limited flying on several days in January, the CCTF squadrons flew nearly every day, flying 60 percent more hours during January and delivering 55 percent more supplies and personnel than in December and reaching a total of 44,645 tons—more than four times the amount delivered during October. With IV Corps now fully engaged in the advance, the amount of supplies delivered to IV Corps units doubled. The liaison squadrons were equally busy, flying 5,000 missions during

January—26 percent more than in December—and evacuating 2,716 casualties. The *64th Hikōsentai* struck again on January 12, this time finding No. 435 Squadron's Dakotas over an advanced landing ground at Onbauk, shooting down two aircraft and destroying two more on the ground. After this incident the transports took to flying to the forward airfields at treetop level as a precaution.[94]

Once again the C-46s of the 4th CCG proved their worth, carrying 19,593 tons of supplies and personnel, nearly half the CCTF's total for the month. As the distances from the supply points to the front increased, the transport squadrons would fly supplies to a field midway between the supply base and the front lines, where other transport aircraft would pick the supplies up for delivery to the front. Toward the end of December the 4th CCG moved from Sylhet to the RAF airfield at Argartala. This move greatly improved the efficiency of the group's operations, since Argartala was near a railhead, allowing supplies to be brought easily to the airfield. A 14th Army RAMO moved to the airfield to speed delivery and loading of supplies. During the night, the RAMO personnel would arrange for delivery of requested supplies to the airfield and load the C-46s for the first supply run of the morning. The airfield had an ideal layout, with a loading ramp parallel to the runway. As returning empty C-46s completed their landing run, they would turn right off the runway onto the loading ramp, where the RAMO crews would load them up again; the loading procedure took about an hour. The loaded C-46s would continue down the loading ramp to turn back onto the runway and take off again. Although the C-46 was less adept at airdropping, heavy rains during the first week of January turned some of the forward airfields into seas of mud, preventing the C-46s from landing. Instead they resorted to dropping supply packs by parachute and bags of rice by free fall. When the control tower on the strip at Indainggale complained that the packs were dropped over too wide an area, one of the C-46 pilots came in and aimed right for the tower, getting the packs within 10 yards.[95]

As the advance progressed, what had been forward airfields became rear-area landing grounds and dropped off the CCTF's itinerary as new fields opened up closer to the front. During January, landing fields became available at Shwebo, Ye-U, and then Kan, though under the constant pounding of repeated landings and takeoffs the fields soon turned into rutted and uneven strips with heavy layers of dust that added to the wear and tear on engines. The dust reduced the engine life of Pratt & Whitney R-2800 engines on C-46s from 600 hours to 450 hours, compounding the demands on maintenance staff and ground crews. At Shwebo, engineers had to build a new runway after only three weeks of intensive use. Often there were as many as 40 CCTF transports circling in the area around these forward fields waiting to land. As the supply trips became longer, the 4th CCG moved again at the end of January, this time to Patenga airfield, a few miles outside Chittagong, which boasted two long runways and adequate ramp space. Chittagong was a major port, so supplies could be delivered by sea, or by rail and road from Calcutta, speeding delivery to the airfield.[96]

As February began, the CCTF could look back on an impressive record, not least the fourfold increase in supplies delivered each month from October 1944 to January 1945 despite having five fewer squadrons available. The month would bring an even-greater effort as the CCTF squadrons supported XXXIII Corps' attack on Mandalay and the IV Corps' daring race for Meiktila. In early January, Lt. Gen. Leese, commanding Allied Land Forces, Southeast Asia, and Stratemeyer told Mountbatten that 14th Army's planned advance would require an additional 100 transport aircraft, with 40 more aircraft required to support the civilian population in the soon-to-be-liberated areas of Burma.[97] To obtain these aircraft, Mountbatten requested that Wedemeyer return two of the three combat cargo squadrons sent to China by 1 February 1945. Wedemeyer agreed to this, and the 2nd and 4th Combat Squadrons returned to India at the end of January to rejoin the 3rd Combat Cargo Squadron, supporting 14th Army. Two additional RAF transport squadrons joined the CCTF, and the RAF agreed to increase the aircraft complement of its transport squadrons from 25 to 30 aircraft.[98] This brought the total of added transport aircraft to 145; enough to allow the plans for the upcoming battles for Mandalay and Meiktila to proceed with greater confidence.

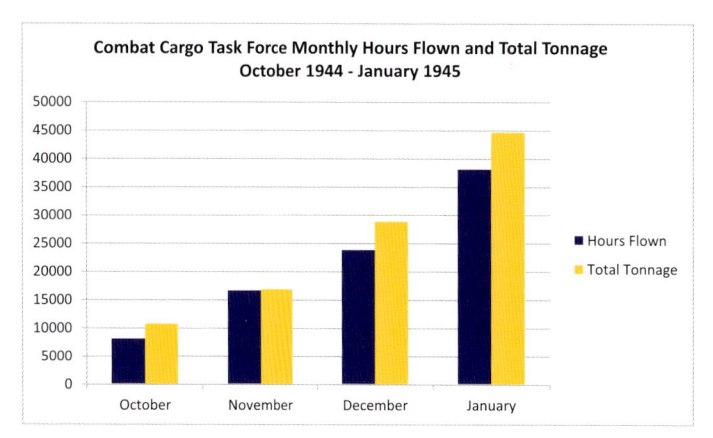

Table 10: (Combat Cargo Task Force, History 15 September 1944-31 May 1945)

Maintenance facilities were basic to say the least. Ground crew from the 4th Combat Cargo Group prepare to change an engine on one of the group's C-46s. Dust from the rough airstrips in Burma reduced engine life and forced more-frequent engine changes. *3A-35864, NARA*

Indirect Support for 14th Army

From the decisive defeat of the Japanese *15th Army* at Imphal until the start of Slim's Extended CAPITAL operation, airpower continued to play a vital role in supporting 14th Army's advance into central Burma. With the steady decline in numbers and capability of the Japanese fighter force in Burma, more of the air effort went to supporting the ground forces either on close air support against targets the ground forces designated, or against the Japanese lines

After the Battle of Imphal, the Royal Air Force began converting its Hurricane fighter-bomber squadrons in India to the more capable Republic Thunderbolt (P-47D) obtained through Lend-Lease. No. 135 Squadron was one of the first to reequip, receiving the Thunderbolt I—the razorback version—while other RAF squadrons took on the bubble canopy version designated the Thunderbolt II. *CF_001242, IWM*

based at Chittagong, had three squadrons of Hurricane Mk II, two squadrons of Spitfire Mk VIII, one Vengeance squadron, and a squadron of Beaufighters. More fighter squadrons had gone back to India for a rest period and were temporarily nonoperational. During July and August the Vengeance dive-bomber squadrons began converting to the more capable Mosquito Mk VI twin-engine fighter, while the Hurricane squadrons progressively reequipped with the Thunderbolt I (P-47D).[101] To enhance the striking power of the air units supporting 14th Army, Stratemeyer assigned several Army Air Force units to 3rd Tactical Air Force and No. 224 Group. Initially these were the 12th Bomb Group and the 459th Fighter Squadron, with the 5th and 6th Fighter Squadrons (Commando) and the Air Commando Night Intruder Section added after their activation (though the Air Commando units remained under the CCTF). The Army Air Force fighter squadrons joined the 12th Bomb Group in attacks on the Japanese lines of communication and supplies and participated in counterair operations that continued along with missions in support of the army.

Air Marshal Baldwin, commanding 3rd Tactical Air Force, had been pressing for some time to transfer the 12th Bomb Group from the Strategic Air Force to 3rd Tactical Air Force, so that the group's efforts could be more closely and more appropriately coordinated with the tactical air effort.[102] Stratemeyer agreed to the transfer and made it part of the June reorganization of Eastern Air Command, placing the 12th Bomb Group directly under 3rd Tactical Air Force. In mid-July the group's squadrons moved to new stations, with the 81st, 82nd, and 83rd Squadrons taking up residence at Feni, while the 434th Squadron went to Comilla. For most of the month, the 12th Group flew in support of Stilwell's force at Myitkyina, but toward the end of July the group began flying missions in support of 14th Army.

of communication to isolate the battlefield, and supply dumps to destroy what supplies continued to get through.[99] Following the reorganization of Eastern Air Command in June 1944, the 3rd Tactical Air Force had two groups providing support for 14th Army.[100] At Imphal, No. 221 Group, with three squadrons of Spitfire Mk VIII fighters, seven squadrons of Hurricane Mk IIc and Mk IV fighters for close air support, and one squadron of Vengeance dive-bombers, worked with IV and XXXIII Corps around Imphal. No. 224 Group,

A B-25J from the 82nd Bomb Squadron, 12th Bomb Group, bombing Japanese positions near Kalewa, on the Chindwin River, in December 1944. The 12th Bomb Group joined the 3rd Tactical Air Force in June 1944 and after the end of the monsoon began flying missions in support of 14th Army. *3A-37575, RG342, NARA*

THE TENTH AIR FORCE IN WORLD WAR II

The monsoon weather interfered on some missions, but the group's squadrons began bombing the Japanese supply areas supporting *15th Army* divisions as they retreated back to the Chindwin River, hitting Tiddim, Kalewa, and Sittaung. The benefit of having the 12th Bomb Group available was its ability to saturate a target with bombs of different types. On September 17, the 81st and 82nd Squadrons hit the town of Mawleik on the Chindwin, dropping 144 100-pound demolition bombs and 144 100-pound incendiary bombs into the target area. Two days later the group sent all four squadrons to bomb Monywa, farther down the Chindwin, with the 81st Squadron dropping 102 250-pound bombs, the 82nd Squadron dropping 40 1,000-pound bombs, and the 434th Squadron dropping 88 500-pound bombs (the 83rd Squadron had to turn back because of bad weather). In early October the 82nd and 83rd Squadrons went back to bomb Kalewa, dropping 232 250-pound bombs and another 32 250-pound bombs with 12-to-36-hour-delay fuses to hinder repair efforts. The Chindwin River also became a target, with B-25s dropping mines that floated 8 feet below the river's surface to disrupt river traffic. Flights of three bombers made regular sweeps down the river during the day, bombing and strafing any rivercraft they came across. As the 14th Army divisions neared the Chindwin, the group flew deeper into central Burma to hit other Japanese supply areas, usually with two or more squadrons bombing the target. The squadrons normally bombed from medium altitudes (4,000 to 9,000 feet), bombing in boxes of six aircraft in elements of three bombers and most often dropping 250- and 500-pound bombs.[103]

Next to Japanese supply areas, the group's bombing effort went against the Japanese railroad system, bombing railroad yards, rail bridges, and railroad tracks. From mid-August through mid-December the group kept up regular attacks against railroad targets, beginning with an attack on the marshaling yards at Thazi—one of the more important railroad junctions—on August 16, returning a month later to bomb the yards again on September 16 and 23, while on the last mission dropping 242 100-pound bombs into the target area. In a group effort, in mid-November 48 aircraft bombed the railroad yards at Ywataung with 310 250-pound bombs and 18 500-pound bombs. This was one of eight marshaling yards hit during the month. The group concentrated on the railroad yards where supplies for *15th Army* passed through on their way north. In between attacks on the railroad yards, the group carried out attacks on sections of the railroad line between stations. On these missions the squadrons would split up into elements of three aircraft, each element taking a section of the railroad line and dropping 250-pound spike bombs to tear up sections of track and strafing any rolling stock they could find along the way. On one of these early railroad missions, the 81st Squadron lost its commanding officer, Maj. Warren Sutton, when ground fire apparently hit his B-25, setting one engine on fire. The bomber flew on past the tracks to crash into a wooded area beyond, killing all onboard. It was one of the squadron's few combat losses and hit doubly hard, since the entire crew were combat veterans. Sutton was a veteran of North Africa, Sicily, and Italy and was on his 127th combat mission when he was killed.[104]

The 12th Group went after railroad bridges regularly with mixed results, and with the same frustrations that other medium- and heavy-bomb squadrons faced. On almost all missions against bridges, the squadrons chose to bomb from medium altitudes, sometimes bombing in boxes of six aircraft, sometimes by individual elements of three bombers, and sometimes bombing individually. The

Railroad yards were an important target for the 12th Bomb Group. An attack by two or three squadrons of B-25s could saturate a target with combinations of general-purpose and fragmentation bombs. Here a B-25H from the 82nd Bomb Squadron flies over the railroad yard at Kinu in Burma on 12 November 1944.
3A-37580, RG342, NARA

Unlike the 490th Bomb Squadron, the 12th Bomb Group usually bombed bridge targets from medium altitude, using combinations of bombs of different weights with mixed results. On a mission to bomb the Mu River bypass bridge on 23 September 1944, the group got a rare direct hit on the bridge. The bomb craters around the bypass bridge, and the main bridge above it, are an indication of what difficult targets narrow bridges were to hit from nearly any altitude. *3A-37668, RG342, NARA*

Maintenance crews working on a 75 mm cannon from a 12th Bomb Group B-25H in an open revetment. Like other Army Air Force B-25 units flying over Burma, the 12th Bomb Group found the 75 mm cannon to be effective against larger targets such as buildings, locomotives, and rivercraft. *Author's collection*

squadrons tried varying the approach to a bridge to come in at different angles or bombing in trail, as well as using different combinations of 250-, 500-, and 1,000-pound bombs. The results were often disappointing. There was the "straddle" problem, when a string of bombs would hit just to each side of a bridge but miss the bridge structure. If the bombing was slightly off, the bombs might hit the railroad tracks leading up to the bridge or away from it, but again miss the bridge. The squadrons frequently returned from a bridge-bombing mission believing they had damaged a bridge but, as they turned away from the target, would see the bridge still standing. On November 28, group commander Col. Lloyd Dalton Jr. went out with other B-25s from the 81st Squadron to try a low-level attack, bombing the bridge at Natmauk with 1,000-pound bombs from 900 feet. On this mission the pilots had success, destroying one span of the bridge. The 81st Squadron tried another low-level attack on December 7, with three aircraft knocking out a span of one of the bridges from an altitude of 600 feet and damaging a second from low altitude. While these results might have been seen as encouraging a change in method, the squadrons appear to have kept on bombing from medium altitudes, sometimes getting good hits that would knock out a bridge, but more often not. As the 81st Squadron reported from a bridge mission on December 24, "the less said about this raid the better. 'Structure sighted—straddled same.'" The 434th Squadron tried a low-level attack on 24 January 1945, knocking out one bridge, and again on January 30, when five aircraft knocked out two bridges in low-level attacks, but the low-level method does not seem to have replaced medium-altitude bombing. It is curious that with the publicity and success the 490th Bomb Squadron received for its "glip" bombing technique that the 12th Bomb Group did not attempt something similar earlier on.[105]

The bombers ran into Japanese fighters on only one occasion. On 6 October 1944 the 83rd Bomb Squadron was on its way to bomb a bridge at Nyaungyan, near Mandalay. Approaching the target, around a dozen Ki-43 fighters from the *64th Hikōsentai* operating out of Meiktila jumped the bomber formation and began a fight that lasted for an hour and 15 minutes. Jettisoning their bombs, the bombers turned back toward their base as the Oscars came in to attack. Capt. Saburo Nakamura, commanding the *1st Chutai*, and a second pilot made a head-on attack against the formation, damaging three aircraft slightly but hitting a fourth in the starboard engine. The plane left the formation and lost height, going down to crash below. Nakamura made a second attack from behind the formation, but return fire hit him in the head, killing him instantly. His Ki-43 went into a dive and disintegrated, throwing the pilot out, his parachute opening automatically. The remaining fighters continued to make methodical head-on attacks on the formation as the B-25 gunners fought back, but apparently without inflicting much more damage to the bombers. In a final effort, one of the Oscars received several hits and broke off the attack. The bomber gunners claimed three fighters destroyed and four probably destroyed, while the Japanese pilots claimed two B-25s shot down. Nakamura was the *64th Hikōsentai*'s leading ace at the time of his death.[106]

While most of the 12th Bomb Group's missions in support of 14th Army went to attacks on the Japanese lines of communication and stores, the group did provide close support to ground forces when requested. For several days toward the end of October and in early November, the 14th Army called on the 12th Group to hit Japanese troop concentrations in the mountains that were the last barrier to the Kabaw Valley and the Chindwin River. On one mission on November 2, the 81st, 82nd, and 434th Squadrons dropped 216 500-pound bombs on a target area around Kennedy Peak, getting nearly every bomb into the designated target area.[107] In early December, as part of the preparations to support XV Corps' advance

THE TENTH AIR FORCE IN WORLD WAR II

B-25s from the 12th Bomb Group approaching a target on the Mayu peninsula in support of XV Corps' advance in the Arakan. The group provided close support for British and Indian units, bombing Japanese positions ahead of Allied troops. *3A-37495, RG342, NARA*

in the Arakan in Operations ROMULUS and TALON, Stratemeyer transferred the 12th Bomb Group to No. 224 Group's operational control.[108] The group's mission was to provide support to the advance and to the amphibious operations, and to strike targets in southern Burma that supported the *28th Army*, defending the Arakan.[109] The advance down the Mayu Peninsula began on December 12. The 12th Group began flying missions to the Arakan the next day, with a three-squadron attack on troop concentrations, the ferry siding, and stores areas around Kyauktaw, taking out similar targets at Myohaung, to the south, the day after. The squadrons usually dropped several hundred 100-pound demolition or incendiary bombs to saturate the target area, but added 250- and 500-pound demolition bombs and 325-pound depth charges to the mix. For three days at the end of December, the group made a concerted effort against strong concentrations of Japanese troops around Thayettabin, sending out three squadrons twice a day.

As an example of the diversity of bombs used, the afternoon mission on December 29 saw the 81st, 83rd, and 434th Squadrons dropping 72 325-pound depth charges, 132 260-pound M-81 fragmentation bombs, and 242 100-pound demolition bombs. The next afternoon the 81st, 82nd, and 83rd Squadrons went back and dropped 144 250-pound demolition bombs, 48 500-pound demolition bombs, and 24 55-gallon oil drums rigged to explode when they hit the ground. Over the three days of bombing, the group dropped more than 2,200 bombs of different sizes in the target area. The group continued bombing Japanese positions in the Arakan during January. Following the successful and unopposed capture of Akyab on January 3, the group flew missions on January 7 and 8 against Japanese positions and on January 12 bombed Myebon just before Royal Marine Commandos began an amphibious assault on the town. After the mission, Air Commodore the Earl of Bandon, commanding No. 224 Group, commended the squadrons for a very successful attack. In the days that followed, the group struck other areas as *28th Army* began to retreat toward southern Burma. On January 21 the group bombed Japanese positions at Kangaw, to the east of Myebon, in preparation for an attack a few days later on January 26, when the group participated in a massive air attack with

In the attacks on Japanese positions in the Arakan, the 12th Bomb Group dropped incendiary bombs made locally from 55-gallon oil drums. The drums contained a napalm mixture and had two white phosphorus bombs attached, with the tail fin from a large general-purpose bomb strapped to the top of the oil drum. They were effective against large area targets where accuracy wasn't as critical. *3A-33923, RG342, NARA*

B-24s and Liberators in support of another amphibious landing. All four squadrons in the group participated in an afternoon mission, dropping 102 1,000-pound bombs and 48 500-pound bombs from

Clouds of dark, black smoke rise up from incendiary oil drum bombs exploding on Japanese positions near Thayettabin in the Arakan in January 1945. The B-25s would saturate a designated area with combinations of demolition bombs, fragmentation bombs, depth charges, and incendiaries. *3A-37795, RG342, NARA*

between 4,000 and 4,700 feet over the target area. Later in January the group transferred to No. 221 Group's operational control to support 14th Army's advance on Mandalay and Meiktila.[110]

The fighter-bombers contributed to the attacks on the Japanese lines of communication when not engaged in escorting bombers or flying counterair missions. The 459th Fighter Squadron had begun bombing missions in May, carrying out their first mission on 1 May 1944, when four P-38s went out to dive-bomb a Japanese supply dump with 1,000-pound bombs, with two fighters flying top cover. During the monsoon the squadron began regular bombing missions when weather permitted, attacking bridges, railroad facilities, and railroad tracks in central Burma. The P-38s would carry one 1,000-pound bomb under the right wing and a 165-gallon drop tank under the left wing for extra range, with one or two flights acting as the bombers while one flight flew top cover. During August and September, weather limited the number of missions, but the bombing missions the squadron did fly were not always easy, as one of the pilots recorded in his diary after a bombing mission on September 8:

> So far this month things have really been rough, and today certainly adds to it. I went on a dive-bombing mission to Monywa on the east bank of the Chindwin River; our target was the waterfront warehouse in the railroad yards. We took off (12 ships) at 8:30 and arrived over the target at 9:35. I was the fourth man in the first flight and observed two hits on the target. The ack-ack was pretty intense but not heavy. I spotted five positions on the ground, and I could see the orange flashes coming out of the gun muzzles. Lt. Moore, one of our new pilots who joined the Squadron last month, was flying Captain Klumb's wing, and it seems that Moore got too close to Klumb on the dive run; therefore, the ack-ack bursting behind Klumb hit Moore's ship. Moore was at 700' when I heard him say over the radio that he was going to belly in because he could not hold flying speed. . . . That was the last we heard. We spent about a half hour looking for him, but the search was in vain. This was Moore's third mission. [Fortunately, Moore survived the crash landing and months as a prisoner of war in Rangoon.][111]

The 459th Fighter Squadron was assigned to No. 224 Group, which provided air support to XV Corps. The squadron flew many interdiction missions in support of the advance in the Arakan, joining medium bombers in attacks on Japanese stores, lines of communication, and bridges, in addition to flying sweeps over Japanese airfields in central Burma. The armament crew load a depth charge onto 1st Lt. William Baumeister's P-38J "Irish Lassie." Baumeister failed to return from a clash with Japanese fighters over the airfield at Zayatkwin on 19 November 1944. *3A-33878, RG342, NARA*

With the end of the monsoon in early October, the squadron went back to flying sweeps over the Japanese airfields in Burma and flying escort to the B-24s and B-25s on their bombing missions. The squadron would take up more bombing missions in 1945.[112]

THE TENTH AIR FORCE IN WORLD WAR II

Five airplanes went out the morning of November 30 but failed to get any hits on the bridge. Squadron commander Capt. Roland Lynn was determined to knock the bridge down. In the afternoon, he and another pilot went out carrying two 1,000-pound bombs each—the first time the squadron had used this weight of bomb. Lynn got two direct hits on the center span of the bridge, knocking it out. In addition to bridges, the squadron went after locomotives, rolling stock, rivercraft, motor vehicles, and bullock carts the Japanese used to haul supplies. The squadron lost one pilot on these missions when his P-47 flew through antiaircraft fire during an attack on Monywa. At the end of the month, the 5th Fighter Squadron returned to Asansol.[113]

The 6th Fighter Squadron (Commando) replaced the 5th Squadron at Feni on 1 December 1944 and began flying the same types of missions: escorting the 12th Bomb Group's B-25s, bombing bridges, and strafing locomotives, rolling stock, and rivercraft when they could be found. Beginning with an attack on the Mu River Bridge bypass on December 4, the squadron dive-bombed several bridges but found good targets hard to come by, since other squadrons had knocked out most of the important bridges within dive-bombing range. The squadron hit the Mu River Bridge bypass on seven missions, going back every few days when repairs made the bridge serviceable again. The first attack on December 4 scored two direct

The two newly organized Air Commando fighter squadrons began operations in November 1944, adding their weight to attacks on Japanese lines of communications and carrying 1,000-pound bombs for attacks on bridges. 1st Lt. William Burghardt's crew chief, SSgt. Cebrelli, leans on a 1,000-pound bomb attached to Burghardt's aircraft prior to the 5th Fighter Squadron (Commando) taking off on another mission against bridges in Burma. *Courtesy, William Burghardt*

The two Air Commando fighter squadrons began making their contribution in November, when the 5th Fighter Squadron (Commando) moved from the main Air Commando base at Asansol to Feni—home of the 12th Bomb Group—for several weeks of combat operations supporting the 12th Group beginning on 10 November 1944. While the squadron flew 19 missions into central Burma escorting the bombers, the squadron also carried out attacks on the lines of communications. Like the 459th, the 5th Squadron went after railroad bridges. The squadron's first bridge target was the infamous Mu River Bridge, which became known as "Old Faithful." The squadron flew missions to the bridge on November 16, failing to get any hits in two missions, but four aircraft returned the next day and got two direct hits on the bridge. Using 500-pound bombs, the squadron went after a number of bridges and bypass bridges during the month, knocking out several with direct hits and damaging others with near misses. Some of the bridges were difficult targets. The equally famous Myitnge Bridge proved hard to knock out. On November 28 there, P-47s went out in the morning to bomb the bridge but failed to get any hits. Four aircraft went back in the afternoon but damaged only the tracks leading to the bridge. The next morning, seven aircraft bombed the bridge, getting three to four direct hits in the center, but while the bridge superstructure was badly twisted, the bridge itself remained standing. Another attack that afternoon, again with seven aircraft, finally knocked out the two center spans of the bridge. By the end of the month, the squadron received intelligence that repairs to the Mu River Bridge were nearly done.

A pilot from one of the Air Commando fighter squadrons stands next to a P-47 named "Durable Doll." The pilot is wearing the 1st Air Commando Group insignia on his leather A-2 jacket. The Thunderbolt has a deep-blue ring around the front of the cowl, part of the theater markings for fighter aircraft (white on camouflaged aircraft and deep blue on natural-metal aircraft). *Author's collection*

hits, with two more on a mission two days later. An attack with eight P-47s on December 7 managed only one direct hit. Three days later, when reconnaissance indicated that repairs to the bypass bridge were nearly complete, 10 aircraft went out and scored six direct hits, knocking out nearly half the bridge structure. The pilots noticed that on every bombing mission to the bypass bridge they could see flatbed railroad cars loaded with lumber, waiting to repair the damage from the latest attack. Strafing targets were few, but repeated sweeps yielded twelve trucks and two tank cars destroyed, two locomotives severely damaged, and numerous small rivercraft and bullock carts. Since the Burmese used bullock carts daily, the pilots had instructions to strafe carts only in areas where the Japanese were known to be using these carts to haul military supplies. On the squadron's first combat mission—escorting B-25s to the Meiktila area—the flights went down to strafe after the bombers turned back to base. One flight found a string of boxcars north of the town. On his first combat mission, 2nd Lt. Brent Lowry was on his strafing run when a huge explosion erupted around his airplane, sending it crashing to the ground. This was the squadron's only combat loss during the month.

One of the choicer targets, when it could be found, was a Japanese gasoline supply dump. The Japanese had taken to storing their gasoline drums in small ravines off the main roads. The Air Commandos found that one airplane, usually the flight leader, flying low along the road could look up these ravines and valleys and often spot the camouflaged drums. 1st Lt. Jack Klarr, a pilot with the 6th Fighter Squadron, remembered what would happen when the flight leader found a cache of gasoline drums. The flight leader would, he recalled, "come back and give it a squirt and then the rest of the flight would come in and strafe. That was always a lot of fun, when you'd find one of these. They'd go up with a big bang."[114] The squadron flew its last mission on December 22, dive-bombing a road bridge and knocking out two spans. A few days later the squadron returned to Asansol and the 5th Fighter Squadron moved to Feni for its next round of operations.[115]

When the 5th Fighter Squadron arrived at Feni at the end of December, Roland Lynn, recently promoted to major, announced that during its time at Feni the squadron would better the 6th Squadron's record of 440 sorties. The squadron got off to a good start, flying 114 sorties over the last three days of December and bombing several Japanese-occupied towns along the Irrawaddy River and bridges and troop concentrations in the Arakan area for XV Corps' advance. On a late-evening patrol, two P-47s were lucky to find two locomotives and several motor vehicles that they strafed and damaged. On the first day of the new year, the squadron flew four missions and, during the third mission, established what was believed to be a record for the P-47. Frustrated with the limited effect 500-pound bombs had on bridge targets, Maj. Lynn tried 1,000-pound bombs against the Mu River Bridge on one of the November missions. Lynn thought that if he could get a 1,000-pound bomb in the right spot, he could take out a bridge. Having tried two 1,000-pound bombs, he decided to try three. He contacted Maj. Younger Pitts, recently appointed commander of the 6th Squadron back at Asansol, and asked Pitts about the idea. Pitts thought it would be possible and tested a P-47 to prove that it could take off and fly with three 1,000-pound bombs: one under each wing and one under the belly. On January 1, Lynn and his operations officer, 1st Lt. Malcom Wilkins, took off to bomb the railroad bridge near Taungdwingyi, 60 miles south of Meiktila on the Rangoon-Mandalay railroad line, a round trip of 700 miles. Lynn recalled that it took a

Maj. Roland Lynn, commanding the 5th Fighter Squadron (Commando), decided to try carrying three 1,000-pound bombs—equivalent to the bombload of a medium bomber—to have more chances when attacking a bridge. Lynn proved it could be done, knocking out a bridge with one of his three bombs, but the sacrifice in range to carry 3,000 pounds of bombs made this combination impractical. *3A-33916, RG342, NARA*

lot longer to get the P-47 off the ground with a bombload that equaled the normal bombload of a B-25. Over the bridge, Lynn went in first, dropping the two underwing bombs in his first attack and the bomb under the fuselage in a second pass. One of his bombs scored a direct hit, knocking out one span of the bridge, while his other bombs, and Wilkins's three bombs, were all near misses. Lynn and Wilkins proved the P-47 could carry this load of bombs successfully, but the sacrifice in range made this heavy of a bombload impractical, and the experiment was not repeated.[116]

The squadron devoted most of its missions during January to continuing attacks on rail and road bridges and the rail and road network in central Burma. On the final mission of 1 January 1945 the squadron again had good luck, damaging three locomotives. The squadron destroyed or damaged more rolling stock, motor vehicles, and tank cars over the month, in addition to numerous rivercraft. Bridge targets required repeated visits. As usually happened, the Japanese would make rapid repairs to a bridge after a dive-bombing mission, and as soon as the repairs were finished the squadron would go back to the same target to knock it down or damage the repair work. The squadron carried on escorting the 12th Bomb Group to targets in central Burma, on two missions flying ahead of the bombers to dive-bomb the Japanese antiaircraft positions just before the bombers arrived over the target. The squadron continued bombing Japanese-held towns and villages and ended the month having flown 58 missions and 702 sorties, achieving Lynn's objective of breaking the 6th Fighter Squadron's sortie record by a substantial margin.[117]

With Allied aircraft now roaming over much of central Burma during the day, the Japanese army could not risk running trains or motor vehicle convoys in daylight and turned to making supply runs along the rail lines and the roads by night. As a result, the 5th and 6th Fighter Squadrons' bag of locomotives, rolling stock, and motor vehicles was modest compared to prior months. The B-25s of the 1st Air Commando Night Intruder section had better luck. It is unclear how the 1st Air Commandos came to have the Night Intruder section, but it became operational in November 1944 with

The Air Commando Bomber Section was reorganized as the Night Intruder Section and received new B-25H aircraft to carry out night intruder missions over Burma. The section's airplanes do not appear to have received any camouflage to make them less conspicuous during their night attacks on Japanese truck convoys and trains, who by this point in the war could operate only at night. 3A-33714, RG342, NARA

a complement of seven B-25H aircraft operating out of Chittagong for ten days to two weeks during periods of moonlight. The section took on the task of sweeping the roads and railroad lines over much of central Burma by night, ranging from 18 to 23 degrees latitude and 94 to 98 degrees longitude—roughly an area from Yeu in the north down to Pegu in the south, and from the Kabaw Valley in the west to the east of Mandalay. The section flew its first operation on November 25, when three B-25s dropped fragmentation bombs and incendiary bombs on Pakokku and Monywa and strafed a locomotive. Over the next 11 days the section went out on six nights, dropping more fragmentation and incendiary bombs on towns and villages and doing great damage to locomotives, rolling stock, and motor vehicle convoys moving at night. On the night of December 1, three B-25s strafed and damaged a locomotive and rolling stock in the yards at Shwebo, exploded a locomotive boiler, hit more rolling stock in another yard, and strafed several motor vehicle convoys. The 75 mm cannon on the B-25H did considerable damage in these strafing attacks. During these missions, antiaircraft fire inflicted minor damage on a few aircraft. With the period of moonlight ending, the section returned to Asansol.[118]

Capt. Frank Merchant (center) and his crew had a narrow escape when their B-25 ran into antiaircraft fire while attacking Japanese truck convoys on 29 December 1944, hitting the left engine. Merchant had to shut down the damaged engine but made it back to Allied lines flying on his one remaining engine, ordering the crew to bail out when they spotted a British truck convoy with its lights on. Author's collection

The Night Intruder section returned to Chittagong for another round of intruder patrols during the period from 23 December 1944 to 3 January 1945. With a shortage of crews, the section could not carry out missions every night or fly duplicate sweeps over an area at intervals during the night. Instead, the section assigned a larger area to each individual crew to sweep during a night mission, sending out three or four B-25s on each night mission. The section noted a marked increase in Japanese activity during their missions, coming across a number of large truck convoys. The bombers also experienced increasing antiaircraft fire this time, particularly from machine guns. The Japanese would begin firing whenever they heard an airplane nearing the area. Five aircraft suffered minor damage, but on December 29 Capt. Frank Merchant had his left engine shot up as he completed a strafing run. Climbing for altitude, Merchant headed back toward base, with the engine losing oil. With the engine shut down, Merchant ordered the crew to bail out when they came over a truck convoy showing headlights. This proved to be a British convoy, and the crew made contact within a few hours. During this second period the section flew missions on 10 nights, dropping 330 parafrag clusters and 66 clusters of incendiaries while firing 57,160 rounds of .50-caliber ammunition and 31 rounds from the 75 mm cannon. The section found and destroyed 11 locomotives and damaged a further 13, destroyed 72 motor vehicles and damaged 138, and knocked out 41 railroad cars, with another 131 damaged, in sharp contrast to the results of the day fighters.[119]

The section went back to Chittagong for another ten days of operations from 21 to 31 January 1945. For the first few days, Japanese activity was intensive but then dropped off rapidly, probably as a result of the B-25 strikes. All motor vehicle convoys traveled without lights and were more widely separated, making damage more difficult. Japanese gunners also switched to firing their machine guns without tracers, opening fire indiscriminately whenever a B-25 came near. Often the crews would not know they were being fired on until their airplane received a hit. During the period, six aircraft received damage from antiaircraft fire, but only one seriously, and that airplane made it back to Chittagong. The section flew missions on nine nights, carrying more fragmentation and incendiary bombs by doubling the clusters together. These lighter bombs proved to be more effective than the heavier 500-pound bombs in the type of attacks the section carried out over Burma. The 75 mm cannon proved most effective, with the section's pilots achieving great accuracy with experience. On several missions the section tried using flares, dropping these at 1,500 feet above a suspected area.

ARMY AIR FORCE UNITS SUPPORTING 14TH ARMY OPERATIONS

Armorers preparing to load fragmentation bombs onto a Night Intruder Section B-25H at their base at Chittagong. The section found that fragmentation bombs were more effective in their attacks on trains and truck convoys than heavier general-purpose bombs. Catching the Japanese by surprise at night, the section ran up an impressive score of locomotives and trucks destroyed. *3A-33914, RG342, NARA*

The crews found that this gave them enough time to carry out two strafing runs on a target, and if they managed to hit an operating locomotive, the steam escaping from the punctured boiler was enough to guide the bomber back for another pass after the flares went out. The results were once again impressive, with the section destroying 13 locomotives, 44 rolling stock, and 76 motor vehicles while damaging 3 locomotives, 84 rolling stock, and 179 motor vehicles. On two occasions the B-25s destroyed entire trains: one carrying ammunition and one carrying gasoline and oil. These efforts contributed to the relentless attrition battle against the Japanese lines-of-communication system, a battle that the Japanese could ill afford and were now losing.[120]

Capt. Harry Sealy with his ground crew in front of his P-38 "Haleakala II." The majority of his victories while with the 459th Fighter Squadron were Japanese airplanes destroyed on the ground in strafing attacks. His last air victory came on 20 October 1944, when he claimed a Ki-43 damaged during a sweep over the Rangoon airfields. *Dwayne Tabatt; courtesy, Carl Molesworth*

Counterair Missions

The Army Air Force fighter squadrons assigned to 3rd Tactical Air Force participated in regular counterair operations during the monsoon until the end of the year, though as previously noted, these operations had a disproportionate return for the effort involved.[121] While the *5th Hikōshidan* had received some reinforcements to build up its strength to around 100 aircraft, the Japanese now faced more than 1,000 Allied aircraft.[122] Although a much-smaller force, the Japanese fighters still had the ability to disrupt air supply operations through attacks on the transport aircraft and so had to be neutralized. With around 75 fighter aircraft in the *50th* and *64th Hikōsentai*—most based in the airfields around Rangoon but able to use a larger number of airfields in central Burma—this proved a difficult task for the 3rd Tactical Air Force. The *5th Hikōshidan*'s policy of avoiding contact with Allied fighters to conserve its forces added to the problem. AAF and RAF fighter squadrons carried out regular sweeps of the main airfields in central and southern Burma, but often with little to show for their efforts compared to the attrition inflicted on the *5th Hikōshidan* during the first six months of the year.

During the monsoon, weather limited the number of missions. The 459th Fighter Squadron flew several sweeps over the Burma airfields but found Japanese aircraft on only one occasion, when during a sweep of Rangoon on 13 September 1944, Capt. Harry Sealy shot down an Oscar from the *64th Hikōsentai*. As the weather began to improve in early October, Eastern Air Command planned a major three-day offensive sweep of the Rangoon airfields at Mingaladon, Hmawbi, and Zayatkwin, where Allied intelligence estimated the Japanese based 45–55 fighters.[123] Designated Operation L, the objective was to force the Japanese fighters into battle. The attacks were scheduled to coincide with the American landings on Leyte, in the Philippines, in the hope of preventing Japanese fighters from leaving Burma. This was a combined AAF/RAF operation, with the RAF providing Beaufighter and Mosquito twin-engine fighters and a composite squadron of RAF Thunderbolts drawn from No. 146 and No. 261 Squadrons. The 58th Fighter Squadron contributed 24 P-47s, while the 5th and 6th Fighter Squadrons (Commando), on their first combat mission since their activation, also formed a composite squadron, with each squadron contributing 12 pilots. The Lightnings of the 459th also joined. The Air Commandos and the 58th Fighter Squadron used Chittagong as a forward base for the missions. As a diversionary attack the 12th Bomb Group sent three squadrons to bomb the airfield at Meiktila to put it out of commission before the main fighter sweep on Rangoon. On the morning of October 18, the RAF Beaufighters and Mosquitos went in to the Rangoon airfields first, with one Beaufighter falling to the Ki-43s. The 58th Fighter Squadron came in 45 minutes later to attack Mingaladon and Hmawbi, claiming four aircraft destroyed on the ground and two shot down in the air.[124]

The 5th and 6th Fighter Squadrons went to Mingaladon. Then Capt. Roland Lynn, commanding the 5th Fighter Squadron, led the mission, with Capt. Olin Carter leading the 6th Fighter Squadron. Lynn had Carter put his 12 aircraft at the front of the formation, while Lynn had the 5th Fighter Squadron above and behind. The 6th Squadron would go in first to strafe the airfield, pulling up to provide top cover for the 5th Squadron when they went in to strafe. Approaching Mingaladon, Carter took his squadron down to 2,000 feet to begin their run, and as he did so, one of his pilots alerted him to approaching Japanese fighters. Knowing that Lynn was in position above him, Carter ordered his pilots to continue their dive. Coming across the field, Carter fired on a Ki-43 that exploded under his fire. On his

The 5th and 6th Fighter Squadrons (Commando) joined other Army Air Force and Royal Air Force squadrons on several days of sweeps against the Japanese airfields in the Rangoon area. Equipped with two 165-gallon drop tanks under the wings, Air Commando Thunderbolts head for Rangoon. The squadrons had not yet had time to paint their aircraft with the required theater markings of dark-blue bands on the nose, vertical and horizontal stabilizers, and wings. *GP-A-CMDO-1-SU-OP, AFHRA*

Capt. Olin Carter commanding the 6th Fighter Squadron (Commando) during the Rangoon fighter sweeps. Flying his P-47D "Little Kitten II," Carter claimed four Japanese aircraft destroyed on the ground and another damaged to add to his claims from his time with the Air Commando Fighter Section supporting the second Wingate expedition. *Courtesy, Olin Carter*

next pass Carter fired on two more aircraft in revetments, but he and his pilots found few other targets. After completing his strafing attack, 1st Lt. Everett Kelly and his wingman were pulling away from the field when Kelly's wingman yelled that he had a Japanese fighter coming in on his tail, and asked Kelly for help. "We went into a dive," Kelly reported; "I swerved to the right, cut inside the Oscar and after firing into him, I saw the plane start to give off smoke. I followed his trail down to 700'. The Oscar was totally aflame, but the pilot was able to bail out and land in the marshes below."[125] Kelly achieved the distinction of shooting down an enemy aircraft on his first combat mission. Roland Lynn took his squadron in on the approaching Japanese fighters. Lynn closed in on an Oscar that had turned into him, but waited a bit too long to open fire. Lynn gave the Japanese fighter a burst, nearly colliding with the fighter as it dove beneath him and went down spinning. Lynn received credit for a probable. He fought two other fighters—one Japanese pilot fighting aggressively with Lynn for 20 minutes—but without result. 2nd Lt. Marion Bell, like Kelly on his first combat mission, also had a successful engagement, damaging one of the Oscars. The 459th Squadron made the final attack of the day, strafing Mingaladon, where the pilots claimed one bomber destroyed and two fighters damaged, then engaged in an inconclusive combat with a formation of Ki-43s.[126]

The offensive to the Rangoon airfields resumed on October 20. On this day, the RAF Thunderbolts went to strafe Mingaladon, while the AAF squadrons went to all three airfields, with the Air Commando fighter squadrons covering Mingaladon and Zayatkwin, the 58th Fighter Squadron taking Hmawbi, and the 459th Fighter Squadron sending 17 fighters to Mingaladon and seven others to Hmawbi and Zayatkwin. Seven 6th Fighter Squadron P-47s attacked Zayatkwin, with Capt. Carter claiming a Ki-46 and a Ki-43 destroyed on the ground and other pilots claiming three more single-engine fighters destroyed. Carter led his flight to attack nearby Hmawbi, where he claimed another Ki-43 damaged. The main fighting for the Air Commandos took place over Mingaladon. Arriving over the airfield, they found around 16 Japanese fighters in the air above the field. In a short fight the Air Commandos made several claims.

On only his second combat mission, Marion Bell got separated from his element leader but, coming out of some clouds, found an Oscar directly beneath him, which he promptly attacked, setting the Japanese aircraft on fire and receiving credit for one aircraft destroyed. Capt. Lynn claimed another fighter as damaged, as did 2nd Lt. "Moon" Mullins, who also claimed another fighter damaged on the ground. Two 5th Fighter Squadron pilots and four from the 6th Fighter Squadron claimed aircraft destroyed on the ground. The 58th Fighter Squadron found nothing at Hmawbi and did not attack. The 459th Squadron was flying top cover when they found Japanese fighters flying above them. The Lightning pilots outmaneuvered their opponents, and in the combat Capt. W. G. Broadfoot shot down one *64th Hikōsentai* fighter, while two other pilots each claimed a Japanese fighter damaged. The Air Commando composite squadron emerged as the high scorer of the two-day offensive, receiving credit for nine aircraft destroyed in the air and on the ground and seven more damaged. In terms of the weight of effort, 164 Allied aircraft reached Rangoon to destroy 5 Japanese aircraft in the air and 12 on the ground, with a further 13 damaged—not the punishing success that had been hoped for.[127] A report on Operation L was critical of the results of the offensive, attributing the dearth of success to the lack of aggressiveness of the 58th and 459th Fighter Squadrons, but singling out the Air Commandos for praise. The report stated, "it was amazing to see a squadron composed of inexperienced pilots flying over unfamiliar territory achieve success that was better than twice the combined efforts of other units participating."[128]

Eastern Air Command decided to make a second attempt to knock out the Japanese aircraft at the Rangoon airfields, combining this with a heavy-bomber attack on the Mahlwagon marshaling

The 459th Fighter Squadron had better luck on an escort mission to Rangoon on 4 November 1944, claiming three Japanese fighters shot down and several more damaged. The squadron had taken the nickname the "Assam Dragons" and painted the engine cowls of their P-38s with a dramatic dragon representation. *3A-35794, RG342, NARA*

yards by B-29s of the XX Bomber Command in their first attack on Rangoon. The first mission took place on November 3, with the 459th Fighter Squadron going in ahead of the bombers to sweep Hmawbi, claiming two fighters damaged. While 44 B-29s bombed the marshaling yards, the 5th and 6th Fighter Squadrons carried out sweeps over the airfields. The 5th Fighter Squadron drew a blank over Mingaladon, while the 6th Fighter Squadron claimed one Ki-21 bomber destroyed and another damaged, as well as damaging a type 3 fighter (Ki-61 Tony) belonging to the *8th Rensei Hikōtai*, an operational training unit based at Rangoon. The next day, RAF Liberators bombed the Insein locomotive workshops with escort from two RAF Thunderbolt squadrons, the 459th Fighter Squadron, and the 5th and 6th Fighter Squadrons. While the 6th Fighter Squadron remained with the Liberators, the 5th Fighter Squadron carried out a sweep over Zayatkwin and Hmawbi, where Capt. P. K. Oram claimed one Ki-43 shot down. The 459th Squadron ran into more Japanese fighters; Maj. Verl Luehring, squadron commander, claimed an Oscar shot down, as did 1st Lt. Oscar Garland. 1st Lt. Donald Russell claimed a Tojo, which was in fact one of the *50th Hikōsentai*'s new Ki-84 Frank fighters, and damaged another Oscar. Two other pilots each claimed a Japanese fighter damaged.[129]

Over the next two months there were few encounters with Japanese aircraft in the air or the ground, but the sweeps of Japanese airfields in central and southern Burma continued, as did escort missions to Rangoon. The 5th Fighter Squadron carried out a sweep over the airfield at Nawnglikio on November 11, destroying a Ki-43 on the ground. The next day the squadron went to Laihka, claiming a Ki-21 destroyed, but lost one P-47 to ground fire near Meiktila. On a sweep over the Rangoon area on November 13, the 459th Fighter Squadron ran into a formation of 20 Japanese fighters, claiming one Ki-44 shot down and a Ki-43 as a probable. Six days later the 459th Squadron joined RAF Thunderbolts to escort a formation of RAF Liberators and B-24s from the 7th Bomb Group on a mission to bomb the Mokpolin railroad yards in Rangoon. Japanese fighters attacked the bombers but the 459th drove them off, claiming one Ki-43 damaged while apparently losing two P-38s that failed to return from the mission. Accompanying the mission as additional escort, the 5th Fighter Squadron claimed one fighter damaged when the P-47s went down to strafe Hmawbi. When the 6th Fighter Squadron replaced the 5th Squadron at Feni in early December, among the first missions was a sweep of the airfields in central Burma, but the P-47s found nothing. On December 13, the 6th Squadron was helping to escort a formation of RAF Liberators bombing targets in the Arakan when Capt. Younger Pitts, the squadron commander, noticed a formation of Japanese fighters to the left of the bombers. He ordered 1st Lt. Jack Klarr to go after them. Klarr came in on the leader of the Japanese formation and opened fire, causing the Oscar to emit a stream of smoke and dive for the deck. Klarr's wingman attacked a second Oscar, knocking pieces off. The medium bombers of the 12th Bomb Group contributed to the effort, making two missions in mid-December to bomb Japanese airfields at Magwe, Thedaw, and Kangang, covering the fields with 500-pound bombs. The last engagement with Japanese fighters occurred in January, while the 459th Fighter Squadron was escorting Royal Navy ships supporting the landing at Myebon. A formation of eight Ki-43s from the *64th Hikōsentai*, carrying bombs, attempted to bomb the ships, with another formation of eight Ki-43s as escort. The Lightnings went after the Oscars, claiming two shot down and a third damaged.[130] These results were not overwhelming, but the continued sweeps of the Japanese airfields forced the *5th Hikōshidan* to pull its fighter aircraft back to the Rangoon area, limiting the use of its airfields in central Burma and thus restricting its operational flexibility. The attrition of pilots and aircraft occurred as the Japanese Army Air Force was pulling units from Sumatra and Malaya back to the Philippines and the home islands, reducing the number of aircraft in Southeast Asia and thus the number of replacement aircraft available for the *5th Hikōshidan*.[131]

Strategic Air Force Operations

The mission of the Strategic Air Force to destroy the Japanese rail, road, and water lines of communication into Burma, ports and supply facilities, and Japanese air force installations supported the Chinese and American forces in the NCAC and the 14th Army in their advances into northern and central Burma. Allied intelligence had estimated that the Japanese army and air force in Burma required the railroad system—the principal means of getting supplies to the front lines—to carry between 600 and 700 tons of supplies a day. To have an impact on Japanese military operations, the air campaign had to cut this delivery capacity by 50 percent or more.[132] By the beginning of the 1944 monsoon season, the Strategic Air Force had eliminated Rangoon as a working port and, through attacks on bridges, had severely disrupted the movement of supplies along the railroad lines running from Rangoon to Mandalay and beyond. During the monsoon season, the weather, the departure of the 7th Bomb Group to haul gasoline to China, the transfer of the 12th Bomb Group and the 490th Bomb Squadron to the 3rd Tactical Air Force, and the need to support the ground forces fighting at Imphal caused

A B-24J from the 7th Bomb Group landing at a base in India. During the 1944 monsoon, the 7th Group shifted from bombing to flying gasoline to China in support of the Fourteenth Air Force. For three months the crews had no practice in bombing or flying in formation, and the lack of training became apparent on the group's return to the Strategic Air Force. *3A-33739, RG342, NARA*

a significant decline in Strategic Air Force operations. Even after the end of the monsoon in October, strategic-bombing operations did not resume their intensity until early December due to the need for special training both for AAF and RAF squadrons and the conversion of the last remaining RAF Wellington squadrons to the more capable Liberator.[133]

The 7th Bomb Group did not return to the Strategic Air Force's operational control until 1 October 1944. For three and a half months the group flew gasoline to China for the Fourteenth Air Force.[134] After receiving orders from Stratemeyer and Davidson to switch from bombing to hauling gasoline, the 7th Group's four squadrons swapped bases with the 12th Bomb Group, the 436th, 492nd, and 493rd Bomb Squadrons moving to Tezgaon and the 9th Bomb Squadron going to Kurmitola—both bases closer to Chittagong, the receiving port for gasoline going to China. The maintenance crews fitted three

The 7th Bomb Group's B-24s had rubber fuel tanks fitted into their bomb bays to carry as much gasoline to China as possible. To allow the B-24s to carry even more gasoline, gun turrets were taken out of the bombers to save weight, and the gunners and bombardiers were removed from the crews. *7th Bombardment Group (H) Historical Foundation, USAFA McDermott Library*

420-gallon fuel tanks into the bomb bays of the B-24s and, to save weight, removed the belly turrets. The group cut the crew size from ten men to five (pilot, copilot, navigator, flight engineer, and radio operator), leaving bombardiers and gunners with little to do, to their frustration. With a full load of gasoline, the B-24s weighed close to 72,000 pounds—well above the emergency maximum gross weight of 64,000 pounds listed in the B-24J pilot's manual. Getting off the runways at Tezgaon and Kurmitola was a challenge. Flying the Hump in a heavily overloaded bomber wasn't easy either. For their first run over the Hump, every crew flew with an experienced Hump pilot, but after that they were on their own. Shortly after the switch to the new mission, the 7th Group received replacement crews in numbers that allowed each squadron to finally have a full complement of combat crews. The squadrons also gained more aircraft, so that each squadron now had an average of 16 B-24Js. The combination of more crews and more planes allowed the group to fly an average of 18 planes a day to China once the tempo of operations picked up. Flying the Hump came as a rude shock to young pilots trained in the clearer skies of the United States, while pushing through thunderstorms was a far cry from sitting in a link trainer. One pilot, recalling his first instrument flight over the Hump, with his previous link training as his only experience of instrument flying, said, "The Hump made you an instrument pilot or a casualty."[135]

And there were casualties. In the three and half months the 7th Bomb Group spent flying gasoline to China, the squadrons lost 14 aircraft along the Hump route and several more in landing and takeoff accidents. This was more than twice the number of aircraft the group lost while flying as part of the Strategic Air Force from December 1943 to June 1944. The 492nd fared the worst, losing six aircraft. Fortunately, many of the crews bailed out successfully and got back to an airbase in China or India, but 31 men lost their lives. The pressure to get as much gas to the Fourteenth Air Force as possible meant little time for training. The planes flew to China individually, giving the newer pilots little practice in formation flying. The group did set up a training regime for the gunners, with an intensive ground school but little practice in actual aerial firing. The bombardiers received no training in their specialized skill while the group was on the gasoline run. There were no airplanes to spare for training bombardiers, and few training devices for practice.[136]

Over the period from June 20—when the group began flying gasoline—until the end of September, the group carried two million gallons of aviation gasoline to China, as well as 800 P-40 drop tanks (filled with fuel when there weren't enough bomb bay fuel tanks) and 45,000 pounds of supplies. The group's efforts won accolades from Chennault, Davidson, Stratemeyer, and Arnold in Washington, all of whom were effusive in their praise of the group's performance. Arnold acknowledged that the crews might well consider their mission a "dull and thankless one," but expressed his sincere appreciation for an outstanding performance.[137] In thanking the group, Stratemeyer noted his long association with and interest in the 7th Bomb Group, saying that the assignment the group had completed so successfully was one of the most important in the group's history.[138] The mission was vitally important. The Fourteenth Air Force desperately needed gasoline for its fighters and medium bombers struggling to contain the Japanese *ICHI-GO* offensive. Airpower alone could not stop the Japanese divisions, and Chinese armies proved incapable of doing so. The Fourteenth Air Force's important base at Hengyang fell on August 8 after a 49-day siege. The base at Ling-ling fell on September 4, Kweilin on November 10, and Liuchow on November 11, leaving only a small number of

Having commanded the 7th Bomb Group during the 1930s, Maj. Gen. Stratemeyer took a keen interest in the group's operations and visited the group's squadrons on numerous occasions, meeting here with crews from the 436th Bomb Squadron. Aware of the frustrations of many crews after being taken off bombing operations, Stratemeyer tried to impress on the group the importance of the mission of hauling gasoline to China, and his gratitude for a job well done. *SU-Bomb-11-SU-PH, AFHRA*

bases farther to the east for the Fourteenth Air Force. Ironically Chennault had achieved his goal of obtaining 500 airplanes for his air force, but instead of beginning an air offensive against the Japanese in China as he had planned, his force was now fully committed to supporting the Chinese armies.[139]

A few weeks after the 7th Bomb Group returned to the Strategic Air Force on 1 October 1944, Air Commodore Mellersh, SAF commander, received a new directive from Eastern Air Command stating that the mission of the SAF was to "assist in the destruction and expulsion of all Japanese forces at the earliest date from Burma."[140] Although they were now few and far between, naval and merchant vessels remained the priority target for the SAF, but Operational Directive No. 16 now called for a major effort against the Japanese lines of communication coming into Burma from Thailand, setting out the objective of attacks as follows:

(ii) Communications into and within Burma, with continued sustained attacks against the BANGKOK/PEGU RAILWAY and PARALLEL RAILWAY in order to render them inoperable to the maximum extent, paying particular attention to the destruction of locomotives and rolling stock. Continued air attacks against CHIENGRAI/KENTUNG lines of communication giving particular attention to the BAN DARA BRIDGE on the BANGKOK/LAMPANG RAIL ROAD and other critical points along this line.[141]

Eastern Air Command assigned SAF responsibility for an area running south of Mandalay and as far to the east and south of this line as the combat radius of the force's aircraft would allow. The SAF added three more Liberator squadrons to the force. No. 99 and 215 Squadrons gave up their aged Wellingtons for Liberators, providing five RAF squadrons with Liberators. With the return of the 7th Bomb Group by November, the SAF had a total of around 100 B-24/Liberator bombers assigned to the force. To maximize the attacks on the Japanese lines of communications, Eastern Air Command had decided earlier that the SAF would shift to daylight bombing, since the few remaining Japanese fighters in Burma now posed less

Air Commodore F. J. Mellersh took over command of the Strategic Air Force when Maj. Gen. Howard Davidson was appointed to command the Tenth Air Force when the Tenth became an operational command again. In addition to the 7th Bomb Group, by December 1944 Mellersh had under his command six RAF bomber squadrons all equipped with Liberator bombers. *Author's collection*

With Japanese airpower rapidly diminishing, the RAF Liberator squadrons abandoned night bombing and, after a period of intensive training, converted to daylight operations. The generally small targets in Burma proved difficult to hit by night. Converting the Liberator squadrons to daylight operations gave Mellersh a more powerful force to bear against the Japanese. *CF_05053, IWM*

THE TENTH AIR FORCE IN WORLD WAR II

of a threat.[142] The SAF implemented an intensive training program in daylight operations for the RAF Liberator squadrons during October and November 1944, the squadrons undergoing four to six weeks of training in formation flying, gunnery, and bombing.[143]

The 7th Bomb Group also went back to training, since its first bombing missions did not go as well as expected. With a greater number of new crews with no combat experience and having had a three-and-a-half-month layoff from bombing, it is not surprising that the squadrons were rusty. On returning to the SAF the group began an intensive training program, but the first combat mission came before the squadrons could complete their training. On October 19 the group sent out 24 B-24s to join RAF Liberators in an attack on the jetties at Moulmein. The bombing was mixed, with only one squadron getting its bombs into the designated target area. The bombers returned to Moulmein on October 22, bombing from 8,000 feet and getting more bombs on the target. Coming off the target, a formation of *50th* and *64th Hikōsentai* fighters attacked the 7th Bomb Group formation. The 493rd Bomb Squadron lost three aircraft: one to the Japanese fighters and two to a midair collision when one damaged bomber collided with another. A mission to bomb the railroad yards at Paliek, near Ye-U, resulted in another case of only fair bombing. Clearly the group needed more practice and more intensive training. The group flew several more missions to lightly defended targets, but Stratemeyer was apparently not pleased with the group's performance and arranged for a new commanding officer to take over the group. Stratemeyer moved Col. Harvey Alness, who had served under Stratemeyer as a young

The Ban Dara Bridge collapsed in the river below following 1st Lt. James Nemecek's final attack on the bridge. His bombardier sighted on the central span and scored a direct hit with his three remaining bombs. *File 825.08, AFHRA*

The attack on the important Ban Dara Bridge in northern Thailand. Four aircraft with volunteer crews went out to bomb the bridge at dusk. This photo shows the bridge still standing after several attacks. *File 825.08, AFHRA*

lieutenant in the prewar 7th Bomb Group, to take command, with instructions to get the group back into form.[144]

Ironically, a few days later the group flew one of its most demanding bombing missions. Mellersh asked the group to knock out the important Ban Dara Bridge on the railroad line from Bangkok to northern Thailand, one of the priority targets assigned in Eastern Air Command's Directive No. 16. Lt. Col. William Delahay, temporarily commanding the group until Alness's arrival, and his operations officer Maj. Richard Henning decided to carry out the mission, with four airplanes attacking the bridge at low level at dusk, and in case that failed, to send 36 B-24s in a conventional attack. The group had a model of the bridge built to work out the best approaches. A call went out for volunteers—one from each squadron—since the mission was considered more than normally dangerous. The four B-24s took off on the morning of 1 November 1944, arriving over the Ban Dara Bridge an hour before dusk. Each bomber carried five 1,000-pound bombs to be dropped on individual runs on the bridge. The first two aircraft missed the bridge with their bombs, while the third aircraft got two hits on the central structure despite numerous hits from machine gun fire. 1st Lt. James Nemecek, from the 436th Bomb Squadron, was the last to attack. His first runs failed to hit the bridge. On the last run, the crew decided to drop all three bombs at once. The bombardier aimed at the central pillar of the bridge and scored a direct hit, dropping the central span into the river. As Nemecek made his final run nearby, machine gun fire shot out the bomber's hydraulic system. Nemecek's copilot, an instrument flying instructor with Eastern Air Command who had volunteered to go on the mission, made a successful night landing without brakes back at Madhaiganj, the 436th Squadron's base.[145]

Under Alness's leadership the 7th Group set up a new training regime, pulling out two squadrons at a time for two weeks of intensive training for every member of the aircrew and putting in a lot of flying practice in formation and low-level flying. The bombardiers finally got motorized bombing-training devices to practice their skills while the gunners attended a special group gunnery school. The 9th and 493rd Squadrons at Pandaveswar trained from November 7 to 22, with the 436th and 492nd Squadrons following, completing their program on December 5. As soon as they finished their training, the squadrons went back to bombing, beginning what became

ARMY AIR FORCE UNITS SUPPORTING 14TH ARMY OPERATIONS

known within the group as the "Battle of the Bridges": a full-scale assault on the railroad line running from Thailand into Burma. From November 1944 until May 1945 the 7th Bomb Group struck the bridges along this line repeatedly. The 457-mile-long railroad line from Bangkok to Pegu in Burma, via Moulmein, crossed more than 271 bridges, with 98 bridges more than 200 feet in length. The line from Bangkok north to Chiang Mai and beyond, running 458 miles, had 112 bridges. The most promising section of the Thailand-Burma railroad system for air attack was the 245-mile single-track line running between Banpong in Thailand to Thanbyuzayat in Burma. This line ran through a section of jungle-covered hills where there were no roads. Breaking bridges along this stretch not only disrupted traffic but compounded the difficulties of repair. Just as in Burma, the Japanese became adept at making speedy repairs to damaged bridges, keeping teams of prisoners of war and local laborers nearby to work on building new bypass bridges and repairing damaged ones. The bombers had to return again and again to the same targets as soon as photoreconnaissance confirmed a bridge was back in operation.[146]

During November and December, the 7th Bomb Group carried out seven attacks on bridges in Thailand and Burma, with the mixed results that had been a feature of most of the group's attacks on bridges. The group tried bombing from low level and medium level, sometimes getting good hits that destroyed or severely damaged a bridge, but sometimes missing the bridge entirely. The most frustrating target during this time was Bridge #277 on the Bangkok-Moulmein rail. The bridge became infamous within the group because of its apparent ability to resist whatever the squadrons threw at it. "Old 277," as it came to be called, was a strong concrete-and-steel bridge the Japanese had built during 1943. On a mission on November 29, two squadrons bombed in a tight pattern from 8,500 feet but failed to damage the bridge. Two weeks later the squadrons tried again, with four aircraft attempting to bomb the bridge from low level with 2,000- and 1,000-pound bombs while 12 B-24s bombed from 8,000 feet. Weather disrupted the attack, but most of the bombs went near the bridge. When the smoke and dust cleared, Old 277 was still standing. At the end of December, the 7th Bomb Group found the answer to destroying bridges when a new weapon made its debut in Burma: the Azon bomb.[147]

In addition to hitting railroad bridges, the 7th Group attacked railroad yards and other railroad facilities, making six attacks on yards in Burma and Thailand. In a few instances when bombing bridges, the B-24s went down to strafe locomotives and rolling stock. To support the advance of 14th Army into central Burma and the XV Corps in the Arakan, the group bombed Japanese supply dumps supporting the *15th* and *28th Army*. In the midst of these bombing missions the Fourteenth Air Force called on the Tenth Air Force again for support. Although Chennault had lost his main airfields in central China, he retained a small number of airfields to the east that were critical to maintaining attacks on Japanese shipping and supporting the Chinese army. Supplying these airfields required a flight over Japanese-held territory. When this was deemed too dangerous for unarmed transports, the Fourteenth Air Force requested the 7th Bomb Group to send a detachment to China to fly aviation gasoline from a base near Kunming to the eastern airfield at Suichwan. Each of the group's squadrons sent ten combat crews and four or five aircraft to the detachment and began flying gasoline on 16 December 1944. The 7th Group's detachment spent six weeks flying gasoline to the Fourteenth Air Force's eastern airfields until these, too, fell to a renewed Japanese offensive, with Suichwan falling on 27 January 1945. Each squadron lost one of its aircraft during the assignment to China, though two of the crews bailed out successfully behind Japanese lines and made it back after a monthlong journey. The flying was demanding. Bradley Hamlett, a newly arrived copilot, recalled that the 7th Group was notorious for ignoring the recommended 65,000-pound gross weight for the B-24J:

Flying out of Luliang we were grossed at 68,500 lbs. We would set the turbos to develop 51 in. of manifold pressure. The manual recommended 40. The book also said to raise the nose at 80 mph and it would start flying. Being over-grossed, in order to get the '24 to fly we had to get all the airspeed we could. We did this by raising the nose just enough for the nose wheel to clear the runway. At the end of the runway you would gently ease back on the control column and hope the SOB would fly. If you came back too fast on the control it could develop a high speed stall that you would not be able to recover from.[148]

During the final months of 1944, the 7th Bomb Group carried out missions against bridges in Burma and Thailand by using a variety of techniques, including bombing from low level. A B-24J from the 436th Bomb Squadron pulls away from a bridge it has just knocked down after a low-level attack. *3A-37525, RG342, NARA*

The 24th Combat Mapping Squadron flew the Consolidated F-7, a special reconnaissance version of the B-24 Liberator. The 24th Squadron carried out solitary, unescorted missions to photograph large sections of Burma, Thailand, and China to provide the basis for detailed maps of these areas for the Allied air forces and armies, using special cameras. *GP-PHOTO-8-HI, AFHRA*

The 8th Photographic Reconnaissance Group was another Army Air Force unit that supported 14th Army and the Chinese American forces in the NCAC. Moving to India in February–March 1944, the 8th Group became part of the Photo Reconnaissance Force under Eastern Air Command, taking on the Army Air Force reconnaissance units already in the theater. The 9th Photographic Reconnaissance Squadron had begun operations with F-4 photoreconnaissance airplanes in December 1942, while the 20th Tactical Reconnaissance Squadron started at the end of January 1944. The 24th Combat Mapping Squadron, flying the F-7 (the photoreconnaissance version of the B-24, with cameras in the nose and the bomb bay), arrived in India in December 1943 to carry out long-range photo coverage used to prepare detailed maps of Burma. Initially the three squadrons formed part of the 5306th Photographic and Reconnaissance Group (Provisional) until 17 January 1944, when they came under the Tenth Air Force, transferring to the 8th Photo Reconnaissance Group in April 1944. The 40th Photographic Reconnaissance Squadron arrived in India in June 1944, adding a second squadron flying the Lockheed F-4/F-5 to the 8th Photo Group in July.[149]

As the Allied armies advanced into Burma, the demands for photographic coverage expanded exponentially. Working alongside their RAF counterparts, the 8th Photo Group's squadrons flew more sorties and prepared more aerial prints for the air and ground forces. The Strategic Air Force needed coverage of targets before and after bombing to determine the amount of damage done. The 9th and 40th Squadrons flew regular photoreconnaissance missions over all the Japanese airfields in Burma to track the movement of aircraft and the operational status of the airfields. In addition, the photo squadrons regularly covered the rail and road bridges in Burma and Thailand to keep track of the speed of repairs. The ground forces needed coverage of the areas ahead of the advance, to gain an appreciation of the terrain and Japanese positions and to locate targets for airstrikes. To keep up with the demand for photos over such a broad area and diverse targets, the photo squadrons divided their aircraft and crews into detachments located at different bases. The 9th Photo Squadron operated detachments from Tingkawk Sakan and Myitkyina supporting the NCAC forces, and at Chittagong supporting 14th Army before the entire squadron moved to Myitkyina in early December. The 20th Tactical Reconnaissance Squadron was fully committed to the NCAC, operating from Dinjan with a detachment at Tingkawk Sakan, moving to Tingkawk Sakan in June 1944 with a forward detachment at Myitkyina, and then moving the entire squadron to Myitkyina in early November. Similarly, the 40th Photo Reconnaissance Squadron had its main base at Alipore, with a detachment at Cox's Bazar supporting the XV Corps and 14th Army,

The 40th Photographic Reconnaissance Squadron arrived in India and joined the 8th Photo Reconnaissance Group in July 1944. Flying versions of the Lockheed F-5 photoreconnaissance version of the Lightning, the 40th Squadron flew many missions deep into southern Burma to provide regular coverage of Japanese activities. *Author's collection*

Maj. William Bailey, 40th Photo Reconnaissance Squadron commander, fills out forms upon his return from a mission over Burma in his F-5E "It's a Lulu" in 1945. Bailey had flown a tour as a photoreconnaissance pilot in the Southwest Pacific early in the war and returned for another tour, flying out of India. *Courtesy, William Bailey*

moving the entire squadron to Cox's Bazar in January 1945. The 9th Photo Squadron concentrated on covering airfields, while the 40th Photo Squadron produced photo coverage of particular areas of Burma. The 24th Combat Mapping Squadron's aircraft flew individual long-range missions to cover large areas of Burma and Thailand for precision mapping. To process the tens of thousands of photos, each squadron had its own photo lab, and the group had the 3rd Photo Technical Unit and the 7th Photo Technical Squadron attached, and the 17th Photo Interpretation Detachment to do the vital work of interpreting the photos to glean as much intelligence as possible. The 9th Photo Squadron used a few B-25C and D aircraft to run a courier service between the different squadron detachments and Photo Reconnaissance Force headquarters, using pilots who had completed their combat tours and were waiting to return to the United States. As an example of the group's effort, in October 1944 the group's squadrons and photo tech units produced 317,698 prints of aerial photographs. In December the total reached 432,372 prints and 34,508 mosaics covering 17,343 square miles in Burma. For the number of sorties carried out, losses were slight. Though photoreconnaissance aircraft frequently saw Japanese fighters during their missions, the fighters rarely attacked, and the F-5 pilots easily evaded the few attempts at interception. Most losses were due to mechanical failure, pilot error, or unknown causes. Between October and December the 8th Photo Group lost 12 aircraft and five crews. Operations in support of the final offensives in Burma would keep the 8th Photo Group's squadrons just as busy until the coming of the monsoon in May.[150]

CHAPTER 13

VICTORY IN BURMA

February–April 1945

Slim's Master Stroke: The Battle for Meiktila

As 14th Army prepared for the advance across the Chindwin River, Eastern Air Command underwent one last reorganization while Air Command, Southeast Asia, gained a new commander. In formulating plans for the advance into Burma, it became apparent that both the forces in the NCAC and 14th Army would be heavily dependent on close air support, and especially air supply. This would require the closest possible coordination between the ground forces and the air units supporting them.[1] The air commanders of the groups within the 3rd Tactical Air Force (until June 1944, No. 221 and 224 Groups, and the 5320th Air Defense Wing [Prov.] / Northern Air Sector Force) had a responsibility for the air defense of their areas, as well as an offensive role. In the coming battles these formations needed to concentrate their entire effort on supporting the ground forces without having to worry about air defense of their rear areas. A further complication to coordination was the need at times for ground commanders to communicate with three levels of air force command: the groups, 3rd Tactical Air Force, and Eastern Air Command. When Mountbatten received approval from the Combined Chiefs of Staff in November to create Allied Land Forces, Southeast Asia, to oversee 14th Army and the NCAC, it seemed appropriate for the air command to adopt a similar and equivalent structure. To allow Slim to concentrate all his efforts on Operation CAPITAL, Lt. Gen. Leese, commanding ALFSEA, relieved 14th Army of responsibility for XV Corps in the Arakan, leaving Slim with IV and XXXIII Corps. Since it was planned for No. 221 Group and No. 224 Group to move forward with the ground forces they were supporting—as the Tenth Air Force had done in the NCAC—this left no real role for 3rd Tactical Air Force. On 1 December 1944 Stratemeyer disbanded 3rd Tactical Air Force so that No. 221 Group could work directly with 14th Army and its two corps, and No. 224 Group with XV Corps, in the Arakan. Air Marshal W. A. Coryton, who had taken over command of 3rd Tactical Air Force from Air Marshal Baldwin, moved over to become Stratemeyer's deputy at Eastern Air Command. Coryton took command of a new formation (RAF Bengal-Burma) responsible for the air defense of Calcutta and administrative services in Bengal.[2]

After nearly three years in the Far East, Peirse returned to England at the end of November. Peirse had the difficult task of helping the RAF in India recover from the 1942 defeat, rebuilding the force into a powerful air weapon in the face of immense challenges and shortages of men and equipment, much like his American counterparts. Although initially skeptical of air force integration, he had come to form an excellent relationship with Stratemeyer and Davidson. When Stratemeyer learned that Peirse would be leaving, he asked Mountbatten if Peirse's assignment could be extended, telling Mountbatten that Peirse "had been a wonderful chief to work for, and that his removal would break up a very fine Anglo-American family party."[3] Peirse had been engaged in an affair with Lady Auchinleck, wife of Gen. Sir Claude Auchinleck, commander in chief of the Indian army, and the affair had become public, affecting Peirse's position. Mountbatten felt he had to replace Peirse, despite his loyalty and diligence.[4] As his replacement Portal appointed Air Chief Marshal Trafford Leigh-Mallory, who had commanded Allied air forces in Operation OVERLORD, but Leigh-Mallory was killed when the plane carrying him out to India crashed in the French Alps. In his place, Portal selected Air Chief Marshal Sir Keith Park, now RAF commander in chief, Middle East, and former commander of No. 11 Group during the Battle of Britain, though Park would not arrive in India until 24 February 1945. In the interim, Air Marshal Sir Guy Garrod, who had been Peirse's deputy, took over temporary command of ACSEA until Park's arrival.[5]

Toward the end of December, Slim and his commanders firmed up their plans for the capture of Mandalay and Meiktila and the decisive battle for central Burma. Slim assigned the 2nd British

Air Chief Marshal Sir Richard Peirse awards Maj. Gen. Stratemeyer the Companion of the Order of the Bath (CB) shortly before Peirse relinquished his post as the head of Air Command, Southeast Asia, in November 1944. Peirse and Stratemeyer formed a sound working relationship as ACSEA expanded and intensified its operations over Burma during 1944. *3A-34067, RG-342, NARA*

Air Chief Marshal Sir Keith Park, who replaced Peirse as commander of Air Command, Southeast Asia, meets Brig. Gen. Frank Evans, commander of the Combat Cargo Task Force, after Park's arrival in February 1945. *File 824.6867, AFHRA*

Division, 19th and 20th Indian Divisions, the 268th Indian Brigade, and the 254 Indian Tank Brigade to XXXIII Corps under the command of Lt. Gen. M. G. N. Stopford, with orders to close up on the Irrawaddy River north and south of Mandalay, cross the river, and move on the city. To IV Corps, with Lt. Gen. Frank Messervy commanding, Slim allotted the 7th and 17th Indian Divisions, the 28th East African Brigade, the Lushai Brigade, and the Sherman tanks in the 255th Indian Tank Brigade, leaving the 5th Indian Division in reserve. Slim's plan for the battle was brilliant but carried great logistical risks. While XXXIII Corps advanced to the Irrawaddy and Mandalay, Slim planned to have IV Corps move secretly down the Myittha River valley to Pauk and on to Pakokku on the Irrawaddy. Here he planned to have 7th Division cross the river and seize a bridgehead. Once this had been done, 17th Division and 255th Tank Brigade would cross the river and strike out for Meiktila as rapidly as possible to seize the town before the Japanese became aware of the threat to their administrative and supply center. To reach the Irrawaddy River, IV Corps divisions and brigades would have to travel a distance of 328 miles from their base at Tamu to Pakokku over a dirt track, relying entirely on air supply, and would have to arrive at their jumping-off point without the Japanese becoming aware of their presence. The approach to the Irrawaddy and the crossing of the river would require complete secrecy, while the seizure of Meiktila would take "speed, surprise, and punch" to ensure that the town could be taken before *Burma Area Army* could react.[6]

To give 17th Division the ability to move fast over the open country of the central plain, Slim accepted Messervy's suggestion to reorganize the division to be both mechanized and air transportable to create a highly mobile striking force.[7] The division's 48th and 63rd Brigades gave up all their pack animals for motor vehicles, while the 99th Brigade acquired a small number of Jeeps as its only form of transport so that transport aircraft could fly in the entire brigade when needed. The division reduced its standard allowance of supplies and ammunition to travel lightly, relying instead on frequent air supply for replenishment. Division artillery fitted their 25-pounder guns with narrower axles so they would fit into a C-47. Slim ordered the 5th Indian Division—his reserve force—to undertake the same reorganization to make it air transportable. To provide more-effective air support, the 14th Army and the RAF took some of the techniques of close air support the RAF teams with Wingate's Special Force developed and created visual control posts (VCP) consisting of a small team of Army and RAF officers with radio operators to control the fighter-bombers providing close air support. Rather than assign an RAF team at the corps level—some distance from the front lines—each brigade in a division had its own VCP team to identify targets for the close-air-support aircraft, adjust the attacks, divert fighter-bombers to other targets, direct aircraft flying in a cab rank waiting for a target, and control medium-bomber operations. In the battles for Mandalay and Meiktila the hurriedly trained VCP teams proved to be an outstanding success.[8]

Air support for the crossing of the Irrawaddy and the seizure of Meiktila would be critical. On 26 January 1945, as IV Corps was advancing down the Myittha River valley, Air Vice-Marshal Stanley Vincent, commanding No. 221 Group (supporting IV and XXXIII Corps), convened a meeting to work up a plan for air support to IV Corps. Representatives from 14th Army and the Combat Cargo Task Force joined Col. Clinton Gaty, commanding the 1st Air Commando Group; Col. Arthur DeBolt, the 2nd Air Commando Group commander; and DeBolt's operations officer, Lt. Col. Levi Chase, an experienced fighter pilot and 10-victory ace from the North African campaign, to work out an air plan.[9] The attendees decided to assign the two Air Commando groups directly to IV Corps to provide close air support, air defense over the battlefield, air supply with transports and gliders, casualty evacuation, artillery spotting, and liaison, using the mixed fighter, bomber, transport, and liaison squadrons of the two Air Commando groups.[10] This would provide IV Corps with a fighter force of 50 P-47s and 50 P-51s, with the small 1st Air Commando Night Intruder section's B-25Hs in support, two C-47 squadrons with some 30 aircraft, and the six liaison squadrons—a sizeable force. The CCTF would provide backup support to fly in troops and supplies, while No. 221 Group agreed to allocate a few squadrons for air defense. Assigning the Air Commandos to IV Corps would allow No. 221 Group to concentrate its effort on supporting the three divisions in XXXIII

Two 1st Air Commando P-47Ds sit near 2nd Air Commando P-51Ds at the RAF airfield at Cox's Bazar in early 1945. Stratemeyer combined the 5th and 6th Fighter Squadrons (Commando) and the Night Intruder Section from the 1st Air Commando Group with the 1st and 2nd Fighter Squadrons (Commando) from the 2nd Air Commando Group into the First Provisional Fighter Group under the Combat Cargo Task Force, providing a powerful striking force to support 14th Army's advance into central Burma. *Courtesy, W. R. Eason*

THE TENTH AIR FORCE IN WORLD WAR II

Corps in their attack on Mandalay. After the meeting, Stratemeyer combined the four Air Commando fighter squadrons and the Night Intruder section into the 1st Provisional Fighter Group, with Levi Chase commanding, and the 317th and 319th Troop Carrier Squadrons (Commando) into the 1st Provisional Troop Carrier Group, under Maj. Neil Holm of the 1st Air Commando Group.[11] Stratemeyer also allocated the 12th Bomb Group to No. 221 Group's operational control. The meeting set February 8 as the target date for 7th Division's crossing of the Irrawaddy and February 20 as the date for 17th Division to begin its race to Meiktila with the 48th and 63rd Brigades and the 255th Tank Brigade.[12] As soon as the division could seize an airfield near Meiktila, the Air Commandos would fly in engineering equipment and a radio control team to make the field ready for the Air Commando and CCTF transports to fly in the division's 99th Brigade. This was the type of operation that Arnold had envisioned when he created the Air Commandos, using airpower to leap over enemy lines to provide greater mobility to the ground forces.

IV Corps began its advance on 19 January 1945. Two days before, Slim had given detailed instructions for seizing the bridgehead across the Irrawaddy and preparing 17th Division for its rapid advance on Meiktila. Remarkably, and fortunately, the Japanese failed to detect IV Corps' advance. Slim used the 28th East African Brigade and the Lushai Brigade to lead the advance, in the hope that the Japanese would think these units were part of XXXIII Corps and simply guarding the corps' flank. When the Lushai Brigade ran into stiff resistance at Gangaw on the track toward Pauk, IV Corps asked for air support. The 12th Bomb Group sent all four B-25 squadrons to attack the village with 108 500-pound bombs and 72 1,000-pound bombs in what the British called an "Earthquake" attack, with one squadron of RAF Thunderbolts and two squadrons of RAF rocket-carrying Hurricane fighters coming in directly after the bombers.[13] Following the airstrike, the Lushai Brigade occupied the village without opposition. By the end of January, 7th Division was in sight of the Irrawaddy and preparing to seize Pakokku. To the east, XXXIII Corps had advanced to the Irrawaddy, with 19th Division crossing the river to establish two bridgeheads north of Mandalay, 2nd Division nearing Sagaing on the Irrawaddy southwest of the city, and 20th Division seizing Myinmu, just west of Sagaing. As Slim had hoped, XXXIII Corps' advance to the Irrawaddy drew in Japanese forces. *Burma Area Army* deployed four divisions for the defense of Mandalay and to counter what appeared to be imminent crossings of the Irrawaddy southwest of the city. Fortuitously, at this juncture *Southern Army* ordered *Burma Area Army* to begin transferring the *2nd Division*, which Kimura had planned to use to defend the Meiktila area, to French Indochina along with the *5th Hikōshidan*, which pulled several air base units out of the Meiktila airfields. Slim now had the strategic initiative and was about to impose his will on *Burma Area Army*.[14]

IV Corps' crossing of the Irrawaddy and seizure of Meiktila became Operation MULTIVITE, divided into four phases:

1 "Vitamin A": The concentration of IV Corps, less 17th Division, in the area around Pauk
2 "Vitamin B": Securing a bridgehead across the Irrawaddy in the vicinity of Nyangu
3 "Vitamin C": Concentrating 17th Division's two motorized brigades within the 7th Division's bridgehead
4 "Vitamin D": The rapid advance to seize Meiktila and an airfield in the area to fly in the 99th Brigade[15]

In preparation for supporting the Irrawaddy crossing, the 5th and 6th Fighter Squadrons had returned to their main base at Asansol, where they received more aircraft to bring each squadron's complement up to 30 P-47s. The squadron's aircraft received newer VHF radios to replace the older HF sets, but each flight leader retained an HF set in his airplane. This was important, since the VCP teams had only HF radio sets. Because the Mustangs of the 1st and 2nd Fighter Squadrons had only VHF sets, the 5th and 6th Squadrons took over the close-air-support role. The VCP teams could call one of the flight leaders on their HF sets, provide instructions on the assigned

Senior British and American officers receive a briefing on Operation MULTIVITE shortly before the operation begins. Coordinating the movement of several divisions up to the west bank of the Irrawaddy River and then launching an opposed river crossing required detailed planning and nearly flawless execution. The operation could not have been conducted without total Allied air superiority. *3A-37406, RG342, NARA*

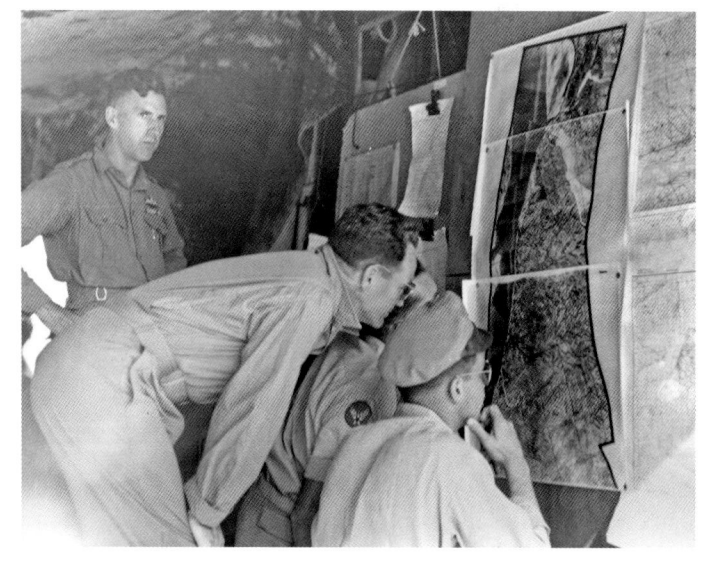

Air liaison officers from the 1st and 2nd Air Commando Groups study a map of the operational area to set objectives for close air support for IV Corps. The Air Commando fighter squadrons began flying missions a few days before 7th Indian Division began crossing the Irrawaddy on 14 February 1945. *3A-37407, RG342, NARA*

VICTORY IN BURMA

Visual control posts (VCP) operating close to the front lines directed close-air-support missions in support of British and Indian troops. The VCP teams were in radio contact with the Air Commando fighters flying in cab rank above the front lines, directing the fighters to bomb and strafe targets forward infantry units had identified. *3A-37410, RG342, NARA*

British and Indian troops from 7th Indian Division moving across a sandbar on the Irrawaddy River to the opposite bank the morning of 14 February 1945. The crossing caught the Japanese by surprise. *3A-35685, RG342, NARA*

British and Indian officers watch 1st Air Commando P-47s attacking a target near the Irrawaddy River bridgehead under control of a VCP team. The 5th and 6th Fighter Squadrons kept patrols over the bridgehead throughout the day. *3A-37410, RG342, NARA*

target, and have the flight leader brief the other airplanes in his flight over his VHF set. The system worked in practice. On 8–9 February 1945 a small group of officers from the CCTF and the 1st and 2nd Air Commando Groups joined IV Corps headquarters near Pauk to control the air operations during the different phases of Operation MULTIVITE. On February 10 the 5th and 6th Squadrons transferred to Hay Field—a long, grass-covered airfield near Cox's Bazar—where the 1st and 2nd Fighter Squadrons arrived three days later. The 5th Fighter Squadron flew the 1st Provisional Fighter Group's first mission that same day, with 14 P-47s undertaking a bombing and strafing mission under VCP control. The next day the 6th Fighter Squadron joined the 5th Squadron in two more attacks on targets IV Corps had designated in the Pakokku area, returning to the area over the next two days to attack Japanese-held villages and gun positions, dive-bombing with 500-pound bombs and making repeated strafing passes.[16]

"Vitamin B" (7th Division's crossing of the Irrawaddy) began at 0530 on 14 February 1945, opposite Nyaungu. At 0505, two C-64 light transport aircraft from the 1st Air Commando Group's 166th Liaison Squadron began flying up and down the river over the crossing site so that their engines would drown out the noise of the many outboard motors starting up on the boats carrying the troops across the river. After the crossing began, three B-25s from the Night Intruder section arrived to bomb and strafe Japanese positions around Nyaungu, with smoke shells indicating the target areas. The bombers dropped fragmentation clusters and strafed with their .50-caliber machine guns and 75 mm cannon. At 0745, P-47s from the 6th Fighter Squadron arrived over the bridgehead area to maintain cab rank patrols that lasted until 1930 that evening, with the squadron flying 49 cab rank sorties during the day. While in some ways an extravagant use of aircraft, the distance between Hay Field and the bridgehead would have considerably lengthened the time between requests for air support and the arrival of the fighters. Chase estimated that it would take two hours for fighters at Hay Field and Cox's Bazar to respond to a request for air support. Using the cab rank system, aircraft would arrive over a target within minutes of a request for an airstrike. Flights of four P-47s arrived in the area, armed with two 500-pound bombs and a belly fuel tank and patrolled for an hour and 15 minutes before heading back to base. An unanticipated benefit of the cab rank patrols turned out to be the suppression of Japanese artillery fire, the Japanese gunners proving reluctant to open fire when armed P-47s were flying overhead. That same day the 2nd Air Commando Group's fighter squadrons flew their first combat mission when Levi Chase led four P-51s from the 1st Fighter Squadron to bomb Japanese positions still resisting near Pakokku.[17]

For the next several days, the 5th and 6th Fighter Squadrons flew cab rank patrols over the bridgehead while the Mustangs of the 1st and 2nd Fighter Squadrons flew patrols over the wider area and strikes on designated targets, bombing Japanese-held villages, troop concentrations, and gun positions. The 1st and 2nd Squadrons each had several F-6D Mustangs equipped with cameras for tactical reconnaissance. These aircraft flew regular missions over the area around Meiktila to search for targets and assess the damage from fighter strikes. When the fighters couldn't contact a VCP team, they went to secondary targets in the surrounding areas, bombing and strafing targets of opportunity. Road and rail sweeps south of Meiktila

Armorers loading a 500-pound bomb onto a P-51D from the 1st Fighter Squadron in preparation for the 2nd Air Commando Group's first combat mission on 14 February 1945. The Mustang in the background has a three-round rocket launcher mounted under the wing and will likely have a 500-pound bomb added. *WWII Air Commando Association*

A B-25H from the 1st Air Commando Group's Night Intruder Section returning from having just bombed the town of Chauk on the Irrawaddy River (burning in the background) on 17 February 1945. The Night Intruder Section's B-25s joined the 5th and 6th Fighter Squadrons in providing close air support to the 7th Indian Division, holding the bridgehead across the Irrawaddy. *3A-37552, RG342, NARA*

The 1st and 2nd Fighter Squadrons each had a few F-6D Mustangs assigned for tactical reconnaissance. The F-6Ds would participate in air strikes, carrying combinations of bombs and rockets like the other Mustangs, and would then take poststrike photos of the targets for analysis of the results. *WWII Air Commando Association*

to keep the Japanese army supply system under constant pressure brought some claims for locomotives, rolling stock, and motor vehicles. The Night Intruder section's B-25s joined the fighters bombing Japanese positions. The *5th Hikōshidan* responded to the crossings along the Irrawaddy, sending out small formations of Ki-43s from the *64th Hikōsentai* to attack British positions and equipment, with 13 fighters attacking the newly built airstrips at Pakokku and Nyaungyan on February 17, shooting down an Air Commando L-5. To counter these attacks the Air Commando squadrons began carrying out regular sweeps over the Japanese airfields in central Burma, bombing and strafing the installations around the fields but not seeing any aircraft.

Although several of the Air Commando fighters returned to base with damage from ground fire, the squadrons suffered no losses during their first week of combat. Then their run of good luck came to an end. On February 19, five *64th Hikōsentai* Ki-43s jumped a flight of four 6th Fighter Squadron P-47s carrying out a sweep of the railroad line south of Meiktila. The P-47s had been strafing the marshaling yards at Thazi and were low on ammunition and fuel. 1st Lt. Marion Ball saw one of the pilots having trouble dropping his belly tank as an Oscar came in on his tail firing, getting hits on the P-47's wing. Ball and his wingman did a 360-degree turn and came in on the Oscar, Ball firing as he closed in to 200 yards, seeing strikes on the engine cowling. The Oscar dove away trailing black smoke, and the P-47s hit the deck to get away. One P-47 went missing when the pilot broke away from Ball's flight to join another flight strafing rolling stock, becoming a victim of Capt. Hideo Miyabe, the *64th Hikōsentai*'s executive officer. That same morning the 6th Squadron lost a pilot when 2nd Lt. Keith Hughes ran into ground fire on his strafing run, his P-47 crashing into the ground and exploding.

The 6th Squadron ran into Japanese fighters on February 26, when a flight of four P-47s saw four Oscar fighters above them. When the Oscars came down on them, the P-47 pilots jettisoned their bombs and belly tanks and prepared to fight. The leading Japanese fighter, Capt. Takeo Miyabe, made a pass on 1st Lt. Charles Posten and his wingman, 1st Lt. Glen Feickert, but broke off to dive after other Allied fighters below. Posten and Feickert went after the leader's wingman, both firing on the Oscar, which went down in a spin to crash in the jungle. Posten and Feickert each received credit for one fighter destroyed. That same morning, Col. Gaty, although not an experienced fighter pilot, borrowed a P-47 to join a 6th Squadron formation on a cab rank patrol. He never returned from the flight and was likely the victim of two other *64th Hikōsentai* pilots patrolling in the area. The 5th Fighter Squadron lost a pilot that day who disappeared on a dive-bombing mission, while Glen Feickert was killed on February 27 when heavy Japanese machine gun fire hit his P-47 on his third strafing pass on a Japanese roadblock holding up the advance on Meiktila. The 2nd Fighter Squadron lost two Mustangs on February 25 and 26, but both pilots survived. On February 25, after learning that a pilot had bailed out behind enemy lines, Maj. Charles Gordon, a 1st Fighter Squadron officer serving temporarily as air liaison with IV Corps, commandeered an L-5

Having received a hit in an oil line from ground fire, an Air Commando P-47 makes an emergency landing on the airfield at Thabutkon shortly after the airfield was captured. Two liaison airplanes are already on the field near the makeshift radio control center, operating out of a jeep. *3A-37425, RG342, NARA*

and flew out to rescue him, landing in a field near the downed pilot, who raced over to the waiting L-5. Taking off, Gordon hit a tree but made it back. Later that afternoon another Mustang went down near British lines. Gordon tried for another rescue in an L-5, but this time while trying to land near British troops in the darkness, he crashed into a tree and broke his leg. The downed Mustang pilot hid in the brush and waited for a British patrol that rescued him the next morning.[18]

Anxious to begin "Vitamin D" and get 17th Division on the way to Meiktila, Messervy ordered the division to begin crossing over into the 7th Division bridgehead on February 17. Four days later the division struck out for Meiktila, with 48th Brigade leading. The advance was swift, quickly overcoming disorganized Japanese resistance. On the afternoon of February 26, tanks and infantry captured the airfield at Thabutkon, one of the airfields in the Meiktila group. Bulldozers traveling with the mechanized columns quickly filled in bomb craters on the airfield to prepare it for flying in the 99th Brigade. While waiting for the alert for the fly-in, the two Air Commando transport squadrons had been making daily supply runs to forward airfields for 7th and 17th Divisions, bringing in 1,396 tons of supplies. After getting the alert from 17th Division to begin the fly-in, an Air Commando C-47 towed a glider to Thabutkon, loaded with radio and runway lighting equipment, early on the morning of February 27. After checking over the airfield, a transport officer radioed to the Air Commando transport squadrons waiting at the airfield at Palel, giving them the go-ahead. The CCTF had temporarily assigned 10 C-47s from the 2nd and 4th Combat Cargo Squadrons to the 1st Provisional Transport Group and arranged for seven RAF Dakotas to join the force for a short period. By the end of the day, 63 transports had flown into the field, carrying troops and two antiaircraft units. Despite intermittent Japanese mortar and machine gun fire, only one airplane received damage, when the pilot overshot the runway on landing. On February 28 the transports flew 108 sorties, and on March 1 they completed 208 sorties, with 116 airplanes landing and taking off between 0645 and 1015. The Air Commando transports completed the fly-in the next day, having carried in 3,947 troops and 293 tons of supplies, with the two Combat Cargo squadrons flying in another 591 troops. The round trip from Palel to Thabutkon took four hours, and some crews made three trips a day. While the 1st Provisional Transport Group had responsibility for flying in the 99th Brigade, other Combat Cargo, RAF, and RCAF transport squadrons also used the airfield at Thabutkon to fly in supplies for 17th Division, carrying in gasoline, oil, and ammunition for the tanks and motor vehicles, and food, ammunition, and medical supplies for the troops. Thabutkon remained open for five days, then shut down after the final sorties on March 3, with 17th Division, now three brigades strong, already moving on to Meiktila. Once the division abandoned Thabutkon it became entirely dependent on air drops for all supplies until it could open the airfield at Meiktila.[19]

By the evening of February 27, advance units of 63rd Brigade were 6 miles from Meiktila. Leapfrogging its sister brigade, 48th

A row of C-47s from the 1st Air Commando Group's 319th Troop Carrier Squadron at Thabutkon airfield. These were the first transports to arrive on 27 February 1945—the day after 17th Indian Division had captured the airfield—bringing in troops from the Division's 99th Brigade to support the advance on Meiktila. *3A-37427, RG342, NARA*

THE TENTH AIR FORCE IN WORLD WAR II

A column of tanks and other vehicles from 17th Division on the road to Meiktila. The division's rapid advance on the town caught the Japanese by surprise. The division's columns of more than 3,000 vehicles moved under cover of Air Commando and RAF fighters, who provided protection from Japanese air attack. Remarkably, Japanese airplanes never attacked the advance, probably due to poor intelligence on Allied movements. *SE_003071, IWM*

A P-51D and an F-6D from the 2nd Air Commando Group's 1st Fighter squadron prepare to take off from Cox's Bazar, armed with 500-pound bombs on a mission in support of 17th Indian Division's advance on Meiktila. While the 1st Air Commando Group's P-47s flew cab rank patrols, the 2nd Air Commando Group's Mustangs attacked Japanese lines of communications leading to Meiktila and Japanese positions in the surrounding towns. *WWII Air Commando Association*

Brigade took the lead on February 28, and by evening the troops were just short of 2 miles from the town. At 0700 on March 1, Maj. Gen. Cowan, commanding 17th Division, ordered the attack on the town to begin. The Air Commando fighter squadrons continued patrolling over the advancing 17th Division columns as they neared Meiktila. The columns contained some 3,000 motor vehicles and tanks and never came under Japanese air attack. While the P-51s of the 1st and 2nd Fighter Squadrons kept up steady attacks on the towns and villages in the area around Meiktila, where the Japanese were concentrating their forces and continued to sweep the road and rail lines, the 5th and 6th Fighter Squadrons patrolled above the advancing columns, providing cab rank flights during the day and responding to calls from VCP teams to strike Japanese positions ahead of the advance. Meiktila itself became a target, with the P-47s and P-51s bombing selected areas of the town. When the 5th and 6th Squadrons left to escort the 7th Bomb Group on a mission to Mingaladon on February 28, four P-47s remained behind to patrol Meiktila with the P-51s from the 1st and 2nd Squadrons, the P-47 pilots using their HF and VHF radios to transmit instructions from the VCP teams to the Mustangs. The VCP teams arranged for colored smoke to mark targets for the fighters, and used gridded mosaics as references to direct the fighters onto the target area, radioing instructions to direct the bombing and strafing for better effect.

On March 1, as the battle for Meiktila began, IV Corps asked the Air Commando fighter squadrons to strike the oil production facilities at Yenangyaung, where *Burma Area Army* obtained all its supplies of gasoline. On the first mission around noon, 20 P-51s went in first, dropping napalm, followed by the P-47s dropping 500-pound bombs. At the end of the day, 25 P-51s and 15 P-47s went back for a second strike, the Mustangs approaching out of the setting sun and opening fire as they approached and dropping more napalm, with the P-47s right behind dropping their 500-pound bombs. For the next three days the squadrons concentrated on supporting the troops and tanks assaulting Meiktila. The fighters kept a cab rank over the town throughout the day. The troops called in the fighters when needed to blast Japanese bunkers and buildings containing machine guns and snipers, sometimes only a few hundred feet from their own positions. On the evening of March 3, Cowan reported to Messervy that the town was clear. By the next evening, 17th Division had consolidated its hold on the town and had captured Meiktila's main airfield. The combination of aggressive and well-led troops, Sherman tanks, artillery, and airstrikes destroyed the Japanese garrison in only three days. Operation MULTIVITE was a complete success. Slim's forces had captured *Burma Area Army's* main supply center in central Burma and now sat astride the Japanese communications network linking Mandalay and Meiktila with southern Burma. Within Meiktila, 17th Division and 255th Tank Brigade—now cut off from the 7th Division bridgehead and entirely dependent on air supply—prepared to defend the town against the Japanese attacks they knew would soon begin.[20]

The capture of Meiktila caught *Burma Area Army* by surprise. Confused reports of an enemy column with some 200 vehicles

1st Lt. William Burghardt's P-47D "Southern Belle" waits to take off on another cab rank mission over Meiktila, armed with two 500-pound bombs and a drop tank. During the battle for Meiktila the 5th and 6th Fighter Squadrons maintained cab rank patrols over the town throughout the day, bombing Japanese troop concentrations, gun positions, and stores under direction from VCP teams using grid map coordinates and colored smoke to identify targets. *Courtesy, William Burghardt*

VICTORY IN BURMA

moving toward Meiktila contributed to the belief that this was simply a raiding party and not a full divisional attack.[21] When Kimura, commanding *Burma Area Army*, learned of the town's capture, he realized he had to retake Meiktila if he was to hold Mandalay and prevent 14th Army from advancing into southern Burma. He immediately ordered the *18th Division*, assigned to reinforce *15th Army* for the battle around Mandalay, to move to Meiktila, and for the *49th Division*, then at Toungoo to the south, to move as rapidly as possible to join in the attack. Initially placed in charge of the attack on Meiktila, the commander of *18th Division* decided not to wait for all the promised reinforcements to arrive, but initiated his attacks on the town and on the 7th Division bridgehead around Nyaungu as soon as Japanese units arrived in the area. On March 14, Kimura placed Lt. Gen. Masaki Honda, the commander of *33rd Army*, then at Lashio, in overall command of the effort to recapture Meiktila. Honda arrived on March 18 and ordered the *18th Division* to attack from the north and *49th Division* from the east. For the next 10 days there was intensive fighting around Meiktila as the Japanese tried to break through into the town. The combined Japanese forces assigned to retake Meiktila outnumbered 17th Division, but the Japanese threw in their units piecemeal, with little coordination in their attacks.[22] Cowan had decided that his best option to retain his hold on Meiktila was to mount an offensive defense. Leaving one brigade to defend the town, he divided his other two brigades and the 255th Tank Brigade into strong columns of Sherman tanks and infantry, with close air support that aggressively sought out the Japanese units as they arrived in the area to disrupt their attacks and destroy them before they could consolidate their positions. To the north, *15th Army* was under intense pressure around Mandalay, where 19th Division began its assault on the city on the night of March 8. The 2nd and 20th Divisions had crossed the Irrawaddy and were advancing to the south and west of Mandalay.

In the bitter fighting from Meiktila to Mandalay, the Japanese were losing men and equipment faster than they could be replaced.[23]

With the successful completion of Operation MULTIVITE, the Air Commando fighter squadrons ended their support for IV Corps and shifted to other missions. The 5th and 6th Fighter Squadrons continued to provide cab rank patrols and attack targets with direction from the VCP teams with 7th and 17th Divisions in the areas around Meiktila until March 13, when they shifted to the operational control of No. 224 Group. The priority for the 5th and 6th Fighter Squadrons became long-range strikes against the Japanese lines of communications in southern Burma, particularly road and rail bridges. In carrying out these missions, each squadron would lose a pilot before the end of the month. To provide close air support to IV Corps, No. 224 Group transferred No. 905 Wing with four Thunderbolt squadrons to No. 221 Group's operational control.[24] These squadrons took over the cab rank patrol duties over 17th Division. The 1st and 2nd Fighter Squadrons left off their strikes on behalf of IV Corps and took on the task of seeking out and destroying the Japanese air force units still active over Burma. On their departure from this assignment, Cowan sent a message to the squadrons saying, on behalf of 17th Division, "The direct support so willingly given to us by our American Allies was of a very high order throughout and contributed in no small measure to our victory. Well done. Thank you."[25]

The 1st Provisional Transport Group continued to support IV Corps as part of the Combat Cargo Task Force, flying in supplies and troops. With the battle for Meiktila at a critical point as *Burma Area Army* marshaled more troops to throw against 17th Division, Slim decided to reinforce Cowan's forces with 9th Indian Brigade, the 5th Division's air-transportable brigade. The CCTF assigned the task of flying in the brigade to the 1st Provisional Transport Group, with its 27 C-47s, under the odd designation Operation BETTY, scheduled to start the morning of March 15 and to take three days. CCTF and IV Corps planners were unaware that the Japanese had chosen to open their attack on Meiktila during the night of March

Troops and tanks from 17th Indian Division seek out Japanese troops trying to break through to Meiktila. Maj. Gen. Cowan, division commander, mounted an aggressive defense of the town, sending out armored columns to break up the Japanese before they could mass for an attack on the town. The Air Commandos flew cab rank patrols over these 17th Division columns. *SE_003095, IWM*

Reserve troops from the 9th Brigade, 5th Indian Division, prepare to board a 2nd Air Commando C-47 at Palel to fly into Meiktila to reinforce 17th Division. Having broken through Japanese lines to capture the town, 17th Division was surrounded and became entirely dependent on air supply. This was in many ways the type of operation that Gen. Arnold had envisioned for the Air Commando and Combat Cargo groups. *3A-37204, RG342, NARA*

While en route from Palel to Meiktila, the transports received word that the airfield at Meitkila was under attack. They diverted temporarily to a hastily built airstrip at Nyaungu, where they waited for the all clear. 3A-33674, RG342, NARA

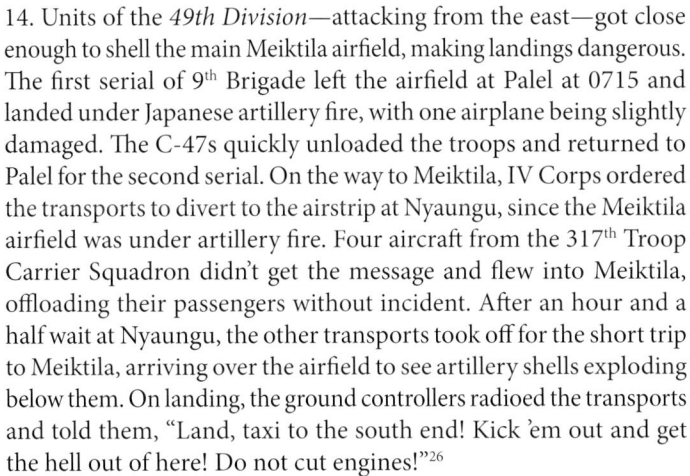

A C-47 from the 1st Air Commando Group's 319th Troop Carrier Squadron lands on the dusty Meiktila airfield. For several days in mid-March, Japanese troops infiltrated close enough to the airfield to bring the transports under fire as they landed. Men from the RAF Regiment and troops from the 5th and 17th Divisions would have to clear the airfield of Japanese soldiers every morning to allow the transports to land with their vital supplies. SE_003273, IWM

14. Units of the *49th Division*—attacking from the east—got close enough to shell the main Meiktila airfield, making landings dangerous. The first serial of 9th Brigade left the airfield at Palel at 0715 and landed under Japanese artillery fire, with one airplane being slightly damaged. The C-47s quickly unloaded the troops and returned to Palel for the second serial. On the way to Meiktila, IV Corps ordered the transports to divert to the airstrip at Nyaungu, since the Meiktila airfield was under artillery fire. Four aircraft from the 317th Troop Carrier Squadron didn't get the message and flew into Meiktila, offloading their passengers without incident. After an hour and a half wait at Nyaungu, the other transports took off for the short trip to Meiktila, arriving over the airfield to see artillery shells exploding below them. On landing, the ground controllers radioed the transports and told them, "Land, taxi to the south end! Kick 'em out and get the hell out of here! Do not cut engines!"[26]

At dawn the next morning, patrols found that a sizeable Japanese force had come in during the night and had dug in on the eastern side of the airfield. A force of RAF regiment troops, 17th Division infantry, and tanks had to clear the area before any aircraft could land. The first serial of troops and supplies on March 16 went to Nyaungu again, but in the afternoon the second serial left Palel at 1400 with orders to proceed directly to Meiktila. The transports landed amid intermittent artillery and mortar fire. As 1st Lt. Roy Burger from the 317th Squadron landed his C-47 on the airfield and began taxiing to the unloading area, a shell struck and collapsed his tail. Pushing the throttles forward, Burger headed for the unloading area, but just as he reached it another shell hit the C-47's right wing, setting it on fire. Burger's crew chief and radio operator made it out through the cargo door with five Indian soldiers, while Burger, his copilot, and three more soldiers went out the top escape hatch just before the flames reached the cockpit. Despite the loss of a C-47, the air lift continued the next day once the RAF regiment, infantry, and tanks had again cleared the field of Japanese troops who had infiltrated during the night. On this day the transports encountered only scattered shelling and sniper fire that did not interfere with the unloading. After dropping off their troops, 10 transports went back to Nyaungu to pick up supplies that had been dropped off the previous day. The fly-in of 9th Brigade ended on the evening of March 18, with the operation costing only one aircraft lost and five damaged but quickly repaired. The 317th and 319th Squadrons had flown in 4,000 men of the brigade and their equipment in 210 sorties from Palel.[27]

The CCTF flew a record number of hours and delivered a record tonnage of supplies supporting IV and XXXIII Corps during February 1945, only to surpass those records in March. In February the CCTF had nine operational Army Air Force squadrons and six RAF squadrons. These squadrons flew 55,005 hours during the month, delivering 54,327 tons of supplies and 40,610 personnel while evacuating 11,378 casualties for the loss of nine aircraft and 19 crew killed. The operations during March reflected the intensity of the fighting around Mandalay and Meiktila and the commitment of six divisions and two tank brigades to the fighting, all of whom were almost completely dependent on air supply: 77,611 hours flown, 66,155 tons of supplies and 56,972 personnel delivered, and 19,888 casualties evacuated for the loss of 16 aircraft, 6 crew, and 19 passengers. Once again, the inestimable value of the 4th Combat Cargo Group and its C-46s was clearly evident, the group's four squadrons delivering 40 percent of all the supplies and troops carried to the front during February and March. The C-46s could carry roughly 40 percent more cargo than the C-47. Had the C-46s not been available, the CCTF would have had to work its C-47 squadrons even harder or try to find more squadrons from other theaters, which simply weren't available. During these two months the squadrons were flying their aircraft an average of seven hours a day for nearly every day of the month. This was well above the level that the CCTF had defined as "intensive," and put a great strain on pilots, crews, and aircraft, allowing minimal time for maintenance. In January, Mountbatten had authorized the use of transport aircraft above their sustained rate to overcome the shortage of aircraft for all the needs of 14th Army and the NCAC.[28] The liaison squadrons were just as active. In February the 1st Air Commando Group's three liaison squadrons flew 9,803 trips and evacuated 4,189 casualties. The 2nd Air Commando Group's three liaison squadrons began operations in March, and together the six squadrons flew 13,157 trips and evacuated 8,309 casualties—double the number in February and a reflection on the intensity of the fighting on the ground. Once

Combat Cargo Task Force C-46s lining up to take on cargo to fly to the front. During February and March 1945 the Combat Cargo Task Force provided supplies for six infantry divisions and two armored brigades fighting around Mandalay and Meiktila. The C-46s of the 4th Combat Cargo Group made an invaluable contribution to 14th Army's advance into central Burma and the capture of Mandalay and Meiktila. Carrying 40 percent more than a C-47, the C-46s considerably enhanced the capacity of the CCTF to support 14th Army in a campaign where 14th Army was almost entirely dependent on air supply. *3A-37231, RG342, NARA*

again, it is important to note that despite the large numbers of transports flying back and forth to the front lines every day, the CCTF lost no transport aircraft to Japanese fighters. The few Japanese fighters available in the *64th Hikōsentai*—the last remaining Japanese fighter unit in Burma—persisted with ineffective attacks on British and Indian troops in their forward positions under orders from *Burma Area Army*, while their aerial lifeline flew unmolested a few miles away.[29]

The 12th Bomb Group and the 459th Fighter Squadron provided direct and indirect support to IV and XXXIII Corps during the battles for Mandalay and Meiktila. While attached to No. 221 Group for operations, the B-25s continued flying missions against bridges in central and southern Burma, concentrating on the vital Rangoon-Mandalay line. Supply dumps in the area south of Meiktila and Mandalay were also frequent targets. As the IV and XXXIII closed on the Irrawaddy River, they called on the 12th Bomb Group for support, requesting attacks on Japanese positions, troop concentrations, and supply dumps in the villages and towns along both sides of the river from Mandalay to Chauk. Normally two to three squadrons went to a designated target, but for some missions the group sent all four squadrons to saturate an area. On February 11, the group bombed the town of Sagaing, on the Irrawaddy River southwest of Mandalay, dropping 634 100-pound incendiary bombs on the town, with devastating effect. After the crossings of the Irrawaddy, the 12th Group's squadrons struck targets the IV or XXXIII Corps had designated, but sometimes worked with the VCP teams, with these teams arranging for smoke shells to mark the target area and directing the bombers onto the target. The squadrons bombed concentrations of Japanese troops gathering for attacks against IV and XXXIII Corps bridgeheads, and the supply dumps supporting these units. Sometimes radio intercepts located the position of a Japanese headquarters, so the B-25s would go out to bomb the suspected area. When the 19th Indian Division ran into strong opposition from Japanese troops inside Fort Dufferin at Mandalay, XXXIII Corps called in the 12th Group to bomb the area with 286 100-pound fragmentation bombs, while four bombers went in at 300 feet to try to breach the walls of the fort with 2,000-pound bombs. The 12th Group responded whenever called on. After a particularly successful strike on the village of Kyauktalon, west of Sagaing on the Irrawaddy, Slim and Vincent sent a congratulatory message to the group, saying, "Thanks for the cooperation of the forces under your command are giving us in the present battle. It is magnificent."[30]

The 459th Fighter Squadron remained under the operational control of No. 224 Group during the battle for central Burma. The

XXXIII Corps called on the 12th Bomb Group to bomb the walls surrounding the old Mandalay palace, where the Japanese were holding out, and Japanese positions within the walls. Repeated bombings by the B-25s and RAF Thunderbolts and artillery shelling finally forced the Japanese to abandon the palace area. *3A-37632, RG342, NARA*

THE TENTH AIR FORCE IN WORLD WAR II

The 459th Fighter Squadron provided close support to the 19th Indian Division during its attack on Mandalay, hitting Japanese positions along the Irrawaddy River. Here, armorers load a large depth charge onto a 459th Squadron P-38. The Lightnings could easily carry a 165-gallon drop tank and a 1,000-pound bomb or heavy depth charge on missions into central Burma. *3A-36022, RG342, NARA*

squadron's contribution was more in the form of indirect support. With their longer range and ability to carry two 1,000-pound bombs, the 459th Squadron continued their own campaign against bridges in central and southern Burma. Dive-bombing with 1,000-pound bombs, the squadron knocked out a good number of bridges during February and March, hitting both road and rail bridges, with their fair share of near misses. One of the squadron's best days was on February 17, when three missions went out to attack three different bridges, knocking out all three in dive-bombing attacks. When not going after bridges, the squadron escorted B-24s and B-25s on their missions. Escorting the bombers on a mission to bomb supply dumps at Victoria Lake near Rangoon, Capt. Hampton Boggs, on his second tour with the squadron, came upon a single-engine Japanese airplane flying near the bombers. From a position above the Japanese aircraft, Boggs dove down with his flight and came in from behind, opening fire from directly astern. The Japanese airplane, which Boggs tentatively identified as a Jill (the Imperial Navy's Nakajima B6N2 Tenzan attack bomber) exploded under his fire. This was in fact another Ki-61 Tony from the *8th Rensei Hikōtai*. Boggs had scored the 459th Squadron's first aerial victory on 1 December 1943, and this was to be his and the squadron's last aerial victory of World War II. After the first crossings of the Irrawaddy, the 459th Squadron joined the attacks on Japanese positions along the river, dropping 1,000-pound bombs and depth charges. On several missions the P-38s escorted the B-25s but, with little likelihood of encountering Japanese fighters, took along 1,000-pound bombs, going in ahead of the bombers to hit antiaircraft positions.[31]

The Japanese kept hammering at 17th Division's positions around Meiktila, but without success, though they cut the link between Meiktila and the 7th Division's bridgehead, isolating 17th Division in the town. Constant pressure against Meiktila's main airfield forced the CCTF to turn to dropping supplies for 17th Division when the transports couldn't land on the main airfield. Japanese losses were severe. By March 25, Honda estimated that the *18th Division* had lost half its artillery, with heavy losses of men, while losses in the *49th Division* were even worse. Mandalay had fallen to 19th Division

on March 20, forcing *15th Division* to withdraw to the south. On March 21, elements of the 2nd Division occupied the town of Myitnge and made contact with the lead elements of 19th Division. To the west, 20th Division had also crossed the Irrawaddy and was pushing toward a link-up with 7th and 17th Divisions. In their advance, all three divisions inflicted heavy casualties on the Japanese divisions attempting to block their way. The shattered elements of *15th Army* were now in full retreat. On March 28, *Burma Area Army*'s chief of staff visited Honda and, after reviewing the situation, agreed with Honda in abandoning the offensive to take Meiktila. Instead, *33rd Army* was to cover *15th Army*'s withdrawal to the east and prevent Allied forces moving south from Meiktila. The battles for Mandalay and Meiktila had ended in a punishing defeat for *Burma Area Army*. In two months of fighting, *15th* and *33rd Army* had an estimated 12,912 casualties, with 6,513 killed.[32] The *18th Division* lost a third of its strength, while the *49th Division*, having begun the battle with a strength of 10,000, suffered 6,500 casualties and lost 45 out of 48 artillery pieces.[33] At Imphal and Kohima, Slim and his divisions had inflicted on the Japanese army the worst defeat it ever suffered. Once again Slim had shattered the forces of his Japanese opponent. He had taken huge risks in advancing IV Corps to capture Meiktila, but the gamble paid off. After the war, Gen. Kimura admitted that Slim's attack on Meiktila was "the masterpiece of Allied strategy" in the war for Burma.[34] The road to Rangoon lay open.[35]

At the height of the battle, disaster beckoned, but from a different direction. In February 1945 Chiang Kai-shek and Wedemeyer requested the return of the Chinese divisions fighting in the NCAC, as well as the Mars Task Force. Wedemeyer particularly wanted the Mars Task Force to move to China immediately so that the experienced American troops could train Chinese units for Wedemeyer's planned offensive in eastern China. Mountbatten and the British Chiefs of Staff had agreed to this, with the proviso that any movement of these troops not take transport aircraft away from what would be needed to support 14th Army and the remaining NCAC forces at this critical juncture

C-46s of the 4th Combat Cargo Group taking on supplies. Air transport was vital to the successful battles in central Burma. Gen. Slim could not have conducted his campaign and the destruction of *Burma Area Army* in the battles for Mandalay and Meiktila without Allied air transports to fly in the supplies his men needed for battle. The threatened withdrawal of American transport squadrons to China could well have been a disaster and brought Prime Minister Churchill to appeal directly to Gen. Marshall. *3A-33662, RG342, NARA*

VICTORY IN BURMA

in the campaign. Mountbatten believed that all transport aircraft supporting the Allied armies in Burma should be viewed as a single force and should be available to support any part of these armies as needed.[36] He had already cut air supply to XV Corps in the Arakan to free up transports to support 14th Army's advance into central Burma. Chiang's refusal to allow his Chinese forces to advance beyond their current positions was allowing the Japanese to withdraw forces from the NCAC sector to reinforce *15th* Army around Mandalay and Meiktila, placing added burdens on IV and XXXIII Corps and requiring more supplies and men that could come only by air. When 36th Division—on the NCAC's right flank—transferred back to 14th Army's control, Mountbatten expected that the Tenth Air Force transport squadrons supporting 36th Division would shift to the Combat Cargo Task Force and continue this support. He considered it unacceptable that 14th Army should have to take over responsibility for providing for NCAC's remaining commitments when its own resources were being stretched to the limit.[37]

Mountbatten was thus astonished to learn that on March 20 the Joint Chiefs of Staff had instructed Sultan to move the Mars Task Force to China, using transport aircraft assigned to either NCAC, the Air Transport Command, or the Fourteenth Air Force. The next day, Mountbatten instructed Sultan not to pull any aircraft out of NCAC pending a meeting to discuss the problem. After meeting with Leese, Slim, Sultan, Stratemeyer, and Keith Park, Mountbatten informed the British Chiefs of Staff that unless he could have access to all the transport aircraft allocated to SEAC, it would not be possible for Slim to maintain the six divisions and two armored brigades he had fighting with IV and XXXIII Corps. This would put the entire campaign in jeopardy. Mountbatten argued for the "necessity of treating the campaign in Burma as a whole and the need to regard transport aircraft as interchangeable between the different sectors of the front as the progress of the campaign demands."[38] He asked that he be allowed to retain all transport aircraft to sustain his operations. The Chiefs of Staff immediately contacted the Joint Chiefs of Staff and asked them to assure that Mountbatten could retain the transport aircraft he needed. To support this request, Churchill sent a personal message to Marshall, saying:

> *As General Marshall will remember from our talks at "Octagon," we greatly disliked the prospect of a large-scale campaign in the jungles of Burma and I have always had other ideas myself. But the United States Chiefs of Staff attached the greatest importance to this campaign against the Japanese and especially to the opening of the Burma Road. We therefore threw ourselves into the campaign with the utmost vigor.... The very considerable battle upon such difficult communications, which is now being fought with the main Japanese army in Burma, is important not only for Burma and as a preliminary to the capture of Rangoon, but plays its part in the general wearing-down of the military and particularly the air-power of Japan.... I feel therefore entitled to appeal to General Marshall's sense of what is fair and right between us, in which I have the highest confidence, that he will do all in his power to let Mountbatten have the comparatively small additional support which his air force requires to enable the decisive battle now raging in Burma to be won.[39]*

This episode illustrates the ongoing tensions arising from the different national interests between America and Britain, which were never completely resolved, with the American preoccupation with China and suspicion of British desire to regain its colonies in Southeast Asia, and the British interests in achieving just that end.[40] Stratemeyer, for example, was apparently skeptical that the British truly intended to seize Rangoon before the monsoon (despite the logistical nightmare that would have confronted 14th Army had it failed to do so), and suspected that the British wanted to remove air units from Burma for an operation against Phuket Island in southern Thailand to provide an air base for an invasion of Malaya.[41] Marshall responded positively to Churchill's plea, replying that "there is complete agreement on the American side with your desire to continue the momentum of Admiral Mountbatten's present offensive to effect the early capture of Rangoon."[42] Mountbatten had indicated to the Combined Chiefs of Staff that if allowed to keep the transport aircraft he needed, he believed he could capture Rangoon by June 1. On the basis of this statement, the Joint Chiefs of Staff agreed not to remove US air forces from Burma before the fall of Rangoon or June 1—whichever came earlier—although still reserving the right to remove these aircraft if Mountbatten's forces did not capture Rangoon before the monsoon. The Joint Chiefs believed that rather than letting these American aircraft remain in Burma over the monsoon period, it would be more important to transfer them to China, particularly in view of preparations for the final assault on the Japanese homeland.[43] An agreement on a revised schedule for the withdrawal of Chinese and all American forces from Burma, now including all Army Air Force units in addition to the Mars Task Force and the Chinese divisions, came two weeks later, tentatively as follows:

April 1945:	The rest of the Mars Task Force
May 1945:	Advanced echelon headquarters, US air forces
15th May:	One Chinese division
June 1945:	The rest of headquarters, US air forces; two US combat cargo groups
June 1:	One Chinese division
June 15:	One Chinese division
July 1945:	Various US air forces
August 1945:	Various US air forces
September 1945:	The rest of US air forces[44]

This greatly relieved Mountbatten's and Slim's anxiety about their ability to retain the transport aircraft 14th Army desperately needed to sustain IV and XXXIII Corps in central Burma, but replaced this anxiety with another: 14th Army now had to capture Rangoon before the onset of the monsoon. The race to Rangoon took on even-greater urgency.

Down but Not Out: Counter Air Force Operations, March–April 1945

From the end of the monsoon in early October 1944, the ability of the *5th Hikōshidan* to counter the Allied assault on northern and central Burma steadily diminished. Attrition took its toll, as did the transfer of aircraft and units to other fronts. At that time the *5th Hikōshidan* had three fighter *hikōsentai* assigned to the *4th Hikōdan*, its one remaining air brigade in Burma (the *50th* with the newer Type 4 Fighter [Frank], and the *64th* and *204th* with the Ki-43 Mk II and Mk III) with the *8th Hikōsentai* still equipped with the Type 99 Light Bomber (Ki-48 Lily), and the *81st Hikōsentai* with the Type 100 Command Reconnaissance Plane (Ki-46 Dinah). This force had approximately 115 aircraft: 80 fighters, 20 bombers, and 15 reconnaissance aircraft. There were an additional 48 aircraft allo-

JAPANESE AIRFIELDS IN THAILAND

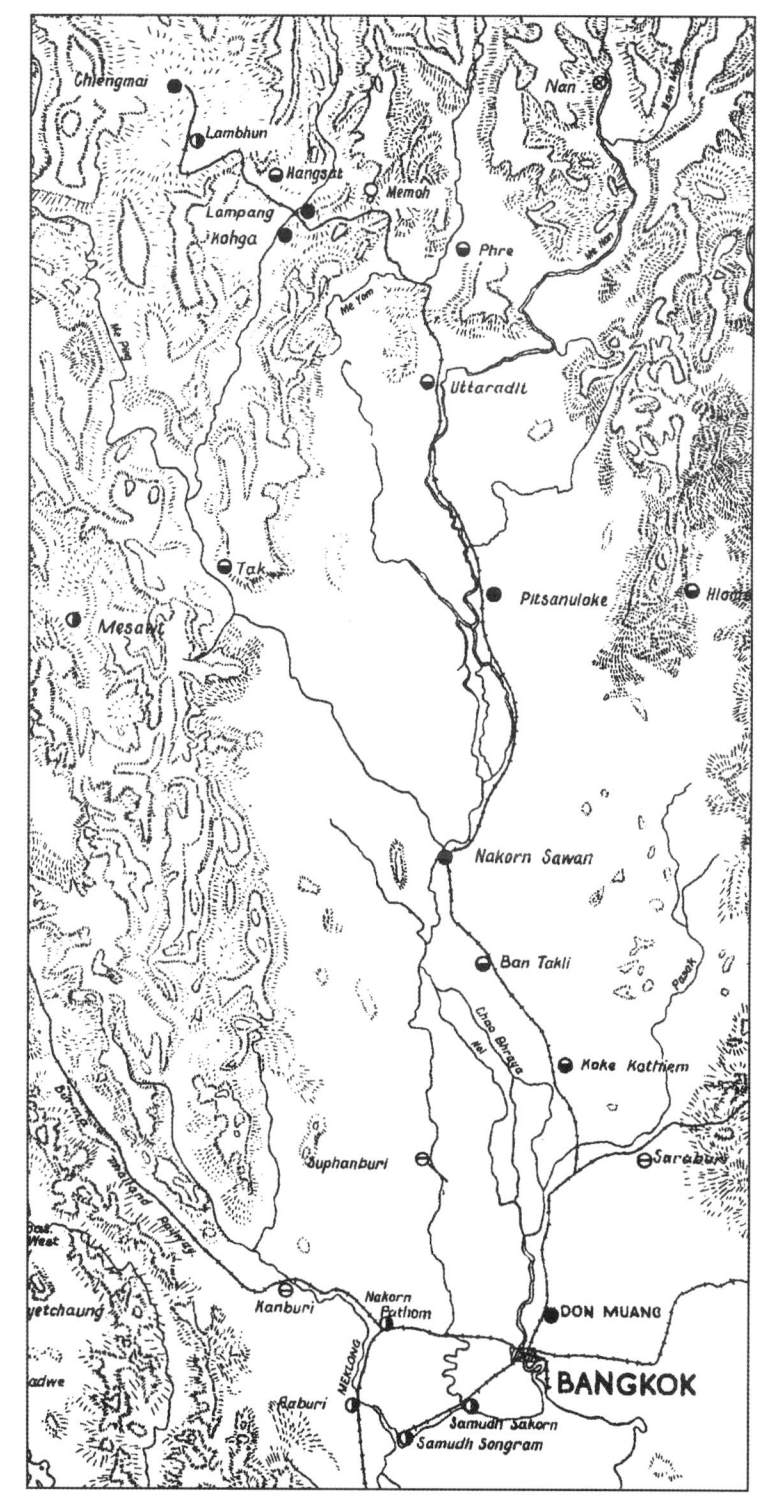

Source: Public Records Office

cated to Thailand and French Indochina, while *3rd Air Army* maintained 60 combat aircraft in Malaya and 259 in the Netherlands East Indies in operational training units, and for the defense of the oil refineries at Palembang. Airplanes from this force could be flown into Burma within a few days. As American forces neared Japan, the Japanese Army Air Force called on units from Southeast Asia to bolster Japan's defenses. The *204th Hikōsentai* was the first to go, transferring to the Philippines just before the invasion of Leyte. In mid-January 1945, following US Navy carrier strikes on Saigon, the *50th Hikōsentai* moved there for the defense of southern Indochina, leaving the veteran *64th Hikōsentai* as the last fighter unit in Burma. By early March, Allied intelligence estimated that the *5th Hikōshidan* had around 49 fighters, 10 bombers, and 8 reconnaissance aircraft in southern Burma, with another 35 bombers in Thailand and 60 fighters and 19 bombers in French Indochina. The drawdown of aircraft assigned to *3rd Area Army* had reduced the numbers in Malaya and the Netherlands East Indies to around 106 combat aircraft. For the *5th Hikōshidan*, the 14th Army's push to Mandalay and Meiktila meant the loss of most of the airfields in central Burma, pushing the Japanese fighters and bombers back to airfields to the south. Japanese air activity was now limited to small groups of Oscar fighters strafing advancing Allied mechanized columns, and infrequent night-bombing raids with the Lily bombers staging in from Thailand to airfields around Rangoon, without much apparent coordination in the attacks.[45]

Although diminished, the threat remained that the Japanese fighters might at any time abandon their attacks on the British and Indian columns and turn on the vulnerable transport aircraft. Despite the numerous Allied fighters flying over the front on defensive and offensive missions, it was still possible for a few Japanese fighters to slip through the net and attack the transports, as the *64th Hikōsentai* had done in the 12 January 1945 attack on No. 435 Squadron's Dakotas at Onbauk. Eastern Air Command needed to keep pressure on the remaining Japanese aircraft operating in Burma. With the end of Operation MULTIVITE, Eastern Air Command decided to assign the counter air force mission to the Mustang squadrons of the 2nd Air Commando Group, allowing the 5th and 6th Fighter Squadrons and the RAF Thunderbolt and Hurricane squadrons to concentrate on close air support and attacks on the Japanese lines of communications. The P-51Ds had the range to strike at any airfield in southern Burma and the performance to overcome any Japanese fighter.[46]

The 1st and 2nd Fighter Squadrons began their counter air force effort on 7 March 1945, providing an escort for a force of 75 7th Bomb Group B-24s and RAF Liberators bombing the dock area at Martaban, but this proved uneventful. The next day, Levi Chase led the squadrons on a sweep of the Rangoon airfields. Chase took 14 Mustangs from the 1st Fighter Squadron to Mingaladon, while 16 Mustangs from the 2nd Fighter Squadron went to Hmawbi. Chase fired on one Oscar he found on the field, setting the Japanese aircraft on fire, then damaged a second, while Capt. Robert Eason damaged two more. The 2nd Squadron found nothing at Hmawbi. The squadrons escorted the bombers to Rangoon to bomb supply dumps on March 9 and 11, hoping for a repeat of the February mission when the Japanese fighters had attempted to intercept the bombers. Once again the mission proved uneventful. Unknown to Allied intelligence, because of the overwhelming odds

VICTORY IN BURMA

1st Lt. Bob Spann in his P-51D "Big Gas Bird" prepares to lead off the 1st Fighter Squadron's third flight for the attack on Don Muang airfield in Thailand on 15 March 1945, a round trip of more than 1,600 miles. Lt. Col. Levi Chase convinced Lt. Gen. Stratemeyer that the mission deep into Thailand was possible. *WWII Air Commando Association*

facing the few remaining Japanese fighters and the difficulty of getting replacement aircraft the *5th Hikōshidan* had ordered a ban on aerial combat.[47]

The results of these first few missions had been disappointing, but Chase had come up with an idea for a more effective means of attacking the *5th Hikōshidan*: using the P-51D's great range. Allied intelligence knew that the *4th Hikōdan* had been withdrawing its aircraft back to Thailand, using the airfields in southern Burma to stage raids against Allied forces and quickly pulling the aircraft back to their Thai bases, where they considered themselves secure from Allied fighters. On March 4, photoreconnaissance of the main airfield at Don Muang, outside Bangkok—which the Japanese shared with the Royal Thai Air Force—showed more than 50 Japanese aircraft around the airfield.[48] With this information, Chase flew to Eastern Air Command headquarters in Calcutta to propose that the 1st and 2nd Fighter Squadrons carry out a long-range strike against the Japanese aircraft at Don Muang. The distance from the Air Commando base at Cox's Bazar to Don Muang was 780 miles, involving a round trip of nearly 1,600 miles—the longest fighter mission ever undertaken in the CBI. The staff of Eastern Air Command were skeptical, but Chase made a persuasive case for the mission, arguing that with long-range drop tanks and careful fuel management, the P-51s could fly to Don Muang, attack the field, and make it back to Cox's Bazar. With Eastern Air Command's approval, Chase had the two Air Commando fighter squadrons each prepare 20 P-51Ds to carry two 110-gallon drop tanks. The night before the mission, Chase and the 2nd Air Commando Group's intelligence officer gave the pilots selected for the mission a careful briefing, providing element leaders maps with indicated courses and target photos of Don Muang.[49]

Chase led the formation off at 1019 on 15 March 1945, leading the 1st Fighter Squadron, while Maj. Roger Pryor led the 2nd Fighter Squadron. Just under three hours later, Chase arrived at the designated initial point: the town of Ayutthaya on the Chao Phraya River north of Bangkok—a remarkable piece of navigation. When they were 10 miles from Don Muang, the pilots jettisoned their drop tanks, and

Gun camera footage showing one of the two Ki-43s that Lt. Col. Chase and his wingman, 1st Lt. Hadley Dixon, encountered as they approached Don Muang airfield. Although given credit for shooting down one of the Japanese fighters, Chase's intended victim, Capt. Masao Hara, evaded Chase's fire. Dixon apparently shot down Hara's wingman, Sgt. Maj. Tadao Sasaki. *WWII Air Commando Association*

THE TENTH AIR FORCE IN WORLD WAR II

when 2 miles away went to full throttle. Coming in on the airfield, Chase found two Oscar fighters flying ahead of him and immediately went after them with his wingman, 1st Lt. Hadley Dixon. Chase fired at the leader, getting hits and seeing the aircraft break to the right and go down smoking; he claimed this fighter as destroyed. Dixon came in on the wingman, firing until he had to pull up when he got too low. Chase's opponent was Capt. Masao Hara, who actually evaded Chase's fire, though taking several hits. Breaking away, Hara came back in on the 1st Fighter Squadron formation and attacked the leader of the fourth flight, Capt. Warren Modine, when Modine's P-51 crossed his sights, setting the P-51 on fire. Modine crashed to his death on the airfield. Dixon shot down Sgt. Maj. Tadao Sasaki, who was also killed when his airplane hit the field.[50]

The Air Commandos achieved complete surprise and found an airfield lined with Japanese airplanes. Despite the risk of making a second pass over the field, Chase ordered another run when he found no antiaircraft fire. Nearly every pilot in the 1st Fighter Squadron submitted claims for Japanese aircraft damaged or destroyed. 1st Lt. Bobby Spann was the high scorer, submitting claims for five aircraft. Coming in across the field, Spann found a row of twin-engine KI-48 Lily bombers directly in his path and proceeded to shoot up five in a series of repeated climbing and diving attacks. Coming off his strafing run, he saw a Ki-21 Sally bomber that had the misfortune to take off just as the attack began. Spann fired on the bomber, sharing in its destruction with Maj. William Buxton, 1st Squadron commander, and 2nd Lt. William Holman. Leading the 2nd Fighter Squadron, Pryor shot up two Ki-61 fighters parked close together in a revetment, initially claiming his kills as a twin-engine aircraft, after which his pilots jokingly named him "Weak-Eyes Yokum" after a character in the popular cartoon strip *Li'l Abner*. When the squadrons returned to Cox's Bazar, the pilots submitted claims for three airplanes shot down in the air and 28 destroyed on the ground, with five probably destroyed and eight damaged, the majority being twin-engine aircraft. While subsequent photoreconnaissance found only 11 aircraft destroyed on the airfield, this was still a severe loss to the *5th Hikōshidan*. That same day, 18 P-38s from the 459th Fighter Squadron flew into Thailand to strafe the airfield at Ban Takli, north of Bangkok, but found nothing. In the days that followed, congratulations came in from Mountbatten, Stratemeyer, and others for the 2nd Air Commando Group's achievement.[51]

Three days later the squadrons went back to sweep the Rangoon airfields, taking off before dawn by the light of flare pots in the hopes of catching Japanese aircraft before they could take off to return to bases in Thailand. Bob Eason led the 1st Fighter Squadron to Mingaladon, where the squadron found several Ki-43s on the field, with Eason damaging two, and two other pilots one each. The 2nd Fighter Squadron found nothing at Hmawbi—their designated target—so moved on to nearby Hlegu, where Capt. Edward Atha saw a twin-engine aircraft in the air as he approached the field. This turned out to be a Ki-46 Dinah, which he promptly shot down. A sweep of airfields in northern Thailand yielded little except a single-engine Fairchild 24 belonging to the Aerial Transport Company of Thailand—the country's small domestic airline—which was shot down. Sweeps of the airfields south of Rangoon on March 21 resulted in the destruction of a bomber and the probable destruction of an Oscar. The *4th Hikōdan* organized a raid on British navy vessels in Akyab harbor on the night of March 25, sending out three Ki-21 bombers from the *58th Hikōsentai* (possibly flown up from Malaya), four Ki-48 bombers from the *8th Hikōsentai*, and seven Ki-43s from the *64th Hikōsentai*. British intelligence detected that the Ki-43s had returned to Hmawbi after the attack and alerted the 1st Provisional Fighter Group.[52]

Reasoning that the Japanese fighters would most likely fly back to Thailand soon after dawn, Chase quickly organized a sweep of the Rangoon airfields for the next morning. Taking off at 0440 to get to Hmawbi just after dawn, Chase flew with 1st Lt. Harold Hettema as his wingman, with Bobby Spann leading the second element in the flight. Coming in on Hmawbi from the north at 1,000 feet, Chase saw three Oscar fighters approaching him head-on. Seeing the oncoming Mustangs, the Japanese flight leader did an immediate

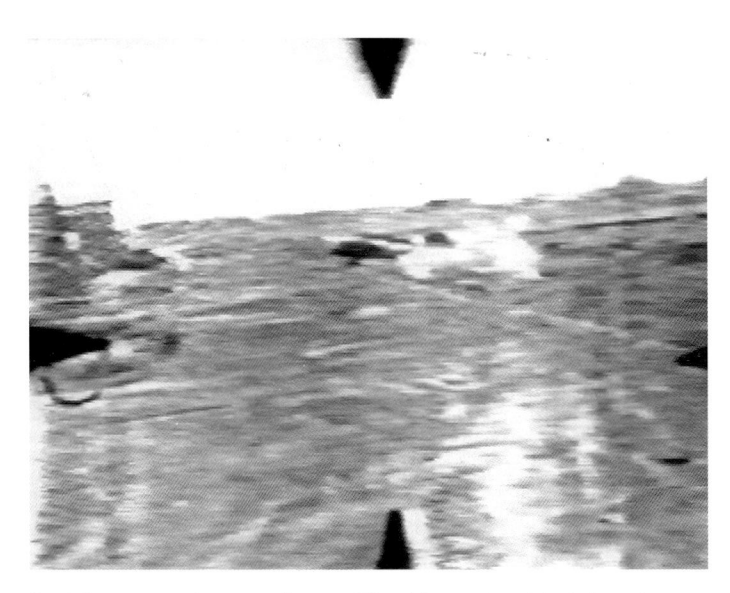

Studying reconnaissance photos of Don Muang the night before the raid, 1st Lt. Bob Spann noticed a row of Japanese bombers on the field. By coincidence, his approach to the airfield brought him directly in line with the bombers he had seen in the photograph. Flying down the line, he claimed five of the bombers destroyed and two more damaged. This blurred photo from his gun camera shows his attack on one of the bombers. *WWII Air Commando Association*

1st Lt. Harold Hettema shot down one of the three Oscar fighters that Lt. Col. Chase, 1st Lt. Spann, and Hettema attacked over Hwmabi airfield early in the morning of 26 March 1945. This shows Hettema in the cockpit of his P-51D, with a Japanese flag for his air victory and two rising-sun flags for two bombers destroyed on the ground in the strafing attack on Don Muang airfield. The 1st and 2nd Fighter squadrons used different Japanese flags to distinguish between air and ground claims. *Courtesy, Harold Hettema*

steep-climbing chandelle and dove toward the south in an attempt to get away. Chase pulled in behind the leader, Capt. Yoshio Nakano, while Hettema came in behind the Oscar on the left and Spann came in on the aircraft on the right. The three Mustang pilots opened fire at the same time, hitting all three Oscars, sending them down to strike the ground in a V formation; Nakano, Warrant Officer Kokichii Kitajima, and Lt. Shinitchiro Kato were all killed. As Chase pulled away, Bob Eason called to warn him that his P-51 was leaking coolant. As he was crossing over Hmawbi, a lucky shot had hit Chase's Mustang in the cooling system. Within minutes, Chase's engine began to run rough and he made a successful crash landing in a field 20 miles west of Hmawbi. At about the same time, Roger Pryor was leading the 2nd Fighter Squadron across Mingaladon, where he, too, got hit in the cooling system, bailing out north of Chase's position.[53]

After seeing Chase walk away from his airplane and learning that Pryor had bailed out, Eason and Spann flew to a newly opened airfield on Ramree Island, where they commandeered two L-5 liaison aircraft and filled them with gas cans, planning to go back and rescue Chase and Pryor. With their wingmen providing cover, Eason and Spann flew back to the area where Chase had gone down. Chase had walked to a nearby village, but with the Japanese in close proximity the villagers were leery of aiding him. Hearing the noise of an airplane engine, Chase saw a P-51 flying overhead. Heading back to the site of his belly landing, he saw an L-5 flying overhead:

I was really surprised. I got out my mirror and flashed at everything. . . . I thought I saw an L-5 land some distance away, and finally found it on the ground about three miles from the village. I threw my jungle kit away as I was too tired to carry it, and a captain from my outfit [Bob Eason] came out and got hold of me. We cut back to the L-5 which had just been loaded with gas. The ground was very bad and all three wheels were stuck. The field was hard mud and dirt, with a lot of holes into which the wheels had run. We tried, but couldn't get the aircraft out.

Then a lieutenant [Spann] landed in another L-5. He got out and started to load gas into it. I saw two or three natives coming toward us, and also thirty to forty more of them coming from the village. I then got into the aircraft, and by all sorts of saluting and salaaming and a fair distribution of rupees the captain got them to help him move the L-5 out to a better place.

We started down the field, and it was a hell of a ride. I thought we might not make it but at least we were going to try. We bumped along for a good distance; the captain was moving the stick around a lot and finally pulled it back, and we left the ground. . . . We climbed up and circled above the other L-5 until he got off, and then headed for Ramree Island. We landed at Ramree and found that the tail wheel was driven up through the metal tubing and into the tail assembly. The elevators were dragging on the ground and we really bumped along. We had only one gallon of gas left when we reached Ramree.[54]

After getting his L-5 off the ground, Spann went to look for Pryor but, after an extended search, failed to find any sign of him. The Japanese had captured Pryor soon after he landed. For their daring in flying 200 miles behind enemy lines to rescue their commander, Eason and Spann were each awarded the Silver Star.[55]

None the worse for his experience, Chase led the two fighter squadrons on a long but again uneventful bomber escort mission to Bangkok the next day. On the return flight Maj. William Hawkins spotted a Lily bomber on the airfield at Pegu and dove down to strafe it with his wingman, who received credit for destroying the airplane. Continuing the counter air force mission, the two squadrons went to Mingaladon on April 1 to bomb and strafe the installations around the field with 500-pound bombs and tanks of napalm. The next day the squadrons went on a sweep of airfields in central

A happy Lt. Col. Levi Chase stands between his two rescuers, Capt. W. R. "Bob" Eason (*right*) and recently promoted Capt. Bob Spann (*left*). On several occasions the 1st and 2nd Fighter Squadrons used liaison aircraft to rescue their pilots from behind Japanese lines, but never so deep into enemy territory as Eason and Spann did during their daring rescue of Chase. *Courtesy, W. R. Eason*

Two P-51Ds from the 2nd Fighter Squadron taking off for the 2nd Air Commando Group's second raid on Don Muang airfield on 9 April 1945. The 1st and 2nd Fighter Squadrons claimed 30 Japanese aircraft destroyed at Don Muang and the Japanese airfield at Nakhon Pathom but lost three Mustangs shot down. Fortunately, Thai police captured the pilots and not the Japanese. *WWII Air Commando Association*

THE TENTH AIR FORCE IN WORLD WAR II

Thailand, hitting Nakhon Sawan, Ban Takhli, and Koke Kathiem, destroying one Sally bomber. When photoreconnaissance photos indicated more Japanese aircraft arriving at Don Muang, Chase took the 2nd Air Commando fighter squadrons back to Thailand on April 9, leading 32 fighters in an attack on Don Muang, while two flights from the 2nd Fighter Squadron attacked the field at Nakhon Pathom, west of Bangkok. Chase decided to have the flights spread out as they neared Don Muang and make a single pass over the field. This time the Japanese reacted with speed, opening fire almost as soon as the Mustangs came over the airfield. There were fewer Japanese airplanes at Don Muang, but a good number of fighters. Several of the Air Commando pilots returned with multiple claims. Antiaircraft fire hit three of the Mustangs, and three pilots bailed out to become prisoners of the Thai police, who had jurisdiction for any Allied airman shot down over Thailand and who proved to treat their captives far better than the Japanese did. The strike on Don Muang resulted in claims for nine twin-engine aircraft and 17 fighters destroyed, with four more fighters claimed at Nakhon Pathom. The Air Commando fighter squadrons flew one more counter air force mission to Thailand on April 29. A force of 16 Mustangs from the two squadrons hit the airfield at Koke Kathiem, while eight aircraft from the 1st Fighter Squadron strafed the field at Nakon Sawan. The field at Nakon Sawan was empty, but at Koke Kathiem the pilots found several fighters on the ground, claiming a Ki-61 Tony, a possible Ki-44, and one other unidentified fighter destroyed. The 459th Fighter Squadron again accompanied the Air Commandos, hitting the field at Ban Takli, where they destroyed another Ki-61 and an unidentified twin-engine bomber for the squadron's last claims for Japanese aircraft. The last mission was a sweep of the airfield at Moulmein, where the 1st Squadron strafed one unidentified aircraft—most likely derelict by this point—without observing any result.[56]

In two months of counter air force missions, the 1st and 2nd Fighter Squadrons claimed eight Japanese aircraft destroyed in the air and 52 destroyed on the ground, with an additional six probables and 32 damaged in strafing attacks. While there was no doubt of some overclaiming, these were losses the *5th Hikōshidan* could not afford, since replacement aircraft and spare parts were by now difficult to obtain. At this point, damaging a Japanese aircraft on the ground was almost as effective as destroying one, because in all likelihood it could not be easily repaired. For his leadership of the raids on Don Muang, Chase received the Silver Star, while the two fighter squadrons and their supporting 327th Aerodrome Squadron received a Distinguished Unit Citation for their mission to Don Muang on March 15. Japanese air opposition effectively ended in April. The light bombers carried out two night raids with pairs of Ki-48 bombers, while the *50th Hikōsentai*, flying in from French Indochina, joined the *64th Hikōsentai* in four attacks on Allied columns moving south toward Rangoon. On April 29, the *5th Hikōshidan* ordered Hmawbi airfield destroyed, and withdrew completely from Burma. After three and a half years of continuous combat, the Allies now dominated the skies over Burma.[57]

Azon and the Battle of the Bridges

During the final months of the Burma campaign, the battle of the bridges that the 7th Bomb Group had been fighting for two years intensified, but with far-more-gratifying results.

The operations of the Strategic Air Force from the beginning of 1945 were intended to support 14th Army's advance under Operation CAPITAL. The main objective of these operations was to cut the flow of supplies coming into Burma over the railroad lines from Thailand, and once the bombers had cut the railroad lines, to destroy the Japanese army's supplies in Burma. The SAF would also be made available to 14th Army for direct support as needed. At a meeting held at Eastern Air Command headquarters on 20 December 1944, the EAC and SAF staffs decided to concentrate all SAF attacks during the first part of January on the Bangkok-Moulmein railroad line, with the goal of rendering large sections of the line unserviceable. After two years of attacking the Japanese lines-of-communication system, it had become accepted doctrine that the most-vulnerable points in the system, and thus the most-productive targets, were the many rail and road bridges along the routes into Burma from Thailand and within Burma to the north. While the medium bombers and fighter-bombers took on the bridges within the range of their respective aircraft, the longer-range B-24s and RAF Liberators had responsibility for the bridges in southern Burma and Thailand. By this time, practical experience had shown that attacking bridges from high altitude was a waste of effort, while bombing from medium and lower altitudes brought somewhat better results. The most effective means of destroying a bridge was to bomb at very low altitude, as the 490th Bomb Squadron had proven time and again, but this method was not foolproof and exposed the bombers to antiaircraft fire. Fortuitously, a new weapon arrived from the United States just in time for this new assault on the railroad system, which provided both greatly improved accuracy and protection from most of the antiaircraft fire the bombers would be exposed to during their attacks on bridges.

As the March 1945 edition of *Impact* (the Army Air Force's confidential intelligence publication) stated in an article on the new weapon, "There is probably no bombardier in the world who, having made an imperfect release, has not watched his bombs go down wide of the target without wishing there were some way he could change their course in the air."[58] The Army Air Force had begun experimenting with guided bombs before the outbreak of World War II. After the start of the war, the Army Air Force's Air Technical Service Command developed a radio-controlled guided bomb

The Azon bomb consisted of a special tail assembly attached to a regular 1,000-pound general-purpose bomb. The tail device was fitted with a radio control device that controlled the movement of the fins by using a servomotor. A powerful flare attached to the fin ignited after the Azon bomb was dropped, so the bombardier could follow the bomb and guide its progress toward the target. *7th Bombardment Group Historical Foundation*

VICTORY IN BURMA

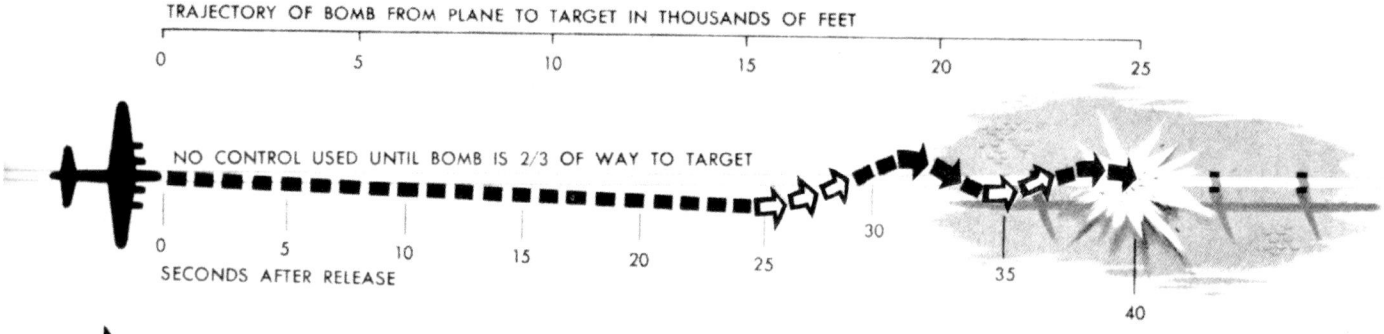

TRAJECTORY OF BOMB FROM PLANE TO TARGET IN THOUSANDS OF FEET

⇦ LEFT CONTROL
⇨ RIGHT CONTROL
■ NO CONTROL

This diagram taken from an issue of the Army Air Force's *Impact* magazine illustrates how a bombardier could control the right-to-left movement of an Azon bomb as it fell toward the target. Long, straight bridges were ideal targets for the Azon bomb. The clear weather of the dry season and relative lack of heavy antiaircraft guns around the bridges along the Burma-Thailand railroad contributed to the success of the Azon bomb as a weapon. *Impact via the author*

known as the VB-1 Azon, for "*Azimuth Only*."[59] The Azon bomb fitted a special tail device with a radio-controlled servomotor connected to movable rudders on the fins of the tail assembly. This enabled the bombardier to steer the bomb by remote control with a small steering device to the left or right of his intended target. The tail assembly could be fitted to a regular M-65 1,000-pound bomb. On the approach to the target, the bombardier would line up the target in his Norden bombsight and release the bomb normally. About eight to ten seconds after release, a one-million-candle-power flare fixed to the tail assembly would ignite, enabling the bombardier to follow the path of the bomb toward the target. Using the remote control steering device, the bombardier could correct azimuth errors, steering the bomb directly to the target. The Azon was ideal for long, narrow targets such as bridges.[60]

Davidson had learned about the Azon bomb in early 1944 and in March submitted a request for 10 B-24s fitted with the radio-transmitting devices and 300 Azon tail assembly units. Although the bombers and the devices arrived in the theater, it took several months for the 7th Bomb Group to put them to use, partly due to some initial skepticism about the Azon bomb's effectiveness and the group's diversion to flying gasoline to China. The first Azon mission took place on 27 December 1944, when three Azon-equipped B-24s went to bomb the key railroad bridge at Pynmana on the Rangoon-Mandalay railroad line, with three standard B-24s going along carrying 2,000-pound bombs. The Azon B-24s went in at altitudes ranging from 8,800 to 9,450 feet. On the first run on the bridge, the bombardier in the lead Azon B-24 got a direct hit, knocking one span off its supports. The second Azon bomb knocked a second span into the dry riverbed below the bridge. Two more Azon bombs scored direct hits, rendering the bridge completely unserviceable. The standard bombs failed to hit the bridge at all. Three days later, the Azon bombers went after the Nyaungchidauk

The first use of the Azon bomb in the CBI theater on 27 December 1944, when the 493rd Bomb Squadron carried out an attack on a railroad bridge at Pynmana. The photograph shows two Azon bombs falling toward the bridge with their flares alight, allowing the bombardiers to easily track their path. *3A-37736, RG342, NARA*

THE TENTH AIR FORCE IN WORLD WAR II

One of the Azon bombs scores a direct hit on the bridge. The craters surrounding the area around the bridge speak to the difficulty of knocking out these narrow targets with conventional bombing. After seeing the results of a few Azon bombing missions, the commander of the 7th Bomb Group requested that all replacement B-24s for the group be equipped for Azon bombing. *3A-37737, RG342, NARA*

Bridge, the Nyaungchidauk bypass bridge, and the Taungup Bridge. Four Azon B-24s knocked out the Nyaungchidauk Bridge with six direct hits. On the fourth pass on the bridge, the bombardier on the second aircraft had just dropped his Azon bomb when he saw that the other bombs had knocked out the main bridge. Using his control stick, he steered his bomb to the bypass bridge alongside the main bridge, knocking this out with a direct hit. With bombs left over, the Azon B-24s knocked out two more bridges, getting three out of four direct hits on their last target, the Taungup Bridge. Now sold on the value of the Azon bomb, Col. Alness requested that all bombardier replacements have Azon training and that all replacement B-24s have the transmitting equipment for Azon bombs. Within the 7th Bomb Group, the 493rd Bomb Squadron became the specialized Azon bombing unit. Alness placed all the Azon-trained bombardiers and Azon-equipped aircraft in the 493rd Squadron.[61]

While the 493rd Bomb Squadron concentrated on Azon bomb attacks against bridges, the 7th Bomb Group's other three squadrons went after bridges along the Burma-Thailand railroad line with conventional bombs; in the absence of Japanese fighters and with only light antiaircraft fire, they descended to low level for many of their attacks. Here a flight of B-24s from the 436th Bomb Squadron prepares to attack the bridge seen in the background. *SQ-BOMB-436-HI, January 1945, AFHRA*

VICTORY IN BURMA

Bombs exploding on the railroad yard at Jumbhorn, deep in southern Thailand. The 7th Bomb Group and RAF Liberators carried out the attack, in what was the longest bombing mission ever flown up to that time, covering a distance of nearly 2,500 miles. *SQ-BOMB-436-HI, February 1945, AFHRA*

Conditions over Burma and Thailand at this time proved ideal for bombing with Azon bombs. The weather during the dry season was usually clear, with bright, sunny, and cloudless skies. The Japanese had only light antiaircraft guns to defend the more important bridges, and these could not reach the bombers flying at 8,000 feet or above. The combination of clear weather and little risk of antiaircraft fire or interception from Japanese fighters allowed long, straight approaches to the bridge targets, giving the bombardiers plenty of time to line up a bridge in their Norden bombsights. During the January "Blitz" on the Bangkok-Moulmein railroad line, the Azon B-24s knocked out two out of four bridges on January 8 and two more on January 9, and two on January 11. Following the Japanese fighter attack on Allied transport aircraft in mid-January, the 7th Bomb Group took a hiatus from bridge bombing to join other SAF squadrons bombing Japanese airfields in Burma. Then it was back to the battle of the bridges. While the 493rd Squadron continued using Azon bombs, the other squadrons in the group used low-level bombing, dropping 1,000-pound bombs from 300 feet. Where there were known Japanese antiaircraft positions, the group began sending in one squadron to make repeated runs at 3,000 feet to locate and drop fragmentation bombs on the gun emplacements to allow the other squadrons to bomb the bridge at very low level. This was dangerous work. As the 9th Bomb Squadron reported in its monthly history for January, "even at 180–190 mph indicated, B-24s are simply huge clay pigeons."[62] The repeated attacks on the Bangkok-Moulmein line severely disrupted traffic along the route. The 7th Bomb Group and the RAF Liberator squadrons knocked out an average of four bridges a day along the line. Allied intelligence estimated that the average daily tonnage over the line dropped from 700/800 tons a day to perhaps a third of that amount—much less than *Burma Area Army*'s daily requirements. A new problem for the Japanese was the disappearance of local native labor. Allied bombers began dropping leaflets all along the railroad line, warning the local populace that the railroad tracks, bridges, and stations would be subject to attack without warning. The now-daily attacks on the railroad system proved the leaflets were correct. The Japanese began to experience a shortage of labor as railroad workers and local laborers disappeared.[63]

With the railroad system damaged, the SAF turned to bombing Japanese supply dumps in southern Burma and in the Mandalay-Meiktila to put maximum pressure on *Burma Area Army* as IV and XXXIII Corps were preparing their crossings of the Irrawaddy River. On 11 February 1945 the SAF arranged the largest bombing mission ever undertaken in Burma. A force of 84 RAF Liberators and 7th Bomb Group B-24s accompanied 59 XX Bomber Command B-29s to bomb the Japanese supply dumps at Victoria Lake near Rangoon. These dumps contained an estimated 50 to 70 percent of *Burma Area Army*'s supplies. For the next two weeks the SAF bombers went after Japanese supply dumps, artillery positions, and troop concentrations for 14th Army. The 7th Bomb Group set a record for the heaviest bombload carried by a B-24 in the CBI. In an attack on supply dumps at Myittha, south of Mandalay, on February 21, 12 B-24s carried a bombload of 10,400 pounds in each airplane, cramming in twelve 500-pound bombs, four 1,000-pound bombs, and four 100-pound bombs. Two more supply dump missions followed, then on February 25 the 436th Bomb Squadron sent three airplanes to bomb the dumps at Taunggyi, carrying a staggering load of 11,000 pounds of bombs, substituting four 250-pound bombs for the four 100-pound bombs carried on the earlier missions. At the beginning of February the group flew its longest mission to date, joining RAF Liberators on 3 February 1945 in an attack on the railroad yards at Jumbhorn, just a few hundred miles from the Thai border with Malaya, and a round trip of close to 2,500 miles. The 493rd Squadron carried Azon bombs on the mission to knock out a key bridge on the Bangkok-Singapore railroad line.[64]

THE TENTH AIR FORCE IN WORLD WAR II

While the other 7th Group squadrons supported 14th Army, the 493rd Bomb Squadron continued to go after bridges with their Azon bombs with small formations of four to six aircraft. The squadron's best day during February was on the 17th, when four bridges went down under Azon bombs. On February 25, the squadron went back to the Ban Dara Bridge in northern Thailand and knocked out the new bypass bridge with four direct hits. The 493rd Squadron had perfected the technique of dropping Azon bombs. The flight would approach a bridge target in trail formation at 30-second intervals, setting up a circular pattern around the bridge, with each airplane making individual runs and dropping one Azon bomb on each run. The radio control equipment in the tail assembly had only five channels, making it difficult to drop a number of Azon bombs at one time, while the bombardiers found it easier and more effective to control a single bomb on each run. The results from Azon bombing were impressive compared to standard bombing. Between December 27 and March 3, the 493rd bombed 36 bridges, dropping 415 Azon bombs and getting 87 hits, or one hit for every four bombs. These attacks knocked out or rendered unserviceable 23 bridges. In comparison, with standard bombing the 492nd Squadron dropped 438 bombs and got 20 hits on bridges, or one hit for every 22 bombs dropped.[65]

The 7th Bomb Group continued to support 14th Army with attacks on Japanese supply dumps, but the group's main effort during March went against bridges. Between March 3 and 31, the 7th Group bombed 30 bridges, destroying 12 and severely damaging 12 more, mostly through the efforts of the 493rd Squadron and the Azon bomb. The group beat its own records for the longest mission and heaviest bombload set in February. On March 19, the 9th and 493rd Squadrons flew more than 2,700 miles to Surat Thani, several hundred miles beyond Jumbhorn, to bomb targets on the Bangkok-Singapore railroad line, while RAF Liberators went to the Jumbhorn area. The crews spent nearly 19 hours in the air, having knocked out several bridges with Azon and standard bombs. The 436th and 492nd Squadrons went to the same area the next day, destroying a bridge, tearing up sections of railroad track, and strafing locomotives and rolling stock. The squadrons took great pride in completing the mission, noting that the distance was only 300 miles less than the longest B-29 mission flown to that date. For completing these missions of unprecedented distance, the 7th Bomb Group received its second Distinguished Unit Citation. In early March the group had begun removing the belly turrets from its B-24s, since the group had encountered so few Japanese fighters on its recent missions over southern Burma and given the availability of sufficient numbers of long-range P-38s and P-51s to serve as escorts to the bombers. The belly turret and fixtures weighed in at around 1,000 pounds, which could be converted to carrying more fuel or bombs. When the SAF planned a mission to bomb a suspected *Burma Area Army* headquarters near Rangoon at the end of March, the 436th Squadron went for a new record, sending out 10 aircraft each carrying 12,000 pounds of bombs—possibly a record for the B-24.[66]

The final weeks of the battle of the bridges saw the 7th Bomb Group's B-24s in a role few could have conceived of earlier. The SAF launched a major attack on locomotives, rolling stock, and railroad installations along the Bangkok-Moulmein line and sections of the Bangkok–Chiang Mai line on March 22. The 436th Squadron went out that day with the B-24s flying like fighter-bombers, going down to low level to strafe whatever they could find along the route and bombing sections of the track. The group began its own intensive 12-day attack on the Bangkok-Moulmein line on April 1. Taking off before dawn to catch locomotives and rolling stock before the

A photo of a bridge the 492nd Bomb Squadron knocked out in April 1945. During March and April 1945 the 7th Bomb Group carried out an intensive attack on bridges along the Burma-Thailand railroad line, using Azon bombs and conventional bombs in low-level attacks similar to the "glip" bombing tactic the 490th Bomb Squadron had perfected. On 24 April 1945 the group claimed 30 bridges knocked out or made unserviceable, during one of its most effective missions of the war. *SQ-BOMB-492-HI, April 1945, AFHRA*

Japanese could hide them, the squadrons took sections of the railroad line, assigning shorter sections to individual aircraft. Once again the B-24s went down on the deck to strafe, shooting up a number of locomotives and tearing up the track with bombs. The squadrons made repeated attacks against bridges, adding to their growing score of bridges knocked out or rendered unserviceable. By mid-April the group had destroyed 98 bridges, but there were many more along the route. Looking for a new method to knock out a bridge, Alness proposed using a variation of the technique the 490th Bomb Squadron had pioneered. His idea was to have a B-24 begin a 20-to-25-degree glide from around 1,500 feet, aiming directly at a bridge, releasing the bombs at 200 feet while pulling out of the glide attack. Several experimental flights proved that the technique would work, and during April, Alness had all pilots practice the new method between missions against a 200-foot-long mockup of a bridge.[67]

The group's first opportunity to try the new technique came on 24 April 1945, in what Eastern Air Command's Weekly Intelligence Summary said "may well be described as the most effective bomber mission ever staged in this Theater."[68] The group sent out 41 B-24s to attack the Bangkok-Moulmein railroad line, with the 9th, 436th, and 492nd Squadrons trying the new method and the 493rd Squadron using Azon bombs. Each squadron took a section of the line. By the end of the day, the squadrons had claimed 30 bridges destroyed or unserviceable, another six probably destroyed, and the approaches to seven more bridges severely damaged. The 436th Squadron claimed 19 bridges destroyed or damaged, with one pilot and his crew claiming three bridges for the high score of the day. Air Commodore Mellersh sent his congratulations to the group, saying, "This mission, planned and executed by the 7th Bomb Group (H), is deserving of the highest praise. Undoubtedly the resulting damage and destruction to the rail line surpassed all previous records for an equal number of sorties on similar targets in this or any other theater."[69] An intelligence assessment of the impact of the repeated attacks by 7th Bomb Group B-24s and RAF Liberators on the railroad line estimated that for April there were an average of 11.7 breaks along the line every day, with a peak of 24 breaks on one single day. There had been no through train along the line since February. At every break, the Japanese had to offload a train and transfer supplies to another train farther along the line—a slow and tedious process. The daily traffic over the line dropped to between 100 to 200 tons a day, a third of what *Burma Area Army* needed for its forces in Burma.[70]

The SAF alternated attacks on the railroad line with attacks on the main Japanese army supply dumps in southern Burma, carrying out five attacks on the dumps at Rangoon. These missions provided a striking contrast with previous missions. After a mission to bomb the Rangoon dumps on April 5, the 492nd Squadron remarked that "there once was a thing called 'Rangoon-jitters,' but that feeling has been put away with moth balls for historical purposes only. Our former respect for this Burma 'hot spot' has dwindled to a low ebb and our bombing altitude over this target has taken a similar nose dive. We began the current Rangoon campaign in February from a height of 16,000 feet, but this mission found us poking our noses in at 9,000 feet in spite of accurate flak."[71] With an even-greater sense of history, the 9th Bomb Squadron—originators of the "Goon at Noon" club back in early 1943—commented that "there is a great deal of satisfaction on the part of all personnel that we are now able to 'Drive over the Goon' just about any time we feel like it without encountering a swarm of enemy fighters—a situation that used to obtain during the hectic months of November and December 1943. One begins to see real progress in the war, and our part becomes more real."[72] There was perhaps no better demonstration of the complete Allied dominance of the air over Burma than the 7th Bomb Group's final mission to Rangoon on 27 April 1945, when the B-24s and RAF Liberators came in to bomb the supply dumps at 2,300 feet.[73]

The Race to Rangoon

As the battle for Meiktila came to an end toward the end of March, Slim was already planning for the next stage of the fight with *Burma Area Army*: the capture of Rangoon. He was under no illusions as to the difficulty of the task, nor the immense logistical challenges 14th Army faced as it marched south toward Rangoon and even farther away from its supply bases. As he recalled in his great memoir of the war in Burma:

> *It would be a race, and a stern one, against two tough competitors, the enemy and the monsoon. The Japanese, in spite of the hammering we had given them, were still numerous and formidable; the shadow of the monsoon loomed over us, only seven or eight weeks away. If we did not take Rangoon before it broke, we should, with landing grounds out, even dropping hazardous, roads dissolving and health deteriorating, find ourselves in a desperate situation with the prospect of a disastrous withdrawal.*[74]

Slim planned a three-stage advance to the south. In the first stage, IV Corps was to consolidate its hold on the area around Meiktila-Thazi area, cutting off the Japanese lines of communication from Thazi to the south. In the second stage, 14th Army would regroup, with some exchanges of units between IV and XXXIII Corps and areas of operation in preparation for the third stage. Slim planned for IV Corps to advance south down the railway corridor to take Rangoon, while XXXIII Corps would advance on Rangoon

Indian troops on their way to Rangoon. After smashing *Burma Area Army* in the battles around Meiktila, 14th Army began a race to Rangoon, hoping to capture the city before the arrival of the monsoon rains turned its forward airfields into seas of mud, leaving the army stranded without supplies. SE_003776, IWM

following the Irrawaddy River to the delta area. To reduce the administrative burden, Slim planned to withdraw two of his British divisions back to India, while limiting supplies for No. 221 Group's forward squadrons and supplies for engineering units, thus squeezing every ounce he could get to provide IV Corps and XXXIII Corps with supplies over the badly stretched supply system. Slim realized that the intense fighting around Meiktila had delayed his progress and that there was a chance he might not reach Rangoon in time before the monsoon broke. At a meeting with Leese, Christison, Sultan, and Stratemeyer on March 19, he proposed that there be an amphibious attack on Rangoon in early May, before the monsoon.[75]

Leese approached Mountbatten with Slim's proposal. With his planning staff working on the idea of a smaller, modified Operation DRACULA, the crisis over removing American transport aircraft erupted and was resolved, but Mountbatten knew that he would have the American transports only until the capture of Rangoon, and none after June 1. With the urgent need to seize the city to support 14th Army, he decided to mount the amphibious operation in the first week of May, using one division from XV Corps and a parachute battalion to capture the Japanese defenses at Elephant Point, at the opening of the Rangoon River, to allow landing craft to move upriver to the city. Dropping the parachute battalion would require two transport squadrons. Mountbatten was reluctant to withdraw squadrons from those supporting 14th Army, but in the end had little choice. With their experience of air landings, the Air Commando troop carrier squadrons got the task, but Stratemeyer insisted that they would need at least two weeks of training for the operation and would have to be taken off their regular air supply duties. The loss of the two squadrons for training would put added strain on the CCTF, but this could not be helped.[76]

Burma Area Army hoped that the *15th* and *33rd Army* could hold a line across southern Burma to prevent 14th Army from reaching Rangoon before the monsoon. Each army was to cover the withdrawal of the other, with both moving to the area north of Toungoo, where Kimura wanted them to bring 14th Army's advance to a halt. But the Japanese divisions had lost so heavily in the Mandalay-Meiktila battles that their battered divisions had little chance against an enemy equipped with strong armor and artillery with overwhelming air support. The strength of *33rd Army* was now down to less than a single division. IV Corps had begun its push from Meiktila, with 17th Division leading, at the end of March, and by April 9 the division had surrounded the town of Pyawbwe, where Kimura had initially hoped to establish a defensive line, having fought numerous small actions inflicting more casualties on the weakened Japanese units now withdrawing in haste. The garrison in the town fought to the last man, leaving 1,110 dead. To the west, XXXIII Corps made progress down the Irrawaddy valley so that by mid-April, 14th Army had five divisions spread across a line below Meiktila. For those who have never been to Burma (now Myanmar) in March and April, these are the hottest months of the year. Afternoon temperatures in Meiktila in April average 101°F. The heat and the dust are enervating. During April the premonsoon rains began to arrive, turning the dirt tracks into mud and leaving behind steaming heat. Just marching would have been a feat of endurance, let alone fighting.[77]

The British and Indian divisions, along with their tank brigades, kept pushing south. Day by day, towns fell that a few months before had been targets for the heavy and medium bombers of the Tenth Air Force: Chauk, the oil fields at Yenangyaung, Pyinmana, Taungup, Prome, and Toungoo. XXXIII Corps' advance forced the *28th Army*

A Royal Navy landing craft travels up the Rangoon River to the city during Operation DRACULA. The troops arrived to find that the Japanese had already abandoned Rangoon and were retreating to the east toward Thailand. *SE_003954, IWM*

to withdraw from the Arakan in an attempt to retreat to the east and into Thailand. After the capture of Pyawbwe, IV Corps gave the retreating Japanese no rest, pushing infantry and armored columns south toward Toungoo, where fighters based at the complex of airfields in the Toungoo area could provide air support for the capture of Rangoon. While 17th Division mopped up Japanese forces around Pyawbwe, the 5th Indian Division passed through the 17th Division to take the lead in the advance to Toungoo. Tanks of the 255th Tank Brigade with 5th Division infantry reached Toungoo on April 22, surprising the Japanese with the speed of their advance (Toungoo lay only 160 miles from Rangoon). On April 29, the 255th Tank Brigade reached Pegu—50 miles from Rangoon—but that day the monsoon chose to arrive three weeks early and made the roads impassable, bringing the advance to a halt. Operation DRACULA was then in progress, with convoys carrying the landing force nearing Rangoon. On May 1, following a massive SAF bombardment by RAF Liberators and 7th Bomb Group B-24s on Japanese gun positions, the 317th and 319th Troop Carrier squadrons dropped 700 Gurkha paratroops over Elephant Point with an escort of P-51s from the 2nd Air Commandos. Flying over Rangoon the next day on a reconnaissance, an RAF wing commander saw a sign on the Rangoon prison reading "Japs Gone" and "Extract Digit"—RAF slang for "get a move on." Taking a chance, he landed his Mosquito at Mingaladon and made his way into the city to find that the Japanese had abandoned the city. The landing forces came up the river and occupied Rangoon without opposition.[78]

Throughout April, the Combat Cargo Task Force and the Army Air Force squadrons assigned to 14th Army continued to provide support for the advance. Apparently some senior officers in IV Corps tried repeatedly to get the 5th and 6th Fighter Squadrons reassigned to providing close air support, but to no avail.[79] The RAF would not agree, preferring to have its own Thunderbolt and Hurricane squadrons take responsibility for the task, leaving the

Air Commando fighter squadrons "to be content with such odd jobs as were left" after RAF fighters using advance bases took over all the close support work.[80] For the 5th and 6th Fighter Squadrons, this meant continuing attacks on the Japanese lines of communication to the south and relentless attacks on Japanese troop concentrations and stores areas, particularly in the area around Toungoo, where Kimura was trying to build up a strong defensive position. For the month of April the two squadrons had responsibility for keeping a section of the Mandalay-Rangoon railroad south of Meiktila unserviceable by dive-bombing railroad bridges and nearby bypass bridges. As fast as the Japanese could repair the bridges, the Air Commandos went back to knock them out again. Toward the end of the month, the squadrons began flying Rhubarb missions over southern Burma, flying as far south as Bassein in the Irrawaddy delta, looking for targets of opportunity and shooting up a few locomotives, rolling stock, and rivercraft.[81]

The 6th Fighter Squadron had its own dramatic rescue behind enemy lines after a mission attacking the railroad station at Thaungdainggon, 10 miles south of Toungoo. Capt. William Hemphill, squadron commander, was leading the mission that day when ground fire hit his P-47. With his engine streaming oil, Hemphill knew he could not make it back, and began looking for a place to land. He called the other fighters and asked them to alert the 166th Liaison Squadron, then based at Meiktila. Hemphill came down in a field 10 miles west of Toungoo, deep behind Japanese lines. When they received the report of a downed Air Commando pilot, Capt. Frank Davis and 1st Lt. Neil Saxon took off in two L-5s to make the rescue with an escort of P-47s. As Davis recalled years later:

I was a C-64 pilot and the Ops. Officer of a Liaison (L-5) Sqd. Two or three P-47 pilots came to our strip at Meiktila and told us Bill Hemphill was down near Toungoo, Burma, about 150 miles south. So Lt. Saxon and I each flew an L-5 down, being escorted by P-47s.

My approach was as slow as I could make it, almost hitting a bunker [the low earthen berm surrounding rice paddies] with the tail wheel. I landed with the brakes on but the field was wet and I couldn't keep from rolling or sliding into a ditch. Bill and I got some natives to help pull the plane back onto level ground. However, after checking things out, I could see there was no way we had enough room for takeoff between the paddy bunkers. As we pondered our problem, some natives came running in, telling us the Japs were coming.

We had no other choice, so we started up. I rev[v]ed it to full throttle, held the brakes as long as I could, and let it go. We hit the first bunker hard, but bounced over it, then went on to hit four more before I finally got it in the air. After landing at Meiktila the plane was not much good.[82]

When not flying counter air force missions, the 1st and 2nd Fighter Squadrons joined the attacks on the Japanese troops and supply dumps. The squadrons began using napalm in their attacks on Japanese positions and Japanese-held villages, with devastating effect. The planners for Operation DRACULA asked the 2nd Air Commando Group to provide low-level photographs of the banks of the Rangoon River, using the F-6Ds assigned to the 1st and 2nd Fighter Squadrons. To provide a diversion for the photoreconnaissance airplanes and allow them to complete the photo mission, the two squadrons went after the antiaircraft positions in the area. As one pilot later commented, it was "a good way to get your ass busted."[83] The 1st Fighter Squadron sent 16 P-51s to join 22 from the 2nd Fighter Squadron. In the attack, antiaircraft fire hit 1st Lt. Herman "Doc" Lyons's Mustang, forcing him to bail out. Bob Eason—Lyons's flight leader—flew to Ramree to organize a rescue, but the L-5 from the group's 127th Liaison Squadron couldn't find Lyons. Two long searches the next day also failed to see any sign of him. After the war, the 1st Squadron learned that the Japanese had quickly captured Lyons and, when they began their retreat from southern Burma, beheaded him.[84]

During the last week of April, the 1st and 2nd Squadrons also began flying Rhubarbs to southern Burma ahead of IV Corps' advance to search for and destroy railroad equipment and any motor vehicles they could find. No. 224 Group had alerted the squadrons that a train was due to leave Rangoon for Thailand loaded with equipment and gasoline. After searching for the train for two days, Lt. Col. William Buxton, commanding the 1st Fighter Squadron, had the good fortune to find the train en route to Pegu. With no antiaircraft fire to contend with, Buxton led his squadron down on repeated strafing passes, completely destroying the train and its cargo. On one of the Rhubarb missions, one of the 2nd Fighter Squadron leaders, having found nothing on his search, came across a field filled with piles of rice straw. Out of boredom, one member of his flight dropped down and strafed one of the piles. To his astonishment, the pile of straw exploded under his fire. The Japanese had placed drums of gasoline all over the field, using the rice straw as camouflage. The flight went back and forth across the field, shooting up every pile they could find. When the Rhubarb missions ended, the two squadrons had destroyed around thirty trucks, five gasoline trucks, four locomotives, three small tankettes, six staff cars, and more than forty ox carts carrying supplies, in addition to damaging more.[85]

The 459th Squadron flew missions throughout the month, keeping up its attacks on bridges and, like the Air Commando fighter squadrons, hitting Japanese troop concentrations and supply dumps in the path of the advancing British and Indian troops. For these attacks the squadron began using napalm to firebomb a designated target area with 110-, 135-, and 165-gallon drop tanks filled with napalm mixture. The squadron used napalm to devastate two railroad stations and the rail yards nearby, taking out a third station with 1,000-pound bombs a few days later. The squadron also used napalm tanks to attack troop concentrations, with 16 P-38s hitting a reported concentration of 4,000 Japanese troops and 20 tanks with 32 110-gallon napalm tanks on April 20. The P-38s ranged widely across southern Burma, hitting targets in the railroad corridor for IV Corps and targets in the Irrawaddy valley ahead of XXXII Corps' advance.[86]

The 12th Bomb Group's squadrons flew missions in support both of IV and XXXIII Corps but toward the end of the month found fewer and fewer targets as the troops neared Rangoon. Like the fighter squadrons, most of the targets the B-25s went after were troop concentrations, supply dumps, and bridges. On many missions the bombers went down to lower altitudes, bombing from 3,000 to 5,000 feet and rarely encountering more than small-arms or machine gun fire that occasionally put a few holes in the bombers but did no serious damage. The B-25s flew many missions to the area around Toungoo, concentrating on Japanese supply dumps and the railroad yards to deny their use to the Japanese. The squadrons did their best to get their bombs into the target area, with the occasional reward of explosions and large columns of smoke rising up as they turned back to base. With little risk of running into Japanese fighters, the squadrons began sending out two or three bombers to search out targets of opportunity. These flights occasionally came across a

"Old Ironsides"—a P-47D from the 5th or 6th Fighter Squadron—waits to go on a mission in support of 14th Army. After turning over the close-air-support role to the RAF, the Air Commando fighter squadrons flew many longer-range interdiction missions into southern Burma to attack Japanese lines of communications, troop concentrations, and targets of opportunity. *Author's collection*

To provide support for 14th Army's advance to Rangoon, the 12th Bomb Group had its squadrons send detachments to operate in rotation out of the airfield at Meiktila to be closer to the front lines. Two B-25s from the 83rd and 434th Bomb Squadrons sit near tents where the aircrews lived while operating out of the airfield. *GP-12-HI-BOMB, AFHRA*

and dust at Meiktila were stifling, the 82nd Squadron reported that "the boys at Meiktila feel as they are really fighting a war now. Living under pup tents and eating mostly K rations, the men have a fair conception of how it feels to be in the infantry."[87] The squadrons flew missions successfully out of Meiktila until April 29, when they returned to Feni.[88]

The month of April saw the squadrons of the Combat Cargo Task Force operating at maximum capacity. The premonsoon weather disrupted operations, with severe thunderstorms over the Arakan hills causing some missions to be aborted or canceled and forcing the transports to take long diversions around the storms to get to the front. The weather claimed at least one aircraft when a C-47 apparently suffered structural failure in a storm, though two C-46s simply went missing for unknown reasons. Nevertheless, every squadron flew missions on every day of the month, despite the weather. The totals for the month exceeded those in March, with the CCTF flying 84,251 total hours, carrying 66,388 tons of supplies and 77,026 personnel. Had the 317th and 319th Troop Carrier Squadrons not been pulled out for training, these totals would have been higher. Squadrons continued to fly their airplanes intensively, averaging seven hours a day. More airfields closer to the front opened up, with engineers repairing captured Japanese airfields and carving out landing grounds from any flat surface long enough to accommodate a C-46 or C-47. This allowed the bulk of supplies to be landed, which was more economical than air dropping. The liaison squadrons also flew more trips but, with the lower intensity of combat, evacuated fewer casualties, instead delivering more personnel and supplies to the frontline units.[89]

In preparing for the advance to Rangoon, 14th Army incorporated plans to use glider-borne aviation engineers to build landing strips close to the front lines, following the advance as it moved farther south. These plans involved the CCTF in two special operations. GUMPTION was the designation for flying in glider-borne aviation engineers, while Operation FREEBORN covered the flying in of a brigade group to the front. In preparation for the first GUMPTION operation, the 317th and 319th Troop Carrier Squadrons towed 40

locomotive or rolling stock, but these targets were few. The squadrons also began using the 75 mm cannon on their B-25H aircraft to damage bridges and railroad tracks; anything to disrupt the flow of supplies. Of their bridge attacks, the 81st Squadron celebrated an attack on April 4 when Maj. Charles Thompson took out the Toungoo railroad bridge, the "nemesis of the 12th Bomb Group and every other outfit operating in that vicinity," as the squadron history described it. Coming in at low level and dropping four 500-pound bombs in trail, Thompson knocked out the center span of the bridge. In something of a role reversal, the bombers often worked with the VCP teams to bomb targets the VCP teams had designated, sometimes within a quarter mile of the front line, bombing and strafing at 300 feet using their cannon and machine guns. The 82nd Bomb Squadron began sending several flights of bombers to operate from Meiktila main airfield as a forward base, beginning their first combat sorties on April 11. The flights flew three to four missions a day out of Meiktila, rotating back to Feni at the end of six days. The 81st Bomb Squadron arrived on April 20. Squadron B-25s shuttled bombs, ammunition, supplies, and personnel back and forth between Meiktila and Feni to keep the flights operational. Though the heat

A B-25H from the 12th Bomb Group pulls away from a double bombing mission against Japanese troops and supply dumps at Taungle and nearby Popaywan in support of 14th Army's advance. Allied intelligence began using radio intercepts to pinpoint the location of Japanese army headquarters for Allied bombers. *Box 146, folder A-2, RG208AA, NARA*

VICTORY IN BURMA

gliders from Palel to Meiktila, where they awaited word to fly south. The 2nd and 4th Combat Cargo Squadrons towed 15 more gliders to Meiktila loaded with engineering equipment. On April 20, 5th Indian Division captured and cleared the Japanese airfield at Lewe, just south of Pyinmana and some 50 miles from Toungoo. British airfield engineers with a detachment of US Army Air Force aviation engineers traveling with the 5th Division columns used bulldozers and a grader to clear a landing strip for gliders that was 150 yards wide and 800 yards long, parallel to the planned transport landing strip and a smaller strip for the L-5s that was 30 by 350 yards. With their work done, the engineers and their equipment rejoined the 5th Division columns, radioing word back that the glider strip was ready.[90]

With the 317th and 319th Squadrons having withdrawn for training in preparation for Operation DRACULA, the 4th Combat Cargo Squadron took over glider-towing duties. At 0445 on April 21, eight C-47s from the 4th CCS took off for Meiktila, towing eight CG-4A gliders from the 2nd Air Commando Group loaded with rations for troops there. After landing and offloading their cargo, the gliders took on the aviation engineers and their equipment, comprising one scraper, one tractor, two bulldozers, a jeep, a trailer, equipment, rations, water, and 19 engineers. Arriving over Lewe between 0955 and 1015, some of the glider pilots failed to see smoke pots marking the glider strip, and landed instead on the L-5 strip. One glider was damaged beyond repair, but fortunately none of the equipment. The engineers got to work, with skirmishing going on near the airfield and sniper fire coming at them, forcing them to stop work at 2300. The next morning at 0700, eight Ki-43s came in over Lewe, strafing the gliders, setting fire to five of them that still had drums of gasoline onboard but missing the engineering area with the vital equipment. The attack did not delay work on the airfield. Ten minutes after the attack, the first transports arrived to air-drop supplies. By noon the transport strip was 4,500 feet long, and at 1600 the first transports landed on the field—RAF Dakotas from No. 62 Squadron bringing in a load of gasoline.[91]

The day the Oscars attacked the airfield at Lewe, an armored advanced guard from 255th Brigade captured Toungoo airfields without opposition. Army engineers following the column chose an airfield named Tennant as the least damaged and easiest to repair, quickly filling in bomb craters on the field. Late that afternoon the 4th CCS received word to fly in gliders to Tennant the next morning. On April 23, six C-47s again flew in supplies to Meiktila, where they picked up six 1st and 2nd Air Commando CG-4A gliders loaded with the same equipment that had been delivered to Lewe. The gliders arrived over Tennant between 1015 and 1045 and landed without incident. The aviation engineers did more grading work to smooth over bomb craters and lengthen the field to 6,000 feet. Three and a half hours after the gliders landed, the first transport came in, a 4th CCS C-47 bringing in airways communication equipment and Army Air Force Airways personnel. The next day, 56 C-46s and C-47s flew supply missions into Tennant, offloading gasoline, rations, ammunition, and other equipment for the forward units. In expectation that a third GUMPTION mission would be required to prepare another airfield farther south, on April 25 a C-47 from the 2nd CCS and two from the 4th CCS made two trips to tow six replacement gliders from Meiktila to Lewe. While waiting for word on the next GUMPTION, the two squadrons flew a complete casualty-clearing station with all its personnel and medical equipment from Meiktila to Tennant in 38 sorties.[92]

In between the second and third GUMPTION operations, the CCTF carried out Operation FREEBORN, flying in a brigade group

A small bulldozer landed by glider works to prepare a landing strip for C-47 transports. At Lewe, on the road to Rangoon, gliders landed an engineering detachment and their equipment by 1015 hours. The engineers got to work and had completed a landing strip by noon the next day. The first RAF Dakotas landed on the airstrip at 1600 hours. *3A-37422, RG342, NARA*

to the Pegu area to block the ability of the Japanese to retreat to the east. On April 27, the 17th Division, having taken over the advance from 5th Division, captured the town of Pyuntaza north of Pegu and before continuing south left a force of infantry to protect engineers laying out a transport strip nearby. By the end of the next day, the strip was ready, and on April 29 the 2nd and 4th CCS flew in a battalion group comprising 1,123 troops and their equipment in 56 sorties. The aviation engineers continued working on the landing strip, lengthening it to accommodate the C-46s of the 4th CCG, who began landing supplies on the strip on April 30. That same day, to the south, engineers traveling with 17th Division columns cleared a new 2,000-

A C-47 from the 2nd Air Commando Group's 317th Troop Carrier Squadron towing a glider over central Burma in early 1945. Gliders carried engineering equipment that enabled American aviation and British army engineers to rapidly build an airstrip for C-47s out of a stretch of flat ground. In this way, air supply could keep up with advancing 14th Army units on their way to Rangoon. *3A-37392, RG342, NARA*

THE TENTH AIR FORCE IN WORLD WAR II

yard landing strip near Payagyi as fighting raged around Pegu some 10 miles to the south. The fly-in of another brigade group began on May 1, using 25 aircraft from the 2nd and 4th CCS. The plan had been to fly in the troops over four days, but the early rains made this impossible. After the first few airplanes landed on the airstrip, the intermittent rain made the field very rough, but the squadrons completed 61 sorties into Payagyi that first day, carrying in 858 troops and 89 tons of equipment. On May 2 the fly-in continued, with the transports flying in another 891 troops and 61 tons of supplies. The last 24 airplanes to reach the field that day had to fly around thunderstorms in the area and through driving rain, landing in deep mud on the now deeply rutted airstrip. Conditions became so bad that the last 22 sorties scheduled for May 3 had to be canceled.[93]

The early arrival of the monsoon slowed the advance and turned these forward airfields into seas of mud, rendering them practically unserviceable for several days. On May 4, engineers reached the airfield complex at Zayatkwin, north of Rangoon, where the Japanese had built three airstrips. The engineers selected an area along the southeast strip for the glider landings. Two days later, C-47s made it into Tennant to pick up the gliders to tow to Zayatkwin. Five C-47s from the 1st CCG and one from No. 117 Squadron towed six gliders loaded with what by now had become the standard set of aviation-engineering equipment. Lewe airfield remained unserviceable until May 8, when the 2nd and 4th CCS could finally get in to pick up the eight CG-4A gliders waiting there. All landed safely except one, which came in after dark and attempted a landing by using the headlights of a jeep to illuminate the field. This was not enough and the glider crashed, destroying the scraper it carried, but the crew escaped without injury. Work was already underway at the field, and earlier that day the first C-47s had landed supplies. The next day the aviation engineers cleared the field for C-46s to land. This completed the CCTF's special operations in support of IV Corps' advance.[94]

Operations GUMPTION and FREEBORN provide examples of the remarkable mobility that air supply gave to the ground forces, and the equally remarkable advances in the capabilities of air supply the Allies developed during the course of the Burma campaign. These two operations in the last two weeks of April 1945 would have been inconceivable three years earlier. In the advance to Rangoon, the divisions in IV and XXXIII Corps pushed forward with the confidence that their supplies would arrive in time and in the necessary quantity. More importantly for the conduct of the battle, when the mechanized infantry and tank columns that Slim introduced entered the open ground in the central plains of Burma, they could move in any direction, knowing that their air support would move with them. As the British official history of the campaign noted, "the fact that the Allied forces could be supplied very largely, and on occasions entirely, by air freed them to a considerable extent from being tied to roads, and enabled them to undertake operations which would otherwise have been impossible to maintain for more than a few days."[95] The history went on to say, "if it is true, as Napoleon said, that armies march on their stomachs, it is equally true that 14th Army was carried to victory on the wings of the Allied air forces."[96]

The AAF and RAF squadrons of the Combat Cargo Task Force made this possible. For the advance into Burma, 14th Army deployed six divisions, two independent brigades, two tank brigades, and corps and army support units totaling around 260,000 men.[97] For much of the final campaign, as the official history noted, rations, ammunition, gasoline, medical supplies, and a host of other items could get to the front lines only by air. To meet this demand, the transport squadrons had to fly their aircraft and their aircrews intensively, and well above normal operational rates. The effort also required the capture of Japanese airfields and the building of new landing strips on the Arakan coast and along the route of the advance in central Burma, which would keep the front lines within economic range of the transports. This required strenuous efforts on the part of Army and aviation engineer battalions. In addition to supplying the daily needs of 14th Army, the CCTF also had to assist in moving 14th Army's reserve supplies forward from the Imphal area closer

Gurkha soldiers board a 4th Combat Cargo Group C-46 to be flown to Mandalay. The ability of the Combat Cargo Task Force to fly men and supplies almost anywhere engineers could build a landing strip gave 14th Army unparalleled mobility and freed the army from dependence on the limited Burmese road network.
3A-37297, RG342, NARA

to the front lines. The coordination of this massive logistical effort was in itself a monumental task of planning and execution that brings great credit to the staff of the CCTF and the squadrons involved, and to the many Army quartermaster and transport units supporting the CCTF. Of the Army Air Force squadrons that supported 14th Army during these final months, none made a greater contribution to the Allied conquest of Burma than the Combat Cargo and Air Commando transport squadrons in the Combat Cargo Task Force.

Combat Cargo Task Force Operations October 1944-April 1945

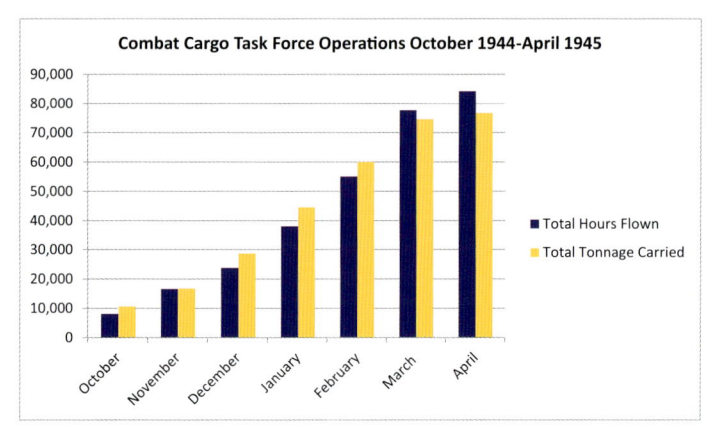

Table 11 Source: CBI: Combat Cargo Task Force, Monthly Histories October 1944-April 1945

CHAPTER 14
ENDGAME

Back to India

For most Army Air Force squadrons in the Tenth Air Force or supporting 14th Army, their participation in the Burma campaign came to an end with the occupation of Rangoon in early May. The Tenth Air Force's fighter groups had begun moving back to India in early May, and the squadrons assigned to Eastern Air Command and the Combat Cargo Task Force soon joined them. The 459th Fighter Squadron flew its last operational mission on May 3, a strafing attack on Japanese troops retreating through Moulmein. On May 14 the P-38s flew in a single formation from Cox's Bazar to the airfield at Dudhkundi in India, where they joined the 33rd and 80th Fighter Groups. A few days later the squadron officially became part of the 33rd Fighter Group, ending the independent existence it had followed since February 1944. In late May the squadron received a number of "Droop Snout" P-38s, a version of the standard P-38J/L with the nose guns removed and replaced with a transparent nose and space for a Norden bombsight and a bombardier. In June, 10 bombardiers joined the squadron to form a Droop Snout flight, with the intention of using these airplanes to drop Azon bombs. The Air Commando fighter squadrons flew patrol missions over Rangoon during the first week of May, covering the landing forces before heading back to India. The 1st and 2nd Fighter Squadrons returned to Kalaikunda—the 2nd Air Commando Group's base—where the heat and humidity made an unpleasant change from the sea breezes at Cox's Bazar. The 5th and 6th Fighter Squadrons returned to the 1st Air Commando Group's base at Asansol. On their return the 5th and 6th Squadron pilots gave up their P-47s to the Air Service Command in exchange for brand-new P-51K Mustangs, accepting the Mustangs with no little trepidation.

After a few days to transition into their new fighters, the squadrons moved to Kalaikunda, where they joined the 1st and 2nd Fighter Squadrons as part of the 1st Provisional Fighter Group.[1]

Stratemeyer had long wanted to reorganize the Air Commando groups into standard fighter, transport, and liaison squadrons under standard tables of organization. In a letter he had his headquarters write to Arnold in March 1945, he stated:

It has long been the opinion of this Headquarters that a task force can be formed, made up of components drawn from a standard table of organization units, to carry out an Air Commando operation, and that the retention of permanent organizations of the Air Commando type constitutes an extravagant use of resources.[2]

Stratemeyer proposed forming a fighter group out of the 1st, 2nd, 5th, and 6th Fighter Squadrons, combining the 317th and 319th Troop Carrier Squadrons into a transport unit and the six Air Commando liaison squadrons into a single liaison group with three squadrons. In the same memo, Stratemeyer recommended converting the three Combat Cargo groups into four standard troop carrier groups with a smaller complement of 64 aircraft in four squadrons. With fewer crews per airplane than the standard troop carrier group, the combat cargo groups had found their period of intensive operations more of a strain on the aircrews. This reorganization would have provided the proposed troop carrier groups with extra crews, allowing for

After withdrawing to India, the 33rd Fighter Group received a number of "droop snout" P-38s, with the guns removed and the nose compartment modified to carry a bombardier and a Norden bombsight to be used for dropping Azon bombs. These modified P-38s were never used for bombing, and one was apparently converted to a high-speed transport for Lt. Gen. Stratemeyer. *Peter M. Bowers Collection, MoF*

The 5th and 6th Fighter Squadrons returned to their base at Asansol in India, where they exchanged their worn P-47Ds for brand-new P-51K Mustangs, though not all pilots were happy with their new mounts, and they gave up their trusted Thunderbolts with some reluctance. The 6th Fighter Squadron painted large black checks on the tails of their Mustangs as an identification feature. *GP-A-CMDO-1-HI, AFHRA*

extended intensive operations. The Plans Division accepted the recommendation in principle but proposed postponing any change until Arnold could review the idea with Stratemeyer on a planned trip to the Far East.[3] Possibly as a result of the decision to defer the proposed reorganization, the 5th and 6th Fighter Squadrons spent only a month at Kalaikunda, returning to Asansol by June 22.[4]

The 12th Bomb Group continued to fly combat missions in support of IV Corps for most of May. After the capture of Rangoon, the 434th Squadron moved to the airfield at Magwe, and the 83rd Squadron to the nearby airfield at Maida Vale, to be closer to the front. Greatly to their disappointment, the group assigned the 81st Squadron to ferrying in gasoline, bombs, ammunition, meat, and ice to Magwe and Maida Vale, where the 434th and 83rd were living in a tent encampment by the side of the airfield. Almost all the missions the two squadrons flew during the month were to provide close air support to the troops pursuing the retreating Japanese heading east toward the Sittang River and Thailand. The squadrons flew three or more missions a day, usually with three airplanes going out on each mission. The Army submitted requests for close air support, providing information on targets. On many of the missions, the bombers worked with the VCP teams, sometimes bombing within 2,000 yards or less of the forward troops. The target areas were usually small (500 by 300 feet), comprising wooded areas believed to be sheltering Japanese troops or sections of a village or town. Initially the squadrons bombed in elements of three, with the two wingmen bombing on the leader, but for greater accuracy they switched to having each aircraft make an individual run over the target area at 1,000 feet. After bombing the target area, the B-25s would return to make three strafing runs with their cannon and machine guns. In a little over two weeks the 83rd Squadron completed 43 missions, dropping 126 tons of bombs and 10 oil drum bombs and firing off 228 rounds of 75 mm cannon and 259,000 rounds of .50 caliber. The forward base operations ended on May 24, when the two squadrons returned to Feni. The 83rd Squadron recorded that the missions flown from the forward base had been some of the most satisfying they had ever flown, causing the most damage to the Japanese. The 81st got in only two missions, joining the 82nd Squadron in attacks on Japanese positions near Sittang and Mokpalin on May 18 and 19 and flying a nearly aborted mission to bomb the airfield at Ban Takli in Thailand. The 82nd Squadron flew several more missions during the middle of the month, but far fewer than the month before. In early June the 81st and 82nd Squadrons moved to Madhaiganj, finding to their delight they would be living in stone buildings as opposed to bamboo bashas. The 83rd Squadron moved to the former 7th Bomb Group base at Pandaveswar, and the 434th Squadron moved back to Feni. Once there, the operations staff began organizing training programs, while the aircrews pondered what the future would bring. One of the great pleasures the squadrons experienced at the time, apart from better food, better living quarters, and time to rest, was the reunion with former squadron members who had been shot down and released from prison in Rangoon. Some who returned had been given up for dead, while others who were thought to have been prisoners had died in captivity at the hands of their captors.[5]

The Combat Cargo Groups continued operating during May, although the onset of the monsoon hampered operations, and the longer distances down to the airfields in southern Burma and around Rangoon meant fewer trips and less tonnage flown during the month. The Joint Chiefs had specified that American transports could be moved after the capture of Rangoon. The two Air Commando transport squadrons returned to their bases in India, the 317th Squadron returning to Kalaikunda and the 319th Squadron to Asansol. The 1st Combat Cargo Group's 2nd, 3rd, and 4th Combat Cargo Squadrons went to Hatazari in India in the middle of the month before moving to Myitkyina and Bhamo to begin air supply operations into southern China. The 4th Combat Cargo Group continued its supply missions into Burma from Chittagong, while the 12th Combat Cargo Squadron returned to the 3rd Combat Cargo Group with the Tenth Air Force. In the northern area, the 443rd Troop Carrier Group and the 315th Troop Carrier Squadron moved from Ledo to Dinjan, the 1st Troop Carrier Squadron joining them there at the end of the month, leaving the 2nd Troop Carrier Squadron at Warazup for the time being. The 1st Troop Carrier Squadron began converting to the C-46. The weight of the American effort in the India-Burma theater began shifting to directly supporting the forces in China. Following the fall of Rangoon, the 443rd Group joined Operation RED DISC, the transfer of the Chinese Sixth Army to China. In early June the three combat cargo groups moved to

A B-25H from the 434th Bomb Squadron at the former RAF airfield at Magwe. The 12th Bomb Group continued to fly missions in support of 14th Army before returning to India toward the end of May. *GP-12-BOMB-HI, AFHRA*

Loading supplies onto a C-47 from the 10th Combat Cargo Squadron for transport to China. After the fall of Rangoon, the transport groups assigned to the Combat Cargo Task Force and the Tenth Air Force began shifting their operations to supporting the India-China Wing of the Air Transport Command, flying troops and supplies to China. *3A-2540, RG342, NARA*

Burma: the 1st and 3rd Groups to Myitkyina, with the 4th CCG going to Namponmao, where they began flying troops and supplies to China in cooperation with what was now the India-China Division of the ATC. Within the Photographic Reconnaissance Force, the 40th Photo Reconnaissance Squadron ceased operations at Akyab and moved back to its main base at Alipore in India. The weight of the American effort was shifting to China.[6]

Formal separation of the integrated Allied air forces took place on 1 June 1945 in accordance with the wishes of the Joint Chiefs of Staff. All American units withdrew from Air Command, Southeast Asia, and on that date, Headquarters, Eastern Air Command, the Strategic Air Force, the Combat Cargo Task Force, and the Photographic Reconnaissance Force all disbanded. The RAF units in these commands reverted to RAF control, and the RAF in Burma went through a complete reorganization. In his Order of the Day, Park gave generous praise to his American colleagues:

Without the support of the American Air Forces in Burma we could not have defeated the Japanese Army as rapidly and as decisively in 1945. All British forces, both land and air, are deeply grateful for the whole-hearted support and complete harmony that existed between American and British Air Force units in the Theater. I am exceedingly proud to have had the American Air Force units in my command.[7]

Overall, the integration of the AAF and the RAF under Eastern Air Command had worked well. The benefits of integration were evident in the successful reconquest of Burma, perhaps best exemplified in the outstanding record of the Combat Cargo Task Force—a case where the whole was truly greater than the sum of its parts. In his later report on the operations of Southeast Asia Command, Mountbatten praised Stratemeyer, who despite his initial misgivings had done so much to make the integration of the two air forces work in practice. Noting that Stratemeyer had won the loyalty of his American and British air commanders, Mountbatten said that Stratemeyer had "provided an outstanding example of how an Allied Air Commander should conduct himself."[8] As the date for the disintegration approached, Mountbatten wrote a personal letter to Stratemeyer to thank him for all his efforts:

The Burma Campaign is nearing its victorious conclusion, and you will soon be transferring your Headquarters from South East Asia to the China Theater.

On this occasion I feel I must express to you my very highest appreciation for all you have done to make the campaign in Burma so great a success.

From the day when I ordered the integration of the British and American Air Forces in this Theater in December 1943, you have labored unceasingly to produce a thoroughly happy and efficiently integrated Air Force in Eastern Air Command.

You have won the respect, trust and admiration of all who I have come across in your command, and I feel sure that goes for all those I have not come across as well.

You have achieved the greatest air supply in history. To make this possible, you first of all obtained complete air supremacy, and through your air action you made it possible to reconquer Burma from the North, which I was told in 1943 by all the Military experts was militarily impossible.[9]

Moving the Tenth Air Force to China

With the capture of Rangoon and the steady withdrawal of *Burma Area Army*'s shattered divisions toward Thailand, the Japanese no longer posed a threat to China or to the Hump route. This brought the differences in national interests to the forefront, but the Allies resolved the underlying tension through a simple parting of the ways.[10] Southeast Asia Command was already planning an operation to begin the reconquest of Malaya (Operation ZIPPER), to take place after the end of the monsoon in October as the first step toward the reconquest of Singapore at the end of 1945. The early capture of Rangoon allowed Mountbatten to accelerate his plans for ZIPPER, scheduling the operation for late August. The United States had no strategic interest in these operations and did not want to be seen as supporting the return of European colonialism in Asia.[11] From its inception, the Tenth Air Force had been intended to support America's primary strategic aim, the support of China and its continued participation in the war. As the war in Europe came to an end, the American strategic focus shifted to the final battles with Japan and the approach to the Japanese home islands. There was still some consideration given to the idea of a landing on the China coast as a preliminary step toward the invasion of Japan. This would require substantially greater American air resources in China. If an amphibious operation on the China coast proved unworkable, there was still a great deal a larger China-based air force could do to support the final advance on Japan.[12]

Stratemeyer and his staff had already been contemplating how to transfer the Tenth Air Force in its entirety to China. In March 1944, Stratemeyer's planning staff had worked on Operation ENTERPRISE, a plan to place substantially all Army Air Forces in the CBI in China, including 13 A-26 groups and six fighter groups, by January 1945.[13] In early January 1945, Stratemeyer had his staff draw up a plan for the redeployment of all Army Air Force units in India and Burma to China after the reconquest of Burma. Stratemeyer presented his plan to Wedemeyer and Sultan at a conference held at Myitkyina on January 15. The basis of the plan was that American tactical air units should remain in Burma until the completion of Phase II of Operation CAPITAL. Once Allied forces had completed Phase II, the American tactical units could shift to China, leaving behind sufficient ground forces to protect the road and pipeline to China. American transport units should remain with ACSEA until the complete reconquest of Burma. The plan envisioned setting up an Army Air Force headquarters in China to command both the Tenth Air Force and the Fourteenth Air Force. Wedemeyer approved Stratemeyer's plan and sent a recommendation to the War Department that the plan be accepted. At the end of January, Wedemeyer decided to take Stratemeyer's plan to transfer the Tenth Air Force to China to Washington, to include the plan in his discussions with the War Department on his own plans for a Chinese offensive in southeastern China aimed at recapturing Kweilin, Liuchow, and Canton on the China coast. Wedemeyer's plan (later designated RASHNESS), which the generalissimo approved, called for the Americans to train and equip 36 Chinese divisions and for a heavy commitment of American tactical air support and air supply. Chennault was against the plan, arguing that the logistical resources then available could not support a buildup of American air forces in China.[14]

Wedemeyer presented his plan to the War Department, receiving a favorable reaction and the promise of more large C-54 transport aircraft to increase the amount of supplies carried over the Hump. On his return to India, Wedemeyer held a conference on April 9 with Stratemeyer and his senior staff from Army Air Forces, India-

The Douglas C-54 Skymaster's greater cargo capacity was essential to plans for increasing the flow of supplies to China. Airfields within India had to be enlarged and expanded to accommodate the number of C-54s that were planned to be assigned to the India-China Wing of the ATC. *3A-1029, RG342, NARA*

Burma, and with Sultan and his staff from the India-Burma theater to confirm details of the ground and air plans. The role of the air forces in China would be to maintain air superiority over southeastern China, isolate the battlefield and interdict the flow of Japanese supplies, and provide close air support to the Chinese divisions on the offensive. The Tenth Air Force would become the tactical air arm of the Army Air Forces in China and would be based in southwestern China to support the campaign. The Fourteenth Air Force would become a strategic air force, moving to the Chengtu area to undertake strategic air operations over China and in coordination with the Far East Air Force in the Philippines. Stratemeyer would move to China to take command of Army Air Forces Headquarters in China, with Davidson commanding the Tenth Air Force and Chennault the Fourteenth Air Force under him. Charles Stone, Stratemeyer's chief of staff in Army Air Forces, India-Burma, and now a brigadier general, had accompanied Wedemeyer to Washington and reported to the conference that the transfer of the Tenth Air Force to China had received Marshall's and Arnold's approval, and that the allocation of C-54s would help solve logistical problems.[15]

The proposed organization of the tactical and strategic air forces would be as follows:

Tactical Air Force
Three fighter groups: 33rd, 80th, 81st Fighter Groups
One medium-bomb group: 12th Bomb Group
One photo flight
One tactical reconnaissance squadron
One P-38 squadron: 459th Fighter Squadron
One troop carrier group: 443rd Troop Carrier Group

Strategic Air Force
Two heavy-bomb groups: 7th and 308th Bomb Groups
One medium-bomb group: 341st Bomb Group
Three fighter groups: 23rd, 51st, 311th Fighter Groups
Two photoreconnaissance squadrons
One P-38 squadron: 449th Fighter Squadron

One troop carrier squadron
One combat cargo squadron
Chinese American Composite Wing (one medium-bomb group, two fighter groups)[16]

On his return to China, Wedemeyer had to tell Chennault that Stratemeyer would become the senior American air officer in China and that Chennault would be subordinate to Stratemeyer in the new command arrangement, a change Chennault was not pleased with.[17] Chennault remained opposed to the Tenth Air Force's planned move to China, arguing that the Fourteenth Air Force already had enough airplanes for current and future operations, and that a better means of increasing American air strength in China was to ensure that the Fourteenth received enough supplies to allow it to operate to its capacity.[18] Bringing more aircraft and units to China would only aggravate existing logistical problems. Nevertheless, Wedemeyer went ahead and issued an order on 1 May 1945, appointing Stratemeyer as commanding general, Army Air Forces, China theater, with the Tenth and Fourteenth Air Forces reporting to him, and authorized plans to begin moving the Tenth Air Force to China. Shortly thereafter Wedemeyer had to revise his plans. The War Department had informed Wedemeyer that due to demands for redeploying forces from Europe to the Pacific, the ATC would not get the large numbers of C-54 transports that had been promised for the India-China Division. The ATC believed that it could still meet the previous estimates of supplies to be flown over the Hump, but when Sultan's and Stratemeyer's staffs reviewed these estimates with the needs in China, they determined that what the ATC promised to fly over the Hump would be much less than what was actually required. The ground forces would need more supplies than had originally been calculated, and the need to use transport aircraft to distribute these supplies within China meant no capacity available for supplying the Tenth Air Force once it was in China.[19]

Despite this setback, Wedemeyer still wanted Stratemeyer to move to China, and offered him a smaller command with Chennault taking on the strategic effort and Davidson commanding an albeit smaller Tenth Air Force.[20] Wedemeyer told Stratemeyer, probably with his recent discussions with Chennault in mind, that "I personally am interested in obtaining the services of officers like you and Davidson whom I know in my heart and mind would be loyal members of our team. I can not be confident of team play under any other possible arrangement."[21] Stratemeyer declined the offer, advising Wedemeyer instead to appoint Stone, recently promoted to major general, as commander of Army Air Forces in China and to bring the "old men"—himself, Chennault, and Davidson—home to the United States. Wedemeyer decided to postpone the decision on command of the Army Air Forces in China but informed the War Department that the transfer of the Tenth Air Force would have to be delayed for several months.[22] He told Chennault that he would continue in command of Army Air Force units in China. At the same time, Stratemeyer wrote to Arnold on May 13, advising him of developments:

As of this writing the command situation in China remains unsettled, and we are endeavoring to obtain the release by 1 June 1945, from Southeast Asia Command of all AAF IBT and Tenth Air Force units in order to implement Hump tonnage to the maximum extent possible. By the time you receive this letter, discussions will have no doubt been made and communicated to you and the War Department for approval. As I now see the picture,

Tenth Air Force and the AAF IBT will proceed towards liquidation. Some transports and perhaps the heavy bombardment group will go on the Hump under the operational control of ATC, the balance of the troop carrier and combat cargo transports being transferred to intra-China distribution of supplies to combat units. One fighter group and attendant service units will be transferred to China and what is left will be available for assignment elsewhere.[23]

Within a few weeks the situation regarding the Tenth Air Force and Army Air Force command in China had reversed. In late May, Stratemeyer's AAF IB Headquarters received word that the promised C-54s would actually be sent to India, reviving hopes that the Tenth would be able to transfer to China after all.[24] Then, on May 28, Stratemeyer found that he had been promoted to lieutenant general. The reason for the promotion became apparent when he met with Arnold in Manila in mid-June. Apparently there was some miscommunication between the theaters and the War Department. When Stratemeyer met with Arnold on June 16, Arnold expressed surprise that Stratemeyer had not yet moved to China, and told him that his promotion to lieutenant general had been done so that he could take command of the Tenth and Fourteenth Air Forces in China.[25] Stratemeyer found that Arnold was determined to avoid the possible command problems that might arise with Chennault's continued presence in China. Stratemeyer left Manila with a letter that Arnold had drafted for Wedemeyer that laid out Arnold's wishes for the Army Air Forces in the China theater going forward:

Dear Al:
It has been evident to me that the situation in China is developing into a war of movement, aimed at isolating the Jap in Indo-China and defeating him or at least containing a substantial bulk of his forces in Southern China. In such a war of movement I know that air must be a most important arm in maintaining your mobility, strengthening your striking power, and eventually destroying the beaten Jap. In order to give you proper advice and to enable your air operation to proceed with a balance and drive that will produce the desired results, you need a senior, experienced air officer, in whom both you and I have confidence. It is my opinion that you should give this job to General Stratemeyer. As you know, he has just completed his mission with Eastern Air Command, culminating in driving back the beaten Jap forces from Burma. This campaign, involving a war of movement and a large scale use of air transports, is similar to the type of campaign with which you are confronted.

General Chennault has been in China for a long period of time fighting a defensive air war with minimum resources. The meagerness of supplies and the resulting guer[r]illa type of war must change to a modern, striking type of offensive airpower. I firmly believe that the quickest and most effective way to change air warfare in your Theater, employing modern offensive thought, tactics and techniques, is to change commanders. I would appreciate your concurrence in General Chennault's early withdrawal from the China Theater. . . .

I understand that the tonnages which I am largely responsible for making available to you have been substantially allocated to the ground forces, thereby reducing the amount of tonnage available to air. This has resulted in your available air striking power being dissipated from India-Burma and China to other theaters and to the United States. There are no plans which I know of for increasing your air forces at a later date and I therefore recommend that you re-evaluate your present situation and create conditions which will permit the redeployment to China of essential air striking power now available in India-Burma. I feel that if you can do this, the Joint Chiefs of Staff will not object to the additional changes in the air plans which will permit you to introduce into China these units, which I feel should be the bulk of those of the Army Air Forces, India-Burma Theater. Any units of the Tenth Air Force which you can program for employment in China can be held in India; the others will be redeployed as soon as we can get the shipping.

I trust that in line with my comments above you will be enabled to put into effect the organization which you recommended to the War Department on your recent visit; that is, that you will have a Commanding General, Army Air Forces, China Theater, directing the employment of the Tenth and Fourteenth Air Forces, one of these forces in a predominantly tactical cooperation with ground forces role, and the other a strategic air force.[26]

Marshall had also expressed puzzlement to Wedemeyer as to why Stratemeyer had not taken up his command. Having received Arnold's letter, Wedemeyer replied to Marshall on June 20, saying he agreed with Arnold's recommendations on the command of his air forces in the China theater with Stratemeyer in overall command and Chennault and Davidson under him. On learning of these plans, Chennault protested vigorously but decided on July 6 to request retirement. Stratemeyer then appointed Stone as the designated commander of the Fourteenth Air Force upon Chennault's departure.[27]

Although there were still many logistical issues to work out, the resolution of the command structure problem finally gave the Army Air Forces, India-Burma sector, and the Tenth Air Force a clear direction. In June a group of AAF IBS officers flew to Chungking to arrange for space near Wedemeyer for what would become Headquarters, Army Air Forces, China theater. On 30 June 1945 Arnold wired formal authority for Stratemeyer to move the Tenth Air Force to China, and that same day, Davidson told his staff that the Tenth Air Force would be going to Kunming. An advanced echelon of Tenth Air Force officers moved to Kunming during the first week of July to set up offices and arrange for quarters. The main body of Tenth Air Force staff flew to Kunming during the last week of July. The Tenth's new headquarters opened on August 1, sharing a building with Wedemeyer's tactical headquarters. In early August the Tenth Air Force headquarters moved again to the airfield at Liuchow, lost to the Japanese on 12 November 1944 but reoccupied on July 1, when Chinese forces took over the area. Despite the fact that the Japanese left a significant number of captured Fourteenth Air Force 500-pound bombs on the runway and destroyed all the airfield buildings, Liuchow was closer than Kunming to the area of southeastern China where the Tenth Air Force expected to operate. The advance party moved to Liuchow, putting up tents to live in and beginning the work of making the base habitable, setting up offices in three damaged buildings and using tarpaulins for covering. This work was still underway when the war came to an end.[28]

The Final Missions

Most of the fighter and bomber units spent the monsoon months in India waiting for word on their fate. Rumors abounded of moves to the Pacific or back to the United States, with the most probable destination being China. Once the new Army Air Force command structure in China became known, the question then became when would the squadron move to China, not if. Many of the veterans who had been overseas for long periods began to rotate back to the United States, with new replacements coming in to fill the squadrons. After the end of the war in Europe, the Army instituted a points system to determine who would be eligible for rotation back to the United States. Soldiers received a certain number of points on the basis of their length of service, their time overseas, their time in combat and combat decorations, and their parental status. Men who had points above a certain level were eligible, while those who had arrived more recently worried about how long it would take them to accumulate the required number of points. But even having enough points was no guarantee of a return home. As the *CBI Roundup*—the CBI theater's newspaper—reminded its readers, "If the Army needs you, you will stay in the Army as long as you are needed."[29]

The Tenth Air Force instituted a flying-training program for the fighter squadrons, requiring the pilots to undergo 90 hours of training in tactical and operational flying in addition to ground lectures covering every aspect of fighter operations. This was a real benefit to the new pilots who lacked operational experience. During June and July the squadrons worked on this training program, the pilots practicing rocket firing, dive-bombing, formation flying, and combat tactics. Mock combats between the P-38s, P-47s, and P-51s provided a welcome diversion. Not so welcome were the orders to all squadrons to undertake physical training and drilling—less than pleasant at the height of the monsoon. Regrettably, several pilots lost their lives during the training program, and, on regular flights, some replacement pilots and some combat veterans died. The death of a veteran often hit squadron morale hard. The 5th and 6th Fighter Squadrons worked on getting used to their new Mustangs. Some pilots appreciated the greater maneuverability of their new fighters, while others longed for the ruggedness of their Thunderbolts. While the training program continued, there were still opportunities for pilots and enlisted men to go on leave to Calcutta or to the rest camps in the hill stations in the foothills of the Himalayas, where they could relax and get away from the heat in Bengal.[30]

On their return to bases in India, the 12th Bomb Group squadrons were delighted to learn they would be converting to the new A-26 Invader. The A-26 was a "hot" ship, considerably faster than the B-25, with the same bombload and a smaller crew of pilot, navigator/bombardier, and gunner. The A-26s began arriving in early July to an enthusiastic reception from the pilots. One pilot in the 81st Squadron called the A-26 "a pilot's dream ship," while another said, "after flying the Invader, no pilot should ever want to handle another ship; it's the hottest twin-engine job in the AAF."[31] As more A-26s arrived, the squadrons passed their older B-25s on to the Air Service Command. The 434th Squadron played host to pilots from the 11th and 22nd Bomb Squadrons from the 341st Bomb Group, who joined

After withdrawing from Burma, the 12th Bomb Group began converting to the Douglas A-26 Invader. Had the war continued, the 12th Group would have returned to combat in China with their new A-26s. This unnamed A-26 has a painting of "Miss Lace" from Milton Caniff's famous *Terry and the Pirates* comic strip. GP-12-HI-BOMB, AFHRA

A P-38J or L at one of the fighter bases in India in July 1945. The airplane is named "Hammer's Destruction Co." and sports five Japanese flags. This appears to be the airplane belonging to 1st Lt. Samuel E. Hammer, who claimed five aerial victories over Burma flying with the 90th Fighter Squadron in the 80th Fighter Group, although at the time the squadron was still flying P-47s. 3A-33693, RG342, NARA

them at Feni to also convert to the A-26. Tragedy struck when one of the A-26s with a crew from one of the squadrons from China crashed, for unknown reasons, into the hills near the air base. Several squadrons experienced accidents with the A-26s as the pilots got used to the greater power and flying characteristics of their new mounts, but all agreed that the A-26 was a honey of an airplane. In August the 341st Group sent the 490th and 491st Squadrons to the 434th Squadron to convert to the A-26.[32]

The 60th Fighter Squadron from the 33rd Fighter Group and the 493rd Bomb Squadron from the 7th Bomb Group were the two squadrons that continued flying combat missions over Burma during the monsoon after the end of Eastern Air Command. In May, when the 33rd Fighter Group's 58th and 59th Fighter Squadrons returned to India, the 60th Fighter Squadron left its forward base at Sahmaw to move to the Myitkyina East airfield, across the Irrawaddy River from Myitkyina, near the village of Waingmaw. Here the squadron began flying patrols over the NCAC front as part of the North Burma Air Task Force, set up to coordinate air support activity after the withdrawal of the Tenth Air Force back to India. When Chiang Kai-shek ordered his Chinese divisions in Burma not to advance beyond the Burma Road at Lashio, then began withdrawing the Mars Task Force and his troops back to China, this left a vacuum in the NCAC area. Although 14th Army had captured Rangoon, there remained a concern over protection for what was now called the Stilwell Road from the remnants of the *18th* and *56th Divisions*. Sultan was concerned that as many as 10,000 Japanese soldiers might retreat to Thailand and regroup to possibly threaten the road and pipeline to China.[33] Sultan wanted Detachment 101, the OSS force of Kachin guerrillas operating in northern Burma, to protect the Stilwell Road and clear the Shan States in northeastern Burma down to the Taunggyi-Kengtung road, around 50 miles beyond the Chinese positions.[34] Detachment 101 had armed and trained the Kachin to operate behind Japanese lines. They had performed invaluable services in support of American, British, and Chinese regular units, providing intelligence on Japanese forces—especially the location of troop concentrations and supply dumps—that was invaluable for airstrikes, guiding Allied forces through the hills of northern Burma, and harassing Japanese support units as they tried to move supplies forward to the front. Detachment 101 raised several battalions of Kachin and Karen to operate in the area south of Lashio to harass retreating Japanese units heading for the Shan States and push them out of the area. These battalions began operating more as conventional forces rather than guerrillas, confronting Japanese troops directly in battle as well as through ambushes. Lacking the heavier weapons of conventional ground forces, the OSS arranged for the 60th Fighter Squadron to be based at Myiktyina to provide air support. For a brief period the 60th Squadron operated from a base deep in Japanese-held territory.[35]

In late May, Detachment 101's battalions captured the town of Laihka, in a small valley east of Katha and Shwebo, where the Japanese had two large storage dumps and had built a small airfield. Detachment 101 officers hired local Shan villagers to repair the airfield, filling in bomb craters and repairing Japanese demolition work by using a captured roller the Shans pulled by hand across the airfield.[36] When the airfield was repaired, Detachment 101's own liaison aircraft, dubbed the Red Ass Squadron, started flying in supplies and evacuating wounded. They flew in Sultan, who came to see the operation for himself. Detachment 101 staff sent a request to the Tenth Air Force asking for P-38s to be stationed at Laihka to support the Kachin and Karen battalions fighting the Japanese. The Tenth Air Force agreed and on June 2 sent twelve pilots and six P-38s from the 60th Fighter Squadron to operate out of Laihka. The field was around 200 miles south of Myitkyina, thereby saving a considerable amount of time in getting to the front. C-47s brought

An American OSS (Office of Strategic Service) officer from Detachment 101 (*right*) with his platoon of Kachin Rangers preparing for a patrol deep behind Japanese lines. These Kachin guerrillas harassed the Japanese units retreating from Burma into Thailand supplied with arms and ammunition from the American Army. *Box 147, folder D, RG208AA, NARA*

Lt. Gen. Dan Sultan stands with a group of Detachment 101 officers on a visit to an advance base in June 1945. Detachment 101 arranged for the 60th Fighter Squadron to be based at Laihka—behind Japanese lines—to provide close air support to the Kachin Rangers. *SC250958, RG111, NARA*

in supplies, gasoline, ammunition, and bombs for the P-38s. The weather shut down the operation fairly soon, with the heavy rain rendering the dirt runway unserviceable, but between June 2 and 10 the 60th Squadron flew 28 missions supporting Detachment 101 battalions. The rest of the squadron flew missions in support of the Kachins from Myitkyina East, flying three to four missions a day to bomb and strafe Japanese supply dumps the Kachin and Karen guerrillas located on their patrols. Many of these missions involved a round trip of 700 miles. The Kachins had been sent to capture the Japanese-held town of Loilem in the Shan States, a 20-minute flight from Laihka. A Japanese force of around 300 soldiers had built strong defensive positions southeast of Loilem, setting up machine gun positions in log-covered bunkers in the hills overlooking the town. When these proved too tough for the Kachin mortars and bazookas to crack, the Detachment 101 officers leading the battalion called in airstrikes. A Detachment 101 officer on the ground used a walkie-talkie radio to contact a pilot in one of the Detachment 101 liaison planes, talking the pilot onto the target area. Coming in low, the liaison pilot would drop smoke grenades right on top of the Japanese positions. The P-38s came in dropping napalm on the marked Japanese positions, returning to make several strafing passes. This went on until the Kachin had taken all the Japanese positions and secured the town. With the runway at Laihka out of commission, the P-38s returned to Myitkyina East.[37]

The 60th Squadron continued to fly missions during July, though the weather frequently interfered. On July 20 the squadron helped a British Force 136 guerrilla force capture the town of Mong-Nai from the Japanese. Six P-38s carrying two 1,000-pound bombs each went in to bomb and strafe the town. Afterward the Force 136 officers radioed, "Many thanks for effort. Our troops now occupy area." For some weeks the squadron had waited for the weather to clear, to allow a mission to bomb the airfield at Lampang in Thailand that the Japanese could have used to launch raids into Burma. Single P-38s went on weather checks to the area to see if a mission could get through. On one of these missions a pilot had to bail out near Lampang when his left engine exploded on fire, but on landing he was put in touch with British agents likely working with the Free Thai movement supporting the Allies, and he came back to friendly territory. The weather cleared sufficiently on July 23 for six P-38s to make it to Lampang. Four aircraft bombed the airfield, getting hits along the runway, while two aircraft went after the railroad yards, bombing the railroad tracks and rolling stock and setting fire to an oil storage tank. The squadron flew its last combat mission of World War II on August 1, when eight P-38s went to bomb and strafe Japanese troop concentrations at Mawkmai, south of Loilem. The bombing was successful, but tragically, for some unknown reason, 2nd Lt. Leland Edwards crashed on his bomb run, his P-38 exploding on the ground. In another tragic accident, 1st Lt. Robert Fulton was on a practice dive-bombing sortie over Myitkyina East when his P-38 went into a vertical dive and crashed near the field, killing him. Fulton was a veteran of 77 missions and already had orders to return to the States. While the loss of any pilot was a blow, the loss of veteran fliers away from combat was especially hard to take.[38]

The 493rd Bomb Squadron gained the distinction of flying what must have been the Tenth Air Force's last operational mission of World War II. After supporting the capture of Rangoon, the 7th Bomb Group stood down from operations and began an intensive training program while waiting to learn what its next assignment would be. At the end of May, as a result of the shortage of the promised C-54 aircraft, Stratemeyer decided to have the 308th Bomb Group in China and the 7th Bomb Group in India work with the Air Transport Command to haul gasoline to China. In the 7th Group, the 9th, 436th, and 492nd Bomb Squadrons took on the gas-hauling mission and moved to the ATC airfield at Tezpur during the first week of June, leaving the 493rd Squadron at Pandaveswar as the group's only operational bomber squadron. As the 9th Bomb Squadron recorded in its monthly history, "no single order ever has effectively depleted, in one stroke, the morale of a unit."[39] The other two squadrons expressed similar sentiments. At Tezpur the group stripped its B-24s of all war-fighting equipment to convert them to

When ordered to return to carrying gasoline to China, the 7th Bomb Group stripped all excess equipment out of its B-24s, removing the upper and lower gun turrets, all guns and armor plate, and anything else that wasn't absolutely necessary. Large rubber fuel tanks went into the bomb bay to carry gasoline. *Author's collection*

To reduce weight further and avoid needless losses, the 7th Bomb Group cut back B-24 crews to the pilot, copilot, navigator, flight engineer, and radio operator. This crew has just arrived at Kunming after flying another load of gasoline from India. At this point in the war, the B-24s could fly along the lower and safer route over Burma to China, avoiding the Himalayan mountains, which had claimed so many airplanes and lives. *Author's collection*

tanker aircraft. The engineering staff removed all top turrets and any remaining ball turrets, took the guns and fixtures out of the nose and tail turrets, stripped out the armor plate, and installed three large bomb bay tanks. With no need for bombardiers or gunners, and mindful of unnecessary losses the year before, crews for the Hump flights consisted of a pilot, copilot, navigator, flight engineer, and radio operator. The squadrons began flying gasoline to China in mid-June.[40]

After the Strategic Air Force disbanded on 1 June 1945, the 493rd Squadron found itself without a mission. Instead the squadron began an intensive training program in all aspects of bombing and operational flying, particularly Azon and radar bombing. A new mission came about in mid-June, when the American Office of War Information (OWI) requested the help of long-range bombers to distribute propaganda leaflets over Thailand. Thailand had allied itself with Japan at the beginning of the war, but opposition to the Japanese within Thailand was growing among the Thai people. The OWI wanted to broaden support for the Allies among the Thai and provide them with news and information on Japan's imminent defeat. This called for airplanes to fly over large areas of Thailand, covering most of the major cities and towns. The 493rd flew its first mission for the OWI on June 18, when three B-24s with an escort of ten P-38s from the 58th Fighter Squadron flew to Bangkok to drop medical supplies over the center of the city, without opposition. As the bombers and fighters pulled away from the drop zone, they saw two submarines moored in the Chao Phraya River, and immediately went down to strafe them.[41]

The 493rd Squadron flew the leaflet-dropping missions deep into Thailand through July and into August. The squadron carried out the 7th Bomb Group's last bombing mission of the war on July 3, when a single B-24 attempted to bomb the Royal Thai Air Force field at Ban Takli through haze that prevented the bombardier from locating the field. Instead he returned to a known checkpoint and with the navigator's assistance dropped his bombs on an estimated ETA. The leaflet missions were long and tiring, averaging 13 hours and often more. During July, one pilot and crew returned to Pandaveswar after having spent 18 hours in the air. Initially the squadron painted the undersides of its B-24s black for night leaflet-dropping missions, but with little risk of fighter interception the squadron began flying into Thailand during daylight. Occasionally the bombers ran into antiaircraft fire, bringing back holes in their aircraft, but in a month of flying over Thailand they never encountered a Japanese airplane. The 493rd flew its last combat mission on 3 September 1945, when four aircraft went to Thailand to drop leaflets over 17 cities and towns. This was the 7th Bomb Group's last combat mission of the war, which for the group had begun with the attack on Pearl Harbor 3 years, 8 months, and 27 days before. The group was one of the few in the Army Air Forces that could claim to have had airplanes in action on the first and the last days of the war.[42]

A B-24 from the 493rd Bomb Squadron prepares for another leaflet-dropping mission over Thailand in August 1945. In anticipation of flying bombing and leaflet-dropping missions by night, the squadron painted the undersides of its B-24s a glossy black. *SQ-BOMB-493-HI, August 1945, AFHRA*

Lt. Dan Shindeldecker (*kneeling, second right*) and his crew after returning from a nearly 15-hour leaflet-dropping mission over Thailand in August 1945. The name of the airplane ("Thai Times") refers to the propaganda and news leaflets the crews dropped on their missions. *SQ-BOMB-493-HI, August 1945, AFHRA*

ENDGAME

A troop transport arrives in the United States carrying men and women from various units. Some men were lucky enough to fly home on aircraft returning to "Uncle Sugar," but most had to take slow transports back home. *Author's collection*

A row of new P-51 Mustangs waiting on a flight line at a base in India after the end of the war. Shipped to India in anticipation of expanded air operations in China, some of these airplanes did end up with the Chinese air force, but most were simply scrapped. *Author's collection*

The End

The Pacific War ended on 15 August 1945, when Japan agreed to accept Allied terms for unconditional surrender outlined in the Potsdam Declaration. On 2 September 1945, representatives of the Japanese government signed the Instrument of Surrender onboard the USS *Missouri* in Tokyo Bay, bringing Japan's attempt to carve out an empire in China and Southeast Asia to an end. On 12 September 1945, Admiral Lord Louis Mountbatten accepted the formal surrender of all Japanese forces in Southeast Asia. Over the next several weeks, Japanese units throughout China and Southeast Asia surrendered to Allied forces. The end of the war removed any need for the Tenth Air Force to transfer to China.

News of Japanese surrender brought joy and relief to the men and women serving in the Tenth Air Force and the Army Air Forces, India-Burma sector. With the war over, joy and relief turned to an intense desire to return home. The US Army started the demobilization process quickly. Men with high points went first, but in early September the Army reduced the number of points required to speed the process. The mass redeployment of soldiers and airmen began on 10 September 1945 and accelerated in the weeks thereafter, with transports carrying the men back to the United States. A fortunate few flew back to the United States, but most returned on Army transport ships. Between September 25 and October 21, 50,000 men and women went back to the United States, and by the end of the year 151,594 men from the India-Burma and China theaters had departed, leaving 78,637 men in the theater. At the end of January the strength was 36,832. Davidson returned to the United States in early September, having turned over command of the Tenth Air Force—"Davidson's Big Ten"

as his men called it—to Maj. Gen. Albert Hegenberger on 1 August 1945. Stratemeyer stayed on in China as commander of Army Air Forces, China theater, until early 1946.[43]

As the men left, so did the units in which they had served. The fighter groups began leaving India in early October. Most reached the United States during November, moving to Camp Kilmer, New Jersey, where they were inactivated. The bomb groups stayed a bit longer, although the 7th Bomb Group had begun flying its B-24s home later in September. The group's engineering staff installed baggage racks in the bomb bays and salvaged metal seats from C-47s and C-87s to fit into the waist compartments to hold additional passengers. The crews made sure to decorate their airplanes with appropriate "artwork" and a record of their achievements. After the planes left, the remaining staff went to work shutting down their bases and completing the paperwork the Army Air Force required. The 7th Group left in early December and reached the United States in early January, where the group was inactivated. The 12th Bomb Group left in December, apparently leaving a number of its B-25s in the theater. Some of the fighters and bombers went to the Chinese

A former Air Commando P-47D gets torn apart in the scrapyard while more Thunderbolts, Mustangs, and B-24s wait their turn. With the war over, there was no longer any need for the thousands of aircraft the American aviation industry had churned out in astonishing numbers. *3A-36907, RG342, NARA*

THE TENTH AIR FORCE IN WORLD WAR II

Adm. Lord Louis Mountbatten reads his order of the day following the formal surrender ceremonies at Singapore on 12 September 1945. Gen. Sir William Slim and Adm. Sir Arthur Power stand on Mountbatten's right, while to his left stand Lt. Gen. R. A. Wheeler, representing US forces, and Air Chief Marshal Sir Keith Park. *CF_000720, IWM*

The American cemetery at Myitkyina in March 1945. This is the resting place for many young American soldiers and airmen who gave their lives serving in India and Burma. More than 700 Americans remain missing in Burma—now Myanmar—to this day. *3A-34007, RG342, NAR*

air force, but most ended up as scrap. It must have galled those who remembered the early days of the Tenth Air Force, when every item of equipment was in short supply, to see rows of new P-51s, P-38s, and B-25s waiting to go to the scrapyard. The Tenth Air Force was inactivated on 6 January 1946.[44]

Only the combat cargo and troop carrier squadrons continued operation. There was a continued need to fly supplies into China and to ferry Chinese troops to the areas the Japanese had occupied, so that the Chinese government could reassert control and resume administration. The 1st and 3rd Combat Cargo Groups had moved to Myitkyina in June to begin operations into China. At the end of August the 1st CCG moved to Liuchow, China, where it was redesignated the 512th Troop Carrier Group, with its squadrons becoming the 326th, 327th, 328th, and 329th Troop Carrier Squadrons. At the same time, the 3rd CCG became the 513th Troop Carrier Group, with its squadrons redesignated as the 330th, 331st, 332nd, and 333rd Troop Carrier Squadrons. As the 513th Troop Carrier Group, the unit moved to Shanghai on 1 November 1945 and remained there until April 1946, flying supply missions within China until it was inactivated. For whatever reason, the 4th Combat Cargo Group did not receive a new designation and remained in India to fly supplies and men into China until it was inactivated in early February 1946. The 443rd Troop Carrier Group also moved to China, initially to Chihkiang at the end of August and then to Hankow in late September. The group received a Distinguished Unit Citation for moving a Chinese army of 30,000 men from Chihkiang to Nanking.[45]

A Summation

The original mission of the Tenth Air Force was to provide direct support to China as part of the American strategic objectives for the ultimate defeat of Japan. These objectives recognized the importance of continuing to contain Japanese forces in China and the possibility of using China as a base for air attacks on Japan, and as a possible base for invasion of the Japanese home islands. The debate between American and British political and military leaders was over China's ability to make a more substantial contribution to the war against Japan, and the heated debate within American leadership was whether this contribution should be through the reform of the Chinese army and a ground offensive, as Stilwell advocated, or through an air campaign that Chennault promoted. The Stilwell-Chennault debate had less of an impact on the mission of the Tenth Air Force than the concurrent debate on how best to get supplies to China: through expanding the air route over the Hump or by building a new land route to China from India. In either case, the mission of the Tenth Air Force would have remained the defense of the supply route to China, though the method of supplying China by air or by land did have a profound impact on the Tenth Air Force's operations. Over time, changes in strategic objectives; the political dynamics among American, British, and Chinese leaders; and the realities of the war in the China-Burma-India theater transformed this mission to the extent that the Tenth Air Force spent the greater part of its existence fighting over Burma and not in China.

The Tenth Air Force's initial objectives in complying with its assigned mission were to provide support to China through the defense of the air ferry operation carrying supplies to China over the Hump route, and the defense of the Assam air bases that were vital to sustaining this operation. During its first year and a half of operations, the Tenth Air Force concentrated successfully on the air defense of the Assam air bases and the destruction of Japanese air and land forces that could threaten the air supply operation. As the strategic debate on Allied strategy for Burma and China progressed, defense of the Assam air bases came to be redefined and expanded into forcing the Japanese army from northern Burma, to remove the threat of Japanese air attack and allow for building the land line of communications to China. These objectives were agreed to at the Quadrant Conference in August 1943 and formed the basis for the first directive issued to Admiral Lord Louis Mountbatten as commander of the new Southeast Asia Command. Following the formation of Southeast Asia Command, the principal role for the units of the Tenth Air Force became the support of Stilwell's Chinese, American, and British forces in their campaign to capture Myitkyina and push construction of the Ledo Road to link up with the Burma Road. To this end, the Tenth Air Force made a vital contribution to the capture of Myitkyina. In the absence of close air support and air supply, it seems doubtful that the siege of Myitkyina could have been won without exorbitant cost. In September 1944 the Combined Chiefs of Staff revised this objective in their

ENDGAME

directive to Mountbatten, calling for the expulsion of Japanese forces from all Burma at the earliest opportunity. This objective became a possibility following the shattering defeat of the Japanese *15th Army* during the battle for Imphal. In the final battles for the defeat of Japanese forces in all of Burma, which removed any threat to the Hump operation, the Tenth Air Force and other Army Air Force units operating as part of Eastern Air Command contributed in no small measure to the ultimate Allied victory.

The Army Air Force and Royal Air Force units in India, operating separately and then in the integrated Air Command, Southeast Asia, had four general objectives for prosecuting the war against the Japanese in Burma:

1. Obtaining air superiority over all of Burma
2. Destroying the Japanese lines of communications into and in Burma to disrupt the flow of supplies to the Japanese ground forces
3. Providing the maximum amount of supplies to the Allied armies for their defense of India and the subsequent advance into Burma
4. Assisting in the destruction of the Japanese ground forces[46]

It took nearly a year and a half after the fall of Burma before the Allies could return to the offensive. For much of this period the Tenth Air Force had a limited ability to strike at the Japanese, with shortages of units, airplanes, men, and equipment. At the end of March 1942, after Brereton had established his Tenth Air Force headquarters in India, he had a force of seven B-17s, one LB-30, and ten P-40 fighters, with 185 officers and 3,025 enlisted men.[47] By December 1943, when the Allies began offensive operations under the new Southeast Asia Command, the American Army Air Forces in India had grown to include 48 heavy bombers, 37 medium bombers, 141 fighters, 51 transports (with another 200-plus transports in the India-China Wing of the Air Transport Command), 10 photoreconnaissance aircraft, and 30 liaison aircraft, with a total, including Service Command and the India-China Wing, of 43,982 officers and men.[48] A little over a year later, in January 1945, the Tenth Air Force and the Army Air Force units operating with Eastern Air Command had 42 heavy bombers (with around a dozen more temporarily in China), 97 medium bombers, 226 fighters, 67 reconnaissance aircraft, and 297 transports.[49] The Army Air Forces, India-Burma sector, now numbered around 80,000 officers and enlisted personnel, with 22,400 serving in the Tenth Air Force and an additional 22,000 working with the Air Transport Command in the India-China Division.[50] As these numbers indicate, it took time for the Army Air Forces in India to build up strength, due to priorities in other theaters of war, but by the last phase of the Burma campaign the Tenth Air Force and Army Air Force units operating with Eastern Air Command had become a powerful striking force.

The battle to establish air superiority over all of Burma was an Allied success, but it was a battle that continued until the very end of the war. For much of the first year and a half after the fall of Burma, the air superiority battle was something of a stalemate.[51] The Allies did not possess aircraft that were qualitatively superior to their Japanese opponents, nor did Allied aircraft have the range to roam deep into Burma to attack Japanese air bases. In northern Burma the fighter units of the Tenth Air Force conducted a successful defense of the Assam air bases against the few Japanese air raids, which did little damage. It remains surprising, given that the Hump route was China's last link to sources of supplies, that the Japanese Army Air Force did not mount a more sustained campaign against the Assam air bases. Nor did the Japanese undertake continued attacks against Allied air transport aircraft later in the war as the Allied armies advanced into Burma. This failure of Japanese initiative was a gift to the Allied air and ground forces.[52] Toward the end of 1943, the AAF and the RAF began to acquire both qualitative and quantitative superiority over the *5th Hikōshidan* with the arrival of Spitfires and the P-38 Lightnings and P-51 Mustangs. With their longer range, the P-38s and P-51s finally gave the Allied air forces the ability to carry out an effective counterair campaign. During March, April, and May 1944, the 459th and 530th Fighter Squadrons and the Fighter Section of the 1st Air Commando Group claimed 224 aircraft destroyed, 29 probably destroyed, and a further 58 damaged.[53] While the actual number of Japanese aircraft destroyed was less than claimed, the damage inflicted put a severe strain on Japanese air operations. Compounding the problems for Japanese air units operating in Burma was the weak logistical system of the Japanese Army Air Force, which made rapid repair of damaged aircraft problematic; the inability of the Japanese aviation industry to produce aircraft in the numbers required; and the drain of aircraft to other battlefields in the Pacific.[54] By the onset of the 1944 monsoon, the Allied air forces had obtained the initiative in the air and, after the end of the monsoon, extended their air superiority throughout the rest of Burma as the Allied armies continued their advance. The *5th Hikōshidan* could carry out only what amounted to nuisance raids against Allied forces. By the fall of Rangoon in May 1945, the Allies had established what amounted to air supremacy over Burma.[55] Air superiority was vital to the success of other air and ground operations, as Air Chief Marshal Sir Keith Park noted in his dispatch on air operations in Southeast Asia from June 1944 to May 1945:

> *It is unnecessary to recount in detail the enormous advantages accruing to both ground and air forces when the enemy air arm is small and misemployed, and when our own squadrons are superior in performance, training and control. It is, however, worth pausing to consider the results had enemy aircraft been allowed unrestricted use of the sky. The air supply on which the whole land campaign hinged would have been impossible, the attrition rate on our close support squadrons, which worked with accuracy and effect, would have been prohibitive, and the disruption caused by our strategic bombers to the enemy's communications far to the rear could not have been such as to have materially influenced the battle.*[56]

As Park stated, air superiority allowed all other air operations to proceed without hindrance from Japanese fighter attack. Allied control of the air over Burma contributed to the success of the second mission of the Allied air forces: the destruction of the Japanese lines of communication to and within Burma. This, too, was a long, drawn-out battle that depended on having a sufficient number of aircraft with the right weapons and tactics to wage an unrelenting battle of attrition against Japanese shipping and the Burmese and Thai railroad systems. In its first month of bombing operations in April 1942, the Tenth Air Force's few bombers dropped 16 tons of bombs on Japanese targets. For much of 1943 the weight of Allied air attacks was not decisive. The Japanese proved adept at making rapid repairs to bridges and railroad yards, and despite the damage done through Allied air attacks, supplies continued to get through to the Japanese armies. Bridges proved to be exceptionally difficult targets to destroy with the tactics then employed. The one clear victory during this year was the denial of Rangoon as a port for Japanese shipping. The combination of the 7th Bomb Group's attacks on shipping and the dock areas at Rangoon and other Burmese ports and the Allied mining campaign against Japanese harbors in Burma and Thailand effectively denied the use of these ports to the Japanese. This put added pressure on the railroad system through Thailand into Burma. After the formation of the Strategic Air Force in December 1943, the weight of the combined AAF/RAF bombing effort grew from 1,550 tons that month to a peak of 10,141 tons in February 1945.[57] The development of new tactics in the campaign against road and rail bridges in Burma and Thailand, especially the low-level tactics the 490th Bomb Squadron perfected and new weapons such as the Azon bomb, enabled Allied air forces to reduce the amount of tonnage carried over the Burmese railroad system to less than 150 tons a day by January 1945—well below the Japanese army's daily requirement of around 600 tons per day.[58] The successful disruption of the Japanese line of communications, though it took months of hard effort to achieve, meant that attacks on Japanese supply dumps, aircraft, artillery, motor vehicles, locomotives, and rolling stock were all that much more effective, since destroyed equipment could not be replaced at the same level, and damaged equipment could not be repaired. To this effort the Allied photoreconnaissance squadrons made a significant contribution, with regular coverage of Japanese targets in Burma to track the destruction from a bombing attack and the rapidity of repair.

In executing their third air force mission—the supply of the materials of war to the Allied armies—the Allied air forces made their greatest contribution to the Allied victory in Burma. As Admiral Mountbatten stated in his report on operations in Southeast Asia under his command, "it was air supply which alone made the campaign in Burma a feasible proposition," though he added that it was the maintenance of Allied air superiority that made air supply possible.[59] As examples of the importance of air supply to the campaign in Burma, Mountbatten listed in his report the support for Wingate's Special Force operations in 1944, in which air supply sustained a division-size force behind enemy lines for three months; the maintenance of five divisions of British and Indian troops during the decisive battle of Imphal; and 14th Army's advance from Imphal to Rangoon in 1944–45. The contribution of air supply was threefold: first, it helped the Allies overcome the nearly complete lack of surface transportation from India into Burma, making the reconquest of Burma possible; second, it gave Allied units the means to defeat the Japanese tactics of encirclement and disruption of land lines of communication that had proven effective in Japanese invasions of Malaya and Burma, as the victories in the Arakan and Imphal in 1944 proved decisively; and third, air supply gave the ground forces unparalleled mobility, as Merrill's Marauders in the campaign for northern Burma and Gen. Slim in his brilliant capture of Meiktila demonstrated.[60] For much of the final phase of the Burma campaign, the Army Air Force provided the bulk of the transport aircraft supporting the Northern Area Combat Command and the 14th Army. It is doubtful that 14th Army's advance into central Burma would have been possible without the AAF squadrons in the Combat Cargo Task Force, since at the time, the RAF did not have enough transport squadrons to replace them. In total, in operations from 15 December 1943 to 1 June 1945, AAF transport squadrons delivered 490,814 tons of supplies into Burma and, together with RAF transport squadrons, airlifted 783,000 troops.[61] It is also important to note the importance of air evacuation to the performance and to the morale of the Allied armies fighting in Burma. The combination of light liaison aircraft flying the wounded back to airstrips where larger C-47s and C-46s could carry them back to hospitals in the rear area no doubt saved the lives of countless Allied soldiers. AAF and RAF squadrons evacuated 135,703 casualties during the same period.[62]

The fourth air force mission—assisting in the destruction of Japanese ground forces—was mainly the task of the fighter squadrons providing close air support to Allied forces, although the medium bombers, and on occasion the heavy bombers, contributed through their attacks on Japanese positions and troop concentrations. For this mission it took time to build up an adequate force with capable aircraft and the proper tactics. The P-40 served the Tenth Air Force from its earliest days to the fall of Myitkyina in August 1944 and helped pioneer the tactics of close air support in the Northern Combat Area Command. Fighter-bombers made up, to some extent, for a lack of artillery and tanks. With experience and good intelligence, fighter pilots became adept at placing their bombs in proximity to Allied troops. The development of air liaison teams in the NCAC and the VCP teams with the 14th Army allowed closer and more-effective coordination between fighter squadrons and ground forces. In this effort the air liaison teams serving with Merrill's Marauders and Wingate's Special Force brigades introduced a number of innovations in close air support, including the use of liaison aircraft as forward air controllers. Perhaps the best example of effective joint air-ground operations was in the fierce fighting around Meiktila, where close coordination among tanks, artillery, infantry, and Air Commando fighter squadrons soundly defeated the attacking Japanese army's attempts to retake the town.

Contributing to the success of these missions was an extensive network of service and support units. The ground crews performed wonders in maintaining aircraft under the most-trying conditions of heat, dust, and rain, with only the most basic facilities and few comforts. The early-warning posts who maintained the alert for intruding Japanese aircraft, the aviation engineer battalions who built and maintained the airfields and the road links, and the quartermaster and trucking companies who provided the packers and the kickers for the air supply effort all contributed to the Allied victory, though few received recognition for their hard work. So, too, in their own way, did the tens of thousands of service troops performing an array of functions from bases stretching from Karachi to Assam, providing replacement parts, food and fuel, mail, communications links, pay, medical services, and every other function a modern air force needed to sustain operations.

Coalitions in war are notoriously difficult to manage. The Allied effort in Burma and China had no end of complications over strategy, command, and conflicts of personalities. The integration of the two Allied air forces in December 1943 was vital to the success of the air war over Burma, and by all accounts it was a success. The creation of Air Command, Southeast Asia, provided for a form of unity of command and economy of force that Clausewitz argued were fundamental principles of war. Even though full integration was never achieved—Mountbatten mentions in his final report the anomaly of having the American XX Bomber Command and the ATC's India-China Wing being beyond his control, and for political reasons the Fourteenth Air Force remained outside Air Command, Southeast Asia, throughout the rest of the war—the extent of integration and cooperation between the Royal Air Force and the Tenth Air Force was of considerable benefit, particularly regarding the allocation of transport aircraft and the direction of the strategic-bombing campaign. Integration was no easy achievement. As the history of the Army Air Forces in World War II noted:

Given the differences of priorities, it is a tribute to the British and American commanders within SEAC and EAC that integration worked so well. Despite many differences in opinion, patience and understanding at the top set a pattern for all elements of the command.[63]

In this respect, Mountbatten's two senior American air commanders (Stratemeyer and Davidson) served him well. Once ordered to follow Mountbatten's decision to integrate the AAF and RAF, Stratemeyer did so wholeheartedly, Mountbatten singling him out for praise in his final report to the Combined Chiefs of Staff.[64] The history of American and British relations in the China-Burma-India theater is a case study of the importance of personalities and personal relationships in coalition warfare.[65] In Stratemeyer, both Arnold and Mountbatten had a loyal commander who could effectively represent the air perspective at senior levels and who had the personality to deal with difficult individuals such as Stilwell and Chennault.[66]

Was it worth the effort? Debate over the correctness and direction of Allied strategy in Burma and China continues to the present day. The reality of Anglo-American strategy in World War II was that the priority given to the defeat of Germany and the decision to undertake an offensive campaign against Japan through the Pacific meant that the war in China and Southeast Asia would always have a lower priority and lesser importance. Whether America and Britain should have limited their offensive operations in Burma, whether the Americans were correct to insist on building the land route to China, whether the entire American Chinese offensive in northern Burma was worth the effort, and whether American strategy in China during World War II was correct are questions that are still asked. Some recent scholarship has been sharply critical of Marshall's and Stilwell's approach to China, America's treatment of China as an ally during the war, and the cost that American strategic initiatives imposed on the Chinese.[67] There is also the view that China's contribution to the victory over Japan was "at best, secondary, despite the hopes and plans of U.S. leaders and the commitment of men and material to aid China."[68] Given the political realities within China of competing political and military factions, the deterioration of the quality of the Chinese armies after years of war, the destruction of much of the Chinese infrastructure and economy, and the loss of territory to provide rice and recruits for the armies, it seems doubtful that Stilwell's goal of creating a large American-equipped, American-trained, and reformed Chinese army would have been possible. Similarly, given the severe logistical problems involved in getting supplies into China, it seems doubtful that a major air campaign against Japan from Chinese bases could have been sustained, or that it would have succeeded, even if the Chinese army had been able to defend the air bases. The far more powerful air forces brought to bear against Germany and Japan failed to bring either to the point of surrender through using conventional weapons.[69] More critically, America's war against Japan was a maritime, not a continental, war. The approach to Japan had to go across the Pacific, since Japan could be invaded only from the sea, not through continental Asia. Arguably, once American forces seized the Mariana Islands as bases for B-29s and US Navy submarines, and with the US Navy's powerful Fast Carrier Task Force freed to roam across the Pacific after defeating the Imperial Japanese Navy in the Battle of the Philippine Sea, China lost its importance in the war against Japan.[70] Had an invasion of Japan been necessary it would have been mounted from Okinawa as planned, not from mainland China. But among the speculative "what ifs" of the history of World War II is the question of how the war in Asia might have been different if Chiang had agreed early in 1942 to the reform of the Chinese army, and if the Americans had been able to equip and train a modern army that could have protected Allied airfields in China and mounted a successful defense against the Japanese ICHI-GO campaign in 1944.[71]

Yet, it is still possible to say that victory over Japan was a victory brought about by a coalition of Allied nations—America, Australia, Britain, China, New Zealand, and Russia—and to argue that China's contribution was still important. For some period of time, China did tie down Japan's forces in the *China Expeditionary Army*, perhaps not so much due to a concerted effort on the part of the Chinese army and more to Japan's reluctance to give up its hold on Chinese territory, but either way the Japanese army remained heavily committed in China until the end of the war. While toward the end the Japanese did pull troops back for defense of the home islands, at the time of Japan's surrender, the Japanese army still had a third of its force—more than a million men—in China and Manchuria. What this meant was that the American and British forces fighting in the Pacific and Burma never had to face anything like the full force of the Japanese army. Had Japan managed to withdraw a greater portion of its forces in China before the depredations of American submarines made this transfer too dangerous, the cost in Allied lives would likely have been far greater.[72]

If China's main contribution to the Pacific War was to contain the Japanese army in China, then an argument can be made that sustaining China's participation in the war was worth the cost in men and material. After the fall of Burma in 1942, China's only lifeline was the airlift over the Hump route. The extent to which the Hump operation helped sustain China's participation in the war is debatable. From one perspective, the supplies delivered over the Hump were not enough to sustain China's war effort; the bulk of the materials delivered via the Hump during 1944 and much of 1945 went to the Fourteenth Air Force, the Twentieth Air Force, and to the small number of Chinese divisions receiving American aid.[73] Certainly the amount of supplies delivered to China were insufficient to prevent the disasters resulting from the *ICHI-GO* offensive. John Plating has argued that as a vehicle for demonstrating American support for China, and thus sustaining Chinese morale, the Hump operation was a success.[74] As Plating argues:

Thus, in early 1942, the alliance [between China and the United States] was nothing more than an agreement on paper, and worth little more, adding no troops and few airplanes to the theater. But once it was shown that cargo planes could ferry supplies from India to China—however meager those first loads were—the airlift took on a new meaning, now able to support Stilwell's and Chennault's plans for China. . . .

[W]ith the achievement of the 10,000 ton goal in December 1943, the airlift began to appropriate a mythic status irrespective of who was getting the tonnage or what was being hauled. All that mattered was that the loads kept coming and that they continued to increase—which they did with great success. By design, all alliances are characterized by the array of contributions the different parties bring to the relationship. The Americans offered war material and advice (solicited or otherwise), and the Chinese offered geographical proximity to the enemy while serving as a grand diversion for the Japanese—with the Hump airlift serving as the nexus of this alliance. In this manner, the Hump was the military operation that sustained the alliance, one that held special importance, as it placed Japan between the looming American threat to the east and an intractable war in the west.[75]

From this perspective, the role of the Tenth Air Force in defending the Assam air bases and the Hump air route to China was important, successful, and clearly worthwhile. In supporting the Hump operation, the Tenth Air Force's participation in the campaign to capture Myitkyina was perhaps its greatest contribution to the American war effort in China and Southeast Asia.[76] The benefit of the capture of Myitkyina to the Hump operation, as difficult as that battle was, is without question. The capture of the town and its airfield removed much of the threat of Japanese fighter attack against the transports of the India-China Division, allowing them to fly a more direct route to Kunming at lower and safer altitudes, carrying more cargo. In the first month following Myitkyina's capture, tonnage over the Hump route more than doubled and had nearly doubled again five months later.[77] Whether the campaign in northern Burma should have continued beyond Myitkyina is a legitimate question.[78] From the fall of 1944, the Allies could have remained on the defensive in northern Burma, and the buildup of Myitkyina as a base for the Hump operation could have continued with limited risk of Japanese interference. With the capture of the Marianas, China's importance to the war against Japan was diminishing. As the British, and Chennault, argued at the time, and as scholars have argued since, the completion of the Ledo road came too late to affect the outcome of the war.[79]

After the defeat of *15th Army* at Imphal, the American Joint Chiefs of Staff argued for the offensive to continue to allow the Ledo Road to link up with the Burma Road to Kunming. At the same time, Mountbatten's senior commanders all argued for pursuing the retreating Japanese forces relentlessly to ensure their destruction.[80] Allied air superiority and air supply made possible the continuation of the campaign in northern Burma and the advance into central Burma that led to Slim's brilliant defeat of *Burma Area Army* in the battles around Mandalay and Meiktila. These final battles in northern and central Burma, in which the Tenth Air Force and the Army Air Force units assigned to Eastern Air Command played a prominent part, ensured the security of the Hump operation and reopened the port of Rangoon. And in these battles it is important to repeat that the contribution of American air transports to sustaining the Allied armies in their advance was critical. It is somewhat ironic that while the application of airpower in China did not achieve all that was hoped, its application in the "forgotten war" in Burma through the integrated Air Command, Southeast Asia "provided a classic demonstration of what air power could do when dedicated to joint operations with the Army and the Navy."[81]

GLOSSARY

AAF	Army Air Forces
AAF, IBS	Army Air Forces, India-Burma sector
ABCFC	Assam-Burma-China Ferry Command
ABDACOM	American-British-Dutch-Australian Command
ACSEA	Air Command, South East Asia
ATC	Air Transport Command
AVG	American Volunteer Group
CAMCO	Central Aircraft Manufacturing Company
CATF	China Air Task Force
CBI	China-Burma-India theater
CCP	Chinese Communist Party
CCTF	Combat Cargo Task Force
CNAC	China National Aviation Corporation
EAC	Eastern Air Command
IATF	India Air Task Force
IB	India-Burma theater
ICW	India-China Wing
KMT	Kuomintang (Nationalist Party)
NCAC	Northern Area Combat Command
OSS	Office of Strategic Services
RAF	Royal Air Force
RCAF	Royal Canadian Air Force
RIAF	Royal Indian Air Force
SAF	Strategic Air Force
SEAC	South East Asia Command
TAF	Tactical Air Force
TCC	Troop Carrier Command
TIFC	Trans-India Ferry Command
VCP	Visual Control Post

APPENDIX 1

TENTH AIR FORCE AIRCRAFT CODE NAMES

HEAVY BOMBERS

B-24D	Loon
B-24E	Pewee
B-24J	Gander
B-29	Fly

LIAISON

L-1A	Canary
L-1C	Brant
L-4B	Fowl
L-5	Turkey
OA-10	Duck
YR-4	Hummer

TRAINERS

AT-16	Tody
PT-17	Kite
PT-22	Tern

GLIDERS

CG-4A	Martin
TG-5A	Condor

MEDIUM BOMBERS

B-25C	Gull
B-25D	Crow
B-25G	Fisher
B-25H	Pigeon
B-25J	Siskin

FIGHTER-BOMBERS

RA-24	Piper
A-36-1	Lory
P-51A-1	Myna
P-51A-5	Owl
P-51A-10	Taha
P-51B-1	Parrot
P-51B-2	Cuckoo
P-51B-7	Flicker
P-51B-10	Sparrow
P-51B-12	Vireo
P-51C	Starling

TRANSPORT

C-39	Snipe
C-43B	Quail
C-45B	Crane
C-46	Stork
C-47	Goose
C-48B	Robin
C-53	Heron
C-54	Raven
C-57	Finch
C-60	Egret
C-87	Eagle
UC-61	Swift
UC-64A	Macaw
UC-78	Grebe

FIGHTERS

P-38G-10	Rook
P-38G-15	Ruff
P-38H	Thrush
P-38J-5	Chat
P-38J-10	Oriole
P-38J-15	Veery
P-40B	Hawk
P-40E	Coot
P-40E-1	Lark
P-40K-1	Teal
P-40K-5	Bird
P-40M-1	Cock
P-40M-5	Dart
P-40M-5	Kiwi (Stripped)
P-40N-1	Rail
P-40N-5	Ibis
P-40N-10	Hen
P-40N-15	Bat
P-40N-20	Poll
P-47D	Junco

PHOTORECONNAISSANCE

F-4	Dove
F-5A-10	Swan
F-5B-1	Willet
F-5C-1	Puffin
F-5E	Chimey
F-7	Chippy
P-40F-6	Waxer
P-40M-6	Flea
P-40N-11	Jay
P-40N-21	Chick
P-40N-26	Curlew

APPENDIX 2

TENTH AIR FORCE ORDER OF BATTLE

January 1943

China Air Task Force

23rd Fighter Group
    74th Fighter Squadron   P-40E/K
    75th Fighter Squadron   P-40E/K
    76th Fighter Squadron   P-40E/K
    16th Fighter Squadron   P-40E/K (from 51st Fighter Group)

11th Bombardment Squadron   B-25C/D (from 341st Bombardment Group (M))

9th Photographic Reconnaissance Squadron   F-4 (Detachment)

India Air Task Force

51st Fighter Group
    25th Fighter Squadron   P-40E/K
    26th Fighter Squadron   P-40E/K

341st Bombardment Group (Medium)
    22nd Bombardment Squadron (M)   B-25C/D
    490th Bombardment Squadron (M)   B-25C/D
    491st Bombardment Squadron (M)   B-25C/D

7th Bombardment Group (Heavy)
    9th Bombardment Squadron   B-24D
    436th Bombardment Squadron   B-24D
    492nd Bombardment Squadron   B-24D
    493rd Bombardment Squadron   B-24D

9th Photographic Reconnaissance Squadron   F-4

Source: Christopher Shores, *Air War for Burma: The Allied Air Forces Fight Back in South-East Asia, 1942–1945* (London: Grub Street, 2005), 383–84.

APPENDIX 3

DIRECTIVE ON INTEGRATION OF BRITISH & UNITED STATES AIR FORCES

11th December 1943

Directive from Lord Louis Mountbatten, Supreme Allied Commander, S.E.A.C. to Air Chief Marshal Sir Richard Peirse, Air Commander-in-Chief, S.E.A.C.; Lieut.-General J. W. Stilwell, Deputy Supreme Allied Commander; and Major-General G. E. Stratemeyer, Commanding General, U.S.A.A.F., India-Burma Sector, dated 11th December 1943

S.E.A.C. Directive No. 5

Pursuant to agreements reached in conference and discussions at SEXTANT with the Commanding General, U.S. Army Air Forces (General H. H. Arnold), the U.S. Chief of Staff (General George C. Marshall), and the British Chief of Air Staff (Sir Charles Portal), I am publishing the following:

1. In order to ensure the effective operational direction of the R.A.F. and the U.S.A.A.F. in this theatre, I have decided to integrate certain elements of the 10th U.S. Air Force and the R.A.F., based upon the following premises:
(a) The 10th U.S. Air Force and the R.A.F. are hereby placed under the unified command of the Air Commander-in-Chief.
(b) The combined air forces so integrated will form a subordinate air command to be known as the Eastern Air Command, consisting initially of the R.A.F. Bengal Command, and the 10th U.S. Air Force. The Commanding General U.S.A.A.F., I.-B. Sector, C.B.I. Theatre, is designated to command the Eastern Air Command.
2. The command of the 14th U.S. Air Force will remain under the Deputy Supreme Allied Commander.
3. Within the Eastern Air Command there will be included:
(a) A Tactical Air Force under the operational command of the present Air Officer Commanding, Bengal Command.
(b) A Strategical Air Force under the operational control of the Commanding General, 10th U.S. Air Force.
(c) Such other grouping as the Air Commander, Eastern Air Command, desires to make.
4. In exercising operational control of these integrated forces, the respective commanders will observe the following principles:
(a) The integrity of U.S.A.A.F. Groups and R.A.F. Wings will be retained.
(b) Administrative control and responsibilities for supply will remain under the respective U.S. and R.A.F. commanders.
5. The Air Commander-in-Chief in exercising his operational control, is specifically given the responsibility for the defence of all U.S. Air Transport Command facilities in the I.-B. Sector of S.E.A.C.
6. Co-ordination of planning and the operations between Commanding General, Eastern Air Command, and the 14th U.S. Air Force will be arranged through the Deputy Supreme Allied Commander and the Air Commander in Chief.

Source: Vice-Admiral the Earl Mountbatten of Burma, *Report to the Combined Chiefs of Staff by the Supreme Allied Commander South-East Asia, 1943–1945*, Appendix E, p. 229.

APPENDIX 4

EASTERN AIR COMMAND, GENERAL ORDERS NO. 1

15 December 1943

Headquarters Eastern Air Command, 15 December 1943
General Orders No. 1

1. Pursuant to instructions contained in South East Asia Command Directive No. 5, Headquarters S.E.A.C., dated 12 December 1943, and Policy Directive No. 1, Headquarters, Eastern Air Command, dated 15 December 1943, I hereby assume command of Eastern Air Command.
2. The Eastern Air Command will consist of units of the Tenth Air Force and units of the Bengal Air Command.
3. The Eastern Air Command will be organized into four components:
   a. A Strategic Air Force under the operational control of Brigadier General Howard C. Davidson.
   b. A Tactical Air Force under the operational control of Air Marshal Sir John Baldwin.
   c. A Troop Carrier Command under the operational control of Brigadier General William D. Old.
   d. A Photographic Reconnaissance Force under the operational control of (to be announced).
4. The missions of the respective components of Eastern Air Command are as follows:
   a. Strategic Air Force: The commander, Strategic Air Force, will conduct strategic air offensive over Burma and adjacent territory in conformity with a general plan to destroy enemy air forces and air installations; selected rail, river, and road communications; depots and other maintenance facilities.
   b. Tactical Air Force: The commander, Tactical Air Force, is charged with full responsibility for the defence of Calcutta and adjacent industrial areas, the Assam area and the Air Transport Command India-China transport route, and in addition has full responsibility for the air support of Army and Amphibious operations.
   c. Troop Carrier Command: The commander, Troop Carrier Command, will provide air transportation for airborne and air transit forces in the support and training of the Army Group and other land or air forces involved in operations in Burma.
   d. Photographic Reconnaissance Force: The commander, Photographic Reconnaissance Force, will conduct photographic and tactical reconnaissance as required for the support of the Strategic Air Force, the Tactical Air Force or the Army Group forces. Individual units of the Photographic Reconnaissance Force will be attached to and placed under the operational control of the commanders Strategic and Tactical Air Forces as required.
5. In exercising operational control of these integrated forces, the respective commanders will observe the following principles:

a. Administrative control and responsibilities for supply and maintenance will remain under the respective USAAF and RAF commanders.
b. The integrity of USAAF Groups and RAF Wings will be retained.
c. The operational staffs of the respective force commanders will consist of USAAF and RAF personnel in such proportion as deemed necessary and desirable by the respective force commanders.
6. The Strategic Air Force, Tactical Air Force, Troop Carrier Command and Photographic Reconnaissance Force will consist initially of the units listed in Inclosure 2 attached. Station locations and certain unit designations, as listed in Inclosure 2, are tentative and may necessarily be changed by Force Commanders as circumstances require.
7. It is desired that military personnel of this command, both RAF and AAF, comply with customary rules of military courtesy in their dealings with one another. Personnel of the USAAF will render the salute to RAF personnel and it is the wish of the commander, Eastern Air Command, that RAF do likewise to USAAF personnel.

8. A resourceful, wily and able enemy must be blasted from the jungles of Burma and driven from its skies in the days to come. His line of communication must be obliterated, his shipping destroyed, his will to resist crushed. Against the inevitable day of retribution when Japan's cities will meet the fate of Berlin, our life line to China must be strengthened and protected. Every ounce of energy of every man in this Command will be required to accomplish this purpose. We must merge into one unified force, in thought and in deed—a force neither British nor American, with the faults of neither and the virtues of both. There is no time for distrust or suspicion.

   I greet the forces of the Bengal Air Command, and their Commander, Air Marshal Baldwin, as comrades in battle, as brothers in the air. A standard of cooperation which we must strive to surpass has been set by the inspiring example of joint achievement of our colleagues in the Northwest African Air Force. We must establish in Asia a record of Allied victory of which we can all be proud in the years to come. Let us write it now in the skies over Burma.

George E. Stratemeyer
Major General, U.S.A.
Commanding

Source: Air 23/1933, National Archives, Kew, UK.

APPENDIX 5

EASTERN AIR COMMAND ORDER OF BATTLE

12 December 1943

Headquarters, Air Command, SEA (Air Chief Marshal Sir Richard Peirse, R.A.F.)
Eastern Air Command (Maj. Gen. George Stratemeyer, U.S.A.A.F.)
3rd Tactical Air Force (Air Marshal Sir John Baldwin, R.A.F.)
221 Group, Imphal (Air Commodore H. V. Rowley, R.A.F.)
168 Wing
42 Squadron   Hurricane IV
45 Squadron   Vengeance
84 Squadron   Vengeance
110 Squadron   Vengeance
170 Wing
5 Squadron   Hurricane IIc
28 Squadron   Hurricane IIb
34 Squadron   Hurricane IIc
155 Squadron   Mohawk IV
224 Group, Chittagong (Air Commodore A. Gray, R.A.F.)
165 Wing
20 Squadron   Hurricane IId
6 Indian Air Force Sqd.   Hurricane IIb
261 Squadron   Hurricane IIc
136 Squadron   Spitfire Vc
607 Squadron   Spitfire Vc
166 Wing
79 Squadron   Hurricane IIc
258 Squadron   Hurricane IIc
615 Squadron   Spitfire Vc
167 Wing
82 Squadron   Vengeance
8 Indian Air Force Sqd.   Vengeance
177 Squadron   Beaufighter VI, X
169 Wing
27 Squadron   Beaufighter VI, X
60 Squadron   Hurricane IIc
234 Wing
11 Squadron   Hurricane IIc
293 Wing
67 Squadron   Hurricane
146 Squadron   Hurricane IIb
176 Squadron   Beaufighter NF, Hurricane IIc

Northern Air Sector Force, Dinjan (Col. J. F. Egan, U.S.A.A.F.)
80th Fighter Group
88th, 89th, 90th Fighter Squadrons   P-40N
459th Fighter Squadron   P-38H
311th Fighter-Bomber Group
528th, 529th Fighter-Bomber Squadrons   A-36A/P-51A
530th Fighter-Bomber Squadron   P-51A
71st Liaison Squadron   L-1/L-5
Strategic Air Force (Brig. Gen. Howard C. Davidson, U.S.A.A.F.)
7th Bombardment Group (H)
9th, 436th, 492nd, 493rd Bomb Squadrons   B-24D
341st Bombardment Group (M)
22nd, 490th, 491st Bomb Squadrons   B-25C/D/G
175 Wing
99 Squadron   Wellington III, X
215 Squadron   Wellington III, X
184 Wing
159 Squadron   Liberator III
Troop Carrier Command (Brig. Gen. William D. Old, U.S.A.A.F.)
1st Troop Carrier Squadron   C-47
2nd Troop Carrier Squadron   C-47
31 Squadron   Dakota
62 Squadron   Dakota
117 Squadron   Dakota
194 Squadron   Dakota
Photographic Reconnaissance Force (Grp. Capt. S. G. Wise, R.A.F.)
9th Photographic Reconnaissance Squadron   F-4
171 Wing
681 Squadron   Spitfire IV/XI
684 Squadron   Mosquito IV

Source: Christopher Shores, *Air War for Burma: The Allied Air Forces Fight Back in South-East Asia, 1942–1945* (London: Grub Street, 2005), 388–89.

APPENDIX 6

JAPANESE AIR ORDER OF BATTLE IN BURMA

November 1943

5th Hikōshidan (Air Division)	
33rd Hikōsentai (Fighter)	Type 1 Fighter Mark II (Oscar)
204th Hikōsentai (Fighter)	Type 1 Fighter Mark II (Oscar)
4th Hikōdan (Air Brigade)	
50th Hikōsentai (Fighter)	Type I Fighter Mark II (Oscar)
8th Hikōsentai (Light Bomber)	Type 99 Light Bomber (Lily)
34th Hikōsentai (Light Bomber)	Type 99 Light Bomber (Lily)
7th Hikōdan (Air Brigade)	
64th Hikōsentai (Fighter)	Type I Fighter Mark II (Oscar)
12th Hikōsentai (Heavy Bomber)	Type 97 Heavy Bomber Mark III (Sally)
98th Hikōsentai (Heavy Bomber)	Type 97 Heavy Bomber Mark III (Sally)
81st Hikōsentai (Reconnaissance)	Type 100 Command Reconnaissance Mark II (Dinah)
21st Hikōsentai (Fighter)	Type 2 Two-seater Fighter (Nick)

Source: Major General S. Woodburn Kirby, *The War against Japan*, vol. 3, *The Decisive Battles* (London: Her Majesty's Stationery Office, 1961), appendix 7, p. 463.

APPENDIX 7

EASTERN AIR COMMAND ORDER OF BATTLE

December 1944

Headquarters, Air Command SEA (Air Marshal Sir Guy Garrod, R.A.F.)
Eastern Air Command (Maj. Gen. George Stratemeyer, U.S.A.A.F.)
221 Group, Imphal (Air Vice-Marshal S. F. Vincent, R.A.F.)
906 Wing
1 Indian Air Force Sqd.	Hurricane IIc
42 Squadron	Hurricane IIc
60 Squadron	Hurricane IIc

907 Wing
11 Squadron	Hurricane IIc
152 Squadron	Spitfire VIII

908 Wing
45 Squadron	Mosquito VI

909 Wing
17 Squadron	Spitfire VIII
155 Squadron	Spitfire VIII
607 Squadron	Spitfire VIII
34 Squadron	Hurricane IIc
113 Squadron	Hurricane IIc

910 Wing
79 Squadron	Thunderbolt
146 Squadron	Thunderbolt
261 Squadron	Thunderbolt

224 Group, Cox's Bazar (Air Vice-Marshal the Earl of Bandon, R.A.F.)
901 Wing
27 Squadron	Beaufighter X
177 Squadron	Beaufighter X
211 Squadron	Beaufighter X

902 Wing
9 Indian Air Force Sqd.	Hurricane IIc
30 Squadron	Thunderbolt
135 Squadron	Thunderbolt
459th Fighter Squadron	P-38J
67 Squadron	Spitfire VIII

904 Wing
2 Indian Air Force Sqd.	Hurricane IIc
4 Indian Air Force Sqd.	Hurricane IIc
273 Squadron	Spitfire VIII

905 Wing
134 Squadron	Thunderbolt
258 Squadron	Thunderbolt

Tenth Air Force (Maj. Gen. Howard C. Davidson, U.S.A.A.F.)
80th Fighter Group
88th, 89th, 90th Fighter Squadrons	P-47D

33rd Fighter Group
58th Fighter Squadron	P-38J
59th, 60th Fighter Squadrons	P-47D
490th Bomb Squadron (M)	B-25H/J

3rd Combat Cargo Group
9th, 10th, 11th, 12th Combat Cargo Squadrons	C-47

443rd Troop Carrier Group
1st, 2nd, 315th Troop Carrier Squadrons	C-47

1st Liaison Group (Provisional)
5th Liaison Squadron	L-1/L-5
71st Liaison Squadron	L-1/L-5
115th Liaison Squadron	L-1-L-5

Combat Cargo Task Force (Brig. Gen. F. W. Evans, U.S.A.A.F.)
1st Combat Cargo Group
1st Combat Cargo Squadron	C-47
2nd Combat Cargo Squadron	C-47
3rd Combat Cargo Squadron	C-47
4th Combat Cargo Squadron	C-47

4th Combat Cargo Group
13th Combat Cargo Squadron	C-46
14th Combat Cargo Squadron	C-46
15th Combat Cargo Squadron	C-46
16th Combat Cargo Squadron	C-46

177 (Transport) Wing R.A.F.
31 Squadron	Dakota
62 Squadron	Dakota
117 Squadron	Dakota
194 Squadron	Dakota

1st Air Commando Group
5th Fighter Squadron (Commando)	P-47D
6th Fighter Squadron (Commando)	P-47D
164th Liaison Squadron	L-4/L-5
165th Liaison Squadron	L-4/L-5
166th Liaison Squadron	L-4/L-5
319th Troop Carrier Sqd. (Commando)	C-47

2nd Air Commando Group (Assigned)
1st Fighter Squadron (Commando)	P-51D
2nd Fighter Squadron (Commando)	P-51D
127th Liaison Squadron	L-4/L-5
155th Liaison Squadron	L-4/L-5
156th Liaison Squadron	L-4/L-5
317th Troop Carrier Sqd. (Commando)	C-47

Strategic Air Force (Air Commodore F. J. Mellersh, R.A.F.)
7th Bombardment Group (H)
9th Bombardment Squadron	B-24J
436th Bombardment Squadron	B-24J
492nd Bombardment Squadron	B-24J
493rd Bombardment Squadron	B-24J

12th Bombardment Group (M)

81st Bombardment Squadron	B-25H/J
82nd Bombardment Squadron	B-25H/J
83rd Bombardment Squadron	B-25H/J
434th Bombardment Squadron	B-25H/J
175 Wing	
99 Squadron	Liberator VI
184 Wing	
355 Squadron	Liberator VI
356 Squadron	Liberator VI
185 Wing	
159 Squadron	Liberator VI
215 Squadron	Liberator VI
357 Squadron	Liberator VI

Photographic Reconnaissance Force (Grp. Capt. S. G. Wise, R.A.F.)

8th Photographic Reconnaissance Group	
9th Photographic Reconnaissance Squadron	F-5E/G
20th Tactical Reconnaissance Squadron	P-40N
24th Combat Mapping Squadron	F-7
40th Photographic Reconnaissance Sqd.	F-5E/G
171 Wing	
681 (P.R.) Squadron	Spitfire XI
684 (P.R.) Squadron	Mosquito
293 Wing: Air Defence of Calcutta	
89 Squadron	Beaufighter NF
615 Squadron	Spitfire VIII

Sources: Major General S. Woodburn Kirby, *The War against Japan*, vol. 4, *The Reconquest of Burma* (London: Her Majesty's Stationery Office, 1965), appendix 4, pp. 441–43; Christopher Shores, *Air War for Burma: The Allied Air Forces Fight Back in South-East Asia, 1942–1945* (London: Grub Street, 2005), 394–96.

NOTES

Introduction

1. John Ehrman, *Grand Strategy*, vol. 5, *August 1943–September 1944* (London: Her Majesty's Stationery Office, 1956), 122.
2. Ibid., 129–30.
3. Ibid., 129.
4. Richard M. Leighton and Robert W. Coakley, *Global Logistics and Strategy, 1940–1943*, United States Army in World War II: The War Department (Washington, DC: Office of the Chief of Military History, US Department of the Army, 1955), 537–38; Robert W. Coakley and Richard M. Leighton, *Global Logistics and Strategy, 1943–1945*, United States Army in World War II: The War Department (Washington, DC: Office of the Chief of Military History, US Department of the Army, 1968), 500.
5. Ehrman, *Grand Strategy*, 5:129.
6. Michael Schaller, *The US Crusade in China, 1938–1945* (New York: Columbia University Press, 1979), 94.
7. Christopher Thorne, *Allies of a Kind: The United States, Britain, and the War against Japan, 1941–1945* (London: Hamish Hamilton, 1978), 206–207.
8. Ibid., 226.
9. Ehrman, *Grand Strategy*, 5:126; Thorne, *Allies of a Kind*, 184–86.
10. Chinese Ministry of Information, *China Handbook, 1937–1945* (New York: Macmillan, 1946), 301.
11. Michael A. Barnhart, *Japan Prepares for Total War: The Search for Economic Security, 1919–1941* (Ithaca, NY: Cornell University Press, 1987), 91; Chinese Ministry of Information: *China Handbook, 1937–1945*, 300; F. F. Liu, *A Military History of Modern China, 1924–1949* (Princeton, NJ: Princeton University Press, 1956), 209.
12. Schaller, *US Crusade in China*, 125–26; Wesley M. Bagby, *The Eagle-Dragon Alliance: America's Relations with China in World War II* (Newark: University of Delaware Press, 1992), 39, 46–47.
13. Charles F. Romanus and Riley Sunderland, *United States Army in World War II: China-Burma-India Theater*, vol. 1, *Stilwell's Mission to China* (Washington, DC: Office of the Chief of Military History, Department of the Army, 1953), 34.
14. Hans J. van de Ven, *War and Nationalism in China, 1925–1945* (London: RoutledgeCurzon, 2003), 274–75, 295.
15. Youli Sun, *China and the Origins of the Pacific War, 1931–1941* (New York: St. Martin's, 1993), 90.

CHAPTER 1:
Formation and Early Operations: December 1941–June 1942

1. Schaller, *US Crusade in China*, ix.
2. Ibid., 4.
3. Ibid., 31–32, 36.
4. Romanus and Sunderland, *United States Army in World War II: China-Burma-India Theater*, 1:8.
5. Ibid., p. 8, 11.
6. *New York Times*, 16 March 1941; Maurice Matloff and Edwin M. Snell, *Strategic Planning for Coalition Warfare, 1941–1942*, United States Army in World War II: The War Department (Washington, DC: Center of Military History, US Army, 1953), 63.
7. Romanus and Sunderland, *United States Army in World War II: China-Burma-India Theater*, 1:10.
8. Ibid., 11, fn. 15.
9. Ibid., 12.
10. Romanus and Sunderland, *United States Army in World War II: China-Burma-India Theater*, 1:17–19; Daniel Ford, *Flying Tigers: Claire Chennault and the American Volunteer Group* (Washington, DC: Smithsonian Institution Press, 1991), 54–61.
11. Ford, *Flying Tigers*, 68–70.
12. Romanus and Sunderland, *United States Army in World War II: China-Burma-India Theater*, 1:20.
13. Ibid., 16–17, 25–27.
14. Ibid., 25–30.
15. Ibid., 23.
16. Schaller, 61–63, 90–91.
17. Tomatsu Haruo, "The Strategic Correlation between the Sino-Japanese and Pacific Wars," in *The Battle for China: Essays on the Military History of the Sino-Japanese War of 1937–1945*, eds. Mark Peattie, Edward J. Drea, and Hans van de Ven (Stanford, CA: Stanford University Press, 2011), 423–45.
18. Liu, *A Military History of Modern China*, 209.
19. Ronald H. Spector, *Eagle against the Sun: The American War with Japan* (New York: Macmillan, 1985), 329–30; J. M. Gwyer, *Grand Strategy*, vol. 3, part 1, *June 1941–August 1942* (London: Her Majesty's Stationery Office, 1964), 332.
20. Ehrman, *Grand Strategy*, 5:124.
21. Spector, *Eagle against the Sun*, 326.
22. Ronald Spector, "The Sino-Japanese War in the Context of World History," in *The Battle for China: Essays on the Military History of the Sino-Japanese War of 1937–1945*, eds. Mark Peattie, Edward J. Drea, and Hans van de Ven (Stanford, CA: Stanford University Press, 2011), 467–81.

23. Schaller, *US Crusade in China*, 88.
24. Romanus and Sunderland, *United States Army in World War II: China-Burma-India Theater*, 1:50–51.
25. Ibid., 1:52; Matloff and Snell, *Strategic Planning for Coalition Warfare, 1941–1942*, 86.
26. Romanus and Sunderland, *United States Army in World War II: China-Burma-India Theater*, 1:55–57.
27. Matloff and Snell, *Strategic Planning for Coalition Warfare, 1941–1942*, 87.
28. Ibid., 99,
29. Ibid., 121–22.
30. David Rigby, *Allied Master Strategists: The Combined Chiefs of Staff in World War II* (Annapolis, MD: US Naval Institute, 2012), 49–51.
31. Matloff and Snell, *Strategic Planning for Coalition Warfare, 1941–1942*, 123.
32. Wesley Frank Craven and James Lea Cate, eds., *The Army Air Forces in World War II*, vol. 1, *Plans and Early Operations, January 1939 to August 1942* (Chicago: University of Chicago Press, 1948), 370.
33. Matloff and Snell, *Strategic Planning for Coalition Warfare, 1941–1942*, 123.
34. Romanus and Sunderland, *United States Army in World War II: China-Burma-India Theater*, 1:61–62.
35. Ibid., 62.
36. Ibid., 66.
37. Ibid., 63–65.
38. Ibid., 70.
39. Ibid., 73.
40. Ibid., 74.
41. Ibid., 75.
42. Ford, *Flying Tigers*, 93–94.
43. General of the Air Force Henry H. Arnold, *Global Mission* (New York: Harper, 1949), 279.
44. Martha Byrd, *Chennault: Giving Wings to the Tiger* (Tuscaloosa: University of Alabama Press, 1987), 137–38.
45. China-Burma-India (CBI): USAAF, India-Burma theater (IBT), "History of Air Operations on the Continent of Asia, December 1941–May 1946," vol. 2, section 1, AFHRA 825.01C, A8154, reel 9948, p. 107, frame 850
46. Ibid., 119, frame 863.
47. Byrd, *Chennault*, 140–41.
48. CBI: USAAF, IBT, "History of Air Operations on the Continent of Asia December 1941–May 1946," frame 864.
49. Norman L. R. Franks and Frank W. Bailey, *Over the Front: A Complete Record of the Fighter Aces and Units of the United States and French Air Services, 1914–1918* (London: Grub Street, 1992), 24.
50. Robert P. Fogerty, *Biographical Data on Air Force General Officers, 1917–1952*, vol. 1, *A through K*, US Air Force Numbered Historical Studies 91 (Manhattan, KS: MA/AH, 1953).
51. Byrd, *Chennault: Giving Wings to the Tiger*, 143.
52. Byrd, *Chennault: Giving Wings to the Tiger*, 142; Major General (Ret'd) Claire Lee Chennault, *Way of a Fighter* (New York: G. P. Putnam's Sons, 1949), 170.
53. Arnold, *Global Mission*, 419; CBI: USAAF, IBT, "History of Air Operations on the Continent of Asia, December 1941–May 1946," 122, frame 865.
54. Byrd, *Chennault*, 149.
55. Memorandum for the Chief of Staff, Establishment of an American Air Force in India, Assistant Chief of Air Staff, February 21, 1942, Assistant Chief of Air Staff, Plans (WP-IV-D-4 (India Book I), AFHRA 145.95, A1472, R2900, frame 487, Air Force Historical Research Agency (AFHRA), Maxwell AFB, AL.
56. Colonel Harold L. George, Assistant Chief of Air Staff, Air War Plans, to Lt. General Henry H. Arnold, Chief of Army Air Forces, "Organization of an Air Task Force in India," 19 February 1942, Assistant Chief of Air Staff, Plans (WP-IV-D-4 (India Book I), AFHRA 145.95, A1472, R2900, frame 494.
57. George to Arnold, "Organization of an Air Task Force in India," 19 February 1942.
58. Air Commodore Henry Probert, *The Forgotten Air Force: The Royal Air Force in the War against Japan, 1941–1945* (London: Brassey's, 1995), 108–109.
59. Ibid., 109.
60. Ibid., 110.
61. Ibid., 107.
62. George to Arnold, "Organization of an Air Task Force in India," 19 February 1942.
63. Ibid.
64. Ibid.
65. Craven and Cate, 1:388.
66. Ibid.
67. Ibid.
68. Cable from Maj. General George Brett to Chief, Army Air Forces, ABDA 418, 18 February 1942, Assistant Chief of Air Staff, Plans (WP-IV-D-4 [India Book I]), AFHRA 145.95, A1472, R2900, frame 513.
69. Cable from Maj. General George Brett to Chief, Army Air Forces, ABDA 418, 18 February 1942.
70. Brett's decision is inferred from Air War Plans Division correspondence mentioning Brereton as commander of the proposed Tenth Air Force prior to his official appointment to the position. See Lt. General Henry H. Arnold to Colonel Caleb V. Haynes, Headquarters, Army Air Force, Letter of Instruction, February 21, 1942, Assistant Chief of Air Staff, Plans (WP-IV-D-4 [India Book I]), AFHRA 145.95, A1472, R2900, frames 491–92.
71. Fogerty, *Biographical Data on Air Force General Officers, 1917–1952*, vol. 1, *A through K*.
72. William H. Bartsch, *Doomed at the Start: American Pursuit Pilots in the Philippines, 1941–1942* (College Station: Texas A&M University Press, 1992), 4.
73. Craven and Cate, 1:178, 182–83.
74. Bartsch, William H., *December 8, 1941: MacArthur's Pearl Harbor* (College Station: Texas A&M University Press, 2003), 442; Craven and Cate, 1:366.
75. Lt. General Lewis H. Brereton, *The Brereton Diaries: The War in the Air in the Pacific, Middle East and Europe, 3 October 1941–8 May 1945* (New York: William Morrow, 1946), 88.

76. Brereton, *The Brereton Diaries*, 88, 97–98.
77. Romanus and Sunderland, *United States Army in World War II: China-Burma-India Theater*, 1:92; Major General Brehon Somervell, Assistant Chief of Staff, Memorandum for the Adjutant General, Designation of Commanding General, S.O.S., United States Army Forces in India, 27 February 1942, Assistant Chief of Air Staff, Plans (WP-IV-D-4 [India Book I]), AFHRA 145.95, A1472, R2900, frames 472–75.
78. Major General Brehon Somervell, Assistant Chief of Staff, Memorandum for the Adjutant General, Designation of Commanding General, S.O.S., United States Army Forces in India, 27 February 1942.
79. Romanus and Sunderland, *United States Army in World War II: China-Burma-India Theater*, 1:92.
80. Craven and Cate, 1:396–97.
81. CBI: USAAF, IBT, "History of Air Operations on the Continent of Asia, December 1941–May 1946," vol. 2, section 1, AFHRA 825.01C, A8154, reel 9948, p. 169, frame 928.
82. Adjutant General to Chief of the Army Air Forces, Assignment of Code Designations, 20 February 1942, Assistant Chief of Air Staff, Plans (WP-IV-D-4 [India Book I]), AFHRA 145.95, A1472, R2900, frame 503.
83. Lt. General Henry H. Arnold, Deputy Chief of Staff for Air, to Colonel Caleb V. Haynes, Headquarters, Army Air Forces, 21 February 1942, Assistant Chief of Air Staff, Plans (WP-IV-D-4 [India Book I]), AFHRA 145.95, A1472, R2900, frames 499–500.
84. Arnold to Haynes, 21 February 1942.
85. Memorandum for the Chief of Staff, Establishment of an American Air Force in India, 24 February 1942, Assistant Chief of Air Staff, Plans (WP-IV-D-4 [India Book I]), AFHRA 145.95, A1472, R2900, frames 487–88.
86. Cablegram to General Lewis H. Brereton from Arnold, 25 February 1942, Assistant Chief of Air Staff, Plans (WP-IV-D-4 [India Book I]), AFHRA 145.95, A1472, R2900, frame 465.
87. James W. Walker, *The Liberandos: A World War II History of the 376th Bomb Group (H) and Its Founding Units* (Waco, TX: 376th Heavy Bombardment Group Veterans Association, 1994), 2–3, 10.
88. CBI: USAAF, IBT, "History of Air Operations on the Continent of Asia, December 1941–May 1946," vol. 2, section 1, AFHRA 825.01C, A8154, reel 9948, pp. 170–72, frames 928–31.
89. Colonel Robert L. Scott Jr., *God Is My Co-pilot* (New York: Charles Scribner's Sons, 1943), 47, 50: Craven and Cate, 1:493.
90. Colonel Scott describes this flight in detail in his book *God Is My Co-pilot*; see chapters 8–10, pp. 55–82.
91. Romanus and Sunderland, *United States Army in World War II: China-Burma-India Theater*, 1:78–79.
92. Edward M. Young, *Death from Above: The 7th Bombardment Group in World War II* (Atglen, PA: Schiffer, 2014), 91; William H. Bartsch, *Every Day a Nightmare: American Pursuit Pilots in the Defense of Java, 1941–1942* (College Station: Texas A&M University Press, 2010), 200–201.
93. Walter D. Edmonds, *They Fought with What They Had* (Boston: Little, Brown, 1951), 370.
94. Bartsch, *Every Day a Nightmare*, 275.
95. Brereton, *The Brereton Diaries*, 99.
96. Ibid., 105.
97. Ibid., 105–106.
98. Ibid., 106.
99. Lauchlin Currie to President Roosevelt, Re: The Defense of Burma, 9 December 1941, Assistant Chief of Air Staff, Plans (WP-IV-D-4 [India Book I]), AFHRA 145.95, A1472, R2900, frames 930–31.
100. J. R. M. Butler, *Grand Strategy*, vol. 3, part 2, *June 1941–August 1942* (London: Her Majesty's Stationery Office, 1964), 464.
101. Maj. Gen. S. Woodburn Kirby, *The War against Japan*, vol. 2, *India's Most Dangerous Hour* (London: Her Majesty's Stationery Office, 1958), 26.
102. Ibid., 23, 25.
103. Ibid., 24–26.
104. Ibid.; see chapters 2, 4, and 5 for a description of the loss of lower Burma and Rangoon.
105. Memorandum for the Chief of Staff, Establishment of an American Air Force in India, 24 February 1942, Assistant Chief of Air Staff, Plans (WP-IV-D-4 [India Book I]), AFHRA 145.95, A1472, R2900, frames 482–83.
106. Craven and Cate, 1:493; Brereton, *The Brereton Diaries*, 108; and Assistant Chief of Air Staff, Intelligence, Historical Division, *The Tenth Air Force 1942*, Army Air Forces Historical Studies 12 (1944), 10. The exact number is unclear; Craven and Cate list eight B-17s, while Brereton mentions two B-24s, two LB-30s, and one B-17 as the only planes available in early March 1942. The US Air Force's historical study on the Tenth Air Force in 1942 mentions one LB-30 and seven B-17s.
107. Brereton, *The Brereton Diaries*, 108.
108. Craven and Cate, 1:493.
109. Maj. Gen. Lewis Brereton to Lt. General H. H. Arnold, Chief of the Army Air Forces, War Department, Washington, DC, 6 March 1942, Henry Harley Arnold Papers, Manuscript Division, Library of Congress, Washington, DC (hereinafter referred to as Arnold Papers), reel 200, p. Folder China-Burma-India Theater, 1941–1944.
110. Brereton to Arnold, 6 March 1942.
111. Ibid.
112. Ibid.
113. "51st Fighter Group, Jan 1942–Mar 1943," AFHRA, GP-51-HI, B0145, reel 1249.
114. Headquarters, 25th Fighter Squadron, 51st Fighter Group, Unit History for March 1942, SQ-FI-25-HI, A0727, reel 765, AFHRA.
115. "51st Fighter Group, Jan 1942–Mar 1943."
116. Maj. Gen. Brehon Somervell, Assistant Chief of Staff, Memorandum for the Adjutant General, Designation of Commanding General, SOS, United States Army Forces in India, 27 February 1942.
117. Romanus and Sunderland, *United States Army in World War II: China-Burma-India Theater*, 1:205.

118. Headquarters 7th Bombardment Group (H), "Consolidated History of the Seventh Bombardment Group (H), AAF, Ground and Air Echelons for the Year 1942," GP-7-HI (1942), B0060, reel 1144, AFHRA.
119. "History of Air Operations on the Continent of Asia, December 1941–May 1946," vol. 2, section 1, frame 801.
120. "Consolidated History of the Seventh Bombardment Group (H), AAF, Ground and Air Echelons for the Year 1942."
121. "Consolidated History of the Seventh Bombardment Group (H), AAF, Ground and Air Echelons for the Year 1942."
122. "51st Fighter Group, Jan 1942–Mar 1943."
123. Office of Statistical Control, *Army Air Forces Statistical Digest World War II*, 2nd printing (December 1945), 173.
124. "51st Fighter Group, Jan 1942–Mar 1943"; Lt. Col. John E. Barr to Commanding General 10th Air Force, Report on Special P–40 Mission Project 157, 19 June 1942, 830.01 Tenth Air Force History, A8224A, reel 10019, frames 324–28, AFHRA.
125. Lt. Col. John E. Barr to Commanding General 10th Air Force, Report on Special P–40 Mission Project 157, 19 June 1942.
126. "51st Fighter Group, Jan 1942–Mar 1943"; Craven and Cate, 1:494.
127. Maj. Gen. Lewis Brereton, Cable of 24 March 1942, to AGWAR for AFNAG, Army Air Force, India-Burma Theater, Miscellaneous Correspondence, 825.161, A8157, R9951, frames 649–57, AFHRA.
128. Brereton cable of 24 March 1942; *The Tenth Air Force 1942*, 22–23.
129. Craven and Cate, 1:495.
130. *The Tenth Air Force 1942*, 21–23.
131. Maj. Gen. Lewis Brereton, Tenth Air Force, New Delhi, to Adjutant General, 28 March 1942, Assistant Chief of Air Staff, Plans (WP-IV-D-4 [India Book I]), AFHRA 145.95, A1472, R2900, frames 396–97.
132. Lt. Gen. Henry H. Arnold, Commanding General, Army Air Forces, to General Harmon, Allocation of Planes for Overseas Operations, 2 April 1942, Arnold Papers, reel 124, folder 7, England.
133. Unit History Covering Period from June 26, 1917, to June 1, 1943, 11th Bombardment Squadron (M), 341st Bomb Group (M), 14th Air Force, SQ-Bomb-11-HI, A0538, reel 0561, AFHRA; Historical Data, 22nd Bombardment Squadron (M) AAF, 341st Bomb Group (M) AAF, Squadron History, November 1938–December 1943, SQ-Bomb-22-HI, A0543, reel 0567, AFHRA.
134. Unit History Covering Period from June 26, 1917, to June 1, 1943, 11th bombardment Squadron (M), 341st Bomb Group (M), 14th Air Force, SQ-Bomb-11-HI; Historical Data, 22nd Bombardment Squadron (M) AAF, 341st Bomb Group (M) AAF, Squadron History, November 1938–December 1943, SQ-Bomb-22-HI.
135. Minutes of an Administrative Planning Conference, 15 March 1942, Minutes of Meetings of the Administrative Planning Committee, 15–30 March 1942, 802.151-1 Air Headquarters, India, A8011, reel 9801, AFHRA.
136. Minutes of an Administrative Planning Conference, 15 March 1942.
137. Minutes of the 3rd Meeting of the Administrative Planning Committee, 30 March 1942, Minutes of Meetings of the Administrative Planning Committee, 15–30 March 1942, 802.151-1 Air Headquarters, India, A8011, reel 9801, AFHRA.
138. Probert, *The Forgotten Air Force*, 110–12.
139. Brereton, *The Brereton Diaries*, 116.
140. Romanus and Sunderland, *United States Army in World War II: China-Burma-India Theater*, 1:202–203.
141. *The Tenth Air Force 1942*, 19, 39.
142. *The Tenth Air Force 1942*, 40–41; Minutes of Meeting at Mr. Coates's Office, 19 March 1942, Minutes of Meetings of the Administrative Planning Committee, 15–30 March 1942, 802.151-1 Air Headquarters, India, A8011, reel 9801, AFHRA.
143. Romanus and Sunderland, *United States Army in World War II: China-Burma-India Theater*, 1:116; Brereton, *The Brereton Diaries*, 114.
144. Brereton, *The Brereton Diaries*, 113–14.
145. Message No. 225 AQUILA, April 7, 1942, Assistant Chief of Air Staff, Plans (WP-IV-D-4 [India Book I]), AFHRA 145.95, A1472, R2900, frame 374.
146. Message No. 225 AQUILA, 7 April 1942.
147. Gen. Marshall to Gen. Brereton, 10 April 1942, Assistant Chief of Air Staff, Plans (WP-IV-D-4 [India Book I]), AFHRA 145.95, A1472, R2900, frames 364–65.
148. Kirby, *The War against Japan*, 2:145.
149. Christopher Shores and Brian Cull, with Yasuho Izawa, *Bloody Shambles*, vol. 2, *The Defence of Sumatra to the Fall of Burma* (London: Grub Street, 1993), 349.
150. "Air Vice-Marshal Stevenson's Dispatch on Air Operations, Burma and the Bay of Bengal, 1 January to 22 May 1942," in *Far East Air Operations, 1942–1945*, ed. John Grehan and Martin Mace, Despatches from the Front (Barnsley, UK: Pen & Sword, 2014), 35; Probert, *The Forgotten Air Force*, 92; Shores et al., *Bloody Shambles*, 2:350–55.
151. Shores et al., *Bloody Shambles*, 2:355–60.
152. Air Ministry to Royal Air Force Delegation, Washington, 27 March 1942, US Air Forces in India, Mar–Aug 1942, Air 8/654, Air Ministry and Ministry of Defence, Department of the Chief of the Air Staff: Registered Files, National Archives, Kew, UK.
153. Air Marshal D. C. S. Evill to Lt. Gen. H. H. Arnold, Chief of the Army Air Forces, 14 April 1942, Assistant Chief of Air Staff, Plans (WP-IV-D-4 [India Book I]), AFHRA 145.95, A1472, R2900, frame 354.
154. Royal Air Force Delegation, Washington, to Air Ministry, 29 March 1942; War Office to CinC, India, 31 March 1942, US Air Forces in India, Mar–Aug 1942, Air 8/654, Air Ministry and Ministry of Defence, Department of the Chief of the Air Staff: Registered Files.
155. Brereton, *The Brereton Diaries*, 114.
156. Ibid., 115.

157. Lt. E. O'Donnell, G-3, to Gen. Brereton, "Plan for Employment of One (1) Squadron in Attack on Concentration of Japanese Shipping Vicinity of Port Blair," 27 March 1942, Administrative History Documents for 1942, Army Air Forces, India-Burma, 12 February 1942–December 1945, AFHRA, 825.01, A8153, R9947, frames 342–43.
158. Brereton, *The Brereton Diaries*, 117.
159. Ibid.
160. Major Louis E. Hobbs, "Report Bombing Mission on Port Blair," 3 April 1942, G-2 Files, Memorandum/Unnumbered, 2 April–3 September 1942, Tenth Air Force, 830.3061-1, A8243, reel 10038, frame 73.
161. Young, *Death from Above*, 104.
162. *New York Times*, 6 April 1942: 1.
163. Romanus and Sunderland, *United States Army in World War II: China-Burma-India Theater*, 1:116.
164. Stilwell to Tenth Air Force, 8 April 1942, Administrative History Documents for 1942, Army Air Forces, India-Burma Sector, AFHRA 825.01, A8153, reel 9947, frame 355; *The Tenth Air Force 1942*, 26.
165. Romanus and Sunderland, *United States Army in World War II: China-Burma-India Theater*, 1:116.
166. Air Marshal D. C. S. Evill, British Joint Staff Mission, Washington, DC, to Lt. Gen. H. H. Arnold, Commanding General, Army Air Forces, 14 April 1942, Assistant Chief of Air Staff, Plans (WP-IV-D-4 [India Book I]), 145.95, AFHRA 145.95, A1472, R2900, frame 354; Lt. Gen. H. H. Arnold, Commanding General, Army Air Forces, to Air Marshal D. C. S. Evill, British Joint Staff Mission, 23 April 1942, Assistant Chief of Air Staff, Plans (WP-IV-D-4 [India Book I]), 145.95, AFHRA, A1472, R2900, frame 352.
167. Gen. Brereton, Tenth Air Force, to Gen. Arnold, 23 April 1942, Administrative History Documents for 1942, AFHRA 825.01, A8153, reel 9947, frame 363.
168. *The Tenth Air Force 1942*, 28.
169. Maj. Gen. Lewis Brereton, Tenth Air Force, to Adjutant General, War Department (AGWAR), 3 May 1942, China-Burma-India (CBI), US Army Air Force (USAAF), India-Burma Theater (IBT). Documents for History of Army Air Force in India, 12 February 1942–15 December 1943, Army Air Forces, India-Burma Sector, 825.01, A8153, reel 9947, frame 380.
170. Brereton to AGWAR, 3 May 1942.
171. *The Tenth Air Force 1942*, 30.
172. Notes on the mission of 16 April 1942 in G-2 Files, Memorandum/Unnumbered, 2 April–3 September 1942, Tenth Air Force, 830.3061-1, A8243, reel 10038, frame 71.
173. Captain Rowan T. Thomas, *Born in Battle: Round the World Adventures of the 513th Bomb Squadron* (Philadelphia: John C. Winston, 1944), 82.
174. Brig. Caleb V. Haynes, India Air Task Force, to Lt. Col. Samuel T. Moore, Historian, Tenth Air Force, 20 April 1943, History of the India-China Ferry under the Tenth Air Force, AFHRA 830.01, A8229, reel 10024.
175. Lt. Col. W. Urbach, Adjutant General, Tenth Air Force, 14 August 1942, History, 18 August 1917–December 1942, SQ-Bomb-436-HI, AFHRA, A0614, reel 0643.
176. "Consolidated History of the Seventh Bombardment Group (H), AAF, Ground and Air Echelons for the Year 1942."
177. Air Command, Southeast Asia Operational Research Section, "Bombing Operations 1941–1942 by R.A.F. and U.S.A.A.F. Units Based in India and Burma: Summary," Bombing Operations, April 1942, Air 23/2855, Air Ministry and Ministry of Defence, Royal Air Force Overseas Commands, Reports and Correspondence: Air Command Southeast Asia, National Archives, Kew, UK.
178. Air Command, Southeast Asia Operational Research Section, "Bombing Operations 1941–1942 by R.A.F. and U.S.A.A.F. Units Based in India and Burma: Summary," Bombing Operations May 1942.
179. Report of Bombardment Mission, 3 May 1942, Rangoon Area, G-2 Files, Memorandum/Unnumbered, 2 April–3 September 1942, Tenth Air Force, 830.3061-1, A8243, reel 10038, frame 67.
180. *The Tenth Air Force 1942*, 42; "Bombing Operations 1941–1942 by R.A.F. and U.S.A.A.F. Units Based in India and Burma: Summary"; Bombing Operations May 1942 lists only two B-17s attacking Mingaladon that night.
181. Combat Mission Report, 6 May 1942, Rangoon Area, G-2 Files, Memorandum/Unnumbered, 2 April–3 September 1942, Tenth Air Force, 830.3061-1, A8243, reel 10038, frame 64.
182. There is a discrepancy about the date of this mission. *The Tenth Air Force 1942* has this mission on May 9 (p. 42), while "Bombing Operations 1941–1942 by R.A.F. and U.S.A.A.F. Units Based in India and Burma: Summary," Bombing Operations May 1942, lists this as a daylight attack on 8 May 1942.
183. Col. William D Old to Chief of Staff, 13 May 1942, G-2 Files, Memorandum/Unnumbered, 2 April–3 September 1942, Tenth Air Force, 830.3061-1, A8243, reel 10038, frame 63; *The Tenth Air Force 1942*, 43.
184. Col. William D. Old to Chief of Staff, Combat Mission Report, 14 May and 16 May 1942, G-2 Files, Memorandum/Unnumbered, 2 April–3 September 1942, Tenth Air Force, 830.3061-1, A8243, reel 10038, frame 63; *The Tenth Air Force 1942*, 43.
185. Col. William D. Old to Commanding General, Tenth Air Force, 30 May 1942, Administrative History Documents for 1942, Army Air Forces, India-Burma Sector, AFHRA 825.01, A8153, reel 9947, frames 486–88.
186. Historical Data, 22nd Bombardment Squadron (M) AAF, 341st Bomb Group (M) AAF, Squadron History, November 1938–December 1943, SQ-Bomb-22-HI, A0543, reel 0567, AFHRA.
187. Col. William D Old to Chief of Staff, Combat Mission Reports, 27, 29, 30, 31 May, 1 June, and 4 June 1942, G-2 Files, Memorandum/Unnumbered, 2 April–3 September 1942, Tenth Air Force, 830.3061-1, A8243, reel 10038, frames 53–60, AFHRA; *The Tenth Air Force 1942*, 43–44.
188. Tenth Air Force Operational Diary, 1 June 1942–1 June 1943, Tenth Air Force 830.305-1, A8242, reel 10037, frame 1596, AFHRA.

189. Christopher Shores, *Air War for Burma: The Allied Air Forces Fight Back in Southeast Asia, 1942–1945* (London: Grub Street, 2005), 16.
190. Ibid., 16.
191. Thomas, *Born in Battle*, 119–20.
192. Thomas, *Born in Battle*, 122–26; *The Tenth Air Force 1942*, 44.
193. Maj. Gen. Lewis Brereton, Headquarters, Tenth Air Force, to Lt. General H. H. Arnold, Commander in Chief, Army Air Forces, 24 June 1942, Assistant Chief of Air Staff, Plans (WP-IV-D-4 [India Book I]), 145.95, AFHRA, A1472, R2900, frames 206–207.
194. "Bombing Operations 1941–1942 by R.A.F. and U.S.A.A.F. Units Based in India and Burma: Summary," Bombing Operations June 1942.
195. "Consolidated History of the Seventh Bombardment Group (H), AAF, Ground and Air Echelons for the Year 1942," 9.
196. Col. William D. Old to Chief of Staff, Tenth Air Force, 25 June 1942, G-2 Files, Memorandum/Unnumbered, 2 April–3 September 1942, Tenth Air Force, 830.3061-1, A8243, reel 10038, frame 49.
197. Kirby, *The War against Japan*, 2:210–214.
198. Col. William D. Old to Commanding General, Tenth Air Force, 30 May 1942, Administrative History Documents for 1942, Army Air Forces, India-Burma Sector, AFHRA 825.01, A8153, reel 9947, frames 486–88.
199. Col. William D. Old to Commanding General, Tenth Air Force, 30 May 1942.
200. Romanus and Sunderland, *United States Army in World War II: China-Burma-India Theater*, 1:76.
201. Ibid., 1:77.
202. John D. Plating, *The Hump: America's Strategy for Keeping China in World War II* (College Station: Texas A&M University Press, 2011), 35–36.
203. T. V. Soong, Minister of Foreign Affairs, to John J. McCloy, Assistant Secretary of War, War Department, 30 January 1942, Assistant Chief of Air Staff, Plans (WP-IV-D-4 [India Book I]), 145.95, AFHRA, A1472, R2900, frames 923–24.
204. William M. Leary Jr., *The Dragon's Wings: The China National Aviation Corporation and the Development of Commercial Aviation in China* (Athens, GA: University of Georgia Press, 1976), 150.
205. T. V. Soong to John J. McCloy, 30 January 1942.
206. Romanus and Sunderland, *United States Army in World War II: China-Burma-India Theater*, 1:77–78.
207. Ibid., p. 78.
208. Frank H. Heck, "Airline to China," in *The Army Air Forces in World War II*, vol. 7, *Services around the World*, ed. Wesley Frank Craven and James Lea Cate (Chicago: University of Chicago Press, 1958), 114.
209. Brereton, *The Brereton Diaries*, 109–10.
210. Brereton, *The Brereton Diaries*, 111; *The Tenth Air Force 1942*, 32.
211. "History of Air Operations on the Continent of Asia, December 1941–May 1946," vol. 2, section 1, frame 797; Plating, *The Hump: America's Strategy for Keeping China in World War II*, 42.
212. Maj. Gen. Lewis Brereton, Tenth Air Force, to Adjutant General, Aquila 239, 9 April 1942, Assistant Chief of Air Staff, Plans (WP-IV-D-4 [India Book I]), 145.95, AFHRA, A1472, R2900, frame 370; Gen. George Marshall, Chief of Staff, to Maj. Gen. Lewis Brereton, Tenth Air Force, 10 April 1942, Assistant Chief of Air Staff, Plans (WP-IV-D-4 [India Book I]), 145.95, AFHRA, A1472, R2900, frame 365.
213. Plating, *The Hump: America's Strategy for Keeping China in World War II*, 43.
214. Maj. Gen. Lewis Brereton, Tenth Air Force, to Adjutant General, Washington, 29 March 1942, Assistant Chief of Air Staff, Plans (WP-IV-D-4 [India Book I]), 145.95, AFHRA, A1472, R2900, frames 404–405; History of Air Operations on the Continent of Asia, December 1941–May 1946," vol. 2, section 1, frames 797–98.
215. "History of Air Operations on the Continent of Asia, December 1941–May 1946," vol. 2, section 1, frame 801; "History of the India-China Ferry," Tenth Air Force, 830.04-4, AFHRA, A8229, reel 10024, frame 1271: Brig. Caleb V. Haynes, India Air Task Force, to Lt. Col. Samuel Moore, Historian, Tenth Air Force, 20 April 1943, attachment to "History of the India-China Ferry," Tenth Air Force, 830.04-4, AFHRA, A8229, reel 10024, frame 1283; the website CBI Order of Battle: Lineages and History (www.cbi-history.com/) lists the activation date of the Trans-India Ferry as 7 April 1942, and the activation date of the Assam-Burma-China Ferry as 17 April 1942.
216. "History of the India-China Ferry."
217. "History of Air Operations on the Continent of Asia, December 1941–May 1946," vol. 2, section 1, frames 801–802; "History of the India-China Ferry"; Brig. Caleb V. Haynes, India Air Task Force, to Lt. Col. Samuel Moore, Historian, Tenth Air Force, 20 April 1943.
218. "History of Air Operations on the Continent of Asia, December 1941–May 1946," vol. 2, section 1, frames 801–802; "History of the India-China Ferry"; Brig. Caleb V. Haynes, India Air Task Force, to Lt. Col. Samuel Moore, Historian, Tenth Air Force, 20 April 1943; Shores, *Air War for Burma*, appendix 1, RAF Order of Battle, September 1942, p. 382.
219. "History of the India-China Ferry."
220. Plating, *The Hump: America's Strategy for Keeping China in World War II*, 81; Probert, *The Forgotten Air Force*, 95.
221. Scott, *God Is My Co-pilot*, 112–13.
222. Kirby, *The War against Japan*, 2:213.
223. Brig. Caleb V. Haynes, India Air Task Force, to Lt. Col. Samuel Moore, Historian, Tenth Air Force, 20 April 1943.
224. Kirby, *The War against Japan*, 2:210.
225. Romanus and Sunderland, *United States Army in World War II: China-Burma-India Theater*, 1:140–48.
226. Scott, *God Is My Co-pilot*, 109–10.
227. Scott, *God Is My Co-pilot*, 110–11; Brig. Caleb V. Haynes, India Air Task Force, to Lt. Col. Samuel Moore, Historian, Tenth Air Force, 20 April 1943.

228. Brig. Caleb V. Haynes, India Air Task Force, to Lt. Col. Samuel Moore, Historian, Tenth Air Force, 20 April 1943.
229. Kirby, *The War against Japan*, 2:214.
230. Craven and Cate, 1:511.
231. Notes on Gen. Brereton's Conference, 9–10:30, 8 June 1942, Supporting Documents for History of Army Air Force in India, 12 February 1942–15 December 1943, Army Air Forces, India-Burma Sector, AFHRA 825.01, A8153, reel 9947, frames 169–71.
232. Notes on Gen. Brereton's Conference, 9–10:30, 8 June 1942.
233. Ibid.
234. *The Tenth Air Force 1942*, 46–47.
235. Maj. Gen. Lewis Brereton, Tenth Air Force, to Lt. Gen. H. H. Arnold, Commander, Army Air Forces, 24 June 1942, Assistant Chief of Air Staff, Plans (WP-IV-D-4 [India Book I]), 145.95, AFHRA, A1472, R2900, frames 209–12.
236. Butler, *Grand Strategy*, 3.2:601–605.
237. Craven and Cate, 1:512; Romanus and Sunderland, *United States Army in World War II: China-Burma-India Theater*, 1:157.
238. Butler, *Grand Strategy*, 3.2:607.
239. Butler, *Grand Strategy*, 3.2:607; Romanus and Sunderland, *United States Army in World War II: China-Burma-India Theater*, 1:158.
240. Maj. Gen. Lewis Brereton, Tenth Air Force, to Lt. Gen. H. H. Arnold, Commander, Army Air Forces, 24 June 1942.
241. *The Tenth Air Force 1942*, 48.

CHAPTER 2:
The China Air Task Force: July 1942–March 1943

1. Byrd, *Chennault: Giving Wings to the Tiger*, 137.
2. *The Tenth Air Force 1942*, 30 (see fn 47, and p. 32); Maurer Maurer, ed., *Air Force Combat Units of World War II* (Washington, DC: Office of Air Force History, 1983), 73.
3. Romanus and Sunderland, *United States Army in World War II: China-Burma-India Theater*, 1:91.
4. Ibid., 161.
5. Byrd, *Chennault: Giving Wings to the Tiger*, 138.
6. Ibid., 138.
7. *The Tenth Air Force 1942*, 31.
8. Minutes of an Administrative Planning Conference, 15 March 1942, Minutes of Meetings of the Administrative Planning Committee 15–30 March 1942, 802.151-1 Air Headquarters, India, A8011, reel 9801, AFHRA.
9. "History of Air Operations on the Continent of Asia, December 1941–May 1946," vol. 2, section 1, frame 956.
10. "History of Air Operations on the Continent of Asia, December 1941–May 1946," vol. 2, section 1, frame 957; *The Tenth Air Force 1942*, 49.
11. "History of Air Operations on the Continent of Asia, December 1941–May 1946," vol. 2, section 1, frame 957.
12. *The Tenth Air Force 1942*, 50.
13. Ibid., 50–51.
14. Ibid., 38.
15. Brig. Gen. Earl Naiden, Chief of Staff, Tenth Air Force, to Brig. Gen. Claire L. Chennault, "Air Force Combat Operations in China," 24 June 1942, Operational Correspondence, 1942–43, China Air Task Force, Fourteenth Air Force, 830.311, AFHRA, A8351, reel 10146, frames 516–18.
16. Brig. Gen. Earl Naiden, Chief of Staff, Tenth Air Force, to Brig. Gen. Claire L. Chennault, "Air Force Combat Operations in China," 24 June 1942.
17. Kirby, *The War against Japan*, 2:212.
18. Romanus and Sunderland, *United States Army in World War II: China-Burma-India Theater*, 1:152–57.
19. Schaller, *The US Crusade in China*, 103; Romanus and Sunderland, *United States Army in World War II: China-Burma-India Theater*, 1:158–59, 162, 163–67, 172.
20. Schaller, *The US Crusade in China*, 108–109; Romanus and Sunderland, *United States Army in World War II: China-Burma-India Theater*, 1:172–73.
21. *The Record: The Eleventh Bombardment Squadron (M)* (Richmond, VA, n.d.), 36.
22. Brig. Caleb V. Haynes, India Air Task Force, to Lt. Col. Samuel Moore, Historian, Tenth Air Force, 20 April 1943.
23. *The Record: The Eleventh Bombardment Squadron (M)* (Richmond, VA, n.d.), 36.
24. Ibid.
25. A comment to this effect can be found in the entry for 9 July 1942 in Bomber Command, China Air Task Force, "Journal of Bomber Command in China," China Air Task Force Bomber Command, Tenth Air Force, AFHRA 864.306 1942, A8351, reel 10146, frame 390.
26. Carl Molesworth, *Sharks over China: The 23rd Fighter Group in World War II* (Washington, DC: Brassey's, 1994), 5.
27. "The China Air Task Force," China Air Task Force, Fourteenth Air Force, 830.057, AFHRA, A8351, reel 10146, frames 238–242.
28. Molesworth, Carl: *Sharks Over China: The 23rd Fighter Group in World War II* (Washington, DC, 1994), p. 6–8.
29. "51st Fighter Group, Jan 1942–Mar 1943," AFHRA, GP-51-HI, B0146, reel 1249.
30. Ibid.
31. *The Tenth Air Force 1942*, 51–53; Byrd, *Chennault: Giving Wings to the Tiger*, 151; Chennault, *Way of a Fighter*, 171–72; "History of Air Operations on the Continent of Asia, December 1941–May 1946," vol. 2, section 1, frame 963.
32. Romanus and Sunderland, *United States Army in World War II: China-Burma-India Theater*, 1:200; Brig. Gen. Claire Chennault, China Air Task Force, to Commanding General, Tenth Air Force, "Report of the Commanding General, C.A.T.F., on the Activities of the CATF during the Period July 4, 1942 to December 31, 1942," Army Air Forces, India-Burma Sector, AFHRA 825.01, A8153, reel 9947, frame 62; Chennault, *Way of a Fighter*, 178.

33. "The China Air Task Force," China Air Task Force, Fourteenth Air Force, 830.057, AFHRA, A8351, reel 10146, frame 210; "Report of the Commanding General, C.A.T.F., on the activities of the CATF during the period July 4, 1942 to December 31, 1942," Army Air Forces, India-Burma Sector, AFHRA 825.01, A8153, reel 9947, frame 62.
34. "The China Air Task Force," China Air Task Force, Fourteenth Air Force, 830.057, AFHRA, A8351, reel 10146, frame 238–42.
35. *The Tenth Air Force 1942*, 79.
36. Molesworth, *Sharks over China*, 15–16.
37. "The China Air Task Force," China Air Task Force, Fourteenth Air Force, 830.057, AFHRA, A8351, reel 10146, frame 217.
38. Ibid., frame 218–19.
39. Byrd, *Chennault: Giving Wings to the Tiger*, 154.
40. Romanus and Sunderland, *United States Army in World War II: China-Burma-India Theater*, 1:188.
41. Brig. Gen. Claire L. Chennault, China Air Task Force, to the Commanding General, Tenth Air Force, 11 September 1942, Supporting Documents for Administrative History of the Army Air Forces in India, 12 February 1942 to 15 December 1943, folder number I, AFHRA 825.01, 12 February–15 December 1943, vol. I, A8153, frames 25–26.
42. Military History Section, Headquarters, Army Forces Far East, Japanese Monograph 76, *Air Operations in the China Area (July 1937–August 1945)*, 60–65; Ikuhiko Hata, Yasuho Izawa, and Christopher Shores, *Japanese Army Air Force Fighter Units and Their Aces, 1931–1945* (London: Grub Street, 2002), 61–62.
43. Chennault, *Way of a Fighter*, 187.
44. Bomber Command, China Air Task Force, "Journal of Bomber Command in China," China Air Task Force Bomber Command, Tenth Air Force, AFHRA 864.306 1942, A8351, reel 10146, frames 388–89.
45. Bomber Command, China Air Task Force, "Journal of Bomber Command in China," China Air Task Force Bomber Command, Tenth Air Force, AFHRA 864.306 1942, A8351, reel 10146, frame 389; *The Record: The Eleventh Bombardment Squadron (M)*, 37.
46. Bomber Command, China Air Task Force, "Journal of Bomber Command in China," China Air Task Force Bomber Command, Tenth Air Force, AFHRA 864.306 1942, A8351, reel 10146, frame 389; *The Record: The Eleventh Bombardment Squadron (M)*, 37; Molesworth, *Sharks over China*, 22.
47. Bomber Command, China Air Task Force, Summary of Missions, in "The China Air Task Force," China Air Task Force, Fourteenth Air Force, AFHRA 830.057, A8351, reel 10146, frame 395.
48. "The China Air Task Force," China Air Task Force, Fourteenth Air Force, 830.057, AFHRA, A8351, reel 10146, frame 223.
49. *The Record: The Eleventh Bombardment Squadron (M)*, 38.
50. Ibid.
51. Molesworth, *Sharks over China*, 29; Frank J. Olynyk, *AVG & USAAF (China-Burma-India Theater) Credits for the Destruction of Enemy Aircraft in Air-to-Air Combat World War 2* (Aurora, OH: F. J. Olynyk, 1986), 9.
52. Molesworth, *Sharks over China*, 30–32; Edward H. Sims, *American Aces in Great Fighter Battles of World War II* (New York: Ballantine Books, 1958), 9–16.
53. Molesworth, *Sharks over China*, 34–35; Olynyk, *AVG & USAAF (China-Burma-India Theater) Credits for the Destruction of Enemy Aircraft in Air-to-Air Combat World War 2*, 9; Hata et al., *Japanese Army Air Force Fighter Units and Their Aces, 1931–1945*, 62.
54.
55. Molesworth, *Sharks over China*, 35–37; Olynyk, *AVG & USAAF (China-Burma-India Theater) Credits for the Destruction of Enemy Aircraft in Air-to-Air Combat World War 2*, 9; Hata et al., *Japanese Army Air Force Fighter Units and Their Aces, 1931–1945*, 62.
56. Chennault, *Way of a Fighter*, 192.
57. Major David L. Hill, 75th Fighter Squadron, to Commanding General, China Air Task Force, "Facts Effecting the Operations of the American Air Force in China," 7 September 1942, China Air Task Force, Fourteenth Air Force, AFHRA 864.311, A8351, reel 10146, frames 536–37.
58. Major John Alison, 75th Fighter Squadron, to Commanding General, China Air Task Force, "Fighter Operations in the China Theater," 7 September 1942, China Air Task Force, Fourteenth Air Force, AFHRA 864.311, A8351, reel 10146, frames 538–39.
59. Major John Alison, 75th Fighter Squadron, to Commanding General, China Air Task Force, "Fighter Operations in the China Theater," 7 September 1942; Major David L. Hill, 75th Fighter Squadron, to Commanding General, China Air Task Force, "Facts Effecting the Operations of the American Air Force in China," 7 September 1942.
60. Major John Alison, 75th Fighter Squadron, to Commanding General, China Air Task Force, "Fighter Operations in the China Theater," 7 September 1942.
61. Chennault, *Way of a Fighter*, 193.
62. Bert Kinzey, *P–40 Warhawk in Detail, Part 2: P–40D through XP–40Q*, Detail and Scale 62 (Carrollton, TX: Squadron/Signal, 1999), 14, 58.
63. Hata et al., *Japanese Army Air Force Fighter Units and Their Aces, 1931–1945*, 62.
64. Chennault, *Way of a Fighter*, 193.
65. Molesworth, *Sharks over China*, 38; Olynyk, *AVG & USAAF (China-Burma-India Theater) Credits for the Destruction of Enemy Aircraft in Air-to-Air Combat World War 2*, 9; Hata et al., *Japanese Army Air Force Fighter Units and Their Aces, 1931–1945*, 62.
66. *The Record: The Eleventh Bombardment Squadron (M)*, 38; Bomber Command, China Air Task Force, Summary of Missions, A8351, reel 10146, frames 417–22.

67. *The Record: The Eleventh Bombardment Squadron (M)*, 38; Bomber Command, China Air Task Force, Summary of Missions, A8351, reel 10146, frames 417–22; Olynyk, *AVG & USAAF (China-Burma-India Theater) Credits for the Destruction of Enemy Aircraft in Air-to-Air Combat World War 2*, 0.
68. Scott, *God Is My Co-pilot*, 214.
69. Chennault, *Way of a Fighter*, 195.
70. *The Record: The Eleventh Bombardment Squadron (M)*, 40–41; Bomber Command, China Air Task Force, Summary of Missions, A8351, reel 10146, frames 448–49.
71. *The Record: The Eleventh Bombardment Squadron (M)*, 38; Bomber Command, China Air Task Force, Summary of Missions, A8351, reel 10146, frames 417–22; Olynyk, *AVG & USAAF (China-Burma-India Theater) Credits for the Destruction of Enemy Aircraft in Air-to-Air Combat World War 2*, 10; David Lee "Tex" Hill with Maj. Reagan Schaupp, USAF, *"Tex" Hill: Flying Tiger* (San Antonio, TX: Universal Bookbindery, 2003), 197; Molesworth, *Sharks over China*, 65–67.
72. *The Record: The Eleventh Bombardment Squadron (M)*, 40–41; Bomber Command, China Air Task Force, Summary of Missions, A8351, reel 10146, frames 450–52; Tenth Air Force Operational Diary, Tenth Air Force 1 June 1942–1 June 1943, 830.305-1, A 8242, reel 10037, frame 1630.
73. Tenth Air Force Operational Diary, Tenth Air Force, 1 June 1942–1 June 1943, frame 1636; Japanese merchant shipping losses in World War II can be found at www.ibiblio.org/hyperwar/Japan/IJN/JANAC-Losses/JANAC-Losses-4.html.
74. Tenth Air Force Operational Diary, Tenth Air Force, 1 June 1942–1 June 1943, frame 1637.
75. Molesworth, *Sharks over China*, 73–76.
76. *The Record: The Eleventh Bombardment Squadron (M)*, 43.
77. Molesworth, *Sharks over China*, 74–75; Holloway's claims are listed in Olynyk, *AVG & USAAF (China-Burma-India Theater) Credits for the Destruction of Enemy Aircraft in Air-to-Air Combat World War 2*, 12.
78. Molesworth, *Sharks over China*, 76.
79. *The Tenth Air Force 1942*, 120.
80. Ibid., 124.
81. Shores, *Air War for Burma*, 45.
82. Shores, *Air War for Burma*, 45–46; Molesworth, *Sharks over China*, 81–82.
83. Tenth Air Force Operational Diary, Tenth Air Force, 1 June 1942–1 June 1943 (see frames for dates listed); William H. Greenhalgh, *Foto Jo in CBI: 9th Photographic Reconnaissance Squadron China-Burma-India, 1942–1945* (William H. Greenhalgh, 1990), 23.
84. *The Record: The Eleventh Bombardment Squadron (M)*, 45.
85. Col. Robert L. Scott Jr., 23rd Fighter Group, to Commanding General, China Air Task Force, Report of Operations of Twenty Third Fighter Group for period July 4, 1942 to December 31, 1942, 31 December 1942, Administrative History Documents for 1942, Army Air Forces, India-Burma Sector, AFHRA 825.01, A8153, reel 9947, frames 354–55.
86. Capt. Everett Holstrom, 11th Bombardment Squadron, to Commanding General, China Air Task Force, Summary of Tactical Operations since July 4, 1 January 1943, Administrative History Documents for 1942, Army Air Forces, India-Burma Sector, AFHRA 825.01, A8153, reel 9947, frames 356–58.
87. *The Tenth Air Force 1942*, 124.
88. "History of Air Operations on the Continent of Asia, December 1941–May 1946," vol. 2, section 1, frame 996.
89. Ibid., frame 997. This history contains a chapter covering the relationship between the China Air Task Force and the Tenth Air Force. I have drawn on this history extensively for this section.
90. Romanus and Sunderland, *United States Army in World War II: China-Burma-India Theater*, 1:198–99; Arnold, *Global Mission*, 419.
91. "History of Air Operations on the Continent of Asia, December 1941–May 1946," vol. 2, section 1, frame 986.
92. Byrd, *Chennault: Giving Wings to the Tiger*, 168.
93. Ibid., 154.
94. Ibid., 138.
95. This observation appears in a briefing given to Gen. Henry Arnold on 16 December 1942 on the difficult relationship within the Tenth Air Force between Gen. Bissell and Gen. Chennault. See Henry Harley Arnold Papers, Library of Congress, reel 200, folder China-Burma-India Theater, 1941–1944.
96. "History of Air Operations on the Continent of Asia, December 1941–May 1946," vol. 2, section 1, frame 1006.
97. Byrd, *Chennault: Giving Wings to the Tiger*, 168.
98. "History of Air Operations on the Continent of Asia, December 1941–May 1946," vol. 2, section 1, frame 1006; Byrd, *Chennault: Giving Wings to the Tiger*, 142–43; the 16 December 1942 memo to Gen. Arnold in his papers is interesting in this respect. See also Chennault's opinion of Bissell in Chennault, *Way of a Fighter*, 201.
99. Byrd, *Chennault: Giving Wings to the Tiger*, 169.
100. Chennault, *Way of a Fighter*, 180.
101. Allan R. Millett and Williamson Murray, eds., *Military Effectiveness*, vol. 1, *The First World War*, new ed. (New York: Cambridge University Press, 2010), 16.
102. Arnold, *Global Mission*, 419.
103. Ibid.
104. Byrd, *Chennault: Giving Wings to the Tiger*, 169; "History of Air Operations on the Continent of Asia, December 1941–May 1946," vol. 2, section 1, frame 1008.
105. "History of Air Operations on the Continent of Asia, December 1941–May 1946," vol. 2, section 1, frame 1008.

106. Byrd, *Chennault: Giving Wings to the Tiger*, 169.
107. "History of Air Operations on the Continent of Asia, December 1941–May 1946," vol. 2, section 1, frame 1007; the chapter on relations between the China Air Task Force and the Tenth Air Force in "History of Air Operations on the Continent of Asia, December 1941–May 1946," vol. 2, section 1, provides details of these interactions between Bissell and Chennault.
108. "History of Air Operations on the Continent of Asia, December 1941–May 1946," vol. 2, section 1, frames 1016–22.
109. Ibid., frames 1012–15.
110. Ibid., frames 1014–15; this is certainly the attitude that Chennault himself expresses in his memoir *Way of a Fighter*. See pp. 201–204 for his caustic comments on Bissell and Stilwell.
111. "History of Air Operations on the Continent of Asia, December 1941–May 1946," vol. 2, section 1, frames 1015–16.
112. Chennault, *Way of a Fighter*, 201.
113. Byrd, *Chennault: Giving Wings to the Tiger*, 171.
114. Romanus and Sunderland, *United States Army in World War II: China-Burma-India Theater*, 1:74.
115. Ibid., 176.
116. Ibid., 172–73, 177–79, 182–83, 251, 322.
117. Byrd, *Chennault: Giving Wings to the Tiger*, 108–109.
118. Ibid., 50.
119. Ibid., 50.
120. Romanus and Sunderland, *United States Army in World War II: China-Burma-India Theater*, 1:253.
121. Haruo, "The Strategic Correlation between the Sino-Japanese and Pacific Wars," 431.
122. Schaller, *The US Crusade in China*, 126.
123. Ibid., p. 115.
124. Byrd, *Chennault: Giving Wings to the Tiger*, 180–81.
125. Brig. Gen. Claire Chennault, Headquarters China Air Task Force, to Wendell Willkie, Special Representative of the President, 8 October 1942, Documents for History of Army Air Force in India, 12 February 1942–15 December 1943, Army Air Forces, India-Burma Sector, 825.01, A8153, reel 9947, frames 476–79.
126. CBI: USAAF, IBT. "History of Air Operations on the Continent of Asia December 1941–May 1946," vol. 3, section 2, 825.01C, A8155, reel 9949, frames 23–28.
127. See Romanus and Sunderland, "The Attempt to Plan a Spring Campaign, in *United States Army in World War II: China-Burma-India Theater*, 1:222–61, for a detailed discussion of Stilwell's plans and discussions with the Chinese; Maurice Matloff, *Strategic Planning for Coalition Warfare 1943–1944*, United States Army in World War II: The War Department (Washington, DC: Center of Military History, US Army, 1959), 33–36; Wesley Frank Craven and James Lea Cate, eds., *The Army Air Forces in World War II*, vol. 4, *The Pacific: Guadalcanal to Saipan, August 1942 to July 1944* (Chicago: University of Chicago Press, 1950), 437.
128. Lt. Gen. H. H. Arnold, Commanding General, Army Air Forces, to Chief of Staff, Establishment and Assignment of Mission to Separate Air Force in China, 6 January 1943, Arnold Papers, reel 200, folder China-Burma-India Theater, 1941–1944.
129. Arnold, *Global Mission*, 413; Byrd, *Chennault: Giving Wings to the Tiger*, 182; Craven and Cate, *The Army Air Forces in World War II*, 4:438.
130. Craven and Cate, *The Army Air Forces in World War II*, 4:438–39.
131. Arnold, *Global Mission*, 422.
132. Romanus and Sunderland, *United States Army in World War II: China-Burma-India Theater*, 1:278.
133. CBI: USAAF, IBT, "History of Air Operations on the Continent of Asia, December 1941–May 1946," vol. 3, section 2, 825.01C, A8155, reel 9949, frames 35–37.

CHAPTER 3:
The India Air Task Force: October–December 1942

1. Operations of the Tenth Air Force, 12 February 1942–January 1943, p. 3, Tenth Air Force, 830.306, A8242, reel 10037, frame 2102.
2. Operations of the Tenth Air Force, 12 February 1942–January 1943, p. 3, Tenth Air Force, 830.306, A8242, reel 10037, frame 2102.
3. Air Headquarters India to Air Ministry, 29 August 1942, Air 20/881, Air Ministry and Ministry of Defense, Air Historical Branch, Assistant Chief of Air Staff (Operations). American Fortress Aircraft: Employment in Middle and Far East, National Archives, Kew, UK.
4. Operations of the Tenth Air Force, 12 February 1942–January 1943; 51st Fighter Group, Jan 1942–Mar 1943, GP-51-HI, B0146, reel 1249; *Army Air Forces Statistical Digest World War II*, 173.
5. Kirby, *The War against Japan*, 2:240.
6. Michael Howard, *Grand Strategy*, vol. 4, *August 1942–September 1943* (London: Her Majesty's Stationery Office, 1970), 80.
7. Ibid.
8. Ibid., 83–84.
9. Ibid., 85–87.
10. Kirby, *The War against Japan*, 2:244, 249–51.
11. "History of Air Operations on the Continent of Asia, December 1941–May 1946," vol. 2, section 1, frames 943–44.
12. Ibid., frame 944.
13. Craven and Cate, *The Army Air Forces in World War II*, 1:566–67.
14. Ibid., 1:568–69.
15. Ibid., 1:569.
16. Ibid., 1:568–69.
17. Gen. Wavell to Chief of Staff, No. 16006/C, 5 July 1942, India: Command and Role of US Air Forces, Air 8/680, Air Ministry and Ministry of Defense, Department of the Chief of the Air Staff: Registered Files, National Archives, Kew, UK.

18. RAFDEL to Air Ministry Whitehall, Slessor to Evill, 15 July 1942, India: Command and Role of US Air Forces, Air 8/680, Air Ministry and Ministry of Defense, Department of the Chief of the Air Staff: Registered Files, National Archives, Kew, UK.
19. Air Ministry Whitehall to Armindia, Chiefs of Staff to Gen. Wavell, OZ 1167, 4 September 1942, India: Command and Role of US Air Forces, Air 8/680, Air Ministry and Ministry of Defense, Department of the Chief of the Air Staff: Registered Files, National Archives, Kew, UK.
20. Air Ministry Whitehall to Armindia, Chiefs of Staff to Gen. Wavell, OZ 1496, 9 October 1942, India: Command and Role of US Air Forces, Air 8/680, Air Ministry and Ministry of Defense, Department of the Chief of the Air Staff: Registered Files, National Archives, Kew, UK.
21. Air Command, Southeast Asia Operational Research Section, "Bombing Operations 1941–1942 by R.A.F. and U.S.A.A.F. Units Based in India and Burma: Summary," Bombing Operations July and August 1942; "51st Fighter Group, Jan 1942–Mar 1943," GP-51-HI, B0145, reel 1249, frame 216; Tenth Air Force Operational Diary, 1 June 1942–1 June 1943, Tenth Air Force 830.305-1, A8242, reel 10037, frame 1561.
22. Brig. Gen. Earl Naiden, Tenth Air Force, to Gen. Joseph Stilwell, 24 July 1942, Documents for History of Army Air Force in India, 12 February 1942–15 December 1943, A8153, reel 9947, frames 459–60.
23. Craven and Cate, *The Army Air Forces in World War II*, 4:414–15.
24. Craven and Cate, *The Army Air Forces in World War II*, 7:114–15; "History of Air Operations on the Continent of Asia, December 1941–May 1946," vol. 2, section 1, frame 810.
25. Craven and Cate, *The Army Air Forces in World War II*, 4:411.
26. "History of Air Operations on the Continent of Asia, December 1941–May 1946," vol. 2, section 1, frame 804.
27. Military Analysis Division, *Air Operations in China, Burma, India World War II* (Washington, DC: US Strategic Bombing Survey, 1947), 42; Operations of the Tenth Air Force, 12 February 1942–January 1943, frames 2102–2104.
28. Craven and Cate, *The Army Air Forces in World War II*, 4:414.
29. "History of Air Operations on the Continent of Asia, December 1941–May 1946," vol. 2, section 1, frame 807.
30. Ibid.
31. Craven and Cate, *The Army Air Forces in World War II*, 4:415.
32. Ibid.
33. Ibid., 418.
34. "History of Air Operations on the Continent of Asia, December 1941–May 1946," vol. 2, section 1, frame 809.
35. Craven and Cate, *The Army Air Forces in World War II*, 7:120.
36. "History of Air Operations on the Continent of Asia, December 1941–May 1946," vol. 2, section 1, frame 808.
37. Plating, *The Hump: America's Strategy for Keeping China in World War II*, 102–104.
38. Col. William Ball, Director of Intelligence Service, Office of the Chief of the Air Corps, to Col. A. Williamson, Subject: Air Attack Operations of the 10th Air Force, 25 July 1942, Assistant Chief of Air Staff, Plans (WP-IV-D-4 [India Book I]), frames 213–21.
39. Group History of the 341st Bombardment Group (Medium), 15 September–December 1942, GP-341-(HI)-Bomb, AFHRA, B0284, reel 1417; "Consolidated History of the Seventh Bombardment Group (H), AAF, Ground and Air Echelons for the Year 1942"; Col. Thomas Timberman, Chief, China-India Section, Theater Group, G.P.D., War Department General Staff, to Brig. Clayton Bissell, Commanding General, Tenth Air Force, 16 September 1942, Documents for History of Army Air Force in India, 12 February 1942–15 December 1943, Army Air Forces, India-Burma Sector, frame 539–44.
40. Col. Thomas Timberman, Chief, China-India Section, Theater Group, G.P.D., War Department General Staff, to Brig. Clayton Bissell, Commanding General, Tenth Air Force, 16 September 1942.
41. Ibid.
42. *Army Air Forces Statistical Digest World War II*, 173.
43. "History of Air Operations on the Continent of Asia, December 1941–May 1946," vol. 2, section 1, frames 987–89.
44. Brig. Gen. Clayton Bissell, Commanding General, Tenth Air Force, to C. V. Haynes, Commanding General, India Air Task Force, 2 October 1942, Documents for History of Army Air Force in India, 12 February 1942–15 December 1943, Army Air Forces, India-Burma Sector, frames 86–88.
45. Ibid., 2 October 1942.
46. Bissell to Haynes, 2 October 1942; "History of Air Operations on the Continent of Asia, December 1941–May 1946," vol. 2, section 1, frames 990–92.
47. "History of Air Operations on the Continent of Asia, December 1941–May 1946," vol. 2, section 1, frame 996; Col. Homer Sanders, 51st Fighter Group, to Commanding General, US Air Forces in India and China, 26 August 1942, Documents for History of Army Air Force in India, 12 February 1942–15 December 1943, Army Air Forces, India-Burma Sector, frames 479–81; Brig. Gen. Clayton Bissell, to Commanding General, Army Air Forces, Improvement of Equipment and Organization of the Army, 24 October 1942, Documents for History of Army Air Force in India, 12 February 1942–15 December 1943, Army Air Forces, India-Burma Sector, frames 16–18.
48. Romanus and Sunderland, *United States Army in World War II: China-Burma-India Theater*, 1:232–33; *The Tenth Air Force 1942*, 110.
49. Military History Section, Headquarters, Army Forces Far East, *Burma Air Operations Record, Jan. 1942–Aug. 1945*, Japanese Monograph 64 (Tokyo: Far East Command, US Army, 1946), 28–29.

50. "51st Fighter Group, Jan 1942–Mar 1943," 13–14; Operations of the Tenth Air Force, 12 February 1942–January 1943, entries from 30 September to 17 October 1942.
51. Operations of the Tenth Air Force, 12 February 1942–January 1943, entries for 20 October 1942; Shores, *Air War for Burma*, 29.
52. Shores, *Air War for Burma*, 29–30; "51st Fighter Group, Jan 1942–Mar 1943," 14–15; *The Tenth Air Force 1942*, 112.
53. Shores, *Air War for Burma*, 29–31; "51st Fighter Group, Jan 1942–Mar 1943," 15–16; *The Tenth Air Force 1942*, 112.
54. Shores, *Air War for Burma*, 31–32; "51st Fighter Group, Jan 1942–Mar 1943," 17–18; *The Tenth Air Force 1942*, 112–113.
55. "51st Fighter Group, Jan 1942–Mar 1943," 19; Operations of the Tenth Air Force, 12 February 1942–January 1943, entries for November and December 1942; Military History Section, Headquarters, Army Forces Far East, *Burma Air Operations Record, Jan. 1942–Aug. 1945*, 29.
56. "51st Fighter Group, Jan 1942–Mar 1943," 19; Operations of the Tenth Air Force, 12 February 1942–January 1943, entries for November and December 1942.
57. "51st Fighter Group, Jan 1942–Mar 1943," 20–22.
58. Young, *Death from Above*, 118–119.
59. "Consolidated History of the Seventh Bombardment Group (H), AAF, Ground and Air Echelons for the Year 1942," 10–11.
60. Young, *Death from Above*, 120–23; Operations of the Tenth Air Force, 12 February 1942–January 1943, entries for October and November 1942.
61. Young, *Death from Above*, 126–27; Operations of the Tenth Air Force, 12 February 1942–January 1943, entries for December 1942; "Consolidated History of the Seventh Bombardment Group (H), AAF, Ground and Air Echelons for the Year 1942," 11–12; History of the Tenth Air Force Headquarters, January 1 to May 31, 1943, Tenth Air Force History, 1942–1945, 830.01, A8224, reel 10018, frame 568.
62. *The Record: The Eleventh Bombardment Squadron (M)*, 40–42; Operations of the Tenth Air Force, 12 February 1942–January 1943, entries for December 1942.
63. Group History of the 341st Bombardment Group (M), 15 September–December 1942; Tenth Air Force, 29 October 1942–27 April 1943, Operations from India: Heavy Bombers, AFHRA, 830.3061-4, A8243, reel 10038, frames 1223–25.
64. Group History of the 341st Bombardment Group (M), 15 September–December 1942; 490th Bombardment Squadron (M), History, 16 September 1942–March 1943, SQ-Bomb-490-HI.
65. Maj. Gen. George Stratemeyer, Chief of the Air Staff, Army Air Forces, to Brig. Gen. Clayton Bissell, Commanding General, Tenth Air Force, 11 December 1942, Documents for History of Army Air Force in India, 12 February 1942–15 December 1943, Army Air Forces, India-Burma Sector, frames 706–707.
66. Narrative History, India Air Task Force, November 1942–31 May 1943, India Air Task Force, Tenth Air Force, 827. 306–1, A8221, reel 10015.
67. Operational Research Section, Bombing Operations 1941–1942 by RAF and USAAF Units Based in India and Burma: Summary.
68. Ibid.

CHAPTER 4:
From Casablanca to Trident: Tenth Air Force Operations, January–May 1943

1. Mark A. Stoler, *Allies and Adversaries: The Joint Chiefs of Staff, the Grand Alliance, and U.S. Strategy in World War II* (Chapel Hill: University of North Carolina Press, 2000), 100.
2. Howard, *Grand Strategy*, 4:242, 252.
3. Howard, *Grand Strategy*, 4:241–42, 244.
4. Stoler, *Allies and Adversaries*, 111.
5. Ibid.
6. Howard, *Grand Strategy*, 4:246.
7. Romanus and Sunderland, *United States Army in World War II: China-Burma-India Theater*, 1:270.
8. Ibid., p. 271.
9. Howard, *Grand Strategy*, vol. 4, appendix III (F), 629–30.
10. Romanus and Sunderland, *United States Army in World War II: China-Burma-India Theater*, 1:306.
11. Craven and Cate, *The Army Air Forces in World War II*, 4:469–71.
12. Phillips Payson O'Brien, *How the War Was Won: Air-Sea Power and Allied Victory in World War II* (Cambridge, UK: Cambridge University Press, 2015), 5.
13. This information comes from a report prepared in November 1943 for all officers and enlisted men in the Tenth Air Force. Memorandum: An Appreciation of the Strategic Employment of the Tenth Air Force in Burmese Operations, 14 November 1943, Documents for History of Army Air Force in India, 12 February 1942–15 December 1943, Army Air Forces, India-Burma Sector, frames 676–89; Craven and Cate, *The Army Air Forces in World War II*, 4:471–72.
14. *The Tenth Air Force, 1 January–10 March 1943*, US Air Force Numbered Historical Studies 104 (1944), 29.
15. Ibid., 29–30.
16. Romanus and Sunderland, *United States Army in World War II: China-Burma-India Theater*, 1:315.
17. Air Ministry, Air Historical Branch, *The Campaigns in the Far East*, vol. 3, *India Command September 1939 to November 1943* (London, n.d.), 103–105, 115–18.
18. Air Ministry, Air Historical Branch: *The Campaigns in the Far East*, vol. 3, appendix 13, pp. 2–3, appendix 14, p. 2; Hata et al., *Japanese Army Air Force Fighter Units and Their Aces, 1931–1945*, 49–52, 142, 157; Military History Section, Headquarters, Army Forces Far East, *Burma Air Operations Record, Jan. 1942–Aug. 1945*, 30–32.
19. Brig. Gen. Caleb V. Haynes, India Air Task Force, to Lt. Gen. Henry Arnold, 10th Air Force Evaluation, 9 February 1943, 827. 306–2, A8221, reel 10015, frames 306–10.

20. *The Tenth Air Force 1943*, US Air Force Numbered Historical Studies 117 (1946), 41.
21. Maj. Gen. Clayton Bissell, Tenth Air Force, to Maj. Gen. Karl Truesdell, Command and General Staff School, 2 May 1943, Documents for History of Army Air Force in India, 12 February 1942–15 December 1943, Army Air Forces, India-Burma Sector, frames 122–29.
22. *The Tenth Air Force 1943*, 42–44.
23. Molesworth, *Sharks over China*, 84–85.
24. Ibid., p. 85.
25. Hata et al., *Japanese Army Air Force Fighter Units and Their Aces 1931–1945*, 51.
26. 51st Fighter Group, January 1942–March 1943, B0145, reel 1248, frame 231; 26th Fighter Squadron, SQ-FI-26-HI, A0728, reel 766.
27. 51st Fighter Group, January 1942–March 1943, B0145, reel 1248, frame 231; 26th Fighter Squadron, SQ-FI-26-HI, A0728, reel 766; Shores, *Air War for Burma*, 61.
28. 25th Fighter Squadron, January–October 1943, SQ-FI-25-HI.
29. Carl Molesworth, *P-40 Warhawk Aces of the CBI* (Oxford: Osprey, 2000), 51.
30. 51st Fighter Group, April–December 1943, B0145, reel 1248, frame 498; 26th Fighter Squadron, SQ-FI-26-HI, A0728, reel 766.
31. Gen. H. H. Arnold, Commanding General, Army Air Forces, to Brig. Gen. Clayton L. Bissell, Commanding General, Tenth Air Force, 10 April 1943, Tenth Air Force, 201—Bissell, Clayton L., August 1942–November 1943, 830.289-1, A8242, reel 10037, frame 927.
32. Arnold to Bissell, 10 April 1943, Tenth Air Force, 201—Bissell, Clayton L., August 1942–November 1943, 830.289-1, A8242, reel 10037.
33. Brig. Gen. Clayton L. Bissell, Commanding General, Tenth Air Force, to Gen. H. H. Arnold, Commanding General, Army Air Forces, 2 May 1943, Tenth Air Force, 201—Bissell, Clayton L., August 1942–November 1943, 830.289-1, A8242, reel 10037, frame 1008.
34. 80th Fighter Group, GP-80–HI, January 1942–December 1943, vol. 1, B0165, reel 1271.
35. Gen. H. H. Arnold, Commanding General, Army Air Forces, to Maj. Gen. Clayton L. Bissell, Commanding General, Tenth Air Force, Tenth Air Force, 201—Bissell, Clayton L., August 1942–November 1943, 830.289-1, A8242, reel 10037, frame 935.
36. Romanus and Sunderland, *United States Army in World War II: China-Burma-India Theater*, 1:308–309.
37. 51st Fighter Group, January 1942–March 1943, B0145, reel 1248, frames 228–30; 26th Fighter Squadron, SQ-FI-26-HI, A0728, reel 766; Tenth Air Force Operational Diary, 1 June 1942–1 June 1943.
38. 51st Fighter Group January 1942–March 1943, B0145, reel 1248, frames 230–31, 243–44; 26th Fighter Squadron, SQ-FI-26-HI, A0728, reel 766; Tenth Air Force Operational Diary, 1 June 1942–1 June 1943.
39. Craven and Cate, *The Army Air Forces in World War II*, 4:464.
40. Ibid.
41. Ibid., 465.
42. Bob Phillips, *KC-8 Burma: CBI Air Warning Team, 1941–1942* (Manhattan, KS: Sunflower University Press, 1992), 147–48.
43. Phillips, *KC-8 Burma: CBI Air Warning Team, 1941–1942*, 149–51.
44. 51st Fighter Group, January 1942–March 1943, B0145, reel 1248, frame 245; 26th Fighter Squadron, SQ-FI-26-HI, A0728, reel 766; Tenth Air Force Operational Diary, 1 June 1942–1 June 1943.
45. 51st Fighter Group, January 1942–March 1943, B0145, reel 1248, frame 256.
46. 51st Fighter Group, January 1942–March 1943, B0145, reel 1248, frames 255–56; 25th Fighter Squadron, January–October 1943, SQ-FI-25-HI; 26th Fighter Squadron, SQ-FI-26-HI; *CBI Roundup* 1, no. 29 (1 April 1943), www.cbi-theater.com/roundup/roundup.html.
47. Tenth Air Force Operational Diary, 1 June 1942–1 June 1943; Capt. Luther Davis, "The 'B'-40 over Burma," *Air Force Magazine* 26, no. 10 (October 1943): 5.
48. 51st Fighter Group, Flight Intelligence Report, Mission 405, 17 March 1943, GP-51-SU-OP, B0146, reel 1249, frames 1192–95.
49. Davis, "The 'B'-40 over Burma," 5.
50. 51st Fighter Group, Flight Intelligence Report, Mission 405, 17 March 1943, GP-51-SU-OP, B0146, reel 1249, frames 1181–82.
51. 51st Fighter Group, Flight Intelligence Report, Missions 496, 503, 515, 517, 538, 541, 784, 787, 793, 795 (14, 16, 19 April, 2; 3 May 1943), GP-51-SU-OP, B0146, reel 1249, frames 1061–1130; 51st Fighter Group, April–June 1943, B0145, reel 1248, frame 470.
52. Molesworth, *P-40 Warhawk Aces of the CBI*, 50.
53. 51st Fighter Group, April–June 1943, B0145, reel 1248, frame 480.
54. 51st Fighter Group, April–June 1943, B0145, reel 1248, frame 494.
55. Tenth Air Force Operational Diary, 1 June 1942–1 June 1943.
56. Tenth Air Force Operational Diary, 1 June 1942–1 June 1943; 51st Fighter Group, Flight Intelligence Report, Missions 861–924, 24 May–11 June 1943, GP-51-SU-OP, B0146, reel 1249, frames 995–1033.
57. Craven and Cate, *The Army Air Forces in World War II*, 4:463.
58. Military History Section, Headquarters, Army Forces Far East, *Burma Air Operations Record, Jan. 1942–Aug. 1945*, 30–31.
59. Tenth Air Force Operational Diary, 1 June 1942–1 June 1943; Narrative History, India Air Task Force, November 1942–31 May 1943.
60. United States Strategic Bombing Survey (Pacific War), *Air Operations in China, Burma, India World War II* (Washington, DC, 1945–1947), 18.
61. Ibid., 20.
62. Headquarters, Tenth Air Force, Air Objective Folder 82.2, Burma South Area, 51st Fighter Group, GP-51-SU-OP, B0146, reel 1249, frame 31.
63. Ibid., frames 31–33.

64. History of the Ninth Bombardment Squadron (H) for the Period January 1, 1943, through May 31, 1943, SQ-Bomb-9-HI January–June 1943, A0538, reel 0561, frame 11; details on Japanese shipping losses are from Joint Army-Navy Assessment Committee, *Japanese Naval and Merchant Shipping Losses during World War II by All Causes* (February 1947), www.ibiblio.org/hyperwar/Japan/IJN/JANAC-Losses/JANAC-Losses-4.html.
65. History of the 436th Bombardment Squadron (H) for the Period January 1, 1943, through April 30, 1943, SQ-Bomb-436-HI, A0614, reel 0643; Tenth Air Force Operational Diary, 1 June 1942–1 June 1943; India Air Task Force, Daily Intelligence Extracts 40–97 (1 January–28 February 1943), 98–158 (1 March–30 April, 1943), 159–218 (1 May–30 June 1943), 827.606, A8221, reel 10015.
66. Col. Harold E. Wright, A–2, Tenth Air Force, to Commanding General, Tenth Air Force, 13 January 1943, 10th Air Force Project Low, Tenth Air Force, 830.322-6, A8245, reel 10045, frames 5–7.
67. Bissell to A–2, Memorandum, 31 January 1943, 10th Air Force Project Low, frame 63.
68. Col. Harold E. Wright, A–2, Tenth Air Force, to Commanding General, Tenth Air Force, 28–29 January and 1, 11, 17 February 1943, 10th Air Force Project Low, Tenth Air Force, 830.322-6, A8245, reel 10045, frames 9–24, 53–74.
69. Wright to Bissell, Follow-up of "Low" Project, 6 March 1943, 10th Air Force Project Low, frame 64.
70. Wright to Bissell, Low Project, 25 February 1943, Wright to Bissell, Follow-up of "Low" Project, 6 March 1943, 10th Air Force Project Low, frames 64–65, 74–75; Brig. Gen. Clayton L. Bissell, Headquarters, Tenth Air Force, to Flag Liaison Officer, Naval Headquarters, New Delhi, 6 March 1943, 10th Air Force Project Low, frame 76; Young, *Death from Above*, 137.
71. India Air Task Force, Narrative History, India Air Task Force, November 1942–31 May 1943, Shipping Tonnage Rangoon Chart.
72. Tenth Air Force Operational Diary, 1 June 1942–1 June 1943; India Air Task Force, Daily Intelligence Extracts 40–97 (1 January–28 February 1943), 98–158 (1 March–30 April 1943), 159–218 (1 May–30 June 1943); History of the Ninth Bombardment Squadron (H) for the Period January 1, 1943, through May 31, 1943; History of the 436th Bombardment Squadron (H) for the Period January 1, 1943, through April 30, 1943; History of the 493rd Bombardment Squadron (H) for the Period January 1, 1943, through April 30, 1943, SQ-Bomb-493-HI, A0623, reel 0652.
73. Tenth Air Force Operational Diary, 1 June 1942–1 June 1943; India Air Task Force, Daily Intelligence Extracts 40–97 (1 January–28 February 1943), 98–158 (1 March–30 April 1943), 159–218 (1 May–30 June 1943); History of the Ninth Bombardment Squadron (H) for the Period January 1, 1943, through May 31, 1943; History of the 436th Bombardment Squadron (H) for the Period January 1, 1943, through April 30, 1943; History of the 493rd Bombardment Squadron (H) for the Period January 1, 1943, through April 30, 1943, SQ-Bomb-493-HI, A0623, reel 0652.
74. Tenth Air Force Operational Diary, 1 June 1942–1 June 1943; India Air Task Force, Daily Intelligence Extracts 40–97 (1 January–28 February 1943), 98–158 (1 March–30 April 1943), 159–218 (1 May–30 June 1943); History of the Ninth Bombardment Squadron (H) for the Period January 1, 1943, through May 31, 1943; History of the 436th Bombardment Squadron (H) for the Period January 1, 1943, through April 30, 1943; History of the 493rd Bombardment Squadron (H) for the Period January 1, 1943, through April 30, 1943, SQ-Bomb-493-HI, A0623, reel 0652.
75. Young, *Death from Above*, 134.
76. Operations Analysis Section, HQ, Army Air Force, India Burma Sector, China-Burma-India, "Study of 7th Bomb Group Operations from 1 February 1943 to 31 March 1944," 27 May 1944, Army Air Forces, India Burma Sector, Operational Analysis 825.3101-1, A8203, reel 9997, frames 293–319.
77. "Study of 7th Bomb Group Operations from 1 February 1943 to 31 March 1944," 27 May 1944.
78. Bombardment Statistics of the 7th Bomb Group, Nov. 20 through May 26, India Air Task Force Operation Statistics, India Air Task Force, 827.308, A8221, reel 10015, frame 322.
79. India Air Task Force Reports on Operations November 1942–September 1943, Operations of the 9th Photographic Squadron (L) December 13, 1942, to May 31, 1943, India Air Task Force, 827.306, A8221, reel 10015, frame 92; Shores, *Air War for Burma*, 89.
80. Edward M. Young, *B-24 Liberator vs. Ki-43 Oscar*, Osprey Duel 41 (Oxford: Osprey, 2012), 31.
81. Ibid., 57.
82. Ibid.
83. Headquarters, India Air Task Force, Daily Intelligence Extract for 5 March 1943, C-102, "Enemy Planes and Tactics in the Rangoon Area," India Air Task Force Daily Intelligence Extracts 98–153 (1 March–30 April 1943); Daily Intelligence Extract for 4 March 1943, C-101; Daily Intelligence Extract for 11 March 1943, C-108, India Air Task Force, 827.306, A8221, reel 10015, frames 1011, 1017–1018, 1038.
84. Headquarters, India Air Task Force, Daily Intelligence Extract for 15 March 1943, C-112, India Air Task Force, Daily Intelligence Extracts 98–158 (1 March–30 April 1943), India Air Task Force, 827.306, frame 1055; Young, *Death from Above*, 140.

85. Headquarters, India Air Task Force, Daily Intelligence Extract for 1 April 1943, C-129; Daily Intelligence Extract for 2 May 1943, C-160, India Air Task Force, Daily Intelligence Extracts 98–158 (1 March–30 April 1943), 159–219 (1 May–30 June 1943), India Air Task Force, 827.306, frames 1136, 1262; Young, *Death from Above*, 146.

86. Headquarters, India Air Task Force, Daily Intelligence Extract for 1 April 1943, C-129; Daily Intelligence Extract for 17 May 1943, C-175, India Air Task Force, Daily Intelligence Extracts 159–219 (1 May–30 June 1943), India Air Task Force, 827.306, frame 1322.

87. Office of the Assistant Chief of Air Staff, Intelligence, "B-24 Tactics over Burma and Thailand," *Informational Intelligence Summary* 44-7 (29 February 1944): 2.

88. Alfonso B. Perez, *A B-24 Bombardier "over Burma": The Personal Diary of Lt. Alfonso B. Perez* (privately published, n.d.), 22.

89. United States Strategic Bombing Survey (Pacific War), *Air Operations in China, Burma, India World War II*, 18.

90. Brig. Gen. Caleb V. Haynes, India Air Task Force, to Lt. Gen. Henry Arnold, 10th Air Force Evaluation, 9 February 1943, 827. 306-2, A8221, reel 10015, frames 306–310.

91. *The Tenth Air Force 1943*, 94.

92. IATF Bombing Mission Reports, 1 January–May 31, 1943, India Air Task Force, 827.306, frame 1322.

93. *The Tenth Air Force 1943*, 100–101.

94. Headquarters, India Air Task Force, Daily Intelligence Extract for 8 April 1943 (C-136), 9 April 1943, India Air Task Force, Daily Intelligence Extracts 98–158 (1 March–30 April 1943), India Air Task Force, 827.306, frames 1164, 1173.

95. *The Tenth Air Force 1943*, 101–102.

96. *The Tenth Air Force 1943*, 102; Headquarters, India Air Task Force, Daily Intelligence Extract for 4 April 1932 (C-132), 26 April 1943 (C-154), 11 May 1943 (C-169), 24 May 1943 (C-182), India Air Task Force, Daily Intelligence Extracts 98–158 (1 March–30 April 1943), India Air Task Force, 827.306, frames 1150, 1240, 1300, 1356.

97. Shores, *Air War for Burma*, 72–73.

98. David K. Hayward, ed., *World War II Diary: By the Men of the 22nd Bomb Squadron of the China Burma India Theater* (Huntington Beach, CA: 22nd Bomb Squadron Association, 2002), 118–19.

99. Shores, *Air War for Burma*, 81; Headquarters, India Air Task Force, Daily Intelligence Extract for 9 April 1943, C-137, frame 1170.

100. Shores, *Air War for Burma*, 82–83; Headquarters, India Air Task Force, Daily Intelligence Extract for 21 April 1943, C-149, 9 April 1943, frame 1214.

101. Headquarters Army Air Forces, India Burma Sector, China Burma India Theater, "Japanese Fighter Tactics against B-25s," July 1944, Air 23/2997, Air Ministry and Ministry of Defence, Royal Air Force Overseas Commands, Reports and Correspondence: Strategic Air Force. Japanese Fighter Tactics Against Heavy Bombers; Historical Record 490th Bombardment Squadron (M), AAF, for April 1943, A0621, reel 650, frame 656; Tenth Air Force Operational Diary, 1 June 1942–1 June 1943.

102. *Army Air Forces Statistical Digest World War II*, 174.

103. James M. Vesely, *Unlike Any Land You Know: The 490th Bomb Squadron in China-Burma-India* (Lincoln, NE: Writers Club Press, 2000), 58.

104. Ibid., 58–59.

105. Historical Record 490th Bombardment Squadron (M), AAF, for May 1943, A0621, reel 650, frames 662–63.

106. Historical Record 490th Bombardment Squadron (M), AAF, for May 1943, A0621, reel 650, frames 662–63; Howard Bell and Anthony Strotman, *The Burma Bridge Busters* (Booksurge, 2005), 39–41.

107. Shores, *Air War for Burma*, 90–91; Headquarters, India Air Task Force, Daily Intelligence Extract for 1 April 1943, C-129; Daily Intelligence Extract for 4 June 1943, C-193, India Air Task Force, Daily Intelligence Extracts 159–219 (1 May–30 June 1943), India Air Task Force, 827.306, frames 1392–93.

108. Headquarters, India Air Task Force, Daily Intelligence Extract for 1 April 1943, C-129; Daily Intelligence Extract for 28 May 1943, C-186, India Air Task Force, Daily Intelligence Extracts 159–219 (1 May–30 June 1943), India Air Task Force, 827.306, frames 1365–67.

109. *The Tenth Air Force 1943*, 95.

110. Lt. Col. John R. Sutherland, Headquarters, Tenth Air Force, to Commanding General, Tenth Air Force, 21 April 1943, Inspection Tour of Heavy and Medium Bombardment Units of the Tenth Air Force, Documents for History of Army Air Force in India, 12 February 1942–15 December 1943, Army Air Forces, India-Burma Sector, 825.01, frames 980–83.

111. Lt. Col. John R. Sutherland, Inspection Tour of Heavy and Medium Bombardment Units of the Tenth Air Force.

112. *The Tenth Air Force 1943*, 106–107.

113. Ibid.

114. Air 23/4963, Air Ministry and Ministry of Defence, Royal Air Force Overseas Commands, Reports and Correspondence: Air Command, Southeast Asia. Summary of Operations 1943 by RAF and USAAF Based in India.

115. Air Ministry, Air Historical Branch, *The Campaigns in the Far East*, vol. 3, *India Command September 1939 to November 1943* (London, n.d.), 118.

116. Ibid.

CHAPTER 5:
Trident, Command Changes, and Operations during the Monsoon: June–August 1943

1. Kirby, *The War against Japan*, 2:359.
2. Louis Allen, *Burma: The Longest War, 1941–1945* (London: J. M. Dent, 1984), 113–116; Kirby, *The War against Japan*, 2:385.
3. Air 23/4963, Summary of Operations 1943 by RAF and USAAF Based in India.
4. Romanus and Sunderland, *United States Army in World War II: China-Burma-India Theater*, 1:296–302, 306–307; Plating, *The Hump: America's Strategy for Keeping China in World War II*, 116–26.
5. Kirby, *The War against Japan*, 2:327.
6. Romanus and Sunderland, *United States Army in World War II: China-Burma-India Theater*, 1:303.
7. Kirby, *The War against Japan*, 2:329.
8. Ibid., 362, 368.
9. Ibid., 368–69.
10. Ibid., 369.
11. Ibid.
12. "History of Air Operations on the Continent of Asia, December 1941–May 1946," vol. 3, section 2, frames 54–56.
13. Ibid., frames 53–54.
14. Romanus and Sunderland, *United States Army in World War II: China-Burma-India Theater*, 1:322.
15. Ibid., p. 329.
16. Schaller, *The US Crusade in China, 1938–1945*, 136.
17. Romanus and Sunderland, *United States Army in World War II: China-Burma-India Theater*, 1:327–33.
18. Lt. Gen. Joseph Stilwell to Tenth Air Force, 23 April 1943, Documents for History of Army Air Force in India, 12 February 1942–15 December 1943, frame 132.
19. "History of Air Operations on the Continent of Asia, December 1941–May 1946," vol. 3, section 2, p. 79, frame 86.
20. Ibid., 85, frame 92.
21. Ibid., 87, frame 94.
22. Ibid., 92, frame 99.
23. Maj. Gen. George Stratemeyer, Chief of the Air Staff, to Maj. Gen. Clayton L. Bissell, Commanding, Tenth Air Force, 9 July 1942, Tenth Air Force, 201—Bissell, Clayton L., August 1942–November 1943, 830.289-1, frames 921–22.
24. Fogerty, *Biographical Data on Air Force General Officers, 1917–1952*, 2 vols.
25. "History of Air Operations on the Continent of Asia, December 1941–May 1946," vol. 3, section 2, p. 88, frame 95.
26. Ibid.
27. Ibid., 89–90, frame 97.
28. Craven and Cate, *The Army Air Forces in World War II*, 4:446–47.
29. Ibid., 4:448.
30. Craven and Cate, *The Army Air Forces in World War II*, 4:448–49; Maj. Gen. Clayton L. Bissell, Tenth Air Force, to Brig. Gen. Caleb V. Haynes, Assam American Air Base Command, 12 June 1943, CBI: USAAF, Tenth Air Force, Headquarters Assam American Air Base Command, Dinjan, India, History of Organization, July 1943, 828.011, A8222, reel 10016, frames 343–44; "History of Air Operations on the Continent of Asia, December 1941–May 1946," vol. 3, section 2, p. 81–82, frames 88–89.
31. Craven and Cate, *The Army Air Forces in World War II*, 4:443.
32. Ibid.
33. Ibid., 466, 537.
34. Ibid., 449.
35. Ibid., 450.
36. Ibid.; "History of Air Operations on the Continent of Asia December 1941–May 1946," vol. 3, section 2, p. 103, frame 110.
37. Carl von Clauswitz, *On War*, ed. Michael Howard and Peter Paret (Princeton, NJ: Princeton University Press, 1976), 240.
38. Ibid., 250.
39. War Department, *Command and Employment of Air Power*, War Department Field Manual FM 100–20 (Washington, DC: War Department, 1944), 1.
40. Craven and Cate, *The Army Air Forces in World War II*, 4:450.
41. Ibid.
42. "History of Air Operations on the Continent of Asia, December 1941–May 1946," vol. 3, section 2, p. 105, frame 112.
43. Ibid., 96–100, frames 103–107.
44. Lt. Gen. Joseph Stilwell, US Army Forces, China-Burma-India, to Maj. Gen. Clayton L. Bissell, Tenth Air Force, 15 April 1943, Documents for History of Army Air Force in India, 12 February 1942–15 December 1943, Army Air Forces, India-Burma Sector, frame 896.
45. "History of Air Operations on the Continent of Asia, December 1941–May 1946," vol. 3, section 2, pp. 105–106, frames 112–13.
46. Howard Davidson's biographical data can be found at www.af.mil/AboutUs/Biographies/Display/tabid/225/Article/107292/major-general-howard-calhoun-davidson.aspx, as well as in Fogerty, *Biographical Data on Air Force General Officers, 1917–1952*.
47. "History of Air Operations on the Continent of Asia, December 1941–May 1946," vol. 3, section 2, p. 106, frame 113.
48. Gen. George Marshall, Chief of Staff, to Lt. Gen. Joseph Stilwell, Commanding General, US Army Forces, China-Burma-India, 20 July 1943, copy in the personal diary of Maj. Gen. George Stratemeyer, for 26 July 1943 through 31 December 1943, Papers of Gen. George Stratemeyer, Thomas Overlander–George Stratemeyer Collection, Special Collections, McDermott Library, US Air Force Academy, Colorado Springs, CO.
49. Craven and Cate, *The Army Air Forces in World War II*, 4:451.

50. Entry for 9 August 1943 in the personal diary of Maj. Gen. George Stratemeyer, for 26 July 1943 through 31 December 1943.
51. Entries for 13–16 August 1943, in the personal diary of Maj. Gen. George Stratemeyer, for 26 July 1943 through 31 December 1943.
52. Entries for 18–20 August 1943, in the personal diary of Maj. Gen. George Stratemeyer, for 26 July 1943 through 31 December 1943; Craven and Cate, *The Army Air Forces in World War II*, 4:451–52.
53. Craven and Cate, *The Army Air Forces in World War II*, 4:184, 451–52.
54. Maj. Gen. Clayton Bissell, Tenth Air Force, to All Unit Commanders, Tenth Air Force, 19 August 1943, Tenth Air Force, 201—Bissell, Clayton L., August 1942–November 1943, 830.289-1, frame 905.
55. Byrd, *Chennault: Giving Wings to the Tiger*, 196.
56. Plating, *The Hump: America's Strategy for Keeping China in World War II*, 109.
57. Arnold, *Global Mission*, 419.
58. Ehrman, *Grand Strategy*, 5:131.
59. Col. Cecil Combs, India Air Task Force, to Maj. Gen. Clayton Bissell, Tenth Air Force, 16 June 1943, Tenth Air Force, 201—Bissell, Clayton L., August 1942–November 1943, 830.289-1, frame 973.
60. India Air Task Force, Narrative History, India Air Task Force, November 1942–31 May 1943, 827.306-1, A8221, reel 10015, frame 19.
61. Charles V. Duncan Jr., *B-24 over Burma* (Modesto, CA: C. V. Duncan, 1986), 71.
62. Young, *Death from Above*, 154.
63. Ibid.
64. Headquarters, India Air Task Force, Daily Intelligence Extract for 6 September 1943, C-287, Daily Intelligence Extracts 282–317 (1 September–6 October 1943), India Air Task Force, 827.306, A8222, reel 10016, frame 194.
65. "History of the 492nd Bombardment Squadron (Heavy) for the Month of September 1943," SQ-Bomb-492-HI, A0623, reel 0652.
66. Headquarters, India Air Task Force, Daily Intelligence Extract for 7 September 1943, C-288, Daily Intelligence Extracts 282–317 (1 September–6 October 1943), India Air Task Force, 827.306, A8222, reel 10016, frame 197; Young, *Death from Above*, 157.
67. Greenhalgh, *Foto Joe in CBI*, 36, 38–43; Shores, *Air War for Burma*, 99; Yasuho Izawa, "64th Flying Sentai, Part 3," *Aero Album* 5, no. 4 (Winter 1972): 8.
68. This data is taken from the India Air Task Force Narrative History for June–September 1943 and India Air Task Force Operations Statistics, Tenth Air Force 827.308, A8221, reel 10015, frames 318–572.
69. Tenth Air Force, India Air Task Force, Daily Intelligence Extracts 40–219 (1 January–30 June 1943), 827.606, A8221, reel 10015; India Air Task Force, Daily Intelligence Extracts 220–281 (1 July–31 August 1943), 827.606, A8222, reel 10016; India Air Task Force Operations Statistics, Tenth Air Force 827.308, A8221, reel 10015, frames 318–572.
70. Tenth Air Force, India Air Task Force, Daily Intelligence Extracts 40–219 (1 January–30 June 1943), 827.606, A8221, reel 10015; India Air Task Force, Daily Intelligence Extracts 220–281 (1 July–31 August 1943), 827.606, A8222, reel 10016; India Air Task Force Operations Statistics, Tenth Air Force 827.308, A8221, reel 10015, frames 318–572; Young, *Death from Above*, 151.
71. Tenth Air Force, India Air Task Force, Daily Intelligence Extracts 40–219 (1 January–30 June 1943), 827.606, A8221, reel 10015; India Air Task Force, Daily Intelligence Extracts 220–281 (1 July–31 August 1943), 827.606, A8222, reel 10016; India Air Task Force Operations Statistics, Tenth Air Force 827.308, A8221, reel 10015, frames 318–572; India Air Task Force Narrative History for June–September 1943.
72. Tenth Air Force, India Air Task Force, Daily Intelligence Extracts 40–219 (1 January–30 June 1943), 827.606, A8221, reel 10015; India Air Task Force, Daily Intelligence Extracts 220–281 (1 July–31 August 1943), 827.606, A8222, reel 10016; India Air Task Force Operations Statistics, Tenth Air Force 827.308, A8221, reel 10015, frames 318–572; India Air Task Force Narrative History for June–September 1943; History of the 22nd Bombardment Squadron (Medium) for August 1943, 22nd Bombardment Squadron (M), SQ-Bomb-22-HI, A0543, reel 0567; History of the 491st Bombardment Squadron (Medium) for August 1943, 491st Bombardment Squadron (M), SQ-Bomb-491-HI, A0622, reel 0651.
73. History of the 490th Bombardment Squadron (Medium) for August 1943, 490th Bombardment Squadron (M), SQ-Bomb-490-HI, A0621, reel 0650.
74. Hata et al., *Japanese Army Air Force Fighter Units and Their Aces 1931–1945*, 142, 157; Izawa, "64th Flying Sentai, Part 3," 8.
75. History of the 22nd Bombardment Squadron for July, August, and September 1943, 22nd Bombardment Squadron (M), SQ-Bomb-22-HI, A0543, reel 0567, frames 59–181.
76. Greenhalgh, *Foto Joe in CBI*, 36.
77. History of the 25th Fighter Squadron for June 1943, 25th Fighter Squadron, SQ-FI-25-HI, A0727, reel 765; History of the 26th Fighter Squadron, October 1942–March 1945, 26th Fighter Squadron, SQ-FI-26-HI, A0728, reel 766.
78. History of the 25th Fighter Squadron for June 1943, 25th Fighter Squadron, SQ-FI-25-HI, A0727, reel 765; History of the 26th Fighter Squadron, October 1942–March 1945, 26th Fighter Squadron, SQ-FI-26-HI, A0728, reel 766; India Air Task Force, Daily Intelligence Extracts 232 (July 13), 242 (July 23), 243 (July 24), 245 (July 27), 246 (July 27), India Air Task Force, Daily Intelligence Extracts 220–281 (1 July–31 August 1943); India Air Task Force, Daily Intelligence Extract 306 (September 26), India Air Task Force, Daily Intelligence Extracts 282–317 (1 September–6 October 1943), 827.606, A8222, reel 10016; 51st Fighter Group Information Bulletins for July 1943, GP-51-SU, B0145, reel 1248.

79. General Orders 28, Brig. Gen. B. G. Ferris, Deputy Chief of Staff, Headquarters, US Army Air Forces, China-Burma-India, to 51st Fighter Group, History of the 51st Fighter Group April–December 1943, 51st Fighter Group, GP-51-HI, B0145, reel 1248, frame 433.
80. History of the 51st Fighter Group, April–December 1943, 51st Fighter Group, GP-51-HI, B0145, reel 1248; History of the 89th Fighter Squadron, January 1942–December 1943, 89th Fighter Squadron, SQ-FI-89-HI, A0762, reel 801.
81. "Study of 7th Bomb Group Operations from 1 February 1943 to 31 March 1944," 27 May 1944.

CHAPTER 6:
Air Command, Southeast Asia: Integrating the Allied Air Forces, August–December 1943

1. Howard, *Grand Strategy*, 4:539.
2. Ibid., 4:540–41.
3. Ibid., 4:541–42.
4. Ibid., 4:542.
5. Romanus and Sunderland, *United States Army in World War II: China-Burma-India Theater*, 1:359.
6. Howard, *Grand Strategy*, 4:542.
7. Ibid., 4:546.
8. Ibid., 4:547.
9. Ibid., 4:549.
10. Ibid.
11. Ibid., 4:550.
12. Matloff, *Strategic Planning for Coalition Warfare, 1943–1944*, 232.
13. Romanus and Sunderland, *United States Army in World War II: China-Burma-India Theater*, 1:358–59; Howard, *Grand Strategy*, 4:575; Kirby, *The War against Japan*, 2:422–23.
14. "Final Report to the President and the Prime Minister," 24 August 1943, "The War against Japan, Long-Term Strategy, Section 20.(b)," Howard, *Grand Strategy*, vol. 4, appendix 8, 686.
15. Maj. Gen. S. Woodburn Kirby, *The War against Japan*, vol. 3, *The Decisive Battles* (London: Her Majesty's Stationery Office, 1961), 5.
16. William T. Y'Blood, *Air Commandos against Japan: Allied Special Operations in World War II Burma* (Annapolis, MD: Naval Institute Press, 2008), 10.
17. Y'Blood, *Air Commandos against Japan*, 11, 14–23, 24–26.
18. Howard, *Grand Strategy*, 4:542–43.
19. Ibid., 4:543.
20. Kirby, *The War against Japan*, 2:425.
21. Ibid., 2:424–25.
22. Ibid., 2:426.
23. Romanus and Sunderland, *United States Army in World War II: China-Burma-India Theater*, 1:364.
24. Kirby, *The War against Japan*, 2:425.
25. Romanus and Sunderland, *United States Army in World War II: China-Burma-India Theater*, 1:364.
26. Kirby, *The War against Japan*, 2:425.
27. Ibid., 2:427.
28. Ibid., 2:428–29.
29. Ibid., 2:428–34.
30. Maurer, *Air Force Combat Units of World War II*, 186.
31. Ibid.
32. Ibid.; History of the 530th Fighter-Bomber Squadron March 1942–October 1943, 530th Fighter Squadron, SQ-FI-530-HI, A0875, reel 874.
33. James M. Fielder, *A History of the 459th Fighter Squadron, Twin Dragons CBI 1943–45* (Universal City, TX: James M. Fielder, 1993), 1.
34. *Army Air Forces Statistical Digest World War II*, 34
35. Air Ministry, Air Historical Branch, *The Campaigns in the Far East*, vol. 3, appendix 11.
36. Ibid., appendix 2.
37. Probert, *The Forgotten Air Force*, 147.
38. "History of Air Operations on the Continent of Asia, December 1941–May 1946," vol. 3, section 2, p. 97, frame 84.
39. Vice-Admiral Mountbatten, the Earl Mountbatten of Burma, *Report to the Combined Chiefs of Staff by the Supreme Allied Commander Southeast Asia, 1943–1945* (London: Her Majesty's Stationery Office, 1945), 11.
40. Ibid.
41. Admiral Lord Louis Mountbatten, Supreme Allied Commander, to Gen. Henry Arnold, Commanding General, Army Air Forces, 1 November 1943, MB1/C Mountbatten Papers: Southeast Asia Command, 1943–46: MB1/C11 General Henry Arnold, Papers of Earl Mountbatten of Burma, Special Collections, University of Southampton, UK.
42. Robert S. Ehlers, *The Mediterranean Air War: Airpower and Allied Victory in World War II* (Lawrence: University Press of Kansas, 2015), 266.
43. Ibid., 266–268.
44. Richard G. Davis, *Carl A. Spaatz and the Air War in Europe* (Washington, DC: Center for Air Force History, 1992), 180.
45. Ibid.
46. War Department Field Manual FM 100–20, *Command and Employment of Air Power*, 1.
47. Maj. Gregory M. Cain, "Air Leadership in Joint/Combined Operations: Lt. General George E. Stratemeyer of the Eastern Air Command, 1943–1945," thesis (Maxwell AFB, AL: US Air Force, Air University School of Advanced Airpower Studies, 1998), 20 (www.dtic.mil/cgi-bin/GetTRDoc?AD=ADA391810).
48. David Syrett, "Northwest Africa, 1942–1943," in *Case Studies in the Achievement of Air Superiority*, ed. Benjamin Franklin Cooling (Washington, DC: Office of Air Force History, US Air Force, 1991), 262.
49. Cain, *Air Leadership in Joint/Combined Operations: Lt. General George E. Stratemeyer of the Eastern Air Command, 1943–1945*, 23.
50. Wesley Frank Craven and James Lea Cate, eds., *The Army Air Forces in World War II*, vol. 5, *The Pacific: Matterhorn to Nagasaki, June 1944 to August 1945* (Chicago: University of Chicago Press, 1953), 18–22.

51. Gen. H. H. Arnold, Commanding General, Army Air Forces, to Maj. Gen. George Stratemeyer, Commanding General, US Army Air Forces, India and Burma, 28 August 1943, China-Burma-India (CBI): Eastern Air Command. Correspondence of Gen. Stratemeyer, August 1943–December 1944, 820.161A, A8072, reel 9864, frame 1165.
52. Ibid.
53. Ibid.
54. Craven and Cate, *The Army Air Forces in World War II*, 4:454.
55. Ibid., 455.
56. Ibid.
57. Ibid., 454.
58. Lt. Col. Joseph S. Clark Jr., Deputy Chief of Staff, Headquarters, Army Air Forces, India-Burma Sector, to Chief of Staff, India-Burma Sector, China-Burma-India Theater, 17 September 1943, History of Army Air Forces India-Burma Sector, China-Burma-India Theater, appendix I, CBI: USAAF, IBT, "History of United States Army Air Forces India-Burma Sector," China-Burma-India Theater, 825.01B, A8154, reel 9948, frames 529–30.
59. "Plan for System of Operational Command in Southeast Asia," History of Army Air Forces India-Burma Sector, China-Burma-India Theater, appendix II, CBI: USAAF, IBT, "History of United States Army Air Forces India-Burma Sector," China-Burma-India Theater, 825.01B, A8154, reel 9948, frames 630–31.
60. "Plan for System of Operational Command in Southeast Asia," History of Army Air Forces India-Burma Sector, China-Burma-India Theater, appendix II.
61. Entry for 11 October 1943 in the personal diary of Maj. Gen. George Stratemeyer for 26 July 1943 through 31 December 1943.
62. Air Chief Marshal Sir Guy Garrod, Deputy Air Officer Commanding-in-Chief, India Command, to Maj. Gen. George Stratemeyer, Headquarters US Army Air Force, New Delhi, 13 October 1943, Air 23/2167, Air Ministry and Ministry of Defence, Royal Air Force Overseas Commands, Reports and Correspondence: Air Command, Southeast Asia. Integration of British and American Air Forces under SEAC.
63. Maj. Gen. George Stratemeyer, Headquarters Army Air Forces, India-Burma Sector, to Air Chief Marshal Sir Guy Garrod, Air Headquarters, New Delhi, 14 October, 1943, Air 23/2167, Air Ministry and Ministry of Defence, Royal Air Force Overseas Commands, Reports and Correspondence: Air Command, Southeast Asia. Integration of British and American Air Forces under SEAC.
64. Stratemeyer to Garrod, 14 October 1943.
65. Integration of American and British Air Forces in Southeast Asia Command, Draft for Message from Supreme Commander to Combined Chiefs of Staff, 14 October 1943, Air 23/2167, Air Ministry and Ministry of Defence, Royal Air Force Overseas Commands, Reports and Correspondence: Air Command, Southeast Asia. Integration of British and American Air Forces under SEAC.
66. Entry for 14 October 1943, in the personal diary of Maj. Gen. George Stratemeyer for 26 July 1943 through 31 December 1943.
67. Ibid.
68. Entry for 23 October 1943 in the personal diary of Maj. Gen. George Stratemeyer for 26 July 1943 through 31 December 1943.
69. Charles F. Romanus and Riley Sunderland, *United States Army in World War II: China-Burma-India Theater*, vol. 2, *Stilwell's Command Problems* (Washington, DC: Office of the Chief of Military History, Department of the Army, 1956), 81.
70. Craven and Cate, *The Army Air Forces in World War II* 4:456.
71. Letter Gen. Stratemeyer to Commanding General, US Army Forces, China-Burma-India Theater, 24 October 1943, History of Army Air Forces India-Burma Sector, China-Burma-India Theater, appendix I, frame 562.
72. Entries for 26 and 27 October 1943 in the personal diary of Maj. Gen. George Stratemeyer for 26 July 1943 through 31 December 1943.
73. Air Marshal A. G. R. Garrod to Air Officer Commanding-in-Chief, Integration of British and American Air Forces Within Southeast Asia Command, 26 October 1943, Air 23/2167, Integration of British and American Air Forces under SEAC.
74. Ibid.
75. Air Marshal A. G. R. Garrod to Air Officer Commanding-in-Chief, 27 October 1943, Air 23/2167, Integration of British and American Air Forces under SEAC.
76. Ibid.
77. Ibid.
78. Integration of American and British Air Forces within Southeast Asia Command, Record of Meeting Held in the office of the Supreme Allied Commander, 28 October 1943, Arnold Papers, reel 200, folder China-Burma-India Theater, 1941–1944.
79. Supreme Allied Commander, Memorandum Covering Organization Chart of Integration of American and British Air Forces within Southeast Asia Command, 1 November 1943, Eastern Air Command. Correspondence of Gen. Stratemeyer, August 1943–December 1944, frame 1160.
80. Ibid.; Mountbatten to Gen. Arnold, 1 November 1943.
81. Maj. Gen. George Stratemeyer, Headquarters, Army Air Forces, India-Burma Sector, to Maj. Gen. Wedemeyer, 30 October 1943, Arnold Papers, reel 200, folder China-Burma-India Theater, 1941–1944.
82. Ibid.
83. Ibid.
84. Maj. Gen. George Stratemeyer, Headquarters, Army Air Forces, India-Burma Sector, to General Arnold, 31 October 1943, Arnold Papers, reel 200, folder China-Burma-India Theater, 1941–1944.
85. Ibid.
86. "History of Air Operations on the Continent of Asia, December 1941–May 1946," vol. 3, section 2, p. 97, frame 189.

87. Mountbatten to Arnold, 1 November 1943, MB1/C Mountbatten Papers: Southeast Asia Command, 1943–46: MB1/C11 Gen. Henry Arnold.
88. Ibid.
89. Maj. Gen. Barney M. Giles, Chief of the Air Staff, to Commanding General, Army Air Forces (n.d.), Subject: Attached Letter (Mountbatten) 1 November 1943, Arnold Papers, reel 200, folder China-Burma-India Theater, 1941–1944.
90. Ibid.
91. Air Chief Marshal Sir Richard Peirse, Air Headquarters, India, to Air Chief Marshal Sir Charles Portal, Chief of Air Staff, 5 November 1943, Air 23/2570, Air Ministry and Ministry of Defence, Royal Air Force Overseas Commands, Reports and Correspondence: Air Command, Southeast Asia. Integration of RAF and USAAF: Policy.
92. Ibid.
93. Mountbatten, *Report to the Combined Chiefs of Staff by the Supreme Allied Commander Southeast Asia, 1943–1945*, 19.
94. Ehrman, *Grand Strategy*, 5:157.
95. Ibid., 153.
96. Kirby, *The War against Japan*, 3:55.
97. Ibid., 3:61.
98. Ibid., 3:62.
99. Entries for 22, 23, 24, 25, 27, and 29 November and 3 and 7 December 1943 in the personal diary of Maj. Gen. George Stratemeyer, for 26 July 1943 through 31 December 1943.
100. Maj. Gen. George Stratemeyer, Memorandum for Gen. H. H. Arnold, Subject: Desired Decisions from Sextant Conference, 29 November, 1943, Early Plans for Integration of American and British into Eastern Air Command, China-Burma-India (CBI): Eastern Air Command, 820.201, vol. 1, A8090, reel 9884, frame 1242.
101. Radio message from Maj. Gen. Stratemeyer to Col. Stone, 26 November 1943, CBI: Eastern Air Command, Documentation Establishing Eastern Air Command, December 1943, 820.201, V.3, A8091, reel 9885, frame 73.
102. Letter from Col. Alvin Luedecke, Assistant Chief of Staff, Plans, Operations, Training and Intelligence to Col. Charles Stone, III, Chief of Air Staff, Army Air Forces, India-Burma Sector, 4 December 1943, Correspondence of Gen. Stratemeyer, August 1943–December 1944, frames 1152–53.
103. Message for Wedemeyer from Mountbatten, 1 December 1943, Early Plans for Integration of American and British into Eastern Air Command, 820.201, vol. 1, frame 1217.
104. Message from Aquila to Maj. Gen. Stratemeyer, 4 December 1943, 820.201, vol. 3, frame 83.
105. Maj. Gen. Stratemeyer to Col. Stone, 2 December 1943, Documentation Establishing Eastern Air Command, December 1943, 820.201, vol. 3, frame 51.
106. "Administrative History of Eastern Air Command, 15 December 1943–31 May 1945," in "History of Air Operations on the Continent of Asia December 1941–May 1946," vol. 3, section 2, 825.01C, A8155, reel 9949, frame 198.
107. Admiral Lord Louis Mountbatten to Air Chief Marshal Sir Charles Portal, Chief of the Air Staff, 27 November 1943, MB1/C202, Marshal of the Royal Air Force Sir Charles Portal, CAS, MB1/C Mountbatten Papers: Southeast Asia Command, 1943–46.
108. "Administrative History of Eastern Air Command, 15 December 1943–31 May 1945," frames 198–99.
109. Gen. Henry Arnold, Commanding General, Army Air Forces, to Admiral the Lord Louis Mountbatten, Supreme Allied Commander, Southeast Asia Command, 3 December 1943, MB1/C11 Gen. Henry Arnold, MB1/C Mountbatten Papers: Southeast Asia Command, 1943–46.
110. Gen. George Marshall, Chief of Staff, to Admiral the Lord Louis Mountbatten, Supreme Allied Commander, Southeast Asia Command, 3 December 1943, MB1/C171, Gen. George Marshall, MB1/C Mountbatten Papers: Southeast Asia Command, 1943–46.
111. Admiral Lord Louis Mountbatten, Supreme Allied Commander, Southeast Asia Command, to Gen. H. H. Arnold, Commanding General, Army Air Forces, 9 December 1943, MB1/C11 Gen. Henry Arnold, MB1/C Mountbatten Papers: Southeast Asia Command, 1943–46; Mountbatten, *Report to the Combined Chiefs of Staff by the Supreme Allied Commander Southeast Asia, 1943–1945*, 28.
112. "Administrative History of Eastern Air Command, 15 December 1943–31 May 1945," frame 198.
113. Mountbatten, *Report to the Combined Chiefs of Staff by the Supreme Allied Commander Southeast Asia, 1943–1945*, 28.
114. See entries for 9, 11, and 12 December 1943, in the personal diary of Maj. Gen. George Stratemeyer for 26 July 1943 through 31 December 1943.
115. Entry for 11 December 1943 in the personal diary of Maj. Gen. George Stratemeyer for 26 July 1943 through 31 December 1943.
116. Admiral Lord Louis Mountbatten, Supreme Allied Commander, Southeast Asia Command, to Air Chief Marshal Sir Charles Portal, Chief of Air Staff, 22 December 1943, MB1/C202 Marshal of the Royal Air Force Sir Charles Portal, CAS, MB1/C Mountbatten Papers: Southeast Asia Command, 1943–46.
117. Admiral Lord Louis Mountbatten, Supreme Allied Commander, Southeast Asia Command, to the Combined Chiefs of Staff, 11 December 1943, Air 23/2167, Integration of British and American Air Forces under SEAC.
118. Mountbatten to the Combined Chiefs of Staff, 11 December 1943.

119. Admiral Lord Louis Mountbatten, Supreme Allied Commander, Southeast Asia Command, to Maj. Gen. George Stratemeyer, Commanding General, Army Air Forces, India-Burma Sector, 11 December 1943, MB1/C255 Lt. Gen. George Stratemeyer, MB1/C Mountbatten Papers: Southeast Asia Command, 1943–46.
120. SEAC. Directive 5, 12 December 1943, Air 23/2167, Integration of British and American Air Forces under SEAC.
121. Gen. George Marshall, Chief of Staff, to Admiral Lord Louis Mountbatten, Supreme Allied Commander, Southeast Asia Command, 4 January 1944, MB1/C171, Gen. George Marshall, MB1/C Mountbatten Papers: Southeast Asia Command, 1943–46.
122. "Administrative History of Eastern Air Command, 15 December 1943–31 May 1945," frame 200.
123. Col. Charles Stone III, Chief of Air Staff, to Maj. Gen. Stratemeyer, "Organization of Eastern Air Command, Integration with the R.A.F. and Location of your Headquarters," 13 December 1943, Correspondence of Gen. Stratemeyer, August 1943–December 1944, frames 1126–30.
124. Maj. Gen. George Stratemeyer, Commanding, Army Air Forces, India-Burma Sector, to Air Chief Marshal Sir Richard Peirse, Air Headquarters, New Delhi, 14 December 1943, Correspondence of Gen. Stratemeyer, August 1943–December 1944, frames 1118–22.
125. Air Chief Marshal Sir Richard Peirse, Air Commander-in-Chief, Southeast Asia, Headquarters Air Command, Southeast Asia Policy Directive 1, 15 December 1943, Air 23/2167, Integration of British and American Air Forces under SEAC.
126. Maj. Gen. George Stratemeyer, Commanding, Headquarters Eastern Air Command, General Orders 1, 15 December 1943, Correspondence of Gen. Stratemeyer, August 1943–December 1944, frames 1069–70.
127. "Administrative History of Eastern Air Command, 15 December 1943–31 May 1945," frames 203–204.

CHAPTER 7:
Combat Resumed: Operations, October–December 1943

1. Changes in Organization, India Air Task Force, June–September 1943, CBI: Tenth Air Force, India Air Task Force, June–September 1943, India Air Task Force, 827.201-1, A8221, reel 10015, frame 2.
2. History for September 1943, Headquarters American Air Command No. 1, CBI: Tenth Air Force, Headquarters American Air Command No. 1 History of Organization, 828.011, A8222, reel 10016, frame 363.
3. *The Tenth Air Force 1943*, 54.
4. Ibid., 46.
5. 80th Fighter Group, October 1943–February 1944, GP-80-SU-OP, B0166, reel 1272.
6. Shores, *Air War for Burma*, 104–105.
7. 311th Fighter–Bomber Group, October 1943–February 1944, GP-311-SU-OP, B0230, reel 1343.
8. "A Brief History of AAF India & Burma," personal collection of Maj. Gen. Howard C. Davidson, AFHRA, 168.7266-56, reel 42822, p. 21.
9. 80th Fighter Group, October 1943–February 1944, GP-80-SU-OP, B0166, reel 1272; 311th Fighter–Bomber Group, October 1943–February 1944, GP-311-SU-OP, B0230, reel 1343; History 80th Fighter Group, November 1943, GP-80-HI, B0165, reel 1271.
10. 80th Fighter Group, October 1943–February 1944, GP-80-SU-OP, B0166, reel 1272; 311th Fighter–Bomber Group, October 1943–February 1944, GP-311-SU-OP, B0230, reel 1343; History 80th Fighter Group, November 1943, GP-80-HI, B0165, reel 1271.
11. Japanese Monograph No. 64: *Burma Air Operations Record, Jan. 1942–Aug. 1945*, p. 47–48.
12. *Burma Air Operations Record, Jan. 1942–Aug. 1945*, 48.
13. Shores, *Air War for Burma*, 104.
14. Lt. Col. C. A. Burrows, to Chief of Air Staff, Army Air Forces, India-Burma Sector, 30 November 1943, Subject: Aircraft Losses, Early Plans to Integrate American and British into Eastern Air Command, December 1943, 820.201, vol. 1, frame 1232; Shores, *Air War for Burma*, 104.
15. Lt. Col. C. A. Burrows, Subject: Aircraft Losses, frame 1232; Shores, *Air War for Burma*, 107.
16. Shores, *Air War for Burma*, 108.
17. *The Tenth Air Force 1943*, 55.
18. Ibid.
19. History 80th Fighter Group, November 1943, GP-80-HI, B0165, reel 1271.
20. *The Tenth Air Force 1943*, 56.
21. Ibid.
22. Ibid.
23. 80th Fighter Group, October 1943–February 1944, GP-80-SU-OP, B0166, reel 1272; 311th Fighter-Bomber Group, October 1943–February 1944, GP-311-SU-OP, B0230, reel 1343; History 80th Fighter Group, November 1943, GP-80-HI, B0165, reel 1271.
24. Flight Intelligence Report of 10 December 1943, 80th Fighter Group, October 1943–February 1944, GP-80-SU-OP; Shores, *Air War for Burma*, 129–30.
25. Flight Intelligence Report for 10 December 1943, 311th Fighter-Bomber Group, October 1943–February 1944, GP-311-SU-OP.
26. W. E. Smith, ed., *2nd Troop Carrier Squadron, AAF, CBI, WWII* (Cullman, AL: Gregath, 1987), 46.
27. Smith, *2nd Troop Carrier Squadron, AAF, CBI, WWII*, 32–33.
28. Flight Intelligence Report for 10 December 1943, 311th Fighter-Bomber Group, October 1943–February 1944, GP-311-SU-OP; Shores, *Air War for Burma*, 130.
29. Flight Intelligence Report for 10 December 1943, 311th Fighter-Bomber Group, October 1943–February 1944, GP-311-SU-OP.
30. Shores, *Air War for Burma*, 126.
31. A full description of Philip Adair's combat on 13 December 1943 can be found at www.p40warhawk.com/ww2_era/groups/80th_FG; Shores, *Air War for Burma*, 131.

32. Flight Intelligence Report for 13 December 1943, 311th Fighter-Bomber Group, October 1943–February 1944, GP-311-SU-OP; Shores, *Air War for Burma*, 131–32.
33. Flight Intelligence Report of 13 December 1943, 80th Fighter Group, October 1943–February 1944, GP-80-SU-OP; Shores, *Air War for Burma*, 130–31, 133–42.
34. Romanus and Sunderland, *United States Army in World War II: China-Burma-India Theater*, 2:88–89.
35. Ibid., p. 46–47.
36. "Air Ground Cooperation in Stilwell's North Burma Campaign, October 43–3 August 1944," CBI: Tenth Air Force, 10th Air Force Air Ground Cooperation, 830.4501-4, A8246, reel 10041, frames 726–62; "Development of Joint Air Ground Operations in Northern Burma," January 1945, CBI: Tenth Air Force, 10th Air Force Air Ground Cooperation, 830.4501-2, A8246, reel 10041, frames 658–719.
37. "Special Report: Development of Close Air Support Techniques in North Burma," 5 September 1944, CBI: Tenth Air Force, 10th Air Force Air Ground Cooperation, 830.4501-1, A8246, reel 10041, frames 614–57.
38. "Special Report: Development of Close Air Support Techniques in North Burma," 5 September 1944, p. 1, CBI: Tenth Air Force, 10th Air Force Air Ground Cooperation, 830.4501-1, A8246, reel 10041, frames 614–57.
39. Flight Intelligence Reports, 311th Fighter-Bomber Group, October 1943–February 1944, GP-311-SU-OP; Romanus and Sunderland, *United States Army in World War II: China-Burma-India Theater*, 2:45.
40. Romanus and Sunderland, *United States Army in World War II: China-Burma-India Theater*, 2:97.
41. Ibid.
42. "Chronological History of 10th A.F. Air Supply Operations," February 1943–May 1945, CBI: Tenth Air Force, Operations, 830.3069-1, A8244, reel 10042, frames 53–83.
43. Romanus and Sunderland, *United States Army in World War II: China-Burma-India Theater*, 2:97.
44. Dr. Joe G. Taylor, *Air Supply in the Burma Campaigns*, US Air Force Numbered Historical Studies 75 (1957), 19.
45. "Chronology of the Evolution of the 5320th Air Defense Wing (Prov.), January 1944," WG-5320-HI, C0175, reel 2367.
46. History of the 490th and 491st Bombardment Squadrons (M) for October and November, 1943, 490th Bombardment Squadron (M), SQ-Bomb-490-HI, A0621, reel 0650; 491st Bombardment Squadron (M), SQ-Bomb-491-HI, A0622, reel 0651.
47. Craven and Cate, *The Army Air Forces in World War II*, 4:486.
48. History of the 490th Bombardment Squadron (M) for November and December 1943, 490th Bombardment Squadron (M), SQ-Bomb-490-HI, A0621, reel 0650.
49. History of the 490th and 491st Bombardment Squadrons (M) for October 1943, 490th Bombardment Squadron (M), SQ-Bomb-490-HI, A0621, reel 0650; 491st Bombardment Squadron (M), SQ-Bomb-491-HI, A0622, reel 0651.
50. History of the 341st Bombardment Group (M) for the month of November 1943, 341st Bombardment Group (M), GP-341-HI-(Bomb), B0284, reel 1417.
51. Lt. Col. James Philpott, 341st Bombardment Group (M), to Brig. Gen. Howard Davidson, Tenth Air Force, 1 November 1943, 341st Bombardment Group (M), GP-341-HI-(Bomb), B0284, reel 1417, frame 1266.
52. History of the 490th Bombardment Squadron (M) for November 1943, 490th Bombardment Squadron (M), SQ-Bomb-490-HI, A0621, reel 0650; Craven and Cate, *The Army Air Forces in World War II*, 4:492.
53. Craven and Cate, *The Army Air Forces in World War II*, 4:492.
54. Ibid., 4:493.
55. History of the 9th Bombardment Squadron (H) for October 1943, 9th Bombardment Squadron (H), SQ-Bomb-9-HI, A0538, reel 0561.
56. Hiroshi Ichimura, *Ki-43 "Oscar" Aces of World War 2*, Osprey Aircraft of the Aces 85 (Oxford: Osprey, 2009), 34.
57. Young, *Death from Above*, 168–69.
58. Ibid., 173–74.
59. Craven and Cate, *The Army Air Forces in World War II*, 4:476.
60. Ibid.
61. Personal Diary of Lt. Gen. George Stratemeyer for 12 November 1943.
62. Craven and Cate, *The Army Air Forces in World War II*, 4:477.
63. Ibid., 478.
64. Ibid., 478–79; Shores, *Air War for Burma*, 116–17; History of the 530th Fighter Squadron for November 1943, 530th Fighter Squadron, SQ-FI-530-HI, A0875, reel 874.
65. Brig. Gen. Howard Davidson, Commanding, Tenth Air Force, to Gen. H. H. Arnold, Commanding, Army Air Forces, 10 December 1943, Documents for History of Army Air Force in India, 12 February 1942–15 December 1943, Army Air Forces, India-Burma Sector, frames 1045–46.
66. Shores, *Air War for Burma*, 118–19.
67. Ibid., 124.
68. Ibid., 118–19; Young, *Death from Above*, 177; Headquarters, Tenth Air Force, CBI: Tenth Air Force, 10th AF Operations, "Account of Mission of Bomb Groups," 21 December 1943, Tenth Air Force 830.305-1, A8242, reel 10037, frames 2217–29; History of the 311th Fighter Group, October 1943–February 1944, 311th Fighter Group, GP-311-HI, B0229, reel 1342.
69. Shores, *Air War for Burma*, 119–20; "Account of Mission of Bomb Groups," 21 December 1943; Craven and Cate, *The Army Air Forces in World War II*, 4:481; Young, *Death from Above*, 177–78.

70. Shores, *Air War for Burma*, 124; Young, *Death from Above*, 178–79; Brig. Gen. Howard Davidson, Commanding, Tenth Air Force, to Gen. H. H. Arnold, Commanding, Army Air Forces, 10 December 1943.

71. Shores, *Air War for Burma*, 124; Young, *Death from Above*, 178–79; History of the 311th Fighter Group, October 1943–February 1944, 311th Fighter Group, GP-311-HI, B0229, reel 1342.

72. Brig. Gen. Howard Davidson, Commanding, Tenth Air Force, to Gen. H. H. Arnold, Commanding, Army Air Forces, 10 December 1943.

73. Meeting Notes of 2 December 1943, meeting to discuss the attack over Rangoon, CBI: Tenth Air Force, Notes and Memoranda of Staff Meetings and Conferences, 1943–1944, A8232, reel 10027.

74. Craven and Cate, *The Army Air Forces in World War II*, 4:481–82.

75. Ibid., 482.

76. United States Strategic Bombing Survey (Pacific War), *Air Operations in China, Burma, India World War II*, 22.

77. Air 23/4884, Air Ministry and Ministry of Defence, Royal Air Force Overseas Commands, Reports and Correspondence: Air Command, Southeast Asia. Operational Effort by RAF and USAAF for Period of Japanese War.

CHAPTER 8:
American Fighter Operations under Eastern Air Command: December 1943–June 1944

1. Romanus and Sunderland, *United States Army in World War II: China-Burma-India Theater*, 2:76–77.
2. Ibid., 2:74–75.
3. Ibid., 2:80; Kirby, *The War against Japan*, 3:65.
4. Kirby, *The War against Japan*, 3:66.
5. Romanus and Sunderland, *United States Army in World War II: China-Burma-India Theater*, 2:32–36.
6. Kirby, *The War against Japan*, 3:24, 40.
7. Ibid., 3:50.
8. Romanus and Sunderland, *United States Army in World War II: China-Burma-India Theater*, 2:28.
9. Ibid., 2:28–29.
10. Kirby, *The War against Japan*, 3:51. Air Chief Marshal Peirse, "Air Chief Marshal Sir Richard Peirse's Dispatch on Air Operations in Southeast Asia, 16th November, 1943, to 31 May, 1944," in *Despatches from the Front: Far East Air Operations, 1942–1945*, ed. John Grehan and Martin Mace (Barnsley, UK: Pen & Sword Military, 2014), 46.
11. Air Ministry, Air Historical Branch, *The Campaigns in the Far East*, 4:15.
12. Air 23/1933, Air Ministry and Ministry of Defence, Royal Air Force Overseas Commands, Reports and Correspondence: Air Command, Southeast Asia. Dispatch on Operations of Eastern Air Command 15 December 1943–1 June 1945, 14.
13. Air Ministry, Air Historical Branch, *The Campaigns in the Far East*, 4:15; R. D. Van Wagner, *1st Air Commando Group: Any Place, Any Time, Any Where*, Military History Series 86-1, USAF Air Command and General Staff College (Maxwell AFB, AL: USAF Air Command and General Staff College, 1986), 29.
14. Y'Blood, *Air Commandos against Japan: Allied Special Operations in World War II Burma*, 32–33, 64–65.
15. Air Ministry, Air Historical Branch, *The Campaigns in the Far East*, 4:15–16, appendix 5; Peirse, "Air Chief Marshal Sir Richard Peirse's Despatch on Air Operations in Southeast Asia, 16th November, 1943, to 31 May, 1944," 44, 46.
16. Peirse, "Air Chief Marshal Sir Richard Peirse's Dispatch on Air Operations in Southeast Asia, 16th November, 1943, to 31 May, 1944," 45.
17. CBI: US Army Air Force (USAAF), India-Burma Theater (IBT). "History of United States Army Air Force Operations in the India Burma Theater,1 January to 2 September 1945," January 1944–September 1945, vol. 1, Army Air Forces, India-Burma Sector, 825.01, A8153, reel 9947, frames 1080–81, pp. xi–xii.
18. Air Ministry, Air Historical Branch, *The Campaigns in the Far East*, 4:31.
19. Peter Preston-Hough, *Commanding Far Eastern Skies: A Critical Analysis of the Royal Air Force Air Superiority Campaign in India, Burma and Malaya, 1941–1945* (Solihull, UK: Helion, 2015), 159–64.
20. Ibid., 177.
21. Peirse, "Air Chief Marshal Sir Richard Peirse's Dispatch on Air Operations in Southeast Asia, 16th November, 1943, to 31 May, 1944," 45.
22. Ibid., 61–63.
23. Taylor, *Air Supply in the Burma Campaign*, 141.
24. Peirse, "Air Chief Marshal Sir Richard Peirse's Dispatch on Air Operations in Southeast Asia, 16th November, 1943, to 31 May, 1944," 50.
25. Taylor, *Air Supply in the Burma Campaign*, 141.
26. Ibid.
27. Ibid., 132.
28. Peirse, "Air Chief Marshal Sir Richard Peirse's Dispatch on Air Operations in Southeast Asia, 16th November, 1943, to 31 May, 1944," 45.
29. CBI: Eastern Air Command, Dispatch on the Operations of Strategic Air Force Eastern Air Command for the Period 15 December 1943 to 31 May 1944, 821.04A, A8138, reel 9932, frames 1034–39, pp. 2–5.
30. Craven and Cate, *The Army Air Forces in World War II*, 4:512; CBI: Eastern Air Command, Operations of Strategic Air Force 15 December 1943 to 3 May 1945, 821.04A, A8138, reel 9932, frame 968, p. 11.
31. Craven and Cate, *The Army Air Forces in World War II*, 4:512.
32. Ibid., 4:514.
33. Kirby, *The War against Japan*, vol. 3; chapter 6 goes into Japanese planning in detail.
34. Kirby, *The War against Japan*, 3:78–79; Military History Section, Headquarters, Army Forces Far East, *Burma Air Operations Record, Jan. 1942–Aug. 1945*, 59–60; Izawa, "64th Flying Sentai, Part 3," 11.

35. Romanus and Sunderland, *United States Army in World War II: China-Burma-India Theater*, 2:39–41.
36. Kirby, *The War against Japan*, 3:64–66, 119, 173–74.
37. History of Organization, January, February, March 1943, 5320th Air Defense Wing (Prov), WG-5320–AirDef (Prov), C0174, reel 2366.
38. History for March and April 1943, 20th Tactical Reconnaissance Squadron, SQ-RCN-20-HI, A0908, reel 970; Greenhalgh, *Foto Joe in CBI*, 56.
39. History for December–March 1943, 80th Fighter Group, GP-80-HI, B0165, reel 1271.
40. History for March 1943, 529th Fighter Squadron, SQ-FI-529-HI, A0824, reel 873, frame 1384.
41. Peter C. Smith, *Straight Down! The North American A-36 Dive Bomber in Action* (Manchester, UK: Crécy, 2000), 192.
42. CBI: Tenth Air Force, Operations, "Burma Banshees Dive Bombing Tactics in Northern Burma," Strategical and Tactical Survey of 10 Air Force Efforts, 830.310 tab M, reel 25769.
43. History for December 1943, 80th Fighter Group, GP-80-HI, B0165, reel 1271.
44. CBI: Tenth Air Force, Operations, Headquarters, 311th Fighter-Bomber Group, "Operations: Types of Bombing Attack by Fighter Bombers," 13 January 1944, Strategical and Tactical Survey of 10 Air Force Efforts, 830.310 tab M, reel 25769; CBI: Tenth Air Force, Tenth Air Force (P-51 Tactics over Burma) from 1 November 1943 to 31 May 1944, 830.589-2, A8247, reel 10042.
45. CBI: Tenth Air Force, Tenth Air Force (P-51 Tactics over Burma) from 1 November 1943 to 31 May 1944, 830.589-2, A8247, reel 10042.
46. Romanus and Sunderland, *United States Army in World War II: China-Burma-India Theater*, 2:36–37.
47. Headquarters, 311th Fighter-Bomber Group, Consolidated Flight Intelligence Report for 3 February 1944, History, October 1943–February 1944, 311th Fighter Group, GP-311-HI, B0229, reel 1342.
48. Headquarters, 5320th Air Defense Wing (Prov), Information Bulletin 40, 12 January 1944, 5320th Air Defense Wing (Prov), WG-5320-AirDef (Prov), C0174, reel 2366.
49. Headquarters, 311th Fighter-Bomber Group, Flight Intelligence Reports for 12 February 1944, 311th Fighter Group, GP-311-SU-OP, B0230, reel 1343.
50. Headquarters, 80th Fighter Group, Flight Intelligence Reports for January and February 1944, 80th Fighter Group, GP-80-SU-OP, B0166, reel 1272.
51. Headquarters, 5320th Air Defense Wing (Prov), Information Bulletin 97, 9 March 1944, 5320th Air Defense Wing (Prov), WG-5320-AirDef (Prov), C0174, reel 2366.
52. Romanus and Sunderland, *United States Army in World War II: China-Burma-India Theater*, 2:145.
53. James E. T. Hopkins, *Spearhead: A Complete History of Merrill's Marauder Rangers* (Baltimore: Galahad, 1999), 142.
54. Romanus and Sunderland, *United States Army in World War II: China-Burma-India Theater*, 2:146–47.
55. "Special Report: Development of Close Air Support Techniques in North Burma," 5 September 1944; "Air Ground Cooperation in Stilwell's North Burma Campaign, October 43–3 August 1944."
56. "Special Report: Development of Close Air Support Techniques in North Burma," 5 September 1944; "History of United States Army Air Force Operations in the India Burma Theater, 1 January to 2 September 1945," 45.
57. "Special Report: Development of Close Air Support Techniques in North Burma," 5 September 1944.
58. Headquarters, 80th Fighter Group, Flight Intelligence Reports for 1–9 March 1944, 80th Fighter Group, GP-80-SU-OP, B0166, reel 1272; Headquarters, 311th Fighter-Bomber Group, Flight Intelligence Reports for 1–9 March 1944, 311th Fighter Group, GP-311-SU-OP, B0230, reel 1343; Headquarters, 5320th Air Defense Wing (Prov), Information Bulletins 89, 90, 91, 93, 94, 95, and 97, 1–9 March 1944, 5320th Air Defense Wing (Prov), WG-5320-AirDef (Prov), C0174, reel 2366.
59. Headquarters, 311th Fighter-Bomber Group, History for March 1944, 311th Fighter Group, GP-311-SU-OP, B0230, reel 1343, frame 1724.
60. See R. D. Van Wagner, *Any Time, Any Place, Any Where: The 1st Air Commandos in World War II* (Atglen, PA: Schiffer, 1998); Y'Blood, *Air Commandos against Japan: Allied Special Operations in World War II Burma*; Edward M. Young, *Air Commando Fighters of World War II* (North Branch, MN: Specialty Press, 2000).
61. Kirby, *The War against Japan*, 3:180–85, 205–17.
62. Y'Blood, *Air Commandos against Japan: Allied Special Operations in World War II Burma*, 77–79, 105–106; Report No. 1, US Navy Air Combat Information, Observations of Operational Forces in India Burma, "Direct Air Support to Long Range Penetration Groups of the Third Indian Division in North Burma, Provided by the First Air Commando Group, USAAF," 8 May 1944, GP-A-CMDO-1-HI.
63. Kirby, *The War against Japan*, 3:185–86; Romanus and Sunderland, *United States Army in World War II: China-Burma-India Theater*, 2:198.
64. Romanus and Sunderland, *United States Army in World War II: China-Burma-India Theater*, 2:166–68; Taylor, *Air Supply in the Burma Campaigns*, 54–58.
65. Romanus and Sunderland, *United States Army in World War II: China-Burma-India Theater*, 2:172–75, 192–93; Kirby, *The War against Japan*, 3:246–47.
66. History of the 88th Fighter Squadron for March 1943, 88th Fighter Squadron, SQ-FI-88-HI, A0761, reel 800; History of the 528th Fighter Squadron for March and April 1943, 528th Fighter Squadron, SQ-FI-528-HI, A0823, reel 872.
67. Headquarters, 80th Fighter Group, Flight Intelligence Reports for March 1944, 80th Fighter Group, GP-80-SU-OP, B0166, reel 1272; Headquarters, 311th Fighter-Bomber Group, Flight Intelligence Reports for March 1944, 311th Fighter Group, GP-311-SU-OP, B0230, reel 1343; Romanus and Sunderland, *United States Army in World War II: China-Burma-India Theater*, 2:175–88.

68. Romanus and Sunderland, *United States Army in World War II: China-Burma-India Theater*, 2:188–91; History of the 528th Fighter Squadron for April 1944, 528th Fighter Squadron, SQ-FI-528-HI, A0823, reel 872; Headquarters, 311th Fighter-Bomber Group, Flight Intelligence Reports for March 1944, 311th Fighter Group, GP-311-SU-OP, B0230, reel 1343; Headquarters, 311th Fighter Group, "Summary of Operations, 311th Fighter Group, October 16, 1943–August 14, 1945, 311th Fighter Group," GP-311-SU-OP, B0230, reel 1343, frame 121.

69. Romanus and Sunderland, *United States Army in World War II: China-Burma-India Theater*, 2:204.

70. Ibid., 2:218.

71. This is a brief summary of the material in Romanus and Sunderland, *United States Army in World War II: China-Burma-India Theater*, vol. 2, chapter 6: "The Drive for Myitkyina," 204–23.

72. Headquarters, 80th Fighter Group, History for April and May 1944, 80th Fighter Group, GP-80-HI, B0165, reel 1271; History of the 89th and 90th Fighter Squadrons for April 1944, 89th Fighter Squadron, SQ-FI-89-HI, A0762, reel 801; 90th Fighter Squadron, SQ-FI-90-HI, A0762, reel 801; Headquarters, 311th Fighter Group, History for April and May 1944, 311th Fighter Group, GP-311-HI, B0229, reel 1342; History of the 529th Fighter Squadron for May 1944, 529th Fighter Squadron, SQ-FI-529-HI, A0824, reel 873.

73. Romanus and Sunderland, *United States Army in World War II: China-Burma-India Theater*, 2:225–33.

74. Ibid., p. 218.

75. "History of United States Army Air Force Operations in the India Burma Theater, 1 January to 2 September 1945," 1.

76. Ibid., 2.

77. Preston-Hough, *Commanding Far Eastern Skies*, 179.

78. Air Ministry, Air Historical Branch, *The Campaigns in the Far East*, 4:70.

79. Hata et al., *Japanese Army Air Force Units and Their Aces, 1931–1945*, 56–58.

80. "History of United States Army Air Force Operations in the India Burma Theater, 1 January to 2 September 1945," 2.

81. Ibid., 3–4.

82. Ibid., 6.

83. Ibid., 5.

84. Shores, *Air War for Burma*, 133–37.

85. Osamu Tagaya, "The Imperial Japanese Air Forces," in *Why Air Forces Fail: The Anatomy of Defeat*, ed. Robin Higham and Stephen J. Harris (Lexington: University Press of Kentucky, 2006), 185.

86. *Burma Air Operations Record, Jan. 1942–Aug. 1945*, 59–66.

87. Shores, *Air War for Burma*, 141; Headquarters, 89th Fighter Squadron, A–2 Form for 28 December 1943, History of 89th Fighter Squadron for December 1943, 89th Fighter Squadron, SQ-FI-89-HI, A0762, reel 801.

88. Shores, *Air War for Burma*, 150–51; Headquarters, 311th Fighter Bomber Group, Consolidated Flight Intelligence Report for 18 January 1944, 311th Fighter Group, GP-311-SU-OP, B0230, reel 1343; Headquarters, 89th Fighter Squadron, Flight Intelligence Report for 18 January 1944, 89th Fighter Squadron, SQ-FI-89-HI, A0762, reel 801; Smith, *2nd Troop Carrier Squadron, AAF, CBI, WWII*, 48–51.

89. Dispatch on Operations of Eastern Air Command, 15 December 1943–1 June 1945, 148.

90. This figure is drawn from Christopher Shores's *Air War for Burma*, which lists Japanese losses during January and February 1944. While Allied pilots did claim more than the actual number of airplanes shot down—not surprising in the heat of combat—the Japanese pilots were worse. Shores relates a combat that took place on 4 February 1944 in which two Spitfire sections engaged some 20 Ki-43s, claiming one probably shot down and one damaged, though the Japanese lost no fighters in the combat. The *204th Hikōsentai*, one of the Japanese units involved, claimed 12 Spitfires shot down—three times the number of Spitfires that actually attacked.

91. Shores, *Air War for Burma*, 156.

92. Y'Blood, *Air Commandos against Japan*, 109–10; Shores, *Air War for Burma*, 175.

93. Young, *Air Commando Fighters of World War II*, 25.

94. Shores, *Air War for Burma*, 176–77.

95. Ibid., 177–78; ACSEA Weekly Intelligence Summary 18 for the week of 19 March 1944, China-Burma-India (CBI): Air Command, Southeast Asia, Weekly Intelligence Summary 1–21 (5 December 1943–16 April 1944), 815.607, A8058, reel 9850.

96. Shores, *Air War for Burma*, 178–80, 187; *Burma Air Operations Record, Jan. 1942–Aug. 1945*, 69.

97. Apparently the blunter wing tips of the Type 1 fighter model II (Ki-43-II), which had a slightly reduced wingspan from the Type 1 fighter model I (Ki-43-I), resembled the clipped wings of the Mitsubishi A6M3 Zero-sen fighter, leading to the confusion. See Air Command, Southeast Asia, Weekly Intelligence Summary 16 (5 March 1944) and 17 (12 March 1944), Air Command, Southeast Asia, Weekly Intelligence Summary 1–22 (5 December 1943–16 April 1944), 815.607, A8058, reel 9850.

98. William M. Behrns and Kenneth Moore, *The San Joaquin Siren: An American Ace in WWII's CBI* (Tucson, AZ: Amethyst Moon, 2011), 148–49.

99. Shores, *Air War for Burma*, 190; History of the 459th Fighter Squadron for March 1944, 459th Fighter Squadron, SQ-FI-490-HI, A0812, reel 860.

100. Shores, *Air War for Burma*, 191–92; History of the 89th and 90th Fighter Squadrons for March 1944, 89th Fighter Squadron, SQ-FI-89-HI, A0762, reel 801; 90th Fighter Squadron, SQ-FI-90-HI, A0762, reel 801; History of the 529th and 530th Fighter Squadrons for March 1944, 529th Fighter Squadron, SQ-FI-529-HI, A0824, reel 873; 530th Fighter Squadron, SQ-FI-530-HI, A0875, reel 874; Headquarters, 311th Fighter-Bomber Group, Consolidated Flight Intelligence Reports for 17 March 1944, 311th Fighter Group, GP-311-SU-OP, B0230, reel 1343.

101. Shores, *Air War for Burma*, 197–201; Air Ministry, Air Historical Branch, *The Campaigns in the Far East*, 4:75.
102. Shores, *Air War for Burma*, 205–207; History of the 459th Fighter Squadron for April 1944, 459th Fighter Squadron, SQ-FI-490-HI, A0812, reel 860.
103. CBI: Tenth Air Force, Headquarters, Tenth Air Force Operational Bulletin 8, "P-38 Combat Tactics over Burma from 12 March 1944 to 17 May 1944," 9 July 1944, 830.548-1, A8247, reel 10042.
104. Nicholas Millman, *Ki-44 "Tojo" Aces of World War 2*, Osprey Aircraft of the Aces 100 (Oxford: Osprey, 2011), 30.
105. Shores, *Air War for Burma*, 209–23; *Burma Air Operations Record, Jan. 1942–Aug. 1945*, 74; History of the 459th Fighter Squadron for April 1944, 459th Fighter Squadron, SQ-FI-490-HI, A0812, reel 860.
106. History of the 530th Fighter Squadron for May 1944, 530th Fighter Squadron, SQ-FI-530-HI, A0875, reel 874.
107. Ibid.; Shores, *Air War for Burma*, 225.
108. History of the 530th Fighter Squadron for May 1944, 530th Fighter Squadron, SQ-FI-530-HI, A0875, reel 874.
109. Ibid.; Shores, *Air War for Burma*, 227
110. History of the 530th Fighter Squadron for May 1944, 530th Fighter Squadron, SQ-FI-530-HI, A0875, reel 874; Shores, *Air War for Burma*, 240–41.
111. History of the 530th Fighter Squadron for May 1944, 530th Fighter Squadron, SQ-FI-530-HI, A0875, reel 874.
112. Shores, *Air War for Burma*, 240–41.
113. Preston-Hough, *Commanding Far Eastern Skies*, 215.
114. Dispatch covering operations of Bengal Command, 15 Nov.–17 Dec. 1943, and 3rd Tactical Air Force, 18 December–1 June 1944, 20.
115. Preston-Hough, *Commanding Far Eastern Skies*, 215.
116. United States Strategic Bombing Survey (Pacific War), *Japanese Air Power* (Washington, DC, 1946), 31.
117. See Air Command, Southeast Asia Weekly Intelligence Summary 8 (9 January 1944) and 31 (18 June 1944), Air Command, Southeast Asia, Weekly Intelligence Summary 1–22 (5 December 1943–16 April 1944), 815.607, A8058, reel 9850; and Air Command, Southeast Asia, Weekly Intelligence Summary 23–49 (23 April 1944–22 October 1944), 815.607, A8059, reel 9851.
118. This number is based on counting pilot losses mentioned in Shores, *Air War for Burma*.
119. *Burma Air Operations Record, Jan. 1942–Aug. 1945*, 69–71.
120. Shores, *Air War for Burma*, 237.
121. Dispatch covering operations of Bengal Command, 15 Nov.–17 Dec. 1943, and 3rd Tactical Air Force, 18 December–1 June 1944, 10.
122. "History of United States Army Air Force Operations in the India Burma Theater, 1 January to 2 September 1945."

CHAPTER 9:
Strategic Bombing and Air Supply Operations under Eastern Air Command: December 1943–June 1944

1. CBI: Eastern Air Command, Operations of Strategic Air Force, 15 December 1943 to 3 May 1945, 821.04A, A8138, reel 9932, frames 967–68.
2. Air Ministry, Air Historical Branch, *The Campaigns in the Far East*, 4:231.
3. Operations of Strategic Air Force, 15 December 1943 to 3 May 1945, 821.04A, A8138, reel 9932, frames 967–68.
4. CBI: Eastern Air Command, Dispatch on the Operations of Strategic Air Force Eastern Air Command for the Period 15 December 1943 to 31 May 1944, 821.04A, A8138, reel 9932, frame 1034.
5. Dispatch on the Operations of Strategic Air Force Eastern Air Command for the Period 15 December 1943 to 31 May 1944, frame 1034.
6. Operations of Strategic Air Force 15 December 1943 to 3 May 1945, frame 982.
7. Young, *Death from Above*, 185–86.
8. Ibid., 186.
9. Operations of Strategic Air Force, 15 December 1943 to 3 May 1945, frames 986–87.
10. Young, *Death from Above*, 186–87; Operations of Strategic Air Force, 15 December 1943 to 3 May 1945, frames 987–89; Dispatch on the Operations of Strategic Air Force Eastern Air Command for the Period 15 December 1943 to 31 May 1944, frames 1035–36.
11. Young, *Death from Above*, 188–89.
12. Ibid., 189; Brig. Gen. Howard Davidson to Brig. Gen. Grandison Gardner, Headquarters, AAF Proving Ground, 1 January 1944, CBI: Tenth Air Force, Maj. Gen. Howard Davidson Correspondence, 830.161, A8232, reel 10027.
13. Young, *Death from Above*, 189–91; History of the 493rd Bombardment Squadron for May 1944, 493rd Bombardment Squadron (H), SQ-Bomb-493-HI, A0623, reel 0652.
14. Young, *Death from Above*, 192–94.
15. Dispatch on the Operations of Strategic Air Force Eastern Air Command for the Period 15 December 1943 to 31 May 1944, frame 1062.
16. Ibid., frame 1043; Young, *Death from Above*, 196–98.
17. Mountbatten, *Report to the Combined Chiefs of Staff by the Supreme Allied Commander Southeast Asia, 1943–1945*, 33; Young, *Death from Above*, 195–96.
18. Young, *Death from Above*, 200–201.
19. Romanus and Sunderland, *United States Army in World War II: China-Burma-India Theater*, 2:316–20.
20. Ibid., 2:315.
21. Ibid.
22. Ibid., 2:325.
23. Ibid., 2:326–27.
24. Diary entry for 11 May 1944 in Lt. Gen. George Stratemeyer Personal Diary 1 January 1944 Thru 31 December 1944, Papers of Gen. George Stratemeyer, Thomas Overlander–George Stratemeyer Collection.

25. Diary entry for 23 May 1944 in Lt. Gen. George Stratemeyer Personal Diary 1 January 1944 Thru 31 December 1944, Papers of Gen. George Stratemeyer, Thomas Overlander–George Stratemeyer Collection.
26. This data is taken from appendix 2, Aircraft in Possession of Strategic Air Force, Dispatch on Operations of Eastern Air Command, 15 December 1943–1 June 1945, 134.
27. Diary entry for 4 June and 9 June 1944, in Lt. Gen. George Stratemeyer Personal Diary 1 January 1944 Thru 31 December 1944, Papers of Gen. George Stratemeyer, Thomas Overlander–George Stratemeyer Collection.
28. Dispatch on the Operations of Strategic Air Force Eastern Air Command for the Period 15 December 1943 to 31 May 1944, frames 1036–37.
29. Air 23/4301, Air Ministry and Ministry of Defence, Royal Air Force Overseas Commands, Reports and Correspondence: Air Command, Southeast Asia. Strategic Air Force (Intelligence). Review of operations, Sept 1943–May 1944, tables I and II.
30. History of the 341st Bombardment Group (Medium), 22nd Bombardment Squadron (Medium), 490th Bombardment Squadron (Medium), and 491st Bombardment Squadron (Medium), for December 1943 and January 1944, 341st Bombardment Group (M), GP-341-HI-(Bomb), B0284, reel 1417; 22nd Bombardment Squadron (M), SQ-Bomb-22-HI, A0543, reel 0567; 490th Bombardment Squadron (M), SQ-Bomb-490-HI, A0621, reel 0650; 491st Bombardment Squadron (M), SQ-Bomb-491-HI, A0622, reel 0651; David K. Hayward, ed., *Eagles, Bulldogs & Tigers: History of the 22nd Bomb Squadron in China-Burma-India* (Huntington Beach, CA:22nd Bomb Squadron Association, 1997), 109.
31. Flight Intelligence Report for 2 December 1943, Flight Intelligence Reports, August 1943–August 1944, 490th Bombardment Squadron (M), SQ-Bomb-490-HI, A0621, reel 0650.
32. Flight Intelligence Reports for 1, 6, 12, 14, 21, 22 December, Flight Intelligence Reports, August 1943–August 1944; "The Saga of the 490th Bombardment Squadron: An Epic of Combat Aviation," 490th Bombardment Squadron (M), SQ-Bomb-490-HI, A0621, reel 0650.
33. "The Saga of the 490th Bombardment Squadron: An Epic of Combat Aviation," 490th Bombardment Squadron (M), SQ-Bomb-490-HI, A0621, reel 0650.
34. Ibid.
35. History of the 490th Bombardment Squadron for January 1944, 490th Bombardment Squadron (M), SQ-Bomb-490-HI, A0621, reel 0650.
36. CBI: Tenth Air Force, Headquarters Tenth Air Force, "Attacks on Bridges by 'Bridge Busters' of the 10th Air Force," 1 January 19–May 1944, 830.454-4, A8247, reel 10042, frames 21–22.
37. CBI: Tenth Air Force, Headquarters Tenth Air Force, "Attacks on Bridges by 'Bridge Busters' of the 10th Air Force," 1 January 19–May 1944, 830.454-4, A8247, reel 10042, frame 17.
38. Craven and Cate, *The Army Air Forces in World War II*, 4:492.
39. Bell and Strotman, *The Burma Bridge Busters*, 48.
40. Ibid., 71–72.
41. History of the 490th Bombardment Squadron for April 1944, 490th Bombardment Squadron (M), SQ-Bomb-490-HI, A0621, reel 0650.
42. History of the 490th Bombardment Squadron for May 1944, 490th Bombardment Squadron (M), SQ-Bomb-490-HI, A0621, reel 0650.
43. History of the 490th Bombardment Squadron for February, March, and April 1944, 490th Bombardment Squadron (M), SQ-Bomb-490-HI, A0621, reel 0650.
44. History of the 490th Bombardment Squadron for May and June 1944, "The Saga of the 490th Bombardment Squadron: An Epic of Combat Aviation," 490th Bombardment Squadron (M), SQ-Bomb-490-HI, A0621, reel 0650.
45. This data is taken from appendix 2, "Aircraft in Possession of Strategic Air Force, Dispatch on Operations of Eastern Air Command 15 December 1943–1 June 1945," 134.
46. Diary entry for 25 May 1944 in Lt. Gen. George Stratemeyer Personal Diary 1 January 1944 Thru 31 December 1944, Papers of Gen. George Stratemeyer, Thomas Overlander–George Stratemeyer Collection.
47. Barbara Stahura, *Earthquakers: The 12th Bombardment Group (M)* (Paducah, KY: Turner, 1998); History of the 81st, 82nd, 83rd, and 434th Bombardment Squadrons for March, April, and May 1944, 81st Bombardment Squadron (M), SQ-Bomb-81-HI, A0597, reel 0592; 82nd Bombardment Squadron (M), SQ-Bomb-82-HI, A0597, reel 0592; 83rd Bombardment Squadron (M), SQ-Bomb-83-HI, A0597, reel 0592; 434th Bombardment Squadron (M), SQ-Bomb-434-HI, A0614, reel 0643.
48. This data is taken from appendix 5, "Aircraft in Possession of Strategic Air Force, Dispatch on Operations of Eastern Air Command 15 December 1943–1 June 1945," 137.
49. Appendix C, "Dispatch on the Operations of Strategic Air Force Eastern Air Command for the Period 15 December 1943 to 31 May 1944," frame 1050.
50. Kirby, *The War against Japan*, 3:389.
51. Appendix H, "Dispatch on the Operations of Strategic Air Force Eastern Air Command for the Period 15 December 1943 to 31 May 1944," frame 1062.
52. Dispatch on the Operations of Strategic Air Force Eastern Air Command for the Period 15 December 1943 to 31 May 1944, p. 7, frame 1046.
53. Taylor, *Air Supply in the Burma Campaigns*, 141.
54. Craven and Cate, *The Army Air Forces in World War II*, 4:208.
55. Air Ministry, Air Historical Branch, *The Campaigns in the Far East*, 4:16.

56. Maj. Gen. George Stratemeyer, Commanding, Headquarters Eastern Air Command, General Orders 1, 15 December 1943, Correspondence of General Stratemeyer, August 1943–December 1944, frame 1069–70; "History of United States Army Air Force Operations in the India Burma Theater, 1 January to 2 September 1945," January 1944–September 1945, vol. 1, p. 134, frame 1222.

57. Maurer Maurer, ed., *Combat Squadrons of the Air Force, World War II* (Washington, DC: US Government Printing Office, 1953), 140–41, 384; Maurer, *Air Force Combat Units of World War II*, 317; James J. Halley, *The Squadrons of the Royal Air Force* (Tonbridge, UK: Air-Britain, 1985), 99, 152, 200; "History of United States Army Air Force Operations in the India Burma Theater, 1 January to 2 September 1945," January 1944–September 1945, vol. 1, p. 137, frame 1225.

58. "History of United States Army Air Force Operations in the India Burma Theater, 1 January to 2 September 1945," January 1944–September 1945, vol. 1, pp. 138–42, frame 1226–30; Taylor, *Air Supply in the Burma Campaigns*, 54–65; Air Ministry, Air Historical Branch, *The Campaigns in the Far East*, 4:50–54; tonnage data is taken from appendix 8, "Transport Operations of Eastern Air Command, Dispatch on Operations of Eastern Air Command 15 December 1943–1 June 1945," 140.

59. "History of United States Army Air Force Operations in the India Burma Theater, 1 January to 2 September 1945," January 1944–September 1945, vol. 1, p. 142, frame 1230.

60. "History of United States Army Air Force Operations in the India Burma Theater, 1 January to 2 September 1945," January 1944–September 1945, vol. 1, p. 142–62, frame 1230–54; Taylor, *Air Supply in the Burma Campaigns*, 67–70; Herbert A. Mason Jr., SSgt. Randy G. Bergeron, and TSgt. James A. Renfrew Jr., *Operation Thursday: Birth of the Air Commandos*, The U.S. Army Air Forces in World War II (Washington, DC: Air Force History and Museums Program, 1994), 36; Brig. Gen. William D. Old, to Commanding General, Eastern Air Command, Report on Troop Carrier Command Participation in "Thursday Operation," 16 March 1944, CBI: Eastern Air Command. Correspondence of Gen. Stratemeyer, August 1943–December 1944, 820.161A, A8072, reel 9864, frames 1533–40.

61. "History of United States Army Air Force Operations in the India Burma Theater, 1 January to 2 September 1945," January 1944–September 1945, vol. 1, pp. 162–68, frames 1254–60; Taylor, *Air Supply in the Burma Campaigns*, 70–74.

62. Maj. Gen. George Stratemeyer, Headquarters Army Air Forces India-Burma Sector, to Gen. Henry Arnold, Commanding General, Army Air Forces, 29 March 1944, Air 23/2267, Air Ministry and Ministry of Defence, Royal Air Force Overseas Commands, Reports and Correspondence: Air Command, Southeast Asia. Employment of Air Commando Groups.

63. "History of United States Army Air Force Operations in the India Burma Theater, 1 January to 2 September 1945," January 1944–September 1945, vol. 1, p. 169, frame 1261.

64. Ibid., vol. 1, p. 172, frame 1264.

65. Ibid., vol. 1, p. 173, frame 1265.

66. Air Ministry, Air Historical Branch, *The Campaigns in the Far East*, 4:186.

67. Taylor, *Air Supply in the Burma Campaigns*, 74.

68. Gen. H. H. Arnold, Commanding General, Army Air Forces, to Admiral Louis Mountbatten, Commander-in-Chief, Southeast Asia Command, 24 March 1944, MB1/C Mountbatten Papers: Southeast Asia Command, 1943–46, MB1C/C11, Gen. Henry Arnold.

69. Y'Blood, *Air Commandos against Japan: Allied Special Operations in World War II Burma*, 149–50.

70. Air Ministry, Air Historical Branch, *The Campaigns in the Far East*, 4:93–100; Kirby, *The War against Japan*, 3:187–204; "History of United States Army Air Force Operations in the India Burma Theater, 1 January to 2 September 1945," January 1944–September 1945, vol. 1, pp. 175–76, frames 1267–68.

71. Taylor, *Air Supply in the Burma Campaigns*, 76.

72. Ibid., 76–81; Air Ministry, Air Historical Branch, *The Campaigns in the Far East*, 4:102–103.

73. Taylor, *Air Supply in the Burma Campaigns*, 80.

74. Mountbatten, *Report to the Combined Chiefs of Staff by the Supreme Allied Commander Southeast Asia, 1943–1945*, 55–56.

75. Taylor, *Air Supply in the Burma Campaigns*, 76–77; "History of United States Army Air Force Operations in the India Burma Theater, 1 January to 2 September 1945," January 1944–September 1945, vol. 1, pp. 179–84, frames 1271–76; Air Ministry, Air Historical Branch, *The Campaigns in the Far East*, 4:236; Mountbatten, *Report to the Combined Chiefs of Staff by the Supreme Allied Commander Southeast Asia, 1943–1945*, 61.

76. Taylor, *Air Supply in the Burma Campaigns*, 81–89; "History of United States Army Air Force Operations in the India Burma Theater, 1 January to 2 September 1945," January 1944–September 1945, vol. 1, pp. 188–90, frames 1280–82.

77. Commendation of Units, 21 May 1944, History of the 443rd Troop Carrier Group for May 1944, 443rd Troop Carrier Group, GP-443-HI (TR CARR), B0554, reel 1754.

78. "History of United States Army Air Force Operations in the India Burma Theater, 1 January to 2 September 1945," January 1944–September 1945, vol. 1, pp. 195–97, frames 1287–89; History of the 443rd Troop Carrier Group for April 1944, 443rd Troop Carrier Group, GP-443-HI (TR CARR), B0554, reel 1754.

79. History of the 1st and 2nd Troop Carrier Squadrons for May 1944, 1st Troop Carrier Squadron, SQ-TR-CARR-1-HI, A0966, reel 1039; 2nd Troop Carrier Squadron, SQ-TR-CARR-2-HI, A0966, reel 1039; Taylor, *Air Supply in the Burma Campaigns*, 25–26.

80. Shores, *Air War for Burma*, 229; Smith, *2nd Troop Carrier Squadron, AAF, CBI, WWII*, 105.

81. Smith, *2nd Troop Carrier Squadron, AAF, CBI, WWII*, 103.
82. Taylor, *Air Supply in the Burma Campaigns*, 26.
83. Air Ministry, Air Historical Branch, *The Campaigns in the Far East*, 4:17.
84. Dr. Robert F. Futrell, *Development of Aero-medical Evacuation in the USAF, 1909–1960*, US Air Force Numbered Historical Studies 23 (1960), 71–72, 86–87, 103, 106–107.
85. Ibid., 275–76.
86. Ibid., 279–80.
87. Maurer, *Combat Squadrons of the Air Force World War II*, 262–63; *Air Force Combat Units of World War II*, 142.
88. Futrell, *Development of Aero-medical Evacuation in the USAF, 1909–1960*, 280.
89. Roy Kappel, *Whispering Wings over Burma: The Jungle Angels, 5th Liaison Squadron* (Elk Creek, NE: R. Kappel, 1998), 50.
90. History of the 71st Liaison Squadron for April and May 1944, 71st Liaison Squadron, SQ-LIA-71-HI, A0834, reel 0894; History of the 5th Liaison Squadron for April 1943–October 1944, 5th Liaison Squadron, SQ-LIA-5-HI, A0841A, reel 0892.
91. Y'Blood, *Air Commandos against Japan: Allied Special Operations in World War II Burma*, 11.
92. Ibid., 79–81.
93. Van Wagner, *Any Time, Any Place, Any Where: The 1st Air Commandos in World War II*, 62.
94. Grp. Capt. H. H. Hilliar, SAPSG, "Organization of Command and Control of British and U.S. Forces in Eastern Air Command," 4 May 1944, Air 23/2597, Air Ministry and Ministry of Defence, Royal Air Force Overseas Commands, Reports and Correspondence: Air Command, Southeast Asia. Air Staff. Eastern Air Command: Reorganization.
95. Air Ministry, Air Historical Branch, *The Campaigns in the Far East*, 4:17.
96. Taylor, *Air Supply in the Burma Campaigns*, 54.
97. Air Ministry, Air Historical Branch, *The Campaigns in the Far East*, 4:16.
98. Taylor, *Air Supply in the Burma Campaigns*, 54.
99. Air Ministry, Air Historical Branch, *The Campaigns in the Far East*, 4:17; Diary entry for 3 June 1944 in Lt. Gen. George Stratemeyer Personal Diary, 1 January 1944 Thru 31 December 1944, Papers of Gen. George Stratemeyer, Thomas Overlander–George Stratemeyer Collection.
100. Romanus and Sunderland, *United States Army in World War II: China-Burma-India Theater*, 2:28–29.
101. Ibid., 2:29.
102. Air Ministry, Air Historical Branch, *The Campaigns in the Far East*, 4:17; "History of Air Operations on the Continent of Asia, December 1941–May 1946," vol. 4, section 2, 825.01C, A8155, reel 9949, frames 251–54.
103. Maj. Gen. George Stratemeyer, Air Commander, Eastern Air Command, to Air Commander in Chief, Air Command Southeast Asia, 17 May 1944, Air 23/2597, Air Ministry and Ministry of Defence, Royal Air Force Overseas Commands, Reports and Correspondence: Air Command, Southeast Asia. Air Staff. Eastern Air Command: Reorganization.
104. Ibid.
105. Ibid.
106. Ibid.
107. "History of United States Army Air Force Operations in the India Burma Theater, 1 January to 2 September 1945," January 1944–September 1945, vol. 1, p. 209, frame 1381.

CHAPTER 10:
Myitkyina and Beyond: Operations, Plans, and Preparations, May–August 1944

1. Ehrman, *Grand Strategy*, 5:418–19; Mountbatten, *Report to the Combined Chiefs of Staff by the Supreme Allied Commander Southeast Asia, 1943–1945*, 64.
2. Ehrman, *Grand Strategy*, 5:148.
3. Ibid., 5:423.
4. Ibid.; Matloff, *Strategic Planning for Coalition Warfare 1943–1944*, 434–35, 438; Mountbatten, *Report to the Combined Chiefs of Staff by the Supreme Allied Commander Southeast Asia, 1943–1945*, 30–31.
5. Romanus and Sunderland, *United States Army in World War II: China-Burma-India Theater*, 2:161; Mountbatten, *Report to the Combined Chiefs of Staff by the Supreme Allied Commander Southeast Asia, 1943–1945*, 31.
6. CBI: USAAF, IBT, "History of Air Operations on the Continent of Asia, December 1941–May 1946," vol. 4, section 2, 825.01C, A8155, reel 9949, frame 224.
7. Craven and Cate, *The Army Air Forces in World War II*, 5:203, 276.
8. "History of Air Operations on the Continent of Asia, December 1941–May 1946," vol. 4, section 2, 825.01C, A8155, reel 9949, frame 226.
9. Ibid., reel 9949, frames 235–36.
10. Ehrman, *Grand Strategy*, 5:491.
11. Ibid.
12. "History of Air Operations on the Continent of Asia, December 1941–May 1946," vol. 4, section 2, 825.01C, A8155, reel 9949, frame 236; Diary entry for 23 May 1944 in Lt. Gen. George Stratemeyer Personal Diary 1 January 1944 Thru 31 December 1944, Papers of Gen. George Stratemeyer, Thomas Overlander–George Stratemeyer Collection; Mountbatten, *Report to the Combined Chiefs of Staff by the Supreme Allied Commander Southeast Asia, 1943–1945*, 65.
13. Mountbatten, *Report to the Combined Chiefs of Staff by the Supreme Allied Commander Southeast Asia, 1943–1945*, 55.

14. Romanus and Sunderland, *United States Army in World War II: China-Burma-India Theater*, 2:172.
15. Ibid., 2:200–201.
16. Ibid., 2:202.
17. Ibid., 2:363.
18. Ibid., 2:364.
19. Ehrman, *Grand Strategy*, 5:490.
20. Mountbatten, *Report to the Combined Chiefs of Staff by the Supreme Allied Commander Southeast Asia, 1943–1945*, 65.
21. Romanus and Sunderland, *United States Army in World War II: China-Burma-India Theater*, 2:171–72.
22. Joseph W. Stilwell, *The Stilwell Papers*, ed. Theodore H. White (New York: W. Sloane, 1948), 296.
23. Romanus and Sunderland, *United States Army in World War II: China-Burma-India Theater*, 2:228.
24. Ibid., 2:229.
25. Office of the Chief of Military History, "The Siege at Myitkyina," Center for Military History "Supporting Documents to CBI Volumes," file 270/19/13/6, Record Group 319: Records of the Army General Staff, 1903–2009, National Archives and Records Administration, 19.
26. Romanus and Sunderland, *United States Army in World War II: China-Burma-India Theater*, 2:255.
27. Ibid., 2:233.
28. The following description of Japanese fortifications at Myitkyina is taken from CBI: Tenth Air Force, Headquarters, Tenth Air Force, "Report of Effects of Air Support at Myitkyina," 17 August 1944, 830.55-2, A8247, reel 10042.
29. Romanus and Sunderland, *United States Army in World War II: China-Burma-India Theater*, 2:236.
30. Office of the Chief of Military History, "The Siege at Myitkyina," Center for Military History "Supporting Documents to CBI Volumes," file 270/19/13/6; Information Bulletin 166, 17 May 1944, 5320th Air Defense Wing (Prov), WG-5320-AirDef (Prov), C0174, reel 2366, frame 2244.
31. Office of the Chief of Military History, "The Siege at Myitkyina," Center for Military History "Supporting Documents to CBI Volumes," file 270/19/13/6; Information Bulletin 167, 18 May 1944, 5320th Air Defense Wing (Prov), WG-5320-AirDef (Prov), C0174, reel 2366, frames 2241–42; Shores, *Air War for Burma*, 229.
32. Office of the Chief of Military History, "The Siege at Myitkyina," Center for Military History "Supporting Documents to CBI Volumes," file 270/19/13/6; Information Bulletins 168–78, 18–29 May 1944, 5320th Air Defense Wing (Prov), WG-5320-AirDef (Prov), C0174, reel 2366, frames 2222–40.
33. Office of the Chief of Military History, "The Siege at Myitkyina," Center for Military History "Supporting Documents to CBI Volumes," file 270/19/13/6; Smith, *2nd Troop Carrier Squadron, AAF, CBI, WWII*, 105–106, 142; History of the 443rd Troop Carrier Group for May 1944, 443rd Troop Carrier Group, GP-443-HI (TR CARR), B0554, reel 1754.
34. Romanus and Sunderland, *United States Army in World War II: China-Burma-India Theater*, 2:247, 236–48.
35. "Development of Joint Air Ground Operations in Northern Burma," January 1945, 7.
36. Ibid., 8.
37. Ibid.
38. Office of the Chief of Military History, "The Siege at Myitkyina," 60.
39. "Development of Joint Air Ground Operations in Northern Burma," January 1945, 8–11.
40. Ibid., 11.
41. Ibid., 10; History of the 528th Fighter Squadron for June and July 1944, 528th Fighter Squadron, SQ-FI-528-HI, A0823, reel 872.
42. Kirby, *The War against Japan*, 3:403–404.
43. History of the 528th Fighter Squadron for June, 528th Fighter Squadron, SQ-FI-528-HI, A0823, reel 872; see also "Development of Joint Air Ground Operations in Northern Burma," January 1945, 12–13.
44. Romanus and Sunderland, *United States Army in World War II: China-Burma-India Theater*, 2:251.
45. Maj. Gen. Howard Davidson, Headquarters, Tenth Air Force, to Brig. Gen. Caleb V. Haynes, Headquarters, I Bomber Command, 15 July 1944, 168.72266-40, Davidson, Howard C., Correspondence (Official), 168.7266, reel 42821, Air Force Historical Research Agency, Maxwell AFB, AL.
46. History of the 490th Bomb Squadron for July 1944, 490th Bombardment Squadron (M), SQ-Bomb-490-HI, A0621, reel 0650; History of the 12th Bomb Group for July 1944, 12th Bombardment Group (M), GP-12-HI-(Bomb), B0070–71, reels 1156–57.
47. Shores, *Air War for Burma*, 244–45; Office of the Chief of Military History, "The Siege at Myitkyina," 68–69; History of the 443rd Troop Carrier Group for June 1944, 443rd Troop Carrier Group, GP-443-HI (TR CARR), B0554, reel 1754.
48. Walt Shiel, *Rough War: The Combat Story of Lt. Paul Eastman, a "Burma Banshee" P-40 and P-47 Pilot* (Jacobsville, MI: Jacobsville Books, 2011), 122.
49. History of the 90th Fighter Squadron for July 1944, 90th Fighter Squadron, SQ-FI-90-HI, A0762, reel 801; Narrative of Encounter with Enemy Aircraft, 529th Fighter Squadron, 6 July 1944, 311th Fighter Group, GP-311-SU-OP, B0230, reel 1343.
50. Shores, *Air War for Burma*, 248; Office of the Chief of Military History, "The Siege at Myitkyina," 77.
51. Shores, *Air War for Burma*, 248; Office of the Chief of Military History, "The Siege at Myitkyina," 79–80.
52. History of the 83rd Bomb Squadron for July 1944, 83rd Bombardment Squadron (M), SQ-Bomb-83-HI, A0597, reel 0592; History of the 12th Bomb Group for July 1944, 12th Bombardment Group (M), GP-12-HI-(Bomb), B0070–71, reels 1156–57.
53. Flight Intelligence Report, 9 July 1944, 528th Fighter Squadron, 311th Fighter Group, GP-311-SU-OP, B0230, reel 1343, frames 1918–20.
54. Ibid., frames 1920–21.
55. Ibid., frames 1921–22.

56. Shores, *Air War for Burma*, 248–49.
57. History of the 89th and 90th Fighter Squadrons for July 1944, 89th Fighter Squadron, SQ-FI-89-HI, A0762, reel 801; 90th Fighter Squadron, SQ-FI-90-HI, A0762, reel 801.
58. History of the 88th Fighter Squadron for July 1944, 88th Fighter Squadron, SQ-FI-88-HI, A0761, reel 800.
59. Romanus and Sunderland, *United States Army in World War II: China-Burma-India Theater*, 2:251–53.
60. CBI: Tenth Air Force, Report on Tenth Air Force Operations, 20 June 1944–30 April 1945, Tenth Air Force History 1942–1945, 830.01, A8224, reel 10018.
61. Craven and Cate, *The Army Air Forces in World War II*, 5:220.
62. Maj. Gen. S. Woodburn Kirby, *The War against Japan*, vol. 4, *The Reconquest of Burma* (London: Her Majesty's Stationery Office, 1965), 40.
63. Ibid., 4:40.
64. Maj. Gen. George Stratemeyer, Commanding, Army Air Forces India-Burma Sector, to Maj. Gen. Howard Davidson, Tenth Air Force, 15 August 1944, Davidson, Howard C., Correspondence (Official), 168.7266, reel 42821, Air Force Historical Research Agency, Maxwell AFB, AL.
65. "History of Air Operations on the Continent of Asia, December 1941–May 1946," vol. 4, section 2, p. 287, frame 287.
66. Kirby, *The War against Japan*, 4:1.
67. Ibid.; Charles F. Romanus and Riley Sunderland, *United States Army in World War II: China-Burma-India Theater*, vol. 3, *Time Runs Out in CBI* (Washington, DC: Office of the Chief of Military History, Department of the Army, 1959), 81.
68. Allen, *The Longest War*, 313.
69. Kirby, *The War against Japan*, 4:372; Allen, *The Longest War*, 638.
70. Kirby, *The War against Japan*, 4:2–3.
71. Romanus and Sunderland, *United States Army in World War II: China-Burma-India Theater*, 2:79.
72. Kirby, *The War against Japan*, 4:3.
73. Ibid.
74. Mountbatten, *Report to the Combined Chiefs of Staff by the Supreme Allied Commander Southeast Asia, 1943–1945*, 72.
75. Ibid., 5–76.
76. Ibid., 75; Kirby, *The War against Japan*, 4:4.
77. Mountbatten, *Report to the Combined Chiefs of Staff by the Supreme Allied Commander Southeast Asia, 1943–1945*, 75–76; Kirby, *The War against Japan*, 4:4.
78. Kirby, *The War against Japan*, 4:4.
79. Ibid., 4:5.
80. Romanus and Sunderland, *United States Army in World War II: China-Burma-India Theater*, 3:84–85.
81. Ibid., 3:85.
82. Kirby, *The War against Japan*, 4:12.
83. Ibid., 4:13.
84. Romanus and Sunderland, *United States Army in World War II: China-Burma-India Theater*, 3:85–88; Kirby, *The War against Japan*, 4:113–14.
85. This is a brief summary of a highly contentious and complicated period in American-Chinese relations over the summer and early fall of 1944. A more detailed discussion of these events can be found in the relevant chapters of Romanus and Sunderland, *United States Army in World War II: China-Burma-India Theater*, vol. 2.
86. CBI: Tenth Air Force, Headquarters Tenth Air Force, Daily Intelligence Extracts for 1944, 31 October 1944, 830.6062, A8251, reel 10046, frame 1445.
87. Entry for 30 October 1944 in the personal diary of Lt. Gen. George Stratemeyer, for 1 January 1944 Thru 31 December 1944, Papers of Gen. George Stratemeyer, Thomas Overlander–George Stratemeyer Collection.
88. Entry for 30 October 1944 in the personal diary of Lt. Gen. George Stratemeyer, for 1 January 1944 Thru 31 December 1944.
89. Mountbatten, *Report to the Combined Chiefs of Staff by the Supreme Allied Commander Southeast Asia, 1943–1945*, 80.
90. Romanus and Sunderland, *United States Army in World War II: China-Burma-India Theater*, 3:33, 90–91, 102.
91. Ibid., 3:101.
92. Romanus and Sunderland, *United States Army in World War II: China-Burma-India Theater*, vol. 2—see chapter 9 and pp. 357–59, 424, 435; Romanus and Sunderland, *United States Army in World War II: China-Burma-India Theater*, 3:130–31.
93. Kirby, *The War against Japan*, 4:53–59; Romanus and Sunderland, *United States Army in World War II: China-Burma-India Theater*, 3:99–101.
94. Military History Section, Headquarters, Army Forces Far East: *Burma Air Operations Record, Jan. 1942–Aug. 1945*, 76–86.
95. History of the 311th Fighter Group for August to October 1944, 311th Fighter Group, GP-311-HI, B0229, reel 1342.
96. History of the 88th Fighter Squadron for August 1944, 88th Fighter Squadron, SQ-FI-88-HI, A0761, reel 800.
97. Maj. Gen. Howard Davidson, Commanding, Tenth Air Force, to Gen. H. H. Arnold, Commanding General, Army Air Forces, 15 July 1944, 168.72266-40, Davidson, Howard C., Correspondence (Official), 168.7266, reel 42821.
98. Report on Tenth Air Force Operations, 20 June 1944–30 April 1945; History of the 5th, 71st, and 115th Liaison Squadrons for August–November 1944, 5th Liaison Squadron, SQ-LIA-5-HI, A0841A, reel 0892; 71st Liaison Squadron, SQ-LIA-71-HI, A0834, reel 0894; 115th Liaison Squadron, SQ-LIA-115-HI, A0844, reel 0895.
99. Headquarters, Tenth Air Force, to Commanding General, Eastern Air Command (SEA), Dispatch on Air Operations, 1 June 1944 to 26 Nov 1944 inclusive, 22 December 1944, CBI: Tenth Air Force, 10th Air Force Operations, Dispatch on Air Operations, 1 June to 26 Nov 1944 Inclusive, 830.306-5, A8243, reel 10038.
100. Headquarters, Tenth Air Force, Tenth Air Force Operations Plan No. 1, 1944, 1 December 1944, 830.3221-1, A8245, reel 10040, frame 0317.

CHAPTER 11:
Supporting the NCAC Advance: August 1944–April 1945

1. Craven and Cate, *The Army Air Forces in World War II*, 5:235.
2. Ibid.
3. Preston-Hough, *Commanding Far Eastern Skies*, 221.
4. History of the 89th and 90th Fighter Squadrons for August–September 1944, 89th Fighter Squadron, SQ-FI-89-HI, A0762, reel 801; 90th Fighter Squadron, SQ-FI-90-HI, A0762, reel 801.
5. History of the 58th, 59th, 60th, 89th, and 90th Fighter Squadrons and 490th Bomb Squadron for October 1944–January 1945, 58th Fighter Squadron, SQ-FI-58-HI, A0744–45, reel 782–83; 59th Fighter Squadron, SQ-FI-59-HI, A0745, reel 783; 60th Fighter Squadron, SQ-FI-HI-A0745, reel 783; SQ-FI-89-HI, A0762, reel 801; 90th Fighter Squadron, SQ-FI-90-HI, A0762, reel 801.
6. Shores, *Air War for Burma*, 310; History of the 90th Fighter Squadron for December 1944, 90th Fighter Squadron, SQ-FI-90-HI, A0762, reel 801; Eastern Air Command, Weekly Intelligence Summary 21 (19 January 1945) and 24 (9 February 1945), CBI: Eastern Air Command, Weekly Intelligence Summary 19–28, 820.607, A8120, reel 9914.
7. History of the 58th Fighter Squadron for January 1945, 58th Fighter Squadron, SQ-FI-58-HI, A0744–45, reel 782–83.
8. History of the 490th Bomb Squadron, October–December 1944 and January 1945, 490th Bombardment Squadron (M), SQ-Bomb-490-HI, A0621, reel 0650.
9. Tenth Air Force Operations Plan No. 1, 1944, 1 December 1944.
10. Air Ministry, Air Historical Branch, *The Campaigns in the Far East*, 4:353.
11. History of the 90th Fighter Squadron for December 1944, 90th Fighter Squadron, SQ-FI-90-HI, A0762, reel 801; Shores, *Air War for Burma*, 295.
12. History of the 3rd Combat Cargo Group for December 1944, 3rd Combat Cargo Group, B0726, reel 1913.
13. Headquarters, Air Command Southeast Asia, Weekly Intelligence Summary 51 (5 November 1944), CBI: Air Command, Southeast Asia, Weekly Intelligence Summary 50–68 (29 October 1944–4 March 1945), 815.607, A8060, reel 9852.
14. Shores, *Air War for Burma*, 279.
15. Eastern Air Command, Weekly Intelligence Summary 14 (1 December 1944), CBI: Eastern Air Command, Weekly Intelligence Summary 14–18, 820.607, A8119, reel 9913.
16. Eastern Air Command, Weekly Intelligence Summary 14 (1 December 1944).
17. History of the 427th Night Fighter Squadron for December 1944 and January 1945.
18. Preston-Hough, *Commanding Far Eastern Skies*, 237–38.
19. Air Chief Marshal Sir Keith Park, "Dispatch on Air Operations in Southeast Asia from 1st June 1944 to the Occupation of Rangoon, 2nd May 1945," in *Far East Air Operations, 1942–1945*, ed. John Grehan and Martin Mace, 104.
20. "A Brief History of AAF India & Burma," reel 42822, p. 82.
21. CBI: Tenth Air Force, 10th Air Force Operations, Operations of the 10th Air Force in North Burma, Joint Intelligence Collection Agency Report 499, 10 December 1944, 830.306-1, A8242, reel 10037, p. 7, frame 2130.
22. Report on Tenth Air Force Operations, 20 June 1944–30 April 1945, 24–25.
23. CBI: Tenth Air Force, Operations, Tenth Air Force Plan for Interdiction of Japanese Lines of Communication Generally North of Mandalay, 28 November 1944, 830.3221-2, A8245, reel 10045.
24. Report on Tenth Air Force Operations, 20 June 1944–30 April 1945, 25.
25. Operations of the 10th Air Force in North Burma, Joint Intelligence Collection Agency Report 499, 10 December 1944.
26. History of the 20th Tactical Reconnaissance Squadron for November and December 1944, SQ-RCN-20-HI, A0908, reel 970.
27. History of the 490th Bomb Squadron for August and September 1944, 490th Bombardment Squadron (M), SQ-Bomb-490-HI, A0621, reel 0650.
28. History of the 490th Bomb Squadron for August and September 1944, 490th Bombardment Squadron (M), SQ-Bomb-490-HI, A0621, reel 0650; History of the 12th Bomb Group for September 1944, 12th Bombardment Group (M), GP-12-HI- (Bomb), B0070–71, reels 1156–57.
29. History of the 80th Fighter Group for August and September 1944, 80th Fighter Group, GP-80-HI, B0165, reel 1271.
30. Weekly Analysis of Tenth Air Force Operations for the Week of 3–9 September 1944, CBI: Tenth Air Force, 10th Air Force Operations, Weekly Analysis of Tenth Air Force Operations, 3 September 1944–17 April 1945, 830.3062, A8243, reel 10038.
31. Weekly Analysis of Tenth Air Force Operations for the Week of 3–9 September 1944.
32. Headquarters, Tenth Air Force, Daily Intelligence Extracts for 14 November 1944, CBI: Tenth Air Force, Headquarters Tenth Air Force, Daily Intelligence Extracts for 1944, 830.6062, A8252, reel 10047.
33. History of the 88th and 90th Fighter Squadrons for October 1944, 88th Fighter Squadron, SQ-FI-88-HI, A0761, reel 800; 90th Fighter Squadron, SQ-FI-90-HI, A0762, reel 801.

34. CBI: Tenth Air Force, 10th Air Force Operations, "Bridge Busting: Med. Bombers vs. Fighters," October–November 1944, 830.454-3, A8247, reel 10041; CBI: Tenth Air Force, Headquarters Tenth Air Force, "Summary of Fighter Bomber and Medium Bomber Attacks on Bridges during the Month of December 1944," 12 February 1945, 830.454-1, A8247, reel 10041; Headquarters, 33rd Fighter Group, Analysis of Bridge Attacks from 1 November 1944 through 31 January 1945, in "Bridge Busting in Burma," November 1944–January 1945, 490th Bomb Squadron, 490th Bombardment Squadron (M), SQ-Bomb-490-HI, A0621, reel 0650.

35. Bell and Strotman, *The Burma Bridge Busters*, 65.

36. Maj. Gen. Howard Davidson, Commanding, Tenth Air Force, to all units, 24 November 1944, CBI: Tenth Air Force, Headquarters, 10th Air Force Historical Data for November 1944, Tenth Air Force History 1942–1945, 830.01, A8224, reel 10018.

37. History of the 490th Bomb Squadron for November–December 1944 and January 1945, 490th Bombardment Squadron (M), SQ-Bomb-490-HI, A0621, reel 0650.

38. Ibid.

39. Headquarters, Tenth Air Force, Critical Review [formerly Weekly Analysis], Period 8 to 14 November, 20 November 1944, 5.

40. Ibid., 5–6.

41. Headquarters, Tenth Air Force, Critical Review, Period 24 to 31 October 1944, 5 November 1944, 6; Headquarters, Tenth Air Force, Daily Intelligence Extract for 8 December 1944, MU-40, CBI: Tenth Air Force, Headquarters Tenth Air Force, Daily Intelligence Extracts for 1944, 830.6062, A8252, reel 10047; CBI: Tenth Air Force, 10th Air Force Operations, "10th Air Force Operations Sept–Dec 1944," 830-308-2, A8244, reel 10042, frames 436–64.

42. "Development of Joint Air Ground Operations in Northern Burma," 12.

43. Ibid.

44. CBI: Tenth Air Force, 10th Air Force Air Ground Cooperation, Operations (Close Support), 830.4501, Oct 1944–Apr 1945, A8246, reel 10041, frames 587–613.

45. "Development of Joint Air Ground Operations in Northern Burma," 15–16.

46. Ibid., 16.

47. Ibid., 20–21.

48. Ibid., 18–19.

49. 80th Fighter Group, Consolidated Flight Intelligence Report for 8 December 1944, 12 December 1944, 80th Fighter Group, GP-80-SU-OP, B0166, reel 1272.

50. "Development of Joint Air Ground Operations in Northern Burma," 17.

51. Ibid., 21.

52. Kirby, *The War against Japan*, 4:144–45.

53. 10th Air Force Air Ground Cooperation, Operations (Close Support).

54. Kirby, *The War against Japan*, 4:146–47; Romanus and Sunderland, *United States Army in World War II: China-Burma-India Theater*, 3:114–23.

55. Romanus and Sunderland, *United States Army in World War II: China-Burma-India Theater*, 3:144.

56. Ibid., 3:144–45; Kirby, *The War against Japan*, 4:145.

57. Kirby, *The War against Japan*, 4:148.

58. Ibid., 191.

59. History of the 33rd and 80th Fighter Groups for December 1944 and January 1945, 33rd Fighter Group, GP-33-HI, B0112, reel 1212; 80th Fighter Group, GP-80-HI, B0165, reel 1271.

60. John Ehrman, *Grand Strategy*, vol. 6, *October 1944–August 1945* (London: Her Majesty's Stationery Office, 1956), 190.

61. Kirby, *The War against Japan*, 4:194–97; Romanus and Sunderland, *United States Army in World War II: China-Burma-India Theater*, 3:130–36.

62. "10th Air Force Operations, Sept–Dec 1944."

63. Taylor, *Air Supply in the Burma Campaigns*, 35–36.

64. Ibid., 35–36, 38–39.

65. Ibid., 43–47.

66. Smith, *2nd Troop Carrier Squadron, AAF, CBI, WWII*, 256.

67. Taylor, *Air Supply in the Burma Campaigns*, 50.

68. Ibid., 51.

69. History of the 5th Liaison Squadron for November and December 1944, 5th Liaison Squadron, SQ-LIA-5-HI, A0841A, reel 0892; "10th Air Force Operations, Sept–Dec 1944."

70. CBI: Tenth Air Force, Headquarters, 10th Air Force Historical Data, November 1944, Air Jungle Rescue, 20 March 1945, 830.01, A8224, reel 10018.

71. CBI: Tenth Air Force, Headquarters, 10th Air Force Historical Data, November 1944, Air Jungle Rescue, 20 March 1945, 830.01, A8224, reel 10018; History of the 5th Liaison Squadron for November 1944, 5th Liaison Squadron, SQ-LIA-5-HI, A0841A, reel 0892.

72. Air Jungle Rescue, 20 March 1945.

73. History of the 490th Bomb Squadron for January 1945, 490th Bombardment Squadron (M), SQ-Bomb-490-HI, A0621, reel 0650.

74. Air Jungle Rescue, 20 March 1945.

75. Kirby, *The War against Japan*, 4:275.

76. Ibid.

77. Ibid., 275–78.

78. History of the 80th and 33rd Fighter Groups and 90th Fighter Squadron for February 1945, 80th Fighter Group, GP-80-SU-OP, B0166, reel 1272; 33rd Fighter Group, GP-33-HI, B0112, reel 1212; 90th Fighter Squadron, SQ-FI-90-HI, A0762, reel 801.

79. History of the 490th Bomb Squadron for February 1945, 490th Bombardment Squadron (M), SQ-Bomb-490-HI, A0621, reel 0650.

80. Kirby, *The War against Japan*, 4:278.

81. Ehrman, *Grand Strategy*, 6:185.

82. Kirby, *The War against Japan*, 4:278–81; Romanus and Sunderland, *United States Army in World War II: China-Burma-India Theater*, 3:223–26; Mountbatten, *Report to the Combined Chiefs of Staff by the Supreme Allied Commander Southeast Asia, 1943–1945*, 122–23, 132–33.

83. Mountbatten, *Report to the Combined Chiefs of Staff by the Supreme Allied Commander Southeast Asia, 1943–1945*, 121.
84. Kirby, *The War against Japan*, 4:315–320; Romanus and Sunderland, *United States Army in World War II: China-Burma-India Theater*, 3:226–30.
85. History of the 33rd and 80th Fighter Groups for March 1945, 80th Fighter Group, GP-80-SU-OP, B0166, reel 1272; 33rd Fighter Group, GP-33-HI, B0112, reel 1212.
86. History of the 490th Bomb Squadron for March 1945, 490th Bombardment Squadron (M), SQ-Bomb-490-HI, A0621, reel 0650; History of the 427th Night Fighter Squadron for February and March 1945, 427th Night Fighter Squadron, SQ-FI-427-HI, A0805, reel 853.
87. History of the 5th, 71st, and 115th Liaison Squadrons, 490th Bomb Squadron, 60th Fighter Squadron, 427th Night Fighter Squadron, 3rd Combat Cargo Group, 33rd Fighter Group, and 80th Fighter Group for April 1945, 5th Liaison Squadron, SQ-LIA-5-HI, A0841A, reel 0892; 71st Liaison Squadron, SQ-LIA-71-HI, A0834, reel 0894; 115th Liaison Squadron, SQ-LIA-115-HI, A0844, reel 0895; 490th Bombardment Squadron (M), SQ-Bomb-490-HI, A0621, reel 0650; 60th Fighter Squadron, SQ-FI-HI-A0745, reel 783; 427th Night Fighter Squadron, SQ-FI-427-HI, A0805, reel 853; 3rd Combat Cargo Group, B0726, reel 1913; 33rd Fighter Group, GP-33-HI, B0112, reel 1212; 80th Fighter Group, GP-80-HI, B0165, reel 1271.
88. Maj. Gen. Howard Davidson, Commanding, Tenth Air Force to All Personnel, Tenth Air Force, 24 April 1945, 3rd Combat Cargo Group, B0726, reel 1913, frames 1260–61.

CHAPTER 12:
Army Air Force Units Supporting 14th Army Operations: June 1944–May 1945

1. Mountbatten, *Report to the Combined Chiefs of Staff by the Supreme Allied Commander Southeast Asia, 1943–1945*, 72.
2. Field Marshal Sir William Slim, *Defeat into Victory* (London: Cassell, 1956), 348, 374.
3. Kirby, *The War against Japan*, 4:9.
4. Slim, *Defeat into Victory*, 347.
5. Kirby, *The War against Japan*, 3:277.
6. Kirby, *The War against Japan*, 4:6.
7. Ibid., 4:447.
8. Slim, *Defeat into Victory*, 380–81; Kirby, *The War against Japan*, 4:105–106.
9. Kirby, *The War Against Japan*, 4:106.
10. General Sir William Slim, "Some Aspects of the Campaign in Burma," *Journal of the Royal Central Asian Society* 33, no. 3–4 (1946): 329.
11. Kirby, *The War against Japan*, 4:105.
12. Gerald A. White Jr., *The Great Snafu Fleet: 1st Combat Cargo / 344th Airdrome / 326th Troop Carrier Squadron in World War II's CBI Theater* (Bloomington, IN: Xlibris, 2000), 31.
13. Y'Blood, *Air Commandos against Japan: Allied Special Operations in World War II Burma*, 10–11.
14. Gen. Henry H. Arnold, Commanding General, Army Air Forces, to Admiral Louis Mountbatten, Supreme Allied Commander, Southeast Asia Command, 13 March 1944, WO 203/4719, War Office: Southeast Asia Command: Military Headquarters Papers, Second World War. SOUTH EAST ASIA COMMAND. Air. Provision for air commandos.
15. Gen. H. H. Arnold, Commanding General, Army Air Forces, to Admiral Louis Mountbatten, Commander-in-Chief, Southeast Asia Command, 24 March 1944, MB1/C Mountbatten Papers: Southeast Asia Command, 1943–46, MB1C/C11, General Henry Arnold.
16. Gen. Henry H. Arnold, Commanding General, Army Air Forces, to Admiral the Lord Louis Mountbatten, Supreme Allied Commander, Advanced Headquarters, Southeast Asia, 7 June 1944, MB1/C11, Mountbatten Papers.
17. Gen. H. H. Arnold, Commanding General, Army Air Forces, to Lt. Gen. Joseph Stilwell, 5 June 1944, Records of Assistant Chief of Staff, Plans, AFHRA 145.181, A1379, R2801, frames 515–16.
18. Gen. Arnold to Admiral Mountbatten, 7 June 1944, in MB1/C11, Mountbatten Papers.
19. Air Marshal Sir William Welsh, Royal Air Force Delegation in Washington, DC, to Marshal of the Royal Air Force Sir Charles Portal, Chief of Air Staff, 1 June 1944, TNA, Air 20/5045, Air Commandos in Southeast Asia.
20. Field Marshal Sir John Dill, Chief, Joint Staff Mission, Washington, to Marshal of the Royal Air Force Sir Charles Portal, 29 May 1944, box C, folder 7: Mountbatten, Peirse, Joubert, Garrod, Lord Portal Archive 2, the Viscount Portal Papers, Christ Church, Oxford (Portal Papers).
21. Air Marshal Sir William Welsh, Royal Air Force Delegation in Washington, DC, to Marshal of the Royal Air Force Sir Charles Portal, Chief of Air Staff, TNA, 23 May 1944, Air 20/5045, Air Commandos in Southeast Asia.
22. Field Marshal Sir John Dill to Marshal of the Royal Air Force Sir Charles Portal, 29 May 1944, Portal Papers.
23. Welsh to Portal, 1 June 1944.
24. See letters from Gen. Henry H. Arnold, Commanding General, Army Air Forces, to Admiral the Lord Louis Mountbatten, Supreme Allied Commander, Southeast Asia Command, of 24 March, 7 June, and 22 July 1944, in MB1/C11, Mountbatten Papers.
25. Y'Blood, *Air Commandos against Japan: Allied Special Operations in World War II Burma*, 124; Van Wagner, *1st Air Commando Group: Any Place, Any Time, Any Where*, 102; White, *The Great Snafu Fleet: 1st Combat Cargo / 344th Airdrome / 326th Troop Carrier Squadron in World War II's CBI Theater*, 38, 40.
26. Kirby, *The War against Japan*, 4:439.
27. Ibid.

28. Advanced Headquarters, Southeast Asia Command, Supreme Allied Commander's Meetings, Ninety-Seventh Meeting Minutes, 10 May 1944, TNA, WO 203/4719, Provision of Air Commandos; Marshal of the Royal Air Force Sir Charles Portal to Admiral Lord Louis Mountbatten, 11 April 1944, MB1/C202, Mountbatten Papers; Marshal of the Royal Air Force Sir Charles Portal, Chief of the Air Staff, to Air Chief Marshal Sir Richard Peirse, AOC, Air Command, Southeast Asia, 12 April 1944, Air 8/1158; Marshal of the Royal Air Force Sir Charles Portal, Chief of the Air Staff, to Air Marshal Sir William Welsh, Joint Staff Mission, Washington, DC, 23 May 1944, Air 8/1158, Air Ministry and Ministry of Defense: Department of the Chief of the Air Staff: Registered Files. Air Commandos in Southeast Asia Command.
29. Michael Howard and Peter Paret, eds. and trans., *Carl von Clausewitz: On War* (Princeton, NJ: Princeton University Press, 1984), 213.
30. Maj. Gen. George Stratemeyer, Air Commander, Eastern Air Command, to Air Chief Marshal Sir Richard Peirse, Air Commander-in-Chief, Air Command, Southeast Asia on Reorganization of Eastern Air Command, 17 May 1944, Eastern Air Command, Correspondence of General Stratemeyer, Aug 43–May 45, AFHRA 820.161A, A8072,R9684, frames 981–86.
31. Portal to Mountbatten, 11 April 1944, MB1/C202, Mountbatten Papers.
32. Air Ministry, Air Historical Branch, *The Campaigns in the Far East*, 4:186.
33. Air Chief Marshal Sir Richard Peirse, A.O.C. Air Command, Southeast Asia, to Marshal of the Royal Air Force Sir Charles Portal, Chief of the Air Staff, 1 April 1944, Air 20/5045, Air Ministry and Ministry of Defence: Papers Accumulated by the Air Historical Branch. Assistant Chief of Air Staff (Policy). Air Commandos for Southeast Asia.
34. Maj. Gen. George Stratemeyer, Commanding, Army Air Forces India-Burma Sector, China-Burma-India Theater, to Gen. Henry H. Arnold, Commanding General, Army Air Forces, 19 March 1944, AIR23/2267, Air 23/2267, Air Ministry and Ministry of Defence, Royal Air Force Overseas Commands, Reports and Correspondence: Air Command, Southeast Asia. Employment of Air Commando Groups.
35. Mason et al., *Operation Thursday: Birth of the Air Commandos*, 36.
36. Kirby, *The War against Japan*, 3:133–52, chapter 22.
37. Lt. Gen. Joseph Stilwell, Commanding, US Army Forces China-Burma-India Theater, to Gen. Henry H. Arnold, Commanding General, Army Air Forces, 26 June 1944, Stratemeyer, George E.: Thomas Overlander–George Stratemeyer Collection, MS-28.
38. Maj. Gen. George Stratemeyer, Commanding, Army Air Forces India-Burma Sector, to Gen. H. H. Arnold, Commanding, Army Air Forces, 25 June 1944, Stratemeyer, George E.: Thomas Overlander–George Stratemeyer Collection, MS-28.
39. Ibid.
40. Ibid.
41. Ibid.
42. Maj. Gen. Howard Davidson, Commanding, Tenth Air Force, to Brigadier D. D. C. Tulloch, Headquarters, Third Indian Division, 18 August 1944, Davidson, Howard C., Correspondence (Official), August–September 1944, 168.7266, reel 42821.
43. Ibid.
44. Ibid.
45. See Stratemeyer to Supreme Commander Southeast Asia Command, Subject: 1st Air Commando Force, 26 January 1944, TNA, WO203/4719, Provision of Air Commandos; Stratemeyer to Gen. Arnold, Subject: First Air Commando Group, 29 March, 1944, AIR23/2267, Employment of Air Commando Groups; and Peirse to Portal, 1 April 1944, AIR20/5045, Air Commandos for Southeast Asia. See also comments in Stratemeyer's personal diary for 18 and 28 March 1944. A copy of this diary is in the Overlander-Stratemeyer Collection in series 1, notebook 2.
46. Stratemeyer personal diary entry for 19 May 1944.
47. Maj. Gen. George Stratemeyer, Air Commander, Eastern Air Command, to Air Commander in Chief, Air Command Southeast Asia, 17 May 1944, Air 23/2597.
48. Air Chief Marshal Sir Richard Peirse, Air Officer Commanding, Air Command, Southeast Asia, to Marshal of the Royal Air Force Sir Charles Portal, Chief of the Air Staff, 19 May 1944, TNA, AIR8/1158, Air Ministry and Ministry of Defense: Department of the Chief of the Air Staff: Registered Files. Air Commandos in Southeast Asia Command.
49. Gen. H. H. Arnold, Commanding, Army Air Forces, to Admiral Lord Louis Mountbatten, Supreme Allied Commander, Southeast Asia Command, 7 June 1944, Air Ministry and Ministry of Defense: Department of the Chief of the Air Staff: Registered Files. Air Commandos in Southeast Asia Command.
50. Maj. Gen. George Stratemeyer, Commanding, Army Air Forces India-Burma Sector, to Gen. H. H. Arnold, Commanding, Army Air Forces, 25 June 1944.
51. Admiral Lord Louis Mountbatten, Supreme Allied Commander, Southeast Asia Command, to Gen. H. H. Arnold, Commanding, Army Air Forces, 11 July 1944, in MB1/C11, Mountbatten Papers.
52. Ibid.
53. Mountbatten, *Report to the Combined Chiefs of Staff by the Supreme Allied Commander Southeast Asia, 1943–1945*, 75; Memorandum of 4 August 1944. HQ, USAAF: Assistant Chief of Air Staff, Plans, AFHRA 145.95 (WP–IV–D–1 (Southeast Asia), A1471, reel 2899.
54. Mountbatten, *Report to the Combined Chiefs of Staff by the Supreme Allied Commander Southeast Asia, 1943–1945*, 75.
55. Kirby, *The War against Japan*, 4:12.
56. Park, *Dispatch on Air Operations in Southeast Asia from 1st June 1944 to the Occupation of Rangoon, 2nd May 1945*, 108.
57. Dispatch on Operations of Eastern Air Command, 15 December 1943–1 June 1945, p. 125.
58. Ibid.

59. Headquarters, Combat Cargo Task Force, A Review of CCTF Operations, 8 June 1945, CBI: Combat Cargo Task Force, History 15 September 1944–31 May 1945, 824.01, A8146, reel 9940.
60. White, *The Great Snafu Fleet: 1st Combat Cargo / 344th Airdrome / 326th Troop Carrier Squadron in World War II's CBI Theater*, 49–50, 65.
61. Van Wagner, *Any Time, Any Place, Any Where: The 1st Air Commandos in World War II*, 91.
62. Young, *Air Commando Fighters of World War II*, 35.
63. Van Wagner, *Any Time, Any Place, Any Where: The 1st Air Commandos in World War II*, 91.
64. History of the 1st Combat Cargo Group for August–December 1944, 1st Combat Cargo Group, GP-CCA-1-HI, B0725, reel 1912.
65. Van Wagner, *Any Time, Any Place, Any Where: The 1st Air Commandos in World War II*, 95–96.
66. From the correspondence between the parties involved, it does seem as if Arnold backed off from his insistence on not integrating the air commando and combat cargo units. There is an intriguing possibility that Portal may have persuaded Arnold to give way on this point. Responding to a report from Air Marshal Welsh on Arnold's intransigence on the issue of command and control and his resentment at Stratemeyer and the RAF commanders in ACSEA for their reluctance to adopt his air commando concept with enthusiasm, Portal told Welsh to "let this question rest and I will discuss it with Arnold when I see him." See Marshal of the Royal Air Force Sir Charles Portal, Chief of the Air Staff, to Air Marshal William Welsh, Joint Staff Mission, Washington, DC, 3 June 1944, AIR8/1158. Portal and Arnold met in England shortly after the D-day invasion during meetings of the Combined Chiefs of Staff, but there is no record of their conversations. But following this meeting, the combat cargo and air commando squadrons began regular support operations—perhaps a mere coincidence, but perhaps not.
67. History of the Combat Cargo Task Force for October 1944, CBI: Combat Cargo Task Force, Monthly Histories, September–November 1944, 824.02, A8146, reel 9940; History of the 1st Combat Cargo Group for October 1944, 1st Combat Cargo Group, GP-CCA-1-HI, B0725, reel 1912.
68. Kirby, *The War against Japan*, 4:37.
69. Ibid.
70. Air Ministry, Air Historical Branch: *The Campaigns in the Far East*, 4:306.
71. History of the Combat Cargo Task Force for November 1944, CBI: Combat Cargo Task Force, Monthly Histories, September–November 1944, 824.02, A8146, reel 9940; History of the 1st Combat Cargo Group for November 1944, 1st Combat Cargo Group, GP-CCA-1-HI, B0725, reel 1912; 2nd Air Commandos History of Operations 1945, 2nd Air Commando Group, GP-A-CMDO-2-HI, B0681, reel 1864.
72. Kirby, *The War against Japan*, 4:153–55.
73. Ibid., 150.
74. History of the Combat Cargo Task Force for November 1944, Combat Cargo Task Force, History, 15 September 1944–31 May 1945.
75. Ibid.
76. Y'Blood, *Air Commandos against Japan: Allied Special Operations in World War II Burma*, 129–30.
77. History of the Combat Cargo Task Force for November 1944, Combat Cargo Task Force, History, 15 September 1944–31 May 1945.
78. White, *The Great Snafu Fleet: 1st Combat Cargo / 344th Airdrome / 326th Troop Carrier Squadron in World War II's CBI Theater*, 84.
79. History of the 1st Combat Cargo Group for August–December 1944; Shores, *Air War for Burma*, 282.
80. History of the Combat Cargo Task Force for December 1944, Combat Cargo Task Force, History, 15 September 1944–31 May 1945.
81. Kirby, *The War against Japan*, 4:128–29.
82. Ibid., 130–31.
83. Slim, *Defeat into Victory*, 395–96.
84. Mountbatten, *Report to the Combined Chiefs of Staff by the Supreme Allied Commander Southeast Asia, 1943–1945*, 104.
85. Kirby, *The War against Japan*, 4:63–65.
86. Slim, *Defeat into Victory*, 393–94.
87. Kirby, *The War against Japan*, 4:169; Probert, *The Forgotten Air Force*, 246.
88. Probert, *The Forgotten Air Force*, 247.
89. Kirby, *The War against Japan*, 4:169.
90. Probert, *The Forgotten Air Force*, 249; Mountbatten, *Report to the Combined Chiefs of Staff by the Supreme Allied Commander Southeast Asia, 1943–1945*, 107–108.
91. History of the Combat Cargo Task Force for December 1944, Combat Cargo Task Force, History, 15 September 1944–31 May 1945.
92. Ibid.
93. History of the 4th Combat Cargo Group for December 1944, 4th Combat Cargo Group, B0727, reel 1914; John G. Martin, *It Began at Imphal: The Combat Cargo Story* (Manhattan, KS: Sunflower University Press, 1988), 43–44.
94. History of the Combat Cargo Task Force for January 1944, Combat Cargo Task Force, History, 15 September 1944–31 May 1945; Shores, *Air War for Burma*, 308.
95. History of the 4th Combat Cargo Group for January 1945, 4th Combat Cargo Group, B0727, reel 1914.
96. History of the 4th Combat Cargo Group for January and February 1945, 4th Combat Cargo Group, B0727, reel 1914.
97. Mountbatten, *Report to the Combined Chiefs of Staff by the Supreme Allied Commander Southeast Asia, 1943–1945*, 113.
98. Ibid., 114.
99. Dispatch on Operations of Eastern Air Command, 15 December 1943–1 June 1945, 87–88.
100. See the Order of Battle for No. 221 and No. 224 Groups in Air Ministry, Air Historical Branch, *The Campaigns in the Far East*, 4: appendix 7.

101. Probert, *The Forgotten Air Force*, 230–34.
102. Park, *Dispatch on Air Operations in Southeast Asia from 1st June 1944 to the Occupation of Rangoon, 2nd May 1945*, 117, 126.
103. History of the 12th Bomb Group for August–November 1944, 12th Bombardment Group (M), GP-12-HI-(Bomb), B0071, reel 1157.
104. History of the 12th Bomb Group for August–November 1944, 12th Bombardment Group (M), GP-12-HI-(Bomb), B0071, reel 1157; History of the 81st Bomb Squadron for August 1944, 81st Bombardment Squadron (M), SQ-Bomb–81-HI, A0597, reel 0592.
105. History of the 12th Bomb Group for August–November 1944, 12th Bombardment Group (M), GP-12-HI-(Bomb), B0071, reel 1157; History of the 81st Bomb Squadron for December 1944, 81st Bombardment Squadron (M), SQ-Bomb-81-HI, A0597, reel 0592; History of the 434th Bomb Squadron for January 1945, 434th Bombardment Squadron (M), SQ-Bomb-434-HI, A0614, reel 0643.
106. Shores, *Air War for Burma*, 268–70.
107. History of the 12th Bomb Group for November 1944, 12th Bombardment Group (M), GP-12-HI-(Bomb), B0071, reel 1157.
108. Mountbatten, *Report to the Combined Chiefs of Staff by the Supreme Allied Commander Southeast Asia, 1943–1945*, 108.
109. Ibid.
110. Ibid., 108–12; History of the 12th Bomb Group for December 1944–January 1945, 12th Bombardment Group (M), GP-12-HI-(Bomb), B0071, reel 1157; History of the 434th Bomb Squadron for January 1945, 434th Bombardment Squadron (M), SQ-Bomb-434-HI, A0614, reel 0643.
111. Fielder, *A History of the 459th Fighter Squadron, Twin Dragons CBI, 1943–45*, p. 42–43.
112. Fielder, *A History of the 459th Fighter Squadron: The Twin Dragons, CBI, 1943–45*, 39–50, provides an account of the squadron's missions from June to December 1944.
113. History of the 5th Fighter Squadron (Commando) for November 1944, 5th Fighter Squadron (Commando), SQ-FI-CMDO-5-HI, A0828, reel 877.
114. Young, *Air Commando Fighters of World War II*, 42.
115. History of the 6th Fighter Squadron (Commando) for December 1944, 6th Fighter Squadron (Commando), SQ-FI-CMDO-6-HI, A0828, reel 877.
116. History of the 5th Fighter Squadron (Commando) for December 1944 and January 1945, 5th Fighter Squadron (Commando), SQ-FI-CMDO-5-HI, A0828, reel 877; Y'Blood, *Air Commandos against Japan: Allied Special Operations in World War II Burma*, 142–43: Edward Young, interview with Roland Lynn, Fighter Section, 5th Fighter Squadron (Commando), 1st Air Commando Group, 52nd Reunion, Portland, OR, 18–21 September 1996.
117. History of the 5th Fighter Squadron (Commando) for January 1945, 5th Fighter Squadron (Commando), SQ-FI-CMDO-5-HI, A0828, reel 877.
118. Y'Blood, *Air Commandos against Japan: Allied Special Operations in World War II Burma*, 139; CBI: Eastern Air Command, Summary of Operations for November and December 1944, A8100, reel 9894.
119. Col. C. B. Gatty, Commanding, 1st Air Commando Group, to Commanding Officer, Eastern Air Command, B-25H Night Intruder Missions from the period of 23 December 1944 to 3 January 1945 and 9 January 1945, 1st Air Commando Group, GP-A-CMDO-1-HI, B0680, reel 1863.
120. Col. C. B. Gatty, Commanding, 1st Air Commando Group, to Commanding Officer, Eastern Air Command, B-25H Night Intruder Missions from the period of 21 January to 31 January 1945 and 7 February 1945, CBI: Eastern Air Command, Operational Reports October 1944–May 1945, 820.306, A8097, reel 9891.
121. Preston-Hough, *Commanding Far Eastern Skies*, 221.
122. Ibid.
123. Ibid., 220.
124. Shores, *Air War for Burma*, 272.
125. Eastern Air Command, Weekly Intelligence Summary 14 (1 December 1944).
126. Young, *Air Commando Fighters of World War II*, 36–38; Shores, *Air War for Burma*, 273.
127. CBI: Eastern Air Command, Headquarters Eastern Air Command, Results of Fighter Attacks on Japanese Airfields in the Rangoon Area, 18–20 October, 820.3121, A8106, reel 9900.
128. CBI: Eastern Air Command, A Study of Operation "L," 16–20 October 1944, 820.423–1, A8112, reel 9906. See also Shores, *Air War for Burma*, 274–75; Young, *Air Commando Fighters of World War II*, 38–39; Y'Blood, *Air Commandos against Japan: Allied Special Operations in World War II Burma*, 131–33.
129. Shores, *Air War for Burma*, 279–80; Y'Blood, *Air Commandos against Japan: Allied Special Operations in World War II Burma*, 133.
130. Shores, *Air War for Burma*, 284–85, 295, 309; History of the 5th Fighter Squadron (Commando) for November 1944, 5th Fighter Squadron (Commando), SQ-FI-CMDO-5-HI, A0828, reel 877.
131. Preston-Hough, *Commanding Far Eastern Skies*, 222–26.
132. CBI: Eastern Air Command, Operations of Strategic Air Force, 15 December 1943 to 3 May 1945, 821.04A, A8138, reel 9932, p. 34.
133. Ibid., reel 9932, p. 39.
134. Young, *Death from Above*, 201–204.
135. Ibid., 204.
136. Ibid., 205–206.
137. Ibid., 206.
138. Ibid.
139. Craven and Cate, *The Army Air Forces in World War II*, 5:117.
140. CBI: Eastern Air Command, Dispatch on Operations against the Japanese by the Strategic Air Force from 1st June 1944 to 26th November 1944, 821.04A, A8138, reel 9932, p. 14.

141. Ibid., 15.
142. Ibid., 4.
143. Ibid.
144. Young, *Death from Above*, 210–13.
145. Ibid., 214–15.
146. Ibid., 217–18.
147. Ibid., 220–23.
148. Ibid., 228.
149. Maurer, *Air Force Combat Units of World War II*, 48; Maurer, *Combat Squadrons of the Air Force World War II*, 53, 107–108, 126–27, 188.
150. Greenhalgh, *Foto Jo in CBI*, 69–80; History of the 8th Photographic Reconnaissance Group for October–December 1944, 8th Photographic Reconnaissance Group, GP-Photo-8-HI, A0755, reel 1944; Statistical Summary 8th Photo Reconnaissance Group Operations October–December 1944, GP-Photo-8-SU-OP-S, A0755, reel 1944.

CHAPTER 13:
Victory in Burma: February–April 1945

1. Kirby, *The War against Japan*, 4:34.
2. Ibid., 4:35; Probert, *Forgotten Air Force*, 226–27.
3. Admiral Lord Louis Mountbatten, Southeast Asia Command, to Marshal of the Royal Air Force Sir Charles Portal, Air Ministry, 19th October 1944, Lord Portal Archive 2, box C, folder 7: Mountbatten, Peirse, Joubert, Garrod, the Viscount Portal Papers, Christ Church College, Oxford, England.
4. Probert, *Forgotten Air Force*, 222.
5. Ibid., 223–24.
6. Kirby, *The War against Japan*, 4:180.
7. Ibid., 180–81.
8. Ibid., 181; Slim, *Defeat into Victory*, 386–87, 394; Probert, *Forgotten Air Force*, 236.
9. Y'Blood, *Air Commandos against Japan: Allied Special Operations in World War II Burma*, 144.
10. Ibid.
11. Ibid., 145.
12. Kirby, *The War against Japan*, 4:182.
13. Ibid., 175.
14. Ibid., 184–89.
15. Joint Air-Ground Operations in the Capture of Meiktila, Eastern Air Command Weekly Intelligence Summary 31 (30 March 1945), CBI: Eastern Air Command, Weekly Intelligence Summary 29–38, 820.607, A8121, reel 9915.
16. History of the 5th and 6th Fighter Squadrons (Commando) for February 1945, 5th Fighter Squadron (Commando), SQ-FI-CMDO-5-HI, 6th Fighter Squadron (Commando), SQ-FI-CMDO-6-HI, A0828, reel 877; Young, *Air Commando Fighters of World War II*, 48–50.
17. Headquarters, Combat Cargo Task Force, Intelligence Extract 10: Operation Multivite, 22 March 1945, CBI: Combat Cargo Task Force, History, 15 September 1944–31 May 1945, 824.01, A8146, reel 9940.
18. Ibid.; History of the 5th and 6th Fighter Squadrons (Commando) for February 1945, 5th Fighter Squadron (Commando), SQ-FI-CMDO-5-HI, 6th Fighter Squadron (Commando), SQ-FI-CMDO-6-HI, A0828, reel 877; Young, *Air Commando Fighters of World War II*, 50–54, 67; Shores, *Air War for Burma*, 333–36.
19. Headquarters, Combat Cargo Task Force, Intelligence Extract 10: Operation Multivite, 22 March 1945, CBI: Combat Cargo Task Force, History, 15 September 1944–31 May 1945, 824.01, A8146, reel 9940.
20. Ibid.; History of the 1st, 2nd, 5th, and 6th Fighter Squadrons (Commando) for February–March 1945, 1st Fighter Squadron (Commando), SQ-FI-CMDO-1-HI, A0827, reel 876; 2nd Fighter Squadron (Commando), SQ-FI-CMDO-2-HI, A0828, reel 877; 5th Fighter Squadron (Commando), SQ-FI-CMDO-5-HI, 6th Fighter Squadron (Commando), SQ-FI-CMDO-6-HI, A0828, reel 877; Young, *Air Commando Fighters of World War II*, 50–54, 67.
21. Allen, *The Longest War*, 430–31, 442.
22. Slim, *Defeat into Victory*, 453.
23. This is a brief synopsis of a complicated battle. See Michael Pearson, *Endgame Burma: Slim's Masterstroke at Meiktila* (Barnsley, UK: Pen & Sword Military, 2010), 78–83; Allen, *The Longest War*, 442–58, for more-detailed treatments, as well as chapters 25 and 26 in Kirby, *The War against Japan*, vol. 4.
24. Air Ministry, Air Historical Branch, *The Campaigns in the Far East*, 4:373–74.
25. History of the 5th Fighter Squadron (Commando) for February 1945, 5th Fighter Squadron (Commando), SQ-FI-CMDO-5-HI.
26. Y'Blood, *Air Commandos against Japan: Allied Special Operations in World War II Burma*, 168.
27. Ibid., 168–69; Kirby, *The War against Japan*, 4:307; Report on Operation BETTY, appendix J, "Combat Cargo Task Force, History, 15 September 1944–31 May 1945."
28. Kirby, *The War against Japan*, 4:203.
29. Combat Cargo Task Force, History, 15 September 1944–31 May 1945; CBI: Combat Cargo Task Force, Monthly Histories, February–March 1945.
30. History of the 82nd Bomb Squadron for February 1945, 82nd Bombardment Squadron (M), SQ-Bomb-82-HI, A0597, reel 0592. See also History of the 81st, 83rd, and 434th Bomb Squadrons for February–March 1945, 81st Bombardment Squadron (M), SQ-Bomb-81-HI, 83rd Bombardment Squadron (M), SQ-Bomb-83-HI, A0597, reel 0592; 434th Bombardment Squadron (M), SQ-Bomb-434-HI, A0614, reel 0643.
31. Fielder, *A History of the 459th Fighter Squadron: The Twin Dragons, CBI, 1943–45*, 60–65.
32. Allen, *The Longest War*, 638.
33. Kirby, *The War against Japan*, 4:313.
34. Robert Lyman, *Slim, Master of War: Burma and the Birth of Modern Warfare* (London: Constable, 2004), 252.

35. Again, this is a brief synopsis of a very complex and fast-moving battle. For fuller treatments of Slim's masterful defeat of *Burma Area Army*, see Pearson, *Endgame Burma: Slim's Masterstroke at Meiktila*; Allen, *The Longest War*; and, for the most detailed description of the battle, Kirby, *The War against Japan*, volume 4.
36. Kirby, *The War against Japan*, 4:317.
37. Ibid., 316–17; Mountbatten, *Report to the Combined Chiefs of Staff by the Supreme Allied Commander Southeast Asia, 1943–1945*, 135.
38. Kirby, *The War against Japan*, 4:318.
39. Ehrman, *Grand Strategy*, 6:196.
40. Thorne, *Allies of a Kind: The United States, Britain, and the War against Japan, 1941–1945*, 588–92.
41. Diary entry for 16 March 1945, Maj. Gen. George E. Stratemeyer Personal Diary 1 January 1945 Thru 25 May 1945, Thomas Overlander–George Stratemeyer Collection.
42. Ehrman, *Grand Strategy*, 6:196.
43. Ibid., 6:196–197.
44. Ibid., 6:197.
45. Eastern Air Command, Weekly Intelligence Summary 11 (10 November 1944) and 27 (2 March 1945); Air Ministry, Air Historical Branch, *The Campaigns in the Far East*, 4: appendix 21.
46. Stratemeyer, Dispatch on Operations of Eastern Air Command, 15 December 1943–1 June 1945, 32.
47. Young, *Air Commando Fighters of World War II*, 69–70; Izawa, "64th Flying Sentai, Part 3," 14.
48. Preston-Hough, *Commanding Far Eastern Skies*, 228.
49. Young, *Air Commando Fighters of World War II*, 70.
50. Ibid., 72; Shores, *Air War for Burma*, 340–41.
51. Young, *Air Commando Fighters of World War II*, 72–76; Shores, *Air War for Burma*, 341.
52. Young, *Air Commando Fighters of World War II*, 76; Shores, *Air War for Burma*, 342–43.
53. Young, *Air Commando Fighters of World War II*, 77.
54. Air Command, Southeast Asia, Weekly Intelligence Summary 80 (27 May 1945), CBI: Air Command, Southeast Asia, Weekly Intelligence Summary 69–105 (11 March 1945–21 November 1945), 815.607, A8061, reel 9853.
55. Young, *Air Commando Fighters of World War II*, 78.
56. Ibid., 80–81, 83; Shores, *Air War for Burma*, 348, 350, 357; Eastern Air Command, Daily Operational Summary for 30 April 1945.
57. Young, *Air Commando Fighters of World War II*, 84–85; *Burma Air Operations Record, Jan. 1942–Aug. 1945*, 98.
58. Office of the Assistant Chief of Air Staff, Intelligence, *Impact* 3, no. 3 (March 1945): 33.
59. Dr. Carlo Kopp, *The Dawn of the Smart Bomb*, Technical Report APA-TR-2011-0302, 26 March 2011, Air Power Australia, available at www.ausairpower.net/WW2-PGMs.html, p. 9.
60. *Impact* 3, no. 3 (March 1945): 33.
61. CBI: Tenth Air Force, Azon in India Burma Theater, 20 March 1945, 830.04-3, A8229, reel 10024.
62. Young, *Death from Above*, 235.
63. Azon in India Burma Theater, 20 March 1945; Young, *Death from Above*, 231–36; "History of Air Operations on the Continent of Asia, December 1941–May 1946," vol. 4, section 2, 825.01C, A8155, reel 9949, p. 159.
64. Young, *Death from Above*, 236–40.
65. Azon in India Burma Theater, 20 March 1945; Young, *Death from Above*, 124.
66. Young, *Death from Above*, 244–45, 247.
67. Ibid., 245–52.
68. Weekly Intelligence Summary 35 (27 April 1945), CBI: Eastern Air Command, Weekly Intelligence Summary 29–38, 820.607, A8121, reel 9915.
69. Young, *Death from Above*, 253.
70. CBI: Eastern Air Command, Dispatch on Operations against the Japanese by the Strategic Air Force from 27 November 1944 to 31 May 1945, 821.04C, A8138, reel 9932, p. 25; Park, *Dispatch on Air Operations in Southeast Asia from 1st June 1944 to the Occupation of Rangoon, 2nd May 1945*, 128.
71. Young, *Death from Above*, 250.
72. Ibid.
73. Ibid., 253.
74. Slim, *Defeat into Victory*, 480.
75. Kirby, *The War against Japan*, 4:321–27.
76. Ibid., 4:327–30.
77. Ibid., 355–67.
78. See Kirby, *The War against Japan*, vol. 4, chapters 31 and 32, for a more detailed description of the advance on Rangoon.
79. History of the 6th Fighter Squadron (Commando) for April 1945, 6th Fighter Squadron (Commando), SQ-FI-CMDO-6-HI, A0828, reel 877.
80. Ibid.
81. History of the 5th and 6th Fighter Squadron (Commando) for April 1945, 5th Fighter Squadron (Commando), SQ-FI-CMDO-5-HI, 6th Fighter Squadron (Commando), SQ-FI-CMDO-6-HI, A0828, reel 877.
82. William Burghardt, "Rice Paddy Rescue," copy in the possession of the author; Van Wagner, *1st Air Commando Group: Any Place, Any Time, Any Where*, 139.
83. Young, *Air Commando Fighters of World War II*, 82.
84. Ibid.
85. Ibid., 71; History of the 1st and 2nd Fighter Squadrons (Commando) for April 1945, 1st Fighter Squadron (Commando), SQ-FI-CMDO-1-HI, A0827, reel 876; 2nd Fighter Squadron (Commando), SQ-FI-CMDO-2-HI, A0828, reel 877.
86. Fielder, *A History of the 459th Fighter Squadron: The Twin Dragons, CBI, 1943–45*, 66–67.
87. History of the 82nd Bomb Squadron (M) for April 1945, 82nd Bombardment Squadron (M), SQ-Bomb-82-HI, A0597, reel 0592.
88. History of the 81st, 82nd, 83rd, and 434th Bomb Squadrons (M) for April 1945, 81st Bombardment Squadron (M), SQ-Bomb-81-HI, 82nd Bombardment Squadron (M), SQ-Bomb-82-HI, 83rd Bombardment Squadron (M), SQ-Bomb-83-HI, A0597, reel 0592; 434th Bombardment Squadron (M), SQ-Bomb-434-HI, A0614, reel 0643.

89. CBI: Combat Cargo Task Force, Monthly Histories for April 1945, 824.02, A8146, reel 9940.
90. Intelligence Extract 16, The Gumption and Freeborn Operations, 20 May 1945, CBI: Combat Cargo Task Force, History, 15 September 1944–31 May 1945, 824.01, A8146, reel 9940.
91. Ibid.
92. Ibid.
93. Ibid.
94. Ibid.
95. Kirby, *The War against Japan*, 4:429.
96. Ibid.
97. Ibid., 4:425.

CHAPTER 14:
Endgame

1. Fielder, *A History of the 459th Fighter Squadron: The Twin Dragons, CBI, 1943–45*, 68, 79; History of the 1st, 2nd, 5th, and 6th Fighter Squadrons (Commando) for May 1945, 1st Fighter Squadron (Commando), SQ-FI-CMDO-1-HI, A0827, reel 876; 2nd Fighter Squadron (Commando), SQ-FI-CMDO-2-HI, A0828, reel 877; 5th Fighter Squadron (Commando), SQ-FI-CMDO-5-HI, 6th Fighter Squadron (Commando), SQ-FI-CMDO-6-HI, A0828, reel 877.
2. Lt. Col. K. K. Colledge, Headquarters, Army Air Forces India-Burma Theater, to Commanding General, Army Air Forces, Reorganization of Air Commando & Combat Cargo Units, 17 March 1945, HQ, USAAF, Assistant Chief of Air Staff, Plans, Airborne Study, 145.81-170, A1378, reel 2800.
3. Col. John Stone, Operational Division, to Assistant Chief of Air Staff, Plans, 19 April 1945, HQ, USAAF, Assistant Chief of Air Staff, Plans, Airborne Study, 145.81-170, A1378, reel 2800.
4. 5th Fighter Squadron (Commando), SQ-FI-CMDO-5-HI, 6th Fighter Squadron (Commando), SQ-FI-CMDO-6-HI, A0828, reel 877.
5. History of the 81st, 82nd, 83rd, and 434th Bomb Squadrons (M) for May–June 1945, 81st Bombardment Squadron (M), SQ-Bomb-81-HI, 83rd Bombardment Squadron (M), 82nd Bombardment Squadron (M), SQ-Bomb-82-HI, A0597, reel 0592; SQ-Bomb-83-HI, A0597, reel 0592; 434th Bombardment Squadron (M), SQ-Bomb-434-HI, A0614, reel 0643.
6. See histories for the specific groups and squadrons for May 1945, 1st Combat Cargo Group, GP-CCA-1-HI, B0725, reel 1912; 3rd Combat Cargo Group, B0726, reel 1913; 4th Combat Cargo Group, B0727, reel 1914; 443rd Troop Carrier Group, GP-443-HI (TR CARR), B0554, reel 1754; 8th Photographic Reconnaissance Group, GP-Photo-8-HI, A0755, reel 1944.
7. Probert, *The Forgotten Air Force*, 276–77.
8. Mountbatten, *Report to the Combined Chiefs of Staff by the Supreme Allied Commander Southeast Asia, 1943–1945*, 211.
9. Admiral Lord Louis Mountbatten, Supreme Allied Commander, Southeast Asia Command, to Maj. Gen. George Stratemeyer, Commanding General, Eastern Air Command, 15 May 1945, copy attached to letter from Stratemeyer to Gen. Arnold, 8 June 1945, in CBI: USAAF, IBT, Letters Maj. Gen, George Stratemeyer to Gen. H. H. Arnold, 825.161-2, A8158, reel 9952.
10. Thorne, *Allies of a Kind: The United States, Britain, and the War against Japan, 1941–1945*, 588; Craven and Cate, *The Army Air Forces in World War II*, 5:267.
11. Romanus and Sunderland, *United States Army in World War II: China-Burma-India Theater*, 3:324.
12. Ibid., 3:267.
13. Ibid., 3:203.
14. "History of Air Operations on the Continent of Asia December 1941–May 1946," vol. 4, section 3, 825.01C, A8155, reel 9949, p. 197; Romanus and Sunderland, *United States Army in World War II: China-Burma-India Theater*, 3:169, 330–35; Craven and Cate, *The Army Air Forces in World War II*, 5:268.
15. "History of Air Operations on the Continent of Asia, December 1941–May 1946," vol. 4, section 3, 825.01C, A8155, reel 9949, pp. 203–204; Romanus and Sunderland, *United States Army in World War II: China-Burma-India Theater*, 3:342–43; Craven and Cate, *The Army Air Forces in World War II*, 5:268.
16. "History of Air Operations on the Continent of Asia, December 1941–May 1946," vol. 4, section 3, 825.01C, A8155, reel 9949, pp. 205–206.
17. Romanus and Sunderland, *United States Army in World War II: China-Burma-India Theater*, 3:343.
18. Ibid.; "History of Air Operations on the Continent of Asia, December 1941–May 1946," vol. 4, section 2, p. 210.
19. Romanus and Sunderland, *United States Army in World War II: China-Burma-India Theater*, 3:344–45; "History of Air Operations on the Continent of Asia, December 1941–May 1946," vol. 4, section 3, pp. 211, 213.
20. Romanus and Sunderland, *United States Army in World War II: China-Burma-India Theater*, 3:345; "History of Air Operations on the Continent of Asia, December 1941–May 1946," vol. 4, section 2, p. 211.
21. Romanus and Sunderland, *United States Army in World War II: China-Burma-India Theater*, 3:345; "History of Air Operations on the Continent of Asia, December 1941–May 1946," vol. 4, section 3, p. 212.
22. Romanus and Sunderland, *United States Army in World War II: China-Burma-India Theater*, 3:346.
23. "History of Air Operations on the Continent of Asia, December 1941–May 1946," vol. 4, section 3, p. 214.
24. Craven and Cate, *The Army Air Forces in World War II*, 5:270.
25. Ibid.
26. "History of Air Operations on the Continent of Asia, December 1941–May 1946," vol. 4, section 3, pp. 218–19.
27. Craven and Cate, *The Army Air Forces in World War II*, 5:271.

28. "History of Air Operations on the Continent of Asia, December 1941–May 1946," vol. 4, section 3, pp. 223–24; History of the Tenth Air Force for August 1945, CBI: Tenth Air Force, Monthly History of the Tenth Air Force 1945, 830.01, A8225, reel 10020.
29. *India-Burma Theater Roundup* 3, no. 36, VE-day, 1945, www.cbi-theater.com/roundup/roundup050845.html.
30. Histories of the 1st, 2nd, 5th, 6th, 58th, 59, 88th, 89th, and 90th Fighter Squadrons for June–August 1945, 1st Fighter Squadron (Commando), SQ-FI-CMDO-1-HI, A0827, reel 876; 2nd Fighter Squadron (Commando), SQ-FI-CMDO-2-HI, 5th Fighter Squadron (Commando), SQ-FI-CMDO-5-HI, 6th Fighter Squadron (Commando), SQ-FI-CMDO-6-HI, A0828, reel 877; 58th Fighter Squadron, SQ-FI-58-HI, A0744–45, reels 782–83; 59th Fighter Squadron, SQ-FI-59-HI, A0745, reel 783; 88th Fighter Squadron, SQ-FI-88-HI, A0761, reel 800; 89th Fighter Squadron, SQ-FI-89-HI, 90th Fighter Squadron, SQ-FI-90-HI, A0762, reel 801.
31. History of the 81st Bomb Squadron (M) for July 1945, 81st Bombardment Squadron (M), SQ-Bomb-81-HI, A0597, reel 0592.
32. History of the 81st, 82nd, 83rd, and 434th Bomb Squadrons (M) for June–August 1945, 81st Bombardment Squadron (M), SQ-Bomb-81-HI, 83rd Bombardment Squadron (M), 82nd Bombardment Squadron (M), SQ-Bomb-82-HI, A0597, reel 0592; SQ-Bomb-83-HI, A0597, reel 0592; 434th Bombardment Squadron (M), SQ-Bomb-434-HI, A0614, reel 0643.
33. Troy J. Sacquety, *The OSS in Burma: Jungle War against the Japanese* (Lawrence: University Press of Kansas, 2013), 205.
34. Ibid.; Romanus and Sunderland, *United States Army in World War II: China-Burma-India Theater*, 3:326.
35. Sacquety, *The OSS in Burma: Jungle War against the Japanese*, 206–207.
36. Richard Dunlop, *Behind Enemy Lines: With the OSS in Burma* (New York: Rand McNally, 1979), 432.
37. Ibid.; Sacquety, *The OSS in Burma: Jungle War against the Japanese*, 210; History of the 60th Fighter Squadron for June 1945, 60th Fighter Squadron, SQ-FI-HI-A0745, reel 783.
38. History of the 60th Fighter Squadron for July–August 1945, 60th Fighter Squadron, SQ-FI-HI-A0745, reel 783.
39. Young, *Death from Above*, 256.
40. Ibid., p. 259–61.
41. Ibid., p. 264.
42. Ibid.
43. *India-Burma Theater Roundup* 4, no. 1 (13 September 1945), 4, no. 2 (20 September 1945), 4, no. 31 (11 April 1946).
44. The dates of departure and inactivation of the Tenth Air Force's units are taken from Maurer, *Air Force Combat Units of World War II*; Young, *Death from Above*, 269.
45. Maurer, *Air Force Combat Units of World War II*.
46. "A Brief History of AAF India & Burma," 4.
47. Ibid., 8
48. Ibid., 16, 34.
49. Ibid., 35–36.
50. Romanus and Sunderland, *United States Army in World War II: China-Burma-India Theater*, 3:33; CBI: Tenth Air Force, Tenth Air Force Personnel, 830.217–1, A8239, reel 10034, frames 1324–25.
51. Preston-Hough, *Commanding Far Eastern Skies*, 278.
52. Ibid.
53. "A Brief History of AAF India & Burma," 37.
54. Preston-Hough, *Commanding Far Eastern Skies*, 280–281.
55. Ibid., p. 280.
56. Air Chief Marshal Sir Keith Park, "Air Operations in South East Asia from 1st June, 1944, to the Occupation of Rangoon, 2nd May, 1945," *London Gazette*, Friday, 3rd supplement, 6 April, 1951, p. 1971.
57. Air 23/4884, Air Ministry and Ministry of Defence, Royal Air Force Overseas Commands, Reports and Correspondence: Air Command, Southeast Asia. Operational Effort by RAF and USAAF for Period of Japanese War.
58. "A Brief History of AAF India & Burma," 53.
59. Mountbatten, *Report to the Combined Chiefs of Staff by the Supreme Allied Commander Southeast Asia, 1943–1945*, 211.
60. Taylor, *Air Supply in the Burma Campaigns*, 141.
61. United States Strategic Bombing Survey (Pacific War), *Air Operations in China, Burma, India World War II*, 46.
62. Ibid.
63. Craven and Cate, *The Army Air Forces in World War II*, 5:205.
64. Mountbatten, *Report to the Combined Chiefs of Staff by the Supreme Allied Commander Southeast Asia, 1943–1945*, 211.
65. Cain, "Air Leadership in Joint/Combined Operations: Lt. Gen. George E. Stratemeyer of the Eastern Air Command, 1943–1945," 67.
66. Ibid., 67–68.
67. See particularly van de Ven, *War and Nationalism in China, 1925–1945*, chapter 1; and Rana Mitter, *China's War with Japan, 1937–1945: The Struggle for Survival* (London: Penguin Books, 2013).
68. Spector, "The Sino-Japanese War in the Context of World History," 478.
69. Edward L. Dreyer, *China at War, 1901–1949* (London: Longman, 1995), 276.
70. S. C. M. Paine, *The Wars for Asia, 1911–1949* (Cambridge, UK: Cambridge University Press, 2012), 202.
71. Jay Taylor, "China's Long War with Japan," in *The Cambridge History of the Second World War*, vol. 1, *Fighting the War*, ed. John Ferris and Evan Mawdsley (Cambridge, UK: Cambridge University Press, 2015), 76.
72. Paine, *The Wars for Asia, 1911–1949*, 217.
73. Plating, *The Hump: America's Strategy for Keeping China in World War II*, 238.
74. Ibid., p. 239.
75. Ibid., p. 240.
76. Ibid., p. 243.
77. "A Brief History of AAF India & Burma," 98.

78. Maj. Gen. S. Woodburn Kirby, *The War against Japan*, vol. 5, *The Surrender of Japan* (London: Her Majesty's Stationery Office, 1969), 428.
79. Paine, *The Wars for Asia, 1911–1949*, 203.
80. Kirby, *The War against Japan*, 5:429.
81. Probert, *The Forgotten Air Force*, 309.

REFERENCES CITED

Government Documents

Air Force Historical Research Agency, Maxwell AFB, AL.

9th Bombardment Squadron (H), SQ-Bomb-9-HI, A0538, reel 0561.

11th Bombardment Squadron (M), SQ-Bomb-11-M, SQ-Bomb-11-HI, A0538, reel 0561.

22nd Bombardment Squadron (M), SQ-Bomb-22-HI, A0543, reel 0567.

81st Bombardment Squadron (M), SQ-Bomb-81-HI, A0597, reel 0592.

82nd Bombardment Squadron (M), SQ-Bomb-82-HI, A0597, reel 0592.

83rd Bombardment Squadron (M), SQ-Bomb-83-HI, A0597, reel 0592.

434th Bombardment Squadron (M), SQ-Bomb-434-HI, A0614, reel 0643.

436th Bombardment Squadron (H), SQ-Bomb-436-HI, A0641, reel 0643.

490th Bombardment Squadron (M), SQ-Bomb-490-HI, A0621, reel 0650.

491st Bombardment Squadron (M), SQ-Bomb-491-HI, A0622, reel 0651.

492nd Bombardment Squadron (H), SQ-Bomb-492-HI, A0623, reel 0652.

493rd Bombardment Squadron (H), SQ-Bomb-493-HI, A0623, reel 0652.

1st Fighter Squadron (Commando), SQ-FI-CMDO-1-HI, A0827, reel 876.

2nd Fighter Squadron (Commando), SQ-FI-CMDO-2-HI, A0828, reel 877.

5th Fighter Squadron (Commando), SQ-FI-CMDO-5-HI, A0828, reel 877.

6th Fighter Squadron (Commando), SQ-FI-CMDO-6-HI, A0828, reel 877.

25th Fighter Squadron, SQ-FI-25-HI, A0727, reel 765.

26th Fighter Squadron, SQ-FI-26-HI, A0728, reel 766.

58th Fighter Squadron, SQ-FI-58-HI, A0744–45, reels 782–83.

59th Fighter Squadron, SQ-FI-59-HI, A0745, reel 783.

60th Fighter Squadron, SQ-FI-HI-A0745, reel 783.

88th Fighter Squadron, SQ-FI-88-HI, A0761, reel 800.

89th Fighter Squadron, SQ-FI-89-HI, A0762, reel 801.

90th Fighter Squadron, SQ-FI-90-HI, A0762, reel 801.

459th Fighter Squadron, SQ-FI-490-HI, A0812, reel 860.

528th Fighter Squadron, SQ-FI-528-HI, A0823, reel 872.

529th Fighter Squadron, SQ-FI-529-HI, A0824, reel 873.

530th Fighter Squadron, SQ-FI-530-HI, A0875, reel 874.

427th Night Fighter Squadron, SQ-FI-427-HI, A0805, reel 853.

5th Liaison Squadron, SQ-LIA–5-HI, A0841A, reel 0892.

71st Liaison Squadron, SQ-LIA–71-HI, A0834, reel 0894.

115th Liaison Squadron, SQ-LIA–115-HI, A0844, reel 0895.

9th Photographic Reconnaissance Squadron, SQ-Photo-9-HI, A0871, reel 933.

20th Tactical Reconnaissance Squadron, SQ-RCN-20-HI, A0908, reel 970.

40th Photographic Reconnaissance Squadron, SQ-Photo-40-HI, A0891, reel 953.

1st Troop Carrier Squadron, SQ-TR-CARR-1-HI, A0966, reel 1039.

2nd Troop Carrier Squadron, SQ-TR-CARR-2-HI, A0966, reel 1039.

1st Air Commando Group, GP-A-CMDO-1-HI, B0680, reel 1863.

2nd Air Commando Group, GP-A-CMDO-2-HI, B0681, reel 1864.

7th Bombardment Group (H), GP-7-HI-(Bomb), B0060, reel 1144.

12th Bombardment Group (M), GP-12-HI-(Bomb), B0070–71, reels 1156–57.

341st Bombardment Group (M), GP-341-HI-(Bomb), B0284, reel 1417.

1st Combat Cargo Group, GP-CCA-1-HI, B0725, reel 1912.

3rd Combat Cargo Group, B0726, reel 1913.

4th Combat Cargo Group, B0727, reel 1914.

33rd Fighter Group, GP-33-HI, B0112, reel 1212.

33rd Fighter Group, GP-33–SU-OP, B0113, reel 1213.

51st Fighter Group, GP-51-HI, B0145, reel 1248.

51st Fighter Group, GP-51-SU-OP, B0146, reel 1249.

80th Fighter Group, GP-80-HI, B0165, reel 1271.

80th Fighter Group, GP-80-SU-OP, B0166, reel 1272.

311th Fighter Group, GP-311-HI, B0229, reel 1342.

311th Fighter Group, GP-311-SU-OP, B0230, reel 1343.

8th Photographic Reconnaissance Group, GP-Photo-8-HI, A0755, reel 1944.

443rd Troop Carrier Group, GP-443-HI (TR CARR), B0554, reel 1754.

5320th Air Defense Wing (Prov), WG-5320-AirDef (Prov), C0174, reel 2366.

China-Burma-India (CBI): Air Command, Southeast Asia, Weekly Intelligence Summary 1–22 (5 December 1943–16 April 1944), 815.607, A8058, reel 9850.

CBI: Air Command, Southeast Asia, Weekly Intelligence Summary 23–49 (23 April 1944–22 October 1944), 815.607, A8059, reel 9851.

CBI: Air Command, Southeast Asia, Weekly Intelligence Summary 50–68 (29 October 1944–4 March 1945), 815.607, A8060, reel 9852.

CBI: Air Command, Southeast Asia, Weekly Intelligence Summary 69–105 (11 March 1945–21 November 1945), 815.607, A8061, reel 9853.

CBI: Eastern Air Command. Correspondence of General Stratemeyer, August 1943–December 1944, 820.161A, A8072, reel 9864.
CBI: Eastern Air Command, Early Plans to Integrate American and British into Eastern Air Command, December 1943, 820.201, V.1, A8090, reel 9884.
CBI: Eastern Air Command, Documentation Establishing Eastern Air Command, December 1943, 820.201, V.3, A8091, reel 9885.
CBI: Eastern Air Command, Operational Reports for October 1944–May 1945, 820.306, A8097, reel 9891.
CBI: Eastern Air Command, Headquarters Eastern Air Command, Summary of Operations for August–October 1944, 820.307, A8099, reel 9893.
CBI: Eastern Air Command, Headquarters Eastern Air Command, Summary of Operations for October 1944–January 1945, 820.307, A8100, reel 9894.
CBI: Eastern Air Command, Headquarters Eastern Air Command, Summary of Operations for February–April 1945, 820.307, A8101, reel 9895.
CBI: Eastern Air Command, Headquarters Eastern Air Command, Summary of Operations for May–3 June 1945, 820.307, A8102, reel 9896.
CBI: Eastern Air Command, Headquarters Eastern Air Command, Results of Fighter Attacks on Japanese Airfields in the Rangoon Area, 18–20 October, 820.3121, A8106, reel 9900.
CBI: Eastern Air Command, Headquarters Eastern Air Command, A Study of Operation "L" 16–20 October, 820.423-1, A8112, reel 9906.
CBI: Eastern Air Command, Weekly Intelligence Summary 1–13, 820.607, A8118, reel 9912.
CBI: Eastern Air Command, Weekly Intelligence Summary 14–18, 820.607, A8119, reel 9913.
CBI: Eastern Air Command, Weekly Intelligence Summary 19–28, 820.607, A8120, reel 9914.
CBI: Eastern Air Command, Weekly Intelligence Summary 29–38, 820.607, A8121, reel 9915.
CBI: Eastern Air Command, Dispatch on the Operations of Strategic Air Force Eastern Air Command for the Period 15 December 1943 to 31 May 1944, 821.04A, A8138, reel 9932.
CBI: Eastern Air Command, Operations of Strategic Air Force 15 December 1943 to 3 May 1945, 821.04A, A8138, reel 9932.
CBI: Eastern Air Command, Dispatch on Operations against the Japanese by the Strategic Air Force from 1 June 1944 to 26 November 1944, 821.04A, A8138, reel 9932.
CBI: Eastern Air Command, Dispatch on Operations against the Japanese by the Strategic Air Force from 27 November 1944 to 31 May 1945, 821.04C, A8138, reel 9932.
CBI: Combat Cargo Task Force, History, 15 September 1944–31 May 1945, 824.01, A8146, reel 9940.
CBI: Combat Cargo Task Force, Monthly Histories, September–November 1944, 824.02, A8146, reel 9940.

CBI: US Army Air Force (USAAF), India-Burma Theater (IBT). "History of United States Army Air Force Operations in the India Burma Theater, 1 January to 2 September 1945," January 1944–September 1945, vol. 1, Army Air Forces, India-Burma Sector, 825.01, A8153, reel 9947.
CBI: USAAF, IBT. Documents for History of Army Air Force in India, 12 February 1942–15 December 1943, Army Air Forces, India-Burma Sector, 825.01, A8153, reel 9947.
CBI: USAAF, IBT. "History of United States Army Air Forces India-Burma Sector," China-Burma-India Theater, 825.01B, A8154, reel 9948.
CBI: USAAF, IBT. "History of Air Operations on the Continent of Asia, December 1941–May 1946," vol. 2, section 1, 825.01C, A8154, reel 9948.
CBI: USAAF, IBT. "History of Air Operations on the Continent of Asia, December 1941–May 1946," vol. 3, section 2, 825.01C, A8155, reel 9949.
CBI: USAAF, IBT. "History of Air Operations on the Continent of Asia, December 1941–May 1946," vol. 4, section 2, 825.01C, A8155, reel 9949.
CBI: USAAF, IBT. "Administrative History of Eastern Air Command, 15 December 1943–31 May 1945," in "History of Air Operations on the Continent of Asia, December 1941–May 1946," vol. 3, section 2, 825.01C, A8155, reel 9949.
CBI: USAAF, IBT. Letters, Maj. Gen, George Stratemeyer to Gen. H. H. Arnold, 825.161-2, A8158, reel 9952.
CBI: USAAF, IBT. "Study of 7th Bomb Group Operations from 1 February 1943 to 31 March 1944," Operations Analysis Section, HQ, Army Air Force, India Burma Sector, China-Burma-India, Army Air Forces, India Burma Sector, Operational Analysis 825.3101-1, A8203, reel 9997, frames 293–319.
CBI: Tenth Air Force, India Air Task Force, June–September 1943, India Air Task Force, 827.201-1, A8221, reel 10015.
CBI: Tenth Air Force, India Air Task Force, India Air Task Force Reports on Operations, November 1942–September 1943, India Air Task Force, 827.306, A8221, reel 10015.
CBI: Tenth Air Force, India Air Task Force, Narrative History, India Air Task Force, November 1942–May 31, 1943, 827. 306-1, A8221, reel 10015.
CBI: Tenth Air Force, India Air Task Force, India Air Task Force Operational Statistics, India Air Task Force, 827.308, A8221, reel 10015.
CBI: Tenth Air Force, India Air Task Force, Daily Intelligence Extracts 40–219 (1 January–30 June 1943), 827.606, A8221, reel 10015.
CBI: Tenth Air Force, India Air Task Force, Daily Intelligence Extracts 220–281 (1 July–31 August, 1943), 827.606, A8222, reel 10016.
CBI: Tenth Air Force, India Air Task Force, Daily Intelligence Extracts 282–317 (1 September–6 October 1943), 827.606, A8221, reel 10016.
CBI: Tenth Air Force, Headquarters, Assam American Air Base Command, Dinjan, India, History of Organization, 828.011, A8222, reel 10016.

CBI: Tenth Air Force, History of the Tenth Air Force Headquarters, 1 January to 31 May 1943, Tenth Air Force History, 1942–1945, 830.01, A8224, reel 10018.

CBI: Tenth Air Force, Headquarters, 10th Air Force Historical Data, November 1944, Air Jungle Rescue, 20 March 1945, 830.01, A8224, reel 10018.

CBI: Tenth Air Force, Report on Tenth Air Force Operations, 20 June 1944–30 April 1945, Tenth Air Force History, 1942–1945, 830.01, A8224, reel 10018.

CBI: Tenth Air Force, Monthly History of the Tenth Air Force, 1945, 830.01, A8225, reel 10020.

CBI: Tenth Air Force, Azon in India-Burma Theater, 20 March 1945, 830.04–3, A8229, reel 10024.

CBI: Tenth Air Force, Notes and Memoranda of Staff Meetings and Conferences, 1943–1944, 830.151, A8232, reel 10027.

CBI: Tenth Air Force, Maj. Gen. Howard Davidson Correspondence, 830.161, A8232, reel 10027.

CBI: Tenth Air Force, Personnel, 830.217–1, A8239, reel 10034.

CBI: Tenth Air Force, 201—Bissell, Clayton L., August 1942–November 1943, 830.289–1, A8242, reel 10037.

CBI: Tenth Air Force, 10th Air Force Operations, Tenth Air Force Operational Diary, 1 June 1942–1 June 1943, Tenth Air Force 830.305–1, A8242, reel 10037.

CBI: Tenth Air Force, 10th Air Force Operations, Operations of the 10th Air Force in North Burma, Joint Intelligence Collection Agency Report 499 (10 December 1944), 830.306–1, A8242, reel 10037.

CBI: Tenth Air Force, 10th Air Force Operations, 29 October 1942–27 April 1943, Operations from India: Heavy Bombers, 830.3061–4, A8243, reel 10038.

CBI: Tenth Air Force, 10th Air Force Operations, Dispatch on Air Operations, 1 June to 26 Nov 1944 Inclusive, 830.306–5, A8243, reel 10038.

CBI: Tenth Air Force, 10th Air Force Operations, Weekly Analysis of Tenth Air Force Operations, 3 September 1944–17 April 1945, 830.3062, A8243, reel 10038.

CBI: Tenth Air Force, 10th Air Force Operations, "Chronological History of 10th A.F. Air Supply Operations," February 1943–May 1945, 830.3069–1, A8244, reel 10042.

CBI: Tenth Air Force, 10th Air Force Operations, "10th Air Force Operations Sept–Dec 1944," 830.308–2, A8244, reel 10042, frames 436–464.

CBI: Tenth Air Force, 10th Air Force Operations, "Burma Banshees Dive Bombing Tactics in Northern Burma," Strategical and Tactical Survey of 10 Air Force Efforts, 830.310 tab M, reel 25769.

CBI: Tenth Air Force, 10th Air Force Operations, 10th Air Force Project Low, Tenth Air Force, 830.322–6, A8245, reel 10045.

CBI: Tenth Air Force, 10th Air Force Operations, Tenth Air Force Plan for Interdiction of Japanese Lines of Communication Generally North of Mandalay, 28 November 1944, 830.3221-2, A8245, reel 10045.

CBI: Tenth Air Force, 10th Air Force Air Ground Cooperation, "Special Report: Development of Close Air Support Techniques in North Burma," 5 September 1944, 830.4501-1, A8246, reel 10041, frames 614–657.

CBI: Tenth Air Force, 10th Air Force Air Ground Cooperation, "Development of Joint Air Ground Operations in Northern Burma," 830.4501-2, A8246, reel 10041, frames 628–719.

CBI: Tenth Air Force, 10th Air Force Air Ground Cooperation, "Air Ground Cooperation in Stilwell's North Burma Campaign, October 1943–3 August 1944," 830.4501-4, A8246, reel 10041.

CBI: Tenth Air Force, Headquarters, Tenth Air Force, "Summary of Fighter Bomber and Medium Bomber Attacks on Bridges during the Month of December 1944," 12 February 1945, 830.454-1, A8247, reel 10041.

CBI: Tenth Air Force, 10th Air Force Operations, "Bridge Busting: Med. Bombers vs. Fighters," October–November 1944, 830.454-3, A8247, reel 10041.

CBI: Tenth Air Force, Headquarters, Tenth Air Force, "Attacks on Bridges by 'Bridge Busters' of the 10th Air Force," January 19–May 1944, 830.454-4, A8247, reel 10042.

CBI: Tenth Air Force, Headquarters, Tenth Air Force, "P-51 Tactics over Burma from 1 November 1943 to 31 May 1944," 830.589-2, A8247, reel 10042.

CBI: Tenth Air Force, Headquarters, Tenth Air Force Operational Bulletin 8, "P-38 Combat Tactics over Burma from 12 March 1944 to 17 May 1944," 9 July 1944, 830.548-1, A8247, reel 10042.

CBI: Tenth Air Force, Headquarters, Tenth Air Force, "Report of Effects of Air Support at Myitkyina," 17 August 1944, 830.55-2, A8247, reel 10042.

CBI: Tenth Air Force, Headquarters, Tenth Air Force, Daily Intelligence Extracts for 1944, 830.6062, A8251, reel 10046.

CBI: Tenth Air Force, Headquarters, Tenth Air Force, Daily Intelligence Extracts for 1944, 830.6062, A8252, reel 10047.

CBI: China Air Task Force (CATF). Operational Correspondence, 1942–43, China Air Task Force, Fourteenth Air Force, 860.311, AFHRA, A8351, reel 10146.

HQ, USAAF, Assistant Chief of Air Staff, Plans, Airborne Study, 145.81-170, A1378, reel 2800.

HQ, USAAF: Assistant Chief of Air Staff, Plans, 145.95 (WP-IV-D-1 [Southeast Asia]), A1471, reel 2899.

HQ USAAF: Assistant Chief of Air Staff, Plans, 145.95 (WP-IV-D-4 [India Book I]), A1472, reel 2900.

"A Brief History of AAF India & Burma," personal collection of Maj. Gen. Howard C. Davidson, 168.7266-56, reel 42822.

Office of the Assistant Chief of Air Staff, Intelligence. "B-24 Tactics over Burma and Thailand," *Informational Intelligence Summary* 44–7 (29 February 1944).

Office of the Assistant Chief of Air Staff, Intelligence. "Tactics of a B-24 Squadron over Burma," *Informational Intelligence Summary* 44–4 (30 January 1944).

Office of the Chief of Military History. "The Siege at Myitkyina," Center for Military History "Supporting Documents to CBI Volumes," file 270/19/13/6, Record Group 319: Records of the Army General Staff, 1903–2009, National Archives and Records Administration.

Report 1, US Navy Air Combat Information, Observations of Operational Forces in India Burma, "Direct Air Support to Long Range Penetration Groups of the Third Indian Division in North Burma, Provided by the First Air Commando Group, USAAF," 8 May 1944, GP-A-CMDO-1-HI.

US Air Force Numbered Historical Studies 12: *The Tenth Air Force 1942* (1944).

US Air Force Numbered Historical Studies 23: Futrell, Dr. Robert F., *Development of Aero-medical Evacuation in the USAF, 1909–1960* (1960).

US Air Force Numbered Historical Studies 75: Taylor, Dr. Joe G., *Air Supply in the Burma Campaigns* (1957).

US Air Force Numbered Historical Studies 91: Fogerty, Robert P., *Biographical Data on Air Force General Officers, 1917–1952* (Manhattan, KS: MA/AH, 1953).

US Air Force Numbered Historical Studies 104: *The Tenth Air Force, 1 January–10 March 1943* (1944).

US Air Force Numbered Historical Studies 117: *The Tenth Air Force 1943* (1946).

Joint Army-Navy Assessment Committee, *Japanese Naval and Merchant Shipping Losses during World War II by All Causes* (February 1947).

Office of Statistical Control, *Army Air Forces Statistical Digest World War II*, 2nd printing (December 1945).

United States Strategic Bombing Survey (Pacific War), *Air Operations in China, Burma, India World War II* (Washington, DC, 1945–1947).

United States Strategic Bombing Survey (Pacific War), *Japanese Air Power* (Washington, DC, 1946).

War Department, *Command and Employment of Air Power*, War Department Field Manual FM 100–20 (Washington, DC: War Department, 1944).

The National Archives, Kew, England

Air 8/654, Air Ministry and Ministry of Defence, Department of the Chief of the Air Staff: Registered Files. US Air Forces in India, Mar–Aug 1942.

Air 8/680, Air Ministry and Ministry of Defence, Department of the Chief of the Air Staff: Registered Files. India: Command and Role of US Air Forces.

Air 8/1158, Air Ministry and Ministry of Defence, Department of the Chief of the Air Staff: Registered Files. Air Commandos in Southeast Asia Command.

Air 20/881, Air Ministry and Ministry of Defence, Air Historical Branch, Assistant Chief of Air Staff (Operations). American Fortress Aircraft: Employment in Middle and Far East.

Air 20/5045, Air Ministry and Ministry of Defence, Papers Accumulated by the Air Historical Branch. Assistant Chief of Air Staff (Policy). Air Commandos for Southeast Asia.

Air 23/1933, Air Ministry and Ministry of Defence, Royal Air Force Overseas Commands, Reports and Correspondence: Air Command, Southeast Asia. Dispatch on Operations of Eastern Air Command, 15 December 1943–1 June 1945.

Air 23/2167, Air Ministry and Ministry of Defence, Royal Air Force Overseas Commands, Reports and Correspondence: Air Command, Southeast Asia. Integration of British and American Air Forces under SEAC.

Air 23/2267, Air Ministry and Ministry of Defence, Royal Air Force Overseas Commands, Reports and Correspondence: Air Command, Southeast Asia. Employment of Air Commando Groups.

Air 23/2570, Air Ministry and Ministry of Defence, Royal Air Force Overseas Commands, Reports and Correspondence: Air Command, Southeast Asia. Integration of RAF and USAAF Policy.

Air 23/2597, Air Ministry and Ministry of Defence, Royal Air Force Overseas Commands, Reports and Correspondence: Air Command, Southeast Asia. Air Staff. Eastern Air Command: Reorganization.

Air 23/2855, Air Ministry and Ministry of Defence, Royal Air Force Overseas Commands, Reports and Correspondence: Air Command, Southeast Asia. Operational Research Section. Bombing Operations 1941–1942 by RAF and USAAF Units Based in India and Burma: Summary.

Air 23/4301, Air Ministry and Ministry of Defence, Royal Air Force Overseas Commands, Reports and Correspondence: Air Command, Southeast Asia. Strategic Air Force (Intelligence). Review of operations, Sept. 1943–May 1944.

Air 23/4681, Air Ministry and Ministry of Defence, Royal Air Force Overseas Commands, Reports and Correspondence: Air Officer Commander-in-Chief 3rd Tactical Air Force. Dispatch covering operations of Bengal Command, 15 Nov.–17 Dec. 1943, and 3rd Tactical Air Force, 18 December–1 June 1944.

Air 23/4884, Air Ministry and Ministry of Defence, Royal Air Force Overseas Commands, Reports and Correspondence: Air Command, Southeast Asia. Operational Effort by RAF and USAAF for Period of Japanese War.

Air 23/4963, Air Ministry and Ministry of Defence, Royal Air Force Overseas Commands, Reports and Correspondence: Air Command, Southeast Asia. Summary of Operations 1943 by R.A.F and USAAF, Based in India.

Air 23/2997, Air Ministry and Ministry of Defence, Royal Air Force Overseas Commands, Reports and Correspondence: Strategic Air Force. Japanese Fighter Tactics against Heavy Bombers. Headquarters Army Air Forces, India-Burma Sector, China-Burma-India Theater, "Japanese Fighter Tactics against B-25s," July 1944.

Air Ministry. Air Historical Branch. *The Campaigns in the Far East*. Volume 3, *India Command September 1939 to November 1943* (London, n.d).

Air Ministry. Air Historical Branch. *The Campaigns in the Far East*. Volume 4, *Southeast Asia November 1943 to August 1945* (London, n.d.).

WO 203/4719, War Office, Southeast Asia Command: Military Headquarters Papers, Second World War. South East Asia Command. Air. Provision for air commandos.

Private Papers and Interviews

Henry Harley Arnold Papers, Library of Congress, Washington, DC.

Davidson, Howard C., Correspondence (Official), 168.7266, reel 42821, Air Force Historical Research Agency, Maxwell AFB, AL.

MB1/C Mountbatten Papers: Southeast Asia Command, Papers of Earl Mountbatten of Burma, Special Collections, University of Southampton, UK.

Papers of Air Chief Marshal Sir Richard Edmund Charles Peirse, AC71/13, Royal Air Force Museum, Hendon, London.

The Viscount Portal Papers, Christ Church College, Oxford.

Papers of Gen. George Stratemeyer, Thomas Overlander–George Stratemeyer Collection, Special Collections, McDermott Library, US Air Force Academy, Colorado Springs, CO.

Interview with Roland Lynn, Fighter Section, 5th Fighter Squadron (Commando), 1st Air Commando Group, 52nd Reunion, Portland, OR, 18–21 September 1996, possession of the author.

Interviews with Members of the 1st and 2nd Fighter Squadron, 2nd Air Commando Group, Air Commando Group Reunion, 8 November 1985, possession of the author.

Dissertation/Thesis

Cain, Maj. Gregory M. "Air Leadership in Joint/Combined Operations: Lt. Gen. George E. Stratemeyer of the Eastern Air Command, 1943–1945." Maxwell AFB, AL: US Air Force, Air University School of Advanced Airpower Studies, 1998. www.dtic.mil/cgi-bin/GetTRDoc?AD=ADA391810, 30 April 2016.

Books, Articles, and Memoirs

Allen, Louis. *Burma: The Longest War, 1941–1945*. London: J. M. Dent, 1984.

Arnold, General of the Air Force Henry H. *Global Mission*. New York: Harper, 1949.

Bagby, Wesley M. *The Eagle-Dragon Alliance: America's Relations with China in World War II*. Newark: University of Delaware Press, 1992.

Barnhart, Michael A. *Japan Prepares for Total War: The Search for Economic Security, 1919–1941*. Ithaca, NY: Cornell University Press, 1987.

Bartsch, William H. *Doomed at the Start: American Pursuit Pilots in the Philippines, 1941–1942*. College Station: Texas A&M University Press, 1992.

———. *December 8, 1941: MacArthur's Pearl Harbor*. College Station: Texas A&M University Press, 2003.

———. *Every Day a Nightmare: American Pursuit Pilots in the Defense of Java, 1941–1942*. College Station: Texas A&M University Press, 2010.

Behrns, William M., and Kenneth Moore. *The San Joaquin Siren: An American Ace in WWII's CBI*. Tucson, AZ: Amethyst Moon, 2011.

Bell, Howard, and Anthony Strotman. *The Burma Bridge Busters*. Booksurge, 2005.

Bidwell, Shelford. *The Chindit War: The Campaign in Burma, 1944*. London: Hodder & Stoughton, 1979.

Brereton, Lt. General Lewis H. *The Brereton Diaries: The War in the Air in the Pacific, Middle East and Europe, 3 October 1941–8 May 1945*. New York: William Morrow, 1946.

Butler, J. R. M. *Grand Strategy*. Vol. 3, part 2, *June 1941–August 1942*. London: Her Majesty's Stationery Office, 1964.

Byrd, Martha. *Chennault: Giving Wings to the Tiger*. Tuscaloosa: University of Alabama Press, 1987.

Chennault, Maj. Gen. (Ret'd) Claire Lee. *Way of a Fighter*. New York: G. P. Putnam's Sons, 1949.

Chinese Ministry of Information. *China Handbook, 1937–1945*. New York: Macmillan, 1946.

Clauswitz, Carl von. *On War*. Edited by Michael Howard and Peter Paret. Princeton, NJ: Princeton University Press, 1976.

Coakley, Robert W., and Richard M. Leighton. *The US Army in World War II: The War Department; Global Logistics and Strategy, 1943–1945*. Washington, DC: Office of the Chief of Military History, US Department of the Army, 1968.

Craven, Wesley Frank, and James Lea Cate, eds. *The Army Air Forces in World War II*. Vol. 1, *Plans and Early Operations, January 1939 to August 1942*. Chicago: University of Chicago Press, 1948.

———. *The Army Air Forces in World War II*. Vol. 4, *The Pacific: Guadalcanal to Saipan, August 1942 to July 1944*. Chicago: University of Chicago Press, 1950.

———. *The Army Air Forces in World War II*. Vol. 5, *The Pacific: Matterhorn to Nagasaki, June 1944 to August 1945*. Chicago: University of Chicago Press, 1953.

———. *The Army Air Forces in World War II*. Vol. 7, *Services around the World*. Chicago: University of Chicago Press, 1958.

Daugherty, Leo J., III. *The Allied Resupply Effort in the China-Burma-India Theater during World War II*. Jefferson, NC: McFarland, 2008.

Davis, Capt. Luther. "The 'B'-40 over Burma." *Air Force Magazine* 26, no. 10 (October 1943).

Davis, Richard G. *Carl A. Spaatz and the Air War in Europe*. Washington, DC: Center for Air Force History, 1992.

Dreyer, Edward L. *China at War, 1901–1949*. London: Longman, 1995.

Duncan, Charles V., Jr. *B-24 over Burma*. Modesto, CA: C. V. Duncan, 1986.

Dunlop, Graham. *Military Economics, Culture and Logistics in the Burma Campaign, 1942–1945*. London: Pickering & Chatto, 2009.

Dunlop, Richard. *Behind Enemy Lines: With the OSS in Burma*. New York: Rand McNally, 1979.

Edmonds, Walter D. *They Fought with What They Had*. Boston: Little, Brown, 1951.

Ehlers, Robert S. *The Mediterranean Air War: Airpower and Allied Victory in World War II*. Lawrence: University Press of Kansas, 2015.

Ehrman, John. *Grand Strategy*. Vol. 5, *August 1943–September 1944*. London: Her Majesty's Stationery Office, 1956.

Ehrman, John. *Grand Strategy*. Vol. 6, *October 1944–August 1945*. London: Her Majesty's Stationery Office, 1956.

Fielder, James M. *A History of the 459th Fighter Squadron: The Twin Dragons, CBI, 1943–45*. Universal City, TX: James M. Fielder, 1993.

Ford, Daniel. *Flying Tigers: Claire Chennault and the American Volunteer Group*. Washington, DC: Smithsonian Institution Press, 1991.

Franks, Norman L. R., and Frank W. Bailey. *Over the Front: A Complete Record of the Fighter Aces and Units of the United States and French Air Services, 1914–1918*. London: Grub Street, 1992.

Greenhalgh, William H. *Foto Jo in CBI: 9th Photographic Reconnaissance Squadron China-Burma-India, 1942–1945*. William H. Greenhalgh, 1990.

Grehan, John, and Martin Mace, eds. *Far East Air Operations, 1942–1945*. Despatches from the Front. Barnsley, UK: Pen & Sword Military, 2014.

Gwyer, J. M. *Grand Strategy*. Vol. 3, part 1, *June 1941–August 1942*. London: Her Majesty's Stationery Office, 1964.

Halley, James J. *The Squadrons of the Royal Air Force*. Tonbridge, UK: Air-Britain, 1985.

Hamlett, T. Bradley. *Bombing the Death Railway*. Sun River, MT: Hamlett Ranch, 2002.

Haruo, Tomatsu. "The Strategic Correlation between the Sino-Japanese and Pacific Wars." In *The Battle for China: Essays on the Military History of the Sino-Japanese War of 1937–1945* Edited by Mark Peattie, Edward J. Drea, and Hans van de Ven, 423–45. Stanford, CA: Stanford University Press, 2011.

Hata, Ikuhiko, Yasuho Izawa, and Christopher Shores. *Japanese Army Air Force Fighter Units and Their Aces, 1931–1945*. London: Grub Street, 2002.

Hayward, David K., ed. *Eagles, Bulldogs & Tigers: History of the 22nd Bomb Squadron in China-Burma-India*. Huntington Beach, CA: 22nd Bomb Squadron Association, 1997.

———. *World War II Diary: By the Men of the 22nd Bomb Squadron of the China Burma India Theater*. Huntington Beach, CA: 22nd Bomb Squadron Association, 2002.

Henderson, Lt. Col. W. *From China Burma India to the Kwai*. Waco, TX: Texian, 1991.

Hill, David Lee "Tex," with Major Reagan Schaupp, USAF. *"Tex" Hill: Flying Tiger*. San Antonio, TX: Universal Bookbindery, 2003.

Hopkins, James E. T. *Spearhead: A Complete History of Merrill's Marauder Rangers*. Baltimore: Galahad, 1999.

Howard, Michael. *Grand Strategy*. Vol. 4, *August 1942–September 1943*. London: Her Majesty's Stationery Office, 1970.

Howard, Michael, and Peter Paret, eds. and trans. *Carl von Clausewitz: On War*. Princeton, NJ: Princeton University Press, 1984.

Hunter, Col. Charles Newton. *Galahad*. San Antonio, TX: Naylor, 1963.

Ichimura, Hiroshi. *Ki-43 "Oscar" Aces of World War 2*. Osprey Aircraft of the Aces 85. Oxford: Osprey, 2009.

Izawa, Yasuho. "64th Flying Sentai, Part 3." *Aero Album* 5, no. 4 (Winter 1972).

Kappel, Roy. *Whispering Wings over Burma: The Jungle Angels, 5th Liaison Squadron*. Elk Creek, NE: R. Kappel, 1998.

Kinzey, Bert. *P-40 Warhawk in Detail, Part 2: P-40D through XP-40Q*. Detail & Scale 62. Carrollton, TX: Squadron/Signal, 1999.

Kirby, Major-General S. Woodburn. *The War against Japan*. Vol. 2, *India's Most Dangerous Hour*. London: Her Majesty's Stationery Office, 1958.

———. *The War against Japan*. Vol. 3, *The Decisive Battles*. London: Her Majesty's Stationery Office, 1961.

———. *The War against Japan*. Vol. 4, *The Reconquest of Burma*. London: Her Majesty's Stationery Office, 1965.

———. *The War against Japan*. Vol. 5, *The Surrender of Japan*. London: Her Majesty's Stationery Office, 1969.

Kopp, Dr. Carlo. *The Dawn of the Smart Bomb*. Technical Report APA-TR-2011-0302, 26 March 2011, Air Power Australia. www.ausairpower.net/WW2-PGMs.html.

Leary, William M., Jr. *The Dragon's Wings: The China National Aviation Corporation and the Development of Commercial Aviation in China*. Athens, GA: University of Georgia Press, 1976.

Lee, Ulysses. *The Employment of Negro Troops*. United States Army in World War II: Special Studies. Washington, DC: Office of the Chief of Military History, US Department of the Army, 1966.

Leighton, Richard M., and Robert W. Coakley. *Global Logistics and Strategy, 1940–1943*. United States Army in World War II: The War Department. Washington, DC: Office of the Chief of Military History, US Department of the Army, 1955.

Lewin, Ronald. *Slim: The Standard Bearer*. London: Leo Cooper, 1976.

Liu, F. F. *A Military History of Modern China, 1924–1949*. Princeton, NJ: Princeton University Press, 1956.

Lyman, Robert. *Slim, Master of War: Burma and the Birth of Modern Warfare*. London: Constable, 2004.

Martin, John G. *It Began at Imphal: The Combat Cargo Story*. Manhattan, KS: Sunflower University Press, 1988.

Mason, Herbert A., Jr., SSgt. Randy G. Bergeron, and TSgt. James A. Renfrew Jr. *Operation Thursday: Birth of the Air Commandos*. The U.S. Army Air Forces in World War II. Washington, DC: Air Force History and Museums Program, 1994.

Matloff, Maurice. *Strategic Planning for Coalition Warfare, 1943–1944*. United States Army in World War II: The War Department. Washington, DC: Center of Military History, US Army, 1959.

Matloff, Maurice, and Edwin M. Snell. *Strategic Planning for Coalition Warfare, 1941–1942*. United States Army in World War II: The War Department. Washington, DC: Center of Military History, US Army, 1953.

Maurer, Maurer, ed. *Combat Squadrons of the Air Force World War II*. Washington, DC: US Government Printing Office, 1982.

———. *Air Force Combat Units of World War II*. Washington, DC: Office of Air Force History, 1983.

Military Analysis Division. *Air Operations in China, Burma, India World War II*. Washington, DC: US Strategic Bombing Survey, 1947.

Military History Section, Headquarters, Army Forces Far East. *Burma Air Operations Record, Jan. 1942–Aug. 1945*. Japanese Monograph 64. Tokyo: Far East Command, US Army, 1946.

Military History Section, Headquarters, Army Forces Far East. *Air Operations in the China Area (July 1937–August 1945)*. Japanese Monograph 76. Washington, DC: Office of the Chief of Military History, Department of the Army, 1956.

Millett, Allan R., and Williamson Murray, eds. *Military Effectiveness*. Vol. 1, *The First World War*. New ed. New York: Cambridge University Press, 2010.

Millman, Nicholas. *Ki-44 "Tojo" Aces of World War 2*. Osprey Aircraft of the Aces 100. Oxford: Osprey, 2011.

Mitter, Rana. *China's War with Japan, 1937–1945: The Struggle for Survival*. London: Penguin Books, 2013.

Molesworth, Carl. *Sharks over China: The 23rd Fighter Group in World War II*. Washington, DC: Brassey's, 1994.

———. *P-40 Warhawk Aces of the CBI*. Oxford: Osprey, 2000.

Mountbatten, Vice-Admiral the Earl Mountbatten of Burma. *Report to the Combined Chiefs of Staff by the Supreme Allied Commander Southeast Asia, 1943–1945*. London: Her Majesty's Stationery Office, 1945.

O'Brien, Phillips Payson. *How the War Was Won: Air-Sea Power and Allied Victory in World War II*. Cambridge, UK: Cambridge University Press, 2015.

Olynyk, Frank J. *AVG & USAAF (China-Burma-India Theater) Credits for the Destruction of Enemy Aircraft in Air-to-Air Combat World War 2*. Aurora, OH: F. J. Olynyk, 1986.

Paine, S. C. M. *The Wars for Asia, 1911–1949*. Cambridge, UK: Cambridge University Press, 2012.

Park, Air Chief Marshal Sir Keith. "Air Operations in South East Asia from 1st June, 1944, to the Occupation of Rangoon, 2nd May, 1945." *London Gazette*, 3rd supplement, Friday, 6 April 1951.

Pearson, Michael. *End Game Burma: Slim's Masterstroke at Meiktila*. Barnsley, UK: Pen & Sword Military, 2010.

Peattie, Mark, Edward J. Drea, and Hans van de Ven, eds. *The Battle for China: Essays on the Military History of the Sino-Japanese War of 1937–1945*. Stanford, CA: Stanford University Press, 2011.

Peirse, Air Chief Marshal. "Air Chief Marshal Richard Peirse's Despatch on Air Operations in South East Asia, 16th November, 1943 to 31 May, 1944." In *Far East Air Operations, 1942–1945*. Edited by John Grehan and Martin Mace, 43–94. Despatches from the Front. Barnsley, UK: Pen & Sword Military, 2014.

Perez, Alfonso B. *A B-24 Bombardier "over Burma": The Personal Diary of Lt. Alfonso B. Perez*. Privately published, n.d.

Perrett, Bryan. *Tank Tracks to Rangoon*. London: R. Hale, 1978.

Phillips, Bob. *KC-8 Burma: CBI Air Warning Team, 1941–1942*. Manhattan, KS: Sunflower University Press, 1992.

Plating, John D. *The Hump: America's Strategy for Keeping China in World War II*. College Station: Texas A&M University Press, 2011.

Preston-Hough, Peter. *Commanding Far Eastern Skies: A Critical Analysis of the Royal Air Force Air Superiority Campaign in India, Burma and Malaya, 1941–1945*. Solihull, UK: Helion, 2015.

Probert, Air Commodore Henry. *The Forgotten Air Force: The Royal Air Force in the War against Japan, 1941–1945*. London: Brassey's, 1995.

The Record: The Eleventh Bombardment Squadron (M). Richmond, VA, n.d.

Rigby, David. *Allied Master Strategists: The Combined Chiefs of Staff in World War II*. Annapolis, MD: US Naval Institute, 2012.

Romanus, Charles F., and Riley Sunderland. *United States Army in World War II: China-Burma-India Theater*. Vol. 1, *Stilwell's Mission to China*. Washington, DC: Office of the Chief of Military History, Department of the Army, 1953.

———. *United States Army in World War II: China-Burma-India Theater*. Vol. 2, *Stilwell's Command Problems*. Washington, DC: Office of the Chief of Military History, Department of the Army, 1956.

———. *United States Army in World War II: China-Burma-India Theater*. Vol. 3, *Time Runs Out in CBI*. Washington, DC: Office of the Chief of Military History, Department of the Army, 1959.

Sacquety, Troy J. *The OSS in Burma: Jungle War against the Japanese*. Lawrence: University Press of Kansas, 2013.

Schaller, Michael. *The US Crusade in China, 1938–1945*. New York: Columbia University Press, 1979.

Scott, Colonel Robert L., Jr. *God Is My Co-pilot*. New York: Charles Scribner's Sons, 1943.

Shiel, Walt. *Rough War: The Combat Story of Lt. Paul Eastman, a "Burma Banshee" P-40 and P-47 Pilot*. Jacobsville, MI: Jacobsville Books, 2011.

Shores, Christopher. *Air War for Burma: The Allied Air Forces Fight Back in Southeast Asia, 1942–1945*. London: Grub Street, 2005.

Shores, Christopher, and Brian Cull, with Yasuho Izawa. *Bloody Shambles*. Vol. 2, *The Defence of Sumatra to the Fall of Burma*. London: Grub Street, 1993.

Sims, Edward H. *American Aces in Great Fighter Battles of World War II*. New York: Ballantine Books, 1958.

Slim, Field Marshal Sir William. "Some Aspects of the Campaign in Burma." *Journal of the Royal Central Asian Society* 33, no. 3–4 (1946): 326–40.

———. *Defeat into Victory*. London: Cassell, 1956.

Smith, Peter C. *Straight Down! The North American A-36 Dive Bomber in Action*. Manchester, UK: Crécy, 2000.

Smith, W. E., ed. *2nd Troop Carrier Squadron, AAF, CBI, WWII*. Cullman, AL: Gregath, 1987.

Spector, Ronald H. *Eagle against the Sun: The American War with Japan*. New York: Macmillan, 1985.

———. "The Sino-Japanese War in the Context of World History." In *The Battle for China: Essays on the Military History of the Sino-Japanese War of 1937–1945*. Edited by Mark Peattie, Edward J. Drea, and Hans van de Ven, 467–81. Stanford, CA: Stanford University Press, 2011.

Stahura, Barbara. *Earthquakers: 12th Bombardment Group (M)*. Paducah, KY: Turner, 1998.

Stilwell, Joseph W. *The Stilwell Papers*. Edited by Theodore H. White. New York: W. Sloane, 1948.

Stoler, Mark A. *Allies and Adversaries: The Joint Chiefs of Staff, the Grand Alliance, and US Strategy in World War II*. Chapel Hill: University of North Carolina Press, 2000.

Sun, Youli. *China and the Origins of the Pacific War, 1931–1941*. New York: St. Martin's, 1993.

Syrett, David. "Northwest Africa, 1942–1943." In *Case Studies in the Achievement of Air Superiority*. Edited by Benjamin Franklin Cooling, 223–70. Washington, DC: Office of Air Force History, US Air Force, 1991.

Tagaya, Osamu. "The Imperial Japanese Air Forces." In *Why Air Forces Fail: The Anatomy of Defeat*. Edited by Robin Higham and Stephen J. Harris, 177–202. Lexington: University Press of Kentucky, 2006.

Taylor, Jay. "China's Long War with Japan." In *The Cambridge History of the Second World War*. Vol. 1, *Fighting the War*. Edited by John Ferris and Evan Mawdsley, 51–77. Cambridge, UK: Cambridge University Press, 2015.

Terry, Thurzal Q. *Strangers in Their Land: CBI Bombardier, 1939–1945*. Manhattan, KS: Sunflower University Press, 1992.

Thomas, Geoffrey J. *Eyes for the Phoenix: Allied Aerial Photo-reconnaissance Operations, South-East Asia, 1941–45*. Aldershot, UK: Hikoki, 1999.

Thomas, Captain Rowan T. *Born in Battle: Round the World Adventures of the 513th Bombardment Squadron*. Philadelphia: John C. Winston, 1944.

Thorne, Christopher. *Allies of a Kind: The United States, Britain, and the War against Japan, 1941–1945*. London: Hamish Hamilton, 1978.

van de Ven, Hans J. *War and Nationalism in China, 1925–1945*. London: RoutledgeCurzon, 2003.

Van Wagner, R. D. *1st Air Commando Group: Any Place, Any Time, Any Where*. Military History Series 86-1. Maxwell AFB, AL: USAF Air Command and General Staff College, 1986.

———. *Any Time, Any Place, Any Where: The 1st Air Commandos in World War II*. Atglen, PA: Schiffer, 1998.

Vesely, James M. *Unlike Any Land You Know: The 490th Bomb Squadron in China-Burma-India*. Lincoln, NE: Writers Club Press, 2000.

Walker, James W. *The Liberandos: A World War II History of the 376th Bomb Group (H) and Its Founding Units*. Waco: TX: 376th Heavy Bombardment Group Veterans Association, 1994.

White, Gerald A., Jr. *The Great Snafu Fleet: 1st Combat Cargo / 344th Airdrome / 326th Troop Carrier Squadron in World War II's CBI Theater*. Bloomington, IN: Xlibris, 2000.

Y'Blood, William T. *Air Commandos against Japan: Allied Special Operations in World War II Burma*. Annapolis, MD: Naval Institute Press, 2008.

Young, Edward M. *Air Commando Fighters of World War II*. North Branch, MN: Specialty Press, 2000.

———. *Meiktila: The Battle to Liberate Burma*. Osprey Campaign 136. Oxford: Osprey, 2004.

———. *Merrill's Marauders*. Osprey Warrior 141. Oxford: Osprey, 2009.

———. *B-24 Liberator vs. Ki-43 Oscar*. Osprey Duel 41. Oxford: Osprey, 2012.

———. *Death from Above: The 7th Bombardment Group in World War II*. Atglen, PA: Schiffer, 2014.

INDEX

A

aeromedical evacuation operations, 6, 229–30, 272–76
air ferry operation. *See* Hump route
air superiority, 6, 11, 21, 52–53, 77, 114, 181–82, 198–207, 255–59
air supply operations, 6, 160–61, 182, 191, 221–29, 272–76, 282–304
air support operations for NCAC, 184–98, 255–80, 293, 311–15, 318, 340
Alexander, Brig. Gen. Edward (USAAF), 119
Alexander, Gen. Sir Harold (Royal Army), 19
American forces. *See* United States Army Air Force
American Volunteer Group (AVG), 11–33
ARCADIA Conference, 12–13
Arnold, Lt. Gen. Henry "Hap" (USAAF), 13, 14, 16, 23, 25, 47, 49, 50, 51, 53–54, 58, 60, 61, 63, 78, 86, 112, 114, 115–16, 117–18, 119, 133–34, 140, 143, 144, 146, 148, 223–24, 226, 229, 230, 247, 248, 282–87, 305, 313, 342–43
Assam-Burma-China Ferry, 28–31. *See also* Hump route
Auchinleck, Gen. Sir Claude (Royal Army), 133, 135, 311

B

Baldwin, Air Marshal Sir John (RAF), 145–46, 147, 148, 179, 223, 231, 282–83, 294, 311
Bandon, Air Vice-Marshal the Earl of (RAF), 297–98
battle of the bridges, 327–32
Bissell, Brig. Gen. Clayton (USAAF), 37, 41, 49, 50–52, 54, 60–66, 76, 85, 86, 91, 97, 114, 115–19, 137
bombing operations, 6, 163–76, 208–21. *See also specific military units*
Brady, Brig. Gen. Francis M. (USAAF), 15, 21, 63–64
Brereton, Maj. Gen. Lewis (USAAF), 12, 13, 16–32, 33, 35–36, 37, 50, 58, 59, 219
Brett, Maj. Gen. George (USAAF), 11, 12, 14–16
Britain, interests in CBI theater, 8. *See also* Royal Air Force
British Army units
    11th Army Group, 178, 281
    14th Army, 178–79, 182, 194–95, 213, 221–27, 231–34, 236, 246–47, 248, 251, 265–69, 272, 277–78, 281–322, 327, 330–40, 345, 351
    7th Indian Division, 194, 314, 321
    17th Indian Division, 195, 312, 316–17, 321
    20th Indian Division, 195
    36th British Division, 258, 265, 269–70, 272, 273, 276–78
Burma
    air plan for, 78–82
Allied victory in (Feb to Apr 1945), 311–38
    See also China-Burma-India theater

C

Casablanca Conference, 78–80
Chennault, Lt. Gen. Claire L. (Chinese AF), 10, 13, 30, 32, 33, 35–39, 42–43, 45–54, 64, 114–15, 117–19, 140, 141, 153, 170, 208, 214, 291, 305, 306, 308, 341–43, 349, 352
Chiang Kai-shek, Generalissimo, 8, 10–12, 13, 23, 29, 33, 35–36, 52–54, 58, 78, 115, 117–18, 141–42, 145, 146, 177, 185, 226, 227, 234, 248–49, 269, 272, 321–22, 345, 352
China, as separate theater, 249
China Air Task Force (CATF), 33–54, 356
China-Burma-India theater (CBI), 6–8, 55–254. *See also* India-Burma theater
Chinese Expeditionary Force, 269–70, 273, 277–78
    22nd Chinese Division, 112, 185, 190, 191, 195–97, 267, 268, 269
    30th Chinese Division, 268–70
    38th Chinese Division, 12, 112, 160, 184, 190, 191, 197, 241–42, 267, 268, 270, 276
    50th Chinese Division, 197–98, 268, 270, 278

Churchill, Winston, 8, 12, 57, 78, 113, 115, 132, 133, 134, 234–35, 247–48, 322
Combat Cargo Task Force (CCTF), 281–304, 312–21, 333–38, 339–41, 349
Coryton, Air Marshal W. A. (RAF), 311

D

Davidson, Brig. Gen. Howard C. (USAAF), 118, 119, 144, 146, 147, 148, 161, 168, 172, 175, 208, 211, 212, 214, 218, 220–21, 232, 236, 239, 242, 246, 249, 252, 264, 273, 278–80, 285, 305–6, 328, 342, 343, 348–49
Dill, Field Marshal Sir John (Royal Army), 53–54, 59, 78, 247

E

Eastern Air Command (EAC), 177–233
Eleventh Army Group, 231
    establishment and organization of, 177–84, 357–59, 360, 362–63
    operations under (Dec 1943 to Jun 1944), 184–233
    reorganization of (Jun 1944), 231–33
Third Tactical Air Force, 179, 200, 232, 236, 294
Troop Carrier Command, 180, 221–29, 360
    See also Strategic Air Force
Egan, Col. J. F. (USAAF), 88–89, 111, 128, 130, 161
Evans, Brig. Gen. Frederick W. (USAAF), 286, 312
Evill, Air Marshal DCS (RAF), 23

F

fighter operations, 184–207. See also *specific military units*

G

Garrod, Air Marshal Sir Guy (RAF), 141, 142–43, 145, 311
geography and climate factors, 6–7
Giffard, Gen. Sir George (British Army), 178, 231, 236, 246, 264, 281
Giles, Lt. Gen. Barney (USAAF), 144, 264

H

Haynes, Brig. Gen. Caleb (USAAF), 16–17, 19, 20, 29–30, 35–37, 39, 43, 45, 60, 63–66, 67, 80, 104–5, 111, 117–18, 119, 137, 146, 150
Hegenberger, Maj. Gen. Albert (USAAF), 348
Honda, Lt. Gen. Masaki (IJA), 318
Hump route (air ferry to China), 26, 28–31, 40, 54, 60, 83, 92, 114–15, 152, 153, 154, 177, 200, 235, 245, 305

I

Imperial Japanese Air Force (IJAF)
    5th Hikōshidan (Air Division), 66, 69, 81–82, 83, 84, 92, 101–3, 105, 127, 135, 153, 155, 157, 174, 180, 184, 198, 200–207, 251–52, 258–59, 302, 304, 315, 322–25, 327
    21st Hikōsentai (Fighter), 102, 103, 121, 172, 174
    33rd Hikōsentai (Fighter), 45, 153, 155, 156, 157–58, 184, 200
    62nd Hikōsentai (Bomber), 201–4
    77th Hikōsentai (Fighter), 200–201
    204th Hikōsentai (Fighter), 157–58, 174, 201–4, 206, 207, 238, 243–45, 252, 322
    4th Hikōdan (Air Brigade), 66, 69, 81–83, 92, 101–4, 252, 322, 324, 325
    8th Hikōsentai (Light Bomber), 47, 66, 67–68, 69, 84, 155, 156, 157–58, 184, 202, 204, 252, 258, 322, 325
    14th Hikōsentai (Light Bomber), 66, 67, 69
    34th Hikōsentai (Light Bomber), 157–58

50th Hikōsentai (Fighter), 47, 66, 68, 69, 81–84, 101–2, 104, 106, 107–9, 127, 153, 154, 155, 156–58, 168, 170, 200–204, 206, 207, 243–45, 252, 258, 302, 307, 323
7th Hikōdan (Air Brigade), 66, 81–82, 92, 101–4, 184, 251
12th Hikōsentai (Heavy Bomber), 66, 184, 202, 251
64th Hikōsentai (Fighter), 66, 67, 68, 69, 81–82, 84, 101–3, 104, 107–9, 121, 122, 127, 172–75, 184, 201–4, 206–7, 252, 258, 289, 293, 296, 302, 304, 307, 315, 320, 323, 325
98th Hikōsentai (Heavy Bomber), 66, 84
9th Hikōshidan (Air Division), 200, 205
87th Hikōsentai (Fighter), 200, 205–6
81st Hikōsentai (Reconnaissance), 66, 67, 69, 184, 252, 323
Imperial Japanese Army (IJA)
   Burma Area Army, 135, 184, 193, 194, 248, 251, 281, 313, 317–18, 321
   15th Army, 57, 66, 81, 83, 92, 113, 184, 194–95, 246–47, 251, 281, 321
   15th Division, 135, 184, 281, 321
   18th Division, 86, 160, 251, 318, 321
   31st Division, 184, 251, 281
   33rd Division, 184, 251
   49th Division, 318, 319, 321
   54th Division, 135
   55th Division, 184, 194, 222
   24th Independent Mixed Brigade, 135
   28th Army, 184, 251, 297
   33rd Army, 246–47, 251, 252, 259, 272, 321
   18th Division, 184, 185, 190, 191, 193–98, 321
   56th Division, 184, 237, 251, 261, 272, 277, 278
India Air Task Force (IATF), 55–77, 82–83, 150, 356
India-Burma theater, 249–54, 255–353
interdiction missions for NCAC advance, 259–72

J

Japanese forces. *See* Imperial Japanese Air Force; Imperial Japanese Army

K

Katamura, Lt. Gen. S. (IJA), 251
Kawabe, Lt. Gen. Masakazu (IJA), 135, 184, 194, 281, 291
Kimura, Lt. Gen. (IJA), 291, 321

L

Leese, Lt. Gen. Sir Oliver (British Army), 248, 293, 311, 333
light-plane operations, 229–31. *See also* aeromedical evacuation operations

M

Mao Pang-tzo, Maj. Gen. (Chinese AF), 10
Marshall, Gen. George (US Army), 11, 13, 17, 22, 25, 29, 52, 58–59, 66, 78, 113–14, 115, 117–18, 132, 133, 134, 135, 140, 146, 147–48, 177, 224, 236, 247, 248, 277, 285, 322, 342, 343, 352
Mars Task Force, 249, 269–70, 272, 273, 275, 277–78, 321, 322
Meiktila, Battle for, 311–22
Mellersh, Air Commodore F. J. W. (RAF), 180, 208, 232, 306, 307, 332
Merrill, Brig. Gen. Frank (British Army), 178, 190, 196, 197–98, 213, 221, 227, 236, 237, 245
Messervy, Lt. Gen. Frank (British Army), 312, 316, 317
monsoon, 1943 operations during, 119–31
Mountbatten, Vice-Adm. Lord Louis (Royal Navy), 132, 134–35, 139, 140–49, 177, 182, 195, 196–97, 214, 222, 223–26, 229, 232, 234–36, 246–49, 269, 272, 277–78, 281–87, 289, 291–93, 311, 319, 321–22, 333, 341, 348
Mutaguchi, Lt. Gen. Renya (IJA), 86, 135, 184, 194, 213
Myitkyina, capture of, 197–98, 234–46

N

Naiden, Brig. Gen. Earl (USAAF), 17, 19, 22, 29, 33, 35, 50, 59–60
Northern Combat Area Command, 184–98, 232, 254, 255–80

O

Octagon Conference (Sept. 1944), 247–48
Old, Brig. Gen. William D. (USAAF), 28, 29, 146, 148, 150, 161, 180, 221–23, 227–28, 231

P

Park, Air Chief Marshal Sir Keith (RAF), 259, 311, 312, 350
Peirse, Air Chief Marshal Sir Richard (RAF), 12, 14, 23, 137, 141–46, 148, 170, 179, 180–82, 212, 231, 232, 259, 283–85, 287, 311
Portal, Air Chief Marshal Sir Charles (RAF), 14, 58, 62–63, 115, 140, 146, 247, 283–85, 287, 311

Q

Quadrant Conference (Quebec Conference), 132–35

R

Rangoon missions, 168–76, 332–38
Roosevelt, Franklin D., 9–10, 11, 12, 13, 14, 29, 32, 33, 52, 53–54, 78, 115, 117, 133, 134, 177, 247–48
Royal Air Force (RAF)
   No. 221 Group, 80, 109, 137, 138, 145, 179, 181, 208, 247, 294, 298, 311, 312–13, 318, 320, 333
   No. 222 Group, 145
   No. 224 Group, 80, 109, 137, 138, 145, 179, 201–2, 294, 297–98, 311, 318, 320–21, 334
   No. 231 Group, 180, 208, 232

S

Scoones, Lt. Gen. G. A. P. (British Army), 194, 224
Slim, Field Marshal Sir William (British Army), 30, 178–79, 194–95, 223, 224–27, 231, 234, 236, 246, 277, 281–82, 288–92, 311–13, 317–22, 332–33, 337, 351, 353
Southeast Asia Air Command (SEAC)
   impact on Tenth AF units, 135–49
   Myitkyina plans and operations (May to Aug 1944), 234–46
   operations under EAC, 177–207
   Strategic Air Force under, 141, 143
   Tactical Air Force under, 141, 143
Spaatz, Lt. Gen. Carl (US Army), 139, 140, 141
Stilwell, Lt. Gen. Joseph (USAAF), 12, 13–14, 16, 17, 22, 23–25, 29, 33, 35–36, 38, 49–50, 52–54, 57–59, 61, 63, 78, 79, 112, 113–15, 117–18, 133–36, 140–48, 159, 161, 177–79, 182, 184–85, 190, 192, 194–98, 213–14, 223, 224–27, 230–32, 234, 235–37, 239, 241–42, 246–49, 251, 253, 273, 284–85, 290–91
Stopford, Lt. Gen. M. G. N. (British Army), 312
Strategic Air Force (SAF)
   operations, 182–83, 208–21, 304–10
   organization, 141, 143, 179–80, 232, 347
Stratemeyer, Maj. Gen. George (USAAF), 116–19, 139–49, 170, 179–80, 182, 197–98, 206, 208, 212, 214, 220–23, 225–26, 228, 231–33, 235, 246–47, 249, 283–87, 293–94, 297, 305–7, 311, 312–13, 322, 333, 339, 341–43, 346, 348, 352
Sultan, Lt. Gen. Dan (USAAF), 246, 248–49, 251, 268, 269–70, 272, 277–78, 322, 341–42, 345–46

T

Tedder, Air Chief Marshal Arthur (RAF), 140
Third Tactical Air Force (EAC), 179, 200, 232, 236, 294
Trident Conference, 112–15

U

United States Army Air Force (USAAF)
   Tenth Air Force
     early operations, 14–32
     endgame for military operations in Burma, 339–41
     formation of, Dec 1941 to Jun 1942, 9–14
     going home, 348–49
     introduction, 6–8
     move to China (1945), 341–48
     SEAC reorganization and, 135–49
   Fourteenth Air Force, 113–14, 116, 117, 136, 141, 252, 305–6
   1st Air Commando Group, 134, 179, 180, 194, 201, 202, 206, 223–24, 282–85, 286–87, 299–301, 312–14, 316, 319, 339–40
   5th Fighter Squadron (Commando), 286, 299–300, 302–4, 312–14, 317, 318, 323, 334, 339
   6th Fighter Squadron (Commando), 286, 299–300, 302–4, 312–14, 317, 318, 323, 334, 339

164th Liaison Squadron, 287
165th Liaison Squadron, 287, 288
166th Liaison Squadron, 287, 288, 314
319th Troop Carrier Squadron, 274, 287, 288, 316, 319, 333, 335–36
Night Intruder Section, 300–302, 315
1st Air Force Ferrying Group, 29, 60–61
1st Combat Cargo Group, 226, 282, 283, 286, 287–89, 292, 337, 340–41, 349
1st Combat Cargo Squadron, 286, 288–89
2nd Combat Cargo Squadron, 286, 287–89, 316, 336, 340
3rd Combat Cargo Squadron, 286, 287–89, 292, 293, 340
4th Combat Cargo Squadron, 286, 288–89, 292, 316, 336, 340
1st Liaison Group (Provisional), 253, 274, 275
5th Liaison Squadron, 230–31, 274–75, 279
71st Liaison Squadron, 136, 229–31, 279
115th Liaison Squadron, 231
1st Provisional Fighter Group (Commando), 312–19, 325–26
2nd Air Commando Group, 312, 313–15, 317, 318, 319, 323, 324, 339–40
1st Fighter Squadron, 314, 315–16, 317, 318, 323, 324–27, 334, 339
2nd Fighter Squadron, 314, 317, 318, 323, 324–27, 334, 339
317th Troop Carrier Squadron, 288, 333, 335–36
3rd Combat Cargo Group, 252–53, 258, 272–76, 282, 340–41, 349
10th Combat Cargo Squadron, 258, 340
11th Combat Cargo Squadron, 243
12th Combat Cargo Squadron, 258, 340
4th Combat Cargo Group, 282, 289, 291, 292–93, 319–20, 321, 337, 340–41, 349
13th Combat Cargo Squadron, 289, 292
14th Combat Cargo Squadron, 289
15th Combat Cargo Squadron, 289, 292
16th Combat Cargo Squadron, 289
7th Bomb Group (H), 16, 17, 18–20–22, 24–28, 31–32, 55, 57–59, 62, 63–64, 70–75, 80, 93–105, 111, 117, 120–25, 130, 136, 166, 168–76, 179, 208–14, 220, 281, 304–6, 307–8, 327–32, 333, 340, 346–48
9th Bomb Squadron, 55, 57, 63, 64, 71, 72–75, 93, 94, 97, 102–4, 121, 124, 168, 170–71, 174–76, 209–13, 305, 307–8, 330, 332
436th Bomb Squadron, 63, 64, 71, 72, 74–75, 93, 94, 95, 96, 97–99, 102, 121, 124–25, 168, 175, 209–13, 306, 307–8, 330, 331
492nd Bomb Squadron, 63, 72, 75, 93, 95, 96, 97–100, 102, 121–22, 124, 125, 168, 209–11, 213, 307–8, 331, 332
493rd Bomb Squadron, 63, 72, 75, 93, 96, 97, 99–100, 102, 121, 124–25, 168, 170, 175–76, 209–13, 307–8, 328–29, 331, 332, 345, 346, 347
8th Photo Reconnaissance Group, 309
9th Photo Reconnaissance Squadron, 48, 64, 65, 66, 76, 100–101, 105–6, 117, 122, 128, 185, 188, 262, 266, 309
12th Bomb Group (M), 184, 215, 219–20, 242, 257, 281, 294–98, 299–300, 305, 313, 320, 334–36, 340, 344, 348–49
81st Bomb Squadron, 219–20, 295, 296, 297–98
82nd Bomb Squadron, 219–20, 294, 295, 296, 297–98
83rd Bomb Squadron, 219–20, 244, 296, 297–98, 340
434th Bomb Squadron, 219–20, 295, 296, 297–98, 340
17th Bomb Group (M), 22
19th Bomb Group, 16, 17, 20
20th Tactical Reconnaissance Squadron, 185, 188, 203, 260, 262, 266, 309
23rd Air Depot Group, 116
23rd Fighter Group, 32, 33, 34–49, 51–52
11th Bomb Squadron, 39, 40, 43, 45–49, 55, 58, 59, 75, 80, 86
16th Fighter Squadron, 41, 43, 46–49, 58, 64, 88
74th Fighter Squadron, 37–38, 47
75th Fighter Squadron, 37–38, 40–43, 46–47
76th Fighter Squadron, 37–38, 43, 44, 46–47
33rd Fighter Group, 252, 256–58, 262–65, 268, 276–79, 339
58th Fighter Squadron, 252, 256, 264, 278, 279, 302, 303, 347
59th Fighter Squadron, 252, 256, 264
60th Fighter Squadron, 252, 256, 264, 265, 275, 279, 345
40th Photo Reconnaissance Group, 309–10
51st Fighter Group, 16, 19–21, 32, 35, 37, 41, 55, 64, 66–70, 80, 82–93, 111, 117, 128–30, 151

16th Fighter Squadron, 117
25th Fighter Squadron, 55, 68–70, 84–85, 86–88, 90–93, 128–29
26th Fighter Squadron, 55, 64, 66–67, 68–70, 82, 84–85, 86–93, 128–29
80th Fighter Group, 86, 115, 117, 129, 135–36, 150–51, 152, 153–60, 179, 185, 187, 189–91, 195, 196, 197, 200–201, 237–46, 255–58, 261–65, 266–70, 272, 276–78
88th Fighter Squadron, 129, 158, 189, 191, 237, 238, 240–42, 243–44, 245, 252, 263–64, 266–67, 278
89th Fighter Squadron, 129, 152, 154, 155–56, 189–90, 191, 196, 197, 200, 201, 203, 228, 238, 240, 245, 252, 253, 255–56, 264, 267
90th Fighter Squadron, 129, 152, 195, 197, 203–4, 238, 240, 243, 245, 256–57, 258, 263–64, 267, 269, 277, 344
459th Fighter Squadron, 135, 137, 163, 171, 175, 180, 181, 201–5, 206, 207, 281, 294, 298, 303, 304, 320–21, 327, 334, 339
308th Bomb Group, 153, 168, 170, 171–76
311th Fighter-Bomber Group, 117, 135, 136, 150–54, 156–58, 160, 172, 179, 185–92, 195–96, 197, 237–46, 252
528th Fighter-Bomber Squadron, 135, 151–52, 154, 158, 160, 185, 187, 191, 196, 197, 203, 240, 241–42, 244
529th Fighter-Bomber Squadron, 135, 151–53, 154, 156–58, 185–86, 187, 188–89, 191, 197, 200–201, 203–4, 238, 240, 242, 245
530th Fighter-Bomber Squadron, 135, 151–53, 158, 160, 163, 170, 171, 172, 174, 180, 181, 188–89, 197, 200–201, 203–4, 205–6, 240, 244–45
341st Bomb Group (Medium), 63–64, 66, 75–76, 80, 90, 99, 104, 105–11, 117, 120–28, 130, 136, 150, 161–68, 176, 179, 185, 208, 215–19, 344–45
22nd Bomb Squadron (M), 45, 55, 58, 64, 66, 75–76, 86, 105–7, 124, 125–28, 167, 215
490th Bomb Squadron (M), 64, 75–76, 104, 106, 107–9, 117, 123–24, 125–27, 162, 163–68, 170, 172, 179–80, 191, 215–19, 226, 242, 256–57, 259–61, 264, 277, 278, 279, 327, 332
491st Bomb Squadron (M), 64, 75–76, 105–6, 123–24, 125, 127, 130, 165, 167, 215
427th Night Fighter Squadron, 258, 259, 278
443rd Troop Carrier Group, 180, 221–23, 239, 273–76, 340–41, 349
1st Troop Carrier Squadron, 115, 136, 161, 180, 191, 221, 227–29
2nd Troop Carrier Squadron, 115, 117, 136, 153, 156–57, 161, 180, 191, 200–201, 221, 224–25, 227–29, 272, 273–74
4th Troop Carrier Squadron, 227
11th Troop Carrier Squadron, 227
18th Troop Carrier Squadron, 227
27th Troop Carrier Squadron, 180, 193, 221–22, 224, 225, 227
315th Troop Carrier Squadron, 180, 193, 221–22, 224

W

Wavell, Lt. Gen. Sir Archibald (British Army), 12, 16, 17, 22, 23, 24, 57–59, 79, 112–13, 133, 137
Wedemeyer, Maj. Gen. Albert (US Army), 142–43, 145–47, 247–49, 269, 277, 289, 293, 321, 341–43
Wingate, Maj. Gen. Orde (USAAF), 57, 79, 112–13, 133–34, 135, 145, 148, 161, 177–80, 182, 185–86, 192, 201, 207, 213, 221–24, 226, 229, 230, 231, 241, 251, 284–85, 312, 351
Wingate's Special Force, 79, 134, 179, 180, 185, 186, 192–94, 197, 221, 222–23